The purpose of this extraordinary anthology is made abundantly clear by the editors' stated intention: "to create a living mosaic of essays and stories in which Black men can view themselves, and be viewed without distortion." In this, they have succeeded brilliantly. *Brotherman* contains more than one hundred and fifty selections, some never before published—from slave narratives, memoirs, and social histories, to novels, poems, short stories, biographies, autobiographies, position papers, and essays.

***Brotherman* books us passage to the world that Black men experience as adolescents, lovers, husbands, fathers, workers, warriors, and elders. On this journey they encounter pain, confusion, anger, and love while confronting the life-threatening issues of race, sex, and politics—often as strangers in a strange land. The first collection of its kind, *Brotherman* gathers together a multitude of voices that add a new, unforgettable chapter to American cultural identity.**

More praise for *Brotherman*

"[An] outstanding collection . . . The powerful opening excerpt by Frederick Douglass evokes his boyhood as a slave, and the collection closes with an eloquent discussion of the race problem today by Cornel West. A distinguished addition to black studies."

—*Publishers Weekly* (starred review)

"*Brotherman* is a tribute to the resiliency of African American men's creativity and intellect. . . . Replete with inspired illustrations by artist Tom Feelings, full of heady prose and soul-stirring commentary, it resonates with the wisdom of the sages: men like Douglass, Du Bois, Washington, Garvey, Dunbar, Chesnutt, Hughes, Toomer, Ellison, Robeson, Ellington, and McKay. Then, as counterpoint and corroboration, it virtually erupts with the energy of new voices: names such as Tait, Kenan, Gates, Ellis, McCall, Hemphill, Cose, Ice T, Farrakhan, Kimbro, West, and Copage."

—*Black Issues in Higher Education*

Please turn the page for more rave reviews . . .

"[An] extraordinary collection . . . Through a breadth of concerns, issues, and perspectives, a comprehensive picture emerges of what it means to live as a Black man in America. . . . Timely and powerful, *Brotherman* is destined to claim a place for itself on the shelf of must-read classics of Black literature for this generation and for many to come."

—*The African Times*

"A living legacy . . . Here are black men speaking their minds and speaking from their hearts and their souls about love, family, and work; sports, politics, and the arts. . . . A profound contribution."

—*The Quarterly Black Review of Books*

"Mesmerizing in its diversity . . . The portrait of the African-American male that they have thus created has universal appeal; it is a reminder, like the term 'Brotherman' itself, that 'we have a common fate.' "

—*St. Louis Post-Dispatch*

"No matter who you are, you'll find it's real nice hearing from the brothers."

—*YSB*

"By sampling the diverse works of Frederick Douglass, W. E. B. Du Bois, Malcolm X, Nathan McCall, Ralph Ellison, Walter Mosley, Paul Robeson, Louis Farrakhan and others, *Brotherman* becomes a living mosaic of essays and stories in which black men can view themselves and be viewed without distortion. . . . This time our symphony of manhood, dignity, and freedom will be heard."

—*Raleigh News & Observer*

"The editors have swept widely but sensitively through African American literature, producing not only a forceful anthology but the first one devoted exclusively to male writings."

—*Booklist*

"This anthology is deftly organized and immensely enriched by the editors' comprehensive selections. . . . Reading *Brotherman* is a stimulating experience, like being at a barbershop on Saturday, where brothermen are explaining, declaiming, and riffin' in various accents. Despite their varied voices, they merge into a tone poem expressing various hues of black and embodying the closing lines of Sterling Brown's powerful poem: 'One thing they cannot prohibit—The strong men . . . coming on . . . The strong men gittin' stronger. Strong men . . . STRONGER. . . ."

—*Class*

Brotherman

THE ODYSSEY OF BLACK MEN IN AMERICA

EDITED BY
HERB BOYD
AND
ROBERT L. ALLEN

ILLUSTRATIONS BY TOM FEELINGS

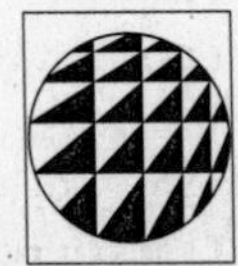

ONE WORLD
BALLANTINE BOOKS • NEW YORK

A One World Book
Published by Ballantine Books

Published in the United States by Ballantine Books, a division of Random House, Inc., New York, and simultaneously in Canada by Random House of Canada Limited, Toronto.

Permission acknowledgments can be found on pages 916–922

Library of Congress Catalog Card Number: 95-94986

ISBN 0-345-38317-6

Cover design by Kristine V. Mills
Cover photo of Denzil Foster and Thomas McElroy of FMob by F. Scott Schafer

Manufactured in the United States of America

First Trade Paperback Edition: February 1996

10 9 8 7 6 5 4 3 2 1

To my father and son—wherever they are

—HERB BOYD

To my grandfather, Joseph Sims (1890–1985)

—ROBERT L. ALLEN

"Being a Black man in America is like having another job."

—ARTHUR ASHE

CONTENTS

Fighting on Two Fronts

Locked In and Locked Out

Color and Class

PART 5: BLACK MAGIC
And Bid Him Sing

Be-Bop, Doo-Wop, Hip-Hop

PART 6: SANKOFA: PAST AS PROLOGUE

Deep Roots

No Justice, No Peace

Black Gold

Return to the Source

Epilogue

ACKNOWLEDGMENTS

It is rather ironic that a book almost exclusively about Black men is in reality the product of a team of gifted women. This project evolved from the genius of our editor, Cheryl D. Woodruff, our agent, Marie Dutton Brown, and was brought to fruition by a staff of devoted and tireless workers at One World Books, especially Leah Odze, Kristine Mills, Brenda Brown, Beverly Robinson, and the uncompromising support of Ballantine president Linda Grey.

And there are other women who made extraordinary sacrifices and lent a helping hand and heart: Katherine Brown, Catherine Boyd, and Elza Boyd. We commend your efforts.

To thank all the men who were steadfast and supportive would be a list as long as our magnificent contributors, to whom we are eternally grateful. A special thanks goes to artist Tom Feelings, whose powerful illustrations say what words cannot.

The next time somebody doubts the possibility of miracles, we will point with pride to *Brotherman*. Above all, we extend our gratitude to all those who prayed for us and the completion of this book. We are sure your special words and commitment turned the tide.

INTRODUCTION

"Brotherman!" is a special greeting among Black men. With that single word a bloodline is invoked, a gender proclaimed. It is a verbal handshake, a shared mantra that expresses much more than a mere hello. This greeting was first heard in the euphoric Sixties. But it still resonates today, carrying a number of meanings for Black men no matter who they are—whether they work in offices in three-piece suits or bop down the street in shredded pants with their caps turned backward. Their coded exchange of "brotherman" signals immediate recognition and rapport. It conveys a message that is at once an affirmation, an affectionate embrace, and a battle cry. It proclaims: *Our blood lines and soulforce are the same and we have a common fate—what happens to one happens to all.*

And that battle cry, that call to arms—though different for each generation—has inspired a multitude of voices during the Black man's long odyssey in America. These voices have cried out in despair, railed against injustice, defied oppression, and have spoken truth with power and eloquence. For every Black man's voice muffled by defeat or hushed by Draconian edicts, hundreds more have soared in triumph, singing endlessly and gloriously about victories over insurmountable odds. When the voice was not disposed to song, then poems, plays, stories, speeches, essays, and narratives reaffirmed our uncompromising manhood, and made resolute demands for freedom, decency, and respect.

These voices now echo from *Brotherman.* Some of them are as old and commanding as the Black men whose blood became the ink of powerful slave narratives. Some are as recent as that gaggle of postmodern writers stepping out beyond hip-hop, New Jack, and neo-retro effusions. *Brotherman* is both a literal and metaphorical map of the Black man's quest for self-affirmation reflected through the multifaceted prism of his fiction and nonfiction writings.

The Black experience in America has been the subject of several significant anthologies, from Alain Locke's *The New Negro*, published in 1925, to the recent *Breaking Ice* by Terry McMillan. Yet none of these books have focused on depicting the singular circumstances of Black men in this country, not even when major anthologies have been dominated by Black male writers. In this regard, *Brotherman* stands alone.

More than a mere charting of the Black man's travails and triumphs—his ceaseless struggle for manhood and dignity—the central purpose of this collection is to create a living mosaic of essays and stories in which Black men can view themselves, and be viewed without distortion. For distortion is only one of the destructive tactics used against us by the powers that be when confronted by our "troubling and threatening presence." When Blacks were not being annihilated, they were often being deceived and burdened with insidious stereotypes. If these measures proved ineffective, Black men then became the target of psychological manipulation, and were made to believe that we and we alone were responsible for our frustrations and failures.

Racism and oppression are responsible for the absence of books like *Brotherman*. On the one hand, our very presence has produced too much inner conflict in American society to allow us to be embraced. And on the other hand, we have not been allowed the luxury of questioning and examining the nature of our relationship to each other or to that larger society. However, unlike W. E. B. Du Bois, who had no answer to his rhetorical question: "How does it feel to be a problem?" we are proposing a few replies to this quandary.

When we told our friends about this project they were shocked to learn there was no other book like *Brotherman* in print. Perhaps one explanation for the appearance of this anthology by and for Black men at this time can be attributed to the remarkable efforts of Black women writers over the last decades. Their genius and determination have created a formidable wedge, widening the discourse for minority voices, and providing Black men with a forum to raise the pressing issues that are unique and integral to their survival.

While *Brotherman* makes no pretense of being the sum total of the Black man's experience, we have tried to select a representative range of fiction and nonfiction. Even so, some of our choices are certain to run counter to some readers' opinions. But this too is our aim. It has always been our intention to stir debate, to be critical and self-critical, to encourage Black men to reflect on where they've been and where they are now, and to offer some options to consider before we decide where we're going.

In *Brotherman*, you will find a variety of responses from Black men covering the spectrum of life experience. Many of these selections have been previously published by authors virtually unknown to readers nowadays. We are pleased to reintroduce them along with others deserving wider recognition from the rich corpus of 150 years of Black literature. We are as proud to include such notables as Paul Laurence Dunbar, W. E. B. Du Bois, Langston Hughes, Richard Wright, James Baldwin, and Ralph Ellison, as we are of introducing Nouk Bassomb, Nathan McCall, Jarvis Masters, Alexs Pate, Michael Eric Dyson, Kevin Powell, Kenneth Meeks, and other emerging writers.

And like the splendid diversity of writers assembled here, the topics and themes they probe run the entire gamut of human emotion and experience. We have cast our nets wide to gather material that speaks to the heart, mind, and soul. Sadly, however, for every writer we chose there were four or five we simply didn't have room to include.

The works you will find in *Brotherman*—the essays, stories, documents, poems, narratives, position papers, and excerpts from novels and autobiographies—form a template of the Black man's endurance, offering deep insights into the complexity of the human condition. Indeed, how Black men experience the passages and episodes of life—as children, young men, lovers, husbands, fathers, workers, artists, athletes, prisoners, partners, activists, and elders—is vital to understanding their roles within the context of family, the community, and the larger society. In these pages you will find Black male writers actively confronting issues of intimacy, vulnerability, pain, confusion, anger, and love. In the process, these intensely engaging and often deeply personal revelations come face-to-face with, and help to clarify, broad social, racial, sexual, and political issues that impinge daily upon African American life in the United States.

Brotherman falls into six major sections. Sterling Brown's poem "Strong Men" in the Prologue opens the book with a potent and powerful voice.

The tone he sets resonates all the way through to the Epilogue, reminding us that African American men "get stronger and stronger."

In Part 1: *Forefathers*, "The Griot's Voice" forms the only subsection. After Harlem's poet, George Edward Tait, declares and defines our mission, the African past is invoked by Nouk Bassomb. Theologian Howard Thurman's meditations are an essential bridge connecting our African heritage to the dreaded "Middle Passage" and the degradation of slavery. Frederick Douglass's slave narrative is indicative of his eloquence, but it is his courageous defiance of the slave-breaker that makes a lasting impression.

Each of the venerable forefathers of African American culture—Douglass, Booker T. Washington, W. E. B. Du Bois, and Marcus Garvey—voice a common demand for the recognition of our manhood, freedom, and humanity. You will find these three themes woven all through *Brotherman*, even though they may be pursued by different strategies and tactics—contrast Washington's moderate mode with the militant stance of Du Bois, and Garvey's separatist convictions. Although these ideologies are refined by each succeeding generation, these defining moments are rooted in our early struggle for justice and equality. Randall Kenan gives Washington's political outlook a fictional turn without minimizing his contributions or defaming his character.

Ralph Ellison's story, "Juneteenth," published here for only the second time, carries a political message, too. The title refers to a Black holiday originally celebrated in Texas. Although slavery was abolished there on June 19, 1862, it did not formally end until 1865. "Juneteenth" is now observed by African Americans as the official emancipation day. In Ellison's skillful hands, this holiday becomes a useful metaphor in the sermon of his protagonist, Rev. Hickman, who himself symbolizes the conjunction of politics and religion. In this extended sermon, Hickman evokes his people's spiritual continuity and their political renewal, while embodying their hopes and aspirations. He is a "keeper of the flame" that burned so brightly in that far away African village where Nouk Bassomb called everyone to the celebration and welcomed us around the fire.

Part 2: *A Son in the Family*, falls into two sections—"Fathers and Sons" and "Boyz 'n the Hood." There is perhaps no more intense or troubled relationship in the Black community than the one between father and son. Originally, the parental tether attached to the sons was intended to keep them safe from the menace of the Ku Klux Klan, rednecks, and the lynch mobs of the South. Even in the North, where the menace was not so apparent, a vestige of this overprotection remained. And, in too many instances, it inhibited, stifled, and suffocated the son, who misunderstood the deep, often unspoken, concern and affection underlying it.

If there's been a lessening of friction between these archetypal figures it's been due to the lessening of parental control that accompanied gains made in the legal and political realm, where relentless civil rights activism helped reduce Jim Crow social and legal restrictions. These gains brought about access to the ballot and increased social latitude for both fathers and sons. Many of these fathers had only a crude, instinctive way of raising their sons, often having had no father of their own as a role model.

The excerpts here from three of the most popular Black male writers—Richard Wright, Langston Hughes, and James Baldwin—are characteristic of the pre-civil rights period. Each of them is either estranged from his father or never really got to know him. We can only speculate about how this lack of fatherly love that they felt affected the art of these literary giants.

Their situation is in direct contrast to contemporary writers such as Quincy Troupe, who is almost devotional in his poem to Quincy, Sr., once a noted baseball player in the old Negro Leagues. Earl Ofari Hutchinson expresses a continuing deep regard for his father. But we get only a glimmer of this adoration from Malcolm X, whose doting father had been a victim of the Klan-like Black Legion. Like Malcolm, Nick Chiles's character, Troy, loses his father at an early age. What he knows of him is gleaned secretly from a batch of love letters written to Troy's mother from Vietnam.

An understanding father, not afraid to reveal his inabilities, and willing to allow his son to express his feelings without censure is found in the warm portraits by Wesley Brown, Louis Edwards, and Henry Louis Gates, Jr. Their tender impressions coincide perfectly with the values found in Haki Madhubuti's "Father's Pledge."

When fathers are not available, and mothers are overburdened, the streets and the "hood" raise the boys, which reminds us of the old African adage: "It takes a village to raise a child." Elements of this practice are very evident in our "Boyz 'n the Hood" section. Here, gang life, peer pressure, and a nihilistic attitude toward life has replaced the less violent initiation rites so common among previous generations. That old, familiar, but relatively stable process of leaving home, acquiring a modicum of education, and then settling into a job demanding only minimum skills no longer exists. An unusually high drop-out rate among African American male students coupled with a distressingly small number of employment opportunities have drastically changed this picture. A minimum wage job at some fast food outlet is about all the large pool of unskilled young Black men can hope for, and it is unrealistic to expect these jobs to compete with the lucrative lure of selling illegal drugs.

On a very basic level, gangs come into being for protection against enemies—real and imagined. With limited ways to assert their authority, gangs resort to controlling a few blocks of turf. Whether in a town like William Demby's "Beetlecreek," or in one of those nameless neighborhoods depicted by William Melvin Kelley in "Enemy Territory" or by Henry Dumas in "Strike and Fade," the gang becomes a predator or a band of conspirators. A lonely outsider must be either quick or smart to avoid a showdown. In Kevin Powell's "Ghetto Bastard," this flight from a fight has a more pressing immediacy.

Nevertheless, maintaining your "cool"—staying calm and unruffled whatever the circumstances—is as necessary for a gang member as his unswerving loyalty to the group. In the selections from Amiri Baraka, Jess Mowry, and Yusef Salaam we see variations of this cool pose. Of course, mixing cool with a little booze and a macho disposition can be dangerous, as Jabari Asim demonstrates in "Two Fools."

It has not been easy to find solutions for these adolescent problems, not even for such astute diviners as Michael Eric Dyson, Roland Gilbert, and Cheo Tyehimba-Taylor. One key element Gilbert and Tyehimba-Taylor propose is the role of male mentors and role models who will counsel and teach young men to take responsibility for their own thoughts, feelings, and actions.

If we are to believe the media, there's a furious war going on between Black men and Black women. We probe this alleged conflict in Part 3: *Relationships.* We examine these rumors of war, seeking the source of the so-called anger, and trying to find out whether the relationship between Black men and women is as complicated and irreconcilable as reported.

According to some accounts, we're at each other's throats so much that we lose sight of the real enemy. This war within a war helps to explain the absence of love themes in Black literature—at least the kind of heavy breathing, romantic love that fills TV and movie screens nowadays. Because Black men and women have rarely had the luxury or time for romantic fantasies, most of the pieces in these sections grapple with real love—not a love scripted for Hollywood, but one based on the kind of life where tenderness and affection must compete against economic and psychological survival.

In the section we call "When a Man Loves a Woman," we examine the way societal changes affect relationships between Black men and women. Charles Chesnutt's Mr. Ryder in "The Wife of His Youth" is a proud, upstanding gentleman who, when presented with a stunning revelation that alters the course of his life, refuses to compromise his integrity or dignity. Ryder's decision to honor the wife of his youth is indicative of a lost era when both men and the society in which they lived were more loving and caring.

We encounter two unforgettably strong wills in the excerpt from Charles Johnson's *Middle Passage.* Rutherford Calhoun is just as single-mindedly set on maintaining his bachelorhood as Isadora Bailey is determined to marry. They are two independent spirits in an old-fashioned Mexican standoff. The potential of mating between equals is realized in Arthur Flowers's *Another Good Loving Blues.* His couple exude a genuine love for each other that only a hoodoo woman and a bluesman could comprehend. Still, you don't need to know anything about herbs and magic to relate to the idyllic love portrayed in James Alan McPherson's *Elbow Room.* The emotions here are as universal as "playing the field," which Trey Ellis's Austin does with great aplomb—and success.

Calvin Hernton's *Sex and Racism in America* created a storm when it first appeared in 1965. But his findings, while startling to some, were nothing new to Chester Himes, who possessed a deft touch in portraying intense scenes between interracial couples. And nobody depicts contemporary African American love and life as realistically and as poignantly as Walter Mosley and Richard Perry. In "Anita," Clarence Major turns an uncensored pen to burning black passion in a relationship too complex to render fully in our chosen excerpt. Passion can also take on a transcendent edge that is quite the opposite of the pain, which Robert Fleming evokes in his poem "Black Women." When it comes to love, says Fleming, Black men cannot afford to continue to look "the wrong way at the wrong things."

And "What's Love Got to Do with It?" Everything! Especially when you realize how many kinds of deep, caring relationships exist outside of the romantic male-female bond. Some of the most dynamic relationships in a man's life occur between him and his grandparents, his siblings, and his children. Gerald Early has a special connection with his daughter, and he subtly reveals that they have something more than sad faces in common. By contrast, Edward Jones's sensitivity toward his daughter is slow in coming—she's long gone before he discovers the error of his ways.

At the end of Ron Stodghill's paean to his grandmother, his fear of losing her fades. Suddenly, he's aware of the cycle of life, realizing that, as one door closes, another opens. Like Stodghill's grandmother, a father clings desperately to life in Alexs Pate's story, "Losing Absalom." But what captivates here is the developing drama between the dying father's son and daughter. Throughout their lives together and apart, Sonny has dominated his sister, Rainy, choosing her boyfriends and governing her decisions, all in the name of brotherly love.

Nathan McCall, Kalamu ya Salaam, and Damu Hakim are bound by a similar pain—estrangement or divorce from the mothers of the children they dearly love. Their reactions to these circumstances range from resignation to near violence. McCall's rage is defused by counseling. Salaam seems to make sense of his personal setback by seeing it in the context of the turbulence and disillusion of the Sixties while Hakim vainly ponders how to negotiate an emotional minefield to see his children.

Ralph Wiley has no pat solutions for relationship dilemmas. He's forced to admit that his list of categories of Black women—as if this might help him make the right choice—is sadly incomplete. Yet conceding that Wiley might be right in saying that love is not for everybody goes against the grain of most Black men. And since they refuse to quit the pursuit, most optimistically view love as a work in progress.

"My Brother's Keeper," the final relationship section, approaches male bonding from several different angles. Sylvester Monroe, Playthell Benjamin, and Kenneth Meeks choose a group setting for their narratives on how Black men relate to each other when the only pressure is whether or not one can withstand a round of taunting, or worse, fraternal hazing. In Rudolph Fisher's "The Walls of Jericho," lighthearted banter keeps Jinx and his partner Bubber in a state of flux as the two men continuously test the flexibility of their friendship.

The very notion of stereotypical Black manhood is challenged in the works of E. Lynn Harris, Melvin Dixon, and Essex Hemphill. Hemphill's encounter with a sensitive stranger is a hopeful sign that maybe homophobia is not as widespread among Black men as it's thought to be. However, the challenge many Black men face in accepting a bisexual or gay comrade is comparatively minor when it comes to embracing someone suffering from AIDS. Woven throughout W. J. Brandy Moore's exhortation is a challenge for Blacks to recognize how AIDS affects the entire Black community. If we are truly our brother's keeper, Moore suggests, then it is time "to act now to save all of our futures."

Survival is a secondary concern in Ernest Gaines's, "A Lesson Before Dying," where a man facing execution learns how to die with dignity and with his manhood intact after he is reluctantly befriended by a teacher. In the end, the doomed man, relishing his newfound humanity and its power to shatter the white sheriff's racist myths, provides a spiritual lesson for both the dying and the living.

Since he was dragged here in chains from Africa, the Black man has found himself in the center of a world of trouble, and in Part 4 we look at "Trouble Man" as he spins off kilter around a globe of permanent racism. The systematic enslavement and destruction of African people by Europeans and Americans during the horrendous Atlantic slave trade established a brutal pattern of exploitation that has simply changed its form from plantation to ghetto. The first section of Part 4 examines "The Permanence of Racism." In Paul Laurence Dunbar's "The Lynching of Jube Benson" we see the most savage expression of racist behavior. Black men hanging from trees, sometimes castrated and their genitals stuffed in their mouths, were not an uncommon sight in the land of Dixie. What a sad paradox to have Supreme Court Justice Clarence Thomas opportunistically charge that his confirmation hearings resembled a "high-tech lynching." Ernie Allen views this comparison as the epitome of cynicism.

While Jean Toomer's *Cane* is often cited for its gothic imagery, evocative scenes, and poetic descriptions, the author also brilliantly depicted the deadly menace of a white mob hungry for a Black death in "Blood Burning Moon." But, as we see in Albert French's "Billy," racist violence is not limited to Black men—Black boys will also do.

Gordon Parks's Hannibal Jones is typical of many Black men who have been denied an opportunity to work simply because of the color of their skin. And as William Strickland concludes in "The Future of Black Men," the inability to obtain employment in a wage-structured society is equivalent to a sentence of spiritual and material death. Strickland's statistics and analyses are irrefutable, and the picture he paints is no less glum than the preceding fictional accounts.

Racism is often viewed as a malignant social disease. Tennis great Arthur Ashe's last words in *Days of Grace* suggest that *racism* is even more sinister and deadly than the AIDS that eventually claimed his life. However, Derrick Bell believes that there is a chance for survival against the scourge of racism, but only if we are "unremitting in our struggle." The lesson, then, for Black men in the future is the same as it was in the past: You must never give up! Derrick Bell closes this section with a call for conviction, courage, and strength for the fight.

In "Fighting on Two Fronts," Bell's words become a motto for the millions of Black men in uniform. The more politically conscious Black servicemen always knew it was necessary to fight on two fronts. These enlightened soldiers saw the enemy both at home and abroad, and they took them on one at a time. This was the meaning of the "Double V Campaign"—the resolve to fight at home and abroad—during World War II.

But before this war to defeat the Nazis in the West and the Japanese invaders in the East, there was World War I. David Levering Lewis vividly captures the image of the Black troops of the 369th Regiment parading down New York's Fifth Avenue to an enthusiastic crowd. They had served with unprecedented distinction and, battle-toughened, they were poised to take on the other foe on the home front.

The troops in John Oliver Killens's *And Then We Heard the Thunder* don't wait to return home to start their fight against racist hostility. The enemy in this World War II tale is in their ranks and must be rooted out. Black munitions handlers at Port Chicago never leave stateside, but nonetheless take a principled stand when it comes to risking their lives unloading dangerous explosives.

When faced with military service, Black men have the choice of either going, conscientiously objecting, or fleeing for the border. But some of them have to hear the bombs and feel the shrapnel before they realize that they've made a terrible mistake. In Wallace Terry's *Bloods*, Specialist 4 Charles Strong sees the horror of the Vietnam War up close and tactically opts for safer ground.

Will there ever come a time when Black men will stand together and refuse to be cannon fodder for Uncle Sam's bloody ventures? This is a question Clyde Taylor poses as he examines military protest and resistance. Part of the answer emerged during the recent Gulf War, when Black soldiers were once more disproportionately represented on the front lines.

Of course, thousands of Black inmates in the nation's penitentiaries don't have to worry about the draft. Too many of them have already waged war against society's laws and lost. Now they find themselves snared in a vicious and unforgiving criminal "injustice" system. When they refuse to heed some white officer's surly commands, these inmates must endure solitary confinement, degradation, inhuman treatment, and other deprivations.

In "Locked In and Locked Out," we find that the first level of survival is to learn how to negotiate your way among fellow prisoners—how to fend off the inevitable rape and daily physical abuse. These are the pertinent topics in both Nathan McCall's "Jim," and Jarvis Masters's "Scars."

Black inmates are often tortured, like the prisoners Albert Race Sample depicts in *Raceboss*, or they're made to suffer interminable humiliation and isolation, as Lloyd Brown shows us in *Iron City*. To be cut off from family and loved ones is particularly painful, and we see some of the bitter results of this separation in *Father Behind Bars*.

The shadows of prison walls sometimes cover more than just the inmates. As John Edgar Wideman explains, our brothers in prison incriminate us all. In effect, if Robert Chrisman is right, we are all prisoners. We all have the obligation to support our brothers behind bars—especially the political prisoners who are so eloquently defended in the piece by Dhoruba Bin Wahad. He writes about two noted political prisoners: Geronimo Pratt, a former Black Panther who has been incarcerated for more than twenty years; and Mumia Abu Jamal, who sits on death row in a Pennsylvania penitentiary.

In "Color and Class," we examine two less obvious ways of being locked in and locked out of mainstream America. "If you had a choice of colors, which one would choose my brother?" goes a line from a Curtis Mayfield song. And this was a real choice Walter White, the renowned civil rights activist, had to make when he succeeded James Weldon Johnson as field secretary of the NAACP. A courageous fighter for racial equality, White declared he was unequivocally a Negro with white skin, blue eyes, and blond hair. However, what White was born with has apparently become an obsessive quest for rock superstar Michael Jackson, although Stanley Crouch says this fixation on pale skin makes sense in the context of minstrelsy and the entertainment world.

"Passing" has always been a popular theme in Black literature, and Langston Hughes's humorous cameo, "Who's Passing for Who?" highlights this tendency. How much of this occurs in reality is anybody's guess, since those who successfully pass aren't about to tip their hands and expose their blood lines. Willard Motley's main character realizes the frustration of the color question when he is rejected by a lover. Ron Hall explores the color complex and notes that, among the nation's ethnic groups, only with Black Americans does one drop of blood really matter. "A German with one drop of French blood is not necessarily French," Hall asserts.

Whether in old sayings such as "If you're white, you're all right; if you're brown stick around; and if you're Black, get back!" to Blue Vein salons or to clubs that apply "brown bag tests," the many shades of Black skin have often brought laughter and pain, ambivalence, and confusion to Black people. Still, color has raised no more profound dilemmas than the diversity of class in the Black community. Social class among African Americans is primarily determined by one's occupation or median income. Thus, it is possible to discern four or five strata—from the underclass to the minuscule upper class.

Not only do these class designations not correspond to white counterparts, but a Black man cannot expect an automatic ally in another Black man of the same class and profession. Brent Wade's protagonist discovers that individual pursuit outweighs group loyalty when he encounters more conflict from one of his own soul brothers than from his white coworkers. Sometimes, as in the selection from Sam Greenlee's *The Spook Who Sat By the Door*, the struggle to overcome the corporate hurdles—this time inside the labyrinth of the CIA—is a lonely endeavor. In fact, it's so lonely that you're forced to internalize the situation and not trust anybody. Introspection guides Stephen Carter through musical presence, with the same scale of influence that Spike Lee has brought in recent years to the film industry.

Lee's skills both in front of and behind the camera are enviable, as demonstrated in *By Any Means Necessary: The Trials and Tribulations of the Making of Malcolm X*, but he's equally adept on the business end, which is something the Black pioneers in rhythm and blues failed to learn. In *The Death of Rhythm and Blues*, Nelson George discloses how whites controlled the music, made the money, and exploited the Black musicians. The lessons of this sad outcome have evidently not been wasted on posse after posse of young rappers. Many of them are becoming extraordinarily proficient as promoters, producers—and like Ice-T, even as authors. The Iceman used rap to get himself out of crime and into rhyme, and he's at the top of his game when he's defining his genre and steps away from the "gangsta" motif.

As we see in the section, "In the Game," Magic Johnson did his best rapping with a basketball, looking one way while passing the other. Throughout his astonishing career, Magic's trademark was always razzle-dazzle. He was still cresting when he tested positive for HIV and said good-bye to the NBA. He had elevated and electrified the game of basketball with his amazing skills and wizardry, and like Jackie Robinson, his personality transcended the arena; his smile won him millions of admirers.

A broad smile, however, is not the most memorable thing about Robinson. Frozen in time is the image of him sliding hard into a base, his face a study in desire. When Robinson broke the color barrier in major league baseball in 1947, it was both a promising beginning and a final inning. Although Blacks were now officially a part of our national pastime, it meant that the old Negro League was on its last legs.

Robinson's steady performance and unflappable demeanor were later adopted by Charlie Sifford on the golf links and Jim Brown on the gridiron. Stifford asks only for a chance to play. Brown, who played nine years without missing a game, never asked for anything—he just ran over or around whoever got in his way.

This common thread of indomitable will and social consciousness was shared by Muhammad Ali and Kareem Abdul Jabbar. Each signaled his strong individuality with a change of name. Their political awareness was collectively realized in the late 1960s when sociologist Harry Edwards coordinated a nationwide revolt of Black athletes. This protest reached its pinnacle in the 1968 Olympics in Mexico when Black track stars mounted the victor's podium and raised their Black-gloved fists in the air. Their audacity would have surprised and probably delighted Satchel Paige who, in his own unhurried way, continually voiced his opposition to the barons of the game.

The final section of *Brotherman*, Part 6, is called *Sankofa—Past as Prologue*. In the Akan culture of West Africa the Sankofa is a bird that faces forward but as he thoughtfully weighs how much affirmative action is good for an individual—what impact it will have on his self-esteem and self-worth.

On a lower rung of the social hierarchy, however, Black workers are trapped in such arduous labor that they would surely welcome some special relief. But the most Hosea Hudson can hope for is a slight raise in pay and a less onerous job. His desperate situation is mirrored by the workers in William Attaway's *Blood on the Forge*. We're not told if these men aspire to become middle class, but Shelby Steele and Ellis Cose seem to be warning us that life as a middle-class African American is not rosy at this level either. One unfortunate consequence of acquiring middle-class values is an inherent disassociation from lower-class Blacks. Their loudest outrage, however, is reserved for their white colleagues who they feel will never accept them as anything more than a "talented nigger," no matter what their accomplishments.

Part 5: *Black Magic* is conjured in four sections. Black men have excelled in every art form: from writing to theater to music and sports. The most significant and influential Black artists seem to know intuitively that they need to buffer their art with political activity. Even those artists who profess to have no interest in things political find it difficult to avoid taking a position on civil rights and the struggle for Black liberation.

In a consistently irreverent satire in "And Bid Him Sing," Ishmael Reed tells how he makes his living as a Black male writer without conceding an inch. For Reed, "Writin' Is Fightin'," and Julius Lester evinces a similar spunk and savvy when declaring his right simply to be a writer—and nothing more.

Reed is not unlike the trickster Cecil Brown imagines in *The Life and Loves of Mr. Jiveass Nigger* in the second section of Part 5, "We Wear the Mask." Ishmael Reed also reminds us of the humorists in Mel Watkins's tome, *On the Real Side*, who know how to laugh at themselves even when the joke's on them. Paul Robeson also wore the mask, blending his remarkable acting talent with his unwavering political convictions. At no point in his illustrious career was he willing to sacrifice either his artistic or political integrity on the altar of American greed and reaction.

Artistic commitment and creative genius are an inextricable part of the lives of the Black musicians featured in "Be-Bop, Doo-Wop and Hip-Hop." Add a touch of elegance to these precious qualities and the stage is set for the magisterial Duke Ellington. Charm and grace were the Duke's calling cards, and like Sidney Bechet, he put nothing else before his love and respect for his music. Miles Davis, the late Prince of Darkness, exemplified these traits with his imcomparable *Black Magic*, and in *Miles*, we experience the man behind the horn. Unlike Bechet, Ellington, and Davis, Quincy Jones has spread his genius across nearly the full expanse of Black music—mastering all forms and constantly inventing new ones. From be-bop to hip-hop, Jones has been a break-

PROLOGUE

STERLING BROWN

Strong Men (Opening Stanzas)

The strong men keep coming—SANDBURG

They dragged you from homeland,
They chained you in coffles,
They huddled you spoon-fashion in filthy hatches,
They sold you to give a few gentlemen ease.

They broke you in like oxen,
They scourged you,
They branded you,
They made your women breeders,
They swelled your numbers with bastards . . .
They taught you the religion they disgraced.

You sang:
    Keep a-inchin' along
    Lak a po' inch worm . . .

You sang:
    Bye and bye
    I'm gonna lay down dis heaby load . . .

You sang:
    Walk togedder, chillen,
    Dontcha git weary . . .
        The strong men keep a-comin' on
        The strong men git stronger.

Brotherman

PART 1

Forefathers

THE GRIOT'S VOICE

GEORGE EDWARD TAIT

I Am a Black Man

I am a Black man
An Afrikan man
My history is that of humanity
My roots predate the calendar
Afrika is my home
My contributions are
    all that is / has been / will be thought (i.e. civilized ideas)
    all that is / has been / will be said (i.e. cultivated words)
    all that is / has been / will be done (i.e. creative actions)

I am a Black man
An Afrikan man
My father's son
My thoughts include his thoughts
My blood and bone and flesh include his
My work include his spirit
I follow in his footsteps
I continue them—
and make my own

I am a Black man
An Afrikan man
Speak not to me of compromise
I am straight line i.e. will
I am upward spiral i.e. growth
I am circle i.e. fulfillment

My goal is perfection
My path is productivity
My vehicle is power

I am a Black man
An Afrikan man
Re-ascending my throne
I tolerate no obstacle
Hindrances do not deter me
I feed on impediments
I shall purge my kingdom

All poachers beware
It's game warden time

I am a Black man
An Afrikan man
Do not attack me with media cries of Chauvinism
(Exploitation is a foreign product—imported by Negroes)
Do not try to change me—I reject the effeminate
Do not ask me to cry—tears are for the trembling and watery eyes anathema
to the warrior
(i.e. the enemy must remain in focus until the enemy no longer remains)
Do not attempt to domesticate me—
I cannot protect you with dishpan hands

I am a Black man
An Afrikan man
In time of war
Present me with harmony but
Speak not to me of peace
Until victory is ours
Present me with unconditional love
That I might
Present us with unconditional liberation

I am a Black man
An Afrikan man
Acknowledge my strength
Offer me not prizes for weakness
Do not encourage the superficial
Tempt me not with diversion
If you are my friend—fight by my side or heal my wounds
If you are my enemy—confess

I am a black man
An Afrikan man
Detained
But not destroyed
Enslaved
But not extinct
Conquered and
Oppressed
But not for long

I am a Black man
An Afrikan man
Fighting for the future / heading for home
Manhood
  Be my momentum
Nationhood
  Be my challenge
Familyhood
  Be my reward

NOUK BASSOMB

IKOP MBOG:

An Account of an African Child's Initiation

My responsibility as a Bassa initiate is to "keep the flame alive in my father's house." "Keep the flame alive in your father's house," are the words I heard over and over again during the three months I spent in the bush learning how to make myself ready to enter adult society. And at the end of this difficult period, the elders said, "Go now, and even if there seems to be no one in the entire compound, keep the flame burning in your father's house." They said it as though I had never heard this injunction before. So this is my duty, my task, my responsibility. When one is assigned such a job, one discovers that the best way to keep a flame alive is to give it away. Everywhere I go, whether in big cities or small villages, people ask me for fire, generally to light a cigarette. I always carry fire with me—a lighter or matches—even though I am not a smoker. I know that when the moment comes and I myself need fire, someone will say, "Here's a light."

"Even if there seems to be no one in the compound, keep the flame alive in your father's house. . . ." But who is my father? Is it my biological father, Bassomb, son of Batama? Is it all the men in my village of my father's age or all the men of his generation throughout the planet? Is it my culture, the culture of the Bassa people, which we call *Mbog Bassa*? African culture? Or human culture, everything human? Or all of the above? Who is my father? Is it purely and simply the Creator? Who is my father? "We give you a container," Samnik Mapuna, my initiator, replied when I asked him these questions. "You fill it up. Whatever you put in it is what will be in there for you. Just go ahead and do the task assigned to you. Fan. Blow. Add dry wood. Remove the ashes. And stay awake."

"But you insisted that the beginning and end of society is in the 'We,' not the 'I,' " I argued when he repeated that each man has to discover for himself what it means to keep the flame alive. "You know what to do, and you do it," he said, but I didn't know what to think. That's when he looked at me as though I were a ghost and, somehow losing his temper, repeated, "Keep talking, boy. In the meantime babies are coughing. Don't you hear the babies coughing? Women will wake up tomorrow morning with sore throats, and elders with pneumonia in their chests. If the people disappear, for whom would you keep the flame alive? We are just praying for the life of the people." He held my hand very paternally, took me aside, and said, "If you want others to accomplish this work for you, why don't you put a goat to roast on the fire? You'll see what will happen. Children will come running. They are always the first to come. And they always come running. Then passersby will stop to rest and have a good meal. Women will also come looking for their children and wondering why the children are drawn to the fire. 'What's going on here?' they will ask, and when they see what's happening, they will take control of the situation. They always do. They will call their daughters and ask them to bring the condiments, all the secret spices and ingredients they keep for great events. Before you know it, the passersby will have water to wash with and quench their thirst. The elders will come also, with kola nuts, palm wine, and lots of stories to tell. Go where you want to go. That fire will stay alive as long as the goat cooks."

Since Africa's contact with the world through Europe, the fire has dimmed. Confronted with the winds of change, it looks as though the fire is dying in my father's house. Young people today are bewildered, especially by the West and its ways. "They seem to have better ways to tie two pieces of wood together," wrote Senegalese writer Sheikh Hamidou Kane, in his noted book *L'Aventure Ambigüe*. "We need to learn how to do this." Learn what, goddammit? "Modern reason, which is science, technique, and technology," answered Senegal's former president and poet, Leopold Sedar Senghor. Perhaps the only good thing about this much-discussed question was the debate, for in embracing the Western view, things fall apart, as Chinua Achebe stated. We have begun to lose our own traditional ways. We have thrown out the baby with the bathwater. This is what makes this adventure, our relationship with the world, especially the West, ambiguous.

If I brought this matter to Samnik Mapuna, he would look at me with that expression I know so well, asking, "Didn't I do a good job with you, O Nouk, son of Bassomb, son of Batama? Didn't you learn anything? Did I waste my time? You talk about the winds of change. Is there wind? Fire has no better friend. Wind? How could wind destroy the fire? That happens only when the fire is covered, overprotected. Expose the fire. The wind will fan and blow it for you. Just add wood. And remove the ashes. Open it up. Today the world is father's compound, the *Mbog* your father's house. Tomorrow the universe will be father's compound, and our planet father's house. Move with the times. Call everyone to the celebration. Welcome everyone around the fire. A people is beaten in battle only when the sons fail to rebuild the shrines which have been destroyed."

HOWARD THURMAN

On Viewing the Coast of Africa

From my cabin window I look out on the full moon, and the ghosts of my forefathers rise and fall with the undulating waves. Across these same waters how many years ago they came! What were the inchoate mutterings locked tight within the circle of their hearts? In the deep, heavy darkness of the foul-smelling hold of the ship, where they could not see the sky, nor hear the night noises, nor feel the warm compassion of the tribe, they held their breath against the agony.

How does the human spirit accommodate itself to desolation? How did they? What tools of the spirit were in their hands with which to cut a path through the wilderness of their despair? If only Death of the body would come to deliver the soul from dying! If some sacred taboo had been defiled and this extended terror was the consequence—there would be no panic in the paying. If some creature of the vast and pulsing jungle had snatched the life away—this would even in its wildest fear be floated by the familiarity of the daily hazard. If Death had come being ushered into life by a terrible paroxysm of pain, all the assurance of the Way of the Tribe would have carried the spirit home on the wings of precious ceremony and holy ritual. But this! Nothing anywhere in all the myths, in all the stories, in all the ancient memory of the race had given hint of this tortuous convulsion. There were no gods to hear, no magic spell of witch doctor to summon; even one's companion in chains muttered his quivering misery in a tongue unknown and a sound unfamiliar.

O my Fathers, what was it like to be stripped of all supports of life save the beating of the heart and the ebb and flow of fetid air in the lungs? In a strange moment, when you suddenly caught your breath, did some intimation from the future give to your spirits a hint of promise? In the darkness did you hear the silent feet of your children beating a melody of freedom to words which you would never know, in a land in which your bones would be warmed again in the depths of the cold earth in which you will sleep unknown, unrealized and alone?

FREDERICK DOUGLASS

Narrative of the Life of Frederick Douglass

I was born in Tuckahoe, near Hillsborough, and about twelve miles from Easton, in Talbot County, Maryland. I have no accurate knowledge of my age, never having seen any authentic record containing it. By far the larger part of the slaves know as little of their ages as horses know of theirs, and it is the wish of most masters within my knowledge to keep their slaves thus ignorant. I do not remember to have ever met a slave who could tell of his birthday. They seldom come nearer to it than planting-time, harvest-time, cherry-time, spring-time, or fall-time. A want of information concerning my own was a source of unhappiness to me even during childhood. The white children could tell their ages. I could not tell why I ought to be deprived of the same privilege. I was not allowed to make any inquiries of my master concerning it. He deemed all such inquiries on the part of a slave improper and impertinent, and evidence of a restless spirit. The nearest estimate I can give makes me now between twenty-seven and twenty-eight years of age. I come to this, from hearing my master say, some time during 1835, I was about seventeen years old.

My mother was named Harriet Bailey. She was the daughter of Isaac and Betsey Bailey, both colored, and quite dark. My mother was of a darker complexion than either my grandmother or grandfather.

My father was a white man. He was admitted to be such by all I ever heard speak of my parentage. The opinion was also whispered that my master was my father; but of the correctness of this opinion, I know nothing; the means of knowing was withheld from me. My mother and I were separated when I was but an infant—before I knew her as my mother. It is a common custom, in the part of Maryland from which I ran away, to part children from their mothers at a very early age. Frequently, before the child has reached its twelfth month, its mother is taken from it, and hired out on some farm a considerable distance off, and the child is placed under the care of an old woman, too old for field labor. For what this separation is done, I do not know, unless it be to hinder the development of the child's affection toward its mother, and to blunt and destroy the natural affection of the mother for the child. This is the inevitable result.

I never saw my mother, to know her as such, more than four or five times in my life; and each of these times was very short in duration, and at night. She was hired by a Mr. Stewart, who lived about twelve miles from my home. She made her journeys to see me in the night, traveling the whole distance on foot, after the performance of her day's work. She was a field hand, and a whipping is the penalty of not being in the field at sunrise, unless a slave has special permission from his or her master to the contrary—a permission which they seldom get, and one that gives to him that gives it the proud name of being a kind master. I do not recollect of ever seeing my mother by the light of day. She was with me in the night. She would lie down with me, and get me to sleep, but long before I waked she was gone. Very little communication ever took place between us. Death soon ended what little we could have while she lived, and with it her hardships and suffering. She died when I was about seven years old, on one of my master's farms, near Lee's Mill. I was not allowed to be present during her illness, at her death, or burial. She was gone long before I knew any thing about it. Never having enjoyed, to any considerable extent, her soothing presence, her tender and watchful care, I received the tidings of her death with much the same emotions I should have probably felt at the death of a stranger.

Called thus suddenly away, she left me without the slightest intimation of who my father was. The whisper that my master was my father, may or may not be true; and, true or false, it is of but little consequence to my purpose whilst the fact remains, in all its glaring odiousness, that slaveholders have ordained, and by law established, that the children of slave women shall in all cases follow the condition of their mothers, and this is done too obviously to administer to their own lusts, and make a gratification of their wicked desires profitable as well as pleasurable; for by this cunning arrangement, the slaveholder, in cases not a few, sustains to his slaves the double relation of master and father.

I know of such cases; and it is worthy of remark that such slaves invariably suffer greater hardships, and have more to contend with, than others. They are, in the first place, a constant offense to their mistress. She is ever disposed to find fault with them; they can seldom do anything to please her; she is never better pleased than when she sees them under the lash, especially when she suspects her husband of showing to his mulatto children favors which he withholds from his black slaves. The master is frequently compelled to sell this class of his slaves, out of deference to the feelings of his white wife; and, cruel as the deed may strike any one to be, for a man to sell his own children to human flesh-mongers, it is often the dictate of humanity for him to do so; for, unless he does this, he must not only whip them himself, but must stand by and see one white son tie up his brother, of but few shades darker complexion than himself, and ply the gory lash to his naked back; and if he lisp one word of disapproval, it is set down to his parental partiality, and only makes a bad matter worse, both for himself and the slave whom he would protect and defend.

Every year brings with it multitudes of this class of slaves. It was doubtless in consequence of a knowledge of this fact, that one great statesman of the south predicted the downfall of slavery by the inevitable laws of population. Whether this prophecy is ever fulfilled or not, it is nevertheless plain that a very different-looking class of people are springing up at the south, and are now held in slavery, from those originally brought to this country from Africa; and if their increase will do no other good, it will do away the force of the argument, that God cursed Ham, and therefore American slavery is right. If the lineal descendants of Ham are alone to be scripturally enslaved, it is certain that slavery at the south must soon become unscriptural; for thousands are ushered into the world, annually, who, like myself, owe their existence to white fathers, and those fathers most frequently their own masters.

I have had two masters. My first master's name was Anthony. I do not remember his first name. He was generally called Captain Anthony—a title which, I presume, he acquired by sailing a craft on the Chesapeake Bay. He was not considered a rich slaveholder. He owned two or three farms, and about thirty slaves. His farms and slaves were under the care of an overseer. The overseer's name was Plummer. Mr. Plummer was a miserable drunkard, a profane swearer, and a savage monster. He always went armed with a cowskin and a heavy cudgel. I have known him to cut and slash the women's heads so horribly, that even master would be enraged at his cruelty, and would threaten to whip him if he did not mind himself. It required extraordinary barbarity on the part of an overseer to affect him. He was a cruel man, hardened by a long life of slaveholding. He would at times seem to take great pleasure in whipping a slave. I have often been awakened at the dawn of day by the most heart-rending shrieks of an own aunt of mine, whom he used to tie up to a joist, and whip upon her naked back till she was literally covered with blood. No words, no tears, no prayers, from his gory victim, seemed to move his iron heart from its bloody purpose. The louder she screamed, the harder he whipped; and where the blood ran fastest, there he whipped longest. He would whip her to make her scream, and whip her to make her hush; and not until overcome by fatigue, would he cease to swing the blood-clotted cowskin. I remember the first time I ever witnessed this horrible exhibition. I was quite a child, but I well remember it. I never shall forget it whilst I remember anything. It was the first of a long series of such outrages, of which I was doomed to be a witness and a participant. It struck me with awful force. It was the blood-stained gate, the entrance to the hell of slavery, through which

I was about to pass. It was a most terrible spectacle. I wish I could commit to paper the feelings with which I beheld it.

This occurrence took place very soon after I went to live with my old master, and under the following circumstances. Aunt Hester went out one night,—where or for what I do not know,—and happened to be absent when my master desired her presence. He had ordered her not to go out evenings, and warned her that she must never let him catch her in company with a young man, who was paying attention to her, belonging to Colonel Lloyd. The young man's name was Ned Roberts, generally called Lloyd's Ned. Why master was so careful of her, may be safely left to conjecture. She was a woman of noble form, and of graceful proportions, having very few equals, and fewer superiors, in personal appearance, among the colored or white women of our neighborhood.

Aunt Hester had not only disobeyed his orders in going out, but had been found in company with Lloyd's Ned; which circumstance, I found, from what he said while whipping her, was the chief offense. Had he been a man of pure morals himself, he might have been thought interested in protecting the innocence of my aunt; but those who knew him will not suspect him of any such virtue. Before he commenced whipping Aunt Hester, he took her into the kitchen, and stripped her from neck to waist, leaving her neck, shoulders, and back, entirely naked. He then told her to cross her hands, calling her at the same time a d——d b——h. After crossing her hands, he tied them with a strong rope, and led her to a stool under a large hook in the joist, put in for the purpose. He made her get upon the stool, and tied her hands to the hook. She now stood fair for his infernal purpose. Her arms were stretched up at their full length, so that she stood upon the ends of her toes. He then said to her, "Now, you d——d b——h, I'll learn you how to disobey my orders!" and after rolling up his sleeves, he commenced to lay on the heavy cowskin, and soon the warm, red blood (amid heart-rending shrieks from her, and horrid oaths from him) came dripping to the floor. I was so terrified and horror-stricken at the sight, that I hid myself in a closet, and dared not venture out till long after the bloody transaction was over. I expected it would be my turn next. It was all new to me. I had never seen anything like it before. I had always lived with my grandmother on the outskirts of the plantation, where she was put to raise the children of the younger women. I had therefore been, until now, out of the way of the bloody scenes that often occurred on the plantation.

(When he was about fifteen years old Douglass was sent by his master to live with and work for a Mr. Covey for a year. It was a bitter experience; young Douglass was frequently and viciously beaten by the depraved Covey.)

I have already intimated that my condition was much worse, during the first six months of my stay at Mr. Covey's, than in the last six. The circumstances leading to the change in Mr. Covey's course toward me form an epoch in my humble history. You have seen how a man was made a slave; you shall see how a slave was made a man. On one of the hottest days of the month of August 1833, Bill Smith, William Hughes, a slave named Eli, and myself, were engaged in fanning wheat. Hughes was clearing the fanned wheat from before the fan, Eli was turning, Smith was feeding, and I was carrying wheat to the fan. The work was simple, requiring strength rather than intellect; yet, to one entirely unused to such work, it came very hard. About three o'clock of that day, I broke down; my strength failed me; I was seized with a violent aching of the head, attended with extreme dizziness; I trembled in every limb. Finding what was coming, I nerved myself up, feeling it would never do to stop work. I stood as long as I could stagger to the hopper with grain. When I could stand no longer, I fell, and felt as if held down by an immense weight. The fan of course stopped; every one had his own work to do; and no one could do the work of the other, and have his own go on at the same time.

Mr. Covey was at the house, about one hundred yards from the treading-yard where we were fanning. On hearing the fan stop, he left immediately, and came to the spot where we were. He hastily inquired what the matter was. Bill answered that I was sick, and there was no one to bring wheat to the fan. I had by this time crawled away under the side of the post and rail-fence by which the yard was enclosed, hoping to find relief by getting out of the sun. He then asked where I was. He was told by one of the hands. He came to the spot, and, after looking at me awhile, asked me what was the matter. I told him as well as I could, for I scarce had strength to speak. He then gave me a savage kick in the side, and told me to get up. I tried to do so, but fell back in the attempt. He gave me another kick, and again told me to rise. I again tried, and succeeded in gaining my feet; but, stooping to get the tub with which I was feeding the fan, I again staggered and fell. While down in this situation, Mr. Covey took up the hickory slat with which Hughes had been striking off the half-bushel measure, and with it gave me a heavy blow upon the head, making a large wound, and the blood ran freely; and with this again told me to get up. I made no effort to comply, having now made up my mind to let him do his worst. In a short time after receiving this blow, my head grew better. Mr. Covey had now left me to my fate. At this moment I resolved, for the first time, to go to my master, enter a complaint, and ask his protection. In order to do this, I must that afternoon walk seven miles; and this, under the circumstances, was truly a severe undertaking. I was exceedingly feeble; made so as much by the kicks and blows which I received, as by the severe fit of sickness to which I had been subjected. I, however, watched my chance, while Covey was looking in an opposite direction, and started for St. Michael's. I succeeded in getting a considerable distance on my way to the woods, when Covey discovered me, and called after me to come back, threatening what he would do if I did not come. I disregarded both his calls and his threats, and made my way to the woods as fast as my feeble state would allow; and thinking I might be overhauled by him if I kept the road, I walked through the woods, keeping far enough from the road to avoid detection, and near enough to prevent losing my way. I had not gone far before my little strength again failed me. I could go no farther. I fell down, and lay for a considerable time. The blood was yet oozing from the wound on my head. For a time I thought I should bleed to death; and think now that I should have done so, but that the blood so matted my hair as to stop the wound. After lying there about three quarters of an hour, I nerved myself up again, and started on my way, through bogs and briers, barefooted and bareheaded, tearing my feet sometimes at nearly every step; and after a journey of about seven miles, occupying some five hours to perform it, I arrived at master's store. I then presented an appearance enough to affect any but a heart of iron. From the crown of my head to my feet, I was covered with blood. My hair was all clotted with dust and blood; my shirt was stiff with blood. My legs and feet were torn in sundry places with briers and thorns, and were also covered with blood. I suppose I looked like a man who had escaped a den of wild beasts, and barely escaped them. In this state I appeared before my master, humbly entreating him to interpose his authority for my protection. I told him all the circumstances as well as I could, and it seemed, as I spoke, at times to affect him. He would then walk the floor, and seek to justify Covey by saying he expected I deserved it. He asked me what I wanted. I told him, to let me get a new home; that as sure as I lived with Mr. Covey again, I should live with but to die with him; that Covey would surely kill me; he was in a fair way for it. Master Thomas ridiculed the idea that there was any danger of Mr. Covey's killing me, and said that he knew Mr. Covey; that he was a good man, and that he could not think of taking me from him; that, should he do so, he would lose the whole year's wages; that I belonged to Mr. Covey for one year, and that I must go back to him, come what might; and that I must not trouble him with any more stories, or that he would himself *get hold of me*. After threatening me thus, he gave me a very large dose of salts, telling me that I might remain in St. Michael's that night (it being quite late), but that I must be off back to Mr. Covey's early in the morning; and that if I did not, he would *get hold of me*, which meant that he would whip me. I remained all night, and, according to his orders, I started off to Covey's in the morning (Saturday morning), wearied in body and broken in spirit. I got no supper that night, or breakfast that morning. I reached Covey's about nine o'clock; and just as I was getting over the fence that divided Mrs. Kemp's fields from ours, out ran Covey with his cowskin, to give me another whipping. Before he could reach me, I succeeded in getting to the cornfield; and as the corn was very high, it afforded me the means of hiding. He seemed very angry, and searched for me a long time. My behavior was altogether unaccountable. He finally gave up the chase, thinking, I suppose, that I must come home for something to eat; he would give himself no further trouble in looking for me. I spent that day mostly in the woods, having the alternative before me,—to go home and be whipped to death, or stay in the woods and be starved to death. That night, I fell in with Sandy Jenkins, a slave with whom I was somewhat acquainted. Sandy had a free wife who lived about four miles from Mr. Covey's; and it being Saturday, he was on his way to see her. I told him my circumstances, and he very kindly invited me to go home with him. I went home with him, and talked this whole matter over, and got his advice as to what course it was best for me to pursue. I found Sandy an old adviser. He told me, with great solemnity, I must go back to Covey; but that before I went, I must go with him into another part of the woods, where there was a certain *root*, which, if I would take some of it with me, carrying it *always on my right side*, would render it impossible for Mr. Covey, or any other white man, to whip me. He said he had carried it for years; and since he had done so, he had never received a blow, and never expected to while he carried it. I at first rejected the idea, that the simple carrying of a root in my pocket would have any such effect as he had said, and was not disposed to take it; but Sandy impressed the necessity with much earnestness, telling me it could do no harm, if it did no good. To please him, I at length took the root, and, according to his direction, carried it upon my right side. This was Sunday morning. I immediately started for home; and upon entering the yard gate, out came Mr. Covey on his way to meeting. He spoke to me very kindly, bade me drive the pigs from a lot near by, and passed on toward the church. Now, this singular conduct of Mr. Covey really made me begin to think that there was something in the *root* which Sandy had given me; and had it been on any other day than Sunday, I could have attributed the conduct to no other cause than the influence of that root; and as it was, I was half inclined to think the *root* to be something more than I at first had taken it to be. All went well till Monday morning. On this morning, the virtue of the *root* was fully tested. Long before daylight, I was called to go and rub, curry, and feed, the horses. I obeyed, and was glad to obey. But whilst thus engaged, whilst in the act of throwing down some blades from the loft, Mr. Covey entered the stable with a long rope; and just as I was half out of the loft, he caught hold of my legs, and was about tying me. As soon as I found what he was up to, I gave a sudden spring, and as I did so, he holding to my legs, I was brought sprawling on the stable floor. Mr. Covey seemed now to think he had me, and could do what he pleased; but at this moment—from whence came the spirit I don't know—I resolved to fight; and, suiting my action to the resolution, I seized Covey hard by the throat; and as I did so, I rose. He held on to me, and I to him. My resistance was so entirely unexpected, that Covey seemed taken all aback. He trembled like a leaf. This gave me assurance, and I held him uneasy, causing the blood to run where I touched him with the ends of my fingers. Mr. Covey soon called out to Hughes for help. Hughes came, and, while Covey held me, attempted to tie my right hand. While he was in the act of doing so, I watched my chance, and gave him a heavy kick close under the ribs. This kick fairly sickened Hughes, so that he left me in the hands of Mr. Covey. This kick had the effect of not only weakening Hughes, but Covey also. When he saw Hughes bending over with pain, his courage quailed. He asked me if I meant to persist in my resistance. I told him I did, come what might; that he had used me like a brute for six months, and that I was determined to be used so no longer. With that, he strove to drag me to a stick that was lying just out of the stable door. He meant to knock me down. But just as he was leaning over to get the stick, I seized him with both hands by his collar, and brought him by a sudden snatch to the ground. By this time, Bill came. Covey called upon him for assistance. Bill wanted to know what he could do. Covey said, "Take hold of him, take hold of him!" Bill said his master hired him out to work, and not to help to whip me; so he left Covey and myself to fight our own battle out. We were at it for nearly two hours. Covey at length let me go, puffing and blowing at a great rate, saying that if I had not resisted, he would not have whipped me half so much. The truth was, that he had not whipped me at all. I considered him as getting entirely the worst end of the bargain; for he had drawn no blood from me, but I had from him. The whole six months afterwards, that I spent with Mr. Covey, he never laid the weight of his finger upon me in anger. He would occasionally say, he didn't want to get hold of me again. "No," thought I, "you need not; for you will come off worse than you did before."

This battle with Mr. Covey was the turning-point in my career as a slave. It rekindled the few expiring embers of freedom, and revived within me a sense of my own manhood. It recalled the departed self-confidence, and inspired me again with a determination to be free. The gratification afforded by the triumph was a full compensation for whatever else might follow, even death itself. He only can understand the deep satisfaction which I experienced, who has himself repelled by force the bloody arm of slavery. I felt as I never felt before. It was a glorious resurrection, from the tomb of slavery, to the heaven of freedom. My long-crushed spirit rose, cowardice departed, bold defiance took its place; and I now resolved that, however long I might remain a slave in form, the day had passed forever when I could be a slave in fact. I did not hesitate to let it be known of me, that the white man who expected to succeed in whipping, must also succeed in killing me.

From this time I was never again what might be called fairly whipped, though I remained a slave four years afterwards. I had several fights, but was never whipped.

BOOKER T. WASHINGTON

Up from Slavery

BOYHOOD DAYS

After the coming of freedom there were two points upon which practically all the people on our place were agreed, and I find that this was generally true throughout the South: that they must change their names, and that they must leave the old plantation for at least a few days or weeks in order that they might really feel sure that they were free.

In some way a feeling got among the coloured people that it was far from proper for them to bear the surname of their former owners, and a great many of them took other surnames. This was one of the first signs of freedom. When they were slaves, a coloured person was simply called "John" or "Susan." There was seldom occasion for more than the use of one name. If "John" or "Susan" belonged to a white man by the name of "Hatcher," sometimes he was called "John Hatcher," or as often "Hatcher's John." But there was a feeling that "John Hatcher" or "Hatcher's John" was not the proper title by which to denote a freeman; and so in many cases "John Hatcher" was changed to "John S. Lincoln" or "John S. Sherman," the initial "S" standing for no name, it being simply a part of what the coloured man proudly called his "entitles."

As I have stated, most of the coloured people left the old plantation for a short while at least, so as to be sure, it seemed, that they could leave and try their freedom on to see how it felt. After they had remained away for a time, many of the older slaves, especially, returned to their old homes and made some kind of contract with their former owners by which they remained on the estate.

My mother's husband, who was the stepfather of my brother John and myself, did not belong to the same owners as did my mother. In fact, he seldom came to our plantation. I remember seeing him there perhaps once a year, that being about Christmas time. In some way, during the war, by running away and following the Federal soldiers, it seems, he found his way into the new state of West Virginia. As soon as freedom was declared, he sent for my mother to come to the Kanawha Valley, in West Virginia. At that time a journey from Virginia over the mountains to West Virginia was rather a tedious and in some cases a painful undertaking. What little clothing and few household goods we had were placed in a cart, but the children walked the greater portion of the distance, which was several hundred miles.

I do not think any of us ever had been very far from the plantation, and the taking of a long journey into another state was quite an event. The parting from our former owners and the members of our own race on the plantation was a serious occasion. From the time of our parting till their death we kept up a correspondence with the older members of the family, and in later years we have kept in touch with those who were the younger members. We were several weeks making the trip, and most of the time we slept in the open air and did our cooking over a log fire out of doors. One night I recall that we camped near an abandoned log cabin, and my mother decided to build a fire in that for cooking, and afterward to make a "pallet" on the floor for our sleeping. Just as the fire had gotten well started a large black snake fully a yard and a half long dropped down the chimney and ran out on the floor. Of course we at once abandoned that cabin. Finally we reached our destination—a little town called Malden, which is about five miles from Charleston, the present capital of the state.

At that time salt-mining was the great industry in that part of West Virginia, and the little town of Malden was right in the midst of the salt-furnaces. My stepfather had already secured a job at a salt-furnace, and he had also secured a little cabin for us to live in. Our new house was no better than the one we had left on the old plantation in Virginia. In fact, in one respect it was worse. Notwithstanding the poor condition of our plantation cabin, we were at all times sure of pure air. Our new home was in the midst of a cluster of cabins crowded closely together, and as there were no sanitary regulations, the filth about the cabins was often intolerable. Some of our neighbours were coloured people, and some were the poorest and most ignorant and degraded white people. It was a motley mixture. Drinking, gambling, quarrels, fights, and shockingly immoral practices were frequent. All who lived in the little town were in one way or another connected with the salt business. Though I was a mere child, my stepfather put me and my brother at work in one of the furnaces. Often I began work as early as four o'clock in the morning.

The first thing I ever learned in the way of book knowledge was while working in this salt-furnace. Each salt-packer had his barrels marked with a certain number. The number allotted to my stepfather was "18." At the close of the day's work the boss of the packers would come around and put "18" on each of our barrels, and I soon learned to recognize that figure wherever I saw it, and after a while got to the point where I could make that figure, though I knew nothing about any other figures or letters.

From the time that I can remember having any thoughts about anything, I recall that I had an intense longing to learn to read. I determined, when quite a small child, that, if I accomplished nothing else in life, I would in some way get enough education to enable me to read common books and newspapers. Soon after we got settled in some manner in our new cabin in West Virginia,

I induced my mother to get hold of a book for me. How or where she got it I do not know, but in some way she procured an old copy of Webster's "blue-back" spelling-book, which contained the alphabet, followed by such meaningless words as "ab," "ba," "ca," "da." I began at once to devour this book, and I think that it was the first one I ever had in my hands. I had learned from somebody that the way to begin to read was to learn the alphabet, so I tried in all the ways I could think of to learn it,—all of course without a teacher, for I could find no one to teach me. At that time there was not a single member of my race anywhere near us who could read, and I was too timid to approach any of the white people. In some way, within a few weeks, I mastered the greater portion of the alphabet. In all my efforts to learn to read my mother shared fully my ambition, and sympathized with me and aided me in every way that she could. Though she was totally ignorant, so far as mere book knowledge was concerned, she had high ambitions for her children, and a large fund of good, hard, common sense which seemed to enable her to meet and master every situation. If I have done anything in life worth attention, I feel sure that I inherited the disposition from my mother.

In the midst of my struggles and longing for an education, a young coloured boy who had learned to read in the state of Ohio came to Malden. As soon as the coloured people found out that he could read, a newspaper was secured, and at the close of nearly every day's work this young man would be surrounded by a group of men and women who were anxious to hear him read the news contained in the papers. How I used to envy this man! He seemed to me to be the one young man in all the world who ought to be satisfied with his attainments.

About this time the question of having some kind of a school opened for the coloured children in the village began to be discussed by members of the race. As it would be the first school for Negro children that had ever been opened in that part of Virginia, it was, of course, to be a great event, and the discussion excited the widest interest. The most perplexing question was where to find a teacher. The young man from Ohio who had learned to read the papers was considered, but his age was against him. In the midst of the discussion about a teacher, another young coloured man from Ohio, who had been a soldier, in some way found his way into town. It was soon learned that he possessed considerable education, and he was engaged by the coloured people to teach their first school. As yet no free schools had been started for coloured people in that section, hence each family agreed to pay a certain amount per month, with the understanding that the teacher was to "board 'round"—that is, spend a day with each family. This was not bad for the teacher, for each family tried to provide the very best on the day the teacher was to be its guest. I recall that I looked forward with an anxious appetite to the "teacher's day" at our little cabin.

This experience of a whole race beginning to go to school for the first time, presents one of the most interesting studies that has ever occurred in connection with the development of any race. Few people who were not right in the midst of the scenes can form any exact idea of the intense desire which the people of my race showed for an education. As I have stated, it was a whole race trying to go to school. Few were too young, and none too old, to make the attempt to learn. As fast as any kind of teachers could be secured, not only were day-schools filled, but night-schools as well. The great ambition of the older people was to try to learn to read the Bible before they died. With this end in view, men and women who were fifty or seventy-five years old would often be found in the night-school. Sunday-schools were formed soon after freedom, but the principal book studied in the Sunday-school was the spelling-book. Day-school, night-school, Sunday-school, were always crowded, and often many had to be turned away for want of room.

The opening of the school in the Kanawha Valley, however, brought to me one of the keenest disappointments that I ever experienced. I had been working in a salt-furnace for several months, and my stepfather had discovered that I had a financial value, and so, when the school opened, he decided that he could not spare me from my work. This decision seemed to cloud my every ambition. The disappointment was made all the more severe by reason of the fact that my place of work was where I could see the happy children passing to and from school, mornings and afternoons. Despite this disappointment, however, I determined that I would learn something, anyway. I applied myself with greater earnestness than ever to the mastering of what was in the "blue-back" speller.

My mother sympathized with me in my disappointment, and sought to comfort me in all the ways she could, and to help me find a way to learn. After a while I succeeded in making arrangements with the teacher to give me some lessons at night, after the day's work was done. These night lessons were so welcome that I think I learned more at night than the other children did during the day. My own experiences in the night-school gave me faith in the night-school idea, with which, in after years, I had to do both at Hampton and Tuskegee. But my boyish heart was still set upon going to the day-school, and I let no opportunity slip to push my case. Finally I won, and was permitted to go to the school in the day for a few months, with the understanding that I was to rise early in the morning and work in the furnace till nine o'clock, and return immediately after school closed in the afternoon for at least two more hours of work.

The schoolhouse was some distance from the furnace, and as I had to work till nine o'clock, and the school opened at nine, I found myself in a difficulty. School would always be begun before I reached it, and sometimes my class had recited. To get around this difficulty I yielded to a temptation for which most people, I suppose, will condemn me; but since it is a fact, I might as well state it. I have great faith in the power and influence of facts. It is seldom that anything is permanently gained by holding back a fact. There was a large clock in a little office in the furnace. This clock, of course, all the hundred or more workmen depended upon to regulate their hours of beginning and ending the day's work. I got the idea that the way for me to reach school on time was to move the clock hands from half-past eight up to the nine o'clock mark. This I found myself doing morning after morning, till the furnace "boss" discovered that something was wrong, and locked the clock in a case. I did not mean to inconvenience anybody. I simply meant to reach that school-house in time.

When, however, I found myself at the school for the first time, I also found myself confronted with two other difficulties. In the first place, I found that all of the other children wore hats or caps on their heads, and I had neither hat nor cap. In fact, I do not remember that up to the time of going to school I had ever worn any kind of covering upon my head, nor do I recall that either I or anybody else had even thought anything about the need of covering for my head. But, of course, when I saw how all the other boys were dressed, I began to feel quite uncomfortable. As usual, I put the case before my mother, and she explained to me that she had no money with which to buy a "store hat," which was a rather new institution at that time among the members of my race and was considered quite the thing for young and old to own, but that she would find a way to help me out of the difficulty. She accordingly got two pieces of "homespun" (jeans) and sewed them together, and I was soon the proud possessor of my first cap.

The lesson that my mother taught me in this has always remained with me, and I have tried as best I could to teach it to others. I have always felt proud, whenever I think of the incident, that my mother had strength of character enough not to be led into the temptation of seeming to be that which she was not—of trying to impress my schoolmates and others with the fact that she was able to buy me a "store hat" when she was not. I have always felt proud that she refused to go into debt for that which she did not have the money to pay for. Since that time I have owned many kinds of caps and hats, but never one of which I have felt so proud as of the cap made of the two pieces of cloth sewed together by my mother. I have noted the fact, but without satisfaction, I need not add, that several of the boys who began their careers with "store hats" and who were my schoolmates and used to join in the sport that was made of me because I had only a "homespun" cap, have ended their careers in the penitentiary, while others are not able now to buy any kind of hat.

My second difficulty was with regard to my name, or rather *a* name. From the time when I could remember anything, I had been called simply "Booker." Before going to school it had never occurred to me that it was needful or appropriate to have an additional name. When I heard the school-roll called, I noticed that all of the children had at least two names, and some of them indulged in what seemed to me the extravagance of having three. I was in deep perplexity, because I knew that the teacher would demand of me at least two names, and I had only one. By the time the occasion came for the enrolling of my name, an idea occurred to me which I thought would make me equal to the situation; and so, when the teacher asked me what my full name was, I calmly told him "Booker Washington," as if I had been called by that name all my life; and by that name I have since been known. Later in life I found that my mother had given me the name of "Booker Taliaferro" soon after I was born, but in some way that part of my name seemed to disappear, and for a long while was forgotten, but as soon as I found out about it I revived it, and made my full name "Booker Taliaferro Washington." I think there are not many men in our country who have had the privilege of naming themselves in the way that I have.

More than once I have tried to picture myself in the position of a boy or man with an honoured and distinguished ancestry which I could trace back through a period of hundreds of years, and who had not only inherited a name, but fortune and a proud family homestead; and yet I have sometimes had the feeling that if I had inherited these, and had been a member of a more popular race, I should have been inclined to yield to the temptation of depending upon my ancestry and my colour to do for me which I should do for myself. Years ago I resolved that because I had no ancestry myself I would leave a record of which my children would be proud, and which might encourage them to still higher effort.

The world should not pass judgment upon the Negro, and especially the Negro youth, too quickly or too harshly. The Negro boy has obstacles, discouragements, and temptations to battle with that are little known to those not situated as he is. When a white boy undertakes a task, it is taken for granted that he will succeed. On the other hand, people are usually surprised if the Negro boy does not fail. In a word, the Negro youth starts out with the presumption against him.

The influence of ancestry, however, is important in helping forward any individual or race, if too much reliance is not placed upon it. Those who constantly direct attention to the Negro youth's moral weaknesses, and compare his advancement with that of white youths, do not consider the influence of the memories which cling about the old family homesteads. I have no idea, as I have stated elsewhere, who my grandmother was. I have, or have had, uncles and aunts and cousins, but I have no knowledge as to what most of them are. My case will illustrate that of hundreds of thousands of black people in every part of our country. The very fact that the white boy is conscious that, if he fails in life, he will disgrace the whole family record, extending back through many generations, is of tremendous value in helping him to resist temptations. The fact that the individual has behind and surrounding him proud family history and connection serves as a stimulus to help him to overcome obstacles when striving for success.

The time that I was permitted to attend school during the day was short, and my attendance was irregular. It was not long before I had to stop attending day-school altogether, and devote all of my time again to work. I resorted to the night-school again. In fact, the greater part of the education I secured in my boyhood was gathered through the night-school after my day's work was done. I had difficulty often in securing a satisfactory teacher. Sometimes, after I had secured someone to teach me at night, I would find, much to my disappointment, that the teacher knew but little more than I did. Often I would have to walk several miles at night in order to recite my night-school lessons. There was never a time in my youth, no matter how dark and discouraging the days might be, when one resolve did not continually remain with me, and that was a determination to secure an education at any cost.

Soon after we moved to West Virginia, my mother adopted into our family, notwithstanding our poverty, an orphan boy, to whom afterward we gave the name of James B. Washington. He has ever since remained a member of the family.

After I had worked in the salt-furnace for some time, work was secured for me in a coal-mine which was operated mainly for the purpose of securing fuel for the salt-furnace. Work in the coal-mine I always dreaded. One reason for this was that anyone who worked in a coal-mine was always unclean, at least while at work, and it was a very hard job to get one's skin clean after the day's work was over. Then it was fully a mile from the opening of the coal-mine to the face of the coal, and all, of course, was in the blackest darkness. I do not believe that one ever experiences anywhere else such darkness as he does in a coal-mine. The mine was divided into a large number of different "rooms" or departments, and, as I never was able to learn the location of all these "rooms," I many times found myself lost in the mine. To add to the horror of being lost, sometimes my light would go out, and then, if I did not happen to have a match, I would wander about in the darkness until by chance I found someone to give me a light. The work was not only hard, but it was dangerous. There was always the danger of being blown to pieces by a premature explosion of powder, or of being crushed by falling slate. Accidents from one or the other of these causes were frequently occurring, and this kept me in constant fear. Many children of the tenderest years were compelled then, as is now true I fear, in most coal-mining districts, to spend a large part of their lives in these coal-mines, with little opportunity to get an education; and, what is worse, I have often noted that, as a rule, young boys who begin life in a coal-mine are often physically and mentally dwarfed. They soon lose ambition to do anything else than to continue as a coal-miner.

In those days, and later as a young man, I used to try to picture in my imagination the feelings and ambitions of a white boy with absolutely no limit placed upon his aspirations and activities. I used to envy the white boy who had no obstacles placed in the way of his becoming a Congressman, Governor, Bishop, or President by reason of the accident of his birth or race. I used to picture the way that I would act under such circumstances; how I would begin at the bottom and keep rising until I reached the highest round of success.

In later years, I confess that I do not envy the white boy as I once did. I have learned that success is to be measured not so much by the position that one has reached in life as by the obstacles which he has overcome while trying to succeed. Looked at from this standpoint, I almost reach the conclusion that often the Negro boy's birth and connection with an unpopular race is an advantage, so far as real life is concerned. With few exceptions, the Negro youth must work harder and must perform his task even better than a white youth in order to secure recognition. But out of the hard and unusual struggle which he is compelled to pass, he gets a strength, a confidence, that one misses whose pathway is comparatively smooth by reason of birth and race.

From any point of view, I had rather be what I am, a member of the Negro race, than be able to claim membership with the most favoured of any other race. I have always been made sad when I have heard members of any race claiming rights and privileges, or certain badges of distinction, on the ground simply that they were members of this or that race, regardless of their own individual worth or attainments. I have been made to feel sad for such persons because I am conscious of the fact that mere connection with what is known as a superior race will not permanently carry an individual forward unless he has individual worth, and mere connection with what is regarded as an inferior race will not finally hold an individual back if he possesses intrinsic, individual merit. Every persecuted individual and race should get much consolation out of the great human law, which is universal and eternal, that merit, no matter under what skin found, is in the long run, recognized and rewarded. This I have said here, not to call attention to myself as an individual, but to the race to which I am proud to belong.

RANDALL KENAN

Let the Dead Bury Their Dead

THIS FAR
or, a Body in Motion

A man who wishes to make a profession of goodness in everything must necessarily come to grief among so many who are not good. Therefore it is necessary for a prince, who wishes to maintain himself, to learn how not to be good, and to use this knowledge and not use it, according to the necessity of the case.

—CHAPTER XV, "OF THE THINGS OF WHICH MEN, ESPECIALLY PRINCES, ARE PRAISED OR BLAMED," *THE PRINCE*, NICCOLÒ MACHIAVELLI

October 20, 1915. You will be dead in less than a month, and though you do not know it you sense It, this crouching, mystery-shrouded doom. It has been your constant companion, a shadow-cloaked marvel, since 1867 when you first stepped inside General Ruffner's house to be a houseboy—a post-Emancipation slave is more accurate; but a life better than life in the salt mines or the coal mines, better than the streets of Malden, West Virginia; better than the smell of urine and rotting garbage and the sounds of drunken men raising hell. People like to think the sweet smell of success drove you, drives you. You know better, don't you? You know who has been at your side all these years.

You are tired and sick and fatigued with fighting, with moving. You have been in constant motion since 1856, *fifty-nine years*, as if from the first day you understood the Newtonian axiom: A body in motion tends to stay in motion. Yet you can't seem to slacken the pace. And why bother?

Your traveling secretary, Nathan Hunt, a Tuskegee product, tells you you are nearing Tims Creek. You wonder: Why? Why did you come? After all these years, why did you make this special trip, out of the way, to see these two, Elihu & Tabitha McElwaine? It has been thirty-three years. Eighteen and seventy-two. Fall. Hampton Normal and Agricultural Institute. You have come so far since then it seems someone else's history, but you have told the tale so many times, so many ways, made the story of the unwashed little peasant boy from the coal mines of West Virginia such a powerful weapon in the battle to become Emperor de facto of the Negro race—the truth, full of duplicity and sin, is of little use to you now. Does it sting to remember?

So ignorant and pitiful you were then, the shame of it still lingers like the smell of shit on the fingers, just like the hunger which still gnaws beneath your wool suit, tailor-made for you in London, beneath the solid-gold watch and chain that dangles from your vest pouch, a gift from E. Julia Emery, one of your many wealthy white patrons—but it gnaws and bites and growls just the same. You cannot rid yourself of it, can you?

You feel the train slow its *chu-chug-chug*, and from the window you note how different the North Carolina forests are from those in Alabama, how like Virginia's, the pines lusher, the undergrowth more sparse. Nathan begins to pack up the papers at which you have stared absently since leaving D.C., your mind wandering, wondering what the two of them will look like after so many years; and how you will look in their eyes.

"Dr. Washington, sir. We've arrived."

I was completely out of money when I graduated. In company with other Hampton students, I secured a place as a table waiter in a summer hotel in Connecticut, and managed to borrow enough money with which to get there. I had not been in this hotel long before I found out that I knew practically nothing about waiting on a hotel table. The head waiter, however, supposed that I was an accomplished waiter. He soon gave me charge of a table at which there sat four or five wealthy and rather aristocratic people. My ignorance of how to wait upon them was so apparent that they scolded me in such a severe manner that I became frightened and left their table, leaving them sitting there without food. As a result of this I was reduced from the position of waiter to that of a dishcarrier.

—CHAPTER IV, "HELPING OTHERS," *UP FROM SLAVERY*

Tims Creek is like so many of the other towns you have stepped into from a train. In 1909 you had fulfilled a commitment to the Standard Oil magnate Henry H. Rogers, touring small Virginia towns from Norfolk to Charleston. Certainly, you hated every minute of it: the poverty, the stench of unclean bodies, the overcooked food, the humidity, the messiah-expectant look of black faces—boys and girls and rheumy-eyed old men—who regarded you as something of a king, a wizard. Wizard, indeed. Did they have any idea how much sacrifice it took to . . . ?

"Dr. Washington. Booker, if I can presume to call you that after so many years. You can't know how glad I am you could come. I knew you would."

"My *good* Tabitha. If you didn't call me Booker, I would be offended. And how on earth could I possibly not come? I'm honored that you asked me."

How do you see her? Thirty-three years is a long time. Perhaps you want to preserve an image of her unaffected by the years: the dark molasses of her slender and dimpled face unsullied by time; her figure still shapely. But you have too keen an eye. You must see time in her face, the comfortable weight of small-town inertia in her hips, the curve of her jaw obscured by gravity. No, at sixty she is not the same; you are not the same. Yet do you sense the same spirit, in her eyes? They absorb you. Yes.

You doff your hat and take her hand and kiss it, and her smile—as you take note, or are you merely beginning to create an illusion?—still quickens you and promises to haunt you late in the evening.

"Booker, old man. It's good to see you again. At last."

The grip of Elihu McElwaine has to be one of the stronger ones you have encountered in years—and you have shaken an incalculable multitude of hands, from Buffalo to Biloxi. His hands are not rough, but they have known tremendous work. Perhaps you see that time has affected him even more deeply than Tabitha. Where once his face had an impish glow, it seems now solidly grave, not unhandsome, in fact very handsome, dark as his sister, with broad features like those masks from the Dark Continent; and unmistakably there lurks behind those jet eyes—you can sense it straightaway—a regal competence and pride. You have always feared Elihu McElwaine, haven't you? And now, your large beige hand vised in his massive midnight fist, despite your titles, your wealth, your influence, your power . . . surely you must flinch inwardly?

"Come, Booker." Tabitha grasps your hand as she did when you were a freshman, walking very near you. Her voice drops to a whisper as if conspiring, and you are engulfed within a calm. "You'll be staying with us, in my father's house. The ceremony is this evening."

That voice. You have had three wives. Fanny, who died in '84; Olivia, who died in '89; and Margaret, sweet, good, witty, clever, eminently competent Margaret, who lectured you severely when she discovered you were making this trip, after the doctors had prescribed rest: rest rest rest rest. Three wives you have had, and none of them with a voice like Tabitha's. You have carried it around with you for thirty-three years; a voice you wish your mother, Janie—that sad, coarse woman, mumbling and swallowing words—had possessed; a husky, night-fluted sound, rimmed by a faint North Carolina curve on the vowels and *g*'s; slow, deliberate, schooled yet soft:

"Again, I want you to know how much this means to the people of Tims Creek. And to me, of course. It's not much of a town, no more than a thousand people. But it's home to some good souls. I know how busy you are, Booker, your schedule has to be an—"

"Yes, Booker." The interjection of Elihu's voice makes you start. "From what I hear, you're practically everywhere at once. Even now you're in New York and London and Paris and Cleveland *and* Tuskegee. Probably even Japan. Quite a feat." Over the years his voice has roughened, no doubt peppered by whiskey and tobacco.

You see him smile, but you know there is an innuendo in his *bon geste*. He has always been a subtle one. In fact, you learned to be subtle from Elihu McElwaine. And from reports you have gotten through "the Machine"—God! how you hate that epithet, but it's so useful, so accurate—he is even more subtle now, more dangerous.

You step into the buggy, Nathan next to you, Tabitha facing you, Elihu driving the team, and you all start down the bumpy road, and perhaps for a moment you have lost sight of It, now that you are spellbound—not by the present but by the steady re-creation of the past you are conjuring; and as you whiff the dray horse odor, you feel that once again you are that frightened boy shunned by the other students, more so even than your fellow Indian students, the same boy shown mysterious kindnesses by these dark and strange twins, benefiting immeasurably from their patience and their plenty—and you feel a twinge of sublimated anger.

Perhaps now, thirty-three years later, you think you will truly discover who they are.

I shall always remember a bit of advice given me by Mr. George W. Campbell, the white man to whom I have referred as the one who induced General Armstrong to send me to Tuskegee. Soon after I entered upon the work Mr. Campbell said to me, in his fatherly way: "Washington, always remember that credit is capital."

—CHAPTER IX, "ANXIOUS DAYS AND SLEEPLESS NIGHTS," *UP FROM SLAVERY*

"But, Dr. Washington, really I must protest."

Emmett's voice has always annoyed you, that thinly disguised Texas drawl. But Emmett J. Scott is damned efficient and as smart as a needle and his memory is infallible and in the end he works even harder than you, *than even you*, which is in itself phenomenal.

For this reason alone you made him your chief lieutenant. But if you had known that he would not be the Board of Trustees' choice for your successor after your death; that he would merely step aside and allow "the Machine" to grind to a halt and allow Tuskegee to become slowly a sad relic of your once-power; that he would betray you, repeatedly, even now as he speaks . . . would you have chosen him? Was the idea of crowning an heir apparent too much of an invitation to that ever-crouching Shadow? Or were you just too busy being busy?

"Mr. Scott. *I'm going to North Carolina*, and that's final."

"But, sir, begging your pardon, there is no particular *reason*. There will be no real publicity as I see it; you will have to cut your meeting in Washington short; you will have to come all the way back here for the board meeting—you know Mr. Carnegie is expected—and then you will have to race back up to Connect—"

"I am fully aware of my obligations, Mr. Scott, and I'm going."

"We will have to arrange guards—"

"No guards."

"But—"

"That will be all, Mr. Scott."

"Yes, sir."

After Emmett left your office that day, did you take out Tabitha's letter? Admire her handwriting—elegant, spidery, precise—which reminded you of how she helped you with your own penmanship, now impeccable? You reread it for probably the fiftieth time, and it thrills you like the first:

> Dear Dr. Washington,
>
> I know it has been some time since our last communication, but I want you to know that you are often in my thoughts. I fondly recall our days at Hampton, and though I know I sound as if I am flattering myself and my brother, I remember our predicting that you would go far in accomplishing great and excellent things, and am happy to see that prediction come to fruition.
>
> As you may remember I am mistress of the colored school here in my hometown and praise God we have almost completed a new three-room structure so that we will no longer need to use the church. I know this is short notice for one so highly sought after, but I was wondering if you might consider coming for the inauguration

in October. Indeed, if you could come I am certain I could with great ease persuade other dignitaries in the state to attend which will in the end insure a bright future for the Tims Creek Colored School.

I in no way intend to compare my modest establishment with your grand institution, but I'm very certain you of all people will appreciate the dire need of support, in all its guises for such endeavors, and that it is of consummate importance for our people.

Please do not look upon this invitation as a nepotistic attempt from those dimly remembered acquaintances of your youth to capitalize on your fame and good fortune; rather envision it as an opportunity to raise up yet another handful of dark good minds into the enlightenment of learning as you and I and others have been so providentially met.

I remain,
most truly
and sincerely
yours,
Tabitha
McElwaine

Surely, your first impulse was to think: McElwaine? She never married! And to wonder: Why? You imagined her voice and her effect on you in those early years, the first woman who made you feel worthy of attention, who made time for you and cleared out a space for you among the minutiae of her life. . . . Did it never occur to you that you might have, at one time, courted or even considered *marrying* her? The very thought now seems ludicrous, somehow striking you as profane.

You have received five letters from her in thirty-three years. Once after the Atlanta speech made headlines; once after your dinner at the White House with Theodore Roosevelt made even more headlines; once after Fanny's death; once after Olivia's death; and this one now.

You said *yes* instantly, not caring about the date or any possible conflicts it might cause—they could be worked out; and when she answered she also informed you that her brother, Elihu, who had been working and traveling all about, would be home, and perhaps you felt a strange rejoicing and loathing, as if you knew this was a summing up, as if you had been sent out from them three decades thence and now had to make an accounting of your deeds.

An accounting. That day in Tuskegee, behind your baronial desk in your baronial office, surrounded by students and workers, a scene in some ways reminiscent of an old-time planter's farm—who had called it "Tuskegee Plantation"?—you sat, absolute master of so many men's fates, covert appointer of judges, deliverer of votes, invisible dispenser of funds. Did you nonetheless struggle with the sensation that you might not measure up? But you have always had that sensation, that you might fail at any given moment, that It might collect you and sweep you away. Haven't you?

This sensation has kept you in motion:

If my life in the past has meant anything in the lifting up of my people and the bringing about of better relations between your race and mine, I assure you from this day it will mean doubly more. In the economy of God there is but one standard by which an individual can succeed—there is but one for a race. . . . We are to be tested in our patience, our forbearance, our power to endure wrong, to withstand temptations, to economize, to acquire and use skill; in our ability to compete, to succeed in commerce, to disregard the superficial for the real, the appearance for the substance, to be great and yet small, learned and yet simple, high and yet the servant of all.

—SPEECH UPON RECEIVING HONORARY DEGREE OF MASTER OF ARTS FROM HARVARD UNIVERSITY, 1896

The little school is packed to overflowing: they spill out the doors, people sit in the windows. As they glare at you in awe perhaps you think of that night in New York, just four years ago, when without provocation or logic a white man burst from his building on West 66th Street and began beating you. All your education and friends and good manners did not stop it, could not spare you the humiliation of arrest by the authorities . . . for why, even in New York City, would they believe a black man's word over the word of a white man? Certainly, this thought makes the presence of these wide-eyed gazers even the more bewildering.

The Governor could not make it, alas, but the Secretary of State of North Carolina brings his greetings along with those of the Speaker of the House, who wanted to attend but couldn't . . . the North Carolina Superintendent of Schools is present, as is a local white Presbyterian minister who said you had been a great inspiration in his ministry—how many white ministers have told you this to date?—and who asked you to sign a copy of *Up From Slavery* . . . there are a number of other whites whose names you have instantly forgotten and who peer at you as if you were John the Baptist himself; they sit in the front row. While behind them seethes the ubiquitous, overwhelming sea of black: coal black, nut black, yellowish black, black black. The faces. Always the same, aren't they, always the look of slavish wonder?

Your act is a magic show. Mesmerizing. Spellbinding. You start out somewhat folksy, down-home—without, of course, losing your magisterial air, without allowing them to forget who you are; you rise in grand oratorical fashion to the heights of Cicero and Seneca, to cadenced, rounded phrases, remembering the lines about the separate fingers and the unified fist, which made you famous, and the nugget about "Cast down your buckets where you are," which made you notorious. In truth you end not too far from where you began, as it is so damnably hot and stuffy in this pathetic little room—closing on the cavalry cry of hope, self-help, self-esteem, work work work work work, the only salvation of the poor, of the race.

As you step down to the cheers and palpitating applause and seek your chair, do you think of your critics and question how far work work work work work will really take these people? Work worked for you because you were ruthless, conniving, unscrupulous, untiring, and always brilliant. Without a doubt you know this. How many Negro men and women did you trample just to hold on? Just to hold on? It seems the more powerful the Machine becomes, the harder it is to remember your original goals. Why have a Machine which requires more and more time and effort to keep oiled and running when it seems to do so little good for the swarthy faces that always confront you?

Perhaps you never ask yourself these questions. You are always so busy going going going going going . . .

Tabitha thanks you and the audience, and now the real work commences: the shaking of the hands, the answering of asinine questions, the kissing of smelly babies. Emmett and Margaret have been trying—in their magical, invisible, effective way—to eliminate this grueling task, to have you whisked away in a twinkling of an eye; but how Du Bois and Trotter would love that! *The imperial Mr. Washington does not even deign to shake the hands of those he has so self-importantly condemned to sharecropping and blacksmithing.* No. You will clasp and grab till your hands are raw and aching, the man of the hour.

But today, as you pump and grin royally, does your mind drift back to Elihu & Tabitha in 1872? They had been a year ahead of you at college, twins of means, dressed always grandly, who cast an aura of mystery and wonder everywhere they went—or so it seemed to you. Whereas you had to work as a janitor and at untold other stinky, sweaty, smelly tasks to earn your keep—it had taken you *two years* to accumulate the money to journey home to Malden—these two went home sometimes twice a semester; leisurely they promenaded about like landed gentlefolk . . . which they were. They clung together like dark trees, never apart. They seemed to read each other's thoughts and to accomplish everything they set out to do. They enchanted you, amazed and bewitched you, you down among your fellow ex-slaves and sons and daughters of ex-slaves and the few penniless Indians who also matriculated at Hampton in a grand "experiment"; but you didn't even have the cachet of being unusual in the eyes of the white missionaries who condescended so prettily to you, *Poor little waif, bright little nigger* . . .

Tabitha & Elihu. They changed your view of the possibilities for Negroes. You had dreamt of it, read of it, of Negroes who had something other than hunger and poverty and debts. But here before your bedazzled eyes were coloreds with a father who could keep *two* children in school, well provided for, and probably not even feel it. What amazing world did they come from? Yet what truly astonished you was the way they treated you: as an equal. You, the poorest among the poor, the first shunned, the last called, were taken under their wing, asked to accompany them at supper, on picnics . . . when you could steal away from work. Nor did they look down from their good fortune onto your nothing. Was it because you were a mulatto and they so dark? But they never once showed signs of being colorstruck; in fact they seemed unaccountably proud of their darkness.

"What do you want to do, Booker"—her voice haunting, mossy—"when you grow up?"

"I'm going to be a preacher. So people'll feed me and I can dress like General Armstrong and people'll look up to me."

The day, Virginia spring-green, just before the twins were to graduate. The new grass smelled of earth, and gnats and bees and beetles buzzed in the ear.

"Now, Booker"—Elihu always seemed to be correcting you, pushing you, and you welcomed it—"do you think you need a Bible and a suit to get people's respect?"

"Well, no. I reckon not. But I ain't gone work at sweating and such."

"*I'm not,*' not 'I ain't.' Think, Booker, before you speak. Remember what Miss Lord taught us about enunciating."

At times you did resent them as much as you envied them—resented them so hard you would cry in your hard bed—but their way won you over, over and over; as ideals or models they held you transfixed; you would be them: you would be better than they . . . or did you even realize how envy motivated and poisoned what you took to be love and devotion?

Hatred is a form of fear. And eventually we come to love that which we fear most. For we have allowed the object of our fear to define us, to have supreme power over us; and the absence of that object would be more than we could bear. We need the fear to create us. Without this fear we are nothing. Often death itself is preferable to the excruciating process of re-creating ourselves against nothing, without our ineffable totem of fear.

—BTW FROM AN UNPUBLISHED DIARY (COURTESY DENABONE ARCHIVES)

When we look at a certain photograph of you, taken by Frances Benjamin Johnston in 1906: those light eyes, the arched eyebrow, the full nose, the prominent elfin ears, the Indian lips—the word "handsome" is impeached by "integrity." A solid dignity. The grey suit, finely cut, the dark tie, the pristine shirt, all collude and tell us: This is a man of profound seriousness and authority. Look at the dark flesh under the eyes—here's a man who's spent many a sleepless night poring over documents and papers to make men free!

Indeed, we see a solid Victorian Citizen in dark relief. But the longer we gaze, and are gazed at by those dark-rimmed eyes—particularly the way the right eye seems to squint oh so slightly—we cannot fight the impression of concentration; and as we gaze it dawns on us how you neither smile nor frown but appear to be considering, to be figuring. Yes, you seem to be calculating. The Calculating Citizen. And though we cannot call the photograph sinister, there is certainly a gravity which goes beyond statuesque solemnity; there exudes, unmistakably, a sense of readiness, a sure understanding of your own power, a sense that if you raised your hand and waved—voilà!—we would disappear.

But do we see the photograph as it was seen in 1906, when we all saw so differently?

How do you look upon the picture now?

W. E. B. DU BOIS

The Souls of Black Folk

After the Egyptian and Indian, the Greek and Roman, the Teuton and Mongolian, the Negro is a sort of seventh son, born with a veil, and gifted with second-sight in this American world,—a world which yields him no true self-consciousness, but only lets him see himself through the revelation of the other world. It is a peculiar sensation, this double-consciousness, this sense of always looking at one's self through the eyes of others, of measuring one's soul by the tape of a world that looks on in amused contempt and pity. One ever feels his twoness,—an American, a Negro; two souls, two thoughts, two unreconciled strivings; two warring ideals in one dark body, whose dogged strength alone keeps it from being torn asunder.

The history of the American Negro is the history of this strife,—this longing to attain self-conscious manhood, to merge his double self into a better and truer self. In this merging he wishes neither of the older selves to be lost. He would not Africanize America, for America has too much to teach the world and Africa. He would not bleach his Negro soul in a flood of white Americanism, for he knows that Negro blood has a message for the world. He simply wishes to make it possible for a man to be both a Negro and an American, without being cursed and spit upon by his fellows, without having the doors of Opportunity closed roughly in his face.

This, then, is the end of his striving; to be a co-worker in the kingdom of culture, to escape both death and isolation, to husband and use his best powers and his latent genius. These powers of body and mind have in the past been strangely wasted, dispersed, or forgotten. The shadow of a mighty Negro past flits through the tale of Ethiopia the Shadowy and of Egypt the Sphinx. Throughout history, the powers of single black men flash here and there like falling stars, and die sometimes before the world has rightly gauged their brightness. Here in America, in the few days since Emancipation, the black man's turning hither and thither in hesitant and doubtful striving has often made his very strength to lose effectiveness, to seem like absence of power, like weakness. And yet it is not weakness,—it is the contradiction of double aims. The double-aimed struggle of the black artisan—on the one hand to escape white contempt for a nation of mere hewers of wood and drawers of water, and on the other hand to plough and nail and dig for a poverty-stricken horde—could only result in making him a poor craftsman, for he had but half a heart in either cause. By the poverty and ignorance of his people, the Negro minister or doctor was tempted toward quackery and demagogy; and by the criticism of the other world, toward ideals that made him ashamed of his lowly tasks. The would-be black *savant* was confronted by the paradox that the knowledge his people needed was a twice-told tale to his white neighbors, while the knowledge which would teach the white world was Greek to his own flesh and blood. The innate love of harmony and beauty that set the ruder souls of his people a-dancing and a-singing raised but confusion and doubt in the soul of the black artist; for the beauty revealed to him was the soul-beauty of a race which his larger audience despised, and he could not articulate the message of another people. This waste of double aims, this seeking to satisfy two unreconciled ideals, has wrought sad havoc with the courage and faith and deeds of ten thousand thousand people,—has sent them often wooing false gods and invoking false means of salvation, and at times has even seemed about to make them ashamed of themselves.

Away back in the days of bondage they thought to see in one divine event the end of all doubt and disappointment; few men ever worshipped Freedom with half such unquestioning faith as did the American Negro for two centuries. To him, so far as he thought and dreamed, slavery was indeed the sum of all villainies, the cause of all sorrow, the root of all prejudice; Emancipation was the key to a promised land of sweeter beauty than ever stretched before the eyes of wearied Israelites. In song and exhortation swelled one refrain—Liberty; in his tears and curses the God he implored had Freedom in his right hand. At last it came,—suddenly, fearfully, like a dream. With one wild carnival of blood and passion came the message in his own plaintive cadences:—

> "Shout, O children!
> Shout, you're free!
> For God has bought your liberty!"

Years have passed away since then,—ten, twenty, forty; forty years of national life, forty years of renewal and development, and yet the swarthy spectre sits in its accustomed seat at the Nation's feast. In vain do we cry to this our vastest social problem:—

"Take any shape but that, and my firm nerves
Shall never tremble!"

The Nation has not yet found peace from its sins; the freedman has not yet found in freedom his promised land. Whatever of good may have come in these years of change, the shadow of a deep disappointment rests upon the Negro people,—a disappointment all the more bitter because the unattained ideal was unbounded save by the simple ignorance of a lowly people.

The first decade was merely a prolongation of the vain search for freedom, the boon that seemed ever barely to elude their grasp,—like a tantalizing will-o'-the-wisp, maddening and misleading the headless host. The holocaust of war, the terrors of the Ku Klux Klan, the lies of carpetbaggers, the disorganization of industry, and the contradictory advice of friends and foes, left the bewildered serf with no new watchword beyond the old cry for freedom. As the time flew, however, he began to grasp a new idea. The ideal of liberty demanded for its attainment powerful means, and these the Fifteenth Amendment gave him. The ballot, which before he had looked upon as a visible sign of freedom, he now regarded as the chief means of gaining and perfecting the liberty with which war had partially endowed him. And why not? Had not votes made war and emancipated millions? Had not votes enfranchised the freedmen? Was anything impossible to a power that had done all this? A million black men started with renewed zeal to vote themselves into the kingdom. So the decade flew away, the revolution of 1876 came, and left the half-free serf weary, wondering but still inspired. Slowly but steadily, in the following years, a new vision began gradually to replace the dream of political power,—a powerful movement, the rise of another ideal to guide the unguided, another pillar of fire by night after a clouded day. It was the ideal of "book-learning"; the curiosity, born of compulsory ignorance, to know and test the power of the cabalistic letters of the white man, the longing to know. Here at last seemed to have been discovered the mountain path to Canaan; longer than the highway of Emancipation and law, steep and rugged, but straight, leading to heights high enough to overlook life.

Up the new path the advance guard toiled, slowly, heavily, doggedly; only those who have watched and guided the faltering feet, the misty minds, the dull understandings, of the dark pupils of these schools know how faithfully, how piteously, this people strove to learn. It was weary work. The cold statistician wrote down the inches of progress here and there, noted also where here and there a foot had slipped or someone had fallen. To the tired climbers, the horizon was ever dark, the mists were often cold, the Canaan was always dim and far away. If, however, the vistas disclosed as yet no goal, no resting-place, little but flattery and criticism, the journey at least gave leisure for reflection and self-examination; it changed the child of Emancipation to the youth with dawning self-consciousness, self-realization, self-respect. In those sombre forests of his striving his own soul rose before him, and he saw himself,—darkly as through a veil; and yet he saw in himself some faint revelation of his power, of his mission. He began to have a dim feeling that, to attain his place in the world, he must be himself, and not another. For the first time he sought to analyze the burden he bore upon his back, that deadweight of social degradation partially masked behind a half-named Negro problem. He felt his poverty; without a cent, without a home, without land, tools, or savings, he had entered into competition with rich, landed, skilled neighbors. To be a poor man is hard, but to be a poor race in a land of dollars is the very bottom of hardships. He felt the weight of his ignorance,—not simply of letters, but of life, of business, of the humanities; the accumulated sloth and shirking and awkwardness of decades and centuries shackled his hands and feet. Nor was his burden all poverty and ignorance. The red stain of bastardy, which two centuries of systemic legal defilement of Negro women had stamped upon his race, meant not only the loss of ancient African chastity, but also the hereditary weight of a mass of corruption from white adulterers, threatening almost the obliteration of the Negro home.

A people thus handicapped ought not to be asked to race with the world, but rather allowed to give all its time and thought to its own social problems. But alas! while sociologists gleefully count his bastards and his prostitutes, the very soul of the toiling, sweating black man is darkened by the shadow of a vast despair. Men call the shadow prejudice, and learnedly explain it as the natural defence of culture against barbarism, learning against ignorance, purity against crime, the "higher" against the "lower" races. To which the Negro cries Amen! and swears that to so much of this strange prejudice as is founded on just homage to civilization, culture, righteousness, and progress, he humbly bows and meekly does obeisance. But before that nameless prejudice that leaps beyond all this he stands helpless, dismayed, and well-nigh speechless; before that personal disrespect and mockery, the ridicule and systematic humiliation, the distortion of fact and wanton license of fancy, the cynical ignoring of the better and the boisterous welcoming of the worse, the all-pervading desire to inculcate disdain for everything black, from Toussaint to the devil,—before this there rises a sickening despair that would disarm and discourage any nation save that black host to whom "discouragement" is an unwritten word.

But the facing of so vast a prejudice could not but bring the inevitable self-questioning, self-disparagement, and lowering of ideals which ever accompany repression and breed in an atmosphere of contempt and hate. Whispering and portents came borne upon the four winds: Lo! we are diseased and dying, cried the dark hosts; we cannot write, our voting is vain; what need of education, since we must always cook and serve? And the Nation echoed and enforced this self-criticism, saying: Be content to be servants, and nothing more; what need of higher culture for half-men? Away with the black man's ballot, by force or fraud,—and behold the suicide of a race! Nevertheless, out of the evil came something of good,—the more careful adjustment of education to real life, the clearer perception of the Negroes' social responsibilities, and the sobering realization of the meaning of progress.

So dawned the time of *Sturm und Drang*: storm and stress today rocks our little boat on the mad waters of the world-sea; there is within and without the sound of conflict, the burning of body and rending of soul; inspiration strives with doubt, and faith with vain questionings. The bright ideals of the past,—physical freedom, political power, the training of brains, and the training of hands,—all these in turn have waxed and waned, until even the last grows dim and overcast. Are they all wrong,—all false? No, not that, but each alone was oversimple and incomplete,—the dreams of a credulous race-childhood, or the fond imaginings of the other world which does not know and does not want to know our power. To be really true, all these ideals must be melted and welded into one. The training of the schools we need today more than ever,—the training of deft hands, quick eyes and ears, and above all the broader, deeper, higher culture of gifted minds and pure hearts. The power of the ballot we need in sheer self-defence,—else what shall save us from a second slavery? Freedom, too, the long-sought, we still seek,—the freedom of life and limb, the freedom to work and think, the freedom to love and aspire. Work, culture, liberty,—all these we need, not singly but together, not successively but together, each growing and aiding each, and all striving toward that vaster ideal that swims before the Negro people, the ideal of human brotherhood, gained through the unifying ideal of Race; the ideal of fostering and developing the traits and talents of the Negro, not in opposition to or contempt for other races, but rather in large conformity to the greater ideals of the American Republic, in order that some day on American soil two world-races may give each to each those characteristics both so sadly lack. We the darker ones come even now not altogether empty-handed: there are today no truer exponents of the pure human spirit of the Declaration of Independence than the American Negroes; there is no true American music but the wild sweet melodies of the Negro slave; the American fairy tales and folk-lore are Indian and African; and, all in all, we black men seem the sole oasis of simple faith and reverence in a dusty desert of dollars and smartness. Will America be poorer if she replaces her brutal dyspeptic blundering with lighthearted but determined Negro humility? or her coarse and cruel wit with loving jovial good humor? or her vulgar music with the soul of the Sorrow Songs?

Merely a concrete test of the underlying principles of the great republic is the Negro Problem, and the spiritual striving of the freedmen's sons is the travail of souls whose burden is almost beyond the measure of their strength, but who bear it in the name of an historic race, in the name of this the land of their fathers' fathers, and in the name of human opportunity.

MARCUS GARVEY

Message of Marcus Garvey to Membership of Universal Negro Improvement Association from Atlanta Prison

August 1, 1925.

Fellow members of the Universal Negro Improvement Association and co-workers in the cause of African Redemption:

It is with feeling of deep love and thoughts of a great future for the Negro race that I address you.

My months of forcible removal from among you, being imprisoned as a punishment for advocating the cause of our real emancipation, have not left me hopeless or despondent; but to the contrary, I see a great ray of light and the bursting of a mighty international political cloud which will bring you complete freedom.

We have gradually won our way back into the confidence of the God of Africa, and He shall speak with the voice of thunder, that shall shake the pillars of a corrupt and unjust world, and once more restore Ethiopia to her ancient glory.

Our enemies have seemingly triumphed for a while, but the final battle when staged will bring us complete success and satisfaction.

The wicked and obstructive elements of our own race who have tried to defeat us shall meet their Waterloo, and when they fall we feel sure they shall not rise again. For many years since our general emancipation, certain elements composed chiefly of a few octoroons and quadroons who hate the blood of our race (although part of us) with greater venom, scorn and contempt than the most prejudiced of other races, have tried to undermine and sell us out to the mighty powers of oppression, and within recent years, they have succeeded in getting the ear of the leading statesmen of the world, and have influenced them to treat the bulk of us Negroes as dogs, reserving for themselves, their kind and class, all the privileges and considerations that, as a race, would have been otherwise granted us and merited.

The National Association for the Advancement of Colored People, although pretending to be interested in and working for the race, is really and truly the active representative of this class. I trust you will not believe that my opposition to the National Association for the Advancement of Colored People is based upon any other motive than that of preventing them from destroying the Negro race that they so much despise and hate.

I am always glad and ever willing to co-operate with all Negro organizations that mean good by the race, but I am perfectly convinced and satisfied that the present executive personnel of the National Association for the Advancement of Colored People is not serious nor honest in intent toward the black race.

When they shall have removed their white and colored officers who believe in the racial extermination of the Negro type, and honestly promote a program for race uplift, then we can co-operate with them for the general good, until then we regard them as among the greatest enemies of our race. They teach race amalgamation and inter-marriage as the means of destroying the moral purity of the Negro race and our absorption within the white race which is nothing less than race suicide.

You must not forget that we have enemies also within our own organization—men whose motives are selfish and who are only seeking the "loaves and fishes" and not honest in heart in serving the people. Yet we have to make the "wheat and tare" grow together till the day of harvest. It is impossible to know all our enemies at one and the same time. Some are our enemies because they do not want to see the Negro rise; some because the organization supplies the opportunity for exploitation; others because they are unable to resist the temptation of the evil one who would have them betray us in our most righteous effort of racial love and freedom.

I feel that my imprisonment has helped to open the eyes of the world to your true position, and has made friends to your cause. Men and women of other races who were mis-informed and deceived by our enemies, are now seeing the light. The graves that the enemies of race pride and purity dug for us may yet entomb them.

Hold fast to the ideal of a dignified Negro race. Let us work together as one people, whether we are octoroons, quadroons, mulattoes or blacks for the making of a nation of our own, for in that alone lies our racial salvation.

The few who do not want to be with us will find out their mistake sooner or later, but as for us, let us all unite as one people. It is no fault of ours that we are what we are—if we are black, brown, yellow or near white, the responsibility for the accident is not ours, but the time has now come for us to get together and make of ourselves a strong and healthy race.

The National Association for the Advancement of Colored People wants us all to become white by amalgamation, but they are not honest enough to come out with the truth. To be a Negro is no disgrace, but an honor, and we of the Universal Negro Improvement Association do not want to become white. We do not seek for the whiteman's company more than he would seek after ours. We are proud and honorable. We love our race and respect and adore our mothers. We are as proud as our fathers were in the days of old, and even though we have passed through slavery in the western world, we shall not hang down our heads, for Ethiopia shall again return to her Glory.

The Universal Negro Improvement Association is a union of all groups within the race. We love each other with pride of race and great devotion and nothing in the world shall come between us.

The truth has to be told so that we may know from whence our troubles cometh. Yet we must never, even under the severest pressure, hate or dislike ourselves. Even though we oppose the present leaders of the National Association for the Advancement of Colored People, we must remember that we are all members of one race, rent asunder by circumstances. Let us help them by advice and conversion. Men like Du Bois need our sympathy. We should teach them to love themselves, at least, have respect for the blood of their mothers—our mothers, who have suffered so much to make us what we are. We should take the truth to the innocent members of the National Association and save them from the mis-leadership of the white and colored persons who seek to destroy our race by miscegenation and use them as a pawn toward that end, and to foster their own class interest. Let us reach out and convert these unfortunate people and thus save them from a grave error. They should not be left to the tender mercies of their vile leaders, for they are good people and of our race, they mean good, but are mis-directed.

I have to return many thanks to you, the members of the Universal Negro Improvement Association, for the loyal support you have given me during my trials and troubles, suffered for you. I can realize that you have at all times done your best for me, even as I have done the best for you, as God has directed me to see. If it were not for you I would have been left helpless and comfortless. I shall never forget you. If it were not for you the members and some of the officers of local divisions, I would have been left penniless and helpless to fight my enemies and the great powers against me, and to even in the slightest way give protection to my wife whom I neglected and cheated for the cause that I so much love.

It is surprising how those we serve and help most can be ungrateful and unkind in our absence, and generally seek to take advantage of the one who cannot help himself. My name I leave with you the people. For you I have built up an organization of international standing. Every sacrifice has been made. My youth, money and ability were freely given for the cause. The cause you now see. It was not made in a day, but it took years of steady work and sacrifice. Others will now try to take advantage of my predicament to rob and exploit you in my name and blame the absent and helpless, but ever remember that, from nothing, I raised up an organization through which you may see the light; let others, if they may, show the ability to carry on that which they have found, and not seek to exploit, to ruin and then blame the absent one as is so easy to do. It was during my absence in the West Indies when I was helpless to act, that the traitors within and enemies without did the deeds of dishonor that placed me for the Black Star Line where I am. Let not the same characters succeed to enrich themselves at the cost of the name of one who cannot protect himself or protect you. You must protect yourselves—the time has come. My full tale of warning is not to be told here, but suffice it to say that on you I rely for the ultimate success of our great effort, and but for you I would have been hopelessly defeated in the great struggle to "keep the fire burning." Probably I should not have expected better for even our Blessed Master feared worse when his chief disciples failed him. I am not complaining, but I warn you against treachery, deceit, self-seeking, dishonesty and racial disloyalty. Personally, as I have so often stated, I counted the cost years ago, but the responsibility is not all mine, but equally that of the one whom I love with great devotion and fondness. You, I feel sure, have done your duty by her and will continue to shield and protect her, while, because of my imprisonment for you, I find it impossible to do my duty.

The God of our Fathers will raise up friends for the cause of Africa, and we who have struggled in the wilderness for all this time shall surely see the promised land.

Hold fast to the Faith. Desert not the ranks, but as brave soldiers march on to victory. I am happy, and shall remain so, as long as you keep the flag flying.

I hope to be with you again with greater energy and force to put the program over. I have yet to let my real voice and soul be heard in Europe, Asia and continental America in plea for the Negro's rights and for a free and redeemed Africa. Yet, I have not spoken. I await the summons of my God for the greater work that must be done. In the meanwhile pray for success and pray for me.

RALPH ELLISON

Juneteenth

No, the wounded man thought, Oh no! Get back to that; back to a bunch of old-fashioned Negroes celebrating an illusion of emancipation, and getting it mixed up with the Resurrection, minstrel shows and vaudeville routines? Back to that tent in the clearing surrounded by trees, that bowl-shaped impression in the earth beneath the pines? . . . Lord, it hurts. Lordless and without loyalty, it hurts. Wordless, it hurts. Here and especially here. Still I see it after all the roving years and flickering scenes: Twin lecterns on opposite ends of the platform, behind one of which I stood on a wide box, leaning forward to grasp the lectern's edge. Back. Daddy Hickman at the other. Back to the first day of that week of celebration. Juneteenth. Hot, dusty. Hot with faces shining with sweat and the hair of the young dudes metallic with grease and straightening irons. Back to that? He was not so heavy then, but big with the quick energy of a fighting bull and still kept the battered silver trombone on top of the piano, where at the climax of a sermon he could reach for it and stand blowing tones that sounded like his own voice amplified; persuading, denouncing, rejoicing—moving beyond words back to the undifferentiated cry. In strange towns and cities the jazz musicians were always around him. Jazz. What was jazz and what religion back there? Ah yes, yes, I loved him. Everyone did, deep down. Like a great, kindly, daddy bear along the streets, my hand lost in his huge paw. Carrying me on his shoulder so that I could touch the leaves of the trees as we passed. The true father, but black, black. Was he a charlatan—am I—or simply as resourceful in my fashion. Did he know himself, or care? Back to the problem of all that. Must I go back to the beginning when only he knows the start . . . ?

Juneteenth and him leaning across the lectern, resting there looking into their faces with a great smile, and then looking over to me to make sure that I had not forgotten my part, winking his big red-rimmed eye at me. And the women looking back and forth from him to me with that bright, bird-like adoration in their faces; their heads cocked to one side. And him beginning:

On this God-given day, brothers and sisters, when we have come together to praise God and celebrate our oneness, our slipping off the chains, let's us begin this week of worship by taking a look at the ledger. Let us, on this day of deliverance, take a look at the figures writ on our bodies and on the living tablet of our heart. The Hebrew children have their Passover so that they can keep their history alive in their memories—so let us take one more page from their book and, on this great day of deliverance, on this day of emancipation, let's us tell ourselves our story. . . .

Pausing, grinning down. . . . Nobody else is interested in it anyway, so let us enjoy it ourselves, yes, and learn from it.

And thank God for it. Now let's not be too solemn about it either, because this here's a happy occasion. Rev. Bliss over there is going to take the part of the younger generation, and I'll try to tell it as it's been told to me. Just look at him over there, he's ready and raring to go—because he knows that a true preacher is a kind of educator, and that we have got to know our story before we can truly understand God's blessings and how far we have still got to go. Now you've heard him, so you know that he can preach.

Amen! They all responded and I looked preacher-faced into their shining eyes, preparing my piccolo voice to support his baritone sound.

Amen is right, he said. So here we are, five thousand strong, come together on this day of celebration. Why? We just didn't happen. We're here and that is an undeniable fact—but how come we're here? How and why here in these woods that used to be such a long way from town? What about it, Rev. Bliss, is that a suitable question on which to start?

God, bless you, Rev. Hickman, I think that's just the place we have to start. We of the younger generation are still ignorant about these things. So please, sir, tell us just how we came to be here in our present condition and in this land. . . .

Not back to that me, not to that six-seven-year-old ventriloquist's dummy dressed in a white evening suit. Not to that charlatan born—must I have no charity for me? . . .

Was it an act of God, Rev. Hickman, or an act of man? . . . Not to that puppet with a memory like a piece of flypaper. . . .

We came, amen, Rev. Bliss, sisters and brothers, as an act of God, but through—I said through, an act of cruel, ungodly man.

An act of almighty God, *my treble echo sounded*, but through the hands of cruel man.

Amen, Rev. Bliss, that's how it happened. It was, as I understand it, a cruel calamity laced up with a blessing—or maybe a blessing laced up with a calamity. . . .

Laced up with a blessing, Rev. Hickman? We understand you partially because you have taught us that God's sword is a two-edged sword. But would you please tell us of the younger generation just why it was a blessing?

It was a blessing, brothers and sisters, because out of all the pain and the suffering, out of the night of storm, we found the Word of God.

So here we found the Word. Amen, so now we are here. But where did we come from, Daddy Hickman?

We come here out of Africa, son; out of Africa.

Africa? Way over across the ocean? The black land? Where the elephants and monkeys and the lions and tigers are?

Yes, Rev. Bliss, the jungle land. Some of us have fair skins like you, but out of Africa too.

Out of Africa truly, sir?

Out of the ravaged mama of the black man, son.

Lord, thou hast taken us out of Africa . . .

Amen, out of our familar darkness. Africa. They brought us here from all over Africa, Rev. Bliss. And some were the sons and daughters of heathen kings . . .

Some were kings, Daddy Hickman? Have we of the younger generation heard you correctly? Some were kin to kings? Real kings?

Amen! I'm told that some were the sons and the daughters of kings . . .

. . . Of Kings! . . .

And some were the sons and daughters of warriors . . .

. . . Of warriors . . .

Of fierce warriors. And some were the sons and the daughters of farmers . . .

Of African farmers . . .

. . . And some of musicians . . .

. . . Musicians . . .

And some were the sons and daughters of weapon makers and of smelters of brass and iron . . .

But didn't they have judges, Rev. Hickman? And weren't there any preachers of the word of God?

Some were judges but none were preachers of the word of God, Rev. Bliss. For we come out of heathen Africa . . .

Heathen Africa?

Out of heathen Africa. Let's tell this thing true; because the truth is the light.

And they brought us here in chains . . .

In chains, son; in iron chains . . .

From half-a-world away, they brought us . . .

In chains and in boats that the history tells us weren't fit for pigs—because pigs cost too much money to be allowed to waste and die as we did. But they stole us and brought us in boats which I'm told could move like the swiftest birds of prey, and which filled the great trade winds with the stench of our dying and their crime . . .

What a crime! Tell us why, Rev. Hickman . . .

It was a crime, Rev. Bliss, brothers and sisters, like the fall of proud Lucifer from Paradise.

But why, Daddy Hickman? You have taught us of the progressive younger generation to ask why. So we want to know how come it was a crime?

Because, Rev. Bliss, this was a country dedicated to the principles of almighty God. That *Mayflower* boat that you hear so much about Thanksgiving Day was a *Christian* ship—Amen! Yes, and those many-named floating coffins we came here in were Christian too. They had turned traitor to the God who set them free from Europe's tyrant kings. Because, God have mercy on them, no sooner than they got free enough to breathe themselves, they set out to bow us down . . .

They made our Lord shed tears!

Amen! Rev. Bliss, amen. God must have wept like Jesus. Poor Jonah went down into the belly of the whale, but compared to our journey his was like a trip to paradise on a silvery cloud.

Worse than old Jonah, Rev. Hickman?

Worse than Jonah slicked all over with whale puke and gasping on the shore. We went down into hell on those floating coffins and don't you youngsters forget it! Mothers and babies, men and women, the living and the dead and the dying—all chained together. And yet, praise God, most of us arrived here in this land. The strongest came through. Thank God, and we arrived and that's why we're here today. Does that answer the question, Rev. Bliss?

Amen, Daddy Hickman, amen. But now the younger generation would like to know what they did to us when they got us here. What happened then?

They brought us up onto this land in chains . . .

. . . In chains . . .

. . . And they marched us into the swamps . . .

. . . Into the fever swamps, they marched us . . .

And they set us to work draining the swampland and toiling in the sun . . .

. . . They set us to toiling . . .

They took the white fleece of the cotton and the sweetness of the sugar cane and made them bitter and bloody with our toil . . . And they treated us like one great unhuman animal without any face . . .

Without a *face*, Rev. Hickman?

Without personality, without names, Rev. Bliss, we were made into nobody and not even *mister* nobody either, just nobody. They left us without names. Without choice. Without the right to do or not to do, to be or not to be . . .

You mean without faces and without eyes? We were eyeless like Samson in Gaza? Is that the way, Rev. Hickman?

Amen, Rev. Bliss, like baldheaded Samson before that nameless little lad like you came as the Good Book tells us and led him to the pillars whereupon the big house stood—Oh, you little black boys, and oh, you little brown girls, you're going to shake the building down! And then, Oh, how you will build in the name of the Lord!

Yes Rev. Bliss, we were eyeless like unhappy Samson among the Philistines—and worse . . .

And WORSE?

Worse, Rev. Bliss, because they chopped us up into little bitty pieces like a farmer when he cuts up a potato. And they scattered us around the land. All the way from Kentucky to Florida; from Louisiana to Texas; from Missouri all the way down the great Mississippi to the Gulf. They scattered us around this land.

How now, Daddy Hickman? You speak in parables which we of the younger generation don't clearly understand. How do you mean, they scattered us?

Like seed, Rev. Bliss; they scattered us just like a dope-fiend farmer planting a field with dragon teeth!

Tell us about it, Daddy Hickman.

They cut out our tongues . . .

. . . They left us speechless . . .

. . . They cut out our tongues . . .

. . . Lord, they left us without words . . .

. . . Amen! They scattered our tongues in this land like seed . . .

. . . And left us without language . . .

. . . They took away our talking drums . . .

. . . Drums that talked, Daddy Hickman? Tell us about those talking drums . . .

Drums that talked like a telegraph. Drums that could reach across the country like a church bell sound. Drums that told the news almost before it happened! Drums that spoke with big voices like big men! Drums like a conscience and a deep heart-beat that knew right from wrong. Drums that told glad tidings! Drums that sent the news of trouble speeding home! Drums that told us *our* time and told us where we were . . .

Those were some drums, Rev. Hickman . . .

. . . Yes and they took those drums away . . .

Away, Amen! Away! And they took away our heathen dances . . .

. . . They left us drumless and they left us danceless . . .

Ah yes, they burnt up our talking drums and our dancing drums . . .

. . . Drums . . .

. . . And they scattered the ashes . . .

. . . Ah, Aaaaaah! Eyeless, tongueless, drumless, danceless, ashes . . .

And a worst devastation was yet to come, Lord God!

Tell us, Rev. Hickman. Blow on your righteous horn!

Ah, but Rev. Bliss, in those days we didn't have any horns . . .

No *horns*? Hear him!

And we had no songs . . .

. . . No songs . . .

. . . And we had no . . .

. . . Count it on your fingers, see what cruel man has done . . .

Amen, Rev. Bliss, lead them . . .

We were eyeless, tongueless, drumless, danceless, hornless, songless!

All true, Rev. Bliss. No eyes to see. No tongue to speak or taste. No drums to raise the spirits and wake up our memories. No dance to stir the rhythm that makes life move. No songs to give praise and prayers to God!

We were truly in the dark, my young brothern and sisteren. Eyeless, earless, tongueless, drumless, danceless, songless, hornless, soundless . . .

And worse to come!

. . . And worse to come . . .

Tell us, Rev. Hickman. But not too fast so that we of the younger generation can gather up our strength to face it. So that we may listen and not become discouraged!

I said, Rev. Bliss, brothers and sisters, that they snatched us out of the loins of Africa. I said that they took us from our mammys and pappys and from our sisters and brothers. I said that they scattered us around this land . . .

. . . And we, let's count it again, brothers and sisters; let's add it up. Eyeless, tongueless, drumless, danceless, songless, hornless, soundless, sightless, dayless, nightless, wrongless, rightless, motherless, fatherless—scattered.

Yes, Rev. Bliss, they scattered us around like seed . . .

. . . Like seed . . .

. . . Like seed, that's been flung broadcast on unplowed ground . . .

Ho, chant it with me, my young brothers and sisters! Eyeless, tongueless, drumless, danceless, songless, hornless, soundless, sightless, wrongless, rightless, motherless, fatherless, brotherless, sisterless, powerless . . .

Amen! But though they took us like a great black giant that had been chopped up into little pieces and the pieces buried; though they deprived us of our heritage among strange scenes in strange weather; divided and divided and divided us again like a gambler shuffling and cutting a deck of cards. Although we were ground down, smashed into little pieces; spat upon, stamped upon, cursed and buried, and our memory of Africa ground down into powder and blown on the winds of foggy forgetfulness . . .

. . . Amen, Daddy Hickman! Abused and without shoes, pounded down and ground like grains of sand on the shores of the sea . . .

. . . Amen! And God—Count it, Rev. Bliss . . .

. . . Left eyeless, earless, noseless, throatless, teethless, tongueless, handless, feetless, armless, wrongless, rightless, harmless, drumless, danceless, songless, hornless, soundless, sightless, wrongless, rightless, motherless, fatherless, sisterless, brotherless, plowless, muleless, foodless, mindless—and Godless, Rev. Hickman, did you say Godless?

. . . At first, Rev. Bliss, he said, his trombone entering his voice, broad, somber and noble. At first. Ah, but though divided and scattered, ground down and battered into the earth like a spike being pounded by a ten-pound sledge, we were on the ground and in the earth and the earth was red and black like the earth of Africa. And as we moldered underground we were mixed with this land. We liked it. It fitted us fine. It was in us and we were in it. And then—praise God—deep in the ground, deep in the womb of this land, we began to stir!

Praise God!

At last, Lord, at last.

Amen!

Oh the truth, Lord, it tastes so sweet!

What was it like then, Rev. Bliss? You read the scriptures, so tell us. Give us a word.

WE WERE LIKE THE VALLEY OF DRY BONES!

Amen. Like the Valley of Dry Bones in Ezekiel's dream. Hoooh! We lay scattered in the ground for a long dry season. And the winds blew and the sun blazed down and the rains came and went and we were dead. Lord, we were dead! Except . . . Except . . .

. . . Except what, Rev. Hickman?

Except for one nerve left from our ear . . .

Listen to him!

And one nerve in the soles of our feet . . .

. . . Just watch me point it out, brothers and sisters . . .

Amen, Bliss, you point it out . . . and one nerve left from the throat . . .

. . . From our throat—right *here*!

. . . Teeth . . .

. . . From our teeth, one from all thirty-two of them . . .

. . . Tongue . . .

. . . Tongueless . . .

. . . And another nerve left from our heart . . .

. . . Yes, from our heart . . .

. . . And another left from our eyes and one from our hands and arms and legs and another from our stones . . .

Amen, Hold it right there, Rev. Bliss . . .

. . . All stirring in the ground . . .

. . . Amen, stirring, and right there in the midst of all our death and buriedness, the voice of God spoke down the Word . . .

. . . Crying Do! I said, Do! Crying Doooo—

These dry bones live?

He said, Son of Man . . . under the ground, Ha! Heatless beneath the roots of plants and trees . . . Son of man, do . . .

I said, Do . . .

. . . I said Do, Son of Man, Dooooo!—

These dry bones live?

Amen! And we heard and rose up. Because in all their blasting they could not blast away one solitary vibration of God's true word . . . We heard it down among the roots and among the rocks. We heard it in the sand and in the clay. We heard it in the falling rain and in the rising sun. On the high ground and in the gullies. We heard it lying moldering and corrupted in the earth. We heard it sounding like a bugle call to wake up the dead. Crying, Dooooo! Ay, do these dry bones live!

And did our dry bones live, Daddy Hickman?

Ah, we sprang together and walked around. All clacking together and clicking into place. All moving in time! Do! I said, Doooo—these dry bones live!

And now strutting in my white tails, across the platform, filled with the power almost to dancing.

Shouting, Amen, Daddy Hickman, is this the way we walked?

Oh we walked through Jerusalem, just like John—That's it, Rev. Bliss, walk! Show them how we walked!

Was this the way?

That's the way. Now walk on back. Lift your knees! Swing your arms! Make your coattails fly! Walk! And him strutting me three times around the pulpit across the platform and back. Ah, yes! And then his voice deep and exultant: And if they ask you in the city why we praise the Lord with bass drums and brass trombones tell them we were rebirthed dancing, we were rebirthed crying affirmation of the Word, quickening our transcended flesh.

Amen!

Oh, Rev. Bliss, we stamped our feet at the trumpet's sound and we clapped our hands, ah, in joy! And we moved, yes, together in a dance, amen! Because we had received a new song in a new land and been resurrected by the Word and Will of God!

Amen! . . .

. . . —We were rebirthed from the earth of this land and revivified by the Word. So now we had a new language and a brand new song to put flesh on our bones . . .

New teeth, new tongue, new word, new song!

We had a new name and a new blood, and we had a new task . . .

Tell us about it, Rev. Hickman . . .

We had to take the Word for bread and meat. We had to take the Word for food and shelter. We had to use the Word as a rock to build up a whole new nation, cause to tell it true, we were born again in chains of steel. Yes, and chains of ignorance. And all we knew was the spirit of the word. We had no schools. We owned no tools; no cabins, no churches, not even our own bodies.

We were chained, young brothers, in steel. We were chained, young sisters, in ignorance. We were school-less, tool-less, cabinless—owned . . .

Amen, Rev. Bliss. We were owned and faced with the awe-inspiring labor of transforming God's word into a lantern so that in the darkness we'd know where we were. Oh God hasn't been easy with us because He always plans for the loooong haul. He's looking far ahead and this time He wants a well-tested people to work his will. He wants some sharp-eyed, quick-minded, generous-hearted people to give names to the things of this world and to its values. He's tired of untempered tools and half-blind masons! Therefore, He's going to keep on testing us against the rocks and in the fires. He's going to heat us till we almost melt and then He's going to plunge us into the ice-cold water. And each time we come out we'll be blue and as tough as cold-blue steel! Ah yes! He means for us to be a new kind of human. Maybe we won't be that people but we'll be a part of that people, we'll be an element in them, Amen! He wants us limber as willow switches and he wants us tough as whit leather, so that when we have to bend, we can bend and snap back into place. He's going to throw bolts of lightning to blast us so that we'll have good foot work and lightning-fast minds. He'll drive us hither and yon around this land and make us run the gauntlet of hard times and tribulations, misunderstanding and abuse. And some will pity you and some will despise you. And some will try to use you and change you. And some will deny you and try to deal you out of the game. And sometimes you'll feel so bad that you'll wish you could die. But it's all the pressure of God. He's giving you a will and He wants you to use it. He's giving you brains and he wants you to train them lean and hard so that you can overcome all the obstacles. Educate your minds! Make do with what you have so as to get what you need! Learn to look at what *you* see and not what somebody tells you is true. Pay lip-service to Caesar if you have to, but put your trust in God. Because nobody has a patent on truth or a copyright on the best way to live and serve almighty God. Learn from what we've lived. Remember that when the labor's back-breaking and the boss man's mean our singing can lift us up. That it can strengthen us and make his meanness but the flyspeck irritation of an empty man. Roll with the blow like ole Jack Johnson. Dance on out of his way like Williams and Walker. Keep to the rhythm and you'll keep to life. God's time is long; and all short-haul horses shall be like horses on a merry-go-round. Keep, keep, keep to the rhythm and you won't get weary. Keep to the rhythm and you won't get lost. We're handicapped, amen! Because the Lord wants us strong! We started out with nothing but the Word—just like the others but they've forgot it . . . We worked and stood up under hard times and tribulations. We learned patience and to understand Job. Of all the animals, man's the only one not born knowing almost everything he'll ever know. It takes him longer than an elephant to grow up because God didn't mean him to leap to any conclusions, for God himself is in the very process of things. We learned that all blessings come mixed with sorrow and all hardships have a streak of laughter. Life is a streak-a-lean—a—streak-a-fat. Ha, yes! We learned to bounce back and to disregard the prizes of fools. And we must keep on learning. Let them have their fun. Even let them eat humming bird's wings and tell you it's too good for you.—Grits and greens don't turn to ashes in anybody's mouth—How about it, Rev. Eatmore? Amen? Amen! Let everybody say amen. Grits and greens are humble but they make you strong and when the right folks get together to share them they can taste like ambrosia. So draw, so let us draw on our own wells of strength.

Ah yes, so we were reborn, Rev. Bliss. They still had us harnessed, we were still laboring in the fields, but we had a secret and we had a new rhythm . . .

So tell us about this rhythm, Rev. Hickman.

They had us bound but we had our kind of time, Rev. Bliss. They were on a merry-go-round that they couldn't control but we learned to beat time from the seasons. We learned to make this land and this light and darkness and this weather and their labor fit us like a suit of new underwear. With our new rhythm, amen, but we weren't free and they still kept dividing us. There's many a thousand gone down the river. Mama sold from papa and chillun sold from both. Beaten and abused and without shoes. But we had the Word, now, Rev. Bliss, along with the rhythm. They couldn't divide us now. Because anywhere they dragged us we throbbed in time together. If we got a chance to sing, we sang the same song. If we got a chance to dance, we beat back hard times and tribulations with a clap of our hands and the beat of our feet, and it was the same dance. Oh they come out here sometimes to laugh at our way of praising God. They can laugh but they can't deny us. They can curse and kill us but they can't destroy us all. This land is ours because we come out of it, we bled in it, our tears watered it, we fertilized it with our dead. So the more of us they destroy the more it becomes filled with the spirit of our redemption. They laugh but we know who we are and where we are, but they keep on coming in their millions and they don't know and can't get together.

But tell us, how do we know who we are, Daddy Hickman?

We know where we are by the way we walk. We know where we are by the way we talk. We know where we are by the way we sing. We know where we are by the way we dance. We know where we are by the way we praise the Lord on high. We know where we are because we hear a different tune in our minds and in our hearts. We know who we are because when we make the beat of our rhythm to shape our day the whole land says, Amen! It smiles, Rev. Bliss, and it moves to our time! Don't be ashamed, my brothern! Don't be cowed. Don't throw what you have away! Continue! Remember! Believe! Trust the inner beat that tells us who we are. Trust God and trust life and trust this land that is you! Never mind the laughers, the scoffers, they come around because they can't help themselves. They can deny you but not your sense of life. They hate you because whenever they look into a mirror they fill up with bitter gall. So forget them and most of all don't deny yourselves. They're tied by the short hair to a run-away merry-go-round. They make life a business of struggle and fret, fret and struggle. See who you can hate; see what you can get. But you just keep on inching along like an old inchworm. If you put one and one and one together soon they'll make a million too. There's been a heap of Juneteenths before this one and I tell you there'll be a heap more before we're truly free! Yes! But keep to the rhythm, just keep to the rhythm and keep to the way. Man's plans are but a joke to God. Let those who will despise you, but remember deep down inside yourself that the life we have to lead is but a preparation for other things, it's a discipline, Rev. Bliss, Sisters and Brothers; a discipline through which we may see that which the others are too self-blinded to see. Time will come round when we'll have to be their eyes; time will swing and turn back around. I tell you, time shall swing and spiral back around. . . .

PART 2

A Son in the Family

OF FATHERS AND SONS

QUINCY TROUPE

Poem for My Father

father, it was an honor to be there, in the dugout
with you, the glory of great black men swinging their lives
as bats, at tiny white balls
burning in at unbelievable speeds, riding up & in & out
a curve breaking down wicked, like a ball falling off a table
moving away, snaking down, screwing its stitched magic
into chitling circuit air, its comma seams spinning
toward breakdown, dipping, like a hipster
bebopping a knee-dip stride, in the charlie parker forties
wrist curling, like a swan's neck
behind a slick black back
cupping an invisible ball of dreams

& you there, father, regal, as an african, obeah man
sculpted out of wood, from a sacred tree, of no name, no place, origin
thick branches branching down, into cherokee & someplace else lost
way back in africa, the sap running dry
crossing from north carolina into georgia, inside grandmother mary's
womb, where your mother had you in the violence of that red soil
ink blotter news, gone now, into blood graves
of american blues, sponging rococo
truth long gone as dinosaurs
the agent-oranged landscape of former names
absent of african polysyllables, dry husk consonants there
now, in their place, names, flat, as polluted rivers

& that guitar string smile always snaking across
some virulent, american, redneck's face
scorching, like atomic heat, mushrooming over nagasaki
& hiroshima, the fever blistered shadows of it all
inked, as etchings, into sizzled concrete
but you, there, father, through it all, a yardbird solo
riffing on bat & ball glory, breaking down the fabricated myths
of white major league legends, of who was better than who
beating them at their own crap game, with killer bats,
as bud powell swung his silence into beauty of a josh
gibson home run, skittering across piano keys of bleachers
shattering all manufactured legends up there in lights
struck out white knights, on the risky edge of amazement
awe, the miraculous truth sluicing through
steeped & disguised in the blues
confluencing, like the point at the cross
when a fastball hides itself up in a slider, curve
breaking down & away in a wicked, sly grin
curved & posed as an ass-scratching uncle tom, who
like old satchel paige delivering his famed hesitation pitch
before coming back with a hard, high, fast one, is slicker
sliding, & quicker than a professional hitman—
the deadliness of it all, the sudden strike
like that of the "brown bomber's" crossing right
of sugar ray robinson's, lightning, cobra bite

& you, there, father, through it all, catching rhythms of chano
pozo balls, drumming, like conga beats into your catcher's mitt
hard & fast as "cool papa" bell jumping into bed
before the lights went out

of the old, negro baseball league, a promise, you were
father, a harbinger, of shock waves, soon come

RICHARD WRIGHT

Black Boy

After my father's desertion, my mother's ardently religious disposition dominated the household and I was often taken to Sunday school where I met God's representative in the guise of a tall, black preacher. One Sunday my mother invited the tall, black preacher to a dinner of fried chicken. I was happy, not because the preacher was coming but because of the chicken. One or two neighbors also were invited. But no sooner had the preacher arrived than I began to resent him, for I learned at once that he, like my father, was used to having his own way. The hour for dinner came and I was wedged at the table between talking and laughing adults. In the center of the table was a huge platter of golden-brown fried chicken. I compared the bowl of soup that sat before me with the crispy chicken and decided in favor of the chicken. The others began to eat their soup, but I could not touch mine.

"Eat your soup," my mother said.

"I don't want any," I said.

"You won't get anything else until you've eaten your soup," she said.

The preacher had finished his soup and had asked that the platter of chicken be passed to him. It galled me. He smiled, cocked his head this way and that, picking out choice pieces. I forced a spoonful of soup down my throat and looked to see if my speed matched that of the preacher. It did not. There were already bare chicken bones on his plate, and he was reaching for more. I tried eating my soup faster, but it was no use; the other people were now serving themselves chicken and the platter was more than half empty. I gave up and sat staring in despair at the vanishing pieces of fried chicken.

"Eat your soup or you won't get anything," my mother warned.

I looked at her appealingly and could not answer. As piece after piece of chicken was eaten, I was unable to eat my soup at all. I grew hot with anger. The preacher was laughing and joking and the grownups were hanging on his words. My growing hate of the preacher finally became more important than God or religion and I could no longer contain myself. I leaped up from the table, knowing that I should be ashamed of what I was doing, but unable to stop, and screamed, running blindly from the room.

"That preacher's going to eat *all* the chicken!" I bawled.

The preacher tossed back his head and roared with laughter, but my mother was angry and told me that I was to have no dinner because of my bad manners.

When I awakened one morning my mother told me that we were going to see a judge who would make my father support me and my brother. An hour later all three of us were sitting in a huge crowded room. I was overwhelmed by the many faces and the voices which I could not understand. High above me was a white face which my mother told me was the face of the judge. Across the huge room sat my father, smiling confidently, looking at us. My mother warned me not to be fooled by my father's friendly manner; she told me that the judge might ask me questions, and if he did I must tell him the truth. I agreed, yet I hoped that the judge would not ask me anything.

For some reason the entire thing struck me as being useless; I felt that if my father were going to feed me, then he would have done so regardless of what a judge said to him. And I did not want my father to feed me; I was hungry, but my thoughts of food did not now center about him. I waited, growing restless, hungry. My mother gave me a dry sandwich and I munched and stared, longing to go home. Finally I heard my mother's name called; she rose and began weeping so copiously that she could not talk for a few moments; at last she managed to say that her husband had deserted her and two children, that her children were hungry, that they stayed hungry, that she worked, that she was trying to raise them alone. Then my father was called; he came forward jauntily, smiling. He tried to kiss my mother, but she turned away from him. I only heard one sentence of what he said.

"I'm doing all I can, Your Honor," he mumbled, grinning.

It had been painful to sit and watch my mother crying and my father laughing and I was glad when we were outside in the sunny streets. Back at home my mother wept again and talked complainingly about the unfairness of the judge who had accepted my father's word. After the court scene, I tried to forget my father; I did not hate him; I simply did not want to think of him. Often when we were hungry my mother would beg me to go to my father's job and ask him for a dollar, a dime, a nickel. . . . But I would never consent to go. I did not want to see him.

My mother fell ill and the problem of food became an acute, daily agony. Hunger was with us always. Sometimes the neighbors would feed us or a dollar bill would come in the mail from my grandmother. It was winter and I would buy a dime's worth of coal each morning from the corner coalyard and lug it home in paper bags. For a time I remained out of school to wait upon my mother, then Granny came to visit us and I returned to school.

At night there were long, halting discussions about our going to live with Granny, but nothing came of it. Perhaps there was not enough money for railroad fare. Angered by having been hauled into court, my father now spurned us completely. I heard long, angrily whispered conversations between my mother and grandmother to the effect that "that woman ought to be killed for breaking up a home." What irked me was the ceaseless talk and no action. If someone had suggested that my father be killed, I would perhaps have become interested; if someone had suggested that his name never be mentioned, I would no doubt have agreed; if someone had suggested that we move to another city, I would have been glad. But there was only endless talk that led nowhere and I began to keep away from home as much as possible, preferring the simplicity of the streets to the worried, futile talk at home.

Finally we could no longer pay the rent for our dingy flat; the few dollars that Granny had left us before she went home were gone. Half sick and in despair, my mother made the rounds of the charitable institutions, seeking help. She found an orphan home that agreed to assume the guidance of me and my brother provided my mother worked and made small payments. My mother hated to be separated from us, but she had no choice.

The orphan home was a two-story frame building set amid trees in a wide, green field. My mother ushered me and my brother one morning into the building and into the presence of a tall, gaunt, mulatto woman who called herself Miss Simon. At once she took a fancy to me and I was frightened speechless; I was afraid of her the moment I saw her and my fear lasted during my entire stay in the home.

The house was crowded with children and there was always a storm of noise. The daily routine was blurred to me and I never quite grasped it. The most abiding feeling I had each day was hunger and fear. The meals were skimpy and there were only two of them. Just before we went to bed each night we were given a slice of bread smeared with molasses. The children were silent, hostile, vindictive, continuously complaining of hunger. There was an over-all atmosphere of nervousness and intrigue, of children telling tales upon others, of children being deprived of food to punish them.

The home did not have the money to check the growth of the wide stretches of grass by having it mown, so it had to be pulled by hand. Each morning after we had eaten a breakfast that seemed like no breakfast at all, an older child would lead a herd of us to the vast lawn and we would get to our knees and wrench the grass loose from the dirt with our fingers. At intervals Miss Simon would make a tour of inspection, examining the pile of pulled grass beside each child, scolding or praising according to the size of the pile. Many mornings I was too weak from hunger to pull the grass; I would grow dizzy and my mind would become blank and I would find myself, after an interval of unconsciousness, upon my hands and knees, my head whirling, my eyes staring in bleak astonishment at the green grass, wondering where I was, feeling that I was emerging from a dream. . . .

During the first days my mother came each night to visit me and my brother, then her visits stopped. I began to wonder if she, too, like my father, had disappeared into the unknown. I was rapidly learning to distrust everything and everybody. When my mother did come, I asked her why had she remained away so long and she told me that Miss Simon had forbidden her to visit us, that Miss Simon had said that she was spoiling us with too much attention. I begged my mother to take me away; she wept and told me to wait, that soon she would take us to Arkansas. She left and my heart sank.

Miss Simon tried to win my confidence; she asked me if I would like to be adopted by her if my mother consented and I said no. She would take me into her apartment and talk to me, but her words had no effect. Dread and distrust had already become a daily part of my being and my memory grew sharp, my senses more impressionable; I began to be aware of myself as a distinct personality striving against others. I held myself in, afraid to act or speak until I was sure of my surroundings, feeling most of the time that I was suspended over a void. My imagination soared; I dreamed of running away. Each morning I vowed that I would leave the next morning, but the next morning always found me afraid.

One day Miss Simon told me that thereafter I was to help her in the office. I ate lunch with her and, strangely, when I sat facing her at the table, my hunger vanished. The woman killed something in me. Next she called me to her desk where she sat addressing envelopes.

"Step up close to the desk," she said. "Don't be afraid."

I went and stood at her elbow. There was a wart on her chin and I stared at it.

"Now, take a blotter from over there and blot each envelope after I'm through writing on it," she instructed me, pointing to a blotter that stood about a foot from my hand.

I stared and did not move or answer.

"Take the blotter," she said.

I wanted to reach for the blotter and succeeded only in twitching my arm.

"Here," she said sharply, reaching for the blotter and shoving it into my fingers.

She wrote in ink on an envelope and pushed it toward me. Holding the blotter in my hand, I stared at the envelope and could not move.

"Blot it," she said.

I could not lift my hand. I knew what she had said; I knew what she wanted me to do; and I had heard her correctly. I wanted to look at her and say something, tell her why I could not move; but my eyes were fixed upon the floor. I could not summon enough courage while she sat there looking at me to reach over the yawning space of twelve inches and blot the wet ink on the envelope.

"Blot it!" she spoke sharply.

Still I could not move or answer.

"Look at me!"

I could not lift my eyes. She reached her hand to my face and I twisted away.

"What's wrong with you?" she demanded.

I began to cry and she drove me from the room. I decided that as soon as night came I would run away. The dinner bell rang and I did not go to the table, but hid in a corner of the hallway. When I heard the dishes rattling at the table, I opened the door and ran down the walk to the street. Dusk was falling. Doubt made me stop. Ought I go back? No; hunger was back there, and fear. I went on, coming to concrete sidewalks. People passed me. Where was I going? I did not know. The farther I walked the more frantic I became. In a confused and vague way I knew that I was doing more running *away* from than running *toward* something. I stopped. The streets seemed dangerous. The buildings were massive and dark. The moon shone and the trees loomed frighteningly. No, I could not go on. I would go back. But I had walked so far and had turned too many corners and had not kept track of the direction. Which way led back to the orphan home? I did not know. I was lost.

I stood in the middle of the sidewalk and cried. A "white" policeman came to me and I wondered if he was going to beat me. He asked me what was the matter and I told him that I was trying to find my mother. His "white" face created a new fear in me. I was remembering the tale of the "white" man who had beaten the "black" boy. A crowd gathered and I was urged to tell where I lived. Curiously, I was too full of fear to cry now. I wanted to tell the "white" face that I had run off from an orphan home and that Miss Simon ran it, but I was afraid. Finally I was taken to the police station where I was fed. I felt better. I sat in a big chair where I was surrounded by "white" policemen, but they seemed to ignore me. Through the window I could see that night had completely fallen and that lights now gleamed in the streets. I grew sleepy and dozed. My shoulder was shaken gently and I opened my eyes and looked into a "white" face of another policeman who was sitting beside me. He asked me questions in a quiet, confidential tone, and quite before I knew it he was not "white" anymore. I told him that I had run away from an orphan home and that Miss Simon ran it.

It was but a matter of minutes before I was walking alongside a policeman, heading toward the home. The policeman led me to the front gate and I saw Miss Simon waiting for me on the steps. She identified me and I was left in her charge. I begged her not to beat me, but she yanked me upstairs into an empty room and lashed me thoroughly. Sobbing, I slunk off to bed, resolved to run away again. But I was watched closely after that.

My mother was informed upon her next visit that I had tried to run away and she was terribly upset.

"Why did you do it?" she asked.

"I don't want to stay here," I told her.

"But you must," she said. "How can I work if I'm to worry about you? You must remember that you have no father. I'm doing all I can."

"I don't want to stay here," I repeated.

"Then, if I take you to your father . . ."

"I don't want to stay with him either," I said.

"But I want you to ask him for enough money for us to go to my sister's in Arkansas," she said.

Again I was faced with choices I did not like, but I finally agreed. After all, my hate for my father was not so great and urgent as my hate for the orphan home. My mother held to her idea and one night a week or so later I found myself standing in a room in a frame house. My father and a strange woman were sitting before a bright fire that blazed in a grate. My mother and I were standing about six feet away, as though we were afraid to approach them any closer.

"It's not for me," my mother was saying. "It's for your children that I'm asking you for money."

"I ain't got nothing," my father said, laughing.

"Come here, boy," the strange woman called to me.

I looked at her and did not move.

"Give him a nickel," the woman said. "He's cute."

"Come here, Richard," my father said, stretching out his hand.

I backed away, shaking my head, keeping my eyes on the fire.

"He is a cute child," the strange woman said.

"You ought to be ashamed," my mother said to the strange woman. "You're starving my children."

"Now, don't you-all fight," my father said, laughing.

"I'll take that poker and hit you!" I blurted at my father.

He looked at my mother and laughed louder.

"You told him to say that," he said.

"Don't say such things, Richard," my mother said.

"You ought to be dead," I said to the strange woman.

The woman laughed and threw her arms about my father's neck. I grew ashamed and wanted to leave.

"How can you starve your children?" my mother asked.

"Let Richard stay with me," my father said.

"Do you want to stay with your father, Richard?" my mother asked.

"No," I said.

"You'll get plenty to eat," he said.

"I'm hungry now," I told him. "But I won't stay with you."

"Aw, give the boy a nickel," the woman said.

My father ran his hand into his pocket and pulled out a nickel.

"Here, Richard," he said.

"Don't take it," my mother said.

"Don't teach him to be a fool," my father said. "Here, Richard, take it."

I looked at my mother, at the strange woman, at my father, then into the fire. I wanted to take the nickel, but I did not want to take it from my father.

"You ought to be ashamed," my mother said, weeping. "Giving your son a nickel when he's hungry. If there's a God, He'll pay you back."

"That's all I got," my father said, laughing again and returning the nickel to his pocket.

We left. I had the feeling that I had had to do with something unclean. Many times in the years after that the image of my father and the strange woman, their faces lit by the dancing flames, would surge up in my imagination so vivid and strong that I felt I could reach out and touch it; I would stare at it, feeling that it possessed some vital meaning which always eluded me.

A quarter of a century was to elapse between the time when I saw my father sitting with the strange woman and the time when I was to see him again, standing alone upon the red clay of a Mississippi plantation, a sharecropper, clad in ragged overalls, holding a muddy hoe in his gnarled, veined hands—a quarter of a century during which my mind and consciousness had become so greatly and violently altered that when I tried to talk to him I realized that, though ties of blood made us kin, though I could see a shadow of my face in his face, though there was an echo of my voice in his voice, we were forever strangers, speaking a different language, living on vastly distant planes of reality. That day a quarter of a century later when I visited him on the plantation—he was standing against the sky, smiling toothlessly, his hair whitened, his body bent, his eyes glazed with dim recollection, his fearsome aspect of twenty-five years ago gone forever from him—I was overwhelmed to realize that he could never understand me or the scalding experiences that had swept me beyond his life and into an area of living that he could never know. I stood before him, poised, my mind aching as it embraced the simple nakedness of his life, feeling how completely his soul was imprisoned by the slow flow of the seasons, by wind and rain and sun, how fastened were his memories to a crude and raw past, how chained were his actions and emotions to the direct, animalistic impulses of his withering body. . . .

From the white landowners above him there had not been handed to him a chance to learn the meaning of loyalty, of sentiment, of tradition. Joy was as unknown to him as was despair. As a creature of the earth, he endured, hearty, whole, seemingly indestructible, with no regrets and no hope. He asked easy, drawling questions about me, his other son, his wife, and he laughed, amused, when I informed him of their destinies. I forgave him and pitied him as my eyes looked past him to the unpainted wooden shack. From far beyond the horizons that bound this bleak plantation there had come to me through my living the knowledge that my father was a black peasant who had gone to the city seeking life, but who had failed in the city; a black peasant whose life had been hopelessly snarled in the city, and who had at last fled the city—that same city which had lifted me in its burning arms and borne me toward alien and undreamed-of shores of knowing.

LANGSTON HUGHES

Father

That summer in Mexico was the most miserable I have ever known. I did not hear from my mother for several weeks. I did not like my father. And I did not know what to do about either of them.

My father was what the Mexicans called *muy americano*, a typical American. He was different from anybody I had ever known. He was interested only in making money.

My mother and step-father were interested in making money, too, so they were always moving about from job to job and from town to town, wherever they heard times were better. But they were interested in making money to *spend*. And for fun. They were always buying victrolas and radios and watches and rings, and going to shows and drinking beer and playing cards, and trying to have a good time after working hours.

But my father was interested in making money to *keep*.

Because it is very hard for a Negro to make money in the United States, since so many jobs are denied him, so many unions and professional associations are barred to him, so many banks will not advance him loans, and so many insurance companies will not insure his business, my father went to Cuba and Mexico, where he could make money quicker. He had had legal training in the South, but could not be admitted to the bar there. In Mexico he was admitted to the bar and practised law. He acquired property in Mexico City and a big ranch in the hills. He lent money and foreclosed on mortgages.

During the revolutions, when all the white Americans had to flee from the Toluca district of Mexico, because of the rising nationalism, my father became the general manager of an electric light company belonging to an American firm in New York. Because he was brown, the Mexicans could not tell at sight that he was a Yankee, and even after they knew it, they did not believe he was like the white Yankees. So the followers of Zapata and Villa did not run him away as they did the whites. In fact, in Toluca, the Mexicans always called my father *el americano*, and not the less polite *el gringo*, which is a term that carries with it distrust and hatred.

But my father was certainly just like the other German and English and American businessmen with whom he associated in Mexico. He spoke just as badly about the Mexicans. He said they were ignorant and backward and lazy.

He said they were exactly like the Negroes in the United States, perhaps worse. And he said they were very bad at making money.

My father hated Negroes. I think he hated himself, too, for being a Negro. He disliked all of his family because they were Negroes and remained in the United States, where none of them had a chance to be much of anything but servants—like my mother, who started out with a good education at the University of Kansas, he said, but had sunk to working in a restaurant, waiting on niggers, when she wasn't in some white woman's kitchen. My father said he wanted me to leave the United States as soon as I finished high school, and never return—unless I wanted to be a porter or a red cap all my life.

The second day out from Cleveland, the train we were on rolled across Arkansas. As we passed through a dismal village in the cotton fields, my father peered from the window of our Pullman at a cluster of black peons on the main street, and said contemptuously: "Look at the niggers."

When we crossed into Mexico at Laredo, and started south over the sun-baked plains, he pointed out to me a cluster of brown peons watching the train slow down at an adobe station. He said: "Look at the Mexicans!"

My father had a great contempt for all poor people. He thought it was their own fault that they were poor.

In Mexico City we went to the Grand Hotel. Then my father took me to call on three charming middle-aged Mexican ladies who were his friends—three unmarried sisters, one of whom took care of his rents in the city. They were very Latin and very Catholic, lived in a house with a charming courtyard, and served the most marvelous dishes at table—roast duck stuffed with pears and turkey with *mole* sauce, a sauce that takes several days to prepare, so complex is its making. And always there were a pile of steaming-hot tortillas, wrapped in a napkin, at one corner of the table.

In their youth, they were very lovely ladies to look at, I vaguely remembered from my trip there as a child. And they still wore their shawls of black lace with dignity and grace. They were all three the color of parchment, a soft, ivory-yellow—the blood of Spain overcast just a little by the blood of Mexico—for they were not Indians. And they were not revolutionists. They had adored the former dictator-president, Porfirio Diaz, and when they wanted to speak of someone as uncouth, they said: *"Muy indio."* Very Indian!

These three aging ladies were, I think, the only people in the whole world who really ever liked my father. Perhaps that was because his property helped to provide them with an income. And perhaps also because they shared many of his aristocratic ideas regarding the peons.

Their only worry about my father concerned his soul. He was not Catholic and never went to mass. The first thing they gave me as a present was a little amulet of the Virgin of Guadalupe. But my father laughed when we got back to the hotel and said he hoped I did not believe in that foolishness. He said greasers and niggers would never get anywhere because they were too religious, always praying.

The following morning, we left for Toluca. I wanted to see my father's tenement houses in Mexico City, but he said I could see them some other time. He was anxious to get back to the plant in Toluca.

Off the big trunk line between the capital and the border, railroad travel in Mexico then was slow and uncomfortable. Many of the coaches had been burned or bullet-ridden in the revolts, so the trains were very crowded. They had a parlor car coach between Mexico City and Toluca, in which one could reserve a seat, but my father was too frugal with money to use this service. So we rode in a crowded second-class coach, with people standing in the aisles, and all over one's feet, and bundles and baskets hanging from everywhere. My father said: "Be careful of pickpockets and thieves. Mexicans steal."

The train wound up and up into the mountains, and finally came down into one of the most beautiful valleys in the world, all lush, green fields and lakes, where water lilies floated, with a snow-capped volcano in the distance, La Nevada de Toluca. We were in the highest inhabitable valley in Mexico. The air was very cool and sweet and the sky a brilliant blue.

We reached Toluca in time for luncheon. My father's *mozo* met us at the station. He was an Indian boy named Maximiliano, with a broad, brown face and black hair that fell into his eyes. He wore the common white trousers and shirt you see all over Mexico, and *huaraches* on his feet. He put all our baggage on his back and secured it in a sort of leather thong about his neck, and trotted on ahead of us toward the house.

My father's house faced a small park near the station. It was a low, blue-white house of one story, all spread out and surrounded by a blue-white wall. As you approached the house, you could see only high adobe walls, rimmed with dull red tile at the top. At one end of the wall, there was a big double door for the horses. At the other end, a small door that led into the patio and the house.

The patio would have been nice, had my father bothered to keep the grass and flowers tended. But he took much better care of the corral at the back of the house, where the horses and chickens were, and the cow.

He had recently foreclosed on the cow. But some shrewd Mexicans must have got the best of him that time, because the cow was ill. She had something hard in her udders; she gave bitter milk, and finally stopped giving milk altogether, as her udders began to petrify. A few weeks after I arrived, she was dead.

But there were two beautiful horses in the corral, and about a hundred large, healthy American chickens, not at all like the scrawny Mexican chickens other people had. My father said he could trade a pair of his chickens any day for a calf or a sheep, and it was true.

My father's housekeeper was a tall Mexican woman with a kind tan-brown face, and two children approaching their teens, whom my father would not permit to eat at our house. But she used to take food home to them at night. My father lived on a rather meagre diet of beef and beans. But the cook and

I soon teamed up against him, and when he was away at the ranch, we would order all kinds of good things to eat from the shops where he traded, and put them on his bill. I would take the blame. My father stormed and said I was just like my mother, always wasting money. So he would usually make a scene whenever he came home from the country, sending the cook flying from the kitchen in tears. But, nevertheless, he would always eat whatever good things were set before him.

Maximiliano, the *mozo*, took care of the horses and the chickens, swept the patio and the corral, and saddled the horses for me or my father. He was a silent boy who spoke but little Spanish, his being an Indian language from the hills. He slept on a pile of sacks in the tool shed, so I asked my father why he didn't give Maximiliano a bed, since there were several old beds around.

He said: "Never give an Indian anything. He doesn't appreciate it."

But he was wrong about that. I gave Maximiliano my spare centavos and cigarettes, and we became very good friends. He taught me to ride a horse without saddle or stirrups, how to tell a badly woven serape from a good one, and various other things that are useful to know in that high valley beneath the white volcanos.

My father paid Maximiliano and the cook almost nothing, but he gave me ten pesos a week allowance, which I used to share with the two servants. There was nothing much to spend money for in Toluca. At least, not knowing anyone and not yet being able to speak Spanish, I found nothing to spend money for, except the movies once a week, on Sundays.

The weekly movie show was a gala occasion for the whole town. Society and its pretty daughters attended and sat in the horseshoe of circular boxes, running from one side of the stage to the other around the ancient auditorium. The young blades and unmarried males of the better families sat in the orchestra proper, and between each reel of bad Hollywood movies, or arty German ones, practically all the males would rise and sweep the circle of boxes with their eyes until they found the girl each liked. Then they would stare at her until the house went dark again. The shows commenced at four o'clock and lasted an ungodly long time, because they had only one projector and had to show each picture reel by reel. When the sun went down, it got very cold in Toluca, and the old theater had no heat, but you gathered your coat about you and stuck it out until the last cowboy had killed the last redskin and smothered the heroine in a kiss. Then you came home through the badly lighted streets, where the meek Indian policemen, huddled in blankets to the eyebrows, slept leaning against adobe corners, a lantern on the ground at their feet.

I began to get very tired of Toluca. My father did not take me to the ranch with him, because he said the roads were infested with bandits, and I could not yet ride well enough. Instead of letting me go about with him to the country or to Mexico City, he put me to learning bookkeeping. I was never very good at figures, and I got hopelessly tangled up in the problems he gave me. My stupidity disgusted him immeasurably, and he would rail at me about the need of acquiring a good business head. "Seventeen and you can't add yet!" he'd cry. Then he would bend over the ledger and show me all over again how to balance the spoiled page, and say: "Now, hurry up and do it! Hurry up! Hurry up!"

"Hurry up!" was his favorite expression, in Spanish or in English. He was always telling the employees under him at the electric light company, the cook at home, or Maximiliano, or me, to hurry up, hurry up and do whatever we were doing—so that we could get through and do something else he always had ready to be done.

Hurry up! My father had tremendous energy. He always walked fast and rode hard. He was small and tough, like a jockey. He got up at five in the morning and worked at his accounts or his mail or his law books until time to go to the office. Then until ten or eleven o'clock at night he would be busy at various tasks, stopping only to eat. Then, on the days he made the long trek to the ranch, he rose at three-thirty or four, in order to get out there early and see what his workers were doing. Every one else worked too slowly for him, so it was always, "Hurry up!"

As the weeks went by, I could think of less and less to say to my father. His whole way of living was so different from mine, his attitude toward life and people so amazing, that I fell silent and couldn't open my mouth when he was in the house. Not even when he barked: "Hurry up!"

I hadn't heard from my mother, even by July. I knew she was angry with me because I had gone to Mexico. I understood then, though, why she had been unable to live with my father, and I didn't blame her. But why had she married him in the first place, I wondered. And why had they had me? Now, at seventeen, I began to be very sorry for myself, in a strange land in a mountain town, where there wasn't a person who spoke English. It was very cold at night and quiet, and I had no money to get away, and I was lonesome. I began to wish I had never been born—not under such circumstances.

I took long rides on a black horse named Tito to little villages of adobe huts, nestled in green fields of corn and alfalfa, little villages, each with a big church with a beautiful tower built a hundred years ago, a white Spanish tower with great bells swinging in the turret.

I began to learn to read Spanish. I struggled with bookkeeping. I took one of the old pistols from my father's desk and fired away in the afternoon at a target Maximiliano had put up in the corral. But most of the time I was depressed and unhappy and bored. One day, when there was no one in the house but me, I put the pistol to my head and held it there, loaded, a long time, and wondered if I would be any happier if I were to pull the trigger. But then, I began to think, if I do, I might miss something. I haven't been to the ranch yet, nor to the top of the volcano, nor to the bullfights in Mexico, nor graduated from high school, nor got married. So I put the pistol down and went back to my bookkeeping.

My father was very seldom at home, but when he was, he must have noticed my silence and my gloomy face, because if I looked the way I felt, I looked woebegone, indeed. One day in August, he told me he was going to Mexico City for a week, and would take me with him for the trip. He said I could see the summer bullfights and Xochimilco. The trip was ten days off, but I began to dream about it, and to press my clothes and get ready.

It seemed that my father couldn't resist saying, "Hurry up," more and more during those ten days, and giving me harder and harder bookkeeping problems to have worked out by the time he got home from the office. Besides, he was teaching me to typewrite, and gave me several exercises to master each evening. "Hurry up and type that a hundred times before you go to bed. Hurry up and get that page of figures done so I can check on it. Hurry up and learn the verb *estar*."

Hurry up . . . hurry up . . . hurry up . . . hurry up, began to ring in my ears like an obsession.

The morning came for us to go to Mexico City. The train left at seven, but unless you reserved parlor-car seats, you had to be in line at the station before dawn to be sure of getting on the train, for the coaches were crowded to capacity. My father did not wish to spend the extra money for parlor-car seats, so he woke me up at four-thirty. It was still dark.

"Hurry up and get dressed," he said through the dark.

At that hour of the morning it is bitter cold in Toluca's high mountain valley. From the well Maximiliano brought us water for washing that was like ice. The cook began to prepare breakfast. We sat down to eat. At the table my father gulped his food quickly, looked across at me, and barked for no reason at all: "Hurry up!"

Suddenly my stomach began to turn over and over. And I could not swallow another mouthful. Waves of heat engulfed me. My eyes burned. My body shook. I wanted more than anything on earth to hit my father, but instead I got up from the table and went back to bed. The bed went round and round and the room turned dark. Anger clotted in every vein, and my tongue tasted like dry blood.

My father stuck his head in the bedroom door and asked me what was the matter.

I said: "Nothing."

He said: "Don't you want to go to Mexico City?"

I said: "No, I don't want to go."

I don't know what else he said, but after a while I heard him telling Maximiliano in Spanish to hurry up with his bags. Then the outside door closed, and he was gone to the train.

The housekeeper came in and asked me what I wanted.

I said: "Nothing."

Maximiliano came back from the station and sat down silently on the tile floor just inside my door, his blanket about him. At noon the cook brought me a big bowl of warm soup, but I couldn't drink it. My stomach kept turning round and round inside me. And when I thought of my father, I got sicker and sicker. I hated my father.

They sent for the doctor. He came and gave me a prescription. The housekeeper took it herself and had it filled, not trusting the *mozo*. But when my father came back after four days in the city, I still hadn't eaten anything. I had a high fever. He sent for the doctor again, and the doctor said I'd better go to the hospital.

This time my father engaged seats in the parlor car and took me to the American Hospital in Mexico City. There, after numberless examinations, they decided I had better remain several weeks, since they thought I had a stomach infection.

The three middle-aged Mexican sisters came to see me and brought a gift of guava jelly. They asked what on earth could have happened to make me so ill. I must have had a great shock, they said, because my eyes were a deep yellow. But I never told them or the doctors that I was sick because I hated my father.

For two or three weeks I got pushed around in a wheelchair in the charming gardens of the American Hospital. When I learned that it was costing my father twenty dollars a day to keep me there, I made no effort to get better. It pleased me immensely to have him spending twenty dollars a day. In September, I went back to Cleveland without having seen Xochimilco, or a bullfight.

JAMES BALDWIN

Notes of a Native Son

On the 29th of July, in 1943, my father died. On the same day, a few hours later, his last child was born. Over a month before this, while all our energies were concentrated in waiting for these events, there had been, in Detroit, one of the bloodiest race riots of the century. A few hours after my father's funeral, while he lay in state in the undertaker's chapel, a race riot broke out in Harlem. On the morning of the 3rd of August, we drove my father to the graveyard through a wilderness of smashed plate glass.

The day of my father's funeral had also been my nineteenth birthday. As we drove him to the graveyard, the spoils of injustice, anarchy, discontent, and hatred were all around us. It seemed to me that God himself had devised, to mark my father's end, the most sustained and brutally dissonant of codas. And it seemed to me, too, that the violence which rose all about us as my father left the world had been devised as a corrective for the pride of his eldest son. I had declined to believe in that apocalypse which had been central to my father's vision; very well, life seemed to be saying, here is something that will certainly pass for an apocalypse until the real thing comes along. I had inclined to be contemptuous of my father for the conditions of his life, for the conditions of our lives. When his life had ended I began to wonder about that life and also, in a new way, to be apprehensive about my own.

I had not known my father very well. We had got on badly, partly because we shared, in our different fashions, the vice of stubborn pride. When he was dead I realized that I had hardly ever spoken to him. When he had been dead a long time I began to wish I had. It seems to be typical of life in America, where opportunities, real and fancied, are thicker than anywhere else on the globe, that the second generation has no time to talk to the first. No one, including my father, seems to have known exactly how old he was, but his mother had been born during slavery. He was of the first generation of free men. He, along with thousands of other Negroes, came North after 1919, and I was part of that generation which had never seen the landscape of what Negroes sometimes call the Old Country.

He had been born in New Orleans and had been a quiet young man there during the time that Louis Armstrong, a boy, was running errands for the dives and honky-tonks of what was always presented to me as one of the most wicked of cities—to this day, whenever I think of New Orleans, I also helplessly think of Sodom and Gomorrah. My father never mentioned Louis Armstrong, except to forbid us to play his records; but there was a picture of him on our wall for a long time. One of my father's strong-willed female relatives had placed it there and forbade my father to take it down. He never did, but he eventually maneuvered her out of the house and when, some years later, she was in trouble and near death, he refused to do anything to help her.

He was, I think, very handsome. I gather this from photographs and from my own memories of him, dressed in his Sunday best and on his way to preach a sermon somewhere, when I was little. Handsome, proud, and ingrown, "like a toe-nail," somebody said. But he looked to me, as I grew older, like pictures I had seen of African tribal chieftains: he really should have been naked, with war-paint on and barbaric mementos, standing among spears. He could be chilling in the pulpit and indescribably cruel in his personal life and he was certainly the most bitter man I have ever met; yet it must be said that there was something else in him, buried in him, which lent him his tremendous power and, even, a rather crushing charm. It had something to do with his blackness, I think—he was very black—with his blackness and his beauty, and with the fact that he knew that he was black but did not know that he was beautiful. He claimed to be proud of his blackness but it had also been the cause of much humiliation and it had fixed bleak boundaries to his life. He was not a young man when we were growing up and he had already suffered many kinds of ruin; in his outrageously demanding and protective way he loved his children, who were black like him and menaced, like him; and all these things sometimes showed in his face when he tried, never to my knowledge with any success, to establish contact with any of us. When he took one of his children on his knee to play, the child always became fretful and began to cry; when he tried to help one of us with our homework the absolutely unabating tension which emanated from him caused our minds and our tongues to become paralyzed, so that he, scarcely knowing why, flew into a rage and the child, not knowing why, was punished. If it ever entered his head to bring a surprise home for his children, it was, almost unfailingly, the wrong surprise and even the big watermelons he often brought home on his back in the summertime led to the most appalling scenes. I do not remember, in all those years, that one of his children was ever glad to see him come home. From what I was able to gather of his early life, it seemed that this inability to establish contact with other people had always marked him and had been one of the things which had driven him out of New Orleans. There was something in him, therefore, groping and tentative, which was never expressed and which was buried with him. One saw it most clearly when he was facing new people and hoping to impress them. But he never did, not for long. We went from church to smaller and more improbable church, he found himself in less and less demand as a minister, and by the time he died none of his friends had come to see him for a long time. He had lived and died in an intolerable bitterness of spirit and it frightened me, as we drove him to the graveyard through those unquiet, ruined streets, to see how powerful and overflowing this bitterness could be and to realize that this bitterness now was mine.

When he died I had been away from home for a little over a year. In that year I had had time to become aware of the meaning of all my father's bitter warnings, had discovered the secret of his proudly pursed lips and rigid carriage: I had discovered the weight of white people in the world. I saw that this had been for my ancestors and now would be for me an awful thing to live with and that the bitterness which had helped to kill my father could also kill me.

He had been ill a long time—in the mind, as we now realized, reliving instances of his fantastic intransigence in the new light of his affliction and endeavoring to feel a sorrow for him which never, quite, came true. We had not known that he was being eaten up by paranoia, and the discovery that his cruelty, to our bodies and our minds, had been one of the symptoms of his illness was not, then, enough to enable us to forgive him. The younger children felt, quite simply, relief that he would not be coming home anymore. My mother's observation that it was he, after all, who had kept them alive all these years meant nothing because the problems of keeping children alive are not real for children. The older children felt, with my father gone, that they could invite their friends to the house without fear that their friends would be insulted or, as had sometimes happened with me, being told that their friends were in league with the devil and intended to rob our family of everything we owned. (I didn't fail to wonder, and it made me hate him, what on earth we owned that anybody else would want.)

His illness was beyond all hope of healing before anyone realized that he was ill. He had always been so strange and had lived, like a prophet, in such unimaginably close communion with the Lord that his long silences which were punctuated by moans and hallelujahs and snatches of old songs while he sat at the living-room window never seemed odd to us. It was not until he refused to eat because, he said, his family was trying to poison him that my mother was forced to accept as a fact what had, until then, been only an unwilling suspicion. When he was committed, it was discovered that he had tuberculosis and, as it turned out, the disease of his mind allowed the disease of his body to destroy him. For the doctors could not force him to eat, either, and, though he was fed intravenously, it was clear from the beginning that there was no hope for him.

In my mind's eye I could see him, sitting at the window, locked up in his terrors; hating and fearing every living soul including his children who had betrayed him, too, by reaching toward the world which had despised him. There were nine of us. I began to wonder what it could have felt like for such a man to have had nine children whom he could barely feed. He used to make little jokes about our poverty, which never, of course, seemed very funny to us; they could not have seemed very funny to him, either, or else our all too feeble response to them would never have caused such rages. He spent great energy and achieved, to our chagrin, no small amount of success in keeping us away from the people who surrounded us, people who had all-night rent parties to which we listened when we should have been sleeping, people who cursed and drank and flashed razor blades on Lenox Avenue. He could not understand why, if they had so much energy to spare, they could not use it to make their lives better. He treated almost everybody on our block with a most uncharitable asperity and neither they, nor, of course, their children were slow to reciprocate.

The only white people who came to our house were welfare workers and bill collectors. It was almost always my mother who dealt with them, for my father's temper, which was at the mercy of his pride, was never to be trusted. It was clear that he felt their very presence in his home to be a violation: this was conveyed by his carriage, almost ludicrously stiff, and by his voice, harsh and vindictively polite. When I was around nine or ten I wrote a play which was directed by a young, white schoolteacher, a woman, who then took an interest in me, and gave me books to read and, in order to corroborate my theatrical bent, decided to take me to see what she somewhat tactlessly referred to as "real" plays. Theater-going was forbidden in our house, but, with the really cruel intuitiveness of a child, I suspected that the color of this woman's skin would carry the day for me. When, at school, she suggested taking me to the theater, I did not, as I might have done if she had been a Negro, find a way of discouraging her, but agreed that she should pick me up at my house one evening. I then, very cleverly, left all the rest to my mother, who suggested to my father, as I knew she would, that it would not be very nice to let such a kind woman make the trip for nothing. Also, since it was a schoolteacher, I imagined that my mother countered the idea of sin with the idea of "education," which word, even with my father, carried a kind of bitter weight.

Before the teacher came my father took me aside to ask *why* she was coming, what *interest* she could possibly have in our house, in a boy like me. I said I didn't know but I, too, suggested that it had something to do with education. And I understood that my father was waiting for me to say something—I didn't quite know what; perhaps that I wanted his protection against this teacher and her "education." I said none of these things and the teacher came and we went out. It was clear, during the brief interview in our living room, that my father was agreeing very much against his will and that he would have refused permission if he had dared. The fact that he did not dare caused me to despise him: I had no way of knowing that he was facing in that living room a wholly unprecedented and frightening situation.

"But as for me and my house," my father had said, "we will serve the Lord." I wondered, as we drove him to his resting place, what this line had meant for him. I had heard him preach it many times. I had preached it once myself, proudly giving it an interpretation different from my father's. Now the whole thing came back to me, as though my father and I were on our way to Sunday school and I were memorizing the golden text: *And if it seem evil unto you to serve the Lord, choose you this day whom you will serve; whether the gods which your fathers served that were on the other side of the flood, or the gods of the Amorites, in whose land ye dwell: but as for me and my house, we will serve the Lord*. I suspected in these familiar lines a meaning which had never been there for me before. All of my father's texts and songs, which I had decided were meaningless, were arranged before me at his death like empty bottles, waiting to hold the meaning which life would give them for me. This was his legacy: nothing is ever escaped. That bleakly memorable morning I hated the unbelievable streets and the Negroes and whites who had, equally, made them that way. But I knew that it was folly, as my father would have said, this bitterness was folly. It was necessary to hold on to the things that mattered. The dead man mattered, the new life mattered; blackness and whiteness did not matter; to believe that they did was to acquiesce in one's own destruction. Hatred, which could destroy so much, never failed to destroy the man who hated and this was an immutable law.

It began to seem that one would have to hold in the mind forever two ideas which seemed to be in opposition. The first idea was acceptance, the acceptance, totally without rancor, of life as it is, and men as they are: in the light of this idea, it goes without saying that injustice is a commonplace. But this did not mean that one could be complacent, for the second idea was of equal power: that one must never, in one's own life, accept these injustices as commonplace but must fight them with all one's strength. This fight begins, however, in the heart and it now had been laid to my charge to keep my own heart free of hatred and despair. This intimation made my heart heavy and, now that my father was irrecoverable, I wished that he had been beside me so that I could have searched his face for the answers which only the future would give me now.

MALCOLM X

Nightmare

When my mother was pregnant with me, she told me later, a party of hooded Ku Klux Klan riders galloped up to our home in Omaha, Nebraska, one night. Surrounding the house, brandishing their shotguns and rifles, they shouted for my father to come out. My mother went to the front door and opened it. Standing where they could see her pregnant condition, she told them that she was alone with her three small children, and that my father was away, preaching, in Milwaukee. The Klansmen shouted threats and warnings at her that we had better get out of town because "the good Christian white people" were not going to stand for my father's "spreading trouble" among the "good" Negroes of Omaha with the "back to Africa" preachings of Marcus Garvey.

My father, the Reverend Earl Little, was a Baptist minister, a dedicated organizer for Marcus Aurelius Garvey's U.N.I.A. (Universal Negro Improvement Association). With the help of such disciples as my father, Garvey, from his headquarters in New York City's Harlem, was raising the banner of black-race purity and exhorting the Negro masses to return to their ancestral African homeland—a cause which had made Garvey the most controversial black man on earth.

Still shouting threats, the Klansmen finally spurred their horses and galloped around the house, shattering every window pane with their gun butts. Then they rode off into the night, their torches flaring, as suddenly as they had come.

My father was enraged when he returned. He decided to wait until I was born—which would be soon—and then the family would move. I am not sure why he made this decision, for he was not a frightened Negro, as most then were, and many still are today. My father was a big, six-foot-four, very black man. He had only one eye. How he had lost the other one I have never known. He was from Reynolds, Georgia, where he had left school after the third or maybe fourth grade. He believed, as did Marcus Garvey, that freedom, independence and self-respect could never be achieved by the Negro in America, and that therefore the Negro should leave America to the white man and return to his African land of origin. Among the reasons my father had decided to risk and dedicate his life to help disseminate this philosophy among his people was that he had seen four of his six brothers die by violence, three of them killed by white men, including one by lynching. What my father could not know then was that of the remaining three, including himself, only one, my Uncle Jim, would die in bed, of natural causes. Northern white police were later to shoot my Uncle Oscar. And my father was finally himself to die by the white man's hands.

It has always been my belief that I, too, will die by violence. I have done all that I can to be prepared.

I was my father's seventh child. He had three children by a previous marriage—Ella, Earl, and Mary, who lived in Boston. He had met and married my mother in Philadelphia, where their first child, my oldest full brother, Wilfred, was born. They moved from Philadelphia to Omaha, where Hilda and then Philbert were born.

I was next in line. My mother was twenty-eight when I was born on May 19, 1925, in an Omaha hospital. Then we moved to Milwaukee, where Reginald was born. From infancy, he had some kind of hernia condition which was to handicap him physically for the rest of his life.

Louise Little, my mother, who was born in Grenada, in the British West Indies, looked like a white woman. Her father *was* white. She had straight black hair, and her accent did not sound like a Negro's. Of this white father of hers, I know nothing except her shame about it. I remember hearing her say she was glad that she had never seen him. It was, of course, because of him that I got my reddish-brown "mariny" color of skin, and my hair of the same color. I was the lightest child in our family. (Out in the world later on, in Boston and New York, I was among the millions of Negroes who were insane enough to feel that it was some kind of status symbol to be light-complexioned—that one was actually fortunate to be born thus. But, still later, I learned to hate every drop of that white rapist's blood that is in me.)

Our family stayed only briefly in Milwaukee, for my father wanted to find a place where he could raise our own food and perhaps build a business. The teaching of Marcus Garvey stressed becoming independent of the white man. We went next, for some reason, to Lansing, Michigan. My father bought a house and soon, as had been his pattern, he was doing freelance Christian preaching in local Negro Baptist churches, and during the week he was roaming about spreading word of Marcus Garvey.

He had begun to lay away savings for the store he had always wanted to own when, as always, some stupid local Uncle Tom Negroes began to funnel stories about his revolutionary beliefs to the local white people. This time, the get-out-of-town threats came from a local hate society called The Black Legion. They wore black robes instead of white. Soon, nearly everywhere my father went, Black Legionnaires were reviling him as an "uppity nigger" for wanting to own a store, for living outside the Lansing Negro district, for spreading unrest and dissention among "the good niggers."

As in Omaha, my mother was pregnant again, this time with my youngest sister. Shortly after Yvonne was born came the nightmare night in 1929, my earliest vivid memory. I remember being suddenly snatched awake into a frightening confusion of pistol shots and shouting and smoke and flames. My father had shouted and shot at the two white men who had set the fire and were running away. Our home was burning down around us. We were lunging and bumping and tumbling all over each other trying to escape. My mother, with the baby in her arms, just made it into the yard before the house crashed in, showering sparks. I remember we were outside in the night in our underwear, crying and yelling our heads off. The white police and firemen came and stood around watching as the house burned down to the ground.

My father prevailed on some friends to clothe and house us temporarily; then he moved us into another house on the outskirts of East Lansing. In those days Negroes weren't allowed after dark in East Lansing proper. There's where Michigan State University is located; I related all of this to an audience of students when I spoke there in January 1963 (and had the first reunion in a long while with my younger brother, Robert, who was there doing postgraduate studies in psychology). I told them how East Lansing harassed us so much that we had to move again, this time two miles out of town, into the country. This was where my father built for us with his own hands a four-room house. This is where I really begin to remember things—this home where I started to grow up.

After the fire, I remember that my father was called in and questioned about a permit for the pistol with which he had shot at the white men who set the fire. I remember that the police were always dropping by our house, shoving things around, "just checking" or "looking for a gun." The pistol they were looking for—which they never found, and for which they wouldn't issue a permit—was sewed up inside a pillow. My father's .22 rifle and his shotgun, though, were right out in the open; everyone had them for hunting birds and rabbits and other game.

After that, my memories are of the friction between my father and mother. They seemed to be nearly always at odds. Sometimes my father would beat her. It might have had something to do with the fact that my mother had a pretty good education. Where she got it I don't know. But an educated woman, I suppose, can't resist the temptation to correct an uneducated man. Every now and then, when she put those smooth words on him, he would grab her.

My father was also belligerent toward all of the children, except me. The older ones he would beat almost savagely if they broke any of his rules—and he had so many rules it was hard to know them all. Nearly all my whippings came from my mother. I've thought a lot about why. I actually believe that as anti-white as my father was, he was subconsciously so afflicted with the white man's brainwashing of Negroes that he inclined to favor the light ones, and I was his lightest child. Most Negro parents in those days would almost instinctively treat any lighter children better than they did the darker ones. It came directly from the slavery tradition that the "mulatto," because he was visibly nearer to white, was therefore "better."

My two other images of my father are both outside the home. One was his role as a Baptist preacher. He never pastored in any regular church of his own; he was always a "visiting preacher." I remember especially his favorite sermon: "That little *black* train is a-comin' . . . an' you better get all your business right!" I guess this also fit his association with the back-to-Africa movement, with Marcus Garvey's "Black Train Homeward." My brother Philbert, the one just older than me, loved church, but it confused and amazed me. I would sit goggle-eyed at my father jumping and shouting as he preached, with the congregation jumping and shouting behind him, their souls and bodies devoted to singing and praying. Even at that young age, I just couldn't believe in the Christian concept of Jesus as someone divine. And no religious person, until I was a man in my twenties—and then in prison—could tell me anything. I had very little respect for most people who represented religion.

It was in his role as a preacher that my father had most contact with the Negroes of Lansing. Believe me when I tell you that those Negroes were in bad shape then. They are still in bad shape—though in a different way. By that I mean that I don't know a town with a higher percentage of complacent and misguided so-called middle-class Negroes—the typical status-symbol-oriented, integration-seeking type of Negroes. Just recently, I was standing in a lobby at the United Nations talking with an African ambassador and his wife, when a Negro came up to me and said, "You know me?" I was a little embarrassed because I thought he was someone I should remember. It turned out that he was one of those bragging, self-satisfied, "middle-class" Lansing Negroes. I wasn't ingratiated. He was the type who would never have been associated with Africa, until the fad of having African friends became a status-symbol for "middle-class" Negroes.

Back when I was growing up, the "successful" Lansing Negroes were such as waiters and bootblacks. To be a janitor at some downtown store was to be highly respected. The real "elite," the "big shots," the "voices of the race," were the waiters at the Lansing Country Club and the shoeshine boys at the state capitol. The only Negroes who really had any money were the ones in the numbers racket, or who ran the gambling houses, or who in some other way lived parasitically off the poorest ones, who were the masses. No Negroes were hired then by Lansing's big Oldsmobile plant, or the Reo plant.

(Do you remember the Reo? It was manufactured in Lansing, and R. E. Olds, the man after whom it was named, also lived in Lansing. When the war came along, they hired some Negro janitors.) The bulk of the Negroes were either on Welfare, or W.P.A., or they starved.

The day was to come when our family was so poor that we would eat the hole out of a doughnut; but at that time we were much better off than most town Negroes. The reason was that we raised much of our own food out there in the country where we were. We were much better off than the town Negroes who would shout, as my father preached, for the pie-in-the-sky and their heaven in the hereafter while the white man had his here on earth.

I knew that the collections my father got for his preaching were mainly what fed and clothed us, and he also did other odd jobs, but still the image of him that made me proudest was his crusading and militant campaigning with the words of Marcus Garvey. As young as I was then, I knew from what I overheard that my father was saying something that made him a "tough" man. I remember an old lady, grinning and saying to my father, "You're scaring these white folks to death!"

One of the reasons I've always felt that my father favored me was that to the best of my remembrance, it was only me that he sometimes took with him to the Garvey U.N.I.A. meetings which he held quietly in different people's homes. There were never more than a few people at any one time—twenty at most. But that was a lot, packed into someone's living room. I noticed how differently they all acted, although sometimes they were the same people who jumped and shouted in church. But in these meetings both they and my father were more intense, more intelligent and down to earth. It made me feel the same way.

I can remember hearing of "Adam driven out of the garden into the caves of Europe," "Africa for the Africans," "Ethiopians, Awake!" And my father would talk about how it would not be much longer before Africa would be completely run by Negroes—"by black men," was the phrase he always used. "No one knows when the hour of Africa's redemption cometh. It is in the wind. It is coming. One day, like a storm, it will be here."

I remember seeing the big, shiny photographs of Marcus Garvey that were passed from hand to hand. My father had a big envelope of them that he always took to these meetings. The pictures showed what seemed to me millions of Negroes thronged in parade behind Garvey riding in a fine car, a big black man dressed in a dazzling uniform with gold braid on it, and he was wearing a thrilling hat with tall plumes. I remember hearing that he had black followers not only in the United States but all around the world, and I remember how the meetings always closed with my father saying, several times, and the people chanting after him, "Up, you mighty race, you can accomplish what you will!"

I have never understood why, after hearing as much as I did of these kinds of things, I somehow never thought, then, of the black people in Africa. My image of Africa, at that time, was of naked savages, cannibals, monkeys and tigers and steaming jungles.

My father would drive in his old black touring car, sometimes taking me, to meeting places all around the Lansing area. I remember one daytime meeting (most were at night) in the town of Owosso, forty miles from Lansing, which the Negroes called "White City." (Owosso's greatest claim to fame is that it is the home town of Thomas E. Dewey.) As in East Lansing, no Negroes were allowed on the streets there after dark—hence the daytime meeting. In point of fact, in those days lots of Michigan towns were like that. Every town had a few "home" Negroes who lived there. Sometimes it would be just one family, as in the nearby county seat, Mason, which had a single Negro family named Lyons. Mr. Lyons had been a famous football star at Mason High School, was highly thought of in Mason, and consequently he now worked around that town in menial jobs.

My mother at this time seemed to be always working—cooking, washing, ironing, cleaning, and fussing over us eight children. And she was usually either arguing with or not speaking to my father. One cause of friction was that she had strong ideas about what she wouldn't eat—and didn't want *us* to eat—including pork and rabbit, both of which my father loved dearly. He was a real Georgia Negro, and he believed in eating plenty of what we in Harlem today call "soul food."

I've said that my mother was the one who whipped me—at least she did whenever she wasn't ashamed to let the neighbors think she was killing me. For if she even acted as though she was about to raise her hand to me, I would open my mouth and let the world know about it. If anybody was passing by out on the road, she would either change her mind or just give me a few licks.

Thinking about it now, I feel definitely that just as my father favored me for being lighter than the other children, my mother gave me more hell for the same reason. She was very light herself but she favored the ones who were darker. Wilfred, I know, was particularly her angel. I remember that she would tell me to get out of the house and "Let the sun shine on you so you can get some color." She went out of her way never to let me become afflicted with a sense of color-superiority. I am sure that she treated me this way partly because of how she came to be light herself.

I learned early that crying out in protest could accomplish things. My older brothers and sister had started to school when, sometimes, they would come in and ask for a buttered biscuit or something and my mother, impatiently, would tell them no. But I would cry out and make a fuss until I got what I wanted. I remember well how my mother asked me why I couldn't be a nice boy like Wilfred; but I would think to myself that Wilfred, for being so nice and quiet, often stayed hungry. So early in life, I had learned that if you want something, you had better make some noise.

Not only did we have our big garden, but we raised chickens. My father would buy some baby chicks and my mother would raise them. We all loved chicken. That was one dish there was no argument with my father about. One thing in particular that I remember made me feel grateful toward my mother was that one day I went and asked her for my own garden, and she did let me have my own little plot. I loved it and took care of it well. I loved especially to grow peas. I was proud when we had them on our table. I would pull out the grass in my garden by hand when the first little blades came up. I would patrol the rows on my hands and knees for any worms and bugs, and I would kill and bury them. And sometimes when I had everything straight and clean for my things to grow, I would lie down on my back between two rows, and I would gaze up in the blue sky at the clouds moving and think all kinds of things.

At five, I, too, began to go to school, leaving home in the morning along with Wilfred, Hilda, and Philbert. It was the Pleasant Grove School that went from kindergarten through the eighth grade. It was two miles outside the city limits, and I guess there was no problem about our attending because we were the only Negroes in the area. In those days white people in the North usually would "adopt" just a few Negroes; they didn't see them as any threat. The white kids didn't make any great thing about us, either. They called us "nigger" and "darkie" and "Rastus" so much that we thought those were our natural names. But they didn't think of it as an insult; it was just the way they thought about us.

One afternoon in 1931 when Wilfred, Hilda, Philbert, and I came home, my mother and father were having one of their arguments. There had lately been a lot of tension around the house because of Black Legion threats. Anyway, my father had taken one of the rabbits which we were raising, and ordered my mother to cook it. We raised rabbits, but sold them to whites. My father had taken a rabbit from the rabbit pen. He had pulled off the rabbit's head. He was so strong, he needed no knife to behead chickens or rabbits. With one twist of his big black hands he simply twisted off the head and threw the bleeding-necked thing back at my mother's feet.

My mother was crying. She started to skin the rabbit, preparatory to cooking it. But my father was so angry he slammed on out of the front door and started walking up the road toward town.

It was then that my mother had this vision. She had always been a strange woman in this sense, and had always had a strong intuition of things about to happen. And most of her children are the same way, I think. When something is about to happen, I can feel something, sense something. I never have known something to happen that has caught me completely off guard—except once. And that was when, years later, I discovered facts I couldn't believe about a man who, up until that discovery, I would gladly have given my life for.

My father was well up the road when my mother ran screaming out onto the porch. *"Early! Early!"* She screamed his name. She clutched up her apron in one hand, and ran down across the yard and into the road. My father turned around. He saw her. For some reason, considering how angry he had been when he left, he waved at her. But he kept on going.

She told me later, my mother did, that she had a vision of my father's end. All the rest of the afternoon, she was not herself, crying and nervous and upset. She finished cooking the rabbit and put the whole thing in the warmer part of the black stove. When my father was not back home by our bedtime, my mother hugged and clutched us, and we felt strange, not knowing what to do, because she had never acted like that.

I remember waking up to the sound of my mother's screaming again. When I scrambled out, I saw the police in the living room; they were trying to calm her down. She had snatched on her clothes to go with them. And all of us children who were staring knew without anyone having to say it that something terrible had happened to our father.

My mother was taken by the police to the hospital, and to a room where a sheet was over my father in a bed, and she wouldn't look, she was afraid to look. Probably it was wise that she didn't. My father's skull, on one side, was crushed in, I was told later. Negroes in Lansing have always whispered that he was attacked, and then laid across some tracks for a streetcar to run over him. His body was cut almost in half.

He lived two and a half hours in that condition. Negroes then were stronger than they are now, especially Georgia Negroes. Negroes born in Georgia had to be strong simply to survive.

It was morning when we children at home got the word that he was dead. I was six. I can remember a vague commotion, the house filled up with people crying, saying bitterly that the white Black Legion had finally gotten him. My mother was hysterical. In the bedroom, women were holding smelling salts under her nose. She was still hysterical at the funeral.

I don't have a very clear memory of the funeral, either. Oddly, the main thing I remember is that it wasn't in a church, and that surprised me, since my father was a preacher, and I had been where he preached people's funerals in churches. But his was in a funeral home.

And I remember that during the service a big black fly came down and landed on my father's face, and Wilfred sprang up from his chair and he shooed the fly away, and he came groping back to his chair—there were folding chairs for us to sit on—and the tears were streaming down his face. When we went by the casket, I remember that I thought that it looked as if my father's strong black face had been dusted with flour, and I wished they hadn't put on such a lot of it.

Back in the big four-room house, there were many visitors for another week or so. They were good friends of the family, such as the Lyons from Mason, twelve miles away, and the Walkers, McGuires, Liscoes, the Greens, Randolphs, and the Turners, and others from Lansing, and a lot of people from other towns, whom I had seen at the Garvey meetings.

We children adjusted more easily than our mother did. We couldn't see, as clearly as she did, the trials that lay ahead. As the visitors tapered off, she became very concerned about collecting the two insurance policies that my father had always been proud he carried. He had always said that families should be protected in case of death. One policy apparently paid off without any problem—the smaller one. I don't know the amount of it. I would imagine it was not more than a thousand dollars, and maybe half of that.

But after that money came, and my mother had paid out a lot of it for the funeral and expenses, she began going into town and returning very upset. The company that had issued the bigger policy was balking at paying off. They were claiming that my father had committed suicide. Visitors came again, and there was bitter talk about white people: how could my father bash himself in the head, then get down across the streetcar tracks to be run over?

So there we were. My mother was thirty-four years old now, with no husband, no provider or protector to take care of her eight children. But some kind of a family routine got going again. And for as long as the first insurance money lasted, we did all right.

HENRY LOUIS GATES, JR.

Colored People

PLAYING HARDBALL

Daddy worked all the time, every day but Sunday. Two jobs—twice a day, in and out, eat and work, work and eat. Evenings, we watched television together, all of us, after I'd done my homework and Daddy had devoured the newspaper or a book. He was always reading, it seemed, especially detective stories. He was a charter subscriber to *Alfred Hitchcock's Magazine* and loved detective movies on TV.

My brother Rocky was the one he was close to. Rocky worshiped sports, while I worshiped Rocky. I chased after him like a lapdog. I wanted to be just like him. But the five years between us loomed like Kilimanjaro. We were always out of phase. And he felt crowded by my adoring gaze.

Rocky and I didn't exactly start off on the right foot. When I was born, my parents moved my brother to Big Mom's house, to live with her and Little Jim, who was our first cousin and Nemo's son and the firstborn male of our generation in the Coleman family. It was not an uncommon arrangement to shift an older child to his or her grandparents', because of crowding. Since we had only three rooms, plus a tiny room with a toilet, my parents thought the move was for the best. And Big Mom's house was only a couple hundred yards straight up the hill. Still, it's difficult to gauge the trauma of that displacement, all these years later. Five years of bliss, ended by my big head popping out.

But Rocky was compensated: he was Daddy's boy. Like the rest of Piedmont, they were baseball fanatics. They knew who had done what and when, how much everyone had hit, in what inning, who had scored the most runs in 1922, who the most rbi's. They could sit in front of a TV for hours at a time, watching inning after tedious inning of baseball, baseball, baseball. Or sit at Forbes Field in Pittsburgh through a doubleheader without getting tired or longing to go home. One night, when I was seven, we saw Sandy Koufax of the Dodgers pitch one game, then his teammate Don Drysdale pitch another. It was the most boring night of my life, though later I came to realize what a feat I had witnessed, two of baseball's greatest pitchers back-to-back.

I enjoyed *going* to the games in Pittsburgh because even then I loved to travel. One of Daddy's friends would drive me. I was fascinated with geography. And since I was even more fascinated with food, a keen and abiding interest of mine, I liked the games for that reason, too. We would stop to eat at Howard Johnson's, going and coming. And there'd be hot dogs and sodas at the games, as well as popcorn and candy, to pass the eternity of successive innings in the July heat. Howard Johnson's was a five-star restaurant in Piedmont.

I used to get up early to have breakfast with Daddy, eating from his plate. I'll still spear a heavily peppered fried potato or a bit of egg off his plate today. My food didn't taste as good as his. Still doesn't. I used to drink coffee, too, in order to be just like Daddy. "Coffee will make you black," he'd tell me, with the intention of putting me off. From the beginning, I used a lot of pepper, because he did, and he did because his father did. I remember reading James Agee's *A Death in the Family* and being moved by a description of the extra pepper that the father's wife put on his eggs the very morning that he is killed in a car. Why are you frying eggs *this* time of day, Mama asked me that evening. Have you seen the pepper, Mama? I replied.

An unathletic child with too great an interest in food—no wonder I was fat, and therefore compelled to wear "husky" clothes.

My Skippy's not *fat*, Mama would lie. He's husky.

But I *was* fat, and felt fatter every time Mama repeated her lie. My mama loved me like life itself. Maybe she didn't see me as fat. But I was. And whoever thought of the euphemism "husky" should be shot. I was short and round—not obese, mind you, but *fat*. Still, I was clean and energetic, and most of the time I was cheerful. And I liked to play with other kids, not so much because I enjoyed the things we did together but because I could watch them be happy.

But sports created a bond between Rocky and my father that excluded me, and, though my father had no known athletic talent himself, my own unathletic bearing compounded my problems. For not only was I overweight; I had been born with flat feet and wore "corrective shoes." They were the bane of my existence, those shoes. While Rocky would be wearing long, pointy-toed, cool leather gentlemen, I'd be shod in blunt-ended, round-toed, fat-footed shoes that nobody but your mother could love.

And Mama *did* love those shoes. Elegant, she'd say. They're Stride-Rite. Stride-wrong, I'd think. Mama, I want some nice shoes, I'd beg, like Rocky's.

Still, I guess they did what they were meant to do, because I have good arches now. Even today, I look at the imprint of my wet foot at a swimming pool, just to make certain that my arch is still arched. I don't ever again want to wear those dull brown or black corrective shoes.

What made it all the more poignant was that Rocky—tall, lean, and handsome, blessed with my father's metabolism—was a true athlete. He would be the first Negro captain of the basketball team in high school and receive "the watch" at graduation. (He was the first colored to do that, too.)

Maybe Mama thought I was husky, but Daddy knew better, and he made no secret of it. "Two-Ton Tony Galento," he and Rocky would say, or they'd call me Chicken Flinsterwall or Fletcher Bissett, Milton Berle's or Jack Benny's character in a made-for-TV movie about two complete cowards. I hated Daddy for doing that and yielded him as unconquerable terrain to my brother, clinging desperately to my mother for protection.

Ironically, I had Daddy's athletic ability, or lack thereof, just as I have his body. (We wear the same size ring, gloves, shoes, shirt, suits, and hat.) And like him, I love to hear a good story. But during my first twelve or so years we were alienated from each other. I despised sports because I was overweight and scared to death. Especially of baseball—hardball, we called it. Yet I felt I had no choice but to try out for Little League. Everyone my age did Little League, after all. They made me a Giant, decided I was a catcher because I was "stout, like Roy Campanella," dressed me in a chest protector and a mask, and squatted me behind a batter.

It's hard to catch a baseball with your eyes closed. Each time a ball came over the plate, I thanked the Good Lord that the batter hadn't confused my nappy head with the baseball that had popped its way into my mitt. My one time at bat was an experience in blindness; miraculously, I wasn't hit in the head. With a 3 and 2 count, I got a ball, so I walked. They put in a runner for me. Everybody patted me on the back like I had just won the World Series. And everybody said nice things about my "eye." Yeah, I thought. My tightly closed eye.

Afterward, Pop and I stopped at the Cut-Rate to get a caramel ice cream cone, then began the long walk up the hill to Pearl Street. I was exhausted, so we walked easy. He was biding his time, taking smaller steps than usual so that I could keep up. "You know that you don't have to play baseball, don't you, boy?" All of a sudden I knew how Moses had felt on Mount Sinai. His voice was a bolt out of the blue. Oh, I want to play, I responded in a squeaky voice. "But you know that you don't *have* to play. I never was a good player. Always afraid of the ball. Uncoordinated, too. I can't even run straight." We laughed. "I became the manager of the team," he said. That caramel ice cream sure tasted good. I held Daddy's hand almost all the way home.

In my one time at bat, I had got on base. I had confronted the dragon and he was mine. I had, I had . . . been absurdly lucky . . . and I couldn't *wait* to give them back their baseball suit. It was about that time that Daddy stopped teasing me about being fat. That day he knew me, and he seemed to care.

Yes, Pop and I had some hard times. He thought that I didn't love him, and I thought he didn't love me. At times, we both were right. I didn't think you wanted me around, he told me much later. I thought that I embarrassed you. He did embarrass me, but not like you might think, not the usual way parents embarrass children in front of their friends, for example. He had a habit of correcting me in front of strangers or white people, especially if they were settling an argument between me and Pop by something they had just said, by a question they had answered. See, I *told* you so, he'd say loudly, embarrassing the hell out of me with a deliberateness that puzzled and vexed me. I hated him when he did that.

And despite my efforts to keep up, he and my brother had somehow made me feel as if I were an android, something not quite a person. I used to dream about going away to military school, and wrote to our congressman, Harley Staggers, for a list of names. I used to devour *McKeever and the Colonel* on Sunday nights and dream about the freedom of starting over, at a high-powered, regimented school away from home. Daddy and Rocky would make heavy-handed jokes about queers and sissies. I wasn't their direct target, but I guess it was another form of masculine camaraderie that marked me as less manly than my brother.

And while I didn't fantasize about boys, I did love the companionship of boys and men, loved hearing them talk and watching their rituals, loved the warmth that their company could bring. I even loved being with the Coleman boys, at one of their shrimp or squirrel feeds, when they would play cards. Generally, though, I just enjoyed being on the edge of the circle, watching and listening and laughing, basking in the warmth, memorizing the stories, trying to strip away illusions, getting at what was really coming down.

I made my peace with sports, by and by, and was comfortable watching Rock and Daddy watch sports. But I could never experience it with the absorption they were capable of, could never live and breathe sports as they did. Oh, I loved to watch all the tournaments, the finals, the Olympics—the ritual events. But my relation to sports was never as visceral and direct as theirs.

After I returned my Little League uniform, I became the team's batboy and then the league's official scorekeeper, publishing our results in a column in the *Piedmont Herald*, our weekly newspaper.

Much more than for sports, I had early on developed an avidity for information about The Negro. I'm not sure why, since Daddy was not exactly a race man. Niggers are crabs in a barrel: if he said that once, he said it to us a thousand times. My father was hard on colored people—and funny about it, too.

Aside from the brief stint as a student in New Jersey, Daddy's major contact with Negro culture from Elsewhere had been in the army, at Camp Lee, Virginia. He used to tell us all kinds of stories about the colored troops at Camp Lee, especially blacks from the rural South. It was clear that the army in World War II had been a great cauldron, mixing the New Negro culture, which had developed in the cities since the great migration of the twenties and thirties, and the Old Negro culture, the remnants of traditional rural black culture in the South.

Camp Lee was where colored soldiers were sent to learn how to be quartermasters—butlers, chefs, and service people, generally. Because the Army replicates the social structure of the larger society it defends, almost all black draftees were taught to cook and clean. Of course, it was usually women who cooked and cleaned outside the Army, but *someone* had to do the work, so it would be black men. Gender and race conflate in a crisis. Even educated black people were put in the quartermasters.

Well, Camp Lee was a circus and my daddy its scribe. He told us stories about how he beat the system, or damn well tried to. The first day, he had raised his hand when an officer asked who knew accounting. How hard could it be? he responded when I laughed. Hell, all you had to be able to do was add and subtract. The one thing I knew, he said, was that an accountant had an office and everybody else had to do basic training. Now, which one would *you* have picked? For two years, he stayed at Camp Lee and avoided being shipped to the front. Everybody else would be processed, then shipped out to Europe. But Daddy became a staff sergeant, serving as secretary and accountant to the commanding officer, who liked him a lot. He sent for Mama, who took a room in a colored home in town. Daddy slept there, too. Mama got a job in a dry cleaners. The pictures that I carry of them in my wallet are from this time, 1942.

The war wouldn't take Pop any farther than Camp Lee, but even that was an experience that stayed with him. There he encountered the customs and sayings, the myths and folklore, of all sorts of black people he had never even heard about. The war did more to recement black American culture, which migration had fragmented, than did any other single event or experience. "War? What is it good for? You tell 'em: absolutely nothing." Nothing for the Negro but the transfer of cultures, the merging of the old black cultures with the new. And the transfer of skills. Daddy was no "race man," but for all his sardonicism, he respected race men and women, the people who were articulate and well educated, who comported themselves with dignity and who "achieved." Being at Camp Lee, an all-colored world, he'd say a decade later, was like watching episodes of *Amos and Andy*.

Hard as Daddy could be on colored people, he was Marcus Garvey compared to *his* father. Pop Gates used to claim that the government should lock up all the niggers in a big reservation in Kansas or Oklahoma or somewhere, feed them, clothe them, and give them two names: John or Mary. Nobody would hurt them, he'd add plaintively when his children would either protest or burst into howls of laughter. Pop Gates *hated* to see black people in loud clothes, and he hated just as much our traditional poetic names, such as Arbadella or Ethelretta. Made-up names, he'd say. Shouldn't be allowed, he'd say.

I was more aggressive around white people than Daddy, and it didn't go down well with him—or anybody else. Especially my Coleman uncles. Daddy, as noted, would almost never take my side in front of others. And if he felt I had violated a boundary, he would name it publicly and side with the boundary. He would do so loudly, even with what struck my child's ears as a certain malice. It tore me up.

He was not always this way with me. At a Little League game when I was ten, I told off a white man, Mr. Frank Price, not for anything he'd done to me, but for the rude way he treated Mr. Stanley Fisher, a black man in his sixties, who was maybe twenty years Price's senior. The details are murky, but Price had been rude to the older man in a way that crossed a line, that made the colored people feel he was a racist.

I do remember that I was unable to control myself, unable to contain my anger. I found myself acting without thinking. I felt the blood rushing to my face, and a flood of nasty words poured out of my mouth, just this side of profanity. Everybody on the first-base side of the Little League field over in Westernport looked up and froze in silence as I stood in front of that big-bellied man's fat red face and told him to leave Mr. Stanley alone. Then I turned to Mr. Stanley and told him not to waste his dignity on that trash: "Don't sweat the small stuff," I said. The colored held their breaths, and Daddy looked like a cat caught between two fighting dogs and not knowing which way to turn. Even Mr. Stanley's face showed surprise at this snot-nosed kid talking right up in some redneck's face. Mr. Stanley must have been more embarrassed by me than reassured.

Daddy stepped in finally, put his arm around my shoulder, and started woofing at Frank Price and giving him those dirty glares of his, all the while pushing me gently up the field toward Stanley and the colored men who always sat together on their lawn chairs out in right field. And we then all walked together up the dusty back road that bordered the Little League field like the rim of a crater, passing the new filtration plant, which made the whole place stink worse than the sulfurous chemicals that it had been built to remove, and all the old colored men were saying what an asshole Frank Price was and always had been, and how he had been rude to Stanley, and how nobody liked or respected him (not even white people), and how nobody within earshot should pay that motherfucker no mind.

Now, you know you are supposed to respect your elders, don't you? Daddy said to me much later, after we had bought a caramel ice cream cone, to go, at the Cut-Rate. And you know you are not supposed to talk back to older people, now don't you? And you know that Stanley Fisher can take care of himself? And you know that you can get in trouble talking back to white people, don't you? Don't you, boy? Boy, you crazy sometimes. That ice cream is dripping down your fingers. Don't let it go to waste.

WESLEY BROWN

Tragic Magic

I turned into my block and saw the car in the driveway. My hands were sweating. As always with my folks and myself, it was time for the battle of wills. I was suddenly very tired. I climbed the steps slowly and rang the bell.

"Welcome home, son." We embraced, but he got the best of it, putting the crush on me before I had a chance to hug back. Pops was short like me, but packed into his runt of a body was about two hundred pounds of muscle swelling inside his pants legs and shirt.

"Melvin's here!"

"You look like you put on some more weight."

"Yeah, that's from all the starch they were feeding me."

"Would you look at this boy!"

"Don't he look good?"

"He sure do. You remember me, don't you, Melvin? I'm your Aunt Clara."

"I remember you, Aunt Clara."

"How you, Melvin?"

"Fine. How are you, Uncle Arthur?" We shook hands and he applied his legendary grip, which brought me to my knees for a moment of silent prayer. When he let me up I saw my mother standing on the steps leading upstairs.

She was much taller than my father, which was something that used to make me wonder how they made it in bed. No doubt they had found a way, just like a Watusi and a Pygmy would if they were strung out on each other. I didn't rush to Moms immediately, but took her in slowly, following the flow of her smooth, prune-juice skin from her face, down her long, bony neck to the branches of her collarbone. My mother had the airs of a giraffe. It wasn't that she felt superior. She was.

"I guess you don't see nobody else, hunh?" It was Debra. She seemed to be more the spitting image of my mother than ever, with just enough of her own unruly spray thrown in for good measure.

"Now that Melvin's here, why don't we eat?"

"Wait a minute, Rachel! The boy just got here. I wanna make a toast first." A bottle of champagne was opened and glasses were passed around to everyone. "I'd like to make this toast to Melvin. We're all glad to have you back home, son. So here's hoping you're on your way now and won't stop. And with a name like Ellington, there ain't no way you can fail!"

There it was. The invocation of the name Ellington. My father was an ardent admirer of Duke Ellington. He had collected almost every record Ellington had ever recorded and raised me on the discography. Pops had played pretty good stride piano when he was younger, but an accident to his left hand at the factory where he worked halted his ambition to become a musician. While he didn't push me to become a musician, Pops encouraged me to adopt the style of our namesake in whatever I did. According to my father, this style was embodied in an Ellington tune entitled "Diminuendo and Crescendo in Blue," and was on the album *Ellington at Newport 1956*. Pops interpreted the side as an expression of what it meant to be blue or really laid low and still sky right out of the blue. He believed that since being blue was one of the cardinal colors of existence, the most important part of life was the middle distance, or what happened between the diminuendo and crescendo of the blues.

This statement was developed in a solo by the tenor saxophone player Paul Gonsalves, who played for twenty-seven straight choruses. Pops said that every one of the choruses that Gonsalves played was a reshuffling of the same old same old, and that the significance of creating twenty-seven possibilities for the way things could go down turned everybody's head around to the extent that after listening nobody could say, "Tell me something I don't already know," but would have to say, "Oh, yeah?"

The older I got, the more Pops urged me to follow the Duke Ellington lead, embodied in the twenty-seven-chorus solo by Paul Gonsalves. He drilled into me that life was a continuous jam session. And that it was only by trading choruses with the vamp of the blues that I would ever learn that freedom is staying loose when time is tight.

I sat down to a table that was definitely a dumping ground for the horn of plenty. The sumptuous spread of meats, vegetables, and freshly baked bread was such a departure from the cut-and-dried grit in prison that for a moment I just feasted on the seasoned steam rising from the table.

"I hope the food tastes all right, Melvin. I cooked all your favorites."

"Everything is really good, Moms."

"Rachel! Is that all you gonna put on his plate?"

"He can get more if he wants it, Walter."

"Here, Melvin, take a piece of this country ham."

"No thanks, Pops."

"What's wrong? Why don't you want any ham?"

"I stopped eating pork while I was away." Jaws locked in the middle of chews.

"Why'd you do that?"

"It didn't agree with me, so I stopped eating it."

"It agreed with you all right before you left."

"Well, I just don't eat it anymore."

"Melvin! You aren't a Muslim, are you?"

"No, Moms, I'm not a Muslim."

"Well, I don't know who you been talkin to," Pops said, "but I can't understand bein all choosy about what you eat. I guess you gonna tell me next that you don't eat no flesh period, and that you done joined some group that eats plants and chews weeds all the time."

"It's all right, Walter. If Melvin doesn't want any ham, he doesn't have to eat any." Moms was definitely trying to be slick, playing a vise closing in on me from the other side of the table. Already I was beginning to feel guilty. But I hung tough and didn't accompany my folks' harangue in support of hog meat by eating any.

"You shouldn't let Daddy get away with some of the things he says to you," Debra said later when we were alone. She had always been much more of a fighter than I was, resisting any unjustified attempts to bridle her. All through grade school she was one of the few girls whom boys would never harass. She had a reputation for fighting with such ferocity and abandon that even boys who were older were not willing to tangle with her.

"What difference would it have made if I had said something?" I said. "You know how Pops is."

"Yeah, I know how he is. That's why I always let him know what's on my mind." She was still too bony to be so brazen, drilling the air with both pinkies and staring with eyes that stung. "I've been that way," she said, "ever since Daddy took me to the hospital to see Uncle Arthur after he had an operation. It was the first time I ever saw an adult who was weak and powerless. It was the best thing that could have ever happened to me. After that, whenever Daddy tried to intimidate me, it just rolled off my back, cause it was like watching Uncle Arthur laid up in the hospital scared to death but trying to order everybody around. If I knew an adult who was sick, I couldn't wait to visit them, especially if it was a man. That's probably one of the reasons I decided to become a nurse. Seeing people humbled by physical ailments helps me to deal with the arrogance of people who have their health and strength. So now if I cater to a man, it's either cause I want to or cause

I'm being well paid. Daddy knows that and doesn't try to tell me what to do anymore. He knows if I wanted to eat veal cutlet through a straw not to say anything to me about it. . . . But anyway, what about you? Are you okay?"

"Yeah, I'm all right."

"I worried about you a lot while you were gone. You've always been so soft-spoken. How did you keep people from messing over you?"

"I just tried to stay out of the way."

"Well, I'm glad you're out of that place. . . . What are you going to do now?"

"Give up masturbation."

"I think you'll come through it all right."

"Coming ain't my problem. What I need is a co-respondent."

"Hey, I wish I could help you, Melvin, but incest just ain't my thing."

"Yeah, I love you, too, sis."

I slipped upstairs to the bathroom to take a piss. When I flushed the toilet there was a knock at the door.

"Who is it?"

"It's your father." When he got all formal like that it was usually the beginning of a long talk.

"I wanna talk to you about somethin."

"What about?"

"Have a seat." Another familiar line. Pops had opened with those same lines (years before) when he had given me my first supply of prophylactics.

"How old are you, now, Melvin?"

"Fifteen."

"I been noticin your sheets lately and it looks like to me you been havin a lot of wet dreams. So I guess you at the age where you gonna wanna make some of them dreams come true. But what you gotta make sure of is that you protect yourself. You know what I mean?" I nodded that I did.

"Now, I'm gonna give you some protection to use and when you run out just tell me and I'll see that you get some more. . . . Now, you got a lot of these fast-tail girls out here that'll tell you not to use nuthin. But you do like I tell you and use the protection. I'm tellin you this now so you won't be comin to me later about some little girl you done knocked up.

"Have you gotten any yet?" he said, stirring his right index finger into a circle made by the thumb and forefinger of his left hand.

"Unh, unh."

"Well, you got plenty of time. No need to rush things. Now, I'm not sayin you shouldn't get a little piece as soon as you can. I'd rather you do that than lose your nature playin with yourself."

I was so proud when he gave me those first prophylactics that I wore one to school every day for about a month. However, it was a long time before I had cause to use a rubber for any other occasion.

I sat down on the toilet seat and wondered what he was going to give me this time.

"I'm sorry about what happened at the dinner table a while ago. I wasn't tryin to give you a hard time. It's just that your mother spent a lot of time fixin all the things you like and when you said you didn't want it, I kind a saw red for a minute."

"That's okay, Pops."

"But that's not what I wanted to talk about. What I really want to talk about is your plans."

"My plans?"

"Yeah, the future. You've had a little setback, but now it's time to plan your next move so you don't make the same mistake again."

"Mistake! What mistake?"

"What I mean is that you'll be wiser the next time. And since every generation gets weaker and wiser, you got to have your wits about you cause you gettin weaker all the time. I'm not just talkin about you. That goes for me, too. You see, when I was comin up, I could only do what there was time for. And there wasn't time for very much. But my generation had to bide our time so your generation could do the things we were never able to do. And when you can take the time to do what you want, you're much wiser than somebody whose time was never their own. You understand what I'm tryin to tell you?"

"Yeah, I see what you mean. But how does being wise make you weak?"

"That's because whenever things change for the better, people tend to get weaker. You need more strength to want something and not have any way of gettin it anytime soon than you do once you get it. That's why you'll never be as strong as me. It's the same with the whole black race. We're a lot wiser than we was in the past, but we're not as strong."

"What do you mean by strong?"

"Acceptin the fact that you can't always have things your own way all the time."

"I know that, Pops!"

"You may know it now, but two years ago you was so hardheaded nobody could tell you nuthin."

"What are you trying to do, sentence me again? I already did my time, Pops."

"But you wouldn't have had to do any time at all if you hadn't done so much talkin in the raw!"

"You're probably right about that, but I'm not going to *if* myself to death over it. I did what I did. And if I can live with it, so should you!"

"All right. I was just checking to see where you situated. I'm a believer that if you say enough out-of-the-way things to somebody, sooner or later they'll get tired of it and set you straight on which way they're headed. . . . Was it rough in that place?"

"It wasn't too bad."

"Nobody did anything to you, did they?"

"A few tried."

"Well, I'm glad it's over with. I knew you'd be all right. You an Ellington . . . You goin out later?"

"Yeah."

"Well, before you go, talk to your mother. She wants to talk to you. But you know how she is. She figures you should come to her. She's probably in the kitchen now. Go talk to her."

LOUIS EDWARDS

Ten Seconds

His family used to go to the beach all the time. Mama and Daddy, Marcus, his older brother, and Jackie, his little sister. The first time they went that he can remember, the time that it happened, he was five years old. Daddy drove a big beige Buick that they jumped into and headed for the beach. It was going to be a picnic because there was food. A large bowl of potato salad was resting in Eddie's lap. Marcus had a pan of seasoned chicken that Daddy would barbecue on one of the pits on the black side of the beach. The side where there were no "Whites Only" signs, the end where the grass was allowed to compete fiercely with the sand for surface space. They parked and Eddie was the first one out of the car, running with the bowl of potato salad to a covered area where there were blue and yellow metal tables and benches. The sand was hot and burned his feet, but it didn't surprise him; this was not his first time here. He couldn't remember the other times, but he had been here before, three or four times maybe. He didn't have to stop and look at the water, wonder at the waves; it was all familiar. He must have been here before. "Edward James Franklin!" his mother yelled. "Boy, if you don't stop all that running." He was laughing, but she could see only his back. Ha. Ha. "Watch out for that bottle glass. And drop that potato salad and I'ma beat your ass." She was always saying she was going to beat his ass for something, and a lot of times she did. Like yesterday when he had said a bad word. Summonabitch! He didn't know what it meant, but Daddy used it all the time. Sometimes he just shouted it at the air when he was angry. Or maybe when he was mad with someone he would use it to talk about them. But sometimes he even used it when he was happy, and it would sort of rumble up out of his chest mixed with laughter. At those times it seemed like such a good word.

But even then Eddie knew that "summonabitch" was a bad word. He had said it once too often when Mama was around. She had promised to beat his ass if she ever heard him use it. So when he said it yesterday after he had dropped his last M&M on the floor, while she was in the same room giving him eyes that were saying you better not pick that up and eat it, and frustration built up in him because with her watching him that way he couldn't even say "God kissed it, the devil missed it" and make it clean, so he couldn't control himself—his last M&M!—couldn't control the way his foot stamped, the way his voice said "Summonabitch!" Yesterday, after that, she rushed over to him like the wind and swatted him on the behind to the rhythm of "What Did I Tell You A-bout Say-ing That Word."

He made it to one of the vacant tables and placed the bowl of potato salad there. The others gathered slowly, his mother carrying two-year-old Jackie, his father with an inflated inner tube he had removed from the trunk of the car, and Marcus carrying the pan of chicken, sulking because Daddy had made him come to the beach with the family. He was old enough to do what he wanted to do. Fifteen! He wanted to stay home and watch TV. When Daddy tried to make him do stuff like this, it really pissed him off. It was just too fuckin' hot outside. And that's when Eddie heard the slapping sound coming from the living room, where they were arguing. Daddy's hand meeting some uncovered part of Marcus. Don't ever get pissed off with Daddy, he had told himself, unless you want to get slapped. And if you do get pissed off with him, you better be careful about what you said to him. "Fuckin" was another one of those words like "summonabitch"; you had to be really careful about when you said it. But Eddie wasn't worried about Marcus right now. Right now he was simply happy and glad to be happy. He ran out onto the sand and did a somersault, landing on his ass, but the pain he felt was sweet, because it was *his* tumble and *his* ass, which today had been neither slapped nor beaten.

"Baby, go ahead and start the fire," Daddy said to Mama. "Me and the boys gonna hit the water."

"Jimmy, can't you see I got this child hanging on me? How the hell am I supposed to start a fire?"

"Put her down. She can walk." Jackie smiled at Daddy. "Or give her to me. Daddy gon teach that baby how to swim." He put his arms out to Jackie and she reached for him. But before they could meet, Mama swerved the baby away.

"James, you must be crazy if you think you takin my baby out in that water," she said.

"I'll start the fire, Mama," Marcus broke in.

"That sounds good to me," Daddy said. He smiled at Marcus, who turned away and walked back to the car to get the charcoal.

"Go on then," Mama said to Daddy and Eddie, motioning toward the water.

Eddie, following the line of her outstretched arm, charged across the sand, feeling free. But he could feel that Daddy was chasing him. The ground quaked beneath his feet from Daddy's heavy trodding. The trembling surface seemed to jump up and meet Eddie's steps halfway, while his knees were still bent, putting an extra strain on the muscles in his little-boy legs, and somehow tickling his stomach, so that he had slowed to a creeping hunched-over walk and was overcome with wild laughter by the time Daddy came up behind him and swooped him up and onto a solid shoulder. It was one of Eddie's favorite spots to sit and he reveled in being placed there now. Daddy was carrying the inflated inner tube on his other shoulder, and Eddie slapped at it with the hand that wasn't gripped around Daddy's neck. Rising up to meet Eddie's nose was Daddy's huffing breath, hot and sweet as it usually was. It was the same hot sweetness that kissed him late at night sometimes while he was dreaming. ("Leave him alone. You gonna wake him up, you drunken fool.") He bobbed up and down on Daddy's shoulder, the water getting closer. Then Daddy splashed in and began to slow down quickly as the water rose to his knees. They continued to move ahead and when the water came up to Daddy's waist, he let the inner tube fall from his shoulder and rest upon the water. He placed Eddie on the inner tube and told him to hold on. The water was cool on Eddie's legs as they dangled in the water through the empty middle of the inner tube. Daddy began pushing Eddie out further into the lake. He looked at Daddy's hand, so big, on the inner tube next to his; he looked across the expansive lake, tiny green-black waves washing toward him; his head fell back, and there was the sky—way, way up. Floating along, he closed his eyes. Everything was so big, so much bigger than he was. You might as well surrender to these forces. A good feeling, being carried. Like when you fell asleep sometimes while watching television in the living room and they came in and tried to wake you up to go get into your bed, but you pretended to be still asleep. They had to pick you up and carry you down the hall to your room, for a second, their eyes all over your face. They were gonna beat your ass if you were faking, but you knew that wasn't true because they kissed you on the neck and laid you on the bed gently, pulled up the covers and kissed you again.

Now Daddy stopped pushing. Eddie opened his eyes, looked back, and saw that the sand was far away. He could barely see Mama, Marcus, and the baby under the covering. The wind turned the inner tube slowly, and he watched as Daddy disappeared underwater with a slurping sound. He was out of sight so long that Eddie began to wonder if he would come back. ("Is he coming back, Mama?" "Yes, baby. Now go on back to bed." "Me, I don't care if he never come back. Always drunk and carrying on. Hmph—tryin to tell me what to do." "Marcus, shut up before I have to hit you." "I guess you have to hit somebody. . . ." "What did you say?" "Nothing." "Don't cry, Mama. Daddy comin back.") Then Daddy whooshed up through the inner tube, filling up the middle with his body and flying water. Eddie felt the big hands locking in his armpits and he kicked his legs in pleasure as he rose high above Daddy's head. "Put me down, put me down," he cried, wanting never to come down. But Daddy did let him down, placed him safely on the floating tube. Then Daddy swam around while Eddie splashed water with his hands. The dark green color of the water intrigued him, so he cupped some in his hands and brought it to his face. It smelled fresh. He stuck out his tongue and dipped it in the water. Salt. The water had a flavor. Clear water tasted like nothing. Green water tasted like salt. Tasting it made him hungry. Watching Daddy swimming and splashing in it made him hungry.

Then Daddy went under again. Eddie watched for him intensely. Where did Daddy go? He wanted to know. Why and how did he always come back? He wanted to know, but he felt powerless. He didn't know how he would ever be able to find out the answers to his questions. But maybe if he could get under the water to follow Daddy, he would have a chance to answer them. It couldn't be very hard to do, going under. It looked so easy, the way Daddy splashed around, going under and coming up as he pleased. But Daddy was big, like the lake; he was too little. How would he ever be able to get under the water to follow Daddy? In frustration he slapped at the surface of the water. Then he kicked at it as hard as he could, but it wouldn't let his legs move through it very fast. It pushed hard back against them. It was a force. He was too little; it was so big. It was a force. He would surrender to it. But since it already knew he was a fighter, he would have to trick it. Pretend to be asleep. It would believe him. They wanted to believe you; they liked to carry you. He pushed himself from his seat on the tube, then let his body go limp. Sliding downward through the middle of the tube, he felt the water hug around him coolly. It was carrying him down, it covered his head, it began to cool his insides, entering through his mouth and through his nose and through his ears. There was a salty burning that soon went quiet. The water flooded his head with waves that washed away Daddy first and then everything else. Then it closed above him in a kiss. Below the surface, it kept carrying him away.

"Lord, have mercy," Mama was saying in a scared, low voice. "The man done killed his own child."

"Shut up, Dorothy," Daddy said, almost directly into Eddie's ear. He was close. "The boy is all right. Don't come running over here with none of your foolishness. I don't wanna hear that shit, woman."

Eddie was struggling to open his eyes.

"Oh, yeah, you gon hear it, all right. You ain't gon kill my child and git away with it."

"Woman, the boy is breathing. Look at here—he just opened up his eyes."

Eddie saw Daddy's face up close, the red eyes that had a wet, sunny sparkle of happiness in them holding his attention. "You all right, Eddie," Daddy assured him in hot sweetness. "You all right, son."

"Well, don't just keep him out here in this hot sun, James. Let's git him in the shade," Mama was saying. "Maybe he need to go to the hospital." Daddy picked Eddie up in his arms, cradling him, and walked toward the covering.

"Daddy, I don't want to know how to swim," Eddie coughed out. Daddy nodded his head okay, okay; he understood. But Eddie would get over it. This was just one bad experience. He wouldn't be afraid of the water forever. Someday he'd want to learn how to swim, and Daddy would teach him. But then that meant that he really did not understand Eddie at all. Eddie wasn't afraid of the water. He meant that he really *didn't* want to know how to swim. Not because he was afraid of the water, but because the drowning was okay. The water could carry you to a good place. He didn't want to learn how to swim, because if he did, he'd be forced to do what Daddy did: keep coming back.

EARL OFARI HUTCHINSON

A Talk with My Father

Like James Baldwin, most of us want to know who is this man we call "father"? Is he the man that he seems or is there something else about HIM that we don't know? We know that he had a life before we were born. But what kind of life?

Most of us will never ask. Partly because we put our fathers on such a distant pedestal that they become larger than life. But then we may not ask because we suspect that there are hidden compartments in their lives where painful secrets are buried deep and truths are blurred in the mists of time.

Our fathers may have done things that they want to forget. We should not be surprised. As Oscar Wilde said, young men must commit terrible sins so that as old men they can have terrible regrets.

Still, if we are lucky and our fathers are still with us, we owe it to ourselves to take them down from the pedestal and talk to them about their lives. I don't mean just listening to them tell of playful reminiscences. I mean their experiences and encounters. This may require a gentle nudge or even a hard push. But it's important because they are not only our fathers. They are our elders. And their past can serve as our signpost to the future.

Whether my father committed terrible sins and now has terrible regrets, I don't know. But I consider myself among those fortunate enough to have him here to ask him. He is now nearing his ninth decade of life. He has seen the triumphs and tragedies of this era. He has witnessed the wars, revolutions, social upheavals and major technological discoveries of the Twentieth Century.

He has lived through the days when African-Americans, in the immortal words uttered by Supreme Court Chief Justice Roger Taney in the Dred Scott decision in 1857, had no rights which a white man was bound to respect. He has seen the great movements of change that have guaranteed African-Americans their rights—at least on paper. He can remember when blacks were called: ex-slaves, colored, negro, Negro, black, Afro-American and African-American; everything, that is, except American.

So we talked. I asked him a few of the same questions I asked the other black fathers I interviewed for *Black Fatherhood*. I believe that scattered among his recollections of yesterday's problems may be, just may be, a few of today's solutions.

But first let me take you on a detour through the personal life of the man that I call "father."

He was born at the turn of the century in the small town of Clarksville, Tennessee, located on the Cumberland and Red Rivers in the Northwest corner of the state. Clarksville not only produced livestock and farm goods, it was a leader in the manufacture of snuff. The town did not have a particularly violent history. In fact, most people there could remember only one lynching. But it was the South and the threat was always there. That was enough for my grandfather.

Jim Hutchinson (everybody called him Jim, never James) was fired by the dream that drove many blacks of his day. He would go North to escape the poverty and violence of the South, find a decent job, and live like a human being. The first chance he got, he took his wife and children and headed North. They settled in St. Louis. It didn't take him long to find out that the dream of freedom in the North was one more dream deferred for blacks.

St. Louis was just as segregated as Clarksville. The schools were just as ill-equipped, neighborhood housing was just as dilapidated, the police were just as brutal, public accommodations were just as closed, health was just as neglected, and blacks were just as poor.

Jim did whatever he could to earn a dollar. He labored in the livestock yards. He planted trees. He sold fruits and vegetables in the streets. It was touch-and-go most of the time for his family, but he persevered.

My father was too young to let racism or poverty disturb the innocence of his youth. After graduating from Sumner High School, which was the only school blacks could attend, he worked at odd jobs—delivery boy, elevator operator, junkyard laborer. Later, he got a job at the Post Office. Even though federal employment was completely segregated then, blacks considered this "a status job."

He might have stayed there, raised a family and settled down to a quiet life in St. Louis. But he had a vague itch, a yearning for more. He had outgrown the narrow provincialism of the St. Louis of those pre-Depression years. He knew there was a bigger world out there and he wanted to see it. For a young black this could only mean one of two places—Harlem or South Side Chicago.

He chose Chicago. He requested a transfer and he waited. When it came through, he said good-bye to his mother, father, three sisters and two brothers. After dutifully promising to keep in touch, visit and even send money occasionally; he boarded the train for Chicago and never looked back.

In the 1920s, Chicago was a rollicking wide open city, under the corrupt administration of Mayor Anton Cermack. Booze, prostitution, gambling and any other conceivable vice ruled the crime-ridden, mob-run city. If you had the cash and connections everything was for sale. But since most blacks had neither, they found themselves nearly as poor and abused as they were on the plantations and farms that most of them had left in Mississippi, Arkansas or Tennessee.

Then the Great Depression hit. Many blacks did not know where their next check or meal would come from. Life for them became a bittersweet dance with survival. My father was lucky. He had a job that paid him in real money, meagre, yes, but real money, not script, as many workers then received.

There were other consolations. Like most blacks on Chicago's South Side, he lived in the area from 29th to 47th Street. The neighborhood was so tight-knit it was said that if you wanted to see a friend or relative from out of town you could stand on the corner of 35th and State Street and sooner or later they'd come by.

But the real delight was 47th Street. My father enjoyed the street's bustling night life, which then was second only to Harlem as the Mecca for black attractions. He could pop in at any one of the dozens of clubs, bars and speakeasies that lined the street.

There was the Grand Theater, the Vendome Theater, the Sunset Cabaret, the Apex Club and the Royal Garden. He could hear the sounds of Count Basie, Earl Hines, Fletcher Henderson, Fess Williams, Walter Barnes, Louis Armstrong, Cab Calloway, Duke Ellington, Muddy Waters or whatever big-name black entertainer who happened to be passing through. Since all the clubs downtown and uptown were closed to blacks, they would play on 47th Street.

I remember seeing a well-preserved picture of him. He was dressed dapperly in a double-breasted suit. He had smooth skin, sparkling eyes and neatly trimmed moustache and what appeared to be a slightly licentious smile across his face. I'm sure he did his thing, and in the words of the ancient blues lament, "had his fun if he didn't get well no mo."

But it was only a matter of time. It happens to every would-be dandy. They meet someone who is just a little hipper, a little wiser, and a little stronger. She pierces the veil of male invincibility and brings him down to earth. It's called love.

When that happens marriage is usually close behind. My father met and married Lucille. Maybe they were too young, maybe they were too dumb, or just maybe it wasn't meant to be. Whatever the reason, it didn't last long.

The end came when my father received a panicky call from his brother who lived close by. He told him to get home right away because Lucille was moving all the furniture out of the house. Only he really knows how he felt. To hear him tell the story, he told his brother, "Let her have the junk, I'm going to get some new furniture anyway."

He had better luck the second time. Thirty-seven years later he was still married to my mother. As Hitler poised to invade Poland, to start World War II, his first child, my sister Earline, was born. A month after the Japanese surrendered on the deck of the U.S.S. *Missouri* to end the war, I was born. I was in the first wave of those who, a quarter century later, society would fawningly call "the baby boomers." Of course, that was years in the future. To my father, I was just another mouth to feed. And if that wasn't enough, my half-brother, Bobby, also lived with us during those years.

As America blissfully slumbered through the bobby soxers, high school hops, Edsels and the anti-Communist McCarthy witch hunts of the 1950s, my father kept his job at the Post Office. On the side, he dabbled in ward politics to gain a few minor perks. With a growing family, he wanted a bigger and better place to live. A home he could call his own. It took some doing, but he finally found the ideal place. It was a three-story apartment building further South.

For any other family it would have been a simple thing, call the moving van, pack up the furniture, load the kids in the car and be on your way. But there was only one hitch. We were not any other American family. The apartment building was located in an all-white neighborhood and we were the first black family to buy there.

In those years, this building, like most others, had a restrictive covenant written into the deed. This meant simply that in perpetuity homeowners could not sell to blacks (one year later in 1948 the Supreme Court would declare restrictive covenants unconstitutional).

My father got around it by finding a "nominee." This was a sympathetic white person who would buy the home in their name and quit claim it over to the black buyer. It was risky business. The nominee might keep the money, the property owner might back out before the deal was closed, or angry homeowners could get an injunction to stop a black family from moving in. If that didn't work, they could resort to violence. In those days, more than one black family fled neighborhoods after their homes were burned and ransacked by white mobs.

Trouble began immediately. There were threats, shouts and even stones thrown at our door. This went on for a year. During that time, two policemen maintained around-the-clock vigil in our lobby, and my father for the first and only time in his life kept a gun close by. Things finally settled down as more blacks moved into the neighborhood. By the time we moved seven years later, the neighborhood was practically all-black.

My father is a passionate music lover. He was a saxophonist for his National Guard band unit. His great joy was the evenings he spent at the Armory practicing with the band. When he took me with him, it was my joy, too. While the men belted out their hot practice numbers on the bandstand, I would roam the cavernous halls of the Armory in an army helmet, military belt and my play rifle, fighting imaginary battles with unseen enemies.

As the years passed, my parents grew restless. They heard stories about a new land of opportunity out west in California. They took a drive out there and fell in love with it. To my parents, the land of sunshine and oranges seemed like paradise. They had found yet another promised land.

When my father retired in the early 1960s, they moved to California. They watched as their children grew to maturity. My brother joined the army. My sister began a career as an artist and a designer, and me, well I would spend a few years trying to figure out what I wanted to do.

But he was a patient man. He had made his peace with the world and was settling in to enjoy the golden years that America says its aging citizens are entitled to after a lifetime of sacrifice and struggle. Then tragedy struck. My mother died of cancer. It was a bitter loss. After nearly a lifetime together, he could not forget her.

There were days when I would drive out to the cemetery with him. He would carefully put flowers on her grave. While I walked back to the car he would linger for a few moments over her grave, I saw his lips faintly moving. They were talking. It was so very private. Only they would ever know what was said. She was very much alive and would always be.

Still, he was no different than any other man. He had physical and emotional needs that memories alone could not satisfy. He hungered for the warmth and caress that only a companion can bring. He got lucky again. He found a lovely lady who gives him the proper doses of affection, attention and when he needs it, his comeuppance. From what I can see, their married years have been good ones.

Now that you know something about this man that I call father, what does he think about some of the problems that face black men today?

INTERVIEW

EARL, JR.—Tell me what works against black men as fathers?

EARL, SR.—*That's easy, no jobs. If a guy doesn't have any income, he can't support his family. Whose fault is that? Doesn't the government have some responsibility to find jobs for its people? It's ridiculous. The government doesn't have any problem finding money to fight wars or take care of people in foreign countries, but it can't even take care of its own.*

Back during the Depression, I remember stepping over guys sleeping on cardboard in Washington Park (on Chicago's South Side). They were everywhere. And they weren't just black, there were plenty of whites, too. They were all in the same boat. They couldn't take care of themselves, so how could they take care of families?

The Democrats saw that the only way they could help these men and their families was to give them something; make jobs for them. They did. Pretty soon, you saw that more families were staying together when the man had a little something, and that was good.

EARL, JR.—Those were different times, they didn't have the problem with drugs, high crime and delinquency that we do today.

EARL, SR.—*Maybe there wasn't a problem with drugs like now, but they did some of the same kind of stuff then. People got drunk, men beat their wives. And remember, if you were black back then, there were no laws to protect you. I mean you were just at the mercy of society. Things were bad and everybody knew it. But I think what made the difference was that we had more of a sense of pulling together. People were more religious then, we prayed a lot. We believed in God.*

Also, we all lived together then. A guy might be a doctor or a lawyer. It didn't make any difference. He lived right next door to a janitor or porter. In the Post Office, we had guys who were college graduates, some even had Master's Degrees. It didn't make any difference. They would be working side by side with a guy who never finished high school. The kids had somebody they could look up to.

EARL, JR.—It seems like people's values were different then.

EARL, SR.—*That's right. People cared more about each other. They took more of an interest in what their friends and neighbors were doing. Your neighbors were almost like part of your family. One time you got into a rock fight with some other kids and the police came and took you all down to the station. A neighbor who saw it called me right away and told me what happened. Right away, I went to the station, I was mad because there was really no reason for them to take you down, you were just kids.*

When I got there several other parents were there too, so evidently somebody had called them. And it was kind of funny to hear everybody shouting at the police. I mean they were raising hell with them. The officers laughed and said they just wanted to scare you and the others a little. It wasn't funny to us, we got all of you out of there fast.

EARL, JR.—How did that sense of caring carry over into your relationship with your wife?

EARL, SR.—*I'm not going to try and say that we didn't have our bad moments, every couple does. People aren't going to always be kissing and hugging each other. There's just too many things that can happen to change a person's attitude and mood. They might have a bad day at work. They might not be feeling well or they could be tired. They may have a problem with money. Anything. And they just don't feel like being lovey dovey. So there's going to be problems. That's just natural.*

It's easy for people to be happy when things are going good, but what happens when the rough times come? That's the real test. If you truly love the other person, then you will respect them. That's important. If you respect them then you will take them seriously when they talk to you. You might not agree with what they have to say, and you might still want to do things your way, but you will listen. What they have to say may sit with you for a while—sometimes things take time to sink in—but eventually you will see that they might have something. Then you can reach some kind of compromise.

EARL, JR.—Did that work with you?

EARL, SR.—*Most of the time. But sometimes, you get it in your head that you just want to get your way. That's natural too. And sometimes you should. But, like I say, if you love and respect the other person then you will come together. One may decide that this is one time when it is better to let the other person have their way even though you don't want to. That's hard, but a mature person can do it. They realize by giving a little here they may gain a lot later. A good general knows when to go forward and when to give ground. He knows that he'll eventually get it back.*

EARL, JR.—That really takes a lot of maturity to understand that?

EARL, SR.—*True, and there's one more thing on that. People would do a lot better if they didn't always expect so much of each other. This is what gets two people in trouble. They see things through their eyes and they try to make the other person see it the same way. They forget that the other person doesn't have the same eyes. I think in my day, we didn't always make those demands on each other and we didn't give the other person a lot of ultimatums.*

EARL, JR.—You did make demands on your children. You wanted them to be the best. Wasn't that why black parents valued education almost as much as they valued the church?

EARL, SR.—*We did. We knew that it was the only thing that really meant anything. There was never any such thing as sending report cards home. We went to pick them up. If there was a problem, we went up to the school the same day. If there was a conference with the teacher, the father went, too. More often than not, there were just as many fathers as there were mothers at school when they had some event.*

In Chicago, a lot of black parents pulled their kids out of the public schools and put them in Catholic schools. I did that with you. The public schools were just so bad and the Catholics had a good reputation then. Many of these parents weren't making much money, and they had to sacrifice a lot to pay that tuition, but we were willing to do it because we knew that in the Catholic schools they were tough, and you would learn something.

EARL, JR.—Speaking of learning something, one of the major problems that still affects African-Americans is lack of health care and information. Now with diseases such as AIDS, it's more important than ever to be informed. I don't know if this was an issue when you were raising your family. . . .

EARL, SR.—*It was an issue. I'm not talking about AIDS, because that wasn't known then. But there was Tuberculosis and Pneumonia and those diseases killed a lot of people. With sex you might get syphilis and gonorrhea, people died from that, too. What made it even worse, remember, was that we didn't have access to doctors and hospitals. People didn't have insurance and even if they could afford it, a lot of companies wouldn't write policies for blacks anyway.*

EARL, JR.—So what did people do?

EARL, SR.—*They used common sense.*

EARL, JR.—What do you mean?

EARL, SR.—*If it was cold they didn't run around wearing a tee-shirt and shorts like you see people doing now. As soon as they felt a little weak, flu or something, they would sit or lie down. They tried not to let themselves get all worked up over every little thing. They knew how to take things in stride and relax.*

They also had a lot of what we called the "remedies." Since most of us came from the South, we knew how to cure ailments at home. We knew how to make cold and hot compacts; how to use herbs, tonics and vegetable roots. We also made lots of soups. When you or your sister got a cold and couldn't breathe, we'd boil a pan of hot water, squeeze some lemon in it, put a towel over your head to keep the steam in, and have you bend over it and breathe deeply the steam.

EARL, JR.—Did it work?

EARL, SR.—*You never complained.*

EARL, JR.—I know drugs weren't a problem, but didn't everybody smoke and drink then?

EARL, SR.—*A lot of people did. I didn't.*

EARL, JR.—Why?

EARL, SR.—*When I was with the band, the guys would always get together afterward and drink. That's just what you were supposed to do. I tried to go along with them a few times, but the whiskey would make me so sick that I just couldn't get past that bad feeling. It was the same with smoking. It just didn't give me a good feeling, even though all my buddies smoked.*

When I look around and see what it can do to you, I guess I was lucky that I didn't like to drink or smoke. It was good also because we never kept much liquor or any cigarettes around the house. You never saw us smoking or drinking. Maybe that's why you didn't pick up the habit.

It seems to me that if kids see their parents smoking and drinking then, unless they're exceptional, they're just naturally going to pick up those habits, too. So I think you were lucky that the stuff did make me sick.

EARL, JR.—We've got another problem. Too many black kids are having kids, years ago that wasn't true. . . .

EARL, SR.—*It was a little different. If a girl got pregnant and she wasn't married it was a big scandal. She almost couldn't be seen in public. Some parents would even send her away to live with an aunt, grandmother or relative in another town. But girls still got pregnant. It just wasn't openly talked about.*

There weren't any classes or teachers that taught things like sex education. People were too afraid to even say the word. So it was something that was supposed to be taken care of in the home.

I don't know if this was good or bad, but many parents tried to put the fear of God in the girls. They'd tell them it was a sin to get pregnant, and God would punish them if they did. They tried to make them feel guilty. Maybe this wasn't the best way, but it seemed to work.

EARL, JR.—It seems like that put the whole burden on girls. It takes two to make a baby. Isn't it just as important, maybe even more important, to get the boys to accept responsibility for their actions?

EARL, SR.—*I'm just telling you that's the way people handled things then.*

EARL, JR.—But today . . . ?

EARL, SR.—*Wait. Even then, if a man made a baby and he wasn't married, it was pretty well understood that the man had to marry the girl. It didn't make much difference how old he was. They had to get married. They called it a "shotgun wedding." The girl's father would find out who the boy was and come looking for him. There were a whole lot of weddings where the boy was dragged to the altar kicking and screaming.*

For some guys it was too much, they might leave home, rather than go through all that. But a lot of times that didn't work. I knew some men who would track the guy to another city and one day show up on his doorstep. I knew a couple of guys who tried to run away and next thing I knew, they were back in Chicago married to the girl.

EARL, JR.—I can't believe that a marriage like that could have any hope of lasting.

EARL, SR.—*You'd be surprised, many did. More often than not, the couple would stay together for years. It's funny how things work. Something you may be forced into and not like, over time you find out that it's right for you. All I know is that some guys I knew that got married like that stayed married and did right by their families.*

EARL, JR.—What if they didn't make it and the man left. You were talking before about jobs being the most important thing for a man to have. He might have to leave because he couldn't support his family.

EARL, SR.—*That's what happened to James [his brother]. He didn't stay married hardly anytime to the woman he got pregnant. I don't know, maybe they weren't right for each other. I know James had the big problem with drinking so that probably had something to do with it too. He was a musician, too, so that didn't help since he was always on the road. But he cared enough about Jimmy [his son] to send money fairly regularly. And that was something then, because remember, there were no laws in those days that forced a man to pay.*

He did something else. Do you remember who Jimmy stayed with while he was growing up?

EARL, JR.—His Grandmother.

EARL, SR.—*That's right. I don't know how James worked it out. He knew that his mother—your grandmother—wanted to take him and so they worked it out. That was probably his way of making sure he was taken care of properly. Jimmy always called her mother. So he had that tie with his father. He never felt abandoned.*

EARL, JR.—So an absentee father can still be a father?

EARL, SR.—*Of course. Just because a man has left the home for good doesn't mean he isn't a father. In fact, when that happens, I would say that he probably should be more of a father than if he were there.*

EARL, JR.—What do you mean?

EARL, SR.—*Children tend to make a father that they don't see regularly bigger than life. A lot of it's fantasy and more often they will be hurt and disappointed if they find out later that he isn't like they imagined him. But if the father shows that he cares, sends money, spends time with them and shows a sincere interest, he becomes part of their lives. They can see the real problems he faces, and that way they get a real taste of life through him. I think this can help them mature better as individuals.*

EARL, JR.—You're talking about boys and their fathers?

EARL, SR.—*I'm talking about boys and girls. They both need their fathers. Certainly a boy needs to have a man around to guide him, be a little tough with him, but a girl needs that same guidance. They are forming their opinions, too. If they grow up and think that all men are no good because those are the only kind of men they see, then that's the attitude that they're going to pass on to their children.*

If they see their father as somebody who's a warm and caring person—I don't mean weak. I think you can be warm, caring and gentle and still be strong. I think that's what's going to come through and that's what girls will pass on.

EARL, JR.—One last question. Was it tough making it through life with your family?

EARL, SR.—*Oh, your mother and I had our share of problems. Sometimes there wasn't enough money. Sometimes there might be bills that we couldn't pay. There were a few times when we couldn't get enough coal to heat the house properly. And, like I said before, we had plenty of disputes about everything.*

But I might work a little longer to earn a few more dollars. Your mother was a talented seamstress, so she would make clothes for friends and neighbors, and they would pay her a little something. She would also make clothes for you and your sister. We had friends whom we always tried to do right by, so when we needed a helping hand, they were there.

We took you to church, to the doctor and to school. When you were really young, you even slept in our bed with us. We always told you that our house was your house. Whatever we had, you had. We made it clear that whenever you had a problem you could come to us. It didn't make any difference what it was.

But the main thing is that your mother and I were a team. We always figured that as long as we worked together the Good Lord would show us a way. And he did.

NICK CHILES

A *Private War*

Troy knew whom the letters were from even before he read the return address—and the thought made him tremble. His father. He squinted at the return address:

PFC Tyler
9th Regiment, U.S. Marine Corps
Danang, Vietnam

Letters from Vietnam, from his father. Probably love letters. The lump in Troy's throat grew immense and threatened to cut off the air to his windpipe any second. He gasped, trying to suck in the room's dusky oxygen, his hand instinctively pressed to his throat to help force it in. He was grateful when he took a deep breath. Tears came quickly. He hadn't been this close to his father in eighteen years, since the days before he died in his sleep one floor below as a relatively young man. Troy held tightly the bunch of letters, wondering how much farther he could go. To read his father's words, the intimate thoughts of this man who hovered over his life like an otherwordly presence, could only fill him with terrible pain. Perhaps it would send him rocketing back seventeen years to when the wounds still festered. Only as an adult did he consider himself over his father's shocking death. Now he had discovered evidence, starkly scrawled and resting ominously in his hands, of his father's presence within him all along. Desperately as a child he had searched for exactly this hidden treasure, groping with his little hands in the most unlikely corners of the house for his father.

Troy slowly slipped one of the letters out of the envelope. He unfolded the still-white sheet covered in ink, noticing how well it had been preserved inside the envelope. He read the first line, and the tears inched down his cheeks.

> Dear Belle,
>
> It's rough over here, but thinking about you helps me keep on going. . . .

Troy put the letter down and closed his eyes to stem the tears. He felt embarrassed, ashamed that he was peeking into the intimate life of his parents—a place no child really wants to go. But he needed to know. He had always starved for anything about his father that he could grab, but his mother had always held it away from him. Now he had his father here in his hands, directly and intimately. He couldn't pass it up. He wanted to take some of these letters with him, to read them slowly in his bed at home, to ponder them, to drink in everything these scrawled words on the page revealed about this distant but deeply affecting figure.

Troy reached down to scoop up a few letters, wondering where he could put them temporarily to keep his little secret hidden from his mother and brother. Maybe he would share them with his brother in due time. But for now he wanted his father to himself.

He noticed a yellowing piece of paper sitting off by itself on the floor, separated from the envelopes in space and appearance. He picked it up and recognized the handwriting from the letters. The words were slightly more scrawled, like the writing of an older person, but they were almost identical to the cursive in the letters from Vietnam. This was from his father also. He looked up in the corner and saw the date: January 8, 1976. Troy frowned. That was the day before his father died. He would never forget that, because it was right after he had started back to school after the holiday break. There was a lot of snow outside—he remembered wondering as he looked out the window if the men carrying the body would slip on the ice. Unconsciously holding his breath, he read the short letter, which was also addressed to Belle, his father's pet name for his mother.

> Belle,
>
> I couldn't take it anymore. I tried real hard, baby. You know I tried. But it still hurts me real bad. Every time I look at him, it hurts me bad. How could I keep on like this?
>
> I know it'll be hard on you, raising the boys by yourself. I'm sorry

about that. But as I see it, I have no choice. It was either this or go crazy. I'd be no good to anybody crazy. Don't take this too hard. You got to keep on going, for the boys. Remember that I love you. I guess that's what made it so hard.

Tell the boys that I'll always love them. Both of them. Good-bye.

Not many things alter a life as drastically as the death of a father. It is an emotional equivalent of a solar eclipse that never ends, denying you the power of those life-giving rays—leaving you no choice but to sprout on your own, laboring intently in the dark. In the months immediately after his father died, Troy suffered deeply, sometimes spending entire days lying on his bed staring at the ceiling, wondering things like whether he would grow up and be a homo if he didn't have a father anymore—or whether he also would die if he fell asleep. His mother had been so worried that she sent him to a child psychologist for a while, but she had to end the sessions after two months because the weekly payments were killing her. Troy remembered being deeply hurt by this, too, because he had started to develop a fondness for the friendly, balding white man with the beard.

To discover your father's suicide note eighteen years after he killed himself is almost as bad as suffering through his death all over again. The discovery grabs everything you had believed and tosses it so unceremoniously out the window. You have to start all over, ordering a new system, a new way of dealing with an absence and longing that had long ago grown faint.

Troy's first thoughts were *Why? What was so painful to him?* His father had purposely taken himself away, of his own free will. He had made a decision to leave Troy and his mother and brother all alone in the world, to fend for themselves. Why hadn't anyone ever told him this, over the years? His mother and her brother, Uncle Bert, and his father's two sisters, Aunt Rose and Auntie Jenny, had all conspired to keep this a secret, amazingly. His father had taken his life, haunted by demons that seemed to cause him constant pain. What did those words mean? Some of them struck Troy as odd—"Every time I look at him it still hurts me bad" . . . "I'll always love them. Both of them." Who is the "him"? Is it Troy? Is it Aaron? Is it someone Troy doesn't know? And why did he feel it necessary to say he loved both Troy and Aaron? Wouldn't that go without saying? He had so many questions; there was so much he didn't know. Troy felt the tears start to slide down his cheeks once again. He made no attempt to stop them.

A slow, broiling, inescapable anger started to build at the tip of Troy's head and spread down through his limbs, gaining much currency in the pit of his stomach. It was almost a wild anger, because it had no clear direction, no target specifically. His father had taken himself away from them. How could he ever deal with that? And the world had allowed him to develop the software to cope with a father's death and still keep going; to fool him into knowing he could get up every morning and rush headlong into a world without a father somewhere, sitting quietly, rocking, waiting to back him up, support him, prop him up when he needed it. How cruel. What this meant was he had never really known his father at all—but how many of us really do? His presence was already shadowy enough in Troy's memories; now it had just taken several steps deeper into the shadows.

Troy needed to read this note again, over and over, until it was seared, branded into his mind, the final words his father coined for consumption. Troy needed to know what it all meant, what was it that had chased his father away from him. He had to know.

When he entered the room and came upon his mother, who was sweeping, he still wondered how he was going to keep everything bottled up. He knew it would be easy enough for him to look like he had just seen a ghost—in a way he had—and his mother could always detect with a remarkable degree of accuracy when something was wrong with her eldest son.

"Did you get all the boxes out of that room up there?" she asked without turning to look at him. "That room was such a mess. It took me a week to get everything up there in them boxes."

"Why are you sweeping, Ma? There's no dirt on this floor," Troy said, looking down at the dark wooden floor in the second-floor room that used to serve as their family room.

Mirabel Tyler turned to look at him, her smooth brown face showing a frown.

"I'm sweeping because it needs to be swept in here, that's why. If I was to wait until you saw dirt before I cleaned something, we'd be growing weeds in the house."

Typically his mother had not readjusted her view of his cleaning habits to account for adulthood, fifteen years of growth. Troy could hear his brother, Aaron, downstairs, talking to the movers. He saw his mother looking at him, but he was not concentrating on a reply. He was wondering whether he should bring up the suicide note.

Seeing that he was not going to respond, Mirabel Tyler turned her small frame around and went back to sweeping. Troy watched the muscles in her forearms tense and relax, tense and relax, as she pulled the broom toward her again and again. Her arms looked so solid, framed by the short sleeves on her old floral-patterned dress—the kind of dress she used to wear a lot when Troy was younger and still at home. For a woman who was a half century on the planet, she was in great shape—Troy could not remember his mother ever really getting sick. As if in a divine revelation, he thought then what awful pain his mother must have endured over the last eighteen years. Not only did her husband leave her to raise two small boys alone, he made a conscious choice to do it. He didn't care for her or for his sons enough to stay with them even in his pain. That reality must have been—and still must be—difficult for her to face. It was difficult enough for Troy to face eighteen years later. He wanted to ask her about it, to get the full story—or just to see how she would react. He didn't want to hurt her necessarily, but he was still angry at her for withholding the information all these years. He wanted to see her shock when he told her that he knew.

"One of the boxes up there fell open when I tried to pick it up," he said to his mother's back. "There were some letters inside of it. Letters that Dad wrote to you when he was in Vietnam."

His mother slowed her sweeping perceptibly. But she didn't turn around yet.

"I also found something else in there, a note. It looked like a suicide note. It was written the day before Dad died."

His mother stopped sweeping now. She bowed her head, but she still was silent. Troy waited to see if she would make him ask, if she was going to make this difficult or easy. After several seconds she started moving the broom back and forth again, this time with an urgency that caused her forearm muscles to strain noticeably. His mother, always the most stubborn member of her family, was going to make him ask.

"Why didn't you tell us, Ma? Why did you, and everybody else, lie to us?"

She spun around quickly, her anger evident already.

"Now, don't you even try to come down here and make me live through all of that again," she said, her brown eyes blazing and her lips pursed in the way they did whenever she was scolding one of them. "I did what I thought was best for you and Aaron. That's what a mother's supposed to do. If you had to find out, I'm sorry you found out this way, but I am not sorry about what I did. What good would it have done to tell a ten-year-old and six-year-old boy that your father just killed himself? How could either of you have understood that? I mean, I didn't even understand it completely. Can you imagine the guilt you would have had to get over if I had told you? No, I will always believe I did the right thing, no matter what you have to say to me now, eighteen years later. You know what they say about hindsight."

Troy realized this was still too sensitive a topic for her to discuss it honestly. To him it looked like she was being defensive. He knew he would not be extracting any apologies from her.

"But, Ma . . . it just seems like you could have told us at some point. Like when we were a little older or something."

"What good would that have done? You had both gotten over it, why bring all those pains back? Like you're doing now."

"I'm sorry if I'm causing you pain, Ma, but I guess you can imagine what it might be like to find out you didn't even know how your father died. That everyone probably knew except you."

"Everybody did not know!" Mirabel said loudly, her anger building. She was leaning on her broom now, pointing a finger at him. This was also a familiar scene. "Only a few people knew besides me. We didn't go around announcing this, Troy."

"Well, can you tell me why he did it, then? I think I can handle it now," Troy asked a little more softly, searching for a tender spot he could exploit.

But his mother shook her head. "No, I don't want to talk about this anymore, Troy. This was none of your business, all of this. This was private, between me and your father. And I'm gonna make sure it stays that way."

Now Troy exploded in anger. "But he was my father! How can you say it's none of my business?! I'm trying to find out how, why, my father died and wasn't around for me when I wanted somebody to teach me how to throw a football, when I wanted to go camping with the Boy Scouts and everybody else was bringing their fathers with them, when I wanted somebody to talk to about girls. It's not private at all! It's part of my family's history."

"Stop yelling at me, boy! I said I don't want to talk about it. Subject is closed. And don't you go talking about all this with your brother. There's no need to get him all turned around just because you found some letters."

She pressed her lips together and turned around to get back to her sweeping. Troy was incredulous. She actually was not going to tell him anything further. And he knew his mother well; she was so stubborn that if she said she was not going to discuss it, there was virtually nothing he could ever do to change her mind. She had an iron will. Troy stood frozen, trying to figure out his next move. If he pestered her about it too much, she would clam up even more. That's just the way she was. He would have better luck with her by letting it go for now and coming back to it another time, maybe sneaking up on her when she was in a good mood. Since she was moving into Harborside, his condo complex at the waterfront, he would have plenty of opportunity.

But he had to know. He couldn't just give up, letting it end here with his mother's wall of silence. Surely there were other ways to dig and get information. He could pretend he was a detective or an investigative reporter—instead of the accountant that he really was—and reconstruct his father's life by talking to old friends and acquaintances. And he had to share it with Aaron; if he didn't, he would be participating in the same awful deception that was perpetrated on them all these years.

As Troy made his way down the stairs to the ground floor, he had no idea of the scale of the adventure on which he was about to embark. And he certainly had no idea of what he would find. He would have been stunned to know it would forever change his life.

"I found some letters from Dad up in the storage room," Troy said to his brother after he had handed him a beer. "They were letters he wrote to Mom when he was in Vietnam."

"Love letters? Why you want to read their love letters, man? Isn't that kind of private?" Aaron asked, reclining on the black leather sofa in Troy's living room and twisting his face into a frown. "I'd be kinda grossed out, personally."

"There was another letter there that he wrote to Mom. I thought you might be interested in this one," Troy said, watching his brother from a chair at his dining-room—or, more accurately, dining-area—table.

"Well, enough of this drama. What is it? Let me see it."

"Okay." Troy got up from the chair and brought the suicide note over to his brother. He sat down at the other end of the couch and watched Aaron closely as he read the note. Aaron's face remained in a frown, even after he looked up at Troy and put the letter down on his lap. He was speechless. He stared past Troy, through the glass doors at the spectacular view of the New York City skyline.

"He killed himself." Aaron said this matter-of-factly, not in a question or with even a hint of surprise or shock. He said it as if it was the final clue in a twisted puzzle he had been unraveling for a long time.

"Yes, he did," Troy said gravely. "All these years of believing he died in his sleep. Of accepting that. Now this. He couldn't deal anymore. He decided to leave us, on his own. It was his decision. I'm still in shock."

"Have you confronted Ma about this?" Aaron asked. Troy was surprised at how well his brother was taking this. No tears. No expressions of anguish. Apparently not even any anger.

"Yeah, I did. She didn't want to deal with it at all. She got very angry, like defensive. She said she didn't tell us what really happened for our own good. She even tried to stop me from telling you about the note. I wanted to ask her what this all meant, all this stuff in the note, but she refused to discuss it anymore. And you know how stubborn Ma can be when she makes up her mind about something."

Aaron nodded his head. The frown had gone away, but now his face was expressionless, as if there was nothing passing through his head. Aaron always prided himself on being so cool under pressure—from somewhere he had gotten the damaged perception that this made him a man—so he didn't allow much display of emotion. Troy usually found himself annoyed at his brother within ten minutes of any conversation. They had never gotten along very well.

"I think she's right," Aaron said. "I don't think this stuff is any of our business. And it doesn't change the fact that he's dead and he's been dead for a very long time. Why bring this stuff back up and put us all through this again?"

Aaron was sounding a lot like his mother, as could be expected. They were very much alike in many ways, especially in their habit of running away from problems, or sticking their head in the sand, as Troy liked to call it. His mother had always been much closer to his younger brother, always more willing to cut Aaron more slack or to lend him assistance, financial or just emotional, in his many times of need. Many times Troy had felt as if they purposely formed their own little world that he couldn't be a part of, that he couldn't understand or appreciate. Consequently he had long harbored a bit of resentment toward his brother, a resentment borne out of his jealousy at what they shared together, these two most important people in his life. Whenever the three of them were together, Troy always had to fight against his suspicions, his insecurities about his place in this family. He wasn't sure why, but he felt this was all somehow connected to his father, or at least by gaining a better understanding of his father's life and his father's death he would have a better perspective from which to make sense of his family geography. But obviously Aaron had no such inclinations. He was comfortable, settled, and he needed to know no more about a distant presence that was no longer even a voice or a face in the hazy bank of his childhood memories. Aaron was only six when his father left. Troy was ten. That made a difference.

"You don't feel like you need to know why he did it, why he left us? Aren't you just the slightest bit curious?" Troy asked, straining to keep the condescension out of his voice. He did not have a great deal of respect for his brother's intellectual curiosity.

"Sure, I'm curious. But I don't think knowing that is worth all the hurt you could cause by digging all this stuff up. Especially the hurt to Ma. If she didn't tell us, I'm quite sure she had very good reasons. Why would you want to disrespect those reasons now?"

"Disrespect? What the hell are you talking about, Aaron? I feel like I'm the one who's been disrespected. I mean, my father killed himself and the world decided I shouldn't know about it? Ever? That does not sit well with me at all. Maybe you can accept it so easily—'I'm sure she had very good reason,' " Troy said, mocking his brother in a nerdy voice, "but that's not good enough for me. I want to know for myself. I need to know."

"Well, whatever you do, my dear brother, keep me out of this, okay? You can chase this ghost all over the country, for all I care. Just don't drag me or Ma into your odyssey, that's all."

"But you are in it, don't you see that? How can you and Ma not be in it? This is our family history. It has everything to do with why we are the way we are. I believe that. Maybe it would explain why you can't seem to get your life together, why you feel like you were supposed to lie up and live off of some woman instead of getting a job."

"Fuck you, Troy!" Aaron screamed, pointing a thin index finger at his brother. "You don't know anything about me, okay?! You don't know what I do every day, what my ambitions are, my dreams. Just because I didn't go to school and become something mindless and boring like an accountant, so I could get a nice car and buy a nice fuckin' sofa"—he slammed his palm down on Troy's leather sofa for emphasis, making a loud splat—"that doesn't mean my life's not together!"

Aaron wiped the spittle from the corner of his mouth and stared angrily at his brother, daring him to continue the challenge. Troy turned away, knowing they might wind up swinging at each other if the conversation continued. Over the years they had ended many a conversation with bloody noses and busted lips.

Aaron lifted his lanky frame from the couch and reached for his leather jacket thrown over a chair. He gave his brother one last glare, but Troy was still turned away from him. Aaron marched to the door and slammed it behind him without another word.

"Well, nobody can say I didn't try," Troy said with a sigh as he picked up Aaron's half-empty beer bottle and brought it into the kitchen. He didn't expect his brother to help him of course, but he thought his brother would be more interested in getting to the truth. Maybe Aaron was scared of the truth. Troy could understand that. He could understand fear because he was dealing with some of it himself. But he feared not the disruption that an investigation into his father's death would cause to kindly, pleasant memories of his father. He feared what his father's suicide would tell him about himself. He couldn't forget that line—"every time I look at him it still hurts me bad." Was his father talking about him?

HAKI R. MADHUBUTI

Father's Pledge

1. I will work to be the best father I can be. Fathering is a daily mission, and there are no substitutes for good fathers. Since I have not been taught to be a father, in order to make my "on the job" training easier, I will study, listen, observe and learn from my mistakes.

2. I will openly display love and caring for my wife and children. I will listen to my wife and children. I will hug and kiss my children often. I will be supportive of the mother of my children and spend quality time with my children.

3. I will teach by example. I will try to introduce myself and my family to something new and developmental each week. I will help my children with their homework and encourage them to be involved in extracurricular activities.

4. I will read to or with my children as often as possible. I will provide opportunities for my children to develop creatively in the arts: music, dance, drama, literature and visual arts. I will challenge my children to do their best.

5. I will encourage and organize frequent family activities for the home and away from home. I will try to make life a positive adventure and make my children aware of their extended family.

6. I will never be intoxicated or "high" in the presence of my children, nor will I use language unbecoming for an intelligent and serious father.

7. I will be nonviolent in my relationships with my wife and children. As

a father, my role will be to stimulate and encourage my children rather than carry the "big stick."

8. I will maintain a home that is culturally in tune with the best of African-American history, struggle and future. This will be done, in part, by developing a library, record/disc, video and visual art collections that reflect the developmental aspects of African people worldwide. There will be *order* and *predictability* in our home.

9. I will teach my children to be responsible, disciplined, fair and honest. I will teach them the value of hard work and fruitful production. I will teach them the importance of family, community, politics and economics. I will teach them the importance of the Nguzo Saba (Black value system) and the role that ownership of property and businesses plays in our struggle.

10. As a father, I will attempt to provide my family with an atmosphere of love and security to aid them in their development into sane, loving, productive, spiritual, hard-working, creative African-Americans who realize they have a responsibility to do well and help the less fortunate of this world. I will teach my children to be *activists* and to *think* for themselves.

BOYZ 'N THE HOOD

WILLIAM DEMBY

Beetlecreek

For many days now Johnny had avoided the boys in the gang. The day of the funeral, Baby Boy came up to him and asked him where he'd been hiding. Johnny told him he'd been busy but that was a lie. The truth was that he was ashamed to see them. He feared their scorn, imagined they had branded him a sissy because of what happened at the shanty.

He had the vague feeling that somehow he had failed a test and for that reason would no longer be suitable for their company.

Once his aunt sent him to the store uptown to get some groceries she had forgotten to buy. He was panic-stricken and walked all the way up the side of the hill over the railroad bridge so that he wouldn't have to pass the gang.

Twice they played whist under the street light near his window and he could hear their yelling. That same night, he imagined hearing one of them say his name and a lot of laughter afterward. This pained him very much and he turned over on the pillow so he wouldn't have to hear their shouts.

Another afternoon, someone knocked at the door while he was all alone in the house. When he went to the door he discovered that it was Baby Boy. He was overjoyed, yet he opened the door only a crack, not daring to let him in the house. Baby Boy wanted him to come over to his house to look at the pigeons. Very much he wanted to go but he was afraid of seeing the rest of the gang.

The night before the funeral, he was left all alone in the house. His uncle had given him enough money to go to the movie but instead he had gone to the A & P and bought a fifteen-cent package of buns with the money. After cutting through the alley behind the store, he climbed the hill that overlooked the valley and the creek.

On the hill, it wasn't quite dark but the valley was already covered by a dusty blue darkness. From up there where he sat, the creek was only an emptiness, a ditch. To one side of the village he could see Bill Trapp's place. There was a single, feeble light burning and even as he watched, the street lights along the creek road went on. From that height, they seemed like a string of weak Christmas tree lights.

The wind blew on the top of the hill and rattled the cellophane wrapper of the buns. He sat crouched with the buns in his lap. Two of them he ate, consuming them rapidly in a few big mouthfuls. It was so quiet, that the sticky chewing sound seemed to come from somewhere outside himself.

Soon it became dark on the hill and the valley below him became level. The sky seemed close to the bushes. For a long time he sat very still, listening to the wind rattle the cellophane, listening to the sealed-in sounds of the valley rise up slowly along the grass.

What was it he was waiting for, he kept asking himself. What did he want? He tried to laugh to see if he could, but when he opened his mouth, the wind blew it away before he could hear it, and he could only feel the laugh on his taut lips.

He thought of girls. He thought of Little Orphan Annie. He thought of a picture in a magazine he had hidden among his things at home—an art photograph of an artist's model in the nude.

The wind blew harder and harder and tried to enter his consciousness and he could hardly breathe.

Afterwards, he ate all the rest of the buns and lay on his back looking at the sky. He was suddenly very tired. He closed his eyes and looked at the colored shapes behind his eyeball. This is all the world, he thought. The eyeball is the world. Maybe the world is God's eyeball. This thought amused him and he squinched his eye trying to make even more colors appear.

What was it he wanted, he kept asking himself. Where was he going? What was he waiting for? He tried to cry but no tears would come nor any sound.

He opened one eye and looked through a tuft of weeds toward the valley. I belong down there, he thought. I am down there and I live there. I am not in Pittsburgh but I am down there in the valley in Beetlecreek, and I am all alone down there.

What if Beetlecreek were a ghost town and he were the only inhabitant. What if, when he went back down to the street, he were to find everybody dead?

He wondered what the gang of boys sure enough thought about him. He didn't care if they did think he was a sissy, he told himself. They weren't anything but a gang of downhome darkies and he was from the city. But the thought of the shanty and the gang made him feel very sad. He was tired of being the weakest one in every gang he was in, the fraidy cat. In Pittsburgh, it was the same way. When it came to choosing up sides, he was always among the last to be picked. And when it came to doing stunts, he was always the one who couldn't ever do anything.

He scraped his fist against the grass and pounded the ground. He felt ashamed of himself. Always he felt ashamed of himself and he was tired of this feeling.

Now he jumped up and ran down the hill. Recklessly he ran, taking a path that could only barely be seen in the reflected light of the moon. Once he tripped and fell. He wanted to cry, but he fought against it, shouting to himself, "You damn sissy! You damn sissy!" And on he ran.

CLAUDE BROWN

Manchild in the Promised Land

There were a lot of real hip young criminals at Warwick. It wasn't like Wiltwyck. For one thing, Wiltwyck only had about a hundred guys, and Warwick had five hundred. And Warwick had guys from all over New York City. They had cats from Brooklyn, the Bronx, Manhattan, Queens, and Richmond—everywhere. There were even cats from small towns upstate and from suburban areas of New York City. And Warwick had real criminals. Nobody at Wiltwyck was there for murder, and they didn't have any cats up there who knew how to steal a car without the keys. But it seemed like just about everybody at Warwick not only knew how to pick locks but knew how to cross wires in cars and get them started without keys. Just about everybody knew how to pick pockets and roll reefers, and a lot of cats knew how to cut drugs. They knew how much sugar to put with heroin to make a cap or a bag. There was so much to learn.

You learned something new from everybody you met. It seemed like just about all the Puerto Rican guys were up there for using drugs. They had a lot of colored cats up there for using drugs, but most of them were jive. Most of these guys were just using drugs to be down and to have a rep as a junkie. You could tell that these cats were jive by the way they went around saying, "Yeah, man, do you shoot stuff?" and all this sort of nonsense, as though they were bragging about it. They would start talking about how much stuff they used a day. I'd look at them and say, "Yeah, like, that's real nice," but they could never make me feel bad or anything, because all I had to do was say my name was Claude Brown. I didn't have to use drugs. I already had a reputation. I'd been other places. I knew people from here, I knew people from there.

Cats had heard about me when I was in Brooklyn gang fighting with K.B. and the Robins. And when I got shot, it was something that everybody seemed to respect me for. I'd only gotten shot with a .32, but the word was out that I'd gotten shot in the stomach with a .38. Cats didn't believe it. They'd come up to me and say, "Man, did you really git shot wit a .38?" and I'd either joke it off or act like they were being silly. I'd say, "Shit, people have gotten shot with .45's, so what?" They would go away marveling.

When we were in the dormitory getting ready to take a shower, the cool guys would say, "Hey, Brown, could I see your scar?" or they would just say, "Man, is that your scar?" I'd say, "Yeah, that's it." If they were hip cats, they might just say something like, "Yeah, man, those bullets can really fuck you up." And I'd say something like, "Yeah, but you can keep gittin' up behind 'em."

Cats used to come up and offer me ins on reefers or horse or anything I wanted. I had two or three flunkies after I'd been there for a month. It was no sweat for me; I was ready to stay there for a long time and live real good. I knew how to get along there. I'd had a place waiting for me long before I came. If I'd known that Warwick was going to be as good as it turned out to be, I would never have been so afraid. As a matter of fact, I might have gotten there a whole lot sooner.

At Warwick, it all depended on you when you went home for a visit. The first time, you had to stay there twelve weeks before you could go home. After that, you could go home for a three-day visit, from Friday to Monday, every eight weeks. That's if you didn't lose any days for fucking up or fighting. This was pretty good, because some people were always going home, and they would see your fellows and bring messages back, and your fellows were always coming up every Friday. A new batch of guys would come up and drugs would come up. When you came back from a weekend home visit, you were searched everywhere. They'd even search in the crack of your ass. You had to go to the doctor and let him look for a dose of clap. But cats would always manage to bring back at least a cap of horse or at least one reefer. Everybody could always manage to smuggle in a little bit of something.

By the time Dunny came up to Warwick, I had a place for him. I was there and ready, sitting pretty. I'd already established myself and was waiting for some of the fellows to come up. I'd been up there about eight weeks when Dunny came. He told me Turk was in the Youth House. They'd gotten busted robbing a hardware store on 145th Street, and for some reason—I guess because he had a worse record than Turk—they sent Dunny right on up, but Turk was still in the Youth House waiting to go to court.

When Dunny came up, I saw him passing by the reception crowd, and I stopped and said something to him before Mr. Jenkins, the cat in charge, told me to go on. Dunny said, "Damn, Sonny, we gon live up here, man; like we gon really run the place!" And I sort of had the feeling it was true, because Dunny was a crazy cat, and he had a whole lot of heart. But I wanted to get a chance to pull his coat about the place called the Annex.

The cats who had a little bit of sense but who were just general fuck-ups were sent to the Annex. At the Annex, you didn't get any visits home, and you could only have a visitor once a month. At Warwick, you could have a visitor every Sunday, if your folks wanted to come and see you. Not too many people actually came up there every Sunday, though. At the Annex, you had to do two years. For all that time, you weren't going to be back on the street, see any girls, go to the places you liked to go, or do the things you liked to do. They said the work was harder too.

Up at Warwick, the cats had never really served any time before. They might have been someplace like Wiltwyck, where you went home only every six months, but they could go home for a visit or could go someplace eventually. In places like Warwick, you find a lot of guys who never had any home to go to, so they didn't mind. One place was just as good as another. For them, Warwick was just one more place until the next stop, which would probably be Coxsackie or Elmira or someplace like that. But to the average cat who hadn't ever served any time, the thought of going to the Annex was something frightening. I hadn't served any time, and I wasn't about to serve any time. I wanted to get back on the streets.

My folks didn't come up too much. Dad would never come any place to see me, and Mama couldn't come often because she didn't have that much money. Dad wouldn't give her any money to come up and see me. The way he felt about it was, "Shit, he got his damn self in that trouble, so let him worry about it himself."

We all came out of Warwick better criminals. Other guys were better for the things that I could teach them, and I was better for the things that they could teach me. Before I went to Warwick, I used to be real slow at rolling reefers and at dummying reefers, but when I came back from Warwick, I was a real pro at that, and I knew how to boost weak pot with embalming fluid. I even knew how to cut drugs, I had it told to me so many times, I learned a lot of things at Warwick. The good thing about Warwick was that when you went home on visits, you could do stuff, go back up to Warwick, and kind of hide out. If the cops were looking for you in the city, you'd be at Warwick.

One of the most interesting things I learned was about faggots. Before I went to Warwick, I used to look down on faggots like they were something dirty. But while I was up there, I met some faggots who were pretty nice guys. We didn't play around or anything like that, but I didn't look down on them any more.

These guys were young cats my age. It was the first time I'd been around guys who weren't afraid of being faggots. They were faggots because they wanted to be. Some cats were rape artists because they wanted to be, some cats were flunkies, some cats were thieves, and some cats were junkies. These guys were faggots because they wanted to be. And some of the faggots up there were pretty good with their hands. As a matter of fact, some of them were so good with their hands, they had the man they wanted just because he couldn't beat them.

At Warwick, there was even a cottage just for faggots. If a cat came up there acting girlish, they'd put him right in there. They had a lot of guys in there—Puerto Ricans, white, colored, everything—young cats, sixteen and under, who had made up their minds that they liked guys, and that's all there was to it.

When I first came up there, I had to go to school for half a day. They put me in a class, and there was a faggot in the class. The cat was about a year older than I was, a real nice-looking guy. As a matter of fact, he was so handsome, I guess it would have been hard for him not to be a faggot. He said that he just liked guys, and that's why he was a faggot. This was the first faggot I had ever talked to, except for Earl, Bucky's brother. His name was Baxter.

He used to give me things and offer me cigarettes. These were things you weren't supposed to have outside of the cottages—cigarettes and candies, stuff like that. One day, I had to talk to him. I said, "Like, look, man, I been talkin' to you, and we been all right, and I like you, but I don't want you givin' me things, 'cause that could be misunderstood. And I suppose sooner or later, you'd be wantin' me to give you somethin' or do somethin' for you, and it's, like, that's just not my way, man. Like, the way I hear it, cats who mess around wit faggots usually come out wit claps or somethin' like that sooner or later."

He looked at me and laughed and said, "No, I don't want anything from you, Brown. I know how you are, but there aren't many guys around here who think they are down who would . . . you know, who I could talk to and who would treat me like I'm somebody or somethin'. It's like, I just like you, and I know we couldn't have anything goin' in that love vein, but, well, I just like you."

I said, "Yeah, well, I like you too, man. And as long as we both understand how things are, there's no reason why we can't go on bein' friends. But, like, it's gotta be friends like this, man, everybody understandin' where he is."

The cats up there I really disliked as a group weren't the faggots but the guys who were afraid somebody might think they were. Warwick made everybody very conscious of his masculinity, and there were a lot of cute guys up there, guys who were real handsome. They were so handsome that if they weren't good with their hands, somebody was liable to try to make a girl out of them. So these guys used to be brutal, dirty. They used to do a whole lot of wicked stuff to cats. They would stab somebody in a minute or hit a cat in his head with something while he was sleeping, all that kind of stuff, because they were afraid guys would think they weren't mean.

WILLIAM MELVIN KELLEY

Dancers on the Shore

I peered over a rotting tree stump and saw him moving, without a helmet, in the bushes. I got his forehead in my sights, squeezed the trigger, and imagined I saw the bullet puncture his head and blood trickle out. "I got you, Jerome. I got you!"

"Awh, you did not."

"I got you; you're dead."

I must have sounded very definite because he compromised. "You only wounded me."

"Tommy? Tommy! Come here." Her voice came from high above me.

I scrambled to my knees. "What, Ma?" She was on the porch of our house, next to the vacant lot where we were playing.

"Come here a minute, dear. I want you to do something for me." She was wearing a yellow dress. The porch was red brick.

I hopped up and ran to the foot of our steps. She came to the top. "Mister Bixby left his hat."

As I had waited in ambush for Jerome, I had seen Mister Bixby climb and, an hour later, chug down the steps. He was one of my father's poker playing friends. It was only after she mentioned it that I remembered Mister Bixby had been wearing, when he arrived, a white, wide-brimmed panama hat with a black band.

Entering my parents' room on the second floor, I saw it on their bed. My mother picked it up. "Walk it around to his house. Now walk, I say. Don't run because you'll probably drop it and ruin it." It was so white a speck of dirt would have shone like a black star in a white sky. "So walk! Let me see your hands."

I extended them palms up and she immediately sent me to the bathroom to wash. Then she gave me the hat. I did not really grip it; rather, with my finger in the crown, I balanced it, as if about to twirl it.

When I stepped onto the porch again, I saw them playing on their corner—Valentine's Gang. Well, in this day of street gangs organized like armies, I cannot rightly call Joey Valentine, who was eight, and his acquaintances, who ranged in age from five to seven, a gang. It was simply that they lived on the next block, and since my friends and I were just at the age when we were allowed to cross the street, but were not yet used to this new freedom, we still stood on opposite sides of the asphalt strip that divided us and called each other names. It was not until I got onto the porch that I realized, with a sense of dread that only a six-year-old can conjure up, that Mister Bixby lived one block beyond Valentine's Territory.

Still, with faith that the adult nature of my mission would give me unmolested passage, I approached the corner, which was guarded by a red fire alarm box, looked both ways for the cars that seldom came, and, swallowing, began to cross over.

They were playing with toy soldiers and tin tanks in the border of dry yellow dirt that separated the flagstones from the gutter. I was in the middle of the street when they first realized I was invading; they were shocked. At the time, I can remember thinking they must have been awed that I should have the unequaled courage to cross into their territory. But looking back, I realize it probably had little to do with me. It was the hat, a white panama hat. A more natural target for abuse has never existed.

I was two steps from the curb when Joey Valentine moved into my path. "Hey, what you got?"

Since he was obviously asking the question to show off, I bit my lips and did not answer. I saw myself as one of my radio heroes resisting Japanese interrogation. I was aloof. However, the white panama hat was not at all aloof. Before I knew it, Joey Valentine reached out a mud-caked hand and knocked the hat off my finger to a resounding chorus of cheers and laughter.

I scooped up the hat before any of them, retreated at a run across the street, and stopped beside the red alarm box. Wanting to save some small amount of my dignity, I screamed at them: "I'll get you guys! I'll get you. I'm not really an American. I'm an African and Africans are friends of the Japs and I'll get them to *bomb your house!*"

But even as I ranted at them, I could see I was doing so in vain. Across the way, Valentine's Gang lounged with the calm of movie Marines listening to Japanese propaganda on the radio. I turned toward my house, inspecting the hat for smudges. There were none; it was as blinding white as ever. Already I felt tears inching down my cheeks.

Not until I was halfway up the porch steps did I see my grandmother sitting in her red iron chair. But before I could say anything, before I could appeal for understanding and comfort, she lifted herself out of the chair and disappeared into the house. She had seen it all—I knew that—and she was too ashamed of me to face me.

Suddenly, she was coming back, holding a broom handle. She had never before lifted a hand to me, but in my state, I felt sure that many things would change. I closed my eyes and waited.

Instead of the crunch of hard wood on bone, I heard her chair creak. I opened my eyes and found the end of the broom handle under my nose.

"You know if you don't go back and deliver that hat, you'll feel pretty bad tonight."

I nodded.

"Well, take this. We don't like you fighting. But sometimes you have to. So now you march down there and tell those boys if they don't let you alone, you'll have to hit them with this. Here." She pushed the broom handle at me.

I took it, but was not very happy about it. I studied her; she looked the same, her white hair bunned at her neck, her blue eyes large behind glasses, her skin the color of unvarnished wood. But something inside must have changed for her actually to tell me to hit someone. I had been in fights, fits and starts of temper that burned out in a second. But to walk deliberately down to the corner, threaten someone, and hit him if he did not move aside, this was completely different, and, as my parents and grandmother had raised me, downright evil. She must have realized what I was thinking.

"You know who Teddy Roosevelt was?"

I nodded.

"Well, he once said: *Speak softly and carry a big stick; you will go far.*"

I understood her, but to do something like this was still alien to my nature. I held back.

"Come on." She stood abruptly and took my hand. We went into the house, down the hall, and into her bedroom. "I have to see to the mulatto rice. You sit on my bed and look at the picture on the wall." She went on to the kitchen. I was still holding the broom handle and now put it down across the bed, and climbed up beside it, surrounded by her room, an old woman's room with its fifty years of perfume, powder, and sweet soap. I felt a long way from the corner and Valentine's Gang.

There were three pictures on the wall and I was not certain which she wanted me to study. The smallest was of my granduncle Wilfred, who lived on Long Island and came to Thanksgiving dinner. The largest was of Jesus, the fingers of His right hand crossed and held up, His left hand baring His chest in the middle of which was His heart, red and dripping blood. In the cool darkness of the room, He looked at me with gentle eyes, a slight smile on His lips. The third was my grandmother's husband, who had died so long before that I had never known him and had no feeling for him as my grandfather. He was light, like my grandmother, but more like some of the short, sallow Italian men who lived on the block. His black hair was parted in the middle. He wore a big mustache which hid his mouth. His jaw was square and dimpled. With black eyes, he seemed to look at something just above my head.

"Well, all right now." My grandmother came in, sweating from standing over the stove, and sat in a small armchair beside the bed. "Did you look at the picture?"

"I didn't know which one." I looked at Jesus again.

"No, not Him this time. This one." She indicated her husband. "I meant him."

Now Pablo [Cortés,] your grandfather—she started—was just like you, as gentle as a milkweed flower settling into honey, and as friendly as ninety-seven puppy-dogs. He was from Cuba, which is an island in the Atlantic Ocean.

He was so kind that he'd meet every boat coming in from Cuba and talk to all of the people getting off, and if he found that one of them didn't have a place to stay, and no money for food, he'd bring him home. He'd lead his new friend into the kitchen and say: "Jennie, this is a countryman. He got no place to sleep, and he's hungry." And I'd sigh and say: "All right. Dinner'll be ready in ten minutes." They'd go into the living room and sing and roll cigars.

That's what he did for a living, roll cigars, working at home. The leaves were spread out all over the floor like a rug and I never did like cigars because I know somebody's been walking all over the leaves, sometimes in barefeet like your mother did when she was a little girl.

Pablo was so friendly he gave a party every day while I was at work. I'd come home and open the door and the cigar smoke would tumble out and through the haze I would see twenty drunken Cubans, most with guitars, others rolling cigars, and all of them howling songs.

So now fifty years ago, I'd come from down South to stay with my brother Wilfred, and I was so dumb that the first time I saw snow I thought somebody upstairs'd broken open a pillow out the window. So my brother Wilfred had to explain a lot of things to me. And the first thing was about the neighborhoods. In those days, New York was all split up into neighborhoods. The Italians lived in one neighborhood, and the Polish in another, and the Negroes and Cubans someplace else. After Pablo and I got married, we lived with the Negroes. And if you walked two blocks one way, you'd come to the Irish neighborhood, and if you were smart, you'd turn around and come back because if the Irish caught you, they'd do something terrible to you.

I don't know if Pablo knew this or not, or if he just thought he was so friendly that everybody would just naturally be friendly right back. But one day he went for a walk. He got over into the Irish neighborhood and got a little thirsty—which he did pretty often—so he went into an Irish bar and asked for a drink. I guess they thought he was new in this country because the bartender gave him his drink. So Pablo, smiling all the time, and waiting for them to smile back, stood there in that Irish bar and drank slow. When he was finished the bartender took the glass and instead of washing it, he smashed it down on the floor and stepped on it and crushed the pieces under his heel. What he meant was that it was pretty bad to be a Cuban and no Irishman would want to touch a glass a Cuban had drunk from.

I don't know if Pablo knew that either. He asked for another drink. And he got it. And after he finished this one, the bartender smashed it in the sink and glared at him.

Pablo was still thirsty and ordered again.

The bartender came and stood in front of him. He was a big man, with a face as red as watermelon. "Say, buddy, can't you take a hint?"

Pablo smiled. "What hint?"

The bartender was getting pretty mad. "Why you think I'm breaking them glasses?"

"I thought you like to break glasses. You must got a high bill on glasses."

The bartender got an ax handle from under the bar. "Get out of here, Cuban!"

So now Pablo knew the bartender didn't want him in the bar. "Now, let me get this straight. If I ask you for drink, and you give me drink, you would break that glass, too?"

"That's right. But you better not order again."

Pablo sighed. He was sad. "Well, then we will pretend I got drunk in this bar." And the next thing anybody knew Pablo was behind the bar, breaking all the glasses he could reach.

"And we will pretend that I look at myself in your mirror." He picked up a bottle and cracked the big mirror they had.

By now there was a regular riot going on with all the men in the bar trying to catch and hold him, and Pablo running around, breaking chairs and tables. Finally just before they caught and tied him up, he tipped over their piano. "We will pretend I played a Cuban song on this piano!"

They called the police and held him until the wagon came. And the next time I saw him was in court the next morning, where the judge kept looking at Pablo like he really didn't believe that a man who seemed so kind and gentle could do such things. But it was plain Pablo had wrecked the Irishman's bar. The judge sentenced him to thirty days in the city jail, and fifty dollars damages, which Pablo couldn't pay. So the judge gave him thirty extra days.

I didn't see Pablo for the next two months. When he came home, he was changed. He wasn't smiling at all, and you remember that he used to smile all the time. As soon as he came in the house he told me he was going out again. I knew where and I got mad. "Do you want to spend another two months in jail? Is that what you want?"

He didn't understand me. "Why you ask me that?"

"Why! You're going over there to that white man's bar and get into a fight and go on back to jail. Did you like it that much? Did jail change you so much?"

"Jennie, don't you see? I try not to change." He picked up five boxes of cigars he'd made before he went to jail and put them into a brown paper bag, and tucked the bag under his arm.

I watched him go out the door and then started to cry. I loved him, you see, and didn't want him back in jail. And I cried because I didn't understand him now and was afraid of that.

When the Irishmen saw him coming into their bar, they were stunned. Their mouths dropped open and they all got very quiet. Pablo didn't pay them any mind, just walked up to the bar and put his foot on the brass rail.

The bartender picked up his ax handle. "What you want here, Cuban? Ain't you had enough?"

"No." Pablo didn't smile. He took the brown paper bag and put it gently on the counter. Cigars, he said, are delicate and shouldn't be tossed around.

The bartender look at the bag. "What you got there?"

"Maybe you find out." He touched the box with his fingers. "I like a drink."

The bartender stared at him for a second and then at the paper bag for a long time. He started to sweat. "All right." He set the drink down in front of Pablo.

For a minute, Pablo just looked at it. Then he lifted it to his lips and drank it down and pushed it across the bar to the bartender.

The bartender picked it up and studied it. Finally, he looked at Pablo again. "What the hell! I had to close up for a week after you was here the first time." He took the glass to the sink, washed it with soap and water, and put it with the other clean glasses. Then he looked at Pablo again. "Satisfied?"

"Not yet." Pablo grabbed the paper bag and started to open it.

"Watch out, fellows!" The bartender yelled in his ear. When Pablo looked up, all the men in the bar were lying on their stomachs covering their heads. The bartender was behind the bar on his knees, his hands over his ears.

Pablo took a cigar box out of the bag, opened it, pulled himself up, and across the bar, and reached the box down to the bartender. "Hey, you want fine, handmade Havana cigar?" He was smiling.

"Are you going back down to that corner?" My grandmother took my hand.

I looked into her face and then at the picture of her husband. He was still studying something just above my head. "I guess so." I did not really want to do it.

"You may not even have to use that." She pointed at the broom handle. "But you should know you can."

I knew this was true and climbed off the bed and picked up the white hat and the broom handle. "Okay."

"I'll be waiting on the porch for you." She smiled, got up, and, sighing, went out to the kitchen.

For a while, I listened to pots knocking and being filled with water. Then I stood in her room and practiced what I would say to Valentine's Gang: "If you guys don't let me go by, I'll have to hit you with this." There was a quake in my voice the first time I said it out loud, but, if I had to, I thought I would actually be able to say it and then use the stick. I went down the hall, onto the porch, and looked down toward the corner.

It was empty. The mothers of the members of Valentine's Gang had summoned them home to supper.

HENRY DUMAS

Strike and Fade

The word was out. Cool it. We on the street, see. Me and Big Skin. We watch the cops. They watch us. People goin and comin. That fire truck still wrecked up side the buildin. Papers say we riot, but we didn't riot. We like the VC, the Viet Cong. We strike and fade. Me and Big Skin, we scoutin the street the next day to see how much we put down on them. Big Skin, he walkin ahead of me. He walkin light, easy, pawin. It daylight but you still got to walk easy on the street. Anytime the Mowhites might hit the block on rubber, then what we do? We be up tight for space, so we all eyes, all feet an easy. You got to do it.

We make it to Bone's place. Bone, he the only blood on the block got a business. Mowhite own the cleaners, the supermarket, the laundry, the tavern, the drugstore, and all the rest. Yeah. But after we burn out half them places, Mowhite he close down his stores for a week.

Our block occupied with cops and National Guard, but the Guard left yesterday. Man, they more cops on the street now than rats. We figure the best thing to do is to kill the cops first so we can get back to killin rats. They watch us. But they got nothin on Big Skin and me. Naw. We clean. They got Sammy, Momo, Walter and his sister too, Doris, Edie, and they even got Mr. Tomkins. He a school teacher. I had him once. He was a nice stud. Me and Big Skin make it to Bone's place. There a lot of guys inside.

We hang around. Listen to talk. I buy a Coke. Big Skin take half. I hold my Coke. Police cars pass outside. They like wolves, cruisin. We inside. Nobody mess with us. A cat name Duke, he talkin.

"You cats got to get more together with this thang. Look at the cats in Brooklyn, Chicago. Birmingham and Cleveland. Look at the cats in Oakland!"

A cat name Mace, he talkin. Mace just got out the Army. "Don't worry, man. It's comin." He point out the window. "This is raw oppression, baby. Look at them mf's. Raw oppression." Mace, he like to use them two words so he sayin them over and over again. He say them words all the time. It ain't funny cause they true. We all look out the window at the cops.

Bone, he behind the counter makin hamburgers. When he get too many orders he can't handle, then one of the cats come behind the counter and give him a hand. Me and Big Skin light up cigarettes. Big Skin pass them around.

I take the last one. I squeeze the pack up so tight, my fingernails cut my hand. I like to make it tight. I throw that pack at the trash can. It bounce in and bounce back. But Duke, he catch it. He throw it in. Not too hard. It stay. He talkin.

"I mean, if every black man in this goddamn country would dedicate one half of a day next week to a boycott. Just don't go to work! Not a black pushin a thing for Charley. Hell, man, we tie it up. We still the backbone, man. We still got this white mf on our backs. What the hell we totin him around for?"

Mace, he talkin.

"Wait. No sooner we make another move, whitey be down on us like rats on warm cheese. It be raw oppression double over. Gestapo. Man, they forget about Hitler after the man come down on us."

Big Skin he talkin.

"They say that the cats in Harlem is gettin together so tight that the Muslims and Martin Luther King got their heads together."

Nobody say nothin. Couple cats laugh. We heard it before. Word been spreadin for all black men to get ready for war. Nobody believe it. But everybody want to. But it the same in Harlem as anywhere else.

Duke he talkin.

"An organized revolution is what the man can't stand. They say it's comin? Man, when it do I be the first to join. If I got to go I take some Chalk Whitey with me and mark him all over hell."

We listen a while. The cats all talkin. We just want to get what's happenin.

We split the scene. Duke, he split too.

We move down the block. It gettin evenin. We meet some cats comin.

We stop and talk. We meet them later on 33rd Street. They pawin like us.

Duke talkin.

"You cats see Tyro yet?"

We say naw. We heard he back in town, but we ain't seen him yet. Tyro was a Green Beret in Viet Nam. But he back. He got no legs and one arm. All the cats been makin it to his pad. They say he got a message for all the cats on the block.

Duke say he makin it to Tyro's now. We walk on. I kick some glass. We see a store that is burnt out. A cop is watching us. We stalkin easy, all eyes, all feet. A patrol car stop alongside us. The gestapos leap out. I see a shotgun. We all freeze.

The Man is talkin.

"You niggers got one hour to get off the street." Then he change his mind. "Against the wall!" There is three of them. Down the street is more. They frisk us. We all clean. One jab the butt of a gun hard on my leg. It give me a cramp in the ball.

They cuss us and tell us to get off the street. We move on. Around the block. Down the street.

I'm limpin. I don't say nothin. I don't curse or nothin. Duke and Big Skin, they mad, cursin and sayin what they gonna do. Me, I'm hurtin too much. I'm lettin my heat go down into my soul. When it come up again, I won't be limpin.

We see some more cats pawin along the block. About fifty. We join. They headin to 33rd. Some cats got heats, some got molotovs. One cat got a sword.

Tyro on 30th Street. We go up. Three other cats come with us. We run up the steps. We pass an old man goin up. He grunt out our way. We say excuse. I'm the last up. The old man scared. We hear a siren outside. The shit done started already.

Tyro's sister open the door. I know her before I dropped out of school. She know me, but she iggin. All the cats move in. I close the door. "We come to see Tyro," I say. She chewin some food, and she wave with her hand. It mean, go on up front. I watch her walk. "You Tina?" She swallow her food. "Yeah. You come to see Tyro, he in there." She turned and went into a door and closed it. I followed the other cats up front. My ball still hurt.

There were six cats already in the room. Six more come in. Somebody pass around a butt. I scoot in a corner. So I am meetin Tyro. He known on the block for years. He used to be the leader of the old Black Unicorns. They broke up by the cops and social workers.

I look at Tyro. He a black stud with a long beard. He sittin in a wheelchair. He wearin fatigues like Fidel Castro. When we paw into the pad, Tyro he talkin.

". . . the Cong are masters at ambush. Learn this about them. When we fell back under fire, we fell into a pincher. They cross-fired us so fast that we didn't know what hit us. Out of sixty men, I was left. I believe they spared me so that I could come back and tell you. The cat that found me was hit himself, but he didn't seem to care. He looked me in my eye . . . for a long time. My legs were busted up from a grenade. This VC stood over my blood. I could tell he was thinkin about somethin. He raised the rifle. I kept lookin him in the eye. It was one of the few times my prayers been answered. The cat suddenly turned and ran off. He had shot several of my buddies already, but he let me go.

"All I can figure is that one day the chips are all comin down. America is gonna have to face the yellow race. Black and yellow might have to put their hands together and bring this thang off. You cats out in the street, learn to fade fast. Learn to strike hard, but don't be around in the explosion. If you don't organize you ain't nothin but a rioter, a looter. These jigs won't hesitate to shoot you.

"Naw. I ain't tellin you to get off the streets. I know like you know. Uncle means you no ultimate good, brothers. Take it for what it is worth. I'm layin it down like it is. I got it from the eagle's beak. That's the way he speak. Play thangs careful. Strike and fade, then strike again, quick. Get whitey outa our neighborhood. Keep women and children off the streets. Don't riot. Rebel.

You cats got this message. Do what you got to do. Stick together and listen for the word to come down. Obey it."

When Tyro finish talkin, some cats get up and shake his hand. Others leave. Out in the street sirens are going. The doorbell rings. Everybody freeze. It some more cats. We all leave.

Down on the street, it like a battlefield. A fire in a store down the block. Cops see us. We fade. I hear shots. Then I know somethin.

The word is out. Burn, baby, burn. We on the scene. The brothers. Together. Cops and people goin and comin. Some people got good loot, some just hoofin it. A police cordon comin. We shadows on the wall. Lights comin toward us. We fade. Somebody struck them. The lights go out. I hear shots. I fall. Glass get my hands. The street on fire now. We yell. 33rd Street here we come! Got to get together!

We move out. Strikin. All feet. All soul. We the VC. You got to be. You got to be.

AMIRI BARAKA

The Screamers

Lynn Hope adjusts his turban under the swishing red green yellow shadow lights. Dots. Suede heaven raining, windows yawning cool summer air, and his musicians watch him grinning, quietly, or high with wine blotches on four-dollar shirts. A yellow girl will not dance with me, nor will Teddy's people, in line to the left of the stage, readying their *Routines*. Haroldeen, the most beautiful, in her pitiful dead sweater. Make it yellow, wish it whole. Lights. Teddy, Sonny Boy, Kenny & Calvin, Scram, a few of Nat's boys jamming long washed handkerchiefs in breast pockets, pushing shirts into homemade cummerbunds, shuffling lightly for any audience.

"The Cross-Over," Deen laughing at us all. And they perform in solemn unison a social tract of love. (With no music till Lynn finishes "macking" with any biglipped Esther screws across the stage. White and green plaid jackets his men wear, and that twisted badge, black turban/on red string conked hair. (OPPRESSORS!) A greasy hip-ness, down-ness, nobody in our camp believed (having social-worker mothers and postman fathers; or living squeezed in lightskinned projects with adulterers and proud skinny ladies with soft voices.) The theory, the spectrum, this sound baked inside their heads, and still rub sweaty against those lesser lights. Those niggers. Laundromat workers, beauticians, pregnant short-haired jail bait separated all ways from "us," but in this vat we sweated gladly for each other. And rubbed. And Lynn could be a common hero, from whatever side we saw him. Knowing that energy, and its response. That drained silence we had to make with our hands, leaving actual love to Nat or Al or Scram.

He stomped his foot, and waved one hand. The other hung loosely on his horn. And their turbans wove in among those shadows. Lynn's tighter, neater, and bright gorgeous yellow stuck with a green stone. Also, those green sparkling cubes dancing off his pinkies. A-boomp bahba bahba, A-boomp bahba bahba, A-boomp bahba bahba, A-boomp bahba bahba, the turbans sway behind him. And he grins before he lifts the horn, at Deen or drunk Becky, and we search the dark for girls.

Who would I get? (Not anyone who would understand this.) Some light girl who had fallen into bad times and ill-repute for dating Bubbles. And he fixed her later with his child, now she walks Orange St. wiping chocolate from its face. A disgraced white girl who learned to calypso in vocational school. Hence, behind halting speech, a humanity as paltry as her cotton dress. (And the big hats made a line behind her, stroking their erections, hoping for photographs to take down south.) Lynn would oblige. He would make the most perverted hopes sensual and possible. Chanting at that dark crowd. Or some girl, a wino's daughter, with carefully vaselined bow legs would drape her filthy angora against the cardboard corinthian, eying past greediness a white man knows, my soft tyrolean hat, pressed corduroy suit, and "B" sweater. Whatever they meant, finally, to her, valuable shadows barely visible.

Some stuck-up boy with "good" hair. And as a naked display of America, for I meant to her that same oppression. A stunted head of greased glass feathers, orange lips, brown pasted edge to the collar of her dying blouse. The secret perfume of poverty and ignorant desire. Arrogant, too, at my disorder, which calls her smile mysterious. Turning to be eaten by the crowd. That mingled foliage of sweat and shadows: *Night Train* was what they swayed to. And smelled each other in The Grind, The Rub, The Slow Drag. From side to side, slow or jerked staccato as their wedding dictated. Big hats bent tight skirts, and some light girls' hair swept the resin on the floor. Respectable ladies put stiff arms on your waist to keep some light between, looking nervously at an ugly friend forever at the music's edge.

I wanted girls like Erselle, whose father sang on television, but my hair was not straight enough, and my father never learned how to drink. Our house sat lonely and large on a half-Italian street, filled with important Negroes. (Though it is rumored they had a son, thin with big eyes, they killed because he was crazy.) Surrounded by the haughty daughters of depressed economic groups. They plotted in their projects for mediocrity, and the neighborhood smelled of their despair. And only the wild or the very poor thrived in Graham's or could be roused by Lynn histories and rhythms. America had choked the rest, who could sit still for hours under popular songs, or be readied for citizenship by slightly bohemian social workers. They rivaled pu with wind-up record players that pumped Jo Stafford into Home E rooms. And these carefully scrubbed children of my parents' friends l on their rhythms until they could join the Urban League or Househo nance and hound the poor for their honesty.

I was too quiet to become a murderer, and too used to extravagance fo their skinny lyrics. They mentioned neither cocaine nor Bach, which was my reading, and the flaw of that society. I disappeared into the slums, and fell in love with violence, and invented for myself a mysterious economy of need. Hence, I shambled anonymously thru Lloyd's, The Nitecap, The Hi-Spot, and Graham's desiring everything I felt. In a new English overcoat and green hat, scouring that town for my peers. And they were old pinch-faced whores full of snuff and weak dope, celebrity fags with radio programs, mute bass players who loved me, and built the myth of my intelligence. You see, I left America on the first fast boat.

This was Sunday night, and the Baptists were still praying in their "fabou-lous" churches. Though my father sat listening to the radio, or reading pulp cowboy magazines, which I take in part to be the truest legacy of my spirit. God never had a chance. And I would be walking slowly toward The Graham, not even knowing how to smoke. Willing for any experience, any image, any further separation from where my good grades were sure to lead. Frightened of post offices, lawyers' offices, doctors' cars, the deaths of clean politicians. Or of the imaginary fat man, advertising cemeteries to his "good colored friends." Lynn's screams erased them all, and I thought myself intrepid white commando from the West. Plunged into noise and flesh, and their form become an ethic.

Now Lynn wheeled and hunched himself for another tune. Fast dancers fanned themselves. Couples who practiced during the week talked over their steps. Deen and her dancing clubs readied *advant-garde* routines. Now it was *Harlem Nocturne*, which I whistled loudly one Saturday in a laundromat, and the girl who stuffed in my khakis and stiff underwear asked was I a musician. I met her at Graham's that night and we waved, and I suppose she knew I loved her.

Nocturne was slow and heavy and the serious dancers loosened their ties. The slowly twisting lights made specks of human shadows, the darkness seemed to float around the hall. Any meat you clung to was yours those few minutes without interruption. The length of the music was the only form. And the idea was to press against each other hard, to rub, to shove the hips tight, and gasp at whatever passion. Professionals wore jocks against embarrassment. Amateurs, like myself, after the music stopped, put our hands quickly into our pockets, and retreated into the shadows. It was as meaningful as anything else we knew.

All extremes were popular with that crowd. The singers shouted, the musicians stomped and howled. The dancers ground each other past passion or moved so fast it blurred intelligence. We hated the popular song, and any freedman could tell you if you asked that white people danced jerkily, and were slower than our champions. One style, which developed as Italians showed up with pegs, and our own grace moved toward bellbottom pants to further complicate the cipher, was the honk. The repeated rhythmic figure, a screamed riff, pushed in its insistence past music. It was hatred and frustration, secrecy and despair. It spurted out of the diphthong culture, and reinforced the black cults of emotion. There was no compromise, no dreary sophistication, only the elegance of something that is too ugly to be described, and is diluted only at the agent's peril. All the saxophonists of that world were honkers, Illinois, Gator, Big Jay, Jug, the great sounds of our day. Ethnic historians, actors, priests of the unconscious. That stance spread like fire thru the cabarets and joints of the black cities, so that the sound itself became a basis for thought, and the innovators searched for uglier modes. Illinois would leap and twist his head, scream when he wasn't playing. Gator would strut up and down the stage, dancing for emphasis, shaking his long gassed hair in his face and coolly mopping it back. Jug, the beautiful horn, would wave back and forth so high we all envied him his connection, or he'd stomp softly to the edge of the stage whispering those raucous threats. Jay first turned the mark around, opened the way further for the completely nihilistic act. McNeely, the first Dada coon of the age, jumped and stomped and yowled and finally sensed the only other space that form allowed. He fell first on his knees, never releasing the horn, and walked that way across the stage. We hunched together drowning any sound, relying on Jay's contorted face for evidence that there was still music, though none of us needed it now. And then he fell backwards, flat on his back, with both feet stuck up high in the air, and he kicked and thrashed and the horn spat enraged sociologies.

That was the night Hip Charlie, the Baxter Terrace Romeo, got wasted right in front of the place. Snake and four friends mashed him up and left him for the ofays to identify. Also the night I had the grey bells and sat in the Chinese restaurant all night to show them off. Jay had set a social form for the poor, just as Bird and Dizzy proposed it for the middle class. On his back screaming was the Mona Lisa with the mustache, as crude and simple. Jo Stafford could not do it. Bird took the language, and we woke up one Saturday whispering *Ornithology*. Blank verse.

And Newark always had a bad reputation, I mean, everybody could pop their fingers. Was hip. Had walks. Knew all about The Apple. So I suppose when the word got to Lynn what Big Jay had done, he knew all the little down cats were waiting to see him in this town. He knew he had to cook. And he blasted all night, crawled and leaped, then stood at the side of the stand, and watched us while he fixed his sky, wiped his face. Watched us to see how far he'd gone, but he was tired and we weren't, which was not where it was. The girls rocked slowly against the silence of the horns, and big hats pushed each other or made plans for murder. We had not completely come. All sufficiently eaten by Jay's memory, "on his back, kicking his feet in the air, Go-ud Damn!" So he moved cautiously to the edge of the stage, and the gritty Muslims he played with gathered close. It was some mean honking blues, and he made no attempt to hide his intentions. He was breaking bad. "Okay, baby," we all thought. "Go for yourself." I was standing at the back of the hall with one arm behind my back, so the overcoat could hang over in that casual gesture of fashion. Lynn was moving, and the camel walkers were moving in the corners. The fast dancers and practicers making the whole hall dangerous. "Off my suedes, motherfucker." Lynn was trying to move us, and even I did the one step I knew, safe at the back of the hall. The hippies ran for girls. Ugly girls danced with each other. Skippy, who ran the lights, made them move faster in that circle on the ceiling, and darkness raced around the hall. Then Lynn got his riff, that rhythmic figure we knew he would repeat, the honked note that would be his personal evaluation of the world. And he screamed it so the veins in his face stood out like neon. "Uhh, yeh, Uhh, yeh, Uhh, yeh," we all screamed to push him further. So he opened his eyes for a second, and really made his move. He looked over his shoulder at the other turbans, then marched in time with his riff, on his toes across the stage. They followed; he marched across to the other side, repeated, then finally he descended, still screaming, into the crowd, and as the sidemen followed, we made a path for them around the hall. They were strutting, and all their horns held very high, and they were only playing that one scary note. They moved near the back of the hall, chanting and swaying, and passed right in front of me. I had a little cup full of wine a murderer friend of mine made me drink, so I drank it and tossed the cup in the air, then fell in line behind the last wild horn man, strutting like the rest of them. Bubbles and Rogie followed me, and four-eyed Moselle Boyd. And we strutted back and forth pumping our arms, repeating with Lynn Hope, "Yeh, Uhh, Yeh, Uhh." Then everybody fell in behind us, yelling still. There was confusion and stumbling, but there were no real fights. The thing they wanted was right there and easily accessible. No one could stop you from getting in that line. "It's too crowded. It's too many people on that line!" some people yelled. So Lynn thought further, and made to destroy the ghetto. We went out into the lobby and in perfect rhythm down the marble steps. Some musicians laughed, but Lynn and some others kept the note, till the others fell back in. Five or six hundred hopped-up woogies tumbled out into Belmont Avenue. Lynn marched right in the center of the street. Sunday night traffic stopped, and honked. Big Red yelled at a bus driver, "Hey, baby, honk that horn in time or shut it off!" The bus driver cooled it. We screamed and screamed at the clear image of ourselves as we should always be. Ecstatic, completed, involved in a secret communal expression. It would be the form of the sweetest revolution, to huckle-buck into the fallen capital, and let the oppressors lindy hop out. We marched all the way to Spruce, weaving among the stalled cars, laughing at the dazed white men who sat behind the wheels. Then Lynn turned and we strutted back toward the hall. The late show at the National was turning out, and all the big hats there jumped right in our line.

Then the Nabs came, and with them, the fire engines. What was it, a labor riot? Anarchists? A nigger strike? The paddy wagons and cruisers pulled in from both sides, and sticks and billies started flying, heavy streams of water splattering the marchers up and down the street. America's responsible immigrants were doing her light work again. The knives came out, the razors, all the Biggers who would not be bent, counterattacked or came up behind the civil servants smashing at them with coke bottles and aerials. Belmont writhed under the dead economy and splivs floated in the gutter, disappearing under cars. But for a while, before the war had reached its peak, Lynn and his musicians, a few other fools, and I, still marched, screaming thru the maddened crowd. Onto the sidewalk, into the lobby, halfway up the stairs, then we all broke our different ways, to save whatever it was each of us thought we loved.

JESS MOWRY

Way Past Cool

Ty was thinking about going home for supper; he could stop at a market and buy as many groceries as he could carry . . . maybe a pack of Popsicles for the kids. His brother Danny wanted a new pair of Nikes, the major-buck kind. Ty wondered what his size was now . . . the little dude was growing so fast. Then Ty saw Deek's eyes flick up to the mirror.

"Shit!" Deek muttered.

Ty glanced in the outside mirror in time to see the cruiser light its strobes, remembering Danny calling it "popping cherries." The .45 was in Ty's lap, along with a half-empty Heineken. He slipped the bottle back into the sixer, laid the gun on top, and covered all with Deek's T-shirt. Deek's face had paled slightly as he swung the car to the curb and stopped. Ty noticed that he cut the front wheels back out again and left the engine running with his foot on the clutch. Maybe it was the beer, but Ty felt cool, even though the Trans-Am's trunk packed mega trouble. Deek was a good driver, and the 'Am had twice the acceleration, cornering grip, and top speed of any city cop car. It was also registered to a blind post-box number. Ty knew Deek wouldn't hesitate a second to abandon it if he had to. The chase might even be fun . . . like an Eddie Murphy movie. The picture of Deek bailing his jiggly lard across some trash-choked vacant lot almost brought a smile to Ty's lips. But then Deek gave a snort of disgust.

"It just *them* suckers! Shit! Hard to believe it been a week already, huh?"

Ty shrugged. "Time warp fast when you havin fun, I spose." He glanced in the mirror again, seeing the white cop waiting in the car. The man's face behind his chrome glasses wore the same sly, shit-eating expression that Danny had put on the day Ty had caught him shoplifting in Pay Less Drugs . . . a goddamn Speak 'N Spell, of all the stupid things to steal! Ty had bought it for him anyway.

The black cop ambled up to Deek's window. Deek ripped open his belt pouch and dug out five hundred-dollar bills. A few people on the sidewalk had slowed their pace as they passed, watching the scene with eyes that were curious, hopeful, or hostile. But Deek's chubby fingers moved fast, hidden between his legs, as he folded the bills and sandwiched them into the Trans-Am's papers.

The big cop leaned casually against the car, his voice pitched to sound routinely bored, but loud enough for the people on the curb to hear. "License, registration, and proof of insurance, please."

The sidewalk people moved on, one or two looking disappointed. A bag lady with a cartful of cans and crap stayed, but she hardly counted as human. Wordlessly, Deek handed the stuff to the man.

Ty's gaze drifted across the street to the burned-out building. He'd seen the skate kids cut in to the doorway, and watched them now as they peered from the shadows behind broken window glass. Ty didn't know much about them . . . just another young dogshit hood gang. The big fat boy was the leader, though he didn't look too bright and it was a miracle he could ride at all. The twins were born followers, hyper to the max and probably a bitch to keep under control, but they'd be fearless and loyal to whoever they respected. There was the small kid with his childlike potbelly and long, tangled dreads: maybe half white, judging by his features and the yellow-brown tones in his hair, and no doubt the mascot who took all the shit and got the dirtiest jobs. Both he and the tall, slender boy were shirtless, and all were cutting school. Ty couldn't blame them much; it had probably been one hell of a morning. Ty tried to get a better look at the slim graceful boy with the big puppy feet and the loose, pawlike hands. For some reason Ty had always been curious about him; it was strange how hard it seemed to see him clearly. Like a ghost in a movie, he never appeared as solid and real as the other boys. Ty sometimes wondered if his pure blackness could somehow shimmer the air around him like heat waves from asphalt. He couldn't really be called girlish, yet was almost more pretty than handsome, and, without a shirt, looked too delicate and fragile to survive in this neighborhood. Of course, the other gang members would protect him. Ty frowned slightly: some boys that age would use a pretty dude until they got the facts of life straight. But Ty didn't think that was happening here. The fat kid might lead, but the slender boy hovered ever at his elbow, and Ty suspected he was the one really in control.

Ty smiled a little, recalling how blown-away those two big boys had been that these kids had shot back. He could guess the gang's thoughts as they peered from behind glass fangs; they would be figuring that the cop had gone back to his car to run Deek's license. They'd be hoping that the 'Am would get searched, found full of rock, and that he and Deek would be slapped around, maybe whacked a few times with the cops' clubs, then handcuffed and hauled away forever. Ty knew this because when he was their age he'd have prayed for the same. He suddenly wanted another beer, but fired one of Deek's Shermans instead and ignored the wistful look the bag lady gave him. One hand strayed to the little medallion on his chest.

Ty closed his eyes, sucking smoke deep and holding it. He remembered back to when Deek was first scheming him out as a bodyguard. They'd been cruisin in the 'Am, just sipping beer and listening to some old Rick James on the CD, when these cops had pulled them over. Till then, Ty wasn't sure about taking the job, as if some small part of him, only half real like a ghost, still stood on the sidewalk clutching his scarred old skateboard and watching the gleaming car pass him by. But seeing Deek casually slip money to the cop, Ty had felt something crumble inside him, and the hungry young ghost on the curb had faded forever.

Now he gazed over at the other young boys and felt only a worn-out sort of sorrow . . . like finding a favorite T-shirt after losing it for months only to discover it just wouldn't fit anymore. In a way those kids were a kind of last defense. Ty felt sympathy, knowing that what they were fighting was so huge and powerful and so far beyond their understanding that they might as well have been trying to stop a tank with BB guns.

Ty himself didn't understand much more, except that there *was* something, and he figured whatever that something was for sure didn't want to be understood. He'd seen a TV special once about the Great Pyramids, and that's how he visualized it: he and Deek were just a couple of bricks on the bottom. On the next level up was the older black dude with the Mercedes and Afro-yuppie suit who Deek scored from about once a week. Above that was only a rumor of a white man uptown. And beyond that the pyramid towered into the clouds and Ty could only imagine what might be hidden up there. Lying awake at night, Ty tried to forget what the pyramid was built on—enough to know what it was made from; power and money and greed. Its cement was probably hate and fear and hopelessness. Ty always pictured the bottom bricks as black.

To Ty, these cops were on no higher a level than his own . . . more likely one row down. Under them were the kids who sold for Deek in the parks and streets and schools. There were about thirty at any time, though the exact number changed almost daily as new ones came in and others got out. Some were busted . . . usually the new ones and often in their first week. Others just quit, and a few just stopped . . . or, as that old antismoking commercial on TV went, *actually*, *technically*, *they died*. Below them were the kids who dealt only to use. Math had never been easy for Ty, but he figured a conservative estimate of 30 × 5 for them. They just *stopped* a lot, more often at the hands of their own burned customers than what they put into their own bodies. And the foundation for the whole structure was the kids who crouched in doorways or stairwells with their pipes and papers and points, begging on the streets for money to "get something to eat," fucking it for the kids who were really starving and *had* to beg, and breaking into cars and apartments and preying on all those younger or weaker . . . or alone.

Without friends.

Ty smoked and watched the boys, thinking how funny it was that everybody outside places like this should be so stupidly amazed that kids wanted guns and banded together in gangs. What in hell else were they supposed to do, go it alone and get picked off one by one? Trouble was, gangs, like individuals, could be bought and used by those smarter and more powerful.

Ty frowned and idly fingered his medallion. Like now. Like those kids over there had no idea how Deek was fitting them into the pyramid . . . the one that was black on the bottom but white on the top.

Ty flipped his half-smoked cigarette out the window, watching as the bag lady scrambled for it. Hell, he thought, didn't those kids watch anything on TV but cartoons? For sure, the facts and figures on the news were mostly lies, but after a while you could *see* them! If you paid attention. If you didn't fuck up your mind. It was plain as dogshit on the sidewalk that if you were rich and white and got caught doing drugs you had a *dependency problem*. You went on TV and told everybody how sorry you were and checked into a place for rich fuckups. A poor black kid with burns on his fingers got dragged into an alley by the cops and beat to a pulp before being hauled off to jail. When are you ever gonna get real, little brothers!

The cop came back to Ty's window and handed him the papers without a word. His face was expressionless behind his chrome mirrors. Ty could see Deek's reflection in silver. It was funny how a dead expression was also a childlike one. Deek said nothing; there was nothing to say that wouldn't have been an even bigger joke. Deek let out the clutch and swung the car away from the curb, not bothering to signal because the cop car stood guard for him.

Ty studied the gang boys as the Trans-Am purred past. Four faces showed sullen hatred for what they couldn't understand. Ty knew the feeling well. It was what would eventually cement them into the pyramid after they were beaten down by banging their heads against it for a few more years. Ty had seen that look in so many eyes for the last few months that he hardly noticed it anymore, even though he knew that, given half a chance, those kids wouldn't waste a second killing Deek and himself on the spot. But there was something different in the fifth face: the fragile features of the slender boy.

Maybe it was the shadows, or the way he always seemed so hard to see. It made Ty uneasy.

Deek saw where Ty was looking. His foot came off the gas and his eyes flicked to the mirror as the cruiser made a squeaky U-turn and dwindled down the block.

"Yo, stupid! How come you never say nuthin? Shit, this's *perfect!*"

Ty shrugged. He picked up his beer and chugged it while Deek cut the car across the street and pulled to the curb, facing the wrong way, directly in front of the gang. Ty could feel the tenseness of the younger boys, trapped as they were in the doorway. He snagged the .45 and flicked off the safety as the fat one reached behind his half-bare butt and the others automatically spread out as wide as they could between the walls. The hate was still there, maybe tempered a little by fear, but the fat boy's jaw was set and the twins' tawny eyes like frozen gold. Only the smallest kid looked uncertain. He pressed against the slender boy, who just seemed to watch with no expression at all. Ty caught a flash of something silver passed from the small kid to the older one, whose long, loose paw closed over it. Ty gave the block a quick checkout; traffic was light, and the cops wouldn't be back. Most people on the sidewalk, at least those under forty who had more than Jell-O for brains, seemed to have found some excuse to cross over to the other side of the street. Only an old lady with a grocery bag walked obliviously between the car and the doorway. Ty slipped out fast and stood, his door left half open while he leaned against the car. His big hands were clasped casually on the roof, cradling the pistol so the boys could see what is. He didn't exactly point it at them, just close enough to signify. Ty knew about their .22, but the silver glint in the slender boy's paw bothered him. He wished that Deek had given him time to snag the short-barreled Uzi carbine from the back seat. Even drunk or stoned Deek was no fool, and he hadn't lived to sixteen by taking these kinds of stupid chances. Ty supposed, as always, he had a reason.

Despite the Heinekens, Ty's senses were sharp, aware of the street life around him. The sparse traffic, both ways, would slow momentarily until the drivers read the word, then speed up to get past. On the opposite sidewalk people were doing the same. Nobody wanted to witness. Even the crazy bag lady moved on, her shopping cart's wheels squealing rustily.

Deek leaned from his window. "Yo, Gordy! What's up, dude?"

Ty saw uncertainty creep into the fat boy's eyes: he might have been ready to die but Deek's cheerfulness took him off guard. The hand hovering back by his butt came slowly to his side. For a moment he hesitated, then took a breath and stepped from the shadows. Even sheathed in rolls of fat his chest was impressive. He came halfway across the sidewalk, warily, like a rat in the open. "So, what you want, Deek? An don't call me Gordy, I hate that!"

Deek put hurt in his voice. "Hey, I'm sorry, Gordon. Didn't know. Just cool to see all you dudes okay."

Ty watched the fat boy's eyes narrow in suspicion. "Why not we be okay, Deek?"

Deek shrugged. "Shitty world, man. That all."

Back in the doorway, Ty noted the twins easing closer to the sunlight, curious now. Only the slender boy remained deep in shadow, his half-naked body blending into the background, hard to see. He seemed to be studying Deek. He'd slipped one arm around the smaller kid, keeping him back, too. His other paw half concealed what Ty now saw was a little silver gun. It was aimed from the hip full at Deek. Ty wondered how good a shot he was. Though small, the gun was bigger than a .22. Ty gave a mental shrug; he'd done the best he could to cover Deek's ass. The rest was in God's hands. That thought caught him by surprise . . . funny thing to think.

As always in these situations Ty felt as if time had slowed. Little details stood out sharp. The sun creeping down the storefront had warmed the broken window glass and a tiny triangle dropped from the frame and hit the concrete with a musical note that seemed loud. The fat boy tensed again. The twins' eyes shifted for an instant. Only the slender dude's gaze never wavered.

There was stubborness in the fat boy's tone. The words came out like they tasted bad. "This *our* ground, Deek! Why you come schemin round here?"

Ty watched the fat boy. There was a hollow triangle in his T-shirt where the twin rolls of chest fat overlapped his belly. That would be a good target, close to the heart, but he'd have to shoot the slender kid first. That wouldn't be easy. Then, to Ty's amazement, Deek popped the door and got out, stretching casually and wiping at the wet under his armpits just like any other kid. Gordon was probably heavier than Deek, and Deek was a good head taller, but Gordon probably had bigger bones. Some kids seemed meant to be fat and looked almost cool that way. Deek wasn't one of them.

Deek's voice was soothing. "Yo, Gordon, I fucked up, okay? Jeez, shoot bullets through me!" He made a vague wave down the street. "What I sayin is, I was just motorin through. How the hell I know them cocksuckin cops gonna curb me? I *sorry*, man. Shit, you *know* I wouldn't try sellin round here without your permission an a righteous cut besides."

Gordon's forehead creased slightly. Two vertical lines appeared over his nose. Ty recalled his mother saying once that those kinds of lines meant a person spent a lot of time trying to figure things out. Somehow you never imagined a fat kid doing much thinking.

Gordon seemed to search for words. He hitched up his sagging jeans. "Well . . ."

Behind him, their toes over the sunlit line, the twins edged forward, eyebrows up, breathing through their mouths. The slender boy stayed where he was. His grip tightened on the small kid. The gang's scent came to Ty's nostrils: dirty jeans, old sport shoes, oily hair, and the bittersweet tang of kid sweat. For a second Ty thought he caught a trace of blood smell, but couldn't be sure.

Gordon finished with a lame "Gots no goddamn right bein here at all, man."

Deek spread chubby pink palms and moved closer to Gordon. "Hey, I hear you, man. An I promise it ain't gonna happen again. Swear to God."

Father of lies, thought Ty. That's what the Bible called the devil.

Gordon seemed to feel the eyes of his gang. His back, curved by the weight of his belly, straightened a little. "Yeah, well . . ."

"Listen up, dude," Deek went on. "Word. I just had to make a little ole detour. What it is, Wesley wanna talk to me."

Gordon was instantly alert. "Bout what?"

Deek's palms spread wider. His own jeans were slipping. Compared to Gordon's big boy-butt Deek had an ass like a girl's, Ty thought.

"Hey, Gordon, you a leader too. You know I can't say. Be breakin the rules, what it is." Deek seemed to think a moment, then stepped even closer to Gordon and laid a big-brother hand on his shoulder. Ty barely heard him whisper. "The Crew maybe havin some drive-by probs, man. Seem Wesley needin some major bucks for scorin himself a decent gun."

Even the twins, closest to Gordon, couldn't have heard. But Ty saw the slender boy's eyes narrow to slits. Gordon looked uncertain for a few seconds, then demanded. "So, what you callin a decent gun, man?"

Ty stiffened as Deek turned with a smile, stepped to the car, and snagged the Uzi from the back seat. All the gang boys tensed. Gordon's hand darted behind his back. The little silver gun gleamed in the slender dude's dark, delicate fingers.

But Deek only held the carbine up sideways for a second or two. "Somethin like this decent enough for ya?"

The twins' eyes went wide as surprised panther cubs. "WAY cool!" breathed one. "PAST," sighed the other. "Word!"

Deek grinned, then casually tossed the gun back into the car. "Word up, you dudes *never* need worry bout nuthin no more, packin one of them! Yo, Gordon, I could make it happen for ya. Straight."

Gordon's mouth had opened slightly. Now it shut with a snap. He snorted. "Uh-huh. Cept how we 'ford bullets for the goddamn thing?"

Deek shrugged. "Aw, there's always ways, man. But what can I say? You just seen the future." He snickered. "State of *the* art. Believe. Just think on it, that all." He smiled again and took the keys from the ignition. "Anyways, like I sayin, I sorry as hell bout crossin your ground out askin first." He walked back and keyed the trunk lid. "Yo! I pay you dudes for me fuckin up."

Gordon came slowly to the rear of the car. The twins crowded close behind him, all caution gone, expecting more wonders. As if on display against the soft black carpet in the Trans-Am's trunk, next to the grocery boxes holding the real merchandise, were two cases of Heineken.

Deek waved a gold-ringed hand as though performing a magic trick. "Hell, they even still cool, Gordon. Shit, I know you an your dudes don't do nuthin else. They both yours, just for lettin me motor through. Deal?"

Ty watched. Street pride was a funny thing; you never knew what rule it would follow, but it was based a lot on practical logic. He caught the flick of the fat boy's eyes to the slim kid's, and saw a slight nod in the shadows. That confirmed what Ty had always suspected about who did a lot of the gang's real thinking, though Ty's respect for the fat boy's brain had risen a point or two. The twins were trembling like eager puppies.

Gordon stepped back and crossed his arms over his chest. "Okay, Deek. One time, *this* time. An that all it for, hear?"

Grinning, Deek moved aside as the twins scrambled for the beer. "Oh, for sure, Gordon. But I just sayin that my offer always open to ya. Course, that just business, you understand?"

"Mm. Spect I unnerstand a lotta shit, man. We let you know, but don't go holdin your breath or nuthin."

The twins carried the cases back to the sidewalk. Still grinning, Deek slammed the trunk lid. "Word. I think hard, I was you, man. Specially if the Crew go an score some major fire." Deek paused a moment, then bent close to Gordon. "Word up, there some big dudes schemin your hood, man. WAY bad dudes! We talkin Gorilla an Cripps class, little brother! Hope you got mega bullets for them two pop toys of yours, man!"

"Shit," muttered Gordon. "Four third-graders kick *anybody's* ass! Little bullet go through big dude easy as small dude! Save your preachin for somebody who give a shit!"

Deek shrugged and twirled his key ring. "Yo! That was for free, Gordon. Everbody gots to have friends!"

"Mmm. I could say somethin, but I won't."

Ty waited until Deek was back in the car before sliding in himself. He watched the slender boy all the while. Their eyes met again for an instant. Ty picked up another beer and popped it as Deek swung the 'Am into the street and squeaked away.

Deek's beeper sounded as they reached the next block. He pulled up next to a corner phone booth that was smothered in spray paint and surrounded by a glittering pool of its own shattered glass. It was still working, though, because Deek talked for a few minutes, then returned to the car looking almost happy for so early in the day.

"Gots a new one wantin a job," he snickered, sliding back into the seat. "Told him to meet us tonight at the Burger King. Always helps to pig em out first, specially the hungry ones." He released the parking brake and shifted into gear, then glanced at Ty. "You figure that black-ass bitch gonna be there?"

Ty frowned and shrugged. "Naw. Too many hours. Child-labor law. Even if she black as sin." He took a swallow of beer, then added, "Like me."

Deek snickered again and shook his head. "Maaaan, it just too fuckin bad there ain't no more Panthers around. You be a natural. Yo! Black pride an brotherhood be a long time dead, stupid, case you ain't figured it out yet. Only black asses you got to worry over is mine an yours!"

JABARI ASIM

Two Fools

Tom-Tom and DeAndre were sitting on the stoop of an abandoned building. Its once-grand exterior was now pocked, pimpled, and peppered with scrawled threats, boasts, and obscenities, courtesy of Tom-Tom's skill and a stolen can of Krylon. Among them:

FOOLS RULE! DEF 2 INS∀NE DOPE GANG!

"Whatchoo feel like gittin into?" Tom-Tom asked his lifelong pal.

DeAndre dug deep into his left nostril, extracted a semisolid glob of green mucus, and thumped it in the general direction of Vandeventer Avenue.

"A bitch is what Ah feel like gittin into," he replied. "A nice, hot nasty bitch."

Tom-Tom laughed, spat, and scratched his crotch. "Well," he said, "since they ain't no bitches roun her, mebbe we could git sump ta eat. Ahm all about grabbin sum grub if ya down fuh it."

This time DeAndre stuck his little finger far into his right ear. He sighed. "Ite den. Wer we gon roll to? We got duh Chinaman's on Greer, duh Chinaman's on Gran, or duh Chinaman's on Gano—hole on, mebbe would check out dat kew shack on Sullivan. You know duh wun dat brutha got?"

"Wer it at? Ah ain't hip ta dat."

"Ya trippin, Dog," DeAndre said, running his tongue across his gold star. Everyone in the gang of Fools sported a gold star on his left front tooth.

"Why Ah gots ta be trippin?"

"Cuz dats wer we got dem Kools duh otha night. Ya know, when Bay wuz runnin sum yang on dat yella bitch go ta Beaumont? Rememba? She uh churleada an shit."

"Aw yeah," said Tom-Tom. His face lit up with memory. "Ahm hip nah. Yeah, Ah rememba duh nigga dat run dat joint. Lil greasy face nigga witta crookit eye."

"Nah ya gittin wittit! How boutta hot link uh sump?"

Tom-Tom shook his head. "Caint hang. Ahm down wit duh five puh-cennuz. Ah aint go fuck wit no pig no mo. Less check out duh Chinaman on Greer and grab sum duck necks."

"Bet," DeAndre said.

The two Fools rose and pimped along the sun-splashed avenue. DeAndre was older than Tom-Tom but a good five inches shorter. His thick mustache and self-assured gait lent him an air of maturity that belied his seventeen years. Tom-Tom, sixteen, was a lean, rangy six feet two. He moved with the long-legged grace of an athlete. It required little imagination to see Tom-Tom clad in the blue-and-gold of Beaumont High, gliding like a gazelle over an array of hurdles. Dreams of athletic glory were already a fast-fading memory for him, for he'd quit school at thirteen, about the same time that he took up smoking.

Only an outsider could fail to see that these two young men were members of the dreaded gang of Fools. Their gold stars, their blue overalls worn with one strap hanging loose, even the distinctive way they scratched and spat—it all spelled "Fool" with a capital *F*.

"Shit, Dog," said DeAndre. "Ah gotta pee."

"Shouldn'ta drank dat foughty ounce. Whatchoo waitin fuh? Go pee."

"Slow up, Dude. Ahm lookin fuh a red ride."

"Word," Tom-Tom said.

Red was the signature color sported by the Dopes, arch-enemies of the Fools. Anything red drove DeAndre and his cohorts into a bright blue rage. Once, in a crowded supermarket, DeAndre had slapped an elderly woman because her red sweater offended him. No one said a word.

Tom-Tom paused when DeAndre found a car that suited his fancy, a spotless red Camaro. Sunlight glinted off DeAndre's five gold finger rings as he splashed the Camaro's gleaming hood.

"Her bout Stinky's old girl?" Tom-Tom asked.

"Naw. Whuh she do?"

Tom-Tom scratched his crotch. "She got hit upsida hay-ed, dats whuh she did. Somebody thode uh brick an caughta owna kitchen. Say she got brain dammitch."

DeAndre zipped his overalls. "Damn, dats fuckt."

"Nah rilly," said Tom-Tom. "Azz me, bitch wuz kinda stupid anyway."

The two old buddies laughed and continued their stroll. Tom-Tom whistled softly as a stylish luxury car sped by. "Lookit dat muhfucka, willya?" he said wistfully. "Wun day dat's go be mah ride."

"Naw it ain't," DeAndre teased.

"Yeah it ils."

"Fuhgit aboudit, Dog. All you go git is uh hoopty."

Tom-Tom froze his friend's laughter with a stern stare. "Ahmo *git* me uh Town Car, you'll see. A baby blue Leenkin Town Car. Gits me dat an Ahm go die wun happy nigga."

"Ah her ya, Homes. Ah wuz juss fuckin witcha."

DeAndre stopped dead in his tracks and signaled for his fellow Fool to do likewise.

"Whassup?" Tom-Tom demanded.

"Trouble, Double-Tee."

"Huh?" Tom-Tom looked around, following DeAndre's gaze until his eyes rested on a red-clad figure standing at a pay phone. The man's back was turned, but there was no mistaking the bright jacket and cap. The red glowed in the sun like a beckoning beacon, taunting the two Fools.

"Whatchoo think?" Tom-Tom asked.

"Aint no thinkin ta do," was DeAndre's quick reply. "Ahmo pull my piece and pop dis punk. Got duh nuts ta warr Dope culluz in *mah* hood. Muhfucka betta git outta Dodge. Goddamn insane Dope gang!"

DeAndre's aim was true. The bark of a gun blast was not unusual in the community, so little notice was paid as the red cap flew into the air above the pay phone. Blood bathed the booth, splattering numerals and coin slot with rich, running red. The receiver dangled like a severed limb.

Later that night DeAndre and Tom-Tom tossed back forty-ounce bottles of malt liquor and watched the news.

"Whatchoo wunna watch dis shit fuh? We could be watchin videos."

DeAndre belched loudly before answering. "Ah like dis new bitch on channel five," he said. "She got pritty ize."

"Probbly contacks," Tom-Tom said. "An ya know all dat hurr own toppa her hay-ed gotta be fake an shit. Ah ain't nevva seena bitch wit dat much rill hurr."

"Ah on't givva fuck," DeAndre said, "juss long azz dat pussy's real. Hey, turn nat uppa sec."

The news announcer told of a random murder. A vendor at the ballpark, a father of three, had been shot in cold blood while calling his wife from a pay phone. He was wearing his work uniform when he was killed.

"Damn!" Tom-Tom shouted. "Dat wuddnt no Dope you popped! Dat wuzza dude who worked fuh duh Pigeons."

The Pigeons were the local professional baseball team. Red and white were the official team colors.

"Shit," Tom-Tom continued. "Dats fuckt."

DeAndre took another sip and shook his head. "Dumb muhfucka shoulda took dat shit off in duh hood. Stupid nigga knew wer he wuz."

"Word," Tom-Tom agreed. "Slide me anutha 'Bull.' "

KEVIN POWELL

Ghetto Bastard

TAKE 1

Chillin' in my Harlem apartment, trying to write. It's all I've wanted to do ever since I was an ill-tempered, snot-nose kid growing up in Jersey City. The omnipresent deadlines are annoying, but I figure several pesty editors beat an empty stomach any day.

Outside, gunshots crack the uptown frost and I think to myself how lucky I am to be young, Black, male, and alive at twenty-five. But that of course doesn't mean I don't think about the precariousness of my life, because I do: each and everyday before I leave my apartment I brace myself for some humiliation (the ultimate would be dying a senseless, meaningless death) at the hands of a racist cop, a condescending employer, an overly watchful store owner, or even another young Black male. Ghetto culture keeps its children on the edge: we are too conditioned to pain to trust anyone fully and too quick to accuse someone of violating our sense of self-worth. Many of my homeboys are dead or in jail somewhere because the ghetto ate them up before they could master the art of survival. After being jumped twice by large groups of Black men (one of those occasions left me with a broken nose), being semihomeless, starving and begging people for help, I cringe when I think what could have happened to me if, as Eric B. and Rakim rap, *I didn't know the ledge* and fell over.

TAKE 2

Thanksgiving Day '91. I trooped across the Hudson River to Jersey City, my hometown, to check out my moms and my aunt Cathy. While glancing at a football game I decided to call my boy, Rashan, who I hadn't spoken with in a while. "What up, dude," he said, kickin' his hardest ghettocentric vernacular. "Ain't nothin', man, just coolin', ya know," I responded, eager to let him know I hadn't forgotten my roots either. After some small talk Rashan told me that Alby died a few weeks ago. Alby. Dead of AIDS. And leukemia. Rashan said Alby was all shriveled up in a hospital bed, cool as ever, still talking " 'bout how he was gonna get a rap contract soon." I felt like one of my relatives had died, 'cause Alby represented for us kids in the 'hood all the possibilities of making something out of nothing. Between our ass-whoopings, reefer pulls, and dice games, Alby strutted his manhood: throwing block parties with his rap crew—Sweet, Slick, and Sly—wearing a big Jackson Five Afro and the latest polyester outfits. No one ever knew how old Alby was, but even senior citizens and the local preachers knew he was the man. Rashan said Alby had gotten into the drug thang and was doing all right until he started taking the stuff himself. Mix that with all the women he was sexin' and you knew Alby's body was destined to crack apart, literally. Damn, Alby, you had it goin' on.

TAKE 3

Me and Darnell use to play stickball every day in the summertime. We were baseball fanatics and we both swore we'd be in the major leagues one day. Carrying long sticks, cheap gloves, and sponge balls, we'd approach P.S. 20 cautiously, looking left and right for the police. School was closed for the summer, so we had to scale the twenty-foot gate to get into the courtyard. Our daily routine was simple: a mad dash to the gate, slipping our gloves and balls and sticks through the bottom and up and over we went. Playing for nickels, dimes, quarters, and dollars—when our paper-route tips were good—each day one of us would go home pissed off because we had lost a game and money.

Like most Black boys in the ghetto, high school graduation was for us less a time to celebrate than a time to contemplate what the huge, terrifying future held for us. Darnell, myself, and most of the homies we grew up with only knew our immediate blocks and the ten blocks in any given direction. Even with this stunted vision we all talked of fleeing the bowels of inner-city living. It was the mid-eighties, the national mood was swinging back toward Jim Crowism, and cocaine and crack were sweeping through the Black communities.

I managed to escape to college due to a sizable financial aid package. A good number of homeys—including my cousin Anthony—opted for the military. That left dudes like Darnell, glued to the ghetto's underbelly but eager to shed their poverty and despair.

Midway into my college career I ran into Darnell on a visit home. He had on a fly suede suit, a pair of suede Ballys, and gold tooth caps punctuated his cocky smile. I couldn't believe this was the same dude I played stickball with only a few years before. We embraced the way old homeboys do, then drifted backward, checking each other out. Here I was, a college boy: loafers with argyle socks and the whole nine, looking like a Cosby kid. On the other hand Darnell looked like he belonged in the community. He had merely cast his bucket where he was and was surviving by whatever means available. "Yeah, man, that's my house over there," he said, pointing proudly to a bright yellow, two-family frame. I was envious. My moms was still paying rent for a dumpy three-room apartment, and Darnell had his mother set up and everything. We rapped a little longer, then melted from each other's consciousness again.

I ran into Darnell late last year. I barely recognized him. He had lost a good deal of weight and was wiping the outside window of a sandwich shop. "Yo, Kev man, whassup?" he asked, his smile revealing a large gap in the center of his mouth. Darnell looked like a ghost of his former self. At twenty-four his body was stooped, his once bright almond-brown skin ashy and peeling, his lips a dark reddish tone, his eyes a dingy yellow. "Whassup with you, man?" I asked, tying a deeper question beneath my response. "Ain't nothin', man, just had some bad luck, youknowwhatahmsayin'? Started taking coke and I got hooked man, my business went downhill. I did have some money saved, but when I got busted for sellin', they frozed my assets, you know. . . ."

And I wasn't listening to Darnell any longer. Only feeling him. We were a few blocks from those summer stickball games, but it seemed like centuries ago. As he talked on and on about jail and getting jumped by drug rivals and how many times he got burned having sex and how he was straightening up his life and how he wanted to play stickball with me, I choked on my disgust and wondered why young Black men swallow suicide when we discover ain't no rainbows in the ghetto. . . .

Unable to quell my anger and frustration, I told Darnell I had to split. "Yo, Kev, what you into, man?" "Yo, I'm just a writer, you know. It ain't easy." Darnell inhaled my words, trying to make sense of what I was doing to survive. "Kev, that's dope, man. Maybe I can get you a job with the *Jersey Journal* or somethin'." "Yeah, that would be mad fly, D." "Ay-ight, Kev man, let's get together so we can play some ball. Can you still pitch like you useta?" I nodded my head yes even though I knew too many fights had destroyed my right shoulder. "Yeah, man, we'll get together." A few weeks later I got word Darnell was dead, shot in the head trying to steal some crack from a drug dealer.

TAKE 4

July '91. New Music Seminar Week. New York City. Naughty By Nature and other groups are performing at the Palladium. It's mad crowded and I'm on the solo tip, sportin' some Girbaud overalls and a white Gap shirt. And scheming on the ladies. I see this dude named Dexter I went to college with. Like a lot of brothers, Dexter hadn't finished school. Last I heard, he was a father, pimpin' women and selling drugs in central Jersey. Wack. His bald head shining brightly—a lot of homeys were gettin' the baldies last summer—Dexter stepped over to me and asked how I was doing. Easing into my male posturing mode, I told him everything was swell. Shifting the conversation, Dexter grew grim and asked if he could speak to me alone. I thought we were already doing that. Nah, take a walk with me. Suddenly distrustful, I told him we could step to the side and rap. Dexter told me he had been carrying a beef against me for the past three years. He claimed I had said some foul shit about him to his ex-girlfriend and he wanted to settle it right there at the Palladium. Stunned, I scanned my memory bank but couldn't find anything so harsh as to warrant his three-year grudge. Dexter figured what I thought wasn't important. I could either be a man or a pussy. Let's step around the corner. Fuck that, I thought to myself, I'm not getting jumped again and this nigga ain't gonna kill me for some dumb ego shit. Thinking quickly, I told Dexter I had to say "peace" to some friends, then I'd be glad to settle this around the corner. He followed me, but I ducked into the crowd. Instantly several other bald-headed homeys popped up and one tried to kick me. I was audi 5000. I ran across Fourteenth Street, narrowly dodging a car. Heading west, I looked across the street and saw at least ten bald heads running parallel to me. Why am I running to my own funeral? I thought aloud, then doubled back toward the Palladium. I ran into a group of cops and they looked at me like I was crazy. Yo, Officer, they might try to kill me. No, I didn't see a gun, but so what. Ah, fuck it. I gotta get out of here. Dexter and his posse lingered behind the police barricade across the street, sure they had me trapped. A cab approached and I hailed it. I jumped in and locked all the doors. The cab wasn't moving. Just go, man, I yelled, ducking down in the backseat. Anywhere! Uh, uh, Forty-second Street, yeah, Port Authority, take me there. Dexter and his boys chased the cab for half a block, then gave up. I asked the driver to take me home to Harlem, shoving my last $25 into his hand. Lying on the backseat, I closed my eyes and pushed the night away.

YUSEF SALAAM

Brer Rabbit Escapes Again, or Brer Fox Bites Off More Than He Can Chew

I was juggling two jobs at the time. I was working the graveyard shift at Harlem Hospital as a patient escort, a nice title for a person who pushes patients around on stretchers or wheelchairs to the X-ray room or the wards. I also had a part-time job as an adjunct English professor at the Borough of Manhattan Community College. I'd hit there around nine-thirty in the morning after clocking out of the hospital at eight A.M. I taught composition three mornings a week; the last class was on Thursday. By then I was dog-tired. I always managed to get some sleep in between transporting patients. My supervisor and I had a special arrangement. We both lived near the hospital, so he'd take a two-hour lunch and go home and rest; I'd cover for him, then I'd go home for two hours and sleep, and he'd cover for me.

One Thursday at BMMC, I collected class assignments, distributed graded papers, and presented an extensive review of material that would be on the final exam. Christmas was about two weeks away, so most of the students, instead of paying attention to me, were dreaming of a white one. We finished around eleven o'clock. I didn't give a homework assignment because I was leaving town for the weekend and didn't want the burden of paperwork when I returned. The students could spend the weekend studying for the final.

Outside, icy winds skied across the nearby Hudson River and splashed on my face. I pulled my coat collar up tighter around my neck. I was in full stride when I hit the sidewalk, trucking toward the Number 2 train, triple tired, homebound for bed. I was halfway to the train station and decided to stop at a discount store to buy a scarf. Got in there and caught a clothes-buying fever; bought two scarfs, a pair of gloves, lumberjack boots, six pair of wool socks, and two army-green wool blankets. I dragged toward the counter with my arms filled. The counter girl tallied up my bill. A fellow with a suitcase bumped into me as he hurried toward the exit. "Excuse me," he muttered, speeding and weaving through the crowd of shoppers with a skill that should have been in a chapter of the professional football running backs' playbook. The counter girl bagged my goods and handed me my change. "Thank you. Please come back."

"Hold it right there!" a voice roared. I spun around. The shake-and-bake running back dropped the suitcase and was trying to scramble out the door. A fat white man grabbed him by the arm, swung him around, and locked him in a full nelson. "I got 'im, Frank!" he shouted. Frank, curly red hair dangling onto his forehead, and eyes as blue as stones in Indian jewelry, faced Robert (I found out his name later) with a bat. The would-be thief's face was twisted in pain, and he was grasping for breath. "Turn me loose, bitch! Damn it!" he gagged. "I said get your hands off me!" The fat fellow eased up a bit, but he kept the full nelson firm. Frank kept pumping that bat; he was ready to slam Robert's head out of the stadium if he would've made a funny move. A female employee retrieved the suitcase while Frank and the fat guy forced the suspect to the back of the store. The fat guy released his hold on Robert and left to call the police. Frank pumped the bat at his detainee, head level. "Don't you move, boy!" he spitted. "My name is Robert, bitch! I got ya', boy, right here!" He grabbed a fistful of his crotch.

Robert's face was round and the color of honey, lashed with lines from the whips of white and black nigger breakers. He raked his hands over his ruffled, short, nappy African locks as he repeatedly growled, "You keep your hands off me."

I stood there watching along with everyone else. I don't get involved in such situations. I'd rather observe from the bleachers, eating popcorn and minding my own business.

"I ain't stole nothing," Robert snapped. "Did I go through that door with anything?" Frank cocked his bat. "No, but you—" "Ain't no 'but' about it. I didn't go through that door with nothing, so the law says I ain't stole nothing." Frank circled Robert, cutting off the path to the door. "You had no intentions of paying for that suitcase. You went past the counter, straight toward the door as fast as you could . . . and as fast as you people run, I wasn't about to let you get too far a head start." "What you mean 'you people'?" Robert asked. Frank looked around. Several of "you people" were staring bullets at him. "I know what you really meant to say. Why don't you go head and say it, you racist!" Frank opened his mouth to respond, blinked his eyes, and Robert broke for the door. Frank's bat swished at the space where Robert had stood. He burned a path halfway to the counter and slammed head-on into a lady coming into the store. He and the woman laid sprawled on the floor. Frank stood over him with the bat raised all the way uptown. As the bat tilted downward, a woman screamed, "Lord, have mercy! Don't kill 'im!" It was a deep, guttural, moan-shout-scream, the kind I've heard at funerals. Frank checked his swing, braking halfway to Robert's head. That bluesy voice had moved me too. "Man, don't kill him," I said calmly. "You'll go to prison for murder." That voice had stirred something in me. I put my hands on Frank's shoulders.

I had heard that woman's voice before. Or one like it. It was my grandma's or aunt's voices when they got the Holy Ghost in church and would moan, cry, and shout about Jesus. I'd heard those blue notes at Harlem Hospital when an employee, a sweet, gentle woman, came screaming clots of mercy pleas downstairs to the emergency room where her son lay dying from gunshot wounds.

"You just hold him until the police comes," I advised Frank. Robert scrambled to his feet. "That's right, brother. He ain't got no business hitting me with no bat." He eased next to me. I shifted away from him. "Look. You tried to steal the man's suitcase. You're wrong. Frank, you should hold him somewhere out of the public's eye until the cops come." Frank nodded. "Downstairs in the basement." He pointed the bat toward the basement and nudged Robert in the side with it, prodding him forward. Robert dragged forward. "Boy, you go on down there with him so they won't hurt him," a voice sang out from the front of the store. It was the same voice that drew me out of the bleachers into Robert and Frank's mess. I followed them into the basement.

The basement was a dim-lit cavity with boxes scattered all over. It was eerily quiet. Frank was holding his position at home plate. Robert was running his mouth, talking loud, saying nothing. I glanced at my watch and yawned, tired from working two jobs, tired of Robert's mouth. He was blowing incoherent blah-blah-blahs until he said, "I'm a good bitch. I done had lovers from Manhattan to Miami. I ain't got to steal no suitcase." Frank winked and smiled at me, rolled his eyes to the sky in ridicule of Robert. I beamed back a smile that showed my disgust with Robert. "I got a little Irish boy out on Long Island who loves this Black stuff," Robert boasted. Frank's face flushed pink. "I know what he likes and I know how to give it to him." Frank looked at me, his eyes questioning. I shrugged my shoulders. "T-t-tell him to stop talking like that." The fat part of the bat rested on his shoulder. I waved my hands to indicate that I was as helpless as he was. "Stop it!" He pumped the bat. "Goddammit, be quiet!"

It was clear to me what was unfolding. Robert was Brer Rabbit, the famous trickster in Black folk tales, who was always outwitting Brer Fox when Brer Fox caught him being mischievous. Or when Brer Fox was trying to bully him. Frank was the powerful fox who'd caught the rabbit trying to steal. Now Robert was attempting to talk his way out of trouble.

In one famous tale Brer Fox catches Brer Rabbit stealing from his garden. He contemplates what kind of punishment to mete out to the rabbit. Brer Rabbit pleads for Brer Fox to do whatever he deems to be the fitting punishment but don't throw him in the dreaded briar patch. Brer Fox, seeing Brer Rabbit's fear of the briar patch, tosses him in the patch, not realizing that the briar patch is the trickster's home.

Every Black man in the USA has had to play Brer Rabbit to a white man/ Brer Fox at one time or another under varying circumstances. Frank was waving the bat. He inched closer to Robert, the bat held high for a head shot.

"I'm gonna show you what you white boys like," Robert proposed, fingering the waist of his pants. Frank rushed at him. "Don't you dare!!" he screamed. Robert dropped his pants, slipped down his underwear. Stood there buck naked. Frank's bat clanked to the floor. Robert turned around, bent over, grabbed the cheeks of his butt. "This is what you white boys love, ain't it now?" He offered. "Goddamn you! You crazy, filthy bastard!" Frank bellowed. His eyes were wide with fright and desperation. He shook his head nervously as if he was about to have a fit and bit his lips hard like he was trying to will himself from thinking compelling, unwanted thoughts. His face, a sad clown mask, pleaded with me that he might be losing his mind.

"Come on, man. Put your clothes on," I urged Robert. "You ain't all that crazy." Robert looked at me. He knew that I was a fellow Brother Rabbit and was aware of the game he was running. He pulled up his underwear and pants as easily as he had dropped them. The sound of two-way radios came from the stairway. And the voices of men talking. Robert began talking loud again, rambling about how much white men loved him and how, when he was younger, he made a Jewish fellow leave his wife. Two pale-faced cops entered. The one with the sergeant stripes asked, "What's the problem, fellows?" He directed the question to me because Frank was out of it. In the midst of Robert's noisy ranting about his white-boy lovers, I tried to explain what had happened. The cops laughed nervously as they picked up on what Robert was saying; inside of their laughter was a hint that I should laugh too. And I faked a laugh that was heartier than theirs. "The guy's a nut," the youngest one observed. I nodded my head in agreement. A store assistant came down and told them the whole story. "Look," the sergeant said. "It's close to Christmas. You don't want to see nobody go to jail. You got your suitcase back, don't ya?" The store assistant nodded. In other words, these white men didn't want Robert in the backseat of their squad car or down at the precinct, which was probably filled with predominately white men, talking like "a nut."

"And you, buddy," the sergeant said, turning to Robert. "If you ever come in this store again, we'll throw you in jail—no questions asked. You understand?" Robert bowed his head and, still babbling, disappeared upstairs.

I caught the Number 2 train. Truly tired. Snored all the way. When the train bellied into my stop on 135th Street in Harlem, I jerked alive.

Brer Rabbits always sleep with one eye open.

MICHAEL ERIC DYSON

Reflecting Black

On a recent trip to Knoxville, I visited Harold's barber shop, where I had gotten my hair cut during college, and after whenever I had the chance. I had developed a friendship with Ike, a local barber who took great pride in this work. I popped my head inside the front door, and after exchanging friendly greetings with Harold, the owner, and noticing Ike missing, I inquired about his return. It had been nearly two years since Ike had cut my hair, and I was hoping to receive the careful expertise that comes from familiarity and repetition.

"Man, I'm sorry to tell you, but Ike got killed almost two years ago," Harold informed me. "He and his brother, who was drunk, got into a fight, and he stabbed Ike to death."

I was shocked, depressed, and grieved, these emotions competing in rapid-fire fashion for the meager psychic resources I was able to muster. In a daze of retreat from the fierce onslaught of unavoidable absurdity, I half-consciously slumped into Harold's chair, seeking solace through his story of Ike's untimely and brutal leave-taking. Feeling my pain, Harold filled in the details of Ike's last hours, realizing that for me Ike's death had happened only yesterday. Harold proceeded to cut my hair with a methodical precision that was itself a temporary and all-too-thin refuge from the chaos of arbitrary death, a protest against the nonlinear progression of miseries that claim the lives of too many black men. After he finished, I thanked Harold, both of us recognizing that we would not soon forget Ike's life, or his terrible death.

This drama of tragic demise, compressed agony, nearly impotent commiseration, and social absurdity is repeated countless times, too many times, in American culture for black men. Ike's death forced to the surface a painful awareness that provides the chilling soundtrack to most black men's lives: it is still hazardous to be a human being of African descent in America.

Not surprisingly, much of the ideological legitimation for the contemporary misery of African-Americans in general, and black men in particular, derives from the historical legacy of slavery, which continues to assert its brutal presence in the untold suffering of millions of everyday black folk. For instance, the pernicious commodification of the black body during slavery was underwritten by the desire of white slave owners to completely master black life. The desire for mastery also fueled the severe regulation of black sexual activity, furthering the telos of Southern agrarian capital by reducing black men to studs and black women to machines of production. Black men and women became sexual and economic property. Because of the arrangement of social relations, slavery was also the breeding ground for much of the mythos of black male sexuality that survives to this day: that black men are imagined as peripatetic phalluses with unrequited desire for their denied object—white women.

Also crucial during slavery was the legitimation of violence toward blacks, especially black men. Rebellion in any form was severely punished, and the social construction of black male image and identity took place under the disciplining eye of white male dominance. This healthy black self-regard and self-confidence were outlawed as punitive consequences were attached to their assertion in black life. Although alternate forms of resistance were generated, particularly those rooted in religious praxis, problems of self-hatred and self-abnegation persisted. The success of the American political, economic, and social infrastructure was predicated in large part upon a squelching of black life by white modes of cultural domination. The psychic, political, economic, and social costs of slavery, then, continue to be paid, but mostly by the descendants of the oppressed. The way in which young black men continue to pay is particularly unsettling.

Black men are presently caught in a web of social relations, economic conditions, and political predicaments that portray their future in rather bleak terms.[1] For instance, the structural unemployment of black men has reached virtually epidemic proportions, with black youth unemployment double that of white youth. Almost one-half of young black men have had no work experience at all. Given the permanent shift in the U.S. economy from manufacturing and industrial jobs to high-tech and service employment and the flight of these jobs from the cities to the suburbs, the prospects for eroding the stubborn unemployment of black men appear slim.[2]

The educational front is not much better. Young black males are dropping out of school at alarming rates, due to a combination of severe economic difficulties, disciplinary entanglements, and academic frustrations. Thus the low level of educational achievement by young black men exacerbates their already precarious employment situation. Needless to say, the pool of high-school graduates eligible for college has severely shrunk, and even those who go on to college have disproportionate rates of attrition.

Suicide, too, is on the rise, ranking as the third leading cause of death among young black men. Since 1960, the number of black men who have died from suicide has tripled. The homicide rate of black men is atrocious. For black male teenagers and young adults, homicide ranks as the leading cause of death. In 1987, more young black men were killed within the United States in a single year than had been killed abroad in the entire nine years of the Vietnam War. A young black man has a one-in-twenty-one lifetime chance of being killed, most likely at the hands of another black man, belying the self-destructive character of black homicide.

Even with all this, a contemporary focus on the predicament of black males is rendered problematical and ironic for two reasons. First, what may be termed the "Calvin Klein" character of debate about social problems—which amounts to a "designer" social consciousness—makes it very difficult for the concerns of black men to be taken seriously. Social concern, like other commodities, is subject to cycles of production, distribution, and consumption. With the dwindling of crucial governmental resources to address a range of social problems, social concern is increasingly relegated to the domain of private philanthropic and nonprofit organizations. Furthermore, the selection of which problems merit scarce resources is determined, in part, by such philanthropic organizations, which highlight special issues, secure the services of prominent spokespersons, procure capital for research, and distribute the benefits of their information.

Unfortunately, Americans have rarely been able to sustain debate about pressing social problems over long periods of time. Even less have we been able to conceive underlying structural features that bind complex social issues together. Such conceptualization of the intricate interrelationship of social problems would facilitate the development of broadly formed coalitions that address a range of social concern. As things stand, problems like poverty, racism, and sexism go in and out of style. Black men, with the exception of star athletes and famous entertainers, are out of style.

Second, the irony of the black male predicament is that it has reached its nadir precisely at the point when much deserved attention has been devoted to the achievements of black women like Alice Walker, Toni Morrison, and Terry McMillan.

The identification and development of the womanist tradition in African-American culture has permitted the articulation of powerful visions of black female identity and liberation. Michele Wallace, Alice Walker, Audre Lorde, and Toni Morrison have written in empowering ways about the disenabling forms of racism and patriarchy that persist in white and black communities. They have expressed the rich resources for identity that come from maintaining allegiances to multiple kinship groups defined by race, gender, and sexual orientation, while also addressing the challenges that arise in such membership.

Thus discussions about black men should not take place in an ahistorical vacuum, but should be informed by sensitivity to the plight of black women. To isolate and examine the pernicious problems of young black men does not privilege their perspectives or predicament. Rather, it is to acknowledge the decisively deleterious consequences of racism and classism that plague black folk, particularly young black males.

The aim of my analysis is to present enabling forms of consciousness that may contribute to the reconstitution of the social, economic, and political relations that continually consign the lives of black men to psychic malaise, social destruction, and physical death. It does not encourage or dismiss the sexism of black men, nor does it condone the patriarchal behavior that sometimes manifests itself in minority communities in the form of misdirected machismo. Above all, African-Americans must avoid a potentially hazardous situation that plays musical chairs with scarce resources allocated to black folk and threatens to inadvertently exacerbate already deteriorated relations between black men and women. The crisis of black inner-city communities is so intense that it demands our collective resources to stem the tide of violence and catastrophe that has besieged them.

I grew up as a young black male in Detroit in the 1960s and 1970s. I witnessed firsthand the social horror that is entrenched in inner-city communities, the social havoc wreaked from economic hardship. In my youth, Detroit had been tagged the "murder capital of the world," and many of those murders were of black men, many times by other black men. Night after night, the news media in Detroit painted the ugly picture of a homicide-ridden city caught in the desperate clutches of death, depression, and decay. I remember having recurring nightmares of naked violence, in which Hitchcockian vertigo emerged in Daliesque perspective to produce gun-wielding perpetrators of doom seeking to do me in.

And apart from those disturbing dreams, I was exercised by the small vignettes of abortive violence that shattered my circle of friends and acquaintances. My next-door neighbor, a young black man, was stabbed in the jugular vein by an acquaintance and bled to death in the midst of a card game. (Of course, one of the ugly statistics involving black-on-black crime is that many black men are killed by those whom they know.) Another acquaintance murdered a businessman in a robbery; another executed several people in a gangland-style murder.

At fourteen, I was at our corner store at the sales counter, when suddenly a jolt in the back revealed a young black man wielding a sawed-off, double-barreled shotgun, requesting, along with armed accomplices stationed throughout the store, that we hit the floor. We were being robbed. At the age of eighteen I was stopped one Saturday night at 10:30 by a young black man who ominously materialized out of nowhere, much like the .357 Magnum revolver that he revealed to me in a robbery attempt. Terror engulfed my entire being in the fear of imminent death. In desperation I hurled a protest against the asphyxiating economic hardships that had apparently reduced him to desperation, too, and appealed to the conscience I hoped was buried beneath the necessity that drove him to rob me. I proclaimed, "Man, you don't look like the type of brother that would be doin' something like this."

"I wouldn't be doin' this, man," he shot back, "but I got a wife and three kids, and we ain't got nothin' to eat. And besides, last week somebody did the same thing to me that I'm doin' to you." After convincing him that I really only had one dollar and thirty-five cents, the young man permitted me to leave with my life intact.

The terrain for these and so many other encounters that have shaped the lives of black males was the ghetto. Much social research and criticism has been generated in regard to the worse-off inhabitants of the inner city, the so-called underclass. From the progressive perspective of William Julius Wilson to the archconservative musings of Charles Murray, those who dwell in ghettos, or enclaves of civic, psychic, and social terror, have been the object of recrudescent interest within hallowed academic circles and governmental policy rooms.[3] In most cases they have not fared well and have borne the brunt of multifarious "blame the victim" social logics and policies.

One of the more devastating developments in inner-city communities is the presence of drugs and the criminal activity associated with their production, marketing, and consumption. Through the escalation of the use of the rock-like form of cocaine known as "crack" and intensified related gang activity, young black men are involved in a vicious subculture of crime. This subculture is sustained by two potent attractions: the personal acceptance and affirmation gangs offer and the possibility of enormous economic reward.

U.S. gang life had its genesis in the Northeast of the 1840s, particularly in the depressed neighborhoods of Boston and New York, where young Irishmen developed gangs to sustain social solidarity and to forge a collective identity based on common ethnic roots.[4] Since then, youth of every ethnic and racial origin have formed gangs for similar reasons, and at times have even functioned to protect their own ethnic or racial group from attack by harmful outsiders. Overall, a persistent reason for joining gangs is the sense of absolute belonging and unsurpassed social love that results from gang membership. Especially for young black men whose life is at a low premium in America, gangs have fulfilled a primal need to possess a sense of social cohesion through group identity. Particularly when traditional avenues for the realization of personal growth, esteem, and self-worth, usually gained through employment and career opportunities, have been closed, young black men find gangs a powerful alternative.

Gangs also offer immediate material gratification through a powerful and lucrative underground economy. This underground economy is supported by exchanging drugs and services for money, or by barter. The lifestyle developed and made possible by the sale of crack presents often irresistible economic alternatives to young black men frustrated by their own unemployment. The death that can result from involvement in such drug- and gang-related activity is ineffective in prohibiting young black men from participating.

To understand the attraction such activity holds for black men, one must remember the desperate economic conditions of urban black life. The problems of poverty and joblessness have loomed large for African–American men, particularly in the Rust Belt, including New York, Chicago, Philadelphia, Detroit, Cleveland, Indianapolis, and Baltimore. From the 1950s to the 1980s, there was severe decline in manufacturing and in retail and wholesale trade, attended by escalating unemployment and a decrease in labor-force participation by black males, particularly during the 1970s.

During this three-decade decline of employment, however, there was not an expansion of social services or significant increase in entry-level service jobs. As William Julius Wilson rightly argues, the urban ghettos then became more socially isolated than at any other time. Also, with the mass exodus of black working- and middle-class families from the ghetto, the inner city's severe unemployment and joblessness became even more magnified. With black track from the inner city mimicking earlier patterns of white flight, severe class changes have negatively affected black ghettos. Such class changes have depleted communities of service establishments, local businesses, and stores that could remain profitable enough to provide full-time employment so that persons could support families, or even to offer youths part-time employment in order to develop crucial habits of responsibility and work. Furthermore, ghetto residents are removed from job networks that operate in more affluent neighborhoods. Thus, they are deprived of the informal contact with employers that results in finding decent jobs. All of these factors create a medium for the development of criminal behavior by black men in order to survive, ranging from fencing stolen goods to petty thievery to drug dealing. For many black families, the illegal activity of young black men provides their only income.

Predictably, then, it is in these Rust Belt cities, and other large urban and metropolitan areas, where drug and gang activity has escalated in the past decade. Detroit, Philadelphia, and New York have had significant gang and drug activity, but Chicago and Los Angeles have dominated of late. Especially in regard to gang-related criminal activity such as homicides, Chicago and L.A. form a terrible one-two punch. Chicago had 47 gang-related deaths in 1987, 75 in 1986, and 60 in 1988. L.A.'s toll stands at 400 for 1988.

Of course, L.A.'s gang scene has generated mythic interpretation in the Dennis Hopper film *Colors*. In the past decade, gang membership in L.A. has risen from 15,000 to almost 60,000 (with some city officials claiming as much as 80,000), as gang warfare claims one life per day. The ethnic composition of the groups include Mexicans, Armenians, Samoans, and Fijians. But gang life is dominated by South Central L.A. black gangs, populated by young black men willing to give their lives in fearless fidelity to their group's survival. The two largest aggregates of gangs, composed of several hundred microgangs, are the Bloods and the Crips, distinguished by the colors of their shoelaces, T-shirts, and bandannas.

The black gangs have become particularly dangerous because of their association with crack. The gangs control more than 150 crack houses in L.A., each of which does over five thousand dollars of business per day, garnering over half a billion dollars per year. Crack houses, which transform powdered cocaine into crystalline rock form in order to be smoked, offer powerful material rewards to gang members. Even young teens can earn almost a thousand dollars a week, often outdistancing what their parents, if they work at all, can earn in two months.

So far, most analyses of drug gangs and the black youth who comprise their membership have repeated old saws about the pathology of black culture and weak family structure, without accounting for the pressing economic realities and the need for acceptance that help explain such activity. As long as the poverty of young black men is ignored, the disproportionate number of black unemployed males is overlooked, and the structural features of racism and classism are avoided, there is room for the proliferation of social explanations that blame the victim. Such social explanations reinforce the misguided efforts of public officials to stem the tide of illegal behavior by state repression aimed at young blacks, such as the sweeps of L.A. neighborhoods resulting in mass arrests of more than four thousand black men, more than at any time since the Watts rebellion of 1965.

Helpful remedies must promote the restoration of job training (such as Neighborhood Youth Corps [NYC] and the Comprehensive Employment and Training Act [CETA]); the development of policies that support the family, such as child-care and education programs; a full employment policy; and dropout prevention in public schools. These are only the first steps toward the deeper structural transformation necessary to improve the plight of African-American men, but they would be vast improvements over present efforts.

Not to be forgotten, either, are forms of cultural resistance that are developed and sustained within black life and are alternatives to the crack gangs. An example that springs immediately to mind is rap music. Rap music provides space for cultural resistance to the criminal-ridden ethos that pervades segments of many underclass communities. Rap was initially a form of musical play that directed the creative urges of its producers into placing often humorous lyrics over the music of well-known black hits.

As it evolved, however, rap became a more critical and conscientious forum for visiting social criticism upon various forms of social injustice, especially racial and class oppression. For instance, Grandmaster Flash and the Furious

Five pioneered the social awakening of rap with two rap records, "The Message" and "New York, New York." These rap records combined poignant descriptions of social misery and trenchant criticism of social problems as they remarked upon the condition of black urban America. They compared the postmodern city of crime, deception, political corruption, economic hardship, and cultural malaise to a "jungle." These young savants portrayed a chilling vision of life that placed them beyond the parameters of traditional African-American cultural resources of support: religious faith, communal strength, and familial roots. Thus, they were creating their own aesthetic of survival, generated from the raw material of their immediate reality, the black ghetto. This began the vocation of the rap artist, in part, as urban griot dispensing social and cultural critique.

Although rap music has been saddled with a reputation for creating violent outbursts by young blacks, especially at rap concerts, most of rap's participants have repeatedly spurned violence and all forms of criminal behavior as useless alternatives for black youth. Indeed rap has provided an alternative to patterns of identity formation provided by gang activity and has created musical vehicles for personal and cultural agency. A strong sense of self-confidence permeates the entire rap genre, providing healthy outlets for young blacks to assert, boast, and luxuriate in a rich self-conception based upon the achievement that their talents afford them. For those reasons alone, it deserves support. Even more, rap music, although its increasing expansion means being influenced by the music industry's corporate tastes and decisions, presents an economic alternative to the underground economy of crack gangs and the illegal activity associated with them.

However, part of the enormous difficulty in discouraging illegal activity among young black men has to do, ironically, with their often correct perception of the racism and classism still rampant in employment and educational opportunities open to upwardly mobile blacks. The subtle but lethal limits continually imposed upon young black professionals, for instance, as a result of the persistence of racist ideologies operating in multifarious institutional patterns and personal configurations, send powerful signals to young black occupants of the underclass that education and skill do not ward off racist, classist forms of oppression.

This point was reiterated to me upon my son's recent visit with me at Princeton near Christmas. Excited about the prospect of spending time together catching up on new movies, playing video games, reading, and the like, we dropped by my bank to get a cash advance on my MasterCard. I presented my card to the young service representative, expecting no trouble since I had just paid my bill a couple of weeks before. When he returned, he informed me that not only could I not get any money, but that he would have to keep my card. When I asked for an explanation, all he could say was that he was following the instructions of my card's bank, since my MasterCard was issued by a different bank.

After we went back and forth a few times about the matter, I asked to see the manager. "He'll just tell you the same thing that I've been telling you," he insisted. But my persistent demand prevailed, as he huffed away to the manager's office, resentfully carrying my request to his boss. My son, sitting next to me the whole time, asked what the problem was, and I told him that there must be a mistake, and that it would all be cleared up shortly. He gave me that confident look that says, "My dad can handle it." After waiting for about seven or eight minutes, I caught the manager's figure peripherally, and just as I turned, I saw him heading with the representative to an empty desk, opening the drawer and pulling out a pair of scissors. I could feel the blood begin to boil in my veins as I beseeched the manager, "Sir, if you're about to do what I fear you will, can we please talk first?" Of course, my request was to no avail, as he sliced my card in two before what had now become a considerable crowd. I immediately jumped up and followed him into his office, my son trailing close behind, crying now, tearfully pumping me with "Daddy, what's going on?"

I rushed into the manager's office and asked for the privacy of a closed door, to which he responded, "Don't let him close the door," as he beckoned three other employees into his office. I angrily grabbed the remnants of my card from his hands and proceeded to tell him that I was a reputable member of the community and a good customer of the bank and that if I had been wearing a three-piece suit (instead of the black running suit I was garbed in) and if I had been a white male (and not a black man) I would have been at least accorded the respect of a conversation, prior to a private negotiation of an embarrassing situation, which furthermore was the apparent result of a mistake on the bank's part.

His face flustered, the manager then prominently positioned his index finger beneath his desk drawer, and pushed a button, while declaring, "I'm calling the police on you." My anger now piqued, I was tempted to vent my rage on his defiant countenance, arrested only by the terrible vision that flashed before my eyes as a chilling premonition of destruction: I would assault the manager's neck; his coworkers would join the fracas, as my son stood by horrified by his helplessness to aid me; the police would come, and abuse me even further, possibly harming my son in the process. I retreated under the power of this proleptic vision, grabbing my son's hand as I marched out of the bank. Just as we walked through the doors, the policemen were pulling up.

Although after extensive protests, phone calls, and the like, I eventually received an apology from the bank's board and a MasterCard from their branch, this incident seared an indelible impression onto my mind, reminding me that regardless of how much education, moral authority, or personal integrity a black man possesses, he is still a "nigger," still powerless in many ways to affect his destiny.

The tragedy in all of this, of course, is that even when articulate, intelligent black men manage to rise above the temptations and traps of "the ghetto," they are often subject to continuing forms of social fear, sexual jealousy, and obnoxious racism. More pointedly, in the 1960s, during a crucial stage in the development of black pride and self-esteem, highly educated, deeply conscientious black men were gunned down in cold blood. This phenomenon finds paradigmatic expression in the deaths of Medgar Evers, Malcolm X, and Martin Luther King, Jr. These events of public death are structured deep in the psyches of surviving black men, and the ways in which these horrible spectacles of racial catastrophe represent and implicitly sanction lesser forms of social evil against black men remains hurtful to black America.

I will never forget the effect of King's death on me as a nine-year-old boy in Detroit. For weeks I could not be alone at night before an open door or window without fearing that someone would kill me, too. I thought that if they killed this man who taught justice, peace, forgiveness, and love, then they would kill all black men. For me, Martin's death meant that no black man in America was safe, that no black man could afford the gift of vision, that no black man could possess an intelligent fire that would sear the fierce edges of ignorance and wither to ashes the propositions of hate without being extinguished. Ultimately Martin's death meant that all black men, in some way, are perennially exposed to the threat of annihilation.

As we move toward the last decade of this century, the shadow of Du Bois's prophetic declaration that the twentieth century's problem would be the color line continues to extend itself in foreboding manner. The plight of black men, indeed, is a microcosmic reflection of the problems that are at the throat of all black people, an idiomatic expression of hurt drawn from the larger discourse of racial pain. Unless, however, there is vast reconstitution of our social, economic, and political policies and practices, most of which target black men with vicious specificity, Du Bois's words will serve as the frontispiece to the racial agony of the twenty-first century, as well.

NOTES

1. For a look at the contemporary plight of black men, especially black juvenile males, see *Young, Black, and Male in America: An Endangered Species*, ed. Jewelle Taylor Gibbs (Dover, Mass.: Auburn House, 1988).

2. See William Julius Wilson, *The Truly Disadvantaged: The Inner City, the Underclass, and Public Policy* (Chicago: University of Chicago Press, 1987).

3. See Wilson, *The Truly Disadvantaged.* For Charles Murray's views on poverty, welfare, and the ghetto underclass, see his influential book, *Losing Ground: American Social Policy, 1950–1980* (New York: Basic Books, 1984).

4. This section on gangs is informed by the work of Mike Davis in his *City of Quartz* (New York: Verso Press, 1991).

ROLAND GILBERT/ CHEO TYEHIMBA-TAYLOR

The Ghetto Solution

THE SIMBA SIX: THE MEN

A lot of what takes place in the Leadership Workshop is sacred. I cannot begin to describe the men's emotional and psychological experiences. For this reason, I'll let them tell you:

Michael Holland, 37, Oakland Police Officer

I was surprised about the sixty-six-hour training. I thought, Hey, I'm a police officer. I'm a responsible individual. What do I need to go through this guy's training for? But later I figured, OK, I'll try it. What do I have to lose?

After that first night, as I walked out, I made a conscious decision that no matter what I had to do that week, I was going to give all of my energy to try to learn everything I could. Those first six hours were overwhelming to me. What we were learning fit so well into all of the things that I understood about the failure of the criminal justice system and why society is going downhill. I had never gotten that much information, that clearly, that quickly, in my life. I've had a couple of psychology classes in college, and they didn't give me anywhere near as clear an understanding about why people function the way they do as this man did in the first six hours of the seminar. After the second night, I was a little intimidated, but I was absolutely determined to come back and learn more about myself.

Here I was, a black man out there trying to help my own people, and they were totally rejecting me because sometimes I had to lock up some of my own people, even though they were the victims. So on the one hand, African-American folks didn't want me to take other African-American folks to jail, but they also wanted me to do something about the guys committing crimes against them. It was sort of a catch-22, and it frustrated the hell out of me.

The story I like to tell is about a lady whose purse got snatched. This little old, African-American woman was walking down the street I'm driving down, and I see this black dude come up and hit her, snatch her purse, and take off. She goes down. I jump out of my car and start chasing him. I'm chasing him through the projects and he goes around a corner and just disappears. He was only twenty feet in front of me and the buildings are two hundred feet long, so there's no way he made it to the other end. He ducked in one of the doors there. I tried to get folks to tell me. "Which way did he go? Which way did he go?" I asked. "Look, this guy just robbed a black woman right here out of your neighborhood. Which way did he go?"

They just stood there and said, "We ain't gonna help you lock a black man up." I was so frustrated by that incident that I asked my sergeant to move me to another beat.

When I went through the leadership workshop, I learned that being a responsible black man meant a hell of a lot more than going to work on time, bringing a paycheck home, paying all of the bills, and not going out and screwing around with other women. When you go through Simba, you learn how to take control of your destiny and help others take control of theirs.

I realized I had an anger "program." It was making me do a lot of drinking. I had gotten to the point with my wife where I felt like arguing didn't do any good, so I just shut up and bottled up all of my anger—which was slowly but surely destroying my marriage. As we continued the training, I got clearer about some of my issues—my self-esteem, my anger, my issues with women, and my fear issue. After the workshop, my relationship with my wife improved and I stopped getting as angry about things I couldn't control.

Simba is the opportunity to meet and get to know the most effective, powerful, and loving man you'll ever meet, and that's the person you see in the mirror everyday. Once you learn how to love, you start to live differently. The bottom line is this: When a man walks away from Simba, he learns how to love, even his enemies.

I think we're creating a new version of the "village" concept. I think there's an Ashanti saying that goes, "It takes an entire village to raise a child." What we're teaching men to do is to be the new village elders. Part of being a village elder for me is to teach—my son, the boys in Simba, I even teach Simba concepts to the officers in my squad, so that they can get an understanding of why a lot of people do what they do out there. There's nothing else in my life that's taught me to be in control of my life like Simba has. And I teach the boys what I've learned . . . what I'm living.

Rashid Shaheed, 32, Consultant

The workshop wasn't anything I expected. It was really a lot of good stuff and it was so personal. That first day, I was excited about the work Roland gave us. By the third day things were getting serious. Intense.

When I was growing up, there was a point where all my family (eleven children, one mother, no father) ate was bread and milk. That's it. We dipped the bread in the milk and that was breakfast, lunch, and dinner. We ate sugar-bread sandwiches and mayonnaise sandwiches. We had one of the smallest houses on the block and when it rained, we would put buckets throughout the house so the floor wouldn't get wet. The front porch was crumbling and broken down. It was definitely a state of poverty, and I internalized it. After going through Simba I learned that I had a poverty "program," which said, "All I need is a quarter, that's all I need. I don't need a hundred dollars, just give me a quarter, and I'll be all right."

Another issue I had during the workshop was the religious aspect. I had to ask myself, is Simba going against my religious teachings? I was the only Muslim brother in my chapter. Everyone else was Christian. The brothers never criticized me or made me feel out of place. We didn't promote our religion, and that was really a good dynamic. When I talk to Muslims about Simba, they say "This is Islam." The teachings are all about self. The Koran speaks about "know thyself" and it's in the African teachings of Kemet also. Simba just solidifies all of those teachings.

Since the seminar, I've learned not to think like a victim, not to blame external circumstances for why I'm feeling a certain way. I understand that certain things happen, but I don't have to let them run my life. Now I know that I am my best friend and that nobody else can determine how I feel unless I allow them to. I'm not going to be a victim. I've found my purpose: to teach African-Americans, particularly the men and boys, not to think like victims.

Simba helped me to see where I was at, why I was getting the results I was getting in my life. I would tell myself I wanted one thing, but my "programs," my habitual ways of thinking, would cause me to react another way.

Simba has given me the ability to say that I am unique. To say that my creator has endowed me with the ability to succeed. It has given me more insight. The seminar allowed me to get real with myself and really check out what was happening with me. I think Simba is a superb way of liberating African-Americans. No other program for African-American boys trains black men to be leaders of self the way Simba does.

It would be a disservice for leaders to get out there and start teaching our boys and not be aware of their own negative programs.

Vernal Martin, 61, Probation Officer

I was born in Dayton, Texas, but I was raised in Houston. My mother died when I was five. I'm the youngest of seven children. I earned a degree in sociology, and I've been married since 1965. I started working for the Alameda County Probation department in 1971.

When I first heard about the leadership workshop, my first reaction was that it was awfully long. I work long hours at work and I thought it was going to take up too much of my time. I didn't go along with it at first, because I didn't think it was necessary for me to help the boys.

On the first day of the workshop, I was late, and I had a lot of excuses as to why I was late. But my excuses weren't any good. He told us that if we gave our word we had to keep it. That the boys would learn from our actions, not from our words. He gave us books to read, and assignments to complete. After I went through the training, I accepted it enough to know that Simba was something I wanted to do. So I committed myself to do it for our boys. In order for us to help the kids, we had to have something to offer them. That workshop gave us something to offer.

When I was in my late twenties, I had auditioned for Count Basie's band. To my surprise, I was accepted, and when Basie left to go on a tour, he said he wanted me to start when he got back. Some of the guys in his band told me that the life of a musician was not all it was cracked up to be and that they would quit if they knew how to do anything else. Count Basie himself told me to think about it, because if I wanted to get married and start a family, I'd have to take into account the traveling lifestyle.

Soon I started making up excuses for why I shouldn't go. I finally came to the conclusion that I wouldn't. I thought I'd just continue singing in the local clubs. I guess I felt like I didn't deserve to sing with Count Basie's band—little ol' me, you know? That's where my low self-esteem came in. It wasn't until I started in Simba that I first talked about this. During the training I found out I had a low self-esteem. I had thought that I was fine. Roland told me that Count Basie was probably thinking that he would be fortunate to get me and there I was thinking that I was not good enough.

I often asked myself, What would it be like if I'd gone to sing with Count Basie's band? What would I be doing now? I guess I'll never know.

During the workshop, Roland gave us something to give to the boys. We needed to get rid of all of the negative programs that we'd learned over the years, so we wouldn't pass them on to the boys. That was the whole idea—having positive things to give to the boys. Simba is the very best program I've ever been in. I've learned things about myself that I probably would never have learned, and I learn things from the kids all the time.

Problems can be solved—we just have to believe we can do it.

We are the problem. Too many of us want somebody else to do it. We think we don't have time. I didn't think I had time, but now I make time. I leave here at 3:30 on Mondays and Wednesdays, I go pick up a little boy, and we go to Simba. I have a lot of work here, but what's more important, our boys or Alameda County's work? I'm doing this for our boys.

Charles Ransom, 50, Real Estate Broker

I'm from Detroit. I moved out to California to go to college. I graduated from San Francisco State with a B.S. in economics. I've been married for two years.

I went to the workshop more out of curiosity and because Roland was bugging me to check it out. Roland and I were in Sunday school class together, so it was kind of hard for me to duck him. At the time, I had just got my second divorce and I was somewhat searching for something to get involved in. I thought maybe this was an opportunity.

I wasn't really sure what to expect. But with all of my sales and management training, I had always been taught to go into a situation trying not to have any preconceived ideas. On the first day of the workshop, Roland gave us enough to make us want to come back.

When we learned about our emotional makeup, I learned that it was all right for me to be emotional. That it was nothing I should be ashamed of, or to try to hide. I've always been emotional and I used to be ashamed of it. One time when I witnessed a fight, I saw a man backhand a kid. The next thing I knew, the police and my friend were pulling me off the man. They had to take me off him because I was about to kill him. If I see somebody in a weak situation, I have a tendency to react. Or if I see a sad situation, I become emotional. The thing is, I can get emotional about anybody but me. When it comes to me, I'm detached.

We were all taught that a man should never show emotions and that a man should always be strong. I can remember as a child that I cried in church when my grandfather died. It was the first time someone close to me had died. My sister and I were crying at the church and my mother looked down at me and shook me and said, "You shouldn't be crying like this; this is not your father. You should be strong."

I got a lot from my mother. She was the matriarch of our family and she felt that she had to be responsible for everybody. I know some of that rubbed off on me. I feel I should be responsible [for everybody], and when I'm not, that's when my guilt comes up. I felt I was responsible for my divorces. I didn't deliberately set out to get divorced, it just happened. But the fact that it happened twice made me feel even more guilt. When I went through Simba, I gradually learned that I had a guilt complex, a guilt "program." The workshop made me realize that I wasn't responsible for my failed marriages. I had done the best that I knew how to do.

In the early days of Simba, before we got the boys, we were meeting every week, and we weren't getting paid. It was all unbelievable. It was amazing to me that when I got to the meetings, we'd all be there. I went because I felt a commitment to go and see it through, even though in the back of my mind I still had doubts if we could pull it off. You could see that Roland was committed. You could see he had a purpose. That is the sign of a good leader—if you can see that the leader is committed, it helps you in your own commitment. He never missed a meeting. He was always full of purpose.

Simba is a long-term commitment to role-modeling for boys. It's something that you have to experience for yourself, and learn about your own negative programs, so that you can be in control enough to give the boys positive programs.

The main thing Simba did for me is make me understand who I am and why I do the things the way I do. I've had a lot of training in sales and everything, but that was more external, about how to deal with other people, not how to deal with myself. What are my weaknesses and my strengths? Most people are too afraid to even analyze themselves in that way. But you can't really grow until you know where you need to grow.

SIMBA'S YOUNG LIONS

Today Keith and Chris are two of the strongest leaders in Simba. Their personal growth as black men and Simba instructors has been tremendous. They know better than anyone else how Simba has affected their lives, so I'm going to let them tell their own stories.

Chris Billups, 24, Simba Instructor

I was born in Los Angeles and raised in Detroit until ninth grade. After that, I moved back to L.A. and graduated from Culver City High School. After high school, I went to the University of California at Berkeley. That's where I met Keith. We knew there was something we wanted to get accomplished for black people and for ourselves, so he and I and a couple other brothers started meeting on campus, trying to form a black-male support group. We had several meetings, and when the semester was over, the group just kind of faded out. I went home for the summer. When I came back, Keith told me about Simba.

We knew it was a group that was about helping African-American men, so we went to an orientation to learn more about the program.

Roland was wearing blue jeans, a white shirt, and some cream-colored loafers. I thought he looked odd. He didn't fit my stereotype of what I thought a black leader should look like. I expected him to look more militant. I thought he'd be wearing some African attire or maybe red, black, and green or something. I also noticed he was light-skinned.

After I went through the first forty hours of the seminar, I thought it was some pretty serious stuff. I knew I wanted to know and do more. And I was amazed by Roland's on-pointness and his focus on what he does. He still amazes me today. During the training, things got very real. I mean there was too much realness in his voice, and realness in people's perceptions of what he was saying, so I knew it wasn't a bunch of psychoanalytical bullshit. I bought into the whole thing right away.

A week after the first forty hours of the Leadership Seminar, I realized that I wasn't in love with my girlfriend. I realized I had a codependency issue with her. One day we got in an argument and she wanted to leave and end the relationship. I didn't want to be without this woman. I didn't want to be alone. I just wanted her to stay. She had been staying with me and I was talking about our ending living together, but she was talking about ending the relationship. We were sitting in my bedroom. At the time, I was taking architecture in school and I had drafting paper and architecture supplies sitting on the table. She was telling me that she was tired of the relationship and I was arguing that I would change, and that I had been trying, but it seemed like she didn't give me credit. But she didn't listen.

We started yelling at each other. I walked over to my desk and grabbed an exacto knife, flipped it up, and just started cutting my left wrist. Then I ran to the bathroom and closed and locked the door. She followed me.

I went to the sink and started cutting. Then I walked back out and showed her. She grabbed my wrists and then went to the phone to call 911. I ran out of the apartment and down the street a couple of blocks. I ran out because I knew if the cops came it would turn into a bigger deal than I wanted it to be. In retrospect, I was just intending to be dramatic. I had cut my wrists, but not badly enough for me to die. My motive was to get attention, I thought that maybe she'd hold on to me or something like that.

Later, the police found me and took me to Highland Hospital, and I remember looking around and thinking: "This is not a place where people get well." They gave me some gauze, put cuffs on my wrists, and took me to the psychiatric ward. It had a big metal door and the cops had to leave their guns behind because some of the people inside might try to grab them. They left me in a room with a brother who was talking crazy, pacing back and forth. After that a doctor came in and asked me questions.

Weeks later, as I finished up my Simba training, I came to realize that I had a fear of abandonment and a shame issue. I had wanted attention and had done this to get it. After I finished the Leadership Seminar, I immediately knew I wanted more. Keith and I had always wanted to do something together and this was something we both felt passionate about. We decided to take the instructors seminar and learn as much as we could, then teach seminars together. When I started my instructor training, a lot of fear came up for me. I questioned my competency. I felt that maybe I wasn't smart enough to be an instructor, partly because the processing in the instructor's training was point-blank range. Questions are asked straight, no-chaser, and it was intense. When we finished, I was overjoyed, just happy to be through with all that stuff. I went through a lot of emotional pressure sitting in a room all those hours, listening to people and watching them make mistakes, making mistakes myself, and finally learning that it was OK.

The biggest thing about the instructor's seminar, to me, is finding out your life's purpose. I began to question myself and ask if this is really what I wanted to do. In March 1990, I decided to stop going to school and do what I really liked doing, working as a Simba Instructor.

Afterwards, Keith and I talked about eventually getting paid and teaching our own seminar. We went to Roland and told him we were ready to teach, ready to do our own chapter. He met with us and took us through the manual. Then we did a seminar for Simba Chapter Five. Chapter Five had about seven men. During the seminar, two things really happened for me. I learned to let go of my need-to-be-right program and my criticism program. The biggest thing that came up for me as an instructor was my age. Some of the brothers in the seminar were twice my age and I had to tell them their shit stank. All types of personal, "father-figure" stuff came up for me. I realized halfway through the process that they were trusting us. Nothing glued them in the chair, they could've left anytime they wanted to. They stayed because they were getting something, and it was working. I thought many of these older brothers were great for trusting people half their age.

Simba has given me an awareness of some of my weaknesses and it empowered me with knowledge that I could use to change them. I also learned that I can help other people change their programs. I learned that as a people, we don't have to settle for less. It woke me from sleeping while my foot was on fire. As a whole, black people's houses are on fire and we're asleep. The concepts in Simba have given me a new outlook.

For example, it's allowed me to now be in a relationship with a woman and not seek revenge for stuff that she has nothing to do with. I now take full responsibility for my actions. I am engaged to be married and I am faithful. I am not codependent. It's allowed me to learn to love me more, and accept myself, regardless of mistakes I've made. I've learned to compare myself less. I've learned to be more honest and share real feelings. As far as my relationship with other brothers, I now have a group of people that I can turn to at anytime and ask for support, cry on their shoulder, whatever. I like to look at us as a big "black mob," out to save our people. Some brothers talk about rolling thirty deep. In Simba, I'm rolling over a hundred deep and we're growing more everyday.

Keith Ragsdale, 25, Simba Instructor

When I was growing up, my father was not around. I had one brother and three older sisters. My mother was an alcoholic and she had a drug problem. She behaved like she didn't want to be in the ghetto. My interpretation of that was that she didn't want to be with me. She tried to kill herself several times. We saw her set herself on fire, more than once. One time after she'd been drinking, she put her hand and arm over the burner of the stove. We stopped her, but not before she had second- and third-degree burns on her wrists and arms. My mother wasn't one to hold her tongue and sometimes she would get drunk and have fights with my uncle. I thought my mother would kick even the devil's ass if he said something wrong to her. She just wasn't afraid to die. She had a very large energy, and when I was a kid, she seemed like a giant to me, even though she was no more than 5′2″.

When I was eleven years old, my mother was killed in a fire. This split up the family. My sisters went to Colorado to live with their father's mother. My brother and I had a different father so we went to stay with relatives on my mother's side. My cousin became my legal guardian and I grew up with her.

The fire happened on a Saturday, January 20, 1979. I was watching TV in my room. My sister came in and asked me to make breakfast. I walked into the kitchen and there was smoke coming from the back porch. My sister ran in and said, "Mom's in there!" Then I heard my mother scream. The door to the back porch was missing a doorknob and it was locked. So my sister got a spoon and opened the door. Big thick, black clouds of smoke came out and I could see the flames. My sister and I both ran out to get help from the next-door neighbor.

We were only gone maybe about two minutes. But by the time the neighbors had gotten to my house, there was a big explosion. It was the water heater and/or the stove. My mother's boyfriend and some other people rushed to the house. When he kicked down the door, the flames rushed out. The fire quickly spread throughout the house, then it burst through the roof.

Then the firemen began to arrive. I stood outside and watched. I began to realize that Mom wasn't coming out of the house. I was scared and I didn't know what would happen. It was overwhelming to walk back into the house after the fire was out. The TV that I'd been watching had melted.

When I went back to school a friend of mine came up to me asking me a whole lot of questions. I told him about the fire and he started shaking his head saying, "See man, if that was me, I'd of had to go back in there. I'd of saved my mother," he said.

It had never occurred to me about saving her. A couple days later, I began to feel some guilt about not getting my mom out.

When I graduated from high school, I was emotionally distraught. I "adopted" many of my friends' moms. Since my mom died when I was real young, I never experienced having real arguments and teenage problems with her. So I tripped when my friends would have problems with their mothers. I had about three of four "moms" during high school. After high school, I was tired of school. I didn't really care where I went. I met a recruiter from U.C. Berkeley and he came down and told me about college. My grades were good, so I got accepted to U.C. Berkeley. I left my guardian and I was happy to leave. I'd never felt like I had a home since the fire.

When I went to Berkeley I realized I was running away from a lot of pain. When I walked on campus I thought I was "Mr. Black." But understand, "Mr. Black" had no connection with Africa. Don't even go there! You got the wrong man! But I knew it all. Whenever a man called me brother, I was like, I hope he means black brother, 'cause I ain't African. One day, somebody came up to me and told me about a brother on campus who was giving a lecture. I went. He was an Egyptologist and he did two slide presentations on African history. One was on the "African Beginnings of Civilization" and the other was on the "African Beginnings of Judeo-Christianity." His presentation showed me pictures of stuff that I'd never seen and if he'd just said it, I would never of believed it, but he had slides and pictures. He took my Bible and showed me passages and pictures of Egypt. I was shocked. To me, my Bible fell out of the sky printed. I had never questioned it. Then I knew and understood that I was African and I was proud. But I was also very angry because I'd been fooled. Everybody knew. Why didn't anybody tell me? How could I have been ignorant for so long? Then I picked up Malcolm X's autobiography. Then I was really angry. I had gotten the book in junior high school, but because he was that evil "hate man," I hadn't read it. So after all these revelations I became "Mr. Africa."

Then one of the brothers brought a Simba flyer to a meeting on campus. The flyer said "rites-of-passage" training. Well, I had never been "initiated" or nothing like that and this was an initiation into manhood. I looked at the date, and I went to the orientation. At the orientation, I was blown away by how serious and focused the men were.

The training was incredible. I learned many things about myself and why I acted the way I did. My big issue had always been self-judgment, especially about my mom. I have been unwilling to forgive myself for her death. It became clear to me that if I forgave myself for what happened to her, it would mean that I didn't love her. So in order for me to love her, I needed to feel bad about not saving her. But after the training, man, I thought I could fly.

I knew I had a choice in everything I did. I felt really empowered. Even my friends could see the difference, and it was helping me with my relationships.

Next, I took the Simba instructor training. I realized I still had a lot of guilt over my mom, which I didn't know I still carried. One day, I was out of agreement, and Roland questioned me. I began to describe the scene where the boy asked me about my mother and I started to cry. Roland said, "You been carrying that around for eleven years?"

"I was supposed to save her," I said.

"Keith, you can't expect an eleven-year-old to know what to do in a situation like that. You did the best that you could do. And you weren't responsible for her. You went to get help and that was good. That was the best you knew how."

After that, I realized that I had to let it go and start living my life without blaming or judging myself.

I grew up in the ghetto and for a long time I had a ghetto state of mind and spirit. Simba has allowed me to choose how I think and to change what I believe about myself and my people. My life's purpose is to teach—to use what I've learned to help our children.

PART 3

Relationships

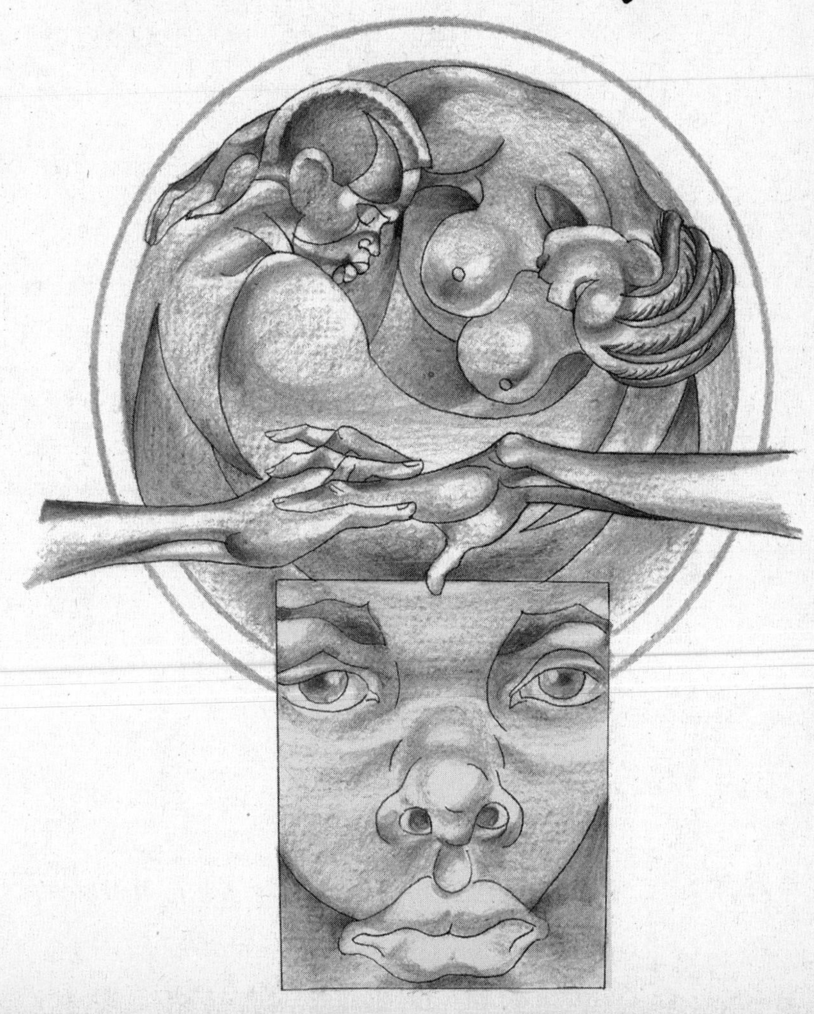

WHEN A MAN LOVES A WOMAN

ROBERT FLEMING

Black Women

Flowers beyond category
they who put lighting over our hands
they who put lightning in our wills

and blow and blow and blow
yourself out   she screamed
shrill   shriek   knives with
their invisible hands cut slice
thin deep lines into the flesh
of the soul

her pain   our pain   her blues our blues

always down low
like a broken radio with a lazy speaker
she   the other part of the unknown
bleeds alone   alone in a shadow room
the crazed cats inside her   whirling
in mid-air   tangled

and blow and blow and blow
yourself out   she screamed

only she sees her self
slide to the floor   moaning
for the wild pieces that never come home

so she cries
over the toilet
so he'll never know

her pain   our pain

even when she stands
hoping to lure us to her face to her heart
we look the wrong way   at the wrong things.

CHARLES JOHNSON

Middle Passage

ENTRY, THE FIRST
June 14, 1830

Of all the things that drive men to sea, the most common disaster, I've come to learn, is women. In my case, it was a spirited Boston schoolteacher named Isadora Bailey who led me to become a cook aboard the *Republic*. Both Isadora and my creditors, I should add, who entered into a conspiracy, a trap, a scheme so cunning that my only choices were prison, a brief stay in the stony oubliette of the Spanish Calabozo (or a long one at the bottom of the Mississippi), or marriage, which was, for a man of my temperament, worse than imprisonment—especially if you knew Isadora. So I went to sea, sailing from Louisiana on April 14, 1830, hoping a quarter year aboard a slave clipper would give this relentless woman time to reconsider, and my bill collectors time to forget they'd ever heard the name Rutherford Calhoun. But what lay ahead in Africa, then later on the open, endless sea, was, as I shall tell you, far worse than the fortune I'd fled in New Orleans.

New Orleans, you should know, was a city tailored to my taste for the excessive, exotic fringes of life, a world port of such extravagance in 1829 when I arrived from southern Illinois—a newly freed bondman, my papers in an old portmanteau, a gift from my master in Makanda—that I dropped my bags and a shock of recognition shot up my spine to my throat, rolling off my tongue in a whispered, *"Here, Rutherford is home."* So it seemed those first few months to the country boy with cotton in his hair, a great whore of a city in her glory, a kind of glandular Golden Age. She was if not a town devoted to an almost religious pursuit of Sin, then at least to a steamy sexuality. To the newcomer she was an assault of smells: molasses commingled with mangoes in the sensually damp air, the stench of slop in a muddy street, and, from the labyrinthine warehouses on the docks, the odor of Brazilian coffee and Mexican oils. And also this: the most exquisitely beautiful women in the world, thoroughbreds of pleasure created two centuries before by the French for their enjoyment. Mulattos colored like magnolia petals, quadroons with breasts big as melons—women who smelled like roses all year round. Home? Brother, for a randy Illinois boy of two and twenty accustomed to cornfields, cow plops, and handjobs in his master's hayloft, New Orleans wasn't home. It was Heaven. But even paradise must have its back side too, and it is here (alas) that the newcomer comes to rest. Upstream there were waterfront saloons and dives, a black underworld of thieves, gamblers, and ne'er-do-wells who, unlike the Creoles downstream (they sniffed down their long, Continental noses at poor, purebred Negroes like myself), didn't give a tinker's damn about my family tree and welcomed me as the world downstream would not.

In plain English, I was a petty thief.

How I fell into this life of living off others, of being a social parasite, is a long, sordid story best shortened for those who, like the Greeks, prefer to keep their violence offstage. Naturally, I looked for honest work. But arriving in the city, checking the saloons and Negro bars, I found nothing. So I stole—it came as second nature to me. My master, Reverend Peleg Chandler, had noticed this stickiness of my fingers when I was a child, and a tendency I had to tell preposterous lies for the hell of it; he was convinced I was born to be hanged and did his damnedest to reeducate said fingers in finer pursuits such as good penmanship and playing the grand piano in his parlor. A Biblical scholar, he endlessly preached Old Testament virtues to me, and to this very day I remember his tedious disquisitions on Neoplatonism, the evils of nominalism, the genius of Aquinas, and the work of such seers as Jakob Böhme. He'd wanted me to become a Negro preacher, perhaps even a black saint like the South American priest Martín de Porres—or, for that matter, my brother Jackson. Yet, for all that theological background, I have always been drawn by nature to extremes. Since the hour of my manumission—a day of such gloom and depression that I must put off its telling for a while, if you'll be patient with me—since that day, and what I can only call my older brother Jackson's spineless behavior in the face of freedom, I have never been able to do things halfway, and I hungered—literally *hungered*—for life in all its shades and hues: I was hooked on sensation, you might say, a lecher for perception and the nerve-knocking thrill, like a shot of opium, of new "experiences." And so, with the hateful, dull Illinois farm behind me, I drifted about New Orleans those first few months, pilfering food and picking money belts off tourists, but don't be too quick to pass judgment. I may be from southern Illinois, but I'm not stupid. Cityfolks lived by cheating and crime. Everyone knew this, everyone saw it, everyone talked ethics piously, then took payoffs under the table, tampered with the till, or fattened his purse by duping the poor. Shameless, you say? Perhaps so. But had I not been a thief, I would not have met Isadora and shortly thereafter found myself literally at sea.

Sometimes after working the hotels for visitors, or when I was drying out from whiskey or a piece of two-dollar tail, I would sneak off to the waterfront, and there, sitting on the rain-leached pier in heavy, liquescent air, in shimmering light so soft and opalescent that sunlight could not fully pierce the fine erotic mist, limpid and luminous at dusk, I would stare out to sea, envying the sailors riding out on merchantmen on the gift of good weather, wondering if there was some far-flung port, a foreign country or island far away at the earth's rim where a freeman could escape the vanities cityfolk called self-interest, the mediocrity they called achievement, the blatant selfishness they called individual freedom—all the bilge that made each day landside a kind of living death. I don't know if you've ever farmed in the Midwest, but if you have, you'll know that southern Illinois has scale; fields like sea swell; soil so good that if you plant a stick, a year later a carriage will spring up in its place; forests and woods as wild as they were before people lost their pioneer spirit and a healthy sense of awe. Only here, on the waterfront, could I recapture that feeling. Wind off the water was like a fist of fresh air, a cleansing blow that made me feel momentarily clean. In the spill of yellow moonlight, I'd shuck off my boots and sink both feet into the water. But the pier was most beautiful, I think, in early morning, when sunlight struck the wood and made it steam as moisture and mist from the night before evaporated. Then you could believe, like the ancient philosopher Thales, that the analogue for life was water, the formless, omnific sea. Businessmen with half a hundred duties barnacled to their lives came to stare, longingly, at boats trolling up to dock. Black men, free and slave, sat quietly on rocks coated with crustacea, in the odors of oil and fish, studying an evening sky as blue as the skin of heathen Lord Krishna. And Isadora Bailey came too, though for what reason I cannot say—her expression on the pier was unreadable—since she was, as I soon learned, a woman grounded, physically and metaphysically, in the land. I'd tipped closer to her, eyeing the beadpurse on her lap, then thought better of boosting it when I was ambushed by the innocence—the alarming trust—in her eyes when she looked up at me. I wondered, and wonder still: What's a nice girl like her doing in a city like this?

She was, in fact, as out of place in New Orleans as Saint Teresa would be at an orgy with de Sade: a frugal, quiet, devoutly Christian girl, I learned, the fourth daughter of a large Boston family free since the Revolutionary War, and positively ill with eastern culture. An educated girl of twenty, she thought it best to leave home to lighten her family's burden, but found no prospects for a Negro teacher, and female at that, in the Northeast. She came south by coach, avoiding the newfangled trains after reading an expert say that traveling at over twenty miles an hour would suffocate all aboard when the speed sucked all the air from the cars. Once in New Orleans, she took a job as a nursery governess for the children of Madame Marie Toulouse, a Creole who had spent her young womanhood as the mistress of first a banker, then a famous actor, a minister, and finally a mortician. Why these four? As Madame Toulouse told Isadora, she'd used the principle of "one for the money, two for the show, three to get ready, and four to go," and they'd left her generous endowments that she invested in a hotel at Royal and Saint Peter's streets. But Isadora was not, I'm afraid, any happier living in a Creole household than I would have been. They were beautiful; she was bookish. They were society here; she was, as a Northerner, the object of polite condescension—the Toulouses, in short, could afford the luxury of stupidity, the blind, cowlike, chin-lifted hauteur of Beautiful People. And such luxury Isadora had never known. You had the feeling, once you knew her, that she'd gambled on knowledge as others gambled on power, believing—wrongly, I think—that she had little else to offer. She let herself get fat, for example, to end the pressure women feel from being endlessly ogled and propositioned. Men hardly noticed her, pudgy as she was, and this suited Isadora just fine. She had a religious respect for Work. She was a nervous eater too, I guess, the sort of lonely, intelligent woman who found comfort in food, or went to restaurants simply to be treated kindly by the waiters, to be fussed over and served, to be asked, "Is everything all right here?"

Yet she *was* pretty in a prim, dry, flat-breasted way. Isadora never used make-up. At age five she had been sentenced to the straightening comb, and since then kept her hair pinned back so tightly each glossy strand stood out like wire, which also pulled back the skin at her temples, pushing forward a nose that looked startingly like a doorknob, and enlarging two watery, moonlike eyes that seemed ever on the verge of tears. No, she wasn't much to look at, nor was the hotel room where she lived with eight one-eyed cats, two three-legged dogs, and birds with broken wings. Most often, her place had a sweet, atticlike odor, but looked like a petshop and sometimes smelled like a zoo. Isadora took in these handicapped strays, unable to see them left unattended, and each time I dropped by she had something new. No, not a girl to tell your friends about, but one reassuring to be with because she had an inner brilliance, an intelligence and clarity of spirit that overwhelmed me.

Generally she spoke in choriambs and iambs when she was relaxed, which created a kind of dimetrical music to her speech. Did I love Isadora? Really, I couldn't say. I'd always felt people fell in love as they might fall into a hole; it was something I thought a smart man avoided.

But some days, after weeks of whoring and card games that lasted three days and nights, I found myself at her hotel room, drunk as Noah, broke and bottomed out, holding a bouquet of stolen flowers outside her door, eager to hear her voice, which was velvety and light like water gently rushing nearby. We'd sit and talk (she abhorred Nature walks, claiming that the only thing she knew about Nature was that it itched), her menagerie of crippled beasts crawling over her lap and mine. Those afternoons of genteel conversation (Isadora wouldn't let me do anything else) we talked of how we both were newcomers to New Orleans, or we took short walks together, or we'd dine at sidewalk cafés, where we watched the Creoles. My earliest impressions of the Cabildo, the fancy-dress quadroon balls and slave auctions arranged by the firm of Hewlett & Bright each Saturday at the new Exchange Market (ghastly affairs, I must add, which made poor Isadora a bit ill), were intertwined with her voice, her reassuring, Protestant, soap-and-water smell. Aye, she was good and honest and forthright, was Isadora. Nevertheless, at other times she was intolerable. She was, after all, a *teacher*, and couldn't turn it off sometimes, that tendency to talk in propositions, or declarative sentences, to correct my southern Illinois accent, with its squashed vowels and missing consonants, and challenge everything I said on, I thought, General Principle.

"Rea-a-ally, Rutherford," she said one afternoon in her sitting room, her back to a deep-silled window where outside a pear tree was in full bloom, its fruit like a hundred green bells draped upon the branches. "You don't think you can keep this up forever, do you? The gambling and girl-chasing?" She gave her gentle, spinster's smile and, as always, looked at me with a steadier gaze than I could look at her. "You have a *mind*. And, if what you tell me is true, you've lacked for nothing in this life. Am I right in saying this? Neither in childhood education nor the nourishment of a sound body and Christian character?"

I gave her a nod, for this was so. Though a slaveholder, Reverend Chandler hated slavery. He'd inherited my brother and me from his father and, out of Christian guilt, taught us more than some white men in Makanda knew, then finally released us one by one, except that Jackson stayed, more deeply bound to our master than any of us dreamed. But I am not ready just yet to talk of Jackson Calhoun.

"So you were," Isadora asked, toying with her teacup, "blessed with reasonably pleasant surroundings and pious counsel?"

I nodded again, squirming a little. Always, and eerily, I had the feeling that Isadora knew more about me than I did.

"Then aren't you obliged, given these gifts, to settle down and start a family so you can give to others in even greater measure?" Her eyes went quiet, closing as if on a vision of her and me at the altar. "My father, you know, was a little like you, Rutherford, or at least my aunties say he was. He stayed in Scolley Square or in the pubs, looking for himself in rum and loose women until he met a woman of character—I mean my mother—who brought out his better instincts."

"What's he doing now?" I rested my teacup on my knee. "Your father?"

"Well . . ." She pulled back, pausing to word this right. "Not much just now. He died last winter, you know, from heart failure."

Wonderful, I thought: The wage of the family man was coronary thrombosis. "And," I said, "he was how old?"

"Forty-nine." Then Isadora hurried to add, "But he had people who *cared* for him, daughters and sons, and a wife who brought him down to earth. . . ."

"Indeed," I said. "Quite far down, I'd say."

"Rutherford!" she yipped, her voice sliding up a scale. "It *hurts* me to see you in such ruin! Really, it does! Half the time I see you, you haven't eaten in two days. Or you're hung over. Or someone is chasing you for money. Or you've been in a fight! You need a family. You're not—not *common*!"

Ah, there it was, revealed at last, the one thing inside Isadora that made me shudder. It was what you heard all your blessed life from black elders and church women in flowered gowns: Don't be common. Comb your hair. Be a credit to the Race. Strive, like the Creoles, for respectability. Class. It made my insides clench. Oh, yes, it mattered to me that Isadora cared, but she saw me as clay. Something she could knead beneath her tiny brown fingers into precisely the sort of creature I—after seeing my brother shackled to subservience—was determined not to become: "a gentleman of color." The phrase made me hawk, then spit in a corner of my mind. It conjured (for me) the image of an Englishman, round of belly, balding, who'd been lightly brushed with brown watercolor or cinnamon.

"No, Isadora." I shook my head. "I don't believe I'll ever get married. There's too much to do. And see. Life is too short for me to shackle myself to a mortgage and marriage." I was a breath away from adding, "And a houseful of gimped cats," but thought it best to bite my tongue.

Her eyes took on a woebegone, persecuted look, a kind of dying-duck expression she had now and then. She stared at me for the longest time, then flashed, "You just won't act *right*, will you?" Touching her handkerchief to the doorknob nose, she stood suddenly, her cat leaping from her enskirted knees and bumping blindly into a candlestand. Isadora took three paces toward the door—I thought she was about to throw me out—then turned to pitch her voice back into the room. "Suppose you *have* to get married, Rutherford Calhoun!" Now her eyes burned. "What about that?"

What Isadora meant by this was a mystery to me. She couldn't be pregnant. Not her. At least not by me—she twisted my fingers whenever I reached for her knee. *Have* to marry her? It made no sense that afternoon, but less than a fortnight later her meaning became horribly clear.

Near the waterfront, after a day of dodging my creditors and shooting craps, I turned a corner and found myself facing a Negro named Santos, a kind of walking wrecking crew who pretty much ran things down on the docks for a Creole gangster known by the name of Philippe "Papa" Zeringue. Some masters, as you know, groomed their slaves to be gladiators: the Africans with a reach, or thickness of skull, or smoldering anger that, if not checked, would result in slave rebellion. So it was with Santos. He'd been a dirt-pit wrestler on a Baton Rouge plantation, and made his master, John Ruffner, a fortune in bare-knuckle fights he arranged for him with blacks from other farms. Freed by Ruffner, undefeated, and itching for trouble, he'd next come to New Orleans, and fell, as many did, into the orbit of life upstream. You have seen, perhaps, sketches of Piltdown man? Cover him with coal dust, add deerskin leggings and a cutaway coat tight as wet leather, and you shall have Santos's younger, undernourished *sister*.

This upright disaster was in the oval light of a lamppost on Royal Street as I passed. He was gnawing a stolen ham. Behind him two policemen stood, tapping their nightsticks on their palms. "Come along now, Santos," said one. "Don't make trouble. That ham'll cost you a month in the Calabozo." Santos went right on chewing, his small, quick eyes half-seeled in gastronomic bliss. And then, without warning, both policemen smashed him full on both sides of his temples with their nightsticks. They'd each taken half steps back too, putting their waists and full weight into the swing. One nightstick broke with a sickening crack, the other vibrated in the officer's hand as if wood had struck wood. As for Santos, he only looked up sleepily. Said, "Now what'd you do that fo'?"

No fools, the policemen flew past me, Santos's eyes on their flapping waistcoats until his gaze lighted upon me. "Illinois!" he said—or, rather his sweaty voice rumbled and rattled windows along the street. "Ain't you Rutherford Calhoun from Illinois?"

I shook my head and took a step backward.

"Dammit, you *are* Calhoun! Don't lie! Papa been lookin' fo' you, boy!"

I touched my chest. "Me?"

"Yes, *you*, nigguh." He came forward, seizing my arm. "He wants to *talk* to you 'bout somethin' you owe him." I told him that surely he was mistaken, that indeed I owed several people within a mile circumference of the city—my landlady Mrs. Dupree; Mr. Fenton the moneylender; and the vendors too—but I'd never *met* Papa. How could I owe him? None of this washed with Santos, a man with whom you didn't argue, because he looked exactly like what he was: an athlete gone slightly to seed, with maybe thirty pounds of muscle alchemizing to fat on his upper body. He'd be dead by forty from the strain on his heart—the extra bulk had scrunched down his spine, I heard, shortening him by two inches, but no matter. He was bigger than me. Silently he steered me, his right hand on the back of my collar, to a tavern owned by Papa on Chartres Street, a one-story building of English-bond brickwork, with sunken, uneven floors, and windows with old, diamond-paned lattices, pushing me through the door to a table at the rear of the room where Papa sat eating a meal of drop-biscuits and blueberries with—my heart jumped!—Isadora! Of a sudden, I had that special feeling of dread that comes when you enter a café and stumble upon two women you used to sleep with—who you'd have sworn were strangers but were now whispering together. About *you*, by God! She looked up as I scuffed jelly-legged to the table, and her eyes, I tell you, were indecipherable.

"Isadora," I gulped, "you *know* these people!"

She gave Papa, in fact, a very knowing smile.

"We just met to discuss a business arrangement that affects you, Rutherford. I'm sure you'll be interested to hear what Mr. Zeringue and I have decided." Isadora touched a napkin to her lips, then stood up. "I'll wait for you outside."

She seemed to take all the available air in the room with her as she sashayed outside, mysteriously happier than I'd seen her in months. For an instant I could not catch my breath. Papa sat with a napkin tucked into his collar. He was holding a soup spoon dripping with blueberry jelly in his right hand when I extended my hand and introduced myself; this spoon he slapped against my palm and, having nothing else to shake, I shook that. Santos roared.

"Sir, you wanted to see me abo—"

"Don't say nothin', Calhoun."

If there were musical instruments that fit this man's voice, that would ring from the orchestra, say, if he appeared on stage, they would be the bull fiddle, tuba, and slide trombone (Isadora was all strings, a soft flick of the lyre), a combination so guttural and brutish, full of grunts and deep-throated notes, that I cannot say his voice put me at ease. Nor this room. It had the atmosphere you feel in houses where some great "Murder of the Age" has taken place. My worst fears about him were confirmed. He was, in every sense of the word, the very Ur-type of Gangster. Fiftyish, a brown-skinned black man with gray-webbed hair, he dressed in rich burgundy waistcoats and had a princely, feudal air about him, the smell of a man who loved Gothic subterfuges and schemes, deceits, and Satanic games of power. Yet, despite his wealth, and despite the extravagant riverboat parties I heard he threw—bashes that made Roman bacchanals look like a backwoods flangdang—he was a black lord in ruins, a fallen angel who, like Lucifer, controlled the lower depths of the city—the cathouses, the Negro press, the gambling dens—but held his dark kingdom, and all within it, in the greatest contempt. He was wicked. Wicked and self-serving, I thought, but why did he want to see me?

"I suppose," said Papa, as if he'd read my mind, "you wanna know why I had Santos bring you heah."

Indeed, I did.

"It's simple—you owe me, Illinois." I started to protest, but his left hand flew up, and he said, "First thing you gotta learn, I reckon, is that it's *rude* to talk when I'm talkin', and that I don't mind gettin' rid of people who have the bad manners to cut me off in mid-sentence. Most people are so confused, you know, 'bout life and what's right that it ain't completely wrong to take it from 'em." He paused as a waiter came to the table, topping off his coffee, then drilled his gaze at me. "Now, you ain't one of them people, I kin tell."

"Nossir," I said.

Papa's brow went dark. "You just did it again, Calhoun."

Quietly, biting my lips, I thought, *Sorry*!

" 'Bout this debt now." He began working a grain of food from his front teeth with his fingernail. "You know that li'l boardinghouse for cullud folks run by Mrs. Dupree?"

I didn't like where this was leading, and found myself disliking him too, but gave him a nod.

"I own it." His eyes narrowed. "Fact is, I own *her*, and she tells me you're three months behind in yo' rent. And that li'l moneylender Fenton—you know him?"

I bobbed my head.

"I own him too, so you might as well say I'm the one holdin' the bad papers, promises, and IOUs that you been handin' out like flyers. It comes to mebbe fifty thousand francs, I figure, and we all know a farthing-and-sixpence hoodlum like you can't even afford the down payment on a glass of lemonade." Looking square at me, he shook his head. "If all cullud men was like you, Calhoun, I 'spect the Race would be extinct by now."

Papa offered me a cigar, but my hands trembled so violently that I used four locofocos before the flame took to the end. "Now, a man *should* pay his debts, it seems to me." He placed a finger thoughtfully on one side of his nose and ordered me to sit down. "That's how worldly things work, Calhoun. The Social Wheel, as I unnerstand it after forty years in business for myself, is oiled by debts, each man owing the other somethin' in a kinda web of endless obligations. Normally," he added, "if a man welched on me like you done, he'd find hisself on the riverbottom. But you are truly blessed, Calhoun. I daresay you have divine protection. You are indeed watched over and loved by one of God's very own angels."

This was all news to me. "I am?"

"Uh-huh. That schoolteacher Miss Bailey has saved yo' behind. Out of the goodness of her heart, she has come forward and offered to liquidate yo' debts with her meager savings, provided you agree—as I know you will—to the simple condition of holy matrimony."

"But that's *blackmail*!"

"Yes," said Papa, nodding. "Yes, it is. I'm acquainted with the technique, son."

"She can't do this!" I sat biting my fingers in rage. "It's . . . it's criminal!"

Santos raised his eyebrows. "Look who's talkin'."

"And it's done," said Papa. "Tomorrow you and Miss Bailey will be wed. I *wouldn't* miss that ceremony, if I was you. It would cancel our arrangement, and I'd have to return Miss Bailey's money, and you'd be in debt again." His eyes bent slowly up to me. "You *do* wanna erase yo' debts don't you?"

"Nossir . . . I mean, yessir!" I eased back off my chair. "But you say the wedding is *tomorrow*?"

"At noon. And I'll be givin' Miss Bailey away. Santos heah will be yo' best man." His factotum grinned. Papa reached his ringed fingers toward my hand and pumped it. "Congratulations, Calhoun. I know you two are gonna be happy together."

For the rest of that day, and most of the night, I had cold shakes and fits of fear-induced hiccuping. Stumbling from the tavern, I felt light-headed, ready to fall, and slapped one hand on the wall outside to steady myself. Isadora came up behind me. She threaded her arm through mine, supporting me as I walked, dazed, toward the waterfront. Yes, I'd underestimated her. She'd wiped my nose with my own handkerchief; with my own bread she'd baked me a tart. "Tell me"—she squeezed my arm—"what you're thinking."

"You are not . . . hic . . . to be *believed*, Isadora!"

"Thank you." She hugged my arm tighter and rested her head on my shoulder. "I'm doing this for your own good, Rutherford."

"The hell you are! I'm *not* getting married! Never!"

"Yes, you are." Her voice was full of finality. "And someday when we are very old, have grandchildren, and you look back upon this rackety free-lance life you've led from the advantage of the comfortable house and family we've built together, you will thank me."

"I will . . . hic . . . *despise* you! Is that what you want? You're twisting my cullions, but you haven't won my consent!" I grabbed her arms and shook her hard enough to dislodge her hat and send her hair flying loose from its pins. "Why are you *doing* this?"

Bareheaded like that, with hair swinging in her eyes, the change came over Isadora, a collapsing of her lips inward against her teeth, the blood rising to her cheeks as if I'd suddenly struck her. One by one, she peeled my fingers off her arms, then stepped away from me, drawing up her shoulders, her hair wilder now than that of a witch.

"Because I love you . . . you fool! . . . and I don't know what to *do* about it because you don't love *me*! I know that! I'm not blind, Rutherford." She began gathering hairpins off the boardwalk, sticking them any which way back into her head. "It's because I'm not . . . not pretty. No, don't say it! That *is* why. Because I'm *dark*. You'd rather have a beautiful, glamorous, light-skinned wife like the women in the theaters and magazines. It's what all men want, someone they can show off and say to the world, 'See, look what *I'm* humping!' But she'd worry you sorely, Rutherford—I know that—you'd be suspicious of every man who came to the house, and your friends too, and she'd be vain and lazy and squander your money on all sorts of foolish things, and she'd hate having children, or doing housework, or being at your side when you're sick, but *I* can make you happy!" We were drawing a crowd, she noticed, and lowered her voice, sniffling a little as she tried to push her hat back into shape. "I'd hoped that you'd *learn* to love me the way I love you . . ."

"Isadora," I struggled. "It's not like that. I *do* love you. It's just that I don't want to marry *anyone* . . ."

"Well, you're getting married tomorrow, or I'm taking back my money." Isadora rammed her hat, hopelessly ruined, down over her ears, her eyes still blazing. "You choose, Rutherford Calhoun, whichever way you like."

And there she left me, standing by the docks in a lather of confusion. Never in my life had anyone loved me so selflessly, as the hag in the Wife of Bath's Tale had loved her fickle knight, but despite this remarkable love, I was not, as I say, ready for marriage. If you must know, I didn't feel *worthy* of her. Her goodness shamed me. I turned into the first pub I found, one frequented by sailors, a darkly lit, rum-smelling room about fourteen feet square, with a well-sanded floor and a lamp that hung within two feet of the tables, stinking of whale oil. The place was packed with seamen. All armed to the eyeballs with pistols and cutlasses, scowling and jabbering like pirates, squirting jets of brown tobacco juice everywhere except in the spittoons—a den of Chinese assassins, scowling Moors, English scoundrels, Yankee adventurers, and evil-looking Arabs. Naturally, I felt pretty much right at home. I sat near the window beside an old mariner in a pair of shag trousers and a red flannel shirt, who was playing with his parrot, an African gray, and drinking hot brandy grog. I ordered a gin twist, then tried to untangle this knot Isadora had tightened around me.

She was as cunning as a Byzantine merchant—that was clear—but I couldn't rightly fault her. She'd known her share of grief, had Isadora. Her mother Viola, she'd told me, died when she was three, which meant that she and her sisters had no one to teach them to think like independent, menless Modern Women—it was something you *learned*, she implied, like learning how to ride a bicycle, or do the backstroke. Certainly her father was no help. Isaiah Bailey was a wifebeater, that's how Viola died, and once she was buried he started punching Isadora and her sisters around on Saturday nights after visiting his still. Yet, miraculously, Isadora had remained innocent. There was no hatred in her. Or selfishness. No vanity, or negativism. Some part of her, perhaps the part she withdrew when Isaiah started whaling on her, remained untouched, a part she fed in the local African Methodist Episcopal Church, and shored up with Scripture: a still, uncorrupted center like the Chinese lotus that, though grown in muck and mud, remained beautifully poised and pure. But shy too. Seeing horses defecate on the street made Isadora blanch. She was constitutionally unable to swear. When she was angry, her lips would form a four-letter word, then freeze, as if she'd been chewing alum. A part of me ached to be with her always, to see that only things of beauty and light came before her. Would marrying her be so bad? That night, a little before dawn, I had a vision of how that union would be in decades to come—eighteen thousand six hundred and ninety-three cups of watery sassafras tea for breakfast, and in each of these I would find cat fur or pigeon feathers. No, it was not a vision to stir a soul that longed for high adventure.

After the gin, five pitchers of beer emptied before me; the sailors thinned out, but still I sat, knowing that each hour brought me closer to the bondage of wedlock. Behind me, I heard first a burp, then the gravelly voice of the now drunken sailor in shag trousers. "Yo-ho, there, young un!" He held up a flagon of grog, his fifth, which he'd only half finished. "Ye can take this, my dear, if you've a mind to. Josiah Squibb's had enough for one night."

"Much obliged . . . Squibb, is it?" I took his flagon in my left hand and his thick, rough hand in my right. "You've put away quite a lot. A man would think you're going to a hanging, friend."

"Worse," said Squibb. "I'm shipping out tomorrow with Captain Ebenezer Falcon. Good as a hangin', that, to hear some men tell it. He's a descendant of Colonel Blood who stole the crown jewels, some say, a buccaneer at heart, and proud of it." Blearily he lit a long-shanked pipe and studied me through eyes too bloodshot, really, to see. "Ye drink a lot y'self, boy. Got problems, have ye?"

"Marriage," I told him. "Tomorrow at noon."

"Blimey!" Squibb sat back, stunned, his chair creaking. "Ye *have* got a problem. Oh, I know about wives all right. Got a couple myself—one in Connecticut, and one in Vermont. That's *why* I ship out. What say I buy yuh a round?"

Josiah Squibb, I learned, had signed on as a cook aboard the *Republic*, a ninety-ton square-rigger that would up-anchor and sail eastward against the prevailing winds to the barracoon, or slave factory, at Bangalang on the Guinea coast, take on a cargo of Africans, and then, God willing, return in three months. "There she be." Squibb stabbed his pipestem toward the window, and the ship he showed me from this distance was strikingly beautiful, a great three-masted, full-rigged bark with a roundtruck hull, grated hatches and bulkheads cut round the deck for circulation. As it turned out, these were the last words from Squibb. Halfway through our last drink, his forehead crashed down upon the table. And his papers . . . ah, these were rolled cylindrically inside his right boot. I thought, *Naw, Calhoun, you can't do that*; but at that selfsame instant I remembered what awaited me at the altar, and I decided most definitely, *Yes, I can*.

"Bad move," said the parrot. "Very bad move."

I said, "Shut up."

Transferring Squibb's papers to my coat, I eased away from the table whilst he snored. "Thief! Thief!" shouted the parrot, but fortunately he could not shatter the cook's heavy-headed sleep. I slipped outside into a shock of cool air and ran down the pier to a cluster of small boats rocking lazily to and fro on the water. I unfastened the rope to one, paddled out toward the *Republic*, then hauled myself hand over hand up a rope ladder to the topgallant bulwark, and over onto a broad empty deck. The crew had not come aboard yet. Standing aft, looking back at the glittering lights ashore, I had an odd sensation, difficult to explain, that I'd boarded not a ship but a kind of fantastic, floating Black Maria, a wooden sepulcher whose timbers moaned with the memory of too many runs of black gold between the New World and the Old; moaned, I say again, because the ship—with its tiered compartments and galleys, like a crazy-quilt house built by a hundred carpenters, each with a different plan—felt conscious and disapprovingly aware of my presence when I pulled back the canvas on a flat-bottomed launch and laid myself down in its hull, which was long and narrow, both hands crossed on my chest. And then waves lapping below the ship gently swung me left then right as in a hammock, sinking me like a fish, or a stone, farther down through leagues of darkness, and mercifully to sleep.

CHARLES W. CHESNUTT

The Wife of His Youth

I

Mr. Ryder was going to give a ball. There were several reasons why this was an opportune time for such an event.

Mr. Ryder might aptly be called the dean of the Blue Veins. The original Blue Veins were a little society of colored persons organized in a certain Northern city shortly after the war. Its purpose was to establish and maintain correct social standards among a people whose social condition presented almost unlimited room for improvement. By accident, combined perhaps with some natural affinity, the society consisted of individuals who were, generally speaking, more white than black. Some envious outsider made the suggestion that no one was eligible for membership who was not white enough to show blue veins. The suggestion was readily adopted by those who were not of the favored few, and since that time the society, though possessing a longer and more pretentious name, had been known far and wide as the "Blue Vein Society," and its members as the "Blue Veins."

The Blue Veins did not allow that any such requirement existed for admission to their circle, but, on the contrary, declared that character and culture were the only things considered; and that if most of their members were light-colored, it was because such persons, as a rule, had had better opportunities to qualify themselves for membership. Opinions differed, too, as to the usefulness of the society. There were those who had been known to assail it violently as a glaring example of the very prejudice from which the colored race had suffered most; and later, when such critics had succeeded in getting on the inside, they had been heard to maintain with zeal and earnestness that the society was a lifeboat, an anchor, a bulwark and a shield,—a pillar of cloud by day and of fire by night, to guide their people through the social wilderness. Another alleged prerequisite for Blue Vein membership was that of free birth; and while there was really no such requirement, it is doubtless true that very few of the members would have been unable to meet it if there had been. If there were one or two of the older members who had come up from the South and from slavery, their history presented enough romantic circumstances to rob their servile origin of its grosser aspects.

While there were no such tests of eligibility, it is true that the Blue Veins had their notions on these subjects, and that not all of them were equally liberal in regard to the things they collectively disclaimed. Mr. Ryder was one of the most conservative. Though he had not been among the founders of the society, but had come in some years later, his genius for social leadership was such that he had speedily become its recognized adviser and head, the custodian of its standards, and the preserver of its traditions. He shaped its social policy, was active in providing for its entertainment, and when the interest fell off, as it sometimes did, he fanned the embers until they burst again into a cheerful flame.

There were still other reasons for his popularity. While he was not as white as some of the Blue Veins, his appearance was such as to confer distinction upon them. His features were of a refined type, his hair was almost straight; he was always neatly dressed; his manners were irreproachable, and his morals above suspicion. He had come to Groveland a young man, and obtaining employment in the office of a railroad company as messenger had in time worked himself up to the position of stationery clerk, having charge of the distribution of the office supplies for the whole company. Although the lack of early training had hindered the orderly development of a naturally fine mind, it had not prevented him from doing a great deal of reading or from forming decidedly literary tastes. Poetry was his passion. He could repeat whole pages of the great English poets; and if his pronunciation was sometimes faulty, his eye, his voice, his gestures, would respond to the changing sentiment with a precision that revealed a poetic soul and disarmed criticism. He was economical, and had saved money; he owned and occupied a very comfortable house on a respectable street. His residence was handsomely furnished, containing among other things a good library, especially rich in poetry, a piano, and some choice engravings. He generally shared his house with some young couple, who looked after his wants and were company for him; for Mr. Ryder was a single man. In the early days of his connection with the Blue Veins he had been regarded as quite a catch, and young ladies and their mothers had manoeuvred with much ingenuity to capture him. Not, however, until Mrs. Molly Dixon visited Groveland had any woman ever made him wish to change his condition to that of a married man.

Mrs. Dixon had come to Groveland from Washington in the spring, and before the summer was over she had won Mr. Ryder's heart. She possessed many attractive qualities. She was much younger than he; in fact, he was old enough to have been her father, though no one knew exactly how old he was. She was whiter than he, and better educated. She had moved in the best colored society of the country, at Washington, and had taught in the schools of that city. Such a superior person had been eagerly welcomed to the Blue Vein Society, and had taken a leading part in its activities. Mr. Ryder had at first been attracted by her charms of person, for she was very good looking and not over twenty-five; then by her refined manners and the vivacity of her wit. Her husband had been a government clerk, and at his death had left a considerable life insurance. She was visiting friends in Groveland, and, finding the town and the people to her liking, had prolonged her stay indefinitely. She had not seemed displeased at Mr. Ryder's attentions, but on the contrary had given him every proper encouragement; indeed, a younger and less cautious man would long since have spoken. But he had made up his mind, and had only to determine the time when he would ask her to be his wife. He decided to give a ball in her honor, and at some time during the evening of the ball to offer her his heart and hand. He had no special fears about the outcome, but, with a little touch of romance, he wanted the surroundings to be in harmony with his own feelings when he should have received the answer he expected.

Mr. Ryder resolved that this ball should mark an epoch in the social history of Groveland. He knew, of course,—no one could know better,—the entertainments that had taken place in past years, and what must be done to surpass them. His ball must be worthy of the lady in whose honor it was to be given, and must, by the quality of its guests, set an example for the future. He had observed of late a growing liberality, almost a laxity, in social matters, even among members of his own set, and had several times been forced to meet in a social way persons whose complexions and callings in life were hardly up to the standard which he considered proper for the society to maintain. He had a theory of his own.

"I have no race prejudice," he would say, "but we people of mixed blood are ground between the upper and the nether millstone. Our fate lies between absorption by the white race and extinction in the black. The one doesn't want us yet, but may take us in time. The other would welcome us, but it would be for us a backward step. ('With malice towards none, with charity for all,' we must do the best we can for ourselves and those who are to follow us. Self-preservation is the first law of nature.)"

His ball would serve by its exclusiveness to counteract leveling tendencies, and his marriage with Mrs. Dixon would help to further the upward process of absorption he had been wishing and waiting for.

II

The ball was to take place on Friday night. The house had been put in order, the carpets covered with canvas, the halls and stairs decorated with palms and potted plants; and in the afternoon Mr. Ryder sat on his front porch, which the shade of a vine running up over a wire netting made a cool and pleasant lounging place. He expected to respond to the toast "The Ladies" at the supper, and from a volume of Tennyson—his favorite poet—was fortifying himself with apt quotations. The volume was open at "A Dream of Fair Women." His eyes fell on these lines, and he read them aloud to judge better of their effect:—

"At length I saw a lady within call,
  Stiller than chisell'd marble, standing there;
A daughter of the gods, divinely tall,
  And most divinely fair."

He marked the verse, and turning the page read the stanza beginning,—

"O sweet pale Margaret,
  O rare pale Margaret."

He weighed the passage a moment, and decided that it would not do. Mrs. Dixon was the palest lady he expected at the ball, and she was of a rather ruddy complexion, and of lively disposition and buxom build. So he ran over the leaves until his eye rested on the description of Queen Guinevere:—

"She seem'd a part of joyous Spring:
A gown of grass-green silk she wore,
Buckled with golden clasps before;
A light-green tuft of plumes she bore
Closed in a golden ring.

. . . . .

"She look'd so lovely, as she sway'd
The rein with dainty finger-tips,
A man had given all other bliss,
And all his worldly worth for this,
To waste his whole heart in one kiss
Upon her perfect lips."

As Mr. Ryder murmured these words audibly, with an appreciative thrill, he heard the latch of his gate click, and a light footfall sounding on the steps. He turned his head, and saw a woman standing before his door.

She was a little woman, not five feet tall, and proportioned to her height. Although she stood erect, and looked around her with very bright and restless eyes, she seemed quite old; for her face was crossed and recrossed with a hundred wrinkles, and around the edges of her bonnet could be seen protruding here and there a tuft of short gray wool. She wore a blue calico gown of ancient cut, a little red shawl fastened around her shoulders with an old-fashioned brass brooch, and a large bonnet profusely ornamented with faded red and yellow artificial flowers. And she was very black,—so black that her toothless gums, revealed when she opened her mouth to speak, were not red, but blue. She looked like a bit of the old plantation life, summoned up from the past by the wave of a magician's wand, as the poet's fancy had called into being the gracious shapes of which Mr. Ryder had just been reading.

He rose from his chair and came over to where she stood.

"Good-afternoon, madam," he said.

"Good-evenin', suh," she answered, ducking suddenly with a quaint curtsy. Her voice was shrill and piping, but softened somewhat by age. "Is dis yere whar Mistuh Ryduh lib, suh?" she asked, looking around her doubtfully, and glancing into the open windows, through which some of the preparations for the evening were visible.

"Yes," he replied, with an air of kindly patronage, unconsciously flattered by her manner, "I am Mr. Ryder. Did you want to see me?"

"Yas, suh, ef I ain't 'sturbin' of you too much."

"Not at all. Have a seat over here behind the vine, where it is cool. What can I do for you?"

" 'Scuse me, suh," she continued, when she had sat down on the edge of a chair, " 'scuse me, suh, I's lookin' for my husban'. I heerd you wuz a big man an' had libbed heah a long time, an' I 'lowed you would n't min' ef I'd come roun' an' ax you ef you'd ever heerd of a merlatter man by de name er Sam Taylor 'quirin' roun' in de chu'ches ermongs' de people fer his wife, 'Liza Jane?"

Mr. Ryder seemed to think for a moment.

"There used to be many such cases right after the war," he said, "but it has been so long that I have forgotten them. There are very few now. But tell me your story, and it may refresh my memory."

She sat back farther in her chair so as to be more comfortable, and folded her withered hands in her lap.

"My name's 'Liza," she began, " 'Liza Jane. W'en I wuz young I us'ter b'long ter Marse Bob Smif, down in ole Missoura. I wuz bawn down dere. W'en I wuz a gal I wuz married ter a man named Jim. But Jim died, an' after dat I married a merlatter man named Sam Taylor. Sam wuz freebawn, but his mammy and daddy died, an' de w'ite folks 'prenticed him ter my marster fer ter work fer 'im 'tel he wuz growed up. Sam worked in de fiel', an' I wuz de cook. One day Ma'y Ann, ole miss's maid, came rushin' out ter de kitchen, an' says she, ' 'Liza Jane, ole marse gwine sell yo' Sam down de ribber.'

" 'Go away f'm yere,' says I; 'my husban' 's free!'

" 'Don' make no diff'ence. I heerd ole marse tell ole miss he wuz gwine take yo' Sam 'way wid 'im ter-morrow, fer he needed money, an' he knowed whar he could git a t'ousan' dollars fer Sam an' no questions axed.'

"W'en Sam come home f'm de fiel' dat night, I tole him 'bout ole marse gwine steal 'im, an' Sam run erway. His time wuz mos' up, an' he swo' dat w'en he wuz twenty-one he would come back an' he'p me run erway, er else save up de money ter buy my freedom. An' I know he'd 'a' done it, fer he thought a heap er me, Sam did. But w'en he come back he did n' fin' me, fer I wuz n' dere. Ole marse had heerd dat I warned Sam, so he had me whip' an' sol' down de ribber.

"Den de wah broke out, an' w'en it wuz ober de cullud folks wuz scattered. I went back ter de ole home; but Sam wuz n' dere, an' I could n' l'arn nuffin' 'bout 'im. But I knowed he'd be'n dere to look fer me an' had n' foun' me, an' had gone erway ter hunt fer me.

"I's be'n lookin' fer 'im eber sence," she added simply, as though twenty-five years were but a couple of weeks, "an' I knows he's be'n lookin' fer me. Fer he sot a heap er sto' by me, Sam did, an' I know he's be'n huntin' fer me all dese years,—'less'n he's be'n sick er sump'n, so he could n' work, er out'n his head, so he could n' 'member his promise. I went back down de ribber, fer I 'lowed he'd gone down dere lookin' fer me. I's be'n ter Noo Orleens, an' Atlanty, an' Charleston, an' Richmon'; an' w'en I'd be'n all ober de Souf I come ter de Norf. Fer I knows I'll fin' 'im some er dese days," she added softly, "er he'll fin' me, an' den we'll bofe be as happy in freedom as we wuz in de ole days befo' de wah." A smile stole over her withered countenance as she paused a moment, and her bright eyes softened into a faraway look.

This was the substance of the old woman's story. She had wandered a little here and there. Mr. Ryder was looking at her curiously when she finished.

"How have you lived all these years?" he asked.

"Cookin', suh. I's a good cook. Does you know anybody w'at needs a good cook, suh? I's stoppin' wid a cullud fam'ly roun' de corner yonder 'tel I kin git a place."

"Do you really expect to find your husband? He may be dead long ago."

She shook her head emphatically. "Oh no, he ain' dead. De signs an' de tokens tells me. I dremp three nights runnin' on'y dis las' week dat I foun' him."

"He may have married another woman. Your slave marriage would not have prevented him, for you never lived with him after the war, and without that your marriage does n't count."

"Would n' make no diff'ence wid Sam. He would n' marry no yuther 'ooman 'tel he foun' out 'bout me. I knows it," she added. "Sump'n's be'n tellin' me all dese years dat I's gwine fin' Sam 'fo' I dies."

"Perhaps he's outgrown you, and climbed up in the world where he wouldn't care to have you find him."

"No, indeed, suh," she replied, "Sam ain' dat kin' er man. He wuz good ter me, Sam wuz, but he wuz n' much good ter nobody e'se, fer he wuz one er de triflin'es' han's on de plantation. I 'spec's ter haf ter suppo't 'im w'en I fin' 'im, fer he nebber would work 'less'n he had ter. But den he wuz free, an' he did n' git no pay fer his work, an' I don' blame 'im much. Mebbe he's done better sence he run erway, but I ain' 'spectin' much."

"You may have passed him on the street a hundred times during the twenty-five years, and not have known him; time works great changes."

She smiled incredulously. "I'd know 'im 'mongs' a hund'ed men. Fer dey wuz n' no yuther merlatter man like my man Sam, an' I could n' be mistook. I 's toted his picture roun' wid me twenty-five years."

"May I see it?" asked Mr. Ryder. "It might help me to remember whether I have seen the original."

As she drew a small parcel from her bosom he saw that it was fastened to a string that went around her neck. Removing several wrappers, she brought to light an old-fashioned daguerreotype in a black case. He looked long and intently at the portrait. It was faded with time, but the features were still distinct, and it was easy to see what manner of man it had represented.

He closed the case, and with a slow movement handed it back to her.

"I don't know of any man in town who goes by that name," he said, "nor have I heard of anyone making such inquiries. But if you will leave me your address, I will give the matter some attention, and if I find out anything I will let you know."

She gave him the number of a house in the neighborhood, and went away, after thanking him warmly.

He wrote the address on the fly-leaf of the volume of Tennyson, and, when she had gone, rose to his feet and stood looking after her curiously. As she walked down the street with mincing step, he saw several persons whom she passed turn and look back at her with a smile of kindly amusement. When she had turned the corner, he went upstairs to his bedroom, and stood for a long time before the mirror of his dressing-case, gazing thoughtfully at the reflection of his own face.

III

At eight o'clock the ballroom was a blaze of light and the guests had begun to assemble; for there was a literary programme and some routine business of the society to be gone through with before the dancing. A black servant in evening dress waited at the door and directed guests to the dressing-rooms.

The occasion was long memorable among the colored people of the city; not alone for the dress and display, but for the high average of intelligence and culture that distinguished the gathering as a whole. There were a number of school-teachers, several young doctors, three or four lawyers, some professional singers, an editor, a lieutenant in the United States army spending his furlough in the city, and others in various polite callings; these were colored, though most of them would not have attracted even a casual glance because of any marked difference from white people. Most of the ladies were in evening costume, and dress coats and dancing pumps were the rule among the men. A band of string music, stationed in an alcove behind a row of palms, played popular airs while the guests were gathering.

The dancing began at half past nine. At eleven o'clock supper was served. Mr. Ryder had left the ballroom some little time before the intermission, but reappeared at the supper-table. The spread was worthy of the occasion, and the guests did full justice to it. When the coffee had been served, the toast-master, Mr. Solomon Sadler, rapped for order. He made a brief introductory speech, complimenting host and guests, and then presented in their order the toasts of the evening. They were responded to with a very fair display of after-dinner wit.

"The last toast," said the toast-master, when he reached the end of the list, "is one which must appeal to us all. There is no one of us of the sterner sex who is not at some time dependent upon woman,—in infancy for protection, in manhood for companionship, in old age for care and comforting. Our good host has been trying to live alone, but the fair faces I see around me to-night prove that he too is largely dependent upon the gentler sex for most that makes life worth living,—the society and love of friends,—and rumor is at fault if he does not soon yield entire subjection to one of them. Mr. Ryder will now respond to the toast,—The Ladies."

There was a pensive look in Mr. Ryder's eyes as he took the floor and adjusted his eye-glasses. He began by speaking of woman as the gift of Heaven to man, and after some general observations on the relations of the sexes he said: "But perhaps the quality which most distinguishes woman is her fidelity and devotion to those she loves. History is full of examples, but has recorded none more striking than one which only to-day came under my notice."

He then related, simply but effectively, the story told by his visitor of the afternoon. He gave it in the same soft dialect, which came readily to his lips, while the company listened attentively and sympathetically. For the story had awakened a responsive thrill in many hearts. There were some present who had seen, and others who had heard their fathers and grandfathers tell, the wrongs and sufferings of this past generation, and all of them still felt, in their darker moments, the shadow hanging over them. Mr. Ryder went on:—

"Such devotion and confidence are rare even among women. There are many who would have searched a year, some who would have waited five years, a few who might have hoped ten years; but for twenty-five years this woman has retained her affection for and her faith in a man she has not seen or heard of in all that time.

"She came to me to-day in the hope that I might be able to help her find this long-lost husband. And when she was gone I gave my fancy rein, and imagined a case I will put to you.

"Suppose that this husband, soon after his escape, had learned that his wife had been sold away, and that such inquiries as he could make brought no information of her whereabouts. Suppose that he was young, and she much older than he; that he was light, and she was black; that their marriage was a slave marriage, and legally binding only if they chose to make it so after the war. Suppose, too, that he made his way to the North, as some of us have done, and there, where he had larger opportunities, had improved them, and had in the course of all these years grown to be as different from the ignorant boy who ran away from fear of slavery as the day is from the night. Suppose, even, that he had qualified himself, by industry, by thrift, and by study, to win the friendship and be considered worthy the society of such people as these I see around me to-night, gracing my board and filling my heart with gladness; for I am old enough to remember the day when such a gathering would not have been possible in this land. Suppose, too, that, as the years went by, this man's memory of the past grew more and more indistinct, until at last it was rarely, except in his dreams, that any image of this bygone period rose before his mind. And then suppose that accident should bring to his knowledge the fact that the wife of his youth, the wife he had left behind him,—not one who had walked by his side and kept pace with him in his upward struggle, but one upon whom advancing years and a laborious life had set their mark,—was alive and seeking him, but that he was absolutely safe from recognition or discovery, unless he chose to reveal himself. My friends, what would the man do? I will presume that he was one who loved honor, and tried to deal justly with all men. I will even carry the case further, and suppose that perhaps he had set his heart upon another, whom he had hoped to call his own. What would he do, or rather what ought he to do, in such a crisis of a lifetime?

"It seemed to me that he might hesitate, and I imagined that I was an old friend, a near friend, and that he had come to me for advice; and I argued the case with him. I tried to discuss it impartially. After we had looked upon the matter from every point of view, I said to him, in words that we all know:—

> 'This above all: to thine own self be true,
> And it must follow, as the night the day,
> Thou canst not then be false to any man.'

Then, finally, I put the question to him, 'Shall you acknowledge her?'

"And now, ladies and gentlemen, friends and companions, I ask you, what should he have done?"

There was something in Mr. Ryder's voice that stirred the hearts of those who sat around him. It suggested more than mere sympathy with an imaginary situation; it seemed rather in the nature of a personal appeal. It was observed, too, that his look rested more especially upon Mrs. Dixon, with a mingled expression of renunciation and inquiry.

She had listened, with parted lips and streaming eyes. She was the first to speak: "He should have acknowledged her."

"Yes," they all echoed, "he should have acknowledged her."

"My friends and companions," responded Mr. Ryder, "I thank you, one and all. It is the answer I expected, for I knew your hearts."

He turned and walked toward the closed door of an adjoining room, while every eye followed him in wondering curiosity. He came back in a moment, leading by the hand his visitor of the afternoon, who stood startled and trembling at the sudden plunge into this scene of brilliant gayety. She was neatly dressed in gray, and wore the white cap of an elderly woman.

"Ladies and gentlemen," he said, "this is the woman, and I am the man, whose story I have told you. Permit me to introduce to you the wife of my youth."

ARTHUR FLOWERS

Another Good Loving Blues

I am Flowers of the delta clan Flowers and the line of O Killens—I am hoodoo, I am griot, I am a man of power. My story is a true story, my words are true words, my lie is a true lie—a fine old delta tale about a mad blues piano player and a Arkansas conjure woman on a hoodoo mission. Lucas Bodeen and Melvira Dupree. Plan to show you how they found the good thing. True love. That once-in-a-lifetime love. Now few folk find the good thing; most folk struggle through life making do—you can learn to love most anybody thats good people. Truth be told its probably best that way because when you find true love my friend its strictly do or die.

My boy Luke Bodeen wasn't even thinking bout no love that bright springly morning he first saw her walking on the dusty little main and only street of Sweetwater Arkansas. But the moment he saw her he wanted her and needed her—she took his breath, she took his heart.

Spring 1918. The Mississippi delta. Bodeen 37 and in his prime. Known to be silver-tongued delta bluesman, Luke Bodeen had left more good women grieving in more towns than he cared to count. But this one touched him. Somewhere deep. Boy didn't know what he was stepping into when he tilted his Stetson just so and crossed her path.

"How do mam, I'm Luke Bodeen. You interested?"

She kept walking, proud little round head cleaving the air. Thick pretty head of hair he couldn't wait to put his fingers into. He matched her stride-for-stride, and their rhythm was a good one. She turned then to look at him and he stumbled into the massive brown galaxies of eyes that saw a mite more than he was comfortable showing.

"A bluesman," he told her, "and a good one too. Outta Memphis Tennessee mostly, but I been around. I come to town with the traveling medicine show."

He paused, poised for an opening.

"Melvira Dupree," she said, "conjure."

He stumbled again. Conjure? Didn't know if he was ready for all that. But he looked her over again and he liked what he saw.

"Well I declare you ain't like no conjure I ever seen."

"Is that so bluesman, and how many have you seen?"

"Oh I seen plenty conjures gal, I'm a well-traveled man, I been to New Orleans, St. Louis and Chicago Illinois, been to New York City, Paris France, Timbucktu and Rio de Janeiro. I done downhome blues wherever the four winds blow. I come back home regular though cause I'm just another good old boy delta born and bred. Warn you up front that I ain't never tossed my shoes under no woman's bed for long. When the blues call I'm liable to answer."

He smiled at her, a bright warm sunny day in the middle of March, a hint of springs to come. She looked him over again with those funny eyes of hers . . . a good spirit, healthy, vigorous . . . she could see that he would be, shall we say, a troublesome man . . . but still . . . there was something about him that spoke to her in that special way. And seeing as she hadn't been any further out of Sweetwater than her traveling spirit had took her, all this talk about getting around intrigued her.

Now Bodeen knew he was being judged, felt her digging. Deep too. Naturally his first urge was to block her, but he found himself just letting her look and hoping she liked what she saw. She, of course, blinked and looked no further—between men and women a degree of mystery is often appropriate.

"I seen hoodoos and conjures of all persuasions," he told her with a downright bodacious grin, "but I ain't never run across one like you. Don't bother me none you understand, I'm here to claim you and if you really conjure, then you know I'm talking true. I likes you gal, I likes your style, really truly I do."

He offered his arm and a big old country courting smile.

She laughed with a newfound pleasure and took them both. Most of the men in Sweetwater were afraid to talk to the woman in her.

"You ain't half bad yourself bluesman."

Her throaty voice was a tickle, a challenge, a music that bewitched him. He preened under her obvious approval like a old bantam rooster and commenced to sing himself a brand-new blues.

I'll bring you sweet southern loving
in a old tin cup

pour it on your body baby
then I'ma lap it all up
everyday
Show you how much I love being your man.

"Gon git you too," he sang, "gon git you good, cause I don't mind working at it."

She just as tickled as she can be.

"Do tell . . . bluesman."

They stopped in front of the Sweetwater General Store and she rested her hand lightly on his arm.

"I thank you for your company Mr. Bodeen, you are kinda cute."

"O I'm a lot more than cute. As you shall see when I come a courting. Course I ain't gon pester you none just now, though. Just enough to put me on your mind some."

She went inside, laughing pertly over a curved brown shoulder bare to the sun.

"You don't know you want to be on my mind bluesman."

"Oh yes I do," he sang after her. "I ain't scared of no conjure, what you gon do, hoodoo a man the blues already claim? I'll be seeing you around Miz Melvira Dupree."

Now it would be safe to say that the good coloredfolk of Sweetwater Arkansas were scandalized and mystified when their conjure woman took up with that bluessinger, when he stayed on after the medicine show left town and moved into her little place out there on Sweetwater Creek.

The local lads were understandably upset with him. They wouldn't have minded a chance with that fox Dupree, but she was known to have a temper, and any old fool know that courting a conjure woman with a temper is a chancy thing. The two of them bickered and fought about as much as they laughed and loved, always mad at each other about something. Any day now folks expected to see that boy hopping round like a toadfrog or wiggling on his belly like a snake. But whatever he was doing, he was doing it right. Melvira Dupree changed up on them. She walked down the street smiling at folks and greeting them good morning just like a regular neighbor. But it was when she started hanging out down at the local jukejoint where Lucas got a job barrellhousing every Friday and Saturday night that folks really commence to commenting. Girl started flouncing that big impressive boodie of hers and having herself much too good of a time for the puritans from the old school, who couldn't quite recall a conjure woman quite like this one. Of course the older Sweetwater women, elders all who didn't miss very much, would poke each others ribs when they saw her walking around town glowing. They knew a recently satisfied woman when they saw one. After all a good man is still hard to find and even conjures appreciate good loving.

And that boy Bodeen, he just as snug as a hog in fresh summer mud. When he wasn't all knotted up mad at her, he could be seen walking around with his thumbs hooked in those red suspenders and grinning proud as a brand-new fool.

Scandalized as they were at their conjure lady taking up with a bluessinger, of all things, you could tell he loved that woman something truly fierce. A buncha Sweetwater women like the way his lean brown fingers caressed music out of those cold piano keys and wondered what music he coaxed from a woman's warm body, but he went home to Melvira Dupree each and every night. Took his money home each and every week, too, like a natchural man, and wasn't never fool enough to try and raise up his hands against her. They did fuss a lot, but folks come to decide that they just liked to fuss.

So the good coloredfolk of Sweetwater Arkansas gave their grudging approval. To this day Sweetwater folk are known for being bighearted, and there just ain't no counting for a conjure's taste noway.

Course what folks saw from the vantage points of their big wraparound porches wasn't the whole story. Never is. Any good story is always at least 4 to 5 stories deep. And since this is a good story, I expect you to pay close attention to the weave of it. Even they couldn't tell the whole story. But what they did come to understand deep down in once starved and lonely souls, is that when you do find yourself some of that real good loving, if you got any sense at all, you hold on to it.

Truth. I swear by all thats holy.

ON THE NATURE OF SWEETWATER LOVING

Blues and women. Women and the blues. According to Lucas Bodeen they come together. The best women to come through a man's life always leave a good blues behind, and Melvira Dupree was the best woman Luke Bodeen ever had. Taught him the best blues he ever sang, you don't know you need it till you've had it and you don't miss it till it's gone. It's an old old song, and Melvira Dupree was the one taught him how to sing it right. Moved in with her out of laziness more than anything else. Always been more comfortable with a woman than without, and she was the one available at that time and place. Simple as that. Even back then he knew she was strange, even more so than women are by nature. But he soon found she had a way with him like no other woman before. She made him feel. She bothered him. Bothered him real bad. Long as he was with her he kept saying that he was just passing through. But a year later he was still there and still comfortable. Satisfied. He likes to think that she was too. Till the rooster crowed.

It was early one morning in the Sweetwater Woods. They were out gathering herbs, specifically Life Everlasting. She always gathered in morning, said morning was best for the earth's medicine. "The earth is stronger then."

Hoodoo talk.

This particular morning he was supposed to be showing her this big batch of Life Everlasting that he had seen when cutting through the woods the other day. He had told her about it because he knew she was always on the lookout for Life Everlasting, and she used it enough for him to know it when he saw it.

It was early on a pretty morning. The woods were a wet and sparkly green and Bodeen was kinda feeling the morning in his soul. He's listening to earlymorning birdsong and he's wondering what blues birds sing. He started whistling, called himself mimicking birdblues about hungry hawks and slithering snakes, about warm southern winds and the fuzzy little feathers that line a she-bird's neck. And what about that first time in flight? Thats got to be nice. A windy blues. Eyes slitting lazily, his arms in front of him, he played with the fingering. Classic air piano.

"Bodeen." Melvira cleared her throat, half amused, half irritated, "my Life Everlasting?"

It took him a minute to focus; right, Life Everlasting. He looked around until he recognized where he was and smiled for effect. "This way for sure, right over the hill here."

They crested the hill and saw the bush below—Life Everlasting. She was pleased. She had been none too sure he knew what he was talking about. She smiled, and when Melvira Dupree smiles the sun beams, flowers bloom and every tree in Tennessee glows crimson with pleasure.

She kissed his jaw, rubbing her lips lightly across the morning stubble. "Bless you Bodeen, that's the finest batch of Life Everlasting I ever seen."

She was singing now, every word a song. She did it all the time, everything she said she sang, thats just the way she spoke, but when she was happy or pleased it really got bad, she could sing the stars out of the sky just by calling out their names. So he's real contented, watching her scramble down the hill, wild mane of her hair billowing out behind her. He's feeling kinda playful and so while she's stuffing Life Everlasting into her burlap tote bag, he ducked off behind a big gnarly oak beside her. He plucked him some little yellow flowers and called himself gon surprise her. Get that, surprise a conjure woman. She was looking dead at him when he stepped out, flowers in hand.

"Thought I'd pick some herbs too," he said. She knew what he was about. Some of that earlymorning sun-kissed loving. She took his flowers from him and looked at them disdainfully. "These are flowers Bodeen, not herbs. What am I supposed to do with flowers?"

He acted like he's offended and reached for them. She snatched them away and popped him across the face. Bright yellow petals explode around his head.

She laughed and darted out of range when he reached for her. "Come back here you."

She darted behind the trunk of that oak behind her and he chased her around it. "Lucas Bodeen you cut it out you hear? Don't you make me drop my Life Everlasting."

She stopped and glared. Pure bluff.

"I'm warning you Bodeen, I'm gonna . . ."

He grabbed. She evaded. Just barely.

"Warning me what? Told you about trying to hoodoo a man the blues already claim."

She laughed. "You mighty sure of yourself ain't you bluesman?"

"Only cause that's the way you like it."

She was laughing so hard he almost caught her. She laughed so rarely. Melvira Dupree was one of those rigid folks that take life strictly serious. Fun had to sneak up and prove itself far as Melvira Dupree was concerned. Bodeen, he was a playful man, make a laugh out of any old thing, good times and bad. Blues training. A magic she found hard to resist. He snatched at her and she stumbled getting away.

"Yeah," she said from the other side of the tree, "I like my men manly, but you way too cocky, I oughta try you boy."

"Try me now whydoncha?"

He grabbed her, "I gotcha now" and, giggling, they tumbled to the ground. Her body writhed with laughter and the effort of evading him, and suddenly she was just laying there, her eyes locking his, her fingers snaking behind his neck and pulling him down onto her parted lips. Sweet lips fresh like they never been kissed. He gave up real quick, letting himself just melt onto her body, when suddenly she flipped him over and she was on top.

"Who got who?" she breathed into the hollow of his throat, and then her tongue was deep in his mouth and her dress was down around her hips when like it was right in his ear he heard a rooster crow, echoes floating through the trees and hanging in the crisp morning air like a old delta fieldholler. Firm tittymeat in his hand, fat growing nipple in his mouth, you know he wasn't hardly paying no attention to no rooster crowing. Till he felt her distraction. Her body went limp and he looked up at her face. She was listening to the echoes of the rooster with a unfocused gaze that he recognized. Another damned Sign. Living with a hoodoo ain't easy. Looked to him sometimes like everything was a Sign with this woman. Everything that happened anywhere in the world meant something. Though what a rooster crowing at six a.m. said beyond Good Morning was beyond him.

He didn't say anything while she pulled loose and rose, brow wrinkled and eyes all out of focus. She pulled her dress up and kissed him absently. "Gotta go Bodeen. Okay?"

He nodded, lucky to get that much. By now he knows better than to question a Sign, so he just laid there with his hands behind his head and watched her dress, thick black hair tangled and laced with leaves and twigs. Strange strange woman this woman of his, he thought, wonder why I always choose the strange ones, seemed like I'da learned by now.

She strided off through the woods and he watched her go. Erect and proud and smooth like young midnight. A force. His. He had to smile. A helluva woman that answers to me. I like that. Always did.

JAMES ALAN McPHERSON

Elbow Room

My dear, dear Gloria, her name was Gweneth Lawson:

She was a pretty, chocolate brown little girl with dark brown eyes and two long black braids. After all these years, the image of these two braids evokes in me all there is to remember about Gweneth Lawson. They were plaited across the top of her head and hung to a point just above the back of her Peter Pan collar. Sometimes she wore two bows, one red and one blue, and these tended to sway lazily near the place on her neck where the smooth brown of her skin and the white of her collar met the ink-bottle black of her hair. Even when I cannot remember her face, I remember the rainbow of deep, rich colors in which she lived. This is so because I watched them, every weekday, from my desk directly behind hers in our fourth-grade class. And she wore the most magical perfume, or lotion, smelling just slightly of fresh-cut lemons, that wafted back to me whenever she made the slightest movement at her desk. Now I must tell you this much more, dear Gloria: whenever I smell fresh lemons, whether in the market or at home, I look around me—not for Gweneth Lawson, but for some quiet corner where I can revive in private certain memories of her. And in pursuing these memories across such lemony bridges, I rediscover that I loved her.

Gweneth was from the South Carolina section of Brooklyn. Her parents had sent her south to live with her uncle, Mr. Richard Lawson, the brick mason, for an unspecified period of time. Just why they did this I do not know, unless it was their plan to have her absorb more of South Carolina folkways than conditions in Brooklyn would allow. She was a gentle, soft-spoken girl; I recall no condescension in her manner. This was all the more admirable because our unrestrained awe of a Northern-born black person usually induced in him some grand sense of his own importance. You must know that in those days older folks would point to someone and say, "He's from the North," and the statement would be sufficient in itself. Mothers made their children behave by advising that, if they led exemplary lives and attended church regularly, when they died they would go to New York. Only someone who understands what London meant to Dick Whittington, or how California and the suburbs function in the national mind, could appreciate the mythical dimensions of this Northlore.

But Gweneth Lawson was above regional idealization. Though I might have loved her partly because she was a Northerner, I loved her more because of the world of colors that seemed to be suspended about her head. I loved her glowing forehead and I loved her bright, dark brown eyes; I loved the black braids, the red and blue and sometimes yellow and pink ribbons; I loved the way the deep, rich brown of her neck melted into the pink or white cloth of her Peter Pan collar; I loved the lemony vapor on which she floated and from which on occasion, she seemed to be inviting me to be buoyed up, up, up into her happy world; I loved the way she caused my heart to tumble whenever, during a restless moment, she seemed about to turn her head in my direction; I loved her more, though torturously, on the many occasions when she did not turn. Because I was a shy boy, I loved the way I could love her silently, at least six hours a day, without ever having to disclose my love.

My platonic state of mind might have stretched onward into a blissful infinity had not Mrs. Esther Clay Boswell, our teacher, made it her business to pry into the affair. Although she prided herself on being a strict disciplinarian, Mrs. Boswell was not without a sense of humor. A round, full-breasted woman in her early forties, she liked to amuse herself, and sometimes the class as well, by calling the attention of all eyes to whomever of us violated the structure she imposed on classroom activities. She was particularly hard on people like me who could not contain an impulse to daydream, or those who allowed their eyes to wander too far away from lessons printed on the blackboard. A black and white sign posted under the electric clock next to the door summed up her attitude toward this kind of truancy: NOTICE TO ALL CLOCKWATCHERS, it read, TIME PASSES, WILL YOU? Nor did she abide timidity in her students. Her voice booming, "Speak up, boy!" was more than enough to cause the more emotional among us, including me, to break into convenient flows of warm tears. But by doing this we violated yet another rule, one on which depended our very survival in Mrs. Esther Clay Boswell's class. She would spell out this rule for us as she paced before her desk, slapping a thick, homemade ruler against the flat of her brown palm. "There ain't no *babies* in here," she would recite. *Thaap!* "Anybody thinks he's still a *baby* . . ." *Thaap!* ". . . should crawl back home to his mama's *titty*." *Thaap!* "You little bunnies shed your *last water* . . ." *Thaap!* ". . . the minute you left home to come in here." *Thaap!* "From now on, you g'on do all your *cryin'* . . ." *Thaap!* ". . . in *church*!" *Thaap!* Whenever one of us compelled her to make this speech it would seem to me that her eyes paused overlong on my face. She would seem to be daring me, as if suspicious that, in addition to my secret passion for Gweneth Lawson, which she might excuse, I was also in the habit of throwing fits of temper.

She had read me right. I was the product of too much attention from my father. He favored me, paraded me around on his shoulder, inflated my ego constantly with what, among us at least, was a high compliment: "You my nigger if you don't get no bigger." This statement, along with my father's generous attentions, made me selfish and used to having my own way. I *expected* to have my own way in most things, and when I could not, I tended to throw tantrums calculated to break through any barrier raised against me.

Mrs. Boswell was also perceptive in assessing the extent of my infatuation with Gweneth Lawson. Despite my stealth in telegraphing emissions of affection into the back part of Gweneth's brain, I could not help but observe, occasionally, Mrs. Boswell's cool glance pausing on the two of us. But she never said a word. Instead, she would settle her eyes momentarily on Gweneth's face and then pass quickly to mine. But in that instant she seemed to be saying, "Don't look back now, girl, but I *know* that bald-headed boy behind you has you on his mind." She seemed to watch me daily, with a combination of amusement and absolute detachment in her brown eyes. And when she stared, it was not at me but at the normal focus of my attention: the end of Gweneth Lawson's black braids. Whenever I sensed Mrs. Boswell watching I would look away quickly, either down at my brown desk top or across the room to the blackboard. But her eyes could not be eluded this easily. Without looking at anyone in particular, she could make a specific point to one person in a manner so general that only long afterward did the real object of her attention realize it had been intended for him.

"Now you little brown bunnies," she might say, "and you black buck rabbits and you few cottontails mixed in, some of you starting to smell yourselves under the arms without knowing what it's all about." And here, it sometimes seemed to me, she allowed her eyes to pause casually on me before resuming their sweep of the entire room. "Now I know your mamas already made you think life is a bed of roses, but in *my* classroom you got to know the footpaths through the *sticky* parts of the rose-bed." It was her custom during this ritual to prod and goad those of us who were developing reputations for meekness and indecision; yet her method was Socratic in that she compelled us, indirectly, to supply our own answers by exploiting one person as the walking symbol of the error she intended to correct. Clarence Buford, for example, an oversized but good-natured boy from a very poor family, served often as the helpmeet in this exercise.

"Buford," she might begin, slapping the ruler against her palm, "how does a tongue-tied country boy like you expect to get a wife?"

"I don't want no wife," Buford might grumble softly.

Of course the class would laugh.

"Oh yes you do," Mrs. Boswell would respond. "All you buck rabbits want wives." *Thaap!* "So how do you let a girl know you not just a bump on a log?"

"I know! I know!" a high voice might call from a seat across from mine. This, of course, would be Leon Pugh. A peanut-brown boy with curly hair, he seemed to know everything. Moreover, he seemed to take pride in being the only one who knew answers to life questions and would wave his arms excitedly whenever our attentions were focused on such matters. It seemed to me his voice would be extra loud and his arms waved more strenuously whenever he was certain that Gweneth Lawson, seated across from him, was interested in an answer to Mrs. Esther Clay Boswell's question. His eager arms, it seemed to me, would be reaching out to grasp Gweneth instead of the question asked.

"Buford, you twisted-tongue, bunion-toed country boy," Mrs. Boswell might say, ignoring Leon Pugh's hysterical armwaving, "you gonna let a cottontail like Leon get a girlfriend before you?"

"I don't want no girlfriend," Clarence Buford would almost sob. "I don't like no girls."

The class would laugh again while Leon Pugh manipulated his arms like a flight navigator under battle conditions. "I know! I know! I swear to *God* I know!"

When at last Mrs. Boswell would turn in his direction, I might sense that she was tempted momentarily to ask me for an answer. But as in most such exercises, it was the worldly-wise Leon Pugh who supplied this. "What do *you* think, Leon?" she would ask inevitably, but with a rather lifeless slap of the ruler against her palm.

"My daddy told me . . ." Leon would shout, turning slyly to beam at Gweneth, ". . . my daddy and my big brother from the Bronx New York told me that to git *anythin'* in this world you gotta learn how to blow your own horn."

"Why, Leon?" Mrs. Boswell might ask in a bored voice.

"Because," the little boy would recite, puffing out his chest, "because if you don't blow your own horn ain't nobody else g'on blow it for you. That's what my daddy said."

"What do you think about that, Buford?" Mrs. Boswell would ask.

"I don't want no girlfriend anyhow," the puzzled Clarence Buford might say.

And then the cryptic lesson would suddenly be dropped.

This was Mrs. Esther Clay Boswell's method of teaching. More than anything written on the blackboard, her questions were calculated to make us turn around in our chairs and inquire in guarded whispers of each other, and especially of the wise and confident Leon Pugh, "What does she mean?" But none of us, besides Pugh, seemed able to comprehend what it was we ought to know but did not know. And Mrs. Boswell, plump brown fox that she was, never volunteered any more in the way of confirmation than was necessary to keep us interested. Instead, she paraded around us, methodically slapping the homemade ruler against her palm, suggesting by her silence more depth to her question, indeed, more implications in Leon's answer, than we were then able to perceive. And during such moments, whether inspired by selfishness or by the peculiar way Mrs. Boswell looked at me, I felt that finding answers to such questions was a task she had set for me, of all the members of the class.

Of course Leon Pugh, among other lesser lights, was my chief rival for the affections of Gweneth Lawson. All during the school year, from September through the winter rains, he bested me in my attempts to look directly into her eyes and say a simple, heartfelt, "hey." This was my ambition, but I never seemed able to get close enough to her attention. At Thanksgiving I helped draw a bounteous yellow cornucopia on the blackboard, with fruits and flowers matching the colors that floated around Gweneth's head; Leon Pugh made one by himself, a masterwork of silver paper and multicolored crepe, which he hung on the door. Its silver tail curled upward to a point just below the face of Mrs. Boswell's clock. At Christmas, when we drew names out of a hat for the exchange of gifts, I drew the name of Queen Rose Phipps, a fairly unattractive squash-yellow girl of absolutely no interest to me. Pugh, whether through collusion with the boy who handled the lottery or through pure luck, pulled forth from the hat the magic name of Gweneth Lawson. He gave her a set of deep purple bows for her braids and a basket of pecans from his father's tree. Uninterested now in the spirit of the occasion, I delivered to Queen Rose Phipps a pair of white socks. Each time Gweneth wore the purple bows she would glance over at Leon and smile. Each time Queen Rose wore my white socks I would turn away in embarrassment, lest I should see them pulling down into her shoes and exposing her skinny ankles.

After class, on wet winter days, I would trail along behind Gweneth to the bus stop, pause near the steps while she entered, and follow her down the aisle until she chose a seat. Usually, however, in clear violation of the code of conduct to which all gentlemen were expected to adhere, Leon Pugh would already be on the bus and shouting to passersby, "Move off! Get away! This here seat by me is reserved for the girl from Brooklyn New York." Discouraged but not defeated, I would swing into the seat next nearest her and cast calf-eyed glances of wounded affection at the back of her head or at the brown, rainbow profile of her face. And at her stop, some eight or nine blocks from mine, I would disembark behind her along with a crowd of other love-struck boys. There would then follow a well-rehearsed scene in which all of us save Leon Pugh, pretended to have gotten off the bus either too late or too soon to wend our proper paths homeward. And at slight cost to ourselves we enjoyed the advantage of being able to walk close by her as she glided toward her uncle's green-frame house. There, after pausing on the wooden steps and smiling radiantly around the crowd like a spring sun in that cold winter rain, she would sing, "Bye, y'all," and disappear into the structure with the mystery of a goddess. Afterward I would walk away, but slowly, much slower than the other boys, warmed by the music and light in her voice against the sharp wet winds of the February afternoon.

I loved her, dear Gloria, and I danced with her and smelled the lemony youth of her and told her that I loved her, all this in a way you would never believe.

TREY ELLIS

Home Repairs

December 18–20, 1981

Jenny

She came for the weekend and just left.

The doorbell rang and Austin Pavlov scurried through his usual routine. I scooted upstairs to my parents' bedroom to reexamine my hair, running on tiptoes to muffle the noise.

Jenny looked the same, and we hugged. She took a cab from the train station but didn't have enough money, so I had to pay the guy. I must admit that in a stupid, old-fashioned sexist way it made me feel like a man.

Immediately we talked and talked and talked. I even turned off the TV. Mom came back and let us use the car. I drove Jenny to the New Haven green, and we walked around the college bars in the cold. Now that I am in college myself, this town seems so dinky. I can't believe I used to worship college students. The drinking age is still eighteen in Connecticut, so we went to the Anchor Bar. In California it's twenty-one, so you can only drink at school parties. We were carded at the door, but luckily Jenny turned eighteen this summer.

She was still full of incredible stories. For her birthday last month she went to Philadelphia and was supposed to meet some friends at a discotheque there but couldn't find them. She was broke and didn't have their number, so she just asked a guy leaving the place if she could crash on his couch. She swears she didn't sleep with him. They just messed around and when she said she had to get to sleep, he was "totally cool about it."

Then this other guy from Haverford College came to Vassar for some party, and by the end of the night he had punched her in the eye. "But, Austin, it was no big deal. He was shitfaced."

Dinner with the family (except Leslie, who was away on a ski trip with her goony jillionaire friends), and Jenny was telling cleaner but nevertheless incredible stories about professors accusing her of cheating right in the middle of class and one about a senior woman sending two hulking field hockey goalies over to her room to tell her to lay off the senior's West Pointer. Mom and Dad hardly touched their food.

"Austin, change the sheets in Leslie's room for your little friend." I hate it when Dad says that. Then the 'rents went to bed.

She helped me stretch and tuck the sheets. I turned on my sister's color TV. I closed us inside my sister's pink room.

"So the TV won't bother my folks." I don't know why I was trying to outsmart her, the queen of seduction. "Would you care for a massage?"

She stretched over my sister's bed as if she had won it. Leslie's *Willard*-era Michael Jackson poster grinned over Jenny's back and my hands. I massaged inside her blouse and purposefully ran into her bra strap again and again, hoping she'd give in and spring her back free. With each pass of my hands, knead of my fingers, she moaned like she was coming. I hoped she didn't notice that I stiffened and angled an ear to the door and inched Leslie's pillow closer to Jenny's open, twisting mouth. She moaned louder, dragged her purple nails up the sides of my jeans.

"Your turn, tiger." I rolled off my T-shirt, and she actually sighed! My boner swelled and swelled in electric waves until I felt this twinge down there. Overstimulated, but who cares. How can you be "over"-stimulated anyway? (I'd find out later.) After rubbing deep into my muscles, she began whispering just the pads of her long fingers down my back. Vast fields of goose bumps miraculously plumped to life behind her electric sweep. My hands swallowed the bedspread. I reached back and caressed her calves as she had mine. Her body stopped. I pushed myself up and was proud of the point my crotch now made.

"Jenny, do you want your birthday present?" I stared at her through my lowered eyebrows, wiggled my head a bit in a sexy way.

I moved in and kissed her without hesitation. Pretty long and with tongues.

"You're a better kisser than I thought."

"Teach me to be better." I kissed her again.

"Not here, this is your own sister's bed."

"Exactly."

"You're sick."

"I know."

"I've got to go brush my teeth. Then let's go downstairs."

We inched out of the room. Sounds from the "Tonight" show and the gray TV light leaked out of the crack at the bottom of my parents' door. Jenny left me for the bathroom in the hallway, and I eased down the creaky stairs.

The TV room's burnt-orange, steel-cone fireplace, Mom's mystery books insulating the walls, the wicker coffee table, and the expired *TV Guide*, they were so much a part of my normal life that to see them there unchanged by my change seemed bizarre.

Somehow I didn't hear her until she was crossing the kitchen.

We lay next to each other on the rug and kissed and kissed and kissed. I caressed her sides, swept down to her butt, then up to her breasts through her shirt. She kissed my neck and chin, and which way was up just then I did not know. She stopped.

"I wonder what's wrong with me?"

"What do you mean? You're fantastic." You never know when Jenny's going to go off the deep end.

"Thanks, I needed to hear that."

My fingers lay between hers, and I noticed we were the identical brown. The peace I felt with her then I had only imagined in Reno.

Then I noticed the nightgown in her hand. She rose to change in the little bathroom off the kitchen. As soon as she was gone I noticed that I wasn't up and that I had to pee. I waited twelve minutes for her to change. Maybe she was new to putting in a diaphragm.

I didn't want to chance creaking back upstairs to the bathroom. I opened the side door to go in the garden, but it was fifteen degrees outside. Pumpkin's kitty litter box sat at the landing to the basement stairs. I peed and peed, until the box looked like a Barbie doll swimming pool. You don't realize how much bigger a human's bladder is than a cat's until something like this comes up. I emptied an entire fresh bag of Kitty Litter on top.

Jenny stepped out of the bathroom.

"Sorry it took so long. We'd better get to sleep. I'll go up first." She kissed me good night and crept away and up. Still, I went to bed more happy than confused.

Yesterday we spent the whole day walking around New Haven. I took her to the British Art Collection and we made fun of the ugly old paintings of pasty women with rosy cheeks fondling bowls of fruit.

(Jenny just called from the Hartford bus terminal. She took a Trailways back up to Springfield, Mass. She said, "Thanks, Austin. I just had to call you. I had a great time. You've got sexy lips."!!!!!)

So anyway, yesterday we did all this stuff, but she was actually a bit cool. I tried to hold her hand, but she wasn't into it. I forgot to mention that after breakfast I tried to sneak a kiss when no one was looking, but no dice.

That night I took her out to eat at Edge of the Green, one of the fanciest places in New Haven. I ordered wine, and we were not even carded. I put my arm around her a few times, but she didn't seem to care. At home I was shitting bricks. Mom was asleep and Dad was at a conference in New York. Jenny and I were lying on the rug downstairs again, but she just kept reading my dad's *GQ* as if I were dead. I put my arm around her and kissed her ear. I tried to rest my head in her lap, but she pushed me away. I drew the magazine out of her fingers and rolled her onto her back. I dangled myself over her and kissed her lips and her neck. I pressed my tongue between her lips. Andover flashed back to me, CPR class when I shot my tongue down the rubber throat of "Resuscitation Annie," the waxy, dead dummy you practice on.

"Isn't this like making out with a log?" Jenny said. "I just don't feel like it." Her voice was weird, entertained. She smiled as she talked. "Look, Austin, yesterday I didn't get the reaction I wanted."

What?? My answer was to try to kiss her some more, but she pinched my face. I extended my lips between her pinch so they looked like a sea creature inside its shell.

"Listen. What do you expect out of this?"

I expect marriage, children, a lifetime of bliss with you, the first and last woman I will ever love.

"Nothing," I said. "Just a nighttime of fun between friends."

I kissed her, and this time she kissed back slightly.

"And what was the matter with last night?"

Her crazy look seemed to say, "You mean, you really don't even *know*!" But this is what she did say:

"Analyze, think, then act or react."

She likes being cryptic and in control. I told her as much, and she agreed.

"Analyze," I said, and screwed closed my brow, focusing my brain on the problem at hand. "Think," I then said with a silent movie-ish pensive scratch of my cheek. "Act or react." I then sprang and smothered her, kissing her whole face. She let me kiss her and responded a tad more, then she got up to get a Pepsi and drank it slowly.

"Hurry up already," I said.

She just flipped only her eyes away from that aluminum can. She finished with a contented "Ahhhh." She rose, snatched up her toothbrush and paste, swung through the TV room door.

She returned, and we were making out for a bit when she said, "Move on top of me." We dry-humped for days and days, she moaned like a porn star, I felt her breasts through her dress, felt her nipples awaken.

"Oh, my pants are ruined." I hadn't really come in my pants, at least not officially, but I guessed that was the "reaction" she had wanted to eke out of me last night. And I guess it worked because she smiled big and locked her legs around mine and play-fucked me hard. I tried sneaking hands down the V of her cleavage, up the slits on the sides of her dress, but it was too tight all around.

"You don't know what to do with my dress, do you?"

I faked a pass for her boobs up her narrow sleeves, and she laughed. I am actually being aggressive and charming, like James Bond or something, I remember thinking. Then she unbuttoned my shirt and tingled my body with her hands.

Just then the front door closed.

"Your dad!" She jumped to the bathroom. I clumsily buttoned one button on my shirt and waited, mummy rigid on the edge of the sofa, to be caught and destroyed. I could hear him standing on the other side of the TV room door, wondering why I was up so late. Then he must have turned and stepped up the stairs to bed.

Jenny peeped out of the bathroom and wouldn't do any more kissing. It literally took more than an hour (from two-fourteen to three-twenty) to get her back to where we were. But now she was wearing her nightgown, so access was eased greatly. The granny nightgown buttoned from toes to clavicle, so I started at the top, each button affording a better and better view of her beautiful brown swells. When I finally saw her small, full breasts and saw her nipples hard as nipples can be just because of me, I wanted to stop my life right then. That's enough, I was thinking. Quit while you're ahead.

I kissed her chest and tasted her nipples, sucked on one as I'd seen in *Deep Throat*. Gently I pinched the other while my other hand squeezed her butt and traced its crack. It was an out-of-body experience, and I saw myself working on her expertly—yes, expertly, I had found a groove, found my calling, and transcended the everyday shittiness of my usual reality. I tried a hand for her panty's elastic.

"Austin, I don't want to get all slimy."

Instead, I retreated to suctioning her breasts, and she clutched my head to her chest.

"Oh, God. Oh, God . . . Sorry, honey, but I have to go to the bathroom." When she returned she said, "Now it's your turn."

I hoped to God she would touch it.

"Actually, Austin, I'm pretty beat."

My eyes flew wide and she smiled. "Psych your mind!"

I smiled until she moved her head down my chest and her hands up my leg.

"You're horny," she said.

"Are you ever horny?"

"I'm horny now."

The touch was almost painful, it was so exquisite. She squeezed everywhere near it, then dragged her head lower and lower until she was nuzzling the waistband of my underwear! Somewhere, alarms went off. Emergency teams scrambled. The impossible suddenly seemed possible. I moved to unbutton my belt, and she suddenly raised her lips from my belly button.

"Don't push it," she said.

Relatching my belt reignited her, and her chin actually brushed my pubic hair. I twitched down there, but it didn't feel as though I'd come. She rose from my stomach.

"Sorry for torturing you like that, sweetheart." But her smile held no apology at all.

For hours we vaguely watched TV, lightly napped in each other's arms, rested easily together. Marriage must be like this, I thought. Once in a while my hand scouted the world near her crotch but was always attacked by her closing legs.

"I haven't had this much fun in a long time, Austin."

I couldn't have paid her to say sweeter words.

"Jenny, I can't believe this is happening." She was lying inside my opened legs. If we were naked, I would have been inside her. I can't remember how many times we told each other we should get some sleep. I looked inside my heart and found there for perhaps the first time in my life nothing but shimmering joy. I kissed through her nightgown just past her belly button, and she jackknifed around my head but urged it away.

"Someday we will make love," she said.

At six twenty-three I tucked her in with a thousand kisses.

Four hours later, after brunch with the 'rents, I drove her to the train station and we kissed on the platform, then kissed through the open window. I prayed some New York-bound friend would have seen me. Our last kiss was the best.

She, an internationally known expert, was supremely turned on. I think I will be a good lover, maybe even great. Unless she was faking it. . . . Naaaah. But I am concerned about not coming. Why am I really excited but semiflaccid? The time with the whore I was also semiflaccid and didn't know when I came.

It's still so unreal. I remember back on the Vineyard, a lifetime ago, biting my pillow and screaming, "I'm in love, I'm in love!" Delectable pain flushed me. I was so shy back then. Could the dark days be through?

CHESTER HIMES

The Lonely Crusade

Lee Gordon walked west on Sunset now, his raincoat buttoned and belted and the collar turned up against the world. The twelve o'clock curfew had long since closed the bars, but still the people filled the streets—servicemen and working women—in their frantic search. But Lee Gordon did not notice them. His face was set in slanting lines and his eyes were luminous with brooding.

It was not so much that she had refused to quit, he thought, as that she had not wanted to. That made the difference. And yet, in this rare lucid moment, he could not really blame her for not wanting to give up the lot she had gained for the little he had to offer. She had no way of knowing what this particular job of hers did to him, that for each development of her own personality he paid a price in loss of self-esteem.

But what really made it hopeless, he thought, was the character of her intentions. He knew that concern for his own welfare was a part of everything she ever did. She was not only convinced of this herself—it was true. So it was doubly unfortunate that the effects she struggled so ardently to achieve never served her purpose. Instead of his being benefited by what she intended to be benefiting, he was injured. Words of encouragement became blows to his pride, actions aimed to inspire his courage nursed his fear, and logic offered to point the goal for him so often confused his purpose. And this was due to the fact that these intentions, while good and noble, grew out of her ignorance of the essential character of his frustrations and became destructive condescensions instead of constructive assistance to the need they were to serve. She deserved credit for trying, he thought, even though her motives were not always unselfish. It was not her fault that in all the things she tried to do for him, she was the one to benefit. And this, he felt, was just. This was right. Yet that did not keep it from being ironic also.

Well—yes, Lee Gordon thought, looking up.

He was at Jackie's. He had walked the seven miles without realizing where he was going. And for an instant he was touched by a sense of omnipresence.

Then of the THEE IN ME *who works behind*
The Veil, I lifted up my hands to find
A Lamp amid the Darkness; and I heard,
As from Without—"THE ME WITHIN THEE BLIND!"

The involution of a mystic, yes, and the actions of a fool, Lee Gordon thought.

"Who is it?" Jackie asked when he knocked upon her door.

"Lee."

She opened the door and stood aside to let him enter, her face showing neither pleasure nor surprise, only a composed complacence as if she had always known that he would come in the night like this.

"Is Kathy asleep?"

She closed the door and locked it. "She's away."

He turned and looked at her ethereal face with open-mouthed wonder and could not breathe at all. Emotions burned through him like flame, and all the things he had always wanted to say to her came clearly worded to his lips. But he said only: "You're beautiful, Jackie," because that said it all.

Now it was in her eyes again, that winning look. Without replying she turned quickly away from him and crossed to close the bedroom door. Watching the natural unaccented pulsing of her hips, he went sick with desire for her and began stripping off his rain coat, tearing at the buttons.

She turned and came back. "What happened, Lee?"

"I'm just tired, Jackie."

"Would you like to go to bed?"

Their gazes hung: his questioning, hers level and unreadable.

"With you?"

She smiled for the first time, friendly, motherly. "Don't be so old-fashioned, Lee. I'm a Communist. If you're tired you may sleep with me. I've slept with many men—" and just before she opened the bedroom door she completed: "who didn't have me." Now matter-of-factly she asked: "Would you like some coffee or something to eat?"

"Well—no. No thanks."

And then he began to undress, excitement beating at his heart and fear throttling him as with a garrote. His common sense tried to inform him that this was no uncommon thing, but his body jerked with a thousand alarms. Jackie had already returned to bed, and when he entered the room without night clothes, she simply turned over and put out the light.

For a moment he lay there away from her, not touching her, and then he said: "Jackie—" in a tone that made it clear.

When she did not immediately reply, he turned, groping, and her breast came alive in his hand. She waited a moment longer, then pushed him gently away.

"You can't have me, Lee."

It went tart, bitter, brackish, and went through him like bile. And suddenly it stilled to a quiet resolution and he said to himself: Yes, yes, I'll do it. I'll sleep naked with this young, beautiful, desirable white woman. And I will not touch her.

When finally he spoke aloud his voice was apologetic. "I might not be able to sleep, but I'll try not to keep you awake."

"You can get so tired you can't go to sleep," she murmured.

"Mine is more mental."

"Would you like for me to play you something?"

"Play me something?"

"Music."

"Oh!—Well—"

"Yes," she finished with a little laugh, snapping on the light and slipping out of bed.

He had the sudden crazy feeling of being hurled through life by the emotions of others, by idiocies and insanities and false values in which he had no part.

And then the opening movement of some unfamiliar symphony sounded with arresting tone. His mind opened and deepened, absorbing the music. Strained and cleared and soared and trod the notes to fantasy in a darkness rocked by Jackie's gentle breathing.

One moment, it was a morning in spring, taking his breath in a burst of newness. And another, taps for the dead, tearing out his heart. It was the merciless cruelty of people, bruising his soul. And then a pastoral scene beside a waterfall, anointing his wounds. It was the majestic march of mountains through his heart, the laughter of the ages in his throat, the roll of man-made thunder in his stomach, a softly played organ in an empty church, and a baby crying in the night.

And his thoughts were like tongueless words, like his black skin trying to speak, like the mute prayers of the dark scared night, like life itself trying to tell him of its mystery in a language never heard, only felt.

It helped more than he could ever say.

Suddenly he began to cry. He buried his face between her breasts and she stroked his kinky hair. He wanted to tell her how much it had helped, but the words still had no tongue.

After a time he stopped crying and turned over away from her looking up into the darkness. "It got me for a moment," he whispered.

She put her arms about him and drew him back to her.

Never so violently responsive, so flagrantly wanton, so completely consuming, but it was not the same. In it was a defiance of the forbidden, shaping it in a way he could not tell.

For a long time afterward they were silent, then she asked: "What's the matter, darling?"

"I'm just unhappy."

"I knew it when I first saw you. You're just frustrated, darling."

"Perhaps I am."

"Frustration always begins with sex, the lack of gratification—"

"But not with you."

And for a long time again they were silent.

"What are you thinking about, darling?" she finally asked.

"You."

"What are you thinking about me, darling?"

"I was wondering how you would be as my wife."

"I would be a wonderful wife to you, darling."

"I bet you would."

"Would you like for me to get up and fix something to eat?" she offered.

"No, kiss me—"

"You're sweet," he said afterward. And a moment later mused: "I wonder why white women are so much more affectionate to Negro men than our own women are."

"It's only in your mind," she said.

"How in my mind?"

"In your mind we are the ultimate."

Lee Gordon vaguely wondered whether to be flattered or insulted, and to avoid deciding, smothered her in his arms.

"And we can give you happiness," she thought triumphantly, offering her body with warm, passionate surrender to another ecstasy.

She could give him this illusion of manhood even while denying that he possessed it, for to her he was the recipient of her grace. But Ruth could give him nothing that to her he did not have. So with Jackie he had these moments that rightfully belonged to Ruth. It could have been wonderful with

Ruth, for she had all that Jackie feigned. But he could never be for her what Jackie could make of him for her own designs.

And yet in the morning when they parted, he had given Jackie infinitely more than she had given him. But he did not know it.

CALVIN C. HERNTON

Sex and Racism in America

I am not absolutely certain at what age I became conscious of my color as a limitation on where I could go, sit, or with whom I could associate. I think it was during my seventh year, for that was when I received my first beating for associating with a white female.

I know I was quite young, because the incident occurred in connection with my long hikes from grammar school, which was about four miles from my house. After traveling half the distance the other Negro children would gradually break off and go their separate ways. I would walk the rest of the way to my house alone. One afternoon, I met another child who had books and was about my age, or at least my size. At first, we did not say anything. But as the days went on, we began to talk to each other, we became friends and made a habit of meeting at the intersection of our similar yet different routes home. Every afternoon we romped up and down the street. I think we argued once—about what I do not recall. I know I hit her because of the argument. She cried. I apologized. After that we became greater friends.

One day my grandmother appeared on the sidewalk before us. I did not know where she came from. She seemed just to *be* there, and, although I did not know what the trouble was, I sensed from the look on her face that something was terribly wrong. My grandmother, who was not yet fifty, caught me by the back of my collar, and literally dragged me all the way home. She did not speak a word. At home, she gave me the beating of my life. I yelled and kicked, and I did not know what I had done . . . yet, I think, on some level of consciousness, I knew that it had something to do with my friend. When Grandmother finished lashing my backside with her belt, bubbles of perspiration stood on her hot, black face. Then she began to lash me with her tongue.

"Boy, is you done gone clean out of your mind!" There was terror in her eyes, and I looked at her dumbly.

"Do you want to git yoself lynched! Messing round wit a *white* gurl! A little, trashy, white heifer. Do you want to git me kilt! Git all the colored folks slaughtered . . ."

On and on she went. Her words put a fear into me that I have never forgotten—the same fear that was instilled so deeply in her that, as she talked, her whole body trembled. I began to tremble also; for, I believe, at that moment I was awakened to a vital part of me that somehow I would have to kill. And it was then, only then, that I began to cry.

No white person knows, really knows, how it is to grow up as a Negro boy in the South. The taboo of the white woman eats into the psyche, erodes away significant portions of boyhood sexual development, alters the total concept of masculinity, and creates in the Negro male a hidden ambivalence towards all women, black as well as white.

I do not know if other black boys had the fear of the white women instilled in their minds through as shocking an incident as I. I do know that they learned it. The particular incident may vary from Negro to Negro, but the lesson is the same: avoid the woman that is white, act as if she does not exist. I learned as a boy, and later as a man, to bow and avert my eyes whenever talking to a white woman. In the South a Negro never looks a white woman straight in the face, never marvels at her figure no matter how attractive she is. On buses, in stores, on crowded streets, the Negro, at all costs, must avoid physical contact with white flesh. In Mississippi and other places in the Deep South, it is reported jokingly that a Negro must step off the sidewalk when a white woman approaches. This is not far from the truth. I know for a fact that it is dangerous in the South for a Negro to be caught (arrested, for instance) with a photograph of a white female in his possession. It would take a lot of nerve for a Negro to express his admiration for a movie star (Marilyn Monroe, Sophia Loren, etc.) in the company of a southern white man. John Dollard, in *Caste and Class in a Southern Town*, tells of an incident where a Negro was afraid to receive a simple letter from a white woman. Even in the North, as I shall show in more detail later, the Negro's fear of the consequences of being familiar with a white woman is not unusual.

Because he must act like a eunuch when it comes to white women, there arises within the Negro an undefined sense of dread and self-mutilation. Psychologically he experiences himself as castrated.

If a Negro acts differently, he runs the risk of being jailed, beaten, or lynched. Nevertheless, many Negroes run this risk. In secrecy, among themselves in pool rooms, on street corners, late at night when no white person is around, you can hear Negro men and teen-agers whispering and sometimes talking aloud about their adventures with white women. Each man who tells a story is laughed at, rebuffed, and "put down." The talk swirls as in a childhood fantasy. Yet every man knows that not all of the stories are lies or pure wishful thinking. Too often the news leaks out about a chauffeur caught redhanded, a handyman escaped North, a teen-ager lynched or electrocuted.

Always the crime is "rape," but everybody, especially the white women, rich or "poor trash," knows better.

I do not propose to evaluate the singular, long-range effects of the beating my grandmother gave me as a result of associating with a white girl. How can I? So much has taken place since then, both *to* me and *in* me. I know this: had my grandmother not discovered my particular transgression against the ethics of segregation when she did, it would have been only a matter of time before someone else would have noticed, and the consequence might or might not have been as severe as a beating. What was important for me—as it is for every Negro boy in the South—was that I gradually learned to fear and hate white girls. My hatred was as immobile as my fear. I feared and hated without understanding. The thought as well as the sight of a white woman completely awed me, and since I knew the white woman was taboo, although not precisely why, an ominous gloom settled upon my mood and lingered throughout my early life.

I remember, during the Depression, standing with my grandmother in long, endless lines with other black folks, waiting for hours, day in and day out, and never reaching the doors of the building inside of which potatoes and fatback meat were being issued. All the while the white women and their children were moving up and onward. When at last, after our legs and faces were frozen from standing all day, and we were inside, the white women behind the counter (who were merely teen-age girls) would tell Grandmother that there was no food. They were arrogant, flippant, and would usher us back out in the cold, empty-handed. Tears would hang in Grandmother's eyes as she would begin to moan the old spiritual about being "A Stranger in Dis Land." And that would seem to comfort her. It did not comfort me.

I knew that my grandmother knew that those girls were lying. There was food, and it was being given to the white women who pushed and shoved us around. I knew Grandmother was a proud, self-willed woman, and I could not understand why she belittled herself before those nasty, lying white girls. I hated those girls. I hated all white women. More important, there arose in me an incipient resentment towards my grandmother, indeed, towards all black women—because I could not help but compare them with white women, and in all phases of public life it was the Negro female who bowed her head and tucked her tail between her legs like a little black puppy.

I think now—no, I *know* now—that this is one of the reasons Negro women encounter so much frustration with their men. Living in a society where the objective social position and the reputed virtues of white women smother whatever worth black women may have, the Negro male is put to judging his women by what he sees and imagines the white woman is. A common expression among Negro males when anything goes wrong between them and their women is to say that a white woman would act differently. Without ever having associated with, let alone having been married to, a white woman, the black man asserts, half-heartedly but significantly, that black women are hell to get along with! The fact that this may be said about all American women does little to alter the black man's depreciatory concept of Negro females. How can it? For the myth of white womanhood has soaked into the Negro's skin. In matters of beauty, manners, social graces, and womanly virtues, the white woman is elevated by American society to the status of a near goddess. Everywhere, the Negro hears about and sees these nymph-like creatures. The Negro's world is thoroughly invaded by the white woman—the mass media, newspapers, magazines, radio, and especially television, bring these lily sirens into the blackness of the Negro's home and mind. It becomes all but impossible for the black man to separate his view of the *ideal* woman from that of the *white* woman. He may do it intellectually, cognitively, but it is a far more difficult feat to achieve emotionally! This is the reason many Negro men feel an estranged resentment towards black women, although they have no alternative but to live with and try to love them.

The human ego is, in large part, a reflection of (or an internalization of) what happens when one person encounters another person. This is especially true when the encounter involves individuals of the opposite sex. Before Grandmother whipped me, a girl was just a girl. After the beating, all females took on a meaning beyond their sex, a meaning symbolized and defined by the color of their skins. And this meaning, this symbolization of pigment severely altered my developing concept of myself as a black boy—a Negro male—in a world of black and white creatures called women. Although I did not understand the ethics of southern Jim Crow, I adhered to them. As long as I attended that school I walked out of my way to avoid my white friend, and I have never seen her again. But in the dream world, in the world of fantasy and nightmare, I saw her—and have seen her—countless times. And this—the autistic, or vicarious, compensation for the injury one suffers in real life—does not make for therapy, but adds to the diseased way in which the Negro male conceives of himself, of white women, and of black women too.

For reasons I consider irrelevant here, I have always wanted a sister. The rest is not irrelevant. Shortly after my first "lesson" in Jim Crow, I began to dream that I had a sister. Sometimes my sister would be colored. Most of the time she would be white—and even the colored sister would be of such light skin that if she wanted to (or if *I* wanted her to) she could pass for white. In both cases, one of the functions of my imaginary sister was to introduce me to imaginary interracial couples. My sister was beautiful, you see, and, of course, not prejudiced. Most of all, she *loved* me. We, my sister, and our interracial friends would do all kinds of things that young people ordinarily do. We played, went to movies, went on bus outings, and so on. We would even fight, but only to make up and become greater comrades. When I say I had such dreams, I do not mean dreaming merely while asleep, I mean daydreaming, outright childhood fantasizing. I made the world *good*; I made black and white people—especially men and women—like and enjoy each other. And yet, there was always the "outside world," a hostile world of blacks and whites of whom we—I, my sister, and friends—had to be cautious. For instance, I fantasized a fabulous apartment left to us by our parents *(you see, our parents were dead)*. And this was where we spent most of our time, hidden from the outside world. When *we* went somewhere in public, we acted in such a way that people could not really tell that we were together. Frequently my dreams assumed a deeper, perhaps more psychiatric, dimension. I would, with her consent, have sex with my sister, the colored one. And always she would turn into the white sister. I would begin to scream and run, thinking she was going to yell and bring down the white community on me and my grandmother. But she never did; instead, she would hold me and reassure me that no one would ever know. I always woke up in a cold sweat.

These dreams and fantasies persisted on an ever widening and deepening level throughout my teens—that is, until I finished high school. At that time I began to date rather seriously. My dates were always light-skinned Negro girls, never dark or black ones, no matter how pretty they might have been. For, I know now, my desire for a girl was affected by the myth and taboo of the white woman. I know now why I enjoyed the envy of other black boys—because I had a light-skinned girl friend. As we walked the streets, all eyes, black and white, would linger or flash quickly upon us. And I was proud. But not proud enough. I felt a partial fulfillment of my ego as a black boy, but it was only partial—because although my girl was very light with long black hair, she was still a Negro. She was, for that alone, not as good as a real white girl. I made up for this also by dreaming. Often while we sat cheek to cheek in the dark of a movie, I would look at her through the depraved eye of my mind and imagine her as white—and sometimes I would even grow afraid to touch her face. At about that time the Negro press had made big headlines of an event in Georgia: a Negro had failed to help a desperate white woman escape from the flaming wreckage of an automobile, because he had been afraid of the consequences of laying his black hands on her flesh in order to pull her free. The woman had perished.

To every Negro boy who grows up in the South, the light-skinned Negro woman—the "high yellow," the mulatto—incites awe. The white woman incites *more* awe. As a boy I was, to say the least, confused. As I grew older, the desire to see what it was that made white women so dear and angelic became a secret, grotesque burden to my psyche. It is that to almost all Negro men, no matter how successfully they hide and deny it. And for these reasons—the absurd idolization of the white woman and the equal absurdity of the taboo surrounding her—there arises within almost all Negroes a sociosexually induced predisposition for white women. The fact that few Negroes will readily admit this is due more to their knowledge that black women and whites in general bitterly disapprove of it, than to their honesty. For if a situation occurs where a white woman makes herself accessible to a black man, the Negro usually takes her. However cautiously, he takes her at once like a grateful baby and like a savage monster. He suffers mixed emotions of triumph, fulfillment, and guilt. At eighteen I had an affair with a white girl in a small town in Alabama. She met me one night in an abandoned railroad yard. I was nervous and scared, not primarily that someone might discover us—although I was scared of that too—but mainly just because she was *white*. I kissed her mouth. I wanted to see if it was different, if it was better than a black mouth. I looked at her for the first time directly and long. It felt like magic—and yet why? Why! I was baffled over whatever white women were supposed to possess that made them objects of grave consequences. Why were they so important? I wondered about her anatomy. I ran my hands over her body. I wanted to know if it was different, if it felt better than black flesh. I kept wanting to find out what made white womanhood *white womanhood*; I wanted to unearth the quality that made her angelic and forbidden.

My search failed. There was nothing objectively or inherently emotional that was *that* different or angelic. Yet there was something—and it was distorted and horrible. There was all of the southern ideology of racism and sex that had been instilled in my mind, in my very skin, and no doubt in hers too. Cautiously, diligently, maddeningly I took her. I hated her for what she made me feel, for the good and bad that she inspired in me; for what she *reduced* me to. I loved her too! But somehow I could not purge myself of the feeling that it was wrong and perverse. I came away not knowing whether I felt elated or outraged.

RICHARD PERRY

No Other Tale to Tell

"Don't go," she said.

He was sitting in the chair she'd cleared for him the day before, legs crossed. He touched a hand to his forehead. She was furious with embarrassment and need, furious that she'd said it.

"I'm not going anywhere, Carla. At least not yet. What is it? Why you hurt so bad?"

She was comforted a little; she was frightened.

"It'll be all right," she said. "It's just been trying."

What a word—*trying*. She tried to smile, but smiling wouldn't come.

"What is it?"

"I'll be all right," she said.

He moved to her across a room cluttered with books and magazines.

"Tell me," he said.

He pulled, she let him; she was in his arms, her face in a curve of throat and shoulder, breathing fish bait, lime aftershave. She took the risk of looking into his eyes. They were brown and curious and kind. They made her want to weep. She'd find a way to explain it. It was only for this little while; she wouldn't give her heart.

"Oh, Lord," she said. "Help me."

"Tell me. How can I help?"

"Hold me." Maybe that would be enough.

He held her. Behind her eyes a humming made her quiver. She was wet, open. Had he been another man, she'd have pulled him to the couch.

"Come to bed with me."

He leaned back, careful. "Is that what you want?"

"Yes."

"You sure?"

"Yes. But only if you want to."

"Is it too quick?"

"I don't know. Not if you want to."

"Okay," Miles said. "I do."

She took his hand, led him upstairs to the room no man had entered, stood while he undressed her. He paused, eyes narrowed, touched her scars.

"The fire," she said. "I . . ."

He pressed a palm to her mouth, kissed her back. His lips were cool. She shivered, lay across the bed, admiring his body as he undressed, the flat, graceful planes, the thickening between his thighs. He was standing the way he'd stood yesterday on her porch, allowing her to look.

She said, "I've got to go to the bathroom."

"Okay."

In the bathroom, leg raised, one foot resting on the tub's edge, she put in her diaphragm. Then she turned to the mirror, holding her shoulders, arms across her breasts. She looked haunted. "He's black," she said. "He's in my bedroom."

She opened the medicine chest, took out cologne, dabbed behind her ears, beneath her breasts, stood wide-legged, left rose scent on her thighs.

When she returned, he was standing naked at the window. She closed the door.

"Miles?"

He turned, held out his hand. She crossed the room, drew him to the bed. Her left breast slipped beneath her arm as he stretched beside her; their knees collided. He touched her face, and when she moved again, they were on their sides, thighs and bellies flush. He had ripples in his stomach, like a washboard. Shifting, she raised her top leg, slung it across his waist; the fit was perfect. She was trying to feel everything at once, but that was impossible, and she focused on the hands stroking her back, thinking how gentle he was, how he touched, the way he moved. The stroking was peeling away the outer layers, the gauzelike protection she was wrapped in. She was warm and almost safe and she tried to give up all the way, to let him touch the core, the wounded infant heart, but it was too frightening, too much like falling into a hole whose only map was depth and darkness. She stiffened, and he held tight until she found a place she could allow him to touch without panic. It was like slipping into a healing sleep, except that here was his smell, here the hard/soft body planes, his hands, and the rigid tube against her belly.

She wasn't sure when it changed, if he moved, or she, but where she'd been warm, now she was burning; he was on top, inside her with a thrust that took her last breath, the one she only now realized that she'd been saving. She wrapped her legs around his waist, squeezed, and found, to her astonishment, that she was coming. Eyes wide, breath whistling in short, hard bursts, she rode out the convulsions, then lay collecting her scattered self.

He waited. When the whistle left her breath, he kissed her, long and hard, and before she could register marvel at what was happening to her lips, he stared into her eyes and moved again.

In her head, words assembled like a song, repeated: *He looked at me, he looked at me.*

Later, without speaking, he massaged her feet. In a little while she went downstairs, made tea, brought it back to bed, where she sat with knees drawn to her chest, watching him through mist the steaming liquid made. She was trying to do two things at once: to hold to the feeling of being connected and yet prepare for his leaving. Things bubbled on her skin, struggled to get inside; she wouldn't let them. Miles set his cup on the night table, touched her thigh, and smiled. She wanted to say: "What's going to become of us, will you stay forever? Move in with me, we'll plant a garden." But if she did, he'd remind her that he couldn't stay, he was on his way to Arizona. Or he'd artfully evade her, or, "Yes, I'll stay," and then Max would come back and she'd have to admit she'd given up the waiting.

Now, in the confusion caused by that thought, she longed to be alone. She looked at him and saw that his eyes were closed.

"Are you sleeping?"

"No," he said. "How you feel?"

"Okay."

"You sure?"

"Uh-huh."

"That story you told me about the birds," he asked lazily. "Was that true?"

"True?"

"I mean," he said, turning, resting his knee against her waist, "Did it really happen?"

"Why's that important?"

"I don't know. Truth matters. Don't it?"

"It's true," she said, "if you think so."

He laughed. "You mean anything's true if you think it?"

"It's a story. Either you believe it or you don't. That's all. There's a shovel in the basement. You need proof, go dig up in the yard. There still might be some bones left."

There was an edge to her voice. Maybe, he thought, you didn't fuck with a storyteller's tale. Maybe you just listened and took from it what you would.

"Well, it's a good story," he said. "You ought to write it down."

"What for?"

"So you won't forget it."

She grunted, moved so they didn't touch. "I won't forget it."

It was a wonder, he thought, that her grunt didn't have an echo. She was lying next to him, but she might have been on the other side of the Grand Canyon. It could, of course, have nothing to do with the story; it could be how she was after sex. He'd known women who were like that. Once their need was met, a shade got pulled across a window, a high wall built. He let his disappointment sweep him. Still, maybe this worked out for the best. He'd already felt too much too soon, and that for a woman who had her share of problems. He didn't know what they were, just that they were more than he could handle. And he wasn't going to try. He didn't do that anymore.

He lay for what felt like a decent time. Then: "Listen, I gotta be going."

She said, indifferently, "I know."

He rose, began to dress. She watched him, male person in her bedroom. He moved to bedside, bent to kiss her. Their foreheads bumped.

"Sorry," he said.

"You'll forgive me if I don't see you to the door."

"I forgive you."

"It's just . . ."

"It's okay," he said. "I'll talk to you."

She nodded and he was leaving, first his back receding, then everything was gone.

WALTER MOSLEY

White Butterfly

Jesus was doing cartwheels across the lawn in the porch light. Little Edna kept herself upright by holding the bars of her crib. She laughed and sputtered at her mute brother. I came in the gate and picked up a football that was nestled in among the dahlia bushes along the fence. I whistled, then threw the ball just when Jesus turned to see me. He caught the football, held it in one hand, and waved to Edna as if he were beckoning her with the other. She rattled her baby bars, bounced on the balls of her feet, and yelled as loud as she could, "Akach yeeee!"

Jesus kicked the ball so hard that it crashed against the far link fence. The jangling of steel was a kind of music for city children.

"What's goin' on out here?" Regina was framed for a moment by the gray haze of the screen door. She came out on the porch and stood in front of our little girl as if protecting her. Edna let out a howl. She couldn't see Jesus and the yard past her mother's skirts.

"Aw, com'on, honey. She's okay," I said as I mounted the three stairs to the porch.

"He could miss a kick out there an' tear her head off!"

Edna let herself fall hard on her diapered bottom. Jesus climbed up into the avocado tree.

"You got to be more careful, Easy," my wife of two years said.

"Eathy," echoed Edna.

I found it hard to answer, because it was always hard for me to think when looking at Regina. Her skin was the color of waxed ebony and her large almond-shaped eyes were a half an inch too far apart. She was tall and slender but, for all that she was beautiful, it was something else that got to me. Her face had no imperfection that I could see. No blemish or wrinkle. Never a pimple or mole or some stray hair that might have grown out of the side of her jaw. Her eyes would close now and then but never blink as normal people do. Regina was perfect in every way. She knew how to walk and how to sit down. But she was never flustered by a lewd comment or shocked by poverty.

I fell in love with Regina Riles each time I looked at her. I fell in love with her before we ever exchanged words.

"I thought it was okay, honey." I reached for her unconsciously and she moved away, a graceful dancer.

"Listen, Easy. Jesus don't know how to think about what's right for Edna. You got to do that for him."

"He knows more than you think, baby. He's been around little children more than most women have. And he understands even if he doesn't talk."

Regina shook her head. "He got problems, Easy. You sayin' that he's okay don't make it so."

Jesus climbed down out of the tree and went to the side of the house to get into his room.

"I don't know what you mean, honey," I said. "Everybody got problems, How you handle your problems means what kinda man you gonna be."

"He ain't no man. Jesus is just a little boy. I don't know what kind of trouble he's had but I do know that it's too much for him, that's why he can't talk."

I let it drop there. I could never bring myself to tell her the real story. About how I rescued the boy from a missing woman's house after he had been bought and abused by an evil man. How could I explain that the man who mistreated Jesus had been murdered and I knew who'd done it, but kept quiet?

Regina hoisted Edna into her arms. The baby screamed. I wanted to grab them both and hug them so hard that all this upset would squeeze out.

Talking to Regina was painful for me sometimes. She was so sure about what was right and what wasn't. She could get me stirred up inside. So much so that sometimes I didn't know if I was feeling rage or love.

I waited outside for a moment after they went in, looking at my house. There were so many secrets I carried and so many broken lives I'd shared. Regina and Edna had no part of that, and I swore to myself that they never would.

I went in finally, feeling like a shadow, stalking himself into light.

"You been drinkin'," Regina said when I walked through the door. I didn't think she could smell it and I hadn't had enough to stagger. Regina just knew me. I liked that, it made my heart kind of wild.

Edna and Regina were both on the couch. When the baby saw me she said, "Eathy," and pulled away to crawl in my direction. Regina grabbed her before she fell to the floor.

Edna hollered as if she had been slapped.

"You been down to the police station?"

"Quinten Naylor wanted to talk with me." I always felt bad when the baby cried. I felt that something had to be done before we could go on. But Regina just held her and talked to me as if there were no yelling.

"Then why you come home all liquored up?"

"Com'on, baby," I said. Everything seemed slow. I felt that there was more than enough time to explain to her, to calm everything down. If only Edna would stop crying, I thought, everything would be okay. "I just took a drink down at the Avalon."

"Musta been a long swallow."

"Yeah, yeah. I needed a drink after what Officer Naylor showed me."

That got her attention, but her stare was still hard and cold.

"He took me over to a vacant lot on a Hundred and Tenth. Dead girl over there. Shot-in-the-head dead. It's the same man killed them other two girls."

"They know who did it?"

I had to suppress my smile. Taking that angry glare off her face made me want to dance.

"Naw," I said, as soberly as I could.

"Then how do they know it's the same man?"

"He crazy, that's why. He marks 'em with a hot cigar."

"Rape?" she asked in a small voice. Edna stopped crying and looked at me with her mother's questioning eye.

"That," I said, suddenly sorry that I had said anything. "And other stuff."

I took Edna to my chest and sat there next to my wife.

"Naylor wanted me to help him. He thought I mighta heard somethin'."

When Regina put her hand on my knee I could have cheered.

"Why'd he think that?"

"I don't know. He knows that I used to get around pretty good. He just thought I might have heard somethin'. I told him that I couldn't help, but by then I needed a drink."

"Who was it?"

"Girl named Bonita Edwards."

Her hand moved to my shoulder.

"I still don't see why a policeman would come here to ask you about it. I mean, unless he thought you had something to do with it."

Regina always wanted to know why. Why did people call me for favors? Why did I feel I had to help certain people when they were in trouble? She never did know how I got her cousin out of jail.

"Well, you know," I said. "He probably thought that I was still in the street a lot. But I told him that I'm workin' for Mofass full-time now and that I don't get out too much."

I had lived a life of hiding before I met Regina. Nobody knew about me. They didn't know about my property. They didn't know about my relationship to the police. I felt safe in my secrets. I kept telling myself that Regina was my wife, my partner in life. I planned to tell her about what I'd done over the years. I planned to tell her that Mofass really worked for me and that I had plenty of money in bank accounts around town. But I had to get at it slowly, in my own time.

The money wasn't apparent in my way of living. So there was no need for her to be suspicious. I intended to tell her all about it someday. A day when I felt she could accept it, accept me for who I was.

"He knows that I get around the neighborhood is all, honey. They found that girl just twelve blocks from here."

"Could you help them?"

Edna stuck her hand down my shirt pocket and drooled on my chest.

"Uh-uh. I didn't know nuthin'. I told him that I'd ask around, though. You know it's an ugly thing."

Regina studied me like a pawnbroker looking for a flaw in a diamond ring. I bounced Edna in my arms until she started to laugh. Then I smiled at Regina. She just shook her head a little and studied me some more.

Edna felt like she weighed a hundred pounds and I laid her across my lap. I lay back myself.

Regina put her cool hand to my cheek. I could count each knuckle. I thought about that poor dead girl and the others.

Edna fell asleep. Regina took her to her crib. And I followed her to our bedroom. A room that was so small it was mostly bed.

She undressed and then moved to put on her nightclothes. But I embraced her before she got to her gown, my pants were down around my ankles. We fell back into the bed with her on top. She tried, weakly, to pull away but I held her and stroked her in the ways she liked. She gave in to my caresses but she wouldn't kiss me. I rolled up on top of her and held her head between my hands. She let my leg slip between hers but when I put my lips to hers she wouldn't open her mouth or her eyes. My tongue pushed at her teeth but that was as far as I got.

Regina let me hold her. She buried her face against my neck while I worked off my shorts and shirt. But when I moved to enter her she turned away from me. All of this was new. Regina wasn't as wild about sex as I was but she would usually come close to matching my ardor. Now it was like she wanted me but with nothing coming from her.

It excited me all the more, and even though I was dizzy with the alcohol in my blood, I cozied up behind her and entered her the way dogs do it.

"Stop, Easy!" she cried, but I knew she meant "Go on, do it!"

She writhed and I clamped my legs around hers. I bucked up against her and she grabbed the night table with such force that it was knocked over on to the floor. The lamp was pulled from the electric plug and the room went dark.

"Oh, God no!" she cried and she came, shouting and bucking and elbowing me hard.

When I relaxed my hold she pushed away and got up. I remember the light coming on and her standing there in the harsh electric glare. There was sweat on her face and glistening in her pubic hair. She looked at me with an emotion I could not read.

"I love you," I said.

I passed into sleep before her answer came.

CLARENCE MAJOR

All-Night Visitors

ANITA

Anita is whipping her tight pussy on me like mad! We are in her dark, beautiful apartment, with a little wine that has warmed her, I think, more than it has me. "I want the light on," I say, and get up, the shock of my sudden movement, leaving her, stuns her. I come back, the bright three-way lamp, a new dimension on her caramel-colored, firm, lean body. The taut little tits with their large rich dark *dark* red berries, some sweet nipples. The gentle yellow lights drive mathematical light sets, like beautiful *tupu* sounds of Coltrane. My spongy, sore, moist sword, as I come back to the bed, dripping her juice along the way, the sweet goodness of it all soothing my limbs; I happily pat my stomach, singing a couple bars from something new by James Brown as I jump on the bed, over her now, growling like a dog, "GGRRRRRRRRRR," and imagining, even how it looks graphically in cartoons, or here, which is also a kind of cartoon of love, my soft black dick, by now completely stunted into a virginal softness, hanging there, and Anita goes, "Lazy nigger, you!" And her wide mouth, those big eyes, sparkling, her white *white* teeth glowing, spotless, virtuous teeth. "I'm dog—GRRRRRRRRR bow-bow! BOW-WOW! BOW-WOW WOW WOW WOW WOW!!!" I am in her face, and her head is turned sideways, she's looking with those big Lil-Armstrong-jazzdays-eyes at me, as if to say, "Who're you supposed to be *now?* What kinda new game is this, little boy? *My my*, men are always boys! Boastful, silly, self-centered little boys, who want somebody to jack them off all the time!"

She giggles, the unclear voice of Donovan carries its weight equal in space, timing our senses, from the FM radio. Her big red tongue shoots out, touches my nose. It is good that I am able to enjoy these moments with Anita, despite all the past contamination between us! She runs her long (she has an *extra* long, extra red, extra *active*) tongue around my cheeks, quickly licks my lips, but I am still a pompous dog ready to bark again, when her hard, long, firm, hand intrudes in the soft, baggy, damp, hairy area of my semen-smelling fruit picker. The conduct of her dry hand always astonishes me, as it delights. She is still giggling. I am delighted, of course, whenever she touches my dick, I like it in a very civil way, not just a natural magnet, magic way. She puts me in large swimming pools of myself weighty with *supreme delight*, despite the slight roughness of her hand. Anita's hand is not rough because she's been washing dishes, sweeping floors, or ironing clothes—they're rough in a *natural* way. She is a creamy thing, *hard* all over. Her little tits are stiff cups that stand firmly, like prudent sentries, looking with dark steadiness in opposite directions. Her stomach is firmer than any stomach, male or female, that I've ever seen. There isn't one inch of fat on her anywhere unless we consider her earlobes fat. Donovan is doing *Mellow Yellow*, as I gently let myself down beside her, she's saying, "Lazzzy lazy nigger, *humhumhum*," still holding my soft copperheaded dick with a kind of playful sense of disgust. For a moment I feel slightly ashamed that my bonanza detector remains, even in her active hand, serene. She is simply shaking it back and forth, and now asking, *"What's this?"* She smells clean, fleshy clean, she always does. So gently soapy-smelling, not strong with some overdose of peakily cheap perfume!

She is already on her elbow, looking down at me by now, smacking her lips, going, "Tut tut tut—What am I gonna do with you, nigger, huh? You're a mess—*won't* it get hard?" "*Be nice* to it, Anita, baby, it'll do anything you want it to do . . ." Yes, it has been a long time since she's given me that sacred rite she is such a master at performing. I'm thinking, why should I torture poor Mr. ex-Perpendicular any longer, tonight, in her dry hole? She gets up to her knees, and I deliberately say nothing because I know from past experience that Anita does not like for me to ask her to suck it, though when she volunteers, she has proven to be unbeatable at getting to the essence of the act. I remember now as she is about to suck it, she knows that at least turning it around in her mouth, swiveling it, whirling it, rotating it with her thick, long tongue, makes it hard as bookends, and vigorous, so powerful, in fact, that I've rocked and almost unhinged her torso from such long, pithy, severe sessions of pure slippery fucking, pushing one juicy hour, to the rhythm of music, into another, right here in this bed. And I suspect now she thinks she'll get me hard and *then* stretch out on her back, her brittle pussy hairs twisting together there, damply, at the mouth of the jewel, hiding that ruthless, hungry merciless gem! that gobbles and gobbles, eats at me—rather, lies more or less in repose, as *I*, out of deep meanings of the self feel compelled to work myself to death, so to speak, to fill up its crater! But that ain't what's happening this time—She doesn't know it yet, but she's going to swivel it, rotate it, nibble it, lick it, gently chew on it, playfully bite it, turn and turn it in the spitkingdom of herself, dance it with her tongue, spank it with juice, excite it to huge precipices without bursting it out of its tense axis of delight, she's going to hold it in honor with both brown hands, as it dips, tosses, as it ascends, in all O all ranges of mind states! Yes, it is my mind! Equal, that is, to every level of myself . . .

I know I can turn her *off* if I say One Word now. That's the last thing in the world I want to do now as I feel the weight of her knees adjusting between mine. "Put this pillow under you—" She's being clinical; O.K., if she wants to be that way, it'll still be good. I feel how I deliberately relax every muscle I can consciously focus on with my mind. She wiggles her firm ass, adjusting it somewhere on her heels, her arms inside the warm soft area of my thighs, I feel the hairs of them. She takes a deep breath, I can smell the air of the ruby we drank drift up to my nostrils. Sound: the slow wet movement of her strong red tongue moving over her lips, mopping away the dryness. Like most of her body's exterior, her lips are usually very dry. Only two spots, exceptions, I can think of: the areas around the edges of her scalp, the crevices between her thighs and where the mound of her pussy begins to rise, are usually warm and moist. As I lift my narrow ass, holding myself in a loop, she slides the big pillow beneath me, I sink down into the conquering softness, her busy automatic-acting fingers tickle the rooty area at the base of this unselfish generative Magic Flute of mine, pull and squeeze my sagging sensitive balls. She coughs, clears her throat. I hear the smack of her tongue between her lips again. I have my eyes closed, soon I'll feel the slow, warm, nerve-racking sweet fuck of the pensive mouth beginning . . .

This hesitation. I know it is coming. Her mouth has not yet touched the ruby head of my *dik*. The moment of waiting, the anxiety of it builds like musical improvisations in my bones, my membranes, the heat, blood energy in me; I continue to try to keep it all very still, cool, I am not even trying to concentrate on hardening up my ecstasy-weapon, this dear *uume* to the emissive glory of life itself! And for once Anita doesn't seem impatient, she isn't pumping it, bungling, and jacking it, trying to make it instantly hard—I suspect she's going to make it really great this time. She can be absolutely wonderful, when she wants to! The anticipation of these moments, of a kind of antagonism of sweet memory of the best times, is overpowering. It takes all the will in my being to lie here, still, the corporeality of myself, in the split-slick heady memory of it . . .

(It is only at these moments, of course, that this particular "movement" of the symphony of life is so beautifully important, all-consuming . . . Equal to the working moments when I am excited by the energetic, rich growth of a concept I am able to articulate! Or my sudden ability to construct bookshelves, or create a silly wacky lovely painting, equal to anything that I do involving the full disclosure of myself! I hesitate to say equal to my ability to handle those firearms in Vietnam, against those nameless human collages that fell in the distance, like things, but maybe even equal to that, too . . .)

The hot nude hole of her mouth, *oh God it is so gooooood!!!* slides now, carelessly, dry at first, but she's excreting saliva, like cunt juice, her firm hands stretching out, in slow-motion, sliding up my flat stomach, my gentle spongy dick blowing up, expanding at a pace equal to the tension in her lips behind the root of her tongue, getting hot as the crevices of her gums, the deliberately slow sinking of her mouth still coming down to the very base of my seed-giver, gently, but firmly engulfing it, in all of its lazy softness, the nerve-ends of my whole ass, my nuts, my thighs are fructifying! The meaty warmth of her velvety lined interior begins to climb just as slowly; Mr. Prick is anxious to quickly reach the full and painful proportion of its promise, but I fight that drive by applying more and more deliberation to my restraint, under the magic, almost weightless touch of her fingers as she adroitly glides them down, tripping through the hairs of my stomach. She need not hold my *uume* with her hands any longer. "He" is trying too hard to make headway in his headiness! He holds himself up, I refuse to let the progressive bastard gristle up to the prolific point where he is like some giant tendon, though Anita might (*if* she weren't usually patient right now) *like* that; O motion, joy, O *shit*, this is TOO MUCH!!! the still missiling motion of the circle of her tight mouth, restrainingly prolonged, up—up! I can feel the inelastic cords of my inner tissues pulling in a complex of nerves, pulling, as her strong big Black Woman, Mighty Nile, African energetic tough lips, the muscles in them quivering, the lengthy moist spongy-porous tongue gently milking the base of my valve, Mr. Hammer's underbelly, milks fruitfully, in a slow rhythm. My eyes are still closed, I am trying not to settle my mind anywhere, it tries for a moment to drift to the greasy magazine of a gun I was examining one day, sitting propped against another guy's back, at the edge of a rice paddy, and I don't know why. I want to *stay* right here, with her, focused on every protrusion, every cord, abstract circle of myself, of her every "feeling," every hurling, every fleshy spit-rich convexity, mentally centered in all the invisible "constructs" of myself, right here, where she and I now form, perform an orchestra she is conducting in juicy floodtides; stay *in* her woman's construction, her work, her togetherness, the rich procreating-like magic of her every touch as—more and more against my will—my *kok* protracts, *swells*, lengthens, perpetuatingly jumpy with fertility, as her permeable mouth decreases its gentle grip in exact ratio to Dick's eminent *strong* polarity. I love her for her reflective, melancholy approach to this fine art! So seldom does she take this much care to do it properly . . .

My serpent is just fatty-hard, but extra long, redundantly so! It is *best* this way, if I can manage to keep it from stiffening to the point where the nerves are minimized somehow. I feel the mouth-motions of her workings, the salivary warmth of her slow, pensive chewing at the *acutely sensitive head*, where the loose skin has slid back, the rich, thick nerve-ends in the thin layers of this loose skin, she lets spit run down slowly around this Bridegroom in his moment of heaven, the warm secreted water from the prolific glands of her tastebud-sensitive mouth, I feel these O so slow careful and skillful movements, the deliberate soft scraping and raking of her beautiful strong teeth across the tender texture of the rim of the head, gently bathing with spit the prepuce's densely nerve-packed walls, which rub these ends of my luckily uninhibited penis. She is concentrating on the head of it, and she can do this for so long it drives me *mad* with porous, beautiful pleasure. She will nibble here, suck one or two times, stop, let it rest limp, aching, in the soft warm cave of her rich dark purple "construct," saliva mixing easily with the slow sebaceous secretion, my own male liquid lubricant, *smegma*, washing around in her grip—a gentle but well-controlled clasp! Then, she might take a gentle but playful plunge *down*, straight down, down, sinking down faster than she's so-far moved, the dick head exploding up into all that wet, warm slime, it's running down, profusely, down the polarity of this *sperma*-generator of love, and all the stinging rich, acute, respirating, the tunnel-sinking sense of it, the sounds of the cool capful of wind speeding away giving way to this cravefeeding, just the hallelujah-warm, narcotic feeling of the drop, as my dick thickens, pushes out—the lengthy pole emitting into her muscles, and tonsils, the juicy soup of my penis glands, the sheath, now in this plunging motion stretched in this hymn of heat to frantic, mad ends! Two more strokes like this and she can finish me. I would shoot a hurricane of seeds into her, falling out convulsively, palmus, in nervous-twitching; *but*

Anita isn't trying to finish me off this time, get it over. She's going to be good to me, but I *cannot* help myself from the submissive fear that she might suddenly bring it to an end, and it can be very painful if it is done incorrectly. Instinctively, Anita knows this. This knowledge is in the very pores of her skin, she is the kind of pussy-woman, the knowledgeable Black Mother of a deep wisdom, intrinsic in every fuse, every chromosome, every crevice of her epidermis, enormous in the internal cavities of her mouth, anus, the atoms of her urethra, the tissues of her every thought, liquid of her nerves, the intelligence of her tracts, digestive system, the energy of her bladder, every foetal tissue of her, every psycho-biological process of her protoplasm!

Yes.

God!!! Yes!

WHAT'S LOVE GOT TO DO WITH IT

GERALD EARLY

First Poem for Linnet

Linnet was seven years old when I wrote my first poem for her. I was then a visiting professor at the University of Kansas on a minority postdoctoral fellowship. I would make the five-hour trip from Lawrence, Kansas, to St. Louis every weekend, for Ida and the girls did not go with me. The first several months were not a particularly good time between Ida and me, though Linnet and Rosalind did not notice it. We have always kept them sheltered from any sense of tension or undercurrent of disruption that may occur in the normal course of a marriage. This was intensely important to the both of us: the girls must not grow up in a bickering, contentious atmosphere. Only once do I remember either Linnet or Rosalind overhearing an argument between me and Ida. Linnet was, I think, two, and Ida and I were arguing about in-laws or money or the quest for social status, frequent topics of disagreement during the early years of our marriage. It had become so heated that Linnet, who was in the bathroom working at her "potty training," emerged, training pants down, face distressed, shouting: "What going on? I want to know! What going on?" So hilarious and so touching it was, that the argument was instantly tabled. It was during these early months in Lawrence (I wound up staying there on the fellowship for two years) that Ida once, rather angrily, almost as if on a dare, asked me to have the children in Lawrence one weekend instead of my coming home.

"But that's crazy," I said. "You'd have to drive up here to drop them off on Thursday and come for them on Sunday."

"I want a weekend to myself," she said, sternly.

So, for that weekend, the children stayed with me in my tiny efficiency.

"Yeah, Daddy, I remember that real well," said Linnet recently. "You slept on the floor and Ros and I slept on your Murphy bed. You cooked for us in this tiny, tiny kitchen. And we watched the PBS children's programs on a black-and-white TV that you had. That was the first time I ever watched a black-and-white TV. We went for walks in the park, to the library. And you couldn't comb our hair right. You kept trying to get it into these barrettes and they kept popping loose, so that, by the end of the day, our hair was all over the place. And you kept muttering, when you were combing our hair, 'How do women do this stuff?' You combed our hair real soft, like you were afraid of hurting us or something, and Ros kept saying, 'Comb harder, Daddy, it's not tight enough.' That was a great weekend, one of the best I ever had."

Because I was alone much of the time while I was in Lawrence, I was able to do a great deal of writing, mostly essays, but also many poems. I thought of making Linnet the subject of an essay, but I could not quite get my mind around the matter. I could not then come to terms with how to write about her in prose. I had written an essay while in Lawrence entitled "Waiting for Miss America" in which both Linnet and Rosalind were mentioned, but they were not the subject of the essay. I had to grow more to learn how to write about them, especially Linnet. In those early years, I did not understand my children, or fully comprehend parenthood, except that, naturally, I was supposed to love my children, which I believe I did, although I was not in any way sure what it was that I was loving. I also felt guilty and deeply uncomfortable whenever I momentarily disliked them. But the poem for Linnet was meant to be a kind of shorthand, a mental place holder to say, "Come back to this when you are older and she is as well."

I wrote it one night on a Montgomery Ward electric typewriter after I had written a rough draft in longhand on my knees with the pad on the bed (a favorite writing position at that time). I did not show it to Linnet for nearly two years; that is, she saw it for the first time when she was probably nine years old. I was afraid she would misunderstand what I wanted to say and, after all, frankly, perhaps I was not at all sure what I was trying to say beneath it all. It had been published nearly a year before I showed it to her. She read it slowly.

"It's nice," she said when finished. "I don't understand it all but I like it. It sounds nice. It sounds like it's about you and me when we take walks together."

She thought for a moment, then asked suddenly, "Why did you write it?"

"There was," I responded, "something I wanted to say to you. I couldn't figure out any other way to say it. I was afraid to show it to you because I thought you might not like a poem about your being slow."

"What's it matter?" she said off-handedly. "Everybody knows I'm dumb."

The pain I felt at that admission was both bitter and deep.

"You're not dumb," I said.

"You got mad at me once and called me dumb," she said.

I hung fire briefly. "If I ever said that to you, I am sorry. But I don't remember ever calling you that. I don't call people names."

"You thought it," she said, looking down.

"If I have ever thought that," I said, "then I am more sorry than words can say."

I have read this poem publicly only once. The occasion was in the spring of 1988, shortly after I had been tenured at Washington University. Jim McLeod, then the chair of African and Afro-American Studies, wanted me to read some poems before a gathering of black students. I did not want to do this as I have always felt a bit uncomfortable doing readings. Moreover, I sensed that the sort of stuff I had written was not likely to impress the students. It wasn't Afrocentric. It wasn't Nikki Giovanni. It wasn't even strikingly good poetry. But I agreed to do it as Jim is a dear colleague. At the last minute I decided to take Linnet with me to the reading.

"This is exciting," she said. "I never heard you read before."

I read for probably twenty minutes and, on impulse, ended with "Dumbo's Ears." I explained to the audience that Linnet was learning disabled and I wrote this poem for her. I am not sure why I decided to read it at all, perhaps to give some reason for bringing my daughter, perhaps to see how she would respond to having her "problem" publicly exposed. I think at that stage in our relationship I was trying to find out something about myself, trying to find out, actually, if I was more deeply bothered by Linnet's learning disability than I had ever been willing to admit to myself, by trying to deal with Linnet's problem publicly. I wanted to understand what being a good parent was, and perhaps there are moments in the relationship when this can be best understood only in some sort of public ritual, some public display. Linnet, in any case, seemed not even to be listening. She was rocking back and forth on a piano bench, making faces, seemingly in her own world. I was a bit horrified by her behavior, reminding me, as it did, of the senseless rocking of a retarded boy I knew in my neighborhood as a child. God, I thought, these people are likely to think she is retarded or something. Why can't she sit there, prim and proper, and listen? They'll think I have an idiot for a daughter. I felt that spasm of shame that she had made me feel so much in the past, and the shame of that shame. I also felt a moment of true annoyance with her. She had let me down as she had several times before, but I instantly felt bad about feeling that way. Am I ever to be worthy of this girl? I thought. She deserves someone so much better as a father than I.

When I finished the poem, I felt, oddly, disarmingly almost, a sense of relief and a fierce sense of pride. Perhaps it was merely a kind of disingenuous public defiance, a public show of wanting to be the good parent, the caring, protective father. But that was only a part of it. This is my daughter, I thought, and I will never disown her for what she is or is not. Whether this was driven entirely by a kind of "audience egotism," it was nonetheless a proper way to feel, the way Linnet deserved to have her father feel. I thought of Augustine's words: I do this for love of your love. I looked at her rocking there, caught her eye, and grinned. Before me sat the image of my own face.

"As a boy," I told her once, "I was called 'Happy.' The other boys called me 'Happy' and it became my nickname when I was about eight years old. I was furious about it at first and I would yell at the boys not to call me that. How dare they give me a name I did not want or like? I was outraged. Besides, it was a degrading name. It was the name of a local TV program called *Happy the Clown*. I hated the name but it stuck for several years, until I was about fourteen."

"Why did they call you that?" Linnet asked.

"Because I was very shy as a boy and people always thought I was sad. But I wasn't really. I was just self-absorbed. I had a sad face just like yours. You know the way everyone says you have a sad face. I had the same face as a child, so the boys thought it would be funny to call me 'Happy.' "

"I hate people thinking you're sad when you're not. I get that all the time. 'Are you unhappy, Linnet?' 'Why are you sad, Linnet?' And I'm not sad. I'm feeling just fine. I wish people would just leave my face alone, stop treating my face like it's their property."

I looked at her when I finished the poetry reading and made the only gesture I could, the one gesture I felt she would appreciate. I threw my arm around her shoulder and we walked out together without another word or even a good-bye.

"Thank you, Daddy, for taking me," she said. "I liked it, especially the last poem."

"Did it make you uncomfortable?" I asked. "I mean, reading that poem? Maybe I shouldn't have read it."

"I'm glad you read it," she said, smiling. "It sounded real good. I thought you read it just for me. Besides, I was real proud. How many of those college kids can say their dads write poems about them and can read them in front of people?"

EDWARD JONES

A *New* Man

One day in late October, Woodrow L. Cunningham came home early with his bad heart and found his daughter with the two boys. He was then fifty-two years old, a conscientious deacon at Rising Star AME Zion, a paid-up lifetime member of the NAACP and the Urban League, a twenty-five year member of the Elks. For ten years he had been the chief engineer at the Sheraton Park Hotel, where practically every employee knew his name. For longer than he could recall, his friends and lodge members had been telling him that he was capable of being more than just the number-one maintenance man. But he always told them that he was contented in the job, that it was all he needed, and this was true for the most part. He would be in that same position some thirteen years later, when death happened upon him as he bent down over a hotel bathroom sink, about to do a job a younger engineer claimed he could not handle.

The afternoon he came home early and discovered his daughter with the boys, he found a letter in the mailbox from his father in Georgia. He read the letter while standing in the hall of the apartment building. He expected nothing of importance, as usual, and that was what he found. "Alice took me to Buddy Wilson funeral just last week," Woodrow read. "I loaned him the shirt they buried him in. And that tie he had on was one that I give him too. I thought I would miss him but I do not miss him very much. Checkers was never Buddy Wilsons game." As he read, he massaged the area around his heart, an old habit, something he did even when his heart was not giving him trouble. "I hope you and the family can come down before the winter months set in. Company is never the same after winter get here."

He put the letter back in the envelope, and as he absently looked at the upside-down stamp taped in the vicinity of the corner, the pain in his heart eased. He could picture his father sitting at the kitchen table, writing the letter, occasionally touching the pencil point to his tongue. A new mongrel's head would be resting across his lap, across thin legs that could still carry the old man five miles down the road and back. Woodrow, feeling better, considered returning to work, but he knew his heart was deceitful. He folded the envelope and stuck it in his back pocket, and out of the pocket it would fall late that night as he prepared for bed after returning from the police station.

Several feet before he reached his apartment door he could hear the boys' laughter and bits and pieces of their man-child conquer-the-world talk. He could not hear his daughter at first. He stopped at his door and listened for nearly five minutes, and in that time he became so fascinated by what the boys were saying that he would not have cared if someone walking in the hall found him listening. It was only when he heard his daughter's laughter, familiar, known, that he put his key in the door. She stood just inside the door when he entered, her eyes accusing but her mouth set in a small O of surprise. Beyond her he could see the boys with their legs draped over the arms of the couch and gray smoke above their heads wafting toward the open window.

He asked his daughter, "Why ain't you in school?"

"They let us out early today," she said. "The teachers had some kinda meetin."

He did not listen to her, because he had found that she lived to lie. Woodrow watched the boys as they took their time straightening themselves up, and he knew that their deliberateness was the result of something his daughter had said about him. Without taking his eyes from the boys, he asked his daughter again why she wasn't in school. When he finally looked at her, he saw that she was holding the stump of a thin cigarette. The smoke he smelled was unfamiliar, and at first he thought that they were smoking very stale cigarettes, or cigarettes that had gotten wet and been dried. He slapped her. "I told you not to smoke in my house," he said.

She was fifteen, and up until six months or so before, she would have collapsed into the chair, collapsed into a fit of crying. But now she picked up the fallen cigarette from the floor and stamped it out in the ashtray on the tiny table beside the easy chair. Her hand shook, the only reminder of the old days. "We just talkin. We ain't doin nothin wrong," she said quietly.

He shouted to the boys, "Get outta my house!" They stood up quickly, and Woodrow could tell that whatever she had told them about him, such anger was not part of it. They looked once at the girl.

"They my guests, Daddy," she said, sitting in the easy chair and crossing her legs. "I invited em over here."

Woodrow took two steps to the boy nearest him—the tall light-skinned one he would spot from a bus window a year or so later—and grabbed him with one hand by the jacket collar, shook him until the boy raised his hands as if to protect his face from a blow. The boy's eyes widened and Woodrow shook him some more. He had been living a black man's civilized life in Washington and had not felt so coiled and bristled since the days when he worked with wild men in the turpentine camps in Florida. "I ain't done nothin," the boy said. The words sounded familiar, similar to those of a wild man ready to slink away into his cabin with his tail between his legs. Woodrow relaxed. "I swear. I don't want no trouble, Mr. Cunningham." The boy had no other smell but that peculiar cigarette smoke, and it was a shock to Woodrow that a body with that smell should know something that seemed as personal as his name. The other, smaller boy had tiptoed around Woodrow and was having trouble opening the door. After the small boy had gone out, Woodrow flung the light-skinned boy out behind him. Woodrow locked the door, and the boys stood for several minutes, pounding on the door, mouthing off.

"Why you treat my guests like that?" Elaine Cunningham had not moved from the chair.

"Clean up this mess," he told her, "and I don't wanna see one ash when you done."

She said nothing more, but instead busied herself tidying the couch cushions. Then Woodrow, after flicking the cushions a few times with his handkerchief, sat in the middle of the couch, and the couch sagged with the familiarity of his weight.

When Elaine had returned the room to what it was, her father said, "I want to know what you was doin in here with them boys."

"Nothin. We wasn't doin nothin. Just talkin, thas all, Daddy." She sat in the easy chair, leaned toward him with her elbows on her knees.

"You can do your talkin down on the stoop," he said.

"Why don't you just say you tryin to cuse me a somethin? Why don't you just come out and say it?"

"If you didn't do things, you wouldn't get accused," he said. He talked without thought, because those words and words like them had been spoken so much to her that he was able to parrot himself. "If you start actin like a young lady should, start studyin and what not, and tryin to make somethin of yourself . . ." Woodrow L. Cunningham bein Woodrow L. Cunningham, he thought.

She stood up quickly, and he was sickened to see her breasts bounce. "I could study them stupid books half the damn day and sit in church the other half, and I'd still get the same stuff thrown in my face bout how I ain't doin right."

"Okay, thas anough a that." He felt a familiar rumbling in his heart. "I done heard enough."

"I wanna go out," she stood with her arms folded. "I wanna go out."

"Go on back to your room. Thas the only goin out you gonna be doin. I don't wanna hear another word outta your mouth till your mother get home." He closed his eyes to wait her out, for he knew she was now capable of standing there till doomsday to sulk. When he heard her going down the hall, he waited for the door to slam. But there was no sound and he gradually opened his eyes. He put a cushion at one end of the couch and took off his shoes and lay down, his hands resting on the large mound that was his stomach. All his friends told him that if he lost thirty or forty pounds he would be a new man, but he did not think that was true. He considered asking Elaine to bring his pills from his bedroom, for he had left the vial he traveled with at work. But he suffered the pain rather than suffer her stirring about. He watched his wife's curtains flap gently with the breeze and the movement soothed him.

"I would not say anything bad about mariage," his father had written to Woodrow after Woodrow called to say he was considering marrying Rita Hadley. "It is easier to pick up and walk away from a wife and a family if you don't like it then you can walk away from your own bad cooking." Woodrow had never been inclined to marry anyone, was able, as he would tell his lodge brothers, to get all the trim he wanted without buying some woman a ring and walking down the aisle with her. "Doin it to a woman for a few months was all right," he would say, sounding like his father, "cause that only put the idea of marryin in their heads. Doin it to them any more than that and the idea take root."

It had never crossed his mind to sleep with any of the women at Rising Star AME, for he had discovered in Georgia that the wrath of church women was greater than that of all others, even old whores. He only went out with Rita because the preacher took him aside one Sunday and told him it was unnatural to go about unmarried and that he should give some thought to promenading with Sister Rita sometime. And, too, he was thirty-six and it was beginning to occur to him that women might not go on forever laying down and opening their legs for him. The second time they went out, he put his arm around Rita and pulled her to him there in the Booker-T Theater. She smacked his hand and that made his johnson hard. "I ain't like that, Mr. Cunningham." He had heard those words before. But when he pulled her to him again, she twisted his finger until it hurt. And that was something he had not experienced before.

His father suffered a mild stroke a week before the wedding. "Do not take this sickness to mean that I do not send my blessing to your mariage to Miss Rita Hadley," his father said in a letter he had dictated to Alice, his oldest daughter. "God took pity on you when he send her your way." Even in the unfamiliarity of Alice's handwriting, the familiarity of his father was there in all the lines, right down to the misspelled words. Until some of his father's children learned in their teens, his father had been the only one in the family who could read and write. "This," he said of his reading and writing, "makes me as good as a white man." And before some of his children learned, discovered there was no magic to it, he enjoyed reading aloud at the supper table to his family, his voice stringing out a long monotone of words that often meant nothing to him and even less to his family because the man read so quickly.

His father read anything he could get his hands on—the words on feed bags, on medicine bottles, on years-old magazine pages they used for wallpaper, just about everything except the Bible. He had a fondness for weeks-old newspapers he would find in the streets when he went to town. No one—not even the squirming small kids—was allowed to move from the supper table until he had finished reading, hooking one word to another until it all became babble. Indeed, it was such a babble that some of his sons would joke behind his back that he was lying about knowing how to read. "Few white men can do what I'm doin right now," he would say. "You go bring ten white men in here and I bet nine couldn't read this. Couldn't read it if God commanded em to." Sometimes, to torment his wife, he would hold a scrap of newspaper close to her face and tell her to read the headlines. "I cain't," she would say. "You know I cain't." No matter how many times he did this, his father would laugh with the pleasure of the very first time. Then he would pass the newspaper among his children and tell them to read him the headlines, and each one would hold it uncomfortably and repeat what their mother had said.

When Woodrow woke, it was nearly five o'clock and his wife was sitting on the side of the couch, asking where Elaine was. "She ain't in her room," his wife said and kissed his forehead. A school cafeteria worker, Rita was a very thin woman who, before she met Woodrow, had lived only for her job and her church activities. She was five years older than he was and had resigned herself to the fact that she was not the type of woman men wanted to marry. "I've put it all in God's hands," she once said to a friend before Woodrow came along, "and left it there."

Rita waited until seven o'clock before she began calling her daughter's friends. "Stop worryin," Woodrow told her after the tenth call, "you know how that girl is." At eight-thirty, they put on light coats and went in search, visiting the same houses and apartments that Rita had called. They returned home about ten and waited until eleven, when they put on their coats again and went to the police station at 16th and V Northwest. They did not call the station because somewhere Woodrow had heard that the law wouldn't begin to hear a complaint unless you stood before it in person.

At the station, the man at the front desk did not look up until they had been standing there for some two minutes. Woodrow wanted to tell him that the police chief and the mayor were now black men and that they couldn't be ignored, but when the man behind the desk looked up, Woodrow could see in his eyes that none of that would have mattered to him.

"Our daughter is missing," Rita said.

"How long?" said the man, a sergeant with an unpronounceable name on his name tag. He pulled a form from a pile to his left and then he took up a pen, loudly clicking out the point to write.

"We haven't seen her since this afternoon," Woodrow says.

The sergeant clicked the pen again and set it on the desk, then put the form back on top with the others. "Not long enough," he said. "Has to be gone forty-eight hours. Till then she's missing, but she's not a missing person."

"She only a baby."

"How old?"

"Fifteen," Woodrow said.

"She's just a runaway," the sergeant said.

"She never run away before," Woodrow said. "This ain't like her, sergeant." Woodrow felt that like all white men, the man enjoyed having attention paid to his rank.

"Don't matter. She's probably waiting for you at home right now, wondering where you two buggied off to. Go home. If she isn't home, then come back when she's a missing person."

Woodrow took Rita's arm as they went back, because he sensed that she was near collapsing. "What happened?" she asked as they turned the corner of U and 10th streets. "Did you say somethin bad to her?"

He told her everything that he could remember, even what Elaine was wearing when he last saw her. Answering was not difficult because no blame had yet been assigned. Despite the time nearing midnight, they became confident with each step that Elaine was just at a friend's they did not know about, that the friend's mother, like any good mother, would soon send their daughter home. Rita, in the last blocks before their apartment, leaned into her husband and his warmth helped to put her at ease.

They waited up until about four in the morning, and then they undressed without words in the dark. Rita began to cry the moment her head hit the pillow, for she was afraid to see the sun come up and find that a new day had arrived without Elaine being home. She asked him again what happened, and he told her again, even things that he had forgotten—the logo of the football team on the light-skinned boy's jacket, the fact that the other boy was bald except for a half-dollar-sized spot of hair carved on the back of his head. He was still talking when she dozed off with him holding her.

Before they had coffee later that morning, about seven thirty, they called their jobs to say they would not be in. Work had always occupied a place at the center of their lives, and there was initially something eerie about being home when it was not a holiday or the weekend. They spent the rest of the morning searching the streets together, and in the afternoon, they separated to cover more ground. They did the same thing after dinner, each spreading out farther and farther from their apartment on R Street. That evening, they called neighbors and friends, church and lodge members, to tell them that their child was missing and that they needed their help and their prayers. Their friends and neighbors began searching that evening, and a few went with Woodrow and Rita the next day to the police station to file a missing person's report. A different sergeant was at the desk, and though he was a white man, Woodrow felt that he understood their trouble.

For nearly three months, Woodrow and Rita searched after they came from work, and each evening after they and their friends had been out, the pastor of Rising Star spoke to a small group that gathered in the Cunninghams' living room. "The world is cold and not hospitable," he would conclude, holding his hat in both hands, "but we know our God to be a kind God and that he has provided our little sister with a place of comfort and warmth until she returns to her parents and to all of us who love and treasure her."

In the kitchen beside the refrigerator, Rita tacked up a giant map of Washington, on which she noted where she and others had searched. "I didn't know the city was this big," she said the day she put it up, her fingertips touching the neighborhoods that she had never heard of or had heard of only in passing—foreign lands she thought she would never set eyes on. Petworth. Anacostia. Lincoln Park. And in the beginning, the very size of the city lifted her spirits, for in a place so big, there was certainly a spot that held something as small as her child, and if they just kept looking long enough, they would come upon that place.

"What happened?" Rita would ask as they prepared for bed. What he told her and her listening replaced everything they had ever done in that bed—discussing what future they wanted for Elaine, lovemaking, sharing what the world had done to them that workday. "What happened?" It was just about the only thing she ever asked Woodrow as the months grew colder. "What happened? Whatcha say to her?" By late February, when fewer and fewer people were going out to search, he had told the whole story, but then he began to tell her things that had not happened. There were three boys, he said at one point, for example. Or, he could see a gun sticking out of the jacket pocket of the light-skinned one, and he could see the outline of a knife in the back pants pocket of the third. Or he would say that the record player was playing so loudly he could hear it from the street. They were small embellishments at first, and if his wife noticed that the story of what happened was changing, she said nothing. In time, with winter disappearing, he was adding more and more so that it was no longer a falseness here and there that was embedded in the whole of the truth, but the truth itself, an ever-diminishing kernel, that was contained in the whole of falseness. And, like some kind of bedtime story, she listened and drifted with his words into a sleep where the things he was telling her were sometimes happening.

RON STODGHILL II

My Sparrow

Three years ago a crack dealer moved into the house next door to my grandmother. He did a good amount of business there. Customers came by during the day and at all times of the night. Many stayed and partied until morning. And while there was occasional gunfire, it was never enough to draw police. But if the drug dealer prospered, my grandmother did not. He and his entourage brought her great stress. In the span of a year my grandmother suffered several strokes, each one pushing her closer to her deathbed.

I was explaining this to Robyn as we pulled up in front of my grandparents' small wooden frame house on Detroit's west side, the place where my mother grew up and where I spent much of my childhood. Robyn and I both lived in New York City. We had been dating several months and had come to a point in our relationship where I thought it best she meet my family. I had not yet brought myself to pop the question, but I wanted to marry Robyn. Two days spent with my mother and sister had introduced her to two of the most important women in my life. Now, as we prepared to meet the third, I could feel my heart pounding in my chest. I took a long, deep breath.

"The strokes and the medication have taken their toll on my grandmother," I said, ringing the doorbell. "Daddy Grady feeds and cleans her, which is real hard on him because he never knows what she wants. Her memory is so bad that she can barely finish a sentence. So don't expect her to say much."

If Robyn was nervous, it didn't show. I searched her big brown eyes for some sign of apprehension, but found nothing but eagerness, I looked for anxiety in her smooth copper face, but saw only a pleasant curl in her full plum lips. Sidling up against her tall, slender body, I gave her hand a gentle squeeze. I noticed her palm was a little moist.

Daddy Grady opened the door with a rueful smile. I hugged him and introduced him to Robyn. Their exchange was warm and brief. He knew our main reason for being there and didn't try to make small talk.

"She's just waking up," he said. "She'll be happy to see you." A quiet, soft-spoken man, Daddy Grady had always been a big physical presence to me. His broad, athletic frame hearkened back to his days as a right offensive tackle for the Tennessee State Tigers in the 1930s, and his large, rugged hands spoke to years of building Cadillacs on General Motors' assembly line. Even after he retired, he had maintained some of his build in chores like cleaning his fishing boat, gardening, or painting around the house. But since my grandmother took ill, his days were spent hovering over the sink, stove, and her bed. Now as he led us upstairs, he looked smallish to me, even frail. His gray polyester slacks sagged off his hips, and his once muscular shoulders were shrunken.

Ascending the staircase, Robyn marveled at the family pictures. While my grandmother had earned her reputation as a civic leader of sorts and professor of education at Wayne State University, she was a historian at heart. Lining the wall at the bottom step were dozens of old sepia-brown photographs that traced my family's lineage back to late 1800s, when my great-grandmother, Mama Hattie, was a young girl. At the top of the stairs were colored Kodaks that included me as a beaming, Afro-wearing grade-school boy.

The bedroom door was closed. From the hallway I could hear music playing softly inside, and recognized it as the mournful croon of Mahalia Jackson. Daddy Grady knocked on the door.

"Margaret," he said. "Ronnie's here."

I had never heard, or perhaps never noticed, my grandfather address my grandmother by her first name. And it dawned on me suddenly, forcefully, that while she had always been my grandmother, she was in fact first his wife. And just as Robyn and I had, William Grady Ashworth and Margaret Crutchfield had also come together while young, dreamy-eyed and full of whatever hope there was back then for black couples in the South. He had stood before a minister and pledged his love for her. Since then she had slept beside him each night, given birth to his three children, cooked many of his best meals, and brought the kind of comfort into his home that only a woman can. She was no grandmother to him. She was his wife, and now he was living out, in its profound entirety, the final words of a vow taken more than a half century before: to stand by this woman in good times and bad, in sickness and in health, till death do they part.

He opened the door. She was lying on the bed beneath a blanket. Her long, thin arms rose slowly to greet us, and her neck, supported by pillows to keep her head upright, craned out toward us. The strokes had damaged many of her muscles, including those in her face, and I could see when she tried to smile that the drooping on the left side of her mouth had worsened since my last visit. Her light-brown skin looked dry and leathery, and the medication had cast a yellow, lifeless pall over her eyes.

It had become fact that no matter how much I prepared myself emotionally for these visits, it was never enough. It always broke my heart to see my grandmother as an invalid. Her own frustration radiated from her helpless, glazed eyes

This time, though, I promised myself that I would keep it together. As I watched Daddy Grady remove the blanket and help her sit up on the edge of the bed, I felt that familiar lump growing in my throat. I fought it back with a hard swallow and stepped over to kiss her cheek.

"I miss you, Mother," I said, running my hand through her feathery gray hair. "I brought someone I want you to meet."

I stepped aside and let Robyn move forward to face my grandmother. I knew how I felt about Robyn the first time I met her. I knew how I was taken by her presence, by the unblemished whites of her eyes, at the rich and deep glow of her copper skin, and her warm yet regal manner. Of course I realized that this was only my opinion. I watched nervously as Robyn stood there before the judging eyes of my grandmother.

"Hello, Grandma," Robyn chirped. "You know, I have heard so much about you."

At first there was no response, only silence and a long stare that seemed to last forever. It was clear that she was checking out Robyn, up and down. Only a grandmother could get away with such a thorough inspection, for anyone else would have been considered rude. Robyn didn't flinch, though. She stared right back at the old lady sitting down in front of her. Then I saw my grandmother's expression begin to change. A smile began working its way to her lips. She reached up, grabbed both of Robyn's hands, and kissed her hard on the cheek. Robyn came up laughing a kind of joyous laugh that comes with deep relief.

I, too, was relieved by my grandmother's reaction. Though a long stare isn't much to go on, I knew my grandmother could be an extremely tough critic. And there were few whose opinion I respected more than hers. I thought about my last visit during the Christmas holiday, just before her ability to converse had broken down completely. I had spoken of my fear of losing her, the backbone of our family.

"Our strength has always come from you," I said.

She had looked surprised to hear me say this. But it was true. Her illness had already set in motion a slow unraveling of our family, at least on the surface. Spared now from her pushing us, we had stopped going to church. Without her leading, the Sunday dinners, holiday get-togethers, and family reunions had become less of a priority. And without her stern hand and wise counsel there seemed a gradual erosion of the basic values and ethics she had imported from Lebanon, Tennessee. We worked less, spent more, and searched for happiness anywhere but in the Church.

"Who," I asked frankly, "will take over when you're gone?"

She grinned knowingly. "We will be fine," she assured me. "You just do your part."

We talked a great deal during that visit. Now as Robyn and I sat at her bedside, my grandmother was mute. She tried to speak a couple of times, but she kept losing track of her thoughts. This frustrated her deeply, so she stopped even trying. For a while I rattled on about a range of things; how grown up my nephews and niece had become, how busy things had been at work, how terrible the city was looking. She seemed to be listening some, but it was clear that her attention was riveted on the soothing voice of Mahalia Jackson wafting from a tape recorder at the foot of her bed. Her eyes were closed and she was swaying back and forth to the music. Robyn also seemed swept up in the melodious gospel song.

"Robyn has a beautiful voice," I heard myself say, turning toward Robyn. "Will you sing for my grandmother?"

The moment I uttered this, I half regretted it. Of course I was telling the truth. Robyn does have a beautiful voice. A velvet-smooth alto, she had recorded a solo album and was working on a demo for a second album. Yet while her work was in R&B, she had learned to sing in a Harlem gospel choir. Still, I knew it was wrong for me to put Robyn on the spot. I was sure she didn't appreciate it.

"I'm sorry, you don't—"

"Sure, I'd love to," Robyn cut in as though she had been hoping for this moment all along. She took my grandmother's hand. "Do you know 'His Eye Is on the Sparrow'?" she asked.

Mother nodded, leaned over and paused the Mahalia Jackson tape. We all sat silently as Robyn's sweet voice began filling the room. She sang as I had never heard her sing before, with a deep and heartfelt emotion that seemed to tremble the walls throughout the house:

> Why should I feel discouraged
> And why should the shadows fall
> Why should my heart feel lonely
> And long for heavenly home
>
> When Jesus is my portion
> A constant friend is he

His eye is on the sparrow
And I know he watches me

As Robyn sang, my grandmother's eyes opened wide and alert. She began to clap her hands and sway as though in a church pew, and Daddy Grady was watching his wife with a face of astonishment. For this moment, as we sat enveloped in the rich and sonorous melody of her song, the air around seemed weightless and ablaze, time felt suspended, and it was as though my grandmother was suddenly unburdened by her illness and she was young again and full of great joy. It was magical, and I felt giddy and proud that I had brought such a gift. For in this moment I would have sworn that Robyn had healed my grandmother, that in the power of her song all my grandmother's pain, fear, and sorrow had been cast away. Robyn peered at the woman and sang gloriously:

His eye is on the sparrow
And I know he watches me
I sing because I'm happy
I sing because I'm free
His eye is on the sparrow
And I know he watches me

Robyn's voice faded. My grandmother clapped softly. Daddy Grady smiled appreciatively. I leaned over and hugged Robyn. And then it was over. The house was quiet again and I could see my grandmother's eyes begin to dim and retreat back into herself. She was gone. For a while we all sat there quietly, awkwardly. I looked over at the clock on the dresser. Soon our flight to New York was leaving. I stood and gave my grandmother a big hug and kiss. So did Robyn. Then Daddy Grady led us out of the room. As he closed the door, I waved. "I'll be back this summer," I said.

Stepping out into the bright daylight, I saw a group of teenagers walking up to the house next door. I took Robyn's hand and walked toward the car. I had many questions. I wondered whether I would ever see my grandmother alive again. I wondered how my family would survive without her strong arms around us. I wondered whether I would ever live out the dreams she had for me, or whether she knew the depths of my love for her.

Still, as I pulled away into traffic, with Robyn sitting close beside me, I felt a great sense of relief surge through me. I was not afraid anymore. For now I knew that if God was taking one great woman out of my life, he had been merciful enough to bless me with another.

ALEXS D. PATE

Losing Absalom

Sonny needed a hand to help brace him for what was ahead. He knew that the man he loved and had lived with for nearly half of his life would not look the same. He took a deep breath and entered Room 1248. But, as soon as he was in the room, his eyes quickly shuttled to his mother. She sat there, on a chair, as if in a trance, staring at an empty, perfectly made-up bed. His father wasn't there.

"Where's Dad?" Sonny stood frozen. How long had it taken him to get there? Was he too late?

"He's not back from surgery." Gwen Goodman looked at her son. When he left home, she had been sorry to see him go. He did something to her. For her. His presence made her feel stronger. For years, she had secretly worried that he would never pull himself free of the spider web hold of North Philly.

Even though she hadn't ever talked about it, Gwen knew very well that on each corner of their dense neighborhood was a living danger. During the sixties, when Sonny was a teenager, street gangs ruled the intersections. Their members were called cornerboys. There was Twenty-fourth and Whither, known as the "2-4 WS." There were the "2-4 RS" on Rednor Street. And the most feared, "2-8," which had extended its turf in so many directions it no longer used its Oxford Street identity. In the 1960s, 2-8 was the power in the hood.

And Gwen knew that every time she sent Sonny out for food or cigarettes, when she used to smoke, or when he was outside playing, that he had to maneuver the best he could around the constant wars that raged on the corners.

In those days it wasn't about drugs. It was about territory. If you lived on Whither you didn't belong on Rednor. And if you were a boy and you couldn't manage to make enough friends for safe passage, you could easily leave the living world on your journey.

Gwen remembered how Sonny always stuck close to home. He spent his share of time on the corner of Twenty-sixth and Whither with his friends. But they weren't gang members. Mostly boys who played basketball and imitated the Miracles and Temptations until they had to go in. As far as she knew, he had never been a gang member. Still, she saw the tension and the pressure that was around him.

She knew it wasn't the same as growing up in the country, like she had.

Gwen had come of age in the small farming community of Newton Grove, North Carolina. And from the moment she picked up her first *Life* magazine, she wanted to move north. Newton Grove wasn't big enough, lively enough. Gwen wanted what the women in the magazines had: a manor and servants.

And in 1946, at twenty-three, one year after her father died, she packed her things and moved north. Her sister had moved to Philadelphia the year before and had cleared a path. Her dreams of society aside, the primary lure was opportunity. With the war industry still in full gear, fueled by new speculations of conflict in Korea and elsewhere, there were plenty of jobs. Gwen found work quickly at the shipyard, working on an assembly line for the navy.

Her first apartment was in a dark, narrow brownstone in North Philly. A cousin from Goldsboro lived in the building and had arranged everything. For the next thirty-four years she lived in North Philadelphia. From 1948 on, she lived with Absalom, on Whither Street, not more than three miles from where she had first set down her suitcase. North Philly became the backdrop to her life.

She watched Sonny intently. He was very uncomfortable, sweating profusely. His suit was beginning to pucker. She hoped he'd be okay, but all of her prayers were for Absalom. Every ounce of emotion, of optimism, of everything she had, had become a legion of soldiers marshaled under Absalom's command. They would fight to the bitter end.

Gwen thought about Absalom and the war they had been waging for his life. They had talked about it openly. Indeed, they had had strategy sessions in which they focused on using their combined energy to stop the growth of the cancer. Gwen was convinced that this was the only way to fight the disease. The doctors seemed to lack confidence in their ability to confront it. She would not wait around passively while Absalom deteriorated. If life was this way, she would adjust.

During the past year her soldiers had provided backup support for his soldiers. In the beginning, this imaginary attempt to heal Absalom seemed to work. Their spirits and his health kicked up a notch. But the enemy, a cancerous growth that fought for the occupation of his brain, continued to widen its field of engagement. It fought on multiple fronts. It defied military logic. And yet, the most devastating thing about the enemy was its persistence. Small defeats did not weaken its ability to rebuild its strength. Gwen looked at Sonny and slowly gave herself, in pieces, over to tears. She was very tired.

Sonny saw her eyes crystallize. He swallowed hard, slowly walked to her, bent down and kissed her on the cheek. Her chocolate-nougat brown skin savaged by winds, worry, and the intensity of life felt cool under the thin coating of cosmetic powder. The weight of her hands sank into his chest. He felt her fingers caress his spine. And slowly his feet disappeared into the floor. He shuddered once and collapsed into a pool of brown water.

He looked into his mother's eyes and saw everything that she had not said to him up to that moment. She was not the type of woman to talk much about the past. Nearly everything happened in the present. And the present was primarily positive. His mother hardly ever played the heavy harp. He walked into her eyes, felt his own reflection and understood that she needed him.

"Has anyone said when he's coming back?"

"No, they just said we should wait here." As Gwen talked, she exhaled a body full of air. "Nothing we can do, I guess, but sit here and wait."

She focused on Sonny. He was heavier now than he was two years ago when she had visited him in Minneapolis. But he was still tall and handsome. She often wondered how he had managed to remain a bachelor for so long. She thought he was more attractive than Absalom was in his prime. Sonny had Absalom's cool, penetrating brown eyes that could explode with a smile, but the rest of his facial features were softened by Gwen's beaming exuberance just beneath his skin.

"Where's Rainy?"

"I don't know. She was supposed to be here by now. But that girl moves so fast, always got so much going on that you can't fully count on her. Do you know what I mean?"

"Yes, Mom." Sonny relaxed. He knew his mother was just warming up. She had picked him up at the airport and had begun to fill in the details on everything. How sick his father was. How Rainy was doing. What kind of hospital they were dealing with. The longer he was with her, the more information he would get. His mother loved to talk and Rainy was her favorite topic.

Gwen had a well of patience for Rainy, confident that Rainy would eventually become something special, just as she thought Sonny had. And to Rainy's credit, she tried to realize her mother's expectation. But something always seemed to go wrong. Rainy's dreams were constantly being put back. Sometimes it was a man who stood in her way, sometimes it was herself.

The way Gwen saw it, Rainy's main problem was laziness—she just didn't work hard enough. If Rainy wanted to be a singer, then Gwen expected her to take singing lessons. But Rainy refused, believing that her connections would give her the ultimate big break. Now, at thirty-six, it seemed unlikely that she would ever pull her life together. Rainy, like so many around her, completely believed that it wasn't hard work that led to success, but people. Who you knew. What contacts you had.

Even though Gwen could see how confused Rainy was, she could never say anything negative. Gwen just listened patiently to everything Rainy had to say, all of her pipe dreams and fantasies, and hoped that things would turn out right.

"But she's getting much better. Much better. Since she's been going out with her new boyfriend, she's been slowing herself down a little." Gwen's words were always clear and well paced. There was little Southern sound in her voice; she had tried to leave that back in North Carolina. When she was tired or angry it would find its way in anyway.

Sonny sat back in the chair and crossed his legs while his mother's words filled the hospital room and transformed it into a parlor with plush overstuffed brocade chairs. He had always loved to hear her talk—he could still see himself, a little boy, listening to her read Mother Goose.

"Who's this new boyfriend?" Sonny asked.

"Some guy she met at the community center. He's real nice, though. I like him. He's smart." Gwen wiggled her body, pulling the material of the beige cotton dress downward. The wiggling was not graceful, but it straightened her dress. "He's smart like you."

Sonny had never heard her say anything positive about any of Rainy's boyfriends, ever. He was shocked. He just stared. This was big news. As smart as his mother thought he was?

Absalom groaned.

"Where did she meet him?" He was going in no particular direction, but he instinctively began a search for the critical weakness. It was inevitable. Sonny believed that all men had an essential, critical weakness that other men could identify with swift precision. It could be a core of coldness in a warm peaceful exterior, a fear, a streak of terror carefully woven into the fabric of bravado, or, worst of all, a dark cynicism carefully tucked away in a hopeful body. To Sonny, the men that Rainy chose, while smooth as Godiva chocolate, were in fact weaker than most.

"She met him in a class she was taking. Some kind of photography class. He treats her real good, too." Gwen knew what Sonny was up to and she wanted him to know that she was on Rainy's side this time. She didn't want to encourage Sonny's habit of picking on Rainy's boyfriends.

When he was younger, still hanging out on the corner of Twenty-sixth and Whither with his friends, Sonny had learned not to trust the smooth ones. In fact, he had come to believe that any sign of smoothness was a telltale danger sign. The Rooster sign.

Rooster, one of Sonny's friends when he was sixteen, was every parent's dream of a best friend for a young boy. He smiled, he was polite. He had surpassed even his television mentor, the character Eddie Haskell from *Leave It To Beaver*, who personified the art of parental deception. Rooster did it better. Absalom and Gwen never suspected he was an accomplished rogue. When things went wrong, no one ever thought about Rooster Jackson, the skinny kid with long, thick hair and an unending smile.

For a while, Rooster and Sonny spent a lot of time together. Away from adults, Rooster was a quicksilver shoplifter, never once getting caught. He would steal leather coats, tennis shoes, watches, jewelry—nearly anything in a department store. Sometimes he'd take the trolley, the subway, and a bus all the way to the Northeast, stand in front of a white school and rob students as they went home.

"Why are you doing this, man? Why are you always trying to get over on people?" Sonny remembered asking.

"How you think we gonna survive this shit, man?" Rooster talked fast. "Anyway, I do it 'cause I can. That's what power is."

Hanging out with Rooster was exhilarating and challenged Sonny daily on the choices he had to make. Sometimes, late on a warm summer night, sitting on the steps in front of Sonny's house, Rooster would make elaborate plans. In the multileveled sounds of night in the city, Rooster and Sonny's conversation created a world beyond the passing cars, the laughing girls, the watchful parents.

"Yeah, Sonny, we could follow the guy who picks up all the money from the PTC. Somebody picks up all that money, from every bus, every subway station, even the el. Man, think how much money that is. I could get a gun—just to scare him, you know—and we could find that guy who collects all that money and we could get in the wind man. Maybe go to Mexico or France or someplace where they can't get us."

Sonny always saw how easily they could be caught. Not Rooster. His success as a shoplifter had inflated an already healthy ego to monstrous proportions.

"Sonny man, I could steal the gold out of old man Benson's mouth without him knowin' it."

"But you're gonna get busted, Rooster."

"They can't bust the Rooster. I'm too cool man. Too cool. Smooth as silk. Soft as butter." Rooster's teeth glistened. "Anyway, you're not perfect. What about the peaches you always steal from Peachy's?"

"I quit that stuff, Rooster, you know that. And you should too. I can't be hanging out with you if you keep this up. It ain't right, man. Your life shouldn't be about ripping off people."

"Yeah, right. Whatever you say, man." Rooster turned his white eyes on Sonny.

Sonny stared back. He didn't care if Rooster didn't like it. Rooster was going in the wrong direction. He knew it. Rooster knew it. He couldn't just sit by and let it happen. That's not what friendship meant—going along. "Count me out, man. Just count me the fuck out. You can't live your whole life shoplifting."

"I'm not, man. Check it out. One day I'm gonna do the big one. I'm gonna get me a bank or something like that."

Sonny shook his head and stepped into a distance between them. They lost contact with each other. A year later Sonny went on to college, leaving Rooster in the grip of North Philly. Six months later, he heard that Rooster had been shot trying to rob a bank in Cheltenham. The adults in the neighborhood were completely shocked and would have sworn that he couldn't have done such a thing. Although paralyzed from the waist down. Rooster still lived in the neighborhood, his smoothness now confined by reality. Rooster's fate had scared Sonny, had caused him to create a mythology about the man.

Sonny distrusted most men. The smoother the talk, the more dangerous he thought them to be. He called it the Rooster sign. He watched for it. He listened for it. He had been close to one. He knew.

"What's he do?"

"Oh, he's a photographer. A very good one too."

"Really?"

"Oh yes. He's a very bright young man. He's very good for Rainy. He's what she's been needing."

Sonny smiled to himself. Just a little more time and information and he'd known exactly what was up. "Sounds great."

"I really think he is. He's a real gentleman. You don't find too many eligible colored men like him." Sonny thought she was laying it on pretty thick. He hadn't even met the guy yet and he was starting to hear crowing.

"What's his name?"

Sonny was watching as his mother averted her eyes and began looking at the floor. He wasn't sure what it meant. In the pause of action, he too looked around the room. He noticed the white sheets and white towels that seemed to be lying everywhere. The small television hanging high over his shoulder reflected a blank screen. Suddenly, he realized that his mother had been perfectly silent for too long.

"You don't know his name?"

"Well, ah . . . I guess I know it."

"Mom, what are you saying? You make this guy sound like he's Jesse Jackson or somebody." He paused to catch his breath and to help her absorb his point. "You don't even know his name?" This was definitely strange.

"Now, I told you." His mother didn't appreciate the attitude. "I do know his name. It's Danny." Gwen opened her purse and hunted for a small package of Kleenex. She felt the perspiration rising to the surface. When she found them, she pulled one tissue out and quickly dabbed her nose. "I think."

"You think? Mom, why do I get the impression you're not being honest with me? First you tell me how great this guy is but when I ask you what his name is you act like there's a brick sticking in your throat." Sonny's smile was full.

Gwen fidgeted. "Well, you know that Rainy. She can't just find a nice boy named George or Willie or even Sampson. That would be too much like right. She had to go and get somebody named Dancer. I know the boy's name. It's Dancer." Gwen was looking for another tissue.

"Dancer?" Sonny paused and looked out the hospital room window. It was a strange building. It was built with a large cortile. The rooms on the outer side of the building faced the streets, the ones on the inner side faced the courtyard and atrium. So as he looked out the window he saw a series of lifeless flags of imaginary countries. Below, a McDonald's peddled sodium burgers.

"You're kidding." A stunted laugh zipped out of his mouth and ran quickly around the room. He leaned forward with a large cantaloupe smile. "Could you please tell me what kind of name is Dancer? That must be a nickname, right?"

"I don't know, Sonny, he's not my son. I can't keep up with everybody and their names. Anyway, what's the big deal?"

"Dancer just doesn't sound like a real name."

"Well, as far as I know, it is. Besides, you don't have a lot of room to question people's names. Sonny ain't exactly the commonest name in the world."

"Well, listen to you. You're the one who gave it to me."

"Don't you go putting that on me. I didn't give you a name like Sonny. Your father did that to you." Gwen chuckled. Her body, seeking comfort, sank deeper into the chair. "I like it now though. It's bright."

"It's bright all right. People think I'm Italian or something."

"Just who are you making fun of?" Gwen was smiling, but Sonny could feel the world's rotation slow to a roll.

"I'm not making fun of anybody. I'm just saying, like I've been saying for forty years, I don't know why you gave me a name like Sonny."

"And I'm telling you, just like I been telling you for the last forty years, that I didn't give you the damn name." Gwen was now focused fully on Sonny. The profanity was out of her mouth so quickly she hadn't had time to reel it in before it broke into the air. "So don't get on my last nerve 'bout no name, boy. Anyway, you know your father gave you that name. And you know why. It ain't like I begged him to name you Sonny."

While his mother was talking, Sonny took a son's step back. He saw his mother sitting before his father's empty hospital bed, tense and edgy, and it made him sad. Sonny turned and looked out over the courtyard, twelve stories below. The south wing of the hospital faced him with its pattern of darkened square indentations. Within that darkness, Sonny imagined, so many people lay, shrouded in a thin hope, struggling for their own voice, singers in recline.

Not Absalom. He would not wait for them to give up on him. Instead he held his own song high above everyone. He encouraged Sonny. Nudged him on. He didn't understand why Gwen liked Dancer so much. She was not usually so easily fooled. But Absalom also knew that Gwen worried about Rainy's chances of getting married as the years passed, and Dancer was the most serious of all of Rainy's recent boyfriends.

"Did they say anything about how long we'd have to wait?" Sonny didn't turn to face his mother.

"Well, no. They said he'd be along in a short while. They wanted to take another look at him. Maybe there was something they missed or something."

Sonny was thinking that he didn't want his father to die before he had a chance to talk to him.

Suddenly the door to the room opened. Sonny's heart stopped. He saw his mother's reflection in the window. He saw the fire of expectation lick the rims of her eyes. As much as he wanted to see his father, he was also afraid to see what he might look like. But he could tell that she wasn't. She was almost smiling with anticipation. As he watched the resolve ripple in his mother's eyes, Sonny realized that he was watching a deep, long-thriving, wildly real bond between two people who had lived through the dark evolution of modern racism. He watched the proof of love reflected in the hospital window—a small, hesitant smile, flickering.

He turned to face the door and saw a sharp mahogany brown leg pierce the air. He smelled the brilliance of Rainy entering the room. Four years younger than Sonny, Rainy overshadowed everyone when she walked into a room. It took every ounce of their mother's energy for her to wrestle back control.

"Rainy. Where have you been? We've been waiting for you for the last hour." Gwen didn't give Rainy a chance to answer. "I'm telling you, I don't know where your head is. Here we are, your father is sick, and you're out hopping around somewhere."

"Hopping around? Mother, your daughter does not hop around. For your information, I was at home." Rainy looked around and broke into a wide grin. "Sonny, baby, I thought you were coming in later on tonight."

"The only flight I could get left this morning." Sonny moved, his arms involuntarily outstretched, his eyes focused on his beautiful sister.

"It's a good thing someone cares enough to get out of bed and come to the hospital to see your father." Gwen opened her purse. Suddenly she felt crowded in the small white room. She wanted to get up and leave the room. She wanted to be somewhere else for a few minutes. Instead she fumbled around in her purse as her two children hugged.

"I'm glad you came back," Rainy said into Sonny's ear. "She needs you."

"And we both need you, Rainy. How are you?"

"I'm fine. But where's Dad?"

Absalom smiled. Altogether they amounted to pure energy. As a whole they helped him understand his life. He liked for them to hug, to touch each other. That was what a family was for.

Gwen closed her purse with a snap and pushed her hair backward and into place. "They said they wanted to take him into the operating room one last time to make sure there wasn't something else they could do."

"Oh God. Whenever these butchers start testing and experimenting you never know what they're going to do."

"Rainy, please." Gwen grabbed Rainy's hand. "Let's think positive."

"I am positive, Mom. But they haven't done a damn thing for Dad since he's been here. I just don't understand why they can't do something for him."

"They're trying, sweetheart. They're trying." Gwen stood up and walked over to Sonny, dragging Rainy with her. They all stood facing the door, looking over the neat empty bed, staring into space.

KALAMU YA SALAAM

What Is *Life?*

In 1985 I was not simply a witness to a death in which I was personally involved, I—and to recognize this was to recognize how "American" I actually was—I became a murderer.

I murdered my marriage. "Murdered" because although I felt too weary to continue the relationship, I was not too weary to willfully put a stop to the relationship. My partner, Tayari, did not want to end it. I did.

Although I had never taken the longevity of my marriage for granted, I never expected the relationship to end. I certainly never envisioned being the one who would walk away from our marriage. But I did, and that walking away both hurt and humbled me.

I would lie awake some nights, staring into the darkness and looking at myself, almost forty years old, stretched out on a bed by a window in the same room I grew up in three decades earlier.

But this was thirty years later. There I was returning to my father's house. He welcomed me. Never questioned why or how I had arrived at where I was. He gave me a lot of space as I wrestled with the eerie notion that my father was not surprised that I left my marriage and returned to his house.

I was hurting, but not in self-pity or guilt. I am instinctively competitive. I hate to lose. But more than that, I hate to give up.

I seldom give up on anything. Once, I was trying to make it to the bank before it closed. I had been working at the computer and had not kept track of the time. When I looked at the clock, it was five minutes before the drive-up window closed that night, and the bank was about ten minutes away. It was already too late to try. But I jumped up and sped into the night anyway. I had nothing but a little gas and twenty minutes to lose, but I had a lot to gain.

As I turned into the bank drive-up, the two neon signs said CLOSED. The curtain was pulled down at the window. But inside the teller's window the lights were still on. Maybe it was two or three minutes after 9:00 P.M. I drove up to the window. Someone peeked from behind it and waved me away. I looked at the guy, rolled my window down, and blew the horn. Another person peeked from behind the curtain; it was a sister whose name I don't know but who recognized me. She pushed the carrier open and served me. I thanked her, made my transaction, thanked her again, and drove off. My spirit of never giving up once again was reinforced by the reality of succeeding after it seemed all hope was gone. I don't give up easily, not at anything.

Many months after I had left home, I was visiting the house talking with our children. Asante, our oldest, a sixteen-year-old junior in high school, was describing a frustrating class situation she faced that semester. She resigned herself to hard times. I told her to slug it out. Her problem was with the teacher and not the material. Later Asante and I were speaking about something else. My relationship with Tayari came up, and she reminded me of our earlier conversation: "Didn't you say that you shouldn't give up?" I knew where it was headed from the way she said it. "Yeah." "Well, why're you giving up?" I looked at her. I told her she was right, but sometimes no matter how hard you try, things don't work out.

"Sometimes, no matter how hard you try, things don't work out." Sometimes life is beyond your control. No matter the popularity of "rugged American individualism," the individual is not lord. The individual, although a powerful force, is limited.

The major problem with the limits is that the fences are invisible. Too often we cannot see what stops us, even as we are stymied, even as we are frustrated, we feel it but we cannot see it. We cannot understand what limits us. What authority? What superior power?

In the face of invisibility sometimes all we can see is our own weakness. Such situations can be debilitations, can take the wind out of you like an unseen cross-body block thrown on you by a crafty opponent as you run full-tilt downfield, your eyes fixed on some distant ball carrier whom you desire to tackle. The person whose block knocked you out and left you gasping for air, your sides aching, your head wondering what happened, that person knew what they were doing. Certain unanticipated situations lurk on the field of life and hit you from the blind side, they hit you squarely, not unfairly, but they get you by surprise, and when you're hit like that, you go down. Don't care how strong you are, how fast you are, you go down.

Perhaps you learn from the incident, perhaps you learn to look the field over as you run so that you won't get caught by a sneak attack again, but that "perhaps" is a later time. Right now you're on the ground, confused, in pain, momentarily out of the game. At such times, down and out, it's hard not to feel foolish. Look how stupid I am to get blocked out and knocked down like this.

I looked at my daughter. I did not say anything else.

I did not plan to return. I was resolved. She knew.

Asante's personality is a lot like mine. We both have heavy problems with authority figures. We both are willing to suffer whatever consequences in our quest to live our lives the way we choose. And suffer we do.

I'd lie in my room hurting because more than any other emotion I was overwhelmed by a sense of failure, even as I was resolved to call it quits.

I was humbled. I have a high level of self-confidence and firmly believe in my own ability to control myself: self-determination.

I don't believe that I can do anything I want to, but I do believe that I can do almost anything. But this was something I couldn't do. I couldn't work out my relationship with Tayari (gradually I came to realize that, as with so many other obstacles in life we fail to cross, part of my failure was not a failure of ability but a failure of will: I really didn't want to do whatever it would have taken to make the relationship work—why I didn't was a whole other set of questions I'm still wrestling to answer).

In the small room with two windows I came to the realization that I was ending a major phase of my adult life and embarking on a new phase.

As I looked at it, almost all of the major relationships I had formed in the past were either ended or down-graded from major to minor. It was then that I began to formulate my theory of death as the dominant reality for African Americans in the eighties.

Before the termination of my marriage I had resigned from Ahidiana, a pan-African nationalist organization (a political formation that had operated a school from the inception of the organization in May 1973, a bookstore for about three years, a printing press/publishing apparatus for five or six years; had organized and instituted cultural programs such as Kwanzaa and a lecture series; and had participated in and initiated community-oriented political activities including antiapartheid demonstrations).

In 1983 I had left the Black Collegian Magazine, a company of which I was a founding member in 1970.

All of those events were milestone markers that turned into tombstones as I ran past them toward the 1990s.

I was born during the postwar optimism of the late forties, went through puberty on picket lines buoyed by the promise of civil rights in the mid-sixties. By the seventies, Black power in my eye, liberation on my mind, I and many, many others of us put all our chips on making momentous change on the mountainous political landscape of America. But mountains, unless blown up, change ever so slowly. We went to the mountain and, by the eighties, found that as much as we changed the mountain, the mountain had also changed us—in fact we had been changed more than the mountain had changed.

Moreover those of us who got to the mountaintop alive, we live to see what generations of African-American mountain climbers have seen as they attempted to scale the heights of America's oppressive power: another mountain. There's always another mountain.

After a sobering peek at reality dissolved the romantic visions that had fueled our climb, we came down slowly. We were shaken by what we had seen. We left friends and comrades, dreams and ideals, broken and too often unburied in the crags and crevices of that mountain that is the 1980s in America. Back in the valley we do not look forward to the next climb (nor to any more climbing for the rest of our lives), but we do not find the valley hospitable either. No rest in the valley. No strength to climb.

Tombstones in the valley and weather-beaten skeletons on the mountain's face mock whatever plans for any future climbs we halfheartedly make. Nevertheless for some of us there is no other choice, we must go on.

Going on will no longer be joyful (sometimes our very grimness alienates those who would help us, who would join us, but what are we to do?—we cannot fake mirth; down to the marrow of our bones we are sad). Young soldiers may look forward to the challenges of war, old soldiers prefer the search for peace even as they heft their weapons and head out on another mission.

Seeing death close up makes you wish for the death of death, but alas death is the only aspect of life that never dies.

For long periods after my father's death I felt like I was drowning in waves of emotions, odd sensations that would wash over me while I sat at a stop light in the car or when I was on the phone talking to someone and someone would say something like, "We're really gonna miss your father," and I would think, *Miss him, sheeit, you don't know—you can't know what missing is about,* and for a couple of seconds I would go blank. I don't feel unique. I don't feel that it's just me being sentimental, but I had never crossed this bridge before, and handling it all was confusing.

I don't care what pop sociology says about Black men as father, Black fathers are very special and very important human beings. To be Black, man, and father in modern America is no small accomplishment. Yet we have had many, many males among us who have somehow managed to be Black and man and father: something akin to sainthood, except they are flesh and blood, emotions and thoughts, and uniformly tough.

Black men who are fathers—strangely none of my initial thoughts were about how my children viewed me, the whole number was concentrated on me looking at my old man and how his passing affected me.

One thought was that I was now the oldest of the Ferdinand men. That thought was a big wave. There were so many expectations and assumed responsibilities tied into being the oldest male, expectations and assumed responsibilities that I had been studiously either refuting or not accepting.

I remember when my mother died and the day my youngest brother "disowned" me. At that moment he wanted a big brother. Someone to take charge and care—somehow neither of us thought of my father doing it all. We were on the front steps of my house on Tennessee Street, and Keith was angry with me. There was something he wanted me to do or thought that I should be doing in relation to my mother's death that I just flat out refused.

I told him, "No, don't put that on me. If you think it ought to be done, then you do it." He said I was not his brother anymore—the expected action was so low-priority in my consciousness that right now I can't even remember what it was, but the repercussions were so deep that I will never forget how Keith reacted—even now, well after we have settled those differences.

I had already moved away from continuing the tradition of the family name, when I changed my name both legally and actually, and though I never asked my father or my mother for permission to do so—at that time everything we did was an act of will, our own will against the world, and we were young and inexperienced enough to believe, to actually believe that our will could carry the day, and if not carry the day, at the very least carry us as far as we felt like going—I never asked my parents. I wasn't living with them at the time, and frankly never even thought about asking them; I just changed my name at a Kwanzaa ceremony in 1970.

So instead of my son being Vallery Ferdinand IV, he was named Mtume ya Salaam. And moreover I believed then and believe now that as our children grow, they should exercise the right to decide whether to keep the names of their birth or choose a name reflective of whatever they want their names to reflect.

I had chosen "Kalamu ya Salaam"—first because it literally meant "Pen of Peace," which was my greatest ambition, to be a writer whose work contributed to real peace for our people. Second because it was a Swahili name, which meant that it was a nontribal language used across national boundaries as a trade language. Swahili is an African language and at that time it was the only African language that was the sole official language of an African country; most of the African countries had European languages as the official language.

Both my mother and my father called me Kalamu, although it was not uncommon to hear them sometimes say (as did most of their friends) "Lil Val" or "Val-ry" (which was the way my birth name was usually pronounced). The people who named me accepted me changing the name they gave me.

This may not seem like much, but at that moment, my mother's death not even a week old, my youngest brother (Kenneth and Keith did not change their names) confronting me—Keith had been in medical school at Howard in D.C. and had left to go back to school just two days before my mother died—at that moment, whether either of us consciously thought about it or not, my change of name was just one very visible example of my break with tradition and my break with my family, a fissure that caused Keith a lot of pain. I guess Keith thought that I didn't care, and certainly he rejected my way of caring, of moving ahead.

In retrospect I had boxed off a lot of traditional-type feelings and was flying ungrounded on the wings of youthful vision of Black people overcoming, uprising. A more truly deep Black consciousness would have found a way to carry tradition with it, but I was young at that time. I did not know deep.

So Keith was rightfully reacting to what he correctly perceived to be his brother's denial of the responsibility of being a "big brother," except in my mind I was not really denying that responsibility. I believed we all had a responsibility to and for each other that stretched far beyond the accidents of birth and outmoded notions of "family" or something equally rational and equally unrealistic.

So now with my father's death, suddenly, like it or not, acknowledge it or not, I was the "head" of the family. I realized with sadness that if continuity and continuance depended on me, then the Ferdinand family was ended. I would not carry that tradition on.

The Ferdinands, like so many, many other Black families, would fragment, the nexus of grandparents, uncles, aunts, cousins, children, mother, and father would become too far-flung and too unrelated in day-to-day ways to be a family any longer in the old sense of the word.

DAMU HAKIM

A *Father's* Lament

My friend and I were in a similar predicament. We had both recently experienced a family breakup through either divorce or separation. His situation was a little rougher than mine. While the mother of my children and I amicably agreed to go our separate ways, my friend and his wife went through bitter divorce proceedings, and a struggle ensued over the custody of the children.

We often talked about our problem of being cut off from our children. My ex-wife had laid no rigid conditions restricting me from seeing my children; she just made it understood that my visitations were not welcomed. Sure, I could see the children, but only under her conditions. To see them, it was often necessary for me to feel my way through an emotional minefield, careful not to say the wrong word or make a wrong move.

I was willing to abide by her rules, "to go along, to get along." My friend was not as passive. One day, after being denied his weekly visit, he went by his ex-wife's house and demanded to see his children. When she refused to open the door, he kicked it down. They argued for several minutes and he threatened to take the children. After he knocked her down, she ran to the bedroom, got her pistol, and shot him in the head. He was dead before emergency medical service arrived.

All of this happened six years ago, but the incident is still fresh in my memory. And it becomes even brighter during those moments when I have to make plans to see or to talk to my children. Though it has been nine years since our separation, my ex-wife retains a chilly disposition and does not encourage any relationship between my children and me. They have never called me, there are no birthday greetings or Christmas gifts from them to me; in no way do they acknowledge my existence.

I wonder what she tells them about me. What kind of picture does she paint? Am I the villain, the bad guy who made her life miserable and whose fault it is that their daddy is not there? When they ask about me, are they silenced? What is her attitude when my name is mentioned; what image of me has she shaped for my children?

On the few occasions when I am lucky enough to talk to my children—we live hundreds of miles apart now—they never ask me anything beyond how I feel, as if they have been well schooled not to pry into my personal affairs. These conversations are usually awkward, and I hang up the telephone depressed, mulling over the many unasked questions.

My situation is by no means unique. From my research I have discovered there are thousands of men who are interested in maintaining ties with their children but have been legally or emotionally thwarted by the courts or their former mates. In the news you hear about all the men who have abandoned their families, leaving their wives and girlfriends to raise their children alone, but what about those of us who want to help nurture and provide for our children? Don't we count?

For far too many of us Men Without Our Children there is no recourse through the courts, nor is it possible to appeal to the mothers. I think the majority of these mothers are interested in their children knowing who their fathers are; they are concerned with them having a relationship. However, there remain a sizable number of mothers who are still nursing some old wounds, who have still not forgiven, who are still determined to hold the children as hostages against the sins of their fathers.

My position on this matter has been to leave my ex-wife alone. I reached the conclusion many years ago that my phone calls and visitations were too unsettling, not wanted, and thus I limited them. She needed neither my money nor my counsel in the raising of the children; sometimes I had the feeling that she wished I were dead. That would certainly make it easier for her to create whatever impression she wanted the children to have of me. Anyway I prayed that with time she would mellow.

There was a period, when the separation was new, when my mother would keep me posted on my estranged family. But then the mother of my children decided that even for them to see my mother was too much of a task. Since our conversations, like those with the children, are confined mostly to greetings, I am still not sure what the problem is and why she continues to be so uncordial and reticent.

Even when some friends we once had in common—some of them unaware of the separation—ask about me, she lets them know that she is not interested in discussing me or my endeavors. I am sure that some of these encounters have been witnessed by the children. It is hard for me to believe that they are impervious to this disdain.

Recently, after going six years without seeing them, I spent some time with my children. Obviously their mother was not at this meeting, which was facilitated by other members of her family. It was clearly understood that the children were not to leave the house with me. No sweat. I was content merely to see them after so many years apart.

The hour or so we spent together was very fulfilling. In several ways we were old friends, checking each other out and recalling half-forgotten events. They were sensible, well-mannered, and quite considered. I learned that they were excellent students. My daughter was a budding flutist, like her father; my son a talented athlete, unlike his father. Their mother had done a fantastic job. And without my help.

It was painful to realize that my children were repeating my experience as a child, who was raised by a single mother. This was one cycle I had promised myself to break. I had quietly pledged not to have my children come up without a father. I had failed. Here in my family was another generation of children without a father. The Nintendo games could not hide my sadness.

After the brief visit I began to ponder my next move. Now that I had seen them, was it possible to go a step farther and ask if they could visit me sometimes? I wanted to get to know them a little better, for them to see the world I lived in, meet some of my friends. It had taken quite a bit of courage and patience to wrangle a visit, I thought; asking for them to come to see me might have to wait a few more years. This is the challenge confronting me now.

Somehow I think the children should have a say in all this. They should be given an opportunity to express their desires. Would their mother be willing to honor this right? It would seem that anyone who had done such a splendid job of raising two remarkable children would not for a moment abrogate their wish to know their father. I am carefully planning the moment when this situation can be discussed.

Indirectly my plight is akin to that brigade of fathers who are struggling for custody of their children, or for the right to have a relationship with them. This problem should not be left up to the courts when it can be decided by common sense. Children and fathers, like the nation's mothers, have rights, and they should not be infringed. If there were a more democratic legal environment for the rights of fathers, there is a strong possibility that the desperate acts committed by my friend and others could be avoided.

NATHAN McCALL

Makes Me Wanna Holler

HELL

I had forgotten how painful life can be. Now, with my divorce pending, it reminds me that life can be very painful, so painful that it becomes a physical ache, a strained feeling in the heart area that can only be relieved by time. I've weathered some tough storms in my 33 years. This one ranks right up there with the toughest of them.

March 11, 1988

Compared to my divorce, doing time in prison was like a day at the beach. Divorce is *hell*, pure and simple, a classic example of how screwed-up and backward-thinking the court system is. More than in any other ordeal in my crazy life, my frustrations with the courts during and after my divorce showed me that the folks running the system don't have a clue.

Nothing in that process works as it should. Nobody has figured out a way to make divorce fair to all concerned. Some women get shafted beyond belief, while others abuse the system and use the courts to slamdunk their men. Some men abandon their parental duties and skip out, certain that the system can't or won't track them down. Those men who *do* try to be responsible for their kids often get pushed aside and financially beaten down, it seems, in retaliation for those who don't. And children get caught in the middle of all that mess.

Divorce. Somebody gets fucked up *real bad*, no matter which way it goes.

Debbie and I had to go through an endless series of hearings and postponements that stretched out for more than a year before the final court appearance. That provided ample time for hostilities between us to simmer and grow. We shared a tension-filled house and nothing more. We slept in the same bed, but barely spoke to each other except to take care of household matters. All the while, Ian and Maya swarmed happily around us, too young to fully understand the depth of the conflict between their parents.

Debbie and I knew we couldn't live together anymore, yet neither of us wanted to leave the house. I wanted to stay because it was *my* house, bought with *my* money. Debbie said she wanted to stay because she had the kids. Actually, her reason was nobler than mine, but I couldn't see past my anger enough to realize that.

Being in the house together created an atmosphere that was volatile and scary at times. One night, when Debbie and I got into an argument, she came charging at me, swinging wildly and banging me with her fists. Ian heard the ruckus and came running from his bedroom into ours. Maya came behind him. Ian started crying, and Maya cried, too.

Ignoring the children, Debbie kept swinging. I grabbed her wrists to keep her from hitting me, and we both fell onto the bed. She got madder then. As the children screamed, she ran to a phone and called the police. By the time the cops showed up, she'd calmed down enough to let me convince her to send them away.

The incident showed me that Debbie knew her greatest weapon against me was the law. After that run-in, I was sure that if anything funky went down, I'd be back in jail.

Whenever I step into a courtroom—for anything—I get flashbacks of the past and see terrifying images of white ghosts sentencing me. I always get ready to bend over because I know I've got it coming. I always think about something we used to say on the block: "Be sure to take a jar of Vaseline with you to court 'cause you gonna get fucked."

On the day of the final hearing, I sat in the courtroom with my palms sweating and my head throbbing, furious that I had to go before an old white man to get permission to dissolve a relationship that was already dead.

I was mad at everybody, including my lawyer. When I'd fallen behind on my legal bills, he stopped working on the case. I went to the bank and got a five-thousand-dollar loan to cover the fee, and he got back on the case again. He made it *real* clear that, first and foremost, he was about money.

Of course, Debbie's family all came to town and sat in on some of the trial. I looked across the room at my wife and her mother and thought about the irony that the same two people pressing for me to get married were now clamoring for my head. *They gonna use the system to punish me 'cause I wouldn't get with the program.*

During one of her trips to the witness stand, Debbie unleashed a bomb that left me nearly floored. She told the judge, "Your Honor, I'm afraid of Nathan. He has been to *prison* for violence."

I was stunned. I considered that the ultimate betrayal. It was clear that she understood racial dynamics well enough to use my prison past to her benefit. I thought, *Go on. Tip off the judge. Let him know there's a dangerous black man here who needs to be controlled.*

I sat there and listened as her lawyer used legalese to call me every kind of no-good motherfucka in the book. "He did willfully" do this and "he maliciously" did that. The thing that bothered me most was that they tried to make it appear that I didn't want to support my children. I kept wondering, *How can they even suggest that? I got married for the sake of the children.*

The case was simple to me. Debbie wanted the house and a thousand dollars a month in child support. I couldn't afford to pay that much, live, and send money for Monroe, too. But it didn't seem to matter what I couldn't do. In the end, I got hit with support obligations that I couldn't possibly meet—five hundred dollars a month in child support. She got to stay in the house and I was ordered to pay the mortgage, nearly seven hundred dollars each month. The total came out to about twelve hundred dollars a month, half of my take-home pay.

When the judge brought down the gavel, I felt like I'd been sentenced to do time all over again. I was crushed. Humiliated. I felt like I was being punished because the marriage didn't work. All I could do was shake my head. *One of the few times in my life when I really tried to do what I thought was right and I get kicked square in the behind.*

On the way out, I asked my lawyer, "What am I supposed to do, go live in a homeless shelter? What about the costs associated with getting a new place after kicking out all those legal fees?"

He said, "You've *got* to pay it or they'll throw you in jail." Then he reminded me that I had to pay him, too.

I said, "But I'm not saying I refuse to pay child support. I'm saying I *can't* pay that full amount and survive. Isn't there somebody I can talk to to explain?!"

"No." Then he looked at me and did what lawyers often do. He shrugged his shoulders and said, "That's just the way it is."

That's just the way it is. People in the system say that all the time. Like there's no way in heaven that a thing can be changed, because they're locked into an established way of doing that thing. Like they can't bring common sense into the system to correct a proven flaw. *That's just the way it is.*

When I left the courtroom and walked through the shiny halls, I saw Debbie's family down at the elevator, skinnin' and grinnin' and congratulating her.

Claxton and Chip went with me to help remove my possessions from the house. Chip and I were in the basement gathering things when Claxton appeared at the top of the stairs and called down to me: "Yo, Nate, there's somebody here to see you."

I went upstairs and saw two policemen standing in the living room. One of the officers said, "Your ex-wife called and said you're taking things from the house that don't belong to you."

Debbie appeared from a back room. The lawman asked her what possessions I was taking that weren't mine. She pointed to a piece of artwork that I'd taken down from the wall. The artwork had been a gift, given to me by Chip and his girlfriend before I got married. I dug into my pocket and whipped out a court-approved list of my possessions and showed the lawman that the artwork in question was included on the list. Seeing that, the cop got mad as hell. He turned to Debbie and got on her case hard for needlessly calling the police on me. "Why would you do something like this?! Don't *ever* do anything like this again!"

Debbie looked sheepishly back at him and kept quiet.

The scene was pitiful. It was so pathetic that I didn't even get mad. When I looked at Debbie standing there, I saw clearly the extremes she'd go to in order to get at me. I felt ashamed that others saw it, too, and that they knew that I'd married someone who would stoop so low.

The cops left, and for a moment the living room was silent. I stood there, looking disgustedly at the woman who was once my wife. She glared defiantly back at me. And Claxton and Chip looked on, shaking their heads in disbelief.

They called it "joint custody." What it really meant was that Debbie got the children and I got to "visit" them every other weekend. I had no say in decisions about where they went to school or in anything else involving their lives. As it turned out, Debbie's parents had more access to Ian and Maya than I did. It was frustrating, and my lawyer kept telling me that there was nothing I could do. *That's just the way it is.*

Even the visitation itself was rife with strains. I never knew what to expect when I went over there, so I'd take Chip along to serve as a witness in case something ugly jumped off. Once, when we got to the house, there was no one home. No note, nothing. I knew Debbie was expecting me because I'd just talked to her by phone.

After that happened more than once, I filed a contempt action to have the judge force her to comply with the visitation order. We got into court, and when the judge learned that I'd fallen behind on child-support payments, he refused to hear my complaint about visitation. I told him I was doing all I could to raise the money needed to catch up. He looked at me coolly and said, "I suggest you file for bankruptcy."

The message from the judge was clear to me: The courts view the father mainly as the money source. *That's just the way it is.*

In no time, I got caught in that recurring cycle that body-slams lots of men after divorce: Every time I fell behind on support payments, Debbie filed an action to take me to court. Every time I went to court, it forced me to spend money on legal fees. (The judge would order me to pay her lawyer, too.) That was money that could have been used to help catch up on support payments.

It went round and round like that until I'd exhausted all my savings on legal fees and support payments, and gone deep into debt. I applied to banks and credit unions, and couldn't get another loan. After getting an apartment, I had no money to live on and had to hit up my parents and friends for money. All the while, I kept wondering about life in the fucking system, which just didn't seem to be working for me.

I knew it was just a matter of time before I fell so far behind that they'd lock me up for failure to pay child support. Desperate and depressed, I began to think illogically. At one point, I thought about dropping everything, just quitting my job and going underground to get white folks off my back.

None of my domestic problems related directly to my race—divorce is a universal hell—but when compounded with all my racial stresses, the divorce and its aftermath took a greater toll. My head was messed up so bad that I'd go for days sometimes without any sleep. Even now—five years later—I still have occasional problems getting to sleep at night.

Sometimes, when I thought about what I was going through, I felt sorry for myself and wondered why I seemed to spend most of my life catching hell. I'd think, *Maybe this is God's way of paying me back for all the hurt and pain I've dished out to other folks. Maybe I need to accept it as divine justice and quietly take my lumps.*

At other times, I looked at it another way: that the anguish was the price I had to pay to be able to live with myself and face the world; that two of my children could say that their parents had been married, no matter how brief and ugly that union had been.

Every now and then, I ran across other dudes who'd been through the same hell as me. We'd spend hours comparing notes and sharing horror tales. Every one of them had a piece of divorce-related advice to give. Sometimes they said things I needed to hear. Like the one friend who told me, "No matter what goes down, take the high road. It's important that you be able to look back on this and feel good about the way you handled yourself."

Sometimes cats told me things I didn't need to hear. Like the tale about one guy who took matters into his own hands when his wife wouldn't let him see his children and the courts refused to do anything to enforce his rights. "He knocked that bitch's front teeth out," a friend told me. "He got thirty days in jail for it, but you know what? Every time he goes round there to get his children now, she hands them over and don't give him no problems."

Those rap sessions carried a lot of weight with me and sometimes affected what I thought and did. I decided that I wanted to do what was right—take the high road—but the notion of knocking out Debbie's teeth also carried some appeal for me.

One day, I went to the house to try to talk with her about calling a truce so that we could stop making lawyers rich. As I sat on the couch, she stood over me, ranting. She went off. Blah, blah, blah, blah . . . I sat there, quietly listening. Suddenly, I couldn't make out what she was saying anymore. Her lips moved and her arms flailed, but I couldn't hear. Without being aware, I'd slipped into a zone. I've been in that zone before. I went into it just moments before I shot Plaz. It's a semi-conscious state where nothing gets absorbed and all logic and reason shut down for the night.

I looked at Debbie and thought about all the anxiety she'd put me through. I thought about the incompetent court system and how it seemed that nobody cared what was happening to me. I thought about taking the high road, then about the cat who'd "knocked that bitch's front teeth out." Something inside me said, *Yeah, knock her front teeth out. You can do thirty days in jail standing on your head.*

That familiar tightness formed in my chest, that fight-or-flight feeling that used to come over me in the old days on the streets. I felt it rising, like vomit just before it convulses you and forces its way out of your mouth. I felt myself about to leap up and punch her in the face. I felt it coming over me, and I got scared. I knew that if I got up from that couch and took one swing—*one swing*—it would get *good* to me and I wouldn't stop. I wouldn't stop until I was completely exhausted or until my ex-wife was stone cold dead. As I sat there, mute, the voices of divorce veterans kept whispering, competing for control: *Knock that bitch's front teeth out. No, take the high road.*

I'd recently read an article about the benefits of counseling. Written by a psychologist, the article said that people don't realize they have to take care of their mental health in the same way they tend to their physical health. The writer said people routinely go to doctors for physical checkups, even when they know there's nothing wrong with them. People should go to counselors, he said, for mental checkups.

That made all the sense in the world to me. I thought about that article as I sat there contemplating whether or not to attack my ex-wife. I decided, then and there, that I needed counseling. I got up from the couch and walked out the door without saying anything, leaving Debbie still in the living room, raising hell.

The next day, I contacted a counselor and went in for therapy. The counselor was a white woman. She seemed to understand right away what I was going through. Seeing how hyped and uptight I was, she prescribed some medication to chill me out. She also gave me her beeper number and said, "Now listen. I want you to put this number in your wallet and keep it with you at all times. I don't care where you are—if that feeling ever comes over you again, call this number and talk to me."

It was comforting to know I had someone to call if I needed advice. That, more than anything, helped me eliminate thoughts about turning violent again. I came close to the edge once or twice after that, but each time, the assurance that I had someone to turn to was enough to calm me. That counselor doesn't know it, but she probably saved Debbie's life.

RALPH WILEY

On the A-Train to Venus with Isis

There are six narrow categories under the broad rubric of *For Black Women Who Are in Close Relationships with Black Men (When the Shower Is Not Enuf)*:

1. Lovely Black
2. Angry Willa
3. Honey Child
4. Black Pearl
5. Down Twala
6. Licorice Chick

Before you start the bonfire, let me explain:

"A nice man will win out over a bowwowwowyippeyoyippeyay."

LOVELY BLACK

Like New York City, love is not for everybody. Many people find they feel, act, and do better outside of it. They tell themselves this after they find they can't deal with it day to day. They can't get work done when they are in love. It flays their nerves. They can't hear themselves think. And it's always so crowded in love, there are so many people on line. Those that aren't on line in love are in line on love. It's hopeless—or it makes them feel that way. It's too big, too busy, dangerous, dirty, overwhelming, so leave me out, I'm better off where I am now, thanks anyway.

One thing that always amazes me about love is how you find it when you're not fishing for it at all and can never locate it when you've got out all the maps looking. There we were waiting to be inhaled by New York City with the rest of its daily breath of flotsam and jetsam, standing on a train platform minding our own business. Like everything else within two hundred miles, we were resigned to our fates.

You know how you laugh to yourself when you meet couples and the man (or the woman these days) says, "I met her (his) fine butt walking down the street!" You know how ridiculous that sounds when somebody like Sir Mix-A-Lot or Bobby Womack or one of your old friends says it. We all know they walked up on a problem walking down the street. Those people who are not properly introduced, who attract each other purely on looks, will never get along. We know this. And when it happens to you, bang-bang, you wonder what took so long as your brain bows to the body of life. People tell me the brain is the key to attraction, and age has proven them to be right. But when you're young, it's hard for your human brain to convince your human body who's boss. It may be true in the end, but the body has a hell of a lobby and can put up a good filibuster, and if you're caught weak or missing, if you are caught being human, there you are, all in lust, hoping it's not love but maybe wanting it to be because we've all seen the same movies, heard the same fairy tales. We've all been asked to dream the same blessed dream.

But that very interior sizer-upper that caused you to be stopped in your tracks by Lovely Black once, eventually may cause you to notice others as well, especially when you are young and your eyes are still good. Just to look, as one looks at the works of art hanging in a good gallery, or an exceptionally long mural. Just to look at their soft, good countenances, upright characters. Their trim constitutions and luscious smiles. But those very people whose qualities stopped you in the past and caused you to compliment and pet them end up becoming upset if you notice the same qualities in others. It's said you get only one true love in life. The hard part is knowing which one. The subway can be confusing if you don't know where you're going in the first place.

"I hate men. And I don't care why anymore."

ANGRY WILLA

Why does your woman ask you if you think some beautiful actress like Halle Berry is fine, and when you say, "Maybe, a little bit," she gets mad? She won't ask, "Do you think Aunt Esther is fine?" Heaven forbid a gimme like that. She won't even ask, "Do you think Halle Berry is smart?" Instead she'll ask, "Do you think Halle Berry is fine?" You hold your hand over your nose so this woman won't see it growing like Pinocchio's, but she sees it anyway and then gets mad and asks, "What you mean, 'a little bit' fine? Oh, you think she's 'a little bit' fine, huh? My friends said if I asked you, you'd tell on yourself. Let's see you go try and get Halle Berry to make you 'a little bit' of dinner."

"Er, sweetheart, you didn't make *any* dinner. And since you brought it up, you haven't made dinner in three months. I'm the cook around here. You said so yourself."

"That's right. Now you know why. And I'm sure not going to make dinner now. So Halle Berry is fine? Well, there's people around town who think *I'm* fine, you know."

"I know, dear. I used to think you were fine myself."

Every time I see a fine sister now, I pause and think to myself, "Somebody, somewhere, is tired of that woman." That can't be my line. But whoever thought of it was a man.

"Thank you."

HONEY CHILD

At least I know it can be done. People can get along. We just shouldn't try to put any time frame around it. Honey Child and I put up with each other for ten years. I never thought I'd do anything for ten years. I always thought that whatever it was, I'd get it done in less time than that.

Honey Child had youth, energy, anger, a sense of humor, good looks, a serviceable brain, and a dead throwing aim on her side. I suppose I take the role of general and supreme commander of my life a little too seriously at times, but this was a good campaign we'd mounted, and Honey Child ended up a general herself, battle decorated. I thought I might get a thank-you for encouraging instead of discouraging her in going back to school for a bachelor's degree or taking classes to get anything from a real estate license to a better understanding of Zen or Mary Kay—you know, things people do and then later wonder how and why they did them, if they are successful. I suppose it could cause resentment when you constantly remind somebody how much you've helped them be successful, and sort of gloss over how they might have helped you. People make their own decisions about what they do in life. Husbands, wives, friends, and lovers only suggest. Honey Child was not beyond saying, "Thank you." Never said it loudly, unless it was much too loudly and slathered with sarcasm, but after ten years, you can tell.

"Nooo, thank you."

BLACK PEARL

Sometimes a woman can help you most by saying no. This happened to me on one occasion before I decided to come and face New York and work there among all my good White folks. "Nooo, thank you," said a fine, talented, experienced friend. "I've been there. I've put up with it before. You'll never be seen for what you are, only for what they'd like for you to be. Which, by the way, isn't very much." When she said it, it intrigued me. I soon learned what she meant.

I'd heard "no" before, when I was young. Young men often hear "no" because they ask questions impossible to answer in the affirmative. Young or old, sometimes men overstep themselves. We want what we can't have, we want to hear what we want to hear. If more women knew this they'd have an easier time keeping us in check. No means no.

It wasn't until later I began to hear a different, more strident and angry kind of no. It was coming from sisters who had been hurt, and it resonated in *For Colored Girls Who Have Considered Suicide (When the Rainbow Is Enuf)* and *The Color Purple*, and other works that cut deeply into the scar tissue of pain. Time passes and heals, but only if you let it. If you stop picking at the wounds of the heart, they have a better chance of healing. A physically abusive man is not a wound but a cancer. But a man who steps on a woman's feelings doesn't always know what he's doing. Sometimes he might be rather clumsily protecting his own feelings.

So what happened was this: I went to a Black-owned television station to be interviewed. The person who was going to interview me was a sister with a lovely hairstyle and a bad disposition. Her smile was not sincere.

"I can't *wait* to hear why you have titled this book *Why Black People Tend to Shout*," she dripped.

"Irony," I begged. "Lady, please, it's irony."

"Yessss," she said. I thought of the serpent god Set.

She was a "senior producer," she said. The show began, and she said, "We had Marita Golden and Terry McMillan and several other Black women authors on our show yesterday, and we all were commenting on how we're *tired* of men *whining*."

"It's going to be hard for me to love this woman as a fellow human being when she's hardly giving me a chance," I thought to myself, but I couldn't show that on my face because the cameras were rolling and the show was live and at the time neither one of us could afford to be completely honest. So I just said, "Well, Miss, we will whine. We are Black men, after all." That tossed her off her high horse for a while, and by then a couple of people had called in to the show who had actually read the book she talked about so very knowingly for someone who had read maybe two pages.

Maybe we'll get along next time, though.

I got along okay with Terry McMillan. You all know Terry. She's the author of books—*Mama*, *Disappearing Acts*, and, most notably, *Waiting to Exhale*—and she does a good job of examining relationships from her perspective. Once we had a brief conversation—again, the conversation took place in televisionstudioland. I was at what is called a "remote" location. I thought it was unfair that Terry and I didn't first get to know each other, or at least get to know each other's delivery, before being asked to be on television together. However, I enjoyed talking to her, and Terry, for her part, allowed I was "better than average" as a man, on sight (I'm not asking for Womanist Papal Dispensation from Terry or anybody—to *hell* with Womanist Papal Dispensation). If women only knew, all any man wants to hear, honestly, is that he is better than average, especially coming from a total stranger. I gave Terry my disarming line about the way many men feel: To far too many of us, commitment is to love what Twain once said golf was to a good walk: "The perfect way to ruin it." Terry laughed like she didn't want to, but had to, and that is a good laugh to pull from somebody. I also mentioned that I'd never heard of "masculine wiles," and Terry seemed to get that one too.

I came upon Terry at yet another made-for-television event, a forum of writers who got together in Washington, D.C., at the behest of the group called Black Issues in Higher Education. On the panel were Marita Golden, the novelist Charles Johnson, Terry, and poet Nikki Giovanni. They discussed some of the few joys and many pitfalls of writing. I admired all of them, for I know what it is, to try and write. I know what it can do to you. Nikki Giovanni was born in Tennessee, but insisted she'd grown up in Ohio, outside Cincinnati, and felt a kinship with her fellow Ohioan Toni Morrison. She wore a rhinestone pin that said JAZZ, a recent Morrison fiction title. I sat in the audience ruminating on all this. Well, I was from Tennessee, and so were Alex Haley and Ishmael Reed and Vernon Jarrett and Carl Rowan. (Maybe I can see Nikki's problem.) And what about Mary Church Terrell and Beverly Guy-Sheftall and the melodic Gloria Wade-Gayles? Ida Wells and Richard Wright were from Mississippi, but found inspiration in the long state. So what could be Nikki's problem with being a writer and coming from Tennessee at the same time? She then hummed a few bars from an old television show that I'd forgotten. "Davy, Davy Crockett," Nikki sang. I found myself completing the chorus under my breath. "King of the wild frontier." I told you, being a writer can make you crazy. The host of the show, Renee Poussaint, mentioned it was odd for Nikki to sing this song when they were supposed to be talking about literature, but Nikki, not one to be cornered, had already put her faux pas behind her without mentioning she had suffered one, which was the way to do it.

Then a Black female student called in to the show and read a portion of a paragraph from Terry's *Waiting to Exhale*, something about a group of women sitting around talking about how most Black men either had no job, were married, or gay, or in jail, or on drugs, or just plain can't fuck (Terry is a good writer who can get raw—and it seems to work for her, too). The female student asked if Terry thought this was advancing a cruel stereotype. Terry didn't have to say a word because the other artists, especially Nikki Giovanni (I have some of her albums, by the way, and *damn* Womanist Papal Dispensation), leaped to her defense, as they certainly should have done as artists. Terry recreates that which is in her to recreate. What else can she do?

Nikki's defense was particularly strident: "Well if you don't like it, change the reality," she said. Not five minutes later, Spike Lee's *Malcolm X* came up. Nikki again piped in. She was beginning to resemble a hungry baby robin in a nest of them, demanding to be fed first. "I hated it, *hated* it," she said. "It was horrible, horrible, this guy acting like he was coming on to Malcolm in prison, and Malcolm looking like some kind of doofus in the barbershop, getting his hair conked, and then kissing this blonde White woman and never kissing his own wife! I hated it. *Hated* it!"

Unfortunately, Nikki had just mounted a tirade about the very images she had defended when coming from Terry. *No job, on drugs, in prison, gay, married, won't fuck.* That was what she had described as hating, although I'm not sure where she saw all this. I'm not sure if she hated the film, or if she hated Spike Lee, or if she hated me. And I was beginning to feel I didn't have a hell of a lot of time left to find out.

After the show I asked Terry why she didn't defend Spike. Terry looked at me. The last time I saw Terry, she was laughing and had a chicken bone in her mouth. And I love her for being her own artist, and *fuck* Male Papal Dispensation.

Professor Derrick Bell left the Harvard Law School faculty in the spring of 1990, on leave until "a woman of color" was granted tenure on the faculty. Two years later he was still on leave, and his job was revoked. I didn't see his kind of male character in sitcoms or popular novels. Just a point.

"Kill the head and the body will die."

DOWN TWALA

There was one outstanding occurrence around the publication of Shahrazad Ali's controversial *The Blackman's Guide to Understanding the Blackwoman*. Sister Ali sold a lot of books. I met her, you guessed it, at a television station. This is getting ridiculous, I thought. They used to say if you wanted to meet a nice woman, go to church. Now if you want to meet any kind of woman, you have to go to a television station. Sister Ali was getting eyes cut at her from the sisters, whom she had pissed off in her book, but I have to say, she didn't let this stop her. So I asked her the real question: "I've heard your book sold 200,000 units. Is that so?" Sister Ali said, "Honey, 200,000 units is low." I immediately became mentally aroused. I wanted to know how to practice that particular kind of togetherness. But Sister Ali wasn't telling me any specifics.

A while later, she came out with *The Blackwoman's Guide to Understanding the Blackman*, which didn't do nearly as well. Black women thought she was just coming down hard on them. Sister doesn't discriminate. If she makes you mad, she figures, you're going to buy her product, or at least talk about it, whereupon someone else might buy it. Later Sister Shahrazad said she had never been invited to speak at the Smithsonian like Terry McMillan or "Roger Wiley." Hmmm. Here's one way to understand the Black man—get his name right. I think the sisters have to get past Sister Ali's book and get to the sensitive spot she rubbed in Black men. We all want to be made to feel special. Some women know this about men and feed that part of the male ego in order to be fed in return, or not, depending on the I.Q. of the man.

"Ragglely."

LICORICE CHICK

I am more likely to fall in love with great talent from afar than with good looks up close. Show me a woman with skill who lives out of state and I'll show you a woman with sex appeal. I also like a woman who can speak a form of dialect that can make me relate and laugh. I'm from the country, no matter what airs I put on, and I like people who can understand my sense of humor. So let's get right to it. When White men and Black women, and Black men and White women, get together, some sisters have been known to point out, somebody's stuff can get "ragglely". But I really have no comment on it either way anymore. It seems as if a large percentage of talented Black people, men and women, end up marrying people other than Black people after they get pseudo-rich and semifamous. I hate to see the talent and the wealth dispersed, but on the other hand, what fool would try to legislate against the power of love? It would be like trying to legislate against a straightening comb.

When people are in love, there's no reasoning with them anyway. We all know this happens, so we might as well applaud when two human beings, whatever color, can get along. We should say, "Great job! Wonderful choice! *Voila!* Bravo! Woof-woof-woof-woof!"

That should make them question what they're doing quick enough. That's what we *should* say, all right. But you know and I know that we are going to listen to the gossip, section off in groups, make a noise and that face like you smell something fishy, and say, "No he/she didn't, girl!"

"I love you."

DEAR JESUS

I must confess here that there is a seventh category of woman, just as there's supposed to be a seventh heaven, a seventh sign, a lucky seven. This Seventh Woman of the Hidden Heart is not so aptly named, though, because meeting any more than two in one lifetime might kill you. The Seventh Woman is that woman who, when you see her, you say, "Damn!" even if you're in church or with your mother. Or she kind of sneaks up on you like a normal everyday woman, and then she smiles at you one day and you see her as you never saw her before and your cold heart feels as though it's been transplanted to Negril. She is the woman you cannot help but love. She warms her way into your soul.

The Seventh Woman is the woman who fits you in all ways, who is your match, whom you love, the one you hit your knees to thank God for sending you—all those things you'd scoff about if you weren't under her influence. All those things you have to convince yourself to do in order to be with other people, you think you already are with her, the operative word here being *think*. Clear thinking seems to go out the window when you are confronted by the Seventh Woman, and then if she tells you she loves you too, well, that's the ball game right there—unless she decides to change her mind, which, after all, is a woman's right.

It's a man's right too, come to think of it, but the Dear Jesus Seventh Woman is not a woman you can leave. You never do leave her, even if she leaves you, or even if you walk away out of abject fear of the power and vulnerability of true intimacy, which scares most men worse than death itself. The Seventh Woman of Life is the woman you meet who then makes you say, "tra-la, tra-la, maybe all that moaning and groaning about real love is true. Maybe I can be happy." Maybe this. Maybe that. It is the "maybe" that makes life worthwhile. You ask me how I know this. I've met the Seventh Woman. Ducking her did no good.

It's up to Black men to provide more than love at this point in history. It's up to Black men to provide a presence, a buttress. We have to get busy working business plans. Love has to wait, not according to me, but according to the way American society has treated Black men and women so far, which is to say to try and get rid of us. Sometimes work comes before love. We do love you sisters, we love you because you brought us here, every walking one of us.

Hang in, hold on, and do what Patti LaBelle says in "Love Never Dies": "You've got to fluff up, baby, I mean fluff up. Beat your face into place, get back in the race . . ." For as Sterling Brown once revealed, "Strong men keep on coming."

"Need some help?"

DARE HAVE A DREAM

Did I say seven categories? Make that eight. No, make that nine . . . no . . .

MY BROTHER'S KEEPER

RUDOLPH FISHER

The Walls of Jericho

In Patmore's the discussion concerned a possible riot in Harlem, a popular topic among these men who loved battle.

Jinx Jenkins and Bubber Brown led the argument on opposite sides, reinforced by continuous expressions of vague but hearty agreement from their partisans:

"Tell 'im 'bout it!"

"That's the time, papa!"

"There now—shake that one off yo' butt!"

Jinx and Bubber worked at the same job every day, moving furniture. At this they got along tolerably, but after hours they were chronic enemies and were absolutely unable to agree upon anything.

Jinx was thin and elongated, habitually stooped in bearing, lean and sinewy, with freckled skin of a slick deep yellow and a chronically querulous voice.

"Fays got better sense," said he. "Never will be no riot no mo' 'round hyeh."

Bubber was as different from Jinx as any man could be, short, round and bulging, with a complexion bordering on the invisible.

" 'Tain't due to be 'round hyeh," he corrected. "It's way over Court Avenue way. Darkey's gonna move in there to-morrer and fays jes' ain't gon' stand fo' it." Bubber spoke with a loose-lipped lisp, perfected by the absence of upper incisors.

"Who he?" Jinx inquired.

"Some lawyer 'n other name' Merrit."

"The one got Pat in that mess with d' gover'ment?"

"Nobody else," said Bubber.

"Well ef he's a lawyer he sho' mus' know what he's doin'."

"Don' matter what he is," argued Bubber. "Ef he move in that neighborhood, fays'll start sump'm sho'—and sho' as they start it, d' boogies'll finish it. Won't make no difference 'bout this Merrit man—he'll jes' be d' excuse—Man, you know that. Every sence d' war, d' boogies is had guns and ammunition they stole from d' army, and they jes' dyin' fo' a chance to try 'em out. I know where they's two machine guns myself, and they mus' be a hund'ed mo' in Harlem."

"Yea," said Jinx. "I've heard 'bout that, too. But I don't think no shine's got no business bustin' into no fay neighborhood."

"He got business bustin' in any place he want to go. Only way for him to git any where is to bust in—ain' nobody gon' *invite* him in."

"Aw, man, whut you talkin' 'bout? Hyeh's a dickty tryin' his damnedest to be fay—like all d' other dickties. When they git in hot water they all come cryin' to you and me fo' help."

"And they git help, what I mean. Any time dickties start fightin', d' rest of us start fightin' too. Got to. Dickties can't fight."

"Jes' 'cause they can't fight ain' no reason how come we got to fight fo' em."

" 'Tain' nothin' else. Fays don' see no difference 'tween dickty shines and any other kind o' shines. One jig in danger is ev'y jig in danger. They'd lick *them* and come on down on *us*. Then we'd have to fight anyhow. What's use o' waitin'?"

"Damn' if you'd ever go out o' yo' way to fight f' no dickties," Jinx taunted.

"Don' know—I might," Bubber said.

"Huh!" discredited Jinx. "You wouldn' go out o' yo' way to fight f' y' own damn self—and you far from a dickty."

"Right," cheerfully agreed Bubber. "I'm far from a dickty, no lie. But I ain' so far from a rat." Jinx missed the meaning of this, so Bubber sidled up close to him and drove it home. "Fact I'm right next to one."

Encircling grins improved Jinx's understanding. "Next to nuthin'!" exploded he, giving the other a rough push.

"Next to nuthin', then," acquiesced Bubber, caroming off. "You know what you is lots better'n I do." Whereupon he did a triumphant little buck and wing step, which ended in a single loud, dust-raising stamp. Dry dust and drier laughter floated irritatingly into Jinx's face. Jinx was long and limber but his restraint was short and brittle. Derision snapped it in two.

"So's yo' whole damn family nuthin'!" he glowered, heedless of the disproportion between the trivial provocation and so violent a reaction. For it is the gravest of insults, this so-called "slipping in the dozens." To disparage a man himself is one thing; to disparage his family is another. "Slipping" is a challenge holding all the potentialities of battle. The present example of it brought Bubber up short and promptly withdrew the bystanders' attention from their gin.

The bystanders began "agitatin' "—uttering comments deliberately intended to urge the two into action. The agitators concealed their grins far up their sleeves, presenting countenances grave with apprehension and speaking in tones resigned to the inevitability of battle.

"Uh-uh! Sho' mus' know each other well!"

"Wha' I come fum, dey fights fo' less 'n dat."

"Ef y' can't stand kiddin', don' kid, I say."

"I don' b'lieve he's gon' hit 'im, though."

"I know what *I'd* do 'f anybody said that 'bout *my* family."

As a matter of fact, the habitual dissension between these two was the symptom of a deep affection which neither, on question, would have admitted. Neither Jinx and Bubber nor any of their associates had ever heard of Damon and Pythias, and frank regard between two men would have been considered questionable to say the least. Their fellows would neither have understood nor tolerated it; would have killed it by derisions, conjectures, suggestions, comments banishing the association to some realm beyond normal manhood. Accordingly their own expression of this affection had to take an ironic turn. They themselves must deride it first, must hide their mutual inclination in a garment of constant ridicule and contention, the irritation of which rose into their consciousness as hostility. Words and gestures which in a different order of life would have required no suppression became with them necessarily inverted, found issue only by assuming a precisely opposite aspect, concealed a profound attachment by exposing an extravagant enmity. And this was a distortion of behavior so completely imposed upon them by their traditions and society that even they themselves did not know they were masquerading.

Bubber, his round face gone ominously blank, drew slowly closer to Jinx, who, face thrust forward a little and scowling, stood with his back to the bar counter, on which both elbows rested.

"Mean—*my* family?" inquired Bubber.

Jinx dared not recant. "All the way back to the apes," he assured him "—and that ain't so awful far back."

"The apes in yo' family is still livin'," said Bubber, "but they's go'n' be one daid in a minute."

"Stay where you at, you little black balloon, or I'll stick a pin in you, you hear?"

By this time Bubber was almost within range and an initial blow was imminent. Absorbed in the impending clash, no one had noticed the arrival of a newcomer. But now this newcomer spoke and his words, soft and low though they were, commanded immediate attention.

"Winner belongs to me."

Everybody looked—spectators holding their drinks, Bubber with his blank black face, Jinx with his murderous scowl. They saw a man at one end of the bar counter, one foot raised upon the brass rail, one elbow resting on the mahogany ledge; a young man so tall that, though he bent forward from the hips in a posture of easy nonchalance, he could still see over every intervening head between himself and the two opponents, and yet so broad that his height was not of itself noticeable; a supremely tranquil young Titan, with a face of bronze, hard, metallic, lustrous, profoundly serene. He repeated his remark in paraphrase:

"I am askin' fo' the winner. I am very humbly requestin' a share in his hind-parts."

It was apparent that the bristling antagonists bristled no longer, had limply lost interest in their quarrel.

"Aw, man," mumbled Jinx, "what you talkin' 'bout?"

"You know what I'm talkin' 'bout, you freckleface giraffe, and so does 'at baby hippopotamus in front of you. We got that Court Avenue job in the mornin', and if I got to break in one rooky on it, I might as well break in two." The voice, too, was like bronze, heavy, rich in tone, uncompromisingly solid, with a surface shadowy and smooth as velvet save for an occasional ironic glint.

"This boogy," explained Bubber, "thinks he's bad. Come slippin' me 'bout my family. He knows I don't play nuthin' like that."

"Need'n git uppity 'bout it," mumbled Jinx sullenly.

"Ain' gittin' uppity. Jes' natchly don' like it, thass all. Keep yo' thick lips off my family ef y' know what's good fo' y'."

He who had interrupted queried blandly, "Ain't there gonna be no fight?"

Jinx said to Bubber— "Aw go 'haid, drabble-tail. Ain' nobody studyin' yo' family."

And this questionable apology Bubber chose to accept. "Oh," said he. "Oh—aw right, then. Thass different."

The atmosphere cleared, attention returned to gin and jest, and Bubber approached the giant, who now was grinning.

"Certainly am sorry th' ain' go'n' be no hostility," sighed the latter. "Been wantin' to spank yo' little black bottom ev'y sence you broke that rope this mornin'."

"Aw go 'haid, Shine. That boogy's shoutin' 'cause you was hyeh to protect 'im. I'm go'n' ketch 'im one these days when you ain' 'round, and I'm go'n' turn 'im ev'y way but loose."

"Don't let 'im surprise y'. He kin wrastle the hell out of a piano."

"Piano don't fight back."

"Don't it? Well—neither will you if he get the same hold on y'."

"Humph. Who the hell's scared o' that—freckle-face giraffe?"

SYLVESTER MONROE

Brothers

Ray Stingley, corporate middle manager, was flying in for the barbecue, an interplanetary traveler descending from a distant world, and his old homies from Prairie Courts formed a welcoming committee to meet his plane. Greg Bronson was up from Tampa, taking a weekend away from his auto showroom; Vest Monroe, Big-Time Vest, had come from Washington between political assignments for Newsweek; *and Steve Steward—well, Steve had all the trappings of success if you didn't know they were borrowed. They were waiting at the gate at Midway Airport when Ray deplaned, his thickset body briefly filling the exit door. He was dressed for the cookout in shorts and a striped polo shirt, but he was carrying a leather portfolio full of ConvaTec business, and he had another plane to catch in a few hours for a meeting on the Coast.*

The rendezvous at Midway was a reunion within a reunion, the first time the four of them had been together since their freshman year at Phillips High, and they greeted one another warmly. They were the ones who got out while there was still time, the achievers who had left the projects and set out in pursuit of the dream twenty years before. All except Steve had achieved a piece of it; they had started out as boys racing one another hungrily through the success stories in their grade school library, and three of them had gone off and written their own—stories of hard work and solid achievement in the American mainstream. Only Steve had stayed behind, home in the projects, where he knew his way around.

"You're looking good," Ray told him, watching him nose Bev's Audi out of the parking lot and start south for Trey-nine.

"That's 'cause my woman takes good care of me," Steve said. "Even though I don't take such good care of her."

Only Vest among the four of them was really at home at Trey-nine, having grown up there. Some of the Thirty-ninth Street brothers were fleetingly irritated with him for having brought the Prairie Courts bunch; the projects had always been suspicious of strangers. "Hey, Vest," one of the picnickers said peevishly, sizing up Greg's careful grooming and his tan baggies, "I thought this was a Trey-nine thing. Who're these outside MF's?" Vest smiled and said they were OK, and the issue was settled; his word was good enough.

Still, there were curious stares, and the visitors moved with the awkward step of tourists in somebody else's country. Ray moved through the crowd, meeting the people, but he was constantly stealing glances at his watch, worrying about his plane and his meeting. Greg stood apart, sipping a beer, a soft-spoken man with a bemused smile and an oddly formal bearing. He was Kamau Akil, citizen of the Republic of New Africa, a warrior in the defense of black people; he could quote Malcolm X and take down an AR-15 rifle, but he lived his daily life in a different world, light-years away from his childhood in the projects. He had just come off the tennis courts, where he had split a match with his father, one set apiece. He had expatriated to another country, far from home.

It was Steve who belonged, though he had never lived in the Taylor Homes. He came from the projects, and while he had been handed a passport out, he had not made it; he had got a few steps across the frontier, but the terrain on the other side had frightened him, and he had retreated to safe ground. He was at ease anywhere there, with his gregarious nature—his outwardness—*and his disarming smile. He had pulled up at Trey-nine early in that gunmetal blue Audi, music up and sunroof back, profiling as if the ride belonged to him, not his woman. Heads turned as he parked and stepped out. Showtime.*

His eyes found Honk in the crowd. They came from different 'hoods, but they had some tastes in common, and their circles intersected.

"Hey, Roy," Steve said, "what's up with you?"

"Hey, brother," Honk said. "You got it."

"I hope these gangsters down here don't F with my ride," Steve said, glancing back at the Audi.

Honk grinned. "We already moved on them MF's," he said. "They know better than to bring that BS around here today."

Steve grinned back, that little I'm-cool smile. He felt as easy at Trey-nine as if he had lived there all his life. He knew where he was.

It was easiest never to leave home. Ghettos were created to hold their inhabitants inside, but their boundaries were a defense perimeter as well, a secured border within which people felt as if they *belonged*. The world beyond that line was terra incognita. The white people who owned and occupied it seemed afraid of young black men and, being afraid, made them feel unwelcome or worse. To walk into a store or hail a cab in the street was to risk humiliation; to apply for a job or a promotion was to invite rejection and never know why; to mingle with whites was to enter a country where a smile could be an open invitation or a coded warning. The projects and the streets could be places of great physical danger, but their perils were mostly known and predictable and were subject in some measure to commonly understood rules. There were, for example, places and situations one avoided and hours of night at which one preferred to be indoors among friends.

The white world downtown didn't operate that way. It had rules, to be sure, but they were like the bylaws of a restricted club: You had to become a member to know them, and you had to know them to become a member. Violating them could, in extreme circumstances, be a corporal or even a capital offense. In the winter of 1986–87, three black men were assaulted by whites for the crime of having stopped for a pizza in a white enclave called Howard Beach in the outboroughs of New York City; one, fleeing the attack, ran into the path of a car and was killed. The vastly more common danger for a young black man was to be judged, silently, by his color and to be prisoner to certain widely held assumptions about it—that he was probably less capable than whites and quite possibly armed and dangerous. The fact that not all white people shared those prejudices was small comfort as against the great number who did—most of them, if one believed one's elders, with their tales of life in the Jim Crow South and in Miss Anne's kitchen. Sorting good whites from bad could be an intractable puzzle, a Rubik's cube rigged against solution. The easiest thing was to give up, put it down, and walk away home.

Most of the Trey-nine brothers had done precisely that; they had surrendered halfway through high school and had led lives outside the frontiers of the white world, with its standards of judgment, risk, and reward. Some had shown promise in school, up to a point. Sonny was quick at his lessons; Honk's drawings hung in the principal's office; Moose had a writer's imagination, in search of words to give it expression. But it took more than intelligence to break out of the cycle of despair. It required the belief that it was *possible* to break out when the stale smell of defeat in the air you breathed told you daily that you could not.

To sustain that belief would have demanded stronger support systems than many of them had, at home, at school, and in the community. Their parents—mothers alone, as often as not—struggled valiantly to feed and clothe them and raise them right. But the fight exhausted whatever small resources of money and hope were available to most ghetto families. It took a particularly stubborn soul to imagine, under the circumstances, that life could or would be much better for one's children. The schools, for the most part, had already surrendered. The peer pressure against learning was furious, and the argument for it—that it would lead somewhere—bumped against the pervasive expectation that it would not. Boys growing up in the ghetto were made aware daily of how little value the larger society placed on the lives and, in a postindustrial age, the labor of poor black men. Their own fathers, too often, were casualties, those who stayed home and those who disappeared. The defeat of one generation begat defeatism in the next.

For most of the Trey-nine brothers, the odds favoring real success in the outside world seemed about the same as the possibility of hitting the Lotto, and the risks were a good deal higher than the price of a dollar ticket. Most preferred the game of chance, even knowing it was mathematically stacked against them; in the other, larger competition, the Man controlled the cards and the rules, and it was accepted as a given in the ghetto that he would never willingly deal black folks into the action—certainly not *poor* black folks.

Accordingly, most chose not to play. It was easier to stay behind and scuffle; in a world conditioned to defeat, merely to survive was a triumph of sorts, and if the payoff was small—service jobs, mostly, for subsistence money—so were the risks of being judged a failure. In the white world, you were made to feel marginal, one in a caste of men consigned by their color to work and to housing that no one else wanted. Among your own, nobody except maybe your woman held you to blame for what kind of job you had or how little you made doing it. You didn't have to be a banker or a brain surgeon. Merely getting by was enough; doing it with a touch of style was, in the eyes of the bloods on Thirty-ninth Street, a triumph.

That any escaped was remarkable. Steve Steward had been handed the keys, thanks to the ABC program, and still hadn't made it. He had walked out into the larger America beyond the ghetto, looked around for a while, and then fled home. He persuaded himself over the ensuing years that there was nothing much out there he wanted anyway. In fact, the world had frightened him. He was fifteen years old when he first glimpsed it at Hanover High; he had wondered all through his boyhood in the ghetto whether white people really existed and then was made suddenly and forcefully aware that *hey!*—they're *predominant*.

He got through his three years among them playing the role he knew by birthright, the tough kid from the projects, an image gentled by his wit and charm; the motto next to his picture in the school yearbook was "Black Power," but the descriptives were "easygoing" and "talkative." The entry further noted that he "likes Chicago," and once he got back there, he stayed, where he grew up at, he liked to say; where he could feel safe. He had never wanted to be more than what he was, and no one in his world demanded it of him, not his doting mother, or his absentee father, or his lovesick women, or his partners on the street. White people and white standards became unreal again. He had traded the danger he felt among them for the security of the reservation, and if he was still role-playing—if his prosperity was borrowed from his ladies and his self-esteem was mortgaged to his drugs—it didn't matter to anyone except himself.

Greg Bronson had ventured even farther from home and had found that he could manage nicely, at least in that daylight world where the deals are done. He took an athlete's pleasure in the game, in closing a hard sale and, in the process, confounding all the white man's European notions of what black men could and could not do. He did not otherwise like being around white people, not unless he was in competition with them; he never lost the sense that every day he spent among them was a day behind enemy lines. The only way he could manage it, psychically, was to armor himself against them and at intervals to secede from their company entirely.

It caused him pain to be thought a racist in reverse. He sometimes wished he could be more flexible on the subject; he even conceded the possibility, out of his own experience, that at least some *few* white people were honest and sincere enough to deal with a black man on terms of mutual respect. The problem, in Greg's suspicious eyes, was that so many could not. In his middle thirties he was still the lonely black teenager in the steel-company office, seeing hostility in the white faces all around him and burning with anger and shame under their gaze. His defense mechanism, then and now, was to act on the working hypothesis that *all* of them were his enemies. It simplified his relationships with them, sparing him the difficult exercise of sorting out which few meant him well. If you shut them all out, none of them could harm you.

His world view was, of course, disabling to his progress and his prospects in corporate America; he could handle any job he was given, but he could not easily work for white people, presuming as he did that they were dedicated to his failure and perhaps his destruction. Not many boys coming of age in the ghetto were immune to doubts about the intentions of the Man; they had the word of their parents and grandparents on it, and the impressions of their own daily lives. Most internalized those feelings and reached a kind of inner accommodation with them, sometimes at great cost. They submitted to the limits on their hopes and possibilities as if they were ordained and maybe even just, the judgment of nature or God.

Greg strained against them. His habit of mind was not surrender but war, and so he entered upon his double life, his three-button daytime persona serving as camouflage for the soldier he became after dark. As Greg Bronson, he was one solitary man, alone and vulnerable. As Kamau Akil, armed, disciplined, and dangerous, he was one with the non-white majority on earth. His anger and his ambitions made a bad match, and there was a price for his militancy, in his life, his career, and his inner peace. Still, he preferred living inside his vision, as a citizen of New Africa; it seemed to him preferable to submission to the ways of a world ordered on the white man's terms. When he and his brother opened Gilead-Angelo Construction, Inc., in the Chicago suburbs in the spring of 1987, it was at once an act of entrepreneurship and a declaration of independence.

He was one of a dozen black teenagers who had set out from the projects of South Side Chicago twenty years before, each in quest of his particular version of the grail. Their hopes had not been very different from those of boys on the far side of the ghetto walls; they aspired to jobs, homes, families, cars, and a little in the bank for a rainy day. But practically all the circumstances of their lives conspired against them, starting with the color of their skin and the poverty of their beginnings. If success means material well-being, a full share in the affluent society, only two or three among them could be said to have achieved it. One had died in a fight, a casualty of the meaningless violence of the ghetto. One was in prison. One was a burned-out basketball player with only his scrapbooks to show for his glory days. One was an underground man, a dropout dependent on drugs and women. One was living in the psychic no-man's-land between his middle-class life-style and his revolutionary black rage. Most were marking time at the margins of the American economy, working-class men in a contracting job market.

And yet there was a measure of victory in most of their lives, not least the fact that they were alive at all; sudden death is a commonplace among young men in the ghetto, and violence is its leading cause. Some had been hustlers and outlaws and had gone straight. Some had been addicted to drugs and had got clean. Practically all were working most of the time. None was on unemployment or the dole. Most had children, and some were trying hard to be fathers to them. The others fit the statistical profile of family life in the ghetto, with its rising numbers of births out of wedlock and families headed by women on welfare. But they did not neatly fit the stereotypes of black men as irresponsible babymakers, uncaring about the love children they had left behind. Those who had failed at fatherhood were only too painfully aware of their failure. They had had neither the money nor the skills to succeed at it, and when they walked away from their women and children, they were not denying their responsibility; they were, rather, conceding defeat.

That some succeeded at life was more extraordinary, given the obstacles in their way. Their stories were the stuff of American myth, the immigrant experience reproduced in the projects of the South Side; they had found hidden springs of strength in the ghetto and in themselves and had made it out into a wider world. Ray was starting up the corporate ladder in marketing; Vest was reporting politics and public affairs out of Washington; Greg was bringing his construction business to a promising launch. Their workaday lives differed in detail, not in kind, from the lives of young, upwardly mobile white men of their generation. They had, of course, to consider the fact of their blackness in moving through the day and make the appropriate course corrections if they were to prosper or even survive. The burden of having to do so was more than Greg, for one, could tolerate, and he seceded from America into his black republic of the mind. Otherwise, the strivers bore a strong family resemblance to the whites they encountered daily in the workplace. Their cares ran to such matters as debt, divorce, child-rearing, and work anxieties, the standard stresses of life in the middle class.

It was not difficult to isolate the advantages they had had, beyond the mysteries of genetics. Each began life with strong, demanding parents, whether a mother alone, as in Vest's case for much of his boyhood, or a married couple, as in Greg's and Ray's. Hope had a high mortality rate in ghetto families, the casualty of poverty and resignation to the way things were. Not many parents protested when their sons slacked off in their studies and finally dropped out of school; the common assumption was that a boy born black in the projects faced a life sentence at hard labor whether he did his lessons or not. The Stingleys, the Bronsons, and Mrs. Monroe were quite aware of what their sons would be up against; they lived in the projects and were not blind. But they had aspirations for something better for their sons than they themselves had known, and they did not merely expect an extra measure of effort—they *required* it. So did a precious few teachers like Leroy Lovelace, gallant men and women whose classrooms were little redoubts of learning in schools where teaching more often resembled a pacification program.

Still, parents and teachers were too often overmatched against the city of destruction; just as Lovelace himself had imagined, the decisive turn for the boys who made it was getting out of the ghetto. Greg's family moved out to the suburbs. Ray's and Vest's could not afford to; their letters of transit were their ABC scholarships to faraway prep schools and then to quality colleges.

The journey was a painful one, since it meant leaving home, and not a little frightening, since it placed them among white people for the first time in their young lives. It was not in fact the company of whites that was redemptive so much as the quality of education and the wide range of options available to them. The doors open to them had largely been closed to the children of the inner city until the black revolt of the early sixties forced them ajar. The youngsters who slipped through might shrink from whites as a class, as Greg did, or move among them easily, as Ray soon discovered he could. In either case, it was important to know them and their folkways—they were, after all, the majority—and it did not hurt to be standing on the same platform when the train to tomorrow pulled in to board passengers.

The ABC boys were the children of the first generation of affirmative action, when the conscience of the nation was still smarting at the situation of the blacks a century after Emancipation. That impulse has cooled since the 1960's, under challenge in the courts and in the journals of modern political and social thought. The fashion twenty years later was to talk more about its failures, like Steve, than about its successes, like Ray and Vest. Success, of course, had never been guaranteed. Programs like ABC promised only the right to play, not to win; the outcome depended on the wit and sinew of the individual player. Ray and Vest had it. Steve did not; the leap from one high school in the ghetto to another in an Ivy college town was measurable, psychically, in light-years and was too long for him. He fell back. The others made it, and so did the great majority of ABC youngsters from the ghettos, the barrios, the reservations, and the white backwaters of poverty in America. Their experience argued for better chances for more people, not fewer; the issue was not whether some might sink but whether any might be helped to survive.

The times no longer favor generosity. We have grown accustomed to, and even comfortable, thinking of the last decades of the twentieth century as an age of limits, on both the resources and the imagination we apply to the ills of our society. We still tend to talk and think, politically, in the vocabulary of the Kennedy era; we tell ourselves that a country capable of putting men on the moon in a decade should be able to buy a solution to this terrestrial problem or that, and when quick results elude us, we give up. The signal of our surrender came when politicians and social scientists began speaking of a "permanent" black underclass. The problems of the inner-city poor may or may not be remediable, but to call them permanent is to surrender without a fight.

We live now in the America that a presidential commission once warned us against: two Americas, really, one black and one white, separate and unequal. The boundary between them is not absolute. We have not entirely abandoned the ghetto and its children to failure as a self-fulfilling prophecy; we have in fact admitted some few achievers to the social and economic midstream of our society. But the gates have never opened wide for the majority of young people growing up poor in our urban black quarters, the Sonny Spruiells and the Pee Wee Fishers and Half Man Carters. They, too, had promise once, but opportunities were scarce, and they had not prepared themselves to seize what chances *were* beginning to materialize. They grew up in isolation from middle-class America, cut off from its choice, its affluence, and even its understanding. All they had in common with whites and well-to-do blacks was their dreams.

Their lives are formed now, as they approach middle age. They existed in their own age of limits, and except for Honk in his prison cell and James Bonner in his unmarked grave, most were doing well—as well, anyway, as their circumstances allow and as well as they are likely to do. Their hope for something more rested with *their* children, little ones coming up, mostly, as their fathers had in the waste and want of the inner city. Their inheritance was not, on its face, a hopeful one, but their challenge to the larger society was plain. It is in the generation of the children that the ideals of America will be tested. It is in their lives that the dreams of the brothers will or will not come true.

PLAYTHELL BENJAMIN

Lush Life

We entered a back room that appeared to be the perfect venue for illicit games of chance. There was a large oak table with a round top directly in the center of the room. A single spotlight with a wide metal visor hung over the table and cast a light on the shady-looking crew, whose deeds probably couldn't stand the light of day. The circular character of the round table made it impossible to discern the headman's position, hence the illusion of equality. Since round is the antithesis of square, it was easy to see why these urban adventurers were at the round table, for there were no squares among them. As we approached the table, Boogie Woogie arose abruptly and shot out his hand with a grin that monopolized his face, and he welcomed us enthusiastically in a country slick southern voice.

"What's happenin, my man? We been waitin on yall." He shook hands with a firm grip and turned to his coconspirators around the table. "This here's my main man, Easy E, and his partner the Professor." He introduced his colleagues individually.

"This here is Hawk . . . Fast Black . . . Honey Comb . . . Snowflakes . . . and Beautiful Cody Jones."

Hawk was a short walnut-brown man with a strong jaw, high cheekbones, thick, shiny eyebrows, and long eyelashes. Though in his forties, his body was trim and powerfully muscled like that of a world-class athlete toned for action. He wore a well-tailored charcoal pinstripe suit of silk and mohair, freaked off with a monogrammed white-on-white shirt and a white panama straw hat. His hair was relaxed and curled. I peeped from jumpstreet that Hawk, despite his handsome exterior, his soft-spoken demeanor and considerable charm, was a cold-blooded gorilla, capable of doing no telling what; he was a straight-up tough guy.

It was easy to see that Fast Black was a sho-nuff gorilla too. He was a big dude: about six foot five, two hundred and thirty-five or forty pounds. He was as black as a mourning coat and looked as rough as a well-worn tractor tire. A razor scar ran from his left earlobe to the bottom of his chin. You can always tell a razor scar by the way it heals. Judging by the length and angle of the cut, it seemed that somebody, somewhere, had made an honest effort to take Fast Black's head. I wondered what he had done to provoke such ill will.

He was dressed in a pair of white pants, white buck shoes, and a long-sleeve white silk shirt—which was open halfway to his navel and revealed a 24-karat gold chain from which hung a gold medallion set with precious stones: diamonds, rubies, and emeralds. His massively muscled body was strikingly displayed in a white see-through silk shirt, and the trousers strained to contain his linebacker thighs. His eyes were bloodshot and his skin was tight against his face, giving it the look of an ebony mask. He struck me right off as a real dangerous muthafucka; mean enough to kill a rock.

Honey Comb was an average-size dude with the build of a tennis player. The cocoa color of his smooth skin highlighted the shiny blackness of his meticulously trimmed mustache and Vandyke beard. He had naturally curly hair that came almost to his shoulders, and his thick lips, toothy smile, and shifty eyes gave him the look of a man you wouldn't want to buy a used car from.

Decked out in navy-blue Bermuda shorts, topsider loafers with white socks, and a colorful short-sleeve print shirt, Honey Comb's well-manicured, bejeweled hands looked like they had never lifted anything heavier than a cocktail glass. His manner was as cool as an autumn breeze in the Bering Strait as he sat there chillin' like a roach on a porch: too smooth to move. From his style and street moniker, I figured him for a sweet mack man.

Snowflakes was blacker than Fast Black, so I knew right off, his nickname had nothing to do with his color. At first I thought Flakes was a coke dealer, but I later discovered that numbers was his game. It was his love for nose candy that had won him his nom de plume. A son of the Jamaican peasantry, he wore the blue-black complexion characteristic of the Afro-Caribbean masses. Though only in his early fifties, Flakes's hair was speckled with spots of premature gray, and he used to tell the squares that's why people called him Flakes. But, then, they were always trying to play off the squares, whatever the deal was. There was an imperious air about him that befitted a policy king, and his big walrus mustache and bushy eyebrows give him the look of a hard man. Flakes wore multicarat diamond rings on each hand and a specially designed wristwatch with a ring of half-carat blue-whites around the face. He was casually dressed in a maroon knit shirt and brown double-knit slacks with white golfers' shoes and cap. He could have passed for a successful lawyer or businessman except for the diamonds, which were rather gaudy and marked him as a player.

Beautiful Cody Jones was a tall, medium-brown, bald-headed rock. Despite his soft voice and easy manner, his physique and attitude were such that I had the feeling this guy was so fearless, he'd tell an all-white jury in Money, Mississippi, to "kiss my black ass, you jive peckerwood muthafuckas" while on trial for raping a white woman. It wasn't that I thought he would strong-arm some pussy; he was too handsome and suave for that—but if wrongly accused, that would be his response. He was dressed in chic tennis whites and sat sort of slouched back in his chair with his arms slung over the back. A huge vein ran down the center of his arms as his pumped-up biceps strained against the elastic in his short shirt sleeves. He had large, wide-set eyes and a smile that revealed a set of teeth so perfect, they looked as if they were created in a laboratory. He sported a diamond stud in his right earlobe, and when he thought deeply, the skin on his forehead folded into layers of ripples like the placid surface of a country lagoon disturbed by rock-throwing kids.

After the introductions Boogie Woogie commenced the meeting in earnest. Pecan tan and pencil thin, his immaculately manicured mustache, squinty eyes, and ever-present, effervescent smile, gave him that look of a quintessential hipster. Choked down in a wide-lapeled white suit, matching burgundy tie and pocket handkerchief, white shirt and wide brim, brown straw hat, he reminded me of Oil Can Harry in the Mighty Mouse comics. A sinister aura hovered about him in spite of his abundant charms. When he spoke, it was obvious that his lack of formal education had not prevented him from developing a sophisticated grasp of the relationship between race, economics, and power in American society.

"Now, brothas, we done got together here today for two reasons, you understan me . . . to help the peoples and make some money. Now, all you know you can't help nobody if you ain't got nothin yoself, know what I'm sayin? Now, everybody in dis room been a soldyar in the war against poverty all of ourwah life . . . cause we know dat the best way to help the po peoples ista not be one of em, you understan what I mean? Now, I don't know about yall, but I done kilt my mule, shot dat muthafucka dead thru the haid befo I left outta the country, so I ain't nevah gone wurk for nobody agin! Understan me? Not nary a livin a ass. Now, I know alla yall feel the same way I do. So, dat means we gotta stop alla dis money from leavin the community . . . deres just too mucha money bein took outta dis community by otha muthafuckas who don live uptown. Now, the way I sees it, you understan me, we ain't nevah gonna own Standard Oil or General Motahs. And we ain't gon control the banks. So, we gotta control the money in ourwah neighborhoods; we gotta do it lak them Guineas be doin it ovah in East Harlem and out in Brooklyn. Now . . . I done been fuckin round out in dese streets for a long time, you understan me, and I know where the money is out heah.

"We gotta control the numbers game and git in the record bizness, too, cause deres mo money in music than in dope. Plus, I don't want nothin ta do with no dope, ceptin the white lady. But I don't wanna git involved with nobody who's fuckin around with no scag . . . cause I believes to my heart dat old scag is gonna destroy ourwah community if things keep goin lak they goin with dem goddam sorry ass junkies runnin round stealin and robbin old ladies and shit lak dat. And now I heah tell dat them dirty desperate muthafuckas be sellin it round the schools and shit . . . So I don't want nothin ta do wit it, you understan what I'm sayin? Now, somma us got kids and we don't want dat dope and shit around dem, so we gone have to do somethin bout it sooner or later.

"We got ta let dese muthafuckas know dat if dey gon be dealin dat scag, dey got to sell it to dem goddam junkies and keep dat shit away from da kids, you understan me? But what we needta do now is ta organize an git us a plan, dats why I invited dese two brothers—Easy E and the Professor—to dis meetin today cause both of dem is real good at organizin. See, dese brothers come out tha civil rights movement and they been organizin in the churches, at the schools and in the community. Fact is, dey been organizin they asses off clear cross the country. I heah tell they the best in the country, now I wanna see if they worth a damn in the city, you know what I'm sayin?" He said it with a shit-eating grin.

I was amazed at how all these slick, tough guys just sat attentively while Boogie Woogie did all the rapping. He was about the smallest one in the group and seemed more charming than threatening. Perhaps, I thought, it was the transparent wisdom of what he was saying that commanded their attention. I wondered if he could compel their allegiance as well. Beautiful Cody Jones was the first to declare himself.

"It sounds like what you're talking about to me is building an army, cause you're gonna haveta go up against the Guineas any way you go," he said in a quiet, businesslike fashion. "But that's cool with me, cause I hate those linguini and mussel eating greaseball muthafuckas. It's bout time we run them dagoes asses back downtown. What you need is some soldiers and money: bottom line. And hey, I'm ready to kick in some of both; you can count me down with the program. What about the rest of you brothers?"

"I useta work for them muthafuckas, ya know, and they'll fight to hold on to their piece of the action uptown," said Hawk. "Do yall really thnk we're ready for a war with the Guineas . . . cause that's what it might come down to."

"Let me tell ya, mon . . . I don't give a fuck about them, you know," Snowflakes asserted. "Anyway it go down is cool wit me, mon. I been itchin to move on these dam dirty dagoes for years, but I nevah could get a big enough crew to stand up wit me. I would jes love to pop off some caps in dem greasy-headed bumba clots. I nevah liked seein em up here runnin round the place. I born in the Garvey movement, ya know, me daddy, was a Garveyite. I always was taught that the black man should control his own . . . and that's what I believe. So, you can count me in."

"Sheeit!" Honey Comb exclaimed, "if Ida heard you niggahs sittin around talkin this kinda shit a year ago, Ida thought all yall needed yall heads examined. But I been listenin to a lotta these Black power peoples here lately and somma that shit they be sayin is right on the money . . . course it look like they be mostly talkin bout gittin mo politicians, but it's the principle of the thing, that's what's happenin. The way I figure it, we actually kinda late at comin to this conclusion. We shoulda been doin somethin like this all along. So whatever the majority decides, I'm down with the program."

"Bu-bu-but is yall ah-ah actually uh-re-ready to k-k-kill some them gui-guineas ah rat now?" Fast Black stuttered, struggling to form his words. There was a coldness in his steely glare as he slowly surveyed each man at the round table. Something in his posture conveyed the message that Fast Black was a true warrior and would throw down at a moment's notice. I wondered if the fact that he had trouble with his rap contributed to his belligerence; I had noticed that about a lot of gorillaish-type dudes I knew. "Ya-ya-yall know w-w-we might ha-haveta wa-war jest as soon ah-as we declare ouwa selfs on this."

"Man, fuck them Guineas!" Boogie Woogie interrupted. "They dont wanna die neither, you understan me? This is a new day; we don seen Black peoples go up against southern sheriffs and shit, and I aint nevah thought I'd live to see no shit lak dat. And dese peoples was janitors and maids and stuff. Now, we sposed to be the bad niggah, the killers, and somma us still makin payoffs to the Guineas, actin lak a bunch of Toms. Fact is, I done seed quite a few of these play-play niggah gangstas Tommin worse than the hankerchief heads. Wanna know what I think, I think the Guineas watch television too;

they done seen how Black peoples have stood up to the police all cross the country, understan me? I dont believe dem muthafuckas is too anxious to git in no fight uptown . . . not no real fight."

"Lo-lo-look Wo-Woogie, I ain't tr-tryin to ta-talk yall outta nothin. My-my name is buck and you know I do-don't give a fu-fu-fuck! Ho-however whicha wa-way it go, I'm do-down with it!" Fast Black declared.

"All we got to do is stan together, mon, that's what the Muslim brothers did; dey don't let the dagoes come nowhere near Muhammad Ali," Snowflakes interjected. "They don't make a dime off the champ, not a fuckin dime, you hear me? And the dagoes dem don't come to dem brudders wit no fuckie; dey don't wanna make the brudders vex, mon, cause dey know dey will have to fight to the death. I think Boogie Woogie is right; what him say is true, the dagoes dem don't really want a real fight. I tell you, mon, all we got to do is jest stick togedder." Snowflakes banged the table, slowly raising one of his thick silver eyebrows, his ebony face glistening with perspiration.

"I sho hope you're right, Flakes," said Hawk. "But I was in the war and I know that you got to be prepared for whatever happens. We need to organize our troops and git us some battle plans. Tell you what, put me in charge and I'll have them muthafuckas sho nuff solderin in no time!"

"Yeah, you and me both, cause I know somethin about makin muthafuckas pump they hearts and act like warriors too. But Hawk is right, we gotta git our troops together before we challenge the Guineas," said Beautiful Cody Jones.

"We gon take care of that and everythng else down the line, you understan?" Boogie Woogie snapped. "But first things first. Right now Easy E and the Professor got some ideas about how we can organize this thing." He turned to me and Father Eubanks. "Well, brothers, you're on!"

KENNETH MEEKS

Pledging Alpha

Three of us pledged Alpha Phi Alpha fraternity in the spring semester of 1983 at Poughkeepsie University, and the constant mind games played on us made campus life difficult. We ran everywhere with a heavy brick in one hand, our school books in the other, and our black-and-gold silk headdress bouncing in the wind. Pledging Alpha made us toys to the big brothers who pledged us; to be made fun of, poked, and jarred.

But even in that crazy world I learned a lesson that would help me through life.

We were supposed to be in the dormitory room belonging to our dean of pledge by five o'clock sharp. It was 5:02. Outside his door, adjusting ourselves before we went in, we prepared for the trouble we would be in.

He told us to come in, and immediately we lined in formation and began our ritual pledgee greeting. In unison we saluted our big brother, stomping one giant step forward, hitting our right fist against our tight chest, and finally over our heads.

"Greetings, big brothers of Alpha Phi Alpha fraternity incorporated, sir!" We ended our greetings in a bow that held us hunched over for as long as our big brothers wanted. "A phi!"

We waited motionless until a big brother said "A"—the acknowledgment that allowed pledgers to stand erect. The whole greeting in unison lasted five seconds.

"A!" said our dean of pledge, a large brute of a six-footer with all muscles. "Sphinxman Number One, you like pledging our fraternity, don't you?"

I was Sphinxman Number One. I hesitated to answer. There were so many trick questions a big brother could ask. And even if I answer right, just being a pledgee makes my answer wrong.

"Number One, are you deaf?" he repeated, annoyance wrapped around his words. "Don't make me repeat myself."

"I love pledging my fraternity!" I finally answered.

I lied. We were only in our second week, and the idea of pledging another six left me haunted.

Another big brother wobbled to stand nose-to-nose with me. He was short and fat, a lot like Porky Pig with an attitude. He'd inhale from his cigarette and defiantly blow smoke in my face.

"Sphinxman Number One," he said to me, his breath still hot. "Did you bring me the tape I wanted?"

The long silence betrayed the fact that I didn't want to loan him my tape. "Yes, sir," I answered without moving.

"Number One, if I dig in your pocket for that tape, I'm going to bust your—"

He started to reach for my pockets, but I beat him to it. I retrieved my ninety-minute TDK cassette with most of my favorite songs on it. He had heard the tape this morning and demanded I have it with me on our next encounter, or else. . . .

He gloated over the tape for a few minutes before he turned sharply toward me with an evil, nemesis grin that puffed his fat cheeks. "I want to keep your tape."

I protested, and that was a mistake.

"What!?" my dean of pledge roared, leaping to his feet. "You have the gall to protest a big brother? Number One, give me twenty push-ups!"

I dropped into position. (But I'd learned a secret to pledging. It was all a mind game, if I let it. Thank Jah for technicalities.) I did a single push-up and called out, "Twenty!"

I was tensed, praying my dean of pledge would let me slide over the push-ups. "Bravo. You got over this time."

I took my place back in line, music pumped through a JVC sound system to the point I could feel the bass strings pounding against my heart.

The wobbling big brother walked back to his place to defiantly blow more smoke in my face. "If you won't let me have this tape, I guarantee neither one of us will listen to it."

I tried to be as polite as possible. "I'm willing to drop the matter now, just take care of my tape."

He wobbled to the far side of the room, where curtains were drawn closed, and held up my TDK tape. With his pudgy Black fingers gripping around the tape's ribbon, he clung to it as he let the plastic shell of the tape drop to the floor. Long, thin strands of ribbon swayed in the air from the air conditioner.

My mouth dropped too. He was destroying my favorite tape. It happened so fast. Before I could protest, he had an open pocket knife in his hand, slicing pieces of ribbon that fell side over side to the floor.

"Now nobody listens to it."

"You son of a bitch," I said.

It's hard for me to remember exactly what happened next, but in a nutshell a scuffle broke out between us. A few fists were flown, but none landed hard enough to damage anyone. We were separated, and somehow I made it to the door.

I do remember declaring that I quit. I yanked the door open, turned, and, looking sharply at the son of a bitch who tore up my tape, said, "You're going to replace my tape, song for song, or I'll kick your ass again."

The door slammed behind me.

I walked to the bathroom to yank my black headdress off. I don't kid around when it comes to my tapes. They were as precious to me as mother's poetry letters slipped between the pages of my English book.

One of the reasons I pledged Alpha fraternity walked into the bathroom, calling me by my pledge name.

"Number One, are you all right?"

"My name is Michael," I said. I was still pissed and almost shaking still. "You don't seem to understand, I quit."

"I know it's frustrating," he said slowly. "This is going to be the hardest six weeks in your life. You just have to stick through it."

"That bastard had no right screwing up my tape," I bitched, with anger keeping me heated on the subject. "Just because I was pledging gave that bastard no right to destroy my favorite tape. It isn't fair."

"Life isn't fair," he answered with that same straight face that read a deeper philosophical meaning that he was noted for. "You roll with the punches, bite the bullet."

"Skip that. That son of a bitch don't have another tape for me tomorrow, I'll kick his ass again. I don't have any beef with you or anybody else. It's between him and me."

"You're going to throw away two weeks of Alpha because one of us messes with your head. I thought you learned to see past the mind games."

By now he was getting too philosophical for me. I was more interested in my shredded tape. I knew he wouldn't replace my music. It took me two days to make that tape with songs in the order I liked. I felt like going back to kick his ass again.

But my friend kept giving me words of encouragement, constantly reminding me that I can make another tape. I knew I would, but that wasn't the point. It was the principle of the matter.

I finally calmed down, and he finally asked, "How about it? Get some air, and come back inside."

"He owes me an apology," I said.

"But you're a Pledge, and he's a big brother," he answered. "You ought to apologize to him and ask him to allow his vote to remain a pledge."

"I don't think so."

He picked up the headdress I had thrown at one point, I don't remember when, and locked his eyes on mine.

"Consider yourself the victim. And I admire the fact that you've never held a grudge on anybody."

After a moment I tied my black silk headdress, gathered the brick, and took a deep breath for balance.

Back inside the room the atmosphere was tense, but tempered. I stepped back in line alongside the rest of my pledge partners and tried hard not to see the smashed remains of my favorite tape. To look at it made my blood boil more, and I was fighting hard to simmer that feeling of wanting to kick his ass again.

"You all right, Number One?" asked my dean of pledge.

"I'm fine."

"Good," he said, and pointed to the mess. "Since it's your tape, you clean it up."

Talking about putting salt in an open wound. I cleaned up the mess, and I wasn't angry over it. He was right about not holding a grudge. It made life easier.

Then I noticed something wrong. I looked closer at the smashed plastic shell to my favorite tape. The TDK trademark was red and new, but something was different—it was a sixty-minute tape.

"I thought—" I tailed off when the wobbly big brother held up an almost identical TDK—my TDK Tape.

"Surprised you, didn't I?" he asked. "Go ahead, you want to laugh too. Don't you, Number One?"

E. LYNN HARRIS

Invisible Life

The football season rolled around, and with it, much cooler weather. Fall was advancing against the backdrop of an immense sky; braids of yellow, red and teal leaves created delicate hues as beautiful as the sweaters worn by my classmates. September flew by, and on the first Friday in October, I was in the locker room at the athletic complex after hitting some tennis balls with one of my frat brothers, Trent Walters. Trent finished his shower and started back to the frat house, where we always gathered before starting the weekend of partying.

This was the weekend of our first home football game, so there would be some serious parties. ΚΑΩ was giving a party too, but this weekend we would be competing with the two other black fraternities for attendees. After I finished dressing, I headed toward the exit of the locker room. I was looking down at my shoes, trying to decide if they needed shining. While trying to adjust my collar from the back, I bumped into a hard body.

"Oh, excuse me," I said, "I wasn't paying attention to where I was going."

"Sure, no problem," the stranger said.

When I looked up at him, my mouth dropped open. It was him! The guy from the party, the guy in my dream.

"Do you have a comb?" he asked.

"Excuse me." I was in a complete state of shock. Was I seeing and hearing him correctly?

"Do you have a comb?" he repeated.

"A comb," I repeated as I tried to regain my composure.

"Yes, a comb."

"I don't think so. Let me look." I suddenly became very nervous. He was staring at me as I frantically looked in my gym bag for a comb.

"It doesn't look like I have one," I said. "I'm sorry."

"No reason to be," he said. "Thanks anyway."

As the stranger walked away, I stood in the same spot, speechless, not knowing what to do next. Suddenly the stranger stopped and turned around toward me.

"Where is the closest place you can buy liquor around here?" he asked.

"Duncan Country, about thirty-five miles away. Do you go to school here?" I asked.

"Yes, unfortunately, I do."

"Why say it like that?"

"Well, this place is different."

"Yes, it is. Where are you from?"

"Philadelphia."

"Philadelphia?" I asked, a bit surprised.

"Ever heard of it?"

"Of course! How did you wind up down here?"

"Football scholarship."

"Oh."

"My name is Kelvin Ellis," he said, extending his massive hand toward me.

"Raymond Tyler," I said as we shook the regular way and then went into the black-power handshake.

"Where are you from, Raymond?"

"Alabama."

"The whole state?" he asked with a smile, exposing almost perfectly white teeth.

"No, I'm from Birmingham."

"I've heard of Birmingham." Kelvin and I had now walked out of the locker room toward the enormous football stadium that anchored the athletic complex while talking about school and the game tomorrow.

"What position do you play?" I asked.

"Defensive back."

"Are you playing tomorrow?"

"No. I sprained my ankle this week. That's why I was down in the locker room in the whirlpool, getting treatment."

"Oh."

"Do you have a car?" he asked.

"Yes."

"How much would you charge to run me down to Duncan? I've got to get a couple of cases of brew."

"Nothing. I have to go down anyway to pick up some beer for my fraternity. What dorm are you in?"

"Westview, the athletic dorm."

"Okay, be outside in about thirty minutes. I'll be in a black Volkswagen."

"Great!"

I got into my car. I wanted to see if Sela wanted to ride to Duncan with me and my new friend. While I was driving, I began thinking about the dream I had had about Kelvin. Should I tell him? No, he would think I was weird. I began to hum the theme music from "The Twilight Zone" to myself as I pulled up in front of the Delta Sigma Theta sorority house. I went inside and asked the girl at the desk to page Sela Richards.

"Sela Richards, Sela Richards, you have a guest downstairs," she called over the loudspeaker. Five minutes later there was no sign of Sela. I left and went to my apartment, changed clothes and headed toward Westview Hall. When I came to Westview, I could see Kelvin standing against the bike rack. He had changed clothes too. As I approached the dorm, I blew my horn and rolled down my window.

"Get in," I said.

"You don't have to say it but once." He smiled.

As we drove down the highway toward Duncan, I could feel Kelvin staring at me. When we talked, he looked me straight in the eyes. I wasn't sure why, but this made me feel a bit uneasy. We talked about sports, school and, of course, females. We stopped at the first liquor store in Duncan. Kelvin purchased a case of beer and I bought two cases, plus a six-pack for the ride back to campus. While our initial conversation started out tense, after the first beer we both appeared to loosen up.

"Are you dating anyone?" Kelvin asked.

"Yes, Sela Richards. She's a Delta and my HTH."

"HTH?"

"Yes. Haven't you heard of *hometown honey*?"

"Hell no," Kelvin laughed. "HTH."

The time seemed to go by so fast. I became comfortable talking with Kelvin; he was very bright for a freshman. He had a deep baritone voice and a wonderful East Coast accent. He was very pleasant and seemed to know exactly what he wanted out of life. Yes, I thought to myself, a perfect ΚΑΩ pledge prospect.

"What about you?" I asked. "Do you have a girlfriend?"

"Yes, back in Philly. The babes here are so country."

"I guess."

I was driving pretty fast. With the sunroof open, the cool October wind breezed through the car. We had drunk a couple of cans of beer and I started to get a slight buzz, plus I had to piss. "Mind if I pull over? This beer has me running."

"No problem. I can use the stretch."

I pulled over along the side of the road and we both let out some of the beer we had consumed. The oyster-colored sky appeared solid as the setting sun shivered against it and the light breeze blew its own way. Kelvin and I sat on the front of my car and continued our conversation. He told me about growing up in Philly. I shared with Kelvin some of my childhood memories growing up in the South. I couldn't believe how comfortable I felt talking with him. I gave Kelvin my opinion of different people and places on campus and of the virtues of pledging ΚΑΩ. Kelvin seemed interested in most of my conversation, but sometimes he appeared to be staring off into never-never land.

"Do you consider yourself open-minded?" he asked as we got back into my car.

"Yeah, I do."

"How open?"

"Pretty open." As we got closer to campus, Kelvin's questions became more personal. I wondered what he meant by "open-minded."

"Do you sleep with your girlfriend regularly?" he asked.

"Often enough. It's hard sometimes with her in a sorority house and me in a one-bedroom apartment with a roommate. But my roommate and I have worked out a system."

"A system?"

"Yeah. We have signals. Like this weekend he has to vacate the premises. He will either break the dorm rules and stay with his girlfriend or he'll stay with one of our fraternity brothers."

"Oh, I see."

"Would you like to come by my apartment and help me finish this beer?" I asked.

"Sure, why not. I'm out of football for a few weeks."

"Okay, man, let's do it."

"I'm game."

Once we reached my apartment, I gave Kelvin another beer. I was putting the rest in the refrigerator when he walked into the kitchen.

"Nice apartment. How much is the rent?"

"Two-fifty."

"Two-fifty? You're kidding."

"No, two-fifty."

"A place like this near Penn would cost three times that."

"It would?"

"Yeah, it would. Raymond, can I ask you something?" He was staring at me again with his light brown eyes with their curling black lashes. There was an ardent look about them. No man had ever looked at me this way.

"Sure."

"What did you think I meant when I asked you if you were open-minded?"

"I don't know. I really didn't think about it."

"You didn't?"

"No, I didn't. What did you mean?"

"Well, I'm not sure the good people of Alabama are going to be able to deal with me."

"Why?" I asked.

"Because I'm bisexual," Kelvin said.

"You're what?" I asked, almost spitting out the beer I had just swallowed.

"Bisexual. I make it with guys and girls. Haven't you heard of it?"

"Yeah, sure, we had sissies at my high school."

"Do I look like a sissy to you?"

"No, of course not, but . . ."

"But what?"

By this time I was getting nervous. Kelvin was standing very close to me, literally blocking my path to the living room and front door. Should I run or should I hit him? I just stood there and continued to talk, trying to change the conversation. "You want to go grab a pizza?"

"You're avoiding my question."

"No, I'm not . . . it's just that . . ."

"It's just what?"

"Well, Kelvin, you're a good-looking guy. You could probably get any girl you want."

"And I do."

"Don't you like girls?"

"I love women. Nobody eats trim better than me."

"Trim?"

"Yeah, you know, pussy."

"Oh. Then tell me, Kelvin, why in the fuck would you want to mess around with a man?"

"Variety is the spice of life."

"If you say so."

"So, Ray, tell me. Have you ever made it with a guy?"

"Hell no!" I protested.

"Don't get bent out of shape, Raymond."

The questions and the conversation were making me agitated. I wanted to appear more sophisticated. Maybe this was an East Coast thing. Did Kelvin guess about the one time I had experimented with my cousin Marcus, when we were both around nine years old? We had really only compared the size of our growing peters. How could he possibly know that?

I looked Kelvin straight in the eyes. "I'm not bent out of shape. That shit's not my style."

"Maybe you haven't run across the right man."

Trying to avoid Kelvin's eyes, I looked down at the gold shag carpet. When I decided to look up, I noticed Kelvin's erection bulging through his jeans and became even more nervous. What had I gotten myself into? This guy was bigger than me. There was a brief, uncomfortable pause. The silence was as heavy as one of my grandma's homemade quilts.

"Well, man, we better head back toward campus," I said.

"Sure. Come here for a second—there's something in your hair."

Without thinking, I moved closer to Kelvin. With the palm of his hands, he softly rubbed my entire face. I quickly pulled back.

"What the fuck are you doing?" I shouted.

A slight smile flickered over his face and he said, "Your skin looked so smooth that I had to touch it."

I didn't respond, silenced by his stare. His eyes were deep-set and defiant. Then he touched my nose and moved his fingers down to my lips. I don't know why, but I didn't stop him as he cupped my face and suddenly kissed my lips. I couldn't believe it, but it felt so natural. It was the first time I had ever kissed a man. I had never felt a spasm of sexual attraction toward a man. Honest to God. But his kiss. I had never kissed anyone like this, not even Sela. Before I was conscious of it, I was kissing Kelvin back and putting my arms around his waist. His force left little room for hesitation or resistance. I felt his strong body press toward mine—and an erection in my Jockey underwear, just aching to come out. I finally managed to pull back when I realized my sex was now full and hard, pressing against my navel. Kelvin looked down at me, gave a half-cocked grin and then pulled me toward him once again. This time there was no resistance.

What was happening? This sinful, sexual longing. This was wrong. Everything in my head screamed *no!* Yet my body was saying *yes*. We stood in the kitchen kissing nonstop for almost an hour.

"Where's your roommate?" Kelvin whispered in my ear.

"Don't worry, he'll call first," I said.

All of a sudden I felt Kelvin's hands touch my sex and then, with a single motion, his hands unzipped my jeans, releasing my throbbing penis. We continued to kiss passionately as he led me to the bedroom. Everywhere he touched became sensitive. My nerves became raw, tingling with unknown enjoyment. The movement of his body against mine felt as sensuous as powdered sheets. Moments later we were both butt-naked, lying on the edge of my twin bed. We managed to stop long enough to push the beds together.

On that night, the first Friday in October, I experienced passion and sexual satisfaction that I had never in my twenty-one years dreamed possible. Until that Friday evening in October, sex with females was all that I knew. I never imagined sex with a male. Sure, I had noticed or envied guys with great bodies while playing high school football, but I never thought of it in a sexual context. I had never before given a man's body such lofty regard as I did with Kelvin. How would I have known that rubbing two male sexual organs together would bring such a complete feeling of ecstasy?

MELVIN DIXON

Vanishing Rooms

Once inside the apartment, I double-locked the door. I went to the window and spent hours looking up and down the street. Night came and swallowed up everything alive. Nothing moved, not even the subway below. I was alone. The rooms stirred empty. The emptiness gave off a chill. My eyes wouldn't cry and wouldn't close. I wanted to scream, but I had no air. I held myself in. I couldn't stop trembling.

God, what had happened? Just yesterday we were standing together at the pier, marveling at the polluted Hudson. Then I had to get to class, dance class. I thought I was late. There was the girl I had danced with. Then the hours and hours I waited for Metro to come home. Suddenly voices filled the outer hallway. Rushing footsteps. Laughter. Banging on doors somewhere. My hands shook again and my stomach tied itself in knots. Where could I hide? But the voices went past my door and up to the last floor of the building. I was sweating. I had to talk to someone. Anyone. I called my parents long-distance but there was no answer. I called again and the line was busy. But what could I tell them? College buddy, roommate, lover dead? Not a chance. Then I fumbled through the telephone directory, found her name, number, and I dialed.

"Ruella, this is Jesse. From dance class, remember? We met yesterday. We danced. Remember?"

"Yes, yes, Jesse. But how did you get my number?" I tried to say something but couldn't. "Jesse? You still there?"

"Listen, something terrible has happened. Metro, my friend. He's been stabbed. He's dead." I couldn't say anything more and she didn't say any more. My breath caught in the phone. "I can't stay here tonight," I said. "Not alone."

"You come right over, honey," she said. "I've got plenty of room."

I took only what I'd need for the night. Once there, I looked at her and she looked at me for a long time before I turned away and searched her windows. She didn't ask any questions. I wanted to talk, to tell her everything. She said there was no rush. I wanted to say that boys named after their mothers are different, that it wasn't for the money that they stabbed Metro; he had all his money on him when his body was found. It was for something else. When I tried to talk my lips started moving faster than the sounds, and I just cried, cried, cried.

Before the morgue's cold darkness had sucked me in, I had seen the gashes like tracks all over Metro's belly and chest. His open eyes were questions I couldn't answer. I couldn't say a word. The officer pulled the sheet all the way back and turned the body over where his ass had been slashed raw. I knew why he had been killed. I tried to scream but had no wind. I needed air. That's when I must have hit the floor. I could still see those gashes. They opened everywhere, grooves of flesh and blood, lips slobbering with kisses.

Ruella put her arms around me. My stomach heaved. I bolted for the toilet and vomited until there was nothing left of the bathroom or me. I woke up in her bed. From then on I called her Rooms.

After that first night she said I could stay longer if I needed to. I told her that guys like me are different.

"Then why did you call me?" she asked.

"Because you were there."

"But why *me*, Jesse?"

"We danced, that's all."

The second night Rooms touched me by accident. I didn't move. The chilly, October night filled the bed space between us. Then her hand crept to mine and held it, caressing and easing out the chill. Slowly, I relaxed but couldn't help remembering the men who had first made me warm. Metro's name came up raw on my tongue. It needed air, more air. "Metro," I said aloud. I kept still.

"Jesse? You all right?"

Rooms drew closer to me. We held each other tight against the dark.

"Jesse? You all right?" Her voice, hovering in the chill.

Something was pricking my scalp. I pulled out one splinter after another, but they were over all of me now, and I scratched and pulled everywhere. Not wood from the warehouse floor or the rickety pier, these were glinting steel blades with my name on them. Faces I'd seen before inched from corners of the room, closing the gap between here and there, now and then. Mouths opened and sneered. Teeth got sharp. Tongues wagged and breath steamed up around me until I sank into the sheets. Now a boy's voice. Then many voices. *"Jesseeeee."* A steel blade getting close. Closer. *"Jesse!"*

"I won't hurt you," said Rooms.

Outside the bedroom window, police sirens hollered up and down the streets. Where the hell were they *then?*

I imagined how Metro came up from the IRT exit and entered our block from the corner of West 12th and Bank Street. He passed the shut newsstand. It was almost morning. Metallic edges of light cut back the night. Metro walked with the same aching sound I knew from my own scuffling feet. I could almost hear the brush of denim between his thighs, see the arch of his pelvis as he swayed arms and hips as if he owned the whole street. His eyes tried to focus on the walk; his head leaned carelessly to the side. As he neared our building he was not alone. Other shapes crawled into the street, filled it. Cigarette smoke trailed out from an alley, and the figures of boys appeared out of nowhere, riding spray-paint fumes, crackling marijuana seeds, and waves of stinking beer.

Four, five, maybe six teenagers. Maybe they were the ones. The same ones I had seen before on my way home from rehearsals. Even then their smell of a quick, cheap high had been toxic. One time they spotted me and yelled, first one, then another until I was trapped.

"Hey, nigger."

"Yeah, you."

"Naw, man, he ain't no nigger. He a faggot."

"Then he a black nigger faggot."

They laughed. I walked faster, almost running, and reached my block in a cold sweat from pretending not to hear them. But I did hear them, and the sweat and trembling in my knees would not go away, not even when I reached the door and locked myself in.

Metro didn't believe it was that bad. But what did he know? A white boy from Louisiana, New England prep schools and college. "Don't worry, baby," he said when I told him what had happened. He held my head and hands until I calmed down. "It'll be all right." And we made love slowly, deliberately, believing we were doing something right. Still, I should have known better than to take so much for granted, even in Greenwich Village where we lived. And I should have known better than to leave him alone by the pier in the condition he was in, just for a dance improvisation. He had a cold, wild look in his eyes. How could I tell how many pills he'd taken? He could have fought back. But then why hadn't I fought back when those Italian kids started yelling. "He a black nigger faggot, yeah, he a faggot, a nigger, too," and shouting and laughing so close they made acid out of every bit of safety I thought we had? Now their hate had eaten up everything.

I could still hear them, making each prove himself a man—"I ain't no faggot. Not me, man"—and drawing blood. And when Metro left the black underground of trains and screeching wheels, when he reached for air in the thick ash of night, they spotted him like found money through the stinking grates of smoke and beer. I imagined how they followed his unsteady walk, his wavering vision, his fatigue. Curses like baseball bats swung out of their mouths. The first ones were on target: "There go a faggot."

"Hey man, you a faggot?"

Metro kept walking. Like I did. *Please keep walking. Please, Metro.*

"I say that man call you a faggot. You a faggot?"

Metro said nothing. Did he even hear them? They came closer. The streets were empty. No witnesses, no help. And I was back home waiting for his knock that never came.

"Yeah, you a faggot all right. Ain't he?"

"Yeah, he a faggot."

And Metro walked faster, skipped into a run, but they caught him. Knives slipped out of their pants. Hands reached for him, caught him in a tunnel of angry metal. They told him to put his wallet back. "This ain't no fucking robbery, man." They knocked him down. Metro sprawled about wet and hurt, couldn't pull himself up.

"Who stuck him?"

"Get up, faggot. We ain't through that easy."

"Look, he's bleeding."

"Who went ahead and stuck him before we all could stick it in? Who?"

They jostled him to his feet, feeling his ass.

"When can the rest of us stick it in? We all wanna fuck him, don't we fellahs?"

"Yeah. When can we fuck him?"

And Metro was wet from the discharged knives. He stopped treading the ground. He swayed back like wood in water, his eyes stiff on the open zippers. The leader of them grinning, his mouth a crater spilling beer, said, *"Now."*

"Why did you call me?" Rooms asked.

I said nothing.

"You think I'm gay, too?"

"No," I said.

"You really loved him," said Rooms.

"Yes."

"That makes all the difference." She held me with her eyes. They cut into me. "There's something else, isn't there? Something you haven't told me."

I tasted blood in my mouth. My head felt hot.

"I can wait," she said.

I went to her window and looked out. A subway rumbled underground, then it was quiet. The lump high in my throat, about to spread all through me since yesterday, eased down for a moment. I went back to my apartment to get the rest of my things.

ESSEX HEMPHILL

In an Afternoon Light

On a recent afternoon in Philadelphia I walked to the corner of 63rd and Malvern Streets to catch a number 10 trolley, *my* imaginary streetcar named Desire. Waiting, when I arrived at the stop was another black man, sipping a bottle of beer and smoking a cigarette. He wore sunshades and was built three sizes larger than my compact frame. I guessed him to be in his thirties though his potbelly suggested an older age or the consumption of too much beer and soul food. A blue hand towel was tossed over his right shoulder. A baseball jacket was draped across his left thigh. He was sitting on the wall I sit on when I wait here. Since there was no trolley in sight, I guardedly walked over and sat at the far end of the wall. He continued to drink his beer as I observed him from the corner of my eye. I pretended to occupy myself with looking for an approaching trolley. He abruptly ended our brief interlude of silence. For no apparent reason he blurted out, "Man, the women's movement is ruling the world. It's turning our sons into faggots and our men into punks."

"What do you mean?" I asked, raising my voice as loudly as he had raised his. Indignation and defensiveness tinged my vocal cords. I thought his remarks were directed specifically at me.

"You see all the cars going by?" he asked, gesturing at the traffic.

"Yeah, so what about it?"

"Well, can't you see that all the drivers in the cars are women—"

"Which only means more women are driving," I interjected.

"—because women have caused major changes in society, brother. Women are ruling more things now. That's why I don't want my son to spend all his time with his mother, his grandmother, and those aunts of his. His mother and I don't live together, but I go visit him and take him downtown or to the movies or down to the Boys' Club to watch basketball games. I think that's important, so he'll know the difference."

"The difference in what?" I asked.

"The difference between a woman and a man. You know . . ."

"Which is supposed to be determined by what—how they use their sex organs? What I do know, brother, is that thirteen and fourteen-year-old black children are breeding babies they can't care for—crack babies, AIDS babies, accidental babies, babies that will grow up and inherit their parents' poverty and powerlessness. The truth is, young people are fucking because they want to fuck. They're encouraged to fuck. Yet we don't talk to them frankly and honestly about sex, sexuality, or their responsibility."

"Okay, brother, hold that thought. You're moving too fast. See, this is what I mean. Suppose you grow up in a home with your father being a minister and your mother is there all the time taking care of the house and kids. You grow up, go off to college, and get a good education. Then you decide you gonna be gay. You like men. I say you learned that. Education did that. Your folks didn't teach you that."

"That's bullshit, and you know it," I insisted. "It's stupid to suggest that women or education can make a man gay. What you fail to understand is that this is the natural diversity of human sexuality no matter what we call it. Also, my father is a minister, my mother was at home raising us before they divorced, and I went to college. And you know what? I'm a faggot."

"No you ain't!"

"Yes I am. In fact, I'm becoming a well-known faggot."

"I don't believe you."

"Why not?"

"Because you ain't switching and stuff."

"Yeah, all you think being gay is about is men switching—but you're wrong. I'm a faggot because I love *me* enough to be who I am. If your son grows up to be a faggot, it won't be because of the way you or his mother raised him. It will be because he learns to trust the natural expression of his sexuality without fear or shame. If he learns anything about courage from you or his mother, then he'll grow up to be himself. You can't blame being straight or gay on a woman or education. The education that's needed should be for the purpose of bringing us all out of sexual ignorance. It's just another tactic to keep us divided—these sex wars we wage. Our sexuality is determined by the will of human nature, and nature *is* the will of God . . ."

He sat there for a moment staring at me, sipping his beer. He lit another cigarette. I realized then that he could beat me to a pulp if he chose to impose his bigger size, his vociferous masculinity on me. But I wasn't afraid for what I had said and revealed. On too many occasions, I have sat silently as men like him mouthed off about gays and women, and I said nothing because I was afraid. But not today. Not this afternoon. The longer I sit silently in my own community, my own home, and say nothing, I condone the ignorance and its by-products of violence and discrimination. I prolong my existence in a realm of invisibility and complicity. I prolong our mutual suffering by saying nothing.

Neither of us spoke another word. In this tense interlude, a bus and trolley approached. I was angry with having to encounter him on such a glorious spring day, but this is the kind of work social change requires. I consoled myself believing this.

When he rose I immediately rose too—a defensive strategy, a precaution.

"It's been good talking to you, brother. I'll think about what you've said." He extended his hand to me just as the bus and the trolley neared. I looked at his hand, known and unknown to me, offered tenuously waiting to clasp my hand.

"Yeah, it was cool talking to you, too," I returned, as I hesitantly shook his hand. He swaggered to the bus and boarded with his beer hidden under the jacket he carried. I walked into the street to meet the trolley in an afternoon light devoid of shame.

W. J. BRANDY MOORE

African-American Males and Survival Against AIDS

For every male of African descent living in America, survival is a guiding factor that accompanies our first breath each morning. We steel ourselves against the painful encounters sure to come once we venture out into the light of day. Survival is often the last thought of the night as we close our eyes, realizing that someone, somewhere, chose another African-American male to victimize. We have little mechanism for determining when we will be in the wrong place at the wrong time! It hurts to face these facts.*

Each day lived without pressure of police violence, drug and alcohol abuse, unemployment, and being in jail is a milestone for male descendants of Africa living in the United States. If we are free from having to prove our manhood or be challenged by family to "fess up" about our private acts, we feel so much better off. Or so we think!

A few of us have become adept at dodging or camouflaging ourselves so that we can live in relative peace. Such peace is hard found, and we find ourselves continually analyzing or explaining what we do, who we are, and why we behave in this or that manner.* It's the price we pay for being born Black in a world that saves all its negativity and boxes it up inside the word *black*.

For most African-American males there is self-doubt and confusion about our ability to survive among other African Americans. We spend too much time covering our tracks while not living up to our personal potential that has been derived from realistic needs and concerns. All in all, African-American males survive wrapped in a bubble of subterfuge because society provides little opportunity for honesty if your skin is dark. We are seldom understood and often not appreciated.

During the last twelve years or so an added burden has crept into our lives. That burden is AIDS! HIV is the virus believed to cause AIDS and other immune-system illnesses. In questionnaires and surveys African Americans still

*Jewelle Taylor Gibbs, ed., *Young, Black and Male in America: An Endangered Species* (Auburn House Publishing Company, Westport, CT, 1988).

*N. A. Day, A. Houston-Hamilton and J. Deslonde, *A Baseline Survey of AIDS Risk Behaviors and Attitudes in San Francisco's Black Communities*. (San Francisco: Polaris Research and Development, 1987, 1989).

seek a cause, a locus for determining why this disease stealthily destroys our youth, and especially males, our protectors? Answers to this question are sporadic and confusing.

HIV has come into the lives of African Americans like a silent warrior in the night. It destroys our plans for the future while it worms its way past our strongest barriers. HIV rambles on through our body, altering genetics and swallowing up cells that are usually expected to save our lives. The disease is most troubling because of the mystery surrounding it. Yet we all must face the fact that HIV/AIDS is with us.

We all know an African-American male who is infected or has succumbed to the ravages of this disease. One recent advertisement suggested, "If you don't know someone with HIV now, you will in two years." Such ideas warn us that something is coming that will have impact throughout our community.

Many of us have become experts on HIV disease because we had to find a way to survive in spite of all the odds. African-American males know the requirements of survival, but many more of us have died because we didn't heed the footsteps of the enemy warrior—AIDS.

We probably know a member of a family who is experiencing grief, disbelief, and feelings of isolation about the stigma brought by AIDS. Yet few of us acknowledge that we don't really understand how the disease works to destroy morale, physical strength, and the will to live among individual Black males. Who gets them through the maze of bureaucracy at clinics and hospitals? Who advocates on their behalf for treatments and care that are appropriate? If they are illiterate or do not comprehend the big words on medical documents, who is there for them? Lastly, who holds them and caresses away their fear and pain in the face of AIDS? Too often there is nobody, and another African-American male exits this life alone. Each and every man of African descent fears that if he is caught by the virus that causes AIDS, he must walk that path alone.

If a man believes that he will soon be dead, he often finds reasons not to plan or dream. If a man can deny his sexuality, whether he is heterosexual, homosexual, or bisexual, then he can pretend that the excessive fevers, the rotting toes and fingers, and the "slight" colds are anything but the wounds of the creeping AIDS warrior. It is difficult to see a future when in such a condition. Media information sources would have us believe that there can be no survival in the face of AIDS. Still more of us find ways to manage our existence with the virus despite the odds.

The reward for too many of us is isolation and lack of support because acknowledgment about male-male sex behaviors must remain a well-kept secret if one is to survive inside the African-American family. Estimates are that more than one-third of African-American males are bisexual and that their behaviors place them at grave risk for HIV disease. We learn early on to deny in order to survive; we expect that those who know about our sexuality will keep it from family and loved ones in our community. After all, community and family are the only refuge allowed African-American males in U.S. society.

The facts today suggest that many African-American males engage in unprotected sexual activities. This is not the same as blaming all Black men for the spread of HIV disease. But the truth is that since we are not all injection-drug users, and since we are relatively certain that Black women and babies are not sleeping with gay white males so as to get AIDS, and since the disease is not airborne or passed by mosquitoes . . . then it is safe to assume that African-American men have some responsibility in the transmission of AIDS in America. To survive HIV, many people living with AIDS look at our behaviors in hindsight and ask, "Why me? How could this have happened?" Those of us living with the virus must acknowledge the import of unprotected sexual activities as we try to educate others and carry out our lives.

AIDS challenges our beliefs when it wipes out 130,000-plus lives with no cure in sight. Approximately one-quarter of these deaths have been among the African-American population. Ninety-three percent of such cases in the Black community were among gay and bisexual males who did not use drugs or share needles. Black males have a tremendous responsibility for making survival a factor in the fight against AIDS. African Americans have quietly witnessed the movement of AIDS across color lines, economic barriers and beyond religious or spiritual teachings. The silent enemy warrior has rattled the walls of our safety such that now we are worried where this dread disease will strike next.*

African-American males have not fared well in the fight against AIDS. Black youth comprise 34 percent of all cases of AIDS among adolescents, and one in seven teenage males will be diagnosed with a sexually transmitted disease this year. AIDS is fast becoming a killer among African-American males and females between the ages of nineteen and twenty-six, especially in the largest urban centers.

We survive now only because of precaution and fear, but it is a confused survival because we deny AIDS as an issue in our lives. On a personal level an African-American man living with the virus must cope with the fear of losing a job, housing, health care, and even burial in the family plot. We present a face of joy in the midst of family and friends, but we tremble inside for fear of exposure to the virus. How do we maintain our integrity in the face of a community that will not openly and honestly discuss sexuality, health, and the impact of disease?

We must acknowledge the pains we feel over isolation and fear and begin to demand that attention be given to our needs and concerns; but we must articulate those needs so that the world knows we are serious. HIV/AIDS

*John Peterson, Ph.D., *High-Risk Sexual Behavior and Condom Use Among African-American Gay and Bisexual Men* (San Francisco: UCSF Center for AIDS Prevention Studies [CAPS], 1991).

takes its toll on those who remain ill informed about its impact upon their lives. African-American males continue to die from this disease because we allow ourselves to be blocked from participation in clinical trials and research, in emotional and practical support programs, and in treatment services. We wait for others to care for us or to create programs for our survival. Must we die alone? A wiser path is to get beyond accommodation and to survive the political, social, and lifestyle challenges without sophistry and pretense. AIDS is a challenge for the entire community of African descendants. We must act now to save all our futures.

ERNEST J. GAINES

A Lesson Before Dying

Miss Emma thought we should all visit Jefferson together as often as we could. I wasn't crazy about the idea of being at the courthouse at the same time as the minister, but one look from my aunt, and I decided that I would go along, at least once. Leaving Irene Cole and Odessa Freeman in charge of classes, I drove to Bayonne with a bag of pecans and peanuts. I remembered my promise to Jefferson, so I dropped by the drugstore for a notebook and a pencil. It was a little after two when I got to the courthouse. The minister, Miss Emma, and my aunt were waiting for me outside. They stood by the minister's car, near the statue of the Confederate soldier and the three flags. The flags hung limp beneath the overcast sky. The minister and my aunt looked at me, and both seemed angry, as if I had kept them waiting deliberately. I had not, of course. If I had not stopped for the notebook and pencil, I probably would have arrived there before they did, but I did not explain this to them. Miss Emma did not feel the same as they did, and that was all that mattered. Both she and my aunt carried food baskets covered with dish towels. As I approached them, Miss Emma pushed herself away from the car and started heavily toward the entrance to the courthouse. My aunt and the minister walked behind her, and I followed.

Paul was not there, and the chief deputy, after searching the food and us, led us out of the office, into the corridor. He walked several paces ahead of us, as if we were not with him. When we came to the rest room marked WHITE MEN, he went inside. We waited for him along the wall. Five minutes later, he came out with another white man. They stood there talking another minute or two before he continued along the corridor. We went up the steps and into the dayroom, and, without a word, he opened the door and left us.

Miss Emma and my aunt spread out a tablecloth on the table, then they placed a pan, a spoon, and a paper napkin in five places. After they had set up everything, they and the minister sat down, but I remained standing.

The first thing you heard were the chains around his ankles, then Jefferson entered the room through the rear door, followed by the deputy. Jefferson wore the same brown wool shirt he'd had on a couple of days before. He had on a pair of faded denims and brogans with no laces. He was dragging his feet to keep the shoes on.

"Here he is," the deputy said. "See y'all at three."

"Paul's not here today?" I asked.

"Mr. Paul's got other duties," the deputy said. He looked at me as if to remind me that I was supposed to say Mister before a white man's name. He stood there eyeing me until he felt that I understood.

"I brought you some good old gumbo," Miss Emma said to Jefferson.

"How's it going, partner?" I said, as I took my seat beside him.

"All right," he said.

"The radio still playing?"

He nodded his head.

"Good," I said.

Miss Emma put rice in each pan, then she poured gumbo over the rice until the pan was nearly full. Besides shrimps, she had put smoked sausage and chicken in the gumbo, and she had seasoned it well with green onions, filé, and black pepper. Gumbo was something you could always eat, even if you were not hungry. I started in. But I was the only one. And I soon realized why.

"May we bow our heads," the minister said, after I had put down my spoon.

Jefferson's head had been bowed from the moment he sat down. I lowered my eyes.

"Our Father who art in Heaven," Reverend Ambrose began. He went through the Lord's Prayer, but that was only for warming up. Then he really got down to praying. He asked God to come down to Bayonne, into the courthouse, into the jail; walk along the cellblock, go into each cell, touch each heart; come into this room and touch the hearts of those here who did not know Him in the pardon of their sins. As he prayed, the minister would slump closer and closer to the table. Then he would jerk his head up and gaze at the ceiling. Miss Emma and my aunt responded with "Amen, Amen, Amen." But Jefferson was quiet, and so was I. Whether or not he was listening, I don't know; but all I was thinking about was the gumbo getting cold.

Finally, Reverend Ambrose brought his prayer-sermon to an end, begging God to bless the gift on the table, which was there to nourish our bodies so that we might do His bidding. Everyone responded with "Amen," except Jefferson.

I started eating. The gumbo was warm but not hot.

"Ain't you go'n eat, Jefferson?" Miss Emma said.

"Ain't hongry."

Miss Emma was not eating either. But the minister and my aunt and I were. I broke off a piece of bread from one of the loaves that Miss Emma had baked. I didn't look at her; I didn't want to see her face.

"The children sent you some more pecans and peanuts," I said to Jefferson. "Did you eat the others I brought you?"

"Some," he said.

"The peanuts too?"

"Few," he said, his head down.

"I brought you that notebook and that pencil," I said. "Do you remember what we talked about?"

He nodded shortly.

"Have you been thinking of questions to ask me?"

He nodded again.

"Do you want to ask me now?"

He didn't say anything. I finished my pan of gumbo.

"There's more there, Grant," Miss Emma said.

"No, ma'am. That was good," I said, glancing at her. I didn't want to look at her too long. I knew what I would find in her face, and I didn't want to see it.

"You want to walk?" I said to Jefferson.

He moved on the bench without answering. You could hear the chains around his ankles as he swung his legs over the bench, then he braced his cuffed hands against the table to push himself up. We started walking around the room. Miss Emma watched us. My aunt and the minister went on eating, but they did not seem to be enjoying their food.

"Jefferson, I want us to be friends," I said. "Not only you and me, but I want you to be friends with your nannan. I want you to be more than a godson to her. A godson obeys, but a friend—well, a friend would do anything to please a friend." We were passing by the table, so I lowered my voice. Jefferson shuffled along beside me, his cuffed hands hanging below his waist, his shoulders too close together, his head down. "A friend does a lot of little things," I went on. "It would mean so much to her if you would eat some of the gumbo." I stopped when we came to the corner of the room. He stopped too, his head still down. "Look at me, Jefferson, please," I said. He raised his head slowly. I smiled at him. "Will you be her friend? Will you eat some of the gumbo? Just a little bit? One spoonful?" He made a slight nod. I smiled at him again.

"Jefferson," I said. We had started walking. "Do you know what a hero is, Jefferson? A hero is someone who does something for other people. He does something that other men don't and can't do. He is different from other men. He is above other men. No matter who those other men are, the hero, no matter who he is, is above them." I lowered my voice again until we had passed the table. "I could never be a hero. I teach, but I don't like teaching. I teach because it is the only thing that an educated black man can do in the

South today. I don't like it; I hate it. I don't even like living here. I want to run away. I want to live for myself and for my woman and for nobody else.

"That is not a hero. A hero does for others. He would do anything for people he loves, because he knows it would make their lives better. I am not that kind of person, but I want you to be. You could give something to her, to me, to those children in the quarter. You could give them something that I never could. They expect it from me, but not from you. The white people out there are saying that you don't have it—that you're a hog, not a man. But I know they are wrong. You have the potentials. We all have, no matter who we are.

"Those out there are no better than we are, Jefferson. They are worse. That's why they are always looking for a scapegoat, someone else to blame. I want you to show them the difference between what they think you are and what you can be. To them, you're nothing but another nigger—no dignity, no heart, no love for your people. You can prove them wrong. You can do more than I can ever do. I have always done what they wanted me to do, teach reading, writing, and arithmetic. Nothing else—nothing about dignity, nothing about identity, nothing about loving and caring. They never thought we were capable of learning these things. 'Teach those niggers how to print their names and how to figure on their fingers.' And I went along, but hating myself all the time for doing so."

We were coming up to the table again, and the ones at the table were quiet and trying to hear what we were saying. I did not start talking again until we had passed them.

"Do you know what a myth is, Jefferson?" I asked him. "A myth is an old lie that people believe in. White people believe that they're better than anyone else on earth—and that's a myth. The last thing they ever want is to see a black man stand, and think, and show that common humanity that is in us all. It would destroy their myth. They would no longer have justification for having made us slaves and keeping us in the condition we are in. As long as none of us stand, they're safe. They're safe with me. They're safe with Reverend Ambrose. I don't want them to feel safe with you anymore.

"I want you to chip away at that myth by standing. I want you—yes, you—to call them liars. I want you to show them that you are as much a man—more a man than they can ever be. That jury? You call them men? That judge? Is he a man? The governor is no better. They play by the rules their forefathers created hundreds of years ago. Their forefathers said that we're only three-fifths human—and they believe it to this day. Sheriff Guidry does too. He calls me Professor, but he doesn't mean it. He calls Reverend Ambrose Reverend, but he doesn't respect him. When I showed him the notebook and pencil I brought you, he grinned. Do you know why? He believes it was just a waste of time and money. What can a hog do with a pencil and paper?"

We stopped. His head was down.

"Look at me, Jefferson, please," I said.

He raised his head. He had been crying. He raised his cuffed hands and wiped one eye, then the other.

"I need you," I told him. "I need you much more than you could ever need me. I need to know what to do with my life. I want to run away, but go where and do what? I'm needed here and know it, but I feel that all I'm doing here is choking myself. I need someone to tell me what to do. I need you to tell me, to show me. I'm no hero; I can just give something small. That's all I have to offer. It is the only way that we can chip away at that myth. You—you can be bigger than anyone you have ever met.

"Please listen to me, because I would not lie to you now. I speak from my heart. You have the chance of being bigger than anyone who has ever lived on that plantation or come from this little town. You can do it if you try. You have seen how Mr. Farrell makes a slingshot handle. He starts with just a little piece of rough wood—any little piece of scrap wood—then he starts cutting. Cutting and cutting and cutting, then shaving. Shaves it down clean and smooth till it's not what it was before, but something new and pretty. You know what I'm talking about, because you have seen him do it. You had one that he made from a piece of scrap wood. Yes, yes—I saw you with it. And it came from a piece of old wood that he found in the yard somewhere. And that's all we are, Jefferson, all of us on this earth, a piece of drifting wood, until we—each one of us, individually—decide to become something else. I am still that piece of drifting wood, and those out there are no better. But you can be better. Because we need you to be and want you to be. Me, your godmother, the children, and all the rest of them in the quarter. Do you understand what I'm saying to you, Jefferson? Do you?"

He looked at me in great pain. He may not have understood, but something was touched, something deep down in him—because he was still crying.

I cry, not from reaching any conclusion by reasoning, but because, lowly as I am, I am still part of the whole. Is that what he was thinking as he looked at me crying?

"Come on," I said. "Let's have some gumbo."

And we went back to the table.

PART 4

Trouble Man

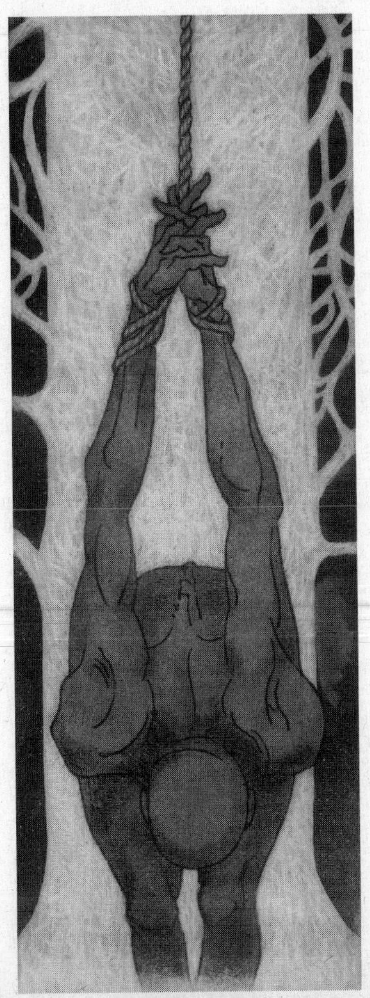

THE PERMANENCE OF RACISM

CLAUDE McKAY

If We Must Die

If we must die, let it not be like hogs
Hunted and penned in an inglorious spot,
While round us bark the mad and hungry dogs,
Making their mock at our accursed lot.
If we must die, O let us nobly die,
So that our precious blood may not be shed
In vain; then even the monsters we defy
Shall be constrained to honor us though dead!
O kinsmen! we must meet the common foe!
Though far outnumbered let us show us brave,
And for their thousand blows deal one deathblow!
What though before us lies the open grave?
Like men we'll face the murderous, cowardly pack,
Pressed to the wall, dying, but fighting back!

PAUL LAURENCE DUNBAR

The Lynching of Jube Benson

Gordon Fairfax's library held but three men, but the air was dense with clouds of smoke. The talk had drifted from one topic to another much as the smoke wreaths had puffed, floated, and thinned away. Then Handon Gay, who was an ambitious young reporter, spoke of a lynching story in a recent magazine, and the matter of punishment without trial put new life into the conversation.

"I should like to see a real lynching," said Gay rather callously.

"Well, I should hardly express it that way," said Fairfax, "but if a real, live lynching were to come my way, I should not avoid it."

"I should," spoke the other from the depths of his chair, where he had been puffing in moody silence. Judged by his hair, which was freely sprinkled with gray, the speaker might have been a man of forty-five or fifty, but his face, though lined and serious, was youthful, the face of a man hardly past thirty.

"What! you, Dr. Melville? Why, I thought that you physicians wouldn't weaken at anything."

"I have seen one such affair," said the doctor gravely; "in fact, I took a prominent part in it."

"Tell us about it," said the reporter, feeling for his pencil and note-book, which he was, nevertheless, careful to hide from the speaker.

The men drew their chairs eagerly up to the doctor's, but for a minute he did not seem to see them, but sat gazing abstractedly into the fire; then he took a long draw upon his cigar and began:

"I can see it all very vividly now. It was in the summer time and about seven years ago. I was practicing at the time down in the little town of Bradford. It was a small and primitive place, just the location for an impecunious medical man, recently out of college.

"In lieu of a regular office, I attended to business in the first of two rooms which I rented from Hiram Daly, one of the more prosperous of the townsmen. Here I boarded and here also came my patients—white and black—whites from every section, and blacks from 'nigger town,' as the west portion of the place was called.

"The people about me were most of them coarse and rough, but they were simple and generous, and as time passed on I had about abandoned my intention of seeking distinction in wider fields and determined to settle into the place of a modest country doctor. This was rather a strange conclusion for a young man to arrive at, and I will not deny that the presence in the house of my host's beautiful young daughter, Annie, had something to do with my decision. She was a girl of seventeen or eighteen, and very far superior to her surroundings. She had a native grace and a pleasing way about her that made everybody that came under her spell her abject slave. White and black who knew her loved her, and none, I thought, more deeply and respectfully than Jube Benson, the black man of all work about the place.

"He was a fellow whom everybody trusted—an apparently steady-going, grinning sort, as we used to call him. Well, he was completely under Miss Annie's thumb, and as soon as he saw that I began to care for Annie, and anybody could see that, he transferred some of his allegiance to me and became my faithful servitor also. Never did a man have a more devoted adherent in his wooing than did I, and many a one of Annie's tasks which he volunteered to do gave her an extra hour with me. You can imagine that I liked the boy, and you need not wonder any more that, as both wooing and my practice waxed apace, I was content to give up my great ambitions and stay just where I was.

"It wasn't a very pleasant thing, then, to have an epidemic of typhoid break out in the town that kept me going so that I hardly had time for the courting that a fellow wants to carry on with his sweetheart while he is still young enough to call her his girl. I fumed, but duty was duty, and I kept to my work night and day. It was now that Jube proved how invaluable he was as a coadjuster. He not only took messages to Annie, but brought sometimes little ones from her to me, and he would tell me little secret things that he had overheard her say that made me throb with joy and swear at him for repeating his mistress's conversation. But, best of all, Jube was a perfect Cerberus, and no one on earth could have been more effective in keeping away or deluding the other young fellows who visited the Dalys. He would tell me of it afterward, chuckling softly to himself. 'An', Doctah, I say to Mistah Hemp Stevens, " 'Scuse us, Mistah Stevens, but Miss Annie, she des gone out," an' den he go outer de gate lookin' moughty lonesome. When Sam Elkins come, I say, "Sh, Mistah Elkins, Miss Annie, she done tuk down," an' he say, "What, Jube, you don' reckon hit de—" Den he stop an' look skeert, an' I say, "I feared hit is, Mistah Elkins," an' sheks my haid ez solemn. He goes outer de gate lookin' lak his bes' frien' done daid, an' all de time Miss Annie behine de cu'tain ovah de po'ch des a-laffin' fit to kill.'

"Jube was a most admirable liar, but what could I do? He knew that I was a young fool of a hypocrite, and when I would rebuke him for these deceptions, he would give way and roll on the floor in an excess of delighted laughter until from very contagion I had to join him—and, well, there was no need of my preaching when there had been no beginning to his repentance and when there must ensue a continuance of his wrong-doing.

"This thing went on for over three months, and then, pouf! I was down like a shot. My patients were nearly all up, but the reaction from overwork made me an easy victim of the lurking germs. Then Jube loomed up as a nurse. He put everyone else aside, and with the doctor, a friend of mine from a neighboring town, took entire charge of me. Even Annie herself was put aside, and I was cared for as tenderly as a baby. Tom, that was my physician and friend, told me all about it afterward with tears in his eyes. Only he was a big, blunt man, and his expressions did not convey all that he meant. He told me how Jube had nursed me as if I were a sick kitten and he my mother. Of how fiercely he guarded his right to be the sole one to 'do' for me, as he called it, and how, when the crisis came, he hovered, weeping, but hopeful, at my bedside, until it was safely passed, when they drove him, weak and exhausted, from the room. As for me, I knew little about it at the time, and cared less. I was too busy in my fight with death. To my chimerical vision there was only a black but gentle demon that came and went, alternating with a white fairy, who would insist on coming in on her head, growing larger and larger and then dissolving. But the pathos and devotion in the story lost nothing in my blunt friend's telling.

"It was during the period of a long convalescence, however, that I came to know my humble ally as he really was, devoted to the point of abjectness. There were times when, for very shame at his goodness to me, I would beg him to go away, to do something else. He would go, but before I had time to realize that I was not being ministered to, he would be back at my side, grinning and puttering just the same. He manufactured duties for the joy of performing them. He pretended to see desires in me that I never had, because he liked to pander to them, and when I became entirely exasperated, and ripped out a good round oath, he chuckled with the remark, 'Dah, now, you sholy is gittin' well. Nevah did hyeah a man anywhaih nigh Jo'dan's sho' cuss lak dat.'

"Why, I grew to love him, love him, oh, yes, I loved him as well—oh, what am I saying? All human love and gratitude are damned poor things; excuse me, gentlemen, this isn't a pleasant story. The truth is usually a nasty thing to stand.

"It was not six months after that that my friendship to Jube, which he had been at such great pains to win, was put to too severe a test.

"It was in the summer time again, and, as business was slack, I had ridden over to see my friend, Dr. Tom. I had spent a good part of the day there, and it was past four o'clock when I rode leisurely into Bradford. I was in a particularly joyous mood and no premonition of the impending catastrophe oppressed me. No sense of sorrow, present or to come, forced itself upon me, even when I saw men hurrying through the almost deserted streets. When I got within sight of my home and saw a crowd surrounding it, I was only interested sufficiently to spur my horse into a jog trot, which brought me up to the throng, when something in the sullen, settled horror in the men's faces gave me a sudden, sick thrill. They whispered a word to me, and without a thought save for Annie, the girl who had been so surely growing into my heart, I leaped from the saddle and tore my way through the people to the house.

"It was Annie, poor girl, bruised and bleeding, her face and dress torn from struggling. They were gathered round her with white faces, an oh! with what terrible patience they were trying to gain from her fluttering lips the name of her murderer. They made way for me and I knelt at her side. She was beyond my skill, and my will merged with theirs. One thought was in our minds.

" 'Who?' I asked.

"Her eyes half opened. 'That black—' She fell back into my arms dead.

"We turned and looked at each other. The mother had broken down and was weeping, but the face of the father was like iron.

" 'It is enough,' he said; 'Jube has disappeared.' He went to the door and said to the expectant crowd, 'She is dead.'

"I heard the angry roar without swelling up like the noise of a flood, and then I heard the sudden movement of many feet as the men separated into searching parties, and, laying the dead girl back upon her couch, I took my rifle and went out to join them.

"As if by intuition the knowledge had passed among the men that Jube Benson had disappeared, and he, by common consent, was to be the object of our search. Fully a dozen of the citizens had seen him hastening toward the woods and noted his skulking air, but, as he had grinned in his old good-natured way, they had, at the time, thought nothing of it. Now, however, the diabolical reason of his slyness was apparent. He had been shrewd enough to disarm suspicion, and by now was far away. Even Mrs. Daly, who was visiting with a neighbor, had seen him stepping out by a back way, and had said with a laugh, 'I reckon that black rascal's a-running off somewhere.' Oh, if she had only known!

" 'To the woods! To the woods!' that was the cry; and away we went, each with the determination not to shoot, but to bring the culprit alive into town, and then to deal with him as his crime deserved.

"I cannot describe the feelings I experienced as I went out that night to beat the woods for this human tiger. My heart smoldered within me like a coal, and I went forward under the impulse of a will that was half my own, half some more malignant power's. My throat throbbed drily, but water nor whiskey would not have quenched my thirst. The thought has come to me since that now I could interpret the panther's desire for blood and sympathize with it, but then I thought nothing. I simply went forward, and watched, watched with burning eyes for a familiar form that I had looked for as often before with such different emotions.

"Luck or ill-luck, which you will, was with our party, and just as dawn was graying the sky, we came upon our quarry crouched in the corner of a fence. It was only half light, and we might have passed, but my eyes caught sight of him, and I raised the cry. We leveled our guns and he rose and came toward us.

" 'I t'ought you wa'n't gwine see me,' he said sullenly; 'I didn't mean no harm.'

" 'Harm!'

"Some of the men took the word up with oaths, others were ominously silent.

"We gathered around him like hungry beasts, and I began to see terror dawning in his eyes. He turned to me, 'I's moughty glad you's hyeah, Doc,' he said; 'you ain't gwine let 'em whup me.'

" 'Whip you, you hound,' I said, 'I'm going to see you hanged,' and in the excess of my passion I struck him full on the mouth. He made a motion as if to resent the blow against such great odds, but controlled himself.

" 'W'y, Doctah,' he exclaimed in the saddest voice I have ever heard, 'w'y, Doctah! I ain't stole nuffin' o' yo'n, an' I was comin' back. I only run off to see my gal, Lucy, ovah to de Centah.'

" 'You lie!' I said, and my hands were busy helping others bind him upon a horse. Why did I do it? I don't know. A false education, I reckon, one false from the beginning. I saw his black face glooming there in the half light, and I could only think of him as a monster. It's tradition. At first I was told that the black man would catch me, and when I got over that, they taught me that the devil was black, and when I had recovered from the sickness of that belief, here were Jube and his fellows with faces of menacing blackness. There was only one conclusion: This black man stood for all the powers of evil, the result of whose machinations had been gathering in my mind from childhood up. But this has nothing to do with what happened.

"After firing a few shots to announce our capture, we rode back into town with Jube. The ingathering parties from all directions met us as we made our way up to the house. All was very quiet and orderly. There was no doubt that it was, as the papers would have said, a gathering of the best citizens. It was a gathering of stern, determined men, bent on a terrible vengeance.

"We took Jube into the house, into the room where the corpse lay. At sight of it he gave a scream like an animal's, and his face went the color of storm-blown water. This was enough to condemn him. We divined rather than heard his cry of 'Miss Ann, Miss Ann; oh, my God! Doc, you don't t'ink I done it?'

"Hungry hands were ready. We hurried him out into the yard. A rope was ready. A tree was at hand. Well, that part was the least of it, save that Hiram Daly stepped aside to let me be the first to pull upon the rope. It was lax at first. Then it tightened, and I felt the quivering soft weight resist my muscles. Other hands joined, and Jube swung off his feet.

"No one was masked. We knew each other. Not even the culprit's face was covered, and the last I remember of him as he went into the air was a look of sad reproach that will remain with me until I meet him face to face again.

"We were tying the end of the rope to a tree, where the dead man might hang as a warning to his fellows, when a terrible cry chilled us to the marrow.

" 'Cut 'im down, cut 'im down; he ain't guilty. We got de one. Cut him down, fu' Gawd's sake. Here's de man; we foun' him hidin' in de barn!'

"Jube's brother, Ben, and another Negro came rushing toward us, half dragging, half carrying a miserable-looking wretch between them. Someone cut the rope and Jube dropped lifeless to the ground.

" 'Oh, my Gawd, he's daid, he's daid!' wailed the brother, but with blazing eyes he brought his captive into the center of the group, and we saw in the full light the scratched face of Tom Skinner, the worst white ruffian in town; but the face we saw was not as we were accustomed to see it, merely smeared with dirt. It was blackened to imitate a Negro's.

"God forgive me; I could not wait to try to resuscitate Jube. I knew he was already past help; so I rushed into the house and to the dead girl's side. In the excitement they had not yet washed or laid her out. Carefully, carefully, I searched underneath her broken finger nails. There was skin there. I took it out, the little curled pieces, and went with it to my office.

"There, determinedly, I examined it under a powerful glass, and read my own doom. It was the skin of a white man, and in it were embedded strands of short, brown hair or beard.

"How I went out to tell the waiting crowd I do not know, for something kept crying in my ears, 'Blood guilty! Blood guilty!'

"The men went away stricken into silence and awe. The new prisoner attempted neither denial nor plea. When they were gone I would have helped Ben carry his brother in, but he waved me away fiercely, 'You he'ped murder my brothah, you dat was *his* frien'; go 'way, go 'way! I'll tek him home myse'f.' I could only respect his wish, and he and his comrade took up the dead man and between them bore him up the street on which the sun was now shining full.

"I saw the few men who had not skulked indoors uncover as they passed, and I—I—stood there between the two murdered ones, while all the while something in my ears kept crying, 'Blood guilty! Blood guilty!' "

The doctor's head dropped into his hands and he sat for some time in silence, which was broken by neither of the men; then he rose, saying, "Gentlemen, that was my last lynching."

JEAN TOOMER

Blood-Burning Moon

1

Up from the skeleton stone walls, up from the rotting floor boards and the solid hand-hewn beams of oak of the pre-war cotton factory, dusk came. Up from the dusk the full moon came. Glowing like a fired pine-knot, it illumined the great door and soft showered the Negro shanties aligned along the single street of factory town.. The full moon in the great door was an omen. Negro women improvised songs against its spell.

Louisa sang as she came over the crest of the hill from the white folks' kitchen. Her skin was the color of oak leaves on young trees in fall. Her breasts, firm and up-pointed like ripe acorns. And her singing had the low murmur of winds in fig trees. Bob Stone, younger son of the people she worked for, loved her. By the way the world reckons things, he had won her. By measure of that warm glow which came into her mind at thought of him, he had won her. Tom Burwell, whom the whole town called Big Boy, also loved her. But working in the fields all day, and far away from her, gave him no chance to show it. Though often enough of evenings he had tried to. Somehow, he never got along. Strong as he was with hands upon the ax or plow, he found it difficult to hold her. Or so he thought. But the fact was that he held her to factory town more firmly than he thought for. His black balanced, and pulled against, the white of Stone, when she thought of them. And her mind was vaguely upon them as she came over the crest of the hill, coming from the white folks' kitchen. As she sang softly at the evil face of the full moon.

A strange stir was in her. Indolently, she tried to fix upon Bob or Tom as the cause of it. To meet Bob in the canebrake, as she was going to do an hour or so later, was nothing new. And Tom's proposal which she felt on its way to her could be indefinitely put off. Separately, there was no unusual significance to either one. But for some reason, they jumbled when her eyes gazed vacantly at the rising moon. And from the jumble came the stir that was strangely within her. Her lips trembled. The slow rhythm of her song grew agitant and restless. Rusty black and tan spotted hounds, lying in the dark corners of porches or prowling around back yards, put their noses in the air and caught its tremor. They began plaintively to yelp and howl. Chickens woke up and cackled. Intermittently, all over the countryside dogs barked and roosters crowed as if heralding a weird dawn or some ungodly awakening. The women sang lustily. Their songs were cotton-wads to stop their ears. Louisa came down into factory town and sank wearily upon the step before her home. The moon was rising towards a thick cloud-bank which soon would hide it.

Red nigger moon. Sinner!
Blood-burning moon. Sinner!
Come out that fact'ry door.

2

Up from the deep dusk of a cleared spot on the edge of the forest a mellow glow arose and spread fan-wise into the low-hanging heavens. And all around the air was heavy with the scent of boiling cane. A large pile of cane-stalks lay like ribboned shadows upon the ground. A mule, harnessed to a pole, trudged lazily round and round the pivot of the grinder. Beneath a swaying oil lamp, a Negro alternately whipped out at the mule, and fed cane-stalks to the grinder. A fat boy waddled pails of fresh ground juice between the grinder and the boiling stove. Steam came from the copper boiling pan. The scent of cane came from the copper pan and drenched the forest and the hill that sloped to factory town, beneath its fragrance. It drenched the men in circle seated around the stove. Some of them chewed at the white pulp of stalks, but there was no need for them to, if all they wanted was to taste the cane. One tasted it in factory town. And from factory town one could see the soft haze thrown by the glowing stove upon the low-hanging heavens.

Old David Georgia stirred the thickening syrup with a long ladle, and ever so often drew it off. Old David Georgia tended his stove and told tales about the white folks, about moonshining and cotton picking, and about sweet nigger gals, to the men who sat there about his stove to listen to him. Tom Burwell chewed cane-stalk and laughed with the others till some one mentioned Louisa. Till some one said something about Louisa and Bob Stone, about the silk stockings she must have gotten from him. Blood ran up Tom's neck hotter than the glow that flooded from the stove. He sprang up. Glared at the men and said, "She's my gal." Will Manning laughed. Tom strode over to him. Yanked him up and knocked him to the ground. Several of Manning's friends got up to fight for him. Tom whipped out a long knife and would have cut them to shreds if they hadnt ducked into the woods. Tom had had enough. He nodded to Old David Georgia and swung down the path to factory town. Just then, the dogs started barking and the roosters began to crow. Tom felt funny. Away from the fight, away from the stove, chill got to him. He shivered. He shuddered when he saw the full moon rising towards the cloud-bank. He who didnt give a godam for the fears of old women. He forced his mind to fasten on Louisa. Bob Stone. Better not be. He turned into the street and saw Louisa sitting before her home. He went towards her, ambling, touched the brim of a marvelously shaped, spotted, felt hat, said he wanted to say something to her, and then found that he didnt know what he had to say, or if he did, that he couldnt say it. He shoved his big fists in his overalls, grinned, and started to move off.

"Youall want me, Tom?"

"Thats what us wants, sho, Louisa."

"Well, here I am—"

"An here I is, but that aint ahelpin none, all th same."

"You wanted to say something? . ."

"I did that, sho. But words is like th spots on dice: no matter how y fumbles em, there's times when they jes wont come. I dunno why. Seems like th love I feels fo yo done stole m tongue. I got it now. Whee! Louisa, honey, I oughtnt tell y, I feel I oughtnt cause yo is young an goes t church an I has had other gals, but Louisa I sho do love y. Lil gal, Ise watched y from them first days when youall sat right here befo yo door befo th well an sang sometimes in a way that like t broke m heart. Ise carried y with me into th fields, day after day, an after that, an I sho can plow when yo is there, an I can pick cotton. Yassur! Come near beatin Barlo yesterday. I sho did. Yassur! An next year if ole Stone'll trust me, I'll have a farm. My own. My bales will buy yo what y gets from white folks now. Silk stockings an purple dresses—course I dont believe what some folks been whisperin as t how y gets them things now. White folks always did do for niggers what they likes. An they jes cant help alikin yo, Louisa. Bob Stone likes y. Course he does. But not th way folks is awhisperin. Does he, hon?"

"I dont know what you mean, Tom."

"Course y dont. Ise already cut two niggers. Had t hon, t tell em so. Niggers always tryin t make somethin out a nothin. An then besides, white folks aint up t them tricks so much nowadays. Godam better not be. Leastawise not with yo. Cause I wouldnt stand f it. Nassur."

"What would you do, Tom?"

"Cut him jes like I cut a nigger."

"No, Tom—"

"I said I would an there aint no mo to it. But that aint th talk f now. Sing, honey Louisa, an while I'm listenin t y I'll be makin love."

Tom took her hand in his. Against the tough thickness of his own, hers felt soft and small. His huge body slipped down to the step beside her. The full moon sank upward into the deep purple of the cloud-bank. An old woman brought a lighted lamp and hung it on the common well whose bulky shadow squatted in the middle of the road, opposite Tom and Louisa. The old woman lifted the well-lid, took hold the chain, and began drawing up the heavy bucket. As she did so, she sang. Figures shifted, restlesslike, between lamp and window in the front rooms of the shanties. Shadows of the figures fought each other on the gray dust of the road. Figures raised the windows and joined the old woman in song. Louisa and Tom, the whole street, singing:

Red nigger moon. Sinner!
Blood-burning moon. Sinner!
Come out that fact'ry door.

3

Bob Stone sauntered from his veranda out into the gloom of fir trees and magnolias. The clear white of his skin paled, and the flush of his cheeks turned purple. As if to balance this outer change, his mind became consciously a white man's. He passed the house with its huge open hearth which, in the days of slavery, was the plantation cookery. He saw Louisa bent over that hearth. He went in as a master should and took her. Direct, honest, bold. None of this sneaking that he had to go through now. The contrast was repulsive to him. His family had lost ground. Hell no, his family still owned the niggers, practically. Damned if they did, or he wouldnt have to duck around so. What would they think if they knew? His mother? His sister? He shouldnt mention them, shouldnt think of them in this connection. There in the dusk he blushed at doing so. Fellows about town were all right, but how about his friends up North? He could see them incredible, repulsed. They didnt know. The thought first made him laugh. Then, with their eyes still upon him, he began to feel embarrassed. He felt the need of explaining things to them. Explain hell. They wouldnt understand, and moreover, who ever heard of a Southerner getting on his knees to any Yankee, or anyone. No sir. He was going to see Louisa to-night, and love her. She was lovely—in her way. Nigger way. What way was that? Damned if he knew. Must know. He'd known her long enough to know. Was there something about niggers that you couldnt know? Listening to them at church didnt tell you anything. Looking at them didnt tell you anything. Talking to them didnt tell you anything—unless it was gossip, unless they wanted to talk. Of course, about farming, and licker, and craps—but those werent nigger. Nigger was something more. How much more? Something to be afraid of, more? Hell no. Who ever heard of being afraid of a nigger? Tom Burwell. Cartwell had told him that Tom went with Louisa after she reached home. No sir. No nigger had ever been with his girl. He'd like to see one try. Some position for him to be in. Him, Bob Stone, of the old Stone family, in a scrap with a nigger over a nigger girl. In the good old days . . . Ha! Those were the days. His family had lost ground. Not so much, though. Enough for him to have to cut through old Lemon's canefield by way of the woods, that he might meet her. She was worth it. Beautiful nigger gal. Why nigger? Why not, just gal? No, it was because she was nigger that he went to her. Sweet . . . The scent of boiling cane came to him. Then he saw the rich glow of the stove. He heard the voices of the men circled around it. He was about to skirt the clearing when he heard his own name mentioned. He stopped. Quivering. Leaning against a tree, he listened.

"Bad nigger. Yassur, he sho is one bad nigger when he gets started."

"Tom Burwell's been on th gang three times fo cuttin men."

"What y think he's agwine t do t Bob Stone?"

"Dunno yet. He aint found out. When he does—Baby!"

"Aint no tellin."

"Young Stone aint no quitter an I ken tell y that. Blood of th old uns in his veins."

"Thats right. He'll scrap, sho."

"Be gettin too hot f niggers round this away."

"Shut up, nigger. Y dont know what y talkin bout."

Bob Stone's ears burned as though he had been holding them over the stove. Sizzling heat welled up within him. His feet felt as if they rested on red-hot coals. They stung him to quick movement. He circled the fringe of the glowing. Not a twig cracked beneath his feet. He reached the path that led to factory town. Plunged furiously down it. Halfway along, a blindness within him veered him aside. He crashed into the bordering canebrake. Cane leaves cut his face and lips. He tasted blood. He threw himself down and dug his fingers in the ground. The earth was cool. Cane-roots took the fever from his hands. After a long while, or so it seemed to him, the thought came to him that it must be time to see Louisa. He got to his feet and walked calmly to their meeting place. No Louisa. Tom Burwell had her. Veins in his forehead bulged and distended. Saliva moistened the dried blood on his lips. He bit down on his lips. He tasted blood. Not his own blood; Tom Burwell's blood. Bob drove through the cane and out again upon the road. A hound swung down the path before him towards factory town. Bob couldnt see it. The dog loped aside to let him pass. Bob's blind rushing made him stumble over it. He fell with a thud that dazed him. The hound yelped. Answering yelps came from all over the countryside. Chickens cackled. Roosters crowed, heralding the bloodshot eyes of southern awakening. Singers in the town were silenced. They shut their windows down. Palpitant between the rooster crows, a chill hush settled upon the huddled forms of Tom and Louisa. A figure rushed from the shadow and stood before them. Tom popped to his feet.

"Whats y want?"

"I'm Bob Stone."

"Yassur—an I'm Tom Burwell. Whats y want?"

Bob lunged at him. Tom side-stepped, caught him by the shoulder, and flung him to the ground. Straddled him.

"Let me up."

"Yassur—but watch yo doins, Bob Stone."

A few dark figures, drawn by the sound of scuffle, stood about them. Bob sprang to his feet.

"Fight like a man, Tom Burwell, and I'll lick y."

Again he lunged. Tom side-stepped and flung him to the ground. Straddled him.

"Get off me, you godam nigger you."

"Yo sho has started somethin now. Get up."

Tom yanked him up and began hammering at him. Each blow sounded as if it smashed into a precious, irreplaceable soft something. Beneath them, Bob staggered back. He reached in his pocket and whipped out a knife.

"Thats my game, sho."

Blue flash, a steel blade slashed across Bob Stone's throat. He had a sweetish sick feeling. Blood began to flow. Then he felt a sharp twitch of pain. He let his knife drop. He slapped one hand against his neck. He pressed the other on top of his head as if to hold it down. He groaned. He turned, and staggered towards the crest of the hill in the direction of white town. Negroes who had seen the fight slunk into their homes and blew the lamps out. Louisa, dazed, hysterical, refused to go indoors. She slipped, crumbled, her body loosely propped against the woodwork of the well. Tom Burwell leaned against it. He seemed rooted there.

Bob reached Broad Street. White men rushed up to him. He collapsed in their arms.

"Tom Burwell. . . ."

White men like ants upon a forage rushed about. Except for the taut hum of their moving, all was silent. Shotguns, revolvers, rope, kerosene, torches. Two high-powered cars with glaring searchlights. They came together. The taut hum rose to a low roar. Then nothing could be heard but the flop of their feet in the thick dust of the road. The moving body of their silence preceded them over the crest of the hill into factory town. It flattened the Negroes beneath it. It rolled to the wall of the factory, where it stopped. Tom knew that they were coming. He couldnt move. And then he saw the searchlights of the two cars glaring down on him. A quick shock went through him. He stiffened. He started to run. A yell went up from the mob. Tom wheeled about and faced them. They poured down on him. They swarmed. A large man with dead-white face and flabby cheeks came to him and almost jabbed a gun-barrel through his guts.

"Hands behind y, nigger."

Tom's wrists were bound. The big man shoved him to the well. Burn him over it, and when the woodwork caved in, his body would drop to the bottom. Two deaths for a godam nigger. Louisa was driven back. The mob pushed in. Its pressure, its momentum was too great. Drag him to the factory. Wood and stakes already there. Tom moved in the direction indicated. But they had to drag him. They reached the great door. Too many to get in there. The mob divided and flowed around the walls to either side. The big man shoved him through the door. The mob pressed in from the sides. Taut humming. No words. A stake was sunk into the ground. Rotting floor boards piled around it. Kerosene poured on the rotting floor boards. Tom bound to the stake. His breast was bare. Nails' scratches let little lines of blood trickle down and mat into the hair. His face, his eyes were set and stony. Except for irregular breathing, one would have thought him already dead. Torches were flung onto the pile. A great flare muffled in black smoke shot upward. The mob yelled. The mob was silent. Now Tom could be seen within the flames. Only his head, erect, lean, like a blackened stone. Stench of burning flesh soaked the air. Tom's eyes popped. His head settled downward. The mob yelled. Its yell echoed against the skeleton stone walls and sounded like a hundred yells. Like a hundred mobs yelling. Its yell thudded against the thick front wall and fell back. Ghost of a yell slipped through the flames and out the great door of the factory. It fluttered like a dying thing down the single street of factory town. Louisa, upon the step before her home, did not hear it, but her eyes opened slowly. They saw the full moon glowing in the great door. The full moon, an evil thing, an omen, soft showering the homes of folks she knew. Where were they, these people? She'd sing, and perhaps they'd come out and join her. Perhaps Tom Burwell would come. At any rate, the full moon in the great door was an omen which she must sing to:

Red nigger moon. Sinner!
Blood-running moon. Sinner!
Come out that fact'ry door.

ALBERT FRENCH

Billy

Mississippi's summer of nineteen thirty-seven faded. Days cooled as long nights chilled. The lights of the Patch flickered again, fires would burn soon. Patch children played in the day. Patch mamas talked in the night, but the stillness that had come in the summer lingered. Patch folks would only whisper about Billy Lee. Their whispers asked questions of days nearing.

Cinder could be seen. Patch folks would watch her, but did not stare, and never looked into her passing eyes. She had become frail with days gone by. Reverend Sims would go to her. Sometimes she let him near and listened to his words, some days Reverend Sims knew to leave her be. He'd tell Katey, "Ya just tell her she gots ta believe."

November's first day came on a Monday. Harvey Jakes put out an extra paper; its headline read "BOY KILLER COMES TO TRIAL." Monday's sun had not risen yet. The courthouse was dark and empty; just the sound of its night could be heard, the shifting of its wood, the scratching of its mice. Sheriff Tom and Deputy Hill led their prisoner through the dark, chilling street. Billy was shivering and flinched from every dog's bark.

First light was first to come. County clerks of habit followed; they wiggled their keys in courthouse doors. Folks from afar who had heard the news had traveled in the night. Banes folks who lived around the corner began making their way.

Patch folks, just a few, were coming on the broken Patch Road. Cinder walked through the shadows the night had left on the road, Katey was by her side. Reverend Sims followed: he had his slavin Bible. His God had told him, "Walk with Cinder this day." Big Jake was coming too, he had told LeRoy, "Ah gots ta go."

Courtroom A was ready, and its bench seats were filling up. Quick whispers burst through the hum of restless chatter: "There he is." "That's him." Sheriff Tom was bringing Billy through the side door. Fingers still pointed at Billy as he slouched down in the big hard chair next to Wilbur Braxton. In the far rear of the courtroom, where coloreds can sit, Cinder sits high in her seat, but she cannot see her child.

Judge Harper called his court to order, then told Matthew Brady to seat the jury. Twelve faces of men filed into their seats. Cinder could see them; she tried to see into their eyes, but the faces were too far away.

Billy kept his head down as Ely Hampton told the jury, "Ah represent the State of Mississippi. Ah represent you, the people of Mississippi. Together we represent Lori Pasko here today." Then his words began to whip and snap at the air: "A knife in the hand of the vicious Nigra boy slashed the life away from Lori. She was just fifteen. . . ."

Billy cringed from the wind of the shouting man's words.

Cinder looked straight into the storm of sounds, tried to see where her child be.

Reverend Sims watched Wilbur Braxton rise and try to turn a wind gone wild. Big Jake listened and nodded his head yes as Wilbur Braxton told Banes folks, "Billy Lee Turner is just ten years old, just a child. A frightened child. What happened at that pond was a tragedy. A tragedy. Not a vicious crime."

Red Pasko's eyes burned red with fire.

Silence was a witness as Wilbur Braxton's words stilled and he took his seat.

Banes folks saw Sheriff Tom take the witness seat and heard him tell Ely Hampton, "Ah found that little girl layin in her mama's bed. She was dead when Ah got there."

Cinder saw the man that keeps her child from her; she did not listen to what he had to say.

Jenny Curran shook when Ely Hampton called her name. She has on her light-blue dress, the one she only wears to church and wore to Lori's funeral. Her long red hair is tied in a pony tail and gently hangs down on her back. Her hand is trembling on Matthew Brady's Bible. Her words are faint when she says, "Ah do."

Banes folks leaned up in their seats as Jenny took her time and told them about the day at the pond when Lori died. Billy kept his head down, but looked up when he heard the red-haired girl crying out, "That's him. That's him right there. That's the nigger that stuck Lori. That's him. He killed Lori. Ah saw him. He stuck her and made her die. Ah hate ya, nigger."

Ginger Pasko sat quietly; tears seeped from her silence.

Banes folks watched Ely Hampton strut and peck before the jury until the noon hour came. Judge Harper looked at his watch, cleared his throat, then announced, "We goin ta take a recess here. We will convene at one-fifteen." The Rosey Gray filled up quickly, but most folks had brought their lunch and just found them a spot in front of the courthouse to eat.

Deputy Hill took Billy back down to Courtroom C and locked the door. Sheriff Tom stood in the hallway talking with Red and Ginger Pasko until he saw Ginger's eyes jerk and stare beyond his shoulder. He turned around and quickly shouted, "Where ya all think ya goin?" Cinder and Katey stopped. Cinder's eyes stilled and just stared at Sheriff Tom. Katey replied, "Theys say Billy be down there in a room. We thinkin maybe theys let us see him. Maybe we be allows ta sits wit him."

Sheriff Tom shouted, "Ya all git out of here. Ya hear me? Git on outside."

Cinder stood still. She gave a quick glance to the redhaired woman standing behind the sheriff. She saw her red eyes and dropped her own. Sheriff Tom shouted again, "Go on, now. Git out of here."

Cinder stood still.

Ginger Pasko reached for Sheriff Tom's arm, tugged at it until he turned around, then she just looked at him. He turned back to Cinder, looked at her, and said, "All right. Down there. Last door. Ya tell Deputy Hill that Sheriff Tom says it's all right." As Cinder passed, she glanced at Ginger Pasko again and their eyes met.

Deputy Hill opened the door when he heard the tapping knock, then let Cinder and Katey in after he looked up the hall and got Sheriff Tom's signal.

Billy jumped up from his chair and ran to his mother, then they sat in the room's noon shadow; the two figures became one shaded sketch. Cinder has Billy in her arms. She has brought him so close that he is her. Billy is snifflin, quiverin, as he says, "Ah wants ta goes home. Mama, they says Ah can't." Katey wiped the tears from her eyes and Deputy Hill looked away.

Cinder whispers, "Mama's here, Mama's here, baby."

Billy pleads again, "Mama, Ah wants ta go home. Ah don't wants ta be in that jail no more."

Cinder sighs as Billy cries and tries to talk through his tearful gasps. "Ah wants ta go home. Ah won't go ta that pond again, Mama."

Cinder closes her eyes, but the dark does not come, just a faint speck of the color green, then the high green grass of green years ago, and Billy can play again, blue is in the sky, Mister Pete singing that old goin-home song, folks let her and her baby be. She kisses Billy, and the breath that carries his words and cries wisps across her lips. "They say Ah go wit ya? They say that?

Ah don't wants ta be in a trial." Cinder is silent, but the dark comes, white face come into the night. Mister Pete's dead, been dead, ain't no sky, ain't no blues, greens die too.

Banes folks watched clocks tick away. The noon hour finally filled with minutes and moments. The courtroom swelled with chatter until Judge Harper called for order.

Billy jumped and looked around when he heard Gumpy's name being called. He heard Gumpy tellin the shoutin man, "He showed me his knife, its have blood on it. He say he stuck her in the titty. He say that too."

Ely Hampton kept pecking at Gumpy: "Where did Billy Lee keep his knife?"

Billy put his head back down and stared at the shades of the table before him. He can hear Gumpy calling, but it is in a different time. "Hey, Billy, can ya's come out? Hey, Billy, ya wants ta go down ta the Catfish wit me?" He can hear the sound of Gumpy's voice, but it is only the sound of his words. Gumpy is telling Ely Hampton, "It's be in his pocket. Cept if he wants ta cuts sumpin. If he gits mad at ya, he chase ya wit it. But he can't catch me. He can't runs like me."

Ely Hampton told Judge Harper, "The State rests its case, Your Honor."

Murmurs sizzled, necks twisted and turned, folks edged far up in their seats. Reverend Sims can see Billy as he jerks away from the sudden outstretched hand with the Bible in it. Then he sees him slowly touch the Bible with the coaxing and whispering of Matthew Brady.

Ginger Pasko shakes her head before turning away.

Cinder's heart pounds a thunderous sound.

Wilbur Braxton nears Billy on the witness stand and whispers something to him. Billy nods his head yes, but does not look up. "Tell the people what your name is, Billy," Wilbur Braxton says.

Billy remains silent.

Wilbur Braxton is patient, he repeats, "Billy, tell the people what your name is."

Billy's lips move, but no sound comes from his mouth.

"Are you afraid, Billy?"

Billy shakes his head no, squirms in the big chair, then nods his head yes.

"Come on, son, I told you there was nothing to be afraid of. Tell the people your name. You can do that."

"Billy Lee my name."

"Now, Billy, tell the people how old you are."

"Ah ten."

"Now, Billy, tell the people why you are here today."

"Ah don't knows. They says it's a trial."

"What's a trial, Billy? Tell the people what a trial is."

"Ah don't know."

"Billy, what happen to you at the pond? What happen, son?"

Billy is silent.

Red Pasko waits for an answer.

"What happen, Billy?"

"Them girls come. They beats me up. Theys bigger."

"Why did they beat you up?"

"Ah don'ts know. Me and Gumpy be in the pond. Theys come and git us."

"Did you try and run from the girls, Billy?"

"Ah runs, but theys catch me. That girl, she bigger than me. She gits me down."

"Billy, what happen when they let you up? Did you try and run again?"

"Ah gits up. She comes and git me agins."

"Did she hit you again?"

"Ah stuck her. Ah make her leave me be."

"Billy, what happen to her?"

"Ah don't know. They says she deads."

"Billy, did you want to hurt her? Did you want to make her die?"

"Ah ain't makes her deads. She comes gits me agins. Ah stuck her. Ah makes her leave me be."

Red Pasko clenches his teeth.

Ely Hampton does not wait for Wilbur Braxton to take his seat before he is up shouting. "Billy Lee. Billy Lee, ya ever see this knife before?"

Billy puts his head down.

Ely Hampton holds the knife up and shouts, "Billy Lee. Look up here. This your knife, boy?"

Billy looks up, nods his head yes, and looks back down.

"Ya say ya stuck her with this knife? How many times you stick her?"

Billy is silent.

"How many times ya stick her, Billy Lee Turner? Ya stuck her pretty hard, didn't ya? Just wasn't a poke, was it? Ya lashed out at her. Ya slashed her arm first, so ya could plunge that knife up in her. Get it in there deep, didn't ya, boy?"

Billy utters, "She beats me up."

Ely Hampton walks away, goes back to his prosecuting table, then comes back to Billy carrying a bag in his hands. He reaches into the bag and pulls out Lori's blood-stained shirt.

Ginger Pasko's gasp cannot muffle her scream.

Ely Hampton holds Lori's shirt up in one hand and Billy's knife in the other and shouts, "Look up here, Billy Lee, look up here."

Slowly Billy looks up.

"This is your knife, Billy Lee, isn't it? This is the shirt Lori had on when ya plunged your knife into her. Isn't it? Answer me, Billy Lee Turner."

Big Jake puts his head down.

Katey utters a desperate whisper, "He ain't means it, Lord."

Billy sees the blood-stained shirt.

November's first day's sun was going down. Its soft yellow rays gently lay across the broken Patch Road. Cinder walked slowly. When she would stop and just stand and quiver, Big Jake was near. Gently he would reach for her, bring her to him so she could lean some of the way.

Katey followed; she was tired of the road and where it went and where it came from. Reverend Sims walked by her side, clutching his slavin Bible, but grasping for the faith he left behind.

Cinder's screams still filled the courthouse; the echoes wouldn't die. Ginger Pasko had heard the cries, but she did not turn around to see, she knew who the woman would be.

Wilbur Braxton was still telling hisself that he had done his best. He had told the jury, "I stand before you respectfully and humbly. Respectfully as you are men, humbly as I am merely a man. We share a heavy burden today; we have that child's life in our hands. My God, that child is no killer."

He had paced back and forth before the twelve faces, he had tried to tell them. "What happened at that pond was a tragedy. Children in fear and anger and a knife at hand. A tragedy in our days. Storms, high waters, winds in the night that blow down homes and shatter lives. We know our tragedies." Ginger Pasko had heard him say, "There is an empty supper seat, Lori's seat; a cup of joy is bare and dry. But there is a mightier force than man that lowers the high waters of the storm, brings flowers to bear where there was only scorn." Twelve silent faces heard him whisper his final plea: "Please don't kill Billy too."

A silent moment had lingered over the court, perhaps too long. Judge Harper cleared his throat and sent his jury away to find its verdict. Banes folks went to waiting, but not too long. Cinder had sat with Reverend Sims; he had told her, "God cans show blind mens to see. He'll show em the rights things ta do. Ya just gots ta believes."

Word of the jury's return spread through the streets and minds before time could gather its composure and pace itself with dignity. Quickly the courtroom filled, then stilled itself as the jury entered. Now only the sound of Matthew Brady's footsteps can be heard as he carries the verdict to Judge Harper. Patiently, the silence in the courtroom waited for Judge Harper to speak, then it ran into the corner and stood with Reverend Sims' God; and put its head down too.

Celebrants' shouts and chatter filled the courtroom until Cinder's screams trampled every sound.

GORDON PARKS

Shannon

Hannibal Jones hadn't gone to Fisk University to become a redcap. He wanted something much better. He had landed his present job two months after the fire at Maude's place; but he kept searching for something better. Yet every job he applied for always required something he didn't have to offer. His professors at Fisk had warned what that qualification would be: a white face. But Hannibal was determined. He kept writing letters to all kinds of places that claimed to need a bright young man who had studied business administration. But Hannibal found no takers.

He saw the ad Meath had put in the New York papers and sent off a letter immediately. He was at a low ebb when the reply came from Galway, inviting him in for an interview. Hannibal was duly impressed to see that the letter was signed by Meath Sullivan, the president of Galway. The instructions were to report directly to him for the interview.

Hannibal arrived at Galway, scrubbed and bright at eight forty-five on the morning of his appointment. His suit, the only one he possessed, was sharply pressed from lying beneath his mattress for a fortnight. He had used this crude, but economical, method during his college days when money was always short. His shoes shone so from polishing that he could see his face reflected in them.

So often he had seen and admired this big industrial complex with its towering smoke stacks and sounds of hissing steam and metal clanking inside those walls that seemed so forbidden to outsiders—especially Negroes.

He made a final inspection of himself before he entered, remembering and checking off everything old Professor Hawkins had told his Negro boys before they departed the hallowed halls of Fisk. "The white man's going to be expecting you to come in dirty. Go in clean, spanking clean. He's going to expect you to come in begging, with your head hung low. Go in proud, with your head held as high as your black neck can stretch. Look at him eyeball to eyeball and say, 'I'm here, white man, clean, educated, and ready—and I hope you're ready for me.' "

Meath's secretary seemed flustered when she looked up and saw Hannibal enter the door. "Yes, can I help you?" she asked, almost too quickly, Hannibal thought.

"I have an appointment with Mr. Sullivan at nine o'clock."

"Mr. Sullivan?"

"Sullivan."

She thumbed her appointment book and looked at it closely. "There's something definitely wrong. Mr. Sullivan has an appointment with a Mr. Jones at nine. I'm sorry—"

"Well, that's me, miss. I'm Mr. Jones, H. R. Jones. His letter said that I was to report to him personally."

"Oh, yes—yes, of course," she said. "I'm terribly sorry. I'll let Mr. Sullivan know you're here." She got up and went through a door behind her. Hannibal checked the time by the wall clock. He was right on the minute: nine sharp. (Always be punctual. The white man's going to expect you to be late. Get there early. Five minutes before is always better than one second after.) Five interminable minutes passed before the secretary returned. "You can come in now," she said most pleasantly.

What an office, Hannibal was thinking as she offered him a chair before the large desk. His shoes sank so deep into the rug he could hardly see their points. "Mr. Sullivan will be right in." She smiled at him before going out and closing the door behind her.

He looked about, bewildered by the opulence. The desk was eight feet long and half as wide. But even it seemed small in so large a room. To the rear, surrounded by a dozen or more big leather chairs was a big important-looking table, where important men surely sat and discussed important things. My God, could I ever become a part of this? he asked himself. He looked up at the painting of a great white yacht skimming the waves of some far-off ocean, focusing in on the letters on the prow. *Liberty*, it read. Scores of other smaller paintings and photographs covered the four walls. Pictures of an attractive woman and beautiful girl—obviously Mr. Sullivan's family, Hannibal thought. A two-foot replica of a bullet stood on a pedestal, with a gold plaque proclaiming first prize in a statewide contest.

Another door opened so softly Hannibal hardly heard it, and Meath stepped into the room. He smiled and extended his hand. Hannibal rose, smiled, and shook it. "You're Mr. Jones, of course. Glad you came."

"Thank you, sir. I'm glad you asked me to come."

"Fine—fine. What does the H. R. stand for?"

"Hannibal Rufus, sir."

"Good name—good name, Hannibal. Named for someone special?"

Hannibal smiled warmly. "Very very special: my great-great-grandfather on my father's side."

"Robust name. Must have been a good man."

"Fine man, sir."

Sullivan started digging through a stack of résumés. "Well now, I'm in need of a first-class administrative assistant—and I assume you're in need of a job or you wouldn't be here. That right?"

"Absolutely," Hannibal answered, stretching his black neck very high. He wanted to say, "And I'm here, ready and able," but it wouldn't come out.

Meath snapped a pince-nez to his nose and pulled out a résumé from the center of the stack. "Ah, here it is." He studied it for a few seconds. "B.A. in business administration, president of Varsity Club—football, basketball, track, and wrestling—Jesus, man, you're a dynamo!" Hannibal beamed (eyeball to eyeball), trying to catch Meath's eye, but Meath's eyes were glued to the paper. "This is impressive, Hannibal, very impressive." He got up and went to the window and gazed out toward a big warehouse adjacent to his office, and began explaining things. "This is a big, big job we're talking about. It's a hell of a responsibility, Hannibal—one hell of a responsibility. A man has to be creative, imaginative, and extremely talented. He has to have great persuasive powers to move a lot of people around to his way of doing things."

"I'm sure I can handle it, Mr. Sullivan. I'm sure I can."

Meath turned abruptly and came back to Hannibal, offering his hand again. "You know, I think you could. Yessir, I think you could." As they shook hands, Meath buzzed for his secretary. She popped in quickly and looked quizzically at her boss, awaiting orders. "We will be in touch with you, Mr. Jones. It may take a few days but you will hear from us. And thanks again for coming in."

"Thank you, sir." And at last Hannibal caught his eye, but the eyeball business was brief, terribly brief—because Sullivan's eyes shot from Hannibal's to his secretary as he bid Hannibal goodbye. "Mabel."

"Yes, Mr. Sullivan."

"After you show Mr. Jones out, have Bert Hansen report to me—immediately."

"Yessir."

Hannibal walked out of the gates with mixed feelings. "Goddamn—Goddamn!" He looked back at all the buildings with smoke and steam rising from them. "Goddamn, Hannibal Jones, you just might be getting your black ass into something real big," he said aloud.

A workman entering the gate turned toward him. "Say something?"

"Just talking to myself," Hannibal said with a smile, and he went on down the street—talking to himself.

Meath gave Bert Hansen his most withering look. "You know something, Bert," he said, picking up Hannibal's résumé and handing it to his assistant. "If you ever cause me another moment—yes, just one more damn moment—of such embarrassment, you will be fired!"

"I don't understand, Mr. Sullivan," Bert said, looking at the résumé. "Just what did I do?"

"What did you do? Well, I'll tell you what you did. You caused me to waste a whole precious half hour of my valuable time on a dumb darky."

"I still don't understand sir."

"Why hell, man, don't you analyze those applications when they come across your desk? Don't you know that Fisk University is a darky school and that H. R. Jones had to be a nigger?"

"I'm sorry, sir. I just didn't know. I never heard of the school before, and his record was quite impressive. I thought—"

"You thought. Pull yourself together, Hansen."

"Yes, sir."

"And Hansen, wait for a few days and send Mr. H. R. Jones a damn nice letter of refusal."

"Yessir."

Two weeks later Hannibal got the reply. When he saw the envelope from Galway with a rifle embossed on it, he closed his eyes, said an earnest prayer and tore it open. It read:

> Mr. H. R. Jones
> Dear Sir,
> Thank you for your visit to Galway Munitions. You impressed me very much during our meeting. You have splendid qualifications. There is no doubt that you have prepared yourself well. Unfortunately, we have decided to postpone establishing the position you applied for. If and when we decide to establish that position, you will certainly be given full consideration. Thank you again for coming in. I wish you continued success.
>
> Sincerely yours,
> M. E. Sullivan, President

"Continued success—shit!" Suddenly he ripped the letter to shreds and threw it to the floor. Then ever so softly he began talking to himself. "When you see Mister White Man, be early and clean and stretch your black neck till your nappy head's high as a goddamned kite and look at Mister White Man eyeball to eyeball and tell him you is ready for him—" Hannibal suddenly began laughing, laughing until he felt like crying.

WILLIAM STRICKLAND

The Future of Black Men

We have survived the Middle Passage and we have survived slavery. We have survived the deadly arbitrariness of Jim Crow and the hypocritical hatefulness of northern discrimination. But now, as we enter the last decade of the twentieth century, we face a danger more covert, more insidious, more threatening and potentially more *final* even than these: the apparently sly conspiracy to do away with Black men as a troublesome presence in America.

A conspiracy may or may not exist, but the potential for the extinction of Black men, and ultimately Black people, is very real indeed. Consider this: Mounting evidence suggests that a near majority of working-age Black men (15 to 44) are alcoholics or drug abusers, are in prison, unemployed, infected with the AIDS virus or suffering from some other life-threatening condition, or are slated to die at the hands of other Black men. We do not know with certainty when this devastation began to set in, but as Jewelle Taylor Gibbs of the University of California at Berkeley reveals in her landmark volume *Young, Black, and Male in America: An Endangered Species* (Auburn House Publishing Co.), more young Black men died from homicide in one year (1977) than died in ten years in the Vietnam War. Reporting on conditions a decade later, *Newsweek* points out that Black men are six times as likely as white men to be murder victims and that they finish last "in practically every socioeconomic measure from infant mortality to life expectancy." In fact, the "dying rate" is so high among our young men today that the life expectancy of Black people as a whole has been declining since 1986. We are suffering therefore from a double-edged holocaust: self-inflicted on the one hand and system-administered on the other. Our young males in America's inner cities, as Gibbs wrote last year in the *Los Angeles Times*, "are . . . endangered. . . , constantly threatened with physical, psychological or social annihilation. They have been miseducated by the educational system, mishandled by the criminal justice system, mislabeled by the mental health system and mistreated by the social welfare system."

Obviously a tree half of whose roots are diseased or dying must ultimately die. Well, Black people are that tree, and Black men half of its imperiled roots. But the very soil on which our tree stands is eroded: America itself is in crisis—in its environment, its politics, its economics, its educational systems, its intellectual life, its heart and soul. Our troubles grow from that soil.

Now, America has always put us down. There is nothing particularly new about that. In antebellum days we were said to be biologically and culturally inferior. Nowadays we are portrayed both as morally inferior and as inherently criminal. Indeed, crime has come to be defined as *Black* and *male*. And it only troubles contemporary America when it is (a) violent and (b) directed against white folks. (So Reagan's, North's and others' trashing the Constitution is not a crime. Exxon's destruction of wildlife and pollution of the Alaska shoreline in the greatest oil spill in American history are not crimes. And the government's 30-year concealment of reactor accidents at its nuclear weapons plants is also not a crime. Meanwhile singer James Brown does six years in the South Carolina slammer.)

The message of "Black male criminality" is a constant refrain, and, sadly, the propaganda—of "wolf packs" and "marauding" and "wilding"—seems to have taken hold among this generation's young Black men. Pummeled by disparaging social commentary, ridiculed by the media and forsaken by Black leaders who should know better, they appear to be internalizing America's negative image and killing themselves in unprecedented numbers. At present, homicide and suicide are two of the three leading causes of death among young Black males between ages 15 and 24, which means that for the first time in our history we are becoming the instruments of our own destruction.

Now, why is this?

If you look at the attitudes of the same age group during the late sixties, as described by one of the most helpful sources, the Report of the National Advisory Commission on Civil Disorders (commissioned by President Lyndon B. Johnson after the Detroit and Newark rebellions of 1967 and headed by Otto Kerner), there is no significant difference between the two groups, even though twenty years have passed, except in the area of racial consciousness and identification. Yet the young man of 1967 was a typical "rioter," and the youth of 1989 appears to be a largely apolitical fatalist.

The rioter, Kerner found, "felt strongly that he deserved a better job and that he was barred from achieving it not because of lack of training, ability, or ambition but because of discrimination by employers." He also "took great pride in his race and was substantially better informed about politics than Negroes who were not involved in the riot."

So a critical difference between then and now is that young Black men of the sixties, socialized by the freedom movement and more solidly grounded in their Black identity, defiantly rejected the vituperation and racist analysis that eats away at the self-confidence of many of our young men today.

YOUTHS ADRIFT

Without a Black struggle to orient them, as it had oriented every generation of Black people since 1619, orphaned by this season's elitist "talented tenth," malignly neglected by the government of the United States, and excluded from the labor force by American business, young Black men have been left to forge their own identities in gangs, out of American television and MTV, and in contention with the dog-eat-dog-get-over-at-any-cost macho street culture.

But left to themselves, they have survived and created. They have invented graffiti art, break dancing, rap and the hip-hop culture, all of which insist on being recognized, protest against being ignored, and are determinedly leaving their mark on a hostile world. Their creators and consumers have moved from the slavish gold chains and designer sweats of a moment ago to red, black and green Africa medallions and African-inspired haircuts, and they have embraced Malcolm X as the symbol—on T-shirts and in slogans—of strong Black manhood (it's not apparent that the substance of his life and work have been considered).

Despite these considerable achievements, they are still youths adrift, hurting and searching and trying, in Spike Lee's words, to "do the right thing," but finding, in the words of Charles Gordone's 1971's classic play, "no place to be somebody." Essentially abandoned, our youths became estranged from the values that held us together through our trials and tribulations in this land—with the results that we now see: cannibalism stalking the inner city of the eighties because of the erosion of racial identity and political clarity, the chemical warfare of the drug culture, and the relaxation of the racial bonds between the Black masses and middle class.

To be fair, I do not think that the Black middle class truly appreciated how absolutely unique the situation was when the sixties movement ended, nor how absolutely crucial was the role that it was now called upon to play. For no Black people had ever before been called upon to teach their children about American racism—only how to overcome it. In the past, one had to learn the mores of the southern caste system or die. And northern racism was only slightly less heavy-handed, as the whole life and work of writer James Baldwin attests.

But in the modern era racism has become structurally covert and universally duplicitous. It hides behind phrases like "reverse discrimination," "qualified employees" and "nonmarketable skills." It is more sophisticated than the old appeals for "law and order" and Reagan's made-up stories about "welfare queens." Instead it offers us "constructive engagement" in South Africa because "sanctions don't work," while it blithely enters into its third decade of sanctions against Cuba. It even denies that the Willie Horton Republican presidential campaign ads were racist. It is without shame.

In this bewildering potpourri of lies, half-truths, rationalizations and deceptions, the best of us needed clearheaded analysis to find our way. We needed at that juncture in our history, and America's, uncompromising truth-tellers, racial advocates who would "tell it like it is." What emerged too frequently instead in the postmovement era were bland racial diplomats, suave compromisers, litigious negotiators, reasonable and, one supposes, well-intentioned go-betweens. But we needed ass-kickers. We needed Frederick Douglass. We needed Sojourner Truth. We needed Malcolm X. But they were gone.

JOBLESSNESS: A WAY OF LIFE

The primary basis of male identity in this country and in human society is work. What you do is who you are (unless you're living off inherited wealth). If you do nothing, you are nothing. And in a wage-structured society where one must sell one's labor to live, the inability to obtain work is both a spiritual and material death sentence. It is a blow struck against one's self-respect, one's identity, one's relations with others and one's sanity.

But work does not fall from the sky. It arises out of the real and perceived needs of an American political economy whose military bases and multinational corporations now straddle the world like a latter-day Rome. In this global economy, Black labor, once indispensable to American rational development, has outlived its usefulness and is merely a superfluous commodity in the international labor market. Witness this July [1989] when a major American car company concluded a $120 million agreement to build a new factory in Europe that would employ nearly 2,000 workers and export the auto components it makes to the car company plants throughout the world. This now common investment of American capital overseas means that the jobs Black men need are now to be found in Europe, Central and South America and Asia—a very long way from Detroit and other job-hungry Black communities.

It is in this global context that we must seek to understand the economic plight of Black men and, in so doing, dispense with the misnomer "Black unemployment" because, given the current spending priorities and allocations of American business and government, most Black men, in most parts of this country, for most of their lives, will never be employed. What we are talking about, then, is Black joblessness as a way of life, a decreed condition handed down through the generations as a form of racist curse.

JOBLESSNESS: GENOCIDE

Joblessness destroys Black men in myriad ways. It starts them on their way to homelessness; it means that able-bodied men can no longer support their families and, lacking the wherewithal, tend to desert them, thereby exacerbating the crisis of our families; it means that some Black men don't get married in the first place, though continuing to father children for whom they only sometimes accept responsibility; it means that Black men don't have health insurance, so that when they finally go to the hospital it is often too late; and it means Black men are under stress unimaginable in larger society. (According to the National Medical Association convention meeting this summer in Orlando, Florida, Black men under 45 are ten times more likely to die of hypertension than whites and have a 45-percent higher rate of lung cancer.) It means that, despairing of living meaningful lives, Black men become alcoholics. Above all, it means that they abuse drugs and get involved in the drug culture.

In all the discussion about drugs, few have addressed the proposition that, at one level, involvement in drugs is also a coping mechanism, a disavowal of the economic meaninglessness to which America has consigned Black men. In decades past, many of our relatives were involved with the numbers racket, which was the underground criminal activity of its day. In these times, however, the choice available to many Black men, banished from the American economy, is the drug economy or nothing.

Add to that the temptation of "easy money" and the societally reinforced version of the *Miami Vice* "good life," then ask yourself: Why would a young man spurn that life to take a $3.35-an-hour job at Wendy's? If he can't be a professional athlete or a musician, the role models for many inner-city youth, why should he take a minimum-wage job when he can make hundreds of dollars a day being a lookout or a delivery boy for a dealer? We have to be for real. The drug economy is the main game in town in the ghetto, and until it is economically replaced, neither Nancy Reagan nor Jesse Jackson nor drug "czar" William Bennett nor all the social workers in the world are going to make it go away.

So there is a straight line from joblessness to the deadly moral chaos of the drug world and its multifaceted destruction of Black men. Drugs fry the brain and turn teenage children into killers. Drugs divert the business acumen and leadership skills that ought to pay off in the straight world to race-destroying criminal ends. Drug money turns beardless children into juvenile emasculators of fathers or mothers struggling to keep a family together, but unable to compete with sons whose drug money makes them the principal family breadwinner. Dealing drugs lands you in prison, where half of those currently incarcerated are Black men. And, above all, drug trafficking elevates money above racial consciousness, dissolving the bonds of solidarity a people require to endure and prevail. Through crack, heroin and cocaine, we are smoking, shooting and snorting away our soul.

Thus genocide need not do its work in concentration camps. It need only destroy a people's life purpose, render the men, in this case, dysfunctional and reduce them, as in the case of the Native American, to a reservation-bound remnant. Like the Native American who succumbed to alcohol and to smallpox-infected blankets, we are under siege from drugs and AIDS-infected needles and anomie. And the result is the same.

We, too, have begun to die out.

OUR AND AMERICA'S CRISIS

I have, only partially tongue-in-cheek, used the concept of conspiracy to suggest the enormous gravity of the crisis facing Black men and the structural underpinnings of that crisis in the American political economy. But the crisis of Black men is really a part of the larger crisis of American society itself: since the Reagan Administration, a crisis of 600,000 farmers who have lost their land; a crisis of poisoned waters and toxic skies; a crisis of befouled oceans and dysfunctional schools; a crisis of aging airplanes falling out of the heavens; and a crisis of overburdened sewer systems discharging lethal waste onto our beaches and into our reservoirs. It is a crisis of leadership and vision so total that Jesse Jackson refers to it as "white leadership having failed white people, and us."

To deal with it, we need a new politics. And we must develop it ourselves.

WHAT IS TO BE DONE

We stand at the crossroads of our future. To ensure it, we must recapture our history for ourselves and our young people and then, standing on that history, we must develop new strategies of struggle adequate to the challenges that now confront us:

• *Reclaim Malcolm X.* We must build bridges back to the inner city. And I can think of no better way to do that than by putting substance to the fascination with Malcolm that already exists there. The year 1990 marks the twenty-fifth anniversary of his assassination and the sixty-fifth anniversary of his birth. This can be the context for reintroducing his real story in a systematic way. Malcolm should be our model not only because of the accuracy of his analysis of America, but also because of his example in overcoming the limitations of oppression through relentless study and rigorous self-discipline. "Malcolm went up against all the forces arrayed against Black men and succumbed to and then transcended them," a friend recently reminded me. Studying Malcolm can give our young men an intellectual understanding of the possibilities of overcoming their circumstances.

• *Communicate.* Before we can begin moving on the solutions to our problems, we must first have some general consensus as to what they are and how we plan to prioritize them. And that means we must begin by talking and communicating with one another. Actually we should go back to the old pre-Civil War practice of holding Negro Conventions. But instead of meeting downtown, we should do so where the people are with whom we need to be in dialogue: in the streets, prisons, churches, schools and so on. We should be meeting city- and statewide, regionally and nationally, and regularly; and we should devise regular methods of communication and knowledge-sharing.

• *Set the agenda.* To set our agenda we need to struggle for our own understanding of the world we live in, which should be a total analysis encompassing what is going on not only with men but with women too, what is going on not only in Black America but in white America too. We also need to understand America's relation to world historical forces, because whatever impacts on America impacts on how it treats or tries to treat us. In short, we must become a race of thinkers, like those who have gone before us—Ida B. Wells, W.E.B. Du Bois, James Baldwin. And we must start now.

• *Hold government accountable.* We must be clear about what we can and should do for ourselves and what government ought to do as part of its responsibility. The point is that significant individual efforts, no matter how well intentioned or praiseworthy, cannot resolve the problems of a whole people against systemic and systematic societal resistance. A fundraiser by a sports star or entertainer to establish, say, a job-retraining program in a given city is highly commendable. But once the program is started, how is it to be maintained? Moreover, we need hundreds of such programs in hundreds of cities, and we need millions of jobs. That is in the sphere of government, and we cannot let them con us out of fulfilling their responsibility.

• *Support programs that work.* We don't need to reinvent the wheel.

Many people are trying to make a difference and should be supported and recognized: in areas from arts and entertainment to the church to education.

• *Create new programs.* For instance, while support for Black colleges is essential, we should also give money for mobile libraries of books, films and supplementary materials in the ghetto. To help develop thinkers who know our history, we should prepare a basic list of books for achieving Black political literacy, which should be obligatory reading for every Black person in the land. And *The Autobiography of Malcolm X* should head the list.

• *Take inventory.* We need an inventory of what folks are doing, what has worked and what hasn't, so we can learn from their experience.

• *Be political.* An agenda for the political emancipation and economic and social development of Black people of necessity requires a political struggle—a battle over state and federal budgets and domestic and foreign priorities. It goes without saying that we should vote and participate in the political processes of this country. And then we must insist that all politicians subject to our influence advance our agenda. Here we can take a page from the book of Israel's supporters, who determine their support for a candidate regardless of party, based on the politician's position on Israel. We need a similar litmus test.

In reality, of course, our agenda is not simply a Black agenda, just as the crisis engulfing Black men and all Black people is not exclusively ours. Jesse Jackson's Rainbow Coalition has proved that the Black agenda and a humane agenda for America are one and the same thing. So the struggle leads us to this: the remaking of America. And to remake this country is to save ourselves, to save Black men—by all the means we have. For the soil of America holds too much of our blood, and of our roots: Harriet Tubman and Fannie Lou Hamer, Jackie Robinson and Joe Louis, Duke and Bird, Malcolm and Martin and all the others. They have held us up this long. The rest is ours to do.

BRENT STAPLES

Parallel Time

I flew to Chicago holding the rucksack on my lap. At takeoff the stewardess had forced me to stow it under the seat, but I snatched it back as soon as she walked away. To let it out of my sight was to risk losing it, and that would be disastrous. The papers inside were proof of who I was.

I was certain that the University of Chicago had already forgotten me and that deans and registrars would greet me blank-faced, without a clue. The germ of this hysteria came from a Ford Foundation communiqué advising me to take along the award letter in case of a mix-up. That was one sentence in one letter in a ream of correspondence. I worried that sentence until it was a hundred pages long. To the cache of letters and newspaper clippings I had added my college transcript just to be on the safe side.

I was certain that my luggage would be sent to a distant city and not returned to me until who knew when. In the rucksack along with my documents I'd packed a shirt and toiletries so I could keep clean until my clothes turned up. All through the flight I worried about the can of spray starch in my duffle bag. It was an aerosol can; surely atmospheric pressure would cause it to explode. The can bore the likeness of an Indian maiden in a buckskin dress, standing beside an ear of corn as tall as she was. As the plane hurtled toward Chicago, I envisioned the can swelling toward explosion, the maiden and the corn growing larger and larger until, *Boom!*, the can blew up, making a jagged, flowering hole in the baggage compartment. When the plane hit a bump in the air, I assumed that the explosion had happened and pressed my nose to the window. There I saw my luggage as clear as day: my army duffel bag and my brown plaid suitcase falling down the sky.

I liked walking at night. During this first week I found the quadrangles tranquil and beautiful after dark, the turrets and towers lit by the autumn moon. On one of these nights, I was nearly given a heart attack when the lawn sprinklers burst into life. The Midway had a separate weather system. When the air on 57th was as still as death, The Midway, two blocks south, was alive with breezes. At night the quiet beauty was mine alone. If I had attended the official tours and lectures of orientation week, perhaps I'd have found out why. People were frightened of crime, and with good reason. Hyde Park was an island of prosperity in a sea of squalor. To the south, beyond the last university buildings, lay what Saul Bellow would later describe as "the edge of ratshit Woodlawn." To the north lay Kenwood, a sliver of rambling Victorian houses, some of whose porches looked out onto the burned-out hovels of 47th Street. Across Washington Park to the west, the ghetto picked up again. Since I'd skipped the tours and lectures to wander on my own, I was ignorant of geography and danger. I had yet to notice the highrise housing projects marching along the western horizon. My only certainties were that the lake was east and that everything was exhilarating, redolent with possibility. The newness excited me to the bone. I sang out loud, leaped and punched at the air. I was hopped up, manic, flying.

I was scanning the course listings when I spotted a talismanic name: Erika Fromm. With no justification at all, I assumed this Fromm to be the daughter of the famous psychiatrist Erich Fromm, who had been a student of Freud's and who, most importantly, had been psychoanalyzed by Freud, and a member of the inner circle. I'd admired Freud, for reasons that were corrupt. I admired him because he granted the analyst absolute power over the patient. In "discovering" the unconscious, Freud had placed the contents of the psyche beyond reach of the person who owned them. The psychoanalyst was part artist, part burglar, part scientist, but mainly a dictator who determined the meaning of every thought and action. People were books that could never understand themselves without us. I had yet to take my first graduate course, but already I thought of myself as a reader of minds.

If I had asked someone, I'd have found that Erika Fromm was not the daughter of Erich Fromm, and only a Fromm by marriage. That's if I'd asked someone, but I didn't. Fromm was a dramatic name. I took it for granted that dramatic facts came with it.

Erika Fromm was teaching "The Psychology of the Ego." Hers was the only course on the menu that required "an interview with the professor." For this interview I put on a shirt.

The woman who met me at the office door looked to be in her sixties, old enough to be a venerable, old enough perhaps to have known Freud himself. She had a Valkyrie's high cheekbones and her hair was swept up and back from her face, in wings. As she turned and crossed the room, I could see that she had begun to stoop from the waist up. She took her place in the leather armchair and motioned me to sit in the plain wooden chair that faced it.

"You vish to study vis me ze psychology off de ego?"

I did.

"Do you know vat ego psychology iss?"

Yes, I said, I did. And I did. I tried to speak, but she cut me off, then lectured me about Anna Freud's breakthroughs in ego psychology. I was drunk on those apple-sized cheekbones, and especially on what I thought to be a Viennese accent, the way she said "zis, zees, zose, and zat."

"I vill admit you," she said.

Nothing could have prepared me for what she said next: "Vee haff been horrible to ze bleck people, ve heff treated zem so badly. Vee haff to mek it up. Vee must make it up. It may take you a little longa to get ze Ph.D., but you vill get it."

We must make it up. . . . It may take you longer to get your degree . . . but you will get it.

I was numb. It seemed Erika had told me that I was a dull child, to be treated with pity and patience, that I should accept condolences in advance for the difficulty I would have. The best I could do was nod until I got my senses back.

It came to me that a clever question might raise her opinion of me. Near the end of the interview, I recovered enough to form the question in my mind, along with the gestures I would use to deliver it. I smiled, leaned forward in my seat and asked it. My voice was hollow and foreign; it was coming not from me but at me, from somewhere across the room. I was still smiling and nodding as she showed me to the door. I vaulted by the students who were waiting in the hallway and rushed out into the quadrangle for air.

Back at the Broadview, I went over my documents yet again. The transcript said "Dean's List, Dean's List, Dean's List." It said Alpha Chi National Scholarship Honor Society. It said Cum Laude graduate, and I cursed myself for falling six one-hundredths of a percentage point short of Magna Cum Laude. I read again the wilted clipping from the Delaware County *Daily Times*—"Brent Staples, son of Mr. and Mrs. Melvin Staples, 316 Ward St., Chester, has won a Danforth Fellowship for advanced study for the Ph.D. degree, according to an announcement from The Danforth Foundation of St. Louis."—and I recalled the rush of happiness I felt when I read those words for the first time. "A frequent Dean's List student throughout the four years at college, he was elected President of his freshman class . . ." Nowhere did the story say that I was a foundling who'd gotten into college by accident. But it came close: ". . . Staples enrolled at Widener as one of 21 academic risks in the Project Prepare Program for educationally disadvantaged students." There it was again: "risk." I wondered if I'd ever be shed of it.

I needed a vote of confidence. I got it from one of the secretaries in the department, a bosomy, brown-skinned woman with a warming smile. Her name was Deloise. The first time we met, she mistook me for one of the construction workers who were jackhammering the sidewalk below her window. I appeared at her door shirtless, in overalls and sandals, a bandana hanging from my back pocket.

"The bathroom is right down the hall," she said.

"I know where the bathroom is," I said.

"Well, the water fountain is right there, next to the bathroom," she said.

"I know where the fountain is, too," I said.

A look of recognition crossed her face: This was the new black doctoral student, the one in those awful overalls.

I applied to Deloise for office space. She produced a ring of keys and told me to follow her. We got off the elevator on the second floor and stopped one door short of Erika Fromm's office. Deloise turned the key, threw open the door, and said, "This is it. You can have this one." The office was vast, the same size as Frau Dr. Fromm's. The window was framed in ivy and overlooked the green tranquility of the social science quadrangle.

Mine was not the customary arrangement. Graduate students just down the hall were crammed three to an office: three desks, and three sets of books, three coffee cups, always one with fungus growing in it. I was alone in this lavish space, and also had heavy neighbors: Erika Fromm on one side, the department chairman on the other.

Deloise gave me a ruler, a stapler, and a dictionary. She apologized that the dictionary was used, and said that requisitioning a new one would take forever. Who needed a new dictionary? The used one was as good as gold. The gift of the office made me feel certified. To celebrate, I threw open the window, smoked the biggest reefer I could roll, and drank a very tall can of beer.

Deloise was brown-skinned Providence. Brown-skinned Providence smiled upon me from every corner of the campus. Secretaries seemed to beam when I came into the room. Administrative assistants cut corners in my favor. Tellers at the University Bank cashed checks that they shouldn't have because my account couldn't cover them. The university as white as it was depended heavily on black women's labor. These women were happy to meet black students and even happier to do them good. They greased the skids in a hundred ways. One of them took me aside and suggested with great tact that I would better represent my people if I ditched the overalls. I welcomed the concern, but overalls and jeans were the only clothes I owned.

I took an apartment across The Midway at the edge of Woodlawn, where nearness to the ghetto had driven down the rents. Five sunny rooms, with a sun porch and a walk-in pantry. I got the apartment illegally. The university had set aside this building and several others for married students and decreed that the single among us would languish in hotel rooms or in studios or in crowded shared apartments. I had not come a thousand miles to live in a shoe box. I needed *lebensraum.*

Brown-skinned Providence reigned at married student housing, too. I was clearly registered as single, but the angels who ran the office spared me the embarrassment of checking. They pointed out the best deals for the money. They cut me a break when the rent was late.

My building was a last outpost of university power. Under my windows middle-class Hyde Park ended and impoverished black Chicago began. The university police cruised east past my dining room and my bedroom, then turned north at my sun porch, back into Hyde Park.

The sun porch was my favorite room. Its windows looked east, along the dead-flat plane of 61st Street, and south on Ingleside Avenue into Woodlawn. I studied there, I ate there and sometimes slept there. The days were punctuated by the screams of children at the elementary school just across 61st Street. At the start of recess they burst from the building as though from jail. First there was a trickle, then a rivulet, then eddies of boys and girls swirling around the school yard, coats and ribbons flying.

At night I let the house go dark so I could watch the street without being seen. The French windows were only eight feet above the ground, and when it was warm I threw them open and listened in on the conversations of passersby. When lovers paused below me I heard the wet sounds of their kissing and the breath coming out of their noses, the rustle of clothing as they rifled each other's bodies. I was invisible to them, but only an arm's length away in the dark.

On the school playground, basketball players carried on after dark. It was too dark to see the game from my porch, but I could hear the ball bouncing on the macadam court, banging off the metal blackboard. Eventually the game petered out. Traffic died down on 61st Street. The neighborhood went to sleep.

One morning before dawn I was startled awake by the voice of a man who sounded like he was in the room.

"You fucked them? You fucked them? They could kill me, you understand that? They could fuckin' kill me!"

Then I heard the muffled cries of a woman, the flat of his hand on her face and head. As I moved in a crouch to the window, I heard people in the apartment above me doing the same.

The woman stumbled backward into 61st Street, her forearm raised against the blows. The pimp was small but squarely built, an inverted triangle from the waist up, in a tight-fitting shirt and pants.

"Where's the money! Where's the money!" There wasn't any. They were detectives. She'd fucked the cops, and hadn't been paid. The pimp batted her around the intersection, then hauled her up Ingleside Avenue. Exit, shouting, stage south.

The pimp was a regular performer at my intersection. On another night I heard his voice. "I want my money! I want my money!" This time he was beating a man with a stick. The stick was big enough to cause pain, but too slight to bring the man down. The man retreated backward into 61st Street, warding off the board. Suddenly he raised his hands into the air and sank to his knees. The pimp dropped the plank and ran back into Woodlawn. The beaten man kneeled like a Muslim at prayer, his palms on the pavement, his bald pate glistening in the headlights of an approaching police car.

The pimp was also a seller of heroin. From my sun porch I watched the buyers who double-parked in front of his building every evening beginning at dusk. The cars queued up on Ingleside Avenue with blinkers flashing, like planes awaiting takeoff at O'Hare. On my side of 61st Street the dealer would have been taken down in no time at all. On my side of 61st you couldn't sneeze without arousing suspicion.

On the other side and southward the crime was worse and so was the supermarket. At the Hyde Park Co-op the food was impeccable and fresh. At the 63rd Street market the meat was unfit for consumption. The produce stank of rot. The 63rd Street "shopping" strip was composed of vacant lots, burned-out buildings. This dismal scene was cast in shadow by the tracks of the Jackson Park el.

At night, I walked to the lakefront whenever the weather permitted. I was headed home from the lake when I took my first victim. It was late fall, and the wind was cutting. I was wearing my navy pea jacket, the collar turned up, my hands snug in the pockets. Dead leaves scuttled in shoals along the streets. I turned out of Blackstone Avenue and headed west on 57th Street, and there she was, a few yards ahead of me, dressed in business clothes and carrying a briefcase. She looked back at me once, then again, and picked up her pace. She looked back again and started to run. I stopped where I was and looked up at the surrounding windows. What did this look like to people peeking out through their blinds? I was out walking. But what if someone had thought they'd seen something they hadn't and called the police. I held back the urge to run. Instead, I walked south to The Midway, plunged into its darkness, and remained on The Midway until I reached the foot of my street.

I'd been a fool. I'd been walking the streets grinning good evening at people who were frightened to death of me. I did violence to them by just being. How had I missed this? I kept walking at night, but from then on I paid attention.

I became an expert in the language of fear. Couples locked arms or reached for each other's hand when they saw me. Some crossed to the other side of the street. People who were carrying on conversations went mute and stared straight ahead, as though avoiding my eyes would save them. This reminded me of an old wives' tale: that rabid dogs didn't bite if you avoided their eyes. The determination to avoid my eyes made me invisible to classmates and professors whom I passed on the street.

It occurred to me for the first time that I was big. I was 6 feet 1½ inches tall, and my long hair made me look bigger. I weighed only 170 pounds. But the navy pea jacket that Brian had given me was broad at the shoulders, high at the collar, making me look bigger and more fearsome than I was.

I tried to be innocuous but didn't know how. The more I thought about how I moved, the less my body belonged to me; I became a false character riding along inside it. I began to avoid people. I turned out of my way into side streets to spare them the sense that they were being stalked. I let them clear the lobbies of buildings before I entered, so they wouldn't feel trapped. Out of nervousness I began to whistle and discovered I was good at it. My whistle was pure and sweet—and also in tune. On the street at night I whistled popular tunes from the Beatles and Vivaldi's *Four Seasons.* The tension drained from people's bodies when they heard me. A few even smiled as they passed me in the dark.

Then I changed. I don't know why, but I remember when. I was walking west on 57th Street, after dark, coming home from the lake. The man and the woman walking toward me were laughing and talking but clammed up when they saw me. The man touched the woman's elbow, guiding her toward the curb. Normally I'd have given way and begun to whistle, but not this time.

This time I veered toward them and aimed myself so that they'd have to part to avoid walking into me. The man stiffened, threw back his head and assumed the stare: eyes dead ahead, mouth open. His face took on a bluish hue under the sodium vapor steetlamps. I suppressed the urge to scream into his face. Instead I glided between them, my shoulder nearly brushing his. A few steps beyond them I stopped and howled with laughter. I called this game Scatter the Pigeons.

Fifty-seventh Street was too well lit for the game to be much fun; people didn't feel quite vulnerable enough. Along The Midway were heart-stopping strips of dark sidewalk, but these were so frightening that few people traveled them. The stretch of Blackstone between 57th and 55th provided better hunting. The block was long and lined with young trees that blocked out the streetlight and obscured the heads of people coming toward you.

One night I stooped beneath the branches and came up on the other side, just as a couple was stepping from their car into their town house. The woman pulled her purse close with one hand and reached for her husband with the other. The two of them stood frozen as I bore down on them. I felt a surge of power: these people were mine; I could do with them as I wished. If I'd been younger, with less to lose, I'd have robbed them, and it would have been easy. All I'd have to do was stand silently before them until they surrendered their money. I thundered, "Good evening!" into their bleached-out faces and cruised away laughing.

I held a special contempt for people who cowered in their cars as they waited for the light to change at 57th and Woodlawn. The intersection was always deserted at night, except for a car or two stuck at the red. *Thunk! Thunk! Thunk!* They hammered down the door locks when I came into view. Once I had hustled across the street, head down, trying to seem harmless. Now I turned brazenly into the headlights and laughed. Once across, I paced the sidewalk, glaring until the light changed. They'd made me terrifying. Now I'd show them how terrifying I could be.

ERNEST ALLEN, JR.

Race and Gender Stereotyping in the Thomas Confirmation Hearings

Much has been said both during and after Judge Clarence Thomas's recent confirmation hearings concerning the use of racial and gender stereotypes in American society. On the one hand, Thomas's supporters generously employed gender stereotypes to discredit the testimony of law professor Anita Hill; on the other, Judge Thomas himself was quite willing to invoke racial stereotypes of the African American male in order to lend greater credibility to his own testimony.

What were these stereotypes, and how were they used? First of all, let's take the one of gender, which is simply this: Males constitute the repository of analytical thought and action, while the ideas and behavior of females are governed by emotion and fancy. In such polarized light, the charges of sexual harassment brought by Anita Hill against Clarence Thomas could be dismissed as the fantasy of a woman who, deep down, desired Thomas sexually. Indeed, this was the gist of one of several of Senator Arlen Specter's discrediting (and now discredited) tactics. This line of attack was reinforced by the egomaniacal testimony of attorney John Doggett III, who testified that, on one occasion, Hill had "fantasized" about his own sexual interest in her—an interest which, he assures us, could not possibly have existed. This bit of stereotyping was dealt with quite adequately this past Sunday by *New York Times* columnist Alessandra Stanley. Clarence Thomas's defenders, she wrote, wished us to believe that Anita Hill was suffering from the characteristically female delusion of erotomania, "a rare mental disorder in which people . . . suffer from the delusion that they are having an affair with someone above their station." But Stanley hypothesizes that, rather than erotomania being at work in this instance, it was more probably an outbreak of the disorder erotomonomania, or the "male delusion that attractive young women are harboring fantasies about them." Erotomonomania, Stanley informs us, is also known as Doggett's Disease, a formulation which has a special poignancy for those of us who suffered through the final evening of the televised hearings.[1]

A second stereotype which surfaced during the hearings was the racial one which holds that, in contrast to the "normal" sexuality of Euro-Americans, people of African descent are possessed of an animal, that is to say a more primitive, a more fecundate sexuality; and that black male genitalia, in particular, are supposedly much larger than those of their white counterparts. This early myth fed into a third and more complex set of stereotypes which developed in the ninteenth-century antebellum South, and which crystallized in the post-Reconstruction era: On the one hand there was the chivalrous white male, whose duty it was to protect the purity of the white female. Because the female was assumed to be the bearer of civilization, and given the danger posed to her by the hypersexual black man, her protection from her own sexuality also meant the safeguarding of the purity of whites as a race—that is, protection from miscegenation. From this conjecture in American culture the lynching of African American males—a genuinely American form of popular entertainment which peaked in the 1890s but which also has continued until very recently—became synonymous with the stereotype of the black male as a rapist of white females. And this despite the fact that, statistically speaking, less than one-third of the thousands of African American males lynched from the 1880s through the 1950s were even *charged* with rape. This complex stereotype, then, harbored numerous dimensions. First, it served to justify the ritual murders of African American political leaders as well as other black individuals who stood up to economic exploitation and disfranchisement. Second, the "pedestaling" of the white female, in turn, resulted in her being stripped of her own self-determination, for protection by white males also implied dependency. Third, invoking the alleged hypersexuality of African American females, it tended to cloak the very real acts of rape of black females by white males. And lastly, it served to obscure the fact that, historically speaking, so-called racial miscegenation in American society was infinitely more the result of liaisons forced upon black women by white men, than white women by black men.

It is with this background that we can more fully analyze Clarence Thomas's assertion, at the beginning of the second round of hearings on October 11, 1991, that he had been subjected to a "high-tech lynching": "I will not provide the rope for my own lynching, or for further humiliation," said Thomas, in a prepared statement.[2] Later in the day he described the proceedings as a "high-tech lynching for uppity blacks who think for themselves."[3] But it was in his October 12 testimony, in a reply to Senator Orrin Hatch, that Thomas attempted to link the stereotypes of sex and race to the accusation of sexual harassment leveled at him:

> And if you want to track through this country in the 19th and 20th century the lynchings of black men, you will see that there is, invariably, or in many instances, a relationship with sex, and an accusation that that person cannot shake off. That is the point that I am trying to make, and that is the point that I was making last night, that this is a high-tech lynching. I cannot shake off these accusations, because they play to the worst stereotypes we have about black men in this country.[4]

Clarence Thomas's attempts to picture himself as a victim of "high-tech lynching" is opportunism of the most cynical stripe—akin to that of George Bush's nomination of him in the first place.[5] First, the connection between the lynching of black males and racial stereotypes had to do with the alleged rape of white females, not the sexual harassment of black ones. I know of no historically recorded instance of a black man's being lynched for sexually harassing or even raping a black female. Second, Thomas's self-description as "uppity" and as "thinking for himself" is as laughable as the support given him by arch-racist Senator Strom Thurmond of South Carolina, who, among other perfidies, has taken as his vocation the attempted blocking of virtually every piece of Civil Rights legislation to pass through Congress since the 1940s. Rather than being "uppity," Clarence Thomas is—if you will forgive my invoking of yet another stereotype—more akin to the contented, favored slave of the master, rather than a rebellious Nat Turner, to say the least. Third, the sordid spectacle posed by the Senate Judiciary Committee hearing from Friday, October 11, through the early hours of Monday, October 14, may have been many things, but it was *not* a lynching. That it eventually and sadly took the form it did—with all its lurid, public details of apparent sexual misconduct—occurred *not* because of racism, but because of the failure of the Senate Judiciary Committee to take charges of sexual harassment seriously. And it was that very failure that led to another round of hearings concerning Thomas's fitness to sit on the Supreme Court. In the improbable case that Anita Hill's charges are not true—and I say this based on the corroborated testimony of Angela Wright, who was disallowed a public hearing at the last moment—the very most that Clarence Thomas might claim in any case is "high-tech character assassination," which is a far cry indeed from a "high-tech lynching." On the other hand, if anyone at the committee hearings was smeared by stereotypical casting, it was Anita Hill.

NOTES

1. Alessandra Stanley, "Erotomania: A Rare Disorder Runs Riot—in Men's Minds," *The New York Times*, November 10, 1991, p. 2E.
2. *The New York Times*, October 12, 1991, p. 10.
3. *Boston Globe*, October 12, 1991, p. 1.
4. *The New York Times*, October 13, 1991, p. 31.
5. In her unsworn testimony Angela Wright "recounts being present when Thomas offered advice to another black in the office on how to cope with his financial difficulty—'mortgage or whatever,' she says. According to Wright, Thomas told him: 'Well, you know why you can't get any money? Because you're not black enough. Now, if you grew an Afro and put on a Dashiki, you would get all the government money you want'." Sidney Blumenthal, "The Higher Hustle," *The New Republic* (November 11, 1991), 46.

ARTHUR ASHE
and ARNOLD RAMPERSAD
Days of Grace

THE BURDEN OF RACE

I had spent more than an hour talking in my office at home with a reporter for *People* magazine. Her editor had sent her to do a story about me and how I was coping with AIDS. The reporter's questions had been probing and yet respectful of my right to privacy. Now, our interview over, I was escorting her to the door. As she slipped on her coat, she fell silent. I could see that she was groping for the right words to express her sympathy for me before she left.

"Mr. Ashe, I guess this must be the heaviest burden you have ever had to bear, isn't it?" she asked finally.

I thought for a moment, but only a moment. "No, it isn't. It's a burden, all right. But AIDS isn't the heaviest burden I have had to bear."

"Is there something worse? Your heart attack?"

I didn't want to detain her, but I let the door close with both of us still inside. "You're not going to believe this," I said to her, "but being black is the greatest burden I've had to bear."

"You can't mean that."

"No question about it. Race has always been my biggest burden. Having to live as a minority in America. Even now it continues to feel like an extra weight tied around me."

I can still recall the surprise and perhaps even the hurt on her face. I may even have surprised myself, because I simply had never thought of comparing the two conditions before. However, I stand by my remark. Race is for me a more onerous burden than AIDS. My disease is the result of biological factors over which we, thus far, have had no control. Racism, however, is entirely made by people, and therefore it hurts and inconveniences infinitely more.

Since our interview (skillfully presented as a first-person account by me) appeared in *People* in June 1992, many people have commented on my remark. A radio station in Chicago aimed primarily at blacks conducted a lively debate on its merits on the air. Most African Americans have little trouble understanding and accepting my statement, but other people have been baffled by it. Even Donald Dell, my close friend of more than thirty years, was puzzled. In fact, he was so troubled that he telephoned me in the middle of the night from Hamburg, Germany, to ask if I had been misquoted. No, I told him, I had been quoted correctly. Some people have asked me flatly, what could *you*, Arthur Ashe, possibly have to complain about? Do you want more money or fame than you already have? Isn't AIDS inevitably fatal? What can be worse than death?

The novelist Henry James suggested somewhere that it is a complex fate being an American. I think it is a far more complex fate being an African American. I also sometimes think that this indeed may be one of those fates that are worse than death.

I do not want to be misunderstood. I do not mean to appear fatalistic, self-pitying, cynical, or maudlin. Proud to be an American, I am also proud to be an African American. I delight in the accomplishments of fellow citizens of my color. When one considers the odds against which we have labored, we have achieved much. I believe in life and hope and love, and I turn my back on death until I must face my end in all its finality. I am an optimist, not a pessimist. Still, a pall of sadness hangs over my life and the lives of almost all African Americans because of what we as a people have experienced historically in America, and what we as individuals experience each and every day. Whether one is a welfare recipient trapped in some blighted "housing project" in the inner city or a former Wimbledon champion who is easily recognized on the streets and whose home is a luxurious apartment in one of the wealthiest districts of Manhattan, the sadness is still there.

In some respects, I am a prisoner of the past. A long time ago, I made peace with the state of Virginia and the South. While I, like other blacks, was once barred from free association with whites, I returned time and time again, under the new rule of desegregation, to work with whites in my hometown and across the South. But segregation had achieved by that time what it was intended to achieve: It left me a marked man, forever aware of a shadow of contempt that lays across my identity and my sense of self-esteem. Subtly the shadow falls on my reputation, the way I know I am perceived; the mere memory of it darkens my most sunny days. I believe that the same is true for almost every African American of the slightest sensitivity and intelligence. Again, I don't want to overstate the case. I think of myself, and others think of me, as supremely self-confident. I know objectively that it is almost impossible for someone to be as successful as I have been as an athlete and to lack self-assurance. Still, I also know that the shadow is always there; only death will free me, and blacks like me, from its pall.

The shadow fell across me recently on one of the brightest days, literally and metaphorically, of my life. On August 30, 1992, the day before the U.S. Open, the USTA and I together hosted an afternoon of tennis at the National Tennis Center in Flushing Meadows, New York. The event was a benefit for the Arthur Ashe Foundation for the Defeat of AIDS. Before the start, I was nervous. Would the invited stars (McEnroe, Graf, Navratilova, et al.) show up?

Would they cooperate with us, or be difficult to manage? And, on the eve of a Grand Slam tournament, would fans pay to see light-hearted tennis? The answers were all a resounding yes (just over ten thousand fans turned out). With CBS televising the event live and Aetna having provided the air time, a profit was assured. The sun shone brightly, the humidity was mild, and the temperature hovered in the low 80s.

What could mar such a day? The shadow of race, and the sensitivity, or perhaps hypersensitivity, to its nuances. Sharing the main stadium box with Jeanne, Camera, and me, at my invitation, were Stan Smith, his wife Marjory, and their daughter Austin. The two little girls were happy to see one another. During Wimbledon in June, they had renewed their friendship when we all stayed near each other in London. Now Austin, seven years old, had brought Camera a present. She had come with twin dolls, one for herself, one for Camera. A thoughtful gesture on Austin's part, and on her parents' part, no doubt. The Smiths are fine, religious people. Then I noticed that Camera was playing with her doll above the railing of the box, in full view of the attentive network television cameras. The doll was the problem; or rather, the fact that the doll was conspicuously a blond. Camera owns dolls of all colors, nationalities, and ethnic varieties. But she was now on national television playing with a blond doll. Suddenly I heard voices in my head, the voices of irate listeners to a call-in show on some "black format" radio station. I imagined insistent, clamorous callers attacking Camera, Jeanne, and me:

"Can you believe the doll Arthur Ashe's daughter was holding up at the AIDS benefit? Wasn't that a shame?"

"Is that brother sick or what? Somebody ought to teach that poor child about her true black self!"

"What kind of role model is Arthur Ashe if he allows his daughter to be brainwashed that way?"

"Doesn't the brother understand *that he is corrupting his child's mind with notions about the superiority of the white woman? I tell you, I thought we were long past that!"*

The voices became louder in my head. Despite the low humidity, I began to squirm in my seat. What should I do? Should I say, To hell with what some people might think? I know that Camera likes her blond dolls, black dolls, brown dolls, Asian dolls, Indian dolls just about equally; I know that for a fact, because I have watched her closely. I have searched for signs of racial partiality in her, indications that she may be dissatisfied with herself, with her own color. I have seen none. But I cannot dismiss the voices. I try always to live practically, and I do not wish to hear such comments on the radio. On the other hand, I do not want Austin's gift to be sullied by an ungracious response. Finally, I act.

"Jeanne," I whisper, "we have to do something."

"About what?" she whispers back.

"That doll. We have to get Camera to put that doll down."

Jeanne takes one look at Camera and the doll and she understands immediately. Quietly, cleverly, she makes the dolls disappear. Neither Camera nor Austin is aware of anything unusual happening. Smoothly, Jeanne has moved them on to some other distraction.

I am unaware if Margie Smith has noticed us, but I believe I owe her an explanation. I get up and go around to her seat. Softly I tell her why the dolls have disappeared. Margie is startled, dumbfounded.

"Gosh, Arthur, I never thought about that. I never *ever* thought about anything like that!"

"*You* don't have to think about it," I explain. "But it happens to us, in similar situations, all the time."

"All the time?" She is pensive now.

"All the time. It's perfectly understandable. And it certainly is not your fault. You were doing what comes naturally. But for us, the dolls make for a bit of a problem. All for the wrong reasons. It shouldn't be this way, but it is."

I return to my seat, but not to the elation I had felt before I saw that blond doll in Camera's hand. I feel myself becoming more and more angry. I am angry at the force that made me act, the force of racism in all its complexity, as it spreads into the world and creates defensiveness and intolerance among the very people harmed by racism. I am also angry with myself. I am angry with myself because I have just acted out of pure practicality, not out of morality. The moral act would have been to let Camera have her fun, because she was innocent of any wrongdoing. Instead, I had tampered with her innocence, her basic human right to act impulsively, to accept a gift from a friend in the same beautiful spirit in which it was given.

Deeply embarrassed now, I am ashamed at what I have done. I have made Camera adjust her behavior merely because of the likelihood that some people in the African American community would react to her innocence foolishly and perhaps even maliciously. I know I am not misreading the situation. I would have had telephone calls that very evening about the unsuitability of Camera's doll. Am I being a hypocrite? Yes, definitely, up to a point. I have allowed myself to give in to those people who say we must avoid even the slightest semblance of "Eurocentric" influence. But I also know what stands behind the entire situation. Racism ultimately created the state in which defensiveness and hypocrisy are our almost instinctive responses, and innocence and generosity are invitations to trouble.

This incident almost ruined the day for me. That night, when Jeanne and I talked about the excitement of the afternoon, and the money that would go to AIDS research and education because of the event, we nevertheless ended up talking mostly about the incident of the dolls. We also talked about perhaps its most ironic aspect. In 1954, when the Supreme Court ruled against school segregation in *Brown v. Board of Education*, some of the most persuasive testimony came from the psychologist Dr. Kenneth Clark concerning his research on black children and their pathetic preference for white dolls over black. In 1992, the dolls are still a problem.

Once again, the shadow of race had fallen on me.

DERRICK BELL

Faces at the Bottom of the Well

Dear Geneva,

Beyond the despair of your final narrative, I am reminded that our forebears—though betrayed into bondage—survived the slavery in which they were reduced to things, property, entitled neither to rights nor to respect as human beings. Somehow, as the legacy of our spirituals makes clear, our enslaved ancestors managed to retain their humanity as well as their faith that evil and suffering were not the extent of their destiny—or of the destiny of those who would follow them. Indeed, we owe our existence to their perseverance, their faith. In these perilous times, we must do no less than they did: fashion a philosophy that both matches the unique dangers we face, and enables us to recognize in those dangers opportunities for committed living and humane service.

The task is less daunting than it might appear. From the beginning, we have been living and working for racial justice in the face of unacknowledged threat. Thus, we are closer than we may realize to those in slavery who struggled to begin and maintain families even though at any moment they might be sold, and separated, never to see one another again. Those blacks living in the pre-Civil War North, though deemed "free," had to live with the ever-present knowledge that the underground railroad ran both ways. While abolitionists provided an illegal network to aid blacks who escaped slavery, Southern "slave catchers" had an equally extensive system that enabled them to kidnap free blacks from their homes or the streets, and spirit them off to the South and a life in bondage.

In those times, racism presented dangers from without that were stark and terrifying, but they were hardly more insidious than those blacks face today in our inner cities—all too often from other blacks. Victimized themselves by an uncaring society, some young blacks vent their rage on victims like themselves, thereby perpetuating the terror that whites once had to invoke directly. We should not be surprised that a society that once legalized slavery and authorized pursuit of fugitive slaves with little concern about the kidnapping of free blacks, now views black-on-black crime as basically a problem for its victims and their communities.

In the context of such a history, played out now as current events, is a long continuum of risks faced and survived, our oppression barring our oppressors from actually experiencing the freedom they so proudly proclaim. The late Harvard historian Nathan Huggins points out in *Black Odyssey*, a book about slavery from the point of view of the slaves: "Uncertainty, the act of being engaged in an unknown and evolving future, was their common fate. In the indefinite was the excitement of the possible. . . . The sense of possibility and that dream have infected all Americans, Africans no less than Europeans. . . . *Yet the dream has been elusive to us all*, white and black, from that first landfall [at] Jamestown where the first twenty Africans landed."

Huggins argues that Americans view history as linear and evolutionary and tend to see slavery and racism as an aberration or pathological condition: "Our national history has continued to amplify the myths of automatic progress, universal freedom, and the American dream without the ugly reality of racism seriously challenging the faith." Those who accept these myths, consider our view that racism is permanent to be despairing, defeatist, and wrong. In so doing, they overlook the fact that the "American dogma of automatic progress fails those who have been marginalized. Blacks, the poor, and others whom the myth ignores are conspicuously in the center of the present, and they call for a national history that incorporates their experience."

Such a new narrative, and the people who make it—among whom are included those who pursue equality through legal means—must find inspiration not in the sacrosanct, but utterly defunct, glory of ideals that for centuries have proven both unattainable and poisonous. Rather, they must find it in the lives of our "oppressed people who defied social death as slaves and freedmen, insisting on their humanity despite a social consensus that they were 'a brutish sort of people.' " From that reality, Huggins takes—as do you and I, Geneva—hope rather than despair. Knowing there was no escape, no way out, the slaves, nonetheless continued to engage themselves. To carve out a humanity. To defy the murder of selfhood. Their lives were brutally shackled, certainly—but *not without meaning despite being imprisoned.*

We are proud of our heroes, but we must not forget those whose lives were not marked by extraordinary acts of defiance. Though they lived and died as captives within a system of slave labor, "they produced worlds of music, poetry, and art. They reshaped a Christian cosmology to fit their spirits and their needs, transforming Protestantism along the way. They produced a single people out of what had been many. . . . Their ordeal, and their dignity throughout it, speaks to the world of the indomitable human spirit."

Perhaps those of us who can admit we are imprisoned by the history of racial subordination in America can accept—as slaves had no choice but to accept—our fate. Not that we legitimate the racism of the oppressor. On the contrary, we can only *de*legitimate it if we can accurately pinpoint it. And racism lies at the center, not the periphery; in the permanent, not in the fleeting; in the real lives of black and white people, not in the sentimental caverns of the mind.

Armed with this knowledge, and with the enlightened, humility-based commitment that it engenders, we can accept the dilemmas of committed confrontation with evils we cannot end. We can go forth to serve, knowing that our failure to act will not change conditions and may very well worsen them. We can listen carefully to those who have been most subordinated. In listening, we must not do them the injustice of failing to recognize that somehow they survived as complete, defiant, though horribly scarred beings. We must learn from their example, learn from those whom we would teach.

If we are to extract solutions from the lessons of the slaves' survival, and our own, we must first face squarely the unbearable landscape and climate of that survival. We yearn that our civil rights work will be crowned with success, but what we really want—want even more than success—is meaning. "Meaningfulness," as the Stanford psychiatrist Dr. Irvin Yalom tells us, "is a by-product of engagement and commitment." This engagement and commitment is what black people have had to do since slavery: making something out of nothing. Carving out a humanity for oneself with absolutely nothing to help—save imagination, will, and unbelievable strength and courage. Beating the odds while firmly believing in, *knowing* as only they could know, the fact that all those odds are stacked against them.

Both engagement and commitment connote service. And genuine service requires humility. We must first recognize and acknowledge (at least to ourselves) that our actions are not likely to lead to transcendent change and may indeed, despite our best efforts, be of more help to the system we despise than to the victims of that system whom we are trying to help. Then, and only then, can the realization and the dedication based on it lead to policy positions and campaigns that are less likely to worsen conditions for those we are trying to help and more likely to remind the powers that be that out there are persons like us who are not only not on their side but determined to stand in their way.

Now there is more here than confrontation with our oppressors. Continued struggle can bring about unexpected benefits and gains that in themselves justify continued endeavor. We can recognize miracles we did not plan and value them for what they are, rather than always measure their worth by their likely contribution to our traditional goals. As a former student, Erin Edmonds, concludes, it is not a matter of choosing between the pragmatic recognition that racism is permanent no matter what we do, or an idealism based on the long-held dream of attaining a society free of racism. Rather, it is a question of *both, and. Both* the recognition of the futility of action—where action is more civil rights strategies destined to fail—*and* the unalterable conviction that something must be done, that action must be taken.

This is, I believe, a more realistic perspective from which to gauge the present and future worth of our race-related activities. Freed of the stifling rigidity of relying unthinkingly on the slogan "we shall overcome," we are impelled *both* to live each day more fully *and* to examine critically the actual effectiveness of traditional civil rights remedies. Indeed, the humility required by genuine service will not permit us to urge remedies that we may think appropriate and the law may even require, but that the victims of discrimination have rejected.

That, Geneva, is the real Black History, all too easily lost in political debates over curricular needs. It is a story less of success than of survival through an unremitting struggle that leaves no room for giving up. We are all part of that history, and it is still unfolding. With you and the slave singers, "I want to be in that number."

Your friend as ever

FIGHTING ON TWO FRONTS

DAVID LEVERING LEWIS

When Harlem Was in Vogue

On a clear, sharp February morning in 1919, on New York's Fifth Avenue, the men of the Fifteenth Regiment of New York's National Guard marched home to Harlem. Their valor under fire (191 unbroken days in the trenches) was legendary. Almost as acclaimed were the triumphs of their regimental band, under the command of Lieutenant James Reese Europe. Big Jim Europe's band, its instruments bought through a tin can millionaire's generosity, had conquered French, Belgian, and British audiences as utterly as his regiment had overwhelmed Germans in battle, leaving crowds delighted and critics mystified by the wail and wah-wah of the "talking trumpet." (So much so that when the proud, skilled musicians of France's Garde Républicaine failed to reproduce these unique sounds, suspicious experts examined one of Europe's horns for some hidden valve or chamber. The logic-bound French concluded that the talking trumpet was a Negro anomaly, musical magic beyond their ken.) European fascination with jazz had started with Jim Europe's band. White America already remembered the band from times before the war, when it had teamed up with Vernon and Irene—the dancing Castles—to make dancing a national pastime and help, as preachers vainly fumed and Puritan parishioners unlimbered, to revolutionize the nation's mores.

But today, February 17, was no occasion for the syncopated beat of ragtime. Lieutenant Europe's men, with Bill "Bojangles" Robinson as regimental drum major, were playing martial music for a victory march, for a heroes' ascent through Manhattan to Harlem. Thirteen hundred black men and eighteen white officers moved in metronome step behind Colonel William Hayward, still limping from a wound suffered at Belleau Wood, out of Thirty-fourth Street into Fifth Avenue. They marched in the tight formation preferred by the French Army, a solid thirty-five-foot square of massed men, sergeants two paces in front of their platoons, lieutenants three paces ahead of sergeants, captains five paces ahead. They had been called "Hell Fighters" by the admiring French in whose 16th and 161st divisions they had served for almost ten months. Officially, they were still the United States 369th Infantry Regiment, the only unit of the war allowed to fly a state flag, the only American unit awarded the Croix de Guerre, and, as the French High Command's supreme mark of honor, the regiment chosen among all Allied forces to lead the march to the Rhine.

New York Mayor John F. Hylan was enjoying the sun in Palm Beach that day and the city fathers had declined to proclaim an official holiday; but high-ranking dignitaries were present and most New Yorkers gave themselves the day off. "I just had to see these boys," one middle-aged white spectator told a reporter. "I will never get another opportunity to see such a sight, and I can get another job."

"Swinging up the Avenue," *The New York Times* front page reported, the men of the 369th "made a spectacle that . . . might explain why the Boches gave them the title of *Blutlustige Schwarze Männer*"—"bloodthirsty black men." Colonel Hayward and Lieutenant Europe (the solo Afro-American officer) were objects of special attention by the crowds, but the hero of the moment was a coal dealer from Albany, Sergeant Henry Johnson, the first American to win the Croix de Guerre. Running out of ammunition, Johnson had killed four of the enemy with a bolo knife and captured twenty-two. The Croix de Guerre (with star and palm) gleamed from the sergeant's tunic as he stood, waving graciously, in the open limousine provided by the city. "New Yorkers," the *Times* continued, "were mightily impressed by the magnificent appearance of these fighting men."

The staccato of leather on Fifth Avenue macadam rose and fell to the deafening counterpoint of applause. At Sixtieth Street, the command of "eyes right" was given as the regiment passed the official reviewing stand. Governor and Mrs. Alfred E. Smith received the salute with appropriate expressions of gravity and pleasure, as did the secretary of state for New York, Francis Hugo, and Acting Mayor Moran. Representing Newton D. Baker, President Wilson's secretary of war, was Emmett Scott, special adviser on Afro-American affairs and the deceased Booker T. Washington's protégé. Rear Admiral Albert Gleaves and General Thomas Barry saluted briskly. Mr. and Mrs. William Randolph Hearst and department store tycoon John Wanamaker applauded. That doyen of plutocrats, Henry Clay Frick, could be seen waving a flag from the window of his Seventy-third Street palace. From another window close by, Mrs. Vincent Astor and several society ladies waved these brave men along to their Harlem neighborhoods.

It was James Weldon Johnson, an official of the National Association for the Advancement of Colored People (NAACP), whose eye and pen gave the parade its best measure in the New York *Age*, one of the Afro-America's leading newspapers:

> The Fifteenth furnished the first sight that New York has had of seasoned soldiers in marching order. There was no militia smartness about their appearance; their "tin hats" were battered and rusty and the shiny newness worn off their bayonets, but they were men who had gone through the terrible hell of war and come back.

The tide of khaki and black turned west on 110th Street to Lenox Avenue, then north again into the heart of Harlem. At 125th Street, the coiled, white rattlesnake insignia of the regiment hissed from thousands of lapels, bonnets, and windows. A field of pennants, flags, banners, and scarves thrashed about the soldiers like elephant grass in a gale, threatening to engulf them. In front of the unofficial reviewing stand at 130th Street, Europe's sixty-piece band broke into "Here Comes My Daddy" to the extravagant delight of the crowd. At this second platform, Harlem notables and returning heroes beheld each other with almost palpable elation and pride. No longer now in the dense, rapid-stepping formation learned from the French, ranks opened, gait loosened. "For the final mile or more of our parade," Major Arthur Little recalled, "about every fourth soldier of the ranks had a girl upon his arm—and we marched through Harlem singing and laughing."

Colonel Hayward shouted a command: the march halted. The Hell Fighters were home. They had come, as thousands of other returning Afro-American soldiers came, with a music, a lifestyle, and a dignity new to the nation—and soon to pervade it.

JOHN OLIVER KILLENS

And Then We Heard the Thunder

The fighting had broken out now all over South Bainbridge, even a few brief skirmishes in the residential section. All day long Celia had sat helpless near her wireless with the reports coming in of concentrated fighting in the commercial district and sporadic outbursts here and there and even now spilling over into North Bainbridge. And she could do nothing but sit and walk up and down and listen to the wireless and go crazy and cry and slowly die and die and die. A few times she went into the street and got into her bomb. The people in the streets were numbed and shellshocked. How in the hell could it possibly happen? How could it happen? A full-scale war in Bainbridge! American soldiers slaughtering each other on the streets of her Bainbridge. It wasn't true—it wasn't true. How could there be such bitterness? Where are you, Solly? Where are you, beloved Solly? Live, my darling, live! Kill if you have to, but please God, live, my bloody darling. Live for your child you've never seen. And live for Her and live for Me. Yes, yes, live for me. Live for all the times you loved me. And live for you—live for you you you! She tried to get through to the Elizabeth Bridge, but by evening the police and the provost marshals had roped off a section that reached six blocks square this side of the bridge and they would not let anybody through. A P.M. stopped her and she turned around and tried to go down another street and another and another, and she tried another bridge, but each time she was thwarted. She came back home after dark and she could hear the war over in the south of her city going on and on and on, and the reddened sky above the city looked like the entire world was burning down. Celia went back into her house and turned on the wireless and turned from station to station, and it was all about the 'Battle of Bainbridge,' they had already given it a 'title for posterity' the Battle of Bainbridge, which was still raging with a fury never witnessed before in the history of modern civilization.

> *This is the anatomy of hate, pure, clean and unadulterated. . . .*

She turned to another station.

> *No wild men ever fought with more sheer ferocity nor with more hatred for the adversary. Both sides are . . .*

She turned the dial.

> *As for the weather it was a balmy day in Bainbridge, made even warmer by the outbreak of hostilities. Bainbridgites are aghast and outraged and still cannot believe that . . .*

She clicked off the wireless and went to the kitchen and got a drink, and she poured it down her throat and felt it spreading through her shoulders and burning up her stomach. How could it possibly be that people could be born in the same country and grow up together side by side and have such hatred for each other? It was the first time she could really even begin to appreciate the anger deep inside of Solly, the anger she had tried so hard to reach and to know and to understand and to feel and to hold and to caress and to soften into tenderness. Because he is a tender man. He is a tender human being. I have known his tenderness.

She went to the telephone for the fifteenth or twentieth time, and she tried to get through to the Farms, she tried to call the Jones Street station. Everywhere the lines were jammed. She finally got somebody to answer at General Jack's headquarters.

She said, 'Why don't you people do something to stop the bloody massacre? Have all of you gone crazy?'

The polite American at the other end said, 'Sorry, lady, we're doing everything we can.' And he politely hung up, and she started to call him again, but she slammed the receiver onto the hook, and she sat on the couch, and she thought, maybe I'm the one who's crazy. Maybe I'm imagining the whole damn thing. It must be my imagination. It's just been too much for me, she tried to think soberly. Losing Pat so suddenly and now Solly is leaving me next week, but I just have to get hold of myself. She saw Solly now as plain as the moonlight, lying dead on a quiet street with his face his dear eyes staring sweetly at the moon, and she knew it was no dream she dreamed, she saw him dead, she saw him dead, and she would never see him alive again. She fell face down on the couch and she cried, 'Don't be dead, Solly! Don't be dead! Don't be dead! Please, dear Solly, don't be dead!'

She reached out and turned the wireless on again.

> *... enraged Australian authorities are moving swiftly now to bring the Americans to their senses ... an insult to the people of Australia ... a slap in the face to the war against fascism ... Efforts to contact General Jack have so far been futile. The word is that he is up north where the other war is continuing. Our authorities have reached all the way to Washington ... Meanwhile the Battle of Bainbridge continues unabated....*

It was after four in the morning and the Battle of Bainbridge was headed toward its second day, and they had battled every inch and every millionth of a second since they came across the King George Bridge, and Solly had lost track of time and space and he thought his back was breaking and his spine would snap in two and he would never sleep again and his eyes would never cry and his shoulder must be broken from the constant kicking of his rifle and the submachine gun, and his trigger hand was fast asleep it seemed, but he was wide awake. They had battled the others block for block, truck to truck, Duck to Duck and Duck to truck, building to building, house to house, hand to hand and man-to-goddamn-crazy-man. He'd seen dead and dying everywhere, but Solly had not gotten a glimpse of Bookworm or the Quiet Man. Scotty was killed near the Jones Street station.

They're all wiped out, he thought. All of them killed and dead and dead and dead, and maybe they were better off than he was, who had not received a single scratch. Worm and Scotty and Quiet Man and Worm and Scott and Quiet Man. They had paid their everlasting dues. He didn't know it, wasn't certain about Worm and Jimmy, but he felt it in the pit of his stomach. All night long he and Samuels and the gunner had shot their way up one street and down the other, not knowing whom they killed or how damn many, and he didn't even know the gunner's name. The gunner was dead now and Scotty was dead, as were soldiers all over the place in every street in every doorway. All night long the guns were talking belching screaming one sweet tune of Peace Everlasting Found in Death's Eternal Tender Sleep. He thought, maybe it's all over now, the Battle of Bainbridge, because he couldn't hear the sound of war any more. His ears were deafened and maybe he would never hear again, or maybe he had also won that Everlasting Peace in Death. Maybe he was dead—he hoped—he almost hoped—

But he shouted to himself, 'I'm still alive! I'm still alive! Fannie Mae, I'm still alive! Tell our son. I'm still alive!' as the crazy Duck dashed madly up a narrow street. They had changed vehicles three times through the night. From Duck to truck to Duck again. The Duck plunged suddenly out onto a broad plaza, made soft and mellow by an unfeeling unromantic orange-colored moonlight spilling all over it, and they had run completely out of the war. And it felt damn good to be alive and feel the cool fresh air like chilled wine rush into his weary lungs. He straightened up and looked round him and he opened his mouth and closed his eyes and drank the air in deeply all inside of him, and it was just like Scotty used to say, 'You close your eyes you lose sight on the world, and you won't ever see again.'

There was an almost imperceptible movement behind a park bench in the plaza as two M-1 rifles took careful aim at Solly, letting him come closer and closer so they could blow his head away. Closer closer closer—they could not miss him if they tried to. He should have never closed his eyes. *Closer-now!*

Samuels felt the movement more than heard it, and he did not hesitate for a why or where or who or by-your-leave. He combed the bench from end to end with a submachine gun he had inherited during an earlier part of the nightmare. Two brief shouts from the mourners' bench and all was peace and quiet there.

Solly hit the floor of the Duck like he was doing a belly-buster. When he finally got his voice again he said, 'Thanks, my friend.' *Time* was the only difference between life and death, and Time could wait and Time could also get impatient.

His friend said, 'It's about time we called each other "friend." We've been working at it long enough.'

Solly laughed weakly into the darkness. Just a hundredth of a second between his living and his dying. 'You're a colored man tonight, old buddy. You have naturally earned your spurs. I'm going to vote you into the club.' The driver softly laughed at them.

Samuels stood up and shouted angrily at Solly, 'I am a white man and I am your friend, and you are a Negro man and you are my best friend, and we are both friends of the human race. Don't hand me any other kind of half-assed nationalistic shit!'

He stared at Samuels through the night, and he tried his best to laugh at Samuels. 'Anything you say, old buddy boy.'

The driver turned toward them and laughed again a kind of harsh and bitter laughter.

Their little tête-á-tête was rudely interrupted as they heard round after round of machine-gun fire sounding off about two blocks beyond the plaza. The driver made a swift U-turn and headed back toward the principal area of the fighting, which had quieted down considerably.

After a while Solly said, 'Maybe everybody has just about run out of ammunition.'

You could only hear sporadic outbursts now. 'Or maybe they just ran out of steam.'

They went wearily up a dark and narrow quiet street.

Samuels said, 'Maybe everybody has reconsidered and realized what fools they've been. Maybe they've had a change of heart.'

The driver said in a thick and dry and Southern voice, 'You must be from up-the-country. A peckerwood is a peckerwood and he gon always be a peckerwood till he become a dead peckerwood.'

Solly laughed and laughed and laughed and laughed. He remembered what Scotty had said a few hours earlier, and he laughed and cried and laughed and cried.

The lines were burning between Washington and Bainbridge, and ears were burning too. And heads of brass would surely roll.

Washington learned about the battle from Australian authorities and they in turn contacted Adeline Street, which was the Supreme Command of the South Pacific.

General Buford Jack was in the Philippines. One of his flunkies, Major General Benson, caught the full wrath of the Pentagon.

'No excuses, Benson! Just stop that goddamn race riot!'

'Sir—'

'Have all of you down there gone completely out of your mind? Don't you know what the war is being fought for?'

'But—'

'No buts, Benson. Stop it immediately, that's all, and get to the bottom of who's responsible, and I don't mean enlisted men. There'll be a full-scale investigation and court-martials and all the rest of it. This is a disgrace to America.'

'Yes, sir—'

'And it better not get into the newspapers or else your head will roll along with the rest. That's no threat, that's a promise, It must get no publicity at all—you understand? I don't care what you have to do to prevent it.'

When General Benson hung up he got in touch with the division commander and ranted and raved and swore at him and threatened. And the division commander called Brigadier General Jefferson Jamison, the base commander at Camp Worthington Farms, and on down the line till it reached the adjutant, Colonel William Bradford the Third.

'What the hell are you doing to stop this race riot?' the base commander asked him. General Jamison was a son of the South like his adjutant, and he was West Point and Regular Army and tall and blue-eyed and overly handsome and fiftyish and graying very hurriedly.

Bradford had just come into the office on the double and was almost out of breath. He said, 'Nothing, sir. I mean we've tried but—'

The general said, 'Nothing!' He stared at the colonel incredulously. 'You mean you have done nothing at all?'

Bradford was not excited yet. As impressive an officer as the general undoubtedly was, it was almost impossible for Bradford to fully respect him, since he slept with the general's wife and knew that the general slept with every fat-assed boy he could lay hands on, even interracially, and from the general's wife he knew other intimate details about the great man.

'Sir, I telephoned you and I spoke to you about it when you got back to camp, and it didn't seem to—I mean I tried to keep them from—We did everything—'

'Listen carefully, Colonel Bradford,' General Jamison said. 'First of all, you had the first opportunity to stop the convoy from going into town—understand? That's when the whole thing should have been halted, but you let the niggers make a fool out of you by your own admission.' The general paused and stared contemptuously at his adjutant. 'Second—you're the one, again by your own admission, who triggered the riot with your idiotic phone calls. If you spent as much thought on Army matters as you do on strategy and tactics of getting into the drawers of every whore from here to Melbourne, you'd be a military genius.'

This bastard knows about me and his wife, the colonel thought, and he's ready to throw me to the pack. He ought to be thankful to me. I'm keeping Martha satisfied while he's running all over the place after every Tom, Dick, and Harry.

General Jamison said, 'You were faced with a simple emergency situation, and instead of using your head, you panicked like a pregnant woman. And you are held entirely responsible for what has happened. Of all the stupid hysterical actions—'

The colonel was so angry he was trembling and his voice failed him temporarily, and he was scared now, because he saw the unveiled hatred in the general's face. And you got me where you want me, you limp-wristed bastard, and you'll feed me gladly to the wolves, and watch them pick me to the bone, and I have nowhere to pass the buck.

When he could talk he said, 'Sir, I have to differ with you, sir, I don't—'

The general had worked himself into a rage. He slapped the desk with the palm of his hand. 'I don't give a damn about your differing or who you're fucking or whose fucking you. Washington has sent the word down. You understand what that means? Somebody's ass is going to burn and it ain't going to be General Jamison's, understand? A race riot in Australia— When I get through with those black Amphibs they'll wish they'd never been born. And you, Colonel, you—'

'I won't be a scapegoat for anybody, General. Not even you, I'll—'

'You shut up and listen to me. I want every white man on this base who is not already over in South Bainbridge. I want them under your command. I want you to take them over the river and peaceably bring that idiocy you started to a halt. I want it done immediately. On second thought I'd better go with you. You might screw it up again. You let me know when you're ready.'

Bradford stared at the general. He had the picture completely before him now. He was to be the scapegoat and the general would be the hero who put out the fire and saved the maiden's honor. And there was nothing he could do to change the story's ending. Nothing—not a goddamn thing—nothing he could do to save his own ass. He would be burned at the stake and General Jamison would get another citation. At the court-martial he could tell it like it happened and let the chips fall every damn where and bring the general down with him. He could do that, and he almost felt consoled by the realization that he had the power to destroy the general. He could pull the building down, even though he himself might be wiped out by the falling debris.

'Get going, Bradford!' the general shouted.

Bradford came to attention and saluted the general and went hurriedly out into the early morning darkness.

'When those damn Amphibs face my court-martial!' the general shouted to the early-morning darkness. 'They want to fight, do they? I'll send the crippled black bastards up north to the goddamn front!'

ROBERT L. ALLEN

The Port Chicago Mutiny

"Remember Port Chicago?"

This was the first sentence of a faded pamphlet I had come across one afternoon ten years ago.

No, I didn't remember Port Chicago, although I vaguely recalled reading about antiwar demonstrations during the Vietnam era at a place in California called Port Chicago. But this pamphlet was dated 1945. What had happened in Port Chicago back then?

The pamphlet told of a terrible explosion that occurred there on July 17, 1944. Port Chicago was a naval ammunition base located on the Sacramento River near its entrance into San Francisco Bay, about thirty miles northeast of the city of San Francisco. The gigantic blast instantly killed over three hundred American sailors, totally destroyed two cargo ships that were tied up at the loading pier, wrecked the base itself, and damaged the small town of Port Chicago, located over a mile away. It was the worst home-front disaster of World War II.

Later I was to learn that of the 320 men killed in the explosion some 202 of them were black men who were ammunition loaders. Indeed, every man handling ammunition at Port Chicago was black and every commissioned officer white—this was standard practice in the segregated Navy at that time. On the cover of the pamphlet was a photograph that showed a group of black sailors handling what appeared to be canisters of ammunition, with a huge wall of such canisters rising behind them. Its title was "Mutiny? The real story of how the Navy branded 50 fear-shocked sailors as mutineers."

What mutiny? I read on, ever more curious.

In August 1944, three weeks after the disaster, 328 of the surviving ammunition loaders were sent to load another ship. The men balked, saying they were afraid, and 258 of them were marched off to a barge and held under guard for several days. Eventually, fifty men were singled out, charged with mutiny, court-martialed, convicted, and handed sentences ranging from eight to fifteen years imprisonment.

This all happened in a matter of a few months. By the end of that year the fifty men were in prison at Terminal Island in Southern California. Swift justice indeed. Perhaps too swift.

The burden of the pamphlet's argument was that the accused sailors were not "depraved" men who refused to do their duty, as the prosecution had argued, but young black men, already demoralized by the Navy's policy of racial discrimination, who had been traumatized by the awful explosion in which so many of their friends died. The men were in shock, the pamphlet contended.

And they were hardly grown men. Many were teenagers like John Dunn, a slender seventeen-year-old, or Charles Widemon, nineteen, who signed up at age seventeen, or Martin Bordenave, eighteen, who managed to enlist when he was only sixteen years old.

Then there was Joseph Small, the man labeled by the prosecution as the ringleader of the mutiny. The pamphlet described Small as a clean-cut, intelligent twenty-three-year-old from New Jersey. Small was accused of organizing a "mutinous assembly" of the black seamen.

The prosecutor in the court-martial was a naval officer by the name of James Frank Coakley. That name rang a bell. Wasn't Coakley the DA in Oakland who prosecuted the Black Panthers and antiwar activists in the 1960s?

Not much was said about the defense attorneys, but the pamphlet did mention that Thurgood Marshall had filed a brief on behalf of the fifty men. He charged that the men had been railroaded to prison because of their race. Marshall, now a U.S. Supreme Court justice, was then chief counsel for the National Association for the Advancement of Colored People (NAACP). The pamphlet was, in fact, published by the NAACP Legal Defense and Educational Fund in March 1945, and it included a coupon for making contributions.

I had stumbled across the pamphlet while doing research on the history of blacks in the U.S. Navy for an article I was writing. I laid the pamphlet aside and continued with my work, but I was fascinated by what it reported and I frequently found myself wondering what was the whole Port Chicago story, and what became of the "mutineers."

Turning to my copy of John Hope Franklin's history of black Americans, *From Slavery to Freedom*, I found only a brief mention of Port Chicago. An afternoon at the local library turned up some newspaper and magazine clippings. The explosion was extraordinarily powerful as one of the two ships tied up at the pier was almost fully loaded with thousands of tons of ammunition, bombs, and other explosives. Photos of the base showed a devastated site with timbers, cars, and equipment strewn crazily about. The disaster made the front page of the *New York Times*, but was quickly replaced by other news of the war.

Here and there I found other accounts, but nothing very substantial. Nevertheless, the more I read the more intrigued I became.

There was also a personal resonance which drew me to this story. I was a draft resister during the Vietnam War, thinking that war illegal and racist. I had marched and demonstrated in the 1960s and eventually refused to be inducted into the Armed Forces. Perhaps a bit self-righteously, I felt my stand was the only moral one to take, although I had no enthusiasm for going to jail, the expected outcome. My parents did not oppose my action, but they were troubled by my decision, especially my father. Like me, he was in his twenties when war broke out, but unlike me during the Vietnam War, he was more than willing, if called to duty, to serve the country as a soldier during World War II. He was called—but after a physical examination he was rejected due to a heart condition. A proud man who previously considered himself physically superior—he was an amateur boxer—I think he took that rejection as a personal failure, which was not helped by the fact that several of his brothers served in the war. Within a year he had started on the downward path toward alcoholism.

I tried to explain to my father why I refused to be drafted, but my talk of illegal American intervention in a civil war in Vietnam did not impress him. I think to him, as to many Americans, the Vietnam War was a matter of stopping communism, as World War II had been a matter of stopping fascism. How could I not understand that? He did not accuse me of cowardice or treason; he respected my decision. For me, his attitude toward World War II was something of a puzzle. I connected more with Malcolm X's questioning of black men who allowed themselves to be drafted by white men to fight against colored men.

My father died in 1972, a victim of too much drink. He was fifty-three years old.

I was saved from doing time in jail when a draft case similar to mine came to trial and was thrown out of court on a technicality. The government decided not to prosecute me.

The Vietnam War affected the men of my generation like no other experience. I wish my father could have understood. Surely the gap between us was not unbridgeable.

For his generation World War II was "the good war," a war in which America was clearly on the side of justice, fighting against fascism and racism—or so the school history texts said. Yet, there was often an undercurrent of bitterness in the war stories told by black veterans, anger at some insult or blatant act of discrimination encountered in the military. For black men, World War II was not unqualifiedly a "good war." No doubt my father well knew this, but that did not make him feel better about having been rejected as "unfit." World War II was still the war in which black men proved their mettle in combat for their country.

As I read the Port Chicago pamphlet I couldn't help but think of my father. These were the men of his generation. Many of them were volunteers who, like him, were anxious to prove themselves. Had he been accepted, he might well have wound up at Port Chicago. If he had survived, how would the experience have affected him? Would he have been one of the "mutineers"? Would it have enabled him to understand my action? I couldn't say, but these questions lurked in the back of my mind, and eventually I found an answer of sorts.

Months passed. I was busy with editing, teaching, and various writing projects. I kept a file of Port Chicago clippings and notes, and through the Navy Judge Advocate General's Office I obtained a copy of the transcript of the mutiny trial. I also applied for a Guggenheim Fellowship to do research on the incident. To my delight, a fellowship was offered, which I readily accepted. Perhaps now I could satisfy my curiosity about what happened at Port Chicago.

I soon learned that many records pertaining to World War II had been declassified in 1972 and were now available to researchers. These included records on the Port Chicago explosion and the mutiny case. The documents were available in various repositories including the National Archives, the Library of Congress, the archives of the U.S. Navy Judge Advocate General's Office, the Navy History Library and Operational Archives at the Washington Navy Yard, the Roosevelt Presidential Library in Hyde Park, New York, the Historical Office of the Navy Construction Battalion at Port Hueneme, California, and the San Bruno (Calif.) Federal Records Center. I visited all of them.

I also discovered that there was a book-length account of the Port Chicago incident. Entitled *No Share of Glory* and authored by Robert E. Pearson, this book—now out of print—was published before many of the primary documents were declassified, and I discovered serious factual errors in it. The book also lacked any substantial treatment of how the black enlisted sailors viewed the situation at Port Chicago. The burden of the book, as suggested by its title, was that, because they refused to load ammunition, the black "mutineers" at Port Chicago deserved no share of glory in the defeat of Japan.

As is evident, material from these sources tended to reflect the official Navy point of view about the matter, and to ignore or give little credence to the viewpoint of the black sailors. Consequently, I realized that I must find at least some of the men who had been there if I wanted to get their story.

The task of locating survivors to interview more than thirty-five years after the event proved to be a challenge. From the transcript of the mutiny court-martial I compiled a list of the fifty "mutineers." I began checking this list against telephone directories in the San Francisco Bay Area, where I lived, in hopes that some of the men might have settled there. I found some similar names in the directories, but they were not the individuals I was seeking.

Since the Navy Judge Advocate General's Office had been helpful in furnishing me with a copy of the trial transcript, I took my problem to them. They informed me that any addresses the Navy might have in its personnel files were not available for public use. However, after checking with the Navy's Bureau of Personnel, I learned that if I provided them with a list of the individuals I wished to locate, and prepared a mailing consisting of an unaddressed outer envelope, a cover letter, and a self-addressed return envelope, the Bureau of Personnel would address the envelopes and mail them to the last known address of any individuals from their files who matched those on my list—a so-called blind mailing. I prepared such a mailing for the fifty names and sent it to the Navy Department. Three weeks later I received the first response, from a man living in New York City. Excitedly, I telephoned him and confirmed that he was indeed a Port Chicago survivor who had been involved in the work stoppage and trial. I asked if I might visit him to conduct an interview and he agreed.

Over the next few weeks I received three more responses from the mailing, from survivors who were now living in Washington, D.C., Charleston, South Carolina, and Montgomery, Alabama. All were followed up with telephone calls and requests for interviews.

Meanwhile, I had placed advertisements in several veterans' publications and perused telephone directories from various cities in hopes of locating additional survivors. My efforts were rewarded.

I wrote to U.S. Supreme Court Justice Thurgood Marshall to ask for an interview. He declined, saying he remembered few details from the event. Fortunately, I was later able to track down the NAACP Legal Defense Fund files in a dusty old warehouse in Manhattan, where I found records of the case, including a copy of Marshall's appeal brief and a verbatim transcript of a meeting he had with Navy officials about the case.

With money from the Guggenheim Fellowship I flew to New York, purchased an unlimited-mileage Greyhound bus ticket, and spent two weeks traveling from New York to New Jersey to Washington, and then south to Charleston and Montgomery. I visited the men at their homes and conducted interviews with them. The interviews concentrated on descriptions of their experiences at Port Chicago in the period before the explosion, the explosion itself, and the ensuing work stoppage and court-martial. The interviews were tape-recorded and generally lasted one and one-half to two hours.

Some months later the Veterans Administration also agreed to do a blind mailing for me. Through this mailing I located four additional survivors, one of whom in turn led me to a tenth survivor. Three of these men lived in Los Angeles, two in New York. All agreed to be interviewed.

Meanwhile, the Navy Department informed me that at least twelve of the fifty men were now deceased, and I suspected that others who could not be located were also deceased. Given that the events in question occurred more than three decades ago, and given the high mortality rate among black males, I would not be surprised to learn that most of the fifty men were now dead. I felt fortunate to be able to locate ten survivors, nine of whom I was able to interview. Five of them were among the fifty charged with mutiny; all but one of them, who was seriously injured in the explosion, had taken part in the work stoppage and had personal knowledge of the events leading up to this confrontation.

All of the men told me that I was the first person who had come to ask them about Port Chicago. They were curious about how I had located them and what my purpose was. Indeed, some were more than curious, they were suspicious, thinking that I had some connection with the Navy or the government. Several expressed concern about possible repercussions to themselves or their families as a result of my research. One man was afraid that his son, who worked for the local police department, might be harassed if it were known that his father had been convicted of mutiny. Another refused to accept my assurances of confidentiality and declined to be interviewed after having initially agreed.

I was not without misgivings myself. After the first interview (with a respondent who did not want his son to overhear us because he had never told him about Port Chicago), I wrote an agonizing memo questioning my own motives. What right had I to pry into these men's lives, to expose them and their painful memories to public scrutiny? Was my motive really anything more than curiosity camouflaged as scholarly interest? Having been a draft resister, did I have some axe to grind? Was I not exploiting their suffering in a misguided debate with my dead father? I had no satisfactory answer to these questions, and they haunted me.

But as more interviews took place I came to believe that the interview process was itself therapeutic, both for myself and for the men, who were often relieved to unburden themselves to a sympathetic listener. Moreover, I and my respondents became bonded by a common desire to tell the whole story about what had transpired at Port Chicago. I did not have to offer them any compensation; for most of them, having the opportunity to finally tell their story in full was reward enough.

I found Joe Small by the easiest of all means—I called Information. From the documents, I knew where he was living when he went into the Navy. On the off chance that he had returned to his hometown and still lived there, I called the Information operator in that town. Yes, there was a J.R. Small listed.

I dialed the number. The voice on the other end of the line was gruff and cautious, but he was the man I was looking for. After some explaining, followed by letters, he agreed to be interviewed. I was ecstatic. Here was the man who the prosecution claimed was the ringleader of the mutiny, and he was willing to talk to me. I was pleased but, like Small, I was also cautious, although for different reasons. Would I get the truth from him? Would he tell me the whole story? Would I get a distorted reconstruction, or even an account of things that never happened? I drew up a list of questions for him that would allow me to test the accuracy and completeness of his memory of those events so many years ago—things I could check against the documents I had. No doubt Joe Small also prepared a set of tests for me to pass.

I first met Joe Small at his home on a winter evening in 1977. He was courteous but understandably reserved. I was nervous. Of medium build and height, with alert eyes in a seasoned dark brown face, Joe Small at age fifty-five was a man who made his living by his wits and his hands. He was a house builder and sometime contractor, a "fix-it" man who understood machines. Oddly, the house in which he lived had not been finished. Due to a zoning dispute he was unable to complete the structure. So he and his family lived in what appeared to be the ground floor or basement of an uncompleted house.

We talked, awkwardly enough at first, getting some sense of each other, then feeling more at ease. He introduced me to his wife, Louise, who welcomed me with a warm smile. I pulled out my tape recorder and we talked for an hour or so.

Over the next several years I went back to visit Joe Small a half dozen times. I was going to write a book, I told him at each of our meetings. "I'm sure you will," he replied, but with waning conviction as the years passed.

Yet the work proceeded, sporadically interrupted by teaching, editing, a divorce, part-time fathering, and a midlife crisis. And somehow, fascinating new developments in the story kept popping up to distract me from finishing the book. For a year or so it took off in a surprising new direction—another writer came up with some circumstantial evidence suggesting that the explosion might have been nuclear in origin. Indeed, the atomic bomb that was dropped on Japan a year later was shipped through Port Chicago. Could there have been an earlier shipment, and something went terribly wrong? The evidence was tantalizing, but after many months of searching, nothing hard could be produced to prove the hypothesis and eventually its proponent concluded that it was untenable.

At one point I simply got fed up with the whole project. I felt it was going nowhere. For two years I pretended that I had never heard of Port Chicago. But I couldn't forget it.

Especially could I not forget Joe Small. I had come to respect him and to admire his ability to survive adversity with a sense of humor. To be sure, what he made of it all was not necessarily what I made of it, but the man had heart and an engaging bullheadedness. He was not my father nor, I think, the man my father might have been had he served at Port Chicago. Joe Small was undisputedly himself, but through him, and the other men I interviewed, I came to see the men of my father's generation with new eyes.

MARTIN LUTHER KING, JR.

Beyond Vietnam

Since I am a preacher by trade, I suppose it is not surprising that I have seven major reasons for bringing Vietnam into the field of my moral vision. There is at the outset a very obvious and almost facile connection between the war in Vietnam and the struggle I, and others, have been waging in America. A few years ago there was a shining moment in that struggle. It seemed as if there was a real promise of hope for the poor—both black and white—through the Poverty Program. There were experiments, hopes, new beginnings. Then came the build-up in Vietnam and I watched the program broken and eviscerated as if it were some idle political plaything of a society gone mad on war, and I knew that America would never invest the necessary funds or energies in rehabilitation of its poor so long as adventures like Vietnam continued to draw men and skills and money like some demonic destructive suction tube. So I was increasingly compelled to see the war as an enemy of the poor and to attack it as such.

Perhaps the more tragic recognition of reality took place when it became clear to me that the war was doing far more than devastating the hopes of the poor at home. It was sending their sons and their brothers and their husbands to fight and to die in extraordinarily high proportions relative to the rest of the population. We were taking the black young men who had been crippled by our society and sending them 8,000 miles away to guarantee liberties in Southeast Asia which they had not found in Southwest Georgia and East Harlem. So we have been repeatedly faced with the cruel irony of watching Negro and white boys on TV screens as they kill and die together for a nation that has been unable to seat them together in the same schools. So we watch them in brutal solidarity burning the huts of a poor village, but we realize that they would never live on the same block in Detroit. I could not be silent in the face of such cruel manipulation of the poor.

My third reason moves to an even deeper level of awareness, for it grows out of my experience in the ghettos of the north over the last three years—especially the last three summers. As I have walked among the desperate, rejected and angry young men I have told them that Molotov cocktails and rifles would not solve their problems. I have tried to offer them my deepest compassion while maintaining my conviction that social change comes most meaningfully through non-violent action. But they asked—and rightly so—what about Vietnam? They asked if our own nation wasn't using massive doses of violence to solve its problems, to bring about the changes it wanted. Their questions hit home, and I knew that I could never again raise my voice against the violence of the oppressed in the ghettos without having first spoken clearly to the greatest purveyor of violence in the world today—my own government. For the sake of those boys, for the sake of this government, for the sake of the hundreds of thousands trembling under our violence, I cannot be silent.

For those who ask the question, "Aren't you a Civil Rights leader?" and thereby mean to exclude me from the movement for peace, I have this further answer. In 1957 when a group of us formed the Southern Christian Leadership Conference, we chose as our motto: "To save the soul of America." We were convinced that we could not limit our vision to certain rights for black people, but instead affirmed the conviction that America would never be free or saved from itself unless the descendants of its slaves were loosed completely from the shackles they still wear. In a way we were agreeing with Langston Hughes, that black bard of Harlem, who had written earlier:

> O, yes,
> I say it plain,
> America never was America to me,
> And yet I swear this oath—
> America will be!

Now, it should be incandescently clear that no one who has any concern for the integrity and life of America today can ignore the present war. If America's soul becomes totally poisoned, part of the autopsy must read Vietnam.

It can never be saved so long as it destroys the deepest hopes of men the world over. So it is that those of us who are yet determined that America *will* be are led down the path of protest and dissent, working for the health of our land.

As if the weight of such a commitment to the life and health of America were not enough, another burden of responsibility was placed upon me in 1964; and I cannot forget that the Nobel Prize for Peace was also a commission—a commission to work harder than I had ever worked before for "the brotherhood of man." This is a calling that takes me beyond national allegiances, but even if it were not present I would yet have to live with the meaning of my commitment to the ministry of Jesus Christ. To me the relationship of this ministry to the making of peace is so obvious that I sometimes marvel at those who ask me why I am speaking against the war. Could it be that they do not know that the good news was meant for all men—for communist and capitalist, for their children and ours, for black and for white, for revolutionary and conservative? Have they forgotten that my ministry is in obedience to the one who loved his enemies so fully that he died for them? What then can I say to the "Viet Cong" or to Castro or to Mao as a faithful minister of this one? Can I threaten them with death or must I not share with them my life?

Finally, as I try to delineate for you and for myself the road that leads from Montgomery to this place I would have offered all that was most valid if I simply said that I must be true to my conviction that I share with all men the calling to be a son of the Living God. Beyond the calling of race or nation or creed is this vocation of sonship and brotherhood, and because I believe that the Father is deeply concerned especially for his suffering and helpless and outcast children, I come tonight to speak for them.

This I believe to be the privilege and the burden of all of us who deem ourselves bound by allegiances and loyalties which are broader and deeper than nationalism and which go beyond our nation's self-defined goals and positions. We are called to speak for the weak, for the voiceless, for victims of our nation and for those it calls enemy, for no document from human hands can make these humans any less our brothers.

WALLACE TERRY

Bloods

SPECIALIST 4
CHARLES STRONG
Pompano Beach, Florida

Machine gunner
Americal Division
U.S. Army
Chu Lai
July 1969–July 1970

This dude, Lieutenant Calley, really didn't do nothing, man. I know, because I use to be in the field. He didn't do that on his own to My Lai. He was told to do that. We killed a whole lot of innocent gooks by mistake, because they were not suppose to be there. The GIs would take them out of their home. But dig this, the people's religion is very strong. They can't leave where they live. So I see why they would come back. I didn't kill any civilians personally. But what I know now, maybe I shot a few. When the stuff happened, it happened so fast, most people got killed in the first fifteen or twenty seconds. That's how fast a fire fight happened.

The war in Vietnam didn't do nothing but get a whole lot of guys fucked up for some money. There may have been a chance of having a base close to Red China. But actually it was fought for money. And the people in the world didn't want it to stop. That marching to stop the war was a whole lot of bullshit. Because, dig this, I seen this with my own eyes, because my MOS was humping the boonies. We found caches that the North Vietnamese got, full of sardines from Maine and even medical supplies from the U.S.

I wish the people in Washington could have walked through a hospital and seen the guys all fucked up. Seventeen-, eighteen-year-olds got casts from head to toes. This old, damn general might walk in and give them a damn Purple Heart. What in the hell do you do with a damn Purple Heart? Dudes got legs shot off and shit, got half their face gone and shit. Anything that you can mention that would make you throw up, that you can possibly dream of, happened.

Can you imagine walking around policing up someone's body? Picking them up and putting them in a plastic bag? Maybe you find his arm here, his leg over there. Maybe you have to dig up somebody's grave. Maybe he been there for a couple of days, and it will start stinking and shit. You dig graves. You open graves. You are an animal. You be out there so long until you begin to like to kill. You know, I even started doing that. I walked over a body of a North Vietnamese, and said, "That's one motherfucker I don't have to worry about." It made me feel good to see him laying there dead. It made me feel good to see a human life laying down there dead.

I was twenty when I went to 'Nam. My people was from South Carolina. We was migrants. We picked string beans in New York. Strawberries in Florida. When my older brothers started to work in the canneries in Florida, we moved to Pompano Beach. My father, he only went to the fourth grade, but I finished high school. I wanted to go into the field of automation and computers at the time. I had saved some money, and my mother had saved some money. I only needed $27 to take this course in a junior college. I asked my brothers and sisters to loan me $27, and they wouldn't do it. So I got a construction job helping carpenters. Then I had a feeling they were going to draft me, because only one of my brothers had been in the Army. They drafted me twenty-nine days before my twentieth birthday. My boy was born when I was in basic training. I don't think she wanted to get pregnant. I just think that we just got carried away. I married her when I got out in '72.

I really didn't have an opinion of the war at first. I was praying that the war would bypass me. I chose not to evade the draft but to conform to it. I figured it was better to spend two years in the service than five years in prison. And I figured that for nineteen years I had enjoyed a whole lot of fruits of this society. I knew that you don't get anything free in this world.

I first arrived in Chu Lai in July 1969. After a week of orientation, I was assigned to the Americal Division, Alpha Company, 1st of the 96th. My company commander was a very good company commander, because he knew his profession and kept us out of a whole lot of crucial incidents. But the second lieutenant—the platoon leader—he was dumb, because he would volunteer us for all kinds of shit details to get brownie points. We would walk point two or three times a week for the whole company. He was literally the word "stupid," because he couldn't read a map. And he would say, "You don't tell me what to do, because they sent me to officers' training school." When we got one or two sniper fire, he would stop right there and call in artillery to saturate the whole area before you could take another step.

One time we had to check out an area. It was during the monsoon season. It rained fifteen days and fifteen nights continuously. We stayed wet fifteen days. We started catching cramps and charley horses. The guys' feet got messed up. Well, they were trying to get supplies in to us. But it was raining so hard, the chopper couldn't get in. After five days, we ran out of supplies. We were so hungry and tired we avoided all contact. We knew where the North Vietnamese were, but we knew that if we got into it, they would probably have wiped a big portion of the company out. We were really dropped there to find the North Vietnamese, and here we was hiding from them. Running because we were hungry. We were so far up in the hills that the place was so thick you didn't have to pull guard at night. You'd have to take a machete to cut even one hundred meters. It could take two hours, that's how thick the shit was. We starved for four days. That was the first time I was ever introduced to hunger.

Then we found some kind of path road down into a little village. And we came to a house that had chickens and stuff there. I think the people abandoned it when they saw us coming. I was the machine gunner, so I had to stay where I was and watch the open area while the guys searched the house. They were city guys who didn't know about utilizing the forest or what they were running into. So they started throwing the rice on the ground. They didn't have the experience that I had. When I was younger, I used to go out for miles of distance into the woods and run the snakes. I told my friend Joe to pick up the rice and get the chickens. So Joe got the stuff. I told them not to worry, so I skinned a chicken. I got a whole mess of heat tabs, and put the chicken in my canteen cup and boiled it for a long time. When I thought the chicken was half done, I put in the rice. And a little salt. It was about the only food we had until the bird came in two days after that. Those guys were totally ignorant. They kept calling rice gook food. That's why they threw it on the ground. I told Joe food is food.

It was a good thing that I didn't run in the house. Because I saw something about an eighth of a mile away. It looked like a little scarecrow out there in the rice paddy. It was sort of like a little sign. I looked at it real hard. I stretched my eye to make sure it wasn't nobody. Then I seen another little dark object, and it was moving. So I opened my fire immediately. I think the Viet Cong was trying to get around behind us so he could ambush us. I just happened to recognize him. I cut off maybe fifty rounds, and the CO hollered, "Hold up there, Charles. Don't just burn the gun up." The rest of the company told me I really got him, so that was the only person that I really was told I actually killed.

My feet was all scriggled up. My skin was raw and coming off. I still carry an infection on my feet right now that I have to visit the VA hospital on a regular basis to take treatment for.

Then I started to take drugs to stop the pain in my feet.

When one of our men was killed the next day, it didn't make a whole lot of difference, because I just felt good that it wasn't me. But it gave me a thrill like you take a drink of alcohol or smoke a cigarette to see a Viet Cong laying dead. It was giving me a good feeling. It stimulated my senses. I thought about it, and I really started to love seeing someone dead. And I started doing more drugs. Now I'm afraid that if someone catches me the wrong way, I would do them really bodily harm. It won't be no fight to prove who the best man is, or to prove manhood. Because of 'Nam, I cannot fight, because if I fight now, I'll fight for life. Someone is gonna die immediately.

But it hurt me bad when they got Joe. Joe was an all right guy from Georgia. I don't know his name. He talked with that "ol' dude" accent. If you were to see him the first time, you would just say that's a redneck, ridge-runnin' cracker. But he was the nicest guy in the world. We used to pitch our tents together. I would give him food. He would share his water. And food and water was more valuable then than paper money. And when we had an opportunity to stand down, he would get sort of drunk and go around the brothers and say, "Hi there, brother man." The brothers would automatically take offense, but I always told them Joe was all right. His accent was just personal.

I remember one night I put my little transistor radio on my pack. We listened to music with the earphones, and he talked about his wife and kids back home on the farm in Georgia. He said he would be glad to see his wife.

The next day he was walking point. I was walking the third man behind him when he hit a booby trap. I think it was a 104 round. It blew him up in the air about eight feet. He came down, and about an inch of flesh was holding his leg to his body. He rested on his buttocks, and his arms were behind him. He was moaning and crying in agony and pain and stuff. What really got to his mind is when he rose himself and saw his leg blown completely off except that inch. He said, "Oh, no, not my legs." I really distinctly remember the look on his face. Then he sort of went into semiconsciousness. He died on the way to the hospital. I had to walk up the trail to guard for the medevac to pick him up. And I remember praying to the Lord to let me see some VC—anybody—jump out on that trail.

After six months, it was approaching Christmas, and we went back through the jungles to the rear area for a standdown. That was when I made up in my mind that I wasn't going back to the field. The officers were dumb, but besides that, before I went to Vietnam, I had three dreams that showed me places in Vietnam. When we were in this one area, it was just like in the first dream. I felt like I had been there before, but I didn't place much value on it. But when I seen the second place, it dawned on me this was the place in the second dream. I said that in my dream, there's supposed to be a foxhole approximately fifteen feet to the left and a little tin can sittin' on it. At the LZ I was in at the time, I walked straight to the place where the foxhole was supposed to be. And there it was. And the can, too. The third dream said that I was going to be crossing a rice paddy, and I was going to get shot in my chest with a sucking wound that I would never recover from. And one of my buddies was holding me in his arms, saying I would be all right until the medevac came in. But it seemed like I never made it out of there. So I wrote my mother and told her that it was time to leave the field, or I would never make it out alive. The first and second dreams came true. It was a sign from the Heavenly Father for me to do something, or the third dream would come true. A Christian never walks into any danger, dumb and blind. Never.

I had three alternatives. One was I could go back to the field. The second was I could go to jail. The third was I could take more time in military service. I chose the third. I enlisted for three years to get out of the field and get trained for welding.

CLYDE TAYLOR

Black Consciousness in the Vietnam Years

We live in days of a Great Change, a shuffling of status and symbols. Yeats's cry "Things fall apart; the centre cannot hold" is good news in the Third World; a ferment rises in the young bloods in the bush. And stepping out of the shelter of their place in the shadows of American exceptionalist rationalizations. Black people in the sixties raised a major opposition to America's violations of human rights. It was about as significant and dramatic a challenge to oppression as any in the century falling short of national revolution. Black Americans became not only beneficiaries of the Great Change, but important agents as well.

One of the nervous tics in the American psyche that led to its stumble into Indochina was probably a not quite conscious reaction to the upsurge of Black people at home. The mentality of American leaders is not above the question whether, hard-pressed by rebellious Blacks into a loss of ego comfort, they were quick to seize a field of action where being white could again be what it once was. The argument has been made that Kennedy listened seriously to advisers who told him that the United States could recoup some face in Vietnam that was lost in the Bay of Pigs. "The average white man feels the shit," says a character in George Davis's novel about the war, *Coming Home*. "First his Chinamen started acting up on him, then his Vietnamese, then his niggers, and now his women."

The Pentagon Papers and other leaks reveal as many sources of the war in the sagging *machismo* of its decision makers as in any printouts of some think-tank systems analysis. One report of leaked secrets has it that the CIA advised Nixon to withdraw from Vietnam (see Chicago *Sun-Times*, June 25, 1971). "On several occasions since coming to office, Nixon has referred to immediate, total U.S. withdrawal from Southeast Asia as 'precipitate' and the equivalent of 'our defeat and humiliation.' " Can you see the phallic defensiveness, the middle-aged sexual insecurity? In the debates, for example, over a slow or quick withdrawal? "Instead of pulling out of Vietnam rapidly, Nixon has withdrawn gradually. . . ."

Those repeated blows upon the flesh of Indochina with assorted military "hardware," the ever-deeper penetrations by enormous B-52s and lean fighter-bombers, continually blasting and pounding the countryside of Vietnam—what are they but the frenzy of aged boy-men, determined to prove that they can still keep it up? The bombardments, the defoliants, the cracking of dikes and blistering of forests with incendiaries, the shots of napalm, mists of air-dropped tear gas and nerve gas, barrages from armor-plated "choppers," the deluge of death blows upon the lightly defended form of Vietnam, which continues, stubbornly, to resist, the shards of fragmentation bombs and "daisy-cutters" splintering into its flanks: these are the phallus-flexings, the hysteric push-pulls of a frigid, twisted male ego, an insane rapist, shocked at not finding love returned for his brutality, desperately plunging in a rain of torture to draw from his victim's body a shivering, piercing cry of suffering and submission and pleading, grateful surrender ("Please, Daddy, you're the best!")—to ward off that inevitable moment of final withdrawal and recognition of its own impotence and limpness.

If the examples of Third-World courage provided a major lesson for this generation's Black awareness, the obscene spectacle of U.S. "intervention" in Vietnam offers a negative reinforcement of that same lesson in the transparent connection of its racism and its imperialism. "If they do that to them, what would they do to us," the thought occurred. One attitude, then, toward the Vietnamese revolutionaries among resistant Black people is "No Vietnamese ever called me nigger!" A more radical reaction is "We are all in the same boat." The most radical response has been "We are allies."

By recognizing a mutuality between a colonized Asian people and themselves, African-Americans merely discover a drift in American national consciousness. White Americans show neither a capacity nor an interest in making real distinctions between peasants in the Philippines or Cuba or Indochina, American Indians, and Black people on a plantation in Louisiana. There is a continuity, not yet charted by historians, between American policy toward "coloreds" abroad and at home. The war in the Philippines at the turn of the century, for example. Some sharp resemblances exist between that war and Vietnam: Anglo-Saxon civilization extending its helping hand to "the little brown brother" and, in the process, forcibly resettling whole populations, killing hundreds of thousands of Filipinos, mostly innocent civilians, and committing dozens of My Lais. And in the states, Republican (and some Democrat) leaders mulled over the inconsistency between the use of ruthless tactics to aid a "backward people" there and finicky concern for the rights of "backward" people here. And these rights were eclipsed more fully then than at any period since slavery.

The most revealing parallel between the two theaters of action is the cut-rate valuation placed on non-white lives by White Americans in both places. Black people sensed in the outcry following the trial and conviction of Lieutenant Calley for the murders at My Lai an upcropping of this racist double valuation. Reporters following the trial uncovered the subterranean issue that never entered the trial record but was familiar in the jargon of Army lawyers and the military as MGR, the "Mere Gook Rule." "Somehow it suggested that life was less valuable to an Oriental, or, put another way, that the laws which protected other human beings did not necessarily apply if the victim happened to be Vietnamese and the killer was an American soldier." (See "This World," San Francisco *Examiner & Chronicle*, March 21, 1971, p. 7.)

The MGR has its domestic counterpart in what could be called the JNR, or "Just a Nigger Rule." (In that celebrated American classic *The Adventures of Huckleberry Finn*, Huck tells of a boat wreck he witnessed. When asked if anyone was killed, he answers, "No'm, just a nigger.") The same week that four white students were killed, during a protest against the Cambodian invasion, at Kent State, Ohio, two Black students were killed at Jackson State, Mississippi. Several months earlier, a massacre took place at Orangeburg, South Carolina, in which state police killed four Black students and wounded dozens in the course of a demonstration to integrate a bowling alley. The Kent State killings received banner headlines, well-publicized hearings, much television coverage, and several books. The Jackson State killings got back-page coverage mostly, and the Orangeburg massacre got hardly any coverage at all.

The man in the middle of all these contradictions is the Black man of fighting age. He is the subject of a subtle rivalry that has existed as long as white men have launched wars and Black men have wanted their freedom. This is the tug of war for his allegiance between the military establishment on the one hand and the Black liberation movement on the other. The young, draft-age leaders of SNCC showed their grasp of this rivalry when they proposed that Black men such as themselves, who were serving in the ranks of the civil rights struggle, be exempted from the draft.

The lures of security and status that the defense establishment can hold out to Black youngsters seem formidable. But the changes in the tone of this contest since World War I suggest some limited but real gains for Black consciousness. Then, Black leaders agitated to get more Black men into the front lines. During the Vietnam War, Black protest forced the Pentagon to limit the number of Black men in front-line elite units such as the paratroopers and the Marines, where they were taking casualties far in excess of their proportions in the military or the national population. In the earlier war, military leaders praised Black officers for "knowing their place." And the 369th Infantry was praised as "possessing black skins, white souls and red blood." Now, the military condones Black-power salutes and Afro hairstyles. The new style of competition with the Black liberation ideal is reflected in the television commercial in which a sister says, "You can be Black and Navy too."

The appeal of the military to Black youth has to be recognized; otherwise, how can we understand the statistics, the high rate of Black enlistment and re-enlistment, often in high-risk elite corps? The Army is obviously an alternative to the disorientation of the Black community. Juvenile courts often make the alternatives clear: the Army or jail, a kind of modern Shanghai recruitment. The choice may also be the Army or unemployment rolls, boredom, futurelessness, collisions with the police, or an uncongenial, woman-dominated household. And Black parents have often acknowledged their own failure and the failure of the Black community with the unreflecting words, "I thought, at least the Army will make a *man* out of him."

But why the heavy choice of elite fighting units? A large part of the explanation is an information lag. "The brother is here, and he's raising hell," said an eighteen-year-old Marine in Vietnam; "we're proving ourselves." The massive record of the fighting courage of Black soldiers in American history is becoming public record, but the news hasn't reached the fresh recruit. As a Black captain pointed out, "They feel they're the first Negroes to fight, because their history books told only of white soldiers, and their movies showed that John Wayne and Errol Flynn won all American wars."

The "prove yourselves worthy" argument is gradually playing itself out along its old lines, but picking up energy under a new face lifting. Where the Black soldier was told, during World War I, that he was inferior fighting material, the recruiting sergeant's new policy is to ride the coattails of the resurgence of Black pride. The defense establishment and the media collaborate eagerly to document the heroism and bravery of the Black fighting man in past wars. And a clutch of grade-school texts are devoted to developing this new image. The Vietnam veteran may have been motivated by the need to live down some mythical history of Black military incompetence; tomorrow's Black recruit is being encouraged to live *up* to a tradition of heroic, and loyal, Black soldiers.

The young Black man is being subjected to a manhood hustle. The military calls and he listens, mostly for the same reasons he listens to the call of big-time sports. The recruiting sergeant and the head coach run the same game on him. On this close-up level, we can see repeated the same process by which American institutions use Black people in time of war. The blood is neglected and despised until the war effort (or team, whatever) needs him. Then the call goes out, offering him an opportunity to prove his individual manhood, become a star. In the heat of the contest, on the front line or the line of scrimmage, he experiences a swelling togetherness feeling with his teammates, exchanges hand slaps, and finds "soul brothers" among white troops. But farther back from the contest, the old system of spoils and status reappears. "Sure, we were buddy-buddy in the Nam," recalls one Black veteran. "There were a couple of guys I was wounded with, crawled around in the mud together, ate out of the same can of beans and drank the same water. But when we got to the stateside hospital they didn't want to know me at all."[1] When the contest is over, or the season, the tour of duty, the eligibility,

[1]Quotations of Black soldiers or veterans, unless otherwise identified, have been taken from a series of articles by Thomas A. Johnson in the *New York Times*, April 28, May 1, and July 29, 1968.

whichever, the not-so-young blood is left on the same corner; likely unemployed and maybe with a forty-dollar habit to feed, and some memories. "Somehow I thought it would be different this time," David Parks wrote in *GI Diary*. "Especially over here, where survival is the thing. But that seems to cut no ice with Mister Pale."

So, faced with American wars, Black people have been caught and continue to be caught in a cycle of hustles, with the implicit promise "This time, it'll be different." This time, it *was* different in that many didn't swallow the Vietnam hustle at all. But even though there has been a paradoxical benefit in an advance of Black consciousness from each of this nation's conflicts, the pattern of Black dependence upon an opportunistic development, frequently at the expense of principles, has not undergone any significant change.

The underground fiber of Black resistance to American oppression endures, however, and has almost certainly been toughened by the experiences of the Vietnam years. It has for sure surfaced more boldly than ever before, and, in the process, subjected itself to important critical self-examination. After the sixties, the concept of Black consciousness begins to include not only an acceptance of one's self, one's negritude, and one's situation in the world, but a determination to advance in the struggle against oppression along lines consistent with the principled struggle for human rights everywhere.

It's anybody's guess when the time will come when Black people will break out of the cycles of random capitalization on American aggressive ventures. That moment can come only after Black love and rage and pride have elevated themselves to a radical Black consciousness, unbending from its principles in any circumstances, whatever its pragmatic tactics. Such a consciousness will be ready to seize the time when American military and political power, confounded in some disastrous undertaking, is at its weakest—as the Algerians did when the French had their hands full with the Vietnamese, or as the Bolsheviks did when the Czars were losing in World War I, or even as the Haitians made a revolution while the French were hip deep in their own revolution. That will be the last occasion when Black consciousness will have to feed itself off the scraps from the fields of America's seasonal bloodlettings.

LOCKED IN AND LOCKED OUT

ALBERT RACE SAMPLE

Racehoss: Big Emma's Boy

When we treat a man as he is, we make him worse than he is. When we treat him as if he is already what he potentially could be, we make him what he should be.

GOETHE

I was sent back to serve the six months remaining on the two years. In 1956, I was sentenced to twenty years for Robbery to run concurrent with the thirty I got for Robbery by Assault. My mind was racing as the transfer truck, "Black Betty," slowly backed inside the gates of Retrieve, one of the twelve prison units comprising the Texas Prison System.

This was it, "the burnin hell," the place that "gits yo heart right" I heard so much about when I served time at the Clemens Unit. Retrieve, formerly an all-white prison unit, had been repopulated a few years previously with the worst, most incorrigible black cons that were in the prison system. Most were multi-recidivists serving heavy-duty sentences. That measly two years I pulled on Clemens was just a drop in the bucket compared to this new thirty year package I was breaking the seal on.

While unloading off the back of the black van, I looked up and saw the numbers inscribed above the red brick archway. 1934 leaped out at me. This widow-maker was born during the depression just like me. What a coincidence, I thought, that was the same year I got "busted" for the first time when Emma went to jail for bootlegging. Going to jail was fun and games back then, but as I stepped into this bastard world of the prison system, I knew growing up with Emma and the time I served on Clemens was just bootcamp for what I was facing now.

Inside the building, there were four separate "tanks" on the lower level and one on the upper level across from the inside picket post. It was late morning and the field hands were still outside working. The tanks were empty, except for the building tenders.

The guard who brought the six of us in hollered up to the inside picket guard, "Boss, open up them Number 3 and 2 tanks. Put half uv these nigguhs in each one uv 'em."

The picket guard threw the levers opening the tank doors, "Awright, you first three nigguhs," pointing us out, "git in that Number 3 tank. Rest uv you git across the hall in Number 2." After we were inside the Number 3 tank, the picket guard hollered, "Got three new 'uns comin in Ol' Bull!"

As the building tender walked toward the front of the tank, the long piece of chain hanging from his belt rattled noticeably. "Got 'em, Boss," Bull hollered while the door was clicking shut. He told us our bunk and locker numbers, what time we'd be fed, and when the lights went out. Then he laid down the tank "laws," "Ain' gon' be no loud talk and no two nigguhs settin on no one bunk. Don' nobody git offa yo bunk at nite afta count time til you holler alley boss, an gits an OK."

When he said that "alley boss" part, it reminded me of the time I was five and had a bad cold. Emma carefully measured out two spoonfuls of castor oil into a cup with a little squeezed orange juice. As I was putting the cup up to my mouth, I pleaded with her not to make me take it. Just the smell was making me nauseous. She told me I'd better drink it and forget about the smell. I turned the cup up and swallowed it, but it wouldn't stay down. I immediately vomited all over the kitchen floor. She grabbed me by my hair and pressed the butcher knife she used to half the orange against my throat. She held it so tight it cut the skin.

"Pick up that bottle and drank ever bit uv it, an you bet not waste a drop. If you utter, I'll pull yo Gotdam, peckerwood head off!" I gulped down the rest of it. She ordered me to get on my cot and "stay there."

In a very short time I needed to go to the outhouse. Since I wasn't supposed to get up, I hollered into the kitchen, "Emma, kin I go outside to do-do, please mam?" My life hadn't changed much. Here I was having to get permission to take a shit again.

I tuned back in to hear Bull saying, "When dey rangs dat bell, be ready ta git ya'll's asses outta dis tank."

The tank had three double deck rows of bunks, with twenty bunks each, and one with twenty-five. Bars that ran from the floor to the ceiling separated Number 3 tank from the one adjacent to it, Number 4. At the front of the tank was an old-fashioned barber chair with silver painted lockers lining the front wall. In the back was a six-sprinkler shower stall, a urinal, a long, eight-faucet face basin which doubled as the tank's drinking fountain. And a row of eight doorless commodes (with those old-timey wooden seats regulating the flushing) faced the front of the tank.

About thirty minutes later, the field workers came in for lunch. They were wet and muddy. Our clean, white clothes tattle-taled we were new arrivals. Some made snide remarks as they rushed for the back to wash up, "Ya'll won' be so priddy an white after dat bell rangs."

Within a few minutes, the picket guard pulled the tank door levers and Bull hollered, "Les go eat!"

The Number 3 and 4 tank (eastside) cons single filed into the messhall along with the cons from the westside tanks (Number 1 and 2). I quickly scanned the messhall hoping to see someone I knew, but didn't. After passing the steam tables, we sat eight cons to a table. While we ate, the building tenders slowly walked up and down the aisles—overseeing. No talking allowed, and fifteen minutes to eat.

When the messhall emptied and we returned to the tanks, the picket guard hollered down, "All you ol' new nigguhs, cum on up to the front," as he opened the Number 2 and 3 tank doors. The six of us stepped out into the area underneath the inside picket. The captain who was waiting there ordered us to line up against the wall. He sized us up and I knew my light complexion made me stand out like a sore thumb against the blackdrop of the other five.

He told the first two men who were both bigger than me, "Ketch that Number 3 hoe, and you ketch that Number 5." I learned on Clemens that the higher the squad number, the better off you were. Judging my size against theirs, I figured I'd probably be put in Number 7 or 6 at least. I was in Number 12 utility squad on Clemens, mending fences, putting in culverts, and had never done field work.

I was next, "You ain't all that big," he said stepping in front of me, "but you wuz big enuff to rob them folks. Got you sum big time this time, didn' you?"

"Yes suh."

"Well, I'm gonna put yore yaller ass where you kin start doin sum uv it. When that Number 1 hoe cums out, you ketch it."

Back on the tank one of the cons said, "Man, Cap'n Smooth put you in a bad-d-d muthafucka! All them nigguhs is wild. An the lead row nigguh they got, Ol' Road Runner, runs wide-open all day long. An Boss Deadeye is a sho nuff number one driver. You betta be ready to hit th' door runnin!"

The turnout bell sounded. I tensed.

"Lemme have 'em, Boss," shouted Cap'n Smooth, who stood at the back door.

"Number 1!" the inside picket boss hollered down, opening all of the lower tank doors.

The Number 1 hoe squad cons from all four tanks ran at full speed down the hall like a herd of buffalos. Bosses on horseback were waiting as we fled out the back door.

Cap'n Smooth counted us and hollered, "Got twenty-seven uv 'em, Boss."

The boss with the patch over his eye rode up behind us and answered loudly, "Thas right! Ol' Road Runner, ya'll git sum grubbin hoes an shovels."

As we left the hoe rack, running behind Road Runner, Boss Deadeye rode at our heels, yelling, "Gitcha Gotdam asses offa this yard an on that turnrow," narrow roads that separate the acres in the field. "Go Head!"

It didn't take much to figure out why they called the lead row man "Ol' Road Runner." He was tall, skinny, and extremely long-legged. He walked so fast the rest of us ran and trotted to keep up with him. His long "drag step" with his feet never leaving the ground made him look like he was walking on a pair of skis.

We must have walked and run five miles down that muddy road behind him. The muscles in my legs cramped and the new brogans were killing my feet.

By the time we reached the "bottoms," my shirt was wringing wet. Road Runner never broke stride until we reached the place to "catch in." I was glad to get there, just so I could stop running.

Boss Deadeye stopped his horse and started yelling, "You nigguhs ketch in heah an start diggin up them tree stumps. Git ever bit uv them roots outta thar."

I started shoveling dirt like a salamander around one of the huge stumps. Even with one eye, Boss Deadeye quickly spotted my shovel-handling ineptitude.

"Ol' new nigguh, cum heah!"

I stopped digging and dropped my shovel. I walked to within ten feet of where he sat astride his horse, and pulled off my flop-down hat. EVERYBODY knew this "rule." I learned that much on Clemens.

"Where you cum from nigguh?"

"I'm frum Longview, Boss."

His next question, "Whut color is yore ol' mammy?"

Before I knew it, I told him she was white and my daddy was a colored man. I saw it in his one eye, he didn't like my answer AT ALL. Angered, he spat tobacco juice at me.

"You know whut nigguh? You mind me uv a big pile uv yaller shit." Some of the cons in the squad started snickering. "Frum now on, I'm gonna call you Ol' Shit-Colored Nigguh. When I call you that, you betta answer me." Leaning forward in his saddle, "Do you unnerstand that nigguh?"

"Yes suh, Boss, but that ain' my name." The cons stopped snickering and giggling, and a hush fell over the squad.

"Why you Gotdam impudent, shit-colored mawdicker!" He spurred his horse and tried repeatedly to hit me with the knotted end of the big rope tied to the horn of his saddle. Avoiding him and his horse, we went around and around. Finally, he gave up.

Thoroughly aggravated, "Gitcha Gotdam ass back over yonder an git ta wek!"

Later a con began to sing in the squad working next to ours. Another con urged him on, "Blow it outcha soul nigguh." As the singing grew louder, I realized the cons in the next squad were cutting trees and hitting their axes in rhythm with the song. I listened to them and kept on digging.

We dug stumps and we dug stumps until, "Dere it is, it's in da air!" Cap'n Smooth, who sat on a horse up ahead, had raised his hat, signalling that the work day was over. We rushed to line up behind Road Runner for the long run back to the building. I was on the back row in the squad right under the nostrils of Deadeye's horse. Each time he snorted, he blew cold slobber on my back. Seems like I was running in slow motion.

Boss Deadeye yelled, "You nigguhs betta git on to that house. Go Head!" Road Runner laid his ears back and took off. He left us struggling to catch up as we trotted wearily behind him with the other seven squads behind us.

On the yard, we stopped by the hoe-rack to put away our tools, then took off again for the backgate. Boss Deadeye rode over to the outside picket and dismounted. He hung his pistol and shotgun on a hook tied to the end of a rope and the backgate picket boss pulled his weapon up into the picket. We stood at the backgate entrance behind Road Runner, eagerly awaiting the signal from Boss Deadeye to "go head."

Instead, he walked over to the side of the squad, evil-eyed me, and said, "Ol' Shit-Colored Nigguh, cum heah."

I didn't move. Cap'n Smooth came out of the small building beside the backgate. Deadeye walked toward him, "Cap'n, I got a ornery ol' nigguh in my squad that laks to play deaf." Then he yelled, "Ol' new nigguh, git yore Gotdam ass over heah."

I stepped out and the rest of my squad went through the backgate. Cap'n Smooth told me, "Stand over yonder," pointing toward the other side of the backgate. I was the first con cut out that evening.

Waiting by the gate, I saw all the other squads. Each one stopped at the backgate and waited for the "go head." They rushed through, stopped midway in the yard, stripped, and were searched. By the time the last squad went through, five of us were standing outside the fence waiting.

After the backgate boss searched us and we had our clothes back on, Cap'n Smooth marched us into the building hallway. He yelled up to the inside picket boss, "Hand me down five pairs uv cuffs, Boss."

When my turn came, Cap'n Smooth took my right wrist and clamped the cuff on tight-tight. Then he backed me up against the iron bars that separated the messhall from the inner hall. With one cuff clamped on my right wrist and my back against the bars, he took the unclosed cuff and looped it through the bars above my head. Then he told me to fold my left arm above my head while he clamped on the other cuff. When he finished, I was left hanging with my toes barely touching the floor.

After an hour, a couple of the cuff hangers started groaning. I bit my lip to keep from crying out too. I thought about what that lying boss told the captain, "All this nigguh's dun all day long is look up in the sky an count birds. Cap'n, I had to beg this nigguh to git him to go to wek." The pains shot through my arms; I dug my teeth deeper into my bottom lip until I tasted the blood inside my mouth.

When the bell rang for supper, none of those who made it in would even look at us as they filed past to enter the messhall. They looked straight ahead. As I listened to their spoons scraping the tin pans behind me, I thought about those big, thumbtack-sized butter beans I passed over at lunch and wished I hadn't.

After "count time," nine o'clock, the lights were dimmed inside the tanks and the hours crept by. I sure had to piss, but the con hanging next to me told me, "We git to piss when they let us down. If you piss in yo britches, thas anutha hour."

"How long will they leave us hung up here?" I asked.

"They lets us down in time to eat an git ready to go to work."

Along about hour six, one of the hangers began moaning louder and louder, violently jerking and pulling against his cuffs. He frantically wiggled and twisted his body around until he was facing the bars. Using his foot to push against them, he reared back, pitching, straining, and pulling as hard as he could. Realizing he couldn't get lose, he bit into his wrists as if they were two chocolate eclairs, growling and gnawing away like a coon with its foot caught in a steel trap.

The blood-splattered con hanging next to him pulled as far away as he could, hollered and yelled for the picket boss.

Looking down from his perch, the picket boss ordered the turnkey, "Run git a bucket an dash sum water on them two crazy nigguhs down on the end."

The dousing worked; he quit mutilating his wrists and contented himself to moaning and groaning out the night like the rest of us.

Finally, the dim lights were turned back to bright. The picket guard handed down the cuff keys to the turnkey, who unlocked us from the bars. After the cuffs were removed, my swollen wrists throbbed like a bad toothache.

The picket boss opened the door to my tank and I headed straight for the back to take a piss and get a drink. I barely sat on my bunk before one of the building tenders shouted, "Les go eat." That walk to the messhall past the bars I had just hung on all night wasn't fast enough for me. I didn't want to look at that place of pain either. As I passed the steam table, I pointed to every food item on it.

LLOYD L. BROWN

Iron City

Cell search comes after Sunday dinner. At the sound of the bell each inmate enters his cell and locks himself in to await the coming of the guards. Nothing will happen to him; he is sure of it. He has nothing to hide; he knows that. In the hours that pass he will tell himself again and again: What do I care? Let them look—there's nothing in here. But why do his eyes keep returning to the cigar box on the shelf until he must jump up from his bunk and look again at the things he knows are there. A couple of letters, a pencil, a toothbrush—nothing wrong about that. And why do his hands continue their restless search, patting his pockets from the outside, slipping in again to make sure? Foolish, of course, and he knows that too. They can always find something if they really want to—a deck of cards, a pair of dice, or even a Jim Kelly, as the inmates call a pocketknife in memory of the old guard, long gone to his reward, who never got through a Sunday search without finding his pearl-handled jackknife in some man's cell. No, it is not that—not the chance of a petty frame-up with maybe a week in the Hole.

But the man is afraid. *The searchers are coming and there is something here that must be hidden.* A sudden panic flares within him at the clash of the key in the range end gate. They are coming! One by one each cell in turn is entered and the murmur of voices draws nearer to where he is trapped. Now his eyes are desperate in their darting search . . . only a moment is left to conceal that which must be kept from them. Now they are crowding into this place that has become a part of the man, and now he stands before them—naked, defenseless, alone.

They find nothing. The secret self of a man, elusive even to love, is forever locked against the men with the keys. Only for the truly damned is there no hiding place.

The three guards who came through Range D that Sunday afternoon were in an amiable mood; and Pee Wee, the new rangeman, who trotted behind them with his clipboard roster, was grinning widely at their high good humor. Their searching this time was little more than a glance within each cell and a snatching off of a few blankets: the only thing they seemed to be looking for was an answering smile to their friendly joshing. They asked Slim where he was hiding that great big ol' razzah, and of Willie, naked except for his socks, they observed that by George this boy could really give some high yallah a good time—now, couldn't he, Pee Wee? One of them asked Paul Harper, with a wink, if the volume by Hugo had some good hot spots in it, and somehow Faulcon reminded another about the one they tell about the old darky preacher and this time he had Mandy up in the hayloft, catch on?, and. . . .

They were still laughing at that when they entered Isaac Zachary's cell.

Zach stood up quickly and turned to unroll his blanket for them, but the one who had told the joke said, "Nah, don't bother with that—guess there aint nothing in there but your smell." He was about to leave when his eye caught the strange markings on the prisoner's back. He whistled sharply through his teeth, then motioned for the other two searchers to come in. "Jesus Christ, look at that!" he said, pointing.

The big man did not turn to face them; now he leaned over the bunk to roll up the ragged covering. They could all see it now—the spatter of scars that streaked like a comet's tail across the dark expanse of his skin.

"Looks like he zigged when he should have zagged."

"Bird-shot, eh?"

"Bird-shot nothing! Wouldn't make holes like that. Looks more like buckshot to me."

"Bet he didn't come back so quick to *that* henhouse. I bet you that."

Zach still had not turned around to smile at their attentions.

"Hey you," said the guard who had come in first.

The broad back seemed to stiffen slightly, but Zach continued with his bed.

"I'm talking to you, nigger—hey!" He nudged the prisoner with his toe.

Zach turned so quickly they barely caught the motion. Facing them now, his eyes were narrow slits, his features drawn tightly immobile except for the quivering nostrils.

"Don't do that!" He let his breath out slowly. He had not spoken loudly and when he spoke again his voice was strangely calm. "I don't want no trouble with you-all. No trouble." He shook his head. "But just don't touch me, that's all. Just don't touch me."

They had drawn back a step at his sudden movement, and now they faced him in silence. The silence filled the tiny place and flowed out through the bars and down the length of the range, flooding the other cells so that even the prisoners who had not heard were engulfed in the surging stillness. Pee Wee stood rigid outside Zach's cell, his grin now a grotesque mask of panic. No man can measure such a moment, for time itself is caught and held in the trap which grips them all.

The guards continued to stare at the man in the cell, blinking against the hatred and fear that seemed to blind them. Abruptly, as though obeying a secret command, they backed out into the runway and one of them motioned to Zach to come out. He hesitated for a second, then strode forward.

"All right," he said quietly. "But just don't touch me!" Then he followed behind as they hurried toward the front gate.

There had been no sound of their going, for Zach's feet were bare and the guards wore rubber soles; and Faulcon and Paul could not be sure that he had been taken away until their cells were opened and they went into Number 8 to find it empty. Only his clothes were there and the letter, propped on his shelf, addressed to Mrs. Annie Mae Zachary.

"Better take his things so they won't get stole." It was Slim, the warden's janitor, and he drew Paul aside to whisper: "You can give me that letter. He aint allowed mail privilege now, but I'll see it gets out."

When Paul gave him the envelope, Slim licked the flap and closed it; and that was strange too, for only the Chief Guard was permitted to seal out-going mail.

The events of the day had left no room for the current events discussion they had planned; too much happening right in here that we got to talk about.

"No, I'm not mad at Zach. Of course, the decision was that we be especially careful to keep out of trouble while the bail question was still up, and I was kind of sorry when it happened that one of us three was the first to mess up. But I guess it had to be one of us instead of the white comrades. A man can't take but so much—and they put so damn much on us." Paul glanced at his friend and a smile broke through the worried look on his lean dark face. "To tell you the truth, Henry, I thought sure it was going to be you. When they were in your cell and telling that joke about the darky preacher, I said to myself: Here it comes—and there goes old Henry to the Hole."

Faulcon chuckled. "Uh uh," he said. "You're forgetting about that old-time song about how 'De ol' sheep, dey know de road—Young lambs must find de way.' Shucks, if you had waited on as many white folks as I did in my days, you'd a heard so much of that stuff you'd never pay it no mind. Oh, I admit there was times when I took exception and mixed a little dirt or maybe a little spit into their soup—not being so politically developed as now—but other than that. . . ."

They looked up to see Slim standing in the door. "Five more minutes," he called and then he was gone before they had a chance to thank him. They jumped up and went out to the walkway where the other men on D were already moving about to stretch their legs and socialize in the last few precious moments before lock-up.

"You know," said Faulcon as they strolled toward the front, "I don't think they're going to allow bail anyway."

Paul nodded. "All we can do is hope for the best and expect the worst. But you may be right."

And Henry Faulcon was right, for twenty minutes after the lock-up bell jangled through the County Jail, the warning buzzer sounded on the giant presses of the Iron City *American*, just four blocks away, and the first morning edition began to roll through, carrying on Page 23 the announcement that the Court of Appeals had approved the ruling of Judge Hanford J. Rupp that the twenty-six convicted Reds were too dangerous to the community to be permitted out on bail pending action on their appeal.

Sunday is a slow day, a day when even the grapevine is slow in getting around from range to range, and it was nearly lock-up before word came to Lonnie James that there had been some trouble down on Range D. It came as a surprise because Murderers' Row was directly above D and if there had been a ruckus down there Lonnie should have heard. But more than the surprise was the worry, for the keyman who brought the news said that the Reds had started raising hell and got thrown into the Hole.

"That's a lot of crap," said Lonnie. "Whitey, what do you want to tell me a lie like that for?"

"Aint lying," said the keyman, a towheaded boy of about eighteen who was doing time for armed robbery; he was standing outside the end gate of Range C, resting a freckled hand on the bars while they talked. "I aint lying," he repeated because he was. "Didn't I see it myself?"

"You sure?"

"Sure I'm sure."

"You're a liar," said Lonnie, for he did not want to believe it.

The white boy was not offended; but now he had lost interest so he said, to end the conversation, "Oh kiss my ass."

Even as he said it Lonnie's hand shot forward and grabbed the keyman's hand. Whitey grinned as his arm was pulled through the bars.

"I ought to break it for you," said Lonnie. "Go ahead and dare me."

"OK—I dare you."

Lonnie smiled now for the first time and let go of the imprisoned arm. "Bet you think I was scared to. Well you're wrong. It's just that I'm going to need you back on first base pretty soon. Remember last year? We really had us some tough games didn't we?"

The keyman nodded, then squatted down to look at the big clock across the middle of the Hub. "Minute more," he announced.

"Hey, Whitey," Lonnie called as the other started down the stairs. "Did they really put all them Reds in the Hole? No kidding now—did they?"

The keyman paused, his head and shoulders showing above the steel bannister: he looked up and now he was frowning. "Just like I said. But what are you worrying about them for anyway."

The bell rang then and Lonnie had to shout after the disappearing head: "I aint worrying about them and you know it, Whitey. I aint worrying about nothing!"

He said that again to himself as he walked from the gate. I aint worrying about a damn thing.

That was not true, of course, no more than was the keyman's eye-witness report; but each had had to lie to the other. Whitey because a keyman is supposed to know everything that goes on in the jail and Lonnie because he must never admit that he was worried: it would show a lack of self-confidence which is never so precious to a man as when no one else has any hope for him.

Crazy Peterson was fast asleep in Number 11 when Lonnie looked in to say goodnight. His wasted cheek, blue-white with the stubble, was pillowed on praying hands; a thin smile marked his idiot's dream. Lonnie grinned, thinking of the old jailhouse joke of unhooking a sleeping man's bunk chains to spill him to the floor.

And I ought to do it, Carl. I really should. Just look at you—sound asleep already, not a thing to bother you. And look at me—now I'll be awake all night wondering if that guy Paul is really in solitary and won't be there to meet me on sick call. Remember how I told you about him and the other two Reds and you said maybe they could help me? Only a fool like you could think of something like that—and them in jail the same as us. Just like last week you said that my lousy no-good lawyer would finally get around to see me and I was crazy enough to believe you. Waiting every day, hardly sleeping nights . . . OK, Carl, I'm going to believe you this one last time and if Paul isn't there in the morning—well, I—

He frowned, not knowing how to end the thought. He closed the door of Peterson's cell, gently, not to waken the innocent murderer who was his friend, who could only listen to him, understanding nothing except their common sorrow, as guiltless of crime as he was of saying the words of hope with which Lonnie had just now charged him.

Then Lonnie James walked into his cell and quickly closed the steel-barred door. Quickly but not in time, for he knew that another long night had slipped in behind him. Another long night that would wait up with him—waiting for another day of life.

ROBERT CHRISMAN

Black Prisoners, White Law

The first black prisoners in America were the Africans brought to these shores in chains in 1619. Like our brothers in prison today—and like ourselves—those African ancestors were victims of the political, economic and military rapacity of white America. Slave camps, reservations and concentration camps; bars, chains and leg irons; Alcatraz, Cummings and Sing Sing: these are the real monuments of America, more so than Monticello or the

Statue of Liberty. They are monuments of a legal inequity which has its roots in the basic laws of the United States and which still endures.

To justify and protect its oppression of blacks, white America developed an ideology of white supremacy which shaped the American state, its politics and all its interlocking cultural institutions—education, church, law. Apartheid, generally attributed to 20th-century South Africa, was developed as an instrument of oppression by this country in the 1600's and has its basis in the laws themselves, in the Constitution itself.

The function of law is to establish and regulate the political and economic franchise of the citizens within a given state. The Constitution, ironically hailed as a magnificent guarantee of human equality and freedom, deliberately refused franchise to black Americans and Indians and granted it only to white Americans of means. Indeed, black people were defined as a source of white franchise, in the infamous 3⁄5 clause. This clause gave the slaveholder a preponderance of political power by apportioning him 3⁄5 constituency for every slave he possessed, *in addition to his own free white constituency*.

The right of slaves to escape bondage was also forbidden: In Article IV, Section 2, "No person held to service or labor in one State, under the laws thereof, escaping into another, shall in consequence of any law or regulation therein, be discharged from such service or labor, but shall be delivered up on claim of the party to whom such service or labor may be due." Escaped slaves were to be returned to the slaveowner—by national decree.

Designed by agrarian slaveholders and northern industrialists and merchants, the Constitution defined the relationship between their economic interests and their political franchise. Hence its preoccupation with finance and the divisions of power. The Bill of Rights, appended 4 years later, is an afterthought, as a concession to human rights.

Black people were governed by the infamous slave codes, which forbade manumission, voting, education, civil status and personal rights and privileges.

The Constitution was an apartheid document that guaranteed the continuance of slavery and racism as permanent institutions and perpetuated them as cultural realities. Despite the elimination by law of slavery and discrimination, we are still the victims of that racism sanctioned and encouraged by the Constitution.

Black people cannot be protected by American law, for we have no franchise in this country. If anything, we suffer double jeopardy: We have no law of our own and no protection from the law of white America which, by its intention and by the very nature of the cultural values which determined it, is inimical to blackness.

In the literal sense of the word, we are out-laws. We are most subject to arrest—and the most frequent victims of crime. Over 40% of the prison inmates in the State of California are black. More blacks than whites are executed in the United States—and this does not include lynchings, "self-defense" or police killings. From 1930–1969, 2066 black people were executed to 1751 whites. Four hundred and five black men were executed for rape, as compared to 48 whites during the same period. In his article, "Black Ecology" (*The Black Scholar*, April 1970) Nathan Hare points out that "blacks are about four times as likely to fall victim to forcible rape and robbery and about twice as likely to face burglary and aggravated assault."

Being outside the law, black Americans are either victims or else prisoners of a law which is neither enforced nor designed for us—except with repressive intent. For example, gun control legislation was enacted by the United States only after black people began buying guns and endorsing the principle of self defense, which is a qualitatively different inspiration than the assassination of individuals such as John F. Kennedy and Malcolm X.

Furthermore, black leaders who address themselves to the fundamental question—that black Americans must have full political and economic franchise—are arrested or harassed. To list just a few black leaders who have been or are political prisoners: W. E. B. Du Bois, Marcus Garvey, Malcolm X, the Honorable Elijah Muhammad, Martin Luther King, as well as some of the currently embattled brothers and sisters: Rap Brown, Bobby Seale, Angela Davis, Ahmed Evans, Ericka Huggins, the Soledad brothers and Cleveland Sellers. The demand for black equality in America exposes its most basic contradiction: that as a democracy it cannot endure or allow the full liberation of its black citizens.

All black prisoners, therefore, are political prisoners, for their condition derives from the political inequity of black people in America. A black prisoner's crime may or may not have been a political action against the state, but the state's action against him is always political. This knowledge, intuitively known and sometimes transcribed into political terms, exists within every black prisoner.

For we must understand that the black offender is not tried and judged by the black community itself, but by the machinery of the white community, which is least affected by his actions and whose interests are served by the systematic subjugation of all black people. Thus the trial or conviction of a black prisoner, *regardless of his offense, his guilt or his innocence*, cannot be a democratic judgment of him by his peers, but a political action against him by his oppressors.

Grand juries, the state and federal judges of the Circuit Courts, Superior Courts and Supreme Courts, are appointed, not elected. This fact alone prejudices a fair trial and precludes black representation, for black people do not have a single official in this country who has the power to appoint a judge or grand jury to the bench. Furthermore, because of the appointive nature of most judgeships, judges have no direct responsibility to the persons they try, through recall or election. Nor do trial juries always reflect the racial and economic compositions of the populations which they represent. If a city has a

40% black population it should have the same percentage on its juries, in its legal staff and in its judges.

It is of course obvious that mugging, theft, pimping and shooting dope are not themselves political actions, particularly when the victims are most often other black people. To maintain that all black offenders are by their actions politically correct is a dangerous romanticism. Black anti-social behavior must be seen in and of its own terms and be corrected for the enhancement of the black community. But it must be understood that the majority of black offenses have their roots in the political and economic deprivation of black Americans by the Euro-American state and that these are the primary causes and conditions of black crime. The individual offender and his black community must achieve this primary understanding and unite for our mutual protection and self-determination.

Thus the matter of black prisoners and white law involves the basic question of self-determination for all black people. Black people must determine when a black person has violated the black community, and that black community must take the corrective action. As we drive for new economic and cultural institutions, we must also create new legal institutions that will accurately reflect the judgment, the social fabric, the conditions of the black community. As it stands now, only the white American community determines when a black person has offended the black community, and this is a colonial imposition and a political injustice.

Most important, the black community outside of bars must never divorce itself from the black community within bars. Freedom is a false illusion in this society; prison is a reality. Black prisoners must be supported by the black community during their incarceration and after they are released.

For the black prisoner is the most vulnerable member of our community—in a naked way he is directly at the mercy of the white power structure. It is also apparent that the black prisoner is one of the most valuable members of our community, as well—the organization, the discipline, the fraternity that black prisoners have developed within prison to survive must be developed by us outside the prison if we are to survive.

We must employ all means necessary to protect and support black people within prison walls. We are all prisoners, and our unwavering task must be the achievement of organization, unity and total liberation.

JOHN EDGAR WIDEMAN

Brothers and Keepers

I heard the news first in a phone call from my mother. My youngest brother, Robby, and two of his friends had killed a man during a holdup. Robby was a fugitive, wanted for armed robbery and murder. The police were hunting him, and his crime had given the cops license to kill. The distance I'd put between my brother's world and mine suddenly collapsed. The two thousand miles between Laramie, Wyoming, and Pittsburgh, Pennsylvania, my years of willed ignorance, of flight and hiding, had not changed a simple truth: I could never run fast enough or far enough. Robby was inside me. Wherever he was, running for his life, he carried part of me with him.

Nearly three months would pass between the day in November 1975 when I learned of my brother's crime and the February afternoon he appeared in Laramie. During that period no one in the family knew Robby's whereabouts. After the initial reaction of shock and disbelief subsided, people in Pittsburgh had settled into the inevitability of a long, tense wait. Prayers were said. As word passed along the network of family and friends, my people, who had long experience of waiting and praying, braced themselves for the next blow. A special watch was set upon those, like my mother, who would be hardest hit. The best was hoped for, but the worst was expected; and no one could claim to know what the best might be. No news was good news. No news meant Robby hadn't been apprehended, that whatever else he'd lost, he still was free. But knowing nothing had its dark side, created a concern that sometimes caused my mother, in spite of herself, to pray for Robby's capture. Prison seemed safer than the streets. As long as he was free, there was a chance Robby could hurt someone or be killed. For my mother and the others who loved them, the price of my brother's freedom was a constant, gnawing fear that anytime the phone rang or a bulletin flashed across the TV screen, the villain, the victim might be Robert Wideman.

Because I was living in Laramie, Wyoming, I could shake loose from the sense of urgency, of impending disaster dogging my people in Pittsburgh. Never a question of forgetting Robby, more a matter of how I remembered him that distinguished my feelings from theirs. Sudden flashes of fear, rage, and remorse could spoil a class or a party, cause me to retreat into silence, lose whole days to gloominess and distance. But I had the luxury of dealing intermittently with my pain. As winter deepened and snow filled the mountains, I experienced a comforting certainty. The worst wouldn't happen. Robby wouldn't be cut down in a wild cops-and-robbers shootout, because I knew he was on his way to find me. Somehow, in spite of everything, we were going to get together. I was waiting for him to arrive. I knew he would. And this certainty guaranteed his safety.

Perhaps it was wishful thinking, a whistling away of the miles and years of silence between us, but I never doubted a reunion would occur.

On a Sunday early in February, huge, wet flakes of snow were falling continuously past the windows of the house on Harney Street—the kind of snow not driven by wolf winds howling in from the north, but soft, quiet, relentless snow, spring snow almost benign in the unhurried way it buried the town. The scale of the storm, the immense quantities of snow it dumped minute after minute, forced me to remember that Laramie was just one more skimpy circle of wagons huddling against the wilderness. I had closed the curtains to shut out that snow which seemed as if it might never stop.

That Sunday I wrote to my brother. Not a letter exactly. I seldom wrote letters and had no intentions of sticking what I was scribbling in an envelope. Mailing it was impossible anyway, since I had no idea where my brother might be. Really it was more a conversation than a letter. I needed to talk to someone, and that Sunday Robby seemed the perfect someone.

So I talked to him about what I'd learned since coming west. Filled him in on the news. Shared everything from the metaphysics of the weather to the frightening circumstances surrounding the premature birth of Jamila, our new daughter. I explained how winter's outrageous harshness is less difficult to endure than its length. How after a tease of warm, springlike weather in late April the sight of a snowflake in May is enough to make a grown man cry. How Laramie old-timers brag about having seen snow fall every month of the year. How I'd almost killed my whole family on Interstate 80 near the summit of the Laramie range, at the beginning of our annual summer migration east to Maine, when I lost control of the Oldsmobile Custom Cruiser and it did a 360 on the icy road in the middle of June.

The letter rambled on and on for pages. Like good talk, it digressed and recycled itself and switched moods precipitously. Inevitably, one subject was home and family. After all, I was speaking to my brother. Whatever the new news happened to be, there was the old news, the deep roots of shared time and place and blood. When I touched on home, the distance between us melted. I could sense Robby's presence, just over my shoulder, a sensation so real I was sure I could have reached out and touched him if I had lifted my eyes from the page and swiveled my chair.

Writing that Sunday, I had no reason to believe my brother was on his way to Laramie. No one had heard from him in months. Yet he was on his way and I knew it. Two men, hundreds of miles apart, communicating through some mysterious process neither understood but both employed for a few minutes one Sunday afternoon as efficiently, effectively as dolphins talking underwater with the beeps and echoes of their sonar. Except that the medium into which we launched our signals was thin air. Thin, high mountain air spangled with wet snowflakes.

I can't explain how or why it happened. Robby was in the study with me, He felt close because he was close, part of him outrunning the stolen car, outrunning the storm dogging him and his partners as they fled from Salt Lake City toward Laramie.

Reach out and touch. That's what the old songs could do. I'd begun that Sunday by reading a week-old *New York Times*. One of the beauties of living in Laramie. No point in frantically striving to keep abreast of the *Times*. The race was over before the paper arrived in town, Thursday after the Sunday it was published. The *Times* was stale news, all its urgency vitiated by the fact that I could miss it when it was fresh and the essential outline of my world, my retreat into willed ignorance and a private, leisurely pace would continue unchanged.

Five minutes of the paper had been enough; then I repacked the sections into their plastic sheath, let its weight pull it off the couch onto the rug. Reach out and touch. Sam Cooke and the Soul Stirrers, the Harmonizing Four, James Cleveland, the Davis Sisters, the Swan Silvertones. I dug out my favorite albums and lined them up against the stereo cabinet. A cut or two from each one would be my Sunday morning service. Deejaying the songs got me off my backside, forced me out of the chair where I'd been sitting staring at the ceiling. With good gospel tunes rocking the house I could open the curtains and face the snow. The sky was blue. Shafts of sunlight filtered through a deluge of white flakes. Snow, sunshine, blue sky, not a ripple of wind deflecting the heavy snow from its straight, downward path. An unlikely conjunction of elements perfectly harmonized. Like the pain and hope, despair and celebration of the black gospel music. Like the tiny body of the baby girl in her isolette, the minuscule, premature, two-pound-fourteen-ounce bundle of bone and sinew and nerve and will that had fought and continued to fight so desperately to live.

The songs had stirred me, flooded me with memories and sensations to the point of bursting. I had to talk to someone. Not anyone close, not anyone who had been living through what I'd been experiencing the past three years in the West. A stranger's ear would be better than a friend's, a stranger who wouldn't interrupt with questions, with alternate versions of events. I needed to do most of the talking. I wanted a listener, an intimate stranger, and summoned up Robby; and he joined me. I wrote something like a letter to wherever my brother might be, to whomever Robby had become.

Wrote the letter and of course never sent it, but got an answer anyway in just two days, the following Tuesday toward the end of the afternoon. I can pinpoint the hour because I was fixing a drink. Cocktail time is as much a state of mind as a particular hour, but during the week five o'clock is when

I usually pour a stiff drink for myself and one for my lady if she's in the mood. At five on Tuesday, February 11, Robby phoned from a bowling alley down the street and around the corner to say he was in town.

Hey, Big Bruh.

Hey. How you doing? Where the hell are you?

We're in town. At some bowling alley. Me and Michael Dukes and Johnny-Boy.

In Laramie?

Yeah. Think that's where we's at, anyway. In a bowling alley. Them nuts is bowling. Got to get them crazy dudes out here before they tear the man's place up.

Well, youall c'mon over here. Which bowling alley is it?

Just a bowling alley. Got some Chinese restaurant beside it.

Laramie Lanes. It's close to here. I can be there in a minute to get you.

Okay. That's cool. We be in the car outside. Old raggedy-ass Oldsmobile got Utah plates. Hey, man. Is this gon be alright?

What do you mean?

You know. Coming by your house and all. I know you heard about the mess.

Mom called and told me. I've been waiting for you to show up. Something told me you were close. You wait. I'll be right there.

In Pittsburgh, Pennsylvania, on November 15, 1975, approximately three months before arriving in Laramie, my youngest brother Robert (whom I had named), together with Michael Dukes and Cecil Rice, had robbed a fence. A rented truck allegedly loaded with brand-new Sony color TVs was the bait in a scam designed to catch the fence with a drawer full of money. The plan had seemed simple and foolproof. Dishonor among thieves. A closed circle, crooks stealing from crooks, with the law necessarily excluded. Except a man was killed. Dukes blew him away when the man reached for a gun Dukes believed he concealed inside his jacket.

Stop. Stop, you stupid motherfucker.

But the fence broke and ran and kept running deaf and dumb to everything except the pounding of his heart, the burning in his lungs, as he dashed crouching like a halfback the fifty feet from the empty rental truck to an office at one corner of his used-car lot. He'd heard the gun pop and pop again as he stumbled and scrambled to his feet but he kept running, tearing open the fatal shoulder wound he wasn't even aware of yet. Kept running and kept pumping blood and pumping his arms and legs past the plate-glass windows of the office, past a boundary of plastic banners strung above one edge of the lot, out into the street, into traffic, waving his arms to get someone to stop. He made it two blocks up Greys Pond Road, dripping a trail of blood, staggering, stumbling, weaving up the median strip between four lanes of cars. No one wanted anything to do with a guy drunk or crazy enough to be playing in the middle of a busy highway. Only when he pitched face first and lay crumpled on the curb did a motorist pull over and come to his aid.

Meanwhile, at the rear of the rental truck, a handful of money, coins, and wadded bills the dying man had flung down before he ran, lay on the asphalt between two groups of angry, frightened men. Black men. White men. No one in control. That little handful of chump change on the ground, not enough to buy two new Sonys at K Mart, a measure of the fence's deception, proof of the game he intended to run on the black men, just as they'd planned their trick for him. There had to be more money somewhere, and somebody would have to pay for this mess, this bloody double double-cross; and the men stared across the money at each other too choked with rage and fear to speak.

By Tuesday when Robby called, the chinook wind that had melted Sunday's snow no longer warmed and softened the air. "Chinook" means "snow-eater," and in the high plains country—Laramie sits on a plateau seven thousand feet above sea level—wind and sun can gobble up a foot of fresh snow from the ground in a matter of hours. The chinook had brought spring for a day, but just as rapidly as it appeared, the mellow wind had swept away, drawing in its wake arctic breezes and thick low-lying clouds. The clouds which had darkened the sky above the row of tacky, temporary-looking storefronts at the dying end of Third Street where Laramie Lanes hunkered.

Hey, Big Bruh.

Years since we'd spoken on the phone, but I had recognized Robby's voice immediately. He'd been with me when I was writing Sunday, so my brother's voice was both a shock and no surprise at all.

Big Brother was not something Robby usually called me. But he'd chimed the words as if they went way back, as if they were a touchstone, a talisman, a tongue-in-cheek greeting we'd been exchanging for ages. The way Robby said "Big Bruh" didn't sound phony, but it didn't strike me as natural either. What I'd felt was regret, an instant, devastating sadness because the greeting possessed no magic. If there'd ever been a special language we shared, I'd forgotten it. Robby had been pretending. Making up a magic formula on the spot. *Big Bruh.* But that had been okay. I was grateful. Anything was better than dwelling on the sadness, the absence, better than allowing the distance between us to stretch further. . . .

On the way to the bowling alley I began to ask questions I hadn't considered till the phone rang. I tried to anticipate what I'd see outside Laramie Lanes. Would I recognize anyone? Would they look like killers? What had caused them to kill? If they were killers, were they dangerous? Had crime changed my brother into someone I shouldn't bring near my house? I recalled Robby and his friends playing records, loud talking, giggling and signifying in the living room of the house on Marchand Street in Pittsburgh. Rob's buddies had names like Poochie, Dulamite, Hanky, and Bubba. Just kids messing around, but already secretive, suspicious of strangers. And I had been a stranger, a student, foreign to the rhythms of their lives, their talk as I sat, home from college, in the kitchen talking to Robby's mother. I'd have to yell into the living room sometimes. Ask them to keep the noise down so I could hear myself think. If I walked through the room, they'd fall suddenly silent. Squirm and look at each other and avoid my eyes. Stare at their own hands and feet mute as little speak-no-evil monkeys. Any question might get at best a nod or grunt in reply. If five or six kids were hanging out in the little living room they made it seem dark. *Do wop, do wop* forty-fives on the record player, the boys' silence and lowered eyes conjuring up night no matter what time of the day I passed through the room.

My father had called them thugs. Robby and his little thugs. The same word he'd used for me and my cut buddies when we were coming up, loafing around the house on Copeland Street, into playing records and bullshucking about girls, and saying nothing to nobody not part of our gang. Calling Rob's friends thugs was my father's private joke. Thugs not because they were incipient criminals or particularly bad kids, but because in their hip walks and stylized speech and caps pulled down on their foreheads they were declaring themselves on the lam, underground, in flight from the daylight world of nice, respectable adults.

My father liked to read the Sunday funnies. In the "Nancy" comic strip was a character named Sluggo, and I believe that's who my father had in mind when he called them thugs. That self-proclaimed little tough guy, snub-nosed, bristle-haired, knuckleheaded Sluggo. Funny, because like Sluggo they were dead serious about the role they were playing. Dead serious and fooling nobody. So my father had relegated them to the funny papers.

Road grime caked the windows of the battered sedan parked outside the bowling alley. I couldn't tell if anyone was inside. I let my motor run, talked to the ghost of my brother the way I'd talked that Sunday, waiting for a flesh-and-blood version to appear.

Robby was a fugitive. My little brother was wanted for murder. For three months Robby had been running and hiding from the police. Now he was in Laramie, on my doorstep. Robbery. Murder. Flight. I had pushed them out of my mind. I hadn't allowed myself to dwell on my brother's predicament. I had been angry, hurt and afraid, but I'd had plenty of practice cutting myself off from those sorts of feelings. Denying disruptive emotions was a survival mechanism I'd been forced to learn early in life. Robby's troubles could drive me crazy if I let them. It had been better to keep my feelings at a distance. Let the miles and years protect me. Robby was my brother, but that was once upon a time, in another country. My life was relatively comfortable, pleasant, safe. I'd come west to escape the demons Robby personified. I didn't need outlaw brothers reminding me how much had been lost, how much compromised, how terribly the world still raged beyond the charmed circle of my life on the Laramie plains.

In my Volvo, peering across the street, searching for a sign of life in the filthy car or the doorway of Laramie Lanes, pieces of my life rushed at me, as fleeting, as unpredictable as the clusters of cloud scudding across the darkening sky.

Rob. Hey, Rob. Do you remember the time we were living on the third floor of Grandma's house on Copeland Street and we were playing and Daddy came scooting in from behind the curtain where he and Mommy slept, dropping a trail of farts, blip, blip, blip, and flew out the door and down the steps faster than anybody'd ever made it before? I don't know what he was doing or what we were doing before he came farting through the room, but I do remember the stunned silence afterward, the five of us kids looking at one another like we'd seen the Lone Ranger and wondering what the hell was that. Was that really Daddy? Were those sounds actually blipping farts from the actual behind of our actual father? Well, we sat on the floor, staring at each other, a couple seconds; then Tish laughed or I laughed. Somebody had to start it. A choked-back, closed-mouth, almost-swallowed, one-syllable laugh. And then another and another. As irresistible then as the farts blipping in a train from Daddy's pursed behind. The first laugh sneaks out then it's all hell bursting loose, it's one pop after another, and mize well let it all hang out. We crack up and start to dance. Each one of us takes a turn being Edgar Wideman, big daddy, scooting like he did across the floor, fast but sneakylike till the first blip escapes and blows him into overdrive. Blip. Blap. Bippidy-bip. And every change and permutation of fart we can manufacture with our mouths, or our wet lips on the back of our hands, or a hand cupped in armpit with elbow pumping. A Babel of squeaky farts and bass farts and treble and juicy and atom-bomb and trip-hammer, machine-gun, suede, firecracker, slithery, bubble-gum-cracking, knuckle-popping, gone-with-the-wind menagerie of every kind of fart we can imagine. Till Mommy pokes her head from behind the curtain and says, That's enough youall. But she can't help grinning her ownself cause she had to hear it too. Daddy trailing that wedding-car tin-can tail of farts and skidding down the steps to the bathroom on the second floor where he slammed the door behind himself before the door on the third floor had time to swing shut. Mom's smiling so we sputter one last fusillade and grin and giggle at each other one more time while she says again, That's enough now, that's enough youall.

Robby crossed Third Street alone, leaving his friends behind in the muddy car. I remember how glad I was to see him. How ordinary it seemed to be meeting him in this place he'd never been before. Here was my brother miraculously appearing from God-knows-where, a slim, bedraggled figure, looking very much like a man who's been on the road for days, nothing like an outlaw or killer, my brother striding across the street to greet me. What was alien, unreal was not the man but the town, the circumstances that had brought him to this juncture. By the time Robby had reached my car and leaned down smiling into the open window, Laramie, robbery, murder, flight, my litany of misgivings had all disappeared.

Rob rode with me from the bowling alley to the Harney Street house. Dukes and Johnny-Boy followed in the Olds. Rob told me Cecil Rice had split back to Pittsburgh to face the music. Johnny-Boy was somebody Robby and Mike had picked up in Utah.

Robby and his two companions stayed overnight. There was eating, drinking, a lot of talk. Next day I taught my classes at the university and before I returned home in the afternoon, Robby and his crew had headed for Denver. My brother's last free night was spent in Laramie, Wyoming. February 11, 1976, the day following their visit, Robby, Mike, and Johnny were arrested in Fort Collins, Colorado. The Oldsmobile they'd been driving had stolen plates. Car they'd borrowed in Utah turned out to be stolen too, bringing the FBI into the case because the vehicle and plates had been transported across state lines. The Colorado cops didn't know the size of the fish in their net until they checked the FBI wire and suddenly realized they had some "bad dudes" in their lockup. "Niggers wanted for Murder One back East" was how one detective described the captives to a group of curious bystanders later, when Robby and Michael were being led, manacled, draped with chains, through the gleaming corridor of a Colorado courthouse.

I can recall only a few details about Robby's last night of freedom. Kentucky Fried Chicken for dinner. Nobody as hungry as I thought they should be. Michael narrating a tale about a basketball scholarship he won to NYU, his homesickness, his ambivalence about the Apple, a coach he didn't like whose name he couldn't remember.

Johnny-Boy wasn't from Pittsburgh. Small, dark, greasy, he was an outsider who knew he didn't fit, ill at ease in a middle-class house, the meandering conversations that had nothing to do with anyplace he'd been, anything he understood or cared to learn. Johnny-Boy had trouble talking, trouble staying awake. When he spoke at all, he stuttered riffs of barely comprehensible ghetto slang. While the rest of us were talking, he'd nod off. I didn't like the way his heavy-lidded, bubble eyes blinked open and searched the room when he thought no one was watching him. Perhaps sleeping with one eye open was a habit forced upon him by the violent circumstances of his life, but what I saw when he peered from "sleep," taking the measure of his surroundings, of my wife, my kids, me, were a stranger's eyes, a stranger's eyes with nothing in them I could trust.

I should have understood why the evening was fragmentary, why I have difficulty recalling it now. Why Mike's story was full of inconsistencies, nearly incoherent. Why Robby was shakier than I'd ever seen him. Why he was tense, weary, confused about what his next move should be. I'm tired, man, he kept saying. I'm tired. . . . You don't know what it's like, man. Running . . . running. Never no peace. Certain signs were clear at the time but they passed right by me. I thought I was giving my guests a few hours' rest from danger, but they knew I was turning my house into a dangerous place. I believed I was providing a respite from pursuit. They knew they were leaving a trail, complicating the chase by stopping with me and my family. A few "safe" hours in my house weren't long enough to come down from the booze, dope, and adrenaline high that fueled their flight. At any moment my front door could be smashed down. A gunfire fight begin. I thought they had stopped, but they were still on the road. I hadn't begun to explore the depths of my naïveté, my bewilderment.

Only after two Laramie Police Department detectives arrived at dawn on February 12, a day too late to catch my brother, and treated me like a criminal, did I know I'd been one. Aiding and abetting a fugitive. Accessory after the fact to the crime of first-degree murder. The detectives hauled me down to the station. Demanded that I produce an alibi for the night a convenience store had been robbed in Utah. Four black men had been involved. Three had been tentatively identified, which left one unaccounted for. I was black. My brother was a suspect. So perhaps I was the fourth perpetrator. No matter that I lived four hundred miles from the scene of the crime. No matter that I wrote books and taught literature and creative writing at the university. I was black. Robby was my brother. Those unalterable facts would always incriminate me.

NATHAN McCALL

Makes Me Wanna Holler

JIM

Two years into my prison stint, Liz had started writing me again, and we talked about the possibility of getting back together. I was also starting to have trouble with my Christian fellowship group. There were too many weirdos joining up to seek protection from the wolves, and it was becoming hard to talk with the Christians about all the things I was learning and thinking about. My mental and spiritual regimen had begun to make me feel whole for the first time in my life, and I wasn't about to give that up just to please some jackleg, wanna-be preachers.

Maybe that's why I started to listen to a guy named Jim, who was the most respected inmate at Southampton. A Richmond native in his mid-thirties, Jim was on the tail end of a life sentence for murder; he'd done close to fifteen years in the joint. He was admired partly because of the way he'd handled his time, but mostly because of his integrity and broad intellect. Unlike so many other dudes, who became mentally passive after years in prison, Jim had somehow remained a freethinker who'd stayed focused on the world beyond that fence. Using his prison time to educate himself, he'd evolved into a self-assured, articulate brother with an unyielding commitment to what he called "black folks' struggle." Administrators were so impressed with his intelligence that they allowed him to teach inmates at the institution's school.

I'd seen him around the yard a lot, but for a long time kept my distance. Jim hated the white man, and I was trying to internalize Christian love. By the summer of '77, I'd begun to fast once weekly, spending those days mostly in my room, praying, thinking, and reading everything from poetry to philosophy to books about nutrition. I read Pearl Buck's novels and Hermann Hesse and *The Prophet*, by Kahlil Gibran. I found myself drawn to the novels of Chaim Potok, including *My Name Is Asher Lev*, a book about a young artist that gave me insight into Jewish culture and whetted my curiosity about art, especially Picasso. I'd never known art could be used so powerfully to make social and political statements.

I experimented with a memory technique and learned how to recall up to one hundred numbers, words, and names in sequential order. There were times I got so deep into reading and fasting that I felt I'd transcended the constraints of prison. In those moments, it seemed not to matter whether I stayed behind bars another year or an eternity.

With all this going on inside me, I think that's why I became more curious about what Jim had to say. Some evenings, he held court on the yard, and guys gathered around and listened to him preach about the white man's evil ways. Eventually, I went with one of my homeboys to check him out. Jim's message reminded me of what I had heard from Chicago, the black revolutionary I'd met in the Norfolk jail, and much of it was similar to the teachings of Malcolm X and the Muslims: "Don't you know white men are the most lying creatures on the face of the earth? They don't care nothing about the truth. They use falsehood to gain dominance over people and they use trickery to maintain that dominance. They run a game on black folks by trying to get them to think bad things about themselves that aren't true and believe good things about white people that are outright lies. Think about it! White folks claim we're lazy and don't wanna work. Our people worked for crackers for two hundred years—for *free*, man!—because white folks were too lazy to work for themselves! Our women cooked, cleaned their houses, and raised their children because whites were too trifling to do their own work, yet they gonna call us lazy?! If you look around today, black folks still do most of the work that whitey don't wanna do!

"Check this out. White folks claim we constantly have illegitimate babies and abandon them. During slavery, they raped black women and fathered more illegitimate children than we can count! Why you think they're so many coffee-brown and light-skinned black folks like me and you? That's because we come from all those children that white men fathered and abandoned, man! And they try to pretend that it's *us* that's got a thing for white women. White men *live* for the day to get a piece a' black meat. Think about it, brother!

"I don't care what we produce or invent, white folks don't want to acknowledge its worth unless they can steal it and take credit for it themselves. Look at all the things black folks invented and had stolen from them! Look at how whites worship Elvis Presley. Black folks been singing soul music for years, and whites wouldn't give them their due, then along comes Elvis, imitating black soul, and they treat him like he's God."

Everything Jim said seemed to have the ring of truth. After he'd finished, I chatted with him and we hit it off real well. When he learned I was a Christian, he challenged me to rethink my commitment to "the white man's religion." He said white folks loved for blacks to embrace Christianity because they use it to control us. He said whites encouraged us to follow Martin Luther King, Jr., because he was a passive Christian, and they urged us to reject Malcolm X because he challenged us to stand up against white oppression.

"If Christianity is such an effective religion, then why hasn't it helped white people become more humane? Most of the white people in this country are Christians and still they're the most hateful, ruthless group of people on the face of the earth. Open your eyes, man! Black Christians are no better. They believe they ain't righteous unless they suffer like Jesus suffered. Christianity got black people thinking we got to be crucified in this life in order to get peace in the next one. I want what's coming to me in *this* life, here and now, man!

"White Christians are also imperialists. Check anywhere in the world and you will find that where there are white people, there is Christianity and there are missionaries. They send the Christian missionaries in first to preach turn-the-other-cheek, then they come with their armies and conquer the people."

I began to see what he was talking about. Books I found in the library told me that whites in South Africa, Britain, France, Portugal, and Spain, not to mention America, had oppressed people of color whenever they encountered them. Practically every place I could identify where there were whites, people of color were suffering at their hands.

Jim was right about something else, too. The prison administration was very supportive of our Christian fellowship group. They knew Christian inmates were the most easily controlled. They made sure they provided space for our activities, often suspending rules to accommodate us. At the same time, the Muslims, who were considered more radical, complained that the administration was less supportive of them. The control issue sealed my split with Christianity. I wanted no part of anything used by white people to control blacks.

In his talks, Jim also focused a lot on history. He said it was important to understand the past because it shapes our present perceptions about ourselves and the rest of the world. He said white people think they're better than everybody else because they are taught a history of distorted facts that always present whites in a positive, superior light. "Think about it, man. They teach you that the white settlers who came over here were heroes, and we celebrate Thanksgiving to commemorate their heroism. But check this out: When the settlers were starving, the Indians helped feed them. The Indians helped them survive through the winter. The settlers repaid them by killing them off and taking their land. Now you tell me, were the white settlers heroes or fucking barbarians?"

I thought about all the lies and the indoctrination I had absorbed all through school. Every year, teachers drilled into our heads myths about the heroic white pioneers who sailed from England and settled Jamestown, Virginia. Relics of that settlement have been preserved through the years to support the myths. I remembered that my fourth- and fifth-grade classes took field trips to the Jamestown settlement, which is about a forty-minute drive from Portsmouth, and visited replicas of the tiny ships the whites rode here. When I was young, I accepted my teachers' version of stories about Jamestown, and everything else I was taught, because there was no reason to question it. I figured that if it was contained in schoolbooks, then it must be true.

Throughout school, except during Black History Week, we were taught more about everybody else than about ourselves. I'll never forget that one of my junior high school history teachers made us memorize all the dynasties of the Chinese empire, from start to finish, in chronological order. Yet the story of Africans brought here as slaves was summed up in our history books in a few short paragraphs, almost as a footnote. On some level, that communicated the message that we were less important than everyone else. I wondered how my black teachers could permit such a thing. I understand now that they taught what was approved for the school system, and that while schools had been integrated for blacks and whites, administrators had still failed to integrate the information passed along to us.

In my reading, I also learned that we'd been grossly misled in school about the Indians. Our textbooks always portrayed Native Americans as primitive heathens who threatened to obstruct the settlers' noble mission. That version of history was promoted by TV westerns that showed "brave" cowboys battling "savage" Indians who attacked them for no apparent reason. When I was young, I thought those Indians were crazy, with their feathered headdresses and painted faces, riding horses and yelling like they had lost their minds. When I learned that those Indians were actually fighting to protect what was rightfully theirs—that *they* were the true heroes and that the settlers were the savages, like Jim said—it made me furious to know that whites so arrogantly distorted the truth.

I reflected on those and other myths that may have influenced my thinking as a child, and I realized that Malcolm X, Chicago, Jim, and so many other cats were right: Black people had been systematically brainwashed, and our parents had paid their tax dollars for the schools, biased textbooks, and curriculums that helped carry that out. Without realizing it, we'd been taught to hate ourselves and love white people, and it was causing us to self-destruct.

Jim and I started exchanging books and talking regularly about the effect of historical myths on blacks. We met on the yard most evenings after chow and talked with other guys who also did a lot of reading. In that group, I met some of the sharpest, most intelligent guys I've known, then or since. Most of them were dropouts who had long before lost interest in formal schooling. But once they got a whiff of some real knowledge—knowledge that was relevant to *them*—they educated themselves far better than any public school could have hoped to do.

We formed our own writers' guild, discussed world affairs and politics, and talked about what we intended to do when we got out. Those were the deepest discussions I'd ever had. We debated theories of the major philosophers: Spinoza, Kant, Hegel, Kierkegaard, and Sartre, among others. We dissected dualism, pantheism, and existentialism, and discussed questions such as: How can you appreciate good until you've known evil? Does essence precede existence, or does existence precede essence? Sometimes, during those conversations, I was struck by the strangeness of former robbers, drug dealers, and murderers standing in the middle of a prison yard, debating the heaviest philosophical questions of all time.

Jim, who also worked constantly to improve his vocabulary, taught me to play the word game Scrabble. He'd memorized many of the two-, three-, and four-letter words in the dictionary to help him score high points. We were often joined in fierce matches by Lee Hargrave, the serial murderer who worked with me in the library. One day, after Hargrave had won a game and left the room, Jim said, "Hey, man, we can't let this white boy beat us on the Scrabble board."

Initially, I didn't get it. "What's the problem?"

"Don't you know this cracker thinks he's smarter than us because he's white and we're black? Can't you tell that? He's always trying to bluff us with medical words he thinks we don't know."

I knew what Jim meant. I got that same feeling when I played whites at chess. I got the feeling that white boys automatically assumed they could beat me on the board because chess was a thinking person's game. I was black and they were white, and therefore they were better thinkers. They never came out and said it, but I could tell by their confident body language and their smug analyses of moves made during games that they assumed they were superior. That's why, whenever I played whites at chess, the fun went completely out of the game. It was war disguised as a game. Every nerve in my body stood on end and my mind focused sharply on every piece on the board; I was like a boxer, eyeing an opponent's every feint and move, ready to use sharply honed reflexes to make him pay dearly for the slightest mistake.

I suspected Hargrave thought he was smarter than everybody at Southampton. He had an elitist air about him. Even after being at Southampton more than a year, he still rarely spoke to more than a few select people and still refused to eat in the cafeteria. While everybody else read *Ebony*, *Jet*, *Time*, *Newsweek*, and other mass-circulation periodicals in the library, Hargrave subscribed to his own—*Town and Country* magazine. Curious, I borrowed an issue from him once and leafed through it. It carried stories and pictures about rich white people who spent their time horseback riding, foxhunting, and managing their stables and shit.

Whenever Hargrave's parents came to visit him, his father wore a business suit and tie and his mother wore a dress. Out of place in the visiting room with all those working-class black people, they looked stiff and formal, like Beaver Cleaver's parents on TV. Every time I went into the visiting room, his parents made it a point to come over to my table to say an artificial hello to my family and me. I sensed they were unaccustomed to interacting with black people, yet they were trying to encourage me to cultivate a relationship with their son. They were well aware that he was in constant danger because of his crimes against elderly people, and I suspected they viewed me as somebody who could help protect him if the need arose. But I wasn't about to let them use me. I knew that if those rich white people passed me on the streets, they would probably roll up their car windows and lock their doors.

After Jim pulled my coat to Hargrave, we came up with a way to cheat him "like white folks cheat us." Jim, who was a great defensive Scrabble player, made sure he sat in front of Hargrave to prevent him from getting openings to score high points. Whenever Hargrave took the lead, Jim and I secretly fed each other key letters to make sure one of us won the game.

Hargrave never won a game after that. I don't know if he caught on, but it didn't matter. No one else in our building played Scrabble. He loved the game, so he *had* to play with us, or not play at all.

In a way, Jim was also similar to Mo Battle, my mentor in the Norfolk jail. When he saw young guys with potential come out of the Receiving Unit, he'd take the time to school them about anything he could. He'd pull them aside and tell them the dos and don'ts of prison life so the wolves couldn't get to them. The wolves resented Jim because of that, but none made a move to do anything about it.

It amazed me to see how much the so-called tough cats respected Jim. Whenever he was around, they cursed less and toned down their macho posturing, as if he were an authority figure or a revered elder. Initially, that kind of deference, which bordered on fear, puzzled me, because Jim didn't carry himself like a knockout artist or anything. Brown-skinned and medium-built, he always dressed neat and spoke softly. He was clean-shaven, and he constantly carried books and newspapers tucked under his arms.

Eventually, I figured out that the characteristics that made him so widely respected had little to do with how he looked; instead, it was his manly demeanor. Ever since I could recall, I and everybody else I knew had associated manhood with physical dominance and conquest of someone else. Watching Jim, I realized we'd gone about it all wrong. Jim didn't have to make a rep for himself as a thumper. He could whip a man with his sharp mind and choice words far more thoroughly than with his fists. The wolves feared his kind of ass-whipping much more than a physical beating, so they kept their distance.

I decided that this was the kind of respect I wanted to command, and I noticed other guys who without being fully aware wanted to be like Jim, too. They strutted on the yard, looking super-macho, like killers, but acted differently in private. In those moments when they weren't profiling with their buddies, some of my tough-acting homies would stop by my perch on the yard or in my cell ask, "What you reading?" I sensed they wanted to improve themselves but didn't want their other homies to see them, because self-improvement wasn't a macho thing. Pearly Blue was one of them. He sometimes tried to draw me into deep private discussions about God and reality while sticking to the tough street vernacular that helped him maintain his macho facade.

As I learned more about our misguided ideas about manhood, I experimented with some of those macho dudes: Whenever I passed them, I looked into their eyes to see what was there. A few had that cold-blooded, killer look about them, but in the eyes of most of them I saw something I hadn't noticed before: fear.

Even in Big Earl. Big Earl was one of the brawniest, most outwardly fearless cats in the place. He was tall and jet-black, his muscles rippled through his T-shirt, and his thighs were so massive that all his pants fit too tight. Big Earl, who was thirtyish, was from a small, off-brand town in rural Virginia, but he didn't need homies to back him up. He walked around the yard, talking loud and intimidating other inmates like he owned the place.

One day, while walking down the long sidewalk on my way to the cafeteria, I spotted Big Earl pimping toward me. (He never said anything to me, Jim, or some of the others who were part of our progressive group.) As he approached, I fixed my eyes on his and kept them locked there. When we got closer, I kept my eyes fastened to his, not in a hostile gaze, but in an expression of serene self-assurance. Initially, he tried to meet my gaze. Then he turned his eyes away and looked toward the ground. I smiled to myself. I would have never been able to back down Big Earl in a rumble, but I had certainly backed him down with my mind.

Several times after that brief, silent encounter, I caught Big Earl watching me curiously. He never said anything. He just watched and turned away whenever he realized I'd caught him staring. I sensed he knew I'd figured that he wasn't as confident of his manhood as he pretended to be, and he felt naked, exposed.

I practiced the piercing eye contact with other guys like Earl and realized that few of the seriously baad cats could meet my gaze. That helped me see my homies and the other toughs at Southampton as they were (and as I had been): streetwise, pseudo baad-asses who were really frightened boys, bluffing, trying to mask their fear of the world behind muscular frames.

Jim made parole in 1977. The word spread fast across the yard that he would soon be leaving. This dude, who had been locked up since 1962—longer than anybody there—was getting out, and it was regarded as a momentous occasion at Southampton.

The day Jim left, hordes of guys lined up along the sidewalk to watch him walk out. The guys in our group, including me, were saddened. It was always that way when good friends left. You were glad they were getting out, yet sorrowful because they had helped you do your time.

Before leaving, Jim chatted with us a few minutes, dropped a few more morsels of advice on us, then said, "Later, man. I'll keep in touch." That was the only time I ever saw a hint of apprehension on his face.

With his arms loaded down with a boxful of books and other possessions, he walked slowly to the administration building. He waved one last time, then turned, his head held high, and disappeared through the door.

JARVIS MASTERS

Scars

I remember the first time my eyes really witnessed the scars on the bodies of almost every one of my fellow prisoners.

I was outside on a maximum custody exercise yard. I stood along a fence, praising the air that the yard gave to my lungs that my prison cell didn't. I wasn't in a rush to pick up a basketball or do anything. I just stood in my own silence.

I looked at the other prisoners on the yard playing basketball or handball, showering and talking to one another. I saw the inmates I felt closest to, John and Pete and David, lifting weights in one corner of the yard.

I noticed the unbelievable similarity of the whip-like scars on their bare skin, shining with sweat from pumping iron in the hot sun.

A deep sense of sadness came over me as I watched these powerful men lift hundreds of pounds of weights over their heads. I looked around the yard to see if the other prisoners besides John, Pete and David had the same types of scars. Sadly enough, they did! There were men on the handball and basketball courts, in the shower, and elsewhere that seemed to have whip marks and deep gashes all over their bodies. It shocked me silent to look behind their legs, on their backs, all over their ribs and see the gruesome evidence of the violence in our lives.

Here, hidden, were America's lost children, surviving in rage and in refuge from society. Most of us were born in the fifties and sixties when there were few laws protecting us from the child abuse that victimized us.

Then, as sudden as a shock, a terrible sense of sadness came over me. I thought of my mother, who had died within that year. "Wow," I thought, "I still wish I had been there when she died."

Suddenly, all the acts of abuse that had taken place in my childhood just came to the surface. I remembered being beaten and whipped by my stepfather and all the silent and lonely nights and days of abandonment by my mother, who was a heroin addict.

Only recently, in the eighties, has this society come to know and realize with some understanding the alarming rate of child abuse in this country.

Yet, what is lost and given up on by society are the men who walk the prison exercise yards throughout the country for horrible crimes often related to the violence done to them as children. No such connection is seen by either the adult in prison who was abused as a child, or by American society at large.

But because our histories were so connected, it was as if we had all had the same parents. I made up my mind that sometime that day, I would bring John and Pete and David together. I wanted to talk about the scars I had noticed and see if I could open them up to think about their abuse as children.

I was a trusted comrade to most of these men, and to a few of them I was their only family. But even so, to dare myself to go into their remembered pain and to convince them that they, like me, had been physically abused by our parents was something out of the ordinary for me.

"Am I crazy?" I wondered, "to have this idea of wanting to open up these men who probably had never spoken openly of their horrible experiences of child abuse. None of these men will ever say that their parents have physically abused them."

They looked hardened to the core as they stood around a weight-lifting bench, proud of their bodies and the images they projected standing there.

It occurred to me, as I approached them, that such a posture of pride symbolized the battle wounds that they had "made their bones" with. This is prison talk for "prove your manhood." Yet my own denials had at one time been similar, when I had been hardened and never wanted to see my parents as the cause and source of the mental and physical scars I wore.

The difficulty in speaking with these men would be to somehow interpret the usual prison language of all of us in sharing our histories. Shucking and jiving is the usual way to talk to cover up sensitive matters with prison humor.

This was how John, a 28-year-old, bulky, 6′3″ tall man serving 25-to-Life for murder, started when I asked him, while others listened, about the scars on his face. He said, "These scars came from kicking ass and in the process getting my ass kicked, which was rare and few."

He continued, "My father taught me how to fight when I was maybe five or six, and I had to learn from him beating on me."

John explained that his father had loved him enough to teach him how to fight when he was only five years old. In a sense, he said, he grew up with a loving fear of his father. He pointed out to me a very noticeable and nasty scar on his upper shoulder. He laughingly went on to say that his father had hit him with a steel rod when John tried to protect his mother from being beaten by his father.

Most of us had seen this scar but never had the nerve to ask about it. As we stared, looking at the imprinted gash, John seemed to feel ashamed. Avoiding us with his eyes, he mumbled a few words before he went on to show us many other scars. I noticed that John had total recall of the smallest of details surrounding these violent events.

I realized, as I should have known, that these experiences in John's childhood haunted him, as many abuse memories do. His detailed accounts somehow told us what he must have really suffered as a child.

Yet, John, as he went on explaining to us, became very rational in his words. He had spent more than half his life in one institutional setting or another, and as a result he projected a very cold and fearsome, even boastful smile on his face. None of what John was sharing did he want us to see, even remotely, as child abuse. He tried with smiles, jokes and jive talk to hide what he himself was feeling in his heart. To him, none of what he had been through was child abuse. And I was afraid to say to him that he was wrong.

This was especially so when he showed us all a gash on his back that was hidden by a tattoo of a dragon. It was a very ugly scar—like I imagined those of a slave who had been whipped.

As John directed me closer to see it, he said, "rub your finger down the dragon's spine." As I did so, I felt what I thought was a thick tight string that moved nastily like a worm beneath the layer of his skin. "Damn, John, what in the hell happened to you?" I asked.

There was something in how I questioned him that made John laugh and the others joined in with him. For that moment, I didn't understand the humor of something so terrible. I forced myself to smile just the same to avoid the sad stare that would have appeared on my face.

John explained that when he was nine or ten his father chased him with a cord. John ran and tried to hide under a bed. He grabbed the springs under the bed and held on as his father pulled him by the legs and hit his back repeatedly with the cord until he fell unconscious and woke up later with a very deep flesh wound. John, again with a cold smile on his face, admitted jokingly that it was the last time he ever ran from his father.

I first met John when we were both in youth homes in Southern California. We were only eleven years old. Throughout the years we traveled together through the juvenile systems until the penitentiary became our final stop.

David and Pete told very similar stories of beatings which occurred at early ages. All of their stories of how they had been abused as children spoke of a life that had a very telling side of how we all came to be in one of the worst prisons in the country.

It scares me to realize that most prisoners will eventually re-enter society and father children and repeat on their own children what has happened to them. With no programs in most prisons that speak to childhood abuse, a high percentage of the prisoners abused as children will ultimately do this. Thus the cycle of abuse and crime will continue.

Not all the scars I saw on men were inflicted in a home setting of abusive parents. Some of them had been put on in callous institutions that further embittered our hearts.

I believe that institutionalization is a kind of refuge for many of the men from the devastating child abuse in their lives. Most prisoners who were abused as children were taken out of the custody of their natural parents at very early ages. The authority figures place them in foster homes, youth homes or juvenile halls to protect the children from further abuse. These settings in most cases were adopted by the children, becoming their protective shield that kept them safe. For most prisoners abused as children, prisons are a continuation of this same process of living in a state of painful refuge.

This was the case with many men in prison that I have spoken with over a number of years. This was equally my own attitude that I unconsciously carried during my more than 15 years of being institutionalized.

Not until I read a series of books on adults who had been abused as children and about healing the shame that binds persons to their pasts, did I truly become committed to the self-examination of my own childhood abuse. I began to unfold and unravel all the hidden causes behind why I just expected to go from one youth institution to the next. I never really tried to stay out of these places and neither did my friends.

What I heard from these men on the exercise yard that day showed me how deeply each of them sought refuge in their denial. They could not allow themselves to openly admit the hidden truth of what they felt or the pain and hurt they've lived with.

As for me, I spoke to them very openly about my parents physically and mentally abusing me. I told how I had been neglected and abandoned by them when I was only five years old. I shared some of the horrors of my past, telling how my mother had left me and my sisters alone for days with our newborn twin brother and sister when I was only four years old. The baby boy died from a crib death which I always believed was my own fault, since I had been made responsible for him. I spoke to them of the pain and hurt that I carried through more than a dozen institutions I had been in. And I told how it was that all of these events ultimately entrapped me in a cycle of lashing out against everything. I never wanted to look inward to face the fact that I was hurting—crying out for help long after the abuse, neglect and abandonment by my parents.

These men were not able to tell, as I had, of their mothers and fathers physically and mentally abusing them. To hear me face something like that openly seemed to sadden them. I think they saw that I was able to accept a truth from my heart they could not.

Hearing me express my own pain and hurt, they all seemed to avoid linking my experiences with theirs. It was as if I had suffered more than they. That wasn't true. What they heard was the voice of their own unspoken stories. This term "abuse" spoke of a hidden truth: we had all been victims of child abuse. This was something that hurt them to agree with.

Instead, we all just fell silent around the weight-lifting bench as each one of us squatted down and thought . . . We all stared across the yard at the other men exercising. The feeling I had was that we were all looking and seeing something that was clear and sad to us all.

John and I spoke again privately later that day, walking together along the fence. Surprisingly, he said to me, "You know something, the day I got used to getting beaten up by my father and by counselors in all those group homes was the day that I knew nothing would ever hurt me again. Everything that I thought could hurt me, I saw as a game. I had nothing to lose and just about everything to gain. A prison cell to me is something that will always be here for me."

I looked at John as he said all this to me, and I didn't know what to say. Then it occurred to me that John was speaking for most of the men I had met in prison.

Secretly, we all like it here. This place welcomes a man who is full of rage and violence. Here, he is not abnormal, not different. Here, his rage is nothing new. Prison lifestyle is an extension of his inner life.

We have learned to abuse and re-abuse ourselves by coming in and out of places like this.

"Look around," I told him. "Look at all these men. Don't we all say that we're men out here on this exercise yard? This prison defines us as such. But there would be much greater power in what you and I can see out here if we could all see ourselves as human beings first. I bet if you truly thought of yourself as one human being, and of me as another, and others out here as more human beings, you would gradually begin to wonder freely and openly about the nature of your life. Try to replace your false manhood impressions," I said to John, "and don't be surprised that you will cry in confronting your past with human love."

Finally, I confided to John what I had thought earlier that morning: that I wished I had been there when my mother died. He asked, "Hey, didn't you say she neglected you?"

John was right; she did, but am I to neglect myself as well by wishing that I wasn't there, that she wasn't my mother, that I didn't still feel a love for her?

ARTHUR HAMILTON, JR., and WILLIAM BANKS

Father Behind Bars

I had my children and my wife. I had a family. I was beginning to feel like a father. The scolding and the coddling, the laughter and the tears, the love and frustration made it real to me. Real and sad. I still didn't have my freedom. And after the last time that my appeal was denied, I fell into depression once more. The dreams of hanging myself started again. It was terrible.

I also began to dream a new dream, about the man I killed and how I killed him.

Over and over I saw his chest explode. I'll never forget the cloud of blue-gray smoke at the end of the shotgun, and the awful silence that followed the deafening blast. I saw his head snap back and his eyes roll back in what was the last moment of his life.

Then my dream would take me where I had never been, but to what must have happened in reality. I saw the man being embalmed, dressed for his funeral, rolled into a church, and then mourned by his family. I was there in the dream every step of the way to the man's grave. I could hear myself yelling: "Self Defense! . . . Self Defense! . . . The man was going to kill *me* . . . It was self defense!" But none of the mourners heard or noticed me. I joined a long line of people who filed past the man's coffin. I was at the very end of the line. When I finally reached the coffin, I looked down and saw the man in the coffin was my brother, Greg.

Of course, I had not killed my brother, but clearly my conscience was telling me I would never forget what I had done. Even though the killing was done in self defense, the man's death was as devastating to his family as Greg's death had been to me.

I concluded that I now had an even greater debt to repay than I had imagined. In addition to my sentence, I had to do something that would make life better for people other than my family. It was clearly a matter of conscience in terms of the torment I was going through, but there was more.

After thinking, praying, and talking with Marilyn, a picture began to develop. I had to do something to help others who were like me, and like the man I killed. These are men who are trapped in lives of crime, poverty, and prison. By doing this, I could morally as well as legally atone for what I had done.

But what to do? I had nothing to give, I thought. What little money I earned from my prison work was sent home to help support my children. Marilyn was now working literally night and day to support our five children and herself.

I sometimes lost track of how much and how hard Marilyn was working. This was because I never saw her come and go to work and because she rarely complained. She was carrying the financial and parental burdens of two people. I didn't have enough of anything for my own family, I realized. How could I seriously consider giving something to others?

Marilyn showed me the way. She explained that she would indeed continue to shoulder the family's financial responsibilities for as long as she had to. She also said that given my circumstances, the small amount of money I was making and sending home was an important contribution that was genuinely needed and appreciated.

Marilyn also pointed me in the direction of this book, *Father Behind Bars*. She told me that I had lived an exceptional life and that others should know how I, or perhaps I should say we, lived, suffered, and survived. Marilyn also encouraged me to get more involved with activities in the prison, in addition to my writing for the paper. This led me to the many other outlets for my desire to make a contribution, one of them being the N.A.A.C.P.

Carl Meritt, Jr., the then president of the Kincross Michigan Chapter of the N.A.A.C.P. asked *me*, an inmate doing time for manslaughter, to become a member of one of the most distinguished and important human rights organizations that has ever existed. Carl didn't know it then but I was deeply moved and honored. The feeling increased when Carl asked me to chair the branch's Press and Publicity Committee. I was in charge of outside communications and the chapter's newsletter. The newsletter is entitled "ECHOES." It won the Thalheimers award in 1993 for ". . . it's dedication to, and the further improvement of, mankind."

From this point, I put together the Kincross prison's Black History Committee, which organized a multicultural Black History Month observance in 1993.

It was the first program of its kind, that I had ever heard of, to be presented. When I was putting it together, I thought it would be useful to make the program something that would help to bring *all* the men in the prison together, not just isolate one group. So on the day of the program, Jews, Muslims, Irish, Italians, and every other ethnic group in the prison *joined* with African Americans to pay tribute to the contributions of black men and women in America.

I also began to feel that something had to be done to help the black family, particularly the families of convicts. This kind of help meant and means keeping those families together. Finally, there it was. I had thought of something that would help me *and* my brothers behind bars, too. It would be more than just a book that would simply tell my story, it would be a living and lasting instrument that could empower other men to create their own stories of success.

And so, after receiving enthusiastic approval and support from the prison authorities, I went to it. Once again the N.A.A.C.P. played a critical part in my efforts. The organization which is today called "Fathers Behind Bars" is at this time set up under the auspices of the N.A.A.C.P. chapter branch here at the prison. Our goals and objectives include: To help fathers in prison reestablish ties with their children and if possible the mothers of their children, to help these men become prepared for family life on the outside, and to give them the confidence and tools to start that process while they are still in prison.

We have really done well so far. We believe that we are giving men hope and the skills they need to be good fathers inside and outside of prison. Other than ourselves, there is no equipment, books, charts, guest speakers, or props—it's just us, confronting our failures and nurturing our potentials as men, and as fathers.

The convicts who have come into the group so far are varied in terms of their ethnic backgrounds and ages. But they are mostly black and mostly young. I am glad about this. Every man needs lessons in fatherhood and family leadership. But for young blacks, it is absolutely critical.

These sessions are intense.

I have seen men come into the group, grapple with issues of fatherhood, family, and personal responsibility just once and then never return. Not because of lack of interest, but because what they found in Fathers Behind Bars was very personal, very strong, and very painful.

But the fact that they felt pain means that they still have pride and sensitivity. And that means, if they build up their personal character and strength, they can still do it—they can still make it as fathers.

The news of Fathers Behind Bars spread, and I got letters from guys in other prisons asking about this concept of having men in prison reclaim and reunite with their families.

The requests for information regarding Fathers Behind Bars, and how to start new chapters in other prisons, got to the point that in addition to this book, the most efficient way to move things forward in this effort was to start a regular newspaper column headed with the organization's name.

Right now, the column is printed in many prison papers around the country. And like the hope I have in my heart, the hope that writing has given me, the momentum is building.

DHORUBA BIN WAHAD

Still Black, Still Strong: Survivors of the U.S. War Against Black Revolutionaries

In the U.S. in particular, political prisoners became a matter of government policy in 1971 as a consequence of a militant Black liberation movement. One of the highlights of this policy was, of course, the assassination of the renowned writer and political activist, George Jackson. He was murdered in San Quentin prison in August of 1971, shot to death. Officials claim he was trying to escape. A number of prison guards were killed. Documents that surfaced under the Freedom of Information Act subsequently showed that George Jackson was a target of the Counterintelligence Program aimed at the Black Panther Party.

George Jackson's murder by the California Adult Authority, the prison system, marked a change in state policy towards political activists who were in prison. This change was codified in a program known as Operation PRISAC—that's an acronym for "prison activists"—instituted in 1973-1974. The government has said that this was terminated in 1976 but we have information that indicates it was continued under a different name up until the 1980's. Operation PRISAC was designed to monitor political activists who were brought to prison as a consequence of the Counterintelligence Program. In 1973-74 the federal government invited all the heads of the various state prison systems to Washington to coordinate their policies in dealing with political prisoners, because this was a different breed of prisoner, a person that had to be isolated and neutralized. It's interesting to note that PRISAC became a necessity because the Counterintelligence Program was so successful in framing political activists. Once these activists—most of them were to become Black political prisoners—were taken off the streets, then a new program had to be designed to isolate them in prison, and monitor the activities of people coming out of prison who may have been influenced through their contact with them. Between 1973 and 1976, many of those who were politicized in prison were mysteriously murdered. To this day no one has been brought to justice for these murders. One individual that comes prominently to mind is a man by the name of Charles Rabbi Parker. He was a well-known political activist in the New York State prison system who had become a member of the Black Panther Party while in prison. He had organized hundreds of prisoners into unions, into a People's Party, he was a leader in the Attica (prison) rebellion in 1971. He was eventually let out of prison in 1976 and by 1978 he had been murdered—mysteriously. People in Europe should understand that the development of political repression in the United States is reflective of the cooptation and the neutralization of legitimate movements for social change, whether it's the anti-war movement that arose out of the Vietnam War, the Black civil rights or Black liberation movement, or the Puerto Rican nationalist movement, the U.S. has carried out a policy of repression, trained other governments in the use of repressive tactics and established a network—a working relationship with the various law enforcement apparatuses in the other states—especially in Europe.

I spent seven years off and on in isolation, solitary confinement. In the United States isolation basically means 23 hours a day confinement to a cell, which is generally 8 feet by 10 feet in size. It's usually a steel cell with a cot, a steel shelf bolted to the wall. When I first went to prison—and I must point out that it was a state prison in New York State, as opposed to a federal prison—every prison had an isolation unit. It was called disciplinary segregation and during the course of my confinement the Department of Correction changed the criteria for confining a prisoner in disciplinary segregation to meet its political needs, to deal with political prisoners.

The United States government is very much "into" the development of techniques, ideas and principles for modifying a person's behavior through sensory deprivation. They have carried out these experiments in many prisons, and Marion, Illinois was the major laboratory for this. The prisoners there are isolated 23.5 hours a day. They are subjected to brutal treatment by prison guards. Many of the prisoners cannot have social visits, they have no personal property to speak of. They are forced to watch television 23.5 hours a day. Investigations have shown that the water system in Marion, which the prisoners drink from, is infected by toxic waste, and the prisoners have been developing various degrees of blood cancer and other ailments, to the point where the prison guards and the prison officals don't drink the water from the prison system. The majority of political prisoners there are Black political prisoners and Puerto Rican nationalist prisoners. They are kept, of course, in the special housing unit, the isolation unit. Many of them have been there for years.

Every prison in New York State now has a prison within a prison, and New York State has built two maximum-maximum security prisons. The first one was in Sullivan County, New York, where as we speak there are five Black political prisoners. Shawanga is unique in the sense that the prisoners' activities are monitored 24-hours-a-day. There are surveillance cameras on the prison gallery, the prison hallway, the prison tier, which the cells open up onto, and the camera moves down the gallery on a track, it's a remote camera. The cell doors are opened by remote control whenever the prisoners are let out of their cells into the close supervision unit and an officer follows them around with a clipboard recording everything they do, every word they say. I guess in comparison to Marion this would be seen as liberal because in Marion the prisoners do not even come out of their cells. But the U.S. government is building another prison in Colorado which will open next year and is being touted as the cutting edge of prison technology. It will use robotics, robots taking care of the prisoners. There will be no human contact between prisoners and guards, even. Unless, of course, they are to be assaulted by them. The prisoners will be locked in their cells 23 hours a day. This prison is employing every means of technology to accomplish this end, and the United States government is very proud of its efforts.

The federal system did not have a maximum-maximum security facility for women, and because a significant number of the political prisoners, especially the white, North American, anti-imperialist political prisoners and Puerto Rican political prisoners were women, the U.S. government had a problem. I think they only had two or three federal women's penitentiaries in the U.S. and only one of them was seriously a maximum security prison. So what they did was take Lexington, which was a prison hospital, and convert a section of it into a maximum security unit for women. They painted this unit all white, they removed any type of sensory stimulation from the environment. The guards were instructed that these individuals were very dangerous terrorists and three women were brought there to "open up" the unit. One was Susan Rosenberg, another Alejandrina Torres, and the other was Silvia Baraldini. What they did not anticipate though was that people on the outside would mobilize against this blatant attempt to isolate political activists, torture them, and bring about their demise by means of sensory deprivation. A campaign was mounted by progressive people and progressive forces to close the Lexington Control Unit. This unit was visited by Amnesty International and other Human Rights Organizations and it was declared, just as the Marion facility was, to be inhumane and to be an institution dedicated to the torture of human beings. Under this national and international pressure, the United States government was forced to close the Lexington Control Unit. However, they only closed it after they had developed an alternative unit in Mariana, Florida. Of course, two of the women who were in the Lexington Unit were ultimately transferred to this maxi-maxi prison in Mariana, Florida, again modelled after Marion, Illinois, where they remain today.

In the United States there are 30 million Black people, but very few people in Europe understand that those people have a particular history, and this history is one of domestic colonialism, internal colonialism. There is a struggle going on in the United States to empower masses of Black people. And the United States government has done everything in its power to sidetrack that struggle, to destroy its most militant advocates, to prop up certain elements in the Black community who support racism and the idea that Black people enjoy the full panoply of rights and privileges all other American citizens enjoy, but simply suffer from social discrimination. In the United States, every aspect of political repression, of racism, has historically been bolstered by the legal system and the law. It was the law that said that Black people were three-fifths of a human being—it was in the Constitution of the United States. When Black people were enslaved, slavery was legal. With Jim Crow, the U.S. version of segregation and apartheid was established after the Civil War, and again it was codified in law. In the United States, Black people's struggle has been at once legal and extra-legal. This is why Black political prisoners in the U.S. are so isolated. People do not understand that the law is used to destroy the legitimate political aspirations of people of color.

Here we come face to face with the contradiction of Amnesty International's policies. Amnesty International does not support movements that advocate the overthrow of the existing political order. What it means is that even if a political order is racist and reactionary, historically discriminatory, the victims have no right to carry out acts of violence against that state. Amnesty International's policies have led it to the ignoble position of not supporting political prisoners in the United States. In fact it did not recognize Nelson Mandela, clearly an individual who was in prison because of his political views and his struggle against the apartheid regime in South Africa.

Amnesty International has only recognized one Black prisoner as a political prisoner and that is Elmer Geronimo Pratt who has been in prison for 21 years. Before him they had recognized the Wilmington 10, the Reverend Ben Chavis and these political prisoners. But other than that, Amnesty International has not dealt with the cases of over 150 political prisoners in the U.S. and this is their shame. As a consequence, the prisoners themselves and the movements from which they come have had an uphill battle in gaining recognition. Our Campaign to Free Black Political Prisoners is often boycotted by particular venues. If we want to do a fund-raising benefit for political prisoners, oftentimes we are denied the use of a huge auditorium because we are not connected to organizations such as Amnesty International. When we say we are from the Campaign to Free Black Political Prisoners in the U.S., they ask us, "Is this for Amnesty International?" And when we say no they say "Well who are these prisoners? We don't have political prisoners in the United States." So Amnesty International plays the part of the legal international opposition to liberal reform in the so-called democracies and the metropoles of the West. The masses of people are not aware that their governments carry out policies of murder, of manipulation of the legal system. In the United States for instance the FBI has carried out a programme called

"Operation Mirage" aimed at targeting Arab Americans in the wake of the Gulf War. Its purpose was, of course, to isolate them from the mainstream society and ultimately lock them up in the detention centers should the war have been a drawn-out affair. So we see that the federal government of the United States becomes emboldened by the failure of independent international bodies to monitor political repression.

We have documented over 150 cases of political imprisonment in the United States, using the criteria as established by the United Nations Commission on Human Rights and the Universal Declaration of Human Rights which defines a political prisoner as an individual who, in pursuit of their political conscience, and as a consequence of their political activity, are imprisoned for those activities. The majority of the political prisoners in the United States are Black. The second largest number are Puerto Rican nationals who consider themselves prisoners-of-war because Puerto Rico is a colony of the United States. As the Universal Declaration of Human Rights makes plain, colonized people have a right to wage armed struggle against the colonizing power for their freedom, and the combatants in this struggle have to be treated as prisoners-of-war. Of course the United States does not consider Puerto Rico a colony and therefore does not treat the Puerto Rican nationalists as prisoners-of-war but rather as criminals. The third largest group of political prisoners in the United States are white anti-imperialist political prisoners. These are individuals who come from the left in the United States and who have carried out support movements, support actions, on behalf of the Black liberation movements and of the Puerto Rican nationalist movement. They have opposed U.S. intervention in the Middle East, the Caribbean, and in Latin America. These individuals are in prison also. And the fourth largest group are Native Americans from the American Indian Movement.

The majority of Black political prisoners come from the Black Panther Party or the Black Liberation Army, and the reason for this is that the majority of Black political prisoners have been in prison for the last 20 years. They were targets of the Counterintelligence Program, like Geronimo Pratt, or they were targets of Operation Newkill, like the New York 3, who were members of the Black Liberation Army, or they were targeted by the government's Joint Anti-Terrorist Task Force, like the Queens 2. Ahmed Abdul Rahman, in Detroit, has been in prison almost 20 years. He was a lieutenant in the Black Panther Party. The reason why these political prisoners are unknown in the United States, aside from the fact that the U.S. has done a magnificent job of concealing its political repression behind criminal law enforcement, is that the organization that they had been members of was destroyed by the United States government. And this is why earlier this year, after my release from prison, we established the Campaign to Free Black Political Prisoners and Prisoners-of-War in the United States. And when we talk about Black prisoners-of-war we are saying that a state of war has existed between the Black community in the United States and the racist power structure of the

United States, and that this state of war has assumed many different forms. One of those forms was of course counterinsurgency. Individuals who had taken up the armed struggle, to arm the resistance against racist police attacks in the Black community, and were captured as a consequence of that resistance, we define as prisoners-of-war.

Mumia Abu-Jamal's case is the most significant case that confronts us today in regards to Black political prisoners. Mumia Abu-Jamal was formerly the Lieutenant of Information in the Philadelphia, Pennsylvania branch of the Black Panther Party. He was an outspoken defender of the poor Black community in Philadelphia. The Philadelphia Police Department is one of the most notorious in the United States. It was headed by a former corrupt politician by the name of Frank Rizzo. The Philadelphia P.D. had murdered and brutalized Black people for a very long time, and recently—a few years ago—this treatment burst upon the national consciousness when the Philadelphia Police Department burned down an entire area in the Black community trying to evict from a house some members of MOVE. MOVE is an organization, or a family, a group of Black activists in the Philadelphia community. Mumia Abu-Jamal was a radio announcer in Philadelphia, and a writer, who in his radio programs and his daily column supported MOVE activists in Philadelphia. He constantly reported police activities in the Black community, reported their treatment of the MOVE prisoners and the MOVE people. This resulted in an attack upon him one evening by police department officials in Philadelphia. They attacked him and his brother who was viciously beaten up by the police. In the melee, one of the police was killed and Mumia Abu-Jamal was arrested for the murder of this policeman. There was no evidence that Mumia had anything to do with the murder of this policeman. However, because of his outspoken advocacy on behalf of the MOVE people, he was put on trial for first-degree murder which is punishable by death. He has exhausted all of his legal remedies under the State and Federal law and he is now facing execution in the Pennsylvania death chamber. And so we are mounting a campaign to stop the State of Pennsylvania from murdering Mumia Abu-Jamal. Political prisoners have been murdered by the state, but all of these murders were conspiracies that were carried out behind the scenes—in dark rooms—they were carried out by officials in secret. Mumia Abu-Jamal's execution of course will not be a secret, it will be something that's codified. So if Mumia Abu-Jamal is murdered by the State of Pennsylvania, this will become a serious precedent for the actual execution, outright legal execution, of political prisoners, of political activists.

It's also useful to note that the death penalty in the United States has always been used as a means of intimidating people of color. In the U.S., 85% of the people on death row are Black, or people of color. Never in the history of the United States has a white person ever been executed for the murder of a Black person, or a person of color. Black men have been executed for rape of white women, some for rapes that were never even proven to have occurred, just on the mere allegation of the charge that they had looked at a white woman, or that they had accosted a white woman. So the death penalty in the United States has historically been used in a racist fashion. And now, if Mumia Abu-Jamal is executed it will have been used not only in a racist fashion, but in a clearly political fashion.

I'm currently working with the Campaign to Free Black Political Prisoners and Prisoners-of-War in the United States. We launched this campaign because we realized that Black political prisoners did not have a national campaign, a coordinated effort to raise public awareness as to their plight. We originally worked within the Freedom Now campaign, a coalition of various activists from different movements who saw the necessity for bringing the issue of political repression to the forefront of the American public. We did not feel that organizations such as Amnesty International or Americas Watch were at all concerned with the issue; they were in fact intimidated by the power of the United States government. During the course of our work, and my travel nationally and internationally for Freedom Now, I realized that it was imperative for the Black community to organize its own efforts around Black political prisoners. Our first objective, of course, is to break through the elaborate fabric of lies woven by the United States government in the international and national community, which conceals the existence of political prisoners. We have mobilized people across the country on scores of college campuses. We have politicized the issue of political repression in areas not previously reached, mainly among Black trade unions, and gained the support of several of them. The Black and Puerto Rican legislative caucus in New York, which consists of over 30 elected officials, have endorsed our campaign. We have established a regular visitation program for political prisoners in New York and elsewhere. We are beginning to coordinate the various activities of the political prisoners' defense in regions of the country so that we can raise funds and focus our attention on particular cases at strategic moments. So the Campaign to Free Black Political Prisoners, while very new, is beginning to make headway.

COLOR AND CLASS

WALTER WHITE

A Man Called White

I am a Negro. My skin is white, my eyes are blue, my hair is blond. The traits of my race are nowhere visible upon me. Not long ago I stood one morning on a subway platform in Harlem. As the train came in I stepped back for safety. My heel came down upon the toe of the man behind me. I turned to apologize to him. He was a Negro, and his face as he stared at me was hard and full of the piled-up bitterness of a thousand lynchings and a million nights in shacks and tenements and "nigger towns." "Why don't you look where you're going?" he said sullenly. "You white folks are always trampling on colored people." Just then one of my friends came up and asked how the fight had gone in Washington—there was a filibuster against legislation for a permanent Fair Employment Practices Committee. The Negro on whose toes I had stepped listened, then spoke to me penitently:

"Are you Walter White of the NAACP? I'm sorry I spoke to you that way. I thought you were white."

I am not white. There is nothing within my mind and heart which tempts me to think I am. Yet I realize acutely that the only characteristic which matters to either the white or the colored race—the appearance of whiteness—is mine. There is magic in a white skin; there is tragedy, loneliness, exile, in a black skin. Why then do I insist that I am a Negro, when nothing compels me to do so but myself?

Many Negroes are judged as whites. Every year approximately twelve thousand white-skinned Negroes disappear—people whose absence cannot be explained by death or emigration. Nearly every one of the fourteen million discernible Negroes in the United States knows at least one member of his race who is "passing"—the magic word which means that some Negroes can get by as whites, men and women who have decided that they will be happier and more successful if they flee from the proscription and humiliation which the American color line imposes on them. Often these emigrants achieve success in business, the professions, the arts and sciences. Many of them have married white people, lived happily with them, and produced families. Sometimes they tell their husbands or wives of their Negro blood, sometimes not. Who are they? Mostly people of no great importance, but some of them prominent figures, including a few members of Congress, certain writers, and several organizers of movements to "keep the Negroes and other minorities in their places." Some of the most vehement public haters of Negroes are themselves secretly Negroes.

They do not present openly the paradox of the color line. It is I, with my insistence, day after day, year in and year out, that I am a Negro, who provokes the reactions to which now I am accustomed: the sudden intake of breath, the bewildered expression of the face, the confusion of the eyes, the muddled fragmentary remarks—"But you do not look . . . I mean I would never have known . . . of course if you didn't want to admit . . ." Sometimes the eyes blink rapidly and the tongue, out of control, says, "Are you sure?"

I have tried to imagine what it is like to have me presented to a white person as a Negro, by supposing a Negro were suddenly to say to me, "I am white." But the reversal does not work, for whites can see no reason for a white man ever wanting to be black; there is only reason for a black man wanting to be white. That is the way whites think; that is the way their values are set up. It is the startling removal of the blackness that upsets people. Looking at me without knowing who I am, they disassociate me from all the characteristics of the Negro. Informed that I am a Negro, they find it impossible suddenly to endow me with the skin, the odor, the dialect, the shuffle, the imbecile good nature, traditionally attributed to Negroes. Instantly they are aware that these things are *not* part of me. They think there must be some mistake.

There is no mistake. I am a Negro. There can be no doubt. I know the night when, in terror and bitterness of soul, I discovered that I was set apart by the pigmentation of my skin (invisible though it was in my case) and the moment at which I decided that I would infinitely rather be what I was than, through taking advantage of the way of escape that was open to me, be one of the race which had forced the decision upon me.

There were nine light-skinned Negroes in my family: mother, father, five sisters, an older brother, George, and myself. The house in which I discovered what it meant to be a Negro was located on Houston Street, three blocks from the Candler Building, Atlanta's first skyscraper, which bore the name of the ex-drug clerk who had become a millionaire from the sale of Coca-Cola. Below us lived none but Negroes; toward town all but a very few were white. Ours was an eight room, two-story frame house which stood out in its surroundings not because of its opulence but by contrast with the drabness and unpaintedness of the other dwellings in a deteriorating neighborhood.

Only Father kept his house painted, the picket fence repaired, the board fences separating our place from those on either side white-washed, the grass neatly trimmed, and flower beds abloom. Mother's passion for neatness was even more pronounced and it seemed to me that I was always the victim of her determination to see no single blade of grass longer than the others or any one of the pickets in the front fence less shiny with paint than its mates. This spic-and-spanness became increasingly apparent as the rest of the neighborhood became more down-at-heel, and resulted, as we were to learn, in sullen envy among some of our white neighbors. It was the violent expression of that resentment against a Negro family neater than themselves which set the pattern of our lives.

On a day in September 1906, when I was thirteen, we were taught that there is no isolation from life. The unseasonably oppressive heat of an Indian summer day hung like a steaming blanket over Atlanta. My sisters and I had casually commented upon the unusual quietness. It seemed to stay Mother's volubility and reduced Father, who was more taciturn, to monosyllables. But, as I remember it, no other sense of impending trouble impinged upon our consciousness.

I had read the inflammatory headlines in the *Atlanta News* and the more restrained ones in the *Atlanta Constitution* which reported alleged rapes and other crimes committed by Negroes. But these were so standard and familiar that they made—as I look back on it now—little impression. The stories were more frequent, however, and consisted of eight-column streamers instead of the usual two- or four-column ones.

Father was a mail collector. His tour of duty was from three to eleven P.M. He made his rounds in a little cart into which one climbed from a step in the rear. I used to drive the cart for him from two until seven, leaving him at the point nearest our home on Houston Street, to return home either for study or sleep. That day Father decided that I should not go with him. I appealed to Mother, who thought it might be all right, provided Father sent me home before dark because, she said, "I don't think they would dare start anything before nightfall." Father told me as we made the rounds that ominous rumors of a race riot that night were sweeping the town. But I was too young that morning to understand the background of the riot. I became much older during the next thirty-six hours, under circumstances which I now recognize as the inevitable outcome of what had preceded.

One of the most bitter political campaigns of that bloody era was reaching its climax. Hoke Smith—that amazing contradiction of courageous and intelligent opposition to the South's economic ills and at the same time advocacy of ruthless suppression of the Negro—was a candidate that year for the governorship. His opponent was Clark Howell, editor of the *Atlanta Constitution*, which boasted with justification that it "covers Dixie like the dew."

Howell and his supporters held firm authority over the state Democratic machine despite the long and bitter fight Hoke Smith had made on Howell in the columns of the rival *Atlanta Journal.*

Hoke Smith had fought for legislation to ban child labor and railroad rate discriminations. He had denounced the corrupt practices of the railroads and the state railway commission, which, he charged, was as much owned and run by northern absentee landlords as were the railroads themselves. He had fought for direct primaries to nominate senators and other candidates by popular vote, for a corrupt practices act, for an elective railway commission, and for state ownership of railroads—issues which were destined to be still fought for nearly four decades later by Ellis Arnall. For these reforms he was hailed throughout the nation as a genuine progressive along with La Follette of Wisconsin and Folk of Missouri.

To overcome the power of the regular Democratic organization, Hoke Smith sought to heal the feud of long standing between himself and the powerful ex-radical Populist, Thomas E. Watson. Tom Watson was the strangest mixture of contradictions which rotten-borough politics of the South had ever produced. He was the brilliant leader of an agrarian movement in the South which, in alliance with the agrarian West, threatened for a time the industrial and financial power of the East. He had made fantastic strides in uniting Negro and white farmers with Negro and white industrial workers. He had advocated enfranchisement of Negroes and poor whites, the abolition of lynching, control of big business, and rights for the little man, which even today would label him in the minds of conservatives as a dangerous radical. He had fought with fists, guns, and spine-stirring oratory in a futile battle to stop the spread of an industrialized, corporate society.

His break with the Democratic Party during the '90's and the organization of the Populist Party made the Democrats his implacable enemies. The North, busy building vast corporations and individual fortunes, was equally fearful of Tom Watson. Thus was formed between reactionary Southern Democracy and conservative Northern Republicanism the basis of cooperation whose fullest flower is to be seen in the present-day coalition of conservatives in Congress. This combination crushed Tom Watson's bid for national leadership in the presidential elections of 1896 and smashed the Populist movement. Watson ran for president in 1904 and 1908, both times with abysmal failure. His defeats soured him to the point of vicious acrimony. He turned from his ideal of interracial decency to one of virulent hatred and denunciation of the "nigger." He thus became a natural ally for Hoke Smith in the gubernatorial election in Georgia in 1906.

The two rabble-rousers stumped the state screaming, "Nigger, nigger, nigger!" Some white farmers still believed Watson's abandoned doctrine that the interests of Negro and white farmers and industrial workers were identical. They feared that Watson's and Smith's new scheme to disfranchise Negro voters would lead to disfranchisement of poor whites. Tom Watson was sent to trade on his past reputation to reassure them that such was not the case and that their own interests were best served by now hating "niggers."

Watson's oratory had been especially effective among the cotton mill workers and other poor whites in and near Atlanta. The *Atlanta Journal* on August 1, 1906, in heavy type, all capital letters, printed an incendiary appeal to race prejudice backing up Watson and Smith which declared:

Political equality being thus preached to the negro in the ring papers and on the stump, what wonder that he makes no distinction between political and social equality? He grows more bumptious on the street, more impudent in his dealings with white men, and then, when he cannot achieve social equality as he wishes, with the instinct of the barbarian to destroy what he cannot attain to, he lies in wait, as that dastardly brute did yesterday near this city, and assaults the fair young girlhood of the south . . .

At the same time, a daily newspaper was attempting to wrest from the *Atlanta Journal* leadership in the afternoon field. The new paper, the *Atlanta News*, in its scramble for circulation and advertising took a lesson from the political race and began to play up in eight-column streamers stories of the raping of white women by Negroes. That every one of the stories was afterward found to be wholly without foundation was of no importance. The *News* circulation, particularly in street sales, leaped swiftly upward as the headlines were bawled by lusty-voiced newsboys. Atlanta became a tinder box.

Fuel was added to the fire by a dramatization of Thomas Dixon's novel *The Clansman* in Atlanta. (This was later made by David Wark Griffith into *The Birth of a Nation*, and did more than anything else to make successful the revival of the Ku Klux Klan.) The late Ray Stannard Baker, telling the story of the Atlanta riot in *Along the Color Line*, characterized Dixon's fiction and its effect on Atlanta and the South as "incendiary and cruel." No more apt or accurate description could have been chosen.

During the afternoon preceding the riot little bands of sullen, evil-looking men talked excitedly on street corners all over downtown Atlanta. Around seven o'clock my father and I were driving toward a mail box at the corner of Peachtree and Houston Streets when there came from near-by Pryor Street a roar the like of which I had never heard before, but which sent a sensation of mingled fear and excitement coursing through my body. I asked permission of Father to go and see what the trouble was. He bluntly ordered me to stay in the cart. A little later we drove down Atlanta's main business thoroughfare, Peachtree Street. Again we heard the terrifying cries, this time near at hand and coming toward us. We saw a lame Negro bootblack from Herndon's barber shop pathetically trying to outrun a mob of whites. Less than a hundred yards from us the chase ended. We saw clubs and fists descending to the accompaniment of savage shouting and cursing. Suddenly a voice cried, "There goes another nigger!" Its work done, the mob went after new prey. The body with the withered foot lay dead in a pool of blood on the street.

Father's apprehension and mine steadily increased during the evening, although the fact that our skins were white kept us from attack. Another circumstance favored us—the mob had not yet grown violent enough to attack United States government property. But I could see Father's relief when he punched the time clock at eleven P.M. and got into the cart to go home. He wanted to go the back way down Forsyth Street, but I begged him, in my childish excitement and ignorance, to drive down Marietta to Five Points, the heart of Atlanta's business district, where the crowds were densest and the yells loudest. No sooner had we turned into Marietta Street, however, than we saw careening toward us an undertaker's barouche. Crouched in the rear of the vehicle were three Negroes clinging to the sides of the carriage as it lunged and swerved. On the driver's seat crouched a white man, the reins held taut in his left hand. A huge whip was gripped in his right. Alternately he lashed the horses and, without looking backward, swung the whip in savage swoops in the faces of members of the mob as they lunged at the carriage determined to seize the three Negroes.

There was no time for us to get out of its path, so sudden and swift was the appearance of the vehicle. The hub cap of the right rear wheel of the barouche hit the right side of our much lighter wagon. Father and I instinctively threw our weight and kept the cart from turning completely over. Our mare was a Texas mustang which, frightened by the sudden blow, lunged in the air as Father clung to the reins. Good fortune was with us. The cart settled back on its four wheels as Father said in a voice which brooked no dissent, "We are going home the back way and not down Marietta."

But again on Pryor Street we heard the cry of the mob. Close to us and in our direction ran a stout and elderly woman who cooked at a downtown white hotel. Fifty yards behind, a mob which filled the street from curb to curb was closing in. Father handed the reins to me and, though he was of slight stature, reached down and lifted the woman into the cart. I did not need to be told to lash the mare to the fastest speed she could muster.

The church bells tolled the next morning for Sunday service. But no one in Atlanta believed for a moment that the hatred and lust for blood had been appeased. Like skulls on a cannibal's hut the hats and caps of victims of the mob of the night before had been hung on the iron hooks of telegraph poles. None could tell whether each hat represented a dead Negro. But we knew that some of those who had worn the hats would never again wear any.

Late in the afternoon friends of my father's came to warn of more trouble that night. They told us that plans had been perfected for a mob to form on Peachtree Street just after nightfall to march down Houston Street to what the white people called "Darktown," three blocks or so below our house, to "clean out the niggers." There had never been a firearm in our house before that day. Father was reluctant even in those circumstances to violate the law, but he at last gave in at Mother's insistence.

We turned out the lights early, as did all our neighbors. No one removed his clothes or thought of sleep. Apprehension was tangible. We could almost touch its cold and clammy surface. Toward midnight the unnatural quiet was broken by a roar that grew steadily in volume. Even today I grow tense in remembering it.

Father told Mother to take my sisters, the youngest of them only six, to the rear of the house, which offered more protection from stones and bullets. My brother George was away, so Father and I, the only males in the house, took our places at the front windows of the parlor. The windows opened on a porch along the front side of the house, which in turn gave onto a narrow lawn that sloped down to the street and a picket fence. There was a crash as Negroes smashed the street lamp at the corner of Houston and Piedmont Avenue down the street. In a very few minutes the vanguard of the mob, some of them bearing torches, appeared. A voice which we recognized as that of the son of the grocer with whom we had traded for many years yelled, "That's where that nigger mail carrier lives! Let's burn it down! It's too nice for a nigger to live in!" In the eerie light Father turned his drawn face toward me. In a voice as quiet as though he were asking me to pass him the sugar at the breakfast table, he said, "Son, don't shoot until the first man puts his foot on the lawn and then—don't you miss!"

In the flickering light the mob swayed, paused, and began to flow toward us. In that instant there opened up within me a great awareness; I knew then who I was. I was a Negro, a human being with an invisible pigmentation which marked me a person to be hunted, hanged, abused, discriminated against, kept in poverty and ignorance, in order that those whose skin was white would have readily at hand a proof of their superiority, a proof patent and inclusive, accessible to the moron and the idiot as well as to the wise man and the genius. No matter how low a white man fell, he could always hold fast to the smug conviction that he was superior to two-thirds of the world's population, for those two-thirds were not white.

It made no difference how intelligent or talented my millions of brothers and I were, or how virtuously we lived. A curse like that of Judas was upon us, a mark of degradation fashioned with heavenly authority. There were white men who said Negroes had no souls, and who proved it by the Bible. Some of these now were approaching us, intent upon burning our house.

Theirs was a world of contrasts in values: superior and inferior, profit and loss, cooperative and noncooperative, civilized and aboriginal, white and black. If you were on the wrong end of the comparison, if you were inferior, if you were noncooperative, if you were aboriginal, if you were black, then you were marked for excision, expulsion, or extinction. I was a Negro; I was therefore that part of history which opposed the good, the just, and the enlightened. I was a Persian, falling before the hordes of Alexander. I was a

Carthaginian, extinguished by the Legions of Rome. I was a Frenchman at Waterloo, an Anglo-Saxon at Hastings, a Confederate at Vicksburg. I was the defeated, wherever and whenever there was a defeat.

Yet as a boy there in the darkness amid the tightening fright, I knew the inexplicable thing—that my skin was as white as the skin of those who were coming at me.

The mob moved toward the lawn. I tried to aim my gun, wondering what it would feel like to kill a man. Suddenly there was a volley of shots. The mob hesitated, stopped. Some friends of my father's had barricaded themselves in a two-story brick building just below our house. It was they who had fired. Some of the mobsmen, still bloodthirsty, shouted, "Let's go get the nigger." Others, afraid now for their safety, held back. Our friends, noting the hesitation, fired another volley. The mob broke and retreated up Houston Street.

In the quiet that followed I put my gun aside and tried to relax. But a tension different from anything I had ever known possessed me. I was gripped by the knowledge of my identity, and in the depths of my soul I was vaguely aware that I was glad of it. I was sick with loathing for the hatred which had flared before me that night and come so close to making me a killer; but I was glad I was not one of those who hated; I was glad I was not one of those made sick and murderous by pride. I was glad I was not one of those whose story is in the history of the world, a record of bloodshed, raping, and pillage. I was glad my mind and spirit were part of the races that had not fully awakened, and who therefore had still before them the opportunity to write a record of virtue as a memorandum to Armageddon.

It was all just a feeling then, inarticulate and melancholy, yet reassuring in the way that death and sleep are reassuring, and I have clung to it now for nearly half a century.

LANGSTON HUGHES

Who's Passing for Who?

One of the great difficulties about being a member of a minority race is that so many kindhearted, well-meaning bores gather around to help you. Usually, to tell the truth, they have nothing to help with, except their company—which is often appallingly dull.

Some members of the Negro race seem very well able to put up with it, though, in these uplifting years. Such was Caleb Johnson, colored social worker, who was always dragging around with him some nondescript white person or two, inviting them to dinner, showing them Harlem, ending up at the Savoy—much to the displeasure of whatever friends of his might be out that evening for fun, not sociology.

Friends are friends and, unfortunately, overearnest uplifters are uplifters—no matter what color they may be. If it were the white race that was ground down instead of Negroes, Caleb Johnson would be one of the first to offer Nordics the sympathy of his utterly inane society, under the impression that somehow he would be doing them a great deal of good.

You see, Caleb, and his white friends, too, were all bores. Or so we, who lived in Harlem's literary bohemia during the "Negro Renaissance," thought. We literary ones in those days considered ourselves too broad-minded to be bothered with questions of color. We liked people of any race who smoked incessantly, drank liberally, wore complexion and morality as loose garments, and made fun of anyone who didn't do likewise. We snubbed and high-hatted any Negro or white luckless enough not to understand Gertrude Stein, Ulysses, Man Ray, the theremin, Jean Toomer, or George Antheil. By the end of the 1920's Caleb was just catching up to Dos Passos. He thought H. G. Wells good.

We met Caleb one night in Small's. He had three assorted white folks in tow. We would have passed him by with but a nod had he not hailed us enthusiastically, risen, and introduced us with great acclaim to his friends, who turned out to be schoolteachers from Iowa, a woman and two men. They appeared amazed and delighted to meet all at once two Negro writers and a black painter in the flesh. They invited us to have a drink with them. Money being scarce with us, we deigned to sit down at their table.

The white lady said, "I've never met a Negro writer before."

The two men added, "Neither have we."

"Why, we know any number of *white* writers," we three dark bohemians declared with bored nonchalance.

"But Negro writers are much more rare," said the lady.

"There are plenty in Harlem," we said.

"But not in Iowa," said one of the men, shaking his mop of red hair.

"There are no good *white* writers in Iowa either, are there?" we asked superciliously.

"Oh yes, Ruth Suckow came from there."

Whereupon we proceeded to light in upon Ruth Suckow as old hat and to annihilate her in favor of Kay Boyle. The way we flung names around seemed to impress both Caleb and his white guests. This, of course, delighted us, though we were too young and too proud to admit it.

The drinks came and everything was going well, all of us drinking, and we three showing off in a high-brow manner, when suddenly at the table just behind us a man got up and knocked down a woman. He was a brownskin man. The woman was blonde. As she rose, he knocked her down again. Then the red-haired man from Iowa got up and knocked the colored man down.

He said, "Keep your hands off that white woman."

The man got up and said, "She's not a white woman. She's my wife."

One of the waiters added, "She's not white, sir, she's colored."

Whereupon the man from Iowa looked puzzled, dropped his fists, and said, "I'm sorry."

The colored man said, "What are you doing up here in Harlem anyway, interfering with my family affairs?"

The white man said, "I thought she was a white woman."

The woman who had been on the floor rose and said, "Well, I'm not a white woman, I'm colored, and you leave my husband alone."

Then they both lit in on the gentleman from Iowa. It took all of us and several waiters, too, to separate them. When it was over, the manager requested us to kindly pay our bill and get out. He said we were disturbing the peace. So we all left. We went to a fish restaurant down the street. Caleb was terribly apologetic to his white friends. We artists were both mad and amused.

"Why did you say you were sorry," said the colored painter to the visitor from Iowa, "after you'd hit that man—and then found out it wasn't a white woman you were defending, but merely a light colored woman who looked white?"

"Well," answered the red-haired Iowan, "I didn't mean to be butting in if they were all the same race."

"Don't you think a woman needs defending from a brute, no matter what race she may be?" asked the painter.

"Yes, but I think it's up to you to defend your own women."

"Oh, so you'd divide up a brawl according to races, no matter who was right?"

"Well, I wouldn't say that."

"You mean you wouldn't defend a colored woman whose husband was knocking her down?" asked the poet.

Before the visitor had time to answer, the painter said, "No! You just got mad because you thought a black man was hitting a *white* woman."

"But she *looked* like a white woman," countered the man.

"Maybe she was just passing for colored," I said.

"Like some Negroes pass for white," Caleb interposed.

"Anyhow, I don't like it," said the colored painter, "the way you stopped defending her when you found out she wasn't white."

"No, we don't like it," we all agreed except Caleb.

Caleb said in extenuation, "But Mr. Stubblefield is new to Harlem."

The red-haired white man said, "Yes, it's my first time here."

"Maybe Mr. Stubblefield ought to stay out of Harlem," we observed.

"I agree," Mr. Stubblefield said. "Good night."

He got up then and there and left the café. He stalked as he walked. His red head disappeared into the night.

"Oh, that's too bad," said the white couple who remained. "Stubby's temper just got the best of him. But explain to us, are many colored folks really as fair as that woman?"

"Sure, lots of them have more white blood than colored, and pass for white."

"Do they?" said the lady and gentleman from Iowa.

"You never read Nella Larsen?" we asked.

"She writes novels," Caleb explained. "She's part white herself."

"Read her," we advised. "Also read the *Autobiography of an Ex-Coloured Man*." Not that we had read it ourselves—because we paid but little attention to the older colored writers—but we knew it was about passing for white.

We all ordered fish and settled down comfortably to shocking our white friends with tales about how many Negroes there were passing for white all over America. We were determined to *épater le bourgeois* real good via this white couple we had cornered, when the woman leaned over the table in the midst of our dissertations and said, "Listen, gentlemen, you needn't spread the word, but me and my husband aren't white either. We've just been *passing* for white for the last fifteen years."

"What?"

"We're colored, too, just like you," said the husband. "But it's better passing for white because we make more money."

Well, that took the wind out of us. It took the wind out of Caleb, too. He thought all the time he was showing some fine white folks Harlem—and they were as colored as he was!

Caleb almost never cursed. But this time he said, "I'll be damned!"

Then everybody laughed. And laughed! We almost had hysterics. All at once we dropped our professionally self-conscious "Negro" manners, became natural, ate fish, and talked and kidded freely like colored folks do when there are no white folks around. We really had fun then, joking about that red-haired guy who mistook a fair colored woman for white. After the fish we went to two or three more night spots and drank until five o'clock in the morning.

Finally we put the light-colored people in a taxi heading downtown. They turned to shout a last good-by. The cab was just about to move off when the woman called to the driver to stop.

She leaned out the window and said with a grin, "Listen, boys! I hate to confuse you again. But, to tell the truth, my husband and I aren't really colored at all. We're white. We just thought we'd kid you by passing for colored a little while—just as you said Negroes sometimes pass for white."

She laughed as they sped off toward Central Park, waving, "Good-by!"

We didn't say a thing. We just stood there on the corner in Harlem dumbfounded—not knowing now *which* way we'd been fooled. Were they really white—passing for colored? Or colored—passing for white?

Whatever race they were, they had had too much fun at our expense—even if they did pay for the drinks.

WILLARD MOTLEY

The Almost White Boy

By birth he was half Negro and half white. Socially he was all Negro. That is when people knew that his mother was a brownskin woman with straightened hair and legs that didn't respect the color line when it came to making men turn around to look at them. His eyes were gray. His skin was as white as Slim Peterson's; his blond hair didn't have any curl to it at all. His nose was big and his lips were big—the only tip-off. Aunt Beulah-May said he looked just like "poor white trash." Other people, black and white, said all kinds of things about his parents behind their backs, even if they were married. And these people, when it came to discussing him, shook their heads, made sucking sounds with their tongues and said, "Too bad! Too bad!" And one straggly-haired Irish woman who had taken quite a liking to him had even gone so far as to tell him, blissfully unmindful of his desires in the matter, "I'd have you marry my daughter if you was white."

One thing he remembered. When he was small his dad had taken him up in his arms and carried him to the big oval mirror in the parlor. "Come here, Lucy," his father had said, calling Jimmy's mother. His mother came, smiling at the picture her two men made hugged close together; one so little and dependent, the other so tall and serious-eyed. She stood beside him, straightening Jimmy's collar and pushing his hair out of his eyes. Dad held him in between them. "Look in the mirror, son," he said. And they all looked. Their eyes were serious, not smiling, not staring, just gloom-colored with seriousness in the mirror. "Look at your mother. . . . Look at me." His dad gave the directions gravely. "Look at your mother's skin." He looked. That was the dear sweet mother he loved. "Look at the color of my skin." He looked. That was his daddy, the best daddy in the world. "We all love each other, son, all three of us," his dad said, and his mother's eyes in the mirror caught and held his father's with something shining and proud through the seriousness; and his mother's arm stole up around him and around his daddy. "People are just people. Some are good and some are bad," his father said. "People are just people. Look—and remember." He had remembered. He would never forget.

Somehow, something of that day had passed into his life. And he carried it with him back and forth across the color line. The colored fellows he palled with called him "the white nigger," and his white pals would sometimes look at him kind of funny but they never said anything. Only when they went out on dates together; then they'd tell him don't let something slip about "niggers" without meaning to. Then they'd look sheepish. Jim didn't see much difference. All the guys were swell if you liked them; all the girls flirted and necked and went on crying jags now and then. People were just people.

There were other things Jim remembered.

. . . On Fifty-eighth and Prairie. Lorenzo with white eyes in a black face. With his kinky hair screwed down tight on his bald-looking head like flies on flypaper. Ruby with her face all shiny brown and her hair in stiff-standing braids and her pipy brown legs Mom called razor-legs. Lorenzo saying, "You're black just like us." Ruby singing out, "Yeah! Yeah! You're a white nigger—white nigger!" Lorenzo taunting, "You ain't no different. My ma says so. You're just a nigger!" Lorenzo and Ruby pushing up close to him with threatening gestures, making faces at him, pulling his straight blond hair with mean fists, both yelling at the same time, "White nigger! White nigger!"

The name stuck.

. . . Women on the sidewalk in little groups. Their lips moving when he walked past with his schoolbooks under his arm. Their eyes lowered but looking at him. "Too bad! Too bad!" He could see them. He knew they were talking about him. "Too bad! Too bad!"

. . . Mom crying on the third floor of the kitchenette flat on Thirty-ninth Street. Mom saying to Dad, "We've got to move from here, Jim. We can't go on the street together without everybody staring at us. You'd think we'd killed somebody."

"What do we care how much they stare or what they say?"

"Even when I go out alone they stare. They never invite me to their houses. They say—they say that I think I'm better than they are—that I had to marry out of my race—that my own color wasn't good enough for me."

Dad saying, "Why can't people mind their own business? The hell with them." Mom crying. No friends. No company. Just the three of them.

. . . Then moving to the slums near Halstead and Maxwell, where all nationalities lived bundled up next door to each other and even in the same buildings. Jews. Mexicans. Poles. Negroes. Italians. Greeks. It was swell there. People changed races there. They went out on the streets together. No more staring. No more name-calling.

He grew up there.

. . . Getting older. And a lot of the white fellows not inviting him to parties at their houses when there were girls from the neighborhood. But they'd still go out of the neighborhood together and pick up girls or go on blind dates or to parties somewhere else. He didn't like to think of the neighborhood parties with the girls and the music and everything, and the door closed to him.

. . . Only once he denied it. He had been going around with Tony for a couple of weeks over on Racine Avenue. They played pool together, drank beer together on West Madison Street, drove around in Tony's old rattling Chevy.

One day Tony looked at him funny and said, point-blank, "Say, what are you anyway?"

Jim got red; he could feel his face burn. "I'm Polish," he said.

He was sorry afterwards. He didn't know why he said it. He felt ashamed.

. . . Then he was finished with school and he had to go to work. He got a job in a downtown hotel because nobody knew what he really was and Aunt Beulah-May said it was all right to "pass for white" when it came to making money but he'd better never get any ideas in his head about turning his back on his people. To him it was cheating. It was denying half himself. It wasn't a straight front. He knew how hard it was for colored fellows to find decent jobs. It wasn't saying I'm a Negro and taking the same chances they took when it came to getting a job. But he did it.

Jim remembered many of these things; they were tied inside of him in hard knots. But the color line didn't exist for him and he came and went pretty much as he chose. He took the girls in stride. He went to parties on the South Side, on Thirty-fifth and Michigan, on South Park. He went dancing at the Savoy Ballroom—and the Trianon. He went to Polish hops and Italian fiestas and Irish weddings. And he had a hell of a swell time. People were just people.

He had fun with the colored girls. But some of them held off from him, not knowing what he was. These were his people. No—he didn't feel natural around them. And with white people he wasn't all himself either. He didn't have any people.

Then all of a sudden he was madly in love with Cora. This had never happened before. He had sometimes wondered if, when it came, it would be a white girl or a colored girl. Now it was here. There was nothing he could do about it. And he was scared. He began to worry, and to wonder. And he began to wish, although ashamed to admit it to himself, that he didn't have any colored blood in him.

He met Cora at a dance at the Trianon. Cora's hair wasn't as blond as his but it curled all over her head. Her skin was pink and soft. Her breasts stood erect and her red lips were parted in a queer little loose way. They were always like that. And they were always moist-looking.

Leo introduced them. Then he let them alone and they danced every dance together; and when it was time to go home Leo had disappeared. Jim asked her if he could take her home.

"I think that would be awfully sweet of you," she said. Her eyes opened wide in a baby-blue smile.

She leaned back against him a little when he helped her into her coat. He flushed with the pleasure of that brief touching of their bodies. They walked through the unwinding ballroom crowd together, not having anything to say to each other, and out onto Cottage Grove, still not having anything to say. As they passed the lighted-up plate-glass window of Walgreen's drugstore Jim asked her, "Wouldn't you like a malted milk?" She didn't answer but just smiled up at him over her shoulder and he felt the softness of her arm in the doorway.

She sipped her malted milk. He sat stirring his straw around in his glass. Once in a while she'd look up over her glass and wrinkle her lips or her eyes at him, friendly-like. Neither of them said anything. Then, when Cora had finished, he held the match for her cigarette and their eyes came together and stayed that way longer than they needed to. And her lips were really parted now, with the cigarette smoke curling up into her hair.

In front of her house they stood close together, neither of them wanting to go.

"It was a nice dance," Cora said; and her fingers played in the hedge-top.

"Yes, especially after I met you."

"I'm going to see you again, aren't I?" Cora asked, looking up at him a little.

Jim looked down at the sidewalk. He hoped he could keep the red out of his cheeks. "I might as well tell you before someone else does—I'm a Negro," he said.

There was a catch in her voice, just a little noise not made of words.

"Oh, you're fooling!" she said with a small, irritated laugh.

"No, I'm not. I told you because I like you."

She had stepped back from him. Her eyes were searching for the windows of the house to see that there was no light behind the shades.

"Please, let me see you again," Jim said.

Her eyes, satisfied, came away from the windows. They looked at the sidewalk where he had looked. Her body was still withdrawn. Her lips weren't parted now. There were hard little lines at the corners of her mouth.

"Let me meet you somewhere," Jim said.

Another furtive glance at the house; then she looked at him, unbelievingly. "You didn't mean that—about being colored?"

"It doesn't matter, does it?"

"No—only—"

"Let me meet you somewhere," Jim begged.

Her lips were parted a little. She looked at him strangely, deep into him in a way that made him tremble, then down his body and back up into his eyes. She tossed her head a little. "Well—call me up tomorrow afternoon." She gave him the number.

He watched her go into the house. Then he walked to the corner to wait for his streetcar; and he kicked at the sidewalk and clenched his fists.

Jim went to meet her in Jackson Park. They walked around. She was beautiful in her pink dress. Her lips were pouted a little bit, and her eyes were averted, and she was everything he had ever wanted. They sat on a bench far away from anybody. "You know," she said, "I never liked nig—Negroes. You're not like a Negro at all." They walked to the other end of the park. "Why do you tell people?" she asked.

"People are just people," he told her, but the words didn't sound real any more.

Twice again he met her in the park. Once they just sat talking and once they went to a movie. Both times he walked her to the car line and left her there. That was the way she wanted it.

After that it was sneaking around to meet her. She didn't like to go on dates with him when he had his white friends along. She'd never tell him why. And yet she put her body up close to him when they were alone. It was all right too when she invited some of her friends who didn't know what he was.

They saw a lot of each other. And pretty soon he thought from the long, probing looks she gave him that she must like him; from the way she'd grab his hand, tight, sometimes; from the way she danced with him. She even had him take her home now and they'd stand on her porch pressed close together. "Cora, I want you to come over to my house," he told her. "My mother and father are swell. You'll like them." He could see all four of them together. "It isn't a nice neighborhood. I mean it doesn't look good, but the people are nicer than—in other places. Gee, you'll like my mother and father."

"All right, I'll go, Jimmy. I don't care. I don't care."

Dad kidded him about his new flame, saying it must be serious, that he had never brought a girl home before. Mom made fried chicken and hot biscuits. And when he went to get Cora he saw Dad and Mom both with dust rags, shining up everything in the parlor for the tenth time; he heard Dad and Mom laughing quietly together and talking about their first date.

He hadn't told them she was a white girl. But they never batted an eye.

"Mom, this is Cora."

"How do you do, dear. Jimmy has told us so much about you." Dear, sweet Mom. Always gracious and friendly.

"Dad, this is Cora." Dad grinning, looking straight at her with eyes as blue as hers, going into some crazy story about "Jimmy at the age of three." Good old Dad. "People are just people."

Dad and Mom were at ease. Only Cora seemed embarrassed. And she was nervous, not meeting Dad's eyes, not meeting Mom's eyes, looking to him for support. She sat on the edge of her chair. "Y-y-yes, sir . . . No, Mrs. Warner." She only picked at the good food Mom had spent all afternoon getting ready. And Jim, watching her, watching Dad and Mom, hoping they wouldn't notice, got ill at ease himself and he was glad when he got her outside. Then they were themselves again.

"Mom and Dad are really swell. You'll have to get to know them," he said, looking at her appealingly, asking for approval. She smiled with expressionless eyes. She said nothing.

On Fourteenth and Halstead they met Slick Harper. Slick was as black as they come. It was sometimes hard, because of his southern dialect and his Chicago black-belt expressions, to know just what he meant in English. He practiced jitterbug steps on street corners and had a whole string of girls—black, brownskin, high-yellow. Everybody called him Slick because he handed his bevy of girls a smooth line and because he wore all the latest fashions in men's clothes—high-waisted trousers, big-brimmed hats, bright sports coats, Cuban heels and coconut straws with gaudy bands. Slick hailed Jim; his eyes gave Cora the once-over.

"Whatcha say, man!" he shouted. "Ah know they all goes when the wagon comes but where you been stuck away? And no jive! Man, ah been lookin' for you. We're throwing a party next Saturday and we want you to come."

Jim stood locked to the sidewalk, working his hands in his pockets and afraid to look at Cora. He watched Slick's big purple lips move up and down as they showed the slices of white teeth. Now Slick had stopped talking and was staring at Cora with a black-faced smirk.

"Cora, this is Slick Harper."

"How do you do." Her voice came down as from the top of a building.

"Ah'm glad to meetcha," Slick said. "You sho' got good taste, Jim." His eyes took in her whole figure. "Why don't you bring her to the party?"

"Maybe I will. Well, we've got to go." He walked fast then to keep up with Cora.

Cora never came over again.

Cora had him come over to her house. But first she prepared him a lot. "Don't ever—ever—tell my folks you're colored. Please, Jimmy. Promise me. . . . Father doesn't like colored people. . . . They aren't broad-minded like me. . . . And don't mind Father, Jimmy," she warned.

He went. There was a cream-colored car outside the house. In the parlor were smoking stands, and knickknack brackets, and a grand piano nobody played. Cora's father smoked cigars, owned a few pieces of stock, went to Florida two weeks every winter, told stories about the "Florida niggers." Cora's mother had the same parted lips Cora had, but she breathed through them heavily as if she were always trying to catch up with herself. She was fat and overdressed. And admonished her husband when he told his Southern stories through the smoke of big cigars: "Now, Harry, you mustn't talk like that. What will this nice young man think of you? There are plenty of fine upright Negroes—I'm sure. Of course I don't know any personally. . . . Now, Harry, don't be so harsh. Don't forget, you took milk from a colored mammy's breast. Oh, Harry, tell them about the little darky who wanted to watch your car—'Two cents a awah, Mistah No'the'nah!' "

Cora sat with her hands in her lap and her fingers laced tightly together. Jim smiled at Mr. Hartley's jokes and had a miserable time. And Jim discovered that it was best not to go to anybody's house. Just the two of them.

Jim and Cora went together for four months. And they had an awful time of it. But they were unhappy apart. Yet when they were together their eyes were always accusing each other. Sometimes they seemed to enjoy hurting each other. Jim wouldn't call her up; and he'd be miserable. She wouldn't write to him or would stand him up on a date for Chuck Nelson or Fred Schultz; then she'd be miserable. Something held them apart. And something pulled them together.

Jim did a lot of thinking. It had to go four revolutions. Four times a part-Negro had to marry a white person before legally you were white. The blood had to take four revolutions. Mulatto—that's what he was—quadroon—octaroon—then it was all gone. Then you were white. His great-grandchildren maybe. Four times the blood had to let in the other blood.

Then one night they were driving out to the forest preserves in Tony's Chevy. "What are you thinking, Jimmy?"

"Oh, nothing. Just thinking."

"Do you like my new dress? How do I look in it?"

"Isn't that a keen moon, Cora?" The car slid along the dark deserted highway. They came to a gravel road and Jim eased the car over the crushed stone in second gear. Cora put her cheek against the sleeve of his coat. The branches of trees made scraping sounds against the sides of the car. Cora was closer to him now. He could smell the perfume in her hair and yellow strands tickled the end of his nose. He stopped the motor and switched the lights off. Cora lifted his arm up over her head and around her, putting his hand in close to her waist with her hand over his, stroking his. "Let's sit here like this—close and warm," she whispered. Then her voice lost itself in the breast of his coat.

For a long time they sat like that. Then Jim said, "Let's take a walk." He opened the door and, half supporting her, he lifted her out. While she was still in his arms she bit his ear gently.

"Don't do that," he said, and she giggled.

Panting, they walked through the low scrub into the woods. The bushes scratched their arms. Twigs caught in Cora's hair. Their feet sank in the earth. Cora kept putting her fingers in Jim's hair and mussing it. "Don't. Don't," he said. And finally he caught her fingers and held them tight in his. They walked on like this. The moon made silhouettes of them, silhouettes climbing up the slow incline of hill.

Jim found a little rise of land, treeless, grassy. Far to the northeast, Chicago sprawled, row on row of dim lights growing more numerous but gentler.

The night was over them.

They sat on the little hillock, shoulder to shoulder; and Cora moved her body close to him. It was warm there against his shirt, open at the neck. They didn't talk. They didn't move. And when Cora breathed he could feel the movement of her body against him. It was almost as if they were one. He looked up at the splash of stars, and the moon clouding over. His arm went around her, shieldingly. He closed his eyes and put his face into her hair. "Cora! Cora!" The only answer she gave was the slight movement of her body.

"Cora, I love you."

"Do you, Jimmy?" she said, snuggling up so close to him that he could feel her heart beat against him.

He didn't move. But after a while she was slowly leaning back until the weight of her carried him back too and they lay full length. They lay like this a long time. He looked at her. Her eyes were closed. She was breathing hard. Her lips were parted and moist.

"Jimmy."

"What?"

"Nothing."

She hooked one of her feet over his. A slow quiver started in his shoulder, worked its way down the length of him. He sat up. Cora sat up.

"There's nobody here but us," she said. Her fingers unbuttoned the first button of his shirt, the second. Her fingers crept in on his chest, playing with the little hairs there.

"There's nobody here but us," she said, and she ran her fingers inside his shirt, over his shoulders and the back of his neck.

"We can't do this, Cora. We can't."

"Do you mean about you being colored? It doesn't matter to me, Jimmy. Honest it doesn't."

"No. Not that. It's because I love you. That's why I can't. That's why I want—"

He sat up straight then. His fingers pulled up some grass. He held it up to the light and looked at it. She had her head in his lap and lay there perfectly still. He could hear her breathing, and her breath was warm and moist on the back of his other hand where it lay on his leg. He threw the grass away, watched how the wind took it and lowered it down to the ground. He lifted her up by the shoulders, gently, until they were close together, looking into each other's eyes.

"I want it to be right for us, Cora," he said. "Will you marry me?"

The sting of red in her cheeks looked as if a blow had left it there; even the moonlight showed that. She sat up without the support of his hands. Her arms were straight and tense under her. Her eyes met his, burning angrily at the softness in his eyes. "You damn dirty nigger!" she said, and jumped up and walked away from him as fast as she could.

When she was gone he lay on his face where he had been sitting. He lay full length. The grass he had pulled stuck to his lips. "People are just people." He said it aloud. "People are just people." And he laughed, hoarsely, hollowly. "People are just people." Then it was only a half-laugh with a sob cutting into it. And he was crying, with his arms flung up wildly above his head, with his face pushed into the grass trying to stop the sound of his crying. Off across the far grass Cora was running away from him. The moon, bright now, lacquered the whiteness of his hands lying helplessly above his head; it touched the blondness of his hair.

STANLEY CROUCH

Man in the Mirror

Because Afro-Americans have presented challenges to one order or another almost as long as they have been here, fear and contempt have frequently influenced the way black behavior is assessed. The controversy over Michael Jackson is the most recent example, resulting in a good number of jokes, articles in this periodical and others, and even the barely articulate letter by the singer himself that was published in *People*. Jackson has inspired debate over his cosmetic decisions because the residue of '60s black nationalism and the condescension of those who would pity or mock black Americans have met over the issue of his face, his skin tone, his hair.

Since the '60s, there has been a tendency among a substantial number of Afro-Americans to promulgate a recipe for the model black person. That model has taken many forms, but all of them are based on presumptions of cultural segregation between black and white Americans. The symbols of that purported segregation were supposed to permeate the ways in which black people lived, dressed, wore their hair, ate, thought, voted, walked, talked, and addressed their African heritage. And though the grip of such nationalism weakened over the years, it continues to influence even those who were lucky enough not to have been adolescents during its period of dominance.

Greg Tate is clearly one who has been taken in, and his recent article on Jackson illustrates the provincialism inherent in such thinking. Jackson alarms Tate, who sees the singer's experience under the scalpel as proof of self-hatred. The trouble with Tate's vision is that it ignores the substance of the American dream and the inevitabilities of a free society. Though no one other than Jackson could know what he seeks, to automatically assume that the pop star's cosmetic surgery was solely intended to eradicate Negroid features in order to "look white" seems far too simple, ignoring both African and American cultural elements.

Présence Africaine published some 20 years ago a compendium of papers delivered in Senegal at the World Festival of Negro Arts. One of the lecturers made note of the fact that a number of African tribes considered the lighter-skinned the more attractive. This vision of beauty was free of colonial influence and probably had more to do with the quality of exoticism that is as central to magnetism as to repulsion. Further, Jackson could just as easily be opting for the mulatto look—if not that of the Latin lover and dandy—that has resulted from the collusion of gene pools whenever light and dark folk have coupled on the Basin Streets of history. Or could he be taken by the keen noses and "refined" features of Ethiopians?

The fact that Michael Jackson not only is a person of African descent but is also an American should never be excluded from a discussion of his behavior. The American dream is actually the idea that an identity can be improvised and can function socially if it doesn't intrude upon the freedom of anyone else. With that freedom comes eccentric behavior as well as the upward mobility resulting from talent, discipline, and good fortune—*and* the downward mobility observed in *some* of those who inhabit the skid rows of this country because they *prefer* the world of poverty and alcoholism to the middle-, upper-middle-, or upper-class backgrounds they grew up in. As one bum who had obviously seen better days said to a waiter as he was being ushered out of the now defunct Tin Palace for panhandling, "People come from all over the world to be bums on the Bowery. Why should I deny myself that right?"

Tate should easily understand this since he is from a well-to-do black family in Washington, D.C., but has chosen to wear dreadlocks in a hairdo that crosses the Rasta world with that of the mohawk and, eschewing the conservative dress of his background, looks as often as not like a borderline homeless person. That Tate is a bohemian by choice rather than birth means that he has plotted out an identity he prefers to that of his social origins and has found the costumes that he feels most appropriate for his personal theatre piece. Though it is much easier for Tate to get another haircut and change his dress than it would be for Jackson to return to his "African physiognomy," each reflects the willingness to opt for imagery that repudiates some aspect of the past.

That sense of improvising an identity shouldn't be thought of as separate from the American—and universal—love of masks. Nor should it be seen as at all separate from the "African retentions" Afro-American cultural nationalists and social anthropologists refer to so frequently. The love of masks, of makeup, and of costumes is often much more than the pursuit of high fashion or the adherence to ritual convention; it is also the expression of that freedom to invent the self and of the literal *fun* Americans have often gotten from scandalizing expectations.

As Constance Rourke observed and as Albert Murray reminds us in his invaluable *The Omni-Americans*, those colonial rebels dressed up as Indians for the Boston Tea Party might have enjoyed the masquerade itself as much as they did dumping the cargo in the ocean. Considered within the spectrum of the happy to hostile masquerade that has since evolved, Michael Jackson's affection for his mirror image veering off from what nature intended places him right in the center of one of the whirlpools of national sensibility.

One needs only to look at any book of photographs from the '60s to see how the connection between protest politics and the love of masks was most broadly played out—SNCC workers donned overalls; hippies took to long hair and tie-dyed outfits; black nationalists wore Figi haircuts and robes; and self-styled Afro-American revolutionaries put on black berets, black leather jackets, black shirts, pants, and shoes, or appropriated the combat dress of Third World military men. And no one who looks at the various costumes worn today, from dotted, yellow "power ties" to gargoyle punk fashions, should have any problem seeing their connection to the masking inclinations rooted in the joy of assumed identities. That love is still so embedded in the national personality that the people of New Orleans are admired as much for the costumes and false faces of Mardi Gras as for their cuisine and their music. And those of us in New York know how much pleasure the greasepaint, sequins, feathers, and satins of the Labor Day parade in Brooklyn bring to spectators and participants.

As far as further African retentions are concerned, it could easily be argued that Michael Jackson is much more in line with the well-documented argument many primitive African cultures have had with the dictates of nature. Have the people of any other cultures so perfectly prefigured plastic surgery or been more willing to accept the pain of traditionally approved mutilation? It is doubtful. In photograph after photograph, Africans are shown wearing plates in their lips to extend them, rings around their necks to lengthen them, plopping red mud in their hair for homemade conks that emulate the manes of lions, filing their teeth, and suffering through the slashes and the rubbed-in ashes that result in spectacular scarification. Whatever one wants to say about "different standards of beauty" and so forth, to conclude that such cultures are at all concerned with "being natural" is to actually reveal one's refusal to see things as they are.

That willingness to suffer under the tribal knife is obviously addressed with much greater technical sophistication in the world of plastic surgery. In fact, the so-called self-hatred of black Americans, whenever it *does* exist, is perhaps no more than a racial variation on the national attitude that has made the beauty industry so successful. In those offices and in those operating rooms where plans are made and carried out that result in millions of dollars in profit, the supposed self-hatred of black Americans has little to do with the wealth earned by plastic surgeons. Far and away, the bulk of their clients are Caucasians in flight from the evidence of age, Caucasians dissatisfied with their profiles, their eyes, their ears, their chins, their necks, their breasts, the fat around their knees, their waists, their thighs, and so forth. Nipped, tucked, carrying implants, and vacuumed free of fat, they face their mirrors with glee.

Where there is so much talk about Afro-Americans fawning over the lighter-skinned among them, what is one to make of all the bottle blondes this country contains and all of those who made themselves sometimes look orange by using lotions for counterfeit tans? It is a certainty that if some Negro American genius were to invent a marketplace procedure that would result in harmlessly emitting the desired levels of melanin for those Caucasians enthralled by tans so that they could remain as dark as they wished throughout the year, his or her riches would surpass those of Bill Cosby. Would this imaginary genius be exploiting Caucasian self-hatred?

Then there is the problem some have with Jackson's apparent softness, his supposed effeminacy. That, too, has a precedent within Afro-American culture itself. The late writer Lionel Mitchell once pointed out that certain black men were bothered about the black church because they were made uncomfortable by those choir directors and pretty-boy lead singers who wore glistening marcelled hair and were obviously homosexual. A friend of Mitchell's extended the writer's position by observing that those very gospel songs were just as often masks through which homosexual romance was crooned. "What do you think is going through their minds when the songs talk about being held close to *His* bosom?" (What a variation on the ways slaves secretly signaled each other through spirituals, planning flight or rebellion!) This is not to say that every homosexual gospel singer thought of things more secular than spiritual when chirping those songs in which love is felt for and from an almighty He or Him, but it is to say that those who feel Jackson has somehow sold out his masculine duties have not looked as closely at their own tradition as perhaps they should.

There is also the fact that Jackson, both as androgynous performer and surgical veteran purportedly seeking to look like Diana Ross, has precursors in the minstrel shows of the middle 19th century. It is there that the tradition of the romantic balladeer actually begins, at least as a phenomenon of mass entertainment. As Robert C. Toll observes in *Blacking Up*, white minstrels became very popular with women because they were able to publicly express tender emotion through the convention of burnt cork and were sometimes able to become national stars for their performances as giddy mulatto beauties. "Female impersonators excited more interest than any other minstrel specialist," writes Toll. "Men in the audience probably were titillated by the alluring stage characters whom they were momentarily drawn to, and they probably got equal pleasure from mocking and laughing at them. . . . At a time when anxiety about social roles was intense, the female impersonator, who actually changed roles, fascinated the public. As a model of properly 'giddy' femininity, he could reassure men that women were in their places while at the same time showing women how to behave without competing with them. Thus, in some ways, he functioned like the blackface 'fool' who educated audiences while also reassuring them that he was their inferior. Neither man nor woman, the female impersonator threatened no one."

Jackson quite clearly bothers more than a few, from Eddie Murphy to the rappers interviewed by Guy Trebay in the article that accompanied Greg Tate's. The pit bull of Murphy's paranoia over pansies has often been unleashed on Jackson and the fact that the rappers were disturbed by Jackson's persona suggests something other than what it seems. Perhaps what bothers them most is that the singer's roots in minstrelsy are so different from their own. As Harry Allen revealed not so long ago, more than a few rappers are actually middle-class Negroes acting out their version of a "gangster aesthetic." Instead of minstrel mugging, you have counterfeit thugging, more than a tad in line with the faddish cracker sensibility of acting bad to bust the ass of the middle class on the rack of rock and roll.

Yet the actual sorrow and the pity of the Michael Jackson story is that he has had to carry the cross of an imposed significance far beyond what his music merits. Jackson comes from rhythm and blues, which is itself a dilution of blues, a descent from the profound emotion of America's first truly adult secular music. As a pop star, Jackson's fame and riches have come from the expression of adolescent passion, but he is also the product of an era in which profundity has been forced on music actually intended to function as no more than the soundtrack for teenage romance and the backbeat for the bouts of self-pity young people suffer while assaulted by their hormones. Rock criticism changed all of that, bootlegging the rhetoric of aesthetic evaluation to elevate the symbols of adolescent frenzy and influencing the way pop stars viewed themselves. So when a man's power is found in an adolescent form, time impinges upon his vitality. If sufficiently spooked, he might be moved to invent a world for himself in which all evidence that he was ever born a particular person at a particular time is removed. That removal might itself become the strongest comment upon the inevitable gloom that comes not of having been given too much too soon but of having been convinced that one is important only so long as he or she is not too old.

RONALD E. HALL

Blacks Who Pass

It was the first meeting of prospective pledges for one of the most respected Black fraternities in America. I was proud. I'd made it to State College and was about to enter the land of the elite. My father—who had only a high school diploma—had often remarked to me, "An education is something no one can take from you." I'd always excelled in school when I wanted to, but joining this fraternity would leave no doubt that I was indeed an educated Black man. The thought excited me so much that I arrived quite early; that left plenty of time for the anxiety to build.

To make a good impression, I had selected my best—and only—suit, a navy-blue single-button wool, a Brooks Brothers model that I had picked up for twenty dollars at a pawnshop before leaving Philadelphia for school. It must have had ghetto written all over it. I walked through the door and struck my best pose, then turned to see the frat brother who had invited me stepping forward. He greeted me and introduced me to other members as they walked in. They were campus stars, and associating with them would increase my status tenfold. I tried frantically to say all the right things to start off on the right foot. After all, these people alone would decide whether or not I became a member of their fraternity. I grew tense with the effort to avoid making some unforgivable error.

AT SIX-FOOT-THREE WITH SMOOTH BROWN SKIN AND DRESSED IN A BROOKS BROTHERS SUIT, HOW COULD I NOT STIR FEMALE HORMONES?

As guests continued to arrive, I sensed the stares beginning to pierce my back. Except for the frat host and me, everyone there had light skin and sharp features. Ordinarily that fact might not have caught my attention, but on this singular evening I felt that all those other prospective pledges had passed a certain test and I had not. This distinction further tried my self-confidence. But the skill of "keeping cool," which I had learned in the ghetto at an early age, enabled me to maintain an outward composure.

Some of the frat brothers came with their girlfriends. They in turn were accompanied by other female friends, who, I supposed, had wanted a chance to meet the single brothers. The darkest of all these young women was much lighter-skinned than I. I glanced about the room trying to catch one of them eyeing me, but they all seemed unaware of my presence. Was that bad? It certainly didn't feel good. Maybe they were behaving with a discretion gauged to these rarefied surroundings? But still, at six-foot-three with smooth brown skin and dressed in a Brooks Brothers suit, how could I not stir female hormones? Surely at least some of these women must want to check me out, I thought. Had they chosen not to out of respect for their boyfriends, or maybe even out of fear of them? Then it happened: A young lady just dark enough to be recognized as Black asked, "Aren't you a little too dark for this fraternity?" In a flash I felt my guts crashing to the floor. I don't remember what I said; I suppose I managed not to make a fool of myself. I was feeling what most Blacks experience when they are the odd "nigger" at a white party, only these were Black people! Needless to say, even though I was asked to join, any hope I had of being accepted vanished immediately. It has been years since I pledged for that fraternity. But I remember that meeting to this day. It was my first exposure to the so-called blue-bloods in Black society, who too often do decide, at some point in their lives, to pass for white.

Eventually I graduated with honors and worked for a while at a mental health clinic before enrolling in a doctoral program. I chose Atlanta University, as it was a mecca for data on Black Americans. While gathering information on skin color for my dissertation, I came to realize that one of the advantages of having brown skin—as distinct from light or dark skin—in the Black community is that you are less likely either to be subjected to a biased attitude or to develop one. You are more readily accepted by Black people in general. Furthermore, quite a lot of Cherokee blood runs in my family, and skin color ranges from very light to very dark and includes everything in between. My identity and self-worth were never tied to skin shade; so although my experience with the fraternity shocked me, it did not truly scar me emotionally. Instead it set me to wondering about something I had long taken for granted—the implications of skin color for identity among Black Americans. I was particularly curious about those who were light enough to pass for white. How often did they cross the color line to avoid the stigma of belonging to a dark-skinned ethnic group? And when they did, why did they not value their Blackness as I had?

Technically any Black person who has mixed parentage can be defined as biracial. Personally I must count myself among that number. I am also among the millions of darker-skinned, technically biracial Black Americans who do not claim such as our identity. When those so-called biracial persons who happen to be lighter-skinned are asked to comment on their identity, their responses differ. Actress Jasmine Guy—whom I used to walk by each morning on my way to class at Atlanta University during the shooting of *School Daze*—has no reservation about referring to herself as Black. She admits that she had some problems, while growing up in Georgia, with lack of acceptance by darker-skinned Blacks; but although her skin was light, her identity as a Black American was rarely questioned by others, perhaps because Jasmine Guy herself never questioned it.

For the light-skinned star of the movie *Flashdance*, identity is not so simple. Jennifer Beals claims that she is neither Black nor white. If she has to fill out a form requesting personal information, she checks the box labeled "Other."

And light-skinned Renee Tenisan, the first "Black" female to be chosen as Playmate of the Year by *Playboy* magazine, believes that calling herself Black is to deny her white ancestry. Her success has obviously brought some measure of pride to both white and Black members of her family. But one wonders how her white relatives might feel about her if she were on welfare, living in the projects. These three examples represent only a few of the responses of light-skinned Blacks to the question of identity.

While I continued my studies at Atlanta University, I discovered additionally that skin color—vis-à-vis self-esteem—seems to be an issue for Black women and Black men in different ways.

Before going to Atlanta I attended the University of Detroit. There I dated a light-skinned Black woman named Crystal, who stimulated my intellect. In those days my budding aspirations to join the mental health profession led me to analyze every person with whom I had more than a casual conversation. Crystal's mother was Black, and her father—I assumed, since I never met him—was white. Regardless, Crystal was certainly light enough to pass. Since she had grown up in the sixties in a Black neighborhood in Detroit, I imagined that her light skin had made life hard for her. And her hair was straight, which also probably brought attacks from her Black peers for being not "Black enough." She had a Black working-class way about her, which contrasted with her reverence for education. One day Crystal sensed that I was analyzing her and remarked, "You aren't as smart as you think you are."

Crystal was a gutsy, tough lady. However, I do remember one tender moment when she revealed her vulnerability. We were seated on the couch in her living room, doing what dating couples tend to do when they are alone. She pointed to the sooty stones in that fireplace and said, "I'd give anything to be as black as that." I was stunned. I don't remember what we'd been talking about; but I do remember that her comment about her skin color was so astonishing because it was utterly out of context. It hit me like a ton of bricks. Crystal had caught me completely off balance. I had believed her to be a street-smart and confident person, only to discover she wore a facade. With all my analyzing and would-be attention to detail, I had missed what might have been obvious to others: Some light-skinned Blacks who can pass for white experience difficulty being accepted by their own people. A brown-skinned Black male, like me, could never have known such an experience as hers. At the time, I could make no sense at all of Crystal's comment. For that moment we were still and the room silent as I searched her eyes for an answer of what to say. She looked away, as I could find nothing appropriate. To this day I have never been so touched and confused simultaneously. I filed that moment in my memory. Not until I was ready to graduate did I truly begin to understand her anguish.

It's well known that most Black people abhor the idea of passing for white. But another aspect of the issue is seldom discussed—the rejection of light-skinned Blacks by those with darker skin. In the same way that whites tend not to accept responsibility for their racism, Blacks do not want to talk about rejection of their own people. Typically it's working-class Blacks—the type in Crystal's background—who are likely to be the most guilty of such behavior. They often do not have a wide range of personal experience with Black people whose skin shades, eye color, facial features, and hair textures vary much from theirs. Such persons, whose white bloodline dates from the antebellum plantations, are almost always associated with the middle class. And so a type of class tension evolved that contributes to the decision of some light-skinned Blacks to pass rather than deal with the racial rejection from Blacks and class rejection from whites. What's more, light-skinned Blacks—again because of class—may have few opportunities to interact with dark-skinned or working-class Blacks in a positive environment. When they do meet, both may have formidable walls to overcome.

Blacks whose skin is light enough to let them pass have presented themselves as white because that act and that identity can improve their quality of life. Dr. Alvin Poussaint, with whom I have corresponded, contends that some light-skinned Black Americans, such as Jennifer Beals and Renee Tenisan, play down their Blackness simply because they do not think there is any advantage in being identified as Black. With their light skin and straight hair they can pass as Greek or Italian, escape the obvious stigmas associated with being Black, and enjoy the privileges of a white person. Even if they choose not to define themselves, they are clearly altering their identity. This is a critical mistake. I can't imagine what it must do to a light-skinned Black person emotionally.

Trying to forgive Blacks who choose to pass for white is difficult for me—even though I understand the advantages they gain. I feel that by passing, they have cursed the memory of every dark-skinned person on their family tree. But the phenomenon is not an issue for me personally, so I must struggle honestly to understand it.

I know that, in the cold calculation of a cost-benefit analysis, to want to be Black in America is crazy. I know, too, intellectually, that once a Black person realizes what is denied him based upon the skin color of his relatives—how he is perceived in the minds not only of bad people but of many people who are fundamentally good—his sense of unfairness may overcome him to the extent that he simply cannot accept that part of himself that has been defined as ugly and inferior. And if such a person has no particular political agenda or ethnic loyalty, passing may seem to be a perfectly logical way of getting what he knows he deserves. But being Black cannot be reduced to an equation or to perfect logic. To live with this decision, many light-skinned Blacks choose professions that offer them ways to benefit Blacks in general—such as law, medicine, and the ministry. In the process they can delude themselves into thinking that their passing for white was and remains necessary for the benefit of Black people.

Furthermore light-skinned Blacks who pass for white but inwardly identify with the Black community suffer. They endure one assault after another upon their dignity and self-worth. And willy-nilly they inflict injury upon themselves. In the company of whites sooner or later they must either laugh off or laugh at the inevitable "nigger" joke. They must hide the remorse that their own laughter causes them and then must wrestle, alone, with their pent-up anger and with the betrayer's guilt they feel. And if they would continue to pass, they must foster the illusion within themselves that such jokes somehow have nothing to do with them. What this can do to the human spirit, I suspect, causes some light-skinned Blacks to hate whites with a flaming passion.

Passing for white inflicts psychological trauma on those who try it, because it requires them to erect a wall between who they are or could be as persons and who they are or try to be amid white society. W.E.B. Du Bois referred to this as dual consciousness, a condition that is rooted in racism.

All Blacks experience dual consciousness to some extent, but dark-skinned Blacks who cannot pass can rely on the support of their communities: In them they can be themselves. Light-skinned Blacks who pass must depersonalize themselves and hold others at a distance to survive. This posture can destroy their relationships with people close to them. Furthermore dark-skinned Blacks may perceive someone who is passing as having a "superior attitude," while whites may perceive him or her as mean or nasty.

In my opinion a belief that light skin is superior prevails worldwide and has an enormous impact upon the decision to pass.

The "mulatto hypothesis" was put forth by early white social scientists. They used it to explain away the few Black individuals who excelled intellectually in business or the sciences. This hypothesis further reinforced the belief that light skin was superior to dark.

One result was that certain jobs were once routinely given or denied Blacks based upon their lightness of skin. For example, civil service jobs were highly sought after by Blacks early in the twentieth century. In Chicago the white officials responsible for filling those positions felt that a Black person with light skin would fit better into an office populated mostly by whites. Also, the menial elevator-operator jobs in the large downtown department stores of northern cities were once reserved for "light-skinned colored girls." Even the Black community, to its simultaneous shame, fame, and economic enrichment, was home to any number of establishments that were owned and operated by Blacks but refused to serve the Black public. In Tulsa, Oklahoma, there was a Black-owned, Black-operated barbecue café that for years did not allow Blacks to eat at its tables. If you weren't light enough to pass, the best you could expect was a plate handed out the back door.

One of the cruelest manifestations of color discrimination in the Black community was the "brown-paper-bag test." The result of this color-comparison test was that dark skin was taxed and light skin was awarded status. For example a campus fraternity or sorority at one of the Black colleges would have a party and charge an admission. Anyone with dark skin who attended would incur an additional tax. Light-skinned guests, usually females, would be admitted free. On those same campuses a dark-skinned Black woman could not have been selected as homecoming queen until the sixties. Whites must have found such behavior a bit peculiar. For light-skinned Blacks, I suppose, it added yet another reason to dissociate themselves from the Black community.

There are in fact many rationales for passing, some of them fascinating. While working on my first book, *The Color Complex*, I came across the intriguing story of a Black woman named Mary Walker. Most of us tend to think that passing is an outdated concept relevant only to a distant and ugly past, when dark-skinned people could be lynched with no outcry from the public; Ms. Walker's case dispels that notion. She grew up during the sixties, at the height of the Black-pride movement, but was raised in an all-white neighborhood of Denver, Colorado. There her parents—both Black—required her and her twelve siblings from birth to pass as white. According to Ms. Walker, her parents believed that life would be better for them if they did not reveal that they were Black. The whole family thus had to guard their secret very carefully: The children were reprimanded if they didn't straighten their hair on schedule or if they used Black slang.

Mary Walker was not particularly bothered by these restrictions until she went off to a small college in the West, where her white cultural norms made her an outcast among Blacks when she tried to join the Black student union on campus. She was told that she was "too white." It was then that she realized that her parents' enforcement of white norms had cost her a major part of her identity. Having no idea what to do about the problem, she decided to ignore it and put her energies into getting her degree.

After graduation Ms. Walker continued to pass until she was in her thirties, when she decided to advocate the hiring of more Black teachers at the school where she was employed and in so doing "came out of the closet" about her own passing. Not too surprisingly the school administration then accused her of trying to take advantage of affirmative action policies by suddenly declaring herself to be Black when she obviously was not. She claims to have been fired from her job as a result, an irony that generated media interest in her story.

Mary Walker's family may in fact have been more white than Black. A Jew who has one drop of Italian blood is not necessarily Italian. A German who has one drop of French blood is not necessarily French. In fact I know of no other ethnic group than Blacks to which the one-drop theory is so important. This essential fact makes the point that to be Black is to be subjected to the most severe discrimination in America.

HOSEA HUDSON

Black Worker in the Deep South

I used to pray to be able to get a job where I could earn a decent wage and work decent hours. I thought it would be wonderful to be paid the tremendous sum of $5 a day which, I was told, a young, strong man could earn in Atlanta, Ga.

I didn't have any trouble getting a common laborer's job in the Nashville, Chattanooga and St. Louis Railroad shop. They told me I would be paid 30 cents an hour for a seven-day week, but they didn't tell me how many hours I would have to put in each day. I found that out for myself.

My job was in and around the coal chute. You could lay off on any day except Sunday. If you made Sunday your day off, you were automatically fired, so I began by being very careful to remember that Sunday was not going to be any day of rest for me, even though I had been taught that it was a sin to work on Sunday. Later on I figured out that "six days shalt thou labor and do all thy work" means that you should rest on *any* one of the seven days so you could have strength to work on the other six.

There were three of us working around the coal chute, all of us Black men. We had to fill the chute, which was a 90-foot-high wooden structure straddling two railroad tracks, one side holding five carloads of coal and the other side, four carloads. Beginning at 7 o'clock in the morning and working until 11 at night some days, our job was to fill up that chute with coal from the open cars. There wasn't any extra-time pay, just straight 30 cents an hour, and it never stormed so furiously nor rained too hard, nor did the sun ever shine too hot nor cold winds whip around us too roughly for us to fill up that coal chute. Picking chunks out of those frozen coal cars was just like picking at stone from the side of a mountain of hard rock.

Around 2:30 p.m. the switch engine was brought out of the roundhouse by the hostler and his helper to be coaled up for the switchman, who had to begin his job switching cars out on to the terminal yard. We would get up on the tender of each one of the engines—I remember hearing people say the tender was the engine's lunchbox and thermos bottle—and we measured the coal with a long steel rod, after which we took our shovels and leveled the coal off even. Then we would tell the straw boss on the ground what number the coal measured up to on the steel rod.

When my Uncle Ned's friend, who was picking cotton along with us, used to tell us that the big driving wheels of the locomotives were made out of pasteboard, I had no way of knowing if he was telling the truth; we children didn't think our grown folks would lie, especially to kids. So when I went to work at the railroad shops I didn't ask anybody what those wheels were made of; I was looking for a chance to find out for myself.

One day the roundhouse foreman took me from the coal chute to help the spring-gang mechanic "shrink the tires" on the driving wheels of one of the old steam engines. And this is how we shrank those "pasteboard" driving wheels with oil, air and fire:

First, we picked up the wheels clear off the tracks. Then the mechanic took his gauge and evened up the rims of the wheels, and we took parts of thin sheets of metal and placed them even, all around the wheel between the tire and the rim. After that we placed a coil of pipe about half an inch thick, with tiny holes on the inner side, next to the rim. At one end of the pipe there was a coupling for another pipe (to be connected); at the other end the pipe was coupled to a rubber hose, which was connected to a 15-gallon oil tank mounted on two wheels. A pipe on the other side of the tank was connected to an air hose. We then put small scraps of rag waste between the coil of pipe and the tire, stuck a lighted match to the rags—after which we turned on the air hose. On the other side of the oil tank, as the air began to blow oil through the tiny holes in the coiled pipe, the steel rim got cherry-red hot, so we cut off the air hose, pulled the coiled pipe off the rim of the driving wheel and turned on the hose pipe of cold water. When the steel rim was cooled, it was welded solid onto that wheel.

And that was how I found out what locomotive wheels were really made of.

On many occasions, after that job with the spring-gang, the roundhouse foreman would come to the coal chute and arrange with the straw boss for me to work for some of the mechanics, who were all white, while their helpers were all Black. A mechanic and his helper, working in close quarters side by side, day after day, month after month, got to know each other's dispositions pretty well. The Black man, dependent on the white mechanic for a chance to make a living, is likely to fall in with the mechanic's disposition or his way of doing things or looking at life.

Since I was six-foot tall and muscular, I got to be called on more and more when one of the mechanic's regular helpers was down sick, or when they had some extra-heavy lifting to do in the roundhouse. When I worked a full day doing a helper's job, I got a helper's pay, $4.68 for an eight-hour day; if I worked only a few hours every day of the week as a helper, I only got the laborer's pay, 30 cents an hour. Sometimes I worked a couple of days before they sent me back to the coal chute. I was not the only one who noticed that whenever an opening came up for a full-time helper, the company master mechanic would hire a new man.

On November 1, 1924, I went to the master mechanic and told him I wanted all my time. He asked what was the matter. Why did I want to quit my job on the coal chute? I told him I was leaving town and going to Birmingham. "If you weren't quitting, I was planning to put you to helping," he said. I told him thanks but I had made my plans to be in Birmingham the next week. I could have told him that I had heard of a Negro earning $5 a day in Birmingham. But I didn't because it had turned out to be too good to be true in Georgia and it could turn out the same way in Alabama.

I didn't have any trouble getting a job at the Stockham Pipe and Fittings plant just outside of Birmingham. And the first thing I learned—after I found that my workday was from six in the morning to six at night—was that I was paid only according to the number of perfect iron molds I produced. No wages at all if I didn't make any molds in a given week, no matter how hard I worked and how much time I put in trying to learn. If I had to learn, some molds would have to be spoiled.

The idea of working in a place where a metal as solid as iron could be melted down to run like water and look like a stream of fire had a kind of stunning effect on me. My foreman took charge of teaching me how to mold iron, beginning with a 4-inch Tee—a pipe joint shaped like the letter *T*. Making molds was a hot and muscle-wearying job, but it was also a highly skilled job in my opinion—the worker must concentrate all his thoughts because molding is not a set pattern of acts, one right after the other. Castings cannot all be made the same way and in the same temper of sand.

The whole interior of the place was hot as the living hell. Most of us would have on just a pair of overalls or some old hip pants; we didn't wear shirts. The water in the drinking pipes at the time was hot enough to take a bath in, and the men were always thirsty for a drink of cool water.

Some of the men would get 20 and 40 gallon barrels and put 100 pounds of ice in each of them, filling them with water; then they would charge everybody 15 cents a week. There were many of us, with sweat running off our half-naked bodies like rain, who didn't seem to know how to stop drinking, once we started. We'd just stand there gulping down that cold, refreshing water, and the next thing we'd know there'd be a fellow or two knocked out with cramps. There was always a stretcher in the box beside the wall, and when a man fell out, a couple of guys ran and got the stretcher, put him on it and hurried him on to the so-called doctor's office. From there they would rush him to the company's hospital. Sometimes, we would get the news the next day that Jim or Big Red or Shorty or Slim was dead.

The company's responsibility—besides furnishing the stretchers—was $500 for the family if the worker died; if he lived and was out two weeks or more, they paid him $9 a week up to nine weeks.

When I went into the Stockham Pipe and Fitting foundry in November 1924, I heard that 1,800 molders were working there and that most of them were Black. There were some whites working on the big box flares, side by side with Negroes. The Blacks were being paid 50 cents an hour and the whites $1.25: $10 a day to white workers, $4 a day to Black workers.

The bulk of Negro common labor was to be found in the wage brackets of 27 to 32 cents an hour in steel plants and in small and large foundries and shops. There were superintendents and assistant-supers in the various departments; in the plants some companies had a super in each department with three assistants and under these assistants there would be the "little" boss, the straw boss, of groups of workers, who would turn the time in for the men under him and also told them what time to report for work.

If the regular time was 7 o'clock, the little boss would tell his men to come in at 4:30 or 5 and these workers often stayed on the job straight through until 6:30 or 7, or even later at night. The regular working time was supposed to be from 7 a.m. to 3 or 3:30 p.m. and the white workers—with a few exceptions—would always start and stop by the official time. But then they were in the skilled and semi-skilled brackets.

On a Friday or Saturday payday when Negro workers went up to the pay window to get their checks, they would in most cases find themselves many hours short in each week's pay. When they told the pay boss at the window how much time they had put in, he would say, "You-all have to see the foreman you work for." And when they looked for their foreman, somebody would call out, "He done went home." But even when they found the straw boss in the shop, now it was his turn to pass the buck. "Wait till Monday," he would tell them, "and I'll get your time straightened out."

Even after this run-around, the workers still had a faint hope they would be paid the balance of their wages on Monday, the day they had promised the grocery man, the furniture man, the rent man, or the insurance-policy man he would get his money. But no such thing; on Monday morning the straw boss told the workers he would see about their time later in the day when he had a chance to go up to the office. Then came the alibis: "Your time got lost and the timekeeper couldn't find it"; or, "Your time will be on your pay slip this coming payday"; or, "I forgot to check with the timekeeper and he's out of the office and won't be back today." The straw boss's answer to the Black worker's complaints depended on how much he liked his looks; how much that worker bowed and pulled off his hat and generally played Uncle Tom. Some of us just couldn't put on that kind of act.

WILLIAM ATTAWAY

Blood on the Forge

Saturday morning Big Mat went to the mill a changed man. A-borning in him was a new confidence. He did not sink into himself when O'Casey singled him out as scapegoat for the mistakes of the crew. He looked the little pit boss in the eye. O'Casey knew men. He knew when to let up. The other men were quick to sense the change. They passed little looks among themselves when O'Casey passed by Big Mat. They began to lag in their work. The pit boss had to do something to save face. Luckily, one of the pouring crew failed to show up. And when the call came for a replacement O'Casey recommended Big Mat.

Bo had said that they put the green men on hot jobs before they knew enough to stay alive. That was true. Black George, one of the men from the red hills, had been slow learning. They had put what was left of him in the ground. But Big Mat proved to be a natural hot-job man. After the first turn he did not have as many burns to grease as had the regulars.

The steel pourers' shelf was just a narrow platform high up against a wall. Around it was a rickety iron railing. Big Mat was told about that railing. One of the pourers said, "It was jest put up lately. 'Fore that a guy who faints rolls right into heaven."

They did faint on the shelf—especially on hot spring days like this one. But

Big Mat welcomed the heat. Through the long, hot hours he would do twice as much work as anybody else. In competition with white men, he would prove himself.

The Bessemers were directly across from the shelf. Through the blinding heat Big Mat saw them in a haze—the blower on the pulpit, watching the tall air-stretched flames, the flaming air pulsing through the white metal, shimmying thirty feet above the live steel, blowing at the sun through holes in the roof. Once Big Mat had thought the holes were there so the flames could light the sky at night. Once the drone of the Bessemers had frightened him. Now his ears did not hear the drone. The steel began to blow noiselessly after he had been a short turn on the shelf.

The blower was an old Irishman. He knew by the color of the flame when it was time to tip a Bessemer. Now he waved his gloved hand at the shelf. Someone let out a warning "Hallo-o-o-o-o-o!" Big Mat followed the example of the men around him and yanked down his dark glasses. The Bessemer sighed, and the place was full of sparks. The furnace was tilted. And almost before the full ladle could move on its overhead tracks to the pourers' shelf another great Bessemer went into its noiseless song.

Hollow molds were moving beneath the shelf. The pourer signaled when the first was in position. He pulled the lever on the full ladle, releasing the white fire. Through his glasses Big Mat could see the red winking eye growing into the bottom of the mold. The stream that fed that eye threw off curtains of sparks, pinpricking his hands and face. He got his signal and threw strips of manganese into the glowing mold. He was continually dodging, but still the sparks fried in the sweat of his chest where the leather apron sagged. The red stream stopped suddenly. Another mold slid underneath the ladle.

Without slowing between molds, they took tests of the steel. The sweat ran into Big Mat's wide-mouthed gloves and made small explosions when it fell on the hot test steel. Big Mat did not flinch. Alone he held the spoon steady. It took two hunkies to hold up a spoon. He smiled behind his expressionless face. His muscles were glad to feel the growing weight of the steel. The work was nothing. Without labor his body would shrivel and be a weed. His body was happy. This was a good place for a big black man to be.

Melody and Chinatown were helping on the floor underneath the Bessemers. Naked to the waist, they worked hard, cleaning a big ladle for relining. The air was stifling. When Melody raised his lips upward to search the thin air he could see Big Mat high above. Pushing up his glasses, he wiped the sweat out of his eyes. He could see the liquid steel hitting the sides of the test spoon, scattering in clouds of white stars over Mat's gloved hands. Even to his hazed eyes, Mat's muscles sang. His own muscles did not sing. They grew weak and cried for long, slow movement. He could not stop them from twitching. It was not the heat and work alone—the rhythms of the machinery played through his body—the stripper, knocking the hardened steel loose from the molds. He couldn't hear it. It would have been a relief to hear it. He felt it inside himself—the heavy rhythm of the piston that used only a stroke to a mold. That rhythm in his body was like pounding out those ingots with a blow of his fist. And he was tired. Twenty-four hours had to pass before he could stagger away to the bunkhouse. Only a thought kept him on the job: next week end he would pleasure himself in Mex Town while some other bastard was baking on the long shift.

Chinatown was inside the big ladle. He could see the sun lancing through cracks in the ceiling high above. The heat of the sun sitting on the roof was nothing to the temperature inside the ladle. But it was just that little added heat that was too much for him to stand. His clothes were wet to his body. Where he squatted there was a wet spot. He was being smothered in a blanket of heat that pressed in from all sides. His lungs ached for moisture. He would have killed somebody for a drink of water. Yet there was water not far away. He had been told not to drink his fill. They had told him to put a tablet of salt on his tongue. The salt was crusted in his throat. He climbed out of the ladle. O'Casey saw him start for the hydrant.

"Just rinse out your mouth and spit," warned O'Casey.

Chinatown fastened his lips to the spigot and turned the water on full force. His lips still clung when the foreman pulled him away. They had to take him out in the yard to untie the knot in his stomach. Then he was sick. Never before had he been so sick. Inside himself he prayed to die if he ever felt like that again.

Between spells Melody and a gray old Slav came out into the yard to watch over Chinatown. The old man's name was Zanski. He looked over the dozing Chinatown to Melody's drooping shoulders.

"You ain't feel so good either?"

"Head turnin'," said Melody.

"Maybe you hold your head far down to the ground . . ."

Melody tried it.

"Do kinda help some."

"Make heat drip out through head."

"Obliged."

"All feller work in heat know that."

They didn't say any more until it was almost time to get back to the floor.

"Sooner be shot in Kentucky than do another turn," groaned Melody.

The old man smiled.

"Don't nothin' git you guys?" asked Melody. "You jest work and work till it git discouragin' to watch."

Zanski pushed his beard away from his lips and gestured at the two men.

"Colored feller alike. Work in mill but ain't feel happy."

Chinatown raised himself on one elbow. He looked at Zanski and scowled.

"Heat liable to git anybody," he broke in defensively.

"Not heat."

"Well, what then?"

"You fellers don't move out of bunkhouse. You got no kids."

"Jest don't want none," said Melody.

"You got no woman. Feller ain't be happy like that."

A thought of Anna flashed into Melody's head. He said nothing.

Chinatown said, "That's where you wrong. You ought to see them boys headed for the cat house of a Saturday."

"That ain't woman."

"You got to git in line for them whores."

"That ain't woman."

"Line reach clear round the mill, I betcha."

"That ain't woman who keep white curtains in a feller's house. Whore girl ain't wash curtains."

Chinatown was puzzled. He did not know what Zanski was talking about. To cover up he said, "Yeah, and they'll roll you if you ain't slick." He settled back to doze again.

The old man went on, "Feller from Ukraine workin'. His woman wash the curtains, and the kids growin' in the yard."

"Hundred o' them," said Melody, because that was the way it looked on washdays.

"Them kids work in the mill sometime. Their kids grow in the yard."

"That makes you feel happy?" mused Melody.

"I think about that when the heat comes," explained Zanski.

"That wouldn't help me none," said Melody.

The old man was silent for a time. Then he spoke as though he knew more than was in a barrelful of books.

"Feller from long way off die like plant put on rock. Plant grow if it get ground like place it come from."

Melody felt the words. But talk faded into nothing in the face of the heat. Under the Bessemers he sweated and gulped the thin air. In his body played the noiseless rhythms of the mill. Before morning he was so worked up that his voice was high and thin, like a knife running over an E string in his throat.

SAM GREENLEE

The Spook Who Sat By the Door

Freeman watched the class reunion from a corner of the common room of the CIA training barracks. It was a black middle-class reunion. They were black bourgeoisie to a man, black nepotism personified. In addition to those who had recruited themselves upon receiving notice that the CIA was now interested in at least token integration, five were relatives or in-laws of civil-rights leaders, four others of Negro politicians. Only Freeman was not middle class, and the others knew it. Even had he not dressed as he did, not used the speech patterns and mannerisms of the Chicago ghetto slums, they would have known. His presence made them uneasy and insecure; they were members of the black elite, and a product of the ghetto streets did not belong among them.

They carefully ignored Freeman and it was as he wished; he had no more love for the black middle class than they for him. He watched them establishing the pecking order as he sat sipping a scotch highball. It was their first day in the training camp after months of exhaustive screening, testing, security checks. Of the hundreds considered, only the twenty-three present in the room had survived and been selected for preliminary training and, constantly reminded of it since they had reported, they pranced, posed and preened in mutual and self-admiration. To be a "Negro firster" was considered a big thing, but Freeman didn't think so.

"Man, you know how much this twelve-year-old scotch cost me in the commissary? Three bills and a little change! Chivhead Regal! As long as I can put my mouth around this kind of whiskey at that price, I'm in love with being a spy."

"You know they call CIA agents spooks? First time we'll ever get paid for that title."

"Man, the fringe benefits—they just don't stop coming in! Nothing to say of the base pay and stuff. We got it made."

"Say, baby, didn't we meet at the Penn Relays a couple of years ago? In that motel on the edge of Philly? You remember that chick you was with, Lurlean? Well, she's teaching school in Camden now and I get a little bit of that from time to time. Now, man, don't freeze on me. I'm married, too, and you know Lurlean don't give a damn. I'll tell her I saw you when we get out of here."

Where'd you go to school, man? Fisk? I went to Morris Brown. You frat? Q? You got a couple brothers here, those two cats over there. What you major in? What your father do? Your mother working, too? Where your wife go to school? What sorority? What kind of work you do before you made this scene? How much bread you make? Where's your home? What kind of car you got? How much you pay for that suit? You got your own pad, or you live in an apartment? Co-op apartment? Tell me that's the new thing nowadays. Clue me in. You got color TV? Component stereo, or console?

Drop those names: doctors I have known, lawyers, judges, businessmen, dentists, politicians, and Great Negro Leaders I have known. Drop those brand names: GE, Magnavox, Ford, GM, Chrysler, Zenith, Brooks Brothers, Florsheim. Johnny Walker, Chivas Regal, Jack Daniels. Imported beer. Du Pont carpeting, wall-to-wall. Wall-to-wall drags with split-level minds, remote-control color TV souls and credit-card hearts.

Play who-do-you-know and who-have-you-screwed. Blow your bourgeois blues, your nigger soul sold for a mess of materialistic pottage. You can't ever catch Charlie, but you can ape him and keep the gap widening between you and those other niggers. You have a ceiling on you and yours, your ambitions; but the others are in the basement and you will help Mr. Charlie keep them there. If they get out and move up to your level, then what will you have?

They eyed Freeman uneasily; he was an alien in this crowd. Somehow, he had escaped the basement. He had moved up to their level and he was a threat. He must be put in his place. He would not last, breeding told, but he should know that he was among his betters.

The tall, good-looking one with the curly black hair and light skin approached Freeman. He was from Howard and wore his clothes Howard-style, the cuffless pants stopping at his ankles. His tie was very skinny and the knot almost unnoticeable, his shoulder-padding nonexistent. He had known these arrogant, Chicago niggers like Freeman before, thinking they owned Howard's campus, moving in with their down-home ways, their Mississippi mannerisms, loud laughter, no manners, elbowing their way into the fraternities, trying to steal the women, making more noise than anyone else at the football games and rallies. One of those diddy-bop niggers from Chicago had almost stolen his present wife.

"Where you from, man? You don't seem to talk much."

"No, I don't."

"Don't what?"

"Don't talk much. I'm from Chicago."

"Chicago? Where you from before that? Wayback, Georgia, Snatchback, Mississippi? You look like you just got off the train, man. Where's the paper bag with your sack of fried chicken?"

Freeman looked at him and sipped his drink.

"No, seriously, my man, where you from? Lot of boys here from the South; how come you got to pretend? I bet you don't even know where State Street and the Loop is. How you sneak into this group? This is supposed to be the cream, man. You sure you don't clean up around here?"

Freeman stood up slowly, still holding his drink. The tall one was standing very close to his armchair and had to step back when Freeman rose.

"Baby, I will kick your ass. Go away and leave me to hell alone."

The tall one opened his mouth to speak; a fraternity brother sidled up, took his arm and led him away. Freeman freshened his drink and sat down in front of the television set. After a lull, the black middle-class reunion resumed.

He had not made a mistake, he thought. All niggers looked alike to whites and he had thought it to his advantage to set himself apart from this group in a way that would make the whites overlook him until too late. They would automatically assume that the others—who looked and acted so much like their black representatives and spokesmen who appeared on the television panels, spoke in the halls of Congress, made the covers of *Time* and *Life* and ran the Negro newspapers and magazines, who formed the only link with the white world—would threaten to survive this test. Both the whites and these saddity niggers, Freeman thought, would ignore him until too late. And, he thought, Whitey will be more likely to ignore a nigger who approaches the stereotype than these others who think imitation the sincerest form of flattery.

He smiled when he thought about walking into his friend's dental office that day.

"Hey, Freebee, what's happening, baby? Ain't seen you in the Boulevard Lounge lately. Where you been hiding? Got something new on the string?"

"No, been working. Look, you know the cap you put on after I got hung up in the Iowa game? I want a new one. With an edge of gold around it."

"Gold? You must be kidding. And where you get that refugee from Robert Hall suit?"

"That's where I bought it. I'm going out to Washington for a final interview panel and I want to please the crackers." His friend nodded. He understood.

Freeman did not spend much time socializing with the rest of the Negro pioneers, those chosen to be the first to integrate a segregated institution. He felt none of the gratitude, awe, pride and arrogance of the Negro "firsts" and he did not think after the first few days that many of them would be around very long; and Freeman had come to stay.

They had calisthenics in the morning and then six hours of classes. Exams were scheduled for each Saturday morning. They were not allowed to leave the area, but there was a different movie screened each night in a plush, small theater. There was a small PX, a swimming pool, a bar and a soda fountain. There was a social area at each end of the building in which they lived that included pool tables, ping-pong, a television room with color TV, chess and checker sets. There was a small library, containing technical material related to their classes and light fiction, magazines and periodicals. There was a music room with a stereo console containing an AM-FM receiver and with records consisting mostly of show tunes from Broadway hits of the last decade. There were Coke machines. It was like a very plush bachelor officers' quarter.

There were basketball courts, badminton courts, a nine-hole golf course, squash courts, a gym, a 220-yard rubberized track, a touch-football field. After the intensive screening which they had undergone prior to their selection, none of the rest thought that the classes and examinations were anything more than window dressing. They settled down to enjoy their plush confinement during the training period after which they would be given offices in the vast building in Langley, Virginia, down by the river.

Freeman combined a program of calisthenics, weight training, isometrics, running and swimming, which never took more than an hour, usually less than half that time. He would watch television or read until dinner, take an hour's nap and then study until midnight.

No one at the training camp, white or colored, thought it strange that Freeman, a product of the Chicago ghetto, where Negroes spend more time, money and care in the selection of their wardrobe than even in Harlem, should be so badly dressed. Or that, although he had attended two first-rate educational institutions, he should speak with so limited a vocabulary, so pronounced an accent and such Uncle Tom humor. They put it down to the fact that he had been an athlete who had skated through college on his fame. Freeman did not worry about the whites because he was being exactly what they wished. The Negroes of the class would be ashamed of him, yet flattered by the contrast; but there might be a shrewd one among them.

There was only one. He approached Freeman several times with penetrating questions. The fraternity thing put him off.

"You a fraternity man, Freeman?" he asked once over lunch.

"Naw. I was once because of the chicks. You had to have that pin, you know. Almost as good as a letter in football. But I thought that kinda stuff was silly. I used to be a Kappa."

He looked at Freeman coldly. "I'm still a Kappa," he said. He finished lunch and never spoke to Freeman again.

Midway through the fourth week, three of the group were cut. They were called into the front office and informed that their grades were not up to standard, and that same evening they were gone. Panic hit the group and there were several conferences concerning what should be done. Several long-distance phone calls were made, three to politicians, five to civil-rights bureaucrats. The group was informed that they were on their own and that after the time, energy, money and effort that had gone into their integration, they should feel obligated to perform up to the highest standards. Freeman had received the best grades in each of the exams, but no one was concerned with that fact.

Two others left the following weekend, although their grades were among the highest in the group. Freeman guessed correctly that it was for homosexuality and became convinced that in addition to being bugged for sound, the rooms were monitored by closed-circuit TV. He was right. The telephones, even the ones in the booths with coin boxes, were bugged as well. The general received a weekly report regarding the progress of the group. It appeared that those intellectually qualified could be cut on physical grounds. They were already lagging at the increasing demands of the morning calisthenics and were not likely to survive the rigors of hand-to-hand combat. The director of the school confidently predicted that not one of the Negroes would survive the ten weeks of the school, which would then be completely free for a new group of recruits presently going through preliminary screening. It was to the credit of Freeman's unobtrusive demeanor that the school's director did not even think of him, in spite of his excellent grades and physical condition, when making his report to the general. If he had, he might have qualified his report somewhat.

The general instructed his school's director to forward complete reports to the full senatorial committee. He intended to head off any possible criticism from Senator Hennington. He could not know that the senator was not in the least concerned with the success or failure of the Negro pioneers to integrate the Central Intelligence Agency. He had won his election and for another six years he was safe.

"When this group is finished, I want you to begin screening another. Don't bother to select Negroes who are obviously not competent; they have already demonstrated their inability to close the cultural gap and no one is in a position seriously to challenge our insistence not to lower standards for anyone. It will cost us a bit to flunk out six or eight a year, but we needn't worry about harassment on this race thing again in the future if we do. It's a sound investment," said the general. He was pleased and again convinced that he was not personally prejudiced. Social and scientific facts were social and scientific facts. He ate a pleasant meal in his club that evening and noted that there were both white and colored present. The whites were members and guests; the Negroes served them. The general did not reflect that this was the proper order of things. He seldom approved of the rising of the sun, either.

BRENT WADE

Company Man

I made an admission to myself this morning. It's taken me some time to gather the resolve, and having done so I'm now left wondering if perhaps Dr. Bond had been right after all. Perhaps there is some courage in reserve somewhere.

What I am now able to admit is that for the last two days I've avoided telling you about Carl Rice. I'm sure you'd figured as much on your own. I'd like to believe that acknowledging my fear portends the eventual completion of this journal, since I have sometimes doubted my willingness to relive it all over again. Dr. Theodore once told me that during therapy, as people get close to their "issues" they often become evasive. I'm sure he said that as an attempt to coax me into talking more—which I wouldn't do. But he was right. Carl is, I suppose, at the heart of all my "issues." That being the case, you might think that I'd know him as well as myself. Yet Carl Rice was more unknowable than anyone I'd ever met, as if he were merely a shadow cast by some smoldering expectation.

He has the body of a sprinter. In fact, that's the most lasting impression I have of Carl—the aging athlete. He moves like a sprinter. There's this curious precision in his walk. Perhaps the swagger of an aging man who knows he still looks good. It always reminded me of the way Ali would walk into the ring toward the end of his career, before the brain damage became apparent.

We were both born in September, Carl on the twentieth—two days and two years behind me. And so we share a house of sorts, if you follow the stars. (Donna tells me that such things are important.) Most of the time, I was never sure where I stood with him. Once, after he had tried unsuccessfully to persuade me to join in the condemnation of the company's hiring practices, he angrily called me a "house nigger." On other occasions I had been an "Oreo," and once a "lackey." (A running argument at that time was over African names—Carl was considering one for himself.) Still, at other times we spoke with that casual familiarity black people share among themselves. He would compliment me on knowing how to "play the game" or kid me about what a "corporate brother" I had become. I can't really say we were friends, though.

Our relationship was in some ways a matter of proximity. There was this terminal awareness of each other's presence. In a business unit of twenty-eight hundred, Carl and I were two of four black managers. We also had the added distinction of having similar high-visibility positions. We ended up working together a lot. At a distance people would sometimes even mistake us for each other. He's also tall, and he shares my affinity for Italian clothes—the Ungaro suits, Armani ties. But of course for Carl it's more than that. He explained to me once how our style of dress is suited for the executive who does not (or cannot) truly aspire to the "pin-striped anonymity of the status quo."

There are other things you should know about Carl, a few telling foibles of the proud brother. He has a fourteen-year-old daughter named Kenya and a twelve-year-old son named Haim, both by his ex-wife, the daughter of an orthodox Jewish printer from New Jersey. Yes, Carl Rice had crossed the color line! I always told myself that one day I would confront Carl with this incongruity. But after the divorce, it didn't seem appropriate. The children now live in California with their mother, the former Marcia Siegel, in a comfortable apartment in West Hollywood. Carl and Marcia have been divorced for six years now. I've never been told just what happened. Carl never let on that they were having problems until the very end. I remember asking him how Marcia's parents had felt about the marriage from the beginning. All he said was, "Well, it wasn't no synagogue wedding." Marcia now works as a publicist for MGM Studios. In Baltimore, she taught contemporary fiction at Goucher College.

They met at NYU, where Carl had gone after being booted out of Howard University. He had protested what he thought was the then elitist mock-white curriculum of the school, by occupying the dean's office in whiteface and a three-piece suit.

Maybe the most important thing you should know is that while I was liked and generally respected at Varitech, Carl was tolerated. The topic, no doubt, of many a hushed discussion. During a meeting I'd heard Len Townes once call him an agitator. (I think he forgot I was there, for as soon as he made his comment and saw me sitting at the back of the room he quickly added a few words about the great job Carl was doing in graphic arts.) Carl is perhaps what a lot of whites would describe, artlessly, as a militant. In truth, though, he had the same fervent views on the failings of the social and corporate worlds of white America that many blacks shared. Only he made no effort to conceal these views whenever the subject arose, although he never invited such discourse. I refused to discuss such things in the plant, but Carl and I would often talk off-site. What had really given Carl his reputation was his well-publicized dissatisfaction with the company's hiring practices. In the end I think it was only the fear of litigation that kept him employed. He was ultimately dispatched to a position of visibility with no chance of advancement. The details of his particular exile are lurid and numerous, but why go into that? You'd never get your questions answered, and besides, I've procrastinated enough.

Now, I think I *had* told you a little about Carl two days ago. Let's see, where had I left you? Oh yes, I had started to tell you about the afternoon I confronted Carl with the CPT fliers. Do you remember? I found myself standing in his office with one of the damned things in my hand. Did I tell you he had known about them all along? Before he even opened his mouth, I knew that. It was the way he looked up at me when I laid the sheet on his desk. He beamed with his old self-satisfied smirk.

"I had expected you to call me as soon as you saw one of those," he said. I told him I hadn't understood the message. He just shook his head. "You knew what CPT meant. That should have told you right off."

Things came back then, in color and sound. The voices first. My grandmother's voice, laughing with Mrs. Francine after church one Sunday.

"Lawd, here they go agin talkin' 'bout choir practice, startin' promptly mind ju, at sebum o'clock. They mean sebum o'clock CPT. I ain't neva seen these Nigros here started nothin' on time."

And there was something I heard your mother say one morning as I waited for you to leave for school.

"Paul, you betta step it up. School don't run on colored people's time."

When the voices toggled off, I was aware of just what I had forgotten. How many years had I not known? I couldn't decide. It was such a requisite thing, a little cultural joke among ourselves. I stood there wondering when it was that I had stopped remembering.

"It's mainly a bulletin," he said. "We want to make sure everybody comes to the meetings. Man, how could you forget CPT? I just don't under—"

"What meetings?"

"Billy, you do work here, don't you? Haven't you been following what's going on? But you don't get out in the shop much, do you? You have to stay close to Mr. Haviland and that nitwit Lloyd Harrow."

"I work for Haviland and I work with Lloyd," I flared. "Why should I be in the shop?"

"Tell me, Billy," Carl asked, "what work does Lloyd Harrow do? There's no job description for his position. He's been down here almost every day this week, wasting my time with his bullshit. You know what he wanted to talk about today? How he believes that Jimi Hendrix was killed by the CIA for playing 'The Star-Spangled Banner' like he did at Woodstock. Says his father has a friend who knows for sure. Can you believe that? Everybody knows it was the FBI that did it."

"The fliers, Carl, what about the fliers?"

"Haven't you heard anything?"

"Believe it or not, my own problems require most of my attention."

"Well the rumors have been rolling around here for the last month. I'm surprised Haviland or your boy Lloyd hasn't asked you about it."

He was about to continue, but someone entered the room. A young man I was sure I recognized, but I couldn't recall from where. Carl greeted him casually, introducing me only as "a brother from executive row."

"Yeah, I seen you around," he responded.

His name was Everett Peale and I had seen him, I suddenly remembered, in the cafeteria. He was one of the people in the kitchen. I'd seen him serving food at the steam tables. But he had another job. As Carl explained, Everett was responsible for distributing the CPT fliers around the shop floor. He had in fact come to Carl for more fliers. Carl took out his desk keys and opened the last drawer on the bottom left side. As he did, Everett turned to me.

"So," he said, "we gonna see you at Fridee's meetin'?"

Before I could answer, Carl quickly interrupted, handing over a stack of fliers as he did.

"He'll be there. Look, you better get out of here before you're seen. And remember, put those up in the morning before six and only in the shop. We don't want to spill this until we're ready."

When he left, Carl poured himself a cup of coffee and lit another Salem. I sat down beside his desk. I couldn't help feeling that Carl had set me up, because now I was involved.

"That boy," Carl said, taking a drag from the cigarette. "I swear, I don't know about him. You know the CPT See Quarter Till thing was all his idea. I had to bite my tongue over that one."

"You lost me, Carl. What do you mean bite your tongue, why?"

"The CPT part was probably a good idea—no white person knows what that means—but the See Quarter Till stuff . . . I hate to hear us talking like that in this day and age." I still didn't know what he was talking about and he must have seen it in my face.

"The fliers," Carl went on, "are a good way to let everyone know when we're meeting. See, we can't be too open about announcing meeting times and places, because that will tip the hat. So what we do is post the fliers when we're going to meet. That way everyone knows we're going to meet, but not when or where. Now, to let everyone know that, we have one person everyone can go to for specific times and places. That person is supposed to be different each time, but this machinist named Earl Gaines has pretty much ended up with the job. I wanted to use a code name or something for Earl, so no one reading the fliers will know who he is. At one of the early meetings, Everett says why don't we use Earl's nickname, Quarter Till. They all thought it was funny. There was nothing I could do."

"Quarter Till?" I said. "So what's that supposed to mean?"

"They call him that because they say he's blacker than quarter to midnight—get it?" He shook his head. "What do you think white people think when they hear us saying things like that? It just saves them from making the insult." He shook his head again. I sometimes believe that Carl cultivated his image with as much care as I did. He pandered to them more than he wanted to admit. He was the angry black man they anticipated.

Having now finished the cigarette, he took a Hershey's bar from his desk, which he ate like a Danish along with the coffee. He still hadn't told me what was going on. What were the fliers and meetings for?

"There's going to be some trouble, Billy. Big trouble. All the brothers in the machinist's union want to walk."

"Walk? From the union, or from the company?"

"Both! A few months ago the union got wind of the new plant the company's building in Mexico. I'm not even going to ask you if you knew about it. But when the union found out, Jack Dulaney goes up to Haviland's office and apparently after a few days of discussion they made a deal. I don't know the specifics of what was said. The bottom line is we got shortchanged. There were some guarantees made about what jobs would be secure and how that would be decided. It's a flat seniority scam, which leaves us high and dry. When the union made the announcement a couple of brothers even went to Dulaney. Here they thought the union was representing their best interests and they get screwed. To top it off all Dulaney does is go into this song and dance about how this deal will be good for everybody. I've dealt with that Irish son of a bitch before. Man, those people are the biggest racists around—you ever notice how many of them belong to these ultra-right-wing political groups? It's them and the Mormons. Now those people, the only thing they want to see black is nightfall. Who is that one glassy-eyed saltine from Utah? I saw him on—"

"Carl, Carl; are you telling me there's going to be a strike?"

"I'm telling you that every black machinist at this company is going to get real loud, real soon. They want to split off from the union, and they want to strike."

Lord, how I wanted to grab Carl and shake him silly. It was such a niggerish mess he'd gotten himself into. I wanted no part of it.

"Who is orchestrating all of this? You? Man, I hope it's not you! They could get rid of you for that. The little piece of a career you have left would be shot."

"Is that concern I hear, Billy? Don't worry, I'm just helping out. You know, supporting my people. All I do is make copies of the fliers and attend the meetings."

"Yeah, so who runs the meetings?"

"You're not collecting information for da massa are you?" He was only half kidding.

"You just laid a lot of shit in my lap, Carl. I want to understand what's going on."

"I guess I'm just overwhelmed by all this concern. I remember last year when the black professionals' association wanted to put together that letter to Haviland decrying this company's piss-poor record of promoting blacks you didn't want any part of it. Is that the same Billy Covington who wants to know what's going on?"

"You're damned right I didn't want any part of it! It wasn't the association that put that letter together. It was you and Curt Reed. And where is he now? He had to leave the company after being stuck in some dead-end job in planning. Your letter did his career a lot of good!"

"That's only because we didn't stick together. There was no show of strength."

"That's because there was no strength in writing that letter. How can you work in a corporation as long as you have and not understand that? It's like changing your name, Carl, it's not going to change anything."

"I'm not even going to get into that with you again. But are you denying that there's a different hiring system for *us*? The system here is not fair, Billy! There are whites in management who don't even have college degrees. They have a job because some white man likes them. They fuck up; they make mistakes—everybody knows we lost that contract with IBM because Jerry Flynn mismanaged the whole project. He had no experience in what he was doing, hadn't even worked on a major winning project since he came to the company, but what do they do? They promote him to contract-development manager under Howie Frost. None of *us* would ever get that kind of break. They'll scrutinize your every credential and still pass you over! And look, they get their children hired in here, their friends, in jobs that don't even get advertised unless they're already filled. And then they complain about affirmative action! And if you have the temerity to mention how racist it all is, they look at you and say, 'Racism? Where, I don't see any? Prove it.' And of course you can never prove it because they control the information! There's always enough of them to form a consensus on anything they want to disbelieve, regardless of fact. I don't understand how you can look at that and not get mad!"

"I don't understand how you can stay in the same job for five years without any real promotion! I don't understand how you can work in a place where you have no credibility. Don't you think that some of these white boys are pissed off too because they got passed over for Flynn? And I'll tell you something else, Carl, if I had a kid you'd best believe I'd get him in here—the same way they do! And the difference between me and you, Carl, is that I could get it done. They'd do it for me. They own the system, Carl! They made it all up just for them; we weren't even a consideration. Can't you see that? You can only work in it! So I don't get into arguments with Len Townes about how sick I think the Elvis cult is and how he wasn't the king of anything, how all he did was rip off a lot of black music and mannerisms and repackage it like it was all his idea. It might have made you feel better to say all that stuff but all it does is piss people off. They don't want to have to know how you feel."

The argument I referred to took place last year in the AV room, where Len, Carl, and I were reviewing slides for a presentation on company operations that Len was to give to an investor review board. Len came as close as I'd ever seen him to losing his facade of control, for he truly loves Elvis.

"Billy, what is this problem you have about pissing white people off?"

We both just sat there, silent, having exhausted the limits of what we could say. A truce. Then Carl took another Hershey's bar from his desk drawer. He offered me a piece, and when I declined he took a big bite. I don't understand how anyone who eats as much junk food as Carl does manages to stay so slim.

We didn't say anything else about unions, fliers, or strikes. We talked around it; we talked about the sales meeting coming up in two weeks, about the wonderful job Meeting Planners (the company I had hired to set the conference up) was doing. I told Carl I'd never been to Atlanta. He was from Athens, Georgia, and had been to Atlanta many times to visit family. For him it was a city that offered no mystery. He showed me the bluelines I'd originally come to see. It would be a nice piece when printed. Carl was a good writer, and while not a graphic artist, he had a fine aesthetic sense.

After I'd approved the bluelines and discussed the print schedule, I left—but not before Carl reminded me again of the Friday meeting. More than anything I was scared, scared that events would overtake me and that I would find no safe haven.

SHELBY STEELE

The Content of Our Character

Not long ago, a friend of mine, black like myself, said to me that the term *black middle-class* was actually a contradiction in terms. Race, he insisted, blurred class distinctions among blacks. If you were black, you were just black and that was that. When I argued, he let his eyes roll at my naïveté. Then he went on. For us, as black professionals, it was an exercise in self-flattery, a pathetic pretension, to give meaning to such a distraction. Worse, the very idea of class threatened the unity that was vital to the black community as a whole. After all, since when had white America taken note of anything but color when it came to blacks? He then reminded me of an old Malcolm X line that had been popular in the sixties. Question: What is a black man with a Ph.D.? Answer: A nigger.

For many years I had been on my friend's side of this argument. Much of my conscious thinking on the old conundrum of race and class was shaped during my high school and college years in the race-charged sixties, when the fact of my race took on an almost religious significance. Progressively, from the mid-sixties on, more and more aspects of my life found their explanation, their justification, and their motivation in my race. My youthful concerns about career, romance, money, values, and even styles of dress became subject to consultation with various oracular sources of racial wisdom. And these ranged from a figure as ennobling as Martin Luther King, Jr., to the underworld elegance of dress I found in jazz clubs on the South Side of Chicago. Everywhere there were signals, and in those days I considered myself so blessed with clarity and direction that I pitied my white classmates who found more embarrassment than guidance in the fact of *their* race. In 1968, inflated by new power, I took a mischievous delight in calling them culturally disadvantaged.

But now, hearing my friend's comment was like hearing a priest from a church I'd grown disenchanted with. I understood him, but my faith was weak. What had sustained me in the sixties sounded monotonous and off-the-mark in the eighties. For me, race had lost much of its juju, its singular capacity to conjure meaning. And today, when I honestly look at my life and the lives of many other middle-class blacks I know, I can see that race never fully explained our situation in America society. Black though I may be, it is impossible for me to sit in my single-family house with two cars in the driveway and a swing set in the backyard and *not* see the role class has played in my life. And how can my friend, similarly raised and similarly situated, not see it?

Yet despite my certainty I felt a sharp tug of guilt as I tried to explain myself over my friend's skepticism. He is a man of many comedic facial expressions and, as I spoke, his brow lifted in extreme moral alarm as if I were uttering the unspeakable. His clear implication was that I was being elitist and possibly (dare we suggest?) anti-black—crimes for which there might well be no redemption. He pretended to fear for me. I chuckled along with him, but inwardly I did wonder at myself. Though I never doubted the validity of what I was saying, I felt guilty saying it. Why?

After he left (to retrieve his daughter from a dance lesson) I realized that the trap I felt myself in had a tiresome familiarity and, in a sort of slow motion epiphany, I began to see its outline. It was like the suddenly sharp vision one has at the end of a burdensome marriage when all the long-repressed incompatibilities come undeniably to light.

What became clear to me is that people like myself, my friend, and middle-class blacks in general are caught in a very specific double bind that keeps two equally powerful elements of our identity at odds with each other. The middle-class values by which we were raised—the work ethic, the importance of education, the value of property ownership, of respectability, of "getting ahead," of stable family life, of initiative, of self-reliance, et cetera—are, in themselves, raceless and even assimilationist. They urge us toward participation in the American mainstream, toward integration, toward a strong identification with the society, and toward the entire constellation of qualities that are implied in the word individualism. These values are almost rules for how to prosper in a democratic, free enterprise society that admires and rewards individual effort. They tell us to work hard for ourselves and our families and to seek our opportunities whenever they appear, inside or outside the confines of whatever ethnic group we may belong to.

But the particular pattern of racial identification that emerged in the sixties and that still prevails today urges middle-class blacks (and all blacks) in the opposite direction. This pattern asks us to see ourselves as an embattled minority, and it urges an adversarial stance toward the mainstream and an emphasis on ethnic consciousness over individualism. It is organized around an implied separatism.

The opposing thrust of these two parts of our identity results in the double bind of middle-class blacks. There is no forward movement on either plane that does not constitute backward movement on the other. This was the familiar trap I felt myself in while talking with my friend. As I spoke about class, his eyes reminded me that I was betraying race. Clearly, the two indispensable parts of my identity were a threat to one another.

Of course when you think about it, class and race are both similar in some ways and also naturally opposed. They are two forms of collective identity with boundaries that intersect. But whether they clash or peacefully coexist has much to do with how they are defined. Being both black and middle-class becomes a double bind when class and race are defined in sharply antagonistic terms, so that one must be repressed to appease the other.

But what is the "substance" of these two identities, and how does each establish itself in an individual's overall identity?

It seems to me that when we identify with any collective we are basically identifying with images that tell us what it means to be a member of that collective. Identity is not the same thing as the fact of membership in a collective; it is, rather, a form of self-definition, facilitated by images of what we wish our membership in the collective to mean. In this sense, the images we identify with may reflect the aspirations of the collective more than they reflect reality, and their content can vary with shifts in those aspirations.

But the process of identification is usually dialectical. It is just as necessary to say what we are *not* as it is to say what we are—so that, finally, identification comes about by embracing a polarity of positive and negative images. To identify as middle-class, for example, I must have both positive and negative images of what being middle-class entails; then I will know what I should and should not be doing in order to be middle-class. The same goes for racial identity. In the racially turbulent sixties the polarity of images that came to define racial identification was very antagonistic to the polarity that defined middle-class identification. One might say that the positive images of one lined up with the negative images of the other, so that to identify with both required either a contortionist's flexibility or a dangerous splitting of the self. The double bind of the black middle-class was in place.

The black middle-class has always defined its class identity by means of positive images gleaned from middle- and upper-class white society and by means of negative images of lower-class blacks. This habit goes back to the institution of slavery itself, when "house" slaves both mimicked the whites they served and held themselves above the "field" slaves. But, in the sixties, the old bourgeois impulse to dissociate from the lower classes (the we/they distinction) backfired when racial identity suddenly called for the celebration of this same black lower class. One of the qualities of a double bind is that one feels it more than sees it, and I distinctly remember the tension and strange sense of dishonesty I felt in those days as I moved back and forth like a bigamist between the demands of class and race.

Though my father was born poor, he achieved middle-class standing through much hard work and sacrifice (one of his favorite words) and by identifying fully with solid middle-class values—mainly hard work, family life, property ownership, and education for his children (all four of whom have advanced degrees). In his mind these were not so much values as laws of nature. People who embodied them made up the positive images in his class polarity. The negative images came largely from the blacks he had left behind because they were "going nowhere."

No one in my family remembers how it happened, but as time went on, the negative images congealed into an imaginary character named Sam who, from the extensive service we put him to, quickly grew to mythic proportions. In our family lore he was sometimes a trickster, sometimes a boob, but always possessed of a catalogue of sly faults that gave up graphic images of everything we should not be. On sacrifice: "Sam never thinks about tomorrow. He wants it now or he doesn't care about it." On work: "Sam doesn't favor it too much." On children: "Sam likes to have them but not to raise them." On money: "Sam drinks it up and pisses it out." On fidelity: "Sam has to have two or three women." On clothes: "Sam features loud clothes. He likes to see and be seen." And so on. Sam's persona amounted to a negative instruction manual in class identity.

I don't think that any of us believed Sam's faults were accurate representations of lower-class black life. He was an instrument of self-definition, not of sociological accuracy. It never occurred to us that he looked very much like the white racist stereotype of blacks, or that he might have been a manifestation of our own racial self-hatred. He simply gave us a counterpoint against which to express our aspirations. If self-hatred was a factor, it was not, for us, a matter of hating lower-class blacks but of hating what we did not want to be.

Still, hate or love aside, it is fundamentally true that my middle-class identity involved a dissociation from images of lower-class black life and a corresponding identification with values and patterns of responsibility that are common to the middle-class everywhere. These values sent me a clear message: Be both an individual and a responsible citizen, understand that the quality of your life will approximately reflect the quality of effort you put into it, know that individual responsibility is the basis of freedom, and that the limitations imposed by fate (whether fair or unfair) are no excuse for passivity.

Whether I live up to these values or not, I know that my acceptance of them is the result of lifelong conditioning. I know also that I share this conditioning with middle-class people of all races and that I can no more easily be free of it than I can be free of my race. Whether all this got started because the black middle-class modeled itself on the white middle-class is no longer relevant. For the middle-class black, conditioned by these values from birth, the sense of meaning they provide is as immutable as the color of his skin.

ELLIS COSE

The Rage of a Privileged Class

Several years ago, discussing lawsuits brought against her paper by minorities and women's groups in the 1970s, the *New York Times* legal counsel told me, "I always felt in the women's case that it was like a divorce or a custody proceeding. . . . There wasn't any of that in the minorities case. And I suppose it's for a very simple reason. There were so few minorities, so few longstanding preexisting relationships, you didn't have the sense of a family being rent asunder. The gap was too wide."

The gap was too wide. The phrase has stayed with me, for it seems to sum up the situation not only at the *New York Times* but across much of America, where whites and minorities—blacks, in particular—stare at each other across a vast (and at points seemingly unbridgeable) chasm. We have become so accustomed to the estrangement that it generally doesn't strike us as strange. As the *Times* executive observed, it is not a rupture between family members but between people who can barely conceive of themselves as belonging to the same tribe or sharing a common heritage. Yet occasionally something happens that makes it clear that this estrangement, however entrenched, is not particularly healthy—at least not for a nation that purports to believe that justice and opportunity should be color-blind.

Through much of 1992 and 1993, many Americans sat before their television sets engrossed in the saga of Rodney King. The videotaped beating, the riot in Los Angeles, and the two trials of the cops who pummeled King into submission provided any number of irresistible television moments; but they also did something more. They forced America to focus, at least briefly, on the problems of racial hostility and interracial alienation. And they highlighted the fact that despite the progress of the past few years, blacks and whites of all social and economic classes will sometimes see the same events in extremely different ways.

Certainly, in a literal sense, blacks and whites saw the same thing: a group of white policemen who repeatedly struck and backed away from the semiprone figure of King. That image was sufficiently powerful and unsettling that people of all races were sickened by it. Yet most whites viewed the beating as a shocking but isolated incident. Indeed, it was so stunning, at least in part, because it was taken to be so unusual. For most blacks, it was confirmation that a brutality many had experienced firsthand reflected a broader problem of brutality and race-based inequity within the criminal justice system.

"In the days after the acquittal of four white Los Angeles police officers charged in the beating of a black man, black and white opinions were uncharacteristically in synch on a racial question," wrote *Washington Post* reporter Lynne Duke in June 1992. "Large majorities of whites and overwhelming majorities of blacks told pollsters that the verdict was wrong. . . . But when asked if the verdict 'shows that blacks cannot get justice in this country,' black and white opinion hit a fork in the road: 78 percent of blacks said yes, compared with only 25 percent of whites."

The following year, during the second trial of the accused policemen, Bobby Doctor, acting director of the U.S. Civil Rights Commission, told me he had witnessed a number of police beatings during his civil rights work in the South. He said that he and other prominent African Americans had long spoken out against police brutality—"but nobody's been listening." With the Rodney King video, "finally, it was there for the country to see, for the world to see."

Wade Henderson, director of the Washington office of the NAACP, also sees King's ordeal as representing much more than the tribulations of one man. He described King as "a black Everyman whose experience with police came to symbolize African-American encounters with law enforcement." Not that King was anyone's idea of a model citizen. He was an ex-con with a penchant for drinking and trouble—hardly a typical, hardworking black American. Many African Americans nonetheless identified strongly with King—not because of who he was but because of what he had been through. No matter whose account of that night in the San Fernando Valley is accepted, no matter what motivation is attributed to the police, King was dealt with, to use Henderson's words, "as something other than a man." In *Presumed Guilty*, his book about the Rodney King encounter, Stacey Koon, the police sergeant in charge at the scene, depicts King as a "huge guy" possessing "superhuman strength" who was completely oblivious to pain. This language strikes Henderson as having less to do with reality than with dehumanizing stereotypes of the sort African Americans have routinely encountered in dealing with law enforcement officers. Many blacks who put themselves in King's place saw him not as a bum who had received rough treatment but as "a glaring reminder that being black in America means that you operate under a different set of rules," as Henderson puts it.

The discrepancy in black and white reactions to the King beating is certainly not surprising. As we have seen, the polling literature is replete with examples of blacks and whites in fundamental disagreement over the most basic facts of American life. In their 1992 survey of Los Angeles County, for instance, researchers at UCLA's Center for the Study of Urban Poverty found that 60 percent of blacks had "not much" confidence in the police, while only 16 percent of whites felt similarly. Eighty percent of blacks agreed with the statement that "blacks usually don't get fair treatment in the courts and criminal justice system," compared to 40 percent of whites. And three-fourths of blacks felt that "American society owes people of my ethnic group a better chance in life than we currently have."

As the astonished UCLA researchers discovered, economic success is no remedy for despair over what blacks perceive as deeply rooted racial inequities. *But why should that be?* Why shouldn't blacks who are affluent, well-educated, and blessed by life acknowledge their good fortune and be content? Why should blacks making six- and seven-figure incomes identify at all with the likes of Rodney King?

Part of the answer lies in David Dinkins's epigram: "A white man with a million dollars is a millionaire, and a black man with a million dollars is a nigger with a million dollars." His obvious point is that many whites have great difficulty differentiating a black go-getter from a black bum, that at night on a lonely stretch of highway a malicious cop is as likely to bash one black head as another. And even if Dinkins doesn't believe his own words, plenty of other blacks do—or at least believe that countless cops see color first and class later, if at all.

Certainly, as police sergeant Don Jackson confirmed during his self-assigned undercover foray into Long Beach, a black skin, in and of itself, can arouse a dangerous degree of suspicion. Numerous others have discovered the same thing. In Reynoldsburg, Ohio, for example, the NAACP claimed that racial hostility was so unrestrained that the police had organized a SNAT—Special Nigger Arrest Team—for the express purpose of harassing blacks. For many black Americans, police abuse is an old story, at least as old as the battle for civil rights. And though the nation was stunned by the police treatment of Rodney King, and even more so by the terrifying riot that followed the acquittal of his assailants, it's worth recalling that this was far from the first instance of conflict between a minority community and the police. Most of the riots of the 1960s were ignited by similar episodes. In 1980, a devastating riot swept Miami when an all-white jury exonerated several white policemen accused of viciously beating a black man following a high-speed chase. Unlike King, Arthur McDuffie died from his injuries. Unlike King, McDuffie, an insurance executive, was a bona fide member of the middle class.

Much of the history of blacks in America is a history of mistreatment and harassment by agents of the state. The so-called Ku Klux Klan Acts, passed by Congress during Reconstruction, were aimed specifically at law enforcement offices who denied newly enfranchised blacks their rights; and though those laws are well over a century old, the U.S. Justice Department continues to find cases that justify their use. Small wonder, then, that in many minority communities reports of police brutality are granted instant (and sometimes unmerited) credibility.

Yet for all the symbolic significance of such cases, it is not thoughts of McDuffie, King, and other African Americans victimized by cops that keep black professionals awake at night. The rage of the black middle class can hardly be laid at the feet of the police. As awful as Rodney King's treatment may have been, most middle-class blacks know that they are not very likely to find themselves on the wrong side of a policeman's baton.

The source of their outrage is generally much more prosaic: colleague, clerk, or prospective neighbor—someone whose only weapons are words and disapproval, and who causes great pain while truly intending no harm. When the senior partner in the big law firm goes to a store and is treated "like I make two cents and am uneducated," he is in exactly the same boat as Dinkins's "nigger with a million dollars." When an accomplished jurist complains of white counterparts who "want you to do well, but not *that* well" and wonders what he might have achieved had he really "been given a fair shot," he is making the same point: that the benefits of material success do not include exemption from being treated as a "nigger." When University of Illinois sociologist Sharon Collins asks whether it is possible for a black person to make race not matter, she is saying, along with the vast majority of other black professionals I interviewed, that America is not nearly as free as it thinks it is of the bigotry that defined its past.

As I write this, the local New York press is reporting on a new study by a Queens College professor showing that blacks in the city, at all income levels, remain extremely segregated from other groups. On my desk sits a huge binder of papers delivered at the 1992 housing conference of the Federal National Mortgage Association (Fannie Mae), reviewing several years of research documenting discrimination encountered by blacks and Hispanic Americans in the housing market. The authors of several of the papers note that when black and Hispanic auditors go into predominantly white areas in search of housing, they are routinely steered into neighborhoods that have more minorities. Other papers focus on trends in lending institutions and on evidence indicating that blacks, whatever their economic profile, have more difficulty getting mortgages than whites. John Kain, a professor of economic and Afro-American studies at Harvard University, offers his opinion (disputed by some other researchers) that "the restriction of black households to massive central-city ghettos, and a few small and isolated black communities located elsewhere in the metropolitan area," denies many African Americans information about and access to jobs and high-quality schools. Anthony Downs, an economist with the Brookings Institution, observes, "Racial and ethnic discrimination is so widespread and has persisted so long in American housing markets that it must be supported by powerful motives and incentives."

Perusing the collection of academic housing studies takes me back to my own first experience looking for an apartment outside of Chicago's black neighborhoods. The tenant of a two-bedroom flat in a trendy North Side area had placed an ad seeking someone to sublet. When I called, her manner was cordial and gregarious; when I arrived a few hours later, she was still polite but decidedly more reserved. She hastily pointed out a few of the apartment's attractions and then excused herself to make a call from the bedroom. It soon became clear that she was talking to the landlord, for in a whisper that I clearly was not supposed to hear, she confided to the person on the other end that a well-dressed black man had answered the ad. Was it all right, she wondered, to show the apartment? The owner, who I later discovered had a black girlfriend, apparently allayed her concerns. The woman returned to the living room with a smile on her face and proceeded to show me around.

My application for the apartment was approved without incident. Still, the woman's behavior made a powerful and unambiguous point: that though the apartment was for rent, it might not be available to someone of my race. And angered as I was at the thought that she—or anyone else—would presume to judge and perhaps reject me simply because of my color, I meekly accepted the treatment as the price to be paid for looking where *my kind* was deemed not to belong.

In *American Apartheid*, sociologists Douglass Massey and Nancy Denton catalogue a multitude of evils tied to racial segregation in housing. Like Harvard's John Kain, they blame it for barring blacks from many jobs and schools, but their indictment goes much further. Segregation isolates blacks politically, they charge, and is responsible for the development of an "oppositional culture" in which "a majority of children are born out of wedlock, . . . most families are on welfare, . . . educational failure prevails, and . . . social and physical deterioration abound." In short, they blame segregation for the existence of a black underclass, and they argue that its deleterious effects are not limited to poor blacks.

"Middle-class households—whether they are black, Mexican, Italian, Jewish, or Polish—always try to escape the poor," they point out. "But only blacks must attempt their escape with a highly segregated, racially segmented housing market. Because of segregation, middle-class blacks are less able to escape than other groups, and as a result are exposed to more poverty. At the same time, because of segregation no one will move into a poor black neighborhood except other poor blacks. Thus both middle-class and poor blacks lose compared with the poor and middle class of other groups: poor blacks live under unrivaled concentrations of poverty and affluent blacks live in neighborhoods that are far less advantageous than those experienced by the middle class of other groups."

The pervasiveness of segregation in America's large cities is beyond dispute, as is the wickedness of a system that exhorts blacks to escape the ghetto and its associated pathologies and then batters them for trying. And as noted in previous chapters, even blacks who do manage to "escape" often encounter problems of another sort. The anger of black suburbanites who are never invited to join private clubs near their homes and the anxiety of black parents trying to raise children in communities where they feel socially isolated say volumes about how pernicious old attitudes can be. And even if residential segregation could be eliminated (which seems an unlikely proposition for the near future), what is to be done about psychological segregation—about the tendency of Americans to force each other into comfortable, separate and racially stereotypical pigeonholes?

The pain of the professionals profiled in the preceding pages is more often than not rooted in feelings of exclusion. In attempting to escape that pain, some blacks end up, in effect, inviting increased isolation. When the successful black lawyer declares that he will "go to my own people for acceptance" because he no longer expects approbation from whites, he is not only expressing solidarity with other members of his race, he is also conceding defeat. He is saying that he is giving up hope of ever being anything but a talented "nigger" to many of his white colleagues, that he refuses to invest emotionally in those who will never quite see him as one of them, whatever his personal and professional attributes.

His white peers would of course be shocked to discover that he finds his workplace a hostile environment and that he feels a need to protect himself from them emotionally. *What,* they would wonder, *can be his problem?* Just as white students on so many college campuses wonder why so many of their black counterparts huddle together adamantly refusing to join "the mainstream."

Whites often take such behavior as a manifestation of irrational antiwhite prejudice. But in most cases, it is perhaps better understood as a reaction similar to that of the lawyer above—as a retreat from a "mainstream" they have come to feel is an irremediably hostile place. Some people would say that they are flat-out wrong, that for blacks willing to meet whites halfway, race no longer has to matter, at least not all that much.

Yet pretending (or convincing ourselves) that race no longer matters (or wouldn't if minorities stopped demanding special treatment) is not quite the same as making it not matter. Creating a color-blind society on a foundation saturated with the venom of racism requires something more than simply proclaiming that the age of brotherhood has arrived. Somehow, as America went from a country concerned about denial of civil rights to one obsessed with "reverse racism" and "quotas" that discriminate against white males, some important steps were missed. Among other things, we neglected as a nation to make any serious attempt to understand why, if racial conditions were improving so much, legions of those who should be celebrating were still singing the blues. To answer that question would have meant, at a minimum, truly listening to what the dissatisfied were saying instead of writing them off as unreasonable whiners.

STEPHEN L. CARTER

Reflections of an Affirmative Action Baby

I got into law school because I am black.

As many black professionals think they must, I have long suppressed this truth, insisting instead that I got where I am the same way everybody else did. Today I am a professor at the Yale Law School. I like to think that I am a good one, but I am hardly the most objective judge. What I am fairly sure of, and can now say without trepidation, is that were my skin not the color that it is, I would not have had the chance to try.

For many, perhaps most, black professionals of my generation, the matter of who got where and how is left in a studied and, I think, purposeful ambiguity. Some of us, as they say, would have made it into an elite college or professional school anyway. (But, in my generation, many fewer than we like to pretend, even though one might question the much-publicized claim by Derek Bok, the president of Harvard University, that in the absence of preferences, only 1 percent of Harvard's entering class would be black.) Most of us, perhaps nearly all of us, have learned to bury the matter far back in our minds. We are who we are and where we are, we have records of accomplishment or failure, and there is no rational reason that anybody—employer, client, whoever—should care any longer whether racial preference played any role in our admission to a top professional school.

When people in positions to help or hurt our careers *do* seem to care, we tend to react with fury. Those of us who have graduated professional school over the past fifteen to twenty years, and are not white, travel career paths that are frequently bumpy with suspicions that we did not earn the right to be where we are. We bristle when others raise what might be called the qualification question—"Did you get into school or get hired because of a special program?"—and that prickly sensitivity is the best evidence, if any is needed, of one of the principal costs of racial preferences. Scratch a black professional with the qualification question, and you're likely to get a caustic response, such as this one from a senior executive at a major airline: "Some whites think I've made it because I'm black. Some blacks think I've made it only because I'm an Uncle Tom. The fact is, I've made it because I'm good."

Given the way that so many Americans seem to treat receipt of the benefits of affirmative action as a badge of shame, answers of this sort are both predictable and sensible. In the professional world, moreover, they are very often true: relatively few corporations are in a position to hand out charity. The peculiar aspect of the routine denial, however, is that so many of those who will bristle at the suggestion that they themselves have gained from racial preferences will try simultaneously to insist that racial preferences be preserved and to force the world to pretend that no one benefits from them. That awkward balancing of fact and fiction explains the frequent but generally groundless cry that it is racist to suggest that some individual's professional accomplishments would be fewer but for affirmative action; and therein hangs a tale.

For students at the leading law schools, autumn brings the recruiting season, the idyllic weeks when law firms from around the country compete to lavish upon them lunches and dinners and other attentions, all with the professed goal of obtaining the students' services—perhaps for the summer, perhaps for a longer term. The autumn of 1989 was different, however, because the nation's largest firm, Baker & McKenzie, was banned from interviewing students at the University of Chicago Law School, and on probation—that is, enjoined to be on its best behavior—at some others.

The immediate source of Baker & McKenzie's problems was a racially charged interview that a partner in the firm had conducted the previous fall with a black third-year student at the school. The interviewer evidently suggested that other lawyers might call her "nigger" or "black bitch" and wanted to know how she felt about that. Perhaps out of surprise that she played golf, he observed that "there aren't too many golf courses in the ghetto." He also suggested that the school was admitting "foreigners" and excluding "qualified" Americans.

The law school reacted swiftly, and the firm was banned from interviewing on campus. Other schools contemplated taking action against the firm, and some of them did. Because I am black myself, and teach in a law school, I suppose the easiest thing for me to have done would have been to clamor in solidarity for punishment. Yet I found myself strangely reluctant to applaud the school's action. Instead, I was disturbed rather than excited by this vision of law schools circling the wagons, as it were, to defend their beleaguered minority students against racially insensitive remarks. It is emphatically not my intention to defend the interviewer, most of whose reported questions and comments were inexplicable and inexcusable. I am troubled, however, by my suspicion that there would still have been outrage—not as much, but some—had the interviewer asked only what I called at the beginning of the chapter the qualification question.

I suspect this because in my own student days, something over a decade ago, an interviewer from a prominent law firm addressed this very question to a Yale student who was not white, and the student voices—including my own—howled in protest. "Racism!" we insisted. "Ban them!" But with the passing years, I have come to wonder whether our anger might have been misplaced.

To be sure, the Yale interviewer's question was boorish. And because the interviewer had a grade record and résumé right in front of him, it was probably irrelevant as well. (It is useful here to dispose of one common but rather silly antiaffirmative action bromide: the old question, "Do you really want to be treated by a doctor who got into medical school because of skin color?" The answer is, or ought to be, that the patient doesn't particularly care how the doctor got *into* school; what matters is how the doctor got *out*. The right question, the sensible question, is not "What medical school performance did your grades and test scores predict?" But "What was your medical school performance?") But irrelevance and boorishness cannot explain our rage at the qualification question, because lots of interviewers ask questions that meet the tests of boorishness and irrelevance.

The controversy is not limited to outsiders who come onto campus to recruit. In the spring of 1991, for example, students at Georgetown Law School demanded punishment for a classmate who argued in the school newspaper that affirmative action is unfair because students of color are often admitted to law school on the basis of grades and test scores that would cause white applicants to be rejected. Several universities have considered proposals that would deem it "racial harassment" for a (white?) student to question the qualifications of nonwhite classmates. But we can't change either the truths or the myths about racial preferences by punishing those who speak them.

This clamor for protection from the qualification question is powerful evidence of the terrible psychological pressure that racial preferences often put on their beneficiaries. Indeed, it sometimes seems as though the programs are not supposed to have any beneficiaries—or, at least, that no one is permitted to suggest that they have any.

And that's ridiculous. If one supports racial preferences in professional school admissions, for example, one must be prepared to treat them like any other preference in admission and believe that they make a difference, that some students would not be admitted if the preferences did not exist. This is not a racist observation. It is not normative in any sense. It is simply a fact. A good deal of emotional underbrush might be cleared away were the fact simply conceded, and made the beginning, not the end, of any discussion of preferences. For once it is conceded that the programs have beneficiaries, it follows that some of us who are professionals and are not white must be among them. Supporters of preferences must stop pretending otherwise. Rather, some large segment of us must be willing to meet the qualification question head-on, to say, "Yes, I got into law school because of racial preferences. So what?"—and, having said it, must be ready with a list of what we have made of the opportunities the preferences provided.

Now, this is a costly concession, because it carries with it all the baggage of the bitter rhetorical battle over the relationship between preferences and merit. But bristling at the question suggests a deep-seated fear that the dichotomy might be real. Indeed, if admitting that racial preferences make a difference leaves a funny aftertaste in the mouths of proponents, they might be more comfortable fighting against preferences rather than for them.

So let us bring some honesty as well as rigor to the debate, and begin at the beginning. I have already made clear my starting point: I got into a top law school because I am black. Not only am I unashamed of this fact, but I can prove its truth.

As a senior at Stanford back in the mid-1970s, I applied to about half a dozen law schools. Yale, where I would ultimately enroll, came through fairly early with an acceptance. So did all but one of the others. The last school, Harvard, dawdled and dawdled. Finally, toward the end of the admission season, I received a letter of rejection. Then, within days, two different Harvard officials and a professor contacted me by telephone to apologize. They were quite frank in their explanation for the "error." I was told by one official that the school had initially rejected me because "we assumed from your record that you were white." (The words have always stuck in my mind, a tantalizing reminder of what is expected of me.) Suddenly coy, he went on to say that the school had obtained "additional information that should have been counted in your favor"—that is, Harvard had discovered the color of my skin. And if I had already made a deposit to confirm my decision to go elsewhere, well, that, I was told, would "not be allowed" to stand in my way should I enroll at Harvard.

Naturally, I was insulted by this miracle. Stephen Carter, the white male, was not good enough for the Harvard Law School; Stephen Carter, the black male, not only was good enough but rated agonized telephone calls urging him to attend. And Stephen Carter, color unknown, must have been white: How else could he have achieved what he did in college? Except that my college achievements were obviously not sufficiently spectacular to merit acceptance had I been white. In other words, my academic record was too good for a black Stanford University undergraduate, but not good enough for a white Harvard law student. Because I turned out to be black, however, Harvard was quite happy to scrape me from what it apparently considered somewhere nearer the bottom of the barrel.

My objective is not to single out Harvard for special criticism; on the contrary, although my ego insists otherwise, I make no claim that a white student with my academic record would have been admitted to any of the leading law schools. The insult I felt came from the pain of being reminded so forcefully that in the judgment of those with the power to dispose, I was good enough for a top law school only because I happened to be black.

Naturally, I should not have been insulted at all; that is what racial preferences are for—racial preference. But I was insulted and went off to Yale instead, even though I had then and have now absolutely no reason to imagine that Yale's judgment was based on different criteria than Harvard's. Hardly anyone granted admission at Yale is denied admission at Harvard, which admits a far larger class; but several hundreds of students who are admitted at

Harvard are denied admission at Yale. Because Yale is far more selective, the chances are good that I was admitted at Yale for essentially the same reason I was admitted at Harvard—the color of my skin made up for what were evidently considered other deficiencies in my academic record. I may embrace this truth as a matter of simple justice or rail against it as one of life's great evils, but being a member of the affirmative action generation means that the one thing I cannot do is deny it. I will say it again: I got into law school because I am black. So what?

PART 5

Black Magic

AND BID HIM SING

COUNTEE CULLEN

Yet Do I Marvel

I doubt not God is good, well-meaning, kind.
And did He stoop to quibble could tell why
The little buried mole continues blind,
Why flesh that mirrors Him must some day die,
Make plain the reason tortured Tantalus
Is baited by the fickle fruit, declare
If merely brute caprice dooms Sisyphus
To struggle up a never-ending stair.
Inscrutable His ways are, and immune
To catechism by a mind too strewn
With petty cares to slightly understand
What awful brain compels His awful hand.
Yet do I marvel at this curious thing:
To make a poet black, and bid him sing!

WALLACE THURMAN

Infants of the Spring

Raymond spent most of the afternoon idly wandering about Central Park, stopping at haphazard intervals to rest on a park bench. He had decided that it was time he was taking stock of himself, time he was casting an appraising and critical eye over his past and present, and perhaps in the muddle find a guide post for the future. He was disturbed and moody. His experiences of the night before and his talk with Stephen this same morning had caused his spirits to become curdled and his mind to become confused. He was going . . . he knew not where. Always he had protested that the average Negro intellectual and artist had no goal, no standards, no elasticity, no pregnant germ plasm. And now he was beginning to doubt even himself.

He wanted to write, but he had made little progress. He wanted to become a Prometheus, to break the chains which held him to a racial rack and carry a blazing beacon to the top of Mount Olympus so that those possessed of Alpine stocks could follow in his wake. He wanted to do something memorable in literature, something that could stay afloat on the contemporary sea of weighted ballast, something which could transcend and survive the transitional age in which he was living. He wanted to accomplish these things, but he was becoming less and less confident that he was possessed of the necessary genius. He did not doubt that he had a modicum of talent, but talent was not a sufficient spring board to guarantee his being catapulted into the literary halls of Valhalla; talent was not a sufficient prerequisite for immortality. He needed genius and there was no assurance that he had it, no assurance that he had done anything more "than learned his lessons well."

Stephen's phrase irritated him, impinged itself upon his consciousness and bored in relentlessly. He was uncertain whether it had been meant to be an aphoristic jest or a sarcastic jibe. Was it a meaty phrase carrying the sting of an adder? Or was it a listless phrase coined to discourage further boring conversation? He did not know, and he had no insight into the machinery which had produced it. But he could not aerate it from his mind. Insistently it flashed across his brain, formed itself into flaming letters before his eyes, and dinned its searing way into his ears.

He soon came to the conclusion that he was cutting a ridiculous figure. On three distinct occasions now, twice with Stephen and once with Lucille, this unwelcome characterization had seemed apt in the light of what they had said on those occasions. He was a self-deluded posturer. A consummate jackass. . . .

Walking through Central Park. Mind chaotic and deranged. Mind tortured, a seething melting pot into which too much unfiltered metal had been poured. Coherence was lacking. Ideas toppled over one another, ideas the result of wide reading and too hasty assimilation. His was an adolescent brain. It had not matured sufficiently to exercise caution and restraint. It had seized upon attractive brilliants, fed upon predigested cereals, and made no use of cauterizing gastric fluids. Yet there was something fundamental there striving for expression and relief, something which protested against unprincipled inundation and unprincipled expression—something which cautioned him to take inventory, and invite maturity.

Despite his superiority complex he was different from most people he knew, precociously different. The difficulty being that he was wont to pervert rather than to train and cultivate this difference. It was something to be paraded rather than something to be carefully nurtured. It was something to release half cocked in order to shock rather than something to utilize essentially. There had been no catharsis, no intellectual metabolism. In pretending to be a dispenser of pearls to swine he had only proved that he, too, sometimes wallowed in the mire.

The struggle to free himself from race consciousness had been hailed before actually accomplished. The effort to formulate a new attitude toward life had become a seeking for a red badge of courage. That which might have emerged normally, if given time, had been forcibly and prematurely exposed to the light. It now seemed as if the Caesarian operation was going to prove fatal both to the parent and to the child.

Futile introspection, desperate flagellations of self which still left him in darkness and despair.

On his way home Raymond tried hard to recall all the various items with which he had concerned himself. He had a confused recollection of having thought about innumerable subjects, innumerable people, but the thoughts were now nebulous and fast fading into obscurity, and there was no key to the dark labyrinth to which they had fled. He had no definite memories, no dominant conclusions. His day of solitude, his day of stock taking, had all been in vain.

"I don't expect to be a great writer. I don't think the Negro race can produce one now, any more than can America. I know of only one Negro who has the elements of greatness, and that's Jean Toomer. The rest of us are merely journeymen, planting seed for someone else to harvest. We all get sidetracked sooner or later. The older ones become warped by propaganda. We younger ones are mired in decadence. None of us seem able to rise above our environment. That donation party the other night is symptomatic of my generation. We're a curiosity . . . even to ourselves. It will be some years before the more forward will be accepted as human beings and allowed to associate with giants. The pygmies have taken us over now, and I doubt if any of us has the strength to use them for a stepladder to a higher plane."

JULIUS LESTER

Falling Pieces of the Broken Sky

When I was twenty-one, I wanted to move to New Hampshire and live haiku. Haiku is more than the three-line, seventeen-syllable poems elementary-school teachers think are appropriate for children. Haiku is a spiritual discipline, a way of Being out of which one writes deceptively simple poems that burst with silence and peel back the layers of perception until the All and Nothingness that is all and evermore is revealed.

That was the life to which I wanted to give myself. I got as close to New Hampshire as western Massachusetts, but I haven't written a haiku in more years than I can recall.

Another reality impinged on my life like an eternal winter of burning winds and snows so white and dazzling that the eyes could find comfort only in blindness. Instead of living and writing haiku, I became a voice of the black collective and wrote books and essays articulating the pain, suffering, and rage of blacks.

Then, one spring afternoon in the early seventies, I learned that the black collective cared only for itself, and its ultimate triumph would be to destroy that singular entity I knew as myself.

I spoke at a high school in Harlem. During the question-and-answer period I was asked: "What should black people do?" The question was repeated with that desperate sincerity which belongs to adolescence.

It was a good question. Richard Nixon was president. The sixties were over and white people were tired of social change. Most of the liberal social programs had been dismantled and the message to blacks was, you are on your own. So what blacks should do was a cogent question.

"I don't know. What do you think we should do?" I answered the question in its many guises.

My refusal to say more seemed to anger them. Finally, someone yelled, "We demand that you lead us!"

I refused the dubious honor.

"Then what good are you?" someone else yelled.

"Absolutely none!" I shot back.

My responsibilities as a black writer did not include being a leader. That would be to sell my birthright.

I must have appeared indifferent and even arrogant in the face of their poverty and desperation, because suddenly the principal was beside me. "I'd better get you out of here." And I was hustled from the auditorium and out of the building.

If I had any response to the afternoon, it was not sympathy or empathy with the students. It was anger that as a black writer I was expected to do more than write. I was made to feel that if all I could do was write, then my words were inadequate to the problem. If I could not be what they needed me to be, they did not want me to be.

That is part of the nature of collectives. The individual is of value only as long as he or she serves the collective in the way the collective demands to be served. The collective has no interest other than itself.

Ten years later I found myself on a panel discussing racism in children's books. One of the black panelists presented examples of books she considered antiblack. When the time came for audience questions, one of the few whites present said, quietly but firmly, "I object to your calling my book racist," and mentioned the name of a book that had been criticized by the panelist.

The black panelist responded, "Your book is one of the most racist books I've ever read," and, producing a sheaf of notes, began citing page numbers and reading passages from the book. All the excerpts were highlighted by prominent use of the word *nigger* and disparaging remarks about same. The black audience responded with mutterings of shock and disapproval. And there the matter rested.

I was not so estranged from the black collective that I did not understand the black panelist's anger. The use of *nigger* and derogatory comments about "niggers" from white characters cannot be read as if we did not live in a society where that word and those comments might not be repeated by a white child to a black one outside the classroom.

I also understood the white author's denial of racism. The book was set in the South at a time when such language and opinions were the norm. If the author was to be true to history, there was no choice but to use the language and opinions of that time and that place. As a writer I would have done the same.

The white author's context was historical; the black panelist's context was today. Was there a way to reconcile the integrity of both?

Almost by definition, the black writer is supposed to be the voice for a people whose cries are not heard, whose laughter is not shared. We are called upon to conjure words, powerful and magical, to counteract those that have flowed and continue to flow from pens held by whites, words that humiliate and disparage us—words whose impact only increases the hatreds that would kill us.

Three examples: The *New York Times Book Review* (December 14, 1980) asked novelist Joyce Carol Oates to reflect on the future of the novel. Among her provocative comments was the following: "I anticipate, in my idealism . . . novels by minorities that range beyond the passionate but delimited concerns of minorities." Who is she to define black suffering as a "delimited concern"? Are black experiences to be cavalierly dismissed because she is "delimited" in her concerns?

The second example is from a *Newsweek* review (January 5, 1981) of a movie starring Goldie Hawn: "Goldie is an incorrigible liberal who defends and brings into her house every oppressed minority: blacks, Chicanos, Indians—and stray dogs. The only ones who don't rip her off are the dogs." Am I being "delimitedly concerned" if I object to being equated with "stray dogs"?

The final example is from a survey of children's literature published in *Time* (December 29, 1980): "All is [not] dragonfree in the world of children's literature. The fragmentation of the nuclear family, the new consciousness of black and women's history and of human rights in general have engendered a series of 'problem books' that confuse as often as they enlighten." Are the sum of the achievements of Virginia Hamilton, Mildred Taylor, John Steptoe, myself, and others to be reduced to "problem books"?

The message of these three excerpts is that neither black writers nor black lives are to be considered seriously. The implication is that the only important values are those considered so by whites. Blacks and women are the dragons in the bountiful garden of children's literature. (And we all know what happens to dragons in children's books.)

Yes, we write "problem books," because we know what a problem whites have created of themselves for us. We write "problem books" because we want *all* children to be better able to grapple with the Hydra-heads of racism than we were at their age.

Hannah Arendt wrote that "it is the poet's task to coin the words we live by." Black writers are engaged in a new minting process that is not exclusive to them. Though our country is racially fragmented, the human condition is not the sole property of any group, despite the impression one might receive from books by many whites.

I wish the black panelist had said to the white writer that there is a fidelity to the human condition deeper than fidelity to the language of a particular time and place. Fidelity to the language of time and place can be a source of pain to blacks because it is part of the reality we must confront in this time and this place. And fidelity to the human condition means to love the soul and its potential for beauty and truth even as that soul seems mired in the worst of the human condition.

I imagine that the white writer would have responded, "That is just what I tried to do," pulled out a copy of the book, and read passages that proved it.

Then the black panelist could have said, "I am so afraid that the language in your book will make a white child feel confirmed in using such language and in expressing such attitudes."

"That is the risk," the white writer might've said.

"But at whose expense?"

"Yours *and* mine," would've come the response. "Yours and mine."

May Sarton was asked once how she wanted to be remembered.

"As wholly human," she responded.

Only to the extent that I am wholly human do I fulfill my responsibility as a black writer, because my responsibility is not to black people only, despite the responsibilities history may impose on a black writer, despite whatever duty one may feel to the black collective.

My responsibility as a black writer is to the ideal of the human. If that is to be the heartbeat of my writing, I cannot succumb to collective definitions and collective ways of Being. To do so is to act irresponsibly in relationship to my gift.

To be responsible as a writer means that every word of mine will have been written truly, as truly as I knew how at the time of the writing. That is only the beginning, however, because writing, though done in solitude, is a social act. It needs the reader to complete it. Writing is a relationship in which I who write and you who read meet in the silent places of your soul. If I have written well and you have read well, we learn a little more about what it means to be wholly human.

Martin Buber wrote that to read a book one "must labor with it hours at a time as with a headstrong horse, until covered with sweat he stands in front of it and reads this book he has tamed."

One who writes needs those who can read, who bring to the act of reading all the levels and nuances of not only mind but feeling that a responsible writer brings to the act of writing. To write and publish is to risk oneself in the world. It is not too much to ask that readers risk themselves when they read.

Being responsible is the act of making a promise to another. As a black writer my promise cannot be made exclusively to blacks. When asked for whom she wrote, Joyce Carol Oates responded, "God." That is my answer, too.

My promise is to that part of you which is beyond and separate from definitions of gender, race, and all the sociological and political descriptions that hang from our limbs and rattle like the chains of Marley's ghost. There is a place of sacred truth in each of us. It is from within that place I seek to write and it is to that place in you my words seek to go.

A black critic wrote of me once that "because he is black he is by virtue of these political and social conditions, a member of a racial collective. He does not have the freedom of defining himself completely outside the boundaries of race and its ramifications. . . . the highly individual nature of his quest ignores his surrounding substantive reality—that of a black man living in Twentieth-century America."

That is too simple. It is also false.

If I take responsibility for that place of sacred truth within, then I know that my "substantive reality" does not differ from that of anyone who has ever existed on the planet. Thus, what I must take responsibility for, ultimately, is the Unseen and the Unknowable.

Reb Simchah Bunam wrote:

The Lord created the world in a state of beginning. The universe is always in an uncompleted state, in the form of its beginning. It is not like a vessel at which the master works to finish it; it requires continuous labor and renewal by creative forces. Should these cease for only a second, the universe would return to primeval chaos.

My responsibility as a black writer does not differ from my responsibility as a human being: to live with reverence toward and responsibility for my soul.

Reb Leib went to see the Maggid of Mezhirich not to hear him discuss Torah but to watch him tie his shoes.

We must learn to tie our shoes.

ISHMAEL REED

Writin' Is Fightin'

In 1953, I was working in a drugstore on William Street in Buffalo, New York. As I left one evening to go home, a man pulled up to the curb and told me that he needed somebody to help him deliver newspapers. There were stacks of them in the backseat of his old brown beat-up Packard, which was just a shade darker than he was. His name was A. J. Smitherman, editor of *The Empire Star Weekly*, a Buffalo newspaper. How would you like to have this job every week? he asked after we'd taken copies of his newspaper to all of the newsstands on his route. I had been writing before then, and date my first commissioned work to 1952, when my mother asked me to write a birthday poem for one of her fellow employees at Satler's Department Store on Fillmore.

As a youngster, living in the projects, I also composed mini-sermons that I'd deliver during Sunday School from the pulpit at Saint Luke's Church, an old Afro-American Episcopal Zion church located on Eagle Street. But working at *The Empire Star* brought me into contact with articulate black people like

Mary Crosby, Mr. Smitherman, and his son, Toussaint. Within a year, they even let me try my hand at writing columns, and I wrote jazz articles in what was to become a pungent writing style.

I drifted away from the *Star* in high school, having other things on my mind and needing more spending money than Mr. Smitherman was able to pay me. He was a relentless man who was barely able to bring out his newspaper every week. When he died, *The Buffalo Evening News* noted that he had to struggle against adversity. That's one of the things I remember about this gentle, intellectual editor and poet. His calm in the face of calamity.

As fate would have it, in 1960, after I'd dropped out of college and found myself, a father, living in the Talbert Mall Projects, attempting to support a family on forty dollars per week, I volunteered to do some work for the *Star*, which was then edited by Joe Walker, a dynamic young militant who was causing a stir in the city because of his fight against segregated schools and on behalf of Black Power. It was then that the lively style of my writing was put to the test. Fighting for a traffic light for my Talbert Mall neighbors (it's still there); debating the current mayor, James Griffith, on the subject of school segregation; defending black prostitutes who'd been brutalized by the police; and, at the same time, writing poetry and plays. The *Star* folded.

An Irish-American poet named David Sharpe liked a play of mine, and I traveled to New York with him one weekend. We spent most of the time at Chumley's, a restaurant located on Bedford Street in the Village. I was impressed. The book jackets of authors who'd drunk there, including Edna Saint Vincent Millay, lined the wall, and years later I felt that I'd arrived because mine went up. A screenwriter read my play standing at the bar (a play that was later lost in an abandoned car); he liked it.

After that, there was no keeping me from New York, and a few weeks later, Dave and I went down on the Greyhound bus. I carried all of my belongings in a blue plastic bag I'd purchased for ten cents at the laundromat, and noticing my embarrassment, Dave carried it for me. It was 1962.

In New York, I joined the Umbra Workshop, to which Amiri Baraka credits the origin of the type of black aesthetic that so influenced the Black Arts Repertory School. It was in that workshop that I began to become acquainted with the techniques of the Afro-American literary style.

In 1965, I ran a newspaper in Newark, New Jersey, where I featured some of the same issues I'd covered in the *Star*, including a controversial piece on a welfare mother, which offended some blacks because she didn't sport the proper coiffure. It was during my tenure as editor of the *Advance* newspaper that I wrote an article about the police. Under heavy criticism, they'd invited members of the community to travel with them as a way of monitoring their activities. Representatives from the local civil rights organizations refused, but, in the interest of fair play, I accompanied them on their rounds one Saturday night, and because I commented that they had a tough job, I was called a right-winger by some black intellectuals.

I don't have a predictable, computerized approach to political and social issues in a society in which you're either for it or agin' it. Life is much more complex. And so for my early articles about black-on-black crime, I've been criticized by the left, and for my sympathy with some "left-wing" causes I've been criticized by the right, though from time to time I've noticed that there doesn't seem to be a dime's worth of difference between the zealotry of the left and that of the right.

I think that a certain amount of philosophical skepticism is necessary, and so regardless of the criticisms I receive from the left, the right, and the middle, I think it's important to maintain a prolific writing jab, as long as my literary legs hold up, because even during these bland and yuppie times, there are issues worth fighting about. Issues that require fresh points of view.

It was quite generous, I thought, for critic Mel Watkins to compare my writing style with that of Muhammad Ali's boxing style. My friend the late Richard Brautigan even saluted me after the publication of *Mumbo Jumbo*, my third novel, with the original front-page description of Jack Johnson's defeat of Jim Jeffries, printed by the *San Francisco Daily*, 4 July 1910. This, too, amounted to overpraise. If I had to compare my style with anyone's it would probably be with that of Larry Holmes. I don't mince my words. Nor do I pull any punches, and though I've delivered some low blows over the years, I'm becoming more accurate, and my punches are regularly landing above the waistline. I'm not a body snatcher like Mike McCallum, and I usually aim for the head.

A black boxer's career is the perfect metaphor for the career of a black male. Every day is like being in the gym, sparring with impersonal opponents as one faces the rudeness and hostility that a black male must confront in the United States, where he is the object of both fear and fascination. My difficulty in communicating this point of view used to really bewilder me, but over the years I've learned that it takes an extraordinary amount of effort to understand someone from a background different from your own, especially when your life doesn't really depend upon it. And so, during this period, when black males seem to be on somebody's endangered-species list, I can understand why some readers and debating opponents might have problems appreciating where I'm coming from.

On a day in the 1940s, the story of the deportation of Jews to European concentration camps was carried in the back pages of a New York newspaper, while news of the weather made the front page. Apparently it was a hot day, and most people were concerned about getting to the beach. And so, during this period when American society begins to resemble those of feudal lore, where the income chasm between the rich and the poor is widening, when downtown developers build concrete and steel vanity monuments to themselves—driving out the writers, the artists, the poor, and leaving the neighborhoods to roaming drug-death squads (since all of the cops are guarding these downtown Brasilias)—it seems that most people are interested in getting to the beach and getting tanned so that they'll resemble the very people the media, the "educational" system, and the cultural leadership have taught them to despise (that's what I meant by blacks being objects of fear and fascination). The widespread adoption of such Afro-American forms as rock and roll can be viewed as a kind of cultural tanning.

And so as long as I can be a professional like Larry Holmes, that is, have the ability to know my way around my craft, I'll probably still be controversial. Arguing on behalf of the homeless, but at the same time defending Atlanta's middle-class leadership against what I considered to be unfair charges made by the great writer James Baldwin (no relation). And as I continue to practice this sometimes uncanny and taxing profession, I hope to become humbler.

I've got a good shot. It's almost a miracle for a black male writer to last as long as I have, and though some may regard me as a "token," I'm fully aware that, regardless of how some critics protect their fragile egos by pretending that black talent is rare, black talent is bountiful. I've read and heard a lot of manuscripts authored by the fellas over the years. The late Hoyt Fuller was right when he said that for one published Ishmael Reed, there are dozens of talented writers in the ghettos and elsewhere, who remain unpublished. And having lasted this long, I've been able to witness the sad demise of a lot of "tokens" who believed what their literary managers told them. Who believed that they were indeed unique and unusual.

Just think of all of the cocky boxers who got punched out by "nobodies" as they took on an unknown to warm up for their fight with the champion. In this business, spoilers are all over the place.

I was shocked to hear Secretary of State George Shultz acknowledge during the Iran-Contragate hearings what our cultural leadership, and "educational" defenders of Western civilization, fail to realize. That people are smart all over the world. I know that. I'm aware of the fellas, writing throughout the country in the back of beat-up trailers, in jails, on kitchen tables, at their busboy jobs, during the rest period on somebody's night shift, or in between term papers. All the guys burnt-out, busted, disillusioned, collecting their hundredth rejection slip, being discouraged by people who say they'll never be a champion, or even a contender. This is for them. Writin' is Fightin'.

WE WEAR THE MASK

CECIL BROWN

The Life and Loves of Mr. Jiveass Nigger

The brothers who had gathered around the table burst out laughing. Of course, it was an old one, but that only made it better. One of the brothers in uniform said y'all know the one about Efan the Bad Nigger and then he said during slavery times every plantation had a bad nigger, and the slave masters would be beefing about who had the baddest nigger, and so this particular slave master named Brian Coker had what he actually thought was the baddest nigger in the South. The nigger's name was something like Kocomo, was about ten feet tall, had muscles like a mule and the general appearance of an ex-gorilla. Now the other slave master he had a nigger named Efan who used to go around bragging to his master and the other slaves or anybody he came in contact with about how bad he was. He was nothin' but a skinny, puny little-bitty fellow, but if you listen to him wolf about himself you'd think he was really bad. He was nothin' but a bullshit artist, see.

Another brother sat down at the table with a beer. He was round like a big, black rubber ball. He turned the chair backwards, straddled it, and threw his head back, laughing. He was wearing a red shirt with huge green and white palm leaves spread over it, and a pair of tan short pants. He said, What did you say that other bad nigger was, an ex-gorilla? Then he howled with laughter. Everybody else, the girls included, laughed too. Yeh, someone said, an ex-gorilla. He sho' musta been bad. Hey, man, go on with the story, some G.I. in uniform said. Anyway, the red-haired storyteller continued, this jiveass called Efan had his master going around thinking he was really bad, and so the master told Brian Coker the owner of that ex-gorilla that . . . The brother who came on like a big black rubber ball was bouncing on the floor . . . told him that he'd bet his plantations that Efan could beat his bad nigger. So the bet was on, 'cause Coker knew his nigger was really bad. They set the date, the place and time, and took care of all the formalities. Then the master went home and took Efan aside, and said, Efan, I have great confidence in you, I have just placed the destiny of not only the life and livelihood of my own family, but also that of your own people, in your hands. You're the baddest nigger in this section of the country, as you yourself have so many times stated, and so I have made it possible for you to use your talent, use it to further the cause of your people. If you beat Brian Coker's nigger next Monday, then we will win a whole plantation, and you'll be set up as overseer. I know you can do it, Efan. Do it for me, and more important—*do it for your people!!* Now, all the while the master was talking this way, Efan was shaking inside because he knew that his mouth had written a check his ass couldn't cash. He was scared but he didn't want the master to know it. He didn't want his master to think he wasn't as bad as he said he was. Efan had a lotta pride. And it was impossible for him to ever go back on his word, even though that *word* was straight from the mouth of Mr. Jiveass Nigger himself. Efan was a man who always backed up his bullshit with action, which explains why he was always getting himself in these impossible situations. So when the master said, I know you will skin the nigger alive, Efan, my man, when he said this, Efan said, Boss, go out there and dig a grave. What for, the master said. Efan said, 'Cause I'm gonna kill him, boss. Wait a minute, boss, you don't have to build no large grave, just a small hole like this. And he made a hole with his two open hands. Just a small hole what you use to bury guts in to keep 'em from the dogs will do, 'cause I'm going crumble that nigger into little bits, I'm gonna pack him into a bucket, boss, like he was dirt. Man, if that master only knew that this skinny nigger was lying!

So for the next five days Efan lived like a king. He had the master working for him. Every morning he'd tell the boss, Boss, you go saddle up your best saddle horse you got there. I'll be down as soon as I take a bath, shave, and get my shoes shined. Hitch the horse out there, comb the mane, and get them brand-new trace chains out. Efan told master if he was gonna beat the nigger he had to eat well, and so he ate six meals a day in the Big House with Miss Ann and the white folks. He wore a white suit, a red handkerchief around his neck, got a haircut, had one of the slaves cleaning out his fingernails and everything. He got so particular that he made the boss get somebody to iron his drawers. 'Cause, boss, he said, I'm gonna beat that joker so he gonna look like a can of beef tripe when I get finish with his no 'count butt. . . . You sho' must be from down home, the way you talk about trace chains, man, a brother said; he had his fingers draped over the breasts of the young, cute girl sitting next to him. Whar' you from, man, the brother said. Let the man finish, someone said. . . . So when that Monday finally came, the poet continued, he took a big swig from the beer mug. When that Monday rolled around, everybody from all over the state, this was Georgia, came to see the Big Fight. That bad nigger Kocomo was already there. He had ripped up some trees by their roots and throw'd them about a couple miles to the side, and was at the time throwing a fifty-pound sledge hammer a mile or so up in the air and every time the hammer came down, it buried itself around five feet in the ground. And big Kocomo would reach down, snatch it up, and send dirt flying everywhichaway.

Thousands of people were standing around watching this and waiting for Efan. Efan was late. Then here come Efan and his master and Miss Ann in a fine golden coach driven by six fine black horses—not white ones, but *black* horses! When Efan saw that bad nigger Kocomo, he start tremblin' all over again. Great God! he thought to himself, if I don't think up somethin', that bad nigger gonna kick my ass and bury *me* in the ground like he doing that sledge hammer. He didn't know what to do, he was trembling so. The crowd was yelling. Efan looked at the bad nigger, and then spat in the dust. Then he climbed out of the coach, and as he stepped out, he flung off his cape. The crowd grew silent. Kocomo was about five times bigger than Efan, but the way Efan was carrying himself had everybody thinking he was bad too. The crowd watched Efan in silence and anticipation, watched Efan stroll calmly over to where this ex-gorilla was standing with the sledge hammer. Efan walked over to the sledge hammer that was lying at Kocomo's feet. He tried to lift it, but it wouldn't budge. But he didn't try too hard because he didn't want everybody to know exactly how weak he was. When he saw that he couldn't possibly lift the thing, he looked up to heaven, and with one hand on the handle of the hammer, he said: St. Peter, you hear me talking to you up there? Well, move over, and tell Sister Mary and them other sisters to move out of the way, okay? And move Baby Jesus too. When Kocomo heard this he start thinking, this sho' must be a bad nigger, to be talking like that. And so he got scared and started trembling a little bit himself. Then Efan reached down like he was gonna pick up the hammer again, but stopped and looked down at his hands. Then he looked over to the coach to where the master and Miss Ann sat, and he started walking over toward them. Everybody's eyes were glued on him as he took his time going over to the coach. Kocomo start to trembling, 'cause he didn't know what that nigger was gonna do next. He was fixin' to run, because he was sorta convinced already that there was something odd about this little-bitty nigger who think he can beat somebody five times his size. Efan finally got to the coach, climbed inside, and took Miss Ann's hand, and led her out so that they were both in full view of the crowd. Then he slapped her across the face. You could hear the slap crack like bullwhip. Efan said, Woman, didn't I tell you not to let me forget my white leather gloves. Where is my gloves at, huh? Now when Kocomo saw this, he jump up and start running. Lord have mercy, he said, any nigger slap a white woman in Georgia is too bad for me. And they never seen that bad Kocomo since.

MEL WATKINS

On the Real Side

Humor is laughing at what you haven't got when you ought to have it. Of course, you laugh by proxy. You're really laughing at the other guy's lacks, not your own.
That's what makes it funny—the fact that you don't know you are laughing at yourself. Humor is when the joke is on you but hits the other fellow first—because it boomerangs. Humor is what you wish in your secret heart were not funny, but it is, and you must laugh. Humor is your unconscious therapy.

—LANGSTON HUGHES

A naive person thinks he has used his means of expression and trains of thought normally and simply, and he has no arrière pensée in mind. . . . it will not surprise us to find that the naive (in humor) occurs far the most often in children, and is then carried over to uneducated adults, whom we may regard as childish. . . . (But) there is the possibility of misleading naïveté. We may assume in the child an ignorance that no longer exists; and children often represent themselves as naive, so as to enjoy a liberty that they would not otherwise be granted.

—SIGMUND FREUD

The ambivalence of comedy reappears in its social meaning, for comedy is both hatred and revel, rebellion and defense, attack and escape. It is revolutionary and conservative. Socially, it is both sympathy and persecution.

—WYLIE SYPHER

Humor—as a folksy Southern relative of mine was fond of saying—is something like a rich man's wallet: it's a hard nut to crack. No one seems able clearly to define it or explain why we laugh.

African-American laughter, in particular, has been something of a mystery, a dilemma, or, quite often, a source of irritation for mainstream Americans from the time blacks first arrived in the Colonies in the seventeenth century. Reports of white Americans' astonishment at the uninhibited display and heartiness of blacks' "cackling laughter" can be found throughout early American writings. In the early nineteenth century, for instance, Washington Irving observed that "the obstreperous peals of the broad-mouthed laughter of the Dutch negroes, who, like other negroes, are famous for their risible powers," could be heard at the Battery of New York even though the blacks were celebrating in a small New Jersey village across the Hudson.

And in the mid-1800s, a Northern visitor to South Carolina wrote:

> At midnight I was awakened by loud laughter, and, looking out, saw that the loading gang of negroes [slaves hired out to the railroad] had made a fire, and were enjoying a right merry repast. Suddenly, one raised such a sound as I never heard before; a long, loud, musical shout, rising, and falling, and breaking into falsetto, his voice singing through the woods in the clear, frosty night air, like a bugle call. . . . When there was silence again, one of them cried out, as if bursting with amusement: "did yer see de dog?—when I began echoing, he turn roun' an' look me straight in der face: ha! ha! ha!" and the whole party broke into the loudest peals of laughter, as if it was the very best joke they had ever heard.

At about the same time, James Fenimore Cooper, perhaps summing up the contemporary contempt for black laughter, wrote of a festive gathering of New York blacks "collected in thousands of . . . fields, beating banjoes, singing African songs, drinking, and worst of all, laughing in a way that seemed to set their hearts rattling within their ribs."

Clearly, the accursed laughter of blacks had early on established itself as one of the race's prominent foibles—still minor, of course, when compared to other more blatantly demeaning stereotypes. By the 1940s white disdain for and, ironically, curiosity about Negro laughter were so well confirmed that Gunnar Myrdal in his massive study of black life in America, *An American Dilemma* (1944), would write confidently that the "Negro's cackling laugh," which "amused the white man and often staved off punishment or brought rewards," was an indication of blacks' ignorance and their "accommodation to class."

Now, interestingly, these writers and most other white observers conspicuously neglected defining or commenting on exactly *what* blacks found so humorous or *why* they were laughing. African-American laughter undoubtedly still causes confusion, consternation, and bafflement among whites. In fact, many whites readily admit that they have experienced some anxiety when confronting a group of blacks laughing uninhibitedly, and many more admit to some curiosity over the timbre and intensity of that revelry. Conversely, most black Americans have felt that their laughter has been interpreted as inappropriate or aggressive by whites or, at least, has been greeted with puzzlement and anxiety. As the African-American presence has increased in mainstream corporations, among blacks it has become a standard joke that when two or more of them gather, any display of joviality could bring an office to a virtual halt. As Richard Pryor has quipped: "White folks get upset when they see us laughing. . . . 'Wha'd'ya think they're doing, Martha? Are they laughing at us?' "

Both the depth of whites' obsession with African-American laughter and blacks' often amused reaction to that obsession are evident in the old "laughing barrel" tale, popular among Southern blacks for decades. As the story goes, whites in a small Southern town were so determined to control black expressiveness that they installed large barrels marked FOR COLORED ONLY in the town square. Negroes who felt the urge to laugh were required immediately to thrust their heads into the barrels. The laughing barrels, as Ralph Ellison facetiously explained, not only "saved many a black a sore behind (and the understaffed police force, energy sorely needed in other areas), [but] performed the far more important function of providing whites a means of saving face before the confounding, persistent, and embarrassing mystery of black laughter."

While in junior high school in Ohio, I was once caught snickering and whispering to the only other black student in the class about the teacher's rigidly formal explanation of a spiritual that we knew in a much less formal manner (much better than he, we thought). In short time, we were loudly reprimanded. But despite trying to hold back our laughter, a minute or so afterward we were at it again. At this point, the teacher, scarlet with anger, approached and, menacingly pointing his finger toward me, screamed in a most outraged voice, "You know, you irk me!" The word *irk*, of course, was not a common term in my working-class home. I had never heard it before, and certainly had never heard anyone express rage in such a curiously restrained manner. If he had shouted that he was "pissed off," I might well have understood and responded accordingly with timidity. Instead, I immediately fell into a fit of laughter that overwhelmed any fear that I might have had of the adult authority figure before me. It was only later, when I had been expelled from the class and given a failing grade that I began to understand the perils of black laughter in an integrated setting.

Whites, of course, did not always regard black laughter as a negative trait. In fact, under certain circumstances, jovial, amusing blacks were a source of comfort. Before Emancipation, lighthearted, grinning slaves were usually preferred to more surly or morose types. The popular 1980s musical maxim, "Don't worry," laugh and "be happy," expresses a mode of behavior that most slave masters favored for their chattel. And by the 1990s, with America becoming more sanguine and ostensibly tolerant of *minor* black cultural eccentricities, black laughter has again lost most of the threatening overtones it once had. In fact, when employed by professional entertainers it may even become a comic signature, a source of comfort and instant recognition for the audience, and a critical part of the entertainer's comic arsenal.

Black minstrel performers such as Billy Kersands—whose uproarious broad-mouthed laugh could be sustained even while he clenched two billiard balls in his jaws—discovered this as early as the nineteenth century. Sammy Davis, Jr.'s, thigh-slapping, foot-stomping laughter was, of course, as broad and expansive as his legendary talents and almost as extravagant as his jewelry. By the 1980s, Eddie Murphy's outrageous, cackling laughter was one of his most striking and effective comic devices, as is the robust, no-holds-barred laugh of late-night television host and comic actor Arsenio Hall. The same may be said of Whoopi Goldberg, Flip Wilson, or Bill Cosby; each has a distinctive manner of laughing and associated body language that enhances and complements their humor. They have made black Americans' hearty, much-maligned laughter an important part of their comic stage presence.

Still, black laughter expresses only one aspect of black American humor (a term that should not be confused with literary "black humor," dark satire, or so-called gallows humor, although they sometimes overlap); its essence lies somewhere underneath the screen of uninhibited mirth. For instance, the hip street persona Murphy affects at the beginning of both his popular *Beverly Hills Cop* films is a slick, apparently frenetic, fast-talking black con man engaged in outthinking and outtalking some dangerous, if somewhat inept, white criminals. This situation, as we will see later, harks back to one of the earliest black comic modes—the black slave outwitting a more powerful and presumably more knowledgeable master, or the even more venerable tradition of the black trickster. In the films, Murphy's quips are distinctively black in character.

Responding to one criminal's accusations that he is an undercover cop, which in fact he is, Murphy averts the danger by turning to his accuser's partner and asserting: "Yeah, I have the money and I *do* wanna do business . . . but with *you.* I ain't doing nothing in front of this dude 'cause this dude is a cop. I know when I smell a *pig* inside the room. I used to be a Muslim, man, and I know there's *po'k* over here . . . [sniffing and, eyes closed, rotating his head in imitation of Stevie Wonder] Yes, *po'k*, man, it's definitely *po'k*. I ain't doing shit around this dude, man. You wanna do business, you know where to find me."

Arsenio Hall's wide-eyed, infectious laugh—sassy one minute, coy the next—helped catapult his late-night show to the top of the television ratings in the 1980s. It also helped take the edge off satirical potshots he aimed at celebrities ranging from Madonna to Jesse Jackson:

I took my bus fare
And went to the state fair.
I had a corn-dog there,
It was medium rare.
Now I need Medicare.
Keep hope alive!

Similarly, the laughter of comic actress Whoopi Goldberg—whether the subtle, ironic laugh that deepens her portrait of the ingenue or the hip titter that distinguishes her characterization of Fontaine, the intellectual junkie—has become a recognizable staple of her stand-up comedy act. But Goldberg's humor, when focused on racial subjects, incorporates other more fundamental aspects of black America's culture and viewpoint. In her 1988 cable television special *Fontaine . . . Why Am I Straight?*, for instance, the hip laugh conceals an irreverence and social awareness common in black humor: "Now Nancy [Reagan], on the other hand, anorexic bitch that she is . . . I don't like her. . . . This is a woman who probably had nothing to do. You know, all the first ladies are supposed to be together with their President husbands, right. And poor Nancy, she didn't know what to do. So somebody probably said, 'Nancy, shit, do drugs.' And, of course, she misunderstood. She's a woman living in an unreal world. Explain to me how you tell an urban teenager who lives in the streets, in the school systems of the real world, 'Just say fucking no!' How do you justify that to a mother who's maybe got six kids and three hundred sixty five bucks a month from welfare and one of those kids is bringing in fifteen grand a week?"

Flip Wilson, one of the first blacks to host a network television variety show, was known almost as much for his cherubic smile and enthusiastic belly laugh ("What you say?") as he was for his hilarious characterization of Geraldine, the down-to-earth black character that he made famous. Yet Wilson's humorous stories were quite often pointedly black in another, more revealing sense. The imposition of black dialect and black attitudes onto famous historical figures was a hallmark of his comedy style. In his version of the discovery of America, Christopher Columbus approaches Queen Isabelle Johnson and informs her that if he doesn't find America there'll be no Benjamin Franklin, no "Star-Spangled Banner" or home of the free, and no Ray Charles. The frantic Queen responds: "Ray Charles! You gon' fine Ray Charles? He in America?" After the Queen agrees to support his venture, Columbus immediately goes out and buys some items that, while not common in Italian households, are recognizably funny to most blacks: "three used ships, two pair of fatigues, some shades, two chicken sandwiches, three cans of Vienna sausages, five cases of Scotch, a small Seven-Up, and a new rag to tie his head with."

Wilson's "Cowboys and Colored People" bit, which involves a dialogue with an Indian named Henry, offers another example of this wry racial humor: "The biggest thing that happened to you Indians is when they put you on the nickel. They put a buffalo on the other side, Henry. If you guys belonged to the NAACP we'd have you on the quarter. Maybe we'd change the name, Henry. Maybe we'd call it the National Association for the Advancement of Colored People Immediately . . . and the Indians on a Gradual Basis."

Bill Cosby, America's most popular sitcom star during the 1980s, is known for his disarming facial contortions and impish, pursed-lipped, chuckle, which helped establish him as one of television's most effective celebrity pitchmen for products ranging from Jell-O to Kodak film. Here again, black laughter and black humor (or, at least, blacks as humorous individuals) become, in the public mind, intrinsically connected.

Still, black laughter is not the most critical ingredient in black humor. After all, some *thing*, some particular set of circumstances, events, acts, or words must induce that laughter. And it's easy to enumerate examples of what most would consider black humor.

It can be as simple as when Moms Mabley walked out onto the Apollo Theatre stage, scanned the audience with a tired, exasperated look, and said, "Yeah, I know how y'all feel . . . Yes chillun, Moms knows."

It is as readily accessible as a group of black schoolboys standing on a corner playing the dozens:

> "Duane, yo momma is like a doorknob, everybody done had a turn."
>
> "I don't play that shit, my man. You better get off my momma . . . cause you know I just left yo house and got off yours."

It can be seen in the comments of two elderly, well-dressed black men who, sitting on a Harlem bench, observed a black teenager hip-hopping by with his baseball cap worn askew, in the nineties' fashion:

> "Look at that boy," one said, "ain't he somethin'."
>
> "Yeah," the other offered, "got his hat all turned around on his head. Fool done forgot where his face is."

Or in the cinema exchange between their fictional counterparts, Sweet Dick Willie (played by comic Robin Harris) and his two middle-aged cronies, who rap and trade quips in Spike Lee's *Do the Right Thing* (1989):

> "You fool, you thirty cents away from having a quarter. How the fuck you goin' get a boat?"
>
> "Don't worry about it."
>
> "You goddamn right, don't worry about it. Look at you! You raggedy as a roach, eat the hole out of a donut . . ."
>
> "I'll be on my feet, soon enough."
>
> "Not in them raggedy-ass shoes. Look at you! Shoes so run over, you got to lay down to put 'em on."

It's also reflected in a remark made by a middle-class businessman upon seeing one of New York City's peripheral, media-anointed "race leaders" pontificating on a television news program. In the time-honored black tradition of naming people with regard to some essential character trait, he immediately dubbed him "Uncle Sharp-Tom."

Or it may be found in the behavior of the bedraggled panhandler who works a corner near Fifth Avenue in lower Manhattan. Speaking with an obsequious black Southern dialect and appearing to have an advanced case of arthritic deformity or cerebral palsy, he never fails to solicit sympathy and a healthy reward with his contortions and slurred pleas for money. The humor surfaces later when, after the rush-hour pedestrians disappear, he reappears with erect posture, precise articulation, and a visibly large wad of bills stuffed into the pocket of his designer jeans.

Certainly, it was apparent in the tales told to me as a child by my next-door neighbor. Known admiringly as the biggest liar in town, he would sit on his front porch or in the local barber shop or nearly anywhere and command an audience with outrageous stories of his war exploits, his battles with the Klan in Mississippi, or his triumphs over his wife (in her absence, of course) or gullible white folks at the bank, his job, the Veterans Administration, and the unemployment office. He was working in a venerable black comic tradition—the tall tale or, simply, *lying.*

The outlandish story or tall tale is a central part of black American comedy (as it is among other ethnic or folk traditions). "I heard most of my early comedy backstage at the Apollo," the late Sammy Davis, Jr., recalled. "We didn't call them jokes at the time, we called them lies. 'That nigger sure can lie' was a common phrase at the time. I would imagine it is still used today." Indeed, it is. If Richard Pryor's down-home raconteur, Mudbone—one of the most eloquent and popular purveyers of the tall tale or big lie in modern comedy—had a real-life prototype, it was surely someone like my irrepressible neighbor. In fact, I believe it was in the mid-fifties when I first heard the line about fighting in World War II at the "battle of Chateaubriand" (used by Pryor, as Mudbone, in the seventies) as my neighbor chronicled his heroic efforts in saving the allies.

By the 1980s, black humor, like black music, had become so much a part of mainstream American culture that it could even be seen on prime-time television sneaker commercials like the popular "Bo [Jackson] Knows" spots or the series of ads that featured the popular young comedian Sinbad. In the Jackson commercial, the superstar athlete demonstrated his skills in various sports (including baseball and football) and representative sports celebrities acknowledged his expertise. Finally, after Jackson was shown flailing away at an electric guitar, blues singer and guitarist Bo Diddley appeared on camera. With a cynical grin on his face, the musician said wryly: "Bo, you don't know diddly!" Sinbad showcased his comic talent in a variety of street corner basketball vignettes. The funniest, which mirrored Eddie Murphy's slick rap in *Beverly Hills Cop*, featured Sinbad introducing a motley crew of playground misfits and castoffs as he tried to talk two foreign television executives into backing televised broadcasts of a schoolyard basketball league.

In short, black humor and its insistent companion black laughter can now be found wherever blacks are found or, in some instances, wherever they might be expected to appear. By the mid-1970s black American humor had come out of the closet or, as it were, the black community. But it continues to provoke some peculiar reactions and curious consequences.

PAUL ROBESON

Here I Stand

In the early days of my career as an actor, I shared what was then the prevailing attitude of Negro performers—that the content and form of a play or film scenario was of little or no importance to us. What mattered was the opportunity, which came so seldom to our folks, of having a part—any part—to play on the stage or in the movies; and for a Negro actor to be offered a *starring* role—well, that was a rare stroke of fortune indeed! Later I came to understand that the Negro artist could not view the matter simply in terms of his individual interests, and that he had a responsibility to his people who rightfully resented the traditional stereotyped portrayals of Negroes on stage and screen. So I made a decision: If the Hollywood and Broadway producers did not choose to offer me worthy roles to play, then I would choose not to accept any other kind of offer. When, during the war years, I had the chance to appear before American audiences in a major Shakespearean production (fifteen years after I had first done so in London), I was deeply gratified to know that my people felt, as Dr. Benjamin Mays put it, that I had "rendered the Negro race and the world a great service in Othello by demonstrating that Negroes are capable of great and enduring interpretations in the realm of the theatre as over against the typical cheap performances that Hollywood and Broadway too often insist on Negroes doing."

Progress has been made and today there are greater opportunities for Negro performers. But it is still a hard struggle to win an equal place for them in the theatre, films, radio and television; and I am very happy and proud to see that so many of our brilliant young actors, singers and dancers are fighting for decent scripts, for roles that are worthy of their artistic talents. Years ago when I refused to sing before a segregated audience the story was headline news, and today I am happy to note that many others also have taken that stand, and that nowadays it is considered news—and bad news, by our people—whenever a prominent Negro artist agrees to perform under Jim Crow arrangements. We have every right to take great pride in the new and rising generation of our artists and we ought to support them in their struggle for equal opportunity. Their notable effort to represent faithfully our people in the arts makes such support a duty for us all.

It was in London, in the years that I lived among the people of the British Isles and traveled back and forth to many other lands, that my outlook on world affairs was formed. This fact is a key to an understanding of why I may differ in certain attitudes from many others of my generation in Negro life.

Having begun my career as a concert singer and actor in the United States, I first went abroad, like many other Negro performers, to work at my profession. If today the opportunities for Negro artists are still very limited in our country, it was many times worse thirty years ago. After several trips back and forth, I decided to stay in Europe and to make my home in London. My reasons were quite the same as those which over the years have brought millions of Negroes out of the Deep South to settle in other parts of the country. It must be said, however, that for me London was infinitely better than Chicago has been for Negroes from Mississippi.

Others have written about the success I achieved in the greater opportunities I found in England, but that is not my story here. I was, of course, deeply gratified to gain a prominent place in the theatre, in films, as concert singer and popular recording artist. Even more gratifying was the friendly welcome I received in English society. At first it was mostly "high society"—the upper-class people who patronized the arts and largely comprised the concert audiences; and I found myself moving a great deal in the most aristocratic circles. Here I was treated (in the old-fashioned phrase that still has meaning in England) as a gentleman and a scholar. My background at Rutgers and my interest in academic studies were given much more weight than such matters are given in America where bankrolls count more than brains and where bookish people are often derided as "eggheads" when they are not suspected of being "subversive." And so I found in London a congenial and stimulating intellectual atmosphere in which I felt at home. And, to an American Negro, the marked respect for law and order which is common among all classes throughout the British Isles was especially pleasing. They simply would not put up with a Faubus over there.

In those happy days, had someone suggested that my home should be "back home" in Jim Crow America I would have thought he was out of his mind. Go *back*—well, what in Heaven's name *for*? Later, when I changed my base in English life and found myself more at home among the common people, I liked that country even better and, beyond an occasional trip to the States, I thought that I was settled for life.

But London was the center of the British Empire and it was there that I "discovered" Africa. That discovery, which has influenced my life ever since, made it clear that I would not live out my life as an adopted Englishman, and I came to consider that I was an African.

Like most of Africa's children in America, I had known little about the land of our fathers, but in England I came to know many Africans. Some of their names are now known to the world—Nkrumah and Azikiwe, and Kenyatta who is imprisoned in Kenya. Many of the Africans were students, and I spent long hours talking with them and taking part in their activities at the West African Students Union Building. Somehow they came to look upon me as one of them; they took pride in my successes; and they made Mrs. Robeson and me honorary members of the Union. Besides these students, who were mostly of princely origin, I also came to know another class of Africans—the seamen in the ports of London, Liverpool and Cardiff. They too had their organizations, and had much to teach me about their lives and their various peoples.

As an artist it was natural that my first interest in Africa was cultural. Culture? The foreign rulers of that continent insisted that there was no culture worthy of the name in Africa. But already musicians and sculptors in Europe were astir with their discovery of African art. And as I plunged, with excited interest, into my studies of Africa at the London School of Oriental Languages, I came to see that African culture was indeed a treasure-store for the world. Those who scorned the African languages as so many "barbarous dialects" could never know, of course, the richness of those languages and of the great philosophy and epics of poetry that have come down through the ages in these ancient tongues.

I studied many of these African languages, as I do to this day: Yoruba, Efik, Twi, Ga and others. Here was something important, I felt, not only for me as a student but for my people at home, and I expressed that thought in an article, "The Culture of the Negro," published in *The Spectator* (June 15, 1934), from which I quote these lines:

"It is astonishing and, to me, fascinating to find a flexibility and subtlety in a language like Swahili, sufficient to convey the teachings of Confucius, for example, and it is my ambition to guide the Negro race by means of its own peculiar qualities to a higher degree of perfection along the lines of its natural development. Though it is a commonplace to anthropologists, these qualities and attainments of Negro languages are entirely unknown to the general public of the Western world and, astonishingly enough, even to Negroes themselves. I have met Negroes in the United States who believed that the African Negro communicated his thoughts by means of gestures, that, in fact, he was practically incapable of speech and merely used sign language!

"It is my first concern to dispel this regrettable and abysmal ignorance of the value of its own heritage in the Negro race itself. . . ."

I felt as one with my African friends and became filled with a glowing pride in these riches, new found to me. I learned that along with the towering achievements of the cultures of ancient Greece and China there stood the culture of Africa, unseen and denied by the imperialist looters of Africa's material wealth. I came to see the roots of my own people's culture, especially in our music which is still the richest and most healthy in America. Scholars had traced the influence of African music to Europe—to Spain with the Moors, to

Persia and India and China, and westward to the Americas. And I came to learn of the remarkable kinship between African and Chinese culture (of which I hope to write at length some day).

My pride in Africa, and it grew with the learning, impelled me to speak out against the scorners. I wrote articles for the *New Statesman and Nation*, *The Spectator* and elsewhere championing the real but unknown glories of African culture. I argued and discussed the subject with men like H. G. Wells, and Laski, and Nehru; with students and savants.

Now, there was a logic to this cultural struggle I was making, and the powers-that-be realized it before I did. The British Intelligence came one day to caution me about the political meaning of my activities. For the question loomed of itself: *If African culture was what I insisted it was, what happens then to the claim that it would take 1,000 years for Africans to be capable of self-rule?*

It was an African who directed my interest in Africa to something he had observed in the Soviet Union. On a visit to that country he had traveled east and had seen the Yakuts, a people who had been classed as a "backward race" by the Czars. He had been struck by the resemblance between the tribal life of the Yakuts and his own people of East Africa. What would happen to a people like the Yakuts now that they had been freed from colonial oppression and were part of the construction of a socialist society?

Well, I went to see for myself and on my first visit to the Soviet Union in 1934 I saw how the Yakuts and the Uzbeks and all the other formerly oppressed nations were leaping ahead from tribalism to modern industrial economy, from illiteracy to the heights of knowledge. Their ancient cultures blooming in new and greater richness. Their young men and women mastering the sciences and arts. A thousand years? No. Less than twenty!

SIDNEY POITIER

This Life

As I say, after being separated out from the Army, I returned to New York City in the winter of 1944–45, fully confident that this time I would be able to manage, armed as I was with an additional year of experience, several hundred dollars, and a frighteningly fresh memory of what the city and the winter had done to a bewildered sixteen-year-old boy. This time they would be faced off against an eighteen-year-old man who knew the score—or so he thought. Alas, it would only be a matter of time before they had me begging for mercy again. My confidence eroded, my new-found manhood turned out to be not nearly so resilient as I had imagined, and my enemies seemed to have awesome powers in reserve just for the purpose of teaching a lesson to cocky little know-it-all bastards like me. They worked me over with a swiftness I'm ashamed to acknowledge, leaving me broke and deflated at the hand-to-mouth existence level, heavily dependent on my accumulated skills as a dishwasher. From my seven-dollar-a-week room on 118th Street I would go to wherever my job happened to be, work my customary eight hours, then back to Harlem, where most of my free time was spent wandering around in the hope of finding someone willing to become my steady girl. I daydreamed a lot about that kind of relationship, hungry for a boy-girl relationship that fitted my fantasies. Dorothy, the girl I'd left behind in Nassau, had by this time married someone else, and of all the girls I met during my Army sojourn, none of them expressed much interest in me beyond a dance, a shared bottle of beer, or the occasional roll in the hay.

One evening, walking along 116th Street, I notice a girl standing alone on the steps of an apartment building, and as I approach, we make and hold eye contact for a few seconds. I read volumes of potential into those few seconds, and as I stroll past her I detect a faint but unmistakable smile, and then she adds a slight movement of her head that seems to be halfway between a friendly nod and an invitation. My heart speeds up, my walk slows down, and I shoot her a smile broader than her own and cap it off with a movement of my head, hoping to leave absolutely no doubt that I'm interested. Oh, God, was I interested! She says, "Hi." I say "Hi" and move toward her. We exchange names and bits of information—I learn, for instance, that she lives in that building on the fifth floor with her father, mother, a sister, and a brother, and that she's in her last year of high school and looking forward to entering the job market. Then I become tongue-tied and can't sustain even a casual conversation without embarrassingly long pauses during which I'm frantically trying to think of something to say. Small talk, cute sayings, funny stories, where the hell are they now that I need them? Afraid that I'm going to scuttle all of this potential on one tongue-tied evening, I lie and say I have an appointment to meet someone and have to go, but would it be possible for me to see her again? She says, "Yes," she'll be at the same place the next evening at about the same time. All of which I take to mean that my tongue-tied stupidity hasn't seriously damaged my chances.

Furious with myself as I walked briskly along 116th Street to keep my bogus appointment I began to think of all the wonderfully witty and impressive things I should have said, instead of standing there like a dummy. What would any girl in the world want with a dodo like you? You can't even talk to them, I thought as I kicked myself all the way home. The next evening I turned up with dozens of well-rehearsed mental notes around which I could build a conversation, if and when it looked as if I was about to fall into one of those long, deep pauses that had almost finished me off the evening before. Her smile was very big this time and I sensed that she'd been looking forward to our meeting again. She was a plump girl, her skin was dark brown, her eyes were misty and soft, and her face was round and pretty with lips I yearned to make contact with. From appearances, this very sweet eighteen-year-old girl fit snugly in the fantasy images I had of what a girlfriend of mine had to be, but our second meeting wasn't much better than the first. Neither was our third or fourth. She obviously liked me in spite of myself, because on our fifth date I took her to a movie and bought her an ice cream cone and she took me home to meet her folks, all of whom drifted off after the introduction into other rooms in the apartment, leaving the two of us to sit and make small talk. I wasn't accustomed to that kind of one-to-one with a girl, and with there being no television at that time to salvage the evening we would just sit there teetering painfully on the brink of those long, deep, embarrassing pauses that left us both feeling insecure and uncomfortable. The relationship fell apart, for obvious reasons.

Through what seemed like an endless winter, psychologically at my lowest point, I moved from 118th Street to 146th Street into the home of a Spanish family from either Puerto Rico or Mexico. They rented me a very nice room for six dollars a week which included fairly liberal kitchen privileges. But the winter and the city had me on the ropes again, off balance and dazed, to the point where I said to myself: I've got to get out of this place and go back home. But I can't go back home. First of all, I can't write to my folks—they don't have the money. In fact, they don't even know where I am—whether I'm alive or dead. Second, it would take at least a hundred dollars to take a bus back to Florida and a boat to Nassau. I have neither the hundred dollars nor any practical way of getting a hundred dollars. Yet I make up my mind to go, because the winter is just too fierce for me. I concede. Hell, I can manage in Nassau—I can go fishing, I can work in the warehouse, something like that. I would rather do something like that than struggle on through a winter that's killing me.

Then one cold evening an idea strikes with lightning force, bringing me to my feet. Standing there in my six-dollar room I look at all sides of this potentially brilliant solution, rerunning it over and over in my mind, weighing its merits against its flaws and coming out each time convinced that it could indeed be a brilliant solution. Convinced by the soundness of the idea, I immediately put it to the test by writing a letter to the President of the United States: "Dear President Roosevelt, my name is Sidney Poitier and I am here in the United States in New York City. I am from the Bahamas. I would like to go back to the Bahamas but I don't have the money. I would like to borrow from you $100. I will send it back to you when I get to the Bahamas. I miss my mother and father and I miss my brothers and sisters and I miss my home in the Caribbean. I cannot seem to get myself organized properly here in America, especially in the cold weather, and I am therefore asking you as an American citizen if you will loan me $100 to get back home. I will send it back to you and I would certainly appreciate it very much. Your fellow American, Sidney Poitier." I sent that letter off and never heard from the cat. Never heard from the cat. And I'm very glad I didn't, because if I had received a hundred-dollar check in a letter, I would have been long gone. I would have spent the next thirty years on a rock with a line in the water, trying to catch me a fish or two. Mantan Moreland would likely have made *Blackboard Jungle*. Eddie "Rochester" Anderson would probably have played in *Guess Who's Coming to Dinner*.

In all sincerity, ignorance, and possibly insanity, my letter was an honest appeal, but there was no response at all from the White House—not a word. I was very displeased about that for a while too. Boy, I would get up every morning and rush down to the mailbox looking for that hundred-dollar check. I even had visions of him sending an Army truck to take me to the train station or the bus station. Finally I gave up—listen, how long can you wait for a hundred dollars? By the time spring arrived, I said, "Well, I'm obviously not going to hear from old President Roosevelt, so I'm back to washing dishes," and that's when I found my way into the American Negro Theatre.

How I stumbled into the theater is something that's been written about a lot, but now I'm going to tell you exactly what it was like. I used to read the *Amsterdam News*, a black paper in New York that carried, among other things, one hell of a good want-ad section from which I could almost always obtain a dishwashing job. One day while browsing through the listings for chauffeurs, maids, dishwashers, porters, janitors, etc., my attention was drawn to the opposite page, the theatrical page, which carried a gossip column, advertisements for movies, night clubs, cocktail lounges, and an article under the heading "Actors Wanted by Little Theatre Group." I said to myself: Hey, here they say actors wanted and on the other page they say dishwashers wanted, janitors wanted, and porters wanted. Well, I've done all those other things, but I've never done acting. Maybe I should go in there and see what that's all about and . . . like I'm carrying on a conversation with myself. And then I said: Yes, I'll drop in there, see how much they're paying, check out the working conditions. They certainly can't be any worse than what I'm into now. So I go down to a place on 135th Street near Lenox Avenue. It was the address of a library that housed the Schomburg Collection on the first floor and the American Negro Theatre downstairs in its basement. I knock on the door of the theater and am admitted by a man who introduces himself as Frederick O'Neal. He says, "Come on in," and I say, "I've come to look after this job that was advertised in the paper." He says, "Are you an actor?" I say, "Yes." He says, "Well, we didn't advertise, exactly. You see, that was an article about us doing a play and we were seeing certain actors. But you *are* an actor?" I say, "Yes, sir." He says, "Okay, where have you acted?" I say, "Oh, a lot of places." He says, "Where?" And I say, "Oh, a lot of places down in Florida and Nassau." He says, "You did?" I say, "Oh, yeah." He says, "Okay, why don't you take this script and go up on the stage and read the part of 'John' on page twenty-seven, and I'll read the other part, but I'll stay down here in the orchestra." I say, "Okay," and go up on the stage.

It is the first time I have ever been on a stage—I didn't even know what a stage looked like—but I'm up there now and I open this "script," but I don't know what it is. It's a book, I think, with a soft cover, but it's called a "script." I turn to page twenty-seven and find an awful lot of writing and I see names right above each little patch of writing, so I figure that's what he wants me to read because he told me to read the part of "John." Everywhere I see "John" I'll read everything under that, so I turn to him and he says, "Any time you're ready." The first person to speak on page twenty-seven is John, so I read his line, and O'Neal reads back his responding line. I read back—but no responding line comes from Frederick O'Neal. I see him sitting in the orchestra staring at me with the most peculiar look. He says, "Boy, get off that stage." I'm always ready to do my number, so I say, "What do you mean?" He says, "Just come on down off that stage and stop wasting my time." I say, "I don't understand." He says, "You're no actor." I say, "Yes, I am." He says, "No, you're not. You don't even know how to read." I say, "I can too read." He says, "You cannot read. Get out of here." He meets me halfway as I'm getting off the stage and he grabs hold of me and leads me to the door and as he pushes me out, he says, "Just go on and get out of here and get yourself a job as a dishwasher or something." How the hell does he know I'm a dishwasher? What the hell is this? Can he read me—is there a sign on me somewhere?

I walk off down the street—O'Neal of course goes back inside the theater, quite justifiably peeved at being messed about like that. I walk off down 135th Street saying to myself: Why would he say that to me? He also said to me, "You can hardly talk. You've got an accent, and that accent—you can't be an actor with an accent like that. And you can hardly read. You can't be an actor and not be able to read." I begin to contemplate what he'd said to me. Now I knew I couldn't read too well, I knew that. And I knew I had an accent—a bad, crippling accent—I knew that because on more than one occasion people would find it funny and would laugh at it. I knew those things, but what I hadn't come to grips with until then was that if I didn't do something about myself, I would be trapped forever as a dishwasher. If he can read that in me through my inexpertness in reading and speech and my general deportment, if he can read that much lack of potential in me, then my life is not going to be worth shit. I'm going to be a dishwasher when I'm forty—and when I'm fifty—and when I'm sixty. Here I am, I'm eighteen years of age, and if I live to be eighty, for the next sixty-two years I'm going to be a dishwasher. I'm not going to be able to impress people. I'm not going to be able to get a hearing from people. No, I'm not going to be able to command attention from anyone unless I'm able to create some idea or present some point of view or successfully put forth some real image of some kind—positive or negative. I am going to be of no consequence for the next sixty-two years. People will walk by me and I won't register. I will always feel inadequate. I will always be a dishwashing nobody, to be dismissed out of hand. Always overlooked. Never considered. That will be my destiny if I do not, by myself, take my life into my own hands and work it into something worthwhile.

But how do you do that? I wonder to myself. And I know right then as I'm walking toward 7th Avenue and 135th Street that I have to find a way to prove that man wrong. To prove—just to him, and by reflection to myself—that I can be more than a dishwasher.

But now the question arises, what more than a dishwasher? What should I start with? Well, the first thing to start with is, I *will* become an actor, because it's around that issue that the challenge originated. First and foremost I have got to prove to him that I can become an actor. Then I'll walk away from it and go on to other things, because once I can prove to him and to myself that I can be more than a dishwasher, the sky's the limit and I can be anything I want to be. But until I get over that first hurdle, he'll be correct in his estimation of me. I saw clearly that this was a crossroad and that I had to make a dramatic choice. And I did. I decided that I was going to be an actor.

Look who's deciding who's going to be an actor—a kid who didn't even know there was such a thing as a book of plays, a kid who had never been in a theater in his life except the once he walked onto a stage and got thrown off. I knew nothing about theater, nothing about acting, knew no actors or actresses except those I had seen in movies and that was different: first of all they were white; second, they were in California; and third, they were mostly working with cows and there were no cows in New York that I knew about. Still, I had to be an actor. But I couldn't start out being an actor until I overcame the handicaps that had caused me to be thrown out of the theater I had just left. He had itemized them for me—he said I could barely read and that I had this horrible accent. Well, I had to rid myself of the accent and I had to learn to read well. How do you rid yourself of an accent? I asked myself. I decided the best way was to listen to the way Americans speak, and to copy it. And what's the best way to listen to Americans speaking? Because I just can't go following people around. A radio, I thought to myself. The best thing for me to do is get me a radio. That very same day I went back to the want-ad section of the *Amsterdam News* and picked out a dishwashing job. Out of the first week's salary, I bought a thirteen-dollar radio. For the next six months, except when I was working or asleep, I listened to that radio morning, noon, and night. Everything I heard, I would repeat, it didn't matter what it was. If the radio said, "This is WOR bringing you the news," then I would say, "This is WOR bringing you the news." WOR, WEAF, WQXR, Lux Radio Theatre of the Air, commercials, soap operas, panel discussions—everything I heard from whoever was speaking, I would repeat. Six months of that and I noticed that my *a*'s were lightening; that my rhythm was changing considerably and I was no longer singsong in my speech pattern as Bahamians generally were. I noticed too that I was developing the pronunciation rhythms most New Yorkers had. Certainly there were still traces of the old accent remaining, but all in all there were some definite signs of improvement.

During the same six months I was working with the radio, I spent as much time as possible reading. One of the restaurants I worked in during that period was in Astoria, Long Island—a big place requiring three dishwashers with machine experience. The work was hard and heavy, but we would almost always have most of the dishes cleared away by 11:00 or 11:15 p.m., and the only dishes after that were a straggly few from the waiters having their own meal after the restaurant was closed. While waiting for the waiters to finish their supper, it was my custom to sit out near the kitchen door and read the *Journal-American*, a fairly conservative newspaper of those days. I didn't have a political view, however, and didn't care if it was conservative, liberal, or what—it just happened to be a big, fat paper. I bought it and read it because it helped me improve my reading. At the waiters' table there was an old Jewish man who used to watch me trying to read that paper. I asked him one night, what does this word mean, and he told me. I thanked him and went back to my paper. He went on watching me for a few seconds and then said, "Do you run across a lot of words that you don't understand?" I said, "A lot—because I'm just beginning to learn to read well," and he said, "Why don't you—I'll sit with you here and I'll work with you for a while." So at about 11:00 p.m. every night when he sat down for his evening meal, I would come out of the kitchen and sit down next to him and read articles from the front page of the *Journal-American*. When I ran into a word I didn't know (and I didn't know half of the article, because anything past a couple of syllables and I was in trouble) he explained the meaning of the word and gave me the pronunciation and then sent me back to the head of the sentence so I could grasp the word in context. In half an hour he would teach me the meaning and pronunciation of twenty-five or thirty words. Then I would take the paper away with me, armed now with the meaning of those words, and reread and reread the article so that the meaning of those words would get locked into my memory. Every evening we did that. He paid no attention to the content of the articles, just dealt with the words, and it was beautiful the way he did it. When I would place the stress on the wrong syllable, he would explain the difference to me, and he didn't have an accent—sometimes I would overemphasize a word and he would say, "You should go softer," or "You should hit this part." From this gentle man I learned about silent letters, abbreviations, words that are pronounced the same but spelled differently, and tricky singulars and plurals like "phenomenon" and "phenomena." This soft-spoken, natural teacher, with thick bifocals, bushy eyebrows, and silver-white hair, sat with me night after night in the twilight of his years and gave me a little piece of himself. I stayed there at that job for about five or six weeks and I learned a pattern from him, then I was off to other things. I have never been able to thank him properly because I never knew then what an enormous contribution he was making to my life. I don't know if he's alive or dead, probably dead by now, but he was wonderful, and a little bit of him is in everything I do.

After my relationship with my teacher, the waiter, I always looked for the meaning of words, and when I ran into words I couldn't pronounce and didn't understand, I would work on them until some sense began to come. I would keep going over and over the sentence they were in, and after a while I would begin to get an idea of what the word meant just by repeating the sentence. That became a habit, as did all the other things he left me with.

Now it's time to go back to the American Negro Theatre—six months later. You ask why would I go back to the American Negro Theatre? I could go anywhere else and try to be an actor. I could find out where there are other theater groups or I could go to a professional agent or something. But I don't even know that there are such things. Besides, I have to go back there to show one man that I can do this. So back I go. But that man isn't there. I'm told he's away for a few days, but that they're soon going to be having auditions for a new class of actors and he'll be one of the men in charge of the auditions. I say, "Terrific, I'd like to audition." They say, "Fine," and tell me when to come.

The American Negro Theatre had by now moved to larger quarters on 127th Street between Lenox and Fifth Avenue, in an Elks' Hall building where they had a larger theater, larger stage, and more classroom space. In other words, the American Negro Theatre was moving up in the world. I arrived at the theater on the afternoon of the auditions to find about seventy-five other people gathered for the same purpose. I sat down in the audience and waited, ready with my material. The clatter in the auditorium came from clusters of auditioners having a last-minute run-through of *their* material. Some like me will be auditioning alone. Some will play scenes with other people. All—unlike me—will be reading from plays. I wonder where the hell they got those plays, because what I've got is a *True Confessions* magazine that I've bought and memorized two paragraphs from, and I'm growing fearful that I may be disqualified for not having a scene from a play for my audition. At that point the lights start down and someone in authority calls the applicants to order and makes a brief welcoming speech in which he explains the aims and aspirations of the American Negro Theatre and officially opens the auditions by calling the first applicant up onto the stage to show his stuff. I think to myself: Hell, it's too late for me to worry about my material now. It's sink or swim with *True Confessions* magazine. I sit there watching intently as other applicants go up on the stage and play out dramatic scenes, comedy scenes, monologues, pantomime . . . and then my turn comes. I hear them say, "Sidney Poitier"—panic! I think: Oh, Lord—here I go now. Do I know how to speak without my accent? I run a few lines in my mind to see if I'm accent-free, and in my mind I say: That's not too bad. Then I go.

The theater holds two hundred or so people. Besides those taking auditions, there are also friends, parents, and others who've come along to lend encouragement and support. Then there are members of the American Negro Theatre's staff, including the president and the drama coaches. The president's name is Abram Hill and, yes, Frederick O'Neal is there, one of the leaders and founders. A lady named Osceola Archer is the drama teacher and head of the drama department, and also present are those heading the body movement and speech classes. So the faculty is well represented.

The bare stage is high, with good depth and width. They're in the middle of doing a play, but the scenery has been moved aside so the applicants can audition on an empty stage lit by two naked lights. I walk up on the stage from the little steps on the side, and immediately I feel self-conscious standing under those two bright lights that seem to accentuate everything and will no doubt accentuate the fact that I'm carrying a *True Confessions* magazine instead of a play. And I'm further disquieted by the fact that, though I'm under the spotlight where everybody can see me, I can't see anybody out in the auditorium. A voice coming from the direction of the faculty table asks, "Sidney Poitier?" "Yes," I reply. "Mr. Poitier, what are you going to do for us?" I say, "I am going to read something from *True Confessions* magazine." I hear a snicker in the audience and I say to myself: Oh, shit! I must have made a mistake, because why would they be laughing? The teacher says, "*True Confessions* magazine?" I say, "Yes, ma'am." She says, "All right. You can begin whenever you're ready." Out of the breast pocket of my suit I pull my magazine. The best suit I've owned to that point in my life is a brown suit, and needless to say, I'm dressed in my brown suit with my brown tie and my brown socks and my brown shoes and my brown shirt. I am dap! Most of the other kids are not as sartorially stunning as I am because, apparently, they are intelligent enough to know that you don't dress up to come to an audition. So I begin to read this *True Confessions* magazine that I've whipped out of my breast pocket. I turn to a page of some innocuous story about "Frank and Melinda." All of these stories are told from a woman's point of view, and in this one Melinda is telling how she first met Frank, and I'm reading this shit. I'm saying, "I met Frank as I walked down the street going towards so-and-so and there coming towards me is this handsome man and I said to myself 'just look at—' " Well, I can feel the people in the audience—I can feel their jaws drop. I can feel them thinking: What the fuck is he doing up there? Such thoughts are reverberating everywhere. Mercifully, Osceola Archer, the drama coach, interrupts. "All right, that's enough," she says. I stop. After a few seconds she says, "Mr. Poitier." I say, "Yes, ma'am." She says, "I would like you to do an improvisation for us. Would you do that?" I say, "Yes, ma'am." Now I don't know what the hell an improvisation is. I just hope that they'll explain it to me so that I won't have to expose my ignorance. She says, "All right, let us presuppose that you are in the jungle . . ." I'm thinking, what the fuck has the jungle got to do with that big word "improvisation." She says, ". . . and you are in the Army and you are in the middle of combat." I'm hearing what she's saying, but I'm trying to put it together to see how the word "improvisation" fits, because I still don't know what the word means. Well, finally it dawns on me what it means. It means that I'm supposed to act out the part of a guy in the Army who's caught in the jungle behind enemy lines and there's no way to escape and the enemy is shooting at me from everywhere and I have to make my last-ditch stand—how do I do it? I say, "All right." She says, "Take a few minutes and think it over and let us know when you're ready." So I turn my back to the audience, because I've seen other people do that to prepare themselves, but I'm not preparing anything. I'm thinking: Oh, shit, now, what am I going to do here? This place ain't no jungle. I don't see no jungle, but now I've got to create all that stuff in my imagination. Well, I think, I'm going to give it a shot because I've seen some movies like this. I turn back around and I say, "I'm ready." She says, "All right, begin." I hold my arms out in the shape of a machine gun and I start looking around—I spin around suddenly as if I'm being surrounded by enemies and I'm saying like James Cagney—that's the only thing that comes into my mind—I'm saying, "Oh, you dirty rats, you can come and get me. I'll kill you." And I go brrr—rrrr—rrrr, bang, bang, bang. I'm carrying on like this and suddenly I get shot in the belly by one of the enemy's bullets and start sinking slowly and agonizingly to the floor—when I suddenly realize that this is a dirty floor and I'm wearing my best suit! My very best suit in all my life! What's going to happen if I fall down on this floor and dirty up my suit! So on the way down to the floor, in the most dramatic moment of my improvisation, I reach out my arm and hold myself half on the floor and half off the floor, and I go on holding that position in the hope that all concerned will realize that I'm supposed to be *on* the floor but am just not going to fuck up my suit doing this improvisation. At which point the drama coach says, "All right, thank you—thank you." I get up and walk off. Now, I don't know whether I've done good or bad. I have a feeling I've done terribly, but I figure I'll brave it out, so I go back and sit in the audience and watch some of the other kids audition, and some of them are really brilliant, but mostly the girls. I finally leave with the understanding that they'll be sending me a card within a week to let me know if I'm accepted or rejected.

A week goes by, and a card arrives that says, "Would you come down and visit with us. We would like to have a talk with you." I dash down there and talk with someone representing the school who says, "We're going to take you on a trial basis for three months. We don't feel that you'll make it, but we want to give you every opportunity. If we feel, at the end of three months, that there hasn't been sufficient improvement we ask you not to continue. Is that understandable, and if so, is it agreeable to you?" I said, "That's understandable and it's agreeable." Little did I realize what the real bottom-line reason for my being accepted on a trial basis was. As it turned out, they had forty students who got passing marks and all forty of them were girls. No men. As rotten as the men were, they had to take ten or twelve of us to fill up the new class, and I was the least likely to succeed among the twelve.

Well, I sure as hell was delighted I was accepted. I set about really determined to learn how to become this actor I needed to be in order to show this guy O'Neal, whom I'm seeing now from time to time around the school, and who, by the way, never acknowledges me. He just passes me by, which makes me feel he's ignoring me because I'm of very little worth. Not realizing that the man has other, more important things to think about than running a judgment on me. Anyway, now I'm in a class, I'm beginning to learn about acting. And right away, because of my accent, I'm being laughed at when I'm playing scenes, so I withdraw a little and I'm reluctant to come out.

There was a brilliant student who was a carryover from another period—he wasn't one of the auditioners—named Richard Jones. He was fabulous—a college graduate, very handsome, a beautiful actor—and he took a liking to me. We became friends, and in time he helped me out of my introverted stance and fear of being ridiculed by playing scenes with me. Also he would very gently explain to people that it wasn't nice to laugh at my accent because "he's trying." After a while he got everybody to kind of cool it, for which I was very grateful because that kind of fun-poking could have developed into something very unpleasant. Richard was instrumental in getting the others off my back. He was brilliant, subtle, and quick of mind. He was also an epileptic. One evening while he and I were playing a scene, whack! he got hit by a seizure—stretched out on the floor, got completely rigid, then started to quiver. Someone who knew about epilepsy said, "Push his pipe into his mouth." I jammed his pipe into his mouth, but he quickly broke it in biting down. After jamming something more substantial in his mouth, we all stood around apprehensively waiting for him to ride through it. In fifteen or twenty minutes he was in control and up on his feet, but he never came back to class. I've never seen him again.

After three months, the faculty of the Theatre School said my first twelve weeks suggested I really wasn't improving and they would rather I didn't come back. I said, "Please! I'm just beginning to get a feel for what it's all about. I realize that there's a hell of a lot more to it than I had thought, but that only strengthens my determination. So please, please reconsider." They said, "No." Devastated at being cut from the class roster, I drifted about in confusion for a week or so before I struck on an idea. I said to myself: Maybe I can barter. I went back to school, searched out Abram Hill, the president, and said, "Mr. Hill, I want to continue to be a student here. What I would like to do is this: You don't have a regular janitor to clean the theater, to sweep down the hallway and take care of the steps and the stage. You leave that haphazardly to students and they don't do a very good job. I will take over the cleaning of the auditorium and I will take over the cleaning of the stage if you will let me continue on for another semester." He said, "Well, I'll think about it. It's unusual, but I'll think about it. You really want to study that badly?" I said, "Yes, sir." He said, "I'll think about it." I came back a few days later and asked if he *had* thought about it and he said, "Yes. We've discussed it and you've got a deal." So back into the class I go, delighted to be back on track again, happily closing out each evening with a little floor scrubbing, stairway mopping, and whatever other janitorial tidbit I laid on the institution under our agreement.

SPIKE LEE with RALPH WILEY

By Any Means Necessary:

The Trials and Tribulations of the Making of Malcolm X

It's big. I mean *Big*. You understand big. Well that's what I see. You gotta have the vision first. You gotta have it, you gotta go through school daze, you gotta do the right thing, and maybe, if you're lucky, you'll get mo' better. But you have to have that vision first. I started seeing it before I was attached to the project, before we made *Mo' Better Blues* and *Jungle Fever*, before *Do The Right Thing*. If I'm diming on myself, giving up the tapes of my own mind, too bad. I've been seeing this film all along in my head. I'd be lying if I said it hasn't been there a long time:

Malcolm X.

Back then I knew the time wasn't right. I wasn't ready and neither was anybody else, probably. But this was the picture *I* was born to make—this was the reason I had become a filmmaker. I learned a lot making those earlier films, my NYU student film, *Joe's Bed-Stuy Barbershop: We Cut Heads* and *She's Gotta Have it* and *School Daze*. There was always a connectedness to this movie that was vague, somewhere off in the future. But one day . . .

Everything I've learned up until now made me feel able, ready to do what needed to be done. *Malcolm X.* Big in scope. Big in scale. Blow it up to 70 millimeters, put it on a thousand plus screens. And no doubt about it, big problems, big headaches to go along with it, but in the end, still a Spike Lee Joint, ya-dig sho-nuff, a film that's gonna be right on top of you, right in your face every minute, frame by frame. I'd always done small stories, but this story had to be more. Much more. I knew it had to be done by an African-American director, and not just any African-American director, either, but one to whom the life of Malcolm spoke very directly. And Malcolm has always been my man. I felt everything I'd done in life up to now had prepared me for this moment. I was down for it, all the way.

I grew up in Brooklyn, in various neighborhoods—Crown Heights, Cobble Hill, and Fort Greene. Saturday afternoons in Cobble Hill was when all the kids, big and little—everybody in the neighborhood who wanted to—would go to the Lido Theater on Court Street for the matinees, the double features, and of course for candy, popcorn, and soda. I can remember my mother, Jacquelyn, taking me to see James Bond movies. She liked them. I used to like old 007 myself. I remember seeing *Help!* with the Beatles and *A Hard Day's Night*.

My mother was always taking me places to see performing arts. I was grounded in the arts. I can remember so clearly how she took me to the Radio City Music Hall one Easter Sunday to see *Bye Bye Birdie*. I also remember her taking me to Broadway to see *The King and I* with Yul Brynner when I was four or five years old, and how I cried until she took me home because I was too scared. Either the music was too loud or I didn't like our seats—last row in the balcony. I'm still afraid of heights. The point of it was this: All this exposure started my interest in visual arts. My siblings and I were exposed to the arts, all of 'em. This happened about as soon as we could walk. I believe exposure makes all the difference in the long run.

Soon I was going on my own to the Lido Theater. One Saturday when we were there checking out the matinee, some construction was going on right next door, and somebody drove a bulldozer through the wall during the movie! I don't remember the movie, but I remember that bulldozer coming. I guess in a way it was prophetic because the Lido is no longer there. And maybe that's one reason I ended up being the kind of filmmaker I became. I figure the competition might be a bulldozer coming through the wall, and I've got to keep my audience involved, or one day I won't be around, either.

Becoming aware of any love of cinema came very late to me. I was not one weaned on Oscar Micheaux or David Lean or anybody else, Black or white, not in any sense that I was conscious of at the time. In fact, way back then, before I read *The Autobiography of Malcolm X*, back in '69-'70, when I was at P.S. 294, Rothschild Junior High in Fort Greene, I had been daydreaming of playing second base for the Mets, of being like my man Joe Morgan (that guy should be a manager in the major leagues!) of the Cincinnati Reds, or maybe like my Brooklyn homeboy, Willie Randolph, who was on his way to eventually becoming the every day second baseman for the Yankees. That was Willie Randolph's daydream I was having.

But then I read the autobiography and—well, just put it this way. I read it and thought, "This is a great Black man, a strong Black man, a courageous Black man who did not back down from anybody, even toward his death. The Man. Malcolm." And then I woke up to other things that were going on around me that had nothing to do with the arts. People had pushed Dr. Martin Luther King's philosophy and his legacy to the forefront—they were both dead by this time, around 1970. Dr. King had gone to Morehouse College in Atlanta. My father Bill Lee was King's classmate there. I would go on to Morehouse myself, in 1975. And Dr. King was chosen for a national holiday. And there are times when Dr. King is a vehicle for my true feelings about the racial situation. But from what I read of Malcolm X, I immediately knew that what he said was much more in line with the way I felt. So it wasn't a question of school loyalty or fellow alumni or knowing I would do a movie about Malcolm X one day. At the time, it was a question of being drawn to his intelligence. So I put King's and Malcolm's respective quotes at the end of *Do The Right Thing*. Many people (white people, that is—it's interesting the things white people question you about that Black people don't) were asking me at that time why I put those particular quotes there, at the end of a film, and which one did I favor more, King's quote or Malcolm's? Here are the quotes:

Violence as a way of achieving racial justice is both impractical and immoral. It is impractical because it is a descending spiral ending in destruction for all. The old law of an eye for an eye leaves everybody blind. It is immoral because it seeks to humiliate the opponent rather than win his understanding: it seeks to annihilate rather than convert. Violence is immoral because it thrives on hatred rather than love. It destroys community and makes brotherhood impossible. It leaves society in monologue rather than dialogue. Violence ends by defeating itself. It creates bitterness in the survivors and brutality in the destroyers.

DR. MARTIN LUTHER KING, JR.

I think there are plenty of good people in America, but there are also plenty of bad people in America and the bad ones are the ones who seem to have all the power and be in these positions to block things that you and I need. Because that is the situation, you and I have to preserve the right to do what is necessary to bring an end to that situation, and it doesn't mean that I advocate violence, but at the same time I am not against using violence in self-defense. I don't even call it violence when it's self-defense, I call it intelligence.

MALCOLM X

What do *you* think?

People asked me if I was advocating violence like Malcolm X did. I laugh at that. What do *you* think?

Is that all Malcolm X was advocating? Or was he advocating a total Black self-respect, a mind to do whatever was necessary to better yourself or uplift the race! Remember that when he came along, Black people were being beaten and lynched and strung from trees by the double digits, brutalized all over the map, treated like the bald-headed stepchildren of America. And Malcolm X was having none of that. He didn't want to hear that. So he said, okay, first things first. By any means necessary. You gotta be alive in order to get ahead, in order to get your rights, don't you? So many times white people have said to me:

"Oh Spike, why did Mookie throw the garbage can through the window of Sal's?"

But I've never, ever had a Black person, an African-American, ask me that question. Not ever, it's understood.

About the quotes at the end, I told people who asked me (by telling me) that they were not really reading that Malcolm quote, which probably meant they had never read or known the man and never wanted to. They said the name, they thought "Malcolm X, oh shit," and they thought violence or nigger or radical or whatever they thought. It doesn't matter. That quote, if you read it thoroughly, it was all about self-defense and that's a lot different from random violence. And it's also important to look at that still picture I used. Malcolm X and Dr. King are shaking hands and smiling. So when I put those two quotes there, it was not a question of either/or, not for me, anyway, just a choice of tactics. I think they were men who chose different paths trying to reach the same destination against a common opponent.

There are a lot of books and tapes and articles out now about Malcolm X. Some of them are revisionist histories, but there was one book I wrote a preface for, called *Malcolm X: The FBI Files*, that I felt important for the public to see. It really showed just how much the government, and especially J. Edgar Hoover, head of the FBI, *hated* Black folks. *Hated* us. With a passion. What he did to King was pitiful. Just pitiful. He would audiotape King, his sexual escapades, and then he let King know he had him on tape. Hoover went in for that sort of thing. Hoover told Dr. King that if he didn't attempt suicide, he was going to send the tapes to his wife Coretta. Dr. King said, "Go ahead." And Hoover sent the tapes to Coretta.

It would be hard to trap Malcolm X like that. He was not like that from what I've been able to learn about him. Once he turned his life around, he was on the straight and narrow. He had been to the bottom, the dregs, and when he rose up, he rose up righteous. Strong. Could not be had just for the asking. Could not be bought by anything or anybody. And Black people, they *sense* that kind of sincerity. He *speaks* to them. It was that evolution that fascinated me about Malcolm X.

They both, Malcolm and King, had eerie premonitions of their deaths. King said, "I've been to the mountaintop, I might not get there with you but we as a people will get to the Promised Land." Malcolm said, "Now is the time for martyrs." So they both knew what they had gotten into for the dignity of their people. That they had to die for what should be a natural human right is the terrible thing. And Malcolm knew he was going to die. He knew. I also think Malcolm was just beaten down. He was tired. He was tired of running, tired of looking over his shoulder, tired of being chased, tired of endangering his family. [I've heard there were a couple of times when brothers from the Nation, the Nation of Islam, were waiting for him in front of his house with knives, and he had to jump over bushes to get into that house.] His own house, in Queens. There's a tape from after his house got bombed on the Sunday in February of 1965, the week before he was assassinated. The next night, Monday, he had to speak in Detroit. I've heard this tape. Malcolm is practically incoherent, and he was never that. The clothes he wore still had that burnt smell and were full of holes, I've been told. People who had been his fellow ministers were now ordering him dead. If Hoover didn't care for Martin Luther King, Jr., you know how he would have felt about Malcolm X. So, you know, my man was almost friendless, and completely worn out. They had won. For a minute.

People should try to learn from both men. They were different, they might have had different means, but they were after the same end. Simple dignity and rights for Black people, and all oppressed people. It's something we could apply to ourselves today, to make it work for today, for the world we live in now. King had his detractors, but Malcolm had many more. I think it was important they came along at roughly the same time, because if King had been the only one out there, there would have been a lot more resistance to him. But it was really white people who had the choice. Malcolm talked about this choice all the time. He would say, "You know, I think I'm helping brother King a lot because it's either me or him. I don't think they want to deal with me right now, so they're more willing to deal with King." They were both after results.

I was definitely not inspired by the blaxploitation film era of the late sixties and early seventies. Except for Melvin Van Peebles' *Sweet Sweetback's Baadasssss Song*, I didn't even watch those films back then, although I've seen almost all of them since. But not back then. I can't explain it; I'm not saying I was a fully developed film connoisseur back then. I suppose it was because I had been weaned on not just art, but the purer forms of art. My father, Bill Lee, is a jazz musician, and he has never played electronically amplified music in his entire life. In some ways I'm like him, in terms of the integrity of my art. In other ways, I'm not like him. My father was never really a businessman. And I'd have to say he really helped me by not being one. What I mean by that is I understood from being my father's son that talent alone is not nearly enough. My father has always been a greatly talented musician, but it takes more than that. You've got to have business sense, too.

I learned that from just seeing how it was with my father. You can't function well as a starving artist—at least, I knew I never wanted to try and do that, and this was long before I became a successful filmmaker. My father would come home with a suit, let's say. He'd say, "Look here, I got this suit for four hundred dollars," swearing he got a bargain. My brothers and I would look at each other and say, "Man, that suit cost fifty dollars, You got robbed! Aw man, Daddy. Not again . . ."

That's my father's story. He was always getting beat. Always. One reason for this is that money never really had any meaning to him. Didn't mean anything to him unless some creditor was asking for it from him. If he had it, fine. If he didn't have it, it was like, well, we'll get some money tomorrow. It doesn't matter. We'll get it. Uh-huh. That's what something in me would say. Uh-huh.

And I never wanted to put myself in that position. So I think I take after my grandmother, Zimmie Shelton, in that I look for value, I'm looking to save, I'm looking to run a tight ship. And since my art turned out to be film, it was also important I wasn't a selfish artist, the kind who is just doing my art for myself, and it doesn't matter if anybody sees it or understands it or not. Film is not really that kind of medium, I don't think. That shit costs too much money for you to just be making films for yourself, unless you're financing it yourself and are a fool who doesn't care about throwing away his or her money. Now if you're a painter or something, that's fine. Cut off your ear, paint for yourself only, suffer in silence.

But film is a different sort of medium. You share in film. So eventually I knew who Oscar Micheaux was, and Gordon Parks, and Melvin Van Peebles, but I didn't become a filmmaker because of them, not at all. I became one because of me. Nothing else was the inspiration for me, and I don't say that with any lack of humility as much as I say it as a statement of fact. My life itself was my artistic inspiration, and my life came from my parents and grandparents. It was what I was s'pose to do. For me, it grew from something I happened to do one summer while I was at Morehouse College, in Atlanta. The summer between my sophomore and junior years there was when I began to love film.

My mother had died the year before of cancer of the liver. I was an undergrad student at Morehouse, and I had chosen mass communications as my major. Mass communications encompassed print journalism, television, radio, and film. I bought my first camera, a Super 8. I didn't have a job, so I began shooting a lot of stuff in New York City so I'd have some stuff to play with when I got back to campus and began to concentrate on the major area of study. Shooting a lot of stuff became shooting all summer, and that's where my love began, I think. Now, that summer just happened to be the summer of the blackout. So I shot that, or people's reactions to it, and felt I was on to something. That was also the first summer of disco and everybody was doing the Hustle, a new dance craze. You could look anywhere in New York City and there was a block party—all these DJ's had their turntables out, right in the street, plugged into the street lamps at night, playing disco music. Folks were doing some serious Hustling! I filmed a lot of those block parties, and then I sort of put those elements together and came up with something I called *Last Hustle in Brooklyn*. I still have it on quarter-inch tape. My coproducer Monty Ross has seen it. It was Monty and myself who sat on my grandmother's porch back when we were in college, eating her fried chicken and drinking her iced tea, visualizing everything we're doing now. So we inspired ourselves. I have to put it that way. And my love of the cinema grew from there, from those spots. When I graduated from Morehouse I realized I still needed more skills to become a filmmaker, so I set out to further my education.

I still live not far from where I grew up. I went to NYU film school (it's a three-year program) after graduating from Morehouse. I won the Student Academy Award for my senior thesis film, *Joe's*.

My first feature film was to be called *The Messenger*. It never got made in spite of intense preparations and borrowing. That almost broke me. But I stayed on the case, and *She's Gotta Have It* was made on a shoestring, $175,000. It came out in August of '86, after being entered in the Cannes Film Festival that May. Then *School Daze* in '88, *Do The Right Thing* in '89, *Mo' Better Blues* in '90, and *Jungle Fever* in '91. But it is *Do The Right Thing* that people seem to remember, or so I've noticed. When I walk the streets in Brooklyn or Manhattan, or go to the Garden for a Knicks game, the people yell to me and say, "Yo, Spike! Do da Right Thing!" That title is going to haunt me to my grave.

I did not put those quotes from King and then Malcolm at the end of *Do the Right Thing* to promote myself as director of *Malcolm X*, necessarily, but it was because of *Do The Right Thing* that a man named Marvin Worth—who had the rights to the material on Malcolm's life—sent me a letter saying that he wanted me to direct the film, or would at least like to discuss with me the possibility of doing it. (I never did receive the letter, but he later showed me a copy of it.) He had bought the rights to the story from Betty Shabazz, Malcolm's widow, and from Alex Haley, who co-wrote *The Autobiography of Malcolm X* more than twenty years ago. But for one reason or another, they had gone through four or five scripts and the film never got made. [I believe there were more than a few reasons for that, and not the smallest is that I believe it wasn't *s'pose* to be made until now. That doesn't make me arrogant. It makes me fortunate.]

Later, people at Warner Brothers suspected me of being behind a letter-writing campaign protesting Norman Jewison directing the film. At that time, right after *Do The Right Thing*, during the shooting of *Mo' Better Blues*, I had made pointed statements in the press about Jewison, the director, who had signed on to the project for Warner Brothers and who'd optioned the rights from Worth. The star of the title role was Denzel Washington, who was brought in before Jewison on the project. Norman and Denzel took a walk on the beach and negotiated a deal. But I never was behind any letter-writing campaign.

I did have serious reservations about a Caucasian directing a film this important to our existence in this country. Playwright August Wilson had the same problem with it. He wrote an article in an issue of *Spin* magazine that I had edited about the same thing, how he wanted a Black director for the movie version of his play *Fences*. Marvin Worth had taken the property from Columbia to Warner Brothers some time ago, and Norman Jewison had signed a deal with Warner Brothers. Norman had asked them at the time what kind of properties they owned. I'd heard he turned down *Bonfire of the Vanities*, but he saw *Malcolm X* and thought it would be a great movie, became very interested in it, and hired Charles Fuller to write a new script. Norman and Charlie are tight because they worked together on *A Soldier's Story*.

Marvin said Norman felt he needed the Black credibility of Charlie to get Betty Shabazz on his side. Norman wanted to feel wanted by the Black community. When it got out that Norman was going to direct this film, that's when I started to speak out about it. So Marvin had gone after me before Norman even came on the scene. Marvin wanted me, Warner Brothers would take me, so it was a matter of how we could make the deal, and let it be Norman's decision to leave, to save face.

I never received the letter from Marvin Worth, and, since he didn't hear from me, there was a long time span when he felt I wasn't interested and didn't know how much I wanted to do the film. Until he started to read statements by me in the paper. And I did go off when I heard the project was up and Norman Jewison was directing it. No way I was going to let it go without saying something about it in public. Let the people know. So eventually Marvin called me and said I really had to stop saying things in the press about Jewison directing. He asked me about the negative mail. Jewison and Warner Brothers thought I was behind it. Like I said, my name is Bennett and I wasn't in it. Marvin and I sat down and talked about me doing the film, and if I was to do it, how to gracefully replace Norman Jewison. Warner Brothers talked to him and, finally, there was a meeting between me, Norman, and Marvin. While all this was happening, Norman was waiting on another draft of a script by Charles Fuller. Norman said he didn't particularly like the second draft of the script, so he just outed with, "I don't know how to do this film, I can't lick it," and then he just wished me luck with it. Just like that.

We didn't want it to seem as if we just Bogarted him or bum-rushed or steamrolled over Jewison, who is a fine director who has done good work. But at that point there was nothing for him to feel attached to with Malcolm X. For me it then became only a matter of choosing which script I wanted to do, whether I wanted to rewrite Marvin Worth's existing script by James Baldwin and a collaborator named Arnold Perl, or one of the others, or whether I wanted to start from scratch, or what. I knew about Malcolm X, but I would have to really get to know him, and those people who knew him intimately, much better before I could feel comfortable shooting the film. I felt that was the only way to do the matter justice.

Why was Warner Brothers willing to make the film? Well, for one thing, Malcolm has been dead for so long, a lot of white folks are less threatened by him—those who are old enough to remember him when he was alive. So I think it had become time for the film to happen, and I give credit to rappers like Chuck D. of Public Enemy, who had given Malcolm X visibility in his music (that was Malcolm saying "No sell out!" at the beginning of *Bring the Noise* back in '87). And, more than twenty-five years after he was murdered, people, especially Black people, still responded to what he was saying, and young people went completely wild over him. I know the challenge in front of me. Malcolm X was so many things to so many people, and then there are the people who think they know all about him, but they don't know anything that's true. And I also know for a fact that around ten million motherfuckers are going to come out of the walls saying that they were down with Malcolm, and that's bullshit. Malcolm X causes a reaction, so there is no way the film won't do the same thing.

The story of Malcolm X belonged to Black film, and there was no other way to look at it. Too many times have the lives of the Martin Luther Kings and Nelson Mandelas ended up as made-for-TV movies. Too many times have the Steven Bikos ended up minor characters in feature films that were supposed to be about them. Too many times have white people controlled what should have been Black films. And there is a reason for this. They still feel—I'm talking about the major Hollywood studios—that white moviegoers here in America are not interested in films with Black subject matter. But, if the major studios are going to finance Black films, for the most part it's two genres: You have the homeboy shoot-'em-up drug movie or you have a hip-hop musical comedy. I think Black film should be broader than that. Don't you?

But the studios have no respect for the buying power of the Black market, no belief that other people are interested in the films we make. They would like for us to believe that the people who are interested in, say, a Spike Lee film, have no idea that they together form a market. We have to prove the same thing over and over to the studios, again and again and again and again.

So as filmmakers we face the same glass ceiling that our brothers and sisters in white corporate America face every day. You've got to be into how much money a studio is going to spend to make your film—unless you're Eddie Murphy—and then how much money they're going to spend to market it effectively. This is not to say Hollywood doesn't want to make Black films at all. If they can keep making *Boyz N the Hood* for six million and take in $57 million, they'll make those forever. But what happens if you want to make films that are beyond those allowable genres? What happens when we want the same amount of money on the production budget, on advertising and marketing our films as for films done by the white boys? That's when we have problems. To this day, I've never had a film that's been in as many as one thousand theaters. The most we had previously was seven hundred, for *Jungle Fever*.

Racism permeates the whole fabric and structure of America, so why should the entertainment industry be unscarred by that? We could go to the Hollywood studios and go right down the line and see how many Black executives there are, number one. Number two, we could see how many Black executives there are *who can green light a picture*. Fox, Universal, Warner Brothers, MGM, Touchstone, Tri-Star, Columbia, Paramount—how many Black executives do they have, and how many can green light a picture? Well, if you did that, and then asked them point-blank, is it racism, they will say no, it's not because of racism, it's really because Hollywood is built on a network, an old boy's system, blah-blah-blah. But you know what the deal is—not to say it's 100 percent racist top to bottom, but that has to account for something there. At least a major percentage of it. So what we have to do is—we as a people have to stop bullshitting and start coming up with financing. I mean, I would love it if some Black investors or foreign investors would totally finance this film. It's a drag, you know, begging.

I don't mean just begging for a reasonable budget for what you want to do. I mean getting to do what you want to do in the first place. Creative control. Black cinema is written, produced, and directed by Black folks, and usually all three of them have to be Black for the film to stay Black. For instance, the motherfuckers behind *Soul Man* think they were giving us a social statement. C. Thomas Howell with blackface. To me that film was an insult to Black people because there is no way any real Black person in that film would not have known this was some idiotic white boy with shoe polish on his face and an Afro rug on his head. It was the same thing with *True Identity*, almost, only reversed. That's Van Peebles' old film *Watermelon Man* being done again and again. That shit is old and tired. *True Identity* was directed by Charles Lane, a brother. I liked his film before that, *Sidewalk Stories*, a lot. But why he wanted to do a film at Touchstone in the first place—now that's a real plantation over there. I would think that with Charles being an independent filmmaker, he'd get room. But they have motherfuckers on their sets every day, checking in. When you finish a shot, they're calling the studio. "All right, they're done with that shot, all right Charles, let's go." That's the way I've heard they make their movies over there. Fuck that.

So Black film is still in a kind of embryonic stage, I believe, partly because of the lack of work opportunity. I mean, it doesn't cost a million dollars to record a song if you're a singer, but the financial needs of a movie have tended to cut us out of the picture in the past. Right now we're just really at the beginning, where we're starting to make our entrée—not to say there weren't Black filmmakers before, but now there seems to be a more concentrated effort by African-Americans to enter this last frontier called movies, cinema, film. The further we move forward, hopefully the better the products will become and we'll have better and better filmmakers eventually. If we could make filmmaking as enticing as some of the other arts, or as popular as sports, we'd get there quicker. In film we haven't produced any Duke Ellingtons or John Coltranes or Michael Jordans or James Baldwins or Zora Neale Hurstons or Ella Fitzgeralds yet. We'll get there, but it's going to be a while coming. And it's only going to happen and happen steady and stay that way when you start to have more and more filmmakers who love cinema, who've seen movies, who know cinema history. If you don't love it, maybe you'll get lucky and make some money, meet some people, bone a leading lady, whatever. But I feel those are not really the right reasons to be in cinema, and it will become obvious in your work. Sooner or later your shit will be exposed as WEAK.

If *She's Gotta Have It* wasn't a hit, there would have been no way I could have made *School Daze*. Not with studio financing anyway. There would not have been this succession of films I've made. Five films in six years would not have happened, and I would not now be doing *Malcolm X* as number six. Or, if I had been doing it, I wouldn't have been doing it as well because my experience and budget would have been more limited. So it was luck, timing, and talent, a combination of those for me. I'm just one writer-producer-director. We've got to have more. We *do* have more.

Daughters of the Dust by Julie Dash is a fine film. And so is *To Sleep with Anger* by Charles Burnett, with Danny Glover. I think Charles makes a kind of art-house movie, which is fine. We need that. But it's like this—Jackie Robinson was not the most talented ballplayer when Branch Rickey picked him to integrate the major leagues. He saw that Jackie had been in the Army, had gone to college, was very disciplined, and he was *fast*, and so they chose him. History chose him. My problem is that a whole lot of those guys who were maybe more talented than Jackie Robinson in the Negro Leagues, instead of supporting Jackie, they were like, "Well, *I'm* better than Jackie." But you can't worry about it. I'm happy for John Singleton and *Boyz N the Hood*, and I hope he gets nominated for Academy Awards for director and screenplay. He should. He's like me in that he came along at the right time.

It's great that we got together, John and I, and found that we saw eye-to-eye on many levels. The reason John and I get along so well is that we recognize good cinema when we see it—we both love cinema, bottom line. And we're too smart to let people try to set us up against each other in any way. I wish I could say the same thing for Matty Rich, who directed *Straight Out of Brooklyn*.

Matty, I think, got some bad advice from some people. I mean, I had just met the brother, and he was telling me how the system was opening up. Opening up? So I was trying to help him. He didn't even know what distributors he could go to. The people he wanted to use, or had been told to use, Samuel Goldwyn, had distributed Charles Burnett's film and I felt they had bungled the release. So I said, "Look Matty, you should call Charles first." This was when he called me before his film was going to come out. I was glad, and glad to talk to him about it. Then Matty told me they were opening his film on the same day as *Jungle Fever*. I told him that was a little crazy and he ought to try and have the date of his opening moved. We'd be splitting the market, and it would hurt his film more than it would hurt mine. The next thing I know, I'm in the *New York Post*: MATTY RICH STEALS SPIKE LEE'S THUNDER. I couldn't believe it. He bought into that shit and came out swinging, attacking me. Was quoted saying I had a big fight with him and was yelling at him and was trying to find out when his film was going to open because I was worried he was going to steal my thunder, and that I had a lot of influence with the selection committee at the Cannes Film Festival and that somehow I had kept him out of the festival. It would take more than Matty's word to get me that kind of power. Matty was tripping.

It doesn't matter, because in my opinion, Matty's not going to be around long as a filmmaker unless he goes into the woodshed and learns his craft. Matty don't love no fucking movies. He don't love cinema. I mean, he brags that he's never taken a class, that he's never been to film school, I ain't got no education in film, I ain't got this, I ain't got that. His movie reflected that shit, too. Not to knock him totally, because anybody that gets a film made should be commended for that, especially at his age. At the same time, I would advise my brother: You'd better go back in the woodshed and learn how to make a movie. Learn the craft of filmmaking.

It's like some of these young Black people run around talking about how doing well in school, or even *going* to school is "acting white." I think it's gotten critical now where you have—I want to say millions, but I'll say a lot of young African-Americans across the country, especially boys, who fail classes on purpose because of peer pressure. Speak "dems, dese, and dose," only because of peer pressure. Seems the fashion is that if you're intelligent, if you do well in school, then you are "acting white." But if you fail classes, if you hang out, if you get high—then you're Black and you're down. That's where ignorance is championed over intelligence, and that's not where we want to be. That's definitely not what Malcolm X was talking about.

It goes back to a value system, and I don't mean a white man's lip service value system either. I mean our own value system, our inherent value system, which doesn't include a lot of meat-eating, incest and disease, and lack of respect for women. Our inherent system of values, down from earliest civilizations in Africa, is not like that at all. So when I say value system, I don't mean Father Knows Best, because father is an alcoholic and is feeling up little Peggy. I mean our own value system. But our whole value system is, how else do I say this, fucked up. It's just completely fucked. When young people will fail classes or belittle their own intelligence to fit in with the rest—what can you say? It's gonna take some strong motherfuckers to say, "You might think I'm trying to be a white boy, but I'm going to get these A's if I can get 'em, and you can kiss my Black ass two times two, which is four, you ignorant-ass motherfuckers!"

They're just going to have to stay strong and not bend to peer pressure. Whether it's staying off unsafe sex, or drugs, or going hard after education, whatever. You just can't be doing shit because everybody else is doing it. And it's bullshit to put it on anybody but ourselves. Malcolm said we're the only ones who are gonna do something positive about our lives, so we have to take responsibility for them. You can't blame it all on the white man—that's part of our problem too. In fact, I think education of our younger brothers and sisters is totally on us and up to us now. You've got to own up to some of this shit we're doing. Sometimes, more often than not in some of these places in the United States, we're the ones killing ourselves. I guess whatever I'm thinking always ends back up with Malcolm X for the time being. By any means necessary. If a book or a film is the means, use it.

My means is filmmaking, and I don't think Warner Brothers knows what they have with this film. The anticipation of it is so high. Somehow they don't know that, or will act like they don't.

Everybody was asking me, even before we started shooting, "When's the film coming out? Spike? When? When? When? I'm going to be there!" White and Black. Cabdriver to mogul. Recently, this one brother on the street asked me when the film was coming out. I told him at that time I thought it would be coming out next Christmas. He told me, "Then I'll be there Christmas Eve!"

And it's not just Black people who want to see this film. It's not just Black people who should see this film. I believe this is going to be a huge, huge film. Big. People have told me some people at Warner Brothers believe this will be their Academy Award film. And they'll probably tell me the same thing. Now let's see if Warner Brothers will back that shit up with money to shoot, promote, and market *Malcolm X*, and I'm talking about the same kind of money they spend on a film like *JFK*.

IN THE GAME

JACKIE ROBINSON

as told to ALFRED DUCKETT

I *Never* Had It *Made*

Quite a while before I signed with Montreal, I had agreed to play on an all-star black team for the American National League that planned to go to Venezuela on a barnstorming tour. Rae and I had planned to be married in February. While I was in South America, we both thought it would be a good chance for Rae to begin to fulfill a lifelong dream of traveling. She wanted to go to New York to see another part of the country. She had a fear that once married she would be stuck in California as both our families were. We both had no idea that our destiny would differ significantly from our parents'. She had saved some money and her family gave her another $100. Rae had been a student nurse for five years, and the prospect of seeing New York excited her. She got a job as a hostess in a swank restaurant on Park Avenue. After a couple of months, she quit because of the way the management treated black patrons and employees. They used every kind of device to let black patrons know they weren't welcome. A black man with a turban on his head could get the best of accommodations because he wasn't a black American in the eyes of the restaurant owner.

Next, Rachel got a job as a nurse at the Hospital for Joint Diseases and lived with a friend of her mother's who had a place in Harlem. Even though she was getting a chance to see New York and had the company of her friend Janice, she was lonely. She was earning a pitifully small salary and usually had her meals at a great little restaurant on Seventh Avenue, called Jenny Lou's. As good as the food was, Rachel and Janice yearned for a home-cooked meal and for the kindness of an invitation to someone's house for dinner. The lady in whose house Rachel and Janice were staying was well-known and had many friends. But none of them thought about asking these young visitors from out of town to come to dinner. Years later, when she returned to New York as Mrs. Jackie Robinson, some of the same people who had known her before as an insignificant girl named Rachel Isum, wanted to do all sorts of things to entertain her. Rae found that quite ironic.

A few weeks after the wedding, we were to fly to Daytona Beach, Florida, where I was to report for spring training with the Montreal farm club. We started out by plane from Los Angeles, arriving at New Orleans quite early in the morning. Upon arrival, I was told to go into the terminal. Rachel waited and waited. Then the stewardess came up to her and suggested that she go into the terminal and take all her things with her. I discovered we had been bumped from our flight owing to military priorities, so they said. We were not alarmed, having been assured that there would be only a brief delay. But as we argued our rights, the plane took off. Another typical black experience. After a few hours we weren't as concerned about the time we were losing as we were about the hunger we felt. Blacks could not eat in the coffee shop but could take food out. We asked where we could find a restaurant. We learned there was one that would prepare sandwiches provided we did not sit down and eat them there. Though we were both weary and hungry, we decided to skip food until we reached a place where we could be treated as human beings.

Our next project was to find a hotel where we could wait until we got another flight. The only accommodations were in a filthy, run-down place resembling a flophouse. A roof over our heads and a chance to lie down, even in a bed of uncertain sanitary condition, was better than nothing. We made the best of it and notified the airport where we could be found. They promised to call. They did. At seven in the evening, exactly twelve hours after we had been told about a "brief delay," we were in the air again. After a short flight, the plane set down at Pensacola, Florida, for fueling. The manager of the Pensacola Airport told me that we were being bumped again. There wasn't any explanation this time. They had simply put a white couple in our seats. A black porter managed to get us a limousine. It stopped at a hotel in Pensacola, and the white driver summoned a black bellboy and asked him where we could get room and board for the night. The bellboy recommended the home of a black family. These were generous and warmhearted people who insisted on taking us in, in spite of the fact that they had a huge family and a tiny home. Their willingness to share made us forget about being sorry for ourselves. Realistically, though, there was just no room for us. We thanked them, telling them we couldn't dream of inconveniencing them and got a ride to the Greyhound bus terminal. We had decided to take the next bus to Jacksonville, thinking that at least we could relax a bit and rest our backs, but we were in for another rude jolt. We had sunk down gratefully into a couple of seats and pushed the little buttons which move you back into a reclining position. The bus was empty when we boarded, and we had taken seats in the middle of the bus. I fell fast asleep. At the first stop, a crowd of passengers got on. The bus driver gestured to us, indicating that we were to move to the back of the bus. The seats at the back were reserved seats—reserved for Negroes—and they were straight-backed. No little button to push. No reclining seats.

I had a bad few seconds, deciding whether I could continue to endure this humiliation. After we had been bumped a second time at the Pensacola Airport, I had been ready to explode with rage, but I knew that the result would mean newspaper headlines about an ugly racial incident and possible arrest not only for me but also for Rae. By giving in to my feelings then, I could have blown the whole major league bit. I had swallowed my pride and choked back my anger. Again, this time it would have been much easier to take a beating than to remain passive. But I remembered the things Rae and I had said to each other during the months we had tried to prepare ourselves for exactly this kind of ordeal. We had agreed that I had no right to lose my temper and jeopardize the chances of all the blacks who would follow me if I could help break down the barriers. So we moved back to the very last seat as indicated by the driver. The bus continued to pick up passengers. They came on board the bus and filled up the choice white seats. The black section was so crowded that every other person sat forward on the edge to create more room. In the dark, Rachel was quietly crying, but I didn't know that until years later. She was crying for me and not out of self-pity. She felt badly because she knew I felt helpless. She hoped I realized that she knew how much strength it took to take these injustices and not strike back.

Finally, the bus pulled into Daytona Beach. We were relieved to reach our destination. But we had not escaped from old man Jim Crow. The white members of the team were living in a hotel; however, Rae and I had "special accommodations" at the home of Joe Harris, a local black political leader. Joe was an activist. He kept in touch with every black voter in his district to make sure they voted. His skill at organizing had enabled him to gain concessions from the power structure. He had persuaded business people in downtown Daytona Beach to treat black customers with respect and had influenced the transit people to hire black drivers on local buses. Joe and his wife Duff treated Rae and me with well-known Southern warmth. They liked to kid us, calling us the lovebirds since we were newlyweds. The one major disadvantage we had at the Harris home was that we could not cook or eat there on a regular basis except for breakfast. For our other meals, we had to depend on greasy-spoon joints.

After staying several days at Daytona Beach, the club was moved to Sanford, Florida. I would have more than two hundred teammates, the majority of them Southern. The first time we met was in the locker room and I remember being quite reticent. Most of the other players seemed intent on doing their own jobs. But there was a mutual wariness between us, a current of tension that I hoped would lessen with time.

I had my first confrontation with the press in camp. Someone asked if I thought I could "make it with these white boys." I said I hadn't had any crucial problems making it with white fellow athletes in the service or at UCLA or at Pasadena. One of the newsmen asked what I would do if one of the white pitchers threw at my head. I replied that I would duck. Noting that I was a shortstop, another newsman made the assumption that this automatically meant I wanted to replace the popular Brooklyn Dodger shortstop, Pee Wee Reese. I pointed out that Pee Wee Reese was after all with the Brooklyn Dodgers and I was trying to make the Montreal Royals. I was not in a position to go after another man's job on another team—I was going to concentrate on securing my berth with Montreal. This confrontation with the press was just a taste of what was to come. They frequently stirred up trouble by baiting me or jumping into any situation I was involved in without completely checking the facts before rushing a story into print.

Clyde Sukeforth, the scout who had taken me to Mr. Rickey, was in camp at Sanford. I was glad to see him. Clyde introduced me to Clay Hopper, the Montreal manager. I had been briefed about Hopper. What I had heard about him wasn't encouraging. A native of Mississippi, he owned a plantation there, and I had been told he was anti-black. There was no outward sign of prejudice in his manner, however, when we first met. Hopper told me I could take it easy, just hit a few and throw the ball around. This relaxed activity—or, rather, lack of activity—went on all that first day and the next. The evening of the second day, the stunning and discouraging word came that Mr. Rickey had ordered me back to Daytona Beach where I had originally reported. Naturally, I was worried about this sudden shift. Officially, I was told I was being sent ahead to Daytona a few days before the rest of the club was to arrive so that Rachel and I would have a chance to settle down. The truth I learned from Wendell Smith when en route to Daytona, was that my presence with the club in Sanford had already created racial tensions. Local civic officials had decided that mixing black and white players was apt to create trouble.

Shortly after Branch Rickey had signed me for Montreal, he had signed John Wright, a black pitcher, for the farm club. Johnny was a good pitcher, but I feel he didn't have the right kind of temperament to make it with the International League in those days. He couldn't withstand the pressure of taking insult after insult without being able to retaliate. It affected his pitching that he had to keep his temper under control all the time. Later I was very sad because he didn't make the Montreal team.

All during that spring training period in Daytona, I was conscious every minute of every day, and during many sleepless nights that I had to make good out there on that ball field. I was determined to prove to our manager, Clay Hopper, that I could make the grade. Perhaps it is a good thing that I didn't know about Hopper's initial reaction to me. Hopper had begged Mr. Rickey not to send me to his club.

"Please don't do this to me," he had pleaded. "I'm white and I've lived in

Mississippi all my life. If you do this, you're going to force me to move my family and my home out of Mississippi." Clay Hopper began to come around only after I demonstrated that I was a valuable property for the club.

During this time of trial, while my fellow players were not overtly hostile to me, they made no particular effort to be friendly. They didn't speak to Wright or to me except in the line of duty, and we never tried to engage them in conversation. They seemed to have little reaction to us, one way or the other.

But the generosity and friendliness of one white teammate during those early days with Montreal stands out vividly. A young and talented player, Lou Rochelli, had been—until my arrival—the number-one candidate for second base. When I got the assignment, it would have been only human for him to resent it. And he had every right to assume that perhaps I had been assigned to second base instead of him because I was black and because Mr. Rickey had staked so much on my success. Lou was intelligent and he was a thoroughbred. He recognized that I had more experience with the left side of the infield than the right, and he spent considerable time helping me, giving me tips on technique. He taught me how to pivot on a double play. Working this pivot as a shortstop, I had been accustomed to maneuvering toward first. Now it was a matter of going away from first to get the throw, stepping on the bag, and then making the complete pivot for the throw to first. It's not an easy play to make especially when the runner coming down from first is trying to take you out of the play. Rochelli taught me the tricks, especially how to hurdle the runner. I learned readily, and from the beginning, my fielding was never in question. But my hitting record was terrible. This was obvious in practice games during that first spring training. After a good hard month of training, I had only two or three decisive hits.

Rae, Mr. Rickey, and Clyde Sukeforth were all great supporters during this period. Rae never missed watching a practice period, and Mr. Rickey became personally involved in helping me. He would stand by the base line and mumble instructions to me.

"Be more daring," he would say.

"Give it all you've got when you run. Gamble. Take a bigger lead."

While Mr. Rickey pushed me, Clyde showed his support and concern by massaging my morale and trying to get me to loosen up.

My supporters were helped by two glorious events that acted like tonic. The first was during the initial Dodgers-Royals game. On the eve of that game I experienced all kinds of mental torture. The grapevine had it that I would not be allowed to play; that the local authorities had been putting terrific pressure on Mr. Rickey. What I didn't know was that the shoe was on the other foot. The Dodger boss was the one exerting the pressure. He had done a fantastic job of persuading, bullying, lecturing, and pulling strings behind the scenes.

I had steeled myself for jeers and taunts and insulting outbursts. To my relief, when I walked out on that field, I heard nothing but a few weak and scattered boos. Holding down second, I felt a mighty surge of confidence and power. I picked up a smoking grounder that seemed certain to be a hit. Pivoting, I made an accurate throw, forcing the runner at second. My arm was in great shape and so were my legs. I had speed to spare.

That game seemed to be a turning point. The next few days in practice and intrasquad play, I began to show significant improvement. I was elated at the happiness my performance brought to Rachel and Mr. Rickey. I got my first base hit, and Rae was delighted. She had made some friends in the Agriculture Department at Bethune-Cookman College, which was close to where we lived. To celebrate, she got special permission from the Harrises to cook a victory dinner of chicken and fresh vegetables given her by her friends at Bethune. It was one of the few times she could cook for me in those days and I really enjoyed it. Our two newspaper friends, Wendell Smith and Billy Rowe of the Pittsburgh *Courier*, were our guests for dinner.

The second inspiring event occurred during the opening game of International League season in Jersey City. It was a major game and Clay Hopper had gambled on me by letting me hold down second base. Through the second inning, we kept the Jersey City team scoreless. My big moment came in our half of the third when with two men on base, I swung and connected. It felt so good I could tell it was a beauty. The ball flew 340 feet over the left field fence. I had delivered my first home run in organized baseball. Through all the cheering, my thoughts went to Rachel, and I knew she shared my joy. This was the day the dam burst between me and my teammates. Northerners and Southerners alike, they let me know how much they appreciated the way I had come through.

All these good and positive things generated a tremendous kind of power and drive inside of me. My next time at bat in the Jersey City game, I laid a bunt down the third base line. I beat it out for a hit. I got the sign to steal second, got a good jump on the pitcher, and made it with ease. When the game ended, I had four hits: a home run and three singles, and I had two stolen bases. I knew what it was that day to hear the ear-shattering roar of the crowd and know it was for me. I began to really believe one of Mr. Rickey's predictions. Color didn't matter to fans if the black man was winner.

My happiness about the three victorious games in Jersey City was soured when we got to Baltimore. There were two racist types sitting behind Rae. As soon as we emerged on the field, they began screaming all the typical phrases such as "nigger son of a bitch." Soon insults were coming from all over the stands. For me on the field it was not as bad as it was for Rae, forced to sit in the midst of the hostile spectators. It was almost impossible for her to keep her temper, but her dignity was more important to her than descending to the level of those ignorant bigots.

On the positive side Rae and I noticed in Florida and in cities like Jersey City that black fans were beginning to turn out in unprecedented numbers despite extremely adverse conditions. Fortunately, there were no racial incidents of consequence. In Southern cities, including Baltimore, segregated seating may have held down racial tension, but it was grossly unfair to blacks who had to take bleachers and outfield seats. But they turned out anyway. Their presence, their cheers, their pride, all came through to me and I knew they were counting on me to make it. It put a heavy burden of responsibility on me, but it was a glorious challenge. On the good days the cries of approval made me feel ten feet tall, but my mistakes, no matter how small, plunged me into deep depression. I guess black, as well as white, fans recognized this, and that is why they gave me that extra support I needed so badly. This was the first time the black fan market had been exploited, and the black turnout was making it clear that baseball could be made even more profitable if the game became integrated.

After Jersey City and Baltimore, the Royals moved to Montreal. It was a fantastic experience. One sportswriter later commented, "For Jackie Robinson and the city of Montreal, it was love at first sight." He was right. After the rejections, unpleasantness, and uncertainties, it was encouraging to find an atmosphere of complete acceptance and something approaching adulation. One of the reasons for the reception we received in Montreal was that people there were proud of the team that bore their city's name.

The people of Montreal were warm and wonderful to us. We rented a pretty apartment in the French-Canadian sector. Our neighbors and everyone we encountered were so attentive and kind to us that we had very little privacy. We were stared at on the street, but the stares were friendly. Kids trailed along behind us, an adoring retinue. To add to our happiness, Rachel shyly told me that very soon there were going to be three of us. There was only one sour note for me at that time. Johnny Wright, the black pitcher Mr. Rickey had signed on, was dropped from the club.

Although he never did anything overtly negative, I felt that Manager Clay Hopper had never really accepted me. He was careful to be courteous, but prejudice against the Negro was deeply ingrained in him. Much, much later in my career, after I had left the Montreal club, the depths of Hopper's bigotry were revealed to me. Very early during my first Montreal season, Mr. Rickey and Hopper had been standing together watching the team work out, when I made an unusually tricky play.

Mr. Rickey said to Hopper that the play I had just executed was "superhuman."

Hopper, astonished, asked Mr. Rickey, "Do you really think a nigger's a human being?" Mr. Rickey was furious, but he made a successful effort to restrain himself and he told me why.

"I saw that this Mississippi-born man was sincere, that he meant what he said; that his attitude of regarding the Negro as a subhuman was part of his heritage; that here was a man who had practically nursed race prejudice at his mother's breast," Mr. Rickey said. "So I decided to ignore the question."

That was one of the incidents I didn't know about, but there were others I was very well aware of because I was right in the center of them. By the time we arrived in Montreal, I had received a classic education in how it felt to be the object of bitter hatred.

Back in spring training I had had some particularly bad experiences. A game with the Jersey City Giants had been scheduled to take place in Jacksonville. But when game time came we were confronted with a padlocked ball park and told the game had been called off. The reason was obvious, and later I learned that my participation would have violated city ordinances.

In De Land, Florida, they announced that we couldn't play a game because the stadium lights weren't working. What this had to do with the fact that the game was to be played in the daytime, no one bothered to explain.

When the Royals came up against Indianapolis in Sanford, the game had begun and the crowd in the ball park had surprised us all by not registering any objection to my playing second base. In fact, the fans rewarded me with a burst of enthusiastic cheers when I slid home early in the game. I was feeling just fine about that until I got back to the dugout. Hopper came over to me and said Wright and I would have to be taken out of the game. He said a policeman had insisted he had to enforce the law that said interracial athletic competition was forbidden.

During the regular season similar incidents occurred over and over again. Surprisingly enough, it was during a game in Syracuse, New York, that I felt the most racial heat. The problem there wasn't from the fans as much as it was from the members of the Syracuse team. During the entire game they taunted me for being black. One of the Syracuse team threw a live, black cat out of the dugout, yelling loudly, "Hey, Jackie, there's your cousin."

The umpire had to call time until the frightened cat had been carried off the field. Following this incident, I doubled down the left field line, and when the next player singled to center, I scored. Passing the Syracuse dugout, I shouted, "I guess my cousin's pretty happy now."

The toll that incidents like these took was greater than I realized. I was overestimating my stamina and underestimating the beating I was taking. I couldn't sleep and often I couldn't eat. Rachel was worried, and we sought the advice of a doctor who was afraid I was going to have a nervous breakdown. He advised me to take a brief rest.

Doctor's orders or not, I just couldn't keep my mind off baseball. Winning the pennant was not a problem. It was virtually in the bag. But the trouble was that if I won the batting crown, people could say afterward that I had stayed out to protect my average. I just had to go back. The rest lasted exactly one day.

At the end of that first season, I did emerge as the league's top batter, and when we returned to play Baltimore again, there were no more taunts and epithets. Instead, I got a big standing ovation after I stole home in one of the games.

Our team won the pennant. They also won the International League playoffs that were held every year among the top four minor league teams. The Louisville Colonels won top honors in their league, the American Association. After that the Royals and Louisville would play off in the crucial little world series. The three games held in Louisville were vital baseball-wise and extremely significant racially. Louisville turned out to be the most critical test of my ability to handle abuse. In a quiet but firm way Louisville was as rigidly segregationist as any city in the Deep South. The tension was terrible, and I was greeted with some of the worst vituperation I had yet experienced. The Louisville club owners had moved to meet anticipated racial trouble by setting a black attendance quota. Many more than the prescribed number of blacks wanted to come to the game since it would be the first instance of interracial competition in baseball in the city's history. As white fans surged through the turnstiles unhampered, numbers of blacks, some of whom had come long distances, were standing outside the gates, unable to gain admittance.

I had been in a deep funk for a few days before the game. Although I didn't expect the atmosphere to be nearly as bad as it turned out to be, I knew that bad trouble lay ahead. To make matters worse I had descended into one of those deadly slumps which are the despair of any player who has ever been afflicted by them. I was playing terrible ball in Louisville. In all three games I managed one hit out of eleven tries. The worse I played, the more vicious that howling mob in the stands became. I had been booed pretty soundly before, but nothing like this. A torrent of mass hatred burst from the stands with virtually every move I made.

"Hey, black boy, go on back to Canada—and stay," a fan yelled.

"Yeah," another one screamed, "and take all your nigger-loving friends with you."

I couldn't hit my stride. With a sick heart, damp hands, a sweaty brow, and nerves on edge, I saw my team go down to defeat in two of the three games. To make up for this, we would have to win three out of four final games to be played in Montreal. When we arrived in that city, we discovered that the Canadians were up in arms over the way I had been treated. Greeting us warmly, they let us know how they felt. They displayed their resentment against Louisville and their loyalty to us on the first day of our return to play the final games by letting loose an avalanche of boos against the Louisville players the minute they came on the field. All through that first game, they booed every time a Louisville player came out of the dugout. It was difficult to be sure how I felt. I didn't approve of this kind of retaliation, but I felt a jubilant sense of gratitude for the way the Canadians expressed their feelings. When fans go to bat for you like that, you feel it would be easy to play for them forever.

I guess the rest of the team felt that way, too. At any rate, we played as if we did. When we came on the field, our loyal Canadians did everything but break the stands down. Louisville showed some spunk as the game opened, jumping to a 2–0 lead in the first inning and going ahead 4–0 by the fifth. After that, the game changed. The confidence and love of those fans acted like a tonic to our team. In a classically hard-fought game, we won the game and tied up the series. We ended up winning three straight to win the championship. My slump had disappeared, and I finished the series hitting .400 and scoring the winning run in the final game.

I was thrilled but I was also in a hurry. I had a reservation on a plane to Detroit to take off on a barnstorming tour. The tour, starting in Detroit, was to last a month. I rushed through the happy Montreal crowd swarming over the field, got into the clubhouse, but before I could shower and dress, an usher came into tell me the fans were still waiting to tell me good-bye. He neglected to mention that there were thousands of them. They grabbed me, they slapped my back. They hugged me. Women kissed me. Kids grinned and crowded around me. Men took me, along with Curt Davis and Clay Hopper, on their shoulders and went around the field, singing and shouting. I finally broke away, showered and dressed, and came out to find thousands still waiting. I managed to plunge through the crowd and was picked up by a private car as I ran down the street. A sportswriter, Sam Martin, described that scene succinctly. He wrote, "It was probably the only day in history that a black man ran from a white mob with love instead of lynching on its mind."

On the plane to Detroit, I had a lot to think about, most of it wonderful. One incident that occurred at the clubhouse during the beautiful madness after the game stood out. Clay Hopper was making last-minute preparations to return to his Mississippi plantation. The Montreal manager came up to me and held his hand out.

"You're a great ballplayer and a fine gentleman," he said, "It's been wonderful having you on the team."

CASSIUS CLAY (MUHAMMAD ALI)

Playboy Interview: Cassius Clay (October 1964)

Interview Conducted for Playboy by Alex Haley

A Candid Conversation with the Flamboyantly Fast-talking, Hard-hitting Heavyweight Champ

It wasn't until 9:55 on a night last February that anyone began to take se-

riously the extravagant boasts of Cassius Marcellus Clay: That was the moment when the redoubtable Sonny Liston, sitting dazed and disbelieving on a stool in Miami Beach's Convention Hall, resignedly spat out his mouthpiece—and relinquished the world's heavyweight boxing championship to the brash young braggart whom he, along with the nation's sportswriters and nearly everyone else, had dismissed as a loudmouthed pushover.

Leaping around the ring in a frenzy of glee, Clay screamed, "I am the greatest! I am the king!"—the strident rallying cry of a campaign of self-celebration, punctuated with rhyming couplets predicting victory, which had rocketed him from relative obscurity as a 1960 Olympic Gold Medal winner to dubious renown as the "villain" of a title match with the least lovable heavyweight champion in boxing history. Undefeated in 100 amateur fights and all 18 professional bouts, the cocky 22-year-old had become, if not another Joe Louis, at least the world's wealthiest poet (with a purse of $600,000), and one of its most flamboyant public figures.

Within 24 hours of his victory, he also became sports' most controversial cause célèbre when he announced at a press conference that he was henceforth to be billed on fight programs only as Muhammad Ali, his new name as a full-fledged member of the Black Muslims, the militant nation-wide Negro religious cult that preaches racial segregation, black supremacy and unconcealed hostility toward whites.

Amidst the brouhaha that ensued—besieged by the world press, berated by more temperate Negro leaders, threatened with the revocation of his title—Cassius preened and prated in the limelight, using his world-wide platform as a pulpit for hymns of self-adulation and sermons on the virtues of Islam. Still full of surprises, he then proceeded to appoint himself as an international goodwill ambassador and departed with an entourage of six cronies on an 8000-mile tour of Africa and the Middle East, where he was received by several heads of state (including Ghana's Nkrumah and Egypt's Nasser), and was accorded, said observers, the warmest reception ever given an American visitor.

We approached the mercurial Muslim with our request for a searching interview about his fame, his heavyweight crown and his faith. Readily consenting, he invited us to join him on his peripatetic social rounds of New York's Harlem, where he rents a three-room suite at the Hotel Theresa (in which another celebrated guest, Fidel Castro, hung his hat and plucked his chickens during a memorable visit to the UN).

For the next two weeks, we walked with him on brisk morning constitutionals, ate with him at immaculate Muslim restaurants (no pork served), sat with him during his daily shoeshine, rode with him in his chauffeured, air-conditioned Cadillac limousine on leisurely drives through Harlem. We interjected our questions as the opportunities presented themselves—between waves and shouts exchanged by the champion and ogling pedestri-

ans, and usually over the din of the limousine's dashboard phonograph, blaring Clay's recording of "I am the Greatest." We began the conversation on our own blaring note.

PLAYBOY: Are you really the loudmouthed exhibitionist you seem to be, or is it all for the sake of publicity?

CLAY: I been attracting attention ever since I been able to walk and talk. When I was just a little boy in school, I caught onto how nearly everybody likes to watch somebody that acts different. Like, I wouldn't ride the school bus. I would *run* to school alongside it, and all the kids would be waving and hollering at me and calling me nuts. It made me somebody special. Or at recess time, I'd start a fight with somebody to draw a crowd. I always liked drawing crowds. When I started fighting serious, I found out that grown people, the fight fans, acted just like those school kids. Almost from my first fights, I'd bigmouth to anybody who would listen about what I was going to do to whoever I was going to fight, and people would go out of their way to come and see, hoping I would get beat. When I wasn't no more than a kid fighter, they would put me on bills because I was a drawing card, because I run my mouth so much. Other kids could battle and get all bloody and lose or win and didn't hardly nobody care, it seemed like, except maybe their families and their buddies. But the minute I would come in sight, the people would start to hollering "Bash in his nose!" or "Button his fat lip!" or something like that. You would have thought I was some well-known pro 10 years older than I was. But I didn't care what they said, long as they kept coming to see me fight. They paid their money, they was entitled to a little fun.

PLAYBOY: How did your first fight come about?

CLAY: Well, on my twelfth birthday, I got a new bicycle as a present from my folks, and I rode it to a fair that was being held at the Columbia Gymnasium, and when I come out, my bike was gone. I was so mad I was crying, and a policeman, Joe Martin, come up and I told him I was going to whip whoever took my bike. He said I ought to take some boxing lessons to learn how to whip the thief better, and I did. That's when I started fighting. Six weeks later, I won my first fight over another boy twelve years old, a white boy. And in a year I was fighting on TV. Joe Martin advised me against trying to just fight my way up in clubs and preliminaries, which could take years and maybe get me all beat up. He said I ought to try the Olympics, and if I won, that would give me automatically a number-ten pro rating. And that's just what I did.

PLAYBOY: When did you hit upon the gimmick of reciting poetry?

CLAY: Somewhere away back in them early fights in Louisville, even before I went to the Olympics, I started thinking about the poetry. I told a newspaperman before a fight, "This guy must be done/I'll stop him in one." It got in the newspaper, but it didn't catch on then. Poetry didn't even catch on with *me* until a lot later, when I was getting ready to fight Archie Moore. I think the reason then was that *he* talked so much, I had to figure up something new to use on him. That was when I told different reporters, "Moore will go in four." When he *did* go down in four, just like I said, and the papers made so much of it, I knew I had stumbled on something good. And something else I found out was how it had bugged Archie Moore. Before the fight, some people got it to me that he was walking around and around in the Alexandria Hotel in Los Angeles, saying over and over, "He's not going to get me in no four, he's not going to get me in no four"—and the next thing he knew, he was getting up off the floor. I been making up things that rhyme for every fight since. . . .

PLAYBOY: After you had scored victories over Archie Moore, Charley Powell, Doug Jones and Henry Cooper, how did you go about your campaign to get a match with Liston?

CLAY: Well, the big thing I did is that until then, I had just been loudmouthing mostly for the *public* to hear me, to build up gates for my fights. I hadn't never been messing personally with whoever I was going to fight—and that's what I started when it was time to go after Liston. I had been studying Liston careful, all along, ever since he had come up in the rankings, and Patterson was trying to duck him. You know what Patterson was saying—that Liston had such a bad police record, and prison record and all that. He wouldn't be a good example for boxing like Patterson would—the pure, clean-cut American boy.

PLAYBOY: You were saying you had been studying Liston . . .

CLAY: Yeah. His fighting style. His strength. His punch. Like that—but that was just part of what I was looking at. Any fighter will study them things about somebody he wants to fight. The big thing for me was observing how Liston acted *out* of the ring. I read everything I could where he had been interviewed. I talked with people who had been around him, or had talked with him. I would lay in bed and put all of the things together and think about them, to try to get a good picture of how his mind worked. And that's how I first got the idea that if I would handle the thing right, I could use psychology on him—you know, needle him and work on his nerves so bad that I would have him beat before he ever got in the ring with me. And that's just what I did!

PLAYBOY: How?

CLAY: I mean I set out to make him think what I wanted him thinking; that all I was was some clown, and that he never would have to give a second thought to me being able to put up any real fight when we got to the ring. The more out of shape and overconfident I could get him to be, the better. The press, everybody—I didn't want nobody thinking nothing except that I was a joke. Listen here, do you realize that of all them ring "experts" on the newspapers, wasn't hardly one that wasn't as carried away with Liston's reputation as Liston was himself? You know what everybody was writing? Saying I had been winning my fights, calling the rounds, because I was fighting "nothing" fighters. Like I told you already, even with people like Moore and

Powell and Jones and Cooper, the papers found some excuse; it never was that maybe I could fight. And when it come to Liston, they was all saying it was the end of the line for me. I might even get killed in there; he was going to put his big fist in my big mouth so far they was going to have to get doctors to pull it out, stuff like that. You couldn't read nothing else. That's how come, later on, I made them reporters tell me I was the greatest. They had been so busy looking at Liston's record with Patterson that didn't nobody stop to think about how it was making Liston just about a setup for me.

PLAYBOY: Would you elaborate?

CLAY: I told you. Overconfidence. When Liston finally got to Patterson, he beat him so bad, plus that Patterson *looked* so bad, that Liston quit thinking about keeping himself trained. I don't care who a fighter is, he has got to stay in shape. While I was fighting Jones and Cooper, Liston was up to his neck in all of that rich, fat ritual of the champion. I'd nearly clap my hands every time I read or heard about him at some big function or ceremony, up half the night and drinking and all that. I was looking at Liston's age, too. Wasn't nothing about him helping him to be sharp for me, whenever I got to him. I ain't understood it yet that didn't none of them "experts" ever realize these things.

What made it even better for me was when Liston just half-trained for the Patterson rematch, and Patterson looked worse yet—and Liston signed to fight me, not rating me even as good as he did Patterson. He felt like he was getting ready to start off on some bum-of-the-month club like Joe Louis did. He couldn't see nothing at all to me but mouth. And you know I didn't make no sound that wasn't planned to keep him thinking in that rut. He spent more time at them Las Vegas gambling tables than he did at the punching bag. He was getting fatter and flabbier every day, and I was steady hollering louder to keep him that way: "I'm going to skin the big bear!" . . . "I'm the greatest!" . . . "I'm so pretty I can't hardly stand to look at myself!" Like that. People can't stand a blowhard, but they'll always listen to him. Even people in Europe and Africa and Asia was hearing my big mouth. I didn't miss no radio or television show or newspaper I could get in. And in between them, on the street, I'd walk up to people and they'd tell one another about what "that crazy Cassius Clay" said. And then, on top of this, what the public didn't know was that every chance I got, I was needling Liston *direct* . . .

PLAYBOY: The press was generally unimpressed with your workouts, and the Liston camp knew it. Was that part of your plan, too?

CLAY: You ain't so stupid. I made sure nobody but my people saw me *really* working out. If anybody else was around, I didn't do no more than go through motions. But look, I'm going to tell you where Liston really lost the fight. Or *when* he lost it. Every day we had been leaking word over there that we were going to pull our raid that day. The Liston people got to the mayor and the police, and we got cautioned that we'd be arrested if we did it. So we made a court case out of it. We requested legal permission to picket Liston's camp, but we were told that a city ordinance prevented carrying signs. We had paid,

I remember, $325 for signs like BIG UGLY BEAR, BEAR-HUNTING SEASON, TOO PRETTY TO BE A FIGHTER, BEAR MUST FALL, and like that. So we taped the signs all over my bus. It wasn't no ordinance against signs on a bus. And we loaded the bus up with people from my camp, and screaming teenage girls, and we drove over there and caused such a commotion that people left off from watching Liston train, and we heard he nearly had a fit. One of his men—I know his name, but I guess I better not call it—even pulled a knife on Howard Bingham. Joe Louis run and asked the guy what in the world was the matter with him. But that's the day Liston lost. We heard he went to pieces. It wasn't long before the weigh-in, where they said *I* was the one went to pieces.

PLAYBOY: One doctor described your conduct at the weigh-in as "dangerously disturbed." Another said you acted "scared to death." And seasoned sportswriters used such terms as "hysterical" and "schizophrenic" in reporting your tantrum, for which you were fined $2500. What was the real story?

CLAY: I would just say that it sounds like them doctors and sportswriters had been listening to each other. You know what they said and wrote them things for—to match in what they expected was about to happen. That's what I keep on telling you. If all of them had had their way, I wouldn't have been allowed in the ring.

PLAYBOY: Had you worked out a fight plan by this time?

CLAY: I figured out my strategy and announced it *months* before the fight: "Float like a butterfly, sting like a bee," is what I said.

PLAYBOY: We read that. But what specifically did you mean?

CLAY: To start with, I knew that Liston, overconfident as he was, and helped by reading what all of the newspapers were saying, he never was going to train to fight more than two rounds. I don't know if you happened to read it later that some of his handlers admitted, after the fight, that this was exactly what he did. So that was my guide how to train, to pace myself. You know, a fighter can condition his body to go hard certain rounds, then to coast certain rounds. Nobody can *fight* fifteen rounds. So I trained to fight the first two rounds, and to protect myself from getting hit by Liston. I knew that with the third, he'd start tiring, then he'd get worse every round. So I trained to coast the third, fourth and fifth rounds. I had two reasons for that. One was that I wanted to prove I had the ability to stand up to Liston. The second reason was that I wanted him to wear himself out and get desperate. He would be throwing wild punches, and missing. If I just did that as long as he lasted on his feet, I couldn't miss winning the fight on points. And so I conditioned myself to fight full steam from the sixth through the ninth round, if it lasted that long. I never did think it would go past nine rounds. That's why I announced I'd take him in eight. I figured I'd be in command by the sixth. I'd be careful—not get hit—and I'd cut him up and shake him up until he would be like a bull, just blind, and missing punches until he was nearly crazy. And I planned that sometime in the eighth, when he had thrown some punch and left himself just right, I'd be all set, and I'd drop him.

Listen here, man, I *knew* I was going to upset the world! You know the only thing I was scared of? I was scared that some of them newspaper "experts" was going to quit praising Liston's big fists long enough to wake up and see what was just as clear as day to me and my camp; and if they printed it, that Liston's camp people might be able to get it into his skull. But I was lucky; that didn't happen. Them newspaper people couldn't have been working no better for me if I had been paying them.

PLAYBOY: Then the fight went about as you had planned?

CLAY: Almost. He came in there at 220 pounds, and untrained to go more than two rounds, and as old as he is—too old—against a kid, and I didn't have an ounce of fat on me. And he didn't have *no* respect for me as a fighter. He was figuring on killing me inside of two rounds. He was a perfect setup. If you remember, I didn't throw many punches, but when I did, they made their mark. I have vicious combinations, and just like I had planned, I hurt his body and I closed his eyes.

PLAYBOY: But Liston did do you some damage, too.

CLAY: You don't expect to fight no fighter without getting hit sometime. But you don't want to get hurt bad, and knocked out—that's the point. Yeah, he hit me some damaging punches. With all the talking I been doing, ain't nobody never heard me say Liston can't hit. He got me in the first with a right to the stomach. In the second, I made the mistake of getting maneuvered on the ropes, and he got in some good shots. And in the last of that second round, after I had cut his eye, he really staggered me there for a minute with a long, hard left. In fact, he did me more damage with that than any other punch. In the fifth, when that stuff—rosin, I guess it was—was in my eyes, and I couldn't see, he hit me with a good left hook to the head.

PLAYBOY: Would you be able to give us a round-by-round account of the fight from your viewpoint?

CLAY: Yeah, I guess I could. The first round, I beat him out, dancing, to keep from getting hit. He was shuffling that way he does, giving me that evil eye. Man, he meant to *kill* me, I ain't kidding! He was jabbing his left—but missing. And I was backpedaling, bobbing, weaving, ducking. He missed with a right hook that would have hurt me. I got away from that, but that was when he got me with that right to my stomach. I just kept running, watching his eyes. Liston's eyes tip you when he's about to throw a heavy punch. Some kind of way, they just flicker. He didn't dream that I'd suddenly stop running when I did, if you remember—and I hit him with a good left and then a flurry of lefts and rights. That was good for points, you know. He nearly flipped, and came after me like a bull. I was hitting and ducking at the same time: that's how neither one of us heard the bell, and was still fighting after it. I remember I got to my corner thinking, "He was supposed to kill me. Well, I'm still alive." Angelo Dundee was working over me, talking a mile a minute. I just watched Liston, so mad he didn't even sit down. I thought to myself, "You gonna wish you had rested all you could when we get past this next round."

I could hear some radio or television expert, all excited, you know the way they chatter. The big news was that I hadn't been counted out yet.

Then, at the second-round bell, just like I knew he would, Liston come at me throwing everything. He was going to make up for looking so bad that I had lasted *one* round. This was when he got me on the ropes, where everybody had said he was supposed to kill me. He hit me some, but I weaved and ducked away from most of his shots. I remember one time feeling his arm grazing the back of my neck and thinking—it was like I shouted to myself—"All I got to do is keep this up." And I got out from under and I caught him with some lefts and rights. Then I saw that first cut, high up on his cheekbone. When a man's first cut, it usually looks a bright pink. Then I saw the blood, and I knew that eye was my target from then on. It was my concentrating on that cut that let me get caught with the hardest punch I took, that long left. It rocked me back. But he either didn't realize how good I was hit or he was already getting tired, and he didn't press his chance. I sure heard the bell *that* time. I needed to get to my corner to get my head clear.

Starting in the third round, I saw his expression, how shook he was that we were still out there and *he* was the one cut and bleeding. He didn't know what to do. But I wasn't about to get careless, like Conn did that time against Joe Louis. This was supposed to be one of my coasting, resting rounds, but I couldn't waste no time. I needed one more good shot, for some more insurance with that eye. So when the bell rang, I just tested him to see was he tiring, and he was; and then I got him into the ropes. It didn't take but one good combination. My left was square on his right eye, and a right under his left eye opened a deep gash. I knew it was deep, the way the blood spurted right out. I saw his face up close when he wiped his glove at that cut and saw the blood. At that moment, let me tell you, he looked like he's going to look 20 years from now. Liston was tiring fast in the fourth, and I was coasting. We didn't neither one do very much. But you can bet it wasn't nobody in there complaining they wasn't getting their money's worth.

Then, in the fifth, all of a sudden, after one exchange of shots, there was a feeling in my eyes like some acid was in them. I could see just blurry. When the bell sounded, it felt like fire, and I could just make it back to my corner, telling Angelo, "I can't see!" And he was swabbing at my eyes. I could hear that excited announcer; he was having a fit. "Something seems to be wrong with Clay!" It sure was something wrong. I didn't care if it was a heavyweight title fight I had worked so long for, I wasn't going out there and get murdered because I couldn't see. Every time I blinked it hurt so bad I said, "Cut off my gloves, Angelo—leave me out of there." Then I heard the bell, and the referee, Barney Felix, yelled to me to get out there, and at the same time Angelo was pushing me up, shouting, "This is the big one, daddy. We aren't going to quit now!" And I was out there again, blinking. Angelo was shouting, "Stay away from him! Stay away!" I got my left in Liston's face and kept it there, kind of staving him off, and at the same time I knew where he was. I was praying he wouldn't guess what was the matter. But he had to see me blinking, and then he shook me with that left to the head and a lot of shots to the body. Now, I ain't too sorry it happened, because it proved I could take Liston's punching. He had found some respect for me, see? He wasn't going so much for the knockout; he was trying to hurt my body, then try for a kill. Man, in that round, my plans were *gone*. I was just trying to keep alive, hoping the tears would wash out my eyes. I could open them just enough to get a good glimpse of Liston; and then it hurt so bad I blinked them closed again. Liston was snorting like a horse. He was trying to hit me square, and I was just moving every which way, because I knew if he connected right, it could be all over right there.

But in the corner after that fifth round, the stuff pretty well washed out of my eyes. I could see again, and I was ready to carry the fight to Liston. And I was gaining my second wind now, as I had conditioned myself, to pace the fight, like I was telling you. My corner people knew it, and they were calling to me, "Get mad, baby!" They knew I was ready to go the next three rounds at top steam, and I knew I was going to make Liston look terrible. I hit him with eight punches in a row, until he doubled up. I remember thinking something like, "Yeah, you old sucker! You try to be so big and bad!" He was gone. He knew he couldn't last. It was the first time in the fight that I set myself flat-footed. I missed a right that might have dropped him. But I jabbed and jabbed at that cut under his eye, until it was wide open and bleeding worse than before. I knew he wasn't due to last much longer. Then, right at the end of the round, I rocked back his head with two left hooks.

I got back to my stool, and under me I could hear the press like they was gone wild. I twisted around and hollered down at the reporters right under me, "I'm gonna upset the world!" I never will forget how their faces was looking up at me like they couldn't believe it. I happened to be looking right at Liston when that warning buzzer sounded, and I didn't believe it when he spat out his mouthpiece. I just couldn't believe it—but there it was laying there. And then something just told me he wasn't coming out! I give a whoop and come off that stool like it was red hot. It's a funny thing, but I wasn't even thinking about Liston—I was thinking about nothing but that hypocrite press. All of them down there had wrote so much about me bound to get killed by the big fists. It was even rumors that right after the weigh-in I had been taken to the asylum somewhere, and another rumor that I had caught a plane and run off. I couldn't think about nothing but all that. I went dancing around the ring, hollering down at them reporters, "Eat your words! Eat! Eat!" And I hollered at the people, "I am the *king*!" . . .

HARRY EDWARDS

The Struggle That Must Be

AN IDEA WHOSE TIME HAD ALMOST COME

Dr. King's assassination and the "days of rage and rivers of fire" that followed momentarily enhanced the legitimacy of the Olympic Project for Human Rights as one of the few unconventional routes of nonviolent Black protest remaining. Further, it was the only route both accessible to Blacks and promising of an *international* protest platform, an escalation long advocated by many of the more militant spokesmen in the Black struggle who saw the oppression of Black Americans, not as a domestic civil rights issue, but as a violation of *international human rights law and principles*. And increasingly in 1968, as the racial situation deteriorated and violent confrontation heightened, people began to see some advantage, however limited, in dramatizing Black America's plight before the international community.

But forces opposing our efforts were not languishing in hand-wringing despair. The Black athletes most likely to qualify for the Olympic Games came under acute pressure.

Money, promises of lucrative professional sports contracts, and allusions to movie, television, and advertising opportunities were all employed to entice potential boycotters to disavow publicly any association with the OPHR effort.

Sprinters who couldn't catch a cold, hurdlers who couldn't catch a peanut with a bushel basket were promised lucrative professional football bonuses and opportunities to try out as flankers and wide receivers—if they participated and did well in the Olympic Games.

Athletes who couldn't hit their plates with their forks were flattered with fantasies of hitting line drives for major league baseball teams and stealing scores of bases.

There were even opportunistic attempts at buying the OPHR on the chance that the whole movement might be for sale. I was offered money on two occasions, totalling in excess of $125,000. In the first instance, a businessman offered me part-interest in a promotional scheme involving a slick travelogue magazine—titled *Holiday at the Olympics*—to be distributed during an eight-month personal-appearance tour of North and South America. My cut was to be a $100,000 minimum against a percentage of the gross take. All I had to do was call off the boycott and pack my bags.

Then there was the intriguing offer of $25,000, cash. All I had to do this time was call off the boycott and publicize the purported role of an aspiring 1968 presidential candidate in "making me see reason." Although politicians campaigning for the office were recruiting Black athletes literally right and left (Nixon with Wilt Chamberlain, Bobby Kennedy with Rosey Grier, Rafer Johnson, and others), I found it insulting that anyone seriously expected me to become involved in that, much less to sell out the political equivalent of an entire franchise for a measly sum of $25,000.

But despite our best efforts to maintain solidarity in the movement, by late spring of 1968 it had become clear that commitment in the ranks was eroding. However, we were not the only ones under increasing pressure. The sports establishment too began to feel the pinch.

On the one hand, those directing the United States Olympic effort could not ignore the potential boycott and risk the humiliation of fielding less than a representative Olympic contingent in Mexico City.

On the other hand, the controlling agencies could not move arbitrarily to eliminate the threat by denying prospective Black Olympians the privilege of participating in the Olympic trials because of their political views. This action would only have precipitated the very outcome that the OPHR was struggling to accomplish.

And so the U.S. Olympic Committee toyed with the idea of having all qualifying athletes sign "patriotic pledges" not to boycott the Games. The OPHR attacked this measure as a blatant infringement upon the athletes' freedom of political expression. When it was determined that the pledge would be legally unenforceable at best and in any event a violation of U.S. constitutional guarantees, consideration of the plan was dropped.

The only option left to the opposition was to develop an expensive, unwieldy, and somewhat embarrassing system of alternates over and above the usual back-up contingent of athletes kept on hand in case of injury or illness.

The OPHR had to make its adjustments too. Gradually, we were losing the struggle in the media. As the games neared, increasingly, the press was printing stories containing alleged quotes from Black athletes publicly identified with the boycott effort that played down the potential of even a token Black boycott, or that intimated the athletes no longer felt that the Olympics "should be used as a political forum." Since we did not have the resources to counter such press coverage, it was decided that we had no option but to manipulate the situation. We asked all athletes firmly within the fold to make as many conflicting statements as possible to the press, preferably to different reporters on the same day. And some athletes didn't have to be asked to contradict themselves. So, while one New York paper was headlining a sports-page story alleging that Lee Evans had bolted the movement, a San Francisco paper and a television station carried a statement by Lee Evans denouncing those athletes who had thus far refused to support the movement. Even I joined in creating the chaos. So while a Los Angeles paper carried a story in which I was commenting on the weakened appeal of the boycott idea, in an interview appearing that same day in a Philadelphia newspaper, I was unequivocally reaffirming the strength and, indeed, the expansion of the movement's appeal.

Finally, I called a press conference in San Francisco, which was extremely well attended. At least forty representatives of the written and electronic media showed up—I am quite certain in anticipation (and for many, in the hope) that I was at last about to call the whole thing off.

They knew that such was not to be when I opened the press conference with the statement: "Ladies and gentlemen of the press, I have asked you here today in order to secure equal time and space in your media—to answer myself . . ."

Pressures from other, more covert sources were much more difficult to dispell or neutralize.

UNITED STATES DEPARTMENT OF JUSTICE

FEDERAL BUREAU OF INVESTIGATION

UPDATE — Office: San Francisco

Harry Thomas Edwards — Date: 10-1-68

Activities

A. Olympic Games Boycott

The "San Francisco Chronicle", a daily San Francisco newspaper, in its issue of July 31, 1968, reported an interview with LEE EVANS, a track athlete from San Jose State College and one of the earliest advocates of the boycott of the Olympic Games. On July 30, 1968, EVANS stated that the boycott was "off". He said that the Black athletes had voted to go to Mexico City, but he felt that some of them would make a protest of an undetermined kind. The "San Francisco Chronicle" issue of August 1, 1968, interviewed HARRY EDWARDS and asked for a comment on the above remarks. EDWARDS replied, "our strategy is chaos". He went on to say that his group desired to give the people picking the team a taste of what the Negro went through living in the United States. EDWARDS then claimed that the athletes might make many conflicting statements about their intentions and this would be in order to create confusion.

The "San Jose Mercury News", a daily San Jose newspaper, in its issue of September 1, 1968, reported from a "New York Times" news service bulletin from Philadelphia, Pennsylvania, that HARRY EDWARDS had told the press that the majority of the athletes would participate.

As my classes at San Jose State reached enrollments upward of four hundred students, rumors increased of student spy recruitment by the FBI and local police intelligence. A friend with sources inside the personnel records department of the college's administration disclosed that FBI agents had made extensive copies of my undergraduate grade transcripts, my health records, and my employee files. When confronted with charges of campus spying, an FBI official declared the charges "outrageous." The college's administration refused to comment at all upon the charges.

"SPYING" CHARGES DENIED BY FBI
by Susy Lydle
SPARTAN DAILY STAFF WRITER

May 22, 1968—A Federal Bureau of Investigation authority denied charges yesterday that an SJS student was asked to "spy" on sociology instructor Harry Edwards and to deliver class notes, tests, and any information on Edwards' activities to the FBI.

According to Rick Brown, news director of SJS' radio-television news center, the report of Edwards' investigation was related to him by the student, who wishes to remain anonymous.

Six weeks ago, according to Brown, the student told a roommate about Edwards' class discussions. The roommate wrote to a friend, a Marine stationed in Washington, D.C., who in turn gave the letter to his commanding officer. The commanding officer sent the letter to San Jose FBI officials, Brown related.

A half hour radio program on the subject, featuring comments from Edwards, campus professors, and other concerned individuals, was aired last night over KSJS-FM and KXUP-AM.

CLASS NOTES

Brown said the FBI contacted the student and asked for all class notes, tests, any information on Edwards' whereabouts over week-ends, and any class discussions where he might have called for student violence and dates for a "Black Revolution."

"The allegations are outrageous," said Bill Kidwell, FBI special agent in San Jose. "The mere idea that we would be involved in such activities is unbeliveable."

"There must be a misunderstanding to say we had enlisted services of a student to spy on a professor," Kidwell continued. "What this student implies is something that just isn't true."

Commenting on Edward's statement that he felt the FBI was sitting in on his classes during the semester, Kidwell said, "It's inconceivable."

Kidwell said he feels that the SJS campus is an integral part of the community. "It is no different than our responsibility at First and Santa Clara," he said.

Information obtained through the Freedom of Information Act ten years later exposed the truth of the situation.

However, the fact that I was not privy to conclusive evidence of unethical, if not illegal spying, at the time did not matter. I, like other Black activists, assumed it to be the case and proceeded accordingly. The assassination of Malcolm X, the murders of at least seven members of the Black Panther party, and most certainly the death of Dr. King had led most of us to regard a healthy dose of paranoia as a necessary, though not sufficient, condition for survival.

FEDERAL BUREAU OF INVESTIGATION

Date: 4/19/68

Transmit the following in ______________________
(Type in plaintext or code)

Via AIRTEL ______ AIRMAIL
(Priority)

To: Director, FBI
From: SAC, San Francisco
Re: Harry Thomas Edwards

[FBI deletion] sent [FBI deletion] information, concerning inflammatory comments that Professor HARRY EDWARDS, San Jose State College, had made in one of his Sociology classes during the present semester.

[FBI deletion] was advised by the Agents that they were not at liberty to divulge FBI sources but that they would be interested in any inflammatory comments that HARRY EDWARDS might have made.

Between the fall of 1967 and the spring of 1968, I received over two hundred written and phoned death threats. And during the NYAC demonstration in New York, a white man approached me with a butcher knife, only to be hustled away by three well-dressed young Blacks who, as it turned out later, were cops. I ate only in cafeteria or smörgasbord restaurants (if the food was already prepared and nobody knew I was coming, my food couldn't be "doctored up"). During lectures, I never drank from water placed at the podium, only straight from a fountain or faucet later.

UNITED STATES GOVERNMENT
MEMORANDUM

Date: 1/31/68

To: Director, FBI
From: SAC, San Francisco
Subject: Harry Thomas Edwards

Source, who made available school records at San Jose State College, was [FBI deletion].

Records at San Jose State College revealed the following descriptive information concerning Edwards:

Name	Harry Thomas Edwards
Race	Negro
Date of Birth	November 22, 1942
Place of Birth	St. Louis, Missouri
Height	6′ 8″
Weight	240 pounds
Hair	Black
Eyes	Brown
Parents	Harry Edwards, Sr. Adlaide [*sic*] Cruise Edwards
Education	Graduated East St. Louis High School, E. St. Louis, January 28, 1960 Attended Fresno, California City College, February 1960–June 1960 Received BA degree, with honors in Sociology, on June 5, 1964 from San Jose State College, San Jose, California Received Master's degree in Sociology, Cornell University, 1966

Such precautions were against the spontaneous or opportunistic assault, since I felt it to be a foregone conclusion that no one and nothing could stop a well-planned effort to put me in the cemetery.

The athletes associated with us also received death threats by the score, and there were official pressures, too.

Tommie Smith, already under surveillance by the FBI and local agencies, was asked to resign from the Reserve Officer's Training Corps (ROTC) at San Jose State by the unit's commanding officer. When Tommie refused, he was given an honorable discharge from the United States Army, although he had never served a day of duty. So, at the height of the 1968 Peace Movement, when hundreds of young Americans were being jailed or forced to flee the country for refusing induction into the military, the army was telling Tommie Smith, "Hell, no! You *can't* go!" (Apparently, the Yankee who took time out from his Vietnam R & R in Japan to give Smith the straight poop was not without his sympathizers in high places in the military.)

And practically everyone associated with the movement began to encounter difficulties of every imaginable sort: difficulties with landlords, the telephone company, mail service, and so forth. After seven years as a licensed California driver, I had received only one ticket for a moving violation. Between the fall of 1967 and the spring of 1968—a period of seven months—I received thirteen tickets for moving violations and numerous tickets for parking violations.

One officer even cited me for failing to signal a turn into my own driveway.

By June, some of the athletes had begun to argue that unless there was complete Black unity—a total Black boycott—there should be no boycott at all. They argued that unless the boycott was total, it would be used by white folks to demonstrate that "niggers couldn't get together on anything." So the movement had continued to erode despite demonstrations at track meets, lectures across the country, and a substantial increase in both the volume and vociferousness of our rhetoric. I was broke financially and physically exhausted after putting in an average of sixteen to eighteen hours a day on the project since October of 1967, as well as teaching a full schedule of classes at San Jose State. I had dropped from 260 pounds to 205 pounds in less than eight months. And I had just recently been informed that my contract with San Jose State would not be renewed (a fact I expected and which was, in any event, irrelevant beyond the principle of the thing since I'd already decided to return to Cornell to complete my Ph.D.). The games were still more than three months away, and it appeared that the OPHR had run completely out of options. So, unable to beat 'em, we decided to join 'em, to maintain the pretense of adamant militancy in pushing for a total boycott only as a shield that would allow us to salvage as much as possible of our protest goals. But, by August, even this tactic seemed of dubious effectiveness.

There was, first of all, the problem of leaks to the press indicating that the boycott had in fact been called off. Though this could have both jeopardized our efforts to devise an alternative protest strategy and eroded the credibility of the movement generally, the actual results were really much less damaging since, by then, no one really knew what to believe.

More serious were the problems that emerged over *what form* a protest at the Olympic Games should take—a refusal to stand on the victory platform during the playing of the national anthem or while the American flag was being raised; a Black Power salute from the victory stand; a refusal to participate in any event after the opening ceremonies since Blacks are systematically left out of the mainstream of American life; a deliberate effort to finish last in every event since we always finished last in American society; crawling out of the starting blocks; blazing right up to the finish line and then sitting down without ever crossing it? Every conceivable option was discussed, with absolutely no agreement, even among the athletes, as to what was appropriate. Part of this dissension was honest, *part of it was paid for*. But, in any event, we had no option but to settle on an agreement that would be a protest. And we left it to the conscience of each athlete as to what method of protest would be employed.

Though I did not wholly agree with the athletes' arguments regarding the imperativeness of unity, I felt nonetheless that the sacrifice of *uniformity* was a relatively small price to pay given the very real threat of a total collapse of the movement under pressures from both disenchanted Black athletes and the sports establishment.

On June 15, 1968, my landlady ordered me out of my apartment after taking the utterly unnecessary precaution of having two police officers on hand to back her up. Since I had already decided to leave San Jose and return to Cornell, I didn't argue, though I could have used another couple of days to complete my packing and other business.

I decided to drive back to Ithaca. This was a near-fatal decision. In Windover, Utah, gale-force winds overturned the pickup-camper unit that had been the mobile headquarters for the OPHR. The unit was a total wreck. It must have rolled over four complete times before finally coming to rest upright. A highway patrolman, upon surveying the scene, commented that it was "a miracle that there were no fatalities."

I bought a car with the insurance settlement and within three days, I was again on my way to Cornell.

I arrived in Ithaca five days later and moved into a rural apartment ten miles outside of town. My traveling, however, was by no means over.

With the games little more than a month away, I set out from Ithaca on one final publicity campaign across the country. My first stop was East St. Louis.

As soon as I arrived, the brothers sponsoring the engagement told me that the site of the lecture was "crawling with agents," and that apparently efforts had been under way for some time to sabotage or disrupt attendance at the speech. There had been absolutely no publicity in the local media; there had been efforts to cancel access to the lecture hall; and a number of people involved in organizing the engagement had been arrested.

To say the least, it was a weird scene when I arrived. There were less than two hundred people in attendance and half of them *looked* like undercover agents, the kind of people who just did not attend radical political rallies.

One guy, with whom I attended junior high school, walked up and—without so much as saying hello after over fifteen years—whispered in my ear, "Walk carefully, man. Everything ain't true that meets the eye, not even me. Don't ever say I didn't do anything for you." With this, on top of an already freaky scene, I began to feel in my bones, intuitively, that there was something heavy afoot. So I decided to drop some diversionary decoys during my speech, some red herrings that would give me an opportunity to escape the situation without getting killed or arrested under one pretext or another.

9/12/68

TELETYPE

TO: SAC, SPRINGFIELD

FROM: DIRECTOR, FBI

HARRY THOMAS EDWARDS

EDWARDS DURING PRIOR SPEECHES, HAS ADVOCATED VIOLENCE AND ADMITTED HE IS A FANATIC REVOLUTIONARY WHEN IT COMES TO SURVIVAL OF HIS PEOPLE. HIS APPEARANCE AT THE EAST ST. LOUIS HIGH SCHOOL SCHEDULED FOR SEPTEMBER FIFTEEN,

NEXT, MUST, THEREFORE, BE ADEQUATELY COVERED TO DETERMINE STATEMENTS WHICH MAY BE MADE IN VIOLATION OF FEDERAL STATUTES OVER WHICH THE FBI HAS INVESTIGATIVE JURISDICTION OR INFLAMMATORY STATEMENTS OF INTEREST TO THE BUREAU. COVERAGE SHOULD INCLUDE [F.B.I. DELETION]

ENDEAVOR TO OBTAIN TAPED RECORDING OR VERBATIM TRANSCRIPTS OF SUBJECT'S REMARKS IF FEASIBLE.

INSURE THAT LOCAL POLICE AUTHORITIES ARE AWARE OF HIS SCHEDULED APPEARANCE.

(Edwards is included in the Agitator Index and is the former professor at San Jose State College who has been leading a proposed Negro boycott of the 1968 Olympics.)

About halfway through a deliberately scatterbrained speech, I began to make allusions to a fictitious engagement in Detroit in hopes that Detroit would appeal to the agents more than my hometown as a possible site for carrying out whatever plans they might have had. Since there were no whites in the audience, I figured that at a minimum, the people involved would have to call in and report the contents of my statements before they could act. (I knew that Dr. King and the SCLC had attacked federal investigative agencies, particularly the FBI, because of a total lack of Blacks in authority positions. It would, therefore, have been extremely unlikely at the time that a Black agent covering one of my rallies would have had the authority to act on his own. In any event, it seemed the only chance I had to get out of what loomed as a very funky situation.) They apparently took the bait on Detroit, and after making a phony reservation on a flight to Detroit, I took the first thing smoking that was headed for anywhere but Detroit. Needless to say, I cancelled the remainder of my lecture tour.

Four days later, I'd finally made my way back to San Jose, mostly by bus and train. I then contacted Louis Lomax and flew to Los Angeles, where I spent the next three days at his Beverly Hills home.

About two weeks later, I did one final lecture at Sacramento State College. Afterward, I began to make preparations to travel to Mexico City.

FBI

Date: 9/19/68

Transmit the following in ____________________
(Type in plaintext or code)

Via AIRTEL ____________________
(Priority)

To: Director, FBI
From: SAC, Detroit
Harry Thomas Edwards

At 6:40 PM, 9/15/68 [FBI deletion] telephonically advised the Detroit Office that subject had just finished making a speech at the East

St. Louis High School, East St. Louis, Ill., and in closing remarks mentioned that he had to leave for Detroit in order to make an 8:00 PM speaking engagement in that city.

Immediately upon receipt of that information from [FBI deletion] the Detroit Office contacted [FBI deletion] and alerted these individuals of the possibility that subject might appear in Detroit, Mich.

[FBI deletion] were able to establish no information indicating that subject arrived in Detroit or the State of Michigan on the night of 9/15/68 or the morning of 9/16/68 [FBI deletion] advised that no incoming flight from St. Louis, Mo. or connecting cities, had a passenger identifiable with the subject.

[FBI deletion] advised there is no indication that subject spoke in Detroit on the evening of 9/15/68 or that subject was scheduled to speak in Detroit, Mich.

FBI

Date: 9-16-68

Transmit the following in ______________________
(Type in plaintext or code)

Via AIRTEL AIR MAIL
(Priority)

TO: DIRECTOR, FBI

FROM: SAC, ST. LOUIS

RE: HARRY THOMAS EDWARDS

On 9-15-68, (FBI Deletion) telephonically contacted TWA Airlines, St. Louis, and determined from (FBI Deletion) that subject EDWARDS held a reservation on TWA Flight #558 departing St. Louis non-stop for Detroit at 5:10 p.m. on 9-15-68. However, he did not use this reservation and as far as TWA records were concerned had made no attempt to renew the reservation for a later flight.

St. Louis on 9-15-68 also contacted American Airlines and determined that subject held no reservation on that airlines for the date of 9-15-68. Delta Airlines was contacted and it was determined that Delta did not fly directly to Detroit but had connecting flights at Chicago, Illinois. Subject held no reservations on Delta Airlines.

No attempt was made to contact other airlines in St. Louis that had flights to other cities with connections for Detroit.

On 9/18/68 the San Francisco Office advised that that office has no information indicating EDWARDS did, in fact, visit Detroit as he indicated he might during his speech in East St. Louis, Ill.

Inasmuch as no information has been developed which would indicate subject visited Detroit, Michigan, Detroit is not submitting a report in this matter and no further investigation will be conducted.

One of the remaining problems that had to be tackled was that of devising alternative plans for implementing what had become an unwieldy program of protest. Furthermore, the Mexican government had its own domestic problems with proposed protests over the games, problems that promised to make any protest a very risky and dangerous affair. Mexican students had vowed to stop the games, deeming them an "ostentatious waste in the midst of dire poverty" in their country. Allegedly, the United States government had provided hundreds of Vietnam-era arms to Mexican troops and police who had vowed

-RAL BUREAU OF INVESTIGATION
. DEPARTMENT OF JUSTICE
MUNICATION SECTION
OCT 4 1968

TELETYPE

FBI WASH DC

FBI SACTO

520 PM 10/4/68

TO: DIRECTOR AND SAN FRANCISCO

FRO: SACRAMENTO

SYMPOSIUM, RACISM IN AMERICA, SACRAMENTO STATE COLLEGE, SACTO, CALIFORNIA, SEPT. TWENTYSEVEN TO OCT. FOUR, SIXTYEIGHT.

HARRY EDWARDS SPOKE AS SCHEDULED THIS DATE BEFORE APPROXIMATELY ONE THOUSAND PEOPLE IN FOOTBALL STADIUM AT SACRAMENTO STATE COLLEGE. HIS MAIN POINT WAS THAT BLACK PEOPLE DO NOT HAVE CONTROL OVER EDUCATION; THAT IN BLACK COMMUNITIES, WASHINGTON, JEFFERSON, AND LINCOLN DEPICTED AS HEROES BUT THIS NOT TRUE; THAT IF CONSTITUTION GOOD ENOUGH FOR WHITES, IT IS GOOD ENOUGH FOR NEGROES. ONLY REFERENCE TO OLYMPICS WAS THAT MEXICAN STUDENTS THERE WOULD PUT A STOP TO IT.

to put down any organized disruptions of the games by force. The situation clearly called for some levelheaded thought, and so I again turned to Brother Lomax for consultation. We talked on the phone briefly, and on October 7, I caught a plane for Los Angeles. As usual, by the time I arrived, Lomax had done his homework and his advice was clean, straightforward, and singular: Don't go to Mexico City.

Lomax was convinced that nothing else could be done from a leadership or organizational capacity insofar as the protests were concerned. Moreoever, through some of his East Coast contacts, he had learned that "it might not be altogether healthy" for either the Black athletes supporting the movement or me if I were in Mexico City when protests erupted. Lomax reasoned that the development of a tragic situation in the wake of Black Olympic protests—a situation "conceivably involving the deaths of some prominent Black athletes"

OPTIONAL FORM NO. 10
MAY 1962 EDITION
GSA FPMR (41 CFR) 101–11.6

UNITED STATES GOVER MENT

Memorandum

TO : DIRECTOR, FBI DATE: 10/14/68

FROM : SAC, ALBANY

SUBJECT: HARRY THOMAS EDWARDS

The following investigation was conducted at Ithaca and Dryden, New York, by (FBI Deletion)

On 10/10/68, (FBI Deletion) Cornell University, Ithaca, N.Y., advised that subject is currently registered in the Cornell Graduate School as a Ph.D candidate with degree expected in 1970. His current residence address is listed as 230 Lake Road, Dryden, N.Y.(which is a small community located approximately 10 miles from Ithaca, N.Y.).

On 10/10/68, a spot check was made at 230 Lake Road, Dryden, N.Y., and it was determined that this address is a small apartment house known as the Bradmere Apartment. While this spot check was being made, subject was observed leaving this residence at which time he entered a blue sedan, foreign make, bearing California registration VXZ 471.

(FBI Deletion) ascertained that subject is residing in Apt. 3 at that apartment house(Bradmere), 230 Lake Road.

and myself—could be "exploited by those who would discredit the entire Black Power Movement." If I were not in Mexico City, "the safety of Black athletes would be the responsibility of the United States Olympic Committee. The USOC would be compelled to see that nothing happened to them."

I had learned to respect Lomax's advice in such matters. Upon learning of Martin Luther King's assassination, he was the first person I'd tried to contact. And it was Lomax who had advised me to get out of the Bay Area one evening in 1967. And so the night that Oakland police officers were involved in a shoot-out with Huey P. Newton (in which Newton was wounded and an officer killed), I was in Los Angeles at Lomax's house. Therefore, when he told me that a trip to Mexico City would be ill advised, I did not take his warning lightly.

I did, however, explore ways of entering Mexico City incognito—no easy task given my size and the publicity I'd received in connection with the movement. After a trip by car from Los Angeles to San Diego and across into Tijuana, where I talked to a number of people about the possibility of air service to inland destinations, I gave up the idea. The costs were prohibitive, the people with whom I would have to deal too seedy (as in pot), and the likelihood of being able to move undetected in Mexico City too remote.

UNITED STATES GOVERNMENT

Memorandum

Mr. W. C. Sullivan - F.B.I. 10/21/68

W. R. Wannall

OLYMPIC GAMES, MEXICO CITY, MEXICO

On 10/19/68 Legal Attache (Legat), Mexico City, telephonically advised that Harry Thomas Edwards was rumored to be in Mexico City and was possibly responsible for unpatriotic action by U. S. Olympic athletes when they gave Black Power sign while U. S. National Anthem was played during presentation awards. Legat requested immediate information as to Edwards' whereabouts, as well as photographs and description of him.

Edwards was the former instructor at San Jose State College in California who was responsible for a movement calling on Negro athletes to boycott the 19th Olympic games in Mexico City. He is a well-known militant among the Black Power advocates and recently transferred to Cornell University at Ithaca, New York. Telephonic inquiry of Assistant Special Agent in Charge (ASAC) at Albany resulted in investigation which disclosed Edwards not at his home but was believed to be at McGill University in Montreal attending a conference of Black Power advocates. A taped television program 10/19/68 confirmed Edwards' attendance at the meeting at McGill but also indicated his plans to travel to Mexico City during the Olympic games.

FD-86 (12-8-67)
UNITED STATES GOVERNMENT

Memorandum

SAC, San Francisco 11/5/68

Director, FBI

HARRY THOMAS EDWARDS

The Immigration and Naturalization Service (INS), Washington, D. C., on 10/23/68, furnished copies of Canadian "Non-Immigrant Arrival-Departure Cards" provided by Canadian immigration authorities on individuals who indicated the purpose of their travel to Canada was to attend the Congress of Black Writers. One such card contained the following information:

Harry Edwards, born 11/22/42, St. Louis, Missouri; residence - 230 Lake Road, Number 3, Dryden, New York.

The above is submitted for your information.

Edwards is included in the Agitator Index and we had prior information that he attended the Black Writers' Congress.

Lomax had told me that "when the Olympic Games start, you should be as far east and north from Mexico City as you can get without going to Canada." But, rather than merely returning to Ithaca, New York (which is what Lomax had in mind), I decided that perhaps I *would* go to Canada, particularly since I had already been invited to address a Black Writer's Conference at McGill University in Montreal. I took my usual precaution of publicly announcing three or four fake destinations as a cover for my real agenda—just to make sure that everybody interested in my travels would have enough to keep them busy.

On the nineteenth of October, 1968, Tommie Smith and John Carlos staged a protest demonstration on the victory podium at the Mexico City Olympic Games that has emerged as a high-water mark in the liberation efforts of Black youth during the 1960s. They didn't need a leader in Mexico City. They were more than capable of carrying on for themselves. Their protest demonstration symbolized the courage, commitment, and growing political sophistication of an entire generation of young Black people. And for their deed, both Tommie Smith and John Carlos were summarily "banished from amateur sport competition for life" by the United States Olympic Committee. Smith and Carlos bore the brunt of the U.S. sports establishment's lust for immediate revenge against everyone associated with the protest effort, against the Black basketball players who boycotted the games entirely, against the "respectable" and "responsible" Blacks who could no longer control or influence the new generation of Black athletes to perform like trained animals on cue, and against me for fomenting everything from the campus athletic revolt to the NYAC boycott to the Olympic Protest for Human Rights.

But most of all, Smith and Carlos were banished for having committed the ultimate Black transgression in a white supremacist society: They dared to become visible, to stand up for the dignity of Black people, to protest from an international platform the racist inhumanity of American society. A total Black boycott of the United States Olympic effort was an idea whose time had *almost* come. But this time almost was not only good enough, it was inspiring and it was historic! And as the Soledad Prison poets say, "History Is a Weapon"—if you can master it.

Meanwhile, George Foreman, the Black U.S. heavyweight boxer, was applauded, celebrated, and praised by U.S. Olympic officials, the white media, and much of the American public, after parading around the ring waving an American flag moments after being declared the gold medalist in the Olympic heavyweight division. But that's sports politics for you.

JIM BROWN

Out of Bounds

I was always much tighter with my offensive lineman than our guys on defense. I didn't know much about the guys on defense. I had to run through those guys every day at practice, and they'd be talking their own talk. My linemen were my lifeblood.

It used to get funny: you could tell by watching our linemen who we were playing that Sunday. Their demeanor told the entire storyline. If we had a game against a team with no defensive line, guys like John Wooten and Gene Hickerson were all laid back, having their fun. Talking big: *I'm gonna kick this guy's ass! Gonna beat him up! Run over me! I'll open the holes!*

Next week we'd have Detroit—Roger and Alex—my boys would be humble! "Damn, I'm gonna need some help. I can't exactly handle this guy straight-on. I think a double team is called for." They'd arrive at practice early, watch film that night until their eyes ached, as serious as accountants. What made it comical was that there wasn't any lying or bullshit about it. Forget the games that athletes and reporters play on each other: when football players get together, discuss what they can and cannot do, they're straight out. Offensive linemen may be the most honest beasts in the jungle. Wooten would watch Roger on film, his eyes would open wide. He'd always say, "Damn, I gotta play against this *big* bitch."

Against a team noted for its pass rush, they'd practically pay the coaches to start our first series with north to south running plays: they wanted to charge straight out and deliver some punishment before we started passing. They knew what defensive linemen would do on pass protection: bash a neck with a fist; probe a groin with a knee; step on a leg, keep running. At the prospect of knocking the living crap out of a quarterback, defensive cats turn evil.

As I recall, our linemen didn't woof much the week of a game with the Rams. The Fearsome Foursome was wicked. Deacon Jones. Secretary of the Defense. Flamboyant. Crazy. Ridiculously quick for a man his size. The guy who made them coin the word Sack. Rosey Grier. Immense. Impossible to defeat with brute force. Sweet and gentle out of shoulder pads. Loved to sing, pick a guitar. Lovely human being. Lamar Lundy. Defined the term Unsung. Steadfast. A mass of muscle. Would have starred on any other team. Merlin Olson. Loved the old-fashioned, man-to-man battles in the Pit. With both hands at once, he would hit guys across the earholes in their helmet for stereo ringing. Put him in the lineup for ten years, worry about something else.

With a line that formidable, the Rams didn't need any assistance from the NFL. They got it anyway, at least I thought so. After Rosey suffered a serious injury, I picked up the paper one morning, read that Detroit had traded Roger Brown to the Rams. I said, Wait. What the hell is that? They still got the Deac and Merlin and Lundy, Rosey gets hurt, boom, they get Roger Brown?

I was sure that trade was bogus. And it wasn't until that trade that I started thinking: yes, pro football is a business. I used to think it was a sport, but it has to be a business. Because no owner, not one, should want Roger Brown, a star, a *300-pound* star, to move to the Rams. With Roger, the Rams are as good as they are with Rosey, perhaps better. And Detroit and Los Angeles are both in the same conference! The league must want the team in Los Angeles to remain strong. A thriving team in a critical market is good for the networks, what's good for the networks is good for the league. Man, these owners are doing some *business.*

As Cleveland Browns, we did a little business of our own: one time we put a bounty on the head of John Henry Johnson. John Henry played fullback for the Pittsburgh Steelers. I considered Detroit, Philadelphia, and Pittsburgh the three dirtiest teams in football—John Henry was Pittsburgh's principal thug. He was a street-brawling SOB who used to drink shots with Bobby Layne. On kickoffs, John Henry had this quaint habit: he'd sneak up on people, break their jaws with his forearm.

One kickoff, John Henry shattered the jaw of our backup fullback, Ed Modzelewski. John Henry broke two different bones, Ed was all fucked up. After the game, our team passed around a hat. Each man stuck $20 in the hat: whoever messed up John Henry would get the pot. Man, they never touched him. He'd dance and move and taunt. If John Henry somehow got cornered, he'd slug it out, or bite people. Though we never stopped trying, we never got John Henry. The ante kept growing.

So did Big Daddy Lipscomb; depending on the time of year, Big Daddy went anywhere from 280 to 320. Amazingly, he was also fast enough to run down halfbacks from behind. Daddy's strength was unrivaled. With most tacklers, even if they had a firm grip on me, I could lean forward, push off the earth with my legs, fall ahead for a few extra yards. Not with Daddy. He would grab me with each of his hands, where my shoulders meet my arms, jerk me up out of my lean, slam me to the ground. Goddamn!

I first opposed Big Daddy in 1959, my third year in the NFL. It was the first time the Cleveland Browns, with me on their side, would play the Baltimore Colts. They had splendid Lenny Moore to run the football, but they also had Johnny Unitas and Raymond Berry, who lived mostly by the pass. We were a ground team, everyone billed it as a classic matchup. The fans were excited, the press was excited, we were excited. Then I wasn't so excited: Daddy decided he would kick my young ass. He announced to the press that he would personally "Get that Cleveland cat."

Other guys had said they would Get Me, but their names weren't Big Daddy. Properly motivated, Daddy could disrupt an entire offense. Watching film didn't cheer me—Wooten kept complaining that he had to face another Big Bitch. I wasn't exactly scared, wasn't exactly stupid. I gave Big Daddy, Sunday's encounter, considerable thought, came up with a plan.

I knew not to make Daddy angry, knew I couldn't whip him physically. I decided to con him. I knew a little bit about Daddy. Though his body was oversized, inside he was a little boy, who hated to be scolded. When he was, he would pout and refuse to perform, and that's why his career was uneven. If you give Big Daddy praise, he was a pussycat. If you gave him enough praise, maybe he wouldn't break you up.

Sunday in Baltimore. Noon. Despite our friendship, I knew Big Daddy had been working up a hate for me. During pregame warmups, I marched right through several Colts, up to Big Daddy.

I said, "Hey, Big Daddy, how you doing? How's your family? You're looking good, man."

Big Daddy was suspicious. I kept on talking and smiling, Mr. Chummy. Finally . . . Daddy smiled. He said it was damn good to see me, too. I told him to have a super game, got the hell out of there. The other Colts were glaring at me.

Well, I had an excellent day. My offensive lineman and I, without the knowledge of the coaches, devised a new blocking scheme: whatever direction their defensive men wanted to go, they would encourage them, push them that way; I would survey the situation, have the option to choose my hole. I'll talk more about this later, because I wish we would have done it my entire career. On that day against the Colts, I wound up scoring five TDs, including a long one for seventy yards. Everyone on the offense was feeling fantastic. Except for poor Bobby Mitchell.

With me out of the picture, hate-wise, Daddy decided to tear up Bobby. Daddy was visibly angry, wanted to hurt Bobby, put him out of the game. Bobby knew it. After Daddy flung him down the first few times, Bobby started scooting out of bounds to avoid him. Daddy only got hotter. On one of Bobby's sweeps, Daddy chased him across the sideline, over the bench, damn near into the stands.

Meanwhile, I did something I never did: kept talking the entire game. "Big Daddy, you're kicking ass. How's that pretty girlfriend? Daddy, we *got* to get together later."

I lugged the ball thirty-two times the day, but Unitas, carving us up, nearly beat us. We held on, 38–31. Poor Daddy never even knew I fooled him.

After the 1963 season, Daddy died. The stories out of Baltimore attributed it to drugs; I believe the papers said he overdosed on heroin. None of the players who knew Daddy believed it. We'd spent time with him—there wasn't one of us who believed he was on drugs. The reports of his death were so mysterious, we suspected wrongdoing. Some guys checked around, they could never prove anything.

A few months before he died, I got to play with Big Daddy. By then he was a Pittsburgh Steeler, we were teammates on the East in the 1962 Pro Bowl. That regular season I had broken my wrist: it was the first time in my career I didn't lead the league in rushing—Jimmy Taylor won it that year. Though I played all year, my wrist didn't begin to heal until the last few weeks of the season. Since my numbers were way down, certain people were suggesting my career was washed up. They happened to be saying the same thing about Daddy.

During Pro Bowl warmups, Allie Sherman, the Giants' head coach, now in charge of the East, walked up to me.

He said, "Jim, I'm gonna use you a lot. I know what people are saying and I know you hurt your wrist. But you're the best runner in the league. Get ready."

I loved Allie for that. I had always liked him, considered him a friend though he was the opposition. His faith in me now, when I was getting dogged, pumped me up. Excited, I went to find Daddy.

I said, "Look, Allie is in my corner. He wants me to have the ball and my wrist is feeling good. I'm gonna win this MVP."

"Jim," Daddy said, "if you got the MVP, I guess I'll go for Lineman of the Game. Shit, I'm still the Daddy."

Once the game began, every time I came to the sidelines I'd give Daddy a pat on the butt. I'd say, "Daddy, you're doing great, man. You're shining. Keep hustling, brother." Then Daddy would come off and ask me, "Jim, how am I doing?" And I'd tell him he was kicking ass. This time it was no con. Daddy was fantastic, going sideline to sideline to drag people down. One time he saved a touchdown, caught Dick Bass from behind.

After the game we both got our trophies. Usually trophies never moved me, this time it did. Back in the locker room I looked at Daddy. He was holding his award to his chest, as a child cradles a puppy. When I think of Daddy, I like to remember that.

CHARLIE SIFFORD

Just Let Me Play: The Story of Charlie Sifford— The First Black PGA Golfer

Getting the card in 1961 wasn't enough. I had to find a way to play in more tournaments. There was no other way around it. In order to keep my Approved Tournament Player's Card and be automatically qualified for each PGA tournament, I had to finish in the top 60 money winners on the whole tour at the end of every year. Some 200 guys were out there competing on the circuit, and I had to beat two-thirds of them in order to continue playing. If I kept giving away 20 tournaments a year to them, how could I possibly make enough money to keep up?

I had paid my $65 dues to the PGA, but that didn't mean I was automatically entered into every tournament. Like any player I still had to send a written application along with an entry fee to each tournament and then wait for a commitment from the sponsors. From where I sat at the beginning of 1961 it didn't look like anything would open up beyond the usual tournaments I'd been playing in, which led me to wonder just how much I'd gained in my battles. Was this another Teddy Rhodes and Bill Spiller job by the PGA, handing me the ATP card and announcing to the media that they'd let the black guys in, only to find a new way to shut me out of the tournaments and the money list?

The first changes to come my way happened in California, where I was invited for the first time ever to enter the Bing Crosby National Pro-Am Tournament and the Palm Springs Golf Classic. For that I had Jackie Robinson to thank, with his wonderful advocacy on my behalf, with assists from Billy Eckstine and Joe Louis. I also played in a new tournament in San Francisco in January, giving me a full slate of seven events that I could enter in the first two months of the year.

I made the cuts in each one of them except for Phoenix and played well enough to finish in the top 15 four times. In San Francisco and Tucson I led after the first rounds with a sweet pair of 65s. For the first time since I'd started playing professional golf I felt like I had a place to go every week, although it was just for a couple of months.

A note of advice here for future pioneers: when you push open a door, you walk softly through it. I had fought to get into the Crosby and the Palm Springs tournaments, and a lot of people had put the pressure on each tournament to put me in there. Harsh words had been spoken, but I didn't go into either one of those places with a chip on my shoulder. I have always felt that if I could just play in a new place, I'd be happy. I don't go in there with an attitude or with some kind of political agenda, and I don't go in there trying to rub the faces of the sponsors and the tournament directors who resisted me. All I want to do is play and be given a chance to make a living, and when that happens, I'm satisfied. I had nothing but good relations with Bing Crosby and the Palm Springs people when I played in their tournaments, and I went back year after year and enjoyed similar cordial treatment. I'd have been a fool to go in there causing trouble, because that would just give them a reason to shut me out the following year.

As I've said before, the only point that I have tried to make is that a black man can play golf just as well as a white man and be just as much of a gentleman on the golf course. The simple fact of my playing, and playing well, was all the point I needed to make. I have never gone into a place and badmouthed the tournament and the sponsors or made inflammatory statements to the press if I was given a fair chance to play golf. It's only when they start stacking the deck against me that I open my mouth.

I actually had quite a nice time going up to Pebble Beach for the Crosby and meeting guys like Bing, Bob Hope, and Dean Martin. Crosby, of course, was the best golfer among them, and he was very serious about his game. For Hope in those days the game seemed like just another opportunity to tell as many jokes as he could shoehorn in. The man loved to entertain, and he was one of these characters who is always on. People asked me back then if I was a little intimidated by being around such big celebrities. Hell, man, I hung out with Billy Eckstine and the greatest jazz musicians in the world for 10 years. No way was I going to get too excited about Dean Martin. I've been around long enough to know that a man is a man, and it doesn't matter how much money he makes or how visible he is. Everyone is entitled to respect.

My game was sharp when I finished fourth at Tucson in the second week of February, but suddenly I was slammed back to reality. The tour went off to the South, and suddenly I was stuck back in California practicing and playing for dollar bets at Western Avenue. The PGA stopped in Baton Rouge; New Orleans; Puerto Rico; Pensacola; St. Petersburg; Palm Beach; and Wilmington, North Carolina, and not one of those places accepted my applications to play.

It looked like I'd be shut out for the entire spring, but unbeknownst to me, something was brewing in Greensboro, North Carolina. The NAACP had taken an interest in my case, and in Greensboro a man named Dr. George Simpson was head of the local chapter and knew the people who ran the Greater Greensboro Open. He worked on them to let me in, and somehow he succeeded. On April 4, a week before the tournament was to start, I got a call: I had been accepted to play at the Sedgefield Country Club as the first black man ever to enter a PGA event in the South.

I can't describe to you the swirling emotions that came over me as I prepared to drive across the country to enter that tournament. I thought about my childhood in Charlotte and about all the white friends I'd made on the golf course. I thought about people like Sutton Alexander, who had helped me out, and the men who had encouraged me to keep playing.

I also thought about the circumstances in which I'd had to leave North Carolina, and about the lynchings. They were killing civil rights workers in the South in those days, and in places like Greensboro they were also fighting bitterly to keep blacks off the public golf courses. How would they feel when I walked into their exclusive country club during the week of their prestigious professional golf event?

The PGA couldn't let anything happen to me out there, could it? I wondered if I might be heading into a very large and dangerous trap: what if something serious happened? Would the PGA and the other golfers come to my defense? Could throwing me to a tipped-off pack of Klansmen be an easy way to get rid of the black man who wouldn't go away?

Everyone in the whole country knew that I was heading to Greensboro. The *New York Times* ran a story about my acceptance to the tournament, and how I had come close to winning in San Francisco and Tucson. Other papers picked up on it. Like Jackie Robinson, I was about to make a very big step for black people, but, unlike Jackie Robinson, I wasn't surrounded by teammates and there were no fences at the golf course to keep back unruly people. Any nut could have decided to make his personal stand against integration by meeting me in Greensboro.

I could envision the headlines: "First Black Golfer Lynched on 14th Tee; PGA Blames Tournament Sponsor." I was alone on this trip, and there is no lonelier feeling than crossing into the Deep South and heading for an all-white country club. Driving across the country I remembered some of the good times with Teddy Rhodes and Zeke Hartsfield and Howard Wheeler when we'd all pile into a car and drive to a new UGA tournament. I'd left all that behind in my pursuit of professional golf, and now I was very much on my own.

I wouldn't have gone at all if it weren't for Rose. When I told her about the invitation, I said that I didn't think I should go. She knew as well as I did that

I could be the victim of violence, and I wasn't so sure that I wanted to take that risk. I had just gotten her and Charles Jr., back with me in California, and now I was going to risk my life for a golf tournament?

But she reassured me. "Nothing's going to happen that you can't handle," she said. "You'll go and you'll do fine. This is what you've been working towards for so many years."

If the good Lord was willing, I'd do fine. All I could do was pray to God that I'd make it, and pray that I'd keep my head if somebody came at me. I remembered what Jackie Robinson had told me several years before. "You can't go after somebody with a golf club if they give you a hard time. If you do that, you'll ruin it for all of the other black players to come."

I hadn't been back in the South for many years. As I drove into North Carolina, it started coming back to me like a bad dream. When I stopped for gas, I couldn't grab a bite to eat in the café. Couldn't use the toilet in some places. In Greensboro, there was no hotel where I could sleep, so Dr. Simpson got me a room at the all-black college, North Carolina A & T. He apologetically said that he'd have put me up in his own house, but it was filled with kids and he didn't have any room. "That's okay," I said in the small, dormitory room. "I'll be fine here."

I was greeted coolly but cordially at the Sedgefield Country Club, and I went about my business signing in and hiring a caddie like I would do at any new tournament. I'm not like Bill Spiller; I didn't have any interest in marching into their locker room to see how far my rights extended. I just wanted to do well on the golf course, and I didn't need any friction or controversy to distract me from my real goal.

The tournament had drawn its usual contingent of top golfers. Sam Snead was there, along with Art Wall, Mike Souchak, Gene Littler, Don Massengale, Jim Ferree, Doug Sanders, and many others. I knew all of them from my years of playing, and to them it was just like any other tournament. They were cordial, too, as they went about the business of hitting balls and putting. Nobody went out of his way to buddy up to me, but that was fine. They were treating me like any other pro, which in itself was a kind of respectful tribute. They were trying to make a living the same as I was, and I didn't expect anyone to pull me aside or make it any easier for me.

The tournament began well for me in the pro-am round, where I tied for third low pro and made $163. My game was sharp and I saw that I could score well on the course. At first I was nervous, wondering if there was trouble brewing, and where it might come from. But as the day wore on it became just another pro-am round with three white businessmen, and I went about my business. A hush would come over groups of people when I walked by, and I heard the whisper ("There's that black player"), but I was used to that. More than anything I think they were curious to see if I could play.

Afterwards I had dinner at Dr. Simpson's house, since I couldn't eat in any local restaurants. The worst thing that day was the college kids in the dormitory. They were so noisy that I didn't get to sleep until past midnight. They were running up and down the halls screaming and yelling so much that I couldn't hear myself think. I decided that the next day I'd accept the offer of a room from George and Betty Lavett, a black family I'd met.

The tournament began the following day, and I had a point to make. I would show them that a black man belonged in that tournament and in every tournament in the country. Many people didn't believe that a black could play as well as Sam Snead and the others, despite my previous accomplishments. A lot was riding on my play that week. If I did well and kept my cool, I could open up the tour a crack for myself and for any other black golfers coming up. If I failed and didn't make the cut, then all of those crackers throughout the South would have an excuse to keep me away from tournaments.

I refused to let the pressure get to me. The course was wet and windy that day, but it didn't bother me any. I went out and put up the best score of the day, a 3 under par 68. My putter came through time and time again, as I one-putted 12 greens and didn't make a bogey the entire round. Suddenly I was the first-round leader of the Greater Greensboro Open. Not bad for a 38-year-old, cigar-chewing black man!

That was the first day that we had any kind of galleries, and once again my nervous early anticipation dissolved as I got into the round. I caught some dirty looks from a few people, but nobody approached me or said anything. I didn't exactly feel embraced by the crowd, but I could handle the little bit of hostility that I felt. This isn't so bad at all, I thought as I was signing my scorecard. If this was as bad as it got, I could play all the time in the South.

At the end of the day I drove over to the Lavetts' house and had dinner. We talked about my playing in the South, and that maybe things had changed enough to allow a black man to make a living at golf without being harassed. I went to bed early in order to be fresh for my morning tee time, but before I fell asleep the phone rang. George knocked on my door and said I had a call.

I thought it was either Rose calling from California or somebody calling to congratulate me for my first round. Instead, it was a voice I'd never heard, but a voice I'll never forget. "Charlie Sifford?" the man asked in a white man's Southern accent.

"That's me."

"You'd better not bring your black ass out to no golf course tomorrow if you know what's good for you, nigger. We don't allow no niggers on our golf course."

The words hit me like a punch in the jaw. I hadn't been called a nigger since I was a kid in Charlotte, and I felt the anger rise up inside me.

"I tee off at 10:15 in the morning," I said. "You do whatever it is you're going to do, because I'll be there."

"You'd just better watch out, nigger," he said, and hung up.

I didn't get much sleep for the rest of that night, and this time I didn't have the college kids to blame. Suddenly things had changed. It wasn't a golf tournament I was in, it was a war zone. I tried to tell myself that it was just some big stupid cracker who gave himself a charge with a crank phone call, but I couldn't shake the fear. I knew how easily black people could disappear in the South, and I knew that if a whole gang of Klansmen were working up the courage at that very moment to pay me a midnight visit, there was nobody around who could stop them.

I thought about not going out there the next day. Maybe I should withdraw from the tournament and go someplace safe. Obviously the South wasn't ready for me yet, and I wasn't so sure that I wanted to risk my life to open up the PGA Tour. I called Rose in Los Angeles and told her what happened. We talked about it for a long time, and she encouraged me to go out there and play. "Just keep moving," she said. "They're not going to hurt you on the golf course, but you make sure that you've got somebody with you when you go to your car."

The next morning I went out to my car with every nerve in my body tingling. Someone called out to me and I must have jumped a foot. It was one of the neighbors wishing me good luck. On the way to the golf course I kept checking my mirrors, wondering if anyone was following me.

I got to the country club and changed my shoes in the car, and as I walked to the practice tee I felt like everyone's eyes were on me. There are always a few hundred people milling around at a tournament: players, sponsors, volunteers, caddies, spectators looking for autographs. Which one of the people who were brushing past me had made the phone call last night? Would a group of them suddenly try to drag me off the course? As I hit my practice balls I tried as hard as I could to calm the butterflies that were in my stomach. "You can't let them get to you," I hissed to myself. "You let this shit affect your game, it means that you're finished with golf."

My tee time was at 10:15, and I stepped to the first tee and hit my drive. The guy I was paired with hit his, and I started to walk down the fairway. And then a familiar voice rang out, a voice that I'd heard over the phone the night before. "Nice shot, Smokey," he yelled. "How ya going to play the next one?"

I looked over and saw a pack of 12 young white men walking down the side of the fairway, as close to me as they could get. They were all taunting me, trying to get my attention by being loud and unruly. I tried to ignore them as I got to my ball and selected a club. They were silent for a moment, but as I began my backswing a voice rang out: "Don't miss it, Darkie."

I pulled the ball to the left of the green and they hooted.

"You can't play for shit."

"Go back to the cotton fields."

"Hey, boy, carry my bag."

They followed me down the fairway again and stood by as I chipped onto the green and putted out, screaming at me with every stroke.

Those creeps followed me from the first tee all the way to the 14th green before the police finally came and took them away. They did everything they could do to disrupt my game. They threatened, they shouted, and one time when I went to look for my ball, I found it surrounded by a pile of beer cans. The rest of the gallery fell silent when those drunken rednecks were around, making their taunts all the more audible. They were dragging the Greater Greensboro Open down to the level of a boxing match, and all of those people watching didn't do a damn thing about it. "You are definitely back in the South," I told myself bitterly. "Ain't no doubt about that."

A buzz went up around the golf course about what was happening, and around the third hole I was joined by a PGA official named George Wash. He saw what was going on, and he stayed with me for the rest of the round. He repeatedly asked the unruly gang to quiet down, and he made sure that he was between me and them the whole way.

Why did it take so long to get them off the course? Man, it was the longest round of golf I've ever played. I don't know how I managed to maintain my poise, because I was scared out there. I didn't know if at any minute those guys were going to come after me or if one of them had a gun in his pocket. It took everything I had to concentrate on the game and not let them get to me. They called me every name in the book, and they added a few about my wife and my parents.

There were times when they were only a few feet away from me, screaming at the top of their lungs. I had to watch them out of the corner of my eye, even as I was lining up a shot. At the same time I wondered what it would feel like to take a swing, just one sweet swing, at one of their heads with a 3-iron. That would shut them up quick, wouldn't it.

But I couldn't do that. I knew that if I blew up, it would all be over. I couldn't solve anything by violence. It would just ensure that all blacks, beginning with me, would be permanently barred from the tour. I just had to learn to handle it, because for all I knew this would happen wherever I went to play golf in the South. They rattled me for sure, but I survived it.

KAREEM ABDUL-JABBAR
and PETER KNOBLER

Giant Steps

UCLA was on the other side of the continent, and that was fine with me. From the moment I announced my intention to attend, held my first press conference, and told them UCLA had "everything I want in a school," I was already out there. School was almost over; my stay at home was short-term. I had my own summer ahead of me for the first time since seventh grade, no Friendship Farm exile. I breezed through finals and said my good-byes to Power like shaking hands on the run; a month later it was a year behind me.

One of the first things UCLA did for me was get me a job. Mike Francovich, a movie producer and loyal alumnus, arranged for me to work at Columbia Pictures in New York. It was not much of a gig, mostly delivering interoffice memos or sitting around soaking up atmosphere, but I took home $125 a week, and that gave me the cash I needed to stay out of my parents' way. I saved what I could for the California days ahead and had some money for dates and music.

But the summer after senior year was really a treat because I could finally play in the Rucker tournament. With no high school restrictions and not yet officially enrolled in college, I signed up and matched up against the legends. Had to see what I could do.

Just to be safe I played under an assumed name, as if they didn't know it was me. I was "El Khan," and I played with Charlie Scott, Earl "the Goat" Manigault, one of the playground immortals, Rick Cobb, and a guy named Onion who hung out with Earl. We did some intense warring with the other young street ballplayers.

We played Brooklyn, with Jim Tillman and Jackie Wilson, and they beat us. Bobby Washington dunked on me twice in a row, which was an intended humiliation. The crowd buzzed, and of course, then I had to do the big payback, so, with everybody on the other team trying to block my way to the hoop, I dunked over all of them. I could play this game!

The Philadelphia equivalent of the Rucker was the Baker League, and it was a matter of civic pride to beat their behinds when, after much preparation and arrangement, the Baker boys rolled into town. There were serious bragging rights at stake, so serious that I wasn't even starting; I didn't have the seniority or the game, they brought me in off the bench.

Philly had brought up two busloads of fans, and as the congregation fanned out, they set up this continuous wail that seemed to be coming from everywhere.

"Where's Jesus?"

"Black Jesus!"

"Where's Jesus?"

"I want to see him!"

We were shooting around, or leaning against the wire mesh fence, and what the hell is going on here? It's Baptist time, where are the folding fans and print dresses?

"Black Jesus!"

Then this dark character, six feet three in ratty shorts and a torn T-shirt, wearing one white low-cut sneaker and one black high-top, ambled onto the court. Supposed to be some kind of star. I'd never heard of him.

The game began. Tip-off. Shot. This guy grabbed the rebound. Strange, instead of pushing it up the court and showing what he's got, maybe putting it in someone's face, whoever this dude thinks he is started spinning with the ball—a herky-jerky, stop-and-go challenge in his own defensive end. One of our guards went after him to cut out this bullshit when, we didn't believe it as we saw it, this motherfucker with his own cheering section jumped into the air, did a 360 and, *while he was spinning* fired an overhand, full-court, topspin pass that bounced at the top of the key and, rising, caught his man in stride on the dead run for an easy lay-up.

The crowd went nuts.

"Black Jesus!"

"I saw him! I saw him!"

He just trotted back to play some D.

After a quarter I got in the game and ultimately our big guys were too tough for them, but the man with the bizarre sense of style played some basketball I had never seen.

Black Jesus. Turns out he was Earl Monroe.

Oscar Robertson was the epitome of the subtle, no-flash ballplayer. He had the game broken down into such fine points that if he got even a half-step on you, you were in big trouble. He kept the game very simple, which was his first secret. All the most effective basketball strategists and players have kept their technique honed to its most lean and essential parts. John Wooden did it in his coaching; Bill Russell did it in his playing, and Oscar was the same way. He didn't have blazing speed, and he didn't do a whole lot of pirouettes, all he did was score, rebound, and dish the ball off. He could handle the basketball well with both hands, using the crossover dribble, first the right hand then the left then back to the right again, to lure his man into going off-balance or leaning in the wrong direction, after which he'd go right by him, and then it was either time for his shot or a pass. If you were going to stop him, you were just going to stop the basics, and you would have to do it perfectly because he could take advantage of any miscue you might make.

At six feet five inches tall, 210 pounds, Oscar was the first big guard. It wasn't obvious because he was so smooth and graceful, but he had tremendous brute strength, and if he bumped into you, he'd knock you back on your heels. On defense he was quick and smart and solid, as easily slap the ball away from his man as be the wall that would not crumble before a drive. On offense he had the consistently effective shot and the absolute will to put it in. His whole thing was access to the basket. When he got ready to shoot, if I could give him even a glimpse of space to work with, he would drive past, leading his defender into my shoulder, which would stop the man, and once past me either hit the lay-up or have the court awareness to hit the teammate whose defender had momentarily left him free while trying to stop Oscar.

He was a master of the three-point play, and he was at his best against guys who played him tough. Oscar versus Jerry Sloan was always a great match-up because Jerry played very physical defense. Jerry would get great position, allowing for no movement, no first step to the hoop, and then let his man run into him and be charged with the foul. Oscar loved that because it played right into his hands. Oscar would always let Jerry set, then fake as if he was going around him. Oscar had the great move so, out of respect, Jerry would react, and as soon as he started, Oscar would bowl Jerry over, go up and hit the jumper, and be on his way to the foul line as the whistle was blowing and the ball was hitting the net. Oscar was so subtle he'd never get called for it. Meanwhile, Oscar was a truck, it was like getting hit by Jim Brown. But Sloan would bounce back up, complain to the refs, and get on with his game. I loved to watch them.

But Oscar was even more valuable as a leader than as a scorer. He was thirty-two years old and had lost maybe a step, but his total mastery enabled him to be just as effective as when he was averaging thirty points a game. By directing and inspiring the rest of us, he enabled the Bucks to play the game the way it was supposed to be played.

We had all the components in place. The Bucks had obtained Lucius Allen in an off-season deal with Seattle—it was good to have my old friend and running mate with me again—and with Lucius, Bobby Dandridge, and Greg Smith, we had three guys who could get up and down the court in a hurry. I was in the middle, and Oscar controlled the ball like he was dishing out compliments. Bobby was deadly from fifteen to twenty feet, and Oscar could spot him the moment he came open. People wouldn't guard Greg Smith, which let him run free under the backboard where he was a terror. Oscar would find him. Lucius and Jon McGlocklin played off Oscar, and both of them could either put the ball on the floor or seem to be careening down the court and then pull up and shoot, which made our fast break effective. All the guys played D, and with Bob Boozer and McCoy McLemore coming off the bench for some board strength, we were a very powerful squad.

Coming out of three consecutive college championships and an NBA semifinal, I was used to winning and assumed it would continue pretty regularly, so I was not as overwhelmed playing with Oscar as I might have been. Had I known that what he added to my game would come only once in my professional lifetime, I might have stopped to savor the pleasure of working with the best. I'd never known anything but the best, though, so while I enjoyed playing with Oscar, it wasn't until several years later that I appreciated him fully.

What the Big O did for me that gave a quantum jump to my game was get me the ball. It sounds simple, and it was—for him. Oscar had this incredible court vision and a complete understanding of the dynamics of the game. Not only did he see guys open on the periphery for a jumper, he knew when each of us would fight through a pick or come open behind a screen, and the ball would arrive and be there like you were taking it off a table.

There is an exact moment when a center, working hard in the pivot for a glimmer of an advantage, has the position he needs for the score. You've run the length of the court, established your ground, defended it against the hands, forearms, elbows, trunks, and knees of another two-hundred-and-fifty-pound zealot who is slapping and bumping and shoving to move you off your high ground. You need the ball right then. It's like a moon shot: Fire too soon and you miss the orbit; fire too late and you're out of range, but let fly when all signals are Go, and you should hit it right on. Oscar had the knack of getting me the ball right at that place and time. Not too high, didn't want to go up in the air and lose the ground you've fought for. Not too low, didn't want to bend for the ball and create a scramble down there. Never wanted to put the ball on the floor where some little guy could steal in and slap it away. Oscar knew all of this, and his genius was, whether two men were in his face trying to prevent him from making the pass or in mine trying to prevent me from receiving it, in getting me the ball chest-high so I could turn and hook in one unbroken motion. No way not to score when Oscar was around. No wonder he has 2,500 more assists than anyone in NBA history.

One night he showed me the whole game. We were playing Golden State, and for some reason Oscar shed ten years and brought out the Big O one last time. Getting old in professional sports doesn't always mean losing your ability all at once, mostly it means only being able to do in unpredictable spurts what you once could call up at will; becoming a miler among sprinters. That night, maybe because he was challenged, maybe because he was angry, maybe simply because he wanted to, Oscar just dominated the floor. He crushed everyone who opposed him on the court; threw hard, precise passes that demanded to be converted; rebounded with a passion, made seventy percent of his shots and scored thirty-seven points before he was lifted. Total mastery. I envy the guys who played with him in his prime. Playing with Oscar was like working with Thomas Edison.

Oscar took the game seriously. All season long if someone screwed up or didn't seem to want to play, he would chew them out for not doing his job. People who weren't rebounding, guys who weren't playing defense, they were in trouble around Oscar. You had to respect him; you were playing with a legend, and he was still doing all of his job; how could you not do yours?

That year I played with a legend and against one. I finally got to go up against Wilt for real. (As with the Babe, Willie, Duke and Oscar, for the greats one name will do.) He had injured his knee and was out my rookie year, but he was very much a presence my second time through.

Wilt held his position in the pro basketball hierarchy with total seriousness. He fought for it the way he went for rebounds, with strength and intimidation. It was his only identity. Finally out from under Russell's shadow, or at least no longer having to read the comparisons in every column and box score, he could have done without my interference. It would have been pleasant for him to rule the roost for a few years before some new young guy knocked him out of the box. And why did it have to be me, the kid he'd taken under his wing? After all, I was the boy he'd loaned his records to, to whom he'd shown the ropes. How could I possibly be threatening to take his place at the top? It took a special will to turn me into the demon threat to his kingdom who had to be defeated. But when the stakes are as high as identity itself, it's amazing what the mind can do.

Wilt had a lot to complain about because, from the start, he couldn't control me. Wilt's entire game was built on strength. He controlled the lane. (In fact, it was because of his dominance that the rules committee widened it by four feet the same way college ball outlawed dunking for me.) He had great timing and excellent spring, and he would routinely reject opponents' shots, either stuffing them while still in the guys' hands or batting them out of the air after they'd been launched. He was very big and very strong, and he would position himself underneath, and you could forget about coming near him. Nobody could move Wilt out of the pivot, and he was ferocious off the boards. (Over the course of his career he grabbed 2,200 more rebounds than Bill Russell and about 8,000 more than I have.) He was the dominant guy in there, with a personality to match.

Wilt has a place of special honor in the history of basketball. He personally made the game progress, brought the big man from clod to controlling factor. If it weren't for Wilt, people wouldn't believe some things were possible—one hundred points by one man in a single game, a fifty-point-per-game average. He led the league in scoring seven times and was the only center ever to lead the NBA in assists.

Wilt was not perfect, however. He wasn't the best competitor; he didn't have the most savvy as far as how to make his team win. Russell seemed to get the more crucial rebounds, and though Wilt won all the scoring titles, Russell came away with eleven championship rings to Wilt's two. (Admittedly, Russell was playing with a superior team around him.) More importantly to me, Wilt was stationary and I was mobile, and I found out fast that he could not handle me on offense. I was eleven years younger than he was, and quicker to begin with. I found my first time down the floor against him that if I let him stand in the pivot and didn't move before I got the ball, he would destroy me. The next time down, however, I saw that if I got even a little movement, I could either fake him left and go up the other way with all the time in the world for a hook, or fake the hook, get him up in the air and drive the other way for a stuff.

Early on, he didn't play me tough, figuring, I guess, that I was just a kid and he could intimidate me with the backboard growl. When that didn't work he tried his usual bag of tricks that had worked on a generation of NBA centers. He'd go for my hands, but find himself a split-second too late, the shot was gone. He'd lay back and try for the in-flight rejection, but I'd get up too high and shoot it over him. That's when it got to be fun. You could see him getting frustrated as my shots kept falling. He would coil and make this tremendous jump, his arms extended like a crane, but I had gauged it, knew exactly how high his outstretched fingers could reach, and put the ball *just* over them. He'd grunt, and it would drop for two.

I worked on a special trajectory shot just for Wilt. I'd start right under the basket, then lean away a tiny bit, and put the ball at the top of the backboard. Wilt would go after it every time. He was determined. It would go past his reach, and I'd know from his body language he'd be thinking, "That's not going in, it's up too high." The ball would squeak against the top of the backboard above the rim and fall right through. Frustrated the hell out of him.

At first, when he would back off me I'd sink the hooks from eight to ten feet. Made it seem like he wasn't playing defense. He hated that. Then the coaches tried to have him muscle me, get all on my back. For a game or two he was reaching up under my armpit and knocking me off balance or batting the ball from my hands. The referees pretty much let this go, and it was fairly successful until I found a countermove. When he threw his arm under my armpit, I'd clamp down on it with my bicep and pin it to my side, then I'd go to the hoop with him. If he pulled it out, it was a foul. If he didn't, I would hold him there while I shot my shot. If he yanked it out while I was shooting, I got my three points. It made him crazy. Jerry West, at the time his teammate on the Lakers and later my coach, told me Wilt would yell at his teammates and complain that they weren't helping him guard me. Jerry says this was the only time he'd ever seen Wilt break down and ask for help.

I never took Wilt for granted, however. You can't ever say that Wilt didn't give his best, or that his best wasn't superlative. Wilt was one of the great centers to play the game, and the next three years we had a very fierce competition. In the years since, he has said I played extra hard against him, as if I had something to prove. He is right; I did play extra hard against him—if I hadn't, he would have dominated me, embarrassed me in front of the league, and undermined my whole game and career. I'd seen him play too long to think I could just go out there and play and not be overwhelmed. Wilt demanded my best, and I gave it to him with a vengeance. I was definitely aware that I was posting up with the man against whom all comparisons would be made. (In airplanes and subways, on movie lines or in the street all big black guys were asked not "Are you Bill Russell?" but, "Are you Wilt?") He was the standard, and because part of his game was intimidation, I had to work especially hard to overcome him.

I think, though, that Wilt feels that beyond playing hard I tried to embarrass him, somehow to build my reputation at his expense, pull him down from his greatness. Make him look small. Wilt's only identity was basketball; it was what made him a man, and he must have seen me—young, full of the future, capable in areas where he'd never been—as a very deep threat. And sometimes, on the court, I did embarrass him, though never intentionally. Toward the end of his career, when he was thirty-six and I was twenty-five, I had it any way I wanted. The Bucks would play his Lakers at the Forum, I'd be getting fifty points against him; he'd try the fadeaway, but I'd be there to block it, and he'd storm out to half-court. With his career, and to Wilt that pretty much meant his life, being closed in his face, he must have taken the defeat to heart. I definitely meant to beat him—I play to win at all times—but never to show him up. From Mr. Donohue on, my coaches had been emphatic about not hot-dogging, and I agreed fully. I try for the victory, and while I'm achieving that I don't try to make anybody feel bad. I'd looked bad for my first fourteen years, and while that might have led some people to inflict it on others, I knew what it felt like and wouldn't dish it out frivolously. Certainly not to a man as important to me as Wilt.

Wilt and I have had our falling outs, however. I started to lose my reverence for him when he supported Richard Nixon for president in 1968. Harlem was in an uproar; black people were struggling for basic human rights, and Wilt was throwing his weight behind an obvious crook who had no regard for us. I became very suspicious of him. As I began to form my own personal philosophy, I found that he and I disagreed on some basics. He was a high-profile, jet-set, trickle-down Republican, and I was a private, community-oriented, share-the-wealth Muslim. Some of the people who hung around him were not my kind of folks, and he wouldn't have had a lot to say to the people I took seriously. We had our own little generation gap going.

Our differences were made perfectly clear when he published his autobiography and in it declared that black women were inferior sexual partners, were generally socially inferior because they were unsophisticated. I knew that was bullshit, and though I should have assumed it would cause trouble, I said so in public. When it got back to him, Wilt was less than pleased; he apparently said that I didn't know what I was talking about. But I did know what I was talking about. I would never have criticized Wilt unless I felt extremely strong in my beliefs; he was not a guy to cross lightly, but I couldn't let that one ride. This was sexuality and capitulation and racial abandonment all in one piece. Wilt was a powerful black man, a symbol to a generation (I had looked up to him myself) and to an entire race; there was no way he should have denigrated his people, particularly in front of a white public guaranteed to seize upon this racist assertion as another means to divide and control us. Wilt the lover had gone too far. I stopped seeing him as a political crossover and began thinking of him as a traitor.

At that point we broke contact. Wilt has a large and very sensitive ego; you just don't put him down. He felt slighted or worse, as if I was repaying his kindness with betrayal. I hadn't betrayed him; I had disagreed with him. To Wilt that was the same thing. From then on he took every opportunity to downgrade my ability, put me on a secondary level in the history of basketball that he found so sustaining. For my part, although I remembered having fun with him and his being a charming and generous man, each slap made me angrier, then calloused. Let the guy talk; I knew what it was about.

It took almost ten years for Wilt and me finally to reestablish communications. We had both been hired to do a television airlines advertisement, and when we entered the studio there was a terrific tension, him and his entourage in one dressing room, me and my friends in another. When we came out, there was an awkward silence. He broke it. "Nice suit," he told me, fingering my lapels. We giants have a hard time getting fitted—forget about buying anything except T-shirts off the rack—and clothing turned out to be a mutual concern. I gave him the name of my tailor, and we started talking.

Turns out he thought I didn't like him. I always liked him, just hated his politics. Thought he was a nice guy. Still do. We shook hands, started joking, got a little loose. The ad, him sitting in his seat, me dwarfing him by three-quarters of an inch, showed our restrained ease with each other. I left the shooting that evening exhilarated and relieved, as if we'd both been battling for a rebound that had never come down.

I'm still glad I kicked his ass on the court, and I would have been perfectly pleased to have gone up against him in his prime. In 1971, my second year in the league and my first against him, he was still playing great. We beat the Lakers in the Western Conference Finals, but after the last game, in Milwaukee, the fans gave him a standing ovation for his performance.

EARVIN "MAGIC" JOHNSON

My Life

When I showed up at my first Laker training camp in Palm Springs, my teammates thought I was crazy. Although the formal start of the season was still a few weeks off, I jumped right in with my usual exuberance. Some guys don't go into overdrive until the playoffs, so I stuck out like a sore thumb.

I could see right off that my intensity was very different from the cool, laid-back style of the NBA. Most professional athletes try to conserve their energy, especially before the season begins. My teammates were shocked to see me diving for loose balls in a meaningless practice, dishing out high fives, and smacking everybody's hand after a little 10-point scrimmage.

"Earvin's running around like a young buck," said Norm Nixon. The name stuck, and from then on my teammates and coaches always called me Buck.

I could see that some of the older guys were rolling their eyes and waiting for me to settle down. They had seen rookies come and go, and I'm sure they expected that my high spirits would fizzle out within a few weeks. But then the Lakers of the late 1970s were not exactly famous for their sparkle and personality. It took a lot to get this team excited. As columnist Jim Murray put it in the *Los Angeles Times* a few weeks before the season began, "I've seen happier faces on guys carrying a casket."

We opened the season in San Diego against the Clippers. Naturally, I maintained my perfect record of screwing up in my first game with every new team. This time, however, I outdid myself: I actually managed to make a fool of myself even before the opening tap.

As the hot new rookie, I was given the honor of leading the Lakers onto the court for the pregame warm-ups. I was supposed to take the ball, dribble to the basket, and dunk it for the first hoop of the new season. That wasn't hard, but I was still nervous. After all, this was the first game of my professional career. The last official game I had played in was back in the spring, against Indiana State. That was only seven months earlier, but it already seemed like another era.

When it was time for the Lakers to come out on the floor, I took the ball, drove to the basket, and—boom!—fell flat on my face. I had tripped over my warm-up pants. I was so anxious that I hadn't bothered to tie them right. They slipped down just enough to send me sprawling onto the floor. My teammates found this absolutely hysterical, and so did the crowd. As I pulled myself up, I did my best to put on a smile. That's because CBS had picked *this* game to kick off their weekly national broadcasts.

Things could only improve from there. At least, that's what I thought. But I played so badly during the first quarter that Coach Jack McKinney took me out after about nine minutes. He brought me back later on, and this time I held my own, and was still on the floor during the final minutes of a very close game.

With eight seconds left, and the Lakers down by one, McKinney called a time-out to set up our final shot. There was only one conceivable play in that situation, and everybody in the building knew exactly what it was: get it to the big guy, and let him shoot. And that's what we did. When Kareem caught the ball at the free-throw line, he put up a long, elegant skyhook that won the game at the buzzer.

As he was running off the court, I was so excited that I leaped into his arms and hugged him. But when I looked up at his face, he clearly wasn't sharing my excitement. What's the big deal? he seemed to be saying. Hitting shots like that is my *job*.

When we got to the locker room he said, "Calm down, Earvin—we've got eighty-one more games to play." But I wasn't about to change my style. I'd always played with passion, and eventually my teammates would get used to it.

Later that same week, in Seattle, I experienced another emotion on the court: fear. Early in the third period, when I was going up for a rebound, somehow my feet got tangled up in Jack Sikma's legs, and I came crashing down to the floor. My knee hurt like hell, and I had to be helped off the court. In the locker room, an orthopedic surgeon gave me a quick exam. "I'm only guessing," he said, "and you'll definitely need X rays. But it doesn't look good. My guess is torn ligaments."

I was devastated. This was only our third game of the season, and if I needed knee surgery I would be out for months—possibly the whole season. It's a good thing I wasn't listening to the radio. When I went down, Chick Hearn, the Lakers' longtime play-by-play announcer, told his listeners that he hoped this wouldn't mean the end of Magic Johnson's career.

Early the next morning, Jerry Buss sent a private jet to fly me back to L.A. for X rays and medical attention. After a long, careful exam, the doctor said, "I'm sorry, Earvin, but we might have to amputate your leg."

I looked up, and he was grinning. It turned out to be nothing worse than a bad sprain. A week later I was back in action.

What happened in Seattle was a real wake-up call about how physical the pro game really was. I had heard about that, but it took some getting used to. And for me there was an even bigger problem—the NBA's intense, one-on-one type of defense. In college we played a zone, and I didn't have much experience guarding individual players. Now, suddenly, I was expected to stop some of the most explosive scorers in the league.

It wasn't fun. In that first game against San Diego, World Free scored something like 40 points against me. The next night, Paul Westphal did the same. In the Seattle game it was Dennis Johnson who killed me. Then came George Gervin. Before long I started to wonder, Can I guard *anyone* in this league? My teammates were probably wondering the same thing.

Coach McKinney helped me understand that my biggest mistake was trying to play every guy the same way. World Free was a one-on-one player who didn't use any picks. He could shoot the ball from anywhere, and he often did. I tried to play Paul Westphal the same way, but Westphal used picks constantly. He never stopped moving without the ball. I had to learn how to fight through a pick and stay with my man, which wasn't easy. In college I had always held my own on defense, but the pro game was a real challenge.

To some extent this problem took care of itself. In that respect it's a little like baseball, where a new pitcher generally has the advantage until the hitters get used to his motion. My first game against just about every team in the NBA was a real struggle. And for the first time in my career I was getting into foul trouble.

A lot of these fouls were called simply because I was new in the league. The officials will never admit it, but every rookie has to pay his dues, just as every star gets a few breaks. When you've got a veteran who makes great moves and excites the fans, the refs go easy on him. After all, nobody pays good money to see Michael Jordan or Larry Bird foul out. By my third year in the league I was making some of the same defensive plays that had gotten me in trouble when I was a rookie, but now I was getting away with them.

I improved a lot just from practicing with my teammates. And the more I played, the better I became. I learned how to get around a pick, how to shade a guy toward his weaker hand, how to get up on a man who shot the jumper well, and how to guard somebody who was quicker than I was.

The guy who really taught me about defense was my teammate Michael Cooper. Coop was my first real friend on the team, and over the years I was closer to him than to anyone else on the Lakers. Although he had arrived a year before me, he tore a ligament in his knee a few weeks before that season started and played in only three games all year, so when I met him he was essentially a second-year rookie.

We became friends during training camp, when Coop was fighting to make the team. I loved his aggressive style and the way he didn't back down from anyone. He reminded me a little of Reggie Chastine, and I quickly became his personal cheerleader. Michael not only made the team; he became our all-important sixth man, the first guy off the bench.

"How do I get more playing time?" he asked Coach McKinney.

"Defense is the ticket," McKinney replied.

"Okay," said Coop. "Then that's how I'm going to make my living."

And he did. The only other guy in the league who was as good on defense was Dennis Johnson, who drove us crazy every time we played against him.

Coop taught me that the key to good defense was mental preparation. After a game at the Forum, he would drive home and watch the videotape—*twice*. Before the game, he'd think about the last time we played that team, and how he could be even more effective against them. He would even think about the officials, because some referees will let you play tighter than others. But mostly he'd focus on the man he was guarding, who was usually the other team's high scorer. Night after night, Coop would come off the bench and shut that guy down.

He was constantly working to make himself better—and not just on defense, either. Coop came into the league without a strong outside shot, and in his early years our opponents used to leave him wide open. He worked his butt off in practice, and he later made himself into one of the best three-point shooters in the league. He still holds the record for the most three-pointers during the playoffs.

Coop could also drive to the hoop. We had a play where I would throw it high above the basket and Coop would slam it down for two points. A classic alley-oop. Only we called it a Coop-a-Loop.

Michael had always been a worker. Back in high school, he built a seven-foot defender out of wood and dragged him around the court so he could pretend somebody was always guarding him.

One reason I had so much success in the NBA was that Coop guarded me in every practice and gave me no slack. The next night, when we played in an actual game, I felt like a prisoner who had just been let out of jail. Nothing an opponent could do could be worse than the moves Coop had already put on me during practice.

The two of us played our hearts out in those scrimmage games, and Coop was all over me. He would pressure me full-court, pushing me and elbowing me all morning. Michael was so skinny and wiry that he could really hurt you. When I went home to take a nap, I'd be feeling Coop all afternoon.

That was another thing I had to get used to as a rookie—taking an afternoon nap whenever I could. It's impossible to fall asleep right after a game, so you end up having a lot of late nights. But there are always morning practices, or early wake-up calls so you can get on the bus to the airport and fly on to the next city. The only way to survive in the NBA is to learn to sleep in the afternoons.

And on airplanes. It took me most of my rookie year to get that right. I finally found a system: I would take a window seat and get myself two pillows. I've been flying that way ever since.

One of the hardest things for a rookie to get used to is the incredibly long and draining NBA season. The college schedule is only 30 games long, but in the pros you play 82—and that's not counting the preseason exhibition games and the playoffs. These days, a team can end up playing as many as 26 postseason games, and every single one is intense and exhausting. The travel and the schedule take their toll on you, and by the middle of January most rookies are ready for their summer vacation. It's depressing when you've already played the equivalent of a full college season and you're not even halfway to the playoffs.

In college there are games where you can coast, but the NBA is a constant battle. Even when your opponent is an expansion team, you're up against men who are playing basketball for their livelihood and are trying to keep their jobs. It's not just a question of talent; these guys are hungry.

It's a good thing I don't mind getting knocked down. I took a real beating that first year, but I played hard, and missed only five games due to injuries. I loved being a member of the Lakers, and I couldn't wait for the games. We were supposed to show up at six o'clock for a seven-thirty home game, but I was always in the locker room by five.

Some rookies have trouble adjusting to the pro game, and I can understand why. You come out of college as a big star, and suddenly you're at the bottom again. You have to learn to be humble. In addition to doing little chores for the veterans, the rookies help carry the equipment on the road, such as the ball bag and the video machine. Some guys mind that, but I didn't. To me it was one more way of being accepted.

The Lakers won 60 games during my rookie season, and you can't ask for more than that. Okay, maybe a *little* more. The Celtics, with brand-new-you-know-who, won 61 games, but who's counting? Besides, Boston lost to Philadelphia in the Eastern Conference Finals. We won our playoff series against Phoenix and Seattle, so it was the Lakers and the 76ers in the championship series.

If my first few minutes as a Laker were a total disaster, the last game of my rookie year more than made up for it. In fact, that final playoff game against Philadelphia was probably the best performance of my life. It was certainly the most dramatic.

Kareem was usually at his best during the playoffs, and he absolutely dominated that series. In the first five games he averaged over 33 points, and his performance in Game Five was just incredible. Both teams had won twice. But during the fifth game, Kareem was forced to leave with a badly sprained ankle. A few minutes later he made a dramatic return, and in the final quarter he scored 14 points to lead us to victory. That gave us a 3–2 lead in the series. Game Six was set for Friday in Philadelphia. The seventh game, if necessary, would be played on Sunday in the Forum.

We were about to board the flight to Philadelphia when Jack Curran told us that Cap, as Kareem was known, would not be making the trip. His ankle was in bad shape, and he couldn't play on it. The hope was that if Cap stayed home and rested, he'd be able to come back for Game Seven. As Curran was handing out the boarding passes, Coach Paul Westhead, who had taken over the team early in the season after McKinney was injured, took me aside. "We'll need you to take over at center," he said.

"I'd love to," I said. "I played some center in high school."

Coach didn't ask me to take over Kareem's leadership role, but that came naturally. I was still a rookie, but I no longer felt like one.

On the plane, I went straight to Kareem's regular spot—the first aisle seat on the left, the bulkhead seat with the most leg room. Then I turned around and announced to the team, "Never fear, E.J. is here." Everybody laughed, but I wasn't kidding.

As soon as we landed in Philadelphia, reporters started asking us about Game Seven in Los Angeles. Without Kareem, nobody thought we had a prayer in Game Six.

That night, we had a team meeting at the hotel. After watching the videotape of Game Five, we all spoke. "I'll be guarding Dawkins," said Jim Chones, our backup center. "I intend to shut down the middle, and you guys can count on it."

That was quite a promise. Darryl Dawkins, who was known as Chocolate Thunder, was one of the most forceful and electrifying players in all of basketball. He was famous for his explosive dunks, and there were so many in his repertoire that he actually gave them names: Earthquake Shaker, Go-Rilla, In Your Face Disgrace, and Rim Wrecker. And then, of course, there was the dunk that he modestly referred to as Chocolate Thunder Flying, Robinzine Crying, Teeth Shaking, Glass Breaking, Rump Roasting, Bun Toasting, Wham Bam, Glass Breaker I Am Jam.

If Jim could do the job on Dawkins, that would go a long way.

"Philadelphia thinks this game is already over," I told my teammates. "But we can use that to our advantage. We can beat them because they'll have a problem matching up against us. But only if we go into this game believing we can win."

Philadelphia was used to trying to deal with Kareem in the low post. But now we had Michael Cooper coming in, which gave us a smaller, faster lineup. Philadelphia had a big size advantage, but we were fast enough to run right by them.

Up until game time, half the population of Pennsylvania still expected Kareem to show up. People were sure that all the talk of his ankle injury was just an elaborate deception. They thought the big guy would suddenly appear at the last minute to drive them crazy.

On the day of the game, there were Kareem sightings all over Philadelphia. A taxi driver told a radio station that he had picked up Kareem at the airport. A woman reported that she had seen him at the Philadelphia Museum of Art. Although Kareem wasn't at our morning shootaround, people still believed he would make a dramatic eleventh-hour appearance at the Spectrum. We didn't invent these stories, but once they started flying we did nothing to discourage them, either. Let people wonder.

The night before the game, I called my dad in Lansing. "Kareem can't be there," I told him. "They've asked me to play center."

"You'll do great," he said. "All you have to do is go back to the kind of game you played in high school." Back at Everett I had been a scorer, shooting the ball from all over the court. It was hard to believe, but that was only three years before.

On Friday night, when I walked out to center court for the opening tap, I was grinning from ear to ear. I had a good feeling about this game. Maybe it was because everybody expected a blowout, and we had nothing to lose. Before the game, people kept saying, "See you in L.A. for Game Seven." They weren't even trying to psyche us out; it just seemed obvious to them.

I smiled when I heard that. But in the back of my mind I was thinking, No way. It's all over tonight.

I felt like we had a terrific joke up our sleeves that the 76ers weren't prepared for. We were going to whip that ball around so fast that they wouldn't know what hit them. Without Kareem, we couldn't afford to play the half-court game and think defensively. Tonight we had to play full-court and take our chances.

I lost the opening tap against Caldwell Jones, but that was no surprise. He was six-eleven, with incredibly long arms. I had already decided that I'd just jump up and down at the start and then go to work on the rest of my game.

We came out smoking and jumped out to a 7–0 lead. Then Philadelphia pulled ahead by eight in the second quarter. At the half, the game was tied, 60–60. Given the expectations, that was already a big psychological edge. I was shooting the lights out, and Philadelphia just couldn't shut me down. They didn't know whether to put a big man on me or a smaller guard, but nothing they tried seemed to work. Caldwell Jones was guarding me, and it seemed like every time he gave me the outside shot, I managed to hit it.

But it wasn't just me. Kareem's absence confused the 76ers, and they never did find the right matchups to cover our guys.

All season long we had dominated teams in the third quarter, and this game was no exception. Before the 76ers even knew what hit them, we ran off 14 straight points. Finally Bobby Jones tapped one in to break the spell. But by then we were just carving up Philadelphia, and getting most of the rebounds. We took their fans right out of the game. Philadelphia knew they were in trouble when their own crowd started booing them after they missed seven shots in a row.

When the third quarter ended we were up by 10. Now we could taste the title.

We knew that Philadelphia would attempt a comeback in the fourth quarter, and of course they did. But each time they came close, we stepped on the gas and pulled away. Three times they closed to within two points. But despite the heroic efforts of Julius Erving, we kept gunning the engine and leaving them behind. The final score was 123–107. For the first time since 1972, the Los Angeles Lakers were world champions.

I had the game of my life. I played forty-seven minutes out of forty-eight, and finished with 42 points, 15 rebounds, and seven assists. I shot 14 free throws and hit every one. "He has played center, forward, and guard in this game," said Brent Musburger on CBS. "He'll pack the uniforms afterward."

I did a lot, but I didn't do it alone. Almost nobody noticed that Jamaal Wilkes finished with 37 points, the most he had scored since high school, and 10 more than Dr. J. Cooper, off the bench, hit for 16. Norm Nixon finished with only four points, but he had nine assists, a game high.

Jim Chones had 10 rebounds, and he kept his promise by holding Darryl Dawkins to 14 points and four rebounds. Dawkins saved his energy for Cooper. In the fourth quarter, he knocked Coop down so hard that we practically had to scrape him off the floor.

"Michael, do you know where you are?" asked the trainer.

"I'm at home, right?" Cooper replied.

Not exactly, Coop. Somehow, Michael stumbled over to the free-throw line and hit both shots.

Usually the winning team's locker room is a wild scene with champagne flying. But ours was strangely quiet, and even I was reserved. We were exhausted. With two minutes left in the game, I had called a time-out just to catch my breath. It was the first time in my career that I had ever done something like that.

We were also stunned. Nobody had expected us to win that game. We knew we could do it, and we were up for the game. But to actually have it happen without the greatest player in the league—that was hard to believe.

But most of all, it just didn't feel right to celebrate this victory without

Kareem. Yes, we had won this game without him, but he was still our leader, and we all knew that he was the one who had carried us to this point.

I knew that he was watching us on TV. "Big Fella," I told him during a postgame interview, "I did it for you."

Kareem had watched the game at home with his sprained left ankle propped up on a coffee table. It was so frustrating for him not to be with us that he had to turn off the sound and chew on a pillow. When Wilkes dunked the ball to give us a 12-point lead in the fourth quarter, Kareem limped out to the backyard and started yelling.

As soon as we got back to the hotel I collapsed on the bed and called my dad. They had let him leave work early to watch the game, which was on tape delay in most of the country. He already knew the outcome, but when I reached him he was still watching it.

When Jim Dart heard that the game wouldn't be shown live, he flew to Philadelphia, took a cab to our hotel, and demanded that I get him a ticket. Jim came into our locker room after the game, and it was great to see him at that moment.

But it's pretty amazing, when you think about it, that as recently as 1980 the Lakers could win the world championship and most fans couldn't see it until the wee hours of the morning. And these were two famous teams with plenty of media appeal! You would have thought that a matchup of Dr. J. and his boys against Kareem's team would have rated a prime-time audience. Could anyone imagine a World Series game on tape delay at 11:30 P.M.? The NBA has come a long way, baby.

I've probably watched that tape a thousand times, and it's always in one or another of the VCRs in my house. Normally, I'm very critical of my own play. But I don't have too many complaints about that incredible night in Philadelphia, when, as Pete Vescey cleverly phrased it, I played center "in Lew of Alcindor."

Lionel Hollins, a guard for Philadelphia, paid me the ultimate compliment after the game. "Magic," he said, shaking his head. "He is his name."

SATCHEL PAIGE

Rules for Staying Young

1. Avoid fried meats, which angry up the blood.

2. If your stomach disputes you, lie down and pacify it with cool thoughts.

3. Keep the juices flowing by jangling around gently as you move.

4. Go very light on the vices, such as carrying on in society—the social ramble ain't restful.

5. Avoid running at all times.

6. And don't look back, something might be gaining on you.

BE-BOP, DOO-WOP, HIP-HOP

EDWARD KENNEDY "DUKE" ELLINGTON

Music Is My Mistress

I am a minstrel, a pedestrian minstrel, a primitive pedestrian minstrel. Sometimes I imagine I paint, with water colors or oils, a crystal-clear lake in the sky reflecting the shadows of invisible trees upside-down beneath sun-kissed, cotton-candy snow. On the fringe, clouds so foamy white—tranquil on top, a raging storm inside . . . "I'll write it," I think, before returning to that half sleep as the plane roars on to Atlanta . . . or is it Atlantis? Plans, plans, the most impossible of enormous plans, pastel or opaque. Sometimes I'll write a play or plot, drama or comedy, revue or re-do. And sometimes I mold a figure, graceful or grotesque, out of whatever material happens to pop into my mind. If it's a chunk of rock or steel, or a trunk of a tree, or maybe just the single petal of a rose, it must be fashioned to the raw, or the ore, according to its dimensions and shape, large or small.

Steel on steel, thousands of miles of steel or tracks, with thousands of round, steel wheels—what a happy marriage! The rhythm of the motion, thirty-nine hours from Chicago to Los Angeles—what a marvel of masculinity, thirty-nine hours, power-stroking all the way. He gave her the high ball in the Loop, stopped in Englewood, and that's all she wrote, grinding up to ninety miles per hour, so hot the steam was bursting out everywhere. She had fine lubrication. You could hear her for miles, whistle-screaming, "Yes, daddy, I'm coming, daddy!" Don't pull that throttle out until you pull into Glendale . . . driving shaft pumping a steady beat . . . long and round, heavin' and strokin' . . . puffin' and smokin' . . . and shovelin' and stokin'. He stopped, let off a little steam. She, out of breath, panted, "Wash up, ready for that red-carpet reception." He got off, glanced over his shoulder at her as she backed out of Union station, out into the yard, with unraised eyelashes, like the dignified lady she was, she who, between departure and arrival, had given her all to a union laborer, opened her throttle wide, and allowed him his every wish. Truly, a tremendous romance.

Should I write this music with the passion they pumped over the track, or should I maybe start with the wheel, the molten steel, or with those burly black arms behind the thrust that drove the spikes into the railroad ties? There's a grunt with every thrust from the owner of those arms, as though he were rehearsing for the cool of the evening, when he and his woman would be together, when he would drag her out of that hot kitchen. Wringing wet with perspiration, she blushes, but she's been wishing for him all day, to come home and pull her out of that hot place. Now she's hotter than the kitchen stove, sexually clobbering this cat, until he thinks she's putting everything on him but . . . do I have to say, "the kitchen stove"?

Raw or ore, gold or gook, or indigo, filigree, or feathers, carve a breach as deep as desire demands, but don't destroy the maidenhead. Blow Cootie up to the ceiling, make Cat go tooting through the roof, jam Sam into a Charleston beat, let Paul go-go, running through the lattice work of brass cacophony, while Jimmy weaves delicate lacework around the edges. Give Harry that "molto profondo," so that Lawrence will cry and wail in the wake of the *après-coup*. Stomp down, those symmetrical after-beats, baby, so that Rab can smelt the melody to smoldering, and over the hush let's hear the broads in the back row whisper, "Tell the story, daddy." Russell's got the kind of wood that Barney had, when Whetsol was playing the unduplicatably dulcet. You can't use Charley Plug or Tricky—one just doesn't, any more. Bubber said it, and he was right! *It don't mean a thing if it ain't got that swing*. Mr. Braud's not going to back away from that mike. Like the great Greer used to tell Freddie Guy—"Take it down from the top, pop, and don't stop for the bop . . .

"Ole Duke used to have a pretty good left hand after he hear James P., The Lion, and Fats," Greer continues, "but then he heard Fletcher, Redman, Whiteman, and Goldkette, and got horn fever . . . *horns, horns, and more horns* . . . Coppin' out and talkin' 'bout 'the band is my instrument.' What would Doc Perry and Lester Dishman say to that? From six pieces to eleven, twelve, fourteen, and fifteen. Then he got up and conducted a symphony of a hundred and ten pieces. After that there was that record album, *The Symphonic Ellington*, with five hundred of the greatest musicians in Europe.

"Will Marion Cook and Henry Grant—they would be pleased. They used to tell Duke to go to the conservatory. Black Bowie used to call him the *phoney duke*, back in Frank Holliday's poolroom. I remember when he was just a yearling, the jive relief piano-plunker. Bill Jones used to be drummin', and he'd catch him out there in those three-four, five-four switches, and scare him stiff. But he'd hang on, and as I said he had a pretty good left hand, and he'd hold the solid deuce till Bill let him off the hook. They raised him with discipline and encouragement music-wise. Those East Coast cats were like that. They had the greatest respect for the book. 'If the man didn't want it played that way,' they said, 'he wouldn't have written it that way.' And so Duke listened, and they laid down the laws, and he listened some more, and I guess that's why he calls himself the world's greatest listener today."

Yes, I am the world's greatest listener. Here I am, fifty years later, still getting cats out of bed to come to work, so that I can listen to them and so that they can make a living for their own families. This, however, does not alter the perspective of the pedestrian peddler, who sometimes imagines that he takes a pair of scissors, and some paper or cardboard, and cuts out shapes of paper dolls. He takes them out on the corner and displays them, bending them and plucking them so that they will make a noise. And of course, the noise is the main thing, because the people hear the noise, and when they like it they say, "Ah, I'll take it . . ." So I let them have it—the noise, that is. And I collect my dolls and go out the next day, to see if I can make other people like the noise. Practically every day I go to a different corner, and sometimes for a change I take my scissors and cut out paper flowers. I wrap them neatly, put them in my pushcart, and take them to the corner. I stand there, plucking them with my third finger to make a noise, hoping it carries an attractive vibration to a passer-by's ear. When he shows interest, I'll do an encore, and when he asks, "How much?", I say: "If you like this little noise, just something in the cup. Don't hurt yourself, Whatever you can stand, and the sound is yours. I can't let you have the flowers. I need them to make more noise. I like to listen myself, you know. I think maybe there's nothing quite like planning and designing at night, and coming out and listening to it next day. I'm impetuous, you know."

There is hardly any money interest in the realm of art, and music will be here when money is gone. After people have destroyed all people everywhere, I see heaping mounds of money strewn over the earth, floating on and sinking into the sea. The animals and fish, who have no use for money, are kicking it out of the way and splattering it with dung. Money and stink, the stink of dung, the stink of money, so foul that in order for the flowers to get a breath of fresh air, the winds will come together and whip the sea into a rage, and blow across the land. Then the green leaves of trees, and grass, will give up their chlorophyll, so that the sea, the wind, the beasts, and the birds will play and sing Nature's old, sweet melody and rhythm. But since you are people, you will not, unfortunately, be here to hear it.

Money is becoming too important. So far as the hazards of the big band are concerned, I give the musicians the money and I get the kicks. Billy Strayhorn said we were exponents of the aural art. Ours is the responsibility of bringing to the listener and would-be listener—as to those unwilling to be listeners—some agreeable vibration that tickles the fancy of the eardrum. Of course, the connoisseur has a much better appreciation of duet and counter-melody than the average would-be listener. Some people think modern means unattractive, whether it's 1905 or 1975, but consonance is in the imagination of the hearer. Maybe a sound gives him a nostalgic nudge, back to the one moment to which he has always wanted to return.

Roaming through the jungle, the jungle of "oohs" and "ahs," searching for a more agreeable noise, I live a life of primitivity with the mind of a child and an unquenchable thirst for sharps and flats. The more consonant, the more appetizing and delectable they are. Cacophony is hard to swallow. Living in a cave, I am almost a hermit, but there is a difference, for I have a mistress. Lovers have come and gone, but only my mistress stays. She is beautiful and gentle. She waits on me hand and foot. She is a swinger. She has grace. To hear her speak, you can't believe your ears. She is ten thousand years old. She is as modern as tomorrow, a brand-new woman everyday, and as endless as time mathematics. Living with her is a labyrinth of ramifications. I look forward to her every gesture.

Music is my mistress, and she plays second fiddle to no one.

SIDNEY BECHET

Treat It Gentle

Well, I put in my eleven months, and when I got out I wasn't allowed to stay in France; so I went back to Germany and played at Haus Vaterland in Berlin where I'd been before, back to that Wild West Bar. While I was there Noble Sissle, who was touring America with his orchestra, wired me to come and join up with his band. And that's how I came back to America. It was late 1929, and that stock market crash had happened by then.

I went back to America and I played with Noble Sissle, but I didn't stay long. We came over to Europe in the summer. Tommy Ladnier, he'd been with Sissle too, and we quit together, in Paris. So I went back to Berlin to Haus Vaterland for three months in the summer of 1931. But I was back with Noble in America during that winter and we played various theatres in New York until I had a disagreement over a salary question. Then, a bit later, in 1932, Tommy and I had a band together. We had our own eight-piece outfit, opening at the Saratoga Club in Harlem. We were only there a few weeks, and then we played three gigs a week in Jersey City and some in White Plains, New York. But in the fall we took a six-piece band into the Savoy in New York City. That was really *the* band. That was the best band. The people liked the band;

it was small and we were all musicians that had a feeling and we understood what Jazz music really meant. We didn't have to make any arrangements or anything like that; we just followed the old school, and just recorded, and we were feeling just that way. We had a fellow named Wilson Myers with us then. He'd played a lot of instruments in his time—clarinet, trombone, drums, banjo and guitar. But around the time Tommy and I were getting that band together, he'd started in to play bass, and he played with us and he certainly played fine bass.

It didn't last too long—we played through till the spring—but while it was still on we had one recording date. We played six numbers that day—*Sweetie Dear, I've Found a New Baby*, Scott Joplin's great number *Maple Leaf Rag*, and the last we cut was *Shag*. I guess by the time we got around to that one we were feeling pretty good because we felt we'd played good and had had a good day; anyway we made it a fine finish up. We were very happy and it was the last piece. That was a fine band, and besides Tommy and me there was Teddy Nixon on trombone, Hank Duncan on piano, Wilson Myers on bass like I said, and Morris Moreland drums.

After my band with Ladnier broke up, I played for a while with Lorenzo Tio at the Nest. Of course, I'd known Lorenzo since I was in short pants. He was a great musicianer, and was a good bit older than me. Well, he came up to New York, and I fixed a number of gigs for him. Then when Tommy and I had finished at the Savoy I had this chance to take a band into the Nest with Lorenzo, and I went because there was a chance to build a band a little bit bigger than the band I'd had at the Savoy. And it was pretty good. Roy Eldridge, he used to come there every day. He was working at Small's, but he came every night to play with the band because we got to working rather late—around five, six, seven in the morning. It was Roy's pleasure to come and sit in with the band. There was a trombonist, too, by the name of Harry White, he played with Cab Calloway's orchestra and the Blue Rhythm Boys; and he worked, too, with Roy at Small's Cabaret. And he also used to come, and he had a lot of fun with us. Well, we stayed there a long while, I guess for about five or six months. That wasn't the last time that he played in New York, because after we had finished our engagement we parted, and he went on and played some place else; then he disappeared. I saw him one time more. I got word from his wife she wanted to see me, you know, and when I went to see her she said that Lorenzo was very ill, and she tried to prove that I owed him some money or something. But I didn't owe him a thing; he was paid just like anyone else. And after that I saw him and related to him what his wife had told me; but he knew—she was just thinking things. I guess she was worried because he was so ill, and she had to do everything she could think of. And that was the last time that I saw Lorenzo, because it wasn't long after that he died right there in New York.

Well, by then things was pretty bad, and for a while there Tommy and I had a tailor shop there up around St. Nicholas Avenue. It wasn't any shop for making suits—just a pressing and repairing place and we called it the Southern Tailor Shop. Tommy, he used to help out shining shoes. We were pretty easy going with the money part of that business, but we got along. A lot of musicianers who didn't have jobs and some who did used to come around and we'd have our sessions right there in back of the shop. That was a good time. It was real enjoyable.

Then around 1934 Noble wired for me to come join the band again, and I went. I tried to talk Tommy into coming with me, but it wasn't what he wanted to do. He had some reason for not wanting to go. He wasn't saying what it was, but I got to see pretty clear that he wouldn't, so I said no more.

I went on out and joined Noble at the French Casino, in Chicago. And then we toured all over for about four years in all. I didn't know the whole story at the time, but it wasn't long before I got the idea, why Tommy wouldn't come with me. Noble hadn't been special about having me, but the man who had the contract for where Noble was working came up to him at one time when I wasn't with the band and said, 'Where's Bechet? This isn't the band I made a contract for. Where's Sidney?' So Noble had to send for me. He was strange in some ways. It wasn't just about me, but about music. He liked music right enough, but that wasn't all of it. Sometimes it was like he was more interested in having his own band than he was in the music.

Well, right away there was trouble for me. It was no time at all before I notice there's this feeling in the reed section; it's feuding with me. One fellow who was there—he played tenor sax—he went up to Noble and said, 'How come Sidney's here?' He didn't want me playing with the band. Noble told him: 'Look, that's all right. You wouldn't be here today if Sidney wasn't playing; you wouldn't have a job.' Then he explained how the man wouldn't give them the contract unless I join up.

But the feuding still went on. That fellow had friends who all the time were fixing numbers that I was supposed to have, giving me hard feature numbers with hardly nothing to them, numbers a man couldn't do nothing with. The reed section there was James Tolliver, Harvey Boone, Ramon Usera and myself. But that Usera and Boone, instead of concentrating on how the music should be played, they were all het up in this jealousy business. But I wouldn't do things that way: I'd seen too much of that. Even after they give me those bad numbers, even when they'd picked out my feature pieces without any regard for my taste about how they should be, I still refused to fight them back. I took what numbers I got and toned them up the best I could. But it's a hell of a thing. There's just no sense to a thing like that: it don't help anyone at all and it just raises hell with the music until there's no enjoyment left to it.

But that James Tolliver, he was my friend; but I didn't know that until later. This group—Usera, Boone, and some others—they got up a meeting in Noble's office and Usera began by complaining how he didn't want to handle my numbers. He was opposed to working on features for me. Usera was doing the arranging for the band and that gave him a power: it got to the point where he'd almost got me out of the band. But just at that time James Tolliver spoke up. 'If you won't arrange for Sidney,' he said, 'I will.' And that's the way it turned out, Tolliver was trying to get away from the bad support and all those off-runs they've been giving me. He really proved to be a friend. The way things were, he'd still have to go back to them sometimes, but now I could begin to feel that the music had a chance of going some.

But the way it worked out, even then it wasn't much good. You can stand a whole lot of double talk for something you really care about, but after a while you can see it spoiled too easy and it isn't worth that. I'd had enough of all that bad feeling; I wasn't looking for any more of that.

There was another thing, too, about being with the band. Touring like that, you're always in a new town. You don't know what place to stay at so you pick the nicest. It comes time to eat—you don't know any of the restaurants so you walk down the street and you pick out the cleanest place you see. That way you're sure you won't be finding last week's menu on your plate. Well, it doesn't take long when you're doing that way—the first thing you know, all your money's gone. And after a little of that, you get fed up. It's just no fun having to scramble all the time and then seeing that nickle disappear and thinking to yourself, 'Had I kept that nickle and the one before it I'd have had me a dime now.' The hell with that. Noble was making the money, and as far as I was concerned he could keep it. It was bad enough just feuding with those others in the band. I quit.

I went back to New York then and it wasn't long before Noble brought the band there too. And just about that time Billy Rose came up to Noble and wanted him to audition for something that Billy was getting together. Right off Noble came after me, begging and pleading. He wanted me to audition with them and after a while I said I would. So we all auditioned, but I was still not with the band and when they went back after the audition, which had been successful and all, Billy said, 'Where's Sidney?'

'He's out of town,' Noble told him.

Well, I wasn't out of town and Noble knew it. What I'd told him was that I wanted more money if I was to play. But he wouldn't say that; there wasn't anything at all said about me in a money way. It was Perry Bradford who told me. He dropped by the hotel where I was staying; he was on his way to visit someone else there and he ran right into me. He was surprised. 'What are you doing here?' he told me. 'I thought you left town.' And that's how it all came out that he told me about the conversation between Noble and Billy in Billy's office.

But a thing like that, that's nothing I take a big accounting of. There's some who are your friends and there's some who are only for themselves and I guess there will always be some of both in this world. What I figure is I got nothing to complain of; I haven't had it bad. I guess I've always been a rolling stone, but there was always somewheres I could stop. There was always something else I could be doing. I told you about that time Tommy Ladnier and I had that tailor shop: that was just one thing, but there'd always be something I could pick up if I had to.

What you really miss, being a rolling stone, it's the things most other people, they have natural. You're always looking for a home somewhere. You're always concerned that you're losing what's the important thing. But that's not the whole story. There's still a thing as big as all of it put together, and that's the music. Having that inside me, I got a lot. No matter what else is happening, the music is the thing to hold to, and it's all mine in a way of speaking: I can be off alone somewheres, I can be sitting here and I can be sad and lonely, but all I got to do is think of some melody and I'm feeling better right off. It's like you could slice up a piece of apple and then you put in a piece of pear, but it doesn't matter about the pear: you still know there's the apple there; you can taste it. That's the way it is with me. I can mix in anything I've got in my life and I've still got the music. I can be damn' near broke but I'm still like the song says—'I'm as rich as Rockefeller in a way of speaking'. There's some people, they're able to be happy watching their money pile up. Well, that's all a matter of your trade, you can say—it's a way you can take your life, if you wish to. What I've wished for, I got. It's the music. There's always those melodies inside me. I can pick and choose them, hear them in my own mind, or put them together—pieces of them—the way Omar used to do when he was making up his feeling, trying to find out what his feeling was. If I've got a trouble, I can answer it right out of my own head. . . . But people are always out to make their judgment about the music from the wrong things. Too many of them, they're more interested in how a musicianer carries on *after* the music. Personality stuff, that's how it is. It's still the way it was back there in New Orleans with Buddy Bolden. People there, they loved that music. And *still* it seemed like they cared more for all those other things Buddy Bolden was doing, all those women he had, all his carrying on. It was something they could point to as if *that* was as much as the music. Even the musicianers themselves get carried away by it. Either they get to feuding for a name for themselves or they get to thinking up some personality thing which has nothing to do with the music.

That's one of the things that make it why a musicianer, if he's real serious about the music, has to have this place inside himself. You've got to say that to yourself. 'I won't have it; I've got the music and I don't give a damn for the rest. Rich or poor, the music is there and that's what I'm for.'

And if you can say that to yourself, if you can say that and mean it, then it doesn't matter so much about whether you're working here or working there; you can fill in some way or another. You're not needing favours from somebody who cares more for a big sign with his name on it than what he cares about the music.

It's like I say: the important thing is to stay with the music, to be honest with it. So when I left Noble Sissle's—that was back around 1937—I wasn't worrying. I wasn't owing any favours, I wasn't missing any meals, and I had the music. I was all right.

So I played here and there, and after a while Herman Rosenberg, he was a good friend of mine, he brought me around to the Hickory House. Joe Marsala was working there; he played clarinet. He had a brother Marty who was there too; Marty played trumpet. And there was Joe Bushkin on piano. I wasn't working then and Herman wanted to bring me around; he was sure they'd be wanting to hire me after they finished hearing me. So I used to work there nights sometimes, but mostly it was Sunday evenings from around four to eight; that was when they had their jam sessions. My pay was mostly from those sessions on Sundays. I wasn't making much in a money way, but the music was real fine. And that's just an example of what I was saying. There's one way or there's another, but if a man really cares for the music, there's always *some* way.

And then one night Herman, he told me to come with him to Nick's. If Nick was to hear me, he said, he was sure to want me. So I went there. They had Bobby Hackett's band at Nick's then: there was Pee Wee Russell on clarinet, Brad Gowans on trombone and sometimes on clarinet too, Eddie Condon on guitar, and Ernie Caceres on baritone. And a friend of mine, Zutty Singleton, he was playing there as a feature. The night I went down there I brought my soprano, and the boys in that band, they were really good, we made it real fine together. Nick, he came in and listened and when we was all through he hired me. After that I was working there for quite a while.

There was some real musicianers there at Nick's. It was something real fine. Eddie Condon was there, and Eddie, he was one of the best. Eddie, he didn't have his own band yet. I could always see, though, that he had the idea. He wanted to do something really sincere to advance Jazz. He had a lot of feeling about how it should be presented, under what conditions. He used to talk to me a lot about that, about how a band should be made up. It was his idea that when you're doing the presenting right you're not giving a name or a colour to a musicianer. What you're doing, you're putting him together with others so that one man in the band helps another find the music, one man working with another. Eddie was always telling me how he'd do if he had a place of his own, and how much he wanted me with him if he had his own band. And ever since that time, if there's been something for the radio or a concert or a job, he's always thought of me and been very happy to see me work with him.

Eddie's a big man now, but he's gotten big in the right way. His interest was always for the music. Even back there at Nick's he was always managing to get work for us between times, helping us get along together. The way he'd say it, helping one is helping another and that way the music, it's helping itself. When he helped me, he saw it as my music he was helping. He saw what I was doing by how I was playing. And it's not been only me: Fats Waller,

Louis Armstrong, Lips Page—he got so much pleasure out of working with them that he did them a lot of good.

Aside from being a real good musicianer, Eddie was a fine manager. And the way things were, somebody like Eddie was needed real bad to help Jazz, to help it get away from all this other business where a man was judged more by how he looked or what he did than by how he played. And there was a need for what he was doing. His work, it was real strong for helping Jazz.

One time I remember I was going to do something with Jelly Roll Morton who was going to make a show, and some fellow who handled the money for it said to Jelly, 'Sidney? Why him, he's an old man! We don't want anybody as old as he is. Just look at him!' But Jelly, he just told that man that if he didn't take me there wouldn't be any outfit. That's the way it happened to Jazz back there. What a man's got in his soul, that's got to be dressed up to meet the public. If he's got white hair you don't allow him a soul.

A man like Eddie Condon, though, what he looked for was the music. He had that inside him and he had the ability to manage things, and that way he did just about the most for helping Jazz to be itself in the way it got to be presented. There's nobody done more than Eddie.

NELSON GEORGE

The Death of Rhythm & Blues

To see how the R&B world began, we need to double back a bit to the war years to see the profound affect they had on the record industry.

Following Japan's attack on Pearl Harbor in 1941, the government halted the manufacture of record players, radios, and other consumer products requiring electronic components, as the war effort took priority. Shellac, the key ingredient in record manufacturing at the time, came from Japanese-controlled Singapore, so there wasn't much around. Yet the misery of the war increased Americans' desire to be entertained, and the music business, like the movie industry, boomed. In 1941, record sales were $50 million. By 1945, they reached $109 million, even though the quality of the pressings had deteriorated, since old records were being scrapped and then reused to satisfy the demand.

This rise was amazing in light of a deep philosophical and economic dispute in the industry. The American Federation of Musicians, the musicians' union, was rightfully fearful that the increasing use of records on radio would eventually put many members out of work, particularly since big bands relied on live broadcasts for so much of their revenue. On August 1, 1942, AFM president James C. Petrillo, in a desperate move, tried to stop progress. He ordered a recording ban, demanded that the record labels give musicians a royalty to compensate for lost revenues from recorded music, and pressured nightclubs to stop using jukeboxes. Records cut prior to the ban, plus some primarily vocal recordings and scattered bootleg sessions (falsely said to have been recorded before the ban), made up the bulk of record releases during the next two years. Decca gave in first, signing a royalty agreement in 1943. Capitol settled soon after, but the big boys, Columbia and Victor (aka RCA), held out until 1944. So Petrillo won . . . sort of.

He could strike and get concessions. He couldn't, however, hold back the forces of economics and technology; nor could he channel audiences' changing enthusiasms. The big-band era and the dominance of swing was over. For lonely GIs and equally lonely women at home, the sentimentality of Frank Sinatra, Peggy Lee, Perry Como, and Nat King Cole was preferred to the frantic rhythms of Gene Krupa and the blasting trumpets of Harry James. Tastes had changed. During the strike, the big-band singers rose to prominence, overshadowing the bandleaders who first exposed them and establishing string-laden vocal recordings as the sound of white pop in the 1950s.

The big bands ran into other economic barriers as well. After the war everything cost more: gasoline, buses, hotel accommodations, and musicians' salaries. And the musicians themselves were changing. During the war those who'd avoided the service grew comfortable, lazy, and, according to accounts from the period, sloppy. Together these factors conspired to make many big-band leaders call it quits in 1946, including Benny Goodman, Woody Herman, Benny Carter, Tommy Dorsey, Les Brown, and Jack Teagarden. Some would later come back in some form to join the remarkably stable organizations of Ellington and Basie as caretakers for the once-vibrant sound of swing.

Creativity in improvisational music had moved in another direction, one that ensured exciting experiments and, ironically, one that enabled rhythm & blues to become the dominant dance music of postwar America.

Like Louis Jordan, a number of ambitious young musicians, including trumpeter Dizzy Gillespie, saxophonist Charlie Parker, and pianist Thelonious Monk, were all big-band refugees. Congregating at Harlem's Minton's Playhouse and other uptown after-hours spots for jam sessions, they were quite consciously creating a new music known, in hep-cat lingo, as bebop. In its purest form, bebop is a complex, rapidly shifting small-group music (two horns, bass, drum, piano) that turned pop melodies into slivers of chords and rhythmic phrases. The rhythm didn't ride on the tom-tom or snare drum, where even poor dancers could find it, but flowed through every instrument. Sure, the drummer kept time, but usually only with a tense, jingling pattern on the cymbals that was impossible for most dancers to follow. This sound made bebop as much a listeners' music as anything heard at Carnegie Hall. Bebop differed from swing and rhythm & blues not just musically but in the players' attitude toward their audience. Cool, self-assured, and, despite widespread drug use among its stars, often dignified in appearance, beboppers made it plain they really didn't care if people—black squares as well as white—understood what they were playing. This was musicians' music, first and foremost. Only those who pledged allegiance to the musicians' brilliance, mesmerized by daredevil improvisations, were welcome.

The most extroverted bebop pioneer was Gillespie, who, with his beret, goatee, constant hep talk, and puffed cheeks when blowing, cut a slyly comic figure. He often clowned onstage, but unlike another great trumpeter, Louis Armstrong, Gillespie escaped an Uncle Tom tag by his ability to simultaneously laugh at his jokes yet maintain his dignity. Despite his humor, Gillespie, like Parker, Monk, and the others, took his music seriously and considered it art as high-minded and elitist as the Western classical music he both envied and despised. The bebop attitude overrode any lingering connection to the black show-business tradition that turned any cultural expression into a potentially lucrative career (though eventually that would happen to the beboppers as well). At this juncture in bebop history, its adherents found it a higher calling than mere entertainment. These musicians were less secular stars than quasi-religious figures, and their fans often referred to them with godly reverence.

For the masses of blacks, after bebop's emergence, jazz was respected, but in times of leisure and relaxation they turned to Louis Jordan and a blend of blues, jump blues, ballads, gospel, and a slew of sax-led instruments and fading black swing orchestras. General black taste in the 1940s can be sampled in Broadcast Music Inc.'s rhythm & blues awards. Decca's Jordan far outdistanced the competition, with one song in 1943 ("Five Guys Named Joe"), one in 1944 ("GI Jive"), two in 1945 ("Caledonia Boogie," "Mop Hop"), six, at the height of his popularity, in 1946 ("Beware Brother Beware," "Buzz Me," "Choo Choo Ch'Boogie," "Don't Worry 'Bout That Mule," "Let the Good Times Roll," and "Stone Cold Dead in the Market," with Ella Fitzgerald), and four in 1947 ("Ain't Nobody Here But Us Chickens," "Boogie Woogie Blue Plate," "Early in the Morning," "Jack You're Dead"). In 1943 and 1944, large black orchestras led by instrumentalists showed strength (vibraphonist Lionel Hampton, trumpeter Erskine Hawkins and saxman Buddy Johnson, trumpeter Cootie Williams), while Nat King Cole, a singer with a crooning big-band vocal style, debuted. Change was quite evident from 1945 to 1947. The orchestras disappeared, replaced first by the rough, gravelly rural voices of Arthur (Big Boy) Crudup and Roosevelt Sykes, then by bluesmen with followings among newly arrived big-city blacks, and finally by smooth, blues-influenced crooners like Private Cecil Gant, Charles Brown, and Ivory Joe Hunter, as well as the astringent tone of Dinah Washington. To some degree that last group of male singers was the black equivalent of the white ex-big-band vocalists (Gant was promoted as "the sepia Sinatra"), though they drew much more overtly on the blues than their white counterparts.

But in 1948 and 1949, there were no white equivalents of Wynonie Harris's

"Good Rockin' Tonight" and "All She Wants to Do Is Rock" on King, two churning, driving records on which Harris was as brash and ballsy as a horny bull. There was no white equivalent of the Ravens' "Bye Bye Baby Blues" on Savoy, with its harmonies and lead-to-chorus interplay that embraced gospel call-and-response in a way the Mills Brothers and Ink Spots, the black harmony stars of the swing era, rarely attempted. There was no white equivalent of the half-crazed shouts, unintelligible words, and stomping beat of John Lee Hooker's "Boogie Chillen" and "Crawling Kingsnake" on Modern. And there was no white equivalent of the honking, stuttering tenor-sax-led hits of Big Jay McNeely ("Deacon's Hop") and Paul Williams ("The Hucklebuck") on Savoy, or the honky-tonk piano-based hits of Amos Milburn on Aladdin (five made the BMI list in 1949, including the raunchy "Chicken Shack Boogie"). The words were bluesy in tone and subject matter, but the rhythms and voices were fresh and new.

So were the labels that recorded, promoted, and distributed these records. Jordan, Cole, and the big bands recorded for large, nationally distributed companies such as Decca, Victor, and Capitol. However, all the new artists were signed to independent labels that began appearing during the war and would proliferate in the next seven years. While the majors had problems identifying the new music—MGM called it "ebony," Decca and Capitol preferred "sepia"—the new labels were rhythm & blues from the start, though bebop, country, electric blues, and gospel were all recorded by the new labels. In 1949, when *Billboard* changed the name of its black pop-music chart from "race" to "rhythm & blues," it wasn't selling a trend, but responding to a phrase and a feeling the independent labels had already made part of the vocabulary.

The biggest surprise on the indies list is that Los Angeles produced the largest number of significant R&B labels. Of the thirty companies, nine called Los Angeles home, including all those inaugurated in 1945. This resulted from an influx of blacks in Southern California, as GIs just back from Asia stayed on and Southern blacks, particularly those from Louisiana, Texas, and Oklahoma, found in sunny California a climate, both atmospherically and socially, more temperate than existed back home. In total about half a million blacks moved to Los Angeles and adjacent cities like Compton during the war years. Their presence made the area a rhythm & blues hot spot, though much of the music released on the Los Angeles indies came from those fertile musical tributaries, New Orleans and Memphis.

I wish it were surprising—but it isn't—that only one of the two Harlem-based labels, Bobby Robinson's Red Robin, was black-owned. Most indies were started by whites, many of them Jewish; blacks weren't the only people kept out of the American business mainstream by discrimination. Unwelcome on Wall Street, many Jewish businessmen looked for places where there were fewer barriers to entrepreneurship. They often turned to black neighborhoods—in some ways paralleling blacks' discovery that their avenues for

LABEL	OWNER	CITY
1942		
Savoy	Herman Lubinsky	Newark
Excelsior (became Exclusive in 1944)	Leon and Otis Rene	Los Angeles
1943		
Apollo	Ike and Bess Berman	New York
1944		
National	Al Greene	New York
Gulf-Gold Star	Bill Quinn	Houston
King	Syd Nathan	Cincinnati
1945		
Modern	Jules, Joe, and Saul Bihari	Los Angeles
Philco-Aladdin	Ed and Leo Mesner	Los Angeles
Bronze	Leroy Hurte	Los Angeles
Four Star	Richard Nelson	Los Angeles
Super Disc	Irving Feld, Viola Marsham	Los Angeles
1946		
Bulleit	Jim Bulleit	Nashville
Specialty	Art Rupe	Los Angeles
Mercury	Irving Green (president)	Chicago
1947		
Atlantic	Herb Abramson, Ahmet Ertegun	New York
Aristocrat-Chess	Leonard and Phil Chess	Chicago
1949		
Freedom	Saul Kaul	Houston
Macy's	Macy Lela Wood	Houston
Peacock	Don Robey	Houston
Imperial	Lew Chudd	Los Angeles

LABEL	OWNER	CITY
1950		
Trumpet	Willard and Lillian McMurry	Jackson, Mississippi
1951		
Dot	Randy Wood, Gene Nobles	Gallatin, Tennessee
Red Robin	Bobby Robinson	New York
Nashboro-Ernie Y	Ernie Young	Nashville
1952		
Duke	James Mattias	Memphis
Sun	Sam Phillips	Memphis
Meteor	Lester Bihari	Los Angeles-Memphis
Vee-Jay	James and Vivian Bracken, Calvin Carter	Chicago-Gary, Indiana

advancement were less barricaded in the world of entertainment. Only two of the black labels on my list, Don Robey's Peacock and family-owned Vee-Jay, would be major forces in the black market, and Vee-Jay was the only one to have a significant impact on the white market.

None of these companies would have had any impact whatsoever without the maturation of black radio. In St. Louis (KXLW), Atlanta (WERD), Louisville (WLOU), Memphis (WDIA), Los Angeles (KRKD), New Orleans (WYLD), Miami (WMBM), and Nashville (WLAC), stations that programmed rhythm & blues, with additional shows catering to blues, gospel, and jazz depending on where they were located, began broadcasting. In addition, there were many programs in the late 1940s still being broadcast on the purchase deals of the past, with powerful deejays still working on two or three stations in a market, though that practice was fading. What was growing, however, was the impact of the deejays, some of whom were as exciting as the performers they promoted. As with the R&B labels, the overwhelming majority of black-oriented stations were white-owned (Atlanta's WERD was one important exception), but the deejays, not the owners, defined the stations and made them profitable. As we'll see, they were paid little relative to the revenues generated, and so they developed a host of hustles, from concert promotion to talent management to payola (pay-for-play). In the rhythm & blues world payola was as common as tacking posters to telephone poles to announce upcoming shows.

What was also accepted, and quite enthusiastically, was the presence of white deejays. Integration would have many unexpected side effects, one of which was the development of a group of whites who, like many in the Jazz Age, were fascinated with black music and black style. Unlike the contemporaries of Fitzgerald, these new Negrophiles embraced black culture to the point that they became "honorary" blacks and, in some cases, subject to the same discrimination as their dark role models. Johnny Otis, a Los Angeles resident of Greek descent, was one of the first of this breed. As a bandleader, songwriter, and talent scout, Otis was a real force in the Los Angeles scene. And in terms of promoting rhythm & blues, these black voices behind white faces would be more important than any single musician.

ALSTON ANDERSON

Dance of the Infidels

I used to listen to jazz all day and most of the night. I'd go to bed by it and wake up with it. Look like nobody else in town was as crazy about it as me; they all said I was 'music happy.' But that was OK by me. They live their life and I live my own.

I used to go to a little cafe on Davis Street a whole lot. There was a big old juke box in the place, and I'd stoop over and put my ear right up against the speaker and listen. That way all I could hear in the whole wide world was music, and that was fine with me. So this night when I walked in the cafe and seen a man doing the same thing—leaning down with his ear against the speaker—I went over and tapped him on the shoulder.

He looked up. I hadn't never seen him before. 'I got that record at home,' I said.

'Oh, yeah?'

'Yeah.'

'Well, that's crazy,' he said, and put his ear to the speaker again. Even while he was stooped over I could tell he was taller than me. When the record was finished and he stood up I noticed that his eyes had a real far-away look in them, like he was used to looking at mountains from a distance.

'You want to go over to my place and listen to records?' I said. He just looked at me, real blank. Then he said, 'Crazy,' and we went outside to the street. He walked like he had springs in the toes of his shoes; like every step he took was going to be a long one, so that you were always surprised at how short they were. All the way to my place he didn't say a word. Most times we walked with enough room between us for a growed woman to walk through. Then one time a man passed us and we had to move together to let him by. Our coat sleeves touched, and he jumped like he'd been burnt. 'What the hell is this?' I thought to myself. I got to thinking right then of how to get rid of him without hurting his feelings.

When we got to my place I offered him a seat, but he didn't sit down. I don't mean to say nothing derogatory about him, but he acted just like a dog acts when he gets to a place he ain't never been in before: he walked all around and sniffed at things. You could almost hear him sniffing out loud.

'You want a drink?' I said.

'You got wine?'

'I ain't got nothing but whisky.'

'No thanks.'

'I can go get some wine, if you want.'

'I'll go get it,' he said.

'No, I'll get it. Make yourself at home.'

I went out and got the wine and when I got back he was sitting in a chair with his legs crossed. I still couldn't figure him out. He looked like he was in a world all his own.

'You blow?' he said.

'Blow?'

'Yeah. You play anything?'

'No. No, I don't play nothing. You?'

'I blow box.'

'You blow what?'

'Piano.'

He sounded irritant because I couldn't understand everything he said.

'You from around here?'

'I'm from The Apple,' he said. Then he knew right off I didn't get it so he said, 'New York. I'm down here visiting my people.'

I poured myself a drink and turned on the record player. Then I remembered that I hadn't opened the wine bottle, so I opened it and poured him a drink. While the record player was warming up I got to leafing through the records. He came over and stood beside me, so I held the records so's he could read the labels. Our coat sleeves touched again and he moved away a little. I handed the records to him and said, 'Here. Why'nt you play what you want?' I said it real soft so's not to offend him and went over and sat on the couch.

He got to looking through the records, and every once in a while he'd say, 'Solid!' Then he got to laughing. Not at me or anything in particular; just laughing.

'Where'd you pick up on these, man?'

'I gets them from a store in New York,' I said. I meant to say The Apple instead of New York, and I was sorry I didn't. He turned around and looked at me, half-smiling, like *he* was the one that was trying to figure *me* out.

He put a record on the player. It was 'Salt Peanuts' by Dizzie Gillespie, with Don Byas on tenor sax. I thought to tell him that that was the first one I bought, that I got it while I was in the Army in New Orleans; but I didn't. He turned the volume up real loud and sat down. I got up and turned it down a little. I knew he'd be disappointed so I said, 'Neighbours.' He nodded.

We sat there listening for a while, neither of us talking. Then he got to riffing Dizzie's solo out loud. 'Well I'll be damn!' I thought. I knew the solo real well myself, so I riffed right along with him. I kept listening for him to make a mistake. He didn't. When the solo was over we looked at one another, both of us smiling. It was like looking at somebody and thinking for a split minute that you was looking at yourself. We both laughed. He got up and came over to me and stretched out his hand.

'Skin,' he said. I slapped his palm real light and he said, 'Solid.' Then we shook hands, and he sat down again. I felt a lot better about his being there. In fact, I felt right then that he could stay there for the rest of his natural life, Amen.

We sat there for about an hour, riffing and listening: Bird, Miles Davis, Dizzie, Bud Powell . . . strictly the kick. He was mostly playing records with Bud on them, so he could listen to the piano. We was having a natural ball.

Then he turned to me and said, 'Do you turn?'

'Do I what?'

'Aw, man,' he said. He looked real disgusted. I'd heard what he said, alright, but I had to have time to figure out what he meant. Then I got it.

'You mean do I smoke?'

'Yeah, man. Yeah.'

'No,' I said, 'but you can go 'head if you want.'

I hadn't never seen anybody smoke marijuana. I'd heard it was bad, so I stayed away from it. But I figured that if he wanted to do it that was his business, not mine. I poured myself another drink and sipped it. He didn't move. When the record was over I got up and took it off. 'What you wanna hear?' I said.

'Play some J.J.,' he said. His mood had done changed, and mine had, too. 'God damn pot head,' I thought. But I liked him—after all, he was the first person I'd met who loved jazz as much as I do—so I was sorry I'd thought it. I found a record by J. J. Johnson and put it on. He still didn't move; just sat there looking down at the floor, like he was thinking. Then he cursed—real soft, but I heard it—and reached in his coat pocket and took out a reefer. He straightened out the ends of it and lit it.

I sat there watching him smoke—taking deep drags and then holding his breath so that no smoke came out—and I thought: what the hell; once won't hurt, will it?

'Gimme a drag,' I said. He handed it to me without a word and I took it. I smoked it just like he had, holding my breath so that the smoke stayed down. We both smoked it, passing it back and forth till it was down to a fraction. Then he put it out and put it in his pocket. 'Gotta save roaches,' he said, and smiled.

For a while I didn't feel anything; just the whisky. Then I got up to change the record—that is I started getting up, because it looked like I'd never stop rising up off that couch—and I knew it had hit me. I took the record off and put on 'Scrapple from the Apple' by Charlie Parker, then sat back down. While I was doing it I noticed that everything in the room looked like it had shifted just a little bit; like somebody had come in and moved everything a little up and to the left.

But it was sitting there listening to Bird and Miles playing in unison that I really got the feel of it. I got up and turned the volume up a little, then sat back down. I got up and turned it up some more. It was just like I'd heard them for the first time. I mean *really* heard them. I turned the record player up full blast. Wail, Bird. I tried to turn it up some more, but the damn thing just wouldn't go any louder. Wail, Bird. To hell with neighbours. To hell with everybody. WAIL, Bird!

We sat there and smoked a couple more sticks and got high as kites. After that he took to coming by my place nearbout every night, and when he ran out of pot it didn't matter. We'd get juiced and have ourselves an A-grade ball, listening and riffing.

I liked the pot. I like it a whole lot. When Ronnie—his name was Ronald Johnson—went back to New York he promised he'd write to me and send me some. Sure enough, about a week after he was gone here come a newspaper addressed to me, all rolled up. I unrolled it real slow, and there was a small package of pot pasted on the inside sheet. On the covering of the package he wrote one word: 'Wail.'

I didn't hear from him after that. I wrote to him and thanked him for the pot, and when he didn't answer I wrote again: nothing. So along about March of the next year I went on up to New York.

I got off the train at Pennsylvania Station and went outside to 34th Street and got a taxi. It was the first time I had ever been to New York. I told the driver where I wanted to go—it was a house on 127th Street near Lenox Avenue—and he took me through the city and through Central Park and then up to Harlem. I liked New York a lot, especially driving through the park. Harlem wasn't nothing like I thought it would be. I'd always imagined there would be lots of shambly houses and all that; but it was all built up, just like the rest of New York. And to this day I've never got over that.

So anyway, me and this taxi go on up to 127th Street and I pay the driver and start up the stairs. I'd checked my bag at the train station, so I didn't have anything to carry. The building was old and dirty and even in the daytime it was dark. I got to Ronnie's apartment and rang the bell. Nothing happened. Instead of ringing it again, like I thought of doing, I just stood there and waited. There was a circle in the upper half of the door and after a while it looked like it moved, so I tried to look through it. I couldn't.

'What do you want?' a man's voice said.

'Do Ronald Johnson live here?'

'What do you want?' the voice said again.

'Do Ronald Johnson—'

The door opened, and a man with hair that looked like it had been pasted down with axle grease poked his head out. He blinked his eyes and said, 'Who're you?'

'I'm Benevolence Delaney,' I said.

'You're *who*?'

I said it again. He kind of smirked and looked me up and down from head to shoes. Then he said, 'He's not here. If you want to see him you can . . .' He looked me up and down again. 'He's at the Y-Bar. You know where that is?'

'No.'

He told me where it was and I found it. It was almost as dark inside it as it had been in the apartment building. I went to the bar and ordered a shot, then looked around. We saw each other at about the same time. He was at the far end of the bar. He got up off his stool real slow, looking like he didn't believe what his eyes was showing him.

'Well, I'll be gaaat-dam,' he said. 'My boy.' We shook hands and looked at one another.

'How you doin'?' I said.

'Aw, man,' he said. He looked me up and down just like his friend had done back at the apartment. I got the feeling he was embarrassed to see me; like I was a third cousin that was born on the wrong side of the river.

'You look good,' I said; but he didn't. He'd lost weight, and his clothes hung on him most like they do on a hatrack. When he talked his eyes kept shifting all around, like any minute he expected somebody to try and hit him.

'Ain't nothing shaking, huss,' he said. 'Nothing but dues, you dig? Kats won't let a man live. I had a gig up at The Track for a while—house band, you dig?—then my habit got me and I had to split but I kicked it and got another gig up in the Bronx. But them square motherhubbers drug me so terrible I had to put that down. West Indians, you dig? I dig what they're sayin', man, but I can't make that time. How *you* doing, man? When'd you fall in town?'

He was talking real fast and looking all around, like I said, and I didn't hardly understand what he was talking about. I asked him what 'The Track' was and he told me it was the nickname for the Savoy Ballroom; only this time he didn't get irritant when I asked him. He was glad to see me, and said it. I told him I'd just got into town and he said, 'You got a pad?'

'No.'

'You could stay at my pad, but I'm sharing it with a stud.'

'I saw him,' I said. 'I reckon I'll get me a room in a hotel.'

'Solid,' he said. 'Let's fall down to the Dewey Square Hotel and get you a pad.'

We walked across town and caught a 7th Avenue bus and went down to the Dewey Square Hotel. I registered and then we went to a little square right near 116th Street and sat on a bench and talked. I asked him if he'd gotten my letters and he said yes. I thanked him again for the pot and said, 'You know where I can get some?'

'Some pot?'

'Yeah.'

'Ain't much shaking. The Man done put the finger on the kats and everybody's layin' low. My boy got busted.'

I looked at him and shook my head. I couldn't hardly understand a word that man said; but I learned to figure it out. He thought for a while and then he said, 'Come on, let's split.' We got up and walked over to 116th Street and 8th Avenue and caught the subway. We rode up to 145th Street and got off and went to a poolroom near the corner.

The poolroom was way bigger than the one back home, with about twelve tables to it. It was packed full of niggers. I followed Ronnie on back to the back of the place, edging by people, and when he stopped I stopped, too. It looked like he got real innerested in one of the games. The man that was shooting was real good. It looked like he was going run 'em all the way, eight-ball and all. I figured that Ronnie and me would be up soon, and I was kinda looking forward to a game. I noticed that nobody in the place was looking at anybody else; just at the pool tables. Then the man that was shooting missed. He cursed and lit a cigarette and moved back to the wall. He was standing right alongside Ronnie. I just barely seen it, I swear, I seen him slip a couple of reefers into Ronnie's hand and Ronnie slipped him some money. They didn't look at one another once the whole time, and not a word was said. Then Ronnie said, 'Come on,' and we edged our way out to the street.

'That was real cool,' I said.

'*Got* to be, man,' he said. 'The Man done put niggers on the police force so they can put the finger on other niggers. And the squares are all happy out of their heads just because they got coloured cops. Ain't that a bitch?'

'Yeah,' I said.

'The only stripes I dig are *pinstripes*, man. I ain't got no eyes atall for them wide ones. Come on, let's fall down to my pad and get happy.'

We caught the 145th Street crosstown bus and rode over to 8th Avenue, and then we caught the 8th Avenue bus and went down to 127th Street and walked across town to his pad. His room-mate wasn't at home. It was the funniest apartment I'd ever seen. As you come in the door the first thing that hits you is a painting of Our Lord and Saviour Jesus Christ with a crown of thorns on His head. His face looked so sad it nearbout scared me. Underneath it there was a sofa with a leopard skin cover. There was a piano against the wall, and even looking at it you could tell the tone wouldn't be so hot; it was old. Through an open doorway you could see a stove with a pot on it.

'Siddown,' Ronnie said. I started to sit on the sofa, but that leopard skin was a little too much for me so I sat in an armchair with a faded green cover on it. I did my best not to look at that leopard skin.

Ronnie went into the kitchen and got to fumbling around. I looked around for something to pass the time and picked up a book. It was *Native Son* by Richard Wright. I read the first page of it and all of a sudden there was a wild sound above my head; a sound of trumpets. It made me jump, and when I looked up Ronnie was standing in the doorway laughing his head off.

'Wake up and live, Bennie!' he said. 'Things to *come*, man!'

I laughed and put the book down. Then I saw that Ronnie'd done had a speaker rigged up in the front room. The record player was in the kitchen. He came in and lit up a stick, or 'a joint,' like he said, and handed it to me. I took a few deep drags and handed it back to him, with the sound of trumpets like drumbeats in my ears.

'You short, black son of a bitch,' Ronnie said, and laughed. He was glad to see me alright. I could tell by his eyes.

So we sat there and got high and listened to records. Then he said his room-mate would be back soon, and since I didn't want to see him I left. I went down to Pennsylvania Station and got my bag out of check, then went to the Dewey Square. It was good to be in New York, and to be high again. It was real good.

I didn't see him for about a week after that. I'd go up to his place—he didn't have a telephone—and either nobody was there or his greasy-head room-mate would tell me he didn't know where Ronnie was. I went to the Y-Bar several times, but I never saw him. So I got to looking around town on my own. I went down to Broadway a few times and looked at all the bright lights and the big Camel advertisement of a man with smoke-rings coming out his mouth. I took in a few movies, and it was sitting in a picture-show one night that I figured out where I might find him. The Dewey Square Hotel is on 117th Street, and right around the corner from it is a nightclub called 'Minton's Playhouse.' Ronnie showed it to me when he first brought me to the hotel. And so, when the movie was over, I went uptown.

My hunch paid off. Minton's was divided into two sections. There was a bar with a juke box in it, just like a regular bar. Then there was a swinging door and when it swung open you could hear live music coming from the inside room. Ronnie wasn't in the bar so I started into the back room. Somebody told me at the door that I'd have to pay more for my drinks in the back, but I said I didn't care and went on in. There was a row of tables on each side of a long room, and near the bandstand there was a dance floor about the size of a big playpen. It was dark inside, but most of the people were wearing dark glasses. I didn't know any of the musicians that were playing, but they were good. I sat at a table and ordered a drink. I didn't recognize Ronnie at first, because I hadn't ever seen him in dark glasses. I picked up my drink and went over and sat beside him. While the band was playing we didn't talk. When they stopped he said, 'Kicks to see you, man.' We shook hands.

'Where you been?' I said.

'Aw, man. I been goofing.'

'Oh, yeah?'

'Yeah, man. Dues, you dig? Gotta pay 'em.'

'I been looking for you,' I said.

'I'm hip.'

The band started up again, so we stopped talking and listened. I noticed he was drinking a coke, and I touched him and asked him by signal if he wanted a drink. He frowned and shook his head. After a long while he turned to me and said, 'You got any bread?'

'I ain't got much,' I said. 'How much you need?'

'Three cents,' he said.

'Three *cents*?'

'Three bucks, man.'

'Oh,' I said. 'Sure, I got that much.' I started to reach for the money but he stopped me. 'Let's split,' he said. I paid the waiter and we went outdoors.

He called a cab and we drove about fifteen blocks uptown. We got out and went to a bar. He just stood inside the doorway and looked all around. He didn't see who or what it was he wanted, so we walked on to another bar. Same thing. We walked about two blocks and crossed the street: same thing. After about three more bars—I was getting kinda tired of this because I wanted a drink—he saw who it was he was looking for. You could tell it the minute he walked in the door. He looked like a great big heavy sack had just been lifted off his shoulders.

'Wait here a minute,' he said. To hell with that, I thought. I went to the bar and ordered a double. Ronnie'd done gone to a booth and was talking to a man in a leather jacket and sky-blue pants. They both got up after a time and

Ronnie signalled to me—all he did was raise his head a little—so I finished the drink and all three of us went outside.

The other man walked just like Ronnie did: with that springy, bouncy step that looked like he was about to take off and fly. We walked on up the block—none of us saying a mumbling word—and around a corner and into a building.

We started up the stairs, me going last, and as we walked past the fifth floor I heard what I thought first was a pigeon cooing and next a baby crying. But it was neither a baby or a pigeon. It was a woman; and she wasn't crying. We walked up to the seventh floor and Ronnie and the man stopped. We was all standing on the stairs, Ronnie on top and then the man and then me. I thought they were going to somebody's apartment, because there was a door right behind Ronnie. But they weren't.

'You got the bread, Bennie?' Ronnie said.

'Oh!' I said. then I remembered that I'd spent all the small bills I had. 'I ain't got nothing but a ten-spot,' I said.

'I ain't got no change for that,' the man said.

'We can get change later,' Ronnie said. I gave the man the ten-spot.

Ronnie took off his jacket and hung it on the doorknob. Then he took off his belt and rolled up the shirtsleeve on his left arm. His skin was grey under the light. The man took a spoon and a little bottle of water out of his jacket pocket. The bottom of the spoon was black. Next he brought out a little brown packet from another pocket and tapped what looked like garlic salt into the spoon from the packet. Then he poured some of the water from the bottle into the spoon, crumpled the empty packet, threw it down the stairs and said, 'Gimme a match.' I lit a match and handed it to him. Ronnie had done wrapped his belt tight around his arm just above the elbow. He was flexing his arm back and forth, and the veins in his forearm were standing out like veins on a dead leaf. The man held the flame to the bottom of the spoon and moved it around so that it heated even. Then he threw the match away and took a hypodermic needle out of his jacket. He sucked all the melted liquid up with the needle, then handed it to Ronnie. Ronnie took it. You could hear him breathing hard. It looked as though he was looking for the right vein. He moved his arm around so that the light would hit it right, meanwhile flexing his fist. I heard the woman on the fifth floor half-shout and half-scream and call a man's name twice. Then her voice sounded like it was muffled in a pillow and the needle was in Ronnie's arm. When the needle hit him he moved back against the wall. But it was so slow that I swear 'fore God it looked just like the wall moved towards him and he was holding it up. When he finished he took the needle from his arm and handed it to the man. He unwrapped the belt and rolled his shirtsleeve down. He was breathing harder now, and beginning to sweat. He was moving now just like a man in a slow-motion movie. He put his belt back on and buckled it and put his jacket on. He went to the door and flung it open. It was then I seen that it was the rooftop, and not somebody's apartment. The other man all this time had taken his jacket off and was going through the same business all over again. I wanted to go outside to see if Ronnie was alright, but the man was fixing himself so I didn't disturb him. I just stood there and watched. All of a sudden there was a loud crash outside. It sounded like a man falling after he'd been hit with a blackjack. I wanted to go outside and look because I didn't know whether the roof was slanted and Ronnie might fall off or if he'd been hit by somebody and was hurt bad and all this time the man had the needle in his arm with the blood coming up dark red into it then going back into his arm real slow as he went tap-tap-tap on top of the needle, and then he was finished and his belt went on loop by loop and he went to the door and looked out.

'Man,' he said. 'That simple motherhubber done fell out.' He put his jacket on and zipped it up and started down the stairs. I stood aside to let him by.

When I got out on the roof Ronnie was laying flat on his back with his legs up like he was about to give birth. His mouth was open and in the dim light his forehead looked exactly like a window pane after a heavy rain. His eyes were wide open, staring up at the stars. I knelt down beside him.

'What's the matter, Ronnie? You OK, man?'

He didn't move. I remembered right then what I'd heard one time in the Army: *When a man takes dope don't let him pass out or he might pass out for good.* So I slapped him. Hard. He didn't move. I slapped him again. He was coming to. I picked him halfway up by the lapels of his jacket and leaned him up against a chimney.

'Ronnie!' I shouted, and shook him. 'Ronnie!' His eyes had closed when I slapped him the first time, and now he opened them. He looked like he was trying hard to focus; like he was looking at me from a distance of eighty miles.

'You OK, man?'

'Huh?'

'You OK?'

'I'm awright, Sugar,' he said. (It was the first time any man had ever called me 'Sugar' in my natural life. What the hell, I thought. Maybe he thinks I'm his wife or girl friend or something. In spite of the situation I couldn't help laughing just a little.) All of a sudden he was alright; or almost alright. He got to his feet by himself. Then he started to slump, so I grabbed him and helped him to the doorway. He shook my arm off. 'I'm straight, Sugar,' he said. I took out my handkerchief and wiped his face. We started down the stairs, and he slumped again. I helped him down a couple flights, then he shook my arm off again. He walked the rest of the way by himself.

When we got to street level he said, 'Git a cab, Sugar.' He sat down on the bottom stair and I went out and got a taxi. When I got back he was spitting. I helped him up and he walked to the taxi by himself. As we were about to start off he turned to me and said, 'Did you get your bread, Sugar?'

'Oh!' I said. I'd forgotten my change from the ten dollars. I started to get out of the cab, but Ronnie stopped me.

'Lemme do it,' he said. 'That's an evil motherhubber.'

He got out of the cab and walked back to the bar. I watched through the rear window to see if he was alright. He was walking just like a man who drinks a lot but can carry his load. In a minute he came back and handed me seven dollars. I thanked him a lot and we drove to his place.

I was sitting in a straight chair—I still couldn't take that leopard-skin couch—and he was sitting in the armchair. His room-mate wasn't there, and I didn't want to leave him until I was sure he was OK. It was about three in the morning by this time, and I was tired. He had one hand to his forehead, and he was beginning to nod. I didn't want to slap him any more, so I decided to talk to keep him awake. So I talked; just rambling on in general. Every once in a while I'd say, 'You listening, man?' and if he answered I'd keep on. If he didn't I'd go over and shake him and he'd say, 'I'm awright, Sugar, I'm listenin'.' So I'd keep on talking.

This went on for about half an hour. Then he got up and went to the piano. He sat there for a long while just looking down at the keys. Then he hit a minor seventh chord with his left hand. He didn't bang, but he hit it hard and kept his hand there. I could hear it echoing into infinity. He hit it again and leaned his head to one side with his left ear close to the keys. Listening. He hit it and hit it and hit it, leaning down lower. His eyes were squinched up real narrow, like he was trying to see the music as well as hear it. It was about then that I seen that what he was really looking at was the leopard-skin couch.

When he talked his voice was real husky, and sounded like he was surprised. 'You know what I see, man?' he said. 'When I look at that couch I see devils dancing in the moonlight. I see angels with skeleton's faces and witches with faces like dogs. And you know what else I see, man? I can see the face of God grinning like a happy nigger.'

He laughed, all of a sudden. Only it wasn't a real laugh. It was kind of a half-crying and half-laughing, as if he'd seen something and couldn't quite express it. Then, just as suddenly, he stopped and got up. I got up, too.

'I got to go,' I said. He looked at me, and his eyes looked just like he'd washed them with some kind of lotion: big and bright.

'Cutting out, huh?' he said.

'Yeah,' I said.

'Fall by tomorrow,' he said.

'I'll be by,' I said. We shook hands and I went downstairs.

It was warm out. I took my tie off and put it in my jacket pocket; then I took the jacket off and slung it over my arm and walked to the Dewey Square Hotel and went to sleep.

MILES DAVIS with QUINCY TROUPE

Miles: The Autobiography of Miles Davis

I arrived in New York City in September 1944, not in 1945 like a lot of jive writers who write about me say. It was almost the end of World War II when I got there. A lot of young guys had gone off to fight the Germans and the Japanese and some of them didn't come back. I was lucky; the war was ending. There were a lot of soldiers in their uniforms all around New York. I do remember that.

I was eighteen years old, wet behind the ears about some things, like women and drugs. But I was confident in my ability to play music, to play the trumpet, and I wasn't scared about living in New York. Nonetheless, the city was an eye-opener for me, especially all the tall buildings, the noise, the cars, and all those motherfucking people, who seemed to be everywhere. The pace of New York was faster than anything I had ever seen in my life; I thought St. Louis and Chicago were fast, but they weren't anything like New York City. So that was the first thing I had to get used to, all the people. But getting around by subway was a gas, it was so fast.

The first place I stayed was at the Claremont Hotel, which was on Riverside Drive right across from Grant's Tomb. The Juilliard School got me a room there. Then I found me a room up on 147th Street and Broadway, in a rooming house run by these people named Bell, who were from East St. Louis and knew my parents. They were nice people and the room was big and clean and cost me a dollar a week. My father had paid for my tuition and had given me some pocket money beyond my rent, enough to last me for about a month or two.

I spent my first week in New York looking for Bird and Dizzy. Man, I went everywhere looking for them two cats, spent all my money and didn't find them. I had to call back home and ask my father for some more money, which he sent me. I still was living clean, not smoking or drinking or using dope. I was just into my music and that was a total high for me. When school started at Juilliard, I would take the subway to 66th Street where the school was located. Right off the bat, I didn't like what was happening at Juilliard. The shit they was talking about was too white for me. Plus, I was more interested in what was happening in the jazz scene; that's the *real* reason I wanted to come to New York in the first place, to get into the jazz music scene that was happening around Minton's Playhouse in Harlem, and what was going on down on 52nd Street, which everybody in music called "The Street." That's what I was really in New York for, to suck up all I could from those scenes; Juilliard was only a smokescreen, a stopover, a pretense I used to put me close to being around Bird and Diz.

After I got to 52nd Street, I found Freddie Webster, who I had met back in St. Louis when he passed through playing in Jimmie Lunceford's band. Then I went and heard the Savoy Sultans at the Savoy Ballroom in Harlem; me and Freddie went to see them. They was badder than a motherfucker. But I was trying to find Bird and Dizzy and, although I was liking what I was seeing, still, it wasn't what I really came to New York to see.

The second thing I looked for was the horse stables. Since my father and grandfather had horses and since I had been riding them most of my life, I loved them as spirits and loved to ride them. I thought they would be in Central Park, so I used to walk up and down the Park, from 110th Street to 59th Street, looking for the horse stables. I never found them. Finally, one day I asked a policeman where I could find them, and he told me they were somewhere on 81st or 82nd Street. I went there and rode me a couple of horses. The attendants looked at me strange, I guess because they weren't used to seeing a black person coming to ride horses. But I just figured that that was their problem.

I went up to Harlem to check out Minton's, on 118th Street between St. Nicholas and Seventh Avenue. Next to Minton's was the Cecil Hotel, where a lot of musicians stayed. It was a hip scene. The first dumb motherfucker I saw on the corner of St. Nicholas and 117th Street was a cat named "Collar." It was in the little park they called Dewey Square, where all the musicians used to sit and get high. I never knew Collar's real name. He was from St. Louis. He used to be the Dexedrine king there and would supply Bird with Dexedrine and nutmeg and shit when he came through St. Louis. So, anyway, here's Collar up in Harlem, clean as a broke-dick dog, white-on-white shirt, black silk suit, his hair all slicked back and down to his shoulders. He said that he was in New York trying to play saxophone at Minton's. But he couldn't play too tough when he was back in St. Louis. He just wanted to be in the life of a musician. He was a *real* funny motherfucker on top of all of this. So here he was, trying to sit in at Minton's, the black jazz capital of the world. He never made it. Nobody never paid no attention to Collar up at Minton's.

Minton's and the Cecil Hotel were both first-class places with a lot of style. The people that went there were the cream of the crop of Harlem's black society. That great, middle-class building across the street from Dewey Square was called Graham Court. A lot of society black people lived in those huge, fabulous apartments; you know, doctors and lawyers and head-nigger-in-charge-type blacks. A lot of people from around the neighborhood, from

Sugar Hill, came to Minton's and the neighborhood was first-class back in those days before the drugs really came in and destroyed it during the 1960s.

People who came to Minton's wore suits and ties because they were copying the way people like Duke Ellington or Jimmie Lunceford dressed. Man, they was cleaner than a motherfucker. But to get into Minton's didn't cost anything. It cost something like two dollars if you sat at one of the tables, which had white linen tablecloths on them and flowers in little glass vases. It was a nice place—much nicer than the clubs on 52nd Street—and it held about 100 or 125 people. It was mainly a supper club and the food was prepared by a great black woman cook named Adelle.

The Cecil Hotel was also a nice place, where a lot of the black musicians visiting from out of town would stay. The rates were reasonable and the rooms were big and clean. Plus, they had a few high-class hustlers and prostitutes who hung around there and so if a cat wanted to get his balls up out of sand he could pay for a fine woman and get himself a room.

Minton's was *the* ass-kicker back in those days for aspiring jazz musicians, not The Street like they're trying to make out today. It was Minton's where a musician *really* cut his teeth and *then* went downtown to The Street. Fifty-second Street was easy compared to what was happening up at Minton's. You went to 52nd to make money and be seen by the white music critics and white people. But you came uptown to Minton's if you wanted to make a reputation among the musicians. Minton's kicked a lot of motherfuckers' asses, did them in, and they just disappeared—not to be heard from again. But it also taught a whole lot of musicians, made them what they eventually became.

I ran into Fats Navarro again up at Minton's and we used to jam up there all the time. Milt Jackson was there. And Eddie "Lockjaw" Davis, the tenor saxophonist, led the house band. He was a motherfucker. See, the great musicians like Lockjaw and Bird and Dizzy and Monk, who were the kings of Minton, never played no ordinary shit. They did this to eliminate a whole lot of people who couldn't play.

If you got up on the bandstand at Minton's and couldn't play, you were not only going to get embarrassed by people ignoring you or booing you, you might get your ass kicked. One night this guy who couldn't play worth shit got up to try and do his thing—bullshit—and style himself off to get some bitches, playing anything. A regular street guy who just loved to listen to all the music was in the audience when this dumb motherfucker got up on the stage to play, so the man just got up quietly from his table and snatched this no-playing cat off the stage, dragged him outside and into the alcove between the Cecil Hotel and Minton's, and just kicked this motherfucker's ass. I mean *real* good. Then he told the dude not to never take his ass up on the bandstand at Minton's again until he could play something worth listening to. That was Minton's. You had to put up or shut up, there was no in between.

A black man named Teddy Hill owned Minton's Playhouse. Bebop started at his club. It was the music laboratory for bebop. After it polished up at Minton's, *then* it went downtown to 52nd Street—the Three Deuces, the Onyx, and Kelly's Stable—where white people heard it. But what has to be understood in all of this is no matter how good the music sounded down on 52nd Street, it wasn't as hot or as innovative as it was uptown at Minton's. The idea was that you had to calm the innovation down for the white folks downtown because they couldn't handle the *real* thing. Now, don't get me wrong, there were *some* good white people who were brave enough to come up to Minton's. But they were few and far between.

I hate how white people always try to take credit for something after *they* discover it. Like it wasn't happening before they found out about it—which most times is always late, and they didn't have nothing to do with it happening. Then, they try to take *all* the credit, try to cut everybody black out. That's what they tried to do with Minton's Playhouse and Teddy Hill. After bebop became the rage, white music critics tried to act like they discovered it—and us—down on 52nd Street. That kind of dishonest shit makes me sick to my stomach. And when you speak out on it or don't go along with this racist bullshit, then you become a radical, a black troublemaker. Then they try to cut you out of everything. But the musicians and the people who really loved and respected bebop and the truth know that the *real* thing happened up in Harlem, at Minton's.

Every night after I finished my classes, I would either go down to The Street or up to Minton's. For a couple of weeks I didn't find Bird or Dizzy nowhere. Man, I was going to the 52nd Street clubs like the Spotlite, the Three Deuces, Kelly's Stable, and the Onyx looking for them. I remember when I went down to the Three Deuces for the first time and saw how little that place was; I thought it was going to be bigger. It had such a big reputation in the jazz scene that I thought it would be all plush and shit. The bandstand wasn't nothing but a little tiny space that could hardly hold a piano and didn't seem like it could ever hold a whole group of musicians. The tables for the customers were all jammed together and I remember thinking that it wasn't nothing but a hole in the wall, and that East St. Louis and St. Louis had hipper-looking clubs. I was disappointed in the way the place looked, but not in the music I heard. The first person I heard there was Don Byas, who was a hell of a tenor saxophone player. I remember listening with awe to him playing all that shit on that little bitty stage.

Then I was finally able to get in touch with Dizzy. I got his number and called him up. He remembered me and invited me over to his apartment on Seventh Avenue in Harlem. It was great to see him. But Dizzy hadn't seen Bird, either, and didn't know how or where to get in touch with him.

I kept looking for Bird. One night I found myself just sort of standing around in the doorway at the Three Deuces when the owner came up and asked me what I was doing there. I guess I looked young and innocent; I couldn't even grow a mustache back then. Anyway, I told him I was looking for Bird and he told me he wasn't there and that I had to be eighteen to come in the club. I told him I *was* eighteen and all I wanted to do was to find Bird. Then the dude start telling me what a fucked-up motherfucker Bird was, about him being a dope addict and all that kind of shit. He asked me where I was from and when I told him, he come telling me that I ought to go on back home. Then he called me, "son," a name I never liked, especially from some white motherfucker who I didn't know. So I told him to go fuck himself and turned around and left. I already *knew* Bird had a bad heroin habit; he wasn't telling me nothing new.

After I left the Three Deuces, I walked up the street to the Onyx Club and caught Coleman Hawkins. Man, the Onyx was jam-packed with people there to see Hawk, who played there regularly. So, because I still didn't know anybody I just hung around the doorway like I had done at the Three Deuces, looking for a face I might recognize, you know, maybe somebody from B's band. But I didn't see anyone.

When Bean—that's what we called Coleman Hawkins—took a break, he came over to where I was, and until this day I don't know why he did this. I guess it was a lucky break. Anyway, I knew who he was and so I spoke to him and introduced myself and told him that I had played with B's band back in St. Louis and that I was in New York going to Juilliard but really trying to find Bird. I told him that I wanted to play with Bird and that he had told me when I got to New York to look him up. Bean kind of laughed and told me that I was too young to get mixed up with somebody like Bird. Man, he was making me mad with all this shit. This was the second time I had heard this that night. I didn't want to hear it no more, even if it came from somebody that I loved and respected as much as Coleman Hawkins. I got a real bad temper, so the next thing I know I'm saying to *Coleman Hawkins* something like, "Well, you know where he is or not?"

Man, I think Hawk was shocked by a young little black motherfucker like me talking to him like that. He just looked at me and shook his head and told me the best place to find Bird was up in Harlem, at Minton's or Small's Paradise. Bean said, "Bird loves to jam in those places." He turned to walk away, then added, "My best advice to you is just finish your studies at Juilliard and forget Bird."

Man, those first weeks in New York were a motherfucker—looking for Bird, and trying to keep up with my studies. Then somebody told me that Bird had friends in Greenwich Village. I went down there to see if I could find him. I went to coffeehouses on Bleecker Street. Met artists, writers, and all these long-haired, bearded beatnik poets. I had never met no people like them in all my life. Going to the Village was an education for me.

I began to meet people like Jimmy Cobb and Dexter Gordon as I moved around Harlem, the Village, and 52nd Street. Dexter called me "Sweetcakes" because I was drinking malted milks and eating cakes, pies, and jelly beans all the time. I was even getting friendly with Coleman Hawkins. He took a liking to me, watched out for me, and helped me all he could to find Bird. By now Bean thought I was really serious about the music and he respected that. But, still no Bird. And not even Diz knew where he was at.

One day I saw in the paper where Bird was scheduled to play in a jam session at a club called the Heatwave, on 145th Street in Harlem. I remember asking Bean if he thought Bird would show up there, and Bean just kind of smiled that slick, sly smile of his and said, "I'll bet *Bird* doesn't even know if he'll really be there or not."

That night I went up to the Heatwave, a funky little club in a funky neighborhood. I had brought my horn just in case I did run into Bird—if he remembered me, he might let me sit in with him. Bird wasn't there, but I met some other musicians, like Allen Eager, a white tenor player; Joe Guy, who played a great trumpet; and Tommy Potter, a bass player. I wasn't looking for them so I didn't pay them hardly no attention. I just found a seat and kept my eye fixed on the door, watching out for Bird. Man, I had been there almost all night waiting for Bird and he hadn't shown up. So I decided to go outside and catch a breath of fresh air. I was standing outside the club on the corner when I heard this voice from behind me say, "Hey, Miles! I heard you been looking for me!"

I turned around and there was Bird, looking badder than a motherfucker. He was dressed in these baggy clothes that looked like he had been sleeping in them for days. His face was all puffed up and his eyes were swollen and red. But he was cool, with that hipness he could have about him even when he was drunk or fucked up. Plus, he had that confidence that all people have when they *know* their shit is bad. But no matter *how* he looked, bad or near death, he still looked good to me that night after spending all that time trying to find him; I was just glad to see him standing there. And when he remembered where he had met me, I was the happiest motherfucker on earth.

I told him how hard it had been to find him and he just smiled and said that he moved around a lot. He took me into the Heatwave, where everybody greeted him like he was the king, which he was. And since I was with him and he had his arm around my shoulder, they treated me with a lot of respect, too. I didn't play that first night. I just listened. And, man, I was amazed at how Bird changed the minute he put his horn in his mouth. Shit, he went from looking real down and out to having all this power and beauty just bursting out of him. It was amazing the transformation that took place once he started playing. He was twenty-four at the time, but when he wasn't playing he looked older, especially off stage. But his whole appearance changed as soon as he put that horn in his mouth. He could play like a motherfucker even when he was almost falling-down drunk and nodding off behind heroin. Bird was something else.

Anyway, after I hooked up with him that night, I was around Bird all the time for the next several years. He and Dizzy became my main influences and teachers. Bird even moved in with me for a while, until Irene came. She came to New York in December 1944. All of a sudden, there she was, knocking on my motherfucking door; my mother had told her to come. So I found Bird a room in the same rooming house, up on 147th and Broadway.

But I couldn't handle Bird's lifestyle then—all the drinking and eating and using dope. I had to go to school in the daytime and he'd be laying up there fucked up. But he was teaching me a lot about music—chords and shit—that I would go and play on the piano when I got to school.

Almost every night I was going somewhere with Diz or Bird, sitting in, soaking up everything I could. And like I said, I had met Freddie Webster, who was a great trumpet player about the same age as me. We would go down to 52nd Street and listen in amazement at how fast Dizzy could play tempos on the trumpet. Man, I hadn't never heard no shit like they was playing on 52nd Street and up at Minton's. That was so good it was scary. Dizzy started showing me shit on the piano so I could expand my sense of harmony.

And Bird introduced me to Thelonious Monk. His use of space in his solos and his manipulation of funny-sounding chord progressions just knocked me out, fucked me up. I said, "Damn, what is this motherfucker doing?" Monk's use of space had a big influence on the way I played solos after I heard him.

Meanwhile I started really getting pissed off with what they was talking about at Juilliard. It just wasn't happening for me there. Like I said, going to Juilliard was a smokescreen for being around Dizzy and Bird, but I did want to see what I could learn there. I played in the school symphony orchestra. We played about two notes every ninety bars, and that was that. I wanted and needed more. Plus, I knew that no white symphony orchestra was going to hire a little black motherfucker like me, no matter how good I was or how much music I knew.

I was learning more from hanging out, so I just got bored with school after a while. Plus, they were so fucking white-oriented and so racist. Shit, I could learn more in one session at Minton's than it would take me two years to learn at Juilliard. At Juilliard, after it was all over, all I was going to know was a bunch of white styles; nothing new. And I was just getting mad and embarrassed with their prejudice and shit.

I remember one day being in a music history class and a white woman was the teacher. She was up in front of the class saying that the reason black people played the blues was because they were poor and had to pick cotton. So they were sad and that's where the blues came from, their sadness. My hand went up in a flash and I stood up and said, "I'm from East St. Louis and my father is rich, he's a dentist, and I play the blues. My father didn't never pick no cotton and I didn't wake up this morning sad and start playing the blues. There's more to it than that." Well, the bitch turned green and didn't say nothing after that. Man, she was teaching that shit from out of a book written by someone who didn't know what the fuck he was talking about. That's the kind of shit that was happening at Juilliard and after a while I got tired of it.

The way I was thinking about music was that people like Fletcher Henderson and Duke Ellington were the real geniuses at arranging music in America. This woman didn't even know who these people were, and *I* didn't have the time to teach her. She was supposed to be teaching me! So, instead of listening to what she and the other teachers said, I was looking up at the clock and thinking about what I would be doing later that night, wondering when Bird and Diz would be going downtown. I was thinking about going home to pick up some clothes to wear over to Bickford's at 145th Street and Broadway, to pick up fifty cents worth of soup so I could have the strength to play later on that night.

On Monday nights at Minton's, Bird and Dizzy would come in to jam, so you'd have a thousand motherfuckers up there trying to get in so they could listen to and play with Bird and Dizzy. But most of the musicians in the know didn't even think about playing when Bird and Dizzy came to jam. We would just sit out in the audience, to listen and learn. The rhythm section for them might be Kenny Clarke on drums and sometimes Max Roach, who I met up there. Curly Russell would be playing bass and Monk was on the piano sometimes. Man, people would be fighting over seats and shit. If you moved you'd lose your seat and have to argue and fight again. It was something. The air was just electric.

The way the shit went down up at Minton's was you brought your horn and hoped that Bird and Dizzy would invite you to play with them up on stage. And when this happened, you'd better not blow it. I didn't. The first time I played there I wasn't great but I was playing my ass off in the style I played, which was different from Dizzy's, although I was influenced by his playing at this time. But people would watch for clues from Bird and Dizzy, and if they smiled when you finished playing, then that meant that your playing was good. They smiled when I finished playing that first time and from then on I was on the inside of what was happening in New York's music scene. So after that I was like an up-and-coming star. I could sit in with the big boys all the time.

That's what I was thinking about in my classes in Juilliard, instead of having my mind on what they was teaching me. That's why I eventually quit Juilliard. They weren't teaching me nothing and didn't *know* nothing to teach me because they were so prejudiced against all black music. And that's what I wanted to learn.

Anyway, after a while I was sitting in up there at Minton's whenever I wanted to and people were coming to hear *me* play. I was getting a reputation. One of the things that surprised me about being in New York was that when I first got there, I thought all the musicians would know more about music than they did. So I was shocked to find out that among the older guys, Dizzy, Roy Eldridge, and long-haired Joe Guy were the only ones I could listen to and learn something from. I expected everybody was going to be a motherfucker and was surprised when I knew a lot more about music than most of them.

Another thing I found strange after living and playing in New York for a little while was that a lot of black musicians didn't know anything about music theory. Bud Powell was one of the few musicians I knew who could play, write, and read all kinds of music. A lot of the old guys thought that if you went to school it would make you play like you were white. Or, if you learned something from theory, then you would lose the feeling in your playing. I couldn't believe that all them guys like Bird, Prez, Bean, all them cats wouldn't go to museums or libraries or borrow those musical scores so they could check out what was happening. I would go to the library and borrow scores by all those great composers, like Stravinsky, Alban Berg, Prokofiev. I wanted to see what was going on in all of music. Knowledge is freedom and ignorance is slavery, and I just couldn't believe someone could be that close to freedom and not take advantage of it. I have never understood why black people didn't take advantage of all the shit that they can. It's like a ghetto mentality telling people that they aren't supposed to do certain things, that those things are only reserved for white people. When I would tell other musicians about all this, they would just kind of shine me on. You know what I mean? So I just went my own way and stopped telling them about it.

I had a good friend named Eugene Hays, who was from St. Louis and studied classical piano at Juilliard with me. He was a genius. If he had been white, he would have been one of the most highly regarded classical pianists in the world today. But he was black and he was ahead of his time. So they didn't give him anything. He and I took advantage of these music libraries. We would take advantage of everything we could.

Anyway, at the time I was hanging out with musicians like Fats Navarro—who everybody called "Fat Girl"—and Freddie Webster, and I had gotten kind of close with Max Roach and J. J. Johnson, the great trombone player from Indianapolis. We was all trying to get our master's degrees and Ph.D.'s from Minton's University of Bebop under the tutelage of Professors Bird and Diz. Man, they was playing so much incredible shit.

One time after the jam session was over and I had gone home to sleep, there was this knock on my door. I got up and went to the door with sleep in my eyes, madder than a motherfucker. I opened the door and there was J. J. Johnson and Benny Carter standing there with pencils and paper in their hands. I asked them, "What do you motherfuckers want this early in the morning?"

J. J. said, " 'Confirmation.' Miles, do 'Confirmation' for me, hum it."

The motherfucker ain't even said hello, right? That's the first thing out of his mouth. Bird had just written "Confirmation" and all the musicians just loved that tune. So, here's this motherfucker at six in the morning. We had just finished jamming "Confirmation" earlier, me and J. J., at the jam session. Now he's talking about humming the tune.

So I started humming it through my sleep, in the key of F. That's what it's written in. Then J. J. says to me, "But Miles, you left out a note. Where's the other note, what's that other note in the tune?" So I remember it and tell him.

He said, "Thanks Miles," wrote something down, and then left. J. J. was a funny motherfucker, man. He used to do that shit to me all the time. He figured I knew what Bird was doing technically because I was going to Juilliard. I'll never forget that first time he did it, and we laugh about it even today. But that's how much everybody was into Bird's and Dizzy's music. We lived and slept it every day.

Me and Fat Girl used to sit in a lot together up at Minton's. He was so big and fat until he lost all that weight right before he died. If he didn't like what some motherfucker was playing up at Minton's, Fat Girl would just block the cat from getting the microphone. He'd just turn sideways and block whoever it was and motion for me to play. Cats used to get mad with Fat Girl, but he didn't care, and whoever he did it to knew they couldn't play. So they'd stay mad for only so long.

But my real main man during those first days in New York was Freddie Webster. I really liked what Freddie was doing on the horn then. He had a style like the players from St. Louis, a big, singing sound, and he didn't play too many notes or play those real fast tempos. He liked medium-tempo pieces and ballads a lot, like I did. I loved the way he played, that he didn't waste notes and had a big, warm, mellow sound. I used to try to play like him, but without the vibrato and "shaking about the notes." He was about nine years older than me, but I used to show him everything they taught me at Juilliard about technique and composition, technical things, which Juilliard *was* good for. Freddie was from Cleveland and grew up playing with Tadd Dameron. We were as close as real brothers and a lot alike. We were about the same size and used to wear each other's clothes.

Freddie had a lot of bitches. Women were his thing, besides music and heroin. Man, people would be coming by telling me about Freddie being a violent cat who carried a .45 gun and shit like that. But everybody who knew him well knew this wasn't true. I mean he didn't take no shit, but he didn't go around fucking with nobody. He even stayed with me for a while after Bird moved out. Freddie spoke his mind and didn't take shit off nobody. He was a complex guy, but we got along real well. We were so close that I paid his rent a lot. Whatever I had was his. My old man was sending me about forty dollars a week, which was a nice amount of money in those days. Whatever I didn't spend on my family I shared with Freddie.

The year 1945 was a turning point in my life. So many things started happening for me and to me. First off, from hanging around with so many musicians and being in so many clubs, I started to drink a little during that year and I started to smoke. And I was playing with more people. Me and Freddie, Fat Girl, J. J., and Max Roach were jamming all over New York and Brooklyn, wherever we could. We'd play downtown on 52nd Street until about twelve or one in the morning. Then, after we finished playing there, we'd go uptown to Minton's, Small's Paradise, or the Heatwave and play until they closed—around four, five, or six in the morning. After we'd be up all night at jam sessions, me and Freddie would sit up even longer talking about music and music theory, about approaches to the trumpet. At Juilliard I'd sleepwalk through them sorry-ass classes, bored to tears, especially in my chorus classes. I'd be sitting there yawning and nodding. Then, after classes, me and Freddie would sit around and talk more music. I hardly slept. And with Irene home, well, I had to be taking care of my husband duties with her sometimes, you know, being with her, shit like that. Then Cheryl would be crying. It was a motherfucker.

During 1945, me and Freddie Webster used to go down almost every night to catch Diz and Bird wherever they were playing. We felt that if we missed hearing them play we were missing something important. Man, the shit they were playing and doing was going down so fast you just had to be there in person to catch it. We really studied what they were doing from a technical point of view. We were like scientists of sound. If a door squeaked we could call out the exact pitch.

There was a white teacher named William Vachiano that I was studying with who helped me. But he was into shit like "Tea for Two" so he'd ask me to play stuff like that for him. We'd have arguments that became legendary among musicians in New York, because he was supposed to be this great teacher of advanced students, like I was. But me and that motherfucker went around on each other's back a lot of times. I would say, "Hey, man, you're supposed to be teaching me something, so do it and cut out the bullshit." Well, when I would say something like that, Vachiano would get madder than a motherfucker and turn all red in the face. But I got my point across to him.

It was playing with Bird that really got my shit to going. I could sit and talk, eat and hang out with Dizzy, because he's such a nice guy. But Bird was a greedy motherfucker. We didn't never have too much to say to each other. We liked playing with each other and that was it. Bird didn't never *tell* you what to play. You learned from him by just watching him, picking up shit that he did. He never did talk about music much when you were alone with him. But we talked a few times about it when he was living with me, and I picked up some things, but mostly I just learned by listening to him play.

Dizzy *liked* to talk a lot about music, though, and I picked up a lot from him in that way. Bird might have been the spirit of the bebop movement, but Dizzy was its "head and its hands," the one who kept it all together. I mean, he looked out for the younger players, got us jobs and shit, talked to us, and it didn't matter that he was nine or ten years older than I was. He never talked down to me. People used to put Dizzy down because he acted so crazy and shit. But he wasn't really crazy, just funnier than a motherfucker and really into the history of black people. He was playing music from Africa and

Cuba a long time before it got popular anywhere else. Dizzy's apartment—at 2040 Seventh Avenue, in Harlem—was the gathering place for many of the musicians in the daytime. There got to be so many of us that his wife, Lorraine, started putting motherfuckers out. I'd be there a lot. Kenny Dorham would be over there, Max Roach, Monk.

It was Dizzy who made me really learn how to play piano. I'd be over there watching Monk doing his weird shit with space and progressive chords. And when Dizzy would practice, man, I would be soaking up all that good shit. But then again, I showed Diz something that I'd learned at Juilliard, the Egyptian minor scales. With the Egyptian scale you just change the flats and sharps where you want the note flatted and where you want it sharp, so you have two flats and one sharp, right? That means you will play E flat and A flat and then the F will be sharp. You put in the note that you want, like in the C scale's minor Egyptian scale. The shit looks funny because you have two flats and a sharp. But it gives you the freedom to work with melodic ideas without changing the basic tonality. So I turned Dizzy on to that; it worked both ways. But I learned way more from him than he did from me.

NATHANIEL MACKEY

Djbot Baghostus's Run

Dear Angel of Dust,

I've been hit by a new round of shattered cowrie shell attacks—a round of attacks whose new wrinkle is that their having to do with vision (the shells' eyelike look when whole) seems now to have to do with putting on a lid. The shells have been replaced by bottle caps. The caps line my forehead, held on by a wire which passes thru the holes punched in them but left with enough play to be able to buzz, vibrate in sympathy with the music piped into my head—not Ornette's "Embraceable You" but Lightnin' Hopkins's "Bottle Up and Go." (Lightnin', you may know, died week before last.) A veritable hive of bottle cap buzzings, my head resonates like a calabash gourd on an mbira. The bottle caps' raspy disbursements make for a cross-accentual "screen," the acoustic rough-equivalent of burlap.

The first attack occurred during the gig we just got back from, a three-night stint at a club called Earl's up north in Albany. It was brought on in part by the news that Monk had suffered a cerebral hemorrhage and was in a coma, which we heard on the local jazz station KJAZ. They were playing a lot of Monk's music, calling it "Monk Watch"—what amounted to a before-the-fact wake. "My God," Penguin muttered, shaking his head, "three years ago Mingus, Marley last May, now Monk." I shook mine as well, saying something about Lightnin' having died the week before. It was then I began to hear "Bottle Up and Go," a faint strain factored into which the play between loose fit and tight fit, bottle cap and coffin lid, conjugated itself at an even fainter, whisperlike remove. It wasn't until later, though, that it hit with full force.

It was Saturday afternoon when we heard the news. We were in Richmond at my cousin Kenny's. He plays baritone mainly, but also alto, soprano, and flute, and there's been talk of him sitting in with us at Earl's. I think it was he who eventually suggested we get something together for the set that night, put together some sort of tribute to Monk. We ended up deciding not to leave it at just Monk but to include the other three who'd come up as well, Mingus, Marley and Lightnin'. We settled on a medley we'd announce under the collective title "Three M's and an H," a medley which would start off with Monk's (yes, you guessed it) "Ask Me Now." From there we'd move on to Marley's "No Woman, No Cry," then to Lambert, *a cappella,* doing "Bottle Up and Go" on harmonica. We'd wrap it up with Mingus's "Free Cell Block F, 'tis Nazi USA." This last we decided to preface with all of us reading in unison the first paragraph of Ellison's novel *Invisible Man*—this to announce an equation of *Nazi* with *not see*.

We didn't have much in the way of rehearsal time but the tunes were all ones we knew so it didn't take much. A quick run-thru during the sound check at the club that evening did it. We deliberately didn't put a lot of polish on it, choosing instead to go after the ragged momentariness the occasion, we felt, required. This we not only went after but largely got. We played the medley during the second set, in the course of which I was hit by the shattered cowrie shell attack, the shattered-cowrie-shell-become-bottle-cap attack.

The medley got off to a good start with Kenny sitting in on alto and doing the soloing on "Ask Me Now." He gave it a sensitive, extended reading which parlayed its lullabylike inflections into inklings and outright glimpses of tensile endurance. This he did largely by way of a tremolo on the spoons to which he resorted every now and then, an abrupt, bothered, headstrong helium-inhalation which made light of all odds or obstruction. The at once wide-eyed, squinting stress on glimpses looked ahead to the Mingus piece, a foreshadowing tack which was lost on none of us. A blue, bruised adumbration of damage done, it was a reading whose wincing regard spoke of loss and resilience. It mourned and put its mourning to rest in the same breath. It etched into its dormant features a see-thru function, the ascendancy of technical-ecstatic squint.

Ever so smoothly, "Ask Me Now," segued into "No Woman, No Cry," another lullaby of sorts. Djamilaa's harmonium gave it a churchical, Eastern feeling, evoked a church or a sacred cave in which it seemed we were gathered. Aunt Nancy had the lead voice on trumpet. She not only saw Kenny's technical-ecstatic squint but raised him a cried-out eye. She let each run break down into a sputter à la Lester Bowie, an extravagant, blubbering collapse whose extravagance mocked itself. Aunt Nancy played sacred clown in the sacred cave it seemed we were in. With each exorbitant, blubbering breakdown more and more people in the audience laughed. Penguin and Lambert on sopraninos and Kenny and I on sopranos comprised a high-pitched, complicit chorus whose giddy insistences complied with Kenny's earlier helium hits. We endorsed and punctuated Aunt Nancy's tragicomic lead with giggly rushes which, a friend who was in the audience told us later, grew possessed of an infectious cartoon quality. We came on—Penguin, Lambert, Kenny and I—like a group of hyperactive chipmunks. What with Aunt Nancy's "quackical" sputter it amounted to a cartoon script and score rolled into one, Donald Duck backed up by Alvin and the Chipmunks.

It was an odd, unexpected treatment of Marley's tune. It caught most of the audience offguard. Chipmunk chatter (chipmunk ecstasy) caught Aunt Nancy a bit offguard as well, though she more than held her own in the fray. Her collapses into "quackical" pathos notwithstanding, she was never long out of touch with the heartfelt resolve and reassurance of the line "Everything's gonna be alright." However much Penguin, Lambert, Kenny and I threatened to take such resolve and reassurance to absurd, overstated heights, she resisted any impulse to follow. Chipmunk sublimity upped the ante on cried-out extravagance but Aunt Nancy had clearly given some thought to these matters, clearly had ideas of her own. More and more she steered a course away from exorbitant collapse as well as away from chipmunk exuberance.

Eventually Aunt Nancy indicated we should back off. We brought "No Woman, No Cry" to a close with a cadenza out of which she emerged with only drum and harmonium accompaniment. She blew nothing but seriously now, a short coda in which when she sputtered she did so poignantly, no longer parodic. She put one in mind of Bill Dixon, so harassed and heartfelt was the winded urgency of her approach, fury so insistently the "note" she resorted to. The dead do live again she implied with an unpitched run of wind which flew like a bat thru the sacred cave. This run she let the piece go out on. Lambert put his harmonica to his mouth, gave the run's echo time to fade and took up from there. The stage lights went down, leaving only a spotlight fixed on him. Sacred cave became deserted crossroads.

So as not to clash with the lullabylike inflections of what had gone before, Lambert gave "Bottle Up and Go" a more laidback reading than usual. He took it slow, gave it a drawn-out feel, made it almost dirgelike. It could've been taps he was playing the way he started out, what with the stage lights going down and all. He gave it a mournful, plaintive sound which spoke of ultimate lights-out, ultimate sleep, reminded us of Lightnin's death. He blew for all he was worth and more, taking deep, gut-swelling inhalations as though breath were both carriage and cure, as though he sought to resuscitate the dead. It was some of the most moving harp we'd ever heard Lambert play. He even threw in a Dixonian touch of his own, interpolating, à la Mingus, Willie Dixon's "I

Want You to Love Me" into "Bottle Up and Go," implicitly stressing the rhyme between the latter's title line and the former's "love your baby slow." He thus recalled Aunt Nancy's coda while obliquely anticipating the Mingus piece. Heartfelt for sure but also exquisitely heady stuff, it went to my head. It was here that the shattered-cowrie-shell-become-bottle-cap attack began to come on.

I immediately noticed the impacted feeling in my forehead to be of a more integral and substantive, less brokenly symbolic sort. The cowrie shells had not only become bottle caps, I noticed, but the bottle caps were unbroken, whole. I was surprised, even a little bit shocked, but, true to my new bottle cap aplomb, took it in stride. I began to hear "Bottle Up and Go" not only coming from Lambert's harmonica but also Lightnin's version piped into my head. The bottle caps buzzed in sympathy with both, "fuzzing" or "dirtying" the sound to such an extent I could've sworn the line Lightnin' sang was "Gotta bottle up a ghost." I immediately thought of Jarred Bottle and even murmured the name under my breath, but the memory of Aunt Nancy's bat-winged run of wind whispered, "Djbot Baghostus," correcting me it seemed. I now knew for sure I'd been hit.

Lambert brought his *a cappella* section to a close and the stage lights came back up. It was now time for the unison reading from *Invisible Man*. Though my head was a corrected cave in which Jarred Bottle had taken a new name, a scarred, unsacred cave in which Aunt Nancy's run of wind still flew, I somehow was able to hold myself together—bottle cap aplomb notwithstanding, barely able. We read the Ellison passage, which only two or three people in the audience seemed to recognize. We then leapt into "Free Cell Block F . . . ," the piece Mingus gave its title after reading an *Ebony* article on southern prisons. It's a piece whose uptown flair and good feeling seem at odds with its political prognosis, a time-lapse equation linking before-the-fact tune with after-the-fact title or intent. The post-equivalent aligning before-the-fact elation with titular afterthought or intent gets made more emphatic by the tune's excursions into 5/4. Perhaps it was this alignment I couldn't quite see. Perhaps it was this which woke me up to the astigmatic strain I now saw to be endemic to the nominal politics the piece pursues. Perhaps the *Nazi/not see* homophony ricocheted from wall to wall with too much force and too little correction within the recesses of the bottle cap cave. Perhaps the ascendency of technical-ecstatic squint to which Kenny had alluded was neither an inverse nor a yielding function so much as a philosophic advocacy of "off-the-wall" inflection. Perhaps it was this which triggered the interception of chimerical wind by chimerical wall inside my head. Whatever it was, I knew I was in trouble after only a few bars.

It all, it seemed, got harder all at once—harder to hold together, harder not to want to, harder to put inside a single frame. The memory of Aunt Nancy's run went on whispering. The air was a delicate fabric her Dixonian tag had made run like a piece of silk. An elated sound which bordered on fanfare,

Mingus's piece was a lit-up cave concentric with the one my head had become, a metallic shell whose putative utopia bat-winged wind only made more remote. A bit more metallic with Kenny sitting in, our rendition had a top-heaviness to it Drennette worked overtime keeping afloat. To me it confirmed and gave added conviction to the bottle caps' cowrie shell conceit, the illusion of sewn lids made more durable, the propped-up incumbency of astigmatic squint.

Penguin soloed first and I followed—him on alto, me on tenor. He took a preacherly tack which made the most of the possibilities for chastisement the equation of *Nazi* with *not see* opened up. Refusing to see, as did looking the other way, came under fire. Tending less toward rhapsody than rant, he put uptown flair and good feeling aside. He harangued and exhorted and even opted at points for a screw-loose, loquacious plea for open eyes, a return to Kenny's wide-eyed squint. It was Penguin to the limit—a bittersweet, biting sound à la Jimmy Lyons without Jimmy's trepidatious phrasing. Penguin went for the big, mouthfilling phrase, straightahead but syntactically loose enough to point to particulars where the need arose. The Greensboro killings came up. The Atlanta child murders came up. The lynching last March in Alabama came up, as did a number of other such "incidents" people choose not, Penguin pointed out, to see for what they are.

The audience appeared to be both chastened and charged up by Penguin's solo. Many sat with their heads bowed, eyes fixed on the floor, nodding every now and then in agreement—some in sad, some in grudging, some in gratified agreement. Others were more vocal in their response, a few shouting out, "Right on," another few, "Amen," another few, "Tell it like it is." Church and political rally rolled into one, Penguin's preacherly tack more than paid off—so much so it had me wondering what if any stone he'd left unturned, what if any ground he hadn't covered, at a loss where to go in my solo.

Penguin ended his solo and there was a long, loud round of applause. Still at a loss, my only chance, I saw, was to somehow predicate the very predicament I was in, to somehow make depletion a virtue, to blow as though beginning from scratch. What came out of the horn recalled Frank Lowe somewhat, a bluesy, gut-bucket croak of a sound I devoted to a single note. I began by playing the same note, C, over and over again, a back-to-basics move or approach by way of which I underscored my start from scratch. I jumped octaves and varied placement and duration but the only note I played was C. I played it long, I played it short, I played it staccato, I played it spaced, I played it soft, I played it loud. C was my letter to the world.

The world's reply was at first a cool one, almost no reply at all. The audience looked on as if perplexed, not knowing what to make of so stark a contrast to what had gone before. The cooler, more noncommittal their response, though, the more insistent I became, the more "scratchical" my tack, as though C were something caught in my throat. "Scratchical" C grew more and more gruff, more and more abrasive. Still, I kept at it. My mind was made up

I'd play nothing but C until the audience responded, showed some sign of catching on. It took a while but finally I saw a few people nod their heads—nod as if to say, "Yeah, I hear you." These few nods proved contagious, or so it seemed, for more and more people began nodding their heads. In no time at all everyone in the club was doing so. A few even yelled out things like "Yeah, break it down" and "That's it, you got it." It was only then that I let go of my "scratchical" fixation, only then that I dared play anything but C, dared acknowledge not-C.

I now played a few other notes. I now extended my insistence on C into a "scratchical" dialectic between it and not-C. Which one would win out I rhetorically asked by way of recourse to a tremolo which "tested" each note. It was then that the audience did something which completely took me by surprise. As if on cue, they each took out a pair of glasses and put them on. They were 3D glasses, the kind made for watching 3D movies. They took them out of bags, they took them out of pocketbooks, they took them out of pockets. Those already wearing glasses took them off to put the 3D glasses on. Almost before I could blink everyone sat bespectacled, staring up at the stage as though "Free Cell Block F . . ." were a 3D movie. I wasn't sure what to make of it. Had they seen my C and raised me a D? What did D mean were that in fact the case? Was 3D the dialectic itself? These and other questions crowded my head.

What I did know, what I couldn't help noticing, was that as soon as they put on the glasses the bottle caps on my forehead gained greater contour. Whereas before they'd been a bit flat, a bit faint, as though they were only a rough draft of themselves, they were now much more sharply defined, were now given greater relief. They were now much more pronounced, more protuberant. (I took a hand off the horn to touch my forehead.) They've been that way ever since.

Yours,
N.

GREG TATE

Silence, Exile, and Cunning: *Miles Davis in Memoriam*

Pronouncing the death of Miles Davis seems more sillyass than sad. Something on the order of saying you've clocked the demise of the blues, the theory of relativity, *Ulysses*, or any other definitive creation of this century. Miles is one of those works of art, science, and magic whose absence might have ripped a chunk out of the zeitgeist big enough to sink a dwarf star into. A friend of mine once said that you could not love being black and not love Miles Davis because Miles was the quintessential African American. African American, not as in two halves thrown together, but a recombinant entity born of sperm and egg to produce a third creature more expansive than either.

Quincy Jones has opined, if someone asks what jazz is, play them *Kind of Blue*. For some of us coming from the African-centric tip, Miles Davis *is* the black aesthetic. He doesn't just represent it, he defines it. Music, poetry, philosophy, fashion, sports, architecture, design, painting, scholarship, politics, film, physics, femininity, even if not feminism—it doesn't matter, Miles is the model and the measure for how *black* your shit really is. Miles rendered black a synonym for the best of everything. To the aristocratic mind of this East St. Louis scion of a pig farmer/dentist, it naturally followed that if you were playing the baadest music on the face of the earth with the baadest musicians living, then of course you were driving the baadest cars, wearing the baadest vines, and intimate with the most regal of women and celebrated of artists, thinkers, and athletes. What black also meant to Miles was supreme intelligence, elegance, creativity, and funk. Miles worked black culture encyclopedically—from the outhouse to the penthouse and back again, to paraphrase brother Stanley Crouch. He rolled up on symphony orchestras with greasy blues phrases and dropped Stockhausen over dopebeats. Like Bessie Smith, he wasn't ashamed to show his ass in high society, or to take his Issey Miyake gear to the toilet stool. (I'm proud to say I nearly bore witness to that shit.)

Accepting Clyde Taylor's definition of black music as "our mother tongue," no artist in history territorialized as many of its multi-accentuated language groups as Miles. And the way he worked these linguistic systems demands we interact as critically with his music as we do with the texts of Baldwin, Baraka, Morrison, or the slave narratives. The music of Miles Davis is the music of a deep thinker on African-American experience.

The reason black music occupies a privileged and authoritative position in black aesthetic discourse is because it seems to croon and cry out to us from a postliberated world of unrepressed black pleasure and self-determination. Black music, like black basketball, represents an actualization of those black ideologies that articulate themselves as antithetical to Eurocentrism. Music and 'ball both do this in ways that are counterhegemonic if not counter-supremacist—rooting black achievement in ancient black cultural practices. In the face of the attempt to erase the African contribution to world knowledge, and the diminution of black intelligence that came with it, the very fact of black talents without precedent or peers in the white community demolishes racist precepts instantaneously. In this war of signifying and countersigning Miles Davis was a warrior king and we were all enthralled.

Paying tribute to the courtly airs of Jean Michel Basquiat, Diego Cortez compared Basquiat's noblesse oblige to Miles's, pointing out how important it was for black culture to have its own aristocrats. George Benson has spoken of how Miles made being a black jazz musician feel like the most exalted honorific one could achieve on this earth. In the business of reinvesting the devalued human stock of chattel slavery with a sense of self-worth, Miles was among the most bullish CEOs in the history of the company. Primarily because he's a blues people's genius.

Obviously, the notion of *black genius* is an oxymoron designed to send Eurocentrists screaming to the mat. Though considered an absurdity by academe, the artistry of a Miles or a Holiday or a Hendrix obliterates that prejudice with a vengeance. That Miles Davis ranks beside Picasso in the modernist pantheon has long been the stuff of journalistic cliché. All things being equal, Miles and Pablo will probably end up sharing a room together in a hell of mirrors being flogged by furies for all the women they dogged. That Miles looms as large as Warhol as far as postmodern thinkers go is an insight for which we can thank Arthur Jafa. Like Warhol, Miles came to use his visual presence and celebrity to manipulate the interpretation of his work and eventually made that stuff a part of the work as well, particularly in the '80s, when his cordial stage demeanor attracted more attention than his band or his horn playing.

Befitting his status as black aesthetic signifier in the flesh, Miles cannot merely be read as a fascinating subject. He's also for many of us an objectified projection of our blackest desires, a model for any black artist who wants to thoroughly interpenetrate Western domains of power and knowledge with Africanizing authority. For those who approach him as a generator of musical systems, metaphors, metaphysics, and gossip, Miles was the premier black romantic artist of this century. It's difficult to say at what point the legend of Miles enveloped his work. The mythologizing process began as early as the mid '50s. You can't interpret Miles's work if you don't acknowledge his syncretism of life and music. This has less to do with trying to read his music through his clothes or his sex life or his choice of pharmaceuticals than with him being, as his biographer Quincy Troupe says, "an unreconstructed black man," a Stagolee figure who makes the modern world deal with him on his terms if it's going to deal with him at all. Few black men receiving their pay from major white corporations could get away with saying they'd like to spend the last minutes of their life choking a white man and suffer no repercussions for it. No one else in jazz could have chucked a following built over a lifetime to pursue the wild and wacky musical course Miles took from *In a Silent Way* onward.

The funny thing is that as disorienting as that period was for his old fans, Miles stepped into the era of black power politics and hippie rebellion like he'd had a hand in creating it all along. He never seemed like the old jazz hand who was trying to get hip to the Youth and Soul movements of the day.

Homeboy came off like he was redefining cool for that generation too. As in the '50s and '60s, in the '70s he emerged as chief prophet of musicality for the next 20 years. Punk, hiphop, house, new jack swing, worldbeat, ambient music, and dub are all presaged in the records Miles cut between 1969 and 1975. There's no other figure whose work can be said to have laid the cornerstone for the advances of Brian Eno, Parliament-Funkadelic, Prince, Public Image Ltd., Talking Heads, Public Enemy, Living Colour, Marshall Jefferson, and Wynton Marsalis. Miles? Yeah, they named that one right. Only thing more to the point might have been Moebius.

On the other hand, the reason Miles was always so fresh was because he was so rooted. When I met Miles for an interview in 1986 it immediately struck me that the person he most reminded me of was my late maternal grandmother. Like her, a barber who spent her last years cutting heads at an Air Force base, Miles not only seemed to be a country person thoroughly wise in the ways of cosmopolitans but the type of country person who seems to become even more country the longer they stay among so-called sophisticates. Not as a ploy, like you'd find in folktales, playing dumb in order to get over on city slickers, but more like recognizing countryness as a state of grace. I imagine this sense of transcendence comes from knowing you are of ancient, enduring, and obdurate stock and that the rest will soon fade.

Lester Bowie once countered Wynton Marsalis's line on the tradition by saying that the tradition in jazz *is* innovation. Perhaps the median between these poles is that you become an innovator by working your way deeper into the tradition rather than by working out of it, recognizing that there's gold in them haunted hills. If the trick is to advance the tradition without refusing, abusing, or deifying it, then Miles wrote the book of love there. You could reduce everything Miles ever played to an obsession with four elements: deep bass, open space, circular time, and blues falsettos. In a mystical or metaphorical sense you could read these constants as earth, air, water, and fire. No matter how avant his music might have seemed to the rear guard, Miles held to those constants. Miles is a nomad, and nomads are famous for being able to re-create their way of life anywhere. I think it was his clarity about where he came from that gave him his urgency to keep moving on, a fugitive for life.

Baraka says black musical tradition implores us to sing and fight. I disagree. I think we'd do that anyway, just out of human necessity. What I do think it teaches us is more Joycean in tenor: silence, exile, and cunning. Miles's music makes you think of Nat Turner, proud without being loud because it was about plotting insurrection. In this sense Miles never changed. His agenda remained the same from day one: stay ahead.

Writers only have their style to leave behind said Nabokov. Miles says he was always looking for musicians who had a style, a voice I think he meant, of their own. In a music built on celebrating democracy and the individual, Miles developed a voice that was not only singular, but critical of all who picked up the instrument afterwards. After Miles, you couldn't just be a good trumpet player. You had to sacrifice your soul and maybe give some blood in the process. Others might have played trumpet from the heart; Miles played it like he was having open heart surgery. At the same time, every note thanked God for putting Louis Armstrong on the planet. Miles's tight-lipped sound conveyed the gaiety of Armstrong's wide vibrato while conjuring up the calculating pockets of dark sarcasm and meanness that at times ruled his spirit.

These qualities were nowhere more apparent than in his treatment of women, if we take him at his word for the gloating accounts of physical and psychological abuse in the as-told-to Troupe biography. Much as I love Miles, I despised him after reading about those incidents. Not because I worshiped the ground he spit on, but because I'd loathe any muhfukuh who violated women the way he did and relished having the opportunity to tell the world about it. Miles may have swung it like a champion but on that score he went out like a roach.

—*1991*

QUINCY JONES

Playboy Interview: Quincy Jones (July 1990)

Interview Conducted for Playboy by Alex Haley

"Back on the Block," the latest hit album from Quincy Jones, may not sell as many copies as "Thriller," the all-time record-setting megahit he produced with Michael Jackson in 1982. It may not have the global impact of "We Are the World," his superstar-studded 1985 musical event, which raised $50,000,000 to fight hunger. It may not earn him another Grammy award, though he has won 20 of them since 1963. But "Back on the Block" is certainly the most historic achievement of Jones's extraordinary career. It's also the story of his life.

A virtuoso blending of bebop, soul, Gospel, rhythm-and-blues, Brazilian and African music, rap and fusion, it's what one critic called "a virtual crash course in black popular music of the 20th Century." In his liner notes for the album, Jones wrote that his intention was "to bridge generations and traverse musical boundaries." Actually, that's what he has been doing ever since he broke into show business at the age of 15 as a trumpet player and arranger for Lionel Hampton.

In the 42 years since then, he has composed, arranged or produced hits for almost every major name in the music business, from such big-band greats as Count Basie and Dizzy Gillespie to modern-day superstars such as Frank Sinatra. He is also credited with helping catalyze the phenomenon of "crossover" by bringing black music across the color line into the musical mainstream. As a vice-president of Mercury Records in the early Sixties, Jones was the first black executive at a major label, and in 1963, he began a second career in Hollywood, where he became the first black to reach the top rank of film composers, with 38 pictures to his credit.

His biggest professional setback came in 1978, when he served as musical director of "The Wiz," a multimillion-dollar flop—but the project solidified a friendship with 20-year-old Michael Jackson (who starred as the Scarecrow) and launched a series of creative collaborations that culminated in "Thriller" and "We Are the World." His first excursion as a movie producer, in 1985, elevated him into the big leagues almost overnight. He persuaded Steven Spielberg to coproduce and direct "The Color Purple," cast Oprah Winfrey and Whoopi Goldberg in the roles that won them Oscar nominations, then supervised the entire production—and, for good measure, wrote the score.

But the strain of living in all those fast lanes, along with the disintegration of his third marriage, to actress Peggy Lipton, drove Jones into a nervous collapse that stirred memories of the near-fatal aneurysm—a hemorrhaging artery in the brain—that had stricken him in 1974 after a similar bout of overwork. This time, he took a month-long "spiritual leave of absence" in Tahiti and returned "in control of my life for the first time."

His eclectic album "Back on the Block" is the harvest of that sabbatical. So is his new company, an entertainment conglomerate partnering Jones and his chief executive, Kevin Wendle, in a co-venture with Time Warner's Bob Pittman, a former MTV executive. And so is the list of honors that have come his way since then—among them this year's Soul Train Heritage Award, which turned into a star-studded 57th-birthday tribute to "Q," as he's known to his hundreds of friends and admirers in the business; a Man of the Year citation at the annual conference of the international music-business association MIDEM; and, most recently, a prestigious Legion of Honor award from the government of France, where he is considered an American national treasure.

Paris was one of the settings for this conversation with Alex Haley, whom he met in 1975 while the author was writing "Roots." Jones was enthralled by the stories Haley told him about his ancestors, and when David Wolper asked Jones to score the first 12 hours of the television miniseries, he and Haley became collaborators as well as friends. When we called Haley with this assignment, he was in the final stages of completing his long-awaited book "Henning," but it's a measure of their friendship that he agreed to take time out for this very special "Playboy Interview." He reports:

"On a desk in Quincy Jones's business office in Los Angeles sits the biggest

Rolodex I've ever seen. It contains, I'm told, the names of more than 5000 friends and associates in the entertainment industry. I believe it. There probably isn't a heavier hitter in the business, or one more universally admired.

"Whatever Quincy's doing, whether it's work or play, he does it with his whole being. And he seems to keep busy pursuing one or the other, in grand style, just about 24 hours a day. My interview with him, appropriately, began on a private jet en route to Manzanillo, Mexico, and continued beside his pool at the spectacular Las Hadas resort hotel, between takes for a feature-length documentary of his life, 'Back on the Block with Quincy Jones,' scheduled for theatrical release in September. Our next session followed a memorable dinner prepared by Quincy's French-Brazilian chef at his showplace Bel Air home, a stone's throw from the Reagans.

"A third session took place last summer in Paris during the bicentennial Bastille Day extravaganza, the orchestral highlight of which Quincy had been imported to conduct. The mayor of Paris headed a parade of Quincy's old friends, who visited him in his flower-banked suite at the Ritz. And after the festivities, before returning home, he and his traveling companions—Time Warner co-C.E.O. Steve Ross and his wife, Courtney, who was a producer of the documentary—decided to stop off in London for dinner with Quincy's pal Dustin Hoffman. As we say in Tennessee, that's tall cotton. But somehow, through it all, success hasn't spoiled Quincy Jones. I wanted to know why. So that's where we began."

PLAYBOY: "Lifestyles of the rich and famous" is a phrase that could have been coined to describe the way you live, Quincy—but you don't seem to have lost your humility. Why not?

JONES: I never forget where I came from, man. When I was seven, I remember my brother Lloyd and I went to spend the summer with my grandmother in Louisville, Kentucky. She was an ex-slave, but she'd moved up in the world since then. The lock on the back door of her little house was a bent nail, and she had a coal stove and kerosene lamps for light, and she used to tell us to go down to the river in the evening and catch us a rat, and we'd take that sucker home in a bag and she'd cook it up for supper. She fried it with onions, and it tasted *good*, man. When you're seven years old and you don't know any better, everything tastes good to you. That kind of memory makes you appreciate everything that much more, because from then on, no matter how good it gets, you never take anything for granted. I've had the whole range of experiences, from rats to *pâté*, and I feel lucky just to be *alive*.

PLAYBOY: Why do you say that?

JONES: In the neighborhood where I was born, on the South Side of Chicago—the biggest ghetto in the world—we used to watch teachers getting killed and policemen shooting black teenagers in the back. Every street was like a territory, and every territory was run by a gang, and everybody used to carry a little switchblade. If I'd stayed there, I'd have been *gone* by now. Because nobody gets out, hardly.

PLAYBOY: But when you were ten, your family moved to Bremerton, Washington, near Seattle. What was it like there?

JONES: The opposite end of the spectrum. My father and my mother had split up back in Chicago, and we moved in with my new stepmother and her three kids in a decent neighborhood in this nice little town where he'd gotten a job as a carpenter down at the naval shipyards. It took me a few months before I realized I didn't have to carry my switchblade anymore. The school I went to was like a model of multi-racial integration, and the kids got along together about as well as they do anywhere in the world. But it's not like we moved to Disneyland. There's no way you're going to live anywhere in America and not feel the pangs of racial prejudice. You still get that *hate* stare from certain kinds of white people, but that's a daily experience from the time you're two years old, and you learn to deal with it.

PLAYBOY: When did you start getting interested in music?

JONES: When I was five or six, back in Chicago. There was this lady named Lucy Johnson who used to play stride piano in the apartment next door, and I listened to her all the time right through the walls. And we used to listen to the songs my other grandmother in St. Louis would play on her old windup Victrola—Fats Waller, Duke Ellington, Billy Eckstine, all the greats. In Bremerton, I joined the school choir and the school band and learned how to play drums, tuba, B-flat baritone horn, French horn, E-flat alto horn, sousaphone and piano. I really wanted to learn trombone, so I could march right behind the drum majorettes. Then my father gave me a trumpet of my own, and soon I was wearing one of those red-and-white derbies and doo-wopping with my plunger mute in the National Guard band. In between the band concerts and singing in a Gospel group, me and my friends would be out playing gigs just about all the time, because this was during World War Two and Seattle had all these Army bases that were the last stop-off before getting shipped out to the Pacific, and that town was *jumpin'*, man.

PLAYBOY: Where did you play those gigs?

JONES: A typical night for us would be from seven to ten at the Seattle Tennis Club in our white tuxedos, playing *Room Full of Roses*, and all that hotsy-totsy stuff for a totally white audience. Then, at ten-thirty, we'd make the rounds of all the black get-down clubs, like the Reverend Silas Groves's Washington Social and Education Club, which was nothing but a juke joint with strippers. Or to the Black and Tan, where we played R&B for an incredible character named Bumps Blackwell, who owned a meat market and a jewelry store and a chain of taxicabs in addition to heading up a band. He's the guy who discovered Sam Cooke and Little Richard. Bumps's band even played for Billie Holiday when she came to town. And we didn't just play *horn* for Bumps. We danced, we sang, we did everything. We had two girl singers, a stripper, four horns, a rhythm section, a male singer and two comedians—that was me and a friend of mine. We doubled as the comedy team of Methedrine and Benzedrine. We put on a *hell* of a show. Anyway, around two A.M., after blowing with Bumps for a few hours, we'd wind up down at the Elks Club playing bebop for ourselves till five or six.

PLAYBOY: Didn't you meet Count Basie around that time?

JONES: I met Basie when I was thirteen years old, when he was playing at the Palomar Theater in Seattle. At that time, he was the biggest and the best big-band leader in the world, but he took me under his wing, and we formed a relationship that lasted the rest of his life. He was my uncle, my father, my mentor, my friend—the dearest man in the world. And his trumpet man, Clark Terry, practically adopted me. He taught me and talked to me and gave me the confidence to get out there and see what I could do on my own. These are the guys who really trained me. They were my idols as musicians, but even more important, they were my role models as human beings. They were more concerned about getting better than about getting over.

PLAYBOY: You've said that Ray Charles was another big early influence on you. When did you meet him?

JONES: When I was about fourteen, I went over to Bumps's house one night, and there he was—this sixteen-year-old blind kid playing the piano and singing *Blowin' the Blues Away*. He was so good he gave me goose bumps. He already had his own apartment, he had all these women, he owned four or five suits. He was doing better than me, and he was *blind*, man. So I just attached myself to him, and he became like a big brother to me. Taught me how to read and write music in Braille and how to voice horns and how to deal with polytonality, and that opened up a golden door for me, because I was fascinated with how all those instruments I'd learned how to play in the band, each of them with its own distinctive sound, could play their own individual variations on the tune and yet interweave them all into the fabric of a song. And from then on, I was hooked on the idea of orchestration and arranging.

PLAYBOY: But it was Lionel Hampton who gave you your first big break. How did that happen?

JONES: I kept hanging out with his band whenever it was in town, until finally, when I was fifteen, he gave me the chance to blow trumpet and write some arrangements for the band. Well, that's all the encouragement I needed to pack up and get on the bus. Only, before we could pull out, his wife, Gladys, caught me on board and yanked me back onto the street. "That boy's gonna finish his schooling before he gets back on this bus," she told Hamp.

So I was *highly* motivated to finish school so I could go join that band. And the moment I graduated from high school—and completed one-semester musical scholarships at Seattle University and Berklee College of Music in Boston—that's exactly what I did. Because Lionel Hampton was a superstar back then. He had the first rock-and-roll band in America—I'm talking about that big-beat sound with the honking tenor sax and the screaming high-note trumpet. Hamp was a *showman*. He even had us wearing these outlandish purple outfits—matching coats and shorts and socks and shoes and Tyrolean hats.

PLAYBOY: Weren't you embarrassed?

JONES: Mortified. But I didn't care, man, because I got to go to New York with the band. I was eighteen, and it was like going to heaven for me, because that's where all my idols were. Oscar Pettiford was like my big brother, and he introduced me to all of them: Miles, Dizzy, Ray Brown, Charlie Parker, Thelonious Monk, Charlie Mingus, all the bebop dudes. They were the new generation of jazz musicians, and they thought it was unhip to be too successful. They said, "We don't want to be entertainers. We want to be artists. We want to explore." But when they went into bebop, we lost some of our greatest warriors, because the public rejected them and they didn't make a dime, not a dime. I mean, they lived from day to day. And they went into this little cocoon and we ended up with a lot of casualties—a lot of people in the gutter, dying from heroin.

PLAYBOY: What was it like touring with Hampton's band?

JONES: It was an education, and not just about music. After we left New York, Hamp's band went on a long tour through the South, 79 one-nighters in a row in the Carolinas alone. It was a grind. And every night was like going into a battle zone. About two thirds of the way through the show, somebody out on the dance floor would start a fight, and before the evening was over, there'd be two or three stabbings. You got used to that kind of thing.

What I didn't get used to was the discrimination. It was on that trip that I got my first real exposure to segregation in the raw, and it just about blew my head apart. Every day and every night, it kept hitting us in the face like a fist. It was like being in enemy territory. The older guys had been on the road for 30 years, and they'd seen it all. They knew just what to say and what not to say around white people down there, where you could stay and where you couldn't stay, where you could eat and where you couldn't eat. We'd show up in some towns and our white bus driver would have to go get us sandwiches and bring them back aboard, because there was no place we could eat. And once, in Texas, we pulled into this little town around five in the morning and there was an effigy of a black person with a rope around his neck hanging from the steeple of the biggest church in town. Man, that just fucked my mind up. I didn't know how to handle it.

But whenever it got to be too much for me, the older guys would say, "Don't feel so bad. It's no different for Lena Horne or Sammy Davis or Harry Belafonte. They may be big stars, but when they play Vegas, they still got to eat in the kitchen, they can't stay in the hotel where they're working, they can't even mingle out front with the people who just paid to see them on the stage." Well, that didn't make me feel any better. But that's the way it was in those days. We've come a long way since then, but back in the Fifties, if you wanted to be treated like a person and appreciated for your musical talent, the older guys said Europe was the place to go.

PLAYBOY: Was there less prejudice there?

JONES: Let's not get carried away, now. You'll run into the same attitudes in Europe as you'll find anywhere else in the world. But in this country, jazz and blues had always been looked down on as the music of the brothel. In Europe, they were mature enough to understand it from the beginning for what it was: one of the true original art forms ever to come from America.

PLAYBOY: You toured Europe with Hampton's band in 1953. How did you go over?

JONES: We were a smash everywhere we went, and while we were in Stockholm, I also got the chance to compose, arrange and conduct four songs in a landmark recording session for Art Farmer, Clifford Brown and the Swedish All-Stars. After it came out, the word about us spread like wildfire all over Europe, and when we got to Paris, they wanted us to record some more albums. We were in Paris, I remember, when I got word from Jeri, my high school sweetheart, that she'd given birth to a little girl named Jolie. We'd gotten married before I left the States, and I didn't get to see either one of them till I got back home to New York. I quit the band to work in the city as a free-lance arranger, so I wouldn't be on the road so much. But we were too young to be married, let alone raising kids, and so it never worked out.

PLAYBOY: Did you make it as an arranger in New York?

JONES: Scuffled around awhile, arranging for James Moody's band, but then Dinah Washington grabbed ahold of me and asked me to start writing arrangements for her. Dinah's material could get pretty raunchy sometimes. One of the songs I arranged for her, I remember, was called *I Love My Trombone Playing Daddy with His Big Long Sliding Thing*. I was ready to move on in 1956 when George Avakian of Columbia Records asked me to write arrangements for the first album by a 20-year-old San Francisco track star named Johnny Mathis. I told him yes, but before I had the chance to do it, Dizzy Gillespie called and asked me to make all the arrangements for a band that the State Department wanted him to take on a good-will tour of the Middle East.

As it turned out, America needed all the good will it could get just then because of the political situation in that part of the world. We arrived in Turkey in the middle of a crisis, and the same people who were stoning the American embassy came to our concert at night. And after the concert, they went rushing up to the stage and grabbed Dizzy, and we were scared to death about what they were gonna do. But they just picked him up on their shoulders and cheered, man, like he was a hero.

When we showed up in Pakistan, they'd never even seen a trumpet or a trombone, but they responded to our music like it was their own. We communicated with them on a level that transcended language and politics and cultural differences. It was on that trip that I felt for the first time the real power and universality of music as a bond among people everywhere.

PLAYBOY: You've said that your next European tours, in 1957 and 1958, were major turning points in your life. In what way?

JONES: The first one was a gas, the second a disaster. In 1957, I was asked to be the musical director of Barclay Records, a very innovative company in Paris that was run by Eddie Barclay and Nadia Boulanger. Before she went into the record business, Nadia had been the musical mentor to some of the greatest composers in the world—guys like Aaron Copland and Igor Stravinsky—and I can't begin to tell you the lessons she taught *me*, not only about music but about living. It was through her that I got to meet incredible people such as James Baldwin, Richard Wright, Françoise Sagan, Josephine Baker, Pablo Picasso, even Porfirio Rubirosa. That year was wonderful.

PLAYBOY: And the next was a bummer?

JONES: They say you learn more from your setbacks than you do from your successes, so I guess I should consider it a triumph. I was asked to become musical director for a Harold Arlen–Johnny Mercer musical called *Free and Easy*, and we took it on the road to Europe with my band. The plan was to tour the Continent for a few months and then pick up Sammy Davis on the way home to star in the show on Broadway. But when we got to Paris, the Algerian crisis had practically paralyzed the country, and the show folded, and we got stranded in Europe for the next 10 months. Every week, I had to scufffle to cover the $5000 payroll, and I wound up hocking all my publishing companies to cover the nut. The pressure of trying to keep everybody afloat finally got so bad that one night, I seriously considered grabbing a handful of pills and just checking out. But that very night, Irving Green of Mercury Records, who was a dear friend of mine, telephoned and gave me the faith and courage I needed to hang in there, and I did, until we finally scraped together enough to get home on.

PLAYBOY: How long did it take you to get back on your feet?

JONES: It was almost seven years before I bought myself out of hock. But I went back to work from the day I got off the boat in New York. Started composing and arranging again for Dinah, who told me to keep an eye on the Reverend C. L. Franklin's young daughter, Aretha. "She's the one, I promise you," Dinah told me. And she was. I organized my own band to play with Billy Eckstine, Johnny Ray and Peggy Lee at Basin Street East, and we went to the Monterey Jazz Festival. By this time, I was beginning to get noticed. In 1961, I won *Jet* magazine's award for best arranger and composer—and my first Grammy nomination, for arranging *Let the Good Times Roll* for Ray Charles.

That's when I got an offer from Irving Green at Mercury to join him as an A&R man. A&R stands for Artists and Repertoire—which means you're in charge of the people you pick and what they sing. So I had to put on a suit and go in to work every day at nine, but I got to do what I love, and I learned a lot about the business side of the music industry, because Irving Green took me to *school*, man. I was producing people like Dizzy, Sarah Vaughan, Art Blakey, and they were getting great records. I was also starting to make good money—but I didn't realize at first that other people who did what I did were getting a percentage of the royalties on top of their salaries, and that's where the real money was. But I found out real fast, and that's when I decided to get into pop music, because I was tired of producing jazz music that got great reviews, only nobody was buying it. So I produced a song—*It's My Party*—for Lesley Gore and it went up to number one on the charts. I did lots of others with her, and they were all hits. Then I started to conduct for Sinatra, and we made a record together, and we worked the Sands in Vegas. . . .

PLAYBOY: You were at the top of your profession in 1974 when you suffered a massive aneurysm that almost killed you. What do you think brought it on?

JONES: I was pushing myself too hard, as usual. I'd been up three days working, and I was at my home in Brentwood, in bed with my wife, when all of a sudden, I felt this blinding pain, like somebody had blown a shotgun through my brain. It was just the worst pain I'd ever felt in my whole life, and I was screaming, and I didn't know what was happening to me. Peggy called the paramedics, but by the time they got there, I had blacked out and gone into a coma. They thought it was a heart attack, and my wife said, "He's strong as a mule, that can't be it." And she called my doctor, Elsie Georgie, who said, "I think I know what it is, but I hope it's not too late," and she took me down to the hospital for a spinal tap and, sure enough, she was right: I'd had an aneurysm. The main artery to my brain had popped and blood was pouring into my brain, which had swollen up so big they had to wait eight days before they could operate on me. Finally, they did, and I woke up and I was still alive.

That was the moment I realized for the first time that I didn't have a three-pronged cord plugged into my body that I could turn on at any time, whenever I wanted. I'd never imagined that I could fall apart like that. And coming through all that—there were actually two aneurysms and two operations a month apart—being blessed enough to come through all that alive, it really was a miracle.

PLAYBOY: You didn't go back to work for several months after the aneurysms. Had they affected your thought processes?

JONES: I was afraid to find out. So for a long time, I didn't even try to work. I was also very weak from the surgery. But finally, I was faced with a decision that would put my recovery and my courage to the test. I had a commitment to tour Japan with a small band and I wasn't sure I should risk it, but Elsie Georgie told me, "You're anemic, but if you baby yourself now, you'll never be OK. So go."

But the surgeon who operated on me warned me not to play the trumpet. He had put a clip on my artery to keep it closed, and he told me that I'd blow off that clip and kill myself if I tried to blow that horn. I didn't believe him, of course, and I decided to take the tour, and I started blowing the horn, and one night, I hit one of those high notes and I felt something crack inside, like my head was gonna break right open. I was scared to death, and I went to the doctor and, sure enough, I'd almost blown off the clip. Well, the doctor didn't have to warn me again. I stopped playing the trumpet and I had to leave the band.

PLAYBOY: How long did it take you to go back to work as a producer?

JONES: Not long. Surviving a second time made me realize that I didn't have anything to be afraid of—except maybe giving up on myself. I got together with two of the guys who'd gone on the tour with me—the Johnson brothers, who had a great sound on guitar and bass—and produced a record with them. We wound up with four hits in a row, and there I was, smack dab back in the record business. It was in the middle of all this that I was at a party in L.A. and ran into this beautiful brother from San Francisco who was writing this book about the story of his family and the history of black people in America, all the way back through slavery to Africa. He called it *Roots*, and it was just about the most moving and powerful story I'd ever heard. Well, it so happened that at the time, I was on a journey of my own, doing research on the evolution of black music, so I felt like it was fated that you and I should meet, Alex.

PLAYBOY: Is it fair to say that you were fanatic about historical authenticity in scoring *Roots* with your African collaborators?

JONES: Letta Mbulu and Caiphus Semenya, yes. Anybody else might say I was fanatical, but to me, it was just trying to tell it like it was, trying to rediscover a heritage that was taken away from us. African music had always been regarded in the West as primitive and savage, but when you take the time to really study it, you see that it's as structured and sophisticated as European classical music, with the same basic components as you'll find in a symphony orchestra—instruments that are plucked, instruments that are beaten and instruments that are blown with reeds. And it's music from the soil—powerful, elemental. Life-force music. Composers from Bizet to Stravinsky have drawn on African influences. And in slave-ship times, it started spreading into the New World, from Brazil all the way up through Haiti to Cuba, through the West Indies, until some of the ships started landing in Virginia and New Orleans. The original African influence had been watered down and assimilated with other sounds along the way, but it was still strong enough that in 1692, the Virginia colony decided to ban the drum, because the slaves used it as a means of communication, and that was threatening to the plantation owners. But that didn't stop the slaves: They started making music with hand claps and foot stomps, anything to keep that spirit alive. The slaves weren't allowed to practice their own religions, either, but the black Christian churches became the keepers of the flame for black music in America: From Gospel, blues, jazz, soul, R&B, rock and roll, all the way to rap, you can trace the roots straight back to Africa. . . .

ICE T

The Ice Opinion

The main misinterpretation and misunderstanding of rap is the dialogue—in the ghetto talk and machismo, even in the basic body language. This is what I call shit talkin'. From the nasty tales of Stagolee in the 1800s to H. Rap Brown in the '60s, most of rap is nothing more than straight-up black bravado. Too many people take shit talkin' seriously because they have no frame of reference.

In the ghetto, a black man will say, "I'll take my dick and wrap it around this room three times and fuck yo' mama." Now, this man cannot wrap his dick around the room three times, and he probably doesn't want to fuck your mother, but this is how he's gonna talk to another brother. It's a black thang. It's machismo. It doesn't mean anything.

When I first started rapping I learned very quickly the political approach couldn't hold a guy's attention, but if I started telling a nasty story, then the audience would really listen. This is no big revelation; sex is used a lot in advertising and the media use it to keep viewers watching until the end of a broadcast. If they advertise "Bikini Stewardesses" at the top of the news, you'll keep watching for a half an hour till they flash the flesh. The media are the worst offenders because when they say, "Oh, look at this. Isn't this awful?" what they are really saying is, "Look at this, look at this, look at this. . . ." All over town sex is used as a teaser to make people go out and pay $7.50 for a movie.

With rap, you quickly learn the trick that you'll get the interest of the audience with sex because they want to know what will happen at the end of the song. They want to see how far I'm gonna take it. If I got onstage and said, "Yeah, I was eating this girl the other night and her pussy tasted like strawberries," everybody in the club would think, "Hooo, shit! This muthafucka's bold." I would get *everybody's* attention and then they would want to know where I could possibly go from there.

The rappers who can hold your attention are either bragging or lying, and most of the stories are lies because if rappers played the moves they talked about—goddamn, they wouldn't have any dicks left.

The art of shit talkin' is responsible for me getting out of crime and getting into rhyme. The best way for me to explain my point of view on hip-hop and its influence on the general public is to give you a brief history of "Ice T the Rapper."

Rapping is just something you pick up growing up in the ghetto. I knew how to write rhymes, because I used to recite rhymes for the gangs. I used to tag, "Crips don't die, they multiply." You've probably heard Bebe's Kids use that phrase. I wrote that slogan, and I'm still waiting for my royalty check.

In the gang, I'd write these slogans on the walls, but they were more hustler-style rhymes. When I heard the record "Rapper's Delight," I thought, "Shit, I can do this." And I tried to rap, but I really wasn't particularly good.

We'd go into this club in L.A. called the Radio, and I would try to rap. The reason I kept trying to rap was my boys. They told me to go rap so we could go the clubs and get some pussy. Once you'd get onstage, the girls would come at you and talk to you. This would be your opportunity to lie and tell 'em you had a record deal. When the film *Breakin'* hit, the director came into the club and told everybody, "Okay, you're gonna be my rapper, you're gonna be my deejay, and you're gonna be my breakers. And I'm going to exploit y'all and make a lot of money."

Now, you've seen that film and that shit was wack. But all y'all know when it came out you were on that shit, "Shabba Doo, yeah." You know you dug it.

So if I was wack, y'all were wack, too.

The movie stylists dressed me up in what they thought breakers and rappers were supposed to wear—things like belts around your crotch and spiked bracelets. I didn't really understand it, and I really didn't want to be in a movie. I didn't have time to be in a movie. The producer told me I was gonna make $500 a day. I told him, "I spend that on sneakers, man."

I did the movie. I tried to rap like New York rappers. I was trying to rap about house parties. "I'll rock the mic, I'll rock the mic, I'll rock the mic." My buddies were all laughing. They would say to me, "Ice, how are you gonna rap about rocking the house parties? We rob parties, man. We're the niggers who come in and say, 'Throw your hands in the air, and leave 'em there.' "

They were right. Nobody was gonna believe it if I didn't rap about the shit I knew. So I wrote this record called "Six in the Morning" about a kid who ran from the police:

> Six in the morning, police at my door
> Fresh Adidas squeak across the bathroom floor.

This song was the beginning of what is now called gangsta rap. I call it reality-based rap, because I used real situations and brought them onto the records. I didn't even think of it as gangsta rap, because I thought of myself as a player. I thought I had a little bit more finesse than the gangsters. I still do.

Then, I recorded "Six in the Morning," and everybody liked it. I came up to the Oakland area, and it was pumping all over the place. I knew I had the ability to do this, and my friends encouraged me. It was like if you get up every morning and cook eggs and somebody told you, "You should sell them eggs, man." People told me, "You can sell that rap." "I could do this all day," I thought. "This is easy. This is just about my life."

That's what I've been doing for a while now. I rap about my life, and I rap about it in the hardest, most blatant sense. I consider what I say as real. This is the way the world I come from is. This is the way I talk and I live. This is the only way I can be.

It took me five years from the release of the "Six in the Morning" single to get an album. For those of you who want to get in the rap business, be patient. It takes a while. Finally, I found Warner Brothers, Sire Records. A man named Seymour Stein signed me. When he called me into his office to meet with him, he was playing calypso music and dancing around in his socks. He asked me if I understood calypso music. I told him no. He quickly went into an explanation of calypso and said, "Just because you don't understand what it means doesn't make it invalid. It just means you don't understand. Just the way I might not understand what you're rapping about, it doesn't make it invalid. So go make your album. I know you know what you're talking about."

He told me I was like the Bob Dylan of the streets. And I knew who Bob Dylan was, so I took that as a compliment, even though I thought he was a little crazy. We made the album *Rhyme Pays*, and then Warner Brothers came to me at the label and said they wanted to put a sticker on the record. I asked why. They explained it was to inform the public some material on the album might offend listeners.

I said, "Fine, that's cool." Then they explained to me the organization behind the stickering was called the Parents' Music Resource Center—the PMRC. I thought, "What a nice organization, what a nice name." Little did I know it was founded and headed by this crazed bitch named Tipper Gore, who has made it her job to put down nearly every artist in the music industry for saying what's on their minds. Gore and the PMRC are wholeheartedly against information exchange. Tipper Gore is the only woman I ever directly called a bitch on any of my records, and I meant that in the most negative sense of the word.

Without her help, the album went gold. No video. No radio. My next album, *Power*, featured the cover photo of my girlfriend in a bikini, which everybody looked at longer than they listened to the album. That went gold and so did my third album, *Freedom of Speech . . . Just Watch What You Say*. The next one, *Original Gangster*, had twenty-eight tracks and really was a double album. By this time, a lot of rappers had started rapping these quick little commercials and calling them songs.

"Yo, what's up?"

"Blam. Blam."

That's two songs, right there. So I didn't get credit for a double album, but the album featured twenty-four complete songs.

After *Original Gangster*, we were really rolling, so we decided to go all out and come out with this group called Body Count. Now Body Count, for those of you who aren't slaves to the press, is a rock group, not a rap group. Body Count was created because I like rock music. I didn't know I wasn't supposed to like rock music. I've been listening to rock music my whole life—Black Sabbath, Blue Oyster Cult, Deep Purple, Black Flag, Circle Jerks, X. I moved into Minor Threat. I listened to No Means No, Cannibal Corpse, Gwar. I was into this whole shit. I liked rock because I like the rage I got out of it. I found rage in Slayer and Megadeth, and used that same rage to make my music.

Everybody should know rock 'n' roll was really started by black artists like Little Richard, who raged on the piano. The music executives then stepped in and had Pat Boone remake all his records. And they decided: White people can rock and black people will do R & B. That's the biggest joke; rock is a state of mind, not a question of color. If you sing about love, and going to school, and drinking milkshakes, and having sex in the missionary position, you're doing pop music. Pop music means popular music. You're attempting to be popular.

The problem with pop is what's popular today will not be popular tomorrow. Talk to Tone Lōc about that shit. Tone is my friend, but he knows he was on some pop shit. "Wild Thing" blew up because it became popular, but now he has to build a core audience, which I know he can do because the man has talent. Your core audience is what's important. Your core audience will buy your records without hearing a single. If you love Prince, and he has an album out, you'll buy that album. You don't wait to hear a song. You just buy Prince. That's your core audience; they don't have to see the video, they just wait until the record's out, and they buy it immediately.

With "Body Count," I knew we didn't want to form an R & B group. To me, R & B goes something like this:

> Baby don't leave me,
> But if you do leave me,
> Don't take the car.
> And if you do take that car,
> Shake that ass on the
> Way out the door.

That's cool music, but where am I gonna get the rage and the anger to attack something with that? Back in the '60s, you had Stevie Wonder and Marvin Gaye, and they were putting out powerful music. Now, it's just "Shake that ass. Shake that ass. Shake that ass."

We knew Body Count had to be a rock band. The name alone negates the band from being R & B. We named the group Body Count because every Sunday night in L.A., I'd watch the news, and the newscasters would tally up the youths killed in gang homicides that week and then just segue to sports. "Is that all I am," I thought, "a body count?"

I ended up being Body Count's lead singer by default. I knew I couldn't sing, but then I thought, "Who *can* sing in rock 'n' roll?" Fuck that. I'm the singer. If you listen to death metal, you don't even know what they're singing. It all sounds like "ARGGGGGGGGGGGGGGGGGGGGGGGGGGGGGGGGGG!" I figured I could do that.

I don't play an instrument, but to me writing music is easy and comes naturally. Most of the best songwriters out there don't even play instruments. And just because you can play an instrument doesn't mean you can write any songs. So all y'all who are good hummers can write songs.

I scored the music and wrote the lyrics for the album with Ernie C., the lead guitarist. We went on tours and people dug us. Little did I know the song titled "Cop Killer" was gonna cause the country to go nuclear. I didn't even think "Cop Killer" was a controversial record, because everybody I know hates the cops. I thought everybody hated the police. And I thought all my fans hate the police—they liked the record, didn't they? Through the "Cop Killer" event, I learned who was really on whose side.

PART 6

Sankofa: Past as Prologue

DEEP ROOTS

DUDLEY RANDALL

A Different Image

The age
requires this task:
create
a different image;
re-animate
the mask.

Shatter the icons of slavery and fear.
Replace
the leer
of the minstrel's burnt-cork face
with a proud, serene
and classic bronze of Benin.

YOSEF BEN-JOCHANNAN

The African Contribution to Technology and Science

I will first express my appreciation for your having me here, and ask that you meticulously follow my comments, because as you know I'm known to be controversial, and that's an understatement. I'm controversial not because something is wrong with my documentation, but because I challenge Western hegemony.

Africa, as the label of my talk, cannot be spoken of in terms of Adam and Eve, because long before they had an *Adam and Eve* there was an *Africa* and *African* people, with concepts that predated Abraham. All of the pyramids of Africa, not only those in Egypt, but those in Sudan, and the two in northern Ethiopia (which the British and the Berlin Conference removed and put into southern Sudan), were built thousands of years before there was an Adam and Eve mentioned anywhere on the planet. When you get to the birth of Abraham, at the same time when the Africans along the Nile are already in their thirteenth dynastic period, there is no Adam and Eve, because the Hebrews gave you the concept of Adam and Eve. Most of you believe that it has something to do with facts, rather than theocracy.

To speak of Africa you would have to revise your concept of the Virgin Mary and understand that it's nothing but a copy of Isis, and her husband God Osiris. You will also have to go to the Nile Valley to the temples there and see that this is thousands of years before Westminster Abbey, and, of course the Vatican in Rome. You can go all over the Nile Valley and elsewhere, and I use the Nile Valley, particularly, in that the oldest records of man are still there in terms of monuments. Of course, there are a lot stolen from Africa here in London, and in Berlin or other such places.

Your ancestors gave to the world the calendar in 10,000 B.C.E. (before the Common "Christian" Era). That is, 7,000 years before Adam and Eve. Your ancestors revised that dating system because of their understanding of the astronomical calculations. It is the science of astronomy that gives the ability to read calendars. Thus 10,000 B.C.E. saw the first calendar. The term is self-explanatory, the solar calendar showing the relationship of the moon and the sun, etc. that gives us the basis of the present calendar, with 364 days corrected each year, instead of 365 days corrected each fourth year. And I will say again that there wasn't a single European society in existence at that time. The first European writer, Homer, had not been born yet. And when Homer was born and finally became literate because of the teachings the Africans gave him, he too started to corroborate the evidence your ancestors had by stating that even the gods of Europe, Greece, in particular, which was then called Pyrrhus, came from Ethiopia.

I'm sure that those of you who have been to college, if not here in England somewhere else, know that I'm quoting from two works of Homer, the *Iliad* and the *Odyssey*, which brought Europe and England into civilization. The African we must talk about is the African that caused people to understand science, medicine, law, engineering, etc. It is common at the universities here to deal with science as if the art of medicine came from a Greek named Hippocrates. We don't have Hippocrates until about 333 B.C.E. Yet we don't need any record other than Hippocrates himself to know that what is being taught at the universities here are lies.

One has to realize that Hippocrates himself, in what is called the Hippocratic Oath, wrote that he had a god named Escalipius, the Greek name for the God Imhotep. Imhotep had died 2500 years before the birth of Hippocrates. Imhotep is the first known multigenius other than the one you call Michelangelo. We don't have Michelangelo until 1609 and he is not known until he does the work of Pope Julius II, who commissioned Michelangelo to paint the ceiling of the Sistine Chapel. Michelangelo used his cousin and other relatives as models for some of the biblical characters that he painted. The basis of engineering was created by Imhotep. He created the first stone structure; that building still stands in a place called Sakkara, about less than an hour north-west of what is today called Cairo. And here you will see the Grand Lodge of Djoser at Sakkara. That modern structure was built in the Third Dynasty, since Djoser was the third pharaoh of the Third Dynasty. Imhotep was the man who gave us the little quip, "eat, drink and be merry for tomorrow we shall die."

The FIRST WORLD western university was the University of Jenne of Timbuktu. But as we continue, we realize that in the universities here you use paper to write on, and if it was not for paper the means of communication would not be as it is today. But in Egypt, Sudan and other such places, and I will remind you that Egypt is still in Africa, the Africans reached such a height in engineering that we even turned the Nile in an *S-turn* to cut down the flow when the inundation period came. That brings us to 2200 B.C. That means at least 1400 years before the first European wrote anything.

Africa, Mother Africa, as I prefer to call her, understanding that the Greeks called her Africa in about 500-400 B.C. I'm talking about the time when the first Greeks who had gone to Pyrrhus, who had come into Egypt by way of Leba (now called Libya) and established their little villages in a little enclave, they then called Africa long before the continent was partitioned by the colonialists. I am speaking about 11.3 or 11.5 million square miles of land, where first the concept of a God and Goddess Nut is shown as the mother of the sky. Symbolically, the God Geb, the god of the earth, lived in a little chapel in the center of Hathor. The African woman is giving birth even to the sun, in the morning through her vagina and receiving the sun back in the evening through her mouth. This shows the whole rotation of the world, long before the world had a beginning and an end. These Africans along the Nile were to do more of this. They were to give us a God Osiris, where people went yearly to pay pilgrimage long before there was a wailing wall in Palestine or a myth of a Jesus born in Bethlehem, which changed at the Nicene Conference of Bishops, ordered by Constantine and removed from a cave in Ethiopia to a manger in Bethlehem.

It is Africa that gave birth to Hadzart Bilal ibn Rahab, who taught Mohammed ibn Abdullah, who was illiterate in his own language, not able to read and write. In spite of what your belief system may be, Hadzart Bilal ibn Rahab became the head of the Moslem embassies under Mohammed ibn Abdullah, Omar the Great, and Abu Bakr. I think that we need to know history before we can quote texts in religious scriptures.

There was a myth of Africa as the home of a people who ate each other and missionaries. I wish we did eat the missionaries, it's never too late! We've got to understand that this Africa we are speaking about even established Europe's greatest universities and first, the University of Salamanca in Spain. The Africa we are speaking about produced the ancestors of the present Queen of England, George III, the German king who spoke no English. We forget that Elizabeth's grandparents and ancestors are related to George III, who was the son of Alexander the Medici, the cardinal of Rome who later became Pope, and an Ethiopian woman by the name of Martha. So I have to say, don't worry too much about it because Elizabeth belongs to the family. The Africa, which you may not know, happened to give birth to Zinjanthropus Boisei by the Africans of Kenya. The Leakey family, Louis and Mary, dated him to 1.7 million years old. Adam is about 4000-5000 years. The Africa you do not know gave birth also to Lucy in Ethiopia dated 3.2 million years old; they are both in Kenyan and Ethiopian museums. And some of us are still ashamed to be Africans! Some of us pay money to have our nose reshaped, our hair fried and boiled and all sorts of things, because we don't know this Africa; we know the Africa of the slave trade with John Hawkins from London and the other little songs.

Yes, that is the phase of Africa. Surely, slavery is a phase of lives past, but slavery is a tiny little bit from 640 A.D. with the Arabs, 1506 A.D. with the Europeans to now as against what I'm talking about; it is minuscule by comparison, because if I wished to go back to Africa, not only when we were performing astronomy, engineering in establishing the pyramids and so forth, but when we gave to the world the fundamental moral concept, "I have not killed man or woman." This is a response to the admonishing of the Goddess Maat. You notice that every time we talk about justice and rights we have an African woman representing the scale of justice. The response to the admonishings which would have stated, "You shall not speak ill of your mother and your father; you shall not kill man nor woman; you shall not hide a light under a bushel," sounds familiar to you because they said some guy named Moses discovered them thousands of years later on Mount Sinai.

Yet they said Moses was born in Goshen. This is the Goshen in Egypt according to the Torah or the Old Testament in the Book of Exodus. Moses had to be trained, and if he was born and lived there (for between age one to eighty-five years of age), according to your Bible, then he must have read this, because he was taught in the Grand Lodge. If he went to the lodge at age seven as a young boy, then he did not come out until he was forty-seven, because it took forty years of training to make a priest in all of the disciplines.

So then, Moses came as nothing but a copy of the Egyptian priests and Teachings of *The Egyptian Mysteries System*.

These same Africans went on to give us the concept of the monotheistic deity. Thus it was that Amenhotep IV, who changed his name to Akhnaton, who gave us the concept of a solitary god by the name of Aten. Akhnaton died long before the birth of Moses. Is it possible for you to come to England, go to kindergarten here, go to elementary school, college, do post-doctoral work and never hear of the English national anthem, the Magna Carta, or Queen Anne's statue? Is it possible, just as it was for Moses to be born in Egypt, a soul brother, because his first wife was Deborah, according to the Bible, and had never heard of Akhnaton.

And it is said that when Moses was running away from the Pharaoh for committing murder (before he got the rod of Mount Sinai), and his brother Aaron was charged for stealing from the Pharaoh's treasury, he met Deborah. It would seem to be that Deborah said, "That Egyptian," pointing to Moses; there was nothing in Moses to tell that he was Jewish; he was not wearing any special clothes; he looked like any other soul brother you can find in London, the Caribbean, Nigeria, Ethiopia, Ghana, the South Pacific. And then you say you are the minority! You are members of the third world. I am not a member of the third world, I am a member of the first world.

When one of the first of the so-called philosophers came to Egypt, we see him before 640 B.C.E. When he was supposed to have released his philosophical thinking, he is in Egypt. From Socrates down to Aristotle, the so-called post-Socratian philosophers, every one of them spent several years in Egypt and of course the only one who couldn't come since he was the creation of Plato's mind, was Socrates. And even he (Socrates) was supposed to have taken the hemlock for teaching African philosophy: "Socrates is an evil doer" was part of the charge against him. Plato had to run (and all the others) for teaching this philosophy. Would you have to run from England for teaching English history? Neither would the Greek government persecute the Greek philosophers for teaching Greek philosophy. It was somebody's philosophy they were teaching, and where did they go to school to know whose philosophy?

It is not until the Persians in 525 B.C.E. allowed them in, and it was not until 323 B.C.E. at the death of Alexander, the son of Philip of Macedonia, that Aristotle was allowed by General Soter (who changed his name to Ptolomy I) to have Tusak to bring those works down, that the Greeks had access to Egyptian works. Those who could study in Egypt for themselves did so, while some were sent over to Greece where they established what they called the Peripatetic schools in what later was called Alexandria, out of African materials.

Is that the Africa you know? It couldn't be, otherwise you couldn't be praising your masters; you would be going back to your educational past and be your own master, at least if not physically, mentally. It is difficult, because colonialism brings to us a kind of history written by the conqueror for the conquered to read and enjoy. When the conquered looks around and finds that even God speaks from the heart of the conqueror, the conquered then becomes suspicious of God. What is God's interest in all of this? It is not the African who said in the Songs of Solomon, Chapter 1, Verses 1-9, and when you get to 8 and 9, it says, "Ye daughters of Canaan look not upon me because I am black, because I'm beautiful. My mother put me in the vineyard, but my sister, she kept indoors," that is why the Queen of Sheba turned black. I thought it was because her mother and father were black! But even in the Bible you find lies, racism and all that. As if we didn't have Bibles. We have "The Book of the Dead" which was changed right here in London from its original name in 1895 at the British Museum. It was called "The Book of Coming Forth By Day and Night." We have the "Book of the Divines," "The Book of Judgment," "The Heart of Judgment," and other such works, that preceded the Old Testament and the Jewish Kabala by thousands of years.

The Africans gave us the concept against murder. When the Shipwats at the Temple of Philos, a Greek word, which means Angelica, by the way, of the Goddess Auset, which the Greeks called Isis, and her son Heru, who the Greeks called Horus, and all the gods viewed the murder of Osiris by his brother Seth. A murder that preceded the Cain and Abel murder by thousands of years, beginning on the island of Angelica, continuing at the Temple of the God Horus, continuing further and you see the Virgin Birth and Immaculate Conception. It is here long before you see it in lifestyle, and you can see in life-size the drama that preceded Greece, showing Horus killing his uncle for the revenge of killing his father, showing his uncle symbolically as a hippopotamus.

This continued to the Temple of Osiris in Abydos, where pictures of the Virgin Birth, the Resurrection, showing Osiris' penis perpendicular to his body, being symbolic to the resurrection. When you go there you will see it all over the place. Those of you who have been to Egypt know that life is shown as the penis coming out of Peta's naval, representative of the extension of the umbilical cord, which is the extension of life, the source of life.

The Africa that I have spoken of, you need to know, and no one can keep you a slave after you know it. In America there is a saying that the mind is a terrible thing to waste. It is said on television all the time by people who call themselves "The Negro College Fund." You can only waste your mind on that one, and by using the term "negro" it indicates they've got no minds, because I have been looking for a negro, and I haven't found one in umpteen years. Because I'm not a Portuguese, I don't create negroes nor Negroland. I'm an African, and that word we need to deal with as having come from the Greeks. I guess some say it has got good connotations. So I beg of you to always carry a mirror, whether you are a man or a woman, to look at yourself daily. Then you've got to have a good feeling about that face you've got, the texture of hair you've got, and all the fine features you've got. I don't know about you, brothers, but when I look at the face of that African woman, I see heaven!

JOHN HENRIK CLARKE

The Africans in the New World: Their Contribution to Science, Invention and Technology

In this short talk on a subject that has many dimensions, and a long untold history, I am really talking about the impact of African people in the opening-up of the Americas and the Caribbean Islands. The appearance outside of Africa of African people in such large numbers tells us something about the greatest and most tragic forced migration of a people in human history. The exploitation of African people made what is called the New World possible, and the African's contribution to the sciences, invention and technology that made this new world possible, is part of a larger untold story. In the United States alone there is supporting literature and volumes of documents on this subject.

We need to examine the events in Africa and in Europe from 1400 through 1600 A.D. This is a pivotal turning point in world history. This was a period when Europe was awakening from the lethargy of its Middle Ages, learning again the maritime concepts of longitude and latitude and using her new skills in the handling of ships to enslave and colonize most of the world.

Europe recovered at the expense of African people. African people were soon scattered throughout the Caribbean, in several areas of South America and in the United States. A neglected drama in the history of dynamic social change had occurred in the year 711 A.D. when a combination of Africans, Arabs and Berbers conquered Spain and ruled the Iberian Peninsula for nearly eight hundred years. The aftermath of the African-Arab loss of Spain and the Arab's use of European mercenaries and equipment wreaked havoc throughout Africa and broke up the independent nations of inner Western Africa, mainly Songhay. This drama had to play itself out and the power of the Africans and the Arabs had to decline before the larger drama of the slave trade and, subsequently, colonialism could get well under way.

Africa was now suffering a second catastrophe. The first catastrophe was the Arab slave trade, which was totally unexpected, and came over six hundred years before the European slave trade. The second catastrophe was the Christian slave trade which started in the fifteenth and sixteenth century. Early Christians could not deal with what African religions were before the advent of Judaism, Christianity and Islam nor could they deal with early Christianity which was a carbon copy of African universal Spirituality. The first thing the Europeans did was to laugh at the African gods. Then they made the Africans laugh at their own gods. Europeans would go on to colonize the world. They not only colonized the world, they would also colonize information about the world, and that information is still colonized. What they would deal with was a carbon copy of Christianity as interpreted by foreigners. This Christian slave trade hit Africa at a moment of internal weakness and Africa was part of the catastrophe before it could recover its strength.

In the Americas and in the Caribbean Islands we find Bartholomew de las Casas, who came on Christopher Columbus' third voyage and who sanctioned the increase of the slave trade with the pretense that this would save the Indian population. When the Pope sent commissions to inquire into what was happening with the Indians, many of the islands did not have one Indian left, they were all dead. It was at Christopher Columbus' suggestion that the slave trade was increased to include more of the Africans, again, under the pretense of saving the Indians. It was the same Christopher Columbus who says in his diary, "As man and boy I sailed up and down the Guinea coast for twenty-three years. . . ." What was he doing up and down the coast of West Africa for twenty-three years? The assumption is that he was part of the early Portuguese slave trade. Now is he still your hero? When you look at the Western hero and how he became a hero, when you look at all those people they called, "The Great," and find out what they were great for you will then have a new concept of history. There are a number of good books on this subject. Two of the more readable are by Eric Williams, late Prime Minister of Trinidad, formerly teacher of political science at Howard University. They are *Capitalism and Slavery*, and his last big book, *The Caribbean from Columbus to Castro*.

The subject of this talk is really "The African Inventor in the New World and His Contribution to Technology, Medicine and Science." While I may be going the long way round, I'll get to the subject. But you will have to know what happened behind the curtain of slavery and the consequences of the Africans' enslavement and to what extent Europe recovered from its lethargy and to what extent Europe exploited people outside of Europe. But the main thing that you have to understand is that the African did not come into slavery culturally empty-handed. In order to stay in luxury, Europe had to have large bodies of people to exploit outside of Europe where they could get land and labor cheap. Where they could get control of other people's resources, cheap or for nothing. This is what apartheid is really all about. It is about Western control of the mineral wealth of the African. Africa is the world's richest continent, full of poor people, people who are poor because someone else is managing their resources. Do you think that if Africans had all the gold and manganese and zinc and bauxite and uranium that comes out of Africa they would be going around begging anybody for anything, drought or no drought? Have you ever sailed down the Congo River and seen all the vast bodies of water flowing into the sea? The Nile River sustained the greatest civilization the world has ever known, and it rarely ever rains in the Nile River. Yet this one river sustained civilizations for thousands of years, because Africans, at that time, knew what to do with water, and how to direct it in the way they needed it.

Still going to my subject, my point is that the African was brought to the Western world and survived through his inventiveness, imagination and his spiritual attitude. Without these he would have not survived. The African was hit harder than the so-called Indian. Where one died the other would survive. It is not that one had spiritual attitude and the other did not, they both had spiritual attitude and they both had culture. But many of the Africans had come out of pluralistic cultures and were more accustomed to the nature of change.

Now, let's get on to the African's inventive mind. The preface to all of this is to deal with the free African craftsman in the Western world and how these craftsmen became free, that is, "free" with a question mark! In the Caribbean where Africans were brought in large numbers, once they were taken over by the British and others their condition as an enslaved people was exploited. A class of Englishmen who had earned no considerable respect in England, came to the Islands as mechanics. Because their white face was a premium and because they were given privileges and guns and land and had access to African women, they considered themselves as belonging to the exploitive class. They literally exhausted themselves. But the Englishmen did not have the skills they found were needed on the islands and they began to disappear, physically, due to death from exhaustion or return to England. The African craftsmen began to replace them. We now see the beginnings of the Africans' inventive mind in the Caribbean Islands. The same thing was happening in parts of South America. Many times the English would bring over English-made furniture and there were some termites in the Caribbean. Some of these termites are still there, and when the termites began to eat up the soft wood in the English-made furniture, the African with his meticulous mind began to duplicate that furniture with local hard wood. This was done especially in Jamaica where they had large amounts of mahogany then. Jamaica does not have mahogany now because the mahogany forests were overcut to the point where Jamaica now has no considerable variety of mahogany. Some of the most beautiful mahogany in the world used to come from Jamaica.

As with the disappearance of the British craftsmen, when the African craftsmen began to emerge, something else began to emerge in the Caribbean Islands. A class of people whose crafts maintained plantations. The Africans saw how important they had become and began to make demands. This is the origin of the Caribbean freeman. These freemen were free enough to communicate with other Africans, free enough to go back to Africa, and free enough to go to the United States. These freemen from the crafts class began to mix friendship with another group of freemen in the United States. Now, how did the freemen become free in the United States? Mostly in the New England states where the winters were so long that it was not economically feasible to support a slave all year round, when they could be used only for four or five months. Slavery would have been just as brutal as it was in the South if the weather permitted. In New England the slaves had become industrial slaves. A large number of them were employed as ship caulkers. In the era of wooden ships, every time a ship came in the caulkers would have to drill something in the holds of the ship to keep it from eroding and to keep it from leaking at sea. A large number of Africans became ship caulkers and a large number became industrial slaves and they began to learn basic industrial skills. Professor Lorenzo Green's book, *The Negro in Colonial New England*, is especially good in explaining the details of this transformation during the period of slavery.

There were also slave inventors, but these slaves could not patent their own inventions. They had to patent them in the name of their masters.

Soon after the latter half of the nineteenth century, when the Africans understood that emancipation was not the reality they had hoped for, they began another resistance movement in the hope of improving their condition. They set up a communication system with all the slaves. There were no "West Indians," no "Black Americans." These were names unknown to us in Africa. We were and we saw ourselves as one people, as African people.

In the nineteenth century the Africans began the inventive period, and before the beginning of the twentieth century Africans had already invented some of the things that made life more comfortable for many in the United States. When you study a list of the numerous inventions of Africans you will find that they would invent things first and foremost to make life better for themselves. Benjamin Banneker was the first notable Black inventor. When the Africans arrived in the United States, in 1619, the year before the Mayflower people arrived, they were not chattel slaves, but indentured slaves. Indentured slaves worked so many years and then they were free. Most of the indentured slaves were whites. Many times whites and Blacks did not see the difference in their lives. They were both exploited, and they both had to work so many years before they were free. Therefore, during this time, there was a period when Africans and whites saw no difference in their plight and this was before prejudice and color differences would set in. Many times they married one another and nobody cared; they were both slaves anyway. Out of these marriages came some people who helped to change the condition of the slaves in the United States. Benjamin Banneker was a product of one of these relationships. In his mother's time if a white woman had a Black lover and because of her whiteness she worked her way out of the indenture ahead of her lover, then she came and bought him out of the indenture and married him. No one took notice.

Benjamin Banneker, literally, made the first clock in the United States. He dabbled in astronomy, he communicated with President Thomas Jefferson and he asked Jefferson to entertain the idea of having a secretary of peace as well as having a secretary of war. He was assistant to the Frenchman L'Enfant who was planning the City of Washington. For some reason L'Enfant got angry with the Washington people, picked up his plans and went back to France. Benjamin Banneker remembered the plans and Benjamin Banneker is responsible for the designing of the City of Washington, one of the few American cities designed with streets wide enough for ten cars to pass at the same time. This was the first of many of the African-American inventors that we have with good records. There will be many to follow and I am only naming a few.

James Forten became one of the first African-Americans to become moderately rich. He made sails and accessories for ships. During the beginning of the winter of the American Revolution it was noticed that the tent cloth they were using for the tents was of better quality than the cloths they had in their britches. James Forten, the sail maker, was approached to use some of the same cloth to make the britches for the soldiers of the American Revolution. These britches, made by this Black man, saved them from that third and last terrible winter of the American Revolution. Now, the role of Blacks in the American Revolution is another lecture in the sense that 5000 Blacks fought against the United States on the side of England in the American Revolution, and the English had to find somewhere for them to go after the war. They sent some of them to Sierra Leone, but some of them went to Nova Scotia.

Jan Ernest Matzeliger, a young man from Guyana, now called Surinam, invented the machine for the mass production of shoes; this invention revolutionized the shoe industry.

In summary, African-Americans continued to create inventions. They revolutionized the American industry. For example, Granville Woods not only revolutionized the electrical concept, but he laid the basis for Westinghouse Electric Company. Elijah McCoy invented a drip coupling for lubrication that revolutionized the whole concept of lubrication. He had over fifty patents to his credit and so many whites stole from Elijah McCoy that anytime a white man took a patent of a lubrication system, or anything that related to it to the patent office, he was asked, "Did you steal it directly from McCoy or did you steal it indirectly from McCoy or is it the real McCoy?" This is how the word came into the English language, "the real McCoy."

In the closing years of the nineteenth century the greatest talent was that of Lewis Latimer. He was not only a draftsman, but he drew up the plans for the telephone. Alexander Graham Bell was the one who invented the telephone, but the patent that had to be drawn up, all the moving parts and all of the vital parts, was done by Lewis Latimer, a Black man. Latimer also did a few other things that don't make me too happy. He improved the Maxim gun that became the forerunner of the present day machine gun. He is also responsible for the fluorescent light. He wrote the first book on the incandescent light that you know as the fluorescent light. He worked with Thomas Edison. He was one of the Thomas Edison pioneers. While Thomas Edison created the principle of the electric light, his light went out in twenty minutes. But the man who created the filament made the light go on indefinitely. That was Lewis Latimer, and he deserves as much credit for the electric light as does Thomas Edison. And he and his accomplishments were completely left out of history. Only Thomas Edison's accomplishments are mentioned.

Not only did African-Americans invent a lot of other things, including labor-saving devices, African-Americans have played a major role in getting America into space. In space medicine the leading doctor is an African-American woman. The person that designed the interior of the ship, including the disposal facility, is an African-American man. When they sent some astronauts up without instructing them in his method of disposal of waste matter, a near catastrophe occurred. The space buggy that they used to walk on the moon was, basically, a Black invention and so is the camera that they used on the trip to the moon.

You might wonder that after all that the African-Americans have contributed in making the United States comfortable, even to the couplings that hold all the weights together when trains are moving around the country, why are they having so much trouble, and why are they still having difficulty? Principally because we were not brought to the United States to be given democracy, to be given Christianity. We were brought to labor and once the labor was done, we were an unwanted population in the United States. We were a nation within a nation searching for a nationality.

When we put all of us together, we are larger, in number, than all of the nations in Scandinavia put together. Their population would not be as large as the African-American population in the United States alone. According to the statistics of the United Nations and the *Jewish Year Book* all the Jews in the world would come to less than one-half the number of African-American population in the United States. Yet Israel gets more financial aid than all of the African nations in the world put together. Principally because we have not developed the political apparatus to put the right pressures on the leaders in the world to make it so.

I see no solution for African peoples, any place in this world, short of Pan-Africanism. Wherever we are on the face of this earth we are an African people. We have got to understand that any problem faced by Africans is the collective problem of all the African people in the world, and not just the problem of the Africans who live in any one part of the world. Once we put all of our skills together, and realize that between the United States, the Caribbean Islands, Brazil and other South American countries there are 150 million African people, and the population of Africa has been counted as 500 million for over fifty years, implying that the African man has been sleeping away from home, and you know that is not true.

In the twenty-first century there are going to be a billion African people on this earth. We have to ask ourselves, "Are we ready for the twenty-first century?" Do we go into the twenty-first century begging and pleading or insisting and demanding? We have to ask and answer that question and we have to decide if we are going to be the rearguard for somebody else's way of life, or do we rebuild our own way of life, or will we be the vanguard to rebuild our own nation.

We have to say to ourselves when we look at our history, the great Nile Valley civilization, the kind of civilizations we built on other rivers, the Niger, the Limpopo, the Zambezi, the kind of civilizations that gave life to the world before the first Europeans wore shoes or had houses that had windows. We need to say to ourselves, with conviction, that, "If I did it once, I will do it again."

J. A. ROGERS

From "Superman" to Man

"Oh, give me liberty,
For were a paradise itself my prison
Still I should long to leap the crystal walls."

—DRYDEN

The next day at noon Dixon was sitting in an end seat contemplating the snow-covered wastes when Passenger No. 2 approached him and sitting in the opposite seat said: "Did I understand you to say you have been in South America?" And the passenger, who had also travelled in South America, engaged him in a conversation about Argentina. The talk gradually led to conditions among the Negroes in the South. Among other things the passenger said, was: "I am a Southerner myself, but I am very much opposed to the South's treatment of the Negro. The South, generally speaking, badly needs an infusion of new ideas. At present it is like an ancestral mansion, whose occupants, sitting behind shuttered windows that barely admit the sunlight, are still basking in the reflection of the dubious glory of the past. The South's pride of race is tragic. Pride of race made Spain what it was—a nation of decayed aristocrats and illiterate superstitious peasants. How I wish my beloved Southland would throw open the windows of its soul and let in the rejuvenating sunlight of truth.

"And the South can never rise higher than the Negro. Black and white in the South are like Siamese Twins who, while they are physiologically distinct beings, are so joined that one of the twins could not harm the other without harming himself, or benefit the other without benefiting himself."

Dixon took occasion to compliment him on his broadmindedness.

"Well," he went on to say, "I've found truth the only thing worth living for. But there is a hard struggle to obtain it. As a rule, we do not like to hear that which doesn't fit with our own ideas. I find that when it comes to unpleasant truths my mind shies like a horse at strange objects. By constant use of the spur, Reason, however, I force my will to accustom itself to strange truths—to overcome prejudice—and so I go on finding each new truth easier to accept."

"Many of our most prominent men, leaders of thought, are conspicuously weak-kneed on this matter of color," he continued. "They dread public opinion. By a good many people I am regarded as a freak or an open enemy. Some even say that I must be a Negro. But I would rather be anything else than a coward or one of those who take opinions from leaders who are out to serve themselves."

"Leaders! There lies the difficulty," said Dixon. "The masses pick their leaders according to their, the masses', own light. Each one picks the way in which he finds the greatest pleasure in giving up his money."

"That's it. It takes money to do anything these days, I know; but if Christ is the typical leader of men how few approach him. There is no record of Christ ever taking up a collection. Leaders, however, are a necessity and they must be supported if they are to work at all. I make it a point never to give a cent to any leader who appeals to me on any ground other than justice for all, regardless of color, creed or class. No segregations. Every American citizen must be free to go anywhere and to do anything that any other law-abiding citizen is free to do. That's my stand. I say with DeFoe:

> " 'He that hath truth on his side is a fool as well as a coward if he is afraid to own it because of the currency or multitude of men's opinion.' "

"I owe a great deal to my Negro mammy," he continued. "I shall never forget her tender care for my mother and me during the hard time after the war, and her forgiving Christian character. More than any other agency, that of my parents not excepted, she has been a power for molding me for good. My people say that the Negro is a hindrance to their progress. Yes, he is, but because of themselves. In other words, he is the prisoner; they are the jailers. No jailer is ever a free man, himself. Thoughts of the Negro, and how to keep him a common laborer predominate in the Southern mind today. Since whatever dwells uppermost in our mind rules us, the South actually has what it dreads most—Negro domination. And ah,—how different things could be!"

Both men exchanged views until the announcement of luncheon. Before leaving for the dining car the passenger said: "The United States, in its treatment of the Negro would do well to imitate the humble oyster, who, when a grit or a worm or whatever it be, gets into his shell, quietly makes the irritant into a pearl. And believe me!" he continued in a voice so kindly, so full of his creed of right doing that it affected Dixon's innermost being and pervaded him with its sincerity, "no other race that I know of possesses the qualities for conversion into human pearls as the Negro—kindly, sunny, faithful!"

That night, while Dixon was cleaning the cuspidors, the senator came in with a newspaper. After reading for a few minutes, he inquired:—"Dixon, I have been wondering why a man of your intelligence should stay in a job like this!" He knew the reason well, but he wanted to hear what the other had to say.

Dixon suspended the cleaning to tell him what he had told the Frenchman. He added: "I recently passed an examination for a secretaryship in the United States Consular service. But," he laughed, "as I had to submit a picture of myself I shall be very much surprised if I get an appointment."

"Have you ever thought of leaving the United States to live abroad?"

"Yes, I have thought of going to Brazil, but on second thoughts, I have decided to remain here. Sometimes I feel as if I am experiencing too much of the acid of color prejudice to keep my temper sweet. But," he added with determination, "this is my country, mine as much as any other American's. My great-great-grandfather died to win the freedom of this country at the battle of Rhode Island, August 29, 1778; my great-grandfather fought to preserve its independence at Lake Erie in 1812; my grandfather fought at Shiloh to preserve its unity, and I myself have seen a little active service. I am an American—a plain American—and one I shall remain in spite of all the attempts to hyphenate me. I am going to fight it out here even as my forefathers did. No one shall make me run."

"Yet, there are many Negroes who hold federal jobs in Washington."

"Yes, some hold fairly good positions," replied Dixon, "but since prejudice is an enemy that will not permit open competition, it is often a matter of the merest chance that they get these often well-merited positions. Color egotism, thus diverting valuable talent into lines of employment that could be filled by persons more fitted for them, is bad economics. A vast amount of Negro talent and genius goes to absolute waste. This woefully short-sighted policy results in a direct loss to the nation."

"But so many Negroes are without any ambition at all," said the senator. "You said that there are better opportunities in the North, but in all the large Northern cities it seems to me that the proportion of Negroes hanging outside saloons and loafing in pool-rooms was far in excess of those white doing the same thing."

"Perhaps so," replied Dixon, "but consider the bad example these have. The educated and ambitious Negro is often forced into competition with his uneducated brother, who, seeing the former faring no better than he, often bossed by one whose chief asset is his complexion, has no incentive to step out. But today at dinner I heard one of the porters say: 'What's the use?

There's Dixon with a good education and he is doing the same porter work as I.' There I was actually setting a bad example to this man! Now, really, can you blame them for this Omar Khayyam outlook? What incentive have they? It might be said that these men had little or no ambition to start with. Perhaps so. But the duty we owe to our fellow-men, is not to throw obstacles in their way, but to encourage them, to fan every spark of ambition. The aspiring Negro is severely handicapped in his desire to accomplish anything. He has to wrestle so long and so hard with prejudice that a great portion of his energy is lost. Take the case of a poor Negro at a university. While the poor white student can get any spare time position, the Negro has to depend on the color whims of the employer. Even the meanest jobs are sometimes refused him. As a student I was once refused a job of taking out soiled dishes in return for my meals on account of color. It is truly disheartening to see Negro youths being graduated, after the severest struggles, to find the door of opportunity closed in their faces. As an instance, take Chicago. Nation-wide experience tells me that the Negro has better opportunities there than anywhere else. Yet the disadvantages colored people suffer in that city, as reported by the Juvenile Protective Association, are unbelievable. I happen to have a clipping from the report in my grip and would like to show it to you."

He left the room returning soon with the clipping, which he handed to the senator. The latter glanced at it a moment and handed it back saying: "Would you mind reading it for me?"

Dixon read:

> " 'In the business world—speaking generally—the discrimination against the Negro is even greater. It grows more and more difficult for a colored man or woman to get work except as a laborer or servant and even in those directions there are serious difficulties. As salespeople, office clerks, and stenographers, there is almost no opportunity for Negroes in Chicago. With one exception the big business colleges discriminate against colored students. There is small encouragement for them to take training in technical courses in public schools. One bright colored boy who graduated from a technical school this year was sent with his classmates to the employment office of a big corporation. 'We don't hire niggers,' said the man in charge.' "

Dixon added, "A conspicuous example of an employer who does the reverse of the above is Henry Ford. In his Detroit plant Negroes work at anything for which they are fit—inventors, designers, machinists, office-work. Ford is a genuine American."

A child's cry was heard in the body of the car. Dixon asked to be excused and hurried in. A few minutes later he returned bringing a baby about eighteen months old.

"His mama has train sickness," explained Dixon.

The youngster, riding on Dixon's knee and tickled by the senator was now laughing and kicking with delight. Dixon, by tossing him and riding him around for the past two days had been spoiling him. Several times he had refused to return to his mother.

The child soon became sleepy again, and nestling in Dixon's arms, was soon sound asleep.

He resumed the reading of the clipping.

> " 'Out of nearly 4,000 men employed by the express companies, only twenty-one are colored men, and fifteen of that number work as porters. There are apparently none at all employed as boot and shoe hands, glovemakers, bindery workers, printers, neck-wear and suspender workers or on the elevated roads. A good many labor unions admit colored men to membership, but these complain that they are discriminated against, at least in the more difficult and better-paid trades, when it comes to getting work.
>
> " 'The result is that the mass of Negroes are forced to seek, in increasing numbers, the less desirable and poorly-paid occupations. More Negro men—nearly 8,000 in all—work as porters and bar helpers in saloons and poolrooms than in any other field.' "

"This report," explained Dixon, "depicts conditions of some years ago, but they are substantially true of all Northern cities now."

"What do you think of the education of the Negro," next asked the senator.

Dixon thought the question vague, but answered, "I do not think it ought to differ from that of any other color of mankind. Every human being regardless of sex, ought to be permitted to develop his or her fullest powers, in his or her own way. Any agency that prevents this is pernicious in the extreme. Is it to the benefit of the state that certain of its citizens be forcibly dwarfed to remain laborers? In the reign of Henry VIII, the lower classes were not permitted to read the Bible, particularly the New Testament. How do we of today view that? Yet, here five hundred years later we find men in authority advocating an analogous thing in non-education of certain citizens."

"But the ignorant Negro is the happy Negro,"—protested the senator. "To educate him is only to make him unhappy."

"Very well," replied Dixon, "here is this sleeping infant. He is ignorant and hence is always happy when healthy, and well-cared for. Would you always keep him at this stage because education and the knowledge of life will make him unhappier as it surely will?

"Again, with the possible exception of the Latin races, the Caucasian is the unhappiest of all peoples. Now, suppose I were to say, 'Do not educate white men any more; to do so is only to make them unhappier,' what would you think of me? Advocates of non-education for Negroes have shown so little regard for us in other vital matters and so much genuine solicitude in this that I have begun to suspect that what they really mean is: Do not educate the Negro and make the unhappy white man, unhappier."

The senator did not reply. Dixon continued: "Moreover, the thinker of any color is often unhappy because education enables him to see the tinsel and the heartaches; the injustices and the greed that go to make up the greater part of our civilization. But, as you say, there is some mercy in this advocacy of non-education of the Negro for while the uneducated Negro of the United States has a far happier lot than any other peasant class perhaps in the world, there is no recognized place in America for the educated Negro. To use an old phrase: he is in advance of his age, that is, so far as conditions are governed by the whites. He lacks that association that helped to make Johnson, Lamb, Coleridge, and Garrick what they were. Solomon said: 'He that increaseth knowledge increaseth sorry.' This statement is especially true of educated Negroes. The ignorant Negro like the ignorant white man will continue to be the happier one until we educate or remove the cause that makes the thinking ones of both races unhappy, namely, the greedy white men and the few greedy Negroes at the top."

"A great many advocate only industrial training for the Negro," said the senator. "What do you think of that? I favor industrial training; since that is the basis of all production, the race will acquire wealth and independence. If the Negro cannot get employment among white people, he must create work for himself. The great trouble with the Negro race is, that it has too many doctors, lawyers, and preachers."

"When you say that the Negro should start out for himself," replied Dixon, "it is equivalent to saying that here amidst this wealth of development, distilled by the human race from the bitter experiences of thousands of years, certain human beings should start in again like troglodytes. In these days of express trains should one be compelled to travel in a prairie schooner until he has learnt to build his own railway? Why impose on us conditions that you'd be the first to kick against if applied to you? It should be just as logical to ask, 'What form of training is preferable for white men?' As no two men are alike human intellect cannot be regimented. Any such attempt, besides preventing full attainment, will cause unhappiness. Everyone, as Shakespeare advises, should study what he most affects. I say let everyone, white as well as black, be permitted to pick out his own occupation and follow it without interference. In this way and this way only will the great curse of civilization—uncongenial employment—be removed.

"You also spoke of the large number of Negro doctors, lawyers and preachers, and the relatively small number in the mechanical pursuits. I happen to have the figures here. The census of 1930 shows: One white doctor for every 726 whites; one Negro doctor for every 3099 Negroes; lawyers, white, one in

686; Negroes, one in 9536; preachers, one for every 869 whites; one for every 471 Negroes."

"Well, I was right about the preachers, anyway."

"According to the white ratio you are. It gives us almost two to one. You see, the Negroes having few of the sweets of this life, have strong hope of getting theirs after they have been put under the sod. The white man's religion promises this very strongly to them, and also to those whites who are similarly deprived. Since the Negro's forte is religion, he is more easily exploited in that field, and since to become a preacher in any group, regardless of race, the chief essential is the gift of gab, the sharpers, who among the whites would be lawyers and speculators, among Negroes simply gravitate to the ministry and also to hair and complexion doctoring."

The train began to slow down as the lights of a town were visible nearby.

"What place is this?" asked the senator.

"Evanston, Wyo."

"How long do we stay?"

"About five minutes. We change engines."

"I think I'll take a walk then."

Dixon took the sleeping child to his mother and went to the drawing-room for the senator's hat and overcoat. Later both left the smoker and went out on the vestibule. As Dixon opened the trap-door a rush of icy air swept in, compelling the senator to button up his overcoat around his neck.

"Pretty cold!" he said, hopping around.

"It gets a bit cold up here on the mountains. It's about 25 below tonight."

The train stopped and both stepped off into the crisp midnight air. The senator saw the sign of the railroad lunchroom.

"Have we time for a cup of coffee?" he asked hurriedly.

"Yes, sir."

"Come along, then," he said, catching Dixon by the coat-sleeve. Dixon left the car in charge of the sleeping-car conductor and both men started on a trot over the crackling snow for the lunch-room.

The senator ordered coffee and sandwiches for Dixon and himself. After a few mouthfuls the senator began to look nervously through the window.

"We've plenty of time, sir," reassured Dixon, guessing the cause of his anxiety. "See! there's the train-conductor just getting his lunch now!"

When the train started again the senator, followed by Dixon, returned to the smoker. Throwing his hat and overcoat on the seat, the senator settled himself comfortably in the chair.

"Let me see," he said after a few contemplative puffs of his cigar, "we were last speaking of Negro education, weren't we? I—I—" he continued haltingly, as a thought struck him like a dart—he had just become conscious of the fact that he had just dined with a Negro! Dixon had been conscious of the incident all along. When the senator recovered his composure he said:

"What do you think of the late leader of your race, Booker T. Washington? I should judge that you are against his policies."

"If it is his policy of advocating the surrender of certain rights of progress in other directions that you mean, sir, I am, on conditions. Booker T. Washington has been much blamed, and is still being blamed, for not standing up more firmly for the rights of his people. A book-agent told me that he had difficulty in selling Washington's book among colored people. Many would-be patrons, he said, refused, saying that they did not like the way in which he had bowed to the white man. But even had Booker T. been endowed with an unbending spirit I cannot see how he could have done otherwise and have carried out his life work. The great majority of the people that needed his help were in the South, where any assertion of Negro rights, would, as you know, not only have been resented, but might have been accompanied with serious results. Had he shown a defiant spirit, there would simply have been no Tuskegee, and schools with the spirit of Tuskegee were, and still are, a necessity for both white and colored. The majority of any race is fit only for industrial pursuits; this would be particularly true of a people but recently freed. And humble as was his manner, there were those whites who complained that Tuskegee, with its thoroughness, was making not servants, but masters, thus threatening white domination. Booker T. Washington has done more than any other person or agency that I know of toward guiding the feet of the crude, struggling mass of freedmen to the first rung of the ladder of progress. It is true that others will have to strive hard to undo the impression he gave of Negro subordination yet the blame for this should be placed on the conditions to which he was forced to adapt himself in order to do his work. But whatever one may say of his methods no one can impugn the honesty of his motives. This was a genuine desire born of the largeness of his heart to do good. Booker T. Washington built his fame on the surest of all foundations—unselfish service. Some object that he made a great deal of money. I sincerely hope he did, for I know of no other American who deserved it better than he. There are a very few of his critics, black or white, indeed, few citizens of any country who would not do well to emulate his unselfishness, his energy, and his persistence."

JOHN HOPE FRANKLIN

A Life of Learning

As I began the task of putting the pieces together that would describe how I moved from one stage of intellectual development to another, I was reminded of a remark that Eubie Blake made as he approached his ninety-ninth birthday. He said, "If I had known that I would live this long I would have taken better care of myself." To paraphrase him, if I had known that I would become a historian I would have kept better records of my own pilgrimage through life. I may be forgiven, therefore, if I report that the beginnings are a bit hazy, not only to me but to my parents as well. For example, they had no clear idea of when I learned to read and write. It was when I was about three or four, I am told.

My mother, an elementary school teacher, introduced me to the world of learning when I was three years old. Since there were no day care centers in the village where we lived she had no alternative to taking me to school and seating me in the rear of her classroom where she could keep an eye on me. I remained quiet but presumably I also remained attentive, for when I was about five my mother noticed that on the sheet of paper she gave me each morning, I was no longer making lines and sketching out some notable examples of abstract art. I was writing words, to be sure almost as abstract as my art, and making sentences. My mother later said that she was not surprised much less astonished at what some, not she, would have called my precocity. Her only reproach—to herself, not me—was that my penmanship was hopelessly flawed since she had not monitored my progress as she had done for her enrolled students. From that point on, I would endeavor to write and, through the written word, to communicate my thoughts to others.

My interest in having some thoughts of my own to express was stimulated by my father who, among other tasks, practiced law by day and read and wrote by night. In the absence of any possible distractions in the tiny village, he would read or write something each evening. This was my earliest memory of him and, indeed, it was my last memory of him. Even after we moved to Tulsa, a real city, and after we entered the world of motion pictures, radio,

This essay was the Charles Homer Haskins Lecture, delivered before the American Council of Learned Societies, New York City, April 14, 1988, and printed in the Council's *Occasional Papers, Number 4* (New York, 1988).

and television, his study and writing habits remained unaffected. I grew up believing that in the evenings one either read or wrote. It was always easy to read something worthwhile, and if one worked at it hard enough he might even write something worthwhile. I continue to believe that.

Two factors plagued my world of learning for all of my developing years. One was race, the other was financial distress; and each had a profound influence on every stage of my development. I was born in the all-Negro town of Rentiesville to which my parents went after my father had been expelled from court by a white judge who told him that no black person could ever represent anyone in his court. My father resolved that he would resign from the world dominated by white people and try to make it among his own people. But Rentiesville's population of less than two hundred people could not provide a poverty-free living even for one who was a lawyer, justice of the peace, postmaster, farmer, and president of the Rentiesville Trading Company which, incidentally, was not even a member of the New York Stock Exchange.

The quality of life in Rentiesville was as low as one can imagine. There was no electricity, running water or inside plumbing. There was no entertainment or diversion of any kind—no parks, playgrounds, libraries, or newspapers. We subscribed to the Muskogee *Daily Phoenix*, which was delivered by the Missouri, Kansas, and Texas Railroad as it made its way southward through the state each morning. The days and nights were lonely and monotonous, and for a young lad with boundless energy there was nothing to do but read. My older sister and brother were away in private school in Tennessee, and one did not even have the pleasure of the company of older siblings. Now and then one went to Checotah, six miles away, to shop. That was not always pleasant, such as the time when my mother, sister, and I were ejected from the train because my mother refused to move from the coach designated for whites. It was the only coach we could reach before the train moved again, so my mother argued that she would not move because she was not to blame if the train's white coach was the only one available when the train came to a halt. Her argument was unsuccessful, and we had to trudge back to Rentiesville through the woods.

There were the rare occasions when we journeyed to Eufala, the county seat, where I won the spelling bee for three consecutive years. There was Muskogee to the north, where I went at the age of five for my first pair of eye glasses—the malady brought on, I was told, by reading by the dim light of a kerosene lamp. It was a combination of these personal and family experiences that forced my parents to the conclusion that Rentiesville was not a viable community. They resolved to move to Tulsa. First, my father would go, find a place, set himself up in the practice of law, and we would follow six months later, in June, 1921, when my mother's school closed for the summer recess.

That June, however, we received word that in Tulsa there was a race riot, whatever that was, and that the Negro section of that highly segregated community was in flames. At the age of six I sensed from my mother's reaction that my father was in danger. We were all relieved several days later, therefore, when a message arrived that he had suffered no bodily harm, but that the property he had contracted to purchase was destroyed by fire. He practiced law in a tent for several months, and our move to Tulsa was delayed by four years.

In the month before I reached my eleventh birthday, we arrived in Tulsa. It was quite a new world, and although a city of less than moderate size at the time, it was to my inexperienced eyes perhaps the largest city in the country. I did not see much of it, however, for racial segregation was virtually complete. I thought that Booker T. Washington, the school where I enrolled in grade seven, was the biggest and best school until one day I saw Central High for whites. It was a massive, imposing structure covering a city block. I was later to learn that it had every conceivable facility such as a pipe organ and a theater-size stage, which we did not have. I also learned that it offered modern foreign languages, and calculus, while our school offered automobile mechanics, home economics, typing, and shorthand. Our principal and our teachers constantly assured us that we need not apologize for our training and they worked diligently to give us much of what was not even in the curriculum.

Now that the family was together again I had the example and the encouragement of both of my parents. My mother no longer taught but she saw to it that my sister and I completed all of our home assignments promptly. Quite often, moreover, she introduced us to some of the great writers, especially Negro authors, such as Paul Laurence Dunbar and James Weldon Johnson, who were not a part of our studies at school. She also told us about some of the world's great music such as Handel's Oratorio "Esther," in which she had sung in college. While the music at school was interesting and lively, especially after I achieved the position of first trumpet in the band and orchestra, there was no Handel or Mozart, or Beethoven. We had a full fare of Victor Herbert and John Philip Sousa, and operettas, in more than one of which I sang the leading role.

Often after school I would go to my father's office. By the time I was in high school, the Depression had yielded few clients but ample time, which he spent with me. It was he who introduced me to ancient Greece and Rome, and he delighted in quoting Plato, Socrates, and Pericles. We would then walk home together and after dinner he went to his books and I went to mine. Under the circumstances, there could hardly have been a better way of life, since I had every intention after completing law school of some day becoming his partner.

It was in secondary school that I had a new and wonderful experience which my parents did not share. It was the series of concerts and recitals at Convention Hall, perhaps even larger than the theater at Central High School which I never saw. As in the other few instances where whites and blacks were under the same roof, segregation was strict, but I very much wanted to go with some of my teachers who always held season tickets. My parents would *never* voluntarily accept segregation, consequently, the concerts were something they chose to forego. Even at court my father refused to accept segregation. Whenever I accompanied him, which was as often as I could, he would send me to the jury box when it was empty or, when there was a jury trial, have me sit at the bench with him. They took the position, however, that if I could beat the humiliation of segregation, I could go to the concerts.

Thus, I could purchase my own tickets with the money I earned as a paper boy. To be more accurate, I was not the paper boy, but the assistant to a white man who had the paper route in the black neighborhood. It was at one of these concerts that I heard Paul Whiteman present Gershwin's "Rhapsody in Blue" while on a nationwide tour in 1927. I also attended the annual performance of the Chicago Civil Opera Company, which brought to Tulsa such stellar singers as Rosa Raisa, Tito Schipa, and Richard Bonelli. I am not altogether proud of going to Convention Hall; there are times, even now, while enjoying a symphony or an opera, when I reproach myself for having yielded to the indignity of racial segregation. I can only say that in the long run it was my parents who knew best, though later I made a conscious effort to regain my self-respect.

There were many sobering experiences at Fisk, which I entered on a tuition scholarship in 1931. The first was my encounter with at least two dozen valedictorians and salutatorians from some of the best high schools in the United States. The fact that I had finished first in my high school class did not seem nearly as important in Nashville as it had in Tulsa. Imagine my chagrin when a whiz kid from Dayton made all A's in the first quarter while I made two B's and a C+. My rather poor grades were somewhat mitigated by my having to hold three jobs in order to pay my living expenses. I was also absolutely certain that the C+ resulted from whimsical grading by the teaching assistants in a course called "Contemporary Civilization." As I think of it now I still become infuriated, and if there was anyone to listen to my case today I would insist that my examinations be reevaluated and my grade raised accordingly! I *was* consoled by my salutatorian girl friend, now my wife of forty-seven years, who over the years has lent a sympathetic ear to my rantings about the injustices in that course. She can afford to be charitable, she received a grade of B+.

Another sobering experience was my first racial encounter in Nashville. At a downtown streetcar ticket window, I gave the man the only money I possessed, which was a $20 bill. I apologized and explained that it was all I had and he could give me my change using any kind of bills he wished. In an outburst of abusive language and using vile racial epithets, he told me that no nigger could tell him how to make change. After a few more similar statements, he proceeded to give me $19.75 in dimes and quarters. From that day until I graduated I very seldom went to Nashville, and when I did I never went alone. It was about as much as a sixteen-year-old could stand. I thought of that encounter some three years later, and felt almost as helpless, when a gang of white hoodlums took a young black man from a Fisk-owned house on the edge of the campus and lynched him. As president of student government I made loud noises and protests to the mayor, the governor, and even President Franklin D. Roosevelt, but nothing could relieve our pain and anguish or bring Cordie Cheek back. Incidentally, the heinous crime he had committed was that, while riding his bicycle, he struck a white child who was only slightly injured.

Still another sobering, even shattering, experience was my discovery at the end of my freshman year that my parents had lost our home and had moved into a four-family apartment building which they had built. I knew that the country was experiencing an economic depression of gigantic proportions, that unemployment had reached staggering figures, and that my father's law practice had declined significantly. I was not prepared for the personal embarrassment that the Depression created for me and my family, and frankly I never fully recovered from it. The liquidation of all debts became an obsession with me, and because of that experience my determination to live on a pay-as-you-go basis is as great today as it was when it was not at all possible to live that way.

Despite these experiences my years in college were pleasant if hectic, rewarding if tedious, happy if austere. Most classes were rigorous, and everyone was proud of the fact that the institution enjoyed an A rating by the Southern Association of Colleges and Secondary Schools. The faculty was, on the whole, first-rate, and they took pride in their scholarly output as well as in their teaching. Although the student body was all black, with the exception of an occasional white exchange student or special student, the faculty was fairly evenly divided between white and black. It was an indication of the lack of interest in the subject that we never thought in terms of what proportion of the faculty was white and what proportion was black.

Since I was merely passing through college en route to law school, I had little interest in an undergraduate concentration. I thought of English, but the chairman of that department, from whom I took freshman English, discouraged me on the ground that I would never be able to command the English language. (Incidentally, he was a distinguished authority in American literature and specialized in the traditions of the Gullah-speaking people of the Sea Islands. I was vindicated some years later when he chaired the committee that awarded me the Bancroft Prize for the best article in the *Journal of Negro History*.) My decision to major in history was almost accidental. The chairman of that department, Theodore S. Currier, who was white, had come into that ill-fated course in contemporary civilization and had delivered the most exciting lectures I had ever heard. I decided to see and hear more of him.

During my sophomore year I took two courses with Professor Currier, and my deep interest in historical problems and the historical process and what he had to say was apparently noted by him. Soon we developed a close personal relationship that developed into a deep friendship. Soon, moreover, I made the fateful decision to give up my plan to study and practice law and to replace it with a plan to study, write, and teach history. My desire to learn more about the field resulted in his offering new courses, including seminars, largely for my benefit. He already entertained the hope that I would go to Harvard, where he had done his own graduate work. I had similar hopes, but in the mid-1930s with the Depression wreaking its havoc, it was unrealistic to entertain such hopes. With a respectable grade point average (that C+ prevented my graduating *summa cum laude*), and strong supporting letters from my professors, I applied for admission to the Harvard Graduate School of Arts and Sciences.

Harvard required that I take an aptitude test that must have been the forerunner to the Graduate Records Examination. It was administered at Vanderbilt University, just across town but on whose grounds I had never been. When I arrived at the appointed place and took my seat, the person in charge, presumably a professor, threw the examination at me, a gesture hardly calculated to give me a feeling of welcome or confidence. I took the examination but cannot imagine that my score was high. As I left the room a Negro custodian walked up to me and told me that in his many years of working there I was the only black person he had ever seen sitting in a room with white people. The record that Fisk made that year was more important. The Association of American Universities placed Fisk University on its approved list. On the basis of this new recognition of my alma mater, Harvard admitted me unconditionally. Apparently this was the first time it had given a student from a historically black institution an opportunity to pursue graduate studies without doing some undergraduate work at Harvard. The University declined, however, to risk a scholarship on me.

Admission to Harvard was one thing, getting there was quite another. My parents were unable to give me more than a very small amount of money and their good wishes. I was able to make it back to Nashville, where Ted Currier told me that money alone would not keep me out of Harvard. He went to a Nashville bank, borrowed $500, and sent me on my way.

Shortly after my arrival in Cambridge in September, 1935, I felt secure academically, financially, and socially. At Fisk I had even taken two modern foreign languages in order to meet Harvard's requirement, and in Currier's seminars I had learned how to write a research paper. Since I was secretary to the librarian at Fisk for four years, I had learned how to make the best use of reference materials, bibliographical aids, and manuscripts. Even when I met my advisor, Professor A. M. Schlesinger, Sr., I did not feel intimated, and I was very much at ease with him while discussing my schedule and my plans. After I got a job washing dishes for my evening meal and another typing dissertations and lectures, a feeling of long-range solvency settled over me. Although

I had a room with a Negro family that had taken in black students since the time of Charles Houston and Robert Weaver, I had extensive contact with white students who never showed the slightest condescension toward me. I set my own priorities, however, realizing that I had the burden of academic deficiencies dating back to secondary school. I had to prove to myself and to my professors that the Association of American Universities was justified in placing Fisk University on its approved list. I received the M.A. degree in nine months and won fellowships with which I completed the Ph.D. requirements.

There were few blacks at Harvard in those days. One was completing his work in French history as I entered. As in Noah's Ark, there were two in the law school, two in zoology, and two in the college. There was one in English and one in comparative literature, there were none in the Medical School and none in the Business School.

The most traumatic social experience I had there was not racist but antisemitic. I was quite active in the Henry Adams Club, made up of graduate students in United States history. I was appointed to serve on the committee to nominate officers for the coming year which, if one wanted to be hypersensitive, was a way of making certain that I would not be an officer. When I suggested the most active, brightest graduate student for president, the objection to him was that although he did not have some of the more reprehensible Jewish traits, he was still a Jew. I had never heard any person speak of another in such terms, and I lost respect not only for the person who made the statement but for the entire group that even tolerated such views. Most of the members of the club never received their degrees. The Jewish member became one of the most distinguished persons to get a degree in United States history from Harvard in the last half-century.

The course of study was satisfactory but far from extraordinary. Mark Hopkins was seldom on the other end of the log, and one had to fend for himself as best he could. I had no difficulty with such a regimen, although I felt that some of my fellow students needed more guidance than the university provided. In my presence, at the beginning of my second year, one of the department's outstanding professors verbally abused a student visiting from another institution and dismissed him from his office because the student's question was awkwardly phrased the first time around. Another professor confessed to me that a doctoral committee had failed a candidate because he did not *look* like a Harvard Ph.D. When the committee told him that he would have to study four more years before applying for reconsideration, the student was in the library the following morning to begin his four-year sentence. At that point, the chairman of the committee was compelled to inform the student that under no circumstances would he be permitted to continue his graduate studies there.

When I left Harvard in the spring of 1939 I knew that I did not wish to be in Cambridge another day. I had no desire to offend my advisor or the other members of my doctoral committee. I therefore respectfully declined suggestions that I seek further financial aid. It was time, I thought, to seek a teaching position and complete my dissertation *in absentia*. I had taught one year at Fisk following my first year at Harvard. With five preparations in widely disparate fields and with more than two hundred students, I learned more history than I had learned at Fisk *and* Harvard. I early discovered that teaching had its own very satisfying rewards. For some fifty-two years, there have been many reasons to confirm the conclusions I reached at Fisk, St. Augustine's, North Carolina College at Durham, Howard, Brooklyn, Chicago, Duke, and short stints in many institutions here and abroad.

After I committed myself to the study, teaching, and writing of history, I was so preoccupied with my craft that I gave no attention to possible career alternatives. Less than two years into my career, however, when I was working on my second book, the president of a small but quite respectable historically black liberal arts college invited me to become dean of his institution. It was at that point that I made a response that was doubtless already in my mind but which I had not yet articulated. I thanked him and respectfully declined the invitation on the grounds that my work in the field of history precluded my moving into college administration. When the president received my letter, he sent me a telegram informing me that he was arriving the following day to explain his offer. During the three hours of conversation with him I had ample opportunity to state and restate my determination to remain a teacher and writer of history. Each time I did so I became more unequivocal in my resistance to any change in my career objectives. I believe that he finally became convinced that he was indeed wrong in offering me the deanship in the first place. From that day onward, I had no difficulty in saying to anyone who raised the matter that I was not interested in deanships, university presidencies, or ambassadorships. And I never regretted the decision to remain a student and teacher of history.

There is nothing more stimulating or satisfying than teaching bright, inquisitive undergraduates. It was puzzling, if dismaying, when a student complained, as one did at Howard that my lengthy assignments did not take into account the fact that his people were only eighty-five years removed from slavery. It was sobering, but challenging when an undergraduate asked, as one did at Brooklyn if I would suggest additional readings since he had already read everything in the syllabus that I distributed on the first day of class. It was reassuring to find that some students, such as those at Chicago, came to class on a legal holiday because I neglected to take note of the holiday in my class assignments. It was refreshing, even amusing, when students requested as some did at Duke, that the date for the working dinner at my home be changed because it conflicted with a Duke-Virginia basketball game. As Harry Golden would say, only in America could one find undergraduates with so much *chutzpah*.

There came a time in my own teaching career when I realized that with all my frantic efforts at research and writing I would never be able to write on all the subjects in which I was deeply interested. If I only had graduate students who would take up some of the problems regarding slavery, free blacks, the Reconstruction era and its overthrow, it would extend my own sense of accomplishment immeasurably. That was a major consideration in my move in 1964 from Brooklyn College to the University of Chicago, where for the next eighteen years I supervised some thirty dissertations of students who subsequently have published more than a dozen books. In view of Chicago's freewheeling attitude toward the time for fulfilling degree requirements, there is a possibility that eight years after retirement, I might have more doctoral students to complete their work and write more books. Meanwhile, I continue to revel in the excitement of teaching in still another type of institution, the law school at Duke University.

I could not have avoided being a social activist even if I had wanted to. I had been barred from entering the University of Oklahoma to pursue graduate studies, and when the National Association for the Advancement of Colored People asked me to be the expert witness for Lyman Johnson, who sought admission to the graduate program in history at the University of Kentucky, I was honored to do so. After all, it was easy to establish the fact that Johnson could not get the same training at the inferior Kentucky State College for Negroes that he could get at the University of Kentucky. Johnson was admitted forthwith. To me it was one more blow against segregation in Oklahoma as well as Kentucky. The defense argument collapsed when the University of Kentucky placed one of its history professors on the stand and asked him about teaching Negroes. He replied soberly that he did not teach Negroes, he taught history, which he was pleased to do.

Then, Thurgood Marshall asked me to serve on his nonlegal research staff when the NAACP Legal Defense Fund sought to eliminate segregation in the public schools. Each week in the late summer and fall of 1953 I journeyed from Washington to New York, where I worked from Thursday afternoon to Sunday afternoon. I wrote historical essays, coordinated the work of some other researchers, and participated in the seminars that the lawyers held regularly, and provided the historical setting for the questions with which they were wrestling. I had little time for relaxing at my home away from home, the Algonquin Hotel, but each time I entered this establishment, I made eye contact with an imaginary Tallulah Bankhead, Agnes DeMille, or Noel Coward, who were among the more famous habitues of its lobby.

The historian, of all people, must not make more of his own role in events, however significant even if it is tempting to do so. It would be easy to claim that I was one of the 250,000 people at the March on Washington in 1963. I was not there and perhaps the truth is even more appealing. Since I was serving as Pitt Professor at the University of Cambridge that year, I was something of a resource person for the BBC-TV. On Richard Dimbleby's popular television program, *Panorama*, I tried to explain to the British viewers what had transpired when James Meredith sought to enter the University of Mississippi. I suspect there was a bit of advocacy even in the tone of my voice. In the summer of 1963 I took British viewers through what the BBC called "A Guide to the March on Washington." Here again, with film clips on Malcolm X, James Baldwin, A. Philip Randolph, and others, I explained why the march was a very positive development in the history of American race relations. Finally, in 1965, I was actually on the Selma march. No, I did not march *with* Martin, as some imaginative writers have claimed. I doubt that Martin ever knew that I was there, far back in the ranks as I was. I was *not* at Pettus Bridge in Dallas County, but joined the march at the city of St. Jude on the outskirts of Montgomery. I took pride in marching with more than thirty historians who came from all parts of the country to register their objection to racial bigotry in the United States. And I want to make it clear that I was afraid, yes, frightened out of my wits by the hate-filled eyes that stared at us from the sidewalks, windows, businesses, and the like. It was much more than I had bargained for.

One must be prepared for any eventuality when he makes any effort to promote legislation or to shape the direction of public policy or to affect the choice of those in the public service. This came to me quite forcefully in 1987 when I joined the others from many areas of activity in opposing the Senate confirmation of Robert H. Bork as associate justice of the Supreme Court of the United States. In what I thought was a sober and reasoned statement, I told the Judiciary Committee of the United States Senate that there was "no indication—in his writings, his teachings, or his rulings—that this nominee has any deeply held commitment to the eradication of the problem of race or even of its mitigation." It came as a shock, therefore, to hear the president of the United States declare that the opponents of the confirmation of Judge Bork constituted a "lynch mob." This was a wholly unanticipated tirade against those activists who had merely expressed views on a subject in which all citizens had an interest.

It was necessary, as a black historian, to have a personal agenda, as well as one dealing with more general matters, that involved a type of activism. I discovered this in the spring of 1939 when I arrived in Raleigh, North Carolina, to do research in the state archives, only to be informed by the director that in planning the building the architects did not anticipate that any Afro-Americans would be doing research there. Perhaps it was the astonishment that the director, a Yale Ph.D. in history, saw in my face that prompted him to make a proposition. If I would wait a week he would make some arrangements. When I remained silent, registering a profound disbelief, he cut the time in half. I waited from Monday to Thursday, and upon my return to the archives I was escorted to a small room outfitted with a table and chair which was to be my private office for the next four years. (I hasten to explain that it did not take four years to complete my dissertation. I completed it the following year, but continued to do research there as long as I was teaching at St. Augustine's College.) The director also presented me with keys to the manuscript collection in order to avoid requiring the white assistants to deliver manuscripts to me. That arrangement lasted only two weeks, when the white researchers, protesting discrimination, demanded keys to the manuscript collection for themselves. Rather than comply with their demands, the director relieved me of my keys and ordered the assistants to serve me.

Nothing illustrated the vagaries of policies and practices of racial segregation better than libraries and archives. In Raleigh alone, there were three different policies. The state library had two tables in the stacks set aside for the regular use of Negro readers. The state supreme court library had no segregation while, as we have seen, the archives faced the matter as it arose. In Alabama and Tennessee, the state archives did not segregate readers, while Louisiana had a strict policy of excluding Negro would-be readers altogether. In the summer of 1945 I was permitted by the Louisiana director of archives to use the manuscript collection since the library was closed in observance of the victory of the United States over governmental tyranny and racial bigotry in Germany and Japan. As I have said elsewhere, pursuing southern history has been for me a strange career.

While World War II interrupted the careers of many young scholars, I experienced no such delay. At the same time, it raised in my mind the most profound questions about the sincerity of my country in fighting bigotry and tyranny abroad. And the answers to my questions shook my faith in the integrity of our country and its leaders. Being loath to fight with guns and grenades in any case, I sought opportunities to serve in places where my training and skills could be utilized. When the United States entered the war in 1941, I had already received my doctorate. Since I knew that several men who had not been able to obtain their advanced degrees had signed on as historians in the War Department, I made application there. I was literally rebuffed without the department giving me any serious consideration. In Raleigh, where I was living at the time, the Navy sent out a desperate appeal for men to do office work, and the successful ones would be given the rank of petty officer. When I answered the appeal, the recruiter told me that I had all of the qualifications except color. I concluded that there was *no* emergency and told the recruiter how I felt. When my draft board ordered me to go to its staff physician for a blood test, I was not permitted to enter his office and was told to wait on a bench in the hall. When I refused and insisted to the draft board clerk that I receive decent treatment, she in turn insisted that the doctor see me forthwith, which he did. By this time, I had concluded that the United States did not need me and did not deserve me. I spent the remainder of the war successfully outwitting my draft board, including taking a position at North Carolina College for Negroes whose president was on the draft appeal board. Each time I think of these incidents, even now, I feel nothing but shame for my country—not merely for what it did to me, but for what it did to the million black men and women who served in the armed forces under conditions of segregation and discrimination.

One had always to be mindful, moreover, that being a black scholar did not exempt one from the humiliations and indignities that a society with more than its share of bigots can heap upon a black person, regardless of education or even station in life. This became painfully clear when I went to Brooklyn College in 1956 as chairman of a department of fifty-two white historians. There was much fanfare accompanying my appointment, including a front-page story with picture in the New York *Times*. When I sought to purchase a home, however, not one of the thirty-odd realtors offering homes in the vicinity of Brooklyn College would show their properties. Consequently, I had to seek showings by owners who themselves offered their homes for sale. I got a few showings including one that we very much liked, but I did not have sufficient funds to make the purchase. My insurance company had proudly advertised that it had $50 million to lend to its policy holders who aspired to home ownership. My broker told me that the company would not make a loan to me because the house I wanted was several blocks beyond where blacks should live. I cancelled my insurance and, with the help of my white lawyer, tried to obtain a bank loan. I was turned down by every New York bank except the one in Brooklyn, where my attorney's father had connections. As we finally moved in after the hassles of more than a year, I estimated that I could have written a long article, perhaps even a small book, in the time expended on the search for housing. The high cost of racial discrimination is not merely a claim of the so-called radical left. It is as real as the rebuffs, the indignities, or the discriminations that many black people suffer.

Many years ago, when I was a fledgling historian, I decided that one way to make certain that the learning process would continue was to write different kinds of history, even as one remained in the same field. It was my opinion that one should write a monograph, a general work, a biography, a period piece, and edit some primary source and some work or works, perhaps by other authors, to promote an understanding of the field. I made no systematic effort to touch all the bases, as it were, but with the recent publication of my biography of George Washington Williams, I believe that I have touched them all. More recently, I have started the process all over again by doing research for a monograph on runaway slaves.

Another decision I made quite early was to explore new areas or fields, whenever possible, in order to maintain a lively, fresh approach to the teaching and writing of history. That is how I happened to get into Afro-American history, in which I never had a formal course, but which attracted a growing number of students of my generation and many more in later generations. It is remarkable how moving or even drifting into a field can affect one's entire life. More recently, I have become interested in women's history, and during the past winter I prepared and delivered three lectures under the general title of "Women, Blacks, and Equality, 1820–1988." I need not dwell on the fact that for me it was a very significant learning experience. Nor should it be necessary for me to assure you that despite the fact that I have learned much, I do not seek immortality by writing landmark essays and books in the field of women's history.

I have learned much from my colleagues both at home and abroad. The historical associations and other learned societies have instructed me at great length at their annual meetings, and five of them have given me an opportunity to teach and to lead by electing me as their president. Their journals have provided me with the most recent findings of scholars and they have graciously published some pieces of my own. Very early I learned that scholarship knows no national boundaries, and I have sought the friendship and collaboration of historians and scholars in many parts of the world. From the time that I taught at the Salzburg Seminar in American Studies in 1951, I have been a student and an advocate of the view that the exchange of ideas is more healthy and constructive than the exchange of bullets. This was especially true during my tenure on the Fulbright Board, as a member for seven years and as the chairman for three years. In such experiences one learns much about the common ground that the peoples of the world share. When we also learn that this country and the western world have no monopoly of goodness and truth or of skills and scholarship, we begin to appreciate the ingredients that are indispensable to making a better world. In a life of learning that is perhaps the greatest lesson of all.

ALEX HALEY

There Are Days When I Wish It Hadn't Happened (March 1979)

Finally after three A.M., practically out on my feet from exhaustion, I locked my hotel-room door behind me, pulled off my clothes down to my underwear and flopped onto the bed for whatever rest I could manage to get before running to catch the next plane at seven. A few hours before, I'd been among the 80,000,000 Americans who had watched the concluding eighth episode of the original *Roots* television miniseries, which had ended with me on camera speaking for several minutes to that unprecedented national audience. Of the earlier seven *Roots* episodes, I'd had to miss six. While they were on, I had been hurrying between airports, hotels and myriad other places in an effort to maintain a blurring schedule of back-to-back appointments in a grueling coast-to-coast promotional tour of interviews, speeches and personal appearances seven days a week, usually from before breakfast to midnight and frequently beyond.

But most assuredly, I wasn't—and still am not—complaining. After some 20 years of having crossed my fingers every time I mailed to editors something I had written, now *Roots*, which represented 12 of those years of work, had already sold close to 1,000,000 hardcover copies, and the television miniseries had collectively attracted the largest audience in the history of the medium. I lay there on the hotel bed, thinking about how lucky I was, no matter what bone weariness it involved, and with those ambivalent thoughts I was drifting into sleep when the loud door buzzer jolted the silence. It couldn't be my wake-up call already! I peered at the night table clock's luminous dial: 3:30! Again the buzzer sounded.

Stumbling to the door in the darkness, I fumbled it open. A young blond-haired bellboy stood there stiffly, his hands at his sides, swallowing hard and looking very solemnly at me standing in the doorway in my underwear, blinking at him.

"Yes?" I managed.

He stuck out his hand. "Sir, I want to thank you for what you've done for America."

He couldn't have been more sincere. That's all he had to say. I wanted to hug him for feeling that way—and to punch him for getting me out of bed. I shook his hand, said I appreciated his saying that, and he marched away.

Then it hit me. So much for anonymity; I guess I'll be having experiences like that now and then for a while; of course, the TV exposure will cause more people to recognize me than did when it was just my picture on the back of the book jacket. . . .

In retrospect, that bellboy pushing the hotel door's buzzer was really kind of a signal that at least major aspects of my life were about to change abruptly, maybe forever. Let me tell you what happened: When I stepped out of my cab at Kennedy Airport later that morning, I got a passing glance from one of the busy skycaps, who practically whirled around, did a double take and exclaimed loudly, *"Alex Haley!"*

Within seconds, I was surrounded by people, jostling, pushing, shoving so hard that I was separated from my bag. I think that skycap must have checked it in for me, for somehow it arrived on the same flight with me in Los Angeles. But right then, that missing bag was the last thing on my mind, amidst all those people yelling my name, shouting, "That's him! That's him!" I was confused, bewildered, I believe for the first time in my life actually afraid that I might be about to get hurt. The people, women especially, were grabbing whatever they could get hold of, tugging at my arms, pulling at my clothes.

I felt someone's hand thrust down inside my collar, then I felt my shirt's top buttons pop off. It was about then that a man in a red American Airlines jacket pushed right alongside me; I heard him say in a low tone, "Stay next to me and follow me," and he began moving. It was like a football play in slow motion. I sensed with great relief that he knew what he was doing, which *I* sure didn't. He'd push with the weight of his body behind his shoulder and thus make a little space, and I'd squeeze into that space right behind him, while constantly exclaiming, "Thank you!" "Yes, ma'am!" "Yes, sir!" with a pen in one hand scribbling some semblance of my name on the pieces of paper that were being thrust at me from all directions. After about five minutes of this, we reached a wall and suddenly the man opened a door I hadn't noticed and we both sort of popped through it, rather like a champagne cork, and the man quickly shut the door behind us. I remember leaning up against the wall and taking a deep breath and demanding of him, "Man, what the hell's *happening*?"

He laughed and said I'd better get used to it, for I'd be seeing a lot more of it. Then he said I'd have to be "preboarded." I hadn't ever heard the expression before. After what had just happened, I followed him without a whimper through various doors and corridors, and suddenly there we were, on the plane, which was still empty. I handed him my ticket. "I'm sorry, Mr. Haley," he said, "but I'd really advise you to upgrade to first class." He saw my expression and began to explain, saying that in the experience of the airlines, VIPs couldn't expect much of a peaceful, relaxed flight if they were surrounded by a couple of hundred passengers. My hackles just rose at that; and I felt embarrassed. Wasn't I the same man I'd been for 50-odd years? I couldn't remember occasioning any public commotions in all that time. But when the fellow insisted, I gave him my credit card and he went to change my ticket.

I won't soon forget sitting alone in that first-class cabin, still needing sleep, astounded at the recent rush of events, my mind racing across the memories of all those years I'd lived alone in a little basement room on Grove Street in Greenwich Village, working through the nights, trying to finish magazine articles to pay the worst bills, taking long walks in the predawn hours and wondering if all of it ever would lead me anywhere. Well, it finally had—beyond my ability even to comprehend it—and I found myself wishing that I still had that little basement room, along with the quiet life that had accompanied it, because if that morning's airport arrival was any evidence, then, just for starters, when in the world was I ever going to be able to sit down again and practice the discipline of being a writer?

Two years later, the blessings have continued to come to me; mixed in among them, though, have been a great many rude awakenings to the hard realities of what fame also brings, including just a few bitter pills.

Through what I might call the early *Roots* days, I still clung hard to the idea that before long, all of the big to-do was going to calm down and I'd discover myself with the dream come true of having the time and the money to write at my own pace, freed forever of the terrible economic pressures I'd known for so many years. Keeping my heavy list of appointments around the country, I also kept it in my head—like a promised lollipop—that before long, just wait and see, I was again going to be able to enjoy good evenings of visiting and chitchat with close family and friends. I was going to have the leisure to take long trips, to investigate the world. I *love* to travel, and I had many journeys in mind. I was going to Egypt to see the Pyramids—and ride a camel. I was going to visit North and East Africa. I was going to get a Eurailpass and indulge myself in the beauty of the European countryside. After my 20-year career in the U.S. Coast Guard, the kind of travel I love most is on shipboard; I was going to sail the seven seas—on slow freighters.

But what happened? That first year, *Roots* continued rather like a roller-coaster ride of talk shows, press conferences, magazine profiles, critical accolades, a few critical attacks, autographing sessions attended by thousands, receiving keys to many cities and more than a dozen honorary doctoral degrees (each one a new thrill for someone who didn't even finish college); being embraced as a friend by celebrities I'd previously written about as a journalist; being a keynote speaker before august assemblies I never imagined would be interested in hearing what I had to say. My lifetime's most moving moments will have to include receiving special citations from the U.S. Senate, as well as from the House of Representatives, to both of which events I had the same internal reaction I've had so many times: wishing fervently that my momma and dad, my grandmas and grandpas—and all the others who came before them, *slaves* all, across the generations all the way back to Kunta Kinte—could have been with me, sharing such a moment. And then I'd realize that they *were*. Like my old cousin Georgia from Kansas City used to say, before she ascended to join them, "They all settin' right up there watchin' what you do, boy!"

In both a serious and a lighter vein, I've also been touched by how many relatives and friends *Roots* has surfaced for me, many of whom I never previously knew I had. As news of my good fortune began circulating, my inundation of mail, telegrams and phone calls included communications not only from dearly remembered old Service buddies but also from "shipmates" who named ships *I* never sailed on. Rather similarly, the relatives ranged from not a few with whom I'd long wanted to have direct contact, and just didn't know where they were, to others who fit best within the proverbial "16th-cousin" category. There is an almost infallibly repetitive pattern in my letters from noship shipmates and the 16th cousins: I am roundly congratulated upon my well-deserved success; they'd always known I'd make it one day—and they're certain I'll wish to manifest my appreciation of their deep faith in some financial manner. Some of them specifically state the appropriate sums, which have ranged to upwards of $100,000—to pay off their debts, to establish them in a business or some other endeavor, to cover medical treatments for themselves or members of their family or any number of other needs, desires or occasionally sheer fantasies.

I don't mean to make light of these requests. Most of them are heartfelt and legitimate. But the point is that I simply haven't the resources to become a charitable institution on a personal basis. And while I'm in this financial area, let me try to point out something very few petitioners ever seem to reflect upon. It's the case not only with me but with any others of us in the free-lance creative positions about whom one hears the great big dollar sums. In the first place, of whatever we may happen to earn through our efforts, a good *half* goes to Uncle Sam. Then come other deductions—substantial ones—of a professional nature. What's left after all that isn't nearly as impressive as it looked at first. I'm surely not crying poor—for, God knows, I never dreamed I'd ever gross what I now net. With it, I have established a foundation to help people to the degree I can afford, especially those in Africa who desperately need assistance of many sorts. Donations to the foundation, along with others last year, amounted to well into six figures. Beyond that, if I tried to supply even half of the funds for which people have asked, I'd very shortly be needing someone to help me. When my replies to money appeals have tried tactfully to explain this, as often as not a return letter merely requests a smaller amount, and when that isn't forthcoming, subsequent letters call me names among which "insensitive" and "stingy bastard" are not uncommon, until I have come to feel that by and large, no matter what you do, or what you try to give, you just can't win nohow.

On the other side of the ledger, I've received many *offers* of money—sometimes a great deal of money—for the use of my name on commercial endorsements, as a sponsor of this or that. Enterprising entrepreneurs have sought the rights to depict me, Kunta Kinte and other *Roots* figures on enough different kinds of products to fill a pretty thick catalog. When I've respectfully declined, they've expressed amazement that I'd have such bad judgment as to pass up profits they knew would exceed my wildest dreams. They ignore my own explanation that I'm proud of what *Roots* has come to mean for a very great many people, and not for any sum would I be likely to host commercial exploitations with their inevitably cheapening results.

If the mail I receive is any evidence, people *everywhere* have been reached by whatever it is that *Roots* has to say. After all this time since the book was published, I still get almost 500 letters a week from all over the world—in every one of the 24 languages in which translations have appeared—and most of them express variations of the same message: They want to tell me personally how *Roots* has changed their attitudes, even their lives, in a positive way.

Once in a while, of course, I'll get an anonymous letter—this kind always is—that lets me know how far we still have to go before the millennium finally arrives. A typical one, which I received the other day, read: "Dear Haley: Now that you have found out who your ancestors are, why don't you go back there and take the rest of your kind with you?" End of letter. That sort of thing would discourage me if there weren't so many more like the one that came in the same mail. It was a deeply touching note from a little boy in Nebraska. From his printing, I'd guess he was about ten years old. He wrote: "Dear Alex Haley, I am sending you some money to put on Kunta Kinte's grave. I'm sorry about what happened to him. Yours truly. . . ." And beneath that, there were 22 cents in coins he had Scotch-taped to the page. The contrast between those two letters were so diametrical, so emblematic, that I had them mounted side by side and hung them in my study, in case I need to be reminded, as I sometimes do, that neither good nor evil has quite triumphed in this world.

NATHAN HARE

The Challenge of a Black Scholar

The first black scholar I ever knew was a professor at a small Negro college in Oklahoma, at the same time mayor of the town (all-Negro) and poet laureate of Liberia (Africa). Though he had only a bachelor's degree, he easily was the superior of his Ph.D. colleagues in debate and discussion (whenever he could corner them) and used to wind up on occasion telling them that they needed to go back to school.

A scholar is a man who contributes original ideas, new insights and information to the existing fund of knowledge—whether or not he has a string of academic degrees or executes his scholarly activities in a manner appropriate to the traditions and conventions of the existing world of scholarship.

But a scholar is even more than that and a black scholar is still another species apart. It will be an irony of recorded history, we have hypothesized, though almost an axiomatic one, that black scholars will provide the catalysts not only for black liberation but perhaps for the ultimate resolution of America's pathology now infecting, in some form or fashion, the entire world.

On the shoulders of the black scholar falls an enormous task. He must decolonize his mind so that he may effectively guide other intellectuals and students in their search for liberation.

The white ruler not only distorted and destroyed the educational development of blacks and colonial peoples but also miseducated himself. Thus the society he dominates is increasingly corrupt and bloody with no clear future. The air is filled with pollution and the land and forests are being destroyed as human alienation and conflict remain on the rise.

The connection between white colonialism and its scholarship has always been apparent to blacks and other victims of it. However, an examination of this relationship is in order.

Thorsten Veblen's observations on white scholarship in such books as *The Theory of the Leisure Class* and *The Higher Learning in America*, though decades old, remain quite applicable today. Veblen described the leisure class mentality of the wealthy class who sought to conspicuously display their apartness from the manual worker through the attachment of prestige to non-productive endeavor. Thus education, which was largely private at the time and afforded only by the well-to-do emphasized the abstract as over against the practical. Much time was spent on such matters as syntax, footnotes (implying the leisure to spend on the reading of many books), and the mastery of lofty jargon which, being incomprehensible, could be taken as profound. Even today a student can pass all of his courses with A's but fail to graduate because he flunks the French test though he may never see Paris and would not know enough to communicate well even if he did. Black scholars today, obeying the dictates of scholarly ritualistic tradition, are compelled to footnote, when writing, say, about the slavery era during which their ancestors were forbidden by law and custom to learn to read and write. They must footnote the white slavemasters or historians acceptable to a society which condoned black slavery.

The forces of production which eventually led to over-urbanization and industrialization have produced a concomitant specialization of learning, and a rise of gadgeteering, but the leisure-class legacy has nevertheless remained.

Neither leisure class education nor specialized education is sufficient to transform black consciousness—or white consciousness for that matter—into a revolutionary, creative instrument for dynamic change. Leisure class education creates dilettantes; specialized education creates pragmatists and moral zombies devoid of imagination or compassion in the exercise of their skills.

Black scholars too, members of the "black bourgeoisie" described by the late E. Franklin Frazier have failed in their roles up to now. Aside from a disproportionate number of "house niggers" descendants among them, most received their early training at Negro colleges where the perfunctory trivia of white academia are mimicked and exaggerated. When I taught at Howard University, for example, there were an average of ten mandatory academic (or cap & gown) processionals yearly.

Now there has developed, out of the black studies call for black professors, a mass migration of many such individuals to the staid milieu of the white college faculty, but mainly what they bring there is their Ph.D. degrees and their social fraternity pins, with the same old style of teaching and attitudes toward matters intellectual. They remain isolated and alienated fundamentally from their non-professional fellows, as well as their students, perhaps to an even greater degree than is characteristic of the white professor. Thus whatever scholarly endeavors they execute are prone to be separated and in discord with the needs of their people's struggle. They pant after professional elevation, conforming to the criteria set forth by white racist administrators, while their people pursue liberation without benefit of a viable ideology or theory.

In the late spring of 1962, E. Franklin Frazier, who had been largely responsible for attracting me to Howard University just before his death, delivered an address at Atlanta University on "The Failure of the Negro Intellectual." This had followed by three decades Carter G. Woodson's *The Miseducation of the American Negro* (based on his experiences in acquiring the master's degree at the University of Chicago and the Ph.D. at Harvard). An expanded and refined version of these two indictments, *The Crisis of the Negro Intellectual*, was published by Harold Cruse. The paradox is that only Cruse, who was not college-trained, has been able, in this era, to write such a book.

Such criticisms have been both well taken and well made, but now is the time to take up the work of Du Bois, who actually sought decades earlier to launch a program of black research and scholarship. In an essay entitled, "Science and Empire," Du Bois told how, when he went to Atlanta University around the turn of the century, he encountered grave problems which not only obstructed his efforts but eventually led to his firing.

> "Social thinkers were engaged in vague statements and were seeking to lay down the methods by which, in some distant future, social law analogous to physical law would be discovered. . . . But turning my gaze from fruitless word-twisting and facing the facts of my own social situation and racial world, I determined to put science into sociology through a study of the conditions and problems of my own group. . . . I entered this primarily with the utilitarian object of reform and uplift; in contrast to Herbert Spencer who had issued ten volumes using biological analyses and the trappings of science but without true scientific results, but nevertheless, I wanted to do the work with scientific accuracy. . . . I did not have any clear conception or grasp of the meaning of that industrial imperialism which was beginning to grip the world. . . .
>
> I tried to isolate myself in the ivory tower of race. I wanted to explain the difficulties of race and the ways in which these difficulties caused political and economic troubles. It was this concentration of thought and action and effort that really, in the end, saved my scientific accuracy and search for truth. . . . continually I was forced to consider the economic aspects of world movements as they were developing at the time. Chiefly this was because the group in which I was interested were workers, earners of wages, owners of small bits of land, servants. The labor strikes interested and puzzled me. They

> were for the most part strikes of workers led by organizations to which Negroes were not admitted.[1]

Eventually, after much persecution from blacks and whites, Du Bois came to the conclusion that knowledge is not enough, that people know pretty much what needs to be done, if they would only act. And so, he switched, in his own words, from science to propaganda. Thus we lost the inestimable value of his scientific inquiry with regard to the way in which we should act and how to move other men to action.

The importance of the intellectual in the struggle for national liberation has always been apparent. In a book titled *Black Intellectuals Come to Power*, for instance, the author told how, in Trinidad,

> When the People's Educational Movement in 1956 became the People's National Movement, more was changed than just one word in the name of the organization, but much in the way of policy and key personnel had already emerged. The period of pre-party activity not only established the dominant themes on which the party platform would be based, but had always been a time in which the norms of leadership and influence within the organization took shape.[2]

The black scholar must recognize and study this and other movements, their successes and failures, as well as the nature of the oppressor and his ways. To date, there has been a tendency to be preoccupied with the study of his own group alone, influenced in part no doubt by the Establishment-sponsored white research to study the victim, as if to say that his own shortcomings, not the policy of oppression, bring on his problems. Thus there are shelves and shelves of books on blacks. Recently, I received a book called *Black On Blue*, and there are studies of "Negroes and Cotton-Picking in South Georgia," "The Correlation Between Negro Unemployment and the Price of Coons in Creek County, Oklahoma" with an increase in insight and understanding of what is necessary for black liberation. A wealthy foundation not long ago gave $10 million to a group of white scholars to study "the Negro." We black scholars at last have recognized that they have been studying the wrong man. We want $10 million, at the least, to study the white man.

The black scholar suffers from the problem of economic dependency and the Establishment's increasing monopoly on the world of grants as well as the publication and dissemination of materials. The black scholar must break free

1. W. E. B. Du Bois, *Dusk of Dawn*, New York: Harcourt, Brace and World, 1940 (Schocken Books Edition, 1968), pp. 50–54.
2. Ivar Oxaal, *Black Intellectuals Come to Power*, Cambridge: Schenkman Publishing Company, 1967, p. 137.

from this dependency as well as his fundamental enslavement to Western concepts of scholarship.

Let's examine a few of those concepts. One case in point is the taboo against taking a stand on matters of right and wrong.[3] Objectively, or its facade, has been made synonymous with neutrality, allowing the scholar to remain ostensibly impartial while catering actually to the wishes of the status quo. Objectivity and impartiality are neither synonymous nor mutually inclusive. As a matter of fact, if a scholar is biased against bias he is possessed by a bias. The belief in neutrality is itself a value-judgment.

On the question of objectivity, the late Louis Wirth, in his prefactory remarks to Karl Mannheim's *Ideology and Utopia*, has written:

> It would be naive to suppose that our ideas are entirely shaped by the objects of our contemplation which lie outside of us or that our wishes and our fears have nothing whatever to do with what we perceive or with what will happen. . . . The most important thing, therefore, that we can know about a man is what he takes for granted, and the most elemental and important facts about a society are those that are seldom debated and generally regarded as settled.[4]

The black scholar must look beneath the surface of things and, wherever necessary and appropriate, take a stand against the bias of white scholarship. He must be biased against white bias, must be an iconoclast, rallying to the call to arms of all the black intelligentsia, to destroy obsolescent norms and values and create new ones to take their place.

> . . . the defetishization of "values," "ethical judgments," and the like, the identification of the social, economic, psychic causes of their emergence, change, and disappearance, as well as the uncovering of the specific interests which they serve at any particular time, represent the greatest single contribution that an intellectual can make to the cause of human advancement.[5]

The black scholar can no longer afford to ape the allegedly "value-free" approach of white scholarship. He must reject absolutely the notion that it is

3. C. Wright Mills, *The Sociological Imagination*, New York: Oxford University Press, 1959, *passim.* See also Pitirim A. Sorokin, *Fads and Foibles in Sociology and Related Sciences*, Chicago: Henry Regnery Company, 1965, *passim.*
4. Karl Mannheim, *Ideology and Utopia*: An Introduction to the Sociology of Knowledge, New York: Harcourt, Brace and World, 1936, pp. xxii, xxiii.
5. Paul M. Sweezy and Leo Huberman, eds., *Paul A. Baran: A Collective Portrait*, New York: Monthly Review Press, 1965, p. 6.

"not professional" ever to become emotional, that it is somehow improper to be "bitter" as a black man, that emotion and reason are mutually exclusive. Anna Freud, in *The Ego and Its Mechanisms of Defense* suggests that it is, on the contrary, normal to be bitter in a bitter situation. If someone sticks a pin in you or a certain portion of your anatomy and you do not yell out, then there is probably something wrong with you or that portion of your anatomy. Emotion and reason may not only go together but may in fact be stimulants to each other. If one is truly cognizant of adverse circumstances, he would be expected, through the process of reason, to experience some emotional response.

To paraphrase racist Rudyard Kipling, if you can keep calm while all around you is chaos, maybe you don't fully understand the situation. If someone points a pistol at you and threatens to gun you down at the count of five (having shot your brother at the count of five, and your mother at the count of five), then gets to three and a half on you and you do not get emotional you probably are guilty of being unreasonable.

In any case, the "ideological fog" of the black scholar, which prevents his endeavors from leading to a central body of knowledge, stems in part from this very aping of psuedo white scholarship camouflaged by grandiosity.

> Scholarship is not realized in the individual in synthesis alone, but also in analysis. No true historical analysis is possible without the constant interpretation of meaning. In order to begin an analysis, there must already be a synthesis present in the mind. A conception of ordered coherence is an indispensable precondition even to the preliminary labor of digging and hewing.[6]

Let us look at an example of the way in which one's perspective or ideology influences interpretation. In the Moynihan Report on the black American family, where a correlation was illustrated between black unemployment and illegitimacy, ideology determines whether one concludes that it is the employment factor which must be changed in order to stabilize the family or, as Moynihan concluded, the family must be stabilized as a prerequisite to economic stability. Ideology enabled him to overlook the fact, though he had the figures showing, that there are thirty-three extra non-white females for every one hundred non-white males between the ages of 25 and 40 in New York City and that that demographic condition itself hampers family stability so long as blacks are impelled to adhere to white Western ideals (practiced only superficially) of monogamy and fidelity. Monogamous fidelity assumes a one-to-one sex ratio else the alternatives of celibacy or infidelity regardless of "moral" ideals.

Therefore, I decided to develop a Hare Report in response to the Moynihan

6. John Huizinga, *Men and Ideas*, New York: Meridian Books, 1968 edition, p. 25.

Report. I sought to make a simple study of marital happiness with the methodological notion of planting tape recorders in the bedrooms of relatives and neighbors. A professor said in horror that that would be both unethical (ideology) and crude (methodology). He instructed me to utilize a scale of intensity under which respondents would be asked if they were very happy, somewhat happy, somewhat unhappy, or very unhappy.

I discovered that some women would say that they were very happy but, should their husbands leave the room, would switch to say that, as a matter of fact, they actually were not happy. When told of this, the professor said that I would have to be methodologically more sophisticated, that people sometimes did not know their own true feelings and also might be reluctant under certain circumstances to tell an interviewer the truth. I must then, he said, construct an index to measure happiness by indirection. He suggested kissing as an indicator of marital happiness (as I thought of Judas), and respondents were asked how many times they kissed their spouses per day. Those who kissed their spouses five times or less a day were regarded as very unhappy; from six to 10 times a day, somewhat unhappy; from 11 to 15 times a day, somewhat happy; and those who kissed their spouses 16 or more times a day were—I felt certain—very tired at the end of the day.

The black scholar must develop new and appropriate norms and values, new institutional structures, and in order to be effective in this regard, he must also develop and be guided by a new ideology. Out of this new ideology will evolve new methodology, though in some regards it will subsume and overlap existing norms of scholarly endeavor.

He must understand the social function of knowledge in general; he must re-assess the traditions, values and mores of Western European scholarship; and finally he must achieve a black perspective of all his training and experience, so that his scholarly tools can become effective instruments for black liberation.

The black scholar must not only develop a new ideology with appropriate methodology, but he must raise new and serious questions even when he cannot immediately find the answers. For "where no clear question is put, no knowledge will give response. Where the question is vague, the answer will be at least as vague."[7]

In Algiers last summer I happened to raise the question to Stokely Carmichael (as a teacher realizing that I could learn from a former student) what he thought the role of a black scholar should be. Stokely replied:

> That is not an easy role, because what the black scholar must now do is to begin to find values that are anti-racist and anti-colonial. That means that the scholars must find a way to promulgate the idea of

7. *Ibid.*, p. 26.

> community where black people are, without actually saying that. Because that's the job of the black scholar, to give black people values very subtly because values people accept most are the most subtle values.
>
> Black scholars must be culture carriers, recognizing that the Europeans living in America are not going to allow them to do that, are going to fight them in every way.

Which all boils down to what Paul A. Baran was speaking of when he observed that a genuine intellectual possesses at least two characteristics—the desire to tell the truth and the courage to do so.

> As such he becomes the conscience of society and the spokesman of such progressive forces as it contains in any given period of history. And as such he is inevitably considered a "troublemaker" and a "nuisance" by the ruling class seeking to preserve the status quo, as well as by the intellect workers in its service who accuse the intellectual of being utopian or metaphysical at best, subversive or seditious at worst.[8]

To conclude, then, the black scholar's main task is to cleanse his mind—and the minds of his people—of the white colonial attitudes toward scholarship and people as well. This includes the icons of objectivity, amoral knowledge and its methodology, and the total demolition of the antisocial attitudes of Ivory-Towerism. Such is the challenge facing the black scholar.

8. Sweezy and Huberman, *op. cit.*, p. 10.

NO JUSTICE, NO PEACE

CHARLES V. HAMILTON

Adam Clayton Powell, Jr.

The Political Biography of an American Dilemma

Powell kept a hyperactive schedule—speaking around the country, engaging in local political party fights in Harlem, preaching at Abyssinian Baptist Church, helping run *The People's Voice.* There was no question that he enjoyed every one of his activities, and he molded them into one piece—projecting himself as the militant, uncompromising fighter for civil rights and liberal socioeconomic causes. One so involved inevitably would make enemies, personal and political. He never hesitated to label whites who disagreed with him as fascists or Dixiecratic racists, and those blacks who fought him as "Uncle Toms." His oratory was becoming even more renown, mixing biblical references with current events, always using the well-developed Baptist-preacher style he had been practicing for almost a decade and a half. After his first term, there was no doubt in anyone's mind that he would seek reelection.

An *Amsterdam News* columnist, Earl Brown (who would be Powell's opponent for the congressional seat twelve years later) realistically assessed the chances of those who thought of challenging Powell. "There is . . . one vast difference between Mr. Powell and the other three [challengers]: he is going to win and they are going to lose. . . . Congressman Powell is still Harlem's political champ."[1] This was patently true, although Brown noted the enigma associated with his conclusion. Powell, Brown said, was really not liked by any of the parties—Democrats, Republicans, American Labor Party, even the Communist Party. "The Democrats would dearly love to ditch him. From President

Truman to Eddie Loughlin, Tammany Hall leader. But they can't because Congressman Powell would win even though neither party backed him. . . . He is one of the few politicians extant who is not wanted by any party, but is sought by practically all of them."[2]

Perhaps. But the Republicans, who had endorsed Powell in 1944, when he captured their primary, decided they would mount a serious campaign against him. Republican governor Thomas E. Dewey was reasonably popular in Harlem and was running for reelection. Perhaps a strong Powell opponent for the congressional seat in the Twenty-second District could be mutually productive—for Dewey, and to unseat Powell. They selected a well-spoken, militant black former army chaplain, with a record of employment with the NAACP in Washington and Cleveland, who was then a student at Columbia University Law School. His name was Grant Reynolds. He was also state commissioner of corrections. His base was not in Harlem politics, but the local black Republicans accepted him as their standard bearer nonetheless. He had come to the attention of the statewide Republicans after a speech he had made at Madison Square Garden on behalf of Governor Dewey in 1944. This was enough for the Harlem Republicans—a man who had access to Dewey. In addition, Reynolds was a very good speaker, tall, and as handsome as Powell. He made a good appearance. More than a few around Harlem began to call the impending contest "the battle of the giants."

Reynolds immediately threw himself into the campaign, confident that he could match Powell on civil rights as well as commitment to public service. He blasted Powell's congressional absentee record—missing fifteen of thirty-two roll-call votes. Reynolds labeled the incumbent "Part-time Powell," and called attention to the enormous speaking fees—five hundred dollars—Powell got through a lecture bureau. For his part, Reynolds was in favor of a seventy-five cent minimum wage (over the current forty cents), low-rent housing, and an end to segregation in the military forces. The latter was a major personal sore point with Reynolds. As an army chaplain, he had suffered innumerable racial indignities on army posts during the war, and he complained publicly and bitterly, finally receiving an honorable discharge after bitter complaints of personal mistreatment as a black officer.

Following his previous strategy, Powell sought the Republican nomination as well as the Democratic. Thus he faced Reynolds in the Republican primary. Reynold's strategy was to engage Powell in a face-to-face public debate, force him to defend and specify his supposedly productive first-term record. Years later, Reynolds reminisced: "I thought that if I could get him on the public platform, I could beat him. He was emotional, and I thought I could get him flustered."[3] But Powell was having none of that. He knew that he had a comfortable lead (in the Democratic primary, at least), and the political adage of not giving your underdog opponent exposure was good enough for him. At various planned forums in the district, Powell either sent a surrogate (one once was Congressman Vito Marcantonio) or simply declined. Reynolds and the *New York Age* tried to make capital with this dodging, but to no avail. Reynolds understood this, but the frustration was no less evident.

Reynolds was also comfortable with his role as a Republican in a predominantly black Democratic district. He was not as enamored with the Roosevelt New Deal as apparently many blacks were. His assessment of the New Deal for blacks was the following:

> We were the only components of the Democratic Party that got the shaft. Labor got rights to organize. The South got agreement that agriculture and domestic servants would not be covered by Social Security. Jews got access. Catholics got support for parochial schools. Blacks got an invitation to go on welfare. I got tremendous applause when I talked about this. The New Deal confined us to a period of dependency that has not been gotten over yet.[4]

The *New York Age* endorsed Reynolds, and the *Amsterdam News* covered his campaign in the same favorable way that *The People's Voice* lent positive space to Powell.

The primary was on August 20, 1946, and on that day Powell easily won the Democratic endorsement to go along with that of the American Labor Party. But he suffered his first electoral defeat in his career at the hands of Grant Reynolds for designation as the Republican nominee. Reynolds nosed him out by five hundred votes in the Republican primary, and this was occasion for blaring headlines in the *Amsterdam News*: "Reynolds Gives Powell 1st Defeat." Reynolds promptly stated: "I regard my nomination as an indication that the people of the 22nd district are sick and tired of buffoonery and showmanship in politics. Furthermore, I regard it as an endorsement of Gov. Thomas E. Dewey and his grand record of achievement which has meant so much to the Negroes of this State."[5]

Powell sent a note to Reynolds: "Congratulations on your primary victory. Your party machine stuck by you." It was a cryptic remark intended to negate the view some might have that Powell was losing his grip on the constituents in Harlem.

The fact is, and many knew it, he was never in serious political trouble. Although the *New York Age* optimistically editorialized several weeks later, during the general election contest, that a Grant Reynolds win was "extremely likely," it was not to be. Powell went on to beat Reynolds in November by a two-to-one vote.[6] He would not have to worry about a serious challenge to his seat in Congress for more than twenty years. His political career in Harlem was confirmed. Apparently, a substantial number of the voters approved of the way he had conducted himself the first term. He now turned his attention to that role and the consolidation of a reputation as Mr. Civil Rights that stuck with him for the next decade and a half.

First, Powell made a decision to sever his ties with *The People's Voice*. In December 1946, he issued a statement that his congressional duties and the pastorate of Abyssinian were more than enough to occupy his time. He was selling his stock in the newspaper and resigning his positions as editor and chairman of the Powell-Buchanan Publishing Corporation effective December 10, 1946. The *New York Times* reported that Powell was advised to leave the newspaper because it had developed a clear reputation as Communist-controlled. He was advised, the *Times* said, "to end his ties with all left-wing groups. Many of Mr. Powell's supporters expressed the view that any connection with organizations of Communist persuasion would handicap his activities in the next Congress, which will be under Republican control."[7] Powell made no reference to this in his resignation statement.

He returned to Congress in January, the father of a new baby boy, Adam Clayton Powell III.

Back in Congress, Powell could be expected to introduce civil rights bills—in favor of a permanent FEPC, antilynching proposals, against segregation in interstate travel—and he did. These moves, however, were not really what made his reputation. In fact, when he would introduce a measure, civil rights supporters either looked for cosponsors or assumed that the bills would likely not get out of committee or even go to hearings. This was not so much a result of the fact that Powell had little political influence as it had to do with the subject of the proposals. In those years, no civil rights bills introduced by anyone were going anywhere. The NAACP, however, had little hope that Congressman Dawson, who at least was liked by the Truman White House, would be of much help. One NAACP letter from its Washington lobbyist, Leslie Perry, to Roy Wilkins stated bluntly: "Dawson can hardly be expected to push any bill."[8] When Powell came to Congress, at least he offered a willing vehicle to have bills introduced. In a report from the Washington NAACP to the director summarizing the status of current bills, Perry wrote that Powell was the sponsor of a bill aimed at ending segregation in interstate travel. The NAACP had sought additional sponsors without success, but "even so," Perry assured the NAACP officials in New York, the organization would fight to have hearings on the bill.[9] Therefore, when another congressman was unavailable, the NAACP, which was the major civil rights interest group on Capitol Hill, could count on Powell to put a proposed bill into the legislative hopper. How hard he would fight for it, or, if he did, how much support he could muster was another matter. But to the legislative in-fighters, the ones who had to count votes, make deals, sway doubters, and craft compromises, in the immediate postwar years into the 1950s, Powell was not particularly useful. Indeed, that was hardly his role. Such tasks were usually performed by more senior people in any case, ones who chaired committees and had built up credit with their colleagues. Few, if any, freshmen legislators had those qualities. Thus Powell's value in those early formative years in Congress was as an outspoken advocate. It was in that capacity that he would make the headlines, command attention, and, in the process, begin to build the reputation as "Mr. Civil Rights."

An illustration of this occurred early in the eightieth congressional session, Powell's second term. Joseph Martin, Republican from Massachusetts, was presiding in the House as Speaker, and a staunch segregationist—Rankin from Mississippi, Powell's old nemesis—was making a speech. Powell knew he would eventually use the word "nigger" as he frequently did in his speeches on the House floor. Indeed, he did, and Powell was on his feet.

Powell: Mr. Speaker, a parliamentary inquiry.
The Speaker: Will the gentleman yield for a parliamentary inquiry?
Rankin: No. I will not yield for that purpose.
Powell: Mr. Speaker, a point of order.
The Speaker: The gentleman will state his point of order.
Powell: Is it within the rules of this Congress to refer to any group of our nation in disparaging terms?
Rankin: It is not disparaging to call them Negroes, as all respectable Negroes know.
Powell: I am addressing the Speaker.
The Speaker: The Chair is not aware of the disparaging term used.
Powell: He used the term "nigger" in referring to a group.
The Speaker: The Chair understood the gentleman to say "Negro."
Rankin: Mr. Speaker, I said what I always say and what I am always going to say when referring to these people.
The Speaker: The gentleman will proceed in order.
Powell: Mr. Speaker, a point of order.
The Speaker: The chair overrules the point of order.[10]

Powell publicized this exchange back in his home district and throughout the nation's Negro press. This was his role. He could speak out, protecting the integrity of people so long denigrated. And he seized every opportunity to do this. On Sunday mornings he would return to the Abyssinian pulpit and deliver his ringing sermons which became a mixture of biblical text, political commentary, and reports from Congress. His basic message was always the same: challenging the society to overcome the American Dilemma, to bring its practices into line with its Creed. This was his theme and his approach as he toured the nation on speaking engagements, projecting himself and being presented as "that dynamic, militant advocate of civil rights, racial justice, and economic advancement for the little people." He was always careful to include the latter point, making it clear that Negroes and whites should stand together in the struggle.

During his first fifteen years in Congress, his reputation as "Mr. Civil Rights" stemmed essentially from two sources: his constant, vigilant championing of the liberal, civil rights cause on platforms around the country as a highly visible speaker from Congress; and the very controversial "Powell Amendment." The reputation was deserved, but it should also be noted that he, of course, was not alone in the civil rights forefront. There were several organizations and individuals devoting their full time and energies to the country's racial problems. The NAACP was the largest group, with its companion legal arm, the NAACP Legal Defense and Educational Fund (LDF). This organization, led by Walter White, Roy Wilkins, and Thurgood Marshall, was probably as well known nationally as Powell, if not as brash and outspoken. A. Philip Randolph continued the fight for a permanent FEPC, and maintained his position as an uncompromising, dignified leader in both the labor movement and in civil rights circles. In time, Clarence Mitchell would become the full-time NAACP lobbyist in Washington, D.C., and would become known as the "101st Senator" because of tireless efforts lobbying in the halls of Congress. And, of course, Mary McLeod Bethune was still active on the civil rights scene into the early fifties. There was Paul Robeson on the left, frequently aligned with the United States Communist Party, along with the aging but still highly regarded W. E. B. Du Bois. This was the period of the NAACP's successful challenge in the courts to overturn legal segregation in the schools and in other areas, notably against restrictive covenants in real estate contracts, and in voting discrimination cases coming out of the South. These people were joined by white liberal allies, and they persistently mounted a legal and political campaign at the national level that served as the backdrop to the more mass-based civil rights struggle that would burst on the scene in the late 1950s. In a few short years, new leaders, especially Dr. Martin Luther King, Jr., would emerge, engaging in mass boycotts, sit-ins, and other protest actions.

But in the first decade or so after World War II, from his highly visible base in Congress, it was Adam Clayton Powell, Jr., who gave flourishing voice to the burgeoning aspirations of millions who wanted to see the country finally and successfully come to grips with the Dilemma—to end racial segregation and discrimination.

NOTES

1. *Amsterdam News*, Earl Brown, "Timely Topics," June 22, 1946, p. 10.
2. *Ibid.*
3. Interview with Grant Reynolds, July 31, 1989, White Plains, New York.
4. *Ibid.*
5. *Amsterdam News*, August 24, 1946, p. 1.
6. Powell received a total of 32,573 votes (22,641 on the Democratic line, and 9,932 on the ALP line) to Reynolds's 19,514 on the Republican line.
7. *New York Times*, December 25, 1946. The FBI duly clipped the *Times* article and one in the *Daily Worker*, but made no comment on the resignation.

8. Letter from Leslie Perry to Roy Wilkins, January 21, 1944. NAACP Papers, Library of Congress, Group II, A-663.

9. Letter from Leslie Perry to Walter White, March 15, 1945. NAACP Papers, Library of Congress, Group II, A-663.

10. *The People's Voice*, March 1, 1947, p. 17. The "Soapbox" column of Powell's in which this appeared was clipped and put in his FBI files. FBI Files. No. HQ 100-51230-A, March 20, 1947.

MARTIN LUTHER KING, JR.

Where Do We Go from Here?

Now, in order to answer the question, "Where do we go from here?" which is our theme, we must first honestly recognize where we are now. When the Constitution was written, a strange formula to determine taxes and representation declared that the Negro was sixty percent of a person. Today another curious formula seems to declare that he is fifty percent of a person. Of the good things in life, the Negro has approximately one half those of whites. Of the bad things in life, he has twice those of whites. Thus half of all Negroes live in substandard housing. And Negroes have half the income of whites. When we view the negative experiences of life, the Negro has a double share. There are twice as many unemployed. The rate of infant mortality among Negroes is double that of whites and there are twice as many Negroes dying in Vietnam as whites in proportion to their size in the population.

In other spheres, the figures are equally alarming. In elementary schools, Negroes lag one to three years behind whites, and their segregated schools receive substantially less money per student than the white schools. One-twentieth as many Negroes as whites attend college. Of employed Negroes, seventy-five percent hold menial jobs.

This is where we are. Where do we go from here? First, we must massively assert our dignity and worth. We must stand up amidst a system that still oppresses us and develop an unassailable and majestic sense of values. We must no longer be ashamed of being black. The job of arousing manhood within a people that have been taught for so many centuries that they are nobody is not easy.

Even semantics have conspired to make that which is black seem ugly and degrading. In Roget's *Thesaurus* there are 120 synonyms for blackness and at least sixty of them are offensive, as for example, blot, soot, grim, devil and foul. And there are some 134 synonyms for whiteness and all are favorable, expressed in such words as purity, cleanliness, chastity and innocence. A white lie is better than a black lie. The most degenerate member of a family is a "black sheep." Ossie Davis has suggested that maybe the English language should be reconstructed so that teachers will not be forced to teach the Negro child sixty ways to despise himself, and thereby perpetuate his false sense of inferiority, and the white child 134 ways to admire himself, and thereby perpetuate his false sense of superiority.

The tendency to ignore the Negro's contribution to American life and to strip him of his personhood is as old as the earliest history books and as contemporary as the morning's newspaper. To upset this cultural homicide, the Negro must rise up with an affirmation of his own Olympian manhood. Any movement for the Negro's freedom that overlooks this necessity is only waiting to be buried. As long as the mind is enslaved, the body can never be free. Psychological freedom, a firm sense of self-esteem, is the most powerful weapon against the long night of physical slavery. No Lincolnian emancipation proclamation or Johnsonian civil rights bill can totally bring this kind of freedom. The Negro will only be free when he reaches down to the inner depths of his own being and signs with the pen and ink of assertive manhood his own emancipation proclamation. And, with a spirit straining toward true self-esteem, the Negro must boldly throw off the manacles of self-abnegation and say to himself and to the world, "I am somebody. I am a person. I am a man with dignity and honor. I have a rich and noble history. How painful and exploited that history has been. Yes, I was a slave through my foreparents and I am not ashamed of that. I'm ashamed of the people who were so sinful to make me a slave." Yes, we must stand up and say, "I'm black and I'm beautiful," and this self-affirmation is the black man's need, made compelling by the white man's crimes against him.

Another basic challenge is to discover how to organize our strength in terms of economic and political power. No one can deny that the Negro is in dire need of this kind of legitimate power. Indeed, one of the great problems that the Negro confronts is his lack of power. From old plantations of the South to newer ghettos of the North, the Negro has been confined to a life of voicelessness and powerlessness. Stripped of the right to make decisions concerning his life and destiny he has been subject to the authoritarian and sometimes whimsical decisions of this white power structure. The plantation and ghetto were created by those who had power, both to confine those who had no power and to perpetuate their powerlessness. The problem of transforming the ghetto, therefore, is a problem of power—confrontation of the forces of power demanding change and the forces of power dedicated to the preserving of the status quo. Now power properly understood is nothing but the ability to achieve purpose. It is the strength required to bring about social, political, and economic change. Walter Reuther defined power one day. He said, "Power is the ability of a labor union like the UAW to make the most powerful corporation in the world. General Motors, say, 'Yes' when it wants to say 'No.' That's power."

Now a lot of us are preachers, and all of us have our moral convictions and concerns, and so often have problems with power. There is nothing wrong with power if power is used correctly. You see, what happened is that some of our philosophers got off base. And one of the great problems of history is that the concepts of love and power have usually been contrasted as opposites—polar opposites—so that love is identified with a resignation of power, and power with a denial of love.

It was this misinterpretation that caused Nietzsche, who was a philosopher of the will to power, to reject the Christian concept of love. It was this same misinterpretation which induced Christian theologians to reject the Nietzschean philosophy of the will to power in the name of the Christian idea of love. Now, we've got to get this thing right. What is needed is a realization that power without love is reckless and abusive, and love without power is sentimental and anemic. Power at its best is love implementing the demands of justice, and justice at its best is power correcting everything that stands against love. And this is what we must see as we move on. What has happened is that we have had it wrong and confused in our own country, and this has led Negro Americans in the past to seek their goals through power devoid of love and conscience.

This is leading a few extremists today to advocate for Negroes the same destructive and conscienceless power that they have justly abhorred in whites. It is precisely this collision of immoral power with powerless morality which constitutes the major crisis of our times.

We must develop a program that will drive the nation to a guaranteed annual income. Now, early in this century this proposal would have been greeted with ridicule and denunciation, as destructive of initiative and responsibility. At that time economic status was considered the measure of the individual's ability and talents. And, in the thinking of that day, the absence of worldly goods indicated a want of industrious habits and moral fiber. We've come a long way in our understanding of human motivation and of the blind operation of our economic system. Now we realize that dislocations in the market operations of our economy and the prevalence of discrimination thrust people into idleness and bind them in constant or frequent unemployment against their will. Today the poor are less often dismissed, I hope, from our consciences by being branded as inferior or incompetent. We also know that no matter how dynamically the economy develops and expands, it does not eliminate all poverty.

The problem indicates that our emphasis must be twofold. We must create full employment or we must create incomes. People must be made consumers by one method or the other. Once they are placed in this position we need to be concerned that the potential of the individual is not wasted. New forms of work that enhance the social good will have to be devised for those for whom traditional jobs are not available. In 1879 Henry George anticipated this state of affairs when he wrote in *Progress and Poverty*:*

The fact is that the work which improves the condition of mankind, the work which extends knowledge and increases power and enriches literature and elevates thought, is not done to secure a living. It is not the work of slaves driven to their tasks either by the task, by the taskmaster, or by animal necessity. It is the work of men who somehow find a form of work that brings a security for its own sake and a state of society where want is abolished.

Work of this sort could be enormously increased, and we are likely to find that the problems of housing and education, instead of preceding the elimination of poverty, will themselves be affected if poverty is first abolished. The poor transformed into purchasers will do a great deal on their own to alter housing decay. Negroes who have a double disability will have a greater effect on discrimination when they have the additional weapon of cash to use in their struggle.

Beyond these advantages, a host of positive psychological changes inevitably will result from widespread economic security. The dignity of the individual will flourish when the decisions concerning his life are in his own hands, when he has the means to seek self-improvement. Personal conflicts among husbands, wives and children will diminish when the unjust measurement of human worth on the scale of dollars is eliminated.

Now our country can do this. John Kenneth Galbraith said that a guaranteed annual income could be done for about twenty billion dollars a year. And I say to you today, that if our nation can spend thirty-five billion dollars a year to fight an unjust, evil war in Vietnam, and twenty billion dollars to put a man on the moon, it can spend billions of dollars to put God's children on their own two feet right here on earth.

Now, let me say briefly that we must reaffirm our commitment to nonviolence. I want to stress this. The futility of violence in the struggle for racial justice has been tragically etched in all the recent Negro riots. Yesterday, I tried to analyze the riots and deal with their causes. Today I want to give the other side. There is certainly something painfully sad about a riot. One sees screaming youngsters and angry adults fighting hopelessly and aimlessly against impossible odds. And deep down within them, you can see a desire for self-destruction, a kind of suicidal longing.

Occasionally Negroes contend that the 1965 Watts riot and the other riots

* Henry George (1839–1897) was the father of the single-tax system, which he set forth in his *Progress and Poverty*, published in 1879. The book argued that the land belonged to society, which created its value and properly taxed that value, not improvements on the land.

in various cities represented effective civil rights action. But those who express this view always end up with stumbling words when asked what concrete gains have been won as a result. At best, the riots have produced a little additional antipoverty money allotted by frightened government officials, and a few water-sprinklers to cool the children of the ghettos. It is something like improving the food in the prison while the people remain securely incarcerated behind bars. Nowhere have the riots won any concrete improvement such as have the organized protest demonstrations. When one tries to pin down advocates of violence as to what acts would be effective, the answers are blatantly illogical. Sometimes they talk of overthrowing racist state and local governments and they talk about guerrilla warfare. They fail to see that no internal revolution has ever succeeded in overthrowing a government by violence unless the government had already lost the allegiance and effective control of its armed forces. Anyone in his right mind knows that this will not happen in the United States. In a violent racial situation, the power structure has the local police, the state troopers, the National Guard and, finally, the army to call on—all of which are predominantly white. Furthermore, few if any violent revolutions have been successful unless the violent minority had the sympathy and support of the nonresistant majority. Castro may have had only a few Cubans actually fighting with him up in the hills, but he could never have overthrown the Batista regime unless he had the sympathy of the vast majority of Cuban people.†

It is perfectly clear that a violent revolution on the part of American blacks would find no sympathy and support from the white population and very little from the majority of the Negroes themselves. This is no time for romantic illusions and empty philosophical debates about freedom. This is a time for action. What is needed is a strategy for change, a tactical program that will bring the Negro into the mainstream of American life as quickly as possible. So far, this has only been offered by the nonviolent movement. Without recognizing this we will end up with solutions that don't solve, answers that don't answer and explanations that don't explain.

And so I say to you today that I still stand by nonviolence. And I am still convinced that it is the most potent weapon available to the Negro in his struggle for justice in this country. And the other thing is that I am concerned about a better world. I'm concerned about justice. I'm concerned about brotherhood. I'm concerned about truth. And when one is concerned about these, he can never advocate violence. For through violence you may murder a murderer but you can't murder murder. Through violence you may murder a liar but you can't establish truth. Through violence you

† In 1956 Fidel Castro landed on the coast of Cuba in the vessel, *Gramma*, to overthrow the despot Fulgencio Batista. Twelve men survived the counterattack and went on to lead the Cuban people to victory over Batista, who fled the island on New Year's Day, 1959, which ushered in the Cuban revolutionary victory.

may murder a hater, but you can't murder hate. Darkness cannot put out darkness. Only light can do that.

And I say to you, I have also decided to stick to love. For I know that love is ultimately the only answer to mankind's problems. And I'm going to talk about it everywhere I go. I know it isn't popular to talk about it in some circles today. I'm not talking about emotional bosh when I talk about love, I'm talking about a strong, demanding love. And I have seen too much hate. I've seen too much hate on the faces of sheriffs in the South. I've seen hate on the faces of too many Klansmen and too many White Citizens Councilors in the South to want to hate myself, because every time I see it, I know that it does something to their faces and their personalities and I say to myself that hate is too great a burden to bear. I have decided to love. If you are seeking the highest good, I think you can find it through love. And the beautiful thing is that we are moving against wrong when we do it, because John was right, God is love. He who hates does not know God, but he who has love has the key that unlocks the door to the meaning of ultimate reality.

I want to say to you as I move to my conclusion, as we talk about "Where do we go from here," that we honestly face the fact that the movement must address itself to the question of restructuring the whole of American society. There are forty million poor people here. And one day we must ask the question, "Why are there forty million poor people in America?" And when you begin to ask that question, you are raising questions about the economic system, about a broader distribution of wealth. When you ask that question, you begin to question the capitalistic economy. And I'm simply saying that more and more, we've got to begin to ask questions about the whole society. We are called upon to help the discouraged beggars in life's marketplace. But one day we must come to see that an edifice which produces beggars needs restructuring. It means that questions must be raised. You see, my friends, when you deal with this, you begin to ask the question, "Who owns the oil?" You begin to ask the question, "Who owns the iron ore?" You begin to ask the question, "Why is it that people have to pay water bills in a world that is two-thirds water?" These are questions that must be asked.

Now, don't think that you have me in a "bind" today. I'm not talking about communism.

What I'm saying to you this morning is that communism forgets that life is individual. Capitalism forgets that life is social, and the kingdom of brotherhood is found neither in the thesis of communism nor the antithesis of capitalism but in a higher synthesis. It is found in a higher synthesis that combines the truths of both. Now, when I say question the whole society, it means ultimately coming to see that the problem of racism, the problem of economic exploitation, and the problem of war are all tied together. These are the triple evils that are interrelated.

If you will let me be a preacher just a little bit—One night, a juror came to Jesus and he wanted to know what he could do to be saved. Jesus didn't get bogged down in the kind of isolated approach of what he shouldn't do. Jesus didn't say, "Now Nicodemus, you must stop lying." He didn't say, "Nicodemus, you must stop cheating if you are doing that." He didn't say, "Nicodemus, you must not commit adultery." He didn't say, "Nicodemus, now you must stop drinking liquor if you are doing that excessively." He said something altogether different, because Jesus realized something basic—that if a man will lie, he will steal. And if a man will steal, he will kill. So instead of just getting bogged down in one thing, Jesus looked at him and said, "Nicodemus, you must be born again."

He said, in other words, "Your whole structure must be changed." A nation that will keep people in slavery for 244 years will "thingify" them—make them things. Therefore they will exploit them, and poor people generally, economically. And a nation that will exploit economically will have to have foreign investments and everything else, and will have to use its military might to protect them. All of these problems are tied together. What I am saying today is that we must go from this convention and say, "America, you must be born again!"

So, I conclude by saying today that we have a task and let us go out with a "divine dissatisfaction." Let us be dissatisfied until America will no longer have a high blood pressure of creeds and an anemia of deeds. Let us be dissatisfied until the tragic walls that separate the outer city of wealth and comfort and the inner city of poverty and despair shall be crushed by the battering rams of the forces of justice. Let us be dissatisfied until those that live on the outskirts of hope are brought into the metropolis of daily security. Let us be dissatisfied until slums are cast into the junk heaps of history, and every family is living in a decent sanitary home. Let us be dissatisfied until the dark yesterdays of segregated schools will be transformed into bright tomorrows of quality, integrated education. Let us be dissatisfied until integration is not seen as a problem but as an opportunity to participate in the beauty of diversity. Let us be dissatisfied until men and women, however black they may be, will be judged on the basis of the content of their character and not on the basis of the color of their skin. Let us be dissatisfied. Let us be dissatisfied until every state capitol houses a governor who will do justly, who will love mercy and who will walk humbly with his God. Let us be dissatisfied until from every city hall, justice will roll down like waters and righteousness like a mighty stream. Let us be dissatisfied until that day when the lion and the lamb shall lie down together, and every man will sit under his own vine and fig tree and none shall be afraid. Let us be dissatisfied. And men will recognize that out of one blood God made all men to dwell upon the face of the earth. Let us be dissatisfied until that day when nobody will shout "White Power!"—when nobody will shout "Black Power!"—but everybody will talk about God's power and human power.

I must confess, my friends, the road ahead will not always be smooth. There will be still rocky places of frustration and meandering points of bewilderment. There will be inevitable setbacks here and there. There will be those moments when the buoyancy of hope will be transformed into the fatigue of despair. Our dreams will sometimes be shattered and our ethereal hopes blasted. We may again with tear-drenched eyes have to stand before the bier of some courageous civil rights worker whose life will be snuffed out by the dastardly acts of bloodthirsty mobs. Difficult and painful as it is, we must walk on in the days ahead with an audacious faith in the future. And as we continue our charted course, we may gain consolation in the words so nobly left by that great black bard who was also a great freedom fighter of yesterday, James Weldon Johnson:

> Stony the road we trod,
> Bitter the chastening rod
> Felt in the days
> When hope unborn had died.
>
> Yet with a steady beat,
> Have not our weary feet
> Come to the place
> For which our fathers sighed?
>
> We have come over the way
> That with tears hath been watered.
> We have come treading our paths
> Through the blood of the slaughtered,
>
> Out from the gloomy past,
> Till now we stand at last
> Where the bright gleam
> Of our bright star is cast.

Let this affirmation be our ringing cry. It will give us the courage to face the uncertainties of the future. It will give our tired feet new strength as we continue our forward stride toward the city of freedom. When our days become dreary with low-hovering clouds of despair, and when our nights become darker than a thousand midnights, let us remember that there is a creative force in this universe, working to pull down the gigantic mountains of evil, a power that is able to make a way out of no way and transform dark yesterdays into bright tomorrows. Let us realize the arc of the moral universe is long but it bends toward justice.

Let us realize that William Cullen Bryant is right: "Truth crushed to earth

This speech was published under the title "New Sense of Direction" in *Worldview* 15 (April 1972): 5ff.

will rise again." Let us go out realizing that the Bible is right: "Be not deceived, God is not mocked. Whatsoever a man soweth, that shall he also reap." This is for hope for the future, and with this faith we will be able to sing in some not too distant tomorrow with a cosmic past tense, "We have overcome, we have overcome, deep in my heart, I did believe we would overcome."

MALCOLM X

Speech to African Summit Conference—Cairo, Egypt*

Their Excellencies
First Ordinary Assembly of Heads of State and Governments
Organization of African Unity
Cairo, U.A.R.

YOUR EXCELLENCIES: The Organization of Afro-American Unity has sent me to attend this historic African Summit Conference as an observer to represent the interests of 22 million African-Americans whose *human rights* are being violated daily by the racism of American imperialists.

The Organization of Afro-American Unity (OAAU) has been formed by a cross section of America's African-American community, and is patterned after the letter and spirit of the Organization of African Unity (OAU).

Just as the Organization of African Unity has called upon all African leaders to submerge their differences and unite on common objectives for the common good of all Africans, in America the Organization of Afro-American Unity has called upon Afro-American leaders to submerge their differences and find areas of agreement wherein we can work in unity for the good of the entire 22 million African-Americans.

Since the 22 million of us were originally Africans, who are now in America, not by choice but only by a cruel accident in our history, we strongly believe that African problems are our problems and our problems are African problems.

YOUR EXCELLENCIES: We also believe that as heads of the independent African states you are the shepherds of *all* African peoples everywhere, whether they are still at home here on the mother continent or have been scattered abroad.

*July 17, 1964.

Some African leaders at this conference have implied that they have enough problems here on the mother continent without adding the Afro-American problem.

With all due respect to your esteemed positions, I must remind all of you that *the Good Shepherd* will leave ninety-nine sheep who are safe at home to go to the aid of the one who is lost and has fallen into the clutches of the imperialist wolf.

We in America are your long-lost brothers and sisters, and I am here only to remind you that our problems are your problems. As the African-Americans "awaken" today, we find ourselves in a strange land that has rejected us, and, like the prodigal son, we are turning to our elder brothers for help. We pray our pleas will not fall upon deaf ears.

We were taken forcibly in chains from this mother continent and have now spent over three hundred years in America, suffering the most inhuman forms of physical and psychological tortures imaginable.

During the past ten years the entire world has witnessed our men, women, and children being attacked and bitten by vicious police dogs, brutally beaten by police clubs, and washed down the sewers by high-pressure water hoses that would rip the clothes from our bodies and the flesh from our limbs.

And all of these inhuman atrocities have been inflicted upon us by the American governmental authorities, the police themselves, for no reason other than we seek the recognition and respect granted other human beings in America.

YOUR EXCELLENCIES: The American Government is either unable or unwilling to protect the lives and property of your 22 million African-American brothers and sisters. We stand defenseless, at the mercy of American racists who murder us at will for no reason other than we are black and of African descent.

Two black bodies were found in the Mississippi River this week; last week an unarmed African-American educator was murdered in cold blood in Georgia; a few days before that three civil rights workers disappeared completely, perhaps murdered also, only because they were teaching our people in Mississippi how to vote and how to secure their political rights.

Our problems are your problems. We have lived for over three hundred years in that American den of racist wolves in constant fear of losing life and limb. Recently, three students from Kenya were mistaken for American Negroes and were brutally beaten by the New York police. Shortly after that two diplomats from Uganda were also beaten by the New York City police, who mistook them for American Negroes.

If Africans are brutally beaten while only visiting in America, imagine the physical and psychological suffering received by your brothers and sisters who have lived there for over three hundred years.

Our problem is your problem. No matter how much independence Africans get here on the mother continent, unless you wear your national dress at all times when you visit America, you may be mistaken for one of us and suffer the same psychological and physical mutilation that is an everyday occurrence in our lives.

Your problems will never be fully solved until and unless ours are solved. You will never be fully respected until and unless we are also respected. You will never be recognized as free human beings until and unless we are also recognized and treated as human beings.

Our problem is your problem. It is not a Negro problem, nor an American problem. This is a world problem; a problem for humanity. It is not a problem of civil rights, but a problem of human rights.

If the United States Supreme Court justice Arthur Goldberg a few weeks ago could find legal grounds to threaten to bring Russia before the United Nations and charge her with violating the human rights of less than 3 million Russian Jews, what makes our African brothers hesitate to bring the United States Government before the United Nations and charge her with violating the human rights of 22 million African-Americans?

We pray that our African brothers have not freed themselves of European colonialism only to be overcome and held in check now by American *dollarism*. Don't let American racism be "legalized" by American dollarism.

America is worse than South Africa, because not only is America racist, but she is also deceitful and hypocritical. South Africa preaches segregation and practices segregation. She, at least, practices what she preaches. America preaches integration and practices segregation. She preaches one thing while deceitfully practicing another.

South Africa is like a vicious wolf, openly hostile toward black humanity. But America is cunning like a fox, friendly and smiling, but even more vicious and deadly than the wolf.

The wolf and the fox are both enemies of humanity, both are canine, both humiliate and mutilate their victims. Both have the same objectives, but differ only in methods.

If South Africa is guilty of violating the human rights of Africans here on the mother continent, then America is guilty of worse violations of the 22 million Africans on the American continent. And if South African racism is not a domestic issue, then American racism also is not a *domestic* issue.

Many of you have been led to believe that the much publicized, recently passed Civil Rights Bill is a sign that America is making a sincere effort to correct the injustices we have suffered there. This propaganda maneuver is part of her deceit and trickery to keep the African nations from condemning her racist practices before the United Nations, as you are now doing as regards the same practices of South Africa.

The United States Supreme Court passed laws ten years ago making America's segregated school system illegal. But the Federal Government cannot enforce the law of the highest court in the land when it comes to nothing but equal-rights to education for African-Americans. How can anyone be so naïve as to think all the additional laws brought into being by the Civil Rights Bill will be enforced?

These are nothing but tricks of this century's leading neocolonialist power. Surely, our intellectually mature African brothers will not fall for this trickery?

The Organization of Afro-American Unity, in cooperation with a coalition of other Negro leaders and organizations, has decided to elevate our freedom struggle above the domestic level of civil rights. We intend to internationalize it by placing it at the level of human rights. Our freedom struggle for human dignity is no longer confined to the domestic jurisdiction of the United States Government.

We beseech the independent African states to help us bring our problem before the United Nations, on the grounds that the United States Government is morally incapable of protecting the lives and the property of 22 million African-Americans. And on the grounds that our deteriorating plight is definitely becoming a threat to world peace.

Out of frustration and hopelessness our young people have reached the point of no return. We no longer endorse patience and turning the other cheek. We assert the right of self-defense by whatever means necessary, and reserve the right of maximum retaliation against our racist oppressors, no matter what the odds against us are.

From here on in, if we must die anyway, we will die fighting back, and we will not die alone. We intend to see that our racist oppressors also get a taste of death.

We are well aware that our future efforts to defend ourselves by retaliating—by meeting violence with violence, eye for eye and tooth for tooth—could create the type of racial conflict in America that could easily escalate into a violent, worldwide, bloody race war.

In the interests of world peace and security, we beseech the heads of the independent African states to recommend an immediate investigation into our problem by the United Nations Commission on Human Rights.

If this humble plea that I am voicing at this conference is not properly worded, then let our elder brothers, who know the legal language, come to our aid and word our plea in the proper language necessary for it to be heard.

One last word, my beloved brothers at this African Summit: "No one knows the master better than his servant." We have been servants in America for over three hundred years. We have a thorough inside knowledge of this man who calls himself "Uncle Sam." Therefore, you must heed our warning. Don't escape from European colonialism only to become even more enslaved by deceitful, "friendly" American dollarism.

May Allah's blessings of good health and wisdom be upon you all.

Asalaam Alaikum
MALCOLM X, Chairman
Organization of Afro-American Unity

JAMES FORMAN

The Making of Black Revolutionaries

While the organization continued its struggle to overcome the internal chaos of late 1964 and early 1965, it also grew more militant. In addition to carrying on extensive action, particularly in Mississippi and Alabama, it began to develop self-defense networks in some areas. I announced SNCC's plan to help organize the Washington, D.C., lobby at a press conference in New York held shortly after the assassination of Brother Malcolm on February 21, 1965. Representatives of the Revolutionary Action Movement (RAM) had come to the conference and asked if they could make a statement after mine. They were under severe pressure, as the result of efforts to divide the black community on the issue of Malcolm's murder, and I agreed that they should speak. The association of SNCC with an organization advocating armed struggle created no problem for most of us in SNCC.

Shortly before his death, Malcolm had said it was the ballot or the bullet. The necessity of advancing from the ballot to the bullet had become clear to me by then; I knew that the ballot would never solve the basic problems of poor people—black people, Puerto Ricans, and Chicanos. For me, as for others, this period marked the approach of an end to any belief in—or willingness to engage in—large, nonviolent demonstrations. But I had one more experience of massive nonviolent action to undergo. This was the Selma-to-Montgomery March.

Selma, Alabama, had become a symbol of black resistance to flagrant denial of the right to vote. Events there in March, 1965, climaxed four years of agitation and finally forced the United States to end some of the abuses of the ballot. But this reform was not just a product of public opinion. The Democratic Party found that its own interests lay in that direction; more black voters meant more Democratic voters, it was believed. Thus the Selma-to-Montgomery March involved some backstage maneuvers by the Johnson administration, together with certain actions by the Southern Christian Leadership Conference of a type that SNCC had encountered before.

SNCC decided not to participate as an organization in the March, which was sponsored by SCLC. We felt that the possibility of violence against the people was too strong and we knew that self-defense would not be allowed on the March. But we did allow individual staff members to participate if they wished. Our fears of intense brutality proved correct on March 9, 1965, when many people were severely beaten and gassed at the Pettus Bridge—including our chairman John Lewis. That incident led us to send a large number of our two-way radio cars to Selma to help the people in whatever way possible, and many staff members also went there.

I arrived in Montgomery on March 11. A new attempt to start the March was scheduled for the next day, but then I discovered that Dr. Martin Luther King had privately acceded to the wish of the Justice Department that it be called off. He told the people at a mass meeting, however, that it would proceed and expectations ran high. I thought this a classic example of trickery against the people, and others also criticized Dr. King, including James Bevel and Hosea Williams of his own staff. Under this pressure, King called Attorney General Nicholas Katzenbach at about four o'clock in the morning to say that he had changed his mind. He could not call off the March, he said.

By nine o'clock that morning, the Justice Department had pressured Judge Johnson into issuing a temporary injunction to stop the March. But SNCC and other people went to work to create a climate of rebellion against the injunction. We had become convinced of the need for the March to proceed and we were certain that Gov. George Wallace would not permit violence by his state troopers this time. H. Rap Brown and other militants were at a private meeting in Washington, D.C., telling President Lyndon B. Johnson to go to hell. The climate across the nation was on our side.

But Dr. King and SCLC had more tricks yet to play. They worked out a deal with the Civil Rights Commission, headed by Leroy Collins, former governor of Florida, by which the thousands of people who had come to Selma from all over the country would march a few feet beyond the Pettus Bridge; Dr. King would kneel and pray, and then turn around to lead the people back into Selma where they would wait for a ruling on the injunction. A favorable ruling had been promised by the U.S. Government. The plan worked.

When the Selma-to-Montgomery March took place, at last, some SNCC people served as marshals but we had generally washed our hands of the affair. Aside from the problems with SCLC, it had become very clear to most of us that mass marches like the March on Washington and the Selma-to-Montgomery March had a cathartic effect. Their size created the impression that "the people" had made a show of power and changes would be forthcoming, but actually they served as a safety valve for the American system by taking the pressure off—pressure created by local activity.

By this time, students from nearby Tuskegee College had begun massive protests in Montgomery and asked for our help. It was there that I met Sammy Younge, Jr., a Tuskegee student who joined SNCC and who, in January of 1966, was murdered by a white gasoline station attendant when he tried to use the "white" toilet. I would later write a book, *Sammy Younge, Jr.: The First Black College Student to Die in the Black Liberation Struggle*, which tells the story of Sammy's life as well as the Montgomery demonstrations and the Selma-to-Montgomery March in detail.

The cycle of black resistance and white repression continued in full swing that summer. In Jackson, Mississippi, the state legislature was holding a special session to pass laws that would liberalize the state's voting requirements. This was a blatant attempt to take the edge off the arguments presented by the Mississippi Freedom Democratic Party in their legal challenge to the seating of the five racist congressmen and their demand for recognition of the MFDP. Demonstrations against the special session led to the arrest of over eight hundred people in June, 1965, and their imprisonment under conditions described by many observers as like a concentration camp. Many were brutally beaten and hospitalized. At the same time, black Mississippians were being arrested in Washington, D.C., for protesting the failure of the clerk of the House of Representatives to have printed the evidence submitted by the MFDP in support of its challenge.

SNCC was deeply involved in helping to mount and lead the Jackson demonstrations. I went there myself at one point, although I had become very leery of such demonstrations and of nonviolence even as a tactic. I had no intention of getting arrested. But at one point, I saw Mrs. Annie Devine, an MFDP leader, being arrested while she stood on the street speaking to a group of demonstrators. It was impossible for me not to take some action, so I walked over and asked the police, "What are you arresting her for? She hasn't done anything." I quickly found myself in the city jail, but that was the last time I got arrested in the Deep South.

SNCC was also active in the Delta again, where a strike of cotton choppers had started that spring and grown until, by early June, over a thousand workers were involved and the Mississippi Freedom Labor Union had been born. Its main demand was a minimum of $1.25 an hour instead of the average pay of $3.00 for work for sunup to sundown. Mechanization and suppression eventually defeated the strike but the fact that it happened at all showed how ready for action our people were—even the most intimidated and controlled elements.

Our project in Arkansas was also active, while over in Georgia SNCC staff member Julian Bond was elected to the state House of Representatives on June 16 as the Democratic candidate, but on an independent and radical platform determined by the black community. A number of SNCC workers campaigned for Julian. His election came about under the Supreme Court's "One Man, One Vote" reapportionment decision, which shifted power in the state legislatures from the rural counties to the metropolitan areas and created many new assembly districts where special elections had to be held—such as Julian's. In these new districts across the South, SNCC saw the possibility of creating bases of support for radical candidates who would use the elections as an opportunity for disruption and the raising of issues. The process of lifting consciousness, of revolutionary development, might thus be accelerated.

Julian's election proved that SNCC could rally mass support and that it had the potential for transforming itself into a political party. This potential was also being revealed in Alabama, under the sign of the black panther.

Near the end of the Selma-to-Montgomery March, a white supporter from Detroit named Mrs. Viola Liuzzo had been killed by Klansmen while she drove through Lowndes County. One night, at a meeting in Montgomery, we decided that SNCC's response to her murder would be to organize in Lowndes—a notoriously racist, terrorized area with an 86 percent black population that was acutely poor and with not one black person registered to vote. Stokely Carmichael became the project director for this county; Bob Mants, Courtland Cox, the Jackson brothers, and Ralph Featherstone were other SNCC staffers working there. I attended two of the early mass meetings in Lowndes but did not go there often. My nerves were in bad shape and, in any case, the other SNCC people had the situation well in hand.

Jack Minnis, head of SNCC's research department, discovered a little-known Alabama law that made it possible for independent political organizations to be formed and run candidates for office under conditions that were technically not difficult to meet. This legal loophole opened the door for the creation later that year of the Lowndes County Freedom Organization, with the black panther as its symbol. Minnis held a number of workshops to explain the whole process. The Alabama people in the Freedom Organization acquired a better understanding of what they were doing, and why, than any other political group that we had thus far developed. A tremendous excitement and new hope began to flow as the black men and women of Lowndes County moved to shake off a hundred years of white supremacy.

All this activity, and especially the birth of the Lowndes County movement, was giving SNCC the sense of a new lease on life when the November, 1965, staff meeting opened. We still faced internal problems, especially those created by individualism and a lack of self-discipline—no doubt about it. A previous staff meeting, in May of the same year, had made this clear enough. One incident centered around the fact that the person responsible for arrangements—room, board, transportation, and so forth—had set up a system of meal cards. It should be noted that the cost of our meetings ran into thousands of dollars; we paid for meals according to the number of people who ate; and there was often confusion caused by many unregistered hangers-on. With the meal cards, given to everyone legitimately attending the meeting for presentation in the dining hall before each meal, the conference coordinator hoped to solve this problem. But a few people raised the cry of "regimentation" and organized a meal card burning. Others, mostly Southern working-class blacks, were prepared to bar this small group from the dining hall, by armed struggle if necessary. A serious confrontation was finally avoided, but the incident revealed the lingering power of destructive individualism.

At the November, 1965, meeting, this problem was intensified by the resentment of some people against the disciplinary letters which they had been sent from the Atlanta office. But, by now, the staff had been sharply reduced in number, and most of the people at this meeting were ready to think in long-range revolutionary terms. We could talk and make plans in an atmosphere relatively free from personal trauma. It was high time—much had happened in the black community, including the Watts rebellion that summer, and if SNCC didn't get itself together, the revolution was going to leave it behind.

For me, the turning point became clear during a talk by Courtland Cox, who had been working in Lowndes County. He was talking about what the people there were trying to do and, at one point, he wrote some words on the blackboard. I think they said, "Get power for black people." And he continued, "The people want power, power to control the courthouse, power to control their lives." As he talked and I looked at the written words, something clicked in me. I felt then that we had emerged from the internal disorder, that we were in a new day, and that I personally could begin to work freely on the basis of my true beliefs—beliefs along the line I had indicated in my Greenwood speech about power.

I went up to the blackboard myself and wrote down, "Power. Education. Organization." "Fundamentally," I said, "the organizer has to see his role as instilling a tremendous political education toward forming basic organizations in order to achieve power." This was the first time that the discussion of power as such had come up in the organization. From that time on, SNCC began to talk more and more about power for black people, organization, and political education. We had attained a whole new level of objectives, we were once again moving in harmony with the needs of the masses of black people.

At the same meeting SNCC also began to discuss the war in Vietnam and to prepare a statement on it. Until that year, most of us—including myself—had considered the war not irrelevant, but simply remote. Its importance to black people had not come home to us. Bob Parris, however, had begun working that summer with some forces in the peace movement. He was concerned that students who had worked in the South—white students in particular—could remain relevant and also continue relating to the black movement in a healthy way after they left the South. His new activity also had roots in a general concern for peace, which had been manifested when he went on a Quaker mission to Japan in the late fifties. Bob worked that summer with the Committee of Unrepresented People, an ad hoc organization which aimed to bring together people from different movements and which held a large gathering in Washington, D.C., to confront the machinery of government with some of the people whose views—especially on the war—it was supposed to represent and did not. Bob also traveled around the country, meeting with various peace groups.

The creation of these and other links between the antiwar movement and what was still called the civil rights movement, together with the expanding consciousness of various SNCC workers, led us to the discussion of Vietnam. It was agreed at the November meeting that a statement should be drafted along certain lines; this work later took place and the statement itself came out in January, 1966—the first time a "civil rights organization" made a public stand against the war.

Release of that declaration was triggered by the murder of Sammy Younge, Jr., in Tuskegee, Alabama, on January 4. The killer was freed by an all-white jury. For myself, Sammy's murder marked the final end of any patience with nonviolence—even as a tactic.

SNCC's statement read:

> The Student Nonviolent Coordinating Committee has a right and a responsibility to dissent with United States foreign policy on an issue when it sees fit. The Student Nonviolent Coordinating Committee now states its opposition to United States' involvement in Vietnam on these grounds:
>
> We believe the United States government has been deceptive in its claims of concern for freedom of the Vietnamese people, just as the government has been deceptive in claiming concern for the freedom of colored people in such other countries as the Dominican Republic, the Congo, South Africa, Rhodesia and in the United States itself.
>
> We, the Student Nonviolent Coordinating Committee, have been involved in the black people's struggle for liberation and self-determination in this country for the past five years. Our work, particularly in the South, has taught us that the United States government has never guaranteed the freedom of oppressed citizens, and is not yet truly determined to end the rule of terror and oppression within its own borders.
>
> We ourselves have often been victims of violence and confinement executed by United States government officials. We recall the numerous persons who have been murdered in the South because of their efforts to secure their civil and human rights, and whose murderers have been allowed to escape penalty for their crimes.
>
> The murder of Samuel Younge in Tuskegee, Ala., is no different than the murder of peasants in Vietnam, for both Younge and the Vietnamese sought, and are seeking, to secure the rights guaranteed them by law. In each case, the United States government bears a great part of the responsibility for these deaths.
>
> Samuel Younge was murdered because United States law is not be-

ing enforced. Vietnamese are murdered because the United States is pursuing an aggressive policy in violation of international law. The United States is no respecter of persons or law when such persons or laws run counter to its needs and desires.

We recall the indifference, suspicion and outright hostility with which our reports of violence have been met in the past by government officials.

We know that for the most part, elections in this country, in the North as well as the South, are not free. We have seen that the 1965 Voting Rights Act and the 1964 Civil Rights Act have not yet been implemented with full federal power and sincerity.

We question, then, the ability and even the desire of the United States government to guarantee free elections abroad. We maintain that our country's cry of "preserve freedom in the world" is a hypocritical mask behind which it squashes liberation movements which are not bound, and refuse to be bound, by the expediencies of United States cold war policies.

We are in sympathy with, and support, the men in this country who are unwilling to respond to a military draft which would compel them to contribute their lives to United States aggression in Vietnam in the name of the "freedom" we find so false in this country.

We recoil with horror at the inconsistency of a supposedly "free" society where responsibility to lend oneself to military aggression. We take note of the fact that 60 percent of the draftees from this country are Negroes called on to stifle the liberation of Vietnam, to preserve a "democracy" which does not exist for them at home.

We ask, where is the draft for the freedom fight in the United States?

We therefore encourage those Americans who prefer to use their energy in building democratic forms within this country. We believe that work in the civil rights movement and with other human relations organizations is a valid alternative to the draft. We urge all Americans to seek this alternative, knowing full well that it may cost them lives—as painfully as in Vietnam.

Our statement caused the liberals and their black flunkies not to mention the racists, to raise a hue and cry against SNCC. These forces claimed that civil rights and the war were two separate issues, not related, and that SNCC as a civil rights organization had no business issuing a statement on the war. Our support among the liberals was sharply curtailed. Julian Bond would soon be denied his seat in the state legislature because he supported the statement. But we continued down the revolutionary path. SNCC began to engage in antidraft activity, and the Atlanta Project conducted demonstrations at the racist draft center in Atlanta, resulting in jail terms for ten people ranging from three years to six months. Later SNCC would create the National Black Anti-War Anti-Draft Union, (NBAWADU). Courtland Cox would go to Europe to represent SNCC on the International War Crimes Tribunal called by Lord Bertrand Russell.

As 1966 began SNCC stood at the end of a period of internal crisis that had lasted less than a year and a half but had shaken the organization profoundly. We had resolved some of our internal contradictions, while others stayed with us. But in the process we had missed a historic opportunity. Too much power had been dissipated. Now we did seem to have entered a new day, and SNCC had clearly begun moving toward Black Power and the anti-imperialist position that it would later apply in all areas. We had also established ourselves in a new headquarters building, with great potential for many activities, and acquired a forty thousand dollar grant for a printing operation that would enable us to proceed full-steam with the propaganda work that I knew we should be doing.

I, and also others, in SNCC felt battered and weakened—but hopeful. We knew that the dynamic of forging revolutionaries in the United States or anywhere is a long and complicated process. People must learn from their own experiences, although study can quicken the pace. We knew how great a handicap was the lack of historical models for our particular group. Radical youth organizations had always been attached in some way to an adult group; we were the first to move on our own and we had no predecessors for guidelines. People said it couldn't work. Our mistakes had to be momentous—and they had to be the mistakes of young people.

The revolutionary organization of our dreams might still emerge I thought.

BOBBY SEALE

Seize the Time: The Story of the Black Panther Party and Huey P. Newton

One day Huey said, "It's about time we get the organization off the ground, and do it now."

This was in the latter part of September 1966. From around the first of October to the fifteenth of October, in the poverty center in North Oakland, Huey and I began to write out a ten-point platform and program of the Black Panther Party. Huey himself articulated it word for word. All I made were suggestions.

Huey said, "We need a program. We have to have a program for the people. A program that relates to the people. A program that the people can understand. A program that the people can read and see, and which expresses their desires and needs at the same time. It's got to relate to the philosophical meaning of where in the world we are going, but the philosophical meaning will also have to relate to something specific."

That was very important with Huey. So, Huey divided it up into "What We Want" and "What We Believe." "What We Want" are the practical, specific things that we need and that should exist. At the same time, we expressed philosophically, but concretely, what we believe. So we read the program one to one. Point One of "What We Want" and Point One of "What We Believe." Point Two of "What We Want" and Point Two of "What We Believe." This is the way the people should look at it. It puts together concisely all the physical needs and all the philosophical principles in some basic instructive thing that they can understand, instead of a bunch of esoteric bullshit.

I don't care what kind of cat is on the block—if he doesn't relate to anything else, he can relate to the ten-point platform and program of the Black Panther Party.

Huey said, "Black people and especially brothers on the block have to have some political consciousness."

We wrote it out and Melvin Newton, Huey's brother, came over and proofed it for corrections in grammar. We put it together, and we took all the paper we needed out of the poverty program supplies late at night at the poverty office. We were writing out the ten-point platform and program inside the back office.

Huey said, "Now, what's the first thing we want?" And Huey answered his own question, "WE WANT FREEDOM."

And I wrote down, "We want freedom."

Then he said, "We want the power to determine the destiny of our black community."

I said, "Right, brother, that's good. What's the next thing?"

"We want full employment for our people."

"What else?"

"Nothing else."

"OK, brother, right."

I thought about it and he was right. That's what we want. We want full employment for our people. This is a basic program for our people, because the people are going to relate to the fact that this is exactly what they want and they ain't going to settle for nothing else—they ain't going to settle for a bunch of esoteric bullshit and a long essay.

Then Huey said, "We want the white racist businessman to end the robbery and exploitation of the black community." So, we wrote that down.

Then we wrote, "We want decent housing, fit for shelter of human beings."

"What else, brother Huey?"

Huey sat there and he thought for a few shakes. He said, "Now we got to get off into the area of education. I think that's important. We got employment, the power of our own community, and decent housing. Now we want decent education that teaches us about the true nature of this decadent American system, and education that teaches us about our true history and our role in present-day society."

After that he went right into, "We want all black men to be exempt from military service."

That's the way we put it. We didn't have to go into anything else because we knew that the black people on the block would understand and that's what we want. Basically nothing else.

Then Huey said, "Look at the racist power structure. We have to deal with that. We have to understand that we want an immediate end to police brutality and murder of black people."

I wrote that exactly like it was.

Huey went on to the next one. "We want all black men and women to be released from the federal, county, state, and city jails and prisons."

I said, "Right," and wrote that down.

Then brother Huey said, "We want every black man brought to trial to be tried in a court by a jury of his peer group as it is defined by the Constitution of this United States."

For a black man this means people from the black community.

Then Huey said, "Let's summarize these points. We want land, we want bread, we want housing, we want education, we want clothing, we want justice, and we want some peace."

That's the way Huey put it and I wrote it down. We went over the ten points and put in our commas and periods, and then we got into "What We Believe." We went through everything we believed that was correlative to everything that we wanted.

Huey said, "This ten-point platform and program is what we want and what we believe. These things did not just come out of the clear blue sky. This is what black people have been voicing all along for over 100 years since the Emancipation Proclamation and even before that. These things are directly related to the things we had before we left Africa."

When we got all through writing the program, Huey said, "We've got to have some kind of structure. What do you want to be," he asked me, "Chairman or Minister of Defense?"

"Doesn't make any difference to me," I said. "What do you want to be, Chairman or Minister of Defense?"

"I'll be the Minister of Defense," Huey said, "and you'll be the Chairman."

"That's fine with me," I told him, and that's just the way that shit came about, how Huey became the Minister of Defense and I became the Chairman of the Black Panther Party. Just like that.

With the ten-point platform and program and the two of us, the Party was officially launched on October 15, 1966, in a poverty program office in the black community in Oakland, California.

We got my wife and Huey's girl friend LaVerne together, and they typed it out for us on stencils inside that poverty program office. The next night we took them and we ran off over a thousand copies of that ten-point platform and program.

Huey said, "The brothers and sisters have to relate to this because this is what they want. This is what they've told me. This is what they've told every other leader in this country."

You always have to understand that Huey understood the difference between reform and revolution. Huey understood that you answer the momentary desires and needs of the people, that you try to instruct them and politically educate them, that these are their basic political desires and needs, and from the people themselves will rage a revolution to make sure that they have these basic desires and needs fulfilled.

That's what Huey P. Newton put forth, and that's what Huey P. Newton understood to be political, and that's what Huey P. Newton understood to be the reason why people who are oppressed will wage a revolution. That's what I remember, that's what I know, that's what I feel, and that's what I'll never forget about Huey. He never forgot about the people. He'd bring it right down to the food, and the bread and employment, decent housing, decent education—the way the motherfuckers, the President, and all, fucked over us in the military service; the pigs, the murder, and brutality; the courts; the brothers who are in jail, how they had to be released.

While he was in jail, a year-and-a-half later, Huey said to add something to Point Ten. He was reading brother Eldridge Cleaver's thing about a black plebiscite in the United States conducted by the United Nations (which is directly related to what Malcolm X said). Huey related not to the personality alone of Malcolm, or Mao Tse Tung, or Fanon. He related to what all these revolutionary leaders of the world said we must do, what we must establish, what we must institutionalize. That's very important. This is the way the program was written. Huey always had the people's desires and political needs in mind. He always had the revolutionary tactics and the revolutionary means in mind as to how the people must go about getting these things, getting these basic desires and needs.

This is where the shit boils down to—to what the people want and not what some intellectual personally wants or some cultural nationalists, like LeRoi Jones, want, or some jive-ass underground RAM motherfucker wants, or what some jive motherfucker in some college studying bullshit says, talking esoteric shit about the basic social-economic structure, and the adverse conditions that we're subjected to so that no black man even understands. Huey was talking about some full employment, some decent housing, some education, about stopping those pigs from brutalizing us and murdering us.

Then Huey came on the street with some guns. About a month and a half after this program was written, Huey P. Newton tried to tell the intellectuals that it's time, it's time to go forth in the revolutionary struggle. That it's no time to be bullshitting. "Pick up some guns and don't be bullshitting." Huey wanted brothers off the block—brothers who had been out there robbing banks, brothers who had been pimping, brothers who had been peddling dope, brothers who ain't gonna take no shit, brothers who had been fighting pigs—because he knew that once they get themselves together in the area of political education (and it doesn't take much because the political education is the ten-point platform and program), Huey P. Newton knew that once you organize the brothers he ran with, he fought with, he fought against, who he fought harder than they fought him, once you organize those brothers, you get niggers, you get black men, you get revolutionaries who are too much.

We went off into this ten-point platform and Huey went forth to take a pulse beat of the black community, using Oakland, California where there's nearly 40 percent blacks and as a black community typical of any other in this nation. I don't give a damn if a black brother's in the South because we have brothers from the South all the way up here in Oakland, and we have brothers from New York, brothers from Chicago, what have you. Huey understood that Oakland was a typical black community, so we took the ten-point platform and program—a thousand copies of it—and went to the black community with them. He didn't just pass out the platform in people's hands. He stopped, talked, and discussed the points on the ten-point platform with all the black brothers and sisters off the block, and with mothers who had been scrubbing Miss Ann's kitchen. We talked to brothers and sisters in colleges, in high schools, who were on parole, on probation, who'd been in jails, who'd just gotten out of jail, and brothers and sisters who looked like they were on their way to jail. They would cite cases. Huey was always interested in any kind of case anyone who looked like he was going to jail had inside of the courts. Huey was always interested in that. Huey would talk about this brother possibly being railroaded off into jail or prison. Huey knew this because he experienced it and because he understood the brother's predicament in terms of the power structure railroading him there.

So, we had a thousand copies of the ten-point platform and program being circulated through the black community by myself and Huey P. Newton. Little Bobby Hutton came along, and for one-and-a-half months, Bobby stuck with me and Huey, helping us articulate this ten-point platform and program, and the fact that we have to arm ourselves against these pigs who've been murdering us and brutalizing us, how we have to arm ourselves against these racists, Birchites, and Ku Klux Klaners infested in the police departments, the pig departments who "occupy our communities," as Huey P. Newton says, "like a foreign troop." We have to defend ourselves against them because they are breaking down our doors, shooting black brothers on the streets, and brutalizing sisters on the head. They are wearing guns mostly to intimidate the people from forming organizations to really get our basic political desires and needs answered. The power structure uses the fascist police against people moving for freedom and liberation. It keeps our people divided, but the program will be what we unite the people around and to teach our people self-defense.

When we started passing the platform around the poverty center there, they'd ask, "Why do you want to be a vicious animal like a panther?"

Huey would break in. "The nature of a panther is that he never attacks. But if anyone attacks him or backs him into a corner, the panther comes up to wipe that aggressor or that attacker out, absolutely, resolutely, wholly, thoroughly, and completely." They didn't *want* to understand that.

Here is the ten-point platform and program as it appears each week in our paper:

OCTOBER 1966
BLACK PANTHER PARTY PLATFORM AND PROGRAM
WHAT WE WANT
WHAT WE BELIEVE

1. We want freedom. We want power to determine the destiny of our Black Community.

We believe that black people will not be free until we are able to determine our destiny.

2. We want full employment for our people.

We believe that the federal government is responsible and obligated to give every man employment or a guaranteed income. We believe that if the white American businessmen will not give full employment, then the means of production should be taken from the businessmen and placed in the community so that the people of the community can organize and employ all of its people and give a high standard of living.

3. We want an end to the robbery by the white man of our Black Community.

We believe that this racist government has robbed us and now we are demanding the overdue debt of forty acres and two mules. Forty acres and two mules was promised 100 years ago as restitution for slave labor and mass murder of black people. We will accept the payment in currency which will be distributed to our many communities. The Germans are now aiding the Jews in Israel for the genocide of the Jewish people. The Germans murdered six million Jews. The American racist has taken part in the slaughter of over fifty million black people; therefore, we feel that this is a modest demand that we make.

4. We want decent housing, fit for shelter of human beings.

We believe that if the white landlords will not give decent housing to our black community, then the housing and the land should be made into cooperatives so that our community, with government aid, can build and make decent housing for its people.

5. We want education for our people that exposes the true nature of this decadent American society. We want education that teaches us our true history and our role in the present-day society.

We believe in an educational system that will give to our people a knowledge of self. If a man does not have knowledge of himself and his position in society and the world, then he has little chance to relate to anything else.

6. We want all black men to be exempt from military service.

We believe that black people should not be forced to fight in the military service to defend a racist government that does not protect us. We will not fight and kill other people of color in the world who, like black people, are being victimized by the white racist government of America. We will protect ourselves from the force and violence of the racist police and the racist military, by whatever means necessary.

7. We want an immediate end to POLICE BRUTALITY and MURDER of black people.

We believe we can end police brutality in our black community by organizing black self-defense groups that are dedicated to defending our black community from racist police oppression and brutality. The Second Amendment to the Constitution of the United States gives a right to bear arms. We therefore believe that all black people should arm themselves for self-defense.

8. We want freedom for all black men held in federal, state, county, and city prisons and jails.

We believe that all black people should be released from the many jails and prisons because they have not received a fair and impartial trial.

9. We want all black people when brought to trial to be tried in court by a jury of their peer group or people from their black communities, as defined by the Constitution of the United States.

We believe that the courts should follow the United States Constitution so that black people will receive fair trials. The Fourteenth Amendment of the U.S. Constitution gives a man a right to be tried by his peer group. A peer is a person from a similar economic, social, religious, geographical, environmental, historical, and racial background. To do this the court will be forced to select a jury from the black community from which the black defendant came. We have been and are being tried by all-white juries that have no understanding of the "average reasoning man" of the black community.

10. We want land, bread, housing, education, clothing, justice, and peace. And as our major political objective, a United Nations-supervised plebiscite to be held throughout the black colony in which only black colonial subjects will be allowed to participate, for the purpose of determining the will of black people as to their national destiny.

When, in the course of human events, it becomes necessary for one people to dissolve the political bands which have connected them with another, and to assume, among the powers of the earth, the separate and equal station to which the laws of nature and nature's God entitle them, a decent respect to the opinions of mankind requires that they should declare the causes which impel them to the separation.

We hold these truths to be self-evident, that all men are created equal; that they are endowed by their Creator with certain unalienable rights; that among these are life, liberty, and the pursuit of happiness. That, to secure these rights, governments are instituted among men, deriving their just powers from the consent of the governed; that, whenever any form of government becomes destructive of these ends, it is the right of the people to alter or to abolish it, and to institute a new government, laying its foundation on such principles, and organizing its powers in such form, as to them shall seem most likely to effect their safety and happiness. Prudence, indeed, will dictate that governments long established should not be changed for light and transient causes; and, accordingly, all experience hath shown, that mankind are more disposed to suffer, while evils are sufferable, than to right themselves by abolishing the forms to which they are accustomed. But, when a long train of abuses and usurpations, pursuing invariably the same object, evinces a design to reduce them under absolute despotism, it is their right, it is their duty, to throw off such government, and to provide new guards for their future security.

SAMUEL F. YETTE

The Choice: The Issue of Black Survival in America

When the decade of the 1970s began, the United States government was officially—but unconstitutionally—in the midst of two wars: (1) a war of "attrition" (genocide) against the colonized colored people of Indochina, and (2) expeditionary "law and order" campaign (repression—selective genocide) against the colonized colored people of the United States.

Although nonaligned, both colonized groups had much in common. As discussed in Part Two, they were, in fact, victims of the *same* war, though in different theaters.

In the United States, as in Indochina, victims of these undeclared wars painfully achieved high visibility during the 1960's. The colonized Blacks inside the United States were the subject of numerous and extensive studies, special programs, White House conferences, and plain gawking curiosity. Occasionally, a collection of what American society regarded as social antiques would present themselves for inspection in the nation's Capital. Such a group arrived in the spring of 1966. A motley collection of Blackpoor, they were a spectacle, even for Lafayette Park, where they spent the night. Rest-broken, poorly clothed, and shivering, the two dozen Mississippi outcasts* could not have been less in tune with the opulence around them. Some still crowded inside and others huddled outside the several tents they had pitched in the park across Pennsylvania Avenue—squarely in front of the White House.

These uninvited campers had braved a bone-chilling mist that shrouded the park. Two years earlier, some of them had dared vote in the Presidential election—for the first time in their many adult years. Others were accused of participating in the "Meredith March Against Fear," a walk quickly interrupted by the blasts of a white man's shotgun that nearly took the life of James Meredith. Some of them might even have joined in that chorus along the Meredith March that gave the first audible shouts of "Black Power!"

Now they were homeless.

They kept explaining that they were *not* the Negroes who had "lived in" at the deactivated Greenville (Mississippi) Air Force Base and were finally dragged out by the military. Instead, they insisted, they had relied on "the people in Washington" to help them work out their needs in an orderly way. All of them had outlived their rights as tenants in the Mississippi feudal system, but they had not outlived their faith in the government. They had been evicted from the land they had worked as sharecroppers, but they still allowed that the failing might be theirs, that it must have been they who had not made clear that their need was great and their cause just.

They hoped that federal antipoverty funds could be arranged for them to build houses and stay in the Delta, for that was home. Paper appeals failing, they brought their bodies to Washington to support their cause and demonstrate their need.

The bureaucratic charades had reduced them to this tent-setting spectacle, a desperate effort to get the attention of President Lyndon B. Johnson, and possibly embarrass him into action on their behalf. The Washington *Post* that morning carried a story of the telegram they sent to the President. It was

* "A young university economics instructor just made a trip to Mississippi and returned convinced that some 100,000 Negro sharecroppers may shortly be thrown off Delta plantations and forced by whites to move north," Marianne Means reported in the New York *World Journal Tribune*, January 31, 1967. "The practical economics of the wage increase (to 84¢ per hour) hardly warrant the sudden eviction of huge numbers of impoverished Negro families . . . but the political realities are something else again. The [instructor's] memorandum points out: 'the incentive [to evict] is rendered particularly strong by the fact that Negroes now constitute a majority of registered voters in a number of Delta counties and all major state and county offices will be up for election this fall.' "

signed "Your Neighbors." Their humor was lost on the President. There was no neighborly response. There was no response at all.

In time, they were driven by harsh weather and dysentery back, hungry and homeless, to the rigors of survival in the Mississippi Delta.

The spectacle of Lafayette Park kept alive the symbolic depravity of an inhumane history. Those anguished inhabitants of the park were truly a dying people. So were their legions of millions left in the valleys of the Black Belt and in the teeming ghettos of Chicago, New York, Los Angeles, Cleveland, and all the other welfare-swelled urban centers of the East, North, and West.

They were obsolete people, described by the then Labor Secretary W. Willard Wirtz as a "human scrap heap":

> We are piling up a human scrap heap of between 250,000 and 500,000 people a year, many of whom never appear in the unemployment statistics.
>
> They are often not counted among the unemployed because they have given up looking for work and thus count themselves out of the labor market. The rate of nonparticipation in the labor force by men in their prime years increased from 4.7 percent in 1953 to 5.2 percent in 1962. The increase has been the sharpest among nonwhites, increasing from 5.3 percent to 8.2 percent in that period.
>
> The human scrap heap is composed of persons who, as a consequence of technological development, of their own educational failures, of environments of poverty and other causes that disqualify them for employment in a skilled economy, cannot and will not find work without special help.
>
> The 115,000 boys who failed the Selective Service educational tests in 1963 are candidates for the human scrap heap.
>
> If we are to turn the human scrap heap into the materials for richer progress and more rewarding lives, then private industry and our private institutions must help us to do the job that government actions have only suggested need doing.*

A people whom the society had always denied social value—personality—had also lost economic value. Theirs was the problem of *all* black America: survival.

Examination of the problem must begin with a single, overpowering socioeconomic condition in the society: black Americans *are* obsolete people.

While this certainly is not accurate in a moral sense, nor, at the moment, biologically, it is true where, in the 1970s, it becomes the issue: it is true in

* Reported in a Department of Labor press release, June 15, 1964, from a lecture by Wirtz to a seminar on automation and technological change in Los Angeles.

the minds and schemes of those who, with inordinate power and authority, control the nation. While it may not be so true among the general population, mass sentiments against oppression and possible genocide are not sufficiently strong to cause these schemes to fail. Black Americans have outlived their usefulness. Their *raison d'être* to this society has ceased to be a compelling issue. Once an economic asset, they are now considered an economic drag. The wood is all hewn, the water all drawn, the cotton all picked, and the rails reach from coast to coast. The ditches are all dug, the dishes are put away, and only a few shoes remain to be shined.

Thanks to old black backs and newfangled machines, the sweat chores of the nation are done. Now the some 25 million Blacks face a society that is brutally pragmatic, technologically accomplished, deeply racist, increasingly overcrowded, and surly. In such a society, the absence of social and economic value is a crucial factor in anyone's fight for a future.

Blacks in America have had 250 years of nationally sanctioned slavery and another hundred years of deceitful enslavement outside the national law. Now they are irreconcilably committed to personal dignity and justice as a people. Their patience, like the oxcart, is gone. But the hope remains that they, *unlike* the oxen, can cease to be driven and can be permitted to stay—on human and civil terms.

They want to survive, but only as men and women—no longer as pawns or chattel. Can they?

This is the most frightful and pressing question facing America in the 1970s. Those who say the most urgent question is the "environment" should recognize that it is Blackness that is unsightly in America. Those who say it is war should face the fact that racism—an arrogance of superiority that seeks economic and military exploitation—is as much the nation's role in Birmingham as it is in Vietnam. And those who say that the most pressing issue is "law and order" should recognize the term for what it is: a euphemism for the total repression and possible extermination of those in the society who cry for justice where little justice can be found.

Whether Blacks have a place in U.S. society is a choice that belongs to the nation. That choice was audaciously called to the attention of white America early in 1960, when four black college students sat down at a North Carolina lunch counter reserved for whites. For the ten raw years of the 1960s, the nation noisily grappled with its choice: freedom or death for Afro-Americans.

By the end of the decade, Blacks were forced to face the evidence heaped painfully upon them. The evidence showed that a choice had been made, and freedom was denied.

True, the decade of the 1960s provided some contrary indications. There were, for example, outpourings of new laws and pronouncements that ostensibly guaranteed not only freedom and security but also socioeconomic progress. Blacks were visibly appointed to a handful of high federal positions. This was a kind of progress, but it was also confusing: it helped obscure from many Blacks and whites alike the true dangers being designed by repressive elements. In significant instances, what appeared to be progress was, in fact, the vehicle of the danger itself. For example, black appointees to high office generally included men of some standing and/or credibility in the black communities. Without that fact, of course, the value of their appointment was greatly, if not totally, diminished. Appointees included such men as Robert C. Weaver as Secretary of Housing and Urban Development, the first nonwhite member of any President's Cabinet; Andrew Brimmer, the first black governor of the Federal Reserve Board; Lisle C. Carter, Jr., as Assistant Secretary of Health, Education, and Welfare; Theodore M. Berry, as community action director of the Office of Economic Opportunity; and Thurgood Marshall as Solicitor General, then Associate Justice of the Supreme Court, both unprecedented.

While the black appointees were highly visible, they were, for the most part, powerless. And their powerless visibility in and around the bureaucratic councils added an aura of legitimacy to illegitimate acts, providing a smokescreen for dirty dealing.

This is neither to criticize nor exonerate the appointees. The fault was not theirs. The fault was in the system—by design. Those who attribute the major fault to the appointees do so mainly out of their failure to grasp the cleverness and ruthlessness in the bureaucratic design to which these men were attached.

This is not to say that those who hoped should not have hoped, and that those who tried should have done otherwise. When the 1960 decade began, there was every reason both to hope and to try.

This cycle of hope, lost hope, promise, aborted promise, then rank oppression began with the election, in 1960, of Senator John F. Kennedy to the Presidency. What with the Freedom Rides in full swing, and with black people singing a bold, new song, what real choice had black people between candidate Richard M. Nixon, who had authored concentration camp legislation, and a superbly glamorous young man who promised to "get America moving again"?

When President Kennedy brought into the White House Andrew Hatcher, the first black White House assistant press secretary, that appointment served to indicate that he was willing to hear the black man's story. Subsequently, he received at the White House the leaders of a massive 1963 march on Washington for "Jobs and Freedom." He promised those leaders—Dr. Martin Luther King, Jr., A. Philip Randolph, Whitney Young, Jr., Roy Wilkins, and John Lewis—a new strategy to attack poverty and injustice.

Less than four months later, President Kennedy was dead, and the decade's first brief hope and promise had died with him. New hope and bigger promises, nonetheless, sprang up in their places.

Kennedy's successor, Lyndon B. Johnson, offered his sequel to President Kennedy's "Let us begin." Said President Johnson: "Let us continue."

The Johnson promise: "The Great Society."

Within a few months after President Kennedy was shot down in Dallas, November 22, 1963, President Johnson announced a new "unconditional war on poverty" and succeeded in getting an aggrieved Congress to pass the Civil Rights Act of 1964 (signed on July 2), and to create, on August 20, the Office of Economic Opportunity (OEO).

Beyond that, President Johnson made highly publicized speeches pledging to open doors for poor Blacks and to help them "walk through those doors" into a "Great Society." Those were the promises of the Great Society. The floods of government promise and black hope both crested at that point in the mid-1960s.

But . . . slowly, almost imperceptibly, the glint began to wear from Uncle Sam's shiny new armor. It tarnished, even while Uncle Sam stood like a colossus in the middle of the poverty and civil rights battlefield, swearing to take on all comers on behalf of Negroes and the poor. Still early in that new day of hope, wary Negroes, straining to see some sign of battle, could not perceive the paralysis that stayed the federal giant.

But as the day wore on, the go-slow motions of the federal giant did not match the fast, rhythmic rhetoric. In time, Negroes began to know that what they heard was aimed *at* them—not for them.

The cruelest hoax since the vain promise of "20 acres and a mule" following the Civil War had been set in motion against Africans transplanted in America. The raised hand of Uncle Sam was swatting poor Negroes while rewarding rich whites with the spoils of black misery. As this truth became known, hope turned to hatred, dedication became disgust, hands raised for help became clenched fists, and eyes searching for acceptance turned inward.

Negroes turned Black.

Blacks could see clearer what Negroes could not: If help would come, they, themselves, would bring it. Beauty was where they found it: Finding beauty meant *being* beautiful. They could win only if the system lost, and vice versa. And what truly was at stake was their natural lives.

And so it went—a decade of freedom rides, promises, public con games, black rebellions, and armed invasions of campus "sanctuaries." Even so, through it all, Blacks did manage more togetherness—whether it was in Vietnam or campsites on this side; the college campus or at wakes for the martyrs; in jail cells or on OEO community action boards.

The black togetherness of the 1960s—the newfound Blackness—produced a new visibility and a grip on the issues affecting black lives. Consequently, through a residue of confidence in the political system, hundreds of Blacks were elected to public office. But even some of them foresaw, as the new decade began, concentration camps and oppression.*

* Reported *Ebony* in its February, 1970, issue (p. 77): "Optimism, guarded, qualified and

Thus, even the Blacks who hoped most and were most rewarded in the tradition of the system saw in the nation's choice a clear and present danger.

The schemes of the 1970s promised new martyrs, bigger jails, more wars (at home and abroad), data banks, wiretaps, and a genuinely regimented society, including the sharp curtailment of black college students, a white establishment take-over of black colleges, and psychological barbed wire around all learning institutions.

In short, the 1970s promised a reversal of those processes that, in the 1960s, tended to bring black people a modicum of socioeconomic advancement.

In the 1970s, for black Americans, it is clearly a question of survival.

JOHN A. WILLIAMS

The Man Who Cried I Am

WINTER. Harry Ames stared out the front window at the bleak street. How did he really feel about winter? He tried to bring his thoughts back to work, but he was waiting with foolish anticipation for Max to stop by. He usually did when he was finished with his rounds. Harry looked down at his shoes and they gave him an idea. He'd take all his shoes out of the closet and polish them. Charlotte's too. All the time he'd be thinking about the unfinished paragraph still in the typewriter. Yes, he would polish shoes. Charlotte would be proud of him.

When he had finished the shoes he returned to the typewriter, snappily pulled up his chair, reread the paragraph which paused at a comma. Listlessly his eyes drifted to the pencils on his table. Jesus! They needed sharpening. How come he hadn't seen that before? He took out the five-and-dime sharp-

very cautious, was the general tone of the responses of a score of the nation's black mayors to a ten-question *Ebony* poll dealing with the status, present and future, of black people in America. . . . As many as 14 of them generally agreed on a single question (that black people will be better off 20 years from now in the United States), but on another issue they were sharply divided (the possibility of black Americans being 'preventively detained' as Japanese-Americans were during World War II). . . . Mayor Carl Stokes of Cleveland predicted a much improved situation for blacks over the next two decades. Mayor Richard Hatcher of Gary foresaw black fortunes plummeting to 'a desperately low level,' unless some unlikely changes are made. The two men agreed that police state-type detention is a very real possibility for blacks and other groups of Americans."

ener and then, one by one, with the utmost care, he sharpened the pencils. Where the hell was Max?

The *New York Times Book Review* lay under some paper, and Harry picked that up and scanned it again, frowning at the picture of a young Negro novelist whom he had never heard of. It gave him a jolt that the review was what they call "a rave." He looked at the picture of the plump novelist. Fat face, eyes like slits. Hmmm. Have to get the book, see what this young boy is putting down. Could be a challenger to the Ames prestige. Them white folks: divide and conquer or, divide and pay less money for talent because everyone's scufflin' to get there and takin' pennies for the project.

Too bad, he continued thinking, that the artists were so terribly distrusted by the Party. The Party people never understood what was what about color in America and never understood painters and writers and musicians, only the workers, and as soon as the workers got theirs, to hell with everything. Labor (workers) was going to be one of the Fattest Cats, Harry guessed, when the smoke of the war finally blew over. It had had the foot way inside the door even when the war broke out. The worst kind of tyrant was the one who once had been a victim.

People Harry had known in the Party were complaining these days about the "Iron Curtain." That Churchill sure had a way of making names stick. Harry's friends complained, but rationalized that the Soviets would soon return to their own borders. They had to stay in those places to help those countries back on their feet, just the way the U. S. was doing. But Harry insisted that the Soviets were there to stay, in Hungary, Poland, Latvia, Estonia and all the other places. He didn't have to rationalize; he wasn't in the Party anymore. To hell with those fools who thought there would be a resurgence of power in America. Nowadays it looked like the Communists were coming back big, riding the coattails of the liberal organizations that were being born with the speed of rabbits fornicating against a stop watch. But there were already blazoning signs that communism was going to catch hell just as after War I when the heady atmosphere of liberalism was becoming just a bit too much to stomach. Americans were afraid to suck every drop of meaning from the words that had given their country birth in the first place.

New liberalism? Look at Max.

Max Reddick was trudging across the street head down.

Max Reddick, a good, competent writer, Harry thought. Ideas to be worked out, a style to be cleaned up and set free. Best reporter the *Democrat* ever had. New liberalism? Look at him. Poor black bastard. All those white boys he knew covering those big stories, that is, the ones who came back in one piece and got their jobs back, were they not liberals? Couldn't they get Max set in a job the way they helped set one another? Uh-uh. No. And Max is still hurting for that girl and a good job. Marriage. By now he may know what kind of marriage it would be. Nothing wrong with the girl, except that she can't do Max no good. All she sees is a house with a white picket fence, a refrigerator and a washing machine. Such a fine-looking broad, too. Jesus! That chick could be so great for Max.

Harry saw Max move out of sight, approaching the house. In a moment he would be ringing the doorbell. Harry was glad Charlotte had a little money. Not a hell of a lot, just enough so they could get by comfortably. And it was getting so that he was commanding larger and larger advances. There had been some talk too about adapting one of his books for the stage. Yeah, it was going all right, so far. But Charlotte. Getting to be a drag, demanding more and more time for other people, places and things. It was as though she wanted to rip him away from the typewriter for good. That was her rival, the machine. But what a rival! It wouldn't scream or fight back. Charlotte hated it all the more. On the spur of the moment, Harry decided to go down and meet Max and pick up the mail. Hastily, he rolled the paper in the typewriter so that only the very top of the page showed. Then he took some blank paper and placed it underneath his unfinished manuscript. With a little skip and a floundering left jab at an unseen enemy, Harry Ames moved to the stairway as the buzzer sounded.

Max Reddick was evil. He wanted to punch out every white face he saw. Evil was beyond anger; it was a constant state, the state of destruction, someone else's. Impatiently he rattled the doorknob. C'mon, Harry, you sonofabitch; let me in from these white folks' streets. He glanced behind him. February. Cold, New York cold where the saline air punched holes in the snow and made it melt faster. Today had been payday for Max. For weeks he had been kept dangling, waiting for the final word to come in on several job applications with newspapers and magazines. He wouldn't have been kept dangling at all had it not been for Kermit Shea.

They had been at Western Reserve at the same time, had met at political meetings often enough to nod to each other, nothing more. Then they had met again while covering the Boatwright case and Max learned that Shea worked for the *Telegram*. They had had coffee and drinks together a few times, again, until Max walked into the *Telegram* office to apply for a job and found Shea in charge of Cityside news. Max knew as he filled out his application that Shea was embarrassed. To hell with him. Shea told him the *Telegram* was full up, but expecting departures momentarily, then steered Max to a number of other editors. The interviews were always the same: colorful newsmen's jabber, changing constantly in order to avoid falling into general use by the public. These were followed by the application-form ritual and, finally (sometimes days later, sometimes at once), the leaning back in the chair, man to man ("You and I are above all this, but the publisher ain't and he's the man who lays out the shekels, right? [The implication being that the Jews were driving the WASPs out of newspaper publishing] but call me next month, right, Max?") And then the handshakes that said that the time wasn't right, but when it is, Max, boy will we call you!

Shock, gracious, pain-absorbing shock came at once and lessened the hurt and surprise. Max, reacting normally for the moment, lit another cigarette, picked through and carefully read Enzkwu's papers.

Yes, there was explosive material here. Enough to unsettle every capital city in the West; enough to force the Africans to cut ties with Europe at once and worry about the consequences later; enough to send black Brazilians surging out of their *favelas* and *barrios* to inundate the sleek beach places of the whites. Wherever white men had been involved with black men, Enzkwu's photostats disclosed a clear and unrelenting danger. Recorded in cold black type were lists of statesmen and diplomats, the records of their deeds, what they planned to do, when, where, why and to whom. The list of people dead, Max knew, and therefore murdered, if their names appeared in Enzkwu's papers, included the residents of four continents. African airfields equipped for the handling of jets and props, along with radio and power stations, the number of men in the army of each country, plus a military critique of those armies, were set down here.

Now Max's hand held another numbered packet, but above the number were the words: THE UNITED STATES OF AMERICA—KING ALFRED. Slowly, he pulled out the sheaf of photostats. So, this is King Alfred, Alfred the Great. He mused, Why is it called King Alfred? Then he saw the answer footnoted at the bottom of the first page.

KING ALFRED*

In the event of widespread and continuing coordinated racial disturbances in the United States, KING ALFRED, at the discretion of the President, is to be put into action immediately.

PARTICIPATING FEDERAL AGENCIES

National Security Council
Central Intelligence Agency
Federal Bureau of Investigation

Department of Justice
Department of Defense
Department of Interior

PARTICIPATING STATE AGENCIES

(Under Federal Jurisdiction)

National Guard Units

State Police

* 849–899 (?) King of England; directed translation from the Latin of the *Anglo-Saxon Chronicle*.

PARTICIPATING LOCAL AGENCIES

(Under Federal Jurisdiction)

City Police | County Police

Even before 1954, when the Supreme Court of the United States of America declared unconstitutional separate educational and recreational facilities, racial unrest and discord had become very nearly a part of the American way of life. But that way of life was repugnant to most Americans. Since 1954, however, that unrest and discord have broken out into widespread violence which increasingly have placed the peace and stability of the nation in dire jeopardy. This violence has resulted in loss of life, limb and property, and has cost the taxpayers of this nation billions of dollars. And the end is not yet in sight. This same violence has raised the tremendously grave question as to whether the races can ever live in peace with each other. Each passing month has brought new intelligence that, despite new laws passed to alleviate the condition of the Minority, the Minority still is not satisfied. Demonstrations and rioting have become a part of the familiar scene. Troops have been called out in city after city across the land, and our image as a world leader severely damaged. Our enemies press closer, seeking the advantage, possibly at a time during one of these outbreaks of violence. The Minority has adopted an almost military posture to gain its objectives, which are not clear to most Americans. It is expected, therefore, that, when those objectives are denied the Minority, racial war must be considered inevitable. When that Emergency comes, we must expect the total involvement of all 22 million members of the Minority, men, women and children, for once this project is launched, its goal is to terminate, once and for all, the Minority threat to the whole of the American society, and, indeed, the Free World.

Chairman, National Security Council

Preliminary Memo: Department of Interior

Under KING ALFRED, the nation has been divided into 10 Regions (See accompanying map).

In case of Emergency, Minority members will be evacuated from the cities by federalized national guard units, local and state police and, if necessary, by units of the Regular Armed Forces, using public and military transportation, and detained in nearby military installations until a further course of action has been decided.

1—Capital region
2—Northeast region
3—Southeast region
4—Great Lakes region
5—South central region

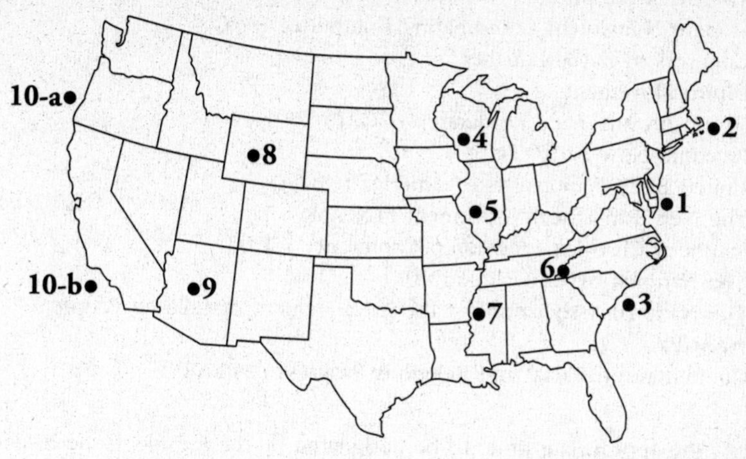

6—Deep South region
7—Deep South region II
8—Great Plains, Rocky Mountain region
9—Southwest region
10—a, b—West Coast region

No attempt will be made to seal off the Canadian and Mexican borders.

Secretary, Department of Interior

Combined Memo: Department of Justice
Federal Bureau of Investigation
Central Intelligence Agency

There are 12 major Minority organizations and all are familiar to nil-lion. Dossiers have been compiled on the leaders of the organizations, and can be studied in Washington. The material contained in many of the dossiers, and our threat to reveal that material, has considerably held in check the activities of some of the leaders. Leaders who do not have such usable material in their dossiers have been approached to take Government posts, mostly as ambassadors and primarily in African countries. The promise of these positions also has materially contributed to a temporary slow-down of Minority activities. However, we do not expect these slow-downs to be of long duration, because there are always new and dissident elements joining these organizations, with the potential power to replace the old leaders. All organizations and their leaders are under constant, 24-hour surveillance. The organizations are:

1—The Black Muslims
2—Student Nonviolent Coordinating Committee (SNCC)
3—Congress of Racial Equality
4—Uhuru Movement
5—Group on Advanced Leadership (GOAL)
6—Freedom Now Party (FNP)
7—United Black Nationalists of America (UBNA)
8—The New Pan-African Movement (TNPAM)
9—Southern Christian Leadership Conference (SCLC)
10—The National Urban League (NUL)
11—The National Association for the Advancement of Colored People (NAACP)
12—Committee on Racial and Religious Progress (CORARP)

NOTE: At the appropriate time, to be designated by the President, the leaders of some of these organizations are to be detained ONLY WHEN IT IS CLEAR THAT THEY CANNOT PREVENT THE EMERGENCY, working with local public officials during the first critical hours. All other leaders are to be detained at once. Compiled lists of Minority leaders have been readied at the National Data Computer Center. It is necessary to use the Minority leaders designated by the President in much the same manner in which we use Minority members who are agents with CENTRAL and FEDERAL, and we cannot, until there is no alternative, reveal KING ALFRED in all its aspects. Minority members of Congress will be unseated at once. This move is not without precedent in American history.

Attorney General

Preliminary Memo: Department of Defense
This memo is being submitted in lieu of a full report from the Joint Chiefs of Staff. That report is now in preparation. There will be many cities where the Minority will be able to put into the street a superior number of people with a desperate and dangerous will. He will be a formidable enemy, for he is bound to the Continent by heritage and knows that political asylum will not be available to him in other countries. The greatest concentration of the Minority is in the Deep South, the Eastern seaboard, the Great Lakes region and the West Coast. While the national population exceeds that of the Minority by more than ten times, we must realistically take into account the following:

1—An estimated 40-50 percent of the white population will not, for various reasons, engage the Minority during an Emergency.
2—American Armed Forces are spread around the world. A breakout of war abroad means fewer troops at home to handle the Emergency.
3—Local law enforcement officials must contain the Emergency until help arrives, though it may mean fighting a superior force. New York City, for

example, has a 25,000-man police force, but there are about one million Minority members in the city.

We are confident that the Minority could hold any city it took for only a few hours. The lack of weapons, facilities, logistics—all put the Minority at a final disadvantage.

Since the Korean War, this Department has shifted Minority members of the Armed Forced to areas where combat is most likely to occur, with the aim of eliminating, through combat, as many combat-trained Minority servicemen as possible. Today the ratio of Minority member combat deaths in Vietnam, where they are serving as "advisers," is twice as high as the Minority population ratio to the rest of America. Below is the timetable for King Alfred as tentatively suggested by the JCS who recommend that the operation be made over a period of eight hours:

1. Local police and Minority leaders in action to head off the Emergency.
2. Countdown to eight hours begins at the moment the President determines the Emergency to be:
   A. National
   B. Coordinated
   C. Of Long Duration — 8th Hour
3. County police join local police. — 7th
4. State police join county and local forces. — 6th
5. Federal marshals join state, county and local forces. — 5th
6. National Guards federalized, held in readiness. — 4th
7. Regular Armed Forces alerted, take up positions; Minority troops divided and detained, along with all white sympathizers, under guard. — 3rd
8. All Minority leaders, national and local, detained. — 2nd
9. President addresses Minority on radio-television, gives it one hour to end the Emergency. — 1st
10. All units under regional commands into the Emergency. — 0

'O' Committee Report:
Survey shows that, during a six-year period, Production created 9,000,000 objects, or 1,500,000 each year. Production could not dispose of the containers, which proved a bottleneck. However, that was almost 20 years ago. We suggest that vaporization techniques be employed to overcome the Production problems inherent in King Alfred.

Secretary of Defense

Max smoked and read, read and smoked until his mouth began to taste like wool and when he finally pushed King Alfred from him, he felt exhausted, as if he had been running beneath a gigantic, unblinking eye that had watched his every move and determined just when movement should stop.

Yeah. Jaja had done his work well. He could have embarrassed and startled a lot of people, blacks and whites, but you have to weed a garden for the flowers to grow. Those dossiers, he knew pretty much what was in them. Well, he had known it; there are always dues to pay. A smoldering anger coursed through Max's stomach. Yes, those leaders clearly had left themselves vulnerable, vulnerable for the hunters who, for a generation and more, sought Communists with such vehemence that they skillfully obscured the growth and power of fascism. How black skins stirred fascists! Perhaps because it was the most identifiable kind of skin; you didn't have to wait until you got up close to see whether a nose was hooked or not; a black skin you could see for a block away. And in the face of the revelations in Jaja's papers, Harry and Jaja's both, made giddy by the presence of that massive, killing evil, had dared to toy with it; had dared to set their pitiable little egos down before that hideous juggernaut. And they had hoped to live. That hope had revealed their inability to accurately measure what was readily measurable. Jaja's for greed, and you, Harry, it's just starting to come. They didn't let their minds go out.

They did not let their minds go out to picture the instability of what seems static; they did not see planets colliding with each other, or picture Sahara or Kalahari as lakes, or picture plains where the Alps, Andes and Rockies now stand; nor did they picture oceans above the sands that crunch softly beneath the feet in the sweet-smelling paths of the Maine or Vermont woods. No, they did not picture the extinction of man and beast and places. If they had, *then* they could see four million dead because they themselves, like the later nine million, refused to see evil rearing up before them, quite discernible, quite measurable. Man is nature, nature man, and all crude and raw, stinking, vicious, evil. And holding that evil lightly because the collective mind refuses to recall the sprint of mountains, the vault of seas and, of course, beside that, the puny murder of millions.

It is still eat, drink and be murderous, for tomorrow I may be among the murdered.

WILLIAM H. GRIER and PRICE M. COBBS

Black Rage

History may well show that of all the men who lived during our fateful century none illustrated the breadth or the grand potential of man so magnificently as did Malcolm X. If, in future chronicles, America is regarded as the major nation of our day, and the rise of darker people from bondage as the major event, then no figure has appeared thus far who captures the spirit of our times as does Malcolm.

Malcolm is an authentic hero, indeed the only universal black hero. In his unrelenting opposition to the viciousness in America, he fired the imagination of black men all over the world.

If this black nobleman is a hero to black people in the United States and if his life reflects their aspirations, there can be no doubt of the universality of black rage.

Malcolm responded to his position in his world and to his blackness in the manner of so many black boys. He turned to crime. He was saved by a religious sect given to a strange, unhistorical explanation of the origin of black people and even stranger solutions to their problems. He rose to power in that group and outgrew it.

Feeding on his own strength, growing in response to his own commands, limited by no creed, he became a citizen of the world and an advocate of all oppressed people no matter their color or belief. Anticipating his death by an assassin, he distilled, in a book, the essence of his genius, his life. His autobiography thus is a legacy and, together with his speeches, illustrates the thrusting growth of the man—his evolution, rapid, propulsive, toward the man he might have been had he lived.

The essence of Malcolm X was growth, change, and a seeking after truth.

Alarmed white people saw him first as an eccentric and later as a dangerous radical—a revolutionary without troops who threatened to stir black people to riot and civil disobedience. Publicly, they treated him as a joke; privately, they were afraid of him.

After his death he was recognized by black people as the "black shining prince" and recordings of his speeches became treasured things. His autobiography was studied, his life marveled at. Out of this belated admiration came the philosophical basis for black activism and indeed the thrust of Black Power itself, away from integration and civil rights and into the "black bag."

Unlike Malcolm, however, the philosophical underpinnings of the new black militancy were static. They remained encased within the ideas of revolution and black nationhood, ideas Malcolm had outgrown by the time of his death. His stature has made even his earliest statements gospel and men now find themselves willing to die for words which in retrospect are only milestones in the growth of a fantastic man.

Many black men who today preach blackness seem headed blindly toward self-destruction, uncritical of anything "black" and damning the white man for diabolical wickedness. For a philosophical base they have turned to the words of Malcolm's youth.

This perversion of Malcolm's intellectual position will not, we submit, be held against him by history.

Malcolm's meaning for us lies in his fearless demand for truth and his evolution from a petty criminal to an international statesman—accomplished by a black man against odds of terrible magnitude—in America. His message was his life, not his words, and Malcolm knew it.

Black Power activism—thrust by default temporarily at the head of a powerful movement—is a conception that contributes in a significant way to the strength and unity of that movement but is unable to provide the mature vision for the mighty works ahead. It will pass and leave black people in this country prouder, stronger, more determined, but in need of grander princes with clearer vision.

We believe that the black masses will rise with a simple and eloquent demand to which new leaders must give tongue. They will say to America simply:

"GET OFF OUR BACKS!"

The problem will be so simply defined.

What is the problem?

The white man has crushed all but the life from blacks from the time they came to these shores to this very day.

What is the solution?

Get off their backs.

How?

By simply doing it—now.

This is no oversimplification. Greater changes than this in the relations of peoples have taken place before. The nation would benefit tremendously. Such a change might bring about a closer examination of our relations with foreign countries, a reconsideration of economic policies, and a reexamination if not a redefinition of nationhood. It might in fact be the only change which can prevent a degenerative decline from a powerful nation to a feeble, third-class, ex-colonialist country existing at the indulgence of stronger powers.

In spite of the profound shifts in power throughout the world in the past thirty years, the United States seems to have a domestic objective of "business as usual," with no change needed or in fact wanted.

All the nasty problems are overseas. At home the search is for bigger profits and smaller costs, better education and lower taxes, more vacation and less work, more for me and less for you. Problems at home are to be talked away, reasoned into nonexistence, and put to one side while we continue the great American game of greed.

There is, however, an inevitability built into the natural order of things. Cause and effect are in fact joined, and if you build a sufficient cause then not all the talk or all the tears in God's creation can prevent the effect from presenting itself one morning as the now ripened fruit of your labors.

America began building a cause when black men were first sold into bondage. When the first black mother killed her newborn rather than have him grow into a slave. When the first black man slew himself rather than submit to an organized system of man's feeding upon another's flesh. America had well begun a cause when all the rebels were either slain or broken and the nation set to the task of refining the system of slavery so that the maximum labor might be extracted from it.

The system achieved such refinement that the capital loss involved when a slave woman aborted could be set against the gain to be expected from forcing her into brutish labor while she was with child.

America began building a potent cause in its infancy as a nation.

It developed a way of life, an American ethos, a national life style which included the assumption that blacks are inferior and were born to hew wood and draw water. Newcomers to this land (if white) were immediately made to feel welcome and, among the bounty available, were given blacks to feel superior to. They were required to despise and depreciate them, abuse and exploit them, and one can only imagine how munificent this land must have seemed to the European—a land with built-in scapegoats.

The hatred of blacks has been so deeply bound up with being an American that it has been one of the first things new Americans learn and one of the last things old Americans forget. Such feelings have been elevated to a position of national character, so that individuals now no longer feel personal guilt or responsibility for the oppression of black people. The nation has incorporated this oppression into itself in the form of folkways and storied traditions, leaving the individual free to shrug his shoulders and say only: "That's our way of life."

This way of life is a heavy debt indeed, and one trembles for the debtor when payment comes due.

America has waxed rich and powerful in large measure on the backs of black laborers. It has become a violent, pitiless nation, hard and calculating, whose moments of generosity are only brief intervals in a ferocious narrative of life, bearing a ferocity and an aggression so strange in this tiny world where men die if they do not live together.

With the passing of the need for black laborers, black people have become useless; they are a drug on the market. There are not enough menial jobs. They live in a nation which has evolved a work force of skilled and semi-skilled workmen. A nation which chooses simultaneously to exclude all black men from this favored labor force and to deny them the one thing America has offered every other group—unlimited growth with a ceiling set only by one's native gifts.

The facts, however, obfuscated, are simple. Since the demise of slavery black people have been expendable in a cruel and impatient land. The damage done to black people has been beyond reckoning. Only now are we beginning to sense the bridle placed on black children by a nation which does not want them to grow into mature human beings.

The most idealistic social reformer of our time, Martin Luther King, was not slain by one man; his murder grew out of that large body of violent bigotry America has always nurtured—that body of thinking which screams for the blood of the radical, or the conservative, or the villain, or the saint. To the extent that he stood in the way of bigotry, his life was in jeopardy, his saintly persuasion notwithstanding. To the extent that he was black and was calling America to account, his days were numbered by the nation he sought to save.

Men and women, even children, have been slain for no other earthly reason than their blackness. Property and goods have been stolen and the victims then harried and punished for their poverty. But such viciousness can at least be measured or counted.

Black men, however, have been so hurt in their manhood that they are now unsure and uneasy as they teach their sons to be men. Women have been so humiliated and used that they may regard womanhood as a curse and flee from it. Such pain, so deep, and such real jeopardy, that the fundamental protective function of the family has been denied. These injuries we have no way to measure.

Black men have stood so long in such peculiar jeopardy in America that a *black norm* has developed—a suspiciousness of one's environment which is necessary for survival. Black people, to a degree that approaches paranoia, must be ever alert to danger from their white fellow citizens. It is a cultural phenomenon peculiar to black Americans. And it is a posture so close to paranoid thinking that the mental disorder into which black people most frequently fall is paranoid psychosis.

Can we say that white men have driven black men mad?

> An educated black woman had worked in an integrated setting for fifteen years. Compliant and deferential, she had earned promotions

and pay increases by hard work and excellence. At no time had she been involved in black activism, and her only participation in the movement had been a yearly contribution to the N.A.A.C.P.

During a lull in the racial turmoil she sought psychiatric treatment. She explained that she had lately become alarmed at waves of rage that swept over her as she talked to white people or at times even as she looked at them. In view of her past history of compliance and passivity, she felt that something was wrong with her. If her controls slipped she might embarrass herself or lose her job.

A black man, a professional, had been a "nice guy" all his life. He was a hard-working non-militant who avoided discussions of race with his white colleagues. He smiled if their comments were harsh and remained unresponsive to racist statements. Lately he has experienced almost uncontrollable anger toward his white co-workers, and although he still manages to keep his feelings to himself, he confides that blacks and whites have been lying to each other. There is hatred and violence between them and he feels trapped. He too fears for himself if his controls should slip.

If these educated recipients of the white man's bounty find it hard to control their rage, what of their less fortunate kinsman who has less to protect, less to lose, and more scars to show for his journey in this land?

The tone of the preceding chapters has been mournful, painful, desolate, as we have described the psychological consequences of white oppression of blacks. The centuries of senseless cruelty and the permeation of the black man's character with the conviction of his own hatefulness and inferiority tell a sorry tale.

This dismal tone has been deliberate. It has been an attempt to evoke a certain quality of depression and hopelessness in the reader and to stir these feelings. These are the most common feelings tasted by black people in America.

The horror carries the endorsement of centuries and the entire lifespan of a nation. It is a way of life which reaches back to the beginnings of recorded time. And all the bestiality, wherever it occurs and however long it has been happening, is narrowed, focused, and refined to shine into a black child's eyes when first he views his world. All that has ever happened to black men and women he sees in the victims closest to him, his parents.

A life is an eternity and throughout all that eternity a black child has breathed the foul air of cruelty. He has grown up to find that his spirit was crushed before he knew there was need of it. His ambitions, even in their forming, showed him to have set his hand against his own. This is the desolation of black life in America.

Depression and grief are hatred turned on the self. It is instructive to pursue the relevance of this truth to the condition of black Americans.

Black people have shown a genius for surviving under the most deadly circumstances. They have survived because of their close attention to reality. A black dreamer would have a short life in Mississippi. They are of necessity bound to reality, chained to the facts of the times; historically the penalty for misjudging a situation involving white men has been death. The preoccupation with religion has been a willing adoption of fantasy to prod an otherwise reluctant mind to face another day.

We will even play tricks on ourselves if it helps us stay alive.

The psychological devices used to survive are reminiscent of the years of slavery, and it is no coincidence. The same devices are used because black men face the same danger now as then.

The grief and depression caused by the condition of black men in America is an unpopular reality to the sufferers. They would rather see themselves in a more heroic posture and chide a disconsolate brother. They would like to point to their achievements (which in fact have been staggering); they would rather point to virtue (which has been shown in magnificent form by some blacks); they would point to bravery, fidelity, prudence, brilliance, creativity, all of which dark men have shown in abundance. But the overriding experience of the black American has been grief and sorrow and no man can change that fact.

His grief has been realistic and appropriate. What people have so earned a period of mourning?

We want to emphasize yet again the depth of the grief for slain sons and ravished daughters, how deep and lingering it is.

If the depth of this sorrow is felt, we can then consider what can be made of this emotion.

As grief lifts and the sufferer moves toward health, the hatred he had turned on himself is redirected toward his tormentors, and the fury of his attack on the one who caused him pain is in direct proportion to the depth of his grief. When the mourner lashes out in anger, it is a relief to those who love him, for they know he has now returned to health.

Observe that the amount of rage the oppressed turns on his tormentor is a direct function of the depth of his grief, and consider the intensity of black men's grief.

Slip for a moment into the soul of a black girl whose womanhood is blighted, not because she is ugly, but because she is black and by definition all blacks are ugly.

Become for a moment a black citizen of Birmingham, Alabama, and try to understand his grief and dismay when innocent children are slain while they worship, for no other reason than that they are black.

Imagine how an impoverished mother feels as she watches the light of creativity snuffed out in her children by schools which dull the mind and environs which rot the soul.

For a moment make yourself the black father whose son went innocently to war and there was slain—for whom, for what?

For a moment be any black person, anywhere, and you will feel the waves of hopelessness that engulfed black men and women when Martin Luther King was murdered. All black people understood the tide of anarchy that followed his death.

It is the transformation of *this* quantum of grief into aggression of which we now speak. As a sapling bent low stores energy for a violent backswing, blacks bent double by oppression have stored energy which will be released in the form of rage—black rage, apocalyptic and final.

White Americans have developed a high skill in the art of misunderstanding black people. It must have seemed to slaveholders that slavery would last through all eternity, for surely their misunderstanding of black bondsmen suggested it. If the slaves were eventually to be released from bondage, what could be the purpose of creating the fiction of their subhumanity?

It must have seemed to white men during the period 1865 to 1945 that black men would always be a passive, compliant lot. If not, why would they have stoked the flames of hatred with such deliberately barbarous treatment?

White Americans today deal with "racial incidents" from summer to summer as if such minor turbulence will always remain minor and one need only keep the blacks busy till fall to have made it through another troubled season.

Today it is the young men who are fighting the battles, and, for now, their elders, though they have given their approval, have not joined in. The time seems near, however, for the full range of the black masses to put down the broom and buckle on the sword. And it grows nearer day by day. Now we see skirmishes, sputtering erratically, evidence if you will that the young men are in a warlike mood. But evidence as well that the elders are watching closely and may soon join the battle.

Even these minor flurries have alarmed the country and have resulted in a spate of generally senseless programs designed to give *temporary summer jobs!!* More interesting in its long-range prospects has been the apparent eagerness to draft black men for military service. If in fact this is a deliberate design to place black men in uniform in order to get them off the street, it may be the most curious "instant cure" for a serious disease this nation has yet attempted. Young black men are learning the most modern techniques for killing—techniques which may be used against *any* enemy.

But it is all speculation. The issue finally rests with the black masses. When the servile men and women stand up, we had all better duck.

We should ask what is likely to galvanize the masses into aggression against the whites.

> Will it be some grotesque atrocity against black people which at last causes one-tenth of the nation to rise up in indignation and crush the monstrosity?
>
> Will it be the example of black people outside the United States who have gained dignity through their own liberation movement?
>
> Will it be by the heroic action of a small group of blacks which by its wisdom and courage commands action in a way that cannot be denied?
>
> Or will it be by blacks, finally and in an unpredictable way, simply getting fed up with the bumbling stupid racism of this country? Fired not so much by any one incident as by the gradual accretion of stupidity into fixtures of national policy.

All are possible, or any one, or something yet unthought. It seems certain only that on the course the nation now is headed it will happen.

One might consider the possibility that, if the national direction remains unchanged, such a conflagration simply might *not* come about. Might not black people remain where they are, as they did for a hundred years during slavery?

Such seems truly inconceivable. Not because blacks are so naturally warlike or rebellious, but because they are filled with such grief, such sorrow, such bitterness, and such hatred. It seems now delicately poised, not yet risen to the flash point, but rising rapidly nonetheless. No matter what repressive measures are invoked against the blacks, they will never swallow their rage and go back to blind hopelessness.

If existing oppressions and humiliating disenfranchisements are to be lifted, they will have to be lifted most speedily, or catastrophe will follow.

For there are no more psychological tricks blacks can play upon themselves to make it possible to exist in dreadful circumstances. No more lies can they tell themselves. No more dreams to fix on. No more opiates to dull the pain. No more patience. No more thought. No more reason. Only a welling tide risen out of all those terrible years of grief, now a tidal wave of fury and rage, and all black, black as night.

RICHARD MAJORS

Cool Pose: The Proud Signature of Black Survival

Just when it seemed that we black males were beginning to recover from past injustices inflicted by the dominant white society, we find once again that we are being revisited in a similar vein. President Reagan's de-emphasis of civil rights, affirmative action legislation and social services programs; the rise of black neoconservatives and certain black feminist groups; harshly critical media events on television (e.g., the CBS documentary "The Vanishing Family—Crisis in Black America") and in films (e.g., *The Color Purple*); and the omnipresent problems of unemployment and inadequate health care, housing, and education—all have helped to shape a negative political and social climate toward black men. For many black men this period represents a *New Black Nadir*, or lowest point, and time of deepest depression.

Black people in general, and the black man in particular, look out on a world that does not positively reflect their image. Black men learned long ago that the classic American virtues of thrift, perseverance and hard work would not give us the tangible rewards that accrue to most members of the dominant society. We learned early that we would not be Captains of Industry or builders of engineering wonders. Instead, we channeled our creative energies into construction of a symbolic universe. Therefore we adopted unique poses and postures to offset the externally imposed "zero" image. Because black men were denied access to the dominant culture's acceptable avenues of expression, we created a form of self-expression—the "Cool Pose."[1-3] Cool Pose is a term that represents a variety of attitudes and actions that serve the black man as mechanisms for survival, defense and social competence. These attitudes and actions are performed using characterizations and roles as facades and shields.

COOL CULTURE

Historically, coolness was central to the culture of many ancient African civilizations. The Yorubas of Western Nigeria (900 B.C. to 200 A.D.) are cited as an example of an African civilization where cool was integrated into the social fabric of the community.[4] Uses of cool ranged from the way a young man carried himself before his peers to the way he impressed his elders during the initiation ritual. Coolness helped to build character and pride for individuals in such groups and is regarded as a precolonial cultural adaptation. With the advent of the modern African slave trade, cool became detached from its indigenous cultural setting and emerged equally as a survival mechanism.

Where the European saw America as the promised land, the African saw it as the land of oppression. Today, reminders of Black America's oppressive past continue in the form of chronic underemployment, inadequate housing, inferior schools, and poor health care. Because of these conditions many black men have become frustrated, angry, confused and impatient.

To help ease the pain associated with these conditions, black men have taken to alcoholism, drug abuse, homicide, and suicide. In learning to mistrust the words and actions of dominant white people, black males have learned to make great use of "poses" and "postures" which connote control, toughness, and detachment. All these forms arise from the mistrust that the black males feel towards the dominant society.

For these black males, particular poses and postures show the white man that although you may have tried to hurt me time and time again, I can take it (and if I am hurting or weak, I'll never let you know). They are saying loud and clear to the white establishment, "I am strong, full of pride, and a survivor." Accordingly, any failures in the real world become the black man's secret.

THE EXPRESSIVE LIFE STYLE

On the other hand, those poses and postures that have an expressive quality of nature have become known in the literature as the "expressive life style."[5] The expressive life style is a way in which the black male can act cool by actively displaying particular performances that emphasize creative expression. Thus, while black people historically have been forced into conciliatory and often demeaning positions in American culture, there is nothing conciliatory about the expressive life style.

This dynamic vitality will not be denied even in limited stereotypical roles—as demonstrated by Hattie McDaniel, the maid in *Gone With the Wind* or Bill "Bojangles" Robinson as the affable servant in the Shirley Temple movies. This abiding need for creative self-expression knows no bounds and asserts itself whether on the basketball court or in dancing. We can see it in black athletes—with their stylish dunking of the basketball, their spontaneous dancing in the end zone, and their different styles of handshakes (e.g., "high fives")—and in black entertainers with their various choreographed "cool" dance steps. These are just a few examples of black individuals in their professions who epitomize this creative expression. The expressive life style is a dynamic—not a static—art form, and new aesthetic forms are always evolving (e.g., "rap-talking" and breakdancing). The expressive life style, then, is the passion that invigorates the demeaning life of blacks in White America. It is a dynamic vitality that transforms the mundane into the sublime and makes the routine spectacular.

A CULTURAL SIGNATURE

Cool Pose, manifested by the expressive life style, is also an aggressive assertion of masculinity. It emphatically says "white man, this is my turf. You can't match me here." Though he may be impotent in the political and corporate world, the black man demonstrates his potency in athletic competition, entertainment and the pulpit with a verve that borders on the spectacular. Through the virtuosity of a performance, he tips the socially imbalanced scales in his favor. "See me, touch me, hear me, but, white man, you can't copy me." This is the subliminal message which black males signify in their oftentimes flamboyant performance. Cool Pose, then, becomes the cultural signature for such black males.

Being cool is a unique response to adverse social, political and economic conditions. Cool provides control, inner strength, stability and confidence. Being cool, illustrated in its various poses and postures, becomes a very powerful and necessary tool in the black man's constant fight for his soul. The poses and postures of cool guard, preserve and protect his pride, dignity and respect to such an extent that the black male is willing to risk a great deal for it. One black man said it well: "The white man may control everything about me—that is, except my pride and dignity. That he can't have. That is mine and mine alone."

THE COST

Cool Pose, however, is not without its price. Many black males fail to discriminate the appropriate uses of Cool Pose and act cool much of the time, without regard to time or space.[6] Needless to say, this can cause severe problems. In many situations a black man won't allow himself to express or show any form of weakness or fear or other feelings and emotions. He assumes a facade of strength, held at all costs, rather than "blow his front," and thus his cool. Perhaps black men have become so conditioned to keeping up their guard against oppression from the dominant white society that this particular attitude and behavior represent for them their best safeguard against further mental or physical abuse. However, this same behavior makes it very difficult for these males to let their guard down and show affection, even for people that they actually care about or for people that may really care about them (e.g., girlfriends, wives, mothers, fathers, "good" friends, etc.).

When the art of being cool is used to put cool behaviors ahead of emotions or needs, the results of such repression of feelings can be frustration. Such frustrations sometimes cause aggression which often is taken out on those individuals closest to such men—other black people. It is sadly ironic, then, that the same elements of cool that allow for survival in the larger society may hurt black people by contributing to one of the more complex problems facing black people today—black-on-black crime.

Further, while Cool Pose enables black males to maintain stability in the face of white power, it may through inappropriate use render many of them unable to move with the mainstream or evolve in healthy ways. When misused, cool can suppress the motivation to learn, accept or become exposed to stimuli, cultural norms, aesthetics, mannerisms, values, etiquette, information or networks that could help them overcome problems caused by white racism. Finally, in a society which has as its credo, "A man's home is his castle," it is ironic that the masses of black men have no castle to protect. Their minds have become their psychological castle, defended by impenetrable cool. Thus, Cool Pose is the bittersweet symbol of a socially disesteemed group that shouts, "We are," in face of a hostile and indifferent world that everywhere screams, "You ain't."

COOL AND THE BLACK PSYCHE

To be fully grasped, Cool Pose must be recognized as having gained ideological consensus in the black community. It is not only a quantitatively measured "social reality" but a series of equally "real" rituals of socialization. It is a comprehensive, officially endorsed cultural myth that became entrenched in the black psyche with the beginning of the slave experience. This phenomenon has cut across all socioeconomic groups in the black community, as black men fight to preserve their dignity, pride, respect and masculinity with the attitudes and behaviors of Cool Pose. Cool Pose represents a fundamental structuring of the psyche of the black male and is manifested in some way or another in the daily activities and recreational habits of most black males. There are few other social or psychological constructs that have shaped, directed or controlled the black male to the extent that the various forms of coolness have. It is surprising, then, that for a concept that has the potential to explain problems in black male and black female relationships, black-on-black crime, and black-on-black pregnancies, there is such limited research on this subject.

In the final analysis, Cool Pose may represent the most important yet least researched area with the potential to enhance our understanding and study of black behavior today.

NOTES

1. Majors, R. G., & Nikelly, A. G., "Serving the Black Minority: A New Direction for Psychotherapy." *J. for Non-white Concerns*, 11:142–151 (1983).

2. Majors, R. G., "The Effects of 'Cool Pose': What Being Cool Means." *Griot*, pp. 4–5 (Spring, 1985).

3. Nikelly, A. G., & Majors, R. G. "Techniques for Counseling Black Students," *Techniques: J. Remedial Educ. & Counseling*, 2:48–54 (1986).

4. Thompson, Robert F., *Flash of the Spirit*. (New York: Random House, 1983).

5. Rainwater, L., *Behind Ghetto Walls*. (Chicago: Aldine, 1970).

6. Majors, R. G., "Cool Pose: A New Hypothesis in Understanding Anti-Social Behavior in Lower SES Black Males," unpublished manuscript.

JESSE JACKSON

Keep Hope Alive

Speech to the 1988 Democratic National Convention

Atlanta, Georgia, July 19, 1988

Tonight we pause and give praise and honor to God for being good enough to allow us to be at this place at this time. When I look out at this convention, I see the face of America, red, yellow, brown, black and white, we're all precious in God's sight—the real rainbow coalition. All of us, all of us who are here think that we are seated. But really we're standing on someone's shoulders. Ladies and gentlemen, Mrs. Rosa Parks.

The mother of the civil rights movement.

I want to express my deep love and appreciation for the support my family has given me over these past months. They have endured pain, anxiety, threat and fear. But they have been strengthened and made secure by a faith in God, in America and in you. Your love has protected us and made us strong.

To my wife Jackie, the foundation of our family; to our five children whom you met tonight; to my mother, Mrs. Helen Jackson, who is present tonight; and to my grandmother, Mrs. Matilda Burns; my brother Chuck and his family; my mother-in-law Mrs. Gertrude Brown, who just last month at age 61 graduated from Hampton Institute, a marvelous achievement; I offer my appreciation to Mayor Andrew Young who has provided such gracious hospitality to all of us this week.

And a special salute to President Jimmy Carter. President Carter restored honor to the White House after Watergate. He gave many of us a special opportunity to grow. For his kind words, for his unwavering commitment to peace in the world, and the voters that came from his family, every member of his family, led by Billy and Amy, I offer him my special thanks, special thanks to the Carter family.

My right and privilege to stand here before you has been won—in my lifetime—by the blood and sweat of the innocent.

Twenty-four years ago, the late Fanny Lou Hamer and Aaron Henry—who sits here tonight from Mississippi—were locked out on the streets of Atlantic City, the heads of the Mississippi Freedom Democratic Party. But tonight, an African American and a white delegation from Mississippi is headed by Ed Cole, an African American, from Mississippi, 24 years later.

Many were lost in the struggle for the right to vote. Jimmy Lee Jackson, a young student, gave his life. Viola Luizzo, a white mother from Detroit, called nigger lover, had her brains blown out at point-blank range.

Schwerner, Goodman and Cheney—two Jews and an African American—found in a common grave, bodies riddled with bullets in Mississippi. The four darling little girls in church in Birmingham, Alabama. They died that we may have a right to live.

Dr. Martin Luther King, Jr. lies only a few miles from us tonight. Tonight he must feel good as he looks down upon us. We sit here together, a rainbow, a coalition—the sons and daughters of slaves sitting together around a common table, to decide the direction of our party and our country. His heart must be full tonight.

As a testament to the struggles of those who have gone before; as a legacy for those who will come after; as a tribute to the endurance, the patience, the courage of our forefathers and mothers; as an assurance that their prayers are being answered, their work has not been in vain, and hope is eternal—tomorrow night my name will go into nomination for the Presidency of the United States of America.

We meet tonight at a crossroads, a point of decision. Shall we expand, be inclusive, or suffer division and impotence?

We come to Atlanta, the cradle of the Old South, the crucible of the New South. Tonight there is a sense of celebration because we are moved, fundamentally moved, from racial battlegrounds by law, to economic common ground. Tomorrow we will challenge to move to higher ground.

Common ground!

Think of Jerusalem—the intersection where many trails met. A small village that became the birthplace for three great religions—Judaism, Christianity and Islam. Why was this village so blessed? Because it provided a crossroads where different people met, different cultures and different civilizations could meet and find common ground.

When people come together, flowers always flourish and the air is rich with the aroma of a new spring. Take New York, the dynamic metropolis. What makes New York so special? It is the invitation of the Statue of Liberty—

give me your tired, your poor, your huddled masses who yearn to breathe free.

Not restricted to English only.

Many people, many cultures, many languages—with one thing in common, the yearning to breathe free.

Common ground!

Tonight in Atlanta, for the first time in this century we convene in the South. A state where governors once stood in school-house doors. Where Julian Bond was denied his seat in the state legislature because of his conscientious objection to the Vietnam War. A city that, through its five African American universities, has graduated more African Americans than any other city in the world. Atlanta, now a modern intersection of the New South.

Common ground! That is the challenge to our party tonight.

Left wing. Right wing. Progress will not come through boundless liberalism nor static conservatism, but at the critical mass of mutual survival. It takes two wings to fly. Whether you're a hawk or a dove, you're just a bird living in the same environment, in the same world.

The Bible teaches that when lions and lambs lie down together, none will be afraid and there will be peace in the valley. It sounds impossible. Lions eat lambs. Lambs sensibly flee from lions. But even lions and lambs find common ground. Why?

Because neither lions nor lambs want the forest to catch on fire. Neither lions nor lambs want acid rain to fall. Neither lions nor lambs can survive a nuclear war. If lions and lambs can find common ground, surely we can as well, as civilized people.

The only time that we win is when we come together. In 1960, John Kennedy, the late John Kennedy, beat Richard Nixon by only 112,000 votes—less than one vote per precinct. He won by the margin of our hope. He brought us together. He reached out. He had the courage to defy his advisors and inquire about Dr. King's jailing in Albany, Georgia. We won by the margin of our hope, inspired by courageous leadership.

In 1964, Lyndon Johnson brought both wings together—the thesis, the antithesis—to create a synthesis, and together we won.

In 1976, Jimmy Carter unified us again and we won. When we do not come together we never win.

In 1968, division and despair in August led to our defeat in November.

In 1980, rancor in the spring and the summer led to Reagan in the fall. When we divide, we cannot win. We must find common ground as a basis for survival and development and change and growth.

Today when we debated, differed, deliberated, agreed to agree, agreed to disagree, when we had the good judgment to argue our case and then not to self-destruct, George Bush was just a little further away from the White House and a little closer to private life.

Tonight, I salute Governor Michael Dukakis. He has run a well-managed and a dignified campaign. No matter how tired or how tried, he always resisted the temptation to stoop to demagoguery.

I've watched a good mind fast at work, with steel nerves, guiding his campaign out of the crowded field without appeal to the worst in us. I've watched his perspective grow as his environment expanded. I've seen his toughness and tenacity close-up. I know his commitment to public service.

Mike Dukakis's parents were a doctor and a teacher; my parents, a maid, a beautician and a janitor.

There is a great gap between Brookline, Massachusetts and Haney Street, the Fieldcrest Village housing project in Greenville, South Carolina. He studied law; I studied theology. There are differences of religion, region and race, differences in experiences and perspectives. But the genius of America is that out of the many, we become one.

Providence has enabled our paths to intersect. His foreparents came to America on immigrant ships; my foreparents on slave ships; we're in the same boat tonight.

Our ships could pass in the night if we have a false sense of independence, or they could collide and crash. We would lose our passengers. But we cannot seek a higher reality and a greater good apart. We can drift on the broken pieces of Reaganomics, satisfy our baser instincts, and exploit the fears of our people. At our highest, we can call upon the noble instincts to navigate this vessel to safety. The greater good is the common good.

As Jesus said, "Not my will, but thine be done." It was his way of saying there's a higher good beyond personal comfort or position.

The good of our nation is at stake—its commitment to working men and women, to the poor and the vulnerable, to the many in the world. With so many guided missiles, and so much misguided leadership, the stakes are exceedingly high. Our choice: full participation in a Democratic government or more abandonment and neglect. And so this night we choose not a false sense of independence, not our capacity to survive and endure.

Tonight we choose interdependency in our capacity to act and unite for the greater good. The common good is finding commitment to new priorities, to expansion and inclusion; a commitment to expanded participation in the Democratic Party at every level; a commitment to new priorities that ensure that hope will be kept alive; a common ground commitment to D.C. statehood and empowerment—D.C. deserves statehood; a commitment to economic set-asides; a commitment to the Dellums bill for comprehensive sanctions against South Africa; a shared commitment to a common direction.

Common ground. Easier said than done. Where do you find common ground—at the point of challenge. This campaign has shown that politics need not be marketed by politicians, packaged by pollsters and pundits. Politics can be a marvelous arena where people come together, define common ground.

We find common ground at the plant gate that closes on workers without notice. We find common ground at the farm auction where a good farmer loses his or her land to bad loans or diminishing markets. Common ground at the schoolyard where teachers cannot get adequate pay, and students cannot get a scholarship and can't make a loan. Common ground at the hospital admitting room where somebody tonight is dying because they cannot afford to go upstairs to a bed that's empty, waiting for someone with insurance to get sick. We are a better nation than that. We must do better.

Common ground. What is leadership if not present help in a time of crisis? And so I met you at a point of challenge in Jay, Maine, where paper workers were striking for fair wages; in Greenfield, Iowa, where family farmers struggle for a fair price; in Cleveland, Ohio, where working women seek comparable worth; in McFarland, California, where the children of Hispanic farm workers may be dying in clusters with cancer; in the AIDS hospice in Houston, Texas, where the sick support one another, 12 of whom are rejected by their own parents and friends. Common ground.

America's not a blanket woven from one thread, one color, one cloth. When I was a child growing up in Greenville, South Carolina, and grandmother could not afford a blanket, she didn't complain and we did not freeze. Instead, she took pieces of old cloth—patches, wool, silk, gabardine, crokersack, only patches—barely good enough to wipe your shoes with.

But they didn't stay that way very long. With sturdy hands and a strong cord, she sewed them together into a quilt, a thing of beauty and power and culture.

Now, Democrats, we must build such a quilt. Farmers, you seek fair prices and you are right, but you cannot stand alone. Your patch is not big enough. Workers, you fight for fair wages. You are right. But your patch, labor, is not big enough. Women, you seek comparable worth and pay equity. You are right. But your patch is not big enough. Women, mothers, who seek Head Start and day care and prenatal care on the front side of life, rather than welfare and jail care on the back side of life, you're right, but your patch is not big enough.

Students, you seek scholarships. You are right. But your patch is not big enough. African Americans and Hispanics, when we fight for civil rights, we are right, but our patch is not big enough. Gays and lesbians, when you fight against discrimination and for a cure for AIDS, you are right, but your patch is not big enough. Conservatives and progressives, when you fight for what you believe, right-wing, left-wing, hawk, dove—you are right from your point of view, but your point of view is not enough.

But don't despair. Be as wise as my grandmama. Pool the patches and the pieces together, bound by a common threat. When we form a great quilt of unity and common ground, we'll have the power to bring about health care and housing and jobs and education and hope to our nation.

We the people can win. We stand at the end of a long dark night of reaction. We stand tonight united in a commitment to a new direction. For almost eight years, we've been led by those who view social good coming from private interest, who viewed public life as a means to increase private wealth. They have been prepared to sacrifice the common good of the many to satisfy the private interest and the wealth of a few. We believe in a government that's a tool of our democracy in service to the public, not an instrument of the aristocracy in search of private wealth.

We believe in government with the consent of the governed—of, for and by the people. We must not emerge into a new day without a new direction.

Reaganomics is based on the belief that the rich had too little money, and the poor had too much. So they engaged in reverse Robin Hood—took from the poor, gave to the rich, paid for by the middle-class. We cannot stand four more years of Reaganomics in any version, in any disguise.

How do I document that case? Seven years later, the richest one percent of our society pays 20 percent less in taxes; the poorest ten percent pay 20 percent more. Reaganomics.

Reagan gave the rich and the powerful a multi-billion dollar party. Now the party is over. He expects the people to pay for the damage. I take this principled position: let us not raise taxes on the poor and the middle class, but those who had the party, the rich and the powerful, must pay for the party!

I just want to take common sense to high places. We're spending $150 billion a year defending Europe and Japan 43 years after the war is over. We have more troops in Europe tonight than we had seven years ago, yet the threat of war is ever more remote. Germany and Japan are now creditor nations—that means they've got a surplus. We are a debtor nation—that means we are in debt.

Let them share more of the burden of their own defense—use some of that money to build decent housing. Use some of that money to educate our children. Use some of that money for long-term health care. Use some of that money to wipe out these slums and put America back to work.

I just want to take common sense to higher places. If we can bail out Europe and Japan, if we can bail out Continental Bank and Chrysler—and Mr. Iacocca makes $8,000 an hour—we can bail out the family farmer.

I just want to make common sense. It does not make sense to close down 650,000 family farms in this country while importing food from abroad subsidized by the U.S. government.

Let's make sense. It does not make sense to be escorting oil tankers up and down the Persian Gulf, paying $2.50 for every $1.00 worth of oil we bring out, while oil wells are capped in Texas, Oklahoma and Louisiana. I just want to make sense.

Leadership must meet the moral challenge of its day. What's the moral challenge of our day? We have public accommodations. We have the right to vote. We have open housing.

What's the fundamental challenge of our day? It is to end economic violence. Plants closing without notice, economic violence. Most poor people are not lazy. They're not black. They're not brown. They're mostly white, female and young.

But whether white, black, brown, the hungry baby's belly turned inside-out is the same color. Call it pain. Call it hurt. Call it agony.

Most poor people are not on welfare. Some of them are illiterate and can't read the want-ad sections. And when they can, they can't find a job that matches their address. They work hard every day. I know. I live among them. I'm one of them.

I know they work. I'm a witness. They catch the early bus. They work every day. They raise other people's children. They work every day. They clean the streets. They work every day. They drive vans and cabs. They work every day. They change the beds you slept in at these hotels last night and can't get a union contract. They work every day.

No more. They're not lazy. Someone must defend them because it's right, and they cannot speak for themselves. They work in hospitals. I know they do. They wipe the bodies of those who are sick with fever and pain. They empty their bedpans. They clean out their commodes. No job is beneath them, and yet when they get sick, they cannot lie in the bed they made up every day. America, that is not right. We are a better nation than that. We are a better nation than that.

We need a real war on drugs. You can't "just say no." It's deeper than that. You can't just get a palm reader or an astrologer; it's more profound than that. We're spending $150 billion on drugs a year. We've gone from ignoring it to focusing on the children. Children cannot buy $150 billion worth of drugs a year. A few high profile athletes—athletes are not laundering $150 billion a year—bankers are.

I met the children in Watts who are unfortunate in their despair. Their grapes of hope have become raisins of despair, and they're turning on each other and they're self-destructing—but I stayed with them all night long. I wanted to hear their case. They said, "Jesse Jackson, as you challenge us to say no to drugs, you're right. And not to sell them, you're right. And not to use these guns, you're right."

And, by the way, the promise of CETA—they displaced CETA. They did not replace CETA. We have neither jobs nor houses nor services nor training—no way out. Some of us take drugs as anesthesia for our pain. Some take drugs as a way of pleasure—both short-term pleasure and long-term pain. Some sell drugs to make money. It's wrong, we know. But you need to know what we know. We can go and buy the drugs by the boxes at the port. If we can buy the drugs at the port, don't you believe the federal government can stop it if they want to?

They say, "We don't have Saturday night specials anymore." They say, "We buy AK-47s and Uzis, the latest lethal weapons. We buy them across the counter at Long Beach Boulevard." You cannot fight a war on drugs unless and until you are going to challenge the bankers and the gun sellers and those who grow the drugs. Don't just focus on the children, let's stop drugs at the level of supply and demand. We must end the scourge on the American culture.

Leadership. What difference will we make? Leadership cannot just go along to get along. We must do more than change presidents. We must change direction. Leadership must face the moral challenge of our day. The nuclear weapons build-up is irrational. Strong leadership cannot desire to look tough, and let that stand in the way of the pursuit of peace. Leadership must reverse the arms race.

At least we should pledge no first use. Why? Because first use begets first retaliation, and that's mutual annihilation. That's not the rational way out. No use at all—let's think this out, and not fight it out, because it's an unwinnable fight. Why hold a card that you can never drop? Let's give peace a chance.

Leadership. We now have this marvelous opportunity to have a breakthrough with the Soviets. Last year, 200,000 Americans visited the Soviet Union. There's a chance for joint ventures into space, not Star Wars and the arms race escalation, but a space development initiative. Let's build in space together and demilitarize the heavens. There's a way out.

America, let us expand. When Mr. Reagan and Mr. Gorbachev met, there was a big meeting. They represented together one-eighth of the human race. Seven-eighths of the human race were locked out of that room: most people in the world tonight—half are Asian, one half of them are Chinese. There are 22 nations in the Middle East. There's Europe, 400 million Latin Americans next door to us, the Caribbean, Africa—a half a billion people. Most people in the world today are yellow or brown or black, non-Christian, poor, female, young, and don't speak English—in the real world.

This generation must offer leadership to the real world. We're losing ground in Latin America, the Middle East, South Africa, because we are not focusing on the real world. We must use basic principles: support international law. We stand the most to gain from it. Support human rights; we believe in that. Support self-determination; we'll build on that. Support economic development; you know it's right. Be consistent, and gain our moral authority in the world.

I challenge you tonight, my friends, let's be bigger and better as a nation and a party. We have basic challenges. Freedom in South Africa—we've already agreed as Democrats to declare South Africa to be a terrorist state. But don't just stop there. Get South Africa out of Angola. Free Namibia. Support the Frontline states. We must have a new, humane human rights assistance policy in Africa.

I'm often asked, "Jesse, why do you take on these tough issues? They're not very political. We can't win that way."

If an issue is morally right, it will eventually be political. It may be political and never be right. Fannie Lou Hamer didn't have the most votes in Atlantic

City, but her principles have outlasted every delegate who voted to lock her out. Rosa Parks did not have the most votes, but she was morally right. Dr. King did not have the most votes about the Vietnam War, but he was morally right. If we're principled first, our politics will fall into place.

Jesse, why did you take these big bold initiatives? A poem by an unknown author went something like this: We mastered the air, we've conquered the sea, and annihilated distance and prolonged life, we were not wise enough to live on this earth without war and without hate.

As for Jesse Jackson, I'm tired of sailing my little boat, far inside the harbor bar. I want to go out where the big boats float, out on the deep where the great ones are. And should my frail craft prove too slight, the waves that sweep those billows o'er, I'd rather go down in a stirring fight than drown to death on the sheltered shore.

We've got to go out, my friends, where the big boats are. And then, for our children, young America, hold your head high now. We can win. We must not lose you to drugs and violence, premature pregnancy, suicide, cynicism, pessimism and despair. We can win.

Wherever you are tonight, I challenge you to hope and to dream. Don't submerge your dreams. Exercise above all else the right to dream. Even on drugs, dream of the day that you are drug-free. Even in the gutter, dream of the day that you will be up on your feet again. You must never stop dreaming. Face reality, yes. But don't stop with the way things are; dream of things the way they ought to be. Dream. Face pain, but love, hope, faith and dreams will help you rise above the pain.

Use hope and imagination as weapons of survival and progress, but you keep on dreaming, young America. Dream of peace. Peace is rational and reasonable. War is irrational in this age and unwinnable.

Dream of teachers who teach for life and not merely for a living. Dream of doctors who are concerned more about public health than private wealth. Dream of lawyers more concerned about justice than a judgeship. Dream of preachers who are more concerned about prophecy than profiteering. Dream on the high road of sound values.

And in America, as we go forth to September, October and November and then beyond, America must never surrender its high moral challenge.

Do not surrender to drugs. The best drug policy is a no first use. Don't surrender with needles and cynicism. Let's have no first use on the one hand or clinics on the other. Never surrender, young America.

Go forward. America must never surrender to malnutrition. We can feed the hungry and clothe the naked. We must never surrender. We must go forward. We must never surrender to illiteracy. Invest in our children. Never surrender, and go forward.

We must never surrender to inequality. Women cannot compromise the ERA or comparable worth. Women are making 67 cents on the dollar to what a man makes. Women cannot buy meat cheaper. Women cannot buy bread cheaper. Women cannot buy milk cheaper. Women deserve to get paid for the work that they do. It's right and it's fair.

Don't surrender, my friends. Those who have AIDS tonight, you deserve our compassion. Even with AIDS you must not surrender. You in your wheelchairs. I see you sitting here tonight. I've stayed with you. I've reached out to you across our nation. Don't you give up. I know it's tough sometimes. People look down on you. It took a little more effort to get here tonight.

And no one should look down on you, but sometimes mean people do. The only justification we have for looking down on someone is that we're going to stop and pick them up. But even in your wheelchairs, don't give up. We cannot forget 50 years ago when our backs were against the wall, Roosevelt was in a wheelchair. I would rather have Roosevelt in a wheelchair than Reagan and Bush on a horse. Don't you surrender, and don't you give up.

Don't surrender and don't give up. Why can I challenge you this way? Jesse Jackson, you don't understand my situation. You be on television. You don't understand. I see you with the big people. You don't understand my situation. I understand. You're seeing me on TV but you don't know what makes me me. They wonder why does Jesse run, because they see me running for the White House. They don't see the house I'm running from.

I have a story. I wasn't always on television. Writers were not always outside my door. When I was born late one afternoon, October 8th, in Greenville, South Carolina, no writers asked my mother her name. Nobody chose to write down our address. My mama was not supposed to make it. You see, I was born to a teenage mother who was born to a teenage mother.

I know abandonment and people being mean to you, and saying you're nothing and nobody, and can never be anything. I understand. Jesse Jackson is my third name. I'm adopted. When I had no name, my grandmother gave me her name. My name was Jesse Burns until I was 12. So I wouldn't have a blank space, she gave me a name to hold me over. I understand when you have no name. I understand.

I wasn't born in the hospital. Mama didn't have insurance. I was born in the bed at home. I really do understand. Born in a three-room house, bathroom in the backyard, slop jar by the bed, no hot and cold running water. I understand. Wallpaper used for decoration? No. For a windbreaker. I understand. I'm a working person's person, that's why I understand you whether you're African American or white.

I understand work. I was not born with a silver spoon in my mouth. I had a shovel programmed for my hand. My mother, a working woman. So many days she went to work early with runs in her stockings. She knew better, but she wore runs in her stockings so that my brother and I could have matching socks and not be laughed at at school.

I understand. At three o'clock on Thanksgiving Day we couldn't eat turkey because mama was preparing someone else's turkey at three o'clock. We had to play football to entertain ourselves and then around six o'clock she would get off the Alta Vista bus when we would bring up the leftovers and eat our turkey—leftovers, the carcass, the cranberries around eight o'clock at night. I really do understand.

Every one of these funny labels they put on you, those of you who are watching this broadcast tonight in the projects, on the corners, I understand. Call you outcast, lowdown, you can't make it, you're nothing, you're from nobody, subclass, underclass—when you see Jesse Jackson, when my name goes in nomination, your name goes in nomination.

I was born in the slum, but the slum was not born in me. And it wasn't born in you, and you can make it. Hold your head high, stick your chest out. You can make it. It gets dark sometimes, but the morning comes. Don't you surrender. Suffering breeds character. Character breeds faith. In the end faith will not disappoint.

You must not surrender. You may or may not get there, but just know that you're qualified and you hold on and hold out. We must never surrender. America will get better and better. Keep hope alive. Keep hope alive. Keep hope alive. On tomorrow night and beyond, keep hope alive.

I love you very much. I love you very much.

MANNING MARABLE

Toward Black American Empowerment

A spectre is haunting Black America—the seductive illusion that equality between the races has been achieved, and that the activism characteristic of the previous generation's freedom struggles is no longer relevant to contemporary realities. In collective chorus, the media, the leadership of both capitalist political parties, the corporate establishment, conservative social critics and public policy experts, and even marginal elements of the Black middle class, tell the majority of African-Americans that the factors which generated the social protest for equality in the 1950s and 1960s no longer exist.

The role of race has supposedly "declined in significance" within the economy and political order. And as we survey the current social climate, this argument seems to gain a degree of credibility. The number of Black elected officials exceeds 6,600, many Black entrepreneurs have achieved substantial gains within the capitalist economic system in the late 1980s; thousands of Black managers and administrators appear to be moving forward within the hierarchies of the private and public sector. And the crowning "accomplishment," the November, 1989, election of Douglas Wilder as Virginia's first Black governor, has been promoted across the nation as the beginning of the transcendence of "racial politics."

WILDER MODEL

The strategy of Jesse Jackson in both 1984 and 1988, which challenged the Democratic Party by mobilizing people of color and many whites around an advanced, progressive agenda for social justice, is dismissed as anachronistic and even "reverse racism." As in the Wilder model, racial advancement is projected as obtainable only if the Negro learns a new political and cultural discourse of the white mainstream. Protest is therefore passe. All the legislative remedies which were required to guarantee racial equality, the spectre dictates, have already been passed.

It is never an easy matter to combat an illusion. There have been sufficient gains for African-Americans, particularly within the electoral system and for sectors of the Black petty bourgeoisie in the 1980s, that elements of the spectre seem true. But the true test of any social thesis is the amount of reality it explains, or obscures. And from the vantage point of the inner-cities and homeless shelters, from the unemployment lines and closed factories, a different reality behind the spectre emerges. We find that racism has not declined in significance, if racism is defined correctly as the systemic exploitation of Blacks' labor power and the domination and subordination of our cultural, political, educational and social rights as human beings. Racial inequality continues albeit within the false discourse of equality. Those who benefit materially from institutional racism now use the term "racist" to denounce Black critics who call for the enforcement of affirmative action and equal opportunity legislation.

Behind the rhetoric of equality exists two crises, which present fundamental challenges to African-Americans throughout the decade of the 1990s. There is an "internal crisis"—that is, a crisis within the African-American family, neighborhood, community, cultural and social institutions, and within interpersonal relations especially between Black males. Part of this crisis was generated, ironically, by the "paradox of desegregation." With the end of Jim Crow segregation, the Black middle class was able to escape the confines of the ghetto. Black attorneys who previously had only Black clients could now move into more lucrative white law firms. Black educators and administrators were hired at predominantly white colleges; Black physicians were hired at white hospitals; Black architects, engineers, and other professionals went into white firms. This usually meant the geographical and cultural schism of elements of Black middle class from the working class and low income African-American population, which was still largely confined to the ghetto.

As Black middle class professionals retreated to the suburbs, they often withdrew their skills, financial resources and professional contacts from the bulk of the African-American community. There were of course many exceptions, Black women and men who understood the cultural obligation they owed to their community. But as a rule, by the late 1980s, such examples became more infrequent, especially among younger Blacks who had no personal memories or experiences in the freedom struggles of two decades past.

The internal crisis is directly related to external, institutional crisis, a one-sided, race/class warfare which is being waged against the African-American community. The external crisis is represented as the conjuncture of a variety of factors, including the deterioration of skilled and higher paying jobs within the ghetto, and the decline in the economic infrastructure; the decline in the public sector's support for public housing, health care, education and related social services for low-to-moderate income people; the demise of the enforcement of affirmative action, equal opportunity laws and related civil rights legislation; the increased racial conservatism of both major political parties and the ideological and programmatic collapse of traditional liberalism; and most importantly, the conscious decision by the corporate and public sector managerial elite to "regulate" the Black population through increasingly coercive means.

VIOLENCE

The major characteristic of the internal crisis is the steady acceleration and proliferation of *violence*, in a variety of manifestations. The most disruptive and devastating type of violence is violent crime, which includes homicide, forcible rape, robbery, and aggravated assault. According to the *Sourcebook of Criminal Justice Statistics* for 1981, the total number of Americans arrested was nearly 9.5 million. Blacks comprise only 12.5 percent of the total U.S. population, but represented 2.3 million arrests, or about *one fourth of all arrests.* Black arrests for homicide and non-negligent manslaughter were 8,693, or about 48 percent of all murders committed in the U.S. For robbery, which is defined by law as the use of force or violence to obtain personal property, the number of Black arrests was 74,275, representing 57 percent of all robbery arrests. For aggravated assault, the number of African-Americans arrested was 94,624, about 29 percent of all arrests in this category. For motor vehicle theft, the number of Blacks arrested and charged was 38,905, about 27 percent of all auto theft crimes. Overall, for all violent and property crimes charged, Blacks totaled almost 700,000 arrests in the year 1979, representing nearly one-third of all such crimes.

One of the most controversial of all violent crimes is the charge of forcible rape. Rape is controversial because of the history of the criminal charge being used against Black men by the white racist legal structure. Thousands of Black men have been executed, lynched and castrated for the imaginary offense of rape. Yet rape or forcible sexual violence is not imaginary when African-American women and young girls are victimized. In 1979, there were 29,068 arrests for forcible rape. Black men comprised 13,870 arrests, or 48 percent of the total. Within cities, where three fourths of all rapes are committed, Blacks total 54 percent of all persons arrested for rape.

The chief victims of rape are not white women, but Black women. The U.S. Department of Justice's 1979 study of the crime of forcible rape established that overall most Black women are nearly *twice* as likely to be rape victims than are white women. The research illustrated that in one year, about 67 out of 100,000 white women would be rape victims; but the rate for Black and other nonwhite women was 115 per 100,000. In the age group 20 to 34 years, the dangers for Black women increase dramatically. For white women of age 20 to 34, 139 out of 100,000 are rape victims annually. For Black women the same age, the rate is 292 per 100,000. For attempted rape, white women are assaulted at a rate of 196 per 100,000; Black women are attacked sexually 355 per 100,000 annually.

There is also a direct correlation between rape victimization and income. In general, poor women are generally the objects of sexual assault; middle class women are rarely raped or assaulted, and wealthy women almost never experience sexual assault. The statistics are clear on this point. White women who live in families earning under $7,500 annually have a 500 percent greater likelihood of being raped than white women who come from households with more than $15,000 income. The gap is even more extreme for African-American women. For Black middle class families, the rate of rape is 22 per 100,000. For welfare and low income families earning below $7,500 annually, the rate for rape is 127 per 100,000. For attempted rape, low income Black women are victimized at a rate of 237 per 100,000 annually.

INTRARACIAL PHENOMENON

Rape is almost always intraracial, not interracial. Nine out of ten times, a white rapist's victim is a white female. Ninety percent of all Black women who are raped have been assaulted by a Black male. Sexual violence within the African-American community, therefore, is not something "exported" by whites. It is essentially the brutality committed by Black men against our mothers, wives, sisters and daughters. It is the worst type of violence, using the gift of sexuality in a bestial and animalistic way, to create terror and fear among Black women.

The type of violence which most directly affects Black men is homicide. Nearly half of all murders committed in any given year are Black men who murder other Black men. But that's only part of the problem. We must recognize, first, that the homicide rate among African-Americans is growing. Back in 1960, the homicide rate for Black men in the U.S. was 37 per 100,000. By 1979, the Black homicide rate was 65 per 100,000, compared to the white male homicide rate of 10 per 100,000. In other words, a typical Black male has a *six to seven times* greater likelihood of being a murder victim than a white male.

The chief victims of homicide in our community are young African-American males. Murder is the fourth leading cause of death for all Black men, and the leading cause of death for Black males of age 20 to 29 years. Today in the U.S., a typical white female's statistical chances of becoming a murder victim are one in 606. For white men, the odds narrow to one chance in 186. For Black women, the odds are one in 124. But for Black men, the chances are one in twenty-nine. For young Black men living in cities who are between age 20 to 29, the odds of becoming a murder victim are *less than one in twenty.* Black young men in American cities today are the primary targets for destruction—not only from drugs and police brutality, but from each other.

SOCIAL COSTS

The epidemic of violence in the Black community raises several related questions. What is the social impact of violence within our neighborhoods? What is the effect of violence upon our children? And most importantly, how do we develop a strategy to reverse the proliferation of Black-against-Black crime and violence?

Violence occurs so frequently in the cities that for many people, it has become almost a "normal" factor. We have become accustomed to burglar alarms and security locks to safeguard our personal property and homes. More than one in three families keeps a gun in their homes. We might try to avoid driving through neighborhoods where crack houses are located. We are trying to avoid the problem, but we're not taking steps to solve it. We need to keep in mind that in most of the violent crime cases, the assailant and the victim live in the same neighborhood, or are members of the same household. Half of all violent deaths are between husbands and wives. Many others include parents killing their children, or children killing parents, or neighbors killing each other. There are hundreds of murders among Blacks for the most trivial reasons—everything from fighting over parking spaces to arguing over five dollars.

Black men are murdering each other in part because of the deterioration of jobs and economic opportunity in our communities. For Black young men, the real unemployment rate exceeds 50 percent in most cities. Overall jobless rates for Black men with less than a high school diploma exceed 15 percent. High unemployment, crowded housing and poor health care all contribute to an environment of social chaos and disruption, which create destructive values and behaviors.

The most tragic victims of violence are Black children. Black children between the ages of one and four have death rates from homicide which are four times higher than for white children the same age. According to the Children's Defense Fund, Black children are arrested at almost seven times the rates for white children for the most serious violent crimes and are arrested at more than twice the white rates for serious property crimes. More than half of the arrests for African-American teenagers are for serious property crimes or violent crimes. For instance, the arrest rate for Black youth aged 11 to 17 for forcible rape is six times higher than for whites. In terms of rates of victimization, non-white females are almost 40 percent more likely than white females to be raped, robbed or victims of other violent crimes.

IDENTITY

How do we understand the acts of violence committed by and against our children? We must begin by focusing on the cultural concept of identity. What is identity? It's an awareness of self in the context of one's environment. Identity is based on the connections between the individual and his or her immediate family and community. We don't exist in isolation of each other. We develop a sense of who we are, of who we wish to become, by interacting with parents, friends, teachers, ministers, co-workers, and others.

Our identity is collective, in that it is formed through the inputs of thousands of different people over many years. If the people relate to an individual in a negative manner, an antisocial or deviant personality will be the result. If children are told repeatedly by teachers or parents that they are stupid, the children will usually do poorly in school, regardless of their natural abilities. If children are told that they are chronic liars and untrustworthy, they will eventually begin to lie and steal. If they are physically beaten by their parents frequently and unjustly, they will learn to resort to physical violence against others. People are not born hateful or violent. There's no genetic or biological explanation for Black-against-Black crime. Violence is *learned* behavior.

Violence between people of color is also directly linked to the educational system. If the curriculum of our public schools does not present the heritage, culture and history of African-Americans, if it ignores or downgrades our vital contributions to a more democratic society, our children are robbed of their heritage. They acquire a distorted perspective about themselves and their communities. If they believe that African-American people have never achieved greatness, in the sciences, art, music, economics and the law, how can they excel or achieve for themselves? Despite the many reforms accomplished to create a more culturally pluralistic environment for learning, most of our public schools are in the business of "miseducation" for people of color. Our children are frequently "cultural casualties" in the ideological warfare against Black people.

The dynamics of violence within the African-American community create such chaos and destructiveness, that they provide a justification for the public and private sectors' retreat from civil rights initiatives. The argument of the dominant white elites proceeds thus: "Blacks must bear the responsibility for their own poverty, crime, illiteracy, and oppression. Affirmative action is consequently harmful to Blacks' interests, since it rewards incompetence and advances individuals not on the basis of merit but race alone. Blacks should stop looking to the government to resolve their problems, and take greater initiatives within the private enterprise system to assist themselves. Through private initiatives, moral guidance and sexual abstinence, the status of the Negro will improve gradually without social dissent and disruption."

SOURCE OF CRISIS

We need to recognize that, fundamentally, there would be no internal crisis among African-Americans if the political economy and social institutions were designed to create the conditions for genuine democracy and human equality. The external crisis of the capitalist political economy is responsible for the internal crisis. All of the private initiatives, and all of the meager self help efforts mounted at the neighborhood level, and the doubling of the number of Black entrepreneurs and enterprises, would not in any significant manner reverse the destructive trends which have been unleashed against our people. Institutional racism and class exploitation since 1619 have always been, and remain, the root causes of Black oppression.

Violence also takes the form of the proliferation of illegal drugs within the African-American community. The political economy of crack cocaine creates many more living victims than those who are killed by the drug. Crack is part of the new urban slavery, a method of disrupting lives and "regulating" the masses of our young people who otherwise would be demanding jobs, adequate health care, better schools and control of their own communities. It is hardly accidental that this insidious cancer has been unleashed within the very poorest urban neighborhoods, and that the police concentrate on petty street dealers rather than those who actually control and profit from the drug traffic. It is impossible to believe that thousands and thousands of pounds of illegal drugs can be transported throughout the country, in airplanes, trucks and automobiles, to hundreds of central distribution centers with thousands of employees and under the so-called surveillance of thousands of law enforcement officers, unless crack represented at a systemic level a form of social control.

SUICIDE RATES

The epidemic of violence, in combination with the presence of drugs, has directly contributed to another type of violence—the growth of African-American suicide rates, especially among the young. From 1950 to 1974, the suicide rate of African-American males soared from 6.8 per 100,000 to 11.4 per 100,000. In the same years, the Black female suicide rate rose from

1.6 per 100,000 to 3.5 per 100,000. A 1982 study by Robert Davis noted that nearly one-half of all suicides among Blacks now occur among people between age 20 to 34 years. Within this group, Black males who kill themselves account for 36 percent of the total number of suicides. Davis also observes that within the narrow age range of 25 to 29, the suicide rate among Black males is higher than that for white males in the same age group. For Black men and women who live in urban areas, the suicide rate is twice that for whites of the same age group who live in cities.

These facts must be understood against the background of social history of African-Americans. Traditionally, suicide was almost unknown within the Black community during slavery and the Jim Crow period. Blacks found ways to cope with stress and the constant disappointments of life, from singing the blues to mobilizing their sisters and brothers to fight against forms of oppression. Frantz Fanon's psychiatric insight, that struggle and resistance for the oppressed is therapeutic, is confirmed by the heritage of the Black liberation movement. But when people lose the will to resist oppression, when they no longer can determine their friends or enemies, they lack the ability to develop the mental and spiritual determination to overcome obstacles. Suicide, once an irrational or irrelevant act, becomes both rational and logical within the context of cultural and social alienation.

DEATH PENALTY

The American legal system in the 1980s and 1990s also contributed to the violence within our communities in several ways. The patterns of institutional racism became far more sophisticated, as former President Reagan pursued a policy of appointing conservative, racist, elitist males to the federal district courts and the U.S. circuit courts of appeals. By 1989 Reagan had appointed over 425 federal judges, more than half of the 744 total judgeships. Increasingly, the criminal justice system was employed as a system of social control, for the millions of unemployed and underemployed African-Americans. The essential element of coercion within the justice system, within a racial context, is of course the utilization of the death penalty.

According to one statistical study by David C. Baldus based on over two thousand murder cases in Georgia during the 1970s, people accused of killing whites were about eleven times more likely to be given the death penalty than those who murdered Blacks. Over half of the defendants in white-victim crimes would not have been ordered to be executed if their victims had been African-Americans. Research on the death penalty in Florida during the 1970s illustrates that Florida Blacks who are accused and convicted of murdering whites are five times more likely to be given the death penalty than whites who murder other whites.

As of 30 June 1989, the nation's entire prison population reached 673,565 inmates, more than double the figure of 1980. At the current rate, just to keep pace with the increased penal population, authorities have to add eighteen hundred new prison beds *each week*. At the current rate, the African-American prisoner population by the year 2000 will exceed 600,000, or about one in sixty African-American men, women, and children.

SOCIAL CONTROL

Under the conditions of race/class domination, prisons are the principal means for group social control, in order to regulate the labor position of millions of Black workers. Our free market system cannot create full employment for all; and the public sector is unwilling to devote sufficient resources to launch an economic reconstruction of the central cities, which in turn would greatly reduce the drug trade. Consequently, prisons become absolutely necessary for keeping hundreds of thousands of potentially rebellious, dissatisfied and alienated African-American youth off the streets.

Between 1973 and 1986, the average real earnings for young African-American males under 25 years fell by 50 percent. In the same period, the percentage of Black males aged 18 to 29 in the labor force who were able to secure full-time, year-round employment, fell from only 44 percent to a meager 35 percent.

Is it accidental that these young Black men, who are crassly denied meaningful employment opportunities, are also pushed into the prison system, and subsequently into permanent positions of economic marginality and social irrelevancy? Within capitalism, a job has never been defined as a human right; but for millions of young, poor Black men and women, they appear to have a "right" to a prison cell or a place at the front on the unemployment line.

STRATEGY

The struggle against violence requires a break from the strategic analysis of the desegregation period of the 1960s. Our challenge is not to become part of the system, but to transform it, not only for our selves, but for everyone. We must struggle against an acceptance of the discourse and perceptions of the dominant white political criminal justice and economic elites, in regards to Black-on-Black violence. If we focus solely on the need to construct more prisons and mandatory sentences for certain crimes, the crisis will continue to exist in our cities and elsewhere. People who have a sense of mastery and control in their lives do not violate their neighbors or steal their property.

An effective strategy for empowerment in the 1990s must begin with the recognition that the American electoral political system was never designed to uproot the fundamental causes of Black oppression. Most of the greatest advances in Black political activism did not occur at the ballot box, but in the streets, in the factories, and through collective group awareness and mobilization. Our greatest leaders in this century—Du Bois, Tubman, Garvey, Malcolm, Martin, and many more—were not elected officials or governmental bureaucrats. Yet because of the electoral focus of most of the current crop of middle class Black elites, we now tend to think of power as an electoral process. But there is also power when oppressed people acquire a sense of cultural integrity and an appreciation of their political heritage of resistance. There is power when we mobilize our collective resources in the media, educational institutions, housing, health care and economic development to address issues. There is power when African-American people and other oppressed constituencies mobilize a march or street demonstration, when we use a boycott or picket line to realize our immediate objectives.

A strategy for African-American empowerment means that Black politicians must be held more closely accountable to the interests of Black people. Power implies the ability to reward and to punish friends and enemies alike. Can Blacks continue to afford to conduct voter registration and education campaigns, and then do nothing to check the voting behavior of our elected officials? Accountability must be measured objectively according to a list of policy priorities, and not determined by political rhetoric at election time. One method to consider could be the creation of "people power" assemblies, popular, local conventions open to the general Black public. Politicians of both major parties would be evaluated and ranked according to their legislative or executive records, and their responses on specific policy questions. Neither the Democratic nor the Republican parties can be expected to provide this level of direct accountability.

FORWARD PATH

We are losing the battle for the hearts and minds of millions of young African-Americans, who have no personal memory of the struggles waged to dismantle the system of Jim Crow segregation. They have no personal experience on the picket lines, in street demonstrations, and in the development of community-based organizations which reinforce and strengthen Black families, Black religious, civic, and social institutions. The path forward is to create a new generation of Black leaders who recognize that the effort to achieve social justice and human equality is unfinished, and that the status of Black people in America could easily deteriorate to a new type of repressive environment comparable to legal segregation in the pre-civil rights South. We must identify and cultivate the leadership abilities of young people who display a potential and interest in progressive social change.

We need to recognize that power in American society is exercised by hierarchies and classes, not by individuals. Part of the price for the individualism and blatant materialism within certain elements of the Black upper-middle class since the 1970s has been their alienation from the dilemmas confronting the Black working class, the poor and unemployed. Class elitism of any type, for a segment of the oppressed community, contributes to a disintegration of solidarity and a sense of common values, goals and objectives. To end the dynamic of violence, we need to recognize that freedom is not rooted within individualism, in isolation from the majority. No single Black woman or man in American will ever transcend the impact of racism and class exploitation unless all of us, and especially the most oppressed among us, also gain a fundamental level of cultural awareness, collective respect, material security and educational advancement. This requires a new vision of the struggle for power, a collective commitment to the difficult yet challenging project of remaking humanity and our social environment, rooted in a vision beyond self-hatred, chemical-dependency, and fratricidal violence. This must be at the heart of our strategy for cultural resistance and empowerment for the 1990s and beyond.

LOUIS FARRAKHAN

A *Torchlight for* America

Nineteen ninety-two marked the quincentennial year of the opening up of the "New World" for the purpose of Western domination. Christopher Columbus is said to have "discovered" this continent in 1492. Since 1492 the Native American people have been misused, abused and then neglected. Since 1555, the black people brought to these shores in chains have also been misused, abused and now remain neglected.

In the official History of the Seal of the United States, published by the Department of State in 1909, Gaillard Hunt wrote that late in the afternoon of July 4, 1776, The Continental Congress resolved that Dr. Benjamin Franklin, Mr. John Adams and Mr. Thomas Jefferson be a committee to prepare a device for a Seal of the United States of America. In the design proposed by the first committee, the obverse (face) of the Seal was a coat of arms in six quarters, with emblems representing England, Scotland, Ireland, France, Germany and Holland, the countries from which the new nation had been peopled. The Eye of Providence in a radiant triangle, and the motto E PLURIBUS UNUM were also proposed for the obverse.

Even though the country was populated by so-called Indians, and black slaves were brought to build the country, the official Seal of the country was never designed to reflect our presence, only that of the European immigrants. The Seal and the Constitution reflect the thinking of the founding fathers that this was to be a nation by white people and for white people. Native Americans, blacks and all other non-white people were to be the burden bearers for the "real" citizens of this nation.

For the reverse (back) of the Seal, the committee suggested a picture of Pharaoh sitting in an open chariot with a crown on his head and a sword in his hand, passing through the divided waters of the Red Sea in pursuit of the Israelites. Hovering over the sea was to be shown a pillar of fire in a cloud, expressive of the Divine presence and command. Rays from this pillar of fire were to be shown beaming on Moses, standing on the shore and extending his hand over the sea, causing it to overwhelm Pharaoh. The motto for the reverse was: REBELLION TO TYRANTS IS OBEDIENCE TO GOD.

The design reveals the spiritual blindness inherent in the genesis of the United States. The founding fathers upheld obedience to God as their symbol while practicing genocide, colonialism and slavery among the native population and our forebears.

It was Thomas Jefferson who said, "I tremble for my country when I reflect that God is just and that His justice cannot sleep forever." It was George Washington who said that he feared the slaves would become a most troublesome species of property before too many years passed over our heads.

America is faced with the political and moral dilemma of reconciling pluralism and the inclusion of non-whites with the democratic ideas espoused by the founding fathers. This is not a democracy in the fullest meaning of the word. Racism has to be overcome in order to gain a full expression of E Pluribus Unum (out of the many, one). Is E Pluribus Unum meant to be interpreted as 'out of the many white ethnic strains, one people," or "out of the many strains, white, black and other, one people?"

Within the walls of this country there are two Americas, separate and unequal, white and black (including other non-whites). In order to reconcile these two Americas, the American people must come to terms with the limited vision of the founding fathers. The founding fathers didn't envision the current population profile, where the numbers of black and Hispanic people are growing, threatening the majority status of whites. Those who desire to maintain the old vision of white rule under the name of democracy and pluralism will no longer be able to continue the subjugation of non-whites. Now is the time for freedom, justice and equality for those who have been deprived of it.

It was made easy for whites to subjugate others because they were taught to see blacks and Native Americans as heathen, savage and sub-human. This, in their minds, justified their not recognizing us as equal citizens in this country. Bearing this in mind, that the original Seal should include a picture of Pharaoh pursuing the Israelites is not without great significance. That it should include a pillar of fire in a cloud, beaming down on Moses, is not without significance for this day and time.

In my judgment, the original Seal was inspired to give America a picture of what her future could become if she did not do justice by the Native Americans and by the blacks who were brought here as her slaves.

Even though America says she wants change and renewal, she must deal with the basis of this country's woes. Either she must evolve from the limited vision of the founding fathers and repudiate that vision, or, America must say that she believes in the true vision of the founding fathers and that the darker people will never be respected as equals inside of this nation.

God has set His hand against this economy as He set His hand against the riches of Egypt. **The only way to fix this economy is to deal with greed, basic immorality and the unwanted presence of 30 million or more black people and 2 million Native Americans whose cry for justice has entered the ears of God.**

Integration, as it has been conceived, is not working to bring true freedom, justice and equality to America's former slaves. It is not working because it was not properly motivated and is not in harmony with the mandate of the time.

We do not want or need that kind of integration that literally results in nothing in terms of economic advancement for our people. The Honorable Elijah Muhammad said that if we wanted better relations between black and white, he could show us how to achieve this. As black people, we first have to come into a knowledge of self that will help us make ourselves worthy of respect and our communities decent places in which to live. We must begin to do something for self. This act on our part will earn the respect of self as well as others. It will ultimately help us to have better relations with those who see us as an unwanted burden in this society.

The focus of black people should be on elevating self, not on trying to force ourselves into the communities of white people. Self-respecting white men do not want to see us with their women. One way to have good race relations is to leave their women and girls alone. Some of us have a false love for the white woman, and some of us have a false love for the white man. Some want the former slavemaster's woman because the former slavemaster has always had free access to our women, and some want the white man because he wields great power in the society.

In a painful recount of the position our freed forebears found themselves in after Emancipation, W. E. B. Du Bois wrote:

> "For the first time he sought to analyze the burden he bore upon his back, that deadweight of social degradation partially masked behind a half-named Negro problem. He felt his poverty; without a cent, without a home, without land, tools, or savings, he had entered into competition with rich, landed, skilled neighbors. To be a poor man is hard, but to be a poor race in a land of dollars is the very bottom of hardships. He felt the weight of his ignorance, not simply of let-

> ters, but of life, of business, of the humanities; the accumulated sloth and shirking and awkwardness of decades and centuries shackled his hands and feet. Nor was his burden all poverty and ignorance. The red stain of bastardy, which two centuries of systematic legal defilement of Negro women had stamped upon his race, meant not only the loss of ancient African chastity, but also the hereditary weight of a mass of corruption from white adulterers, threatening almost the obliteration of the Negro home."

At one time, white folks held up the Cadillac as the symbol of success. We who were not successful, wanted to at least have the symbol of success, so we aspired to own a Cadillac. Likewise, white men have held up white women as the best and most beautiful women on the Earth. To have a loving relationship with her—to marry her or to have sex with her—to many of our black men is the epitome of being accepted and successful.

The Honorable Elijah Muhammad taught us to take our own women and girls and respect, honor and protect them. He taught us to work hard to produce a future for our children; to rid ourselves of alcohol, tobacco, gambling, laziness and dependency; and to work to make our neighborhoods decent places for us to live. This kind of action on our part could lead to a healthier relationship between the races.

Certainly if we look at our females as that which God produced for us, then we would have to expect the white man to leave our women and girls alone. True love, however, transcends color and race. We must ask the question of those who have gone the way of having interracial relations, is the love a true love, or is it merely an acting out of a corrupted fantasy which is held by both black and white? When we, as a people, are healed of our mental, moral and spiritual sickness, then maybe we can look across racial lines and see the true value and worth of one another. However, healing of the deadly diseases of white supremacy and black inferiority has to take place **first**!

I have to stand and speak for the voiceless, whose leadership has often been quiet or weak in the face of an open enemy. Although I have been misrepresented by the media, here is a new opportunity to receive my message and judge it against the criterion of truth.

Am I really an anti-Semite? Am I really a hater? Can these charges really be proven? When people disagree, the intelligent and rational thing to do is to have a dialogue. Perhaps through dialogue differences can be reconciled. If anything that I have said or written is proved to be a lie, then I will retract my words and apologize before the world.

The Honorable Elijah Muhammad taught us that the way to stop back-biting and slander is to gather the parties together and allow them to present their charges and evidence to each other's face, then we will know where the truth rests and where the lie rests. We are willing to sit and meet before the world and discuss our position. We recognize the ability of the American government and business community to help the black community. The Nation of Islam, in turn, can help America solve its problems. But we cannot solve any problems by bowing down to falsehood.

The Honorable Elijah Muhammad pointed out to us that Babylon, that great and wicked city, could have been healed. She was not healed because she refused to listen to guidance coming to her kings from the mouth of one of her Hebrew slaves. He pointed this out to indicate that America, though dying, can also be healed.

In the design for the original Seal for this country, the pillar of fire in a cloud, expressive of the Divine presence and command—that was also written of in the Bible as seen in a vision by Ezekiel—is now a reality in America. In the Seal's design, the reason that Pharaoh was depicted with a sword in his hand is to symbolize America's pursuit of world dominion by way of skilled machinations backed up by force. America has held a whole nation in captivity for over 400 years—even as Pharaoh did in the biblical history of Moses and the ancient Hebrews—and she has done so by use of force and wicked machinations. The beam of light that was seen shining down on the face of Moses in the design for the original Seal of this country is a sign that the light from God is now beaming down on one from among the ex-slaves. In that light is the guidance that can heal America, the modern Babylon and the modern Egypt. Will America be healed?

A man was born in Georgia and was privileged to meet a Master Teacher, Who gave him the keys for liberating the minds of our people to form the true basis of a new world order. He laid the foundation upon which I stand today. On October 7, 1897, in a little town called Sandersville, Georgia, mother Marie (Poole) Muhammad gave birth to a noble black man who was given a great light by his Teacher, Master Fard Muhammad, so that a light would be lifted up in the midst of gross darkness. That light is the teachings of the Honorable Elijah Muhammad, which I am sharing with America right now.

We have the torchlight. America is being challenged to take the bushel basket off the light. Let us sit down and talk about bringing real solutions before the American people, as civilized people should and are obligated to do.

The Kingdom of God is an egalitarian kingdom structured on truth, where each of us will be treated with fairness and justice. America could become the basis for the Kingdom of God. She has within her borders every nation, kindred and tongue. If they could be made peaceful, productive and mutually respecting, you would have the basis for the Kingdom of God right here on earth.

However, what America does not have is the teaching that would make one people out of the many creeds, colors and nationalities that occupy this land. That teaching cannot be the skilled wisdom from the political leadership that subordinates the language and culture of America's diverse members, while lifting the American way of life as the model—which is very racist and white supremacist in nature. The current American way of life can only produce an apparent unity among caucasians, because it negates the diversity and beauty of the non-white population. You can never achieve unity, or E Pluribus Unum, in this country under the doctrine of white supremacy.

America needs a spiritual healing. In the scriptures it reads, *"If my people, which are called by my name, shall humble themselves and pray, and seek my face, and turn from their wicked ways; then will I hear from heaven, and will forgive their sin, and will heal their land."* (II Chronicles 7:14) This is the promise of God for us, and for all of America. Moses and Aaron set two signs before the people, one of life and a blessing, and the other of death and a cursing. He said, *". . . choose life, that both thou and thy seed may live."* (Deuteronomy 30:19) The Honorable Elijah Muhammad and Louis Farrakhan say to America the same.

We need to humble ourselves and pray to Allah, God, so that we might receive that same spiritual message that Paul refers to in his words concerning Christ. Paul said, in Christ, *"There is no Jew nor Greek, there is neither bond nor free, there is neither male nor female: for ye are all one in Christ Jesus."* (Galatians 3:28) Paul envisioned the end of nationalism, the end of classism and the end of sexism. He envisioned it through the true message of the man called Christ.

Even though America claims to be a Christian country, America, evidently, has missed the message of Christ, or has yet to receive His true message. However, once that true message is given, those who truly want righteousness, justice and peace will gravitate toward that message and they could form the basis of the Kingdom of God on earth. This can be achieved by establishing the truth that frees white people from the sickness of white supremacy and frees black people from the sickness of black inferiority, and lifts us up from an inferior condition and mentality—setting a new standard by which we all should live. The new standard is duty to God and service to our fellow man.

The Honorable Elijah Muhammad taught us that the greatest of all religious principles is to follow the Golden Rule: Do unto others as you would have them do unto you, and love for your brother what you love for yourself.

A Torchlight for America can be purchased from The Final Call, 734 West 79th Street, Chicago, IL 60620. The retail price is $12.00, plus $1.50 shipping and handling.

RANDALL ROBINSON

Operation Island Storm?
It's Time U.S.-Led Forces Ended Haiti's Nightmare

We must get ready for military action in Haiti. The United States should unilaterally sever all commercial air links with Haiti and commit itself to assembling a regional military force that would be ready to go into Haiti soon should the Haitian military refuse to step down in compliance with United Nations Resolution 917. The countries opposing intervention like Brazil, Peru, Ecuador and Uruguay are blissfully untouched by refugee flows and drug transshipments from Haiti. Neither the United States nor countries closer to the crisis are.

No reasonable person would advocate military action in Haiti as a first choice. However, in the face of the ongoing brutalization of the Haitian people, Gen. Raoul Cedras and his cohorts are not leaving people of conscience any alternatives. Economically, politically and socially, the United States simply can no longer afford to appease the Haitian military.

Already our pockets are tapped. At a time of fiscal austerity, the U.S. Navy and Coast Guard vessels stationed off Haiti to keep contraband out and boat people in cost in excess of $100 million a year. The Clinton administration's commendable attempt to provide a hearing to all Haitian refugees until other countries agree to participate in the processing of refugees will require even more ships, more personnel and more U.S. taxpayer dollars.

Our political system is also strained. Because the immediate focus of my recent fast was to secure fairer treatment for Haitian refugees, some may assume that I see increased emigration as a solution to the current stalemate. That is not the case. I recognize that the president, as well as normally compassionate state and federal legislators, must now devote their time to figuring out how best to accommodate Haitian refugees—at a time when their full attention should be focused on the needs of their constituents. But we should all recognize that our elected officials are being sucked into this political maelstrom, which often has racial overtones, solely because of the murderous ways of the Haitian military. Recall that when President Jean Bertrand Aristide held office from December 1990 to September 1991, more Haitians returned to that country than left it.

While Americans at all socioeconomic levels are shaken by the fear of crime, much of it drug-related, leading figures in the Haitian military continue to profit from the transshipment of drugs from South America to our shores. Recent hearings in the Senate Foreign Relations subcommittee on terrorism, narcotics and international operations provided abundant documentation of Haiti's role in the cocaine trade.

There is a recent and relevant precedent for addressing the problem of a regional governmental leader being directly involved in the transshipment of illegal narcotics to the United States. Clinton must move forcefully to ensure that those within Haiti's military involved in spreading drugs to our cities and towns be brought swiftly to justice.

What about the possibility that the Haitian military will voluntarily step down? Some believe that the recent action by the U.N. Security Council imposing a commercial embargo and a non-commercial flight ban will produce change in Port-au-Prince. There is no rational basis for expecting this to happen, absent the use of force. Indeed, the officers who have (in the words of a recent U.N. report) "unleashed a reign of terror in Haiti" can probably live with cacophonous international condemnation, secure in the knowledge that their drug dealing and sanctions-busting black market operations guarantee their financial security and material well-being. And the longer they are able to accumulate these ill-gotten gains, the more comfortable will be their life exile, should they ever have to face that eventuality.

Is there political support for a military mission to Haiti? There is now. Reps. Maxine Walers, Cynthia McKinney, Charles Rangel, John Lewis and other members of the Congressional Black Caucus are urging the use of force to end the slow strangulation of the Haitian people. Chairman David Obey and Dan Murtha of the House Appropriations Committee stress the importance of quick and decisive military action to end the prolonged and unnecessary suffering. In Florida, Gov. Lawton Chiles, Sen. Bob Graham and Reps. Alcee Hastings and Carrie Meek all understand the relationship between the brutality of the Haitian military and the arrival of refugees on their state's shores. They are part of the growing chorus that urges the use of force in the event that the Haitian military refuses to step aside.

The tragedy is that President Bush could have halted—but did not—the butchery of the coup leaders in 1991. And there is support from other countries in the hemisphere too—if our leaders are willing to accept it. Last week Michael Manley, the former prime minister of Jamaica, told me of a proposal that he, Canadian Prime Minister Brian Mulroney and Venezuelan President Carlos Andres Perez made after Aristide was overthrown in September 1991. They let it be known officially that they were willing to commit soldiers from each of their countries to an American-led military presence in Haiti for the purpose of restoring Aristide to power. Nothing ever came of their offer. At the time, the Bush administration was training members of the very military that had derailed democracy. (It is against this historical backdrop that one must assess the recent comments of former President Bush that the United States should "move forward and forget about Aristide.") Clinton must be careful not to follow the blood-soaked blueprint of Bush's Haiti policy.

The first step in the reorientation of Haiti policy is to insure that the processing of Haitian refugees now goes forward in accordance with internationally established standards. We need Immigration and Naturalization Service officials who are able to communicate in Creole or have qualified translators to assist them. Lawyers willing to assist the applicants pro bono must be allowed to do so, and the U.N. High Commission for Refugees must be allowed as observers. And we have to persuade other countries to help us process these refugees.

However, at the same time that we prepare for the removal of Haiti's military, we must recommit ourself to the fulfillment of an obligation in the so-called Governors Island accord. This agreement, which we entered into last July and tragically reneged on last fall with the withdrawal of the USS Harlan County, calls on the United States to train those socially salvageable elements of the Haitian military and police. Just like the people of Romania, Albania, Bulgaria, Estonia, Lithuania and other heretofore undemocratic European nations, Haitians deserve patient U.S. support in the development of civilian-controlled armies.

U.S. and regional troops must carry out a carefully designed program of civic and humanitarian assistance that would signal not only our opposition to military rule but also a regional commitment to social and economic normalization in Haiti. Drilling wells, establishing health clinics and removing military barracks from civilian areas—this is the kind of support that U.S. troops have provided to other nations in the face of man-made and natural disasters. We can do the same in Haiti.

U.S. military planners are confident that the mechanics of removing Haiti's military would be swift and relatively cost free. However, because our military has always had cozy relationships with the likes of Cedras in Haiti, there is now great reluctance at the Pentagon to move against old friends. Cedras's men are not highly disciplined or well-trained; unlike the militaries in many other Third World nations, the Haitian armed forces have never seen the U.S. military as an enemy. Indeed, their most potent weapon is their supreme and well-founded confidence that the American defense and intelligence agencies will commit themselves to undermining, rather than being party to, any plan to use force against them in Haiti.

One final word of caution. Clinton committed himself to the restoration of democracy in Haiti and the honoring of the results of the Haitian elections of December 1990. But there are those who, like Bush and Dan Quayle, advocate that the United States either engineer or insist upon new presidential elections rather than allowing Aristide to serve until his term expires in 1995. This would not only fly in the face of basic democratic principles, it would also compromise the task of building public support for decisive action.

Clinton has said that he is committed to promoting democracy abroad. He must begin—and produce results—right next door in Haiti.

KWEISI MFUME

The State of Black America—Congressional Black Caucus (September 1994)

Ladies and gentlemen, we are well aware of the crises that beset the African American community and other communities where minority groups reside. They have been documented by statisticians, lamented by the victimized, and we have seen them reported time and time again on television and in the daily newspapers. But we are here today to redeem a greater sense of progress in the Congress than has ever been the case before on behalf of those African American, Hispanic, and Asian American minorities from whom we labor in coalition.

In this caucus, we have accomplished or exceeded almost all of our legislative goals and priorities for the 103rd Congress. Indeed, key areas of concern in our communities have taken political center stage: crime, unemployment, healthcare reform, minority business development, foreign policy. All of these issues have a sense of freshness about them that has been, in many respects, shaped by the efforts of the men and women of the Congressional Black Caucus in conjunction with like-minded others in the Congress who we have worked with over the last two years. Today, I would like to talk a bit about where we are as a society, what direction we are headed in, and how we can give new meaning to the social contract which we have all subscribed to by virtue of our citizenship in this democracy.

One of the worst problems we face today is the horror of crime. It has gripped our cities in terror and has changed our lives in a very real and sobering way. As such, we have become manifestations of both fear and frustration—physically, mentally, and even economically. In this city and in every big city and small town across this country, crime is an issue. It resonates within our subconscious and it pricks the nerve of our emotions because it is real. We can talk, in abstract terms, about the effect of the deficit, or wonder aloud about the effects of unbridled interest rates on our society, but everyone in this room knows someone else who has felt the sting of crime. It is tangible, it is evident, and it is frighteningly real.

It is argued by some that the media has played a role in stoking the fear among the masses of people. While that may or may not be debatable, the fact remains that ours still is a very violent society. We have created an aggressive pop culture that in turn has created an aggressive subculture. It is a subculture that devalues life, depreciates work, and dispenses pain. In such an environment, fear is exacerbated and trust becomes the victim of experience. We have a major problem with guns on our streets and guns in our schools, where drugs are more available than textbooks. And while many believe in the right to bear arms of any type or size, many more are begging, in communities across this nation, for freedom from the fear that these lethal weapons produce.

The recently passed crime bill, I believe, is a step in the right direction, but I hasten to add that it is only a very small step. Beyond the crime bill, we have to look at the contributors of violence in our society in a frank and open manner if we are to start to address the root causes of the problems as we know them in our country. We must address a variety of issues including income disparity, improved education and living conditions, and consistency with both our domestic policy and our foreign policy. No amount of warehousing of prisoners is really going to solve the problems. It will alleviate the overcrowding, which many states are forced to grapple with on a daily basis, but it will accomplish little else.

And thus, education is always a good place to start. We need to bolster our system of education from the bottom up. This means, in essence, fully funding programs. Head Start, preschool, elementary, and secondary school education—too many of our young people are being promoted through school because of their age and because of their size only to be rewarded at the end of twelve years with certificates of attendance rather than legitimate high school diplomas. These are the same young people who we put out on the streets and who we place in the factories and who we usher off to offices to compete for jobs in an ever-increasing competitive environment. We expect them to do what they are not oftentimes equipped to do because the process from which they have come is in desperate need of repair. And so, then, the student in the end who makes the grade is still the student who comes early and stays late to learn the meaning of the lesson.

The Caucus has worked hard to make sure that every American, from toddler age through graduate school, be given equal access to a decent and affordable education. The Head Start Program was expanded to include younger children. Federal assistance to schools in inner cities was increased and now states are being required to provide disadvantaged students with equal access to high-quality teachers, books, and other resources. That is a direct outgrowth of the work of this organization and of the work of others within the Congress, who recognize that education is indeed the right place to start. The School to Work Program was enacted to help students who do not intend to go to college obtain the skills that they will need today in today's workforce. Finally, the National Service Program—argued for, pushed for and conceived by the Kerry Administration, was enacted with the help of the members of this caucus and others, to in turn help people of any age earn money for college or graduate school while performing community service. Through this program, both students and the communities they come from are winners.

But we also need other systems in place. We have got to come to grips with reviewing this whole notion of competency in teachers. Although some unions disagree with the approach, it is clear that it has benefits for both the teacher and the taught alike. Additionally, alternative educational methods ought to be experimented with and explored for value and not for expediency. And if we are to address the issues in an honest fashion and really look for solutions, then we as a nation don't need to talk in terms of quotas. We need to find jobs for the unemployed, and if we are serious and want to be proactive, the long-term solution is to restore quality education and training programs and to place good people in good jobs.

As many of you know, the Congressional Black Caucus has worked hard to improve tax policy, toward interest and opportunity building for low- and middle-income people. Specifically, issues such as the expansion of the earned income tax credit and the continuation of a targeted jobs tax credit have been priorities of this organization that have harvested great benefits. It has been said by some who choose to mock us and to jeer at us and to criticize without really being critical in a way that is building on what their fears or suspicions or distrusts may be, that we are more anti-business than we are anti-prosperity. I don't know how that assumption has been fostered among those who will criticize our efforts, but I do know what the record is. We look at business differently. We look at business and we see jobs and prosperity and a stable middle class and a chance to raise children with dignity and to provide them with a comfortable home and good healthcare and the calm parental affection that comes from being financially secure. We recognize also that business development in this country is not just about Fortune 500 companies, but it is also about the expansion of minority business opportunity, to create an expansive society that in the process creates more jobs and stimulates more growth, a society then that really is equal in its dispensation of opportunity.

At the historic March on Washington, well over a quarter of a century ago, Martin Luther King, Jr. stood before a quarter of a million people assembled at the memorial of one of our nation's greatest leaders, and on that famous day, Doctor King, heir to Abraham Lincoln, addressed the crowd in these words: He said, "We have come to our nation's capitol to cash a check."

When the architects of the republic wrote the magnificent words of the Constitution and the Declaration of Independence, they were in essence signing a promissory note, to which every American was to fall heir. This note was a promise that all men, and indeed, all women, would be guaranteed the unalienable rights of life, liberty, and the pursuit of happiness. And yet, before the republic was born, it compromised the moral principles and the moral claims articulated in the Declaration of Independence and in the Preamble to the Constitution, and in all the other Preambles that it issued to justify its revolution against tyranny, by having subjected human beings, many of our ancestors, to the bondage of the flesh as well as bondage of the spirit.

In the two hundred plus years since then, we have, in spite of ourselves, and in spite of the shortcomings of the Founding Fathers, created a society that has gone beyond its wildest expectations and aspirations. We have outgrown the deficiencies that were a part of that Constitution that labeled us as three-fifths of an individual, that denied women the right to suffrage, that denied black people the right to citizenship. And we have grown in spite of that.

When we stand today to argue forcibly that our growth must not come to a conclusion, we do that out of the best sense of who we are. That check that Dr. King spoke of has yet to be redeemed by many of our people. They are black and brown and yellow, they reside in little towns and hamlets, in big cities and barrios and reservations across this country. They cry out over and over and over again for the right to be heard, the right to be listened to, and the right to participate. The genius that the Founding Fathers bequeathed was to be, if realized, a form of government based on opportunity.

But measured against the promise of America, we as a nation have fallen short in ways that continue to haunt us, plague us, and divide us. We must also find ways, in our quest to deal with many of the real issues that are before us, to purge bigotry from the national psyche. We must be cognizant of newfangled political fads that often breed intolerance. The Congressional Black Caucus has worked with the Hispanic Caucus and others and will continue to fight the hysteria in Congress over immigration. We cannot afford to allow the country to wallow in the muck of being the purveyors of scapegoatism. We are too big and too diverse as a nation to go down that road again, because as a people we understand the damage more than others of what bigotry can do. We must also build new bonds with those who have been our traditional allies while at the same time opening dialogue with those who have not been. Black people must be allowed the right of assembly, with all of our divergent interests and organizations, if we are ever to come to grips with the problems that beset us. Hopefully this will not come at the expense of those who have historically shared our pain, the pain of being made scapegoats. The most obvious of these new efforts must come with our Jewish brothers and sisters as well. We are co-partners in a long and rich religious history, the Judeo-Christian tradition. Most African Americans and Jewish Americans have a shared passion for social justice both at home and abroad. We must seek a revival of this spirit inspired by new vision with new possibilities. We must find ways to build new bridges while at the same time putting in place a mutual, reciprocal respect. Black leaders in the Congress and, indeed, the Congressional Black Caucus will continue to fight all forms of bigotry wherever they originate and we will continue to reach out to others in our communities to build coalitions to deal with the problems that we face every day.

We've seen progress in our efforts to deal with the images that are brought out of Hollywood—the negative portrayal of African Americans throughout the pop culture, on radio and on T.V. Earlier this year we expressed our concerns about the cancellation of Black-oriented programs, which seemed to be disappearing at an ever increasing rate. Already we are beginning to see remarkable progress this season, by the networks' willingness and desire to expand positive African American programming.

You know, there are a lot of things that fall under the umbrella of this concern that we have. I mentioned minority business development earlier. Let me go back to it for just a moment. Minority businesses have been the creators of jobs within hard-pressed and depressed communities, not Fortune 500 companies. Minority businesses help to buoy and stabilize communities in such a way that economic downturn is diverted or certainly lessened. Minority business development gives not only the owners of the business but the workers a greater sense of independence and dignity and worth because in the process what they are doing is threading and expanding economic opportunity. We must be careful in our approach to these businesses and recognize that when America has a sneeze, these businesses oftentimes get pneumonia. They're not asking for handouts. They don't want any special treatment. They want, and argue for, an equal playing field, an equal opportunity.

We must also understand, when we talk about healthcare reform, and it appears more increasingly so each day that the healthcare reform that many thought would be the case when the president gave his address a year and a half ago, that healthcare reform may not occur as we know it, because of an unwillingness by some to compromise and because of an effort by others to stigmatize the issue and by special interest groups who are most effected playing on the fears of Americans by suggesting that if we reform healthcare, we somehow or another are going to bring down the government.

But in that debate, that larger debate, there must also be smaller debates that go to the heart and to the needs of the people that the men and women of the Congressional Black Caucus represent. There must also be opportunities, under any reform, for minority positions and healthcare providers who have traditionally done the work in communities when others pulled out. There must also be a sense of commitment and shared passion to be serious about finding a cure for the American tragedy of AIDS, the disease that ravages so many in our communities and other communities. We must understand that the healthcare debate will be as we make it or as we choose not to participate, and we therefore cannot shrink from that debate. We will argue to people as we have done forcefully over and over again that healthcare is not relegated to any one segment of the Congress or of the Administration or to the American public, but that all of us play a role in it, and the Congressional Black Caucus refuses to be left out of that debate.

There are inequities in our financial system that we plan to address. It is still a shame in this nation that even with the recently released HUMDA Data on mortgage lending this year and the year before that and the year before that and the year before that, that we continue to see discriminatory transient practices by the financial services industry, in lending to people simply because of their zip code or the color of their skin or the sound of their surname. We will challenge those institutions at every turn, and with every fiber in our bodies to bring about a sense of fairness so that people who work hard and play by the rules, who give to the society, who obey the laws, who raise their families, who want to contribute, have the same opportunity to get a loan from a bank that anyone else would.

And let me say just two other things in closing. The issue of values cannot be left out of any debate, any new commitment for change, any pronouncements about our agenda, any efforts to change America, any efforts to change our communities, because it is too very, very important. What Moses brought down from Mount Sinai was not the Ten Suggestions, but rather a blueprint for life. This caucus will and must, without any equivocation as we embrace the years ahead, be in the forefront of that debate because we understand it in a different way. Most of us who serve in this body, like many of you in this audience, were raised to work hard, play by the rules, love our country, and cherish our faith. We were taught the sacredness of life, how every life counted, why we could not abandon the least of these in our society. We were given as children a healthy respect for our elderly, told to cherish their wisdom and told also to seek their counsel. We developed an appreciation for the fact that work has its rewards and that there's nothing wrong with eight hours a day toiling for yourself or, in some instances, for someone else, if in fact you are contributing properly, you do what you do because you like it, and you have a sense of value when you go home at night. The family structure has oftentimes been talked about politically and for sheer expediency. Today, hopefully in its true light, we must find new ways to embrace and support the family structure.

Unlike many in this room, I came out of a disjointed family structure, grew up in the worst of possible conditions. Set aside and divided from my sisters at an early age, I became hopeless after my mother's death. I hit the streets and dropped out of school. I flirted with every temptation that was around, became a teen parent before my time, felt left out and victimized like many who were also eighteen at that time felt and many feel today. I was lost, unprepared, and without direction; and in the process, because of a miracle, I found myself.

The fact of the matter is, that most of the girls and most of the boys that came out of that situation and that neighborhood are not that much different from boys and girls today, and the fact also is, that just as Moses never found that bridge over troubled water, most of these young people will not be able to develop and to create a productive life unless we find ways to intervene with great dispatch. We have an obligation, despite the circumstance of our own conception, despite how we may have come forward, to reach out and embrace for this generation the basic understanding that families are important, that families are a structure that ought to be nurtured, and that revitalizing family life is a battle that we, in fact, can win.

It means taking responsibility and recognizing that the government can't and won't solve every one of our problems. The basic notion of "do for self" that was advanced in the late fifties by the Honorable Elijah Muhammad has worth, it has value many decades later, because in doing for self, we find a way to enhance self, and to enhance the future for people in this society, in a society that we love, that is diverse and pluralistic, and one that must survive.

In two months, I will be preparing to step down from the Chairmanship of the Congressional Black Caucus. It has been one that was filled with great expectation, great delivery, and one also filled with a great deal of misunderstanding. Misunderstanding on the part of many Americans who see the Congressional Black Caucus as this wide-eyed crazy pinko Communist, liberal, twisted group that can't think for itself, that's out of step with everybody and everything, that has nothing better to do except to stand up and to put forth and advance positions.

How cynical can one be? We exist because we have no choice. We all would like to believe that we could live to see the day that there would not be a need for a Congressional Black Caucus, because we would have in our society and our system a new sensitivity and a new understanding and a new appreciation for the value of diversity. Ladies and gentlemen, that day has not yet arrived, and just as in the 1870s, when eleven or so black members of Congress during the period of Reconstruction informally came together and became for all intents and purposes a Congressional Black Caucus, then, like now, we find ourselves in formation not because of our desire to be a block but because of the necessity, oftentimes, to do so.

Following Reconstruction, as many of you know, particularly those who dabble in history, there was a period of time where changes were overturned and Jim Crow became the order of the day and replaced outright slavery and a number of members of the Caucus, those black members of Congress in the House and Senate dwindled, so that by the year 1901 there were none. We have risen in many respects from that awkward period of our nation's history when we went to zero, the period that former Congressman White talked about when he said that one day, and some way, people of ethnic diversity and indeed, those of African ancestry would find a way to return to the Congress of the United States. We have done that. In the last ninety or so years we stand today as a manifestation not so much of our great abilities or our greatest promises, but as a manifestation of the will of people to believe that they ought to be one person, one vote, that they can make a change by electing people to offices, and that they can make a change by taking them out if they fail to do what is in the best interest of those people and the nation in which we reside.

It has been a good two years, and I would be remiss if I did not thank the thirty-nine other men and women of the Caucus for placing in me their trust and their confidence to do as I oftentimes only could do: Interpret from my own window where we were and what we had to do and how we had to do it. And so I look forward to working with this organization as a member, I look forward in the future to working on the legislative agenda that remains unfinished and will remain unfinished until every American really tastes this notion of equal opportunity under the law.

I look forward also to the blessings of being able, through the simple elements of my own example, to turn around the lives of young people who were like me at nineteen years of age, without a bridge over troubled water, with no one to turn to, and with a disbelief in themselves. I hope that my example will allow them to say, "If you could overcome all of that so can I." I will remind them that "it's not so much about where you live, it's what's living in you." If we do nothing else as an organization, we must find a way to convey that to all young people in this country, regardless of their race or religion, to tell them that the future that we care so much about is a future that really belongs to them, and that they one day must become caretakers if we are to make America the nation that it should and must be.

BLACK GOLD

EARL G. GRAVES

The Men of Black Enterprise

When Eddie Murphy's film *Boomerang* hit theaters across the nation in 1992, Kenneth Turan, a movie critic with the *Los Angeles Times*, took exception to the setting around which the romantic comedy revolves. Turan wrote in a review published in the July 1, 1992 edition of the *Times*: "The most intriguing aspect of *Boomerang* [is] its racial composition, for this film takes pains to create a reverse world from which white people are invisible . . . it feels in its own way as silly and arbitrary as mainstream movies without any people of color on the screen."

Was this film set in the crime ridden 'hood? In 1940s Harlem? In civil rights-era Mississippi? None of the above. The principals of Murphy's film happened to be black executives and professionals at a black-owned, black-run cosmetics company in New York. Despite the existence, for decades, of several such firms (the most prominent of which is Johnson Publishing Co.'s Fashion Fair cosmetics), for Ken Turan and several other movie reviewers, a competitive, professionally run, sophisticated black-owned company is the stuff of fantasy.

Unfortunately, this is the case for too many Americans.

Alonzo Herndon. Arthur G. Gaston Sr. S. B. Fuller. Oscar Micheaux. Berry Gordy. Henry G. Parks. Percy Sutton. John H. Johnson. Joshua I. Smith. Herman J. Russell. David Bing. Edward Lewis. Byron E. Lewis. J. Bruce Llewellyn. George E. Johnson. Reginald F. Lewis. Comer J. Cottrell. Edward G. Gardner. Thomas Burrell. Mel Farr.

Do you know these men? Most Americans—and yes, too many African Americans—would be hard pressed to identify them or to detail their achievements. The tragic truth is that, in our celebration of black historical achievement, while we sing the praises of our civil rights leaders, politicians, athletes, entertainers, and artists, our voices too often fall silent when it comes to our legacy in business. As the publisher of *Black Enterprise*, a magazine dedicated to chronicling the progress of African Americans in business, I believe this must change if we are to meet the challenges that face our people and our nation.

The story of A. G. Gaston, who built a business empire that includes Booker T. Washington Insurance Co. and Citizens Federal Savings Bank in Jim Crow Birmingham, should be as well known as that of Washington himself. Gaston, who celebrated his 102nd birthday on July 4, 1994, provided key behind-the-scenes support to Rev. Martin Luther King during 1963 civil rights demonstrations in Birmingham. Not only did the Gaston Hotel serve as King's headquarters, Gaston also paid the bail of civil rights leaders arrested for marching. Gaston is a living testament to our achievements in business against seemingly insurmountabie odds.

Our appreciation of black business achievement doesn't improve much when it comes to more contemporary entrepreneurial giants. When we speak of the sudden, tragic death of Reginald Lewis, most people think of the talented Boston Celtic forward, not the Harvard-trained lawyer who created the nation's largest black-owned company with his landmark $985 million buyout of Beatrice International Foods in 1987.

We cannot allow this ignorance to continue.

Why?

Because, as we move toward the 21st century, we are well into the latest phase of our struggle for freedom of opportunity in America, the battle for economic empowerment, Our confidence as full shareholders (not just laborers and consumers) in the American economy rests with recognizing that our achievements in business are just as valuable as our accomplishments in entertainment, politics, and sports.

Athletes, singers, and activist preachers can no longer shoulder the burden of being role models for our children by themselves. We need to uphold men like H. J. Russell, whose Atlanta-based construction company is helping to build the new Georgia Dome, not just the Black athletes who will play in the stadium. We need to be as familiar with Berry Gordy, the entrepreneur who created Motown, as we are with the performers, such as the popular Boyz II Men, signed to the label.

No celebration of the contributors of Black men—and women—to this nation and this world is complete without the names of the African Americans who build, acquire, and run successful businesses—the economic foundation of this nation. My good friend, actor Ossie Davis, said it best in a letter published in *BE*: "Despite the prodigious progress we African Americans have already achieved in our heroic fight for freedom in the '60s and '70s, there is still one more river to cross: the river of equality. For that we will need an economic philosophy based not only on sound economic theory in general, but on our own history and capabilities, and addressed to our needs."

To do this, we must know our history, and teach it to the entire nation. The African American business tradition is fact—not the product of wishful imagination.

JOHN H. JOHNSON

with LERONE BENNETT, JR.

Succeeding Against the Odds

After securing my home base, I entered the lucrative post exchange military market—we're now the largest Black vendor in the military—and laid the groundwork for expansion into the European market. And it may be observed at once that the same principles that worked in Chicago and Dallas worked in Paris and London.

The clearest example of this was my whirlwind London campaign, based, like the American and West Indian campaigns, on the peculiar needs of that market.

Before approaching a single store, I surveyed the territory and identified vulnerable points. To help in this effort, I hired a British publicist named Mercia Watkins. After touring our offices, she said she didn't know whether she could sell Fashion Fair but that she was relatively sure she could sell me and the Johnson Publishing Company success story.

"The English," she said, "respect achievement. They respect success. They respect royalty and champions. You're the champion in your field, and the best way to sell Fashion Fair is to sell achievement and a man who succeeded against the odds."

The easiest way to do this, she said, was to bring some of England's top fashion writers to America and expose them to the Johnson Publishing Company-Fashion Fair environment.

All right. But how were we going to get their attention? How were we going to persuade busy and important writers to cross the Atlantic for interviews and briefings?

The solution we came up with was the *Concorde.* The British super-plane was new then, and few journalists could afford the super-fare for the three-hour flight to the States.

We made it affordable, paying all expenses for a group of fifteen writers and editors, Black and White. We flew the group to New York City and put them up at the Helmsley Palace. We got them tickets to the Shubert Theater where they not only saw Broadway's hottest show, *Dreamgirls*, but went backstage to meet the show's stars.

This was the appetizer for a twenty-four-hour extravaganza in Chicago, where they lived at the Ritz Carlton and were carried by limousines to the Johnson Publishing Company headquarters for a tour, luncheon, and interviews and to my Lake Shore Drive apartment for dinner.

The results—a series of glowing stories on the Fashion Fair Miracle—surpassed our expectations and provided the backdrop for a London luncheon that introduced the line to English and French buyers. One writer said that Fashion Fair provided "a foundation shade to blend over every skin from pale to the darkest Caribbean Brown."

We flew the Ebony Fashion Show to London for the luncheon, which was held at the Dorchester Hotel. The theme of the luncheon, "Ebony and Ivory," was reflected in a black and white piano and Black and White models who emphasized that Fashion Fair was for everybody.

This brought immediate orders from London's Harrods and Paris's Printemps, followed by commitments from other high-line stores, including Dickins & Jones and Selfridges in London and Galeries Lafayette in Paris.

While masterminding the Fashion Fair campaign, I was also directing the day-to-day affairs of an insurance company, three radio stations, and three magazines. And although I spent most of my time in this period on Fashion Fair accounts, I had to put on my fireman's hat from time to time to put out fires in other divisions of the company.

One of these fires, a serious one, developed at Supreme Life Insurance Company, where I had installed a master salesman and marketing expert as president. Under his leadership, sales increased. So, unfortunately, did administrative and financial problems. Before things got completely out of hand, I assumed the position of president as well as chairman of the board and reorganized the staff.

This was a delicate operation involving not only the board but the State Insurance Department. To save and preserve the legacy of Pace and other Supreme pioneers, I pulled out all stops and invested additional funds. When the business was reestablished on a sound basis, I named Lloyd G. Wheeler president and installed controls to prevent a recurrence of the problem. Since then, the company has regained lost ground and established new records.

In the midst of this crisis, I confronted and solved two editorial problems. The first was the declining circulation of a new magazine, *Ebony Jr!* The magazine, designed for children between the ages of six and twelve, hit a peak circulation of 100,000 before dropping to 40,000. The major problems—identification of parents with children in the target age groups and city-by-city sales campaigns focused on boards of education—were solvable, but required more time and money than I was willing to give at the time. After investing more than $2 million, I decided to cut my losses and concentrate on the profitable divisions.

The second problem was the *Ebony* format. When I started *Ebony*, the standard picture-magazine size was 13¾″ by 9¾″, the *Life* and *Look* size. After *Life* and *Look* went out of business, all major magazines—*Esquire, Ladies' Home Journal, McCall's*—reduced their sizes to 10⅞″ by 8¼″. *Ebony* bucked the trend and became the last of the big commercial magazines.

This created major advertising and circulation problems, for the whole industry was geared now to the new standard size. I was emotionally tied to the big book. But I couldn't buck the tide of advertisers, who refused to prepare oversized ads. When we lost Ford, Campbell Soup, and General Motors ads in one issue, I bit the bullet, reduced the size, and increased the price.

I was prepared for adverse reader reaction, but circulation increased. It turned out that it was more convenient to handle the standard-sized book. The new *Ebony* also received better display space on the newsstands. All of a sudden, circulation exploded, going from 1.2 million to 1.5 million to the 1.8 million we sell today.

To take up the slack created by the discontinuance of *Ebony Jr!* I created a new magazine, *EM*, addressed to the Ebony man. At the same time, I bought 20 percent of the outstanding stock of *Essence*, a New York–based magazine designed for Black women.

The upshot of all this was a stronger personal and corporate profile, as *Forbes* magazine pointed out in 1982 when it named me to its list of the 400 richest Americans. The magazine said my net worth was $100 million. Two years later, the magazine said I was worth "at least" $150 million.

I've never counted, but I don't quarrel with the figures listed in the Forbes 400—and I don't apologize. Whatever the correct figure, whether it's the $175 or $200 million some analysts cite today, I earned it, and I'm still earning it. I work harder today than I did when I started out. I make more presentations, I call on more clients, I make more speeches and public appearances. In fact, if I were young again, and if I knew then what I know now, I could be even more successful. Young or not, if I get a few more years, I'm going to create a bigger company despite age, despite race, despite the odds.

The Forbes 400 honor was one wave in an unprecedented tide of personal and corporate recognition. There was, to begin with, the national outpouring of acclaim that followed the fortieth anniversary of *Ebony* in November 1985. The company grossed $154,860,000 in that year and was No. 1 for the second straight year on the *Black Enterprise* list of the top one hundred Black businesses. In 1987, when *Black Enterprise* named me Entrepreneur of the Decade, Johnson Publishing Company grossed $173,500,000 from publishing, broadcasting, and TV production and cosmetics, and employed 1,828 persons.

In the same period, the Better Boys Club of Chicago named me Chicagoan of the Year, the first Black so honored. Governor James Thompson and Mayor

Harold Washington were among the civic and corporate leaders who gathered to celebrate what I called a Chicago and an American triumph.

There was also a sentimental trip to my Arkansas City hometown—my first visit in fifty-three years. I don't know what I expected, but I was brought to tears by the Blacks and Whites who hugged and kissed me and welcomed me home. This was the New South, and it took some getting used to, White men and women hugging Black men and women and sassing each other and sharing yesterdays and tomorrows.

What a wonderful thing it was, they said, for a native son to come home in glory after showing the world what Arkansas City folk could do. People who were old enough remembered Miss Gert, as they called my mother. They said it was a shame that she didn't live to see the sun of this day.

In the blinding hot Arkansas sun, remembered from decades ago, I relived the lost years with Dorothy Moore, widow of former sheriff Robert S. Moore, and Nathaniel Hayes, an old friend and former captain in the sheriff's department. We talked about old times and old places and called back the flood and the first picture show and the bakery shop, where my stepfather worked. Then we went into the integrated high school for a Black and White welcoming ceremony attended by every major official in Arkansas City and Desha county, led by Mayor R. C. Bixler, Sheriff Ben Williams, and State Representative Bynum Gibson.

I had no illusions about the meaning of the turnout. The people, Black and White, came to see not a man, not a personality, but a dream and a faith. They had perhaps doubted the dream in their hearts. They had said perhaps that it no longer worked. They came on this day to see with their own eyes that it could still happen and that it could happen to a boy from Arkansas City. And if it could happen to a Black boy from Arkansas City, it could happen to anyone.

After the ceremony, I visited the shotgun house where I was born and the St. John Baptist Church. Before leaving town in a motorcade arranged by Governor Bill Clinton and his aide, Rodney Slater, I walked one last time down the great levee and looked across the Mississippi River with eyes misted by the dreams and hopes and fears of my youth.

All the themes and stations of my life—the Mississippi River, Goin' to Chicago, the welfare roll and the roll of the 400 richest Americans and Gertrude Johnson Williams and *Negro Digest* and *Ebony* and *Jet*—came together when I was inducted into the Junior Achievement's Business Hall of Fame, along with, among others, John E. Swearingen of Standard Oil Company of Indiana, Hyatt hotel magnate A. N. Pritzker, and, posthumously, Gustavus F. Swift (1839–1903), Philip D. Armour (1832–1901), Marshall Field (1834–1906), Colonel Robert R. McCormick (1880–1955), and Julius Rosenwald (1862–1932).

As I sat in Chicago's Museum of Science and Industry, listening to the citations, I had a sudden and unbelievable vision of the great names entombed in this Business Hall of Fame, the Armours, the Rosenwalds, the Fields, marching in the same procession with a Black boy who had walked barefooted in Mississippi mud and dreamed an impossible dream.

When I got up to acknowledge the award, I looked beyond the immediate audience and said to Blacks, to Hispanics, to Asians, to Whites, to dreamers everywhere, that long shots *do* come in and that hard work, dedication, and perseverance will overcome almost any prejudice and open almost any door.

That was my faith then and it's my faith now.

I believe that the greater the handicap the greater the triumph.

I believe that the only failure is failing to try.

I believe that Black, Brown, and White Americans are chained together by tradition, history, and a common market and that what helps one group of Americans helps all Americans.

And if my life has meaning and color and truth, it is because millions of Americans, Black and White, have proved through me that the Dream is still alive and well and working in America.

DENNIS KIMBRO
and NAPOLEON HILL

Think and Grow Rich: A Black Choice

DESIRE: THE STARTING POINT OF ALL ACHIEVEMENT

"Some of us seem to accept the fatalist position, the fatalist attitude, that the Creator accorded to us a certain position and condition, and therefore there is no need trying to be otherwise."

—MARCUS GARVEY

"No one need fear death. We need fear only that we may die without having known our greatest power."

—NORMAN COUSINS

In everyone's life there comes a time of ultimate challenge—a time when all our resources are tested. A time when life seems unfair. A time when our faith, our values, our patience, our compassion, our ability to persist, are all pushed to the limit and beyond. Some have used such tests as opportunities for growth; others have turned away and allowed these experiences to destroy their hopes.

Have you ever wondered what comprises the critical difference in the way we respond to life's challenges? Society has been fascinated by what triggers us to behave the way we do. We would all like to know what sets certain men and women apart from their peers. You may have heard the story of the dehydrated man in the desert, who is weak, sun-worn, and exhausted, and after spotting an oasis miles away, summons unknown inner reserves in an effort to reach his goal.

Obviously, those who stamp their mark in this world are men and women who are motivated by the *desire to achieve.* Unless you *want to* taste the true riches of life—health, love, freedom, and prosperity—you will forever be among those who have *tried* but remained by the shoreline mired in their failure. You must desperately *want to* succeed. You must be consumed with an encompassing *burning desire* to reach a definite objective. You must be obsessed with an overwhelming urge to win.

We face life with only two options: *Either move or be moved.* The battle-tested and determined individual will stand out from the crowd.

The Man Who Desired to Be Rich

Hailing from humbling beginnings, S. B. Fuller was once identified as one of the wealthiest black men in America. In his long life, Fuller owned businesses throughout the country. A fearless believer in individual initiative, he denounced welfare as the enemy of motivation. Fuller dedicated his life to achieving his dreams and helping others realize theirs. He lived by the phrase: "Nothing comes from doing nothing."

Fuller was born in Ouachita Parish, Louisiana, in 1905, the oldest of eight children raised by tenant farmers. He was driving mules at age nine, and quit school after the sixth grade. By the time he was seventeen, his father had left and his family had moved to Memphis.

For the next several years he struggled to make ends meet. As he drifted from job to job, something was gnawing inside. "Why are some people wealthy and others poor?" he constantly thought. Unexpectedly, he found the answer in his mother's dying words.

"We shouldn't be poor, S.B.," the frail black woman said on her deathbed. "And don't let me ever hear you say it's God's will. We're poor only because Father has never developed the desire for anything else." It was his mother, among all other influences, who refused to accept this hand-to-mouth existence, though it was all she had ever known. Fuller's dying mother knew there was something drastically wrong with the idea that her family, *living in a land of plenty*, was barely getting by. In a split moment in time her son became the sounding board and the recipient of her years of wisdom.

The few words passed on to him became deeply ingrained in his mind. Almost immediately they changed his life. Fuller *wanted* to become rich, and his goal soon became an obsession.

There's an important rule that governs the principle of desire. The rule states: You can be, have, or do anything that you want—if only you *want* it hard enough! In other words, you must eagerly long for something—not a mere wishing or wanting, but a *fierce, eager, consuming hunger that knows no defeat and demands satisfaction.*

Just as the great oak, as an embryo, sleeps within the acorn, success begins in the form of an *intense desire.* Out of a strong desire grow the motivating forces that cause men to embrace hopes, initiate plans, develop courage, and stimulate their minds to action in pursuit of a definite plan or purpose. There is nothing behind desire except the impulse through which it may be transformed into action. Anyone who is capable of stimulating his or her own mind to produce intense desire is capable also of the achievement of that desire.

Though no one in his family wanted to be wealthy, Fuller conditioned his mind with such intensity that he was compelled into action. The attainment of his goal became his sole driving force.

After hitchhiking to Chicago in 1928, Fuller held a variety of jobs—but mostly he sold. He sold life insurance until he discovered he could earn more money peddling soap. Said Fuller, "A local magazine printed the names of Chicago's highest paid executives. In 1934, the president of Metropolitan Life earned $50,000. On the other hand, the president of Lever Brothers—a soap company—made nine times as much. At that point, I quit selling insurance and started selling soap."

So intense was Fuller's desire that he took his last few dollars, purchased a case of soap, and began selling toiletries door to door, in Depression-laden Chicago.

He sold soap for pennies a cake and pitched his products for as long as people would listen. "Repetition is the mother of knowledge," he quipped. In 1935, Fuller boasted he would one day own his initial supplier, Boyer National Laboratories, who many times refused to give him credit. A decade later he made good on his promise and bought the struggling company. During his years as a salesman and entrepreneur, Fuller gained the respect and admiration of his peers. By setting aside nearly every penny he had earned, he managed to save $25,000, which he used as a springboard to buy other businesses and expand his empire.

What was Fuller's secret? What power, known or unknown, allowed him to leave the masses of the impoverished and join the ranks of the wealthy *in the teeth of a depression*? Listen as he unveils the key: "I knew exactly what I wanted. *I had to be a millionaire!*"

With only a sixth-grade education, Fuller began reading for self-development. "When you know that you don't know, you've got to read." His favorite books were the Bible, Robert Collier's *Secret of the Ages*, and Napoleon Hill's *Think and Grow Rich.* One day Fuller read a single fact that changed his outlook: Of the 4043 millionaires in America then, 3954 had not finished high school. This helped fuel his desire—"If they can do it, so can I!"

Within five years Fuller had dozens of salespeople and a small factory. He had bought real estate, a drug company, a department store, a string of theaters, and two black newspapers. And yes, he had become a millionaire.

It is important to note that S. B. Fuller started life with few advantages. However, he chose a goal and armed himself with an intense desire and set out to reach it. There is an immense difference between the chances of the man who begins with a thorough understanding of himself, with a resolution to win at all costs, and the individual who sets out with no particular purpose or ambition, and no firm determination that he will reach his objective.

There is all the difference in the world between the prospects of the man who has committed himself to his life's purpose without reservation, has burned all bridges behind him and has taken a secret oath to succeed, has vowed to see his proposition through to the end, no matter what sacrifices he must make or how long it may take, and the man who wavers and goes about his objective halfheartedly.

Not everyone would care to be an S. B. Fuller or any of the other achievers highlighted in this book. Not everyone would choose to pay the price of success. To many, the riches of life are different. But the choice remains yours, and yours alone. The principle through which S. B. Fuller got his millions *is still alive! It is available to you.* Whether success to you means material rewards, as it did to this penniless, uneducated black man, or advancing in your chosen field—whatever it is that you choose *will only come through intense desire.*

Complacency is the enemy of achievement. It makes all the difference in the world whether you undertake a proposition to win—with clenched teeth and a resolute will—having prepared for it thoroughly, and determined at the very outset to hit your mark, or whether you begin your task with indecision and indifference. It is widely believed that the man who has the fortitude and the right mental attitude will, sooner or later, reach his objective.

Now, have you knocked on the door named Desire? Will you accept the torch of opportunity this great nation has to offer? Are you willing to study the principles spelled out in *Think and Grow Rich: A Black Choice*? If you answer yes, chances are this lesson is for you.

The Power of Desire and Motives

Basic motives, moved to action, are all prefaced by the desire for a specific objective. Men and women of ordinary ability become pillars of strength when aroused by desire, stimulated by action. Bring a person face to face with the possibility of death, and, amazingly, he or she will exhibit all kinds of physical strength and prowess. The following story clearly illustrates this point.

> An old African sage, wise and influential, lived on the side of a mountain near a lake. It was common practice for the people of the village to seek his advice. The old man spent many hours sitting in front of

his small hut, where he rocked in a crude rocking chair made of branches and twigs. Hour after hour he sat and rocked as he thought.

One day he noticed a young African warrior walking on the path toward his hut. The young man walked up the hill and stood erect before the sage. "What can I do for you?" the old man said.

The warrior replied, "I was told by those in the village that you are very wise. They said that you can give me the secret of happiness and success."

The old man listened, then gazed at the ground for several moments. He rose to his feet, took the boy by the hand, and led him down the path back toward the lake. Not a word was spoken. The young warrior was obviously bewildered, but the sage kept walking. Soon they approached the lake, but did not stop. Out into the water the old man led the boy. The farther they walked, the higher the water advanced. The water rose from the boy's knees to his waist, then to his chin, but the old man said nothing and kept moving deeper and deeper. Finally the lad was completely submerged. At this point the wise man stopped for a moment, turned the boy around, and led him out of the lake and up the path back to the hut. Still not a word was spoken. The old African sat again in his creaky chair and rocked to and fro.

After several thought-provoking minutes, he looked into the boy's questioning eyes and asked, "Young man, when you were in the lake, underwater, what was it you desired most?"

Openly excited, the boy replied, "Why, you old fool, I wanted to breathe!"

Then the sage spoke these words: "My son, when you want happiness and success in life as badly as you wanted to breathe, you will have found the secret."

This tale provides an excellent analogy. *What is it that you desire more than anything else?* When you pursue your objective with the same state of mind so clearly described in the above tale, then you will reach your goal!

GEORGE C. FRASER

Success Runs in Our Race

IT TAKES A VILLAGE TO RAISE A CHILD

It is better to be part of a great whole than to be the whole of a small part.

FREDERICK DOUGLASS

Like many African Americans, when I entered the white-dominated corporate world for the first time twenty years ago, I did my best to tone down my blackness. I have to laugh now when I remember the internal battle that raged as I would prepare to attend yet another Procter & Gamble formal company dinner. "Do I take my own bottle of hot sauce, or do I leave my cultural tastes at home?"

It was like those days of my youth back in Manhattan. If the Puerto Ricans were whaling away on the blacks, did I try to pass as a Puerto Rican in order to get safely to school or the grocery store, or did I defiantly announce my blackness and suffer the result?

In reflecting upon those days, I see now that I lived, as many African Americans do, a dual existence. I ate white when I was around whites. ("Hold the fatback, please.") And I talked white around whites, to the point that I joked I was "bidialectal," speaking white English and black English, depending on whether I was with the brothers or others.

I make light of this duality, but it goes to the heart of a very serious issue that W. E. B. Du Bois explored in *The Souls of Black Folk* when he wrote:

> It is a peculiar sensation, this double-consciousness, this sense of always looking at one's self through the eyes of others. . . . One feels his two-ness—an American, a Negro; two souls, two thoughts, two unreconciled strivings; two warring ideals in one dark body, whose dogged strength alone keeps it from being torn asunder.

Afrocentrist Anthony J. Mensah, a native of Ghana, refers to this "two-ness" as "the schizoid nature of black existence," which, he says, "arises out of the contention that black people in America do not belong to any one functional, coherent, cohesive culture."

Of course, the truth is we belong to one of the oldest cultures in all of history, that of the people of Africa. Tragically, however, blacks in America have often rejected their own community because they didn't think they could succeed in overcoming racism if they remained linked to the victims of it.

The result of that black flight from our own blackness is evident today in many urban neighborhoods where the exodus of the black middle class has drained hope from the streets. Professor William Julius Wilson of the University of Chicago holds that "the central problem of the underclass is joblessness reinforced by increasing social isolation in impoverished neighborhoods."

When the poor live only with the poor, they have restricted access to opportunities for jobs, education, and role models. They have no "success network" to plug into.

"Thus neighborhoods that have few legitimate employment opportunities, inadequate job information networks, and poor schools not only give rise to weak labor force attachment but also raise the likelihood that people will turn to illegal or deviant activities for income, thereby further weakening their attachment to the legitimate job market," Wilson holds. For many of our inner-city poor, the problem is not only poverty and racism, but hopelessness and a lack of opportunities. In other words, as one inner-city resident said, "The system keeps me in the system."

The situation is prevalent across the country. In Cleveland, where I live, a Cleveland and Rockefeller Foundation study found that if this trend is not reversed, it is projected that three fourths of city neighborhoods will be majority-poor by the turn of the century.

Between 1950 and 1990, Cleveland's population went from 915,000 to 506,000, according to the Cleveland Foundation Commission on Poverty. This exodus of primarily the more affluent city residents into the suburbs and outlying communities led to a decline in housing values, deteriorating housing stock, and a disintegration of the support community for the less affluent. As the middle class moved out, the commission found that with them went positive role models and vital connections to employment opportunities so desperately needed by those striving to break the poverty cycle and better their lives. At the same time, much of the capital necessary to support city services and commercial development is drained, to devastating effect. The commission reported:

> Persistent poverty, the kind that endures over many years and with increasing frequency is passed from one generation to another, tends to be found in neighborhoods marked by a deteriorated social infrastructure—that grassroots network of churches, schools, banks, businesses, neighborhood centers, indeed families themselves—which feeds and nourishes the life of a small community. Where social support systems have broken down, poverty has become for many a permanent condition.

Said another way, many of our young people have nowhere to go and nothing to do. They are looking for jobs, respect, and supervision. Remember when you were a kid? There were Boys' Clubs, Christian youth organizations, church activities, Golden Gloves competitions, Boy and Girl Scouts, high school functions, and two-parent families. There were jobs in the neighborhood—safe and stable jobs that also provided the opportunity for young people to learn from mentors and role models. There was an infrastructure in our communities, a network of support and guidance. There was discipline, dress codes, and an ingrained respect for authority whether in the schools or on the streets. Sex, violence, and drugs may have been present, but they were not as pervasive, nor as glorified in the media.

The sense of hopelessness has been further entrenched by government cutbacks in social programs, the breakup of the family structure, and the lack of employment opportunities for even those who have done the right thing and gone on to college.

Our young people in many areas of the country appear to be confused, despondent, and misguided in their values. Their lives have no meaning to them, and as a result, they have no respect for the value of anyone else's life.

I believe that jobs, jobs, and more jobs are, to a large degree, the solution. There should be a much greater emphasis not only on college training but on technical and vocational training. We need to make an investment in this "at risk" generation.

Not every African American can be, or wants to be, a nuclear physicist, president of Xerox, or a business entrepreneur. But every African American must be encouraged to first graduate from high school and then to consider the opportunities that lie beyond that. Our young people need to prepare themselves for the considerable new job opportunities that will await them in the twenty-first century.

After World War II, the Japanese focused on building the finest work force in the world. They did this by stressing and developing programs to train their citizenry in technical and vocational skills. To that end, they succeeded in dominating world production standards in the automotive and electronic industries.

In coming years, the available pool of workers will be largely dominated by blacks and other minorities, whose numbers have increased in far greater increments than other groups. This means opportunity for those who make themselves valuable by obtaining educations and training. This door will be opened for us. But we have to take the initiative and step up to it by setting an agenda and focusing on vocational and technical training.

The black working and middle classes must shore up the infrastructure in their communities. They can do this by networking together. Strong networks give power to the people in them. And power of this sort provides the strength to break out of the poverty cycle. Employers in the private and public sectors must be enlisted in this movement as well, because they control the resources. We must all be part of the solution, and we must all move beyond the myopia of racism.

Author John Williams said, "Whatever future America will have will be directly related to the solving of its racial dilemma, which is a human dilemma."

The Enemy Within

While there are racial and societal forces at work on us from the outside, a certain portion of our problem lies within. From the days of our enslavement, many of us bought into the slave mentality. We accepted the white man's pronouncement that we were an inferior race, and even when we came to understand that it was a false pronouncement, it continued to dominate our collective psyches; it was a powerful indoctrination.

The following is an infamous and chilling example of how that mentality was ingrained into our ancestors, and into succeeding generations. It is taken from a speech given by Willie Lynch, from whose name the term *lynching* is derived. Lynch was a British slave owner in the West Indies, probably of Jamaican heritage, who used mind-control techniques on his black slaves and then advocated the use of those manipulative techniques to other slave owners. He was invited to the colony of Virginia in 1712 to teach his methods to slave owners there, and these are his words as passed down. I think you will find them haunting:

> Gentlemen: I greet you here on the bank of the James River in the year of Our Lord one thousand seven hundred and twelve. First, I shall thank you The Gentlemen of the Colony of Virginia for bringing me here. I am here to help you solve some of your problems with slaves. Your invitation reached me on my modest plantation in the West Indies where I have experimented with some of the newest and still oldest methods for control of slaves. Ancient Rome would envy us if my program is implemented. As our boat sailed south on the James River, named for our illustrious King, whose version of the Bible we cherish, I saw enough to know that your problem is not unique. While Rome used cords of wood as crosses for standing human bodies along its old highways in great numbers, you are here using the tree and the rope on occasion.
>
> I caught the whiff of a dead slave hanging from a tree a couple miles back. You are not only losing valuable stock by hangings, you are having uprisings, slaves are running away, your crops are sometimes left in the field too long for maximum profit, you suffer occasional fires, your animals are killed, gentlemen, you know what your problems are; I do not need to elaborate. I am not here to enumerate your problems, I am here to introduce you to a method of solving them.
>
> In my bag here, I have a fool proof method for controlling Black

Slaves. I guarantee everyone of you that if installed correctly, it will control the slaves for at least 300 years. My method is simple and members of your family and any Overseer can use it.

I have outlined a number of difference(s) among the slaves; and I take these differences and make them bigger. I use fear, distrust, and envy for control purposes. These methods have worked on my modest plantation in the West Indies and [they] will work throughout the South. Take this simple little list of differences, think about them. On top of my list is "Age" but it is there only because it begins with "A." The second is "Color" or "Shade," there is intelligence, size, sex, size of plantation, status of plantation, attitude of owner, whether the slaves live in the valley, on a hill, East, West, North, or South, have a fine or coarse hair, or are tall or short. Now that you have a list of differences, I shall give you an outline of action but before that, I shall assure you that distrust is stronger than trust and envy is stronger than adulation, respect and admiration.

The Black Slave, after receiving this indoctrination, shall carry on and will become self-refueling and self-generating for hundreds of years, maybe thousands.

Don't forget you must pitch the old black versus the young black and the young black male against the old black male. You must use the dark skin slave vs. the light skin slaves and the light skin slaves vs. the dark skin slaves. You must also have your white servants and overseers distrust all blacks, but it is necessary that your slaves trust and depend on us. They must love, respect and trust only us.

Gentlemen, these Kits are keys to control, use them. Have your wives and children use them, never miss an opportunity. My plan is guaranteed and the good thing about this plan is that if used intensely for one year the slaves themselves will remain perpetually distrustful.

Thank you, gentlemen.

Interestingly on March 17, 1978, a secret memorandum was issued to the president and his Cabinet as part of a "comprehensive review of current developments in Black Africa from the point of view of their possible impacts on the black movement in the United States." It was an analysis of the strategic social, economic, and political ramifications made by then-chairman of the National Security Council Zbigniew Brzezinski under Jimmy Carter.

I was provided a copy of this memorandum by the Reverend Walter E. Fauntroy, who, as chairman of the Congressional Black Caucus, joined numerous national black organizations in expressing outrage over this memorandum. Reverend Fauntroy is now pastor of one of Washington, D.C.'s most influential churches, and chairman of Southern Christian Leadership Conference. He also heads a Washington, D.C.–based consulting firm specializing in international finance and trade.

It was Brzezinski's position at the time that it was not in the best interest of the U.S. to allow any part of the U.S. black movement to show outreach and support for the emerging movement in black Africa.

To that end a "range of policy options" was suggested; at least four of those options reflect Willie Lynch's approach to controlling slaves. They were:

• to elaborate and bring into effect a special program designed to perpetuate division in the black movement to neutralize the most active groups of leftist radical organizations representing different social strata of the black community to encourage divisions in black circles.

• to preserve the present climate which inhibits the emergence from within the black leadership of a personality capable of exerting nationwide appeal.

• to work out and realize preventive operations in order to impede durable ties between US black organizations and radical groups in African states.

• to support actions designed to sharpen social stratification in the black community which would lead to the widening and perpetuation of the gap between successful educated blacks and the poor, giving rise to growing antagonism between different black groups and weakening of the movement as a whole.

Tragically, the infamous Brzezinski memorandum and Lynch's predatory, racist instincts were effective and few of us can deny that the self-defeating mentality that he nurtured among his slaves lives on today. Still, too many blacks prey upon each other, and those who would hold us back watch in delight as the media feeds them with images of conflict within our own families and neighborhoods. All of these preoccupations regarding our differences, plight, and challenges contribute to divisiveness, which makes us all weaker in our battles against racism on the outside. Jealousies within our racial community stifle productive behavior that might benefit us all, and they severely limit our ability to come together for united, positive action in which combined strength and shared resources might elevate our lives. Our enemies delight in our fractured community. They fear unity, trust, and cohesion. We must recognize and resist the insidious "race-lynching" of our own. We have to remove our own hands from the ropes around our own necks before we can begin to effectively battle our common enemies.

RETURN TO THE SOURCE

REGINALD McKNIGHT

I Get On the Bus

I take the bus to the end of the line, all the way to the wharf near Place Leclerc. It is my intention to walk from here to Place de l'Indépendance, the center of town. I simply want to walk in a place I am not known, where people do not greet me, ask me where I am going, how I am doing. I will perhaps go to the expensive boulangerie just off the square, where mainly white and Lebanese teenagers congregate. They will leave me alone. They will not even see me. Then I will go to a good hotel. But suddenly I spot the Gorée Island ferry ticket cage and decide that Gorée would be the perfect place to steep in my loneliness. Gorée was a slave depot many many years ago. Each time I go there I can smell taste touch the very fibers of slavery. The old holding-pen walls, the pebbles on the strand, the air, all vibrate with atoms of dried blood, evaporated sweat, desiccated vomit. It is unlike any other place I know. It is the perfect place for self-pity. There is pain there, but it is not my pain. It is like a chorus for my solo. Perhaps too many years have passed since what, for lack of a better term, I could call my ancestral leave-taking. Perhaps I am no longer African, or African only in the vestigial sense. My senses register the waterless horrors of the island's past as if they were photocopied pictures of paintings. I go there not because of some overpowering emotion that takes hold of me but because the ancient emotion does not overwhelm my own.

I get on the boat. The boat goes to Gorée. I get off the boat. The weather is beautiful, eye-splitting blue sky, deep green cut-glass water. The sunlight is almost audible. Many people, mostly Africans, are swimming, sunbathing. My head starts throbbing. My vision blurs. I see the world as if through water. Wiry African boys, rubbery African girls, move like stop-action figures, jabbering, squealing. I walk past them, to the village, past the village, and up the rocky trail that leads to the cliffs. I always feel nervous when I go to the cliffs alone. There is a legend of an old woman who lives up here. She is a powerful sorceress named Koumba Castelle. They say she rides a white horse around the island at night. They say her power is so sinister and fierce that if you were to meet her while walking in these hills, if you were to see her face, look her in the eye, the bottom half of your face will twist to the left, the top will twist right, and you will spend the rest of your days this way. They say that Koumba owns the island, that she jealously guards every inch. Once, after World War II, they tried to build a bridge connecting Gorée to Dakar. The sorceress did not like this, so she called up a tremendous squall, which tore the bridge like so many matchsticks. They rebuilt the bridge and again she tore it down, this time before it was ever completed. I have seen the remnant of the bridge many times, though I am afraid to approach it. It hangs out a hundred feet or so over the sea. Rays of rusted cable jut from the crumbling cement and asphalt like ribs. They say the bridge is cursed—no doubt it is—and birds, lizards, even weeds, neither thrive nor feed there.

Keeping a good distance from the bridge, I approach the edge of the cliff. I stare down into the water. It is astoundingly beautiful, clear. It shifts from blue to blue: indigo, cobalt, azure, robin's egg. The sunlight cuts into it, glassy blades scraping yellow lines onto the black volcanic rock on the ocean floor. I stare for a long time. I wait for tears. I wait for a great surge of self-pity to storm across the ocean and knock me flat. But nothing comes. Not a thing. Then, slowly as time in hellfire, a dull shame fills my gut. *Oh well is what you said that night, Evan. Oh well. What were you thinking? And who do you think you are? Here. Now. Trying to conjure up tears for yourself. Oh well? What did you mean? Oh well, it is only a dream? Oh well, since I have gone through the trouble of lifting this slab? Oh well, he is only a legless African?* He caressed my face. *So you killed him?* He was poor. *So you killed him?* He was grateful for the two brass coins I gave him. *So you killed him?* I broke bread with him. *So you killed him?* I did not know him. *So you killed him?* I think perhaps I did, but besides the dull shame I feel nothing. It is as though my nerves were spun in webs, wrapped in gauze, sealed in wax. I stand here and gnash my teeth, squeeze my fists, but can call up no real emotion. Instead, my head rocks; the pressure builds at the top of my skull. The high-pitched squeal builds and I hold my head in my hands for fear that my skull will literally explode. I inhale deeply in order to calm myself, and I smell diesel fumes. I hear footsteps behind me, a slow, unsteady gait. I open my eyes but do not turn around. Instead I try to focus on the water. The closer the steps, the deeper I stare into the water. But I can scarcely concentrate. The two pains, the one deep inside my brain, the other boring into the top of my head, alternately become one, then separate. The rhythms are like heartbeat and breath, working to keep something alive.

There is a man standing next to me. I find something familiar about him even before I look up at his face. Worn-out, point-toed sandals, gray khaftan, maroon fez, a bald head. There is nothing remarkable about him at first. Then he turns full face to me. It is the man with the teary egg-white eyes, the blind man to whom I gave alms when on the bus. Perhaps by reflex, I reach into my pocket and pull out a five-hundred-franc note. "Aam," I say to him. "Jerrejeff, jerrejeff, jerrejeff," he says in a flat mumble. He slips the franc note into his pocket, spreads his arms, bends over as if looking for something on the ground, throws his arms forward, and dives off the cliff. He tumbles through the air, head over heels, head over heels, head over heels. My eyes widen, then I close them, and for the briefest moment I feel weightless, as though I, myself, am careening through the air. I hear him hit the water.

I turn and walk back toward the trail, but I become dizzy and sit down on a small boulder. My head is spinning. I am hyperventilating. *I gotta get out of here.* I shut my eyes and turn my face to the sky, breathing in deeply, exhaling, breathing, exhaling. I consider prayer. I consider jumping off the cliff myself. I consider, for a long long time, going back to the U.S. I think of *King Lear*, and what would have happened if Edgar had led Gloucester to the brink of a real cliff. Would Gloucester simply say, "Jerrejeff, jerrejeff, jerrejeff," as he tumbled down? I think about many things, some of them quite stupid, but I keep these thoughts turning to assess my mind's lucidity. Again I hear footsteps. Again I am afraid to look. In fact I put my hands over my face.

"There you are, you asshole."

I open my eyes. It is Allen. He stands before me, red-faced, knuckles on hips, and slightly out of breath.

"Al. What are you doing here?" For a moment, I think I am hallucinating him.

"You remember Cal Whitaker? The guy who runs the—"

"You know him?"

"Yeah, and I guess you know him too. He happens to keep a place here on Gorée and it just so happens Evalyn and I were up here visiting the guy. He's a friend of mine. In fact, if you'll check that basket of fruit you call a brain, you might just remember you and Evalyn and Ruth and I met him at the Embassy for lunch when you first got here."

"I remember. He was probably too drunk to even see me."

"Oh. You think so? Well, guy, it just so happens he saw you just . . . just . . . strolling! Fucking strolling through the village like some goddamn tourist. 'Hey,' he says to me, 'I just saw that weirdo space cadet you been looking for.' And here you are. Goddamn. Son of a bitch. Do you have any idea what you've put us through? You got the cops, the gendarmes, the United-fucking-States State Department—"

"Allen?"

"What!"

"Shut up, man. Ain't it obvious I've quit the Peace Corps? I couldn't care less who's looking for me. And quit calling me names. I might be sick, but I'm still big enough to knock you down."

"Well, shit, Evan, if you wanted to quit, why didn't you just come talk to me?" As he speaks he repeatedly throws his arms into the air and drops them loosely so that his hands smack against his thighs. "You have any idea how many times I've come up here to look for you? I do have other things to do, guy. Everybody was sure you were dead, you big . . . Well, everybody thought you were dead or something."

"I really am sick, Allen."

"You got that right, dude."

"You can't tell by looking at me?"

Allen sits next to me on the boulder. "You know," he says, "maybe if you'd checked into that hospital you wouldn't be so damned sick." He pulls off his glasses and wipes his forehead with the back of his arm. Even though he perspires heavily, his shirt is perfectly creased. "I think you really ought to go back to the States," he says, "get some rest, maybe see a shrink. I think you know that, guy." He holds his glasses by one of the ear pieces, twirls them round and round. "I just don't think you're ready for Africa, Evan."

"May just be that none of us is, but I'm staying for a while."

MAULANA KARENGA

The African American Holiday *of* Kwanzaa: *A Celebration of* Family, Community, *and* Culture

It is out of the common values and practices of Continental African first fruit celebrations, that I began to conceive and develop Kwanzaa. But it was in and through the context of African American life and struggle that I completed its creation. Kwanzaa was created in 1966 to serve several functions in the African American community. First, Kwanzaa was created to reaffirm and restore our African heritage and culture. The encouragement for its creation as an expression of recovery and reconstruction of African culture occurred in the *general* context of the Black liberation movement of the 60s and in the *specific* context of Us organization[1].

In the 60s the Black Movement after 1965 was defined by its thrust to "return to the source," to go "back to Black." It stressed the rescue and reconstruction of African history and culture, redefinition of ourselves and our culture and a restructuring of the goals and purpose of our struggle for liberation and a higher level of human life based on an Afrocentric model[2]. This stress on restoration was evidenced in cultural practices such as renaming of oneself and one's children with African names, wearing the Natural or Afro hair style and African clothes, relearning African languages, especially Swahili, and reviving African life-cycle ceremonies such as naming, nationalization, i.e., initiation or rites of passage [Akika]; wedding [Arusi] and funeral [Maziko].

This restorative thrust also involved the struggle for and establishment of Black Studies [i.e., African and African American Studies] in academia and the building of community institutions which restored and reintroduced African culture, i.e., cultural centers, theatres, art galleries, independent schools, etc. Moreover, there was an emphasis on returning to the Continent permanently or temporarily for cultural revitalization, to reestablish links and build ongoing mutually beneficial and reinforcing relationships. And finally, there was the attempt to recover and begin to live—even relive—African values in the family and community as a way to rebuild and reinforce family, community and culture.

Us, under the leadership of this writer, was and remains a vanguard organization in this process of cultural restoration. In fact upon its founding, it declared itself dedicated to "the creation, recreation and circulation of Black culture". This, Us maintained, would be accomplished by self-conscious construction, institution-building and social struggle which shaped the culture and the people and aided in the creation of a society in which they could live and develop freely. Thus, Us argued, that key to the improvement and enrichment of African American life was the rescue and reconstruction of their culture.

Us defined culture in its fullest sense as the totality of thought and practice by which a people creates itself, celebrates, sustains and develops itself, and introduces itself to history and humanity. Culture for Us, then, is not simply fine art, but the totality of thought and practice of a people which occurs in at least seven fundamental areas: history, religion [spirituality]; social organization; economic organization; political organization; creative production [art, music, literature, dance]; and ethos [the collective psychology which results from activity in the other six areas]. Us further defined culture in terms of its view and value dimensions and the quality of practice that proceeds from these. It maintains that the quality of social practice is directly related to the quality of cultural vision and values. Values here are defined as categories of commitment and priorities which enhance or diminish human possibilities. In a word, what a person determines as important and puts first in his/her life determines the human quality and direction of that life. And as it is with a person, so it is with a people.

Secondly, then, Kwanzaa was created to introduce and reinforce the *Nguzo Saba* [the Seven Principles]. These values were and are a self-conscious contribution to the general Movement call and the specific Us call and struggle for an African [African American] value system. These seven communitarian African values are: Umoja [Unity]; Kujichagulia [Self-determination]; Ujima [Collective Work and Responsibility]; Ujamaa [Cooperative Economics]; Nia [Purpose]; Kuumba [Creativity]; and Imani [Faith]. Their communitarian character was viewed as especially important because of their collective emphasis, positive composition and their rootedness and prevalence in African culture. The Nguzo Saba were thus projected as the moral minimum set of African values that African Americans needed in order to rebuild and strengthen family, community and culture and become a self-conscious social force in the struggle to control their destiny and daily life.

Thirdly, Kwanzaa was created to address the absence of non-heroic holidays in the national African American community. With the possible exception of African American History Month, which itself is essentially organized around heroes and heroines, there was no national holiday to celebrate a communal event of great historic and cultural significance before the creation of Kwanzaa. Even African American History Month, as suggested above, focuses not so much on communal events and issues as on heroic achievement of persons who serve as models. This is clearly important, but it is not a substitute for holidays which call for and cultivate communal rituals around major events and issues in communal history and culture. Thus, Kwanzaa serves an important function as the only nationally celebrated non-heroic African American holiday.

Fourthly, then, Kwanzaa was created to serve as a regular communal celebration which reaffirmed and reinforced the bonds between us as a people. It was designed to be an ingathering to strengthen community and reaffirm common identity, national purpose and ultimate common direction. And finally, Kwanzaa was created as an act of cultural self-determination, as a self-conscious statement of our cultural truth as an African people. That is to say, it was an important way and expression of being African in a European-dominated context. The first act of a self-conscious, self-determining people, Us contended, is to redefine and reshape their world in their own image and interest. This, as stated above, is a cultural project in the full sense of the word, i.e., a total project involving restructuring thought and practice on every level. Moreover, it is a project which requires *recovering lost models and memory, suppressed principles and practices of African culture*, and putting these in their struggle to free themselves and realize their highest aspirations.

The First Fruit Model

The choice of African first fruit celebrations as the focal point and foundation of a new African American holiday was based on several considerations. First, these celebrations were prevalent throughout Africa and thus had the Pan-African character necessary to be defined as African in general as distinct from simply ethnically specific. This was important to Us given its policy of making, whenever possible, a creative and useful synthesis from various African cultural sources rather than choosing only one culture for emulation. Secondly, the core common aspects of these festivals which were discussed above, i.e., ingathering, reverence, commemoration, recommitment and celebration were seen as very relevant to building family, community and culture. This is especially true in terms of their stress on bonding, reaffirmation, restoration, remembrance, spirituality and recommitment to ever higher levels of human life as well as celebration of the Good in general.

Thirdly, the length of the festivals was between seven and nine days for their core celebrations. In Southeastern Africa the festivals are essentially seven days. In West Africa celebrations are sometimes longer and vary from seven to nine days[3]. Among the Yoruba, however, one New Yam Festival, Odun Ijesu, lasts only three days, while the Odwira festival of the Ashanti lasts "a period of one week or more"[4]. The Zulu first fruit celebration, Umkhosi, which played an important part in the conceptualization of Kwanzaa, is a seven-day holiday. This seven-day holiday framework was of value because it complemented and reinforced the decision to make Kwanzaa a seven-day holiday in which each day is dedicated to and representative of one of the Nguzo Saba [The Seven Principles]. Finally, the first fruit celebrations of Southeastern Africa occurred at the end of one year and at the beginning of the next, i.e., in late December and early January[5]. In fact, the Zulu first fruit celebration, Umkhosi, is celebrated roughly about the same time as Kwanzaa and again is seven days. Thus, the first fruit festivals and the time of their celebration, especially in Southeastern Africa, became a model for Kwanzaa. And the dates for its celebrations were established as *26 December–1 January.*

This year-end time period became the choice for the time of celebrating Kwanzaa for several reasons. First, it would answer the concern for cultural authenticity in terms of time correspondence between Continental celebrations and Kwanzaa. Secondly, this time of celebration of Kwanzaa fits into the existing pattern of year-end celebrations in the U.S. and thus allowed us to build on the holiday spirit and orientation already present. Not only were there Christmas and Hanukkah celebrations, there was also the New Year celebration which is an essential feature of African first fruit celebrations. Therefore, celebrants of Kwanzaa, living in a multicultural context, remained participants in the general season of celebration of newness, remembrance and recommitment with the decided advantage of being able to celebrate in their own culturally specific way.

Moreover, this time period was chosen to establish Kwanzaa because the dates, 26 December–1 January, marked the end of the high-priced hustle and bustle of Christmas buying and selling. This allowed for avoidance of the crass commercialism usually associated with this period and for savings on any modest gifts one might want to purchase in the context of Kwanzaa gift-giving guidelines. Finally, the time for Kwanzaa celebration was chosen to give those who wished it a culturally specific holiday alternative to the existing ones. In a word, it was to give African Americans an opportunity to celebrate themselves, their culture and history rather than simply imitate the dominant culture. And placing it in the context of the general celebrations of the season offered a definite chance for a proactive choice at a time when one could clearly be made.

It is important here to make several observations. First, the above opportunity was specifically offered for those who wanted such an alternative either before or after becoming aware of Kwanzaa. It was not meant to deny choice but to allow it. For one can't choose if s/he doesn't have a choice and cultural choice is fundamental to the principle of Self-determination [Kujichagulia]. Secondly, "alternative" here clearly refers to opportunity, option and chance to make a proactive choice as distinct from substitute or reactive choice or posture. Thus, Kwanzaa is not a reaction to or substitute for anything. It is the outgrowth of a normal need of a people to shape its world in its own cultural image and interests.

Thirdly, Kwanzaa is above all a cultural choice as distinct from a religious one. This point is important because when the question arises as to the relation between choosing Kwanzaa or/and Christmas, this distinction is not always made. This failure to make this distinction causes confusion, for it appears to suggest one must give up one's religion to practice one's culture. Whereas this might be true in other cases, it is not so in this case. For here, one can and should make a distinction between one's specific religion and one's general culture in which that religion is practiced. On one hand, Christmas is a religious holiday for Christians, but it is also a cultural holiday for Europeans. Thus, one can accept and revere the religious message and meaning but reject its European cultural accretions of Santa Claus, reindeer, mistletoe, frantic shopping, alienated gift-giving, etc.

This point can be made by citing two of the most frequent reasons Christian celebrants of Kwanzaa give for turning to Kwanzaa. The first reason is that it provides them with cultural grounding and reaffirmation as African Americans. The other reason is that it gives them a spiritual alternative to the commercialization of Christmas and the concurrent move away from its original spiritual values and message. Here it is of value also to note that there is a real and important difference between spirituality as a general appreciation for and commitment to the transcendent and religion which suggests formal structures and doctrines. Kwanzaa is not a religious holiday, but a cultural one with an inherent spiritual quality as with all major African celebrations. Thus, *Africans of all faiths* can and do celebrate Kwanzaa, i.e., Muslims, Christians, Black Hebrews, Jews, Buddhists, and Hindus as well as those who follow the ancient traditions of Maat, Yoruba, Dogon, etc. For what Kwanzaa offers is not an alternative to their religion or faith but *a common ground of African culture* which they all share and cherish. It is this common ground of culture on which they all meet, find ancient and enduring meaning, and by which they are thus reaffirmed and reinforced.

NGUZO SABA
(*The Seven Principles*)

1. UMOJA (Unity)

To strive for and maintain unity in the family, community, nation and race.

2. KUJICHAGULIA (Self-determination)

To define ourselves, name ourselves, create for ourselves and speak for ourselves instead of being defined, named, created for and spoken for by others.

3. UJIMA (Collective Work and Responsibility)

To build and maintain our community together and make our sister's and brother's problems our problems and to solve them together.

4. UJAMAA (Cooperative Economics)

To build and maintain our own stores, shops and other businesses and to profit from them together.

5. NIA (Purpose)

To make our collective vocation the building and developing of our community in order to restore our people to their traditional greatness.

6. KUUMBA (Creativity)

To do always as much as we can, in the way we can, in order to leave our community more beautiful and beneficial than we inherited it.

7. IMANI (Faith)

To believe with all our heart in our people, our parents, our teachers, our leaders and the righteousness and victory of our struggle.

Notes

1. Maulana Karenga. *Kwanzaa: Origin, Concepts, Practice.* Los Angeles: Kawaida Publications, 1977, p. 1B.

2. Afrocentric essentially means African centered or having a quality, character or approach rooted in the cultural image and human interest of African people. See Molefi Asante, *The Afro-Centric Idea.* Philadelphia: Temple University Press, 1987. See also Maulana Karenga, "Black Studies and the Problematic of Paradigm: The Philosophical Dimension," *Journal of Black Studies*, 18.4 (June 1988), pp. 403–404.

3. D. G. Coursey. "The New Yam Festival Among the Ewe," *Ghana Notes and Queries,* 10 (December 1968).

4. J. B. Danquah. *Gold Coast: Akan Laws and Customs and the Abuakwa Constitution.* London: George Rutledge and Sons, Ltd., 1928, p.129.

Ibid. Danquah notes that Odwira generally falls in December or January also. But he sees Odwira as a thanksgiving festival rather than a harvest festival although it is celebrated in some places during the harvest season in July and August. According to him, the real New Yam Festival is Ohum, which occurs in July and August.

5. W. C. Willoughby. *The Soul of the Bantu.* Garden City, NY: Doubleday, Doran & Co., 1928, pp. 235, 237: Max Gluckman, "Social Aspects of First Fruit Celebrations and the South Eastern Bantu," *Africa,* 11. (January, 1938), p. 25; O. F. Raum. "The Interpretation of the Nguni First Fruit Ceremony." *Paideuma.* Vol. 13, 1967.

MOLEFI KETE ASANTE

Afrocentricity

Africans are at the center of American history. Arriving before the pilgrims, we existed before the American nation. A succession of spokespersons, from the 18th Century, have understood as much and have been able to capitalize on this centrality. Whether it was Booker T. Washington imploring whites at the Atlanta Exposition of 1895 to "cast down your buckets where you are" or the early Black Panthers and Vernon Jordan of the Urban League making their separate proposals for coalitions with various groups of whites, we have known this truth and have interpreted it as the interweaving of history in the beautiful but troubled land for nearly four hundred years. It is now time for us to activate our collective will to peace and consciousness.

During slavery our fathers and mothers perfected their predictions of white behavior; they began to tell only what was acceptable and thus concealed their true beliefs, impressions, and ideas behind masks. It was better, in a survival sense, to tell whites what they wanted to hear and continue to live than to tell unpleasant facts and be "sold down the river." Knowing the Europeans' prejudice against Africans, our fathers were cognizant of the inconsistences of white proclamations.

Politics and economics constitute the decisive sectors of black-white confrontation in the rising of our spirits. Undoubtedly other areas will be affected. But the critical juncture in our path to an unprecedented era of productivity will be the crossroads of economic and political actions.

The next age will be a political age. So the reactions of whites will be political and pragmatic. Regardless of the intervening crises of spirit, whether they be in international politics or spiritual values, the essential European mode of response will be practical. The conservative drive to protect what they will appear to be losing, that is, a dominant role in world politics will force Europeans to respond practically. In fact, the loss of European dominance will be made a reality by numerous contending and allying forces. These forces include the rise of our spirits in the United States, the coming to early consciousness in Brazil, the economic strength and flexibility of Japan, the tightening of internal control over oil production by the African and Arab states, the establishment of a Palestinian state, the hegemony of the Peoples Republic of China over Asia, the transfer of petro-dollars to OPEC, the completion of the Pan-African union among African states, and the further decline of Europe, particularly Britain and France, whose wealth and political clout were built upon external holdings. With these ominous signs, historical certainties, made so by the ever progression of contemporary forces and the sureness of change, and barring nuclear madness which would make everything absurd, white Americans, the preeminent children of Europe, will find pragmatism not merely a philosophical tenet, to be accepted or rejected, but a consummate necessity for survival.

Thus, in politics and economics, new arrangements will have to be made, new pledges taken, and different promises given, for example, it is conceivable that Europeans witnessing the birth of a collective Afrocentricity, not realized since ancient time, will reinterpret political concepts and principles to assure as much as possible the cooperation of the races. But you see, race is neither a biological nor an anthropological fact, it is a political concept. Its origin like that of nations and states is rooted in the will to command power over other people, and power is predicated upon distinctions and differences. The exacerbation of these differences was at first a political work, only secondarily was it an anthropological trick. That is precisely why anthropology is also the most political of the social sciences. One does not discover even in political science the underlying premises of anthropology. Much more than political science, anthropology is a European discipline. In its inception and later in its conspiracies with sociology, it attempted to define the rest of the world in relationship to the European world.

Classification schemes created *Negroid, Mongoloid*, and *Caucasoid* races. Definitions, emerging from the Caucasoid perspective with little claim to objectivity (which is a creation of the same western minds), abounded. Among the political tactics was the comparative definition used in the nineteenth century by European writers who wrote statements like "as compared to the Caucasoid race, the Negroid race has thick lips, flat noses, kinky hair, etc."; but it is a game that can be played by any group interested in political and economic exploitation of other people. Had Afrocentric perspectives been applied, the definition would have been "as compared to blacks, whites have undeveloped lips, pointed noses, limp hair, etc." Anthropological terms forced upon us a concept of race that ultimately legitimized oppression, murder, and genocide. Of course, I cannot say that Malinowski, Levy-Bruhl, and others intentionally created these mental atrocities, but they provided the basic European rationale for racial differences. If you figured that someone was your enemy because his eyes looked differently, now you were able to add a qualitative dimension to your judgment and the anthropologists gave a European perspective to a question which had social and political implications.

The practical end of all of this anthropological inquiry is the presence of ethno-this and ethno-that to once again indicate European dominance. Thus, ethno-rhetoric, ethno-musicology, ethno-science and even ethnography are meant to show the other, to study the other as other and, in fact, inferior. In other words, what Africans create becomes ethno-music not real music and so forth.

What does this mean for the Euro-American response to the rise of our spirits? It is simply this, there will be a positive response to the new era because Afrocentricity will reinterpret history and give whites a new way out of their collective dilemma which results from the gathering intellectual and economic forces. The political concept of race will have to be redefined and then dismissed as an obfuscation of the power relationships which in fact hold sway in this country.

Contemporary African biologists talk about gene pools, genotypes, and phenotypes, ideas which make some sense scientifically. On the other hand, the concept "race" must be dealt with in order to dispense with political nonsense. The political concept "race" will be reinterpreted by Afro-Americans because it has no biological or anthropological basis. In the United States the concept of race reached more limits than any place except Brazil or Azania (South Africa). In the United States, eighteenth- and nineteenth-century legislatures wrestled with the problem of codifying a meaningless concept and many settled on "any trace of African blood," "any parent, grandparent, or great-grandparent who was an African," etc. Such schemes which were designed to "keep the white race pure" included keeping white women out of bed with black men because offspring of such unions could only be black. Booker T. Washington aptly noted during one of his swings through the South that "African blood is pretty powerful, just one drop and you are counted on my side." While his white audience roared wild laughter, the point was sharply made that the whole idea of race purity as a concept to be defended is rather absurd.

Strange and weird exchanges occur in such an atmosphere. Whites might even brag, "I'm one fourth Cherokee," because it's considered a bit exotic to be part Indian, after all they don't really constitute any kind of threat; the whites nearly eliminated them. But have you ever heard anyone defined as white say, "I'm one fourth African"? You see, we constitute a potential threat. And quite frankly in those regions of the United States, like the Dakotas, Minnesota, North Carolina, and portions of the Southwest, to claim Indian ancestry is still not considered exotic because in those areas race and group definitions are still political.

What then are the directions of the black reinterpretation? We must first de-politicize race as a concept. There are two steps to this de-politicalization: *dismantling* and *restructuring*. Race can only lose its political potency by attacking the white social sciences that persist in creating myths to further enhance the idea of racial purity and superiority. The periodic rebirth of mad white social scientists who claim the definitive case for white superiority is a direct outgrowth of all the mania and phobia created by the political concept of race. Once we dispense with the artificialities of "race" as a political concept we will have won one of the battles to reorder the social questions. Indeed our people have always understood "enia dudu," "watu weusi," "baiki mutane," and "meedidzee" as social realities.

Restructuring does not mean the setting up of race again as a concept but rather the reorganization of the whole identity question in the United States. For each nation the process of identity is different. Brazil, for example, recognized Afro-Brazilians and Luzo-Brazilians; Nigeria recognizes over two hundred ethnic groups; the Soviet Union over one hundred; the Japanese Islands less than five ethnic groups, etc. In the United States most of the people originally came from some place else. The Navajo, Apache, Creek, Choctaw, and numerous other ethnic and linguistic groups were in America when the first people from Africa and Europe arrived. In some respects it should be easy to reorganize identity labels which would not be reflective of politics but of national or continental origin; in other respects it will be difficult and trying. For example, people identified as Jews often see themselves in both an ethnic and religious sense, so that a person who has no religious inclination is still defined as being a Jew. Furthermore, to use a label which indicates continental or national origin would be misleading in terms of this special gene pool. Because a Jewish person came from Russia to the United States you would not normally call him a Russo-American or if he came from America you would not say he is an Afro-American. As I have indicated, restructuring of identity labels is a problematic undertaking. What Afrocentricity will mean to this process, however, is the coming to terms with national consciousness among the "enia dudu" throughout the world. Such negotiation between a people and their consciousness does not negate or minimize their essential character. Afrocentricity depoliticizes the concept of race and points the way to the restructuring of identity.

Why have I been writing as if politics and economics are separate matters? Because even though they are both functions of power, they manifest themselves differently. And while it is true that the possessors of one usually possess the other, it is not always the case. There are numerous examples of nations whose politicians are controlled by external economic interests. In fact, our community has seen its share of outside economic control even though politicians have been selected by the community.

One of the most important economic rights in the coming decades will be the right to salary. It is very important that we understand the significance of this matter. When one studies or reads United States history, it becomes clear that those who owned the land became big capitalists; land is the basis of all wealth. By the time Africans were emancipated the major landholdings had already been taken. Even the land blacks managed to acquire was often taken from them. So in the rise of the spirits it will not be major landholdings that will help us overcome the economic plight that has plagued us. We shall have to fight the contest for salaries. It is increasingly true with whites also that the security of salary is more important than the right to real estate. The large number of people moving into apartments or already living in apartments attests to the declining interest in and ability to buy real estate. We must struggle to gain a foothold in every sector of the American economy. There will continue to be, as there must be, entrepreneurs who will seek to create profits for themselves and positions for others. But the extent of all black owned businesses for the next four decades will be infinitesimal in the total American economy. Our path to economic survival will not be based upon landholdings but owning secure industries, creative breakthroughs in art and music, exploitation of all fields of athletics and salaried positions based on education and talent.

A society much more diversified than we can even now imagine will provide both unlimited opportunity for success in entrepreneurial activities. Given this configuration, our encounter with whites will intensify in those areas where we have traditionally been underemployed, i.e., electronics, corporation management, legal and administrative areas, the medical profession, particularly in the top echelons of medical services, administration of academic institutions, and various positions in the information industry. The white response to this encounter is, as I have pointed out, predictable. There will be subtle moves to evade the inevitable, new white scientists will rise up with fantastic discoveries about black abilities or inabilities, organizations will be formed to promote competence and familiar words will take on unfamiliar meanings among those who are afraid of us. But in the end our Afrocentricity will insure our victory based upon the products, opportunities, and jobs created by our work, sweat, genius, blood, and durability. Quite fortunately we are a persistent people who know that what our prophets predicted must indeed come to pass. And our encounter with Europeans in the economic arena will generate a more cohesive world dedicated to the expression of spirit and soul, and by that, dignity and integrity.

The encounters we experience in various sectors of society will enhance our collective consciousness. We are only now becoming a collective will, the recession of individuality as our main thrust: one brother working as a clerk in a department store, one sister as an accountant in a corporation, one brother in university administration, one sister in chemical research at a national laboratory. Instead of one who was usually "the first black to . . ." we have a phalanx which is real not imaginary.

When I was a child in Georgia and we got our first black clerk at the five and ten store, whites would come to the door, stare, then exclaim to other whites while pointing at the trying-to-keep-cool brother, "They are even in here now!" Those were the days of an imagined phalanx. We may not all be preparing ourselves in the same way, but we are *preparing* and that is the key to the rise. The general encounter on a wide range of political, social, and economic issues will contribute to our growing awakeness. We will come to terms with consciousness in spite of the American experience and perhaps *because* of our collective encounter with the European's reaction to our search for human peace. That is why I see the potency of rise as an injection into the world of culture. Consciousness is the first sign of vigor and power. Our rising tide of consciousness will wash all as clean as coal. Already it is a *fait accompli* in American music so will it be in other aspects of American life. It is not to be lamented; it is to be accepted as the natural course of historical maturity where the personal infusion of spirit extends materialism and spirituality to form a people level.

Our knowledge, developed out of necessity, helps to ascertain the political and social direction the nation and world is tending. We know full the distrust the rich white has of the poor white and we also know that the poor whites are constantly struggling to hide their origin. But this is only tangentially our problem, that is, we are affected by the discussions and actions that the rich whites take to frustrate the poor whites but ours is a different problem. Class is significant only as an added dimension to the stratification already present. Because we are surrounded by white cultural styles (and have not been completely overwhelmed) we are aware of communication and social behaviors of whites though we do not participate in those behaviors. Use of terms like "minority," "qualified," "standards," "law and order," and "quality control" when dealing with interracial situations reflect a communication bias often found in white language. It is not stretching the point too far to reiterate that we have been able to tell the direction of national politics by the words that emerge from behind closed doors. American politics is money politics and money determines what shall be spoken in public and what shall not be spoken. The impregnable walls of race dictate that Anglo-Saxons rule the economic sector of the United States. These are differences between non-Anglo-Saxon and Anglo-Saxon wealth. The Jewish rich, department store owners, and media tycoons, can seldom sit at the same tables, that is, share the social clubs or status symbols of the Anglo-Saxon rich.

The rise of Africans in America will have its initial impact on the broad middle of American life and society. Only as a tandem influence, combined with other cultural and political thrusts, will it have an impact on the controllers of the economy. We can only affect the controllers of wealth in the production of their products. Most employees are new peasants. The revolt of the employees is the revolt of the new peasants, when the rise introduces, as surely it must, quite new interpretations of value, it will be the collective wills of many segments of society that will react in a major attempt to elevate the employees.

What then is the response of other people likely to be towards Afrocentricity? Certainly there will not be massive participation because Afrocentricity is seen as an antithesis to the architecton set up by Europeans. So the response will be pragmatic, watching the shape of things to come, and deliberate, with good reason for a wait and see attitude. The fact that we will no longer genuflect must not be taken as vindictiveness, it is only another sign of the consciousness that is upon us. Others will find the new epoch to be favorable to their own sense of collective development which will become increasingly like Afrocentricity. Many will embrace it for its humanism and cultural vitality. Each of you know, of course, what we must do.

THE TRANSCENDENT PROCESS

The transcending action which takes us from the traditional to the revolutionary consciousness is complex and intriguing. In its most elemental stage, it may be called the eradication, blotting out, of the old and the opening up to the new. We *breakdown* in order to *breakthrough.*

Each person chooses to become Afrocentric; this is the only way to accomplish it. You experience in the *breakdown* a certain tearing away from mental and psychological habits that held you enslaved to Eurocentric concepts. This is a violent process. It is a separation and all separations are violent. We move away from the lifestyles of oppression and victimization. We reject consciousness of oppression. We dispense with attitudes of defeatism. We turn our backs on those negative race behaviors that conceal the manliness and womanliness we possess. We condemn those deviations of symbols and actions which hark back to the slave mentality. Like a dazzling comet our new self radiates to all those in our presence; we become new people.

ERIC V. COPAGE

Kwanzaa: An African-American Celebration of Culture and Cooking

Before eating, open your mouth.

PROVERB, MAURITANIA

I was never a holiday kind of guy. Perhaps it was because we observed few holiday rituals of any kind. Although we put up a Christmas tree every year, there was no ceremony to it—no drinking of eggnog or listening to carols while hanging ornaments. To me the tree seemed more or less like another piece of furniture. Over the past few years, however, the holiday season has taken on a new meaning for me as my family sits at the dinner table the week following Christmas to celebrate Kwanzaa.

This cultural observance for black Americans and others of African descent was created in 1966 by Maulana (Ron) Karenga, who is currently chairman of black studies at California State University in Long Beach. *Kwanzaa* means "first fruits of the harvest" in Swahili, but there is no festival of that name in any African society. Karenga chose Swahili, the lingua franca of much of East Africa, to emphasize that black Americans come from many parts of Africa. Karenga synthesized elements from many African harvest festivals to create a unique celebration that is now observed in some way by more than 5 million Americans.

When I first told my wife I was thinking about observing Kwanzaa, she barred the way to our attic and said she'd never chuck our Christmas tree lights and antique ornaments. I told her that wouldn't be necessary. Kwanzaa, which runs from December 26 to New Year's Day, does not replace Christmas and is not a religious holiday. (We now celebrate both.) It is a time to focus on Africa and African-inspired culture and to reinforce a value system that goes back for generations.

Like many people, I was introduced to Kwanzaa by chance, in late December a few years back. I was visiting the American Museum of Natural History when I heard the sibilant sound of African rattles. It was coming from a dance performance, part of the Kwanzaa celebration that has been held annually at the museum since 1978. The holiday didn't make much of an impression on me then, but I returned to it after the birth of my son, Evan, in 1987.

I wanted Evan to have a three-dimensional sense of his African heritage. I wanted him to experience the pride of learning about the sublime Russian poet Aleksander Pushkin, the extraordinary American composer Duke Ellington, and Alexandre Dumas, author of *The Three Musketeers.* I wanted Evan to learn about the West African medieval empires—Songhai, Mali, and Ghana—and about the African explorers such as Esteban, who traveled throughout what is now Arizona and New Mexico in the sixteenth century, and about inventors like the mechanical engineer Elijah McCoy (who was the original "real McCoy"). I wanted him to understand that through tenacity, hard work, and purposefulness—all of which are grounded in the African and African-American ethos—blacks have flourished as well as survived. I wanted to train Evan to look for opportunity, and to prepare for it. And I wanted to have a forum for showing him examples of past successes, and for showing him that those people inevitably gave back to the black community in particular and to the general community in which they lived.

But how to do this? I could have made up some ritual. But then we'd miss the communal aspect, the idea that in households similar to ours people were involved in similar activities. We'd miss one of the major reasons for celebrating a cultural holiday, the hoped-for metaphysical bonding with other African-Americans.

There is Black History Month, of course, which I've always enjoyed. I look forward to being enveloped for four weeks in the membrane of black accomplishment as it comes to me from special radio and television programs and is represented in the special displays in bookstores. But this Gatling gun approach to black culture, laudable as it is, seems to lack focus. And unlike other long observances—Lent, for instance, or Ramadan—Black History Month has no agreed-upon ritual, structure, or climax.

I thought about my goals for Evan and decided that Kwanzaa was the best lens through which to view the landscape of the African diaspora and the lessons it has to teach. Because it is only one week long, and because of the ceremony, and because it climaxes with a glorious feast, Kwanzaa has an intensity and focus that provides the perfect atmosphere for my son to experience the joys of being black.

Kwanzaa also has the celebratory aspect that will provide memories for Evan and now my daughter, Siobhán, to savor as adults and to pass on to their children.

If you want to adhere strictly to the Kwanzaa program as Karenga conceived it, here is what you need to have and what they mean:

1. *Mazao:* fruits and vegetables, which stand for the product of unified effort.
2. *Mkeka:* a straw place mat, which represents the reverence for tradition.

3. *Vibunzi:* an ear of corn for each child in the family.

4. *Zawadi:* simple gifts, preferably related to education or to things African or African-influenced.

5. *Kikombe cha umoja:* a communal cup for the libation (I like to look at this as a kind of homage to past, present, and future black Americans).

6. *Kinara:* a seven-branched candleholder, which symbolizes the continent and peoples of Africa.

7. *Mishumaa saba:* the seven candles, each one symbolizing one of the Nguzo Saba, or seven principles, that black Americans should live by on a daily basis and which are reinforced during Kwanzaa.

On each day of Kwanzaa, a family member lights a candle, then discusses one of those seven principles. The principles, along with Karenga's elucidation of them in 1965, are:

1. *Umoja (Unity):* To strive for and maintain unity in the family, community, nation, and race.

2. *Kujichagulia (Self-determination):* To define ourselves, name ourselves, create for ourselves, and speak for ourselves instead of being defined, named, created for, and spoken for by others.

3. *Ujima (Collective Work and Responsibility):* To build and maintain our community together, and to make our sisters' and brothers' problems our problems and to solve them together.

4. *Ujamaa (Cooperative Economics):* To build and maintain our own stores, shops, and other businesses and to profit from them together.

5. *Nia (Purpose):* To make our collective vocation the building and developing of our community in order to restore our people to their traditional greatness.

6. *Kuumba (Creativity):* To do always as much as we can, in whatever way we can, in order to leave our community more beautiful and beneficial than we inherited it.

7. *Imani (Faith):* To believe with all our heart in our people, our parents, our teachers, our leaders, and in the righteousness and victory of our struggle.

The next-to-last day of the holiday, December 31, is marked by a lavish feast, the *Kwanzaa Karamu*, which, in keeping with the theme of black unity, may draw on the cuisines of the Caribbean, Africa, South America . . . wherever Africans were taken. In addition to food, the Karamu is an opportunity for a confetti storm of cultural expression: dance and music, readings, remembrances. Here is Karenga's suggested way of conducting a Karamu as enlarged upon by Cedric McClester:

1. *Kukaribisha (Welcoming)*
   Introductory remarks and recognition of distinguished guests and elders
   Cultural expression through songs, music, dance, unity circles, etc.
2. *Kukumbuka (Remembering)*
   Reflections of a man, a woman, and a child
   Cultural expression
3. *Kuchunguza tena na kutoa ahadi tena (Reassessment and Recommitment)*
   Introduction of distinguished guest lecturer, and short talk
4. *Kushangilia (Rejoicing)*
   Tamshi la tambiko (libation statement)
   Kikombe cha umoja (unity cup)
   Kutoa majina (calling names of family ancestors and black heroes)
   Ngoma (drums)
   Karamu (feast)
   Cultural expression
5. *Tamshi la tutaonana*
   Farewell Statement

When my family lights the black, red, and green Kwanzaa candles the last week of December, we do so with millions of other black Americans around the nation. Major community celebrations are held in just about every city that has any kind of black population: Atlanta, Chicago, Philadelphia, Milwaukee, Dayton, Durham, and Charleston, to name just a few. The people who celebrate Kwanzaa comprise a cross-section of black America. They include Catherine Bailey of Boston, a teacher who has been celebrating since 1969; Saalik Cuevas, a Puerto Rican-American computer programmer who is as proud of his African heritage as he is of his Spanish and Indian backgrounds; and Diana N'Diaye, a folklorist at the Smithsonian Institution. Audie Odum-Stallato, a cooking instructor and caterer, has invited non-African-Americans to Kwanzaa as her way of sharing African culture. There are others for whom the idea of sharing Kwanzaa with anyone other than a fellow African-American would be anathema.

Some people, such as New York City caterers Carol and Norma Jean Darden, "Kwanzafy" their Christmas by using African-inspired Yuletide decorations and ornaments on their Christmas tree. Gwen Foster, an Oakland, California, social worker, also uses African-inspired Christmas decorations—including a straw wreath wrapped with red, black, and green ribbon that she hangs on her front door—in addition to holding a small Kwanzaa ceremony with her family on each of the seven days. Lincoln Pattaway and his family celebrate Kwanzaa in lieu of Christmas. Like Foster, the Pattaways, who live in Houston, also have an intimate family celebration—but on only one night of Kwanzaa. The other nights they do the town.

We meet in different areas: in schools, community centers. One of the reasons we move around is because the city is so vast and you want to make it available to everyone. The historical society I belong to sponsors one night. The other nights are sponsored by other groups. During our last celebration, there were about two hundred people. It was standing-room-only.

There are big banners and beautiful signs. There is also a table set the same way we would set it at home, with the candles, mat, fruit, and vegetables. Most people are dressed in African garb. We're seated in front of the stage. Whoever is conducting the program for that night comes out to introduce themselves and the group. We are given a brief explanation of Kwanzaa. We light one of the candles and somebody speaks about that night's principle. This year we sponsored self-determination (*Kujichagulia*) and our speaker, a local product, was an Egyptologist. After he spoke about Egypt, we had the libation. Then we asked the audience to make a circle. We drank from the unity cup and talked about commitment for the following year.

Because it's a large group and so many people want to participate, we start at 7:00 P.M., and with the entertainment and activities, sometimes we're still there at midnight.

Saalik Cuevas takes a much more intimate approach. Over the past twelve years that Saalik, his wife, Isha, and their two sons, Sha'ir and Na'im, have celebrated Kwanzaa, they have usually kept their observance to a family affair.

We had gotten to a point that we started getting more in touch with our African selves. A good friend invited us to a Kwanzaa celebration. We didn't know anything about it, but were immediately struck by the spirituality of the affair. We made up our minds then and there to incorporate Kwanzaa into our lives. We started reading up on it. That first year everything was homemade. For the kinara, for instance, I used a piece of wood and seven apple juice caps covered with aluminum foil. The unity cup was a gourd we had bought. And that fall we bought what is called Indian corn, to represent our first son.

Our first Kwanzaa consisted of my wife, myself, and our eldest child. The second year we invited a few other family members. By then we had bought a kinara. It's made of wood and lacquered red. It's about 2 feet across and nearly 3 feet high. I got long tapered red, black, and green candles for it. We bought another straw mat that just about covers our whole table. Our unity cup is a white porcelain chalice.

Our Kwanzaa table now takes up the whole server in our dining room. We add to it year after year. We have African sculptures on the table, a basket of fruit, a separate basket with vegetables. The boys came up with the idea of having little baskets of rice and beans and corn. After the seven days of Kwanzaa, we use that rice, beans, and corn to make the first meal of the year.

We spend the whole day after Christmas setting up the Kwanzaa table and decorating the house. By sunset we are dressed in African clothes and ready to light the candle for Umoja. We pour a drop or two of water right on the rug for the ancestors. Then we pass around the cup. Traditionally I start it off since I am the eldest male in the household. We discuss the principle. For instance, I said last year that not only African-Americans need unity, but the entire human race needs unity, so that there won't be war, poverty, and hunger. After that I'll say a short prayer. It could be the Lord's Prayer or an African prayer. Then we snuff out the candles, and that signifies the end of the ceremony for that day. The ceremony lasts about twenty minutes. Then we eat.

Instead of a slew of gifts at the end of Kwanzaa, we give the children a few gifts each day. The first day will be something simple like fruit, books, a dashiki. We want them to get into the feel of this African holiday. The third or fourth day we might give them a cartoon book about the pyramids or Sun Man [a black hero-figure toy like the "He Man" toy] or something like that. On the last day, since this is America and we know that when they go back to school they are going to be asked what they got, we give the more commercial Nintendo, Ninja turtle video, train set–type presents. My wife and I feel that if we try to force Kwanzaa on our two sons, they might push it away. But if we try to incorporate it into our lives, it might take better.

We like to celebrate the last day of Kwanzaa. We might have forty-five people over to our house, close friends and family. What we do is supply basic foods for a mega Kwanzaa buffet and ask other people to bring salads. We go over all the Kwanzaa principles in detail, not just that day's principle. For instance, last year we talked about Mandela as an example of Umoja because with him, it was the first time in a long time that black people had a common focus. This ceremony can last almost an hour.

After the ceremony, we ask people who are creative to do something. My mother-in-law, for instance, is a good speaker, and as an elder she will read from Kahlil Gibran about children. We might have someone who is a good singer lead us in an old spiritual.

As for the recorded music, we always play Sweet Honey in the Rock, who sing a song about the Nguzo Saba. And then we might play Olatunji, Marvin Gaye, the Supremes, or KRS-One. A woman once came up to me and asked me to give her a list of Kwanzaa songs. I gave her a copy of *Billboard* magazine, turned to the R and B charts, and said, "Here, choose any of these." Any of those musics are part of the black experience, as are reggae, traditional African music, Afro-Cuban jazz. . . .

One year we were lucky enough to have someone who was into the traditional African belief system, that of the Yoruba people in particular, and he did a blessing for us. And once we had someone who told traditional stories. Between the playing of music, dancing, and eating, the party can last all night.

The other days of Kwanzaa we snuff out the candles. But on Imani we let the candles burn down. It signifies the end of the holiday.

JAMES E. JACKSON

The Journey of Martin Luther King, Jr.

The twentieth of January, 1986, is a legal "official" holiday, designated in the law of the land as "Martin Luther King, Jr., Day." The enactment into law of this memorial national holiday was the culmination of a five-year struggle for the just recognition of the man and the noble cause of securing the equality of the Afro-American people to which he gave heroic leadership, alongside his devotion to the cause of peace and justice. This is an occasion to memorialize the rather short public life of a very significant personality of our times, the remarkable democrat and fighter for the liberation and equal rights of the Afro-American people, champion of progressive causes generally and outstanding activist in the cause of the struggle for peace—the Rev. Dr. Martin Luther King, Jr.

Martin Luther King, Jr., was loyal and committed to the main task of the years in which he lived, within our country specifically and in the world generally. Within our country the central obstacle, the central brake affecting the motion of the wheel of progress is divisionism among the people along racial lines.

The evil heritage of racism—generated, compounded, left to block the road of progress of the working class of our country and the people—remains a number one item on the agenda of unfinished democratic tasks which are thwarting progress toward socialism.

To this task Martin Luther King, Jr., committed himself with imagination, courage and dedication and, above all, with extraordinary inspiration. People should commit themselves to the cause of the advance of human progress not for the purpose of glory or personal aggrandizement, but in such a way that they help masses to perceive the elementary truth to which they themselves are dedicating their lives. And it is in this sense Martin Luther King, Jr., is remembered best in history—for his galvanic personality and capability of inspiring noble emotion in millions and tens of millions to take some steps toward righting ancient wrongs and contributing something to social, historic progress.

So there is not so much in the matter of unique doctrines that we celebrate in the contribution of Martin Luther King, Jr., but his capacity to make the idea of equality and the brotherhood of peoples a material force to move the feet of millions onto the path of progress and away from the barbarism of racist divisionism. This is a necessary prerequisite to make accomplishments along this road, in order to unleash the big wheel of the working class, the masses, to move toward social progress and socialism in a revolutionary way.

Martin Luther King, Jr., went through a historic progression in his own development of consciousness, of awareness, of what freedom is. Freedom, said Engels, is response to necessity. Engels said, "freedom is the consciousness of necessity," being aware of that which should be done, what is historically on the agenda to be done. An individual who responds to historic, social necessity is a free person—subjectively speaking—and one who turns his eyes away from what should be done at a given time is unfree.

There is a story about Henry David Thoreau, the great American poet and philosopher and outstanding champion of Abolitionism during the period of slavery. Once when he was in prison, a visitor said to him, "Henry, what are you doing in there, behind bars?" And he responded, "What are you doing outside?"

Freedom is not reckoned only in terms of jail bars. The person in prison can be much freer than slaves on the outside. This is the meaning of the famous words of the song, *Die gedanken sind frei*—in any event, my thoughts are free, my mind belongs to no man or woman, it belongs to logic and necessity, and consequently is free.

Martin Luther King, Jr., wasn't born a celebrated champion of peace and freedom. He was a kind of reluctant warrior who, nevertheless, became a very courageous warrior who shook the country, and shook the confidence of the ruling class. Martin Luther King, Jr., made a first step in awareness and acted on that step when he responded to the call of the people of Montgomery, Alabama, to do something about the unrelieved criminality of segregation on the buses of Montgomery.

That movement arose under the inspiration of a heroic Black woman, Ms. Rosa Parks. She decided that she had toiled all day, her feet were tired, and she was not going to get up and go to the back of the bus when some white person came in and chose to sit in her seat. This precipitated the famous Montgomery bus boycott struggle. Martin Luther King, Jr., gave leadership to that, inspired the whole community, neutralized many tens of thousands of whites who were, until then, more or less prejudiced or at least did nothing about segregation. There were efforts to crush the bus boycott by the racists of the whole country. Senator Eastland went to Montgomery, Alabama, and held a mass meeting in the public stadium; the baseball/football park. Ten thousand white people attended that rally, organized by the White Citizens' Council and featuring Senator Eastland. Eastland was one of the most vulgar-mouthed, pornographic racists. But the white people listened, but they did not act.

There is a lesson in that. The style of leadership provided by Martin Luther King, Jr., in that situation united the Black community and neutralized the white community. At times, neutrality in certain situations becomes a form of alliance. There are many forms of alliance. There is an old adage, which is a very good tactic, "Lord, if you don't help me, don't help the bear." That becomes a form of neutrality in the confrontation between an individual and a bear. In this situation, it was a historic form of alliance to simply abstain from actively opposing the bus boycott—the struggle of the Black citizens of Montgomery. And this was historic because it marked the beginning of the end of Dixiecratism and the official status of racism in the South. When the appeal to lynch-mob tradition against Blacks was not acted on by the whites, the whole structure of Dixiecratism began to come apart at the seams.

The second big aspect of Martin Luther King's leadership was evident when the masses confronted the police during the first days of the boycott. Here the courage of the man was exhibited when he simply walked through the police lines without a turn of the head or a bat of an eye. It inspired the others.

The police were the symbol of terror, and the racist patterns of the Deep South were able to be sustained only on the basis of bowing to the terror of the police. I remember, as a small boy we used to say, "Brass buttons, blue coat, can't catch a billy goat." Even the sight of a policeman was a signal to run. They would march on the scene like a herd of elephants and everyone would scatter before them like leaves in the wind. But when people didn't run any more, the police terror had lost its psychological power. There is a famous newspaper picture of a small Black boy in the midst of a group of Ku Kluxers simply leaning against a pole picking his nose. No longer did terrorists among the police represent objects of fear. And when the police lose their capacity to intimidate and cower people, it foreshadows the end of the system. The end of the racist system of jim crowism was fundamentally at hand, though aspects of it remained for many years, already in the bus boycott days in Montgomery of 1960.

Incidentally, the triumphant struggle in Montgomery more or less coincided in time with the first loss of territory by the imperilled system of exploitation in the Americas, the Cuban Revolution.

The ruling class reluctantly accepted the consequences of Montgomery. And they discovered "a new Negro," with a big and lucid mouth. They felt that now with a few dollars he would become their Negro. He had already demonstrated considerable organizing talents. So all kinds of blandishments were offered. They'd give him a bigger church than his father had—he was a preacher and the son of a preacher—and they'd make him president of Morehouse College (where he himself had graduated earlier) and other such inducements.

But the masses of Black people also discovered a personality who could lead effectively. There were bids and invitations for him to come and speak and inspire and help in solving the problems making for unbearable misery throughout the South, and not just the South. And King opted to stay with the people and to turn aside the bribes and offers to go back to a "normal life."

Reflecting on the Montgomery experience, King took a historic second step in consciousness. The importance of King is that what he did personally, he did in a goldfish bowl. He shared the thought processes by which he arrived at a judgment to move a stage higher in his consciousness, and therefore thousands and tens of thousands moved with him.

So he preached that unity of Black people is useful and necessary, and makes it possible to win allies among non-Black people to support the initiatives of Black people. But the unity of Black people is not, of itself, enough to win against such powerful vested interests as U.S. capitalism. Therefore, he said, it is necessary to also find a common bond with the whole population. And so he entered into the struggle for the interests of poor people. And he discovered the working class and its mass organizations.

He became a personality appearing at one trade union convention after another. He became convinced that not only are people oppressed who are Black, but basically and fundamentally, people are oppressed because they are poor. Therefore, notwithstanding the shades of confusion and blindness in the eyes of many people, it is nevertheless a reality that objectively Black people and white people are standing together on class grounds. Consequently, for Blacks to enjoy equal rights and civil rights, it is necessary that they have the material means to enjoy those rights. He asked, "What does it matter if one has the right to ride the front of the bus and have no money to pay the fare?" Consequently the economic struggle is an important element, a decisive element, of the content of freedom.

What is freedom? You can also break it down into material things, and one of those material things is a right to economic equality. Therefore, he took the second step of merging the struggle for freedom with the struggle for bread, jobs, and all the rights of working people.

And then he came to a third level of consciousness: That the struggle for bread and freedom can not be solved within the limitations of one country, from the standpoint of limiting one's vision only to the borders of one's country. To solve even an internal problem, in our times, requires a world view. Therefore, he said, "What if we win economic security, what if we win freedom from racism and the abolition of all the racist, Jim Crow laws, and the world is disintegrated by the foreign policy that is already massacring Vietnamese and confronting the world with the danger of thermonuclear war?" Therefore, the struggle for peace, the struggle for securing and retaining the world, is a necessary basis for creating an environment for improving the living conditions within the world.

Martin Luther King brought this consciousness—that the struggle on the international level, for an end to the war in Vietnam in the interests of world peace and disarmament, was a necessary part of the democratic and economic struggle for rights and livelihood here at home. Consequently, he joined the peace movement with vigor. By doing so he added greatly to the scope of the peace forces. The Women's Strike for Peace, the Women's International League for Peace and Freedom, the Friends, had taken initiatives against the war and stimulated activity, but the result was still too small to fulfill its historic task. When the masses of civil rights marchers took to the streets with the peace forces, organized under common banners for peace and freedom, and merged these two aspects of the political/social struggle, then the peace movement in our country took on really massive dimensions.

One of the first great marches for peace was led by Martin Luther King, Jr., in New York City. Some quarter of a million people marched to the United Nations. From then on the dimensions of the peace movement achieved hundreds of thousands, and soon, it became a majority movement. Soon it became a movement which not even a Johnson or a Nixon could ignore and it became a great material force helping bring an end to the war in Vietnam.

But his principled stand against the immoral war in Vietnam is but one reason we take time now to invoke his sterling example and his unimpeachable legacy. In our celebration of Martin Luther King, Jr.'s birthday, we honor not only a man who was fearless in his commitment to justice and human decency, we pay tribute to one who personified the best we had to offer to correct the jangling discords of our system, to paraphrase one of his most memorable quotes. As we pause to reflect on his contributions, let us be ever mindful of our singular endeavors. Let us struggle to uphold the beliefs and tenets he sacrificed his life for. In our efforts to cherish his memory, we can do no less.

CORNEL WEST

Race Matters

Since the beginning of the nation, white Americans have suffered from a deep inner uncertainty as to who they really are. One of the ways that has been used to simplify the answer has been to seize upon the presence of black Americans and use them as a marker, a symbol of limits, a metaphor for the "outsider." Many whites could look at the social position of blacks and feel that color formed an easy and reliable gauge for determining to what extent one was or was not American. Perhaps that is why one of the first epithets that many European immigrants learned when they got off the boat was the term "nigger"—it made them feel instantly American. But this is tricky magic. Despite his racial difference and social status, something indisputably American about Negroes not only raised doubts about the white man's value system but aroused the troubling suspicion that whatever else the true American is, he is also somehow black.

RALPH ELLISON, "*WHAT AMERICA WOULD BE LIKE WITHOUT BLACKS*" (1970)

What happened in Los Angeles in April of 1992 was neither a race riot nor a class rebellion. Rather, this monumental upheaval was a multiracial, trans-class, and largely male display of justified social rage. For all its ugly, xenophobic resentment, its air of adolescent carnival, and its downright barbaric behavior, it signified the sense of powerlessness in American society. Glib attempts to reduce its meaning to the pathologies of the black underclass, the criminal actions of hoodlums, or the political revolt of the oppressed urban masses miss the mark. Of those arrested, only 36 percent were black, more than a third had full-time jobs, and most claimed to shun political affiliation. What we witnessed in Los Angeles was the consequence of a lethal linkage of economic decline, cultural decay, and political lethargy in American life. Race was the visible catalyst, not the underlying cause.

The meaning of the earthshaking events in Los Angeles is difficult to grasp because most of us remain trapped in the narrow framework of the dominant liberal and conservative views of race in America, which with its worn-out vocabulary leaves us intellectually debilitated, morally disempowered, and personally depressed. The astonishing disappearance of the event from public dialogue is testimony to just how painful and distressing a serious engagement with race is. Our truncated public discussions of race suppress the best of who and what we are as a people because they fail to confront the complexity of the issue in a candid and critical manner. The predictable pitting of liberals against conservatives, Great Society Democrats against self-help Republicans, reinforces intellectual parochialism and political paralysis.

The liberal notion that more government programs can solve racial problems is simplistic—precisely because it focuses *solely* on the economic dimension. And the conservative idea that what is needed is a change in the moral behavior of poor black urban dwellers (especially poor black men, who, they say, should stay married, support their children, and stop committing so much crime) highlights immoral actions while ignoring public responsibility for the immoral circumstances that haunt our fellow citizens.

The common denominator of these views of race is that each still sees black people as a "problem people," in the words of Dorothy I. Height, president of the National Council of Negro Women, rather than as fellow American citizens with problems. Her words echo the poignant "unasked question" of W. E. B. Du Bois, who, in *The Souls of Black Folk* (1903), wrote:

> They approach me in a half-hesitant sort of way, eye me curiously or compassionately, and then instead of saying directly, How does it feel to be a problem? they say, I know an excellent colored man in my town. . . . Do not these Southern outrages make your blood boil? At these I smile, or am interested, or reduce the boiling to a simmer, as the occasion may require. To the real question, How does it feel to be a problem? I answer seldom a word.

Nearly a century later, we confine discussions about race in America to the "problems" black people pose for whites rather than consider what this way of viewing black people reveals about us as a nation.

This paralyzing framework encourages liberals to relieve their guilty consciences by supporting public funds directed at "the problems"; but at the same time, reluctant to exercise principled criticism of black people, liberals deny them the freedom to err. Similarly, conservatives blame the "problems" on black people themselves—and thereby render black social misery invisible or unworthy of public attention.

Hence, for liberals, black people are to be "included" and "integrated" into "our" society and culture, while for conservatives they are to be "well behaved" and "worthy of acceptance" by "our" way of life. Both fail to see that the presence and predicaments of black people are neither additions to nor defections from American life, but rather *constitutive elements of that life.*

To engage in a serious discussion of race in America, we must begin not with the problems of black people but with the flaws of American society—flaws rooted in historic inequalities and longstanding cultural stereotypes. How we set up the terms for discussing racial issues shapes our perception and response to these issues. As long as black people are viewed as a "them," the burden falls on blacks to do all the "cultural" and "moral" work necessary for healthy race relations. The implication is that only certain Americans can define what it means to be American—and the rest must simply "fit in."

The emergence of strong black-nationalist sentiments among blacks, especially among young people, is a revolt against this sense of having to "fit in." The variety of black-nationalist ideologies, from the moderate views of Supreme Court Justice Clarence Thomas in his youth to those of Louis Farrakhan today, rest upon a fundamental truth: white America has been historically weak-willed in ensuring racial justice and has continued to resist fully accepting the humanity of blacks. As long as double standards and differential treatment abound—as long as the rap performer Ice-T is harshly condemned while former Los Angeles Police Chief Daryl F. Gates's antiblack comments are received in polite silence, as long as Dr. Leonard Jeffries's anti-Semitic statements are met with vitriolic outrage while presidential candidate Patrick J. Buchanan's anti-Semitism receives a genteel response—black nationalisms will thrive.

Afrocentrism, a contemporary species of black nationalism, is a gallant yet misguided attempt to define an African identity in a white society perceived to be hostile. It is gallant because it puts black doings and sufferings, not white anxieties and fears, at the center of discussion. It is misguided because—out of fear of cultural hybridization and through silence on the issue of class, retrograde views on black women, gay men, and lesbians, and a reluctance to link race to the common good—it reinforces the narrow discussions about race.

To establish a new framework, we need to begin with a frank acknowledgment of the basic humanness and Americanness of each of us. And we must acknowledge that as a people—*E Pluribus Unum*—we are on a slippery slope toward economic strife, social turmoil and cultural chaos. If we go down, we go down together. The Los Angeles upheaval forced us to see not only that we are not connected in ways we would like to be but also, in a more profound sense, that this failure to connect binds us even more tightly together. The paradox of race in America is that our common destiny is more pronounced and imperiled precisely when our divisions are deeper. The Civil War and its legacy speak loudly here. And our divisions are growing deeper. Today, eighty-six percent of white suburban Americans live in neighborhoods that are less than 1 percent black, meaning that the prospects for the country depend largely on how its cities fare in the hands of a suburban electorate. There is no escape from our interracial interdependence, yet enforced racial hierarchy dooms us as a nation to collective paranoia and hysteria—the unmaking of any democratic order.

The verdict in the Rodney King case which sparked the incidents in Los Angeles was perceived to be wrong by the vast majority of Americans. But whites have often failed to acknowledge the widespread mistreatment of black people, especially black men, by law enforcement agencies, which helped ignite the spark. The verdict was merely the occasion for deep-seated rage to come to the surface. This rage is fed by the "silent" depression ravaging the country—in which real weekly wages of all American workers since 1973 have declined nearly 20 percent, while at the same time wealth has been upwardly distributed.

The exodus of stable industrial jobs from urban centers to cheaper labor markets here and abroad, housing policies that have created "chocolate cities and vanilla suburbs" (to use the popular musical artist George Clinton's memorable phrase), white fear of black crime, and the urban influx of poor Spanish-speaking and Asian immigrants—all have helped erode the tax base of American cities just as the federal government has cut its supports and programs. The result is unemployment, hunger, homelessness, and sickness for millions.

And a pervasive spiritual impoverishment grows. The collapse of meaning in life—the eclipse of hope and absence of love of self and others, the breakdown of family and neighborhood bonds—leads to the social deracination and cultural denudement of urban dwellers, especially children. We have created rootless, dangling people with little link to the supportive networks—family, friends, school—that sustain some sense of purpose in life. We have witnessed the collapse of the spiritual communities that in the past helped Americans face despair, disease, and death and that transmit through the generations dignity and decency, excellence and elegance.

The result is lives of what we might call "random nows," of fortuitous and fleeting moments preoccupied with "getting over"—with acquiring pleasure, property, and power by any means necessary. (This is not what Malcolm X meant by this famous phrase.) Post-modern culture is more and more a market culture dominated by gangster mentalities and self-destructive wantonness. This culture engulfs all of us—yet its impact on the disadvantaged is devastating, resulting in extreme violence in everyday life. Sexual violence against women and homicidal assaults by young black men on one another are only the most obvious signs of this empty quest for pleasure, property, and power.

Last, this rage is fueled by a political atmosphere in which images, not ideas, dominate, where politicians spend more time raising money than debating issues. The functions of parties have been displaced by public polls, and politicians behave less as thermostats that determine the climate of opinion than as thermometers registering the public mood. American politics has been rocked by an unleashing of greed among opportunistic public officials—who have followed the lead of their counterparts in the private sphere, where, as of 1989, 1 percent of the population owned 37 percent of the wealth and 10 percent of the population owned 86 percent of the wealth—leading to a profound cynicism and pessimism among the citizenry.

And given the way in which the Republican Party since 1968 has appealed to popular xenophobic images—playing the black, female, and homophobic cards to realign the electorate along race, sex, and sexual-orientation lines—it is no surprise that the notion that we are all part of one garment of destiny is discredited. Appeals to special interests rather than to public interests reinforce this polarization. The Los Angeles upheaval was an expression of utter fragmentation by a powerless citizenry that includes not just the poor but all of us.

What is to be done? How do we capture a new spirit and vision to meet the challenges of the post-industrial city, post-modern culture, and post-party politics?

First, we must admit that the most valuable sources for help, hope, and power consist of ourselves and our common history. As in the ages of Lincoln, Roosevelt, and King, we must look to new frameworks and languages to understand our multilayered crisis and overcome our deep malaise.

Second, we must focus our attention on the public square—the common good that undergirds our national and global destinies. The vitality of any public square ultimately depends on how much we *care* about the quality of our lives together. The neglect of our public infrastructure, for example—our water and sewage systems, bridges, tunnels, highways, subways, and streets—reflects not only our myopic economic policies, which impede productivity, but also the low priority we place on our common life.

The tragic plight of our children clearly reveals our deep disregard for public well-being. About one out of every five children in this country lives in poverty, including one out of every two black children and two out of every five Hispanic children. Most of our children—neglected by overburdened parents and bombarded by the market values of profit-hungry corporations—are ill-equipped to live lives of spiritual and cultural quality. Faced with these facts, how do we expect ever to constitute a vibrant society?

One essential step is some form of large-scale public intervention to ensure access to basic social goods—housing, food, health care, education, child care, and jobs. We must invigorate the common good with a mixture of government, business, and labor that does not follow any existing blueprint. After a period in which the private sphere has been sacralized and the public square gutted, the temptation is to make a fetish of the public square. We need to resist such dogmatic swings.

Last, the major challenge is to meet the need to generate new leadership. The paucity of courageous leaders—so apparent in the response to the events in Los Angeles—requires that we look beyond the same elites and voices that recycle the older frameworks. We need leaders—neither saints nor sparkling television personalities—who can situate themselves within a larger historical narrative of this country and our world, who can grasp the complex dynamics of our peoplehood and imagine a future grounded in the best of our past, yet who are attuned to the frightening obstacles that now perplex us. Our ideals of freedom, democracy, and equality must be invoked to invigorate all of us, especially the landless, propertyless, and luckless. Only a visionary leadership that can motivate "the better angels of our nature," as Lincoln said, and activate possibilities for a freer, more efficient, and stable America—only that leadership deserves cultivation and support.

This new leadership must be grounded in grass-roots organizing that highlights democratic accountability. Whoever *our* leaders will be as we approach the twenty-first century, their challenge will be to help Americans determine whether a genuine multiracial democracy can be created and sustained in an era of global economy and a moment of xenophobic frenzy.

Let us hope and pray that the vast intelligence, imagination, humor, and courage of Americans will not fail us. Either we learn a new language of empathy and compassion, or the fire this time will consume us all.

HERB BOYD

The Million Man March

October 16, 1995, was an unforgettable day in Washington, D.C. It was the day that the spirit of *Brotherman* sprang to life. As a friend commented: "Hey, Herb, you know what—*Brotherman* is a metaphor, but the Million Man March made it alive, made it real."

Just as the chorus of voices in *Brotherman* was composed of the young and old, rich and poor, liberal and conservative, established and the emerging, this historic gathering demonstrated for the first time in history the collective power of African American men joined by a unified purpose.

At the Million Man March, I watched as tens of thousands of my brothers bonded with deep love and regard, wept openly, and clung desperately to each other, displaying an intimacy that belies the macho image. As a journalist, I try to be reserved, to hold back and remain objective, but at the march, there were times when I just couldn't hold back my own tears.

The Million Man March was a special moment of rare epiphany for men who have endured the effects of chattel slavery, racism, and humiliation, who have been pushed to the margins of society, bruised by an ensemble of negative stereotypes, alienated from affection and respect, and, for the most part, rendered invisible.

But for this brief, affirming moment, we were not invisible, no longer isolated in our own despair, but asserting our manhood in the nation's capital for all the world to see. While Minister Louis Farrakhan of the Nation of Islam issued the call, the response transcended this controversial leader, and many of those gathered at the National Mall and on the streets of Washington, D.C., expressed a personal agenda for attending the march. Hundreds of them were motivated by the same list of reasons given by Reverend Jesse Jackson, who declared he was marching because "our babies die earlier. Why do we march? Because the media stereotyped us. We are projected as less intelligent than we are, less hardworking than we work, less universal than we are, and more violent than we are."

Sylvester Brown, who attended the march in 1963 and brought his son, Nigel, to this one, said he came because he wanted his son to see how thousands of Black men could stand together. "My being here has less to do with Farrakhan and more to do with my own personal needs," said Brown, a resident of Washington, D.C., and a police officer. "This event is larger than Farrakhan and everybody else. It's about Black men bonding with Black men, and being excited about doing something positive with their lives."

While the feeling of comradery and euphoria moved through the massive throng like electricity, white America trembled in anxiety. The visible current of power generated by one million Black men regenerated by the legacy of our forebears from Douglass to Du Bois, from Washington to Garvey, from Martin to Malcolm was incontestable. This phenomenal display of solidarity is one reason the media, law-enforcement officials, and the National Park Service seemed intent on underreporting the size of the turnout. It is simply astounding, but not surprising that, without the threatened legal challenge by the Nation of Islam, the original estimates of 400,000 would have been allowed to stand as the official count. A number of officials who have worked on crowd control in Washington estimated that there were more than two million Black people assembled for the march, making it larger than the record attendance established during the presidential inauguration of Lyndon Baines Johnson in 1965. In recent memory, only the Pope's appearance in the Philippines, which drew five million, attracted greater numbers. And while officials are willing to concede the march is the largest "Black" demonstration in the nation's history, they are unwilling to give it the validation it justly deserves. Of course, this figure will be disputed, much as the Census, the African Holocaust, and other woefully inaccurate tabulations about Black people and our experience have been.

Noted psychologist Dr. A. J. Franklin said such manipulation of numbers is an aspect of "deep denial. This is merely another attempt to keep us invisible," he explained. "You have to understand that it was an ever-shifting crowd, but it maintained its density throughout."

"I have been to Washington, D.C., for several large rallies," said Ron Lockett, a Detroit youth counselor, "and this is by far the largest. They just don't want to have this event as the biggest gathering in the history of the nation's capital. And they certainly don't want it to be something that can be attributed to Minister Farrakhan. No matter how many of us came to the march, I expected the number to be lowered by the police and the media."

Black Americans provided other examples of white America's inability to tell the truth—that white men can't count Black men because they can't see us, or that maybe they still believe that we are only three fifths of a man. "But it's not about numbers—the spirit was the real message," Franklin continued, "and that's the bottom line."

And the spirit was not limited to Black men. Though there was but a sprinkling of Black women at the March—estimated in the thousands—their voices were heard from the podium. This is a vast improvement over the march on Washington in 1963 when only Mahalia Jackson's glorious voice was heard in song. "This is the prettiest scene I have seen in my whole life," said Cora Masters Barry, the wife of host Mayor Marion Barry, gazing at the thousands of Black men amassed from the Capitol Building to the Washington Monument and beyond. "And I want to say to all the sisters who could not be here in spirit and prayer . . . that we must lift up our brothers." She ended her brief remarks by citing a stanza from Sterling Brown's poem about "strong men getting stronger."

"If you think this is a large crowd," Reverend Al Sharpton had said earlier, "wait until we go home and get our sisters." Still, there were a number of notable sisters already there, including the venerable Queen Mother Moore; Dr. Dorothy Height, president of the National Council of Women; Dr. Betty Shabazz, widow of Malcolm X and director of communications at Medgar Evers College in Brooklyn; former Pennsylvania secretary of state and activist against Gangsta Rap, C. Delores Tucker; poet/actress Maya Angelou; E. Faye Williams, a Washington lawyer and chairwoman of the march's local organizing committee, and a number of Black women politicians.

The presence of such a diverse collection of Black women can in part be attributed to the efforts of Chicago activist Conrad Worrill, Maulana Ron Karenga, Haki Madhubuti, cultural activist and talk radio broadcaster Bob Law, Minister Conrad Muhammad of Mosque #7 in Harlem, and activist Ron Daniels. Daniels, in particular, was unwavering in his insistence on forging a partnership with women that would put aside patriarchy. "As some Black women have correctly pointed out . . . the Million Man March should not convey the impression that the crisis in the Black community is simply a crisis of the Black male. The suppression of Black women outside and inside the Black community is also a historical fact of life," Daniels told the march's organizers.

That they listened to his recommendations is evident from the large number of women on the program, and Rosa Parks, often saluted as the "Mother of the Civil Rights Movement," provided not only a bridge from the civil rights movement to the Million Man March, but her words summarized the feelings of so many Black women. Parks, who endorsed the march from its inception, praised it as an opportunity for "men of African heritage to make a change in their lives for the better."

Change was a recurring theme in Reverend Jesse Jackson's speech, especially the need for Black men to change their self-destructive behavior. Jackson, who was soundly rebuked by leading Black clergymen for supporting the march, made it clear that the media and others were mistaken to assert that Farrakhan and the Nation of Islam were principally responsible for bringing so many Black men together. "Did Minister Farrakhan organize the march?" Jackson asked rhetorically. "No, he did not. Clarence Thomas and Newt Gingrich organized the march."

Reverend Jackson was alluding to these men's intolerant attitudes when it comes to dealing with Black America; declaring that it was their blindness to our struggle and our needs that provoked such a massive turnout.

Jackson's implication that the march was larger than Farrakhan was echoed by thousands of participants, and perhaps nowhere better than in an Op-Ed piece published in the *New York Times* by Cornel West, two days before the march. "In casting the demonstration as 'Farrakhan's March,' the mainstream media want to shift the focus from Black pain to white anxiety . . . men who are deeply concerned about Black suffering and are outraged at the nation's right-wing turn, yet are neither Nation of Islam members nor Farrakhan followers," West wrote. He said he was marching because the next major battle in the struggle for Black freedom involves moral and political channeling of the overwhelming Black rage and despair. "To stand on the sidelines and yield the terrain to Minister Farrakhan and other Black nationalists would be to forsake not only my (Martin Luther) King legacy but, more important, my love for Black people," West concluded.

Cultural critic Stanley Crouch, who views Farrakhan as a demagogue, offers an alternative interpretation of Jackson's remark. "One wonders what Jesse Jackson thinks now, since it was he who brought the Nation of Islam into electoral politics when he got Farrakhan to register his followers in 1984," Crouch mused.

Among America's Black organizations and its leading intellectuals, feelings about the march were varied. The National Association for the Advancement of Colored People, the National Urban League, and several prominent Baptist groups withheld endorsements, citing support for the message but not the messenger. In the opinion of Dr. Benjamin Chavis, former executive director of the NAACP and the march's chief coordinator, the two could not be separated. "This is a march for and by Black men, supported by Black women," Chavis bellowed from the podium on this Black Monday. One notable Black woman, however, who did not support the march was Angela Davis, and she was joined by such distinguished leaders and writers as Jewel Jackson McCabe, Michele Wallace, and Marcia Gillespie, all of them contending that the exclusion of women was sexist.

Amiri Baraka, for his own reasons, also cast aspersion on the march, stating that "First of all, I wouldn't go to war and leave half the army at home," which, whether he knew it or not, was an ironic commentary on Farrakhan's pre-march military metaphor "You don't take your woman into the foxhole with you."

It was late in the afternoon when Minister Farrakhan stepped to the podium, facing, as Brotherman Yusef Salaam recounted in the *Amsterdam News*, "a sea of men . . . stretching beyond the horizon, spilling across streets and around government office buildings, clinging to tree branches and standing on monuments, each one silent, calm, and solemn." Farrakhan began his more than two-hour speech amid bewildering mystical references about the height of the Washington Monument, the layout of the city, and Benjamin Banneker's role in this endeavor, the numerical significance of Abraham Lincoln being the sixteenth president, and a welter of baffling Masonic symbolism. Later, he would offer more puzzling esoterica, discussing at length an exegesis on the word "atonement," which was the theme of the march.

But between these intriguing, albeit metaphysical, digressions, Farrakhan lashed America for its racism and white supremacy, suggesting it was a "disease" and how he was just the doctor pointing out the malady. "God brought the idea through me," he said of the march and its genesis. "And he didn't bring it through me because my heart was dark with hatred and anti-Semitism. He didn't bring it through me because my heart was filled with hatred for white people and for the human family on the planet. If my heart were that dark, how is the message so bright, the message so clear, the response so magnificent?" Farrakhan said he did not come to destroy America, but to rescue and reconstruct it. He stressed the need for eight million Black people to register to vote, a responsibility that has only recently been supported by the Nation of Islam. "We're no longer going to vote for somebody just because they're Black," he thundered. "We've tried that. We wish we could. But we got to vote for you if you are compatible to our agenda."

Many of those in attendance were still not satisfied with the march's agenda, feeling that it failed to address a number of pressing social and political issues. For them, not enough was said about what plans could be implemented to halt the forces that are eroding affirmative action, welfare reform, and a so-called criminal justice system that has permanently stigmatized one third of Black men between the ages of twenty and thirty. But as most conceded, no one march or series of marches can heal all the problems Black people face in America. These problems, they insist, are systemic and call for a virtual restructuring of society. Alleynde Baptiste, a twelve-year-old inspirational speaker from Chicago, touched on part of the prescription during his rousing speech:

"When you can pass on to your youth that tradition of struggle," he told his brothermen, ". . . when you take control of your institutions, your schools . . . when you emphasize your economic resources for our benefit, when you stop making excuses, then we can build a new nation of strong people."

Now that the march has been recorded on the pages of history, it remains to be seen whether it will be a keynote or a footnote. Whether it can make a difference in the lives of millions of Black people and become more than an ephemeral flash to make Farrakhan—a master of controversy—increasingly palatable to the American public. "The success of the march," said journalist Don Rojas, "will now compel America's rulers to deal with Farrakhan, not dismiss him. But without a concrete set of demands," Rojas asserted, "and a plan for sustained action to force concessions on those demands, this march may do less to jump-start a faltering civil rights movement and more to catapult Farrakhan into the ranks of major leaders at a time when mainstream Black leadership is in crisis."

It may take months, even years, to determine the ultimate impact of this unprecedented gathering, and even the combined charisma of Colin Powell, Michael Jackson, Denzel Washington, Michael Jordan, Mike Tyson, and O. J. Simpson could not have drawn such a crowd. Pundits often cite the integration of the plants and factories during World War II as a product of the threatened march on Washington in 1941, led by A. Philip Randolph and Bayard Rustin, as an important parallel. They remind us that the march on Washington in 1963 left in its wake the passage of the Civil Rights Act of 1965. Millions of African American men marched on Washington in 1995 as an act of atonement. But the tangible gains of atonement are not easy to predict or to measure.

It is our hope that those assembled displayed enough energy, enough pride, and enough commitment to ignite brothers and sisters around the nation with a renewed sense of purpose. We pray that we can sustain this energy long enough to make ourselves better men. Better men at home and better men in our respective communities. We hope that these better men can spark a resurgence of political activity, mobilize our disaffected, and revitalize an all but moribund civil rights movement. The real legacy of the Million Man March will not be measured in the numbers assembled; rather it will be measured by the lives saved, the futures restored, and the promises kept.

EPILOGUE

STERLING BROWN

Strong Men (Closing Stanzas)

They gave you the jobs that they were too good for,
They tried to guarantee happiness to themselves
By shunting dirt and misery to you.

You sang:
    Me an' muh baby gonna shine, shine
    Me an' muh baby gonna shine.
        The strong men keep a-comin' on
        The strong men git stronger . . .

They bought off some of your leaders
You stumbled, as blind men will . . .
They coaxed you, unwontedly soft-voiced . . .
You followed a way.
Then laughed as usual.

They heard the laugh and wondered;
Uncomfortable;
Unadmitting a deeper terror . . .
        The strong men keep a-comin' on
        Gittin' stronger . . .

What, from the slums
Where they have hemmed you,
What, from the tiny huts

They could not keep from you—
What reaches them
Making them ill at ease, fearful?
Today they shout prohibition at you
"Thou shalt not this"
"Thou shalt not that"
"Reserved for whites only"
You laugh.

One thing they cannot prohibit—
The strong men . . . coming on
The strong men gittin' stronger.
Strong men . . .
STRONGER . . .

AUTHOR INDEX

ABOUT THE CONTRIBUTORS

KAREEM ABDUL-JABBAR (Ferdinand Lewis Alcindor, Jr.) was first in the news as a celebrated high school basketball player who led Power Memorial Academy of New York City to seventy-one consecutive victories. At the University of California, the 7 ft. 2 in. center launched another record-breaking streak as his team won three straight NCAA titles (1967–69). But he gained his greatest fame as a professional for the Milwaukee Bucks (1969–75) and the Los Angeles Lakers (1975–89). He was voted the MVP six times, scored 38,387 points in his career, and led his teams to six NBA titles.

MUHAMMAD ALI (Cassius Clay) promised to "float like a butterfly and sting like a bee" when he took on an opponent, and this he did almost flawlessly during his remarkable career in the ring. His ascent to international acclaim began in 1960 when he won the gold medal as a light-heavyweight in the Olympics. Four years later, he toppled the seemingly invincible Sonny Liston, changed his name to Muhammad Ali, joined the Nation of Islam, and reigned as heavyweight champion of the world until 1967, when he was stripped of his crown for refusing military service on religious grounds. In 1974 he regained the title, using a "rope-a-dope" tactic to exhaust George Foreman before knocking him out in Zaire. Ali, whose record was 55–5, is the only boxer to win the title three times. Though now suffering from Parkinson's syndrome, Ali remains, as he always contended—"The Greatest!"

ERNEST ALLEN, JR. teaches history in the Department of Afro-American Studies at the University of Massachusetts at Amherst. Editor of the academic journal, *Contributions in Black Studies*, he is also contributing and advising editor to *The Black Scholar*, and coeditor of the forthcoming anthology *Unite or Perish: Documents of Black Radicalism and Black Nationalism, 1954–1975.*

ROBERT L. ALLEN is the author of *The Port Chicago Mutiny* and *Black Awakening in Capitalist America*. He coedited *Court of Appeal* with Robert Chrisman. He is senior editor of *The Black Scholar* and is a former board president of the Oakland Men's Project.

ALSTON ANDERSON is a native of Panama who was educated in Kingston, Jamaica. After a stint in the Army (1943–46), he earned a degree from North Carolina College. He did graduate work at Columbia University in philosophy and then studied metaphysics at the Sorbonne in Paris. It was there, inspired by William Faulkner and jazz, that he began to write. His story, "Dance of the Infidels," appears in the anthology *From Blues to Bop: A Collection of Jazz Fiction*.

MOLEFI KETE ASANTE is a professor and chairperson of the Department of African American studies at Temple University in Philadelphia. Widely recognized as the leading proponent of the Afrocentric perspective, Asante is the author of more than twenty books, including *Afrocentricity*, and over one hundred scholarly articles. He edits the *Journal of Black Studies, The Afrocentric Review*, and is a columnist for the *African Concord* magazine.

ARTHUR ASHE (1943–93) was the first African American tennis player to win some of the most coveted singles championship games, including the Wimbledon, the U.S. Open, and the World Cup Finals. He wrote *Hard Road to Glory*, a history of African American athletes. The noted civil rights activist contracted AIDS as a result of a blood transfusion during triple by-pass surgery for a heart ailment, and died of AIDS-related complications. His autobiography, *Days of Grace*, written with Arnold Rampersad, was published posthumously.

JABARI ASIM is book editor of the *St. Louis Post-Dispatch*. He is founding editor of *Eyeball*, a literary arts journal, and an assistant editor of *Drumvoices Revue*. His poetry has appeared in literary magazines including *Black American Literature Forum*, *Obsidian II*, and *Painted Bride Quarterly*. His fiction and poetry are included in *In the Tradition: An Anthology of Young Black Writers*.

WILLIAM ATTAWAY (1911–86) was a novelist, playwright, screenwriter, and songwriter. His books include his first novel, *Let Me Breathe Thunder*, published in 1939, and his last novel, *Blood on the Forge*, published in 1941. He published two later books about music: *Calypso Song Book* and *Hear America Singing*. He also composed songs and arranged tunes for his friend, Harry Belafonte.

JAMES BALDWIN (1924–87) explored a wide range of cultural, sexual, and political topics with unequalled precision and poetic clarity over a forty-year career. Harlem-born, his most notable books include *Notes of a Native Son*, *Nobody Knows My Name*, *Another Country*, *The Fire Next Time*, *No Name in the Street*, and his last novel, *Just Above My Head*. A collection of his nonfiction, *Price of the Ticket*, was published in 1985. He died of cancer at age sixty-three in St. Paul de Vence, France.

WILLIAM BANKS is the director of the Harlem Writers Guild in New York City. He is extremely active in the media and is the producer and host of a televised book review, "In Our Own Words," the only regularly scheduled television program dealing exclusively with black writers in America. Coauthor, with Arthur Hamilton, of *Father Behind Bars* and author of *A Love So Fine*, he reviews books for the *Chicago Tribune*, *Publisher's Weekly*, and the *New York Times*. He lives in New Haven.

AMIRI BARAKA (LeRoi Jones) ranks as one of America's most versatile writers, equally adept as a poet, playwright, essayist, anthologist, historian, and polemicist. His *Blues People* is among the most cited books on Black music, and he has written more than twelve volumes of poetry. He published his autobiography in 1984. For more than thirty years he has uniquely blended his art and politics. His motto: "I see art as a weapon, and a weapon of revolution."

NOUK BASSOMB was born in Cameroon, Africa. He received a Ph.D. in archaeology from the Sorbonne, then moved to the United States, where he set up the Homeless Self-Help Program. His works include a memoir relating his four-year experience in a concentration camp in Cameroon and two volumes of plays on the political situation in his native land, all of which were published in France. He is currently working on an account of the three-month initiation he underwent in the African rain forest in order to enter adult society. He lives in New York City.

SIDNEY BECHET was the product of a musical family in New Orleans and helped to popularize the Dixieland sound. Though proficient on the clarinet, Bechet was recognized mostly for his pioneering work on the soprano saxophone. During the 1920s he traveled extensively in Europe, and later recorded with Louis Armstrong and Jelly Roll Morton. His autobiography, *Treat It Gentle*, is considered among the best ever written by a jazz musician. Bechet died in Paris on May 14, 1959.

DERRICK BELL presently teaches at the New York University School of Law. Formerly a professor at Harvard University's law school, he resigned in protest of the lack of women of color on the law faculty. His books include *Faces at the Bottom of the Well: The Permanence of Racism*, *And We Are Not Saved:*

The Elusive Quest for Racial Justice, and most recently a memoir, *Confronting Authority*.

PLAYTHELL BENJAMIN has been a professional journalist for over a decade. His column is featured twice weekly in the *New York Daily News*, and he frequently writes on art and politics for the *Manchester Guardian*. He also hosts a popular radio show on WBAI-FM in New York City. He has recently completed his first novel.

YOSEF BEN-JOCHANNAN is known mainly for his work as an Egyptologist, having authored such significant books as *Black Men of the Nile and His Family* and *Africa: Mother of "Western Civilization."* Affectionately known as "Dr. Ben," he has taken more than 25,000 people on study trips to the Nile Valley in Egypt. Currently, he is a senior lecturer, Faculty of Language, Al Azhar University in Egypt. During his always engrossing lectures, Dr. Ben uses wit, humor, and common sense to accentuate history and to expose historical distortions.

LERONE BENNETT, JR., a pioneer in the writing of African American history, is the executive editor of *Ebony* magazine in Chicago. He is the author of over ten books, including *Before the Mayflower: A History of Black America*, *Confrontation: Black and White*, *Black Power, U.S.A.: The Human Side of Reconstruction*, *What Manner of Man: A Biography of Martin Luther King, Jr.*, *Pioneers in Protest*, and, with John H. Johnson, *Succeeding Against the Odds.*

CECIL BROWN was educated at Columbia University and the University of Chicago. He is currently a professor at the University of California, Berkeley, and is the author of *The Life and Loves of Mr. Jiveass Nigger* and *Coming Up Down Home: A Memoir of a Southern Childhood.*

CLAUDE BROWN attended night school and Howard University, receiving a bachelor's degree from the latter in 1963. His famous autobiography resulted from an article he was asked to do on Harlem while an undergraduate at Howard. He submitted a 1,500-page manuscript, which was trimmed and published as *Manchild in the Promised Land*. He is also the author of *Children of Ham*.

JIM BROWN played in the rugged National Football League for the Cleveland Browns for nine years and never missed a game. A tough running back, he asked no quarter and gave none. Tackling him, said one player, was like bringing down a raging bull. Brown won the rushing title eight of nine years as a pro, accumulating 12,312 yards and 126 touchdowns. After retiring from the game in 1966, he made a number of action films. Brown has been active in recent years with Amer-I-Can, an organization he started to help gang members and ex-convicts.

LLOYD L. BROWN is a writer and former editor. His 1951 novel, *Iron City*, based upon his experience as a political prisoner, was published in twelve different languages. He served as Paul Robeson's collaborator on his book, *Here I Stand*. A former reporter for the Harlem newspaper *Freedom*, founded by Robeson, Brown's articles have appeared in numerous publications. He lives in New York City.

STERLING BROWN (1901–89), an influential poet and literary critic, attended Williams College and Harvard University. He taught as an English professor for more than fifty years, mainly at Howard University, and served as adviser in Negro Studies for the Federal Writers Project. His book of poetry, *Southern Road*, is considered a classic. His works include *The Negro in Washington*, *The Negro in American Fiction*, *Negro Poetry and Drama*, and *The Negro Caravan*. *The Collected Poems of Sterling Brown* was published in 1980.

WESLEY BROWN teaches literature and creative writing at Rutgers University. He is the author of two novels: *Tragic Magic* and *Darktown Strutters*. He has written two produced plays and has coedited two multicultural anthologies, *Visions of America* (autobiography and essay) and *Imagining America* (short fiction).

STEPHEN L. CARTER, William Nelson Cromwell Professor of Law at Yale University, is among the nation's leading experts on constitutional law. He is the author of *Reflections of an Affirmative Action Baby*, *The Culture of Disbelief*, and *The Confirmation Mess*.

CHARLES W. CHESNUTT (1858–1932) is considered the first African American short story writer to effectively master the form. Self-educated, he started teaching in the North Carolina public schools at sixteen and was appointed principal at age twenty-three. His first short story was published in the *Atlantic Monthly* in 1887. He authored three novels and two short story collections, including *The Wife of His Youth and Other Stories of the Color Line*, *The Marrow of Tradition*, and *The Conjure Woman and Other Tales*.

NICK CHILES is an education reporter for *New York Newsday*, where he won a 1992 Pulitzer Prize. His work has also appeared in the *Washington Post*, *Essence*, and the *Los Angeles Times*. He is the author of two novels, *The Body Hunter* and *A Private War*.

ROBERT CHRISMAN is editor and publisher of *The Black Scholar* and is currently a lecturer in English and Afro-American Studies at the University of

Michigan. He is the author of two volumes of poems, *Minor Casualties, New and Selected Poems*, and *Children of Empire*. He has edited the anthologies *Court of Appeal: The Black Community Speaks out on the Racial and Sexual Politics of Thomas vs. Hill*, *Panafricanism*, and *Contemporary Black Thought*.

JOHN HENRIK CLARKE not only personifies the self-taught scholar, he is viewed by many as the doyen of Black studies. "People often tell me that I am the leading African and African American historian," says Clarke self-effacingly, "but that position belongs to John Hope Franklin or Benjamin Quarles. If I have made any real contribution, it has been in the area of curriculum development and teaching materials." A keen and diligent chronicler of Harlem, he has amassed a library of memorabilia on this famous community. His books *Harlem USA* and *Harlem Voices* have recently been republished. Clarke was a close associate of Malcolm X and helped him outline the constitution for the Organization of Afro-American Unity.

PRICE M. COBBS is assistant clinical professor of psychiatry at the University of California, San Francisco; fellow, American Psychiatric Association; member, Institute of Medicine, National Academy of Sciences; and president, Pacific Management Systems. With William H. Grier, he wrote *Black Rage* and *The Jesus Bag*.

ERIC V. COPAGE, a journalist and editor, is the author of *Kwanzaa: An African-American Celebration of Culture* and the popular meditation book, *Black Pearls.* A former staff reporter for *Life* magazine and the *New York Daily News*, he is currently an editor at the *New York Times Magazine*. His forthcoming books include *Black Pearls Journal* and *Black Pearls for Parents*. He lives in Montclair, New Jersey.

ELLIS COSE, a journalist and writer on public policy issues, is a contributing editor and essayist for *Newsweek*. His first column, about Chicago communities, was published in the *Chicago Sun-Times* when he was nineteen, and in 1976, the *Sun-Times* assigned him to Jimmy Carter's presidential campaign. His books include *A Man's World*, *A Nation of Strangers*, and *The Rage of a Privileged Class*.

STANLEY CROUCH was a jazz critic and staff writer at the *Village Voice* for ten years. The author of *The All-American Skin Game or the Decoy of Race* and the highly acclaimed *Notes of a Hanging Judge*, Crouch received the Whiting Writers Award and is currently a MacArthur Fellow. His articles have appeared in the *New York Times*, *Vogue*, *Downbeat*, the *Amsterdam News*, and the *Village Voice*. He lives in New York City.

COUNTEE CULLEN (1903–46) was a major poet during the Harlem Renaissance, who acknowledged Keats as a central influence. Educated at New York University and Harvard, his collections of verse include *Color*, *Copper Sun*, *The Ballad of the Brown Girl*, and *The Black Christ*. His novel, *One Way to Heaven*, appeared in 1932. He also served as assistant editor of *Opportunity*, which, along with *The Crisis*, was an important medium expression for the writers of the Harlem Renaissance.

MILES DAVIS, known by many jazz lovers as the "Prince of Darkness," was both an elegant stylist on trumpet and an innovator of several musical genres. Raised in a middle-class family, Davis left his hometown of St. Louis ostensibly to study at Juilliard School of Music in New York City. But his real motive was to find his idol, saxophonist Charlie "Yardbird" Parker. Eventually they would, with other musicians, create the mode of bebop, but Davis was always a restless spirit, and during his illustrious career played a pivotal role in the Cool School of jazz, modal, fusion, and hip-hop.

WILLIAM DEMBY is a novelist and educator who lives in Sag Harbor, New York. His works include *Beetlecreek*, which is set in the Clarksburg, Virginia, coal mining region where he grew up, *The Catacombs*, and *Love Story Black*. He graduated from Fisk University in 1947 and worked in Europe as a jazz musician and a writer for film and television. He has also studied painting in Rome.

MELVIN DIXON (1950–92) was a writer of poetry, fiction, and literary criticism, as well as a translator. His works include a collection of poems, *Change of Territory*; two novels, *Trouble the Water* and *Vanishing Rooms*; and a book of criticism, *Ride Out the Wilderness: Geography and Identity in Afro-American Literature*. A former NEA poetry fellow, he was a contributing editor at *Callaloo*. His poetry and short stories have appeared in *Poets for Life: 76 Poets Respond to AIDS*, *Breaking Ice*, and *Men on Men 2*.

FREDERICK DOUGLASS (1818–95) was born a slave but fled bondage and established himself as one of the nineteenth century's most electrifying orators and writers. His three autobiographical narratives, all American classics, are *Narrative of the Life of Frederick Douglass, An American Slave*, published in 1845; *My Bondage and My Freedom*, published ten years later; and *Life and Times of Frederick Douglass*, first published in 1881. A key adviser to President Lincoln, he was appointed Consul General to Haiti six years before his death.

W. E. B. DU BOIS (1868–1963) was one of the founders of the N.A.A.C.P. as well as founder and editor of *The Crisis*. Educated at Fisk University, Harvard University, and the University of Berlin, he served as professor of Economics and

History at Atlanta University and editor of the *Atlanta Studies*. Some of his many notable books include *The Souls of Black Folk*, *The Negro*, *Darkwater: Voices from Within the Veil*, *Africa: Its Place in Modern History*, *Dusk of Dawn*, *Color and Democracy: Colonies and Peace*, *Worlds of Color*, and *The ABC of Color*. He died in Ghana, West Africa, in 1963, just hours before the March on Washington.

HENRY DUMAS (1934–68) was a poet and fiction writer. His works, collected and edited by Eugene B. Redmond, include *Ark of Bones and Other Stories*, *Jonah and the Green Stone* (a novel), and *Goodbye Sweetwater* (an anthology). Dumas died at thirty-four when he was shot in a New York City subway station.

PAUL LAURENCE DUNBAR (1872–1906), considered the first important Black poet in American literature, published several collections of short stories as well as three novels. He also wrote song lyrics and a musical play. His anthologies are *The Best Stories of Paul Laurence Dunbar* and *The Complete Poems of Paul Laurence Dunbar*.

MICHAEL ERIC DYSON is director of the Institute of African American Research and professor of Communication Studies at the University of North Carolina at Chapel Hill. He is the author of *Making Malcolm: The Myth and Meaning of Malcolm X* and the forthcoming *From God to Gangsta' Rap: Notes on Black Culture*. An award-winning journalist, his work has appeared in such publications as *Emerge* and the *New York Times*.

GERALD EARLY is the director of the Department of African American Studies at Washington University in St. Louis. He is the author of several books, including *Daughters: On Fathers and Fatherhood*, *Lure and Loathing: Essays on Race, Identity, and the Ambivalence of Assimilation*, *The Culture of Bruising: Essays on Prize Fighting*, and *Tuxedo Junction: Essays on American Culture*. His honors include a General Electric Foundation Award and the Whiting Writers Award. His articles have appeared in the *Atlantic Monthly*, the *New Republic*, and *Harpers*. He is currently working on a book about Fisk College.

HARRY EDWARDS became a household name after coordinating a boycott of the 1968 summer Olympics, chronicled later in *The Revolt of the Black Athlete*. Later, while working on his doctorate at Cornell University, he helped negotiate a settlement between the administration and African American students who had taken over several campus buildings. *The Struggle That Must Be*, his 1980 autobiography, was widely acclaimed. He is now a professor of sports sociology at the University of California at Berkeley, and a consultant to Major League Baseball, the San Francisco 49ers, and the Golden State Warriors of the NBA.

LOUIS EDWARDS is the author of *Ten Seconds*. He received a B.A. in journalism from Hunter College. Since 1986, he has worked for the public relations office of New Orleans Jazz and Heritage Festival and the JVC JAZZ Festival—New York. He lives in New Orleans.

EDWARD KENNEDY "DUKE" ELLINGTON (1899–1974) has no peer as an American composer. Among his thousand published songs are such standards as "Sophisticated Lady," "Caravan," "Mood Indigo," and "It Don't Mean a Thing." His orchestra, which included such luminaries as Johnny Hodges, Harry Carney, Jimmy Hamilton, and composer/arranger Billy Strayhorn, was not only a lab for his compositions but was reflective of his elegance and gentility—he was in every way the "Duke." He was truly a jazz legend and an American original. At the time of his death in 1974, Duke was seventy-five.

TREY ELLIS attended Phillips Academy, Andover, and Stanford University. He is the author of two novels, *Platitudes* and *Home Repairs*, and his work as a screenwriter was recently showcased in a segment of the 1994 Hudlin Brothers' HBO short film trilogy, *Cosmic Slop*. His articles have appeared in such publications as *Elle*, *Art & Antiques*, *Newsweek*, *The Black Film Review*, *Interview*, and the *Washington Post Review*. He currently lives in Venice, California.

RALPH ELLISON (1914–94) achieved international fame with his first novel, *Invisible Man*, which won the National Book Award in 1953. A collection of political, social, and critical essays, *Shadow and Act*, published in 1964, further enhanced his reputation. Another collection of his essays, *Going to the Territory*, was published in 1986. In later life Ellison was Albert Schweitzer Professor of the Humanities at New York University.

MINISTER LOUIS FARRAKHAN is the charismatic leader of the Nation of Islam and chief organizer of "The Million Man March." Stressing self-reliance and strict codes of behavior, Farrakhan's speeches at major arenas around the country often draw standing room only crowds. His successful ministry has focused primarily on redeeming ex-convicts, drug addicts, and victims of broken lives. Minister Farrakhan's speeches have been collected in *Back Where We Belong* and *A Torchlight for America*.

TOM FEELINGS, a native of Brooklyn, New York, is an award-winning artist and illustrator. In 1971 he was the first African American artist to win the prestigious Caldecott Honor with his illustrations for *Moja Means One*, written by

Muriel Feelings. He has worked with a number of prominent writers, including Maya Angelou, Eloise Greenfield, and John Henrik Clarke. His most recent book, *The Middle Passage: White Ships, Black Cargo*, features drawings that powerfully evoke the Middle Passage during the Atlantic slave trade, with text by John Henrik Clarke. Feelings is presently a professor of Art at the University of South Carolina.

RUDOLPH FISHER (1897–1934) was best known for his two novels of the Black life in Harlem in the 1920s, *The Walls of Jericho* and *The Conjure-Man Dies*, the first mystery novel by a Black American. Fisher's short stories were collected in *The City of Refuge*.

ROBERT FLEMING, a freelance journalist and poet, formerly worked as a reporter for the *New York Daily News*, earning several honors including a New York Press Club Award and a Revson Fellowship in 1990. His articles have appeared in publications including *Essence*, *Black Enterprise*, *U.S. News & World Report*, *Omni*, and *Psychology Today*. His poetry and essays have appeared in *Upsouth* and *In Search of Color Everywhere: A Collection of African American Poetry*. He is the author of *The Wisdom of the Elders*.

ARTHUR FLOWERS is the author of *De Mojo Blues* (1986), which firmly established him as a writer of great promise, and a highly acclaimed second novel, *Another Good Loving Blues*. The Memphis-born novelist is cofounder of the New Renaissance Writers' Guild and the Griot Shop, and has recently moved back to New York City after living briefly on the West Coast.

JAMES FORMAN, a writer and former Civil Rights activist, has published four books: *High Tide of Black Resistance*, *The Making of Black Revolutionaries*, *Sammy Younge, Jr.*, and *Self-Determination of the African-American People*. He is the recipient of many awards and honors, including the 1990 Fannie Lou Hamer Freedom Award from the National Council of Black Mayors, and the 1991 Certificate of Appreciation from the University of Michigan. He lives in Washington, D.C.

JOHN HOPE FRANKLIN, historian, teacher, writer, and editor, authored the most widely used general history of African Americans, *From Slavery to Freedom*, first published in 1947 and recently issued in a seventh edition. His numerous books include *The Militant South, 1800–1861*, *Racial Equality in America*, and *Race & History: Selected Essays, 1938–1988*. Among the books he edited are *Three Negro Classics* and *Color and Race*. He lives in Durham, North Carolina, where he has been professor emeritus of History at Duke since 1985.

GEORGE C. FRASER is president of SuccessSource, a company he founded in 1988. He attended New York University and received an M.B.A. from

Dartmouth. Mr. Fraser is also the creator and publisher of *SuccessGuide: The Networking Guide to Black Resources*, the first publication of its kind in the United States, which was recently selected for a CEBA Award. He has worked in marketing and has won numerous awards for his work on behalf of the community. He is the author of *Success Runs in Our Race: The Complete Guide to Effective Networking in the African American Community.*

ALBERT FRENCH is a writer who lives in Pittsburgh, Pennsylvania. His first novel, *Billy*, was published in 1993. He is also the author of the novel, *Holly*.

ERNEST J. GAINES is best known for his 1971 novel, *The Autobiography of Miss Jane Pittman*, which was made into a television movie. Among Gaines's six novels are his first, *Catherine Carmier*, *A Lesson Before Dying*, *A Gathering of Old Men*, and *In My Father's House*. The recipient of many awards, including a 1971 Guggenheim Fellowship and a 1993 MacArthur Fellowship, his stories have been collected in *Bloodline* (1968) and have appeared in numerous anthologies and periodicals.

MARCUS GARVEY (1887–1940), born in Jamaica, came to the United States in 1916 and organized the largest Black nationalist movement in American history, the Universal Negro Improvement Association. A seminal figure in African American history, Garvey advocated economic independence, race pride, and Pan-Africanism. Many of his writings and speeches were collected in *Philosophy and Opinions of Marcus Garvey*, edited by Amy Jacques Garvey.

HENRY LOUIS GATES, JR. is one of America's most prominent scholars. Currently professor of English and chairman of Afro-American Studies at Harvard University, he has received countless awards, including a MacArthur Prize Fellowship. His works include *The Signifying Monkey: A Theory of Afro-American Literary Criticism*, *Loose Canons: Notes on the Culture Wars*, and, most recently, *Colored People*, a memoir. He has also edited over twenty books, including *The Schomburg Library of Nineteenth-Century Black Women Writers*, and *Bearing Witness: Selections from African American Autobiography in the Twentieth Century*. He is a frequent contributor to publications such as *Harper's*, the *New York Times Book Review*, the *New Yorker*, and the *Village Voice*.

NELSON GEORGE, a journalist and screenwriter, has written extensively on sports, film, art, culture, and politics for publications including *Billboard*, the *Village Voice*, and the *New York Times*. He is also the coauthor and producer of the hit rap film, *CB4*. A prolific writer, he is the author of seven books, including *Buppies, B-Boys, Bops & Bohos*, and *Urban Romance*. His current book, *Blackface: Reflections on African Americans and the Movies*, was published in 1994. He lives in Brooklyn.

ROLAND J. GILBERT founded Simba, Inc., an organization designed to help African American men, in 1988. He holds a B.A. in economics and an M.S. in administration from the University of California, Irvine. A presidential appointee for the U.S. Small Business Administration in Washington, D.C., he retired from private practice in management consulting in 1988 to devote his time to Simba, Inc. Coauthor, with Cheo Tyehimba, of *The Ghetto Solution*, he lives in Oakland, California.

EARL G. GRAVES is president and chief executive officer of Earl G. Graves, Ltd., and publisher of *Black Enterprise* magazine. In 1972, he was named one of the ten most outstanding minority businessmen in the country by the president of the United States, and has won numerous additional awards, including the National Award of Excellence in recognition for his achievements in minority business enterprise. He also serves as chairman and CEO of Pepsi-Cola of Washington, D.C., L.P., the largest minority-controlled Pepsi-Cola franchise in the United States.

SAM GREENLEE is the author of two novels, *The Spook Who Sat By the Door* and *Baghdad Blues* (1976). He writes: "Given the current state of Black publication, I have decided to play the market by writing a new novel under the pseudonym of Cleopatra Sappho Nzingha Jones under the title: *For Cullud Girls Who Have Contemplated Suicide While Waiting to Exhale Because a Raisin in the Sun Ain't Enuff*. Mr. Greenlee lives in Selma, Alabama.

WILLIAM H. GRIER is a former chairman of the Department of Psychiatry at Meharry Medical College and former professor of Psychiatry, Wayne State University. He coauthored *Black Rage* and *The Jesus Bag* with Price M. Cobbs. He lives in San Diego.

DAMU HAKIM is a freelance writer who lives in New York City.

ALEX HALEY (1921–92) earned his status in the American literary world as the author of the 1976 blockbuster novel, *Roots: The Saga of an American Family*. The book sold millions of copies worldwide in thirty-seven languages and became one of the top-rated shows in television history. Taking twelve years to research and write, *Roots* captured many awards, including the Pulitzer Prize. Haley also cowrote *The Autobiography of Malcolm X* with the Black leader in 1965. A veteran journalist, he initiated the *Playboy* interviews for the magazine in 1962 and wrote countless magazine articles as well. His last works, published posthumously, were *Alex Haley: The Playboy Interviews* and *Queen*, cowritten with David Stevens.

RONALD E. HALL is assistant professor in the Department of Social Work at the University of St. Thomas, St. Paul, Minnesota. He received a Ph.D. from Atlanta University. He is regarded as the nation's leading scholar on skin color and, as a result, testified as an expert witness for the first skin color court case in the United States: *Morrow vs. IRS*. He is the author of several books: *Color Complex*, *Cutanco-Chroma*, and *Black Male in America*, as well as a social work study, "Skin Color Bias Among African Americans."

ARTHUR L. HAMILTON, JR. is an editor for the *Lakeland Pen* newspaper in Coldwater, Michigan, where he writes a monthly column, "Fathers Behind Bars" for prison papers around the country. He is the founder of Fathers Behind Bars, Inc., a nonprofit support organization for parents in prison. He is the coauthor, with William Banks, of *Fathers Behind Bars*. Hamilton has won awards for his poetry, and his poem, "Rat Race," was published in *On the Threshold of a Dream: Vol. I.*

CHARLES V. HAMILTON is a professor of Political Science at Columbia University, where he has worked since 1969. His many books include *Black Power: The Politics of Liberation in America* (with Stokely Carmichael), *The Black Experience in American Politics*, and *Adam Clayton Powell, Jr.: The Political Biography of an American Dilemma*.

NATHAN HARE was the first person hired to coordinate a Black studies program in the United States and, in 1968, coined the term "ethnic studies," which replaced "minority studies." Founding publisher of *The Black Scholar* from 1969–75, he has won numerous awards. A pioneer, with his wife, Julia, of the Black male/female relationships movement, he is the author of many books, including *The Black Anglo Saxons* and, with his wife, *The HARE PLAN to Overhaul the Public Schools and Educate Every Black Man, Woman and Child*. He was coeditor, with Robert Chrisman, of *Pan-Africanism and Contemporary Black Thought*, and has published dozens of articles. He holds two Ph.D.s in clinical psychology and sociology, and currently practices psychotherapy in San Francisco.

E. LYNN HARRIS, an honors graduate of the University of Arkansas, Fayetteville, is the author of two bestselling novels, *Invisible Life* and *Just as I Am*. Both books use a rich, thought-provoking storytelling style to examine the controversial contemporary issues of race, bisexuality, and AIDS. A former computer sales executive with IBM, he lives in Atlanta, Georgia.

ESSEX HEMPHILL is the editor of the award-winning anthology, *Brother to Brother: New Writings by Black Gay Men*. He is the author of *Ceremonies: Prose and Poetry* and is the recipient of a National Endowment for the Arts Fellowship in Poetry, and fellowships from the J. Paul Getty Trust and the PEW Charitable Trusts. His poetry has been featured in two controversial, award-winning, Black gay film and video documents: *Looking for Langston* by

Isaac Julien and *Tongues Untied* by Marion Riggs. He lived in Philadelphia until his death in 1995.

CALVIN C. HERNTON has published seven books, including *Sex and Racism in America*, which has been in print for twenty years with more than 200,000 copies sold; and *Scarecrow*, a novel. His most recent book is *The Sexual Mountain and Black Women Writers*, where for the first time a Black male writer, from a literary point of view, analyzes the conflict between Black men and women. Hernton is also a lauded poet, essayist, and social scientist, and for over ten years he has taught African American literature and creative writing at Oberlin College.

CHESTER HIMES (1909–84), the author of novels, short stories, essays, and films, began writing while serving a prison term for armed robbery. His early novels, among them *The Lonely Crusade*, *The Primitive*, and *If He Hollers Let Him Go*, are considered Black classics. His later detective novels such as *Cotton Comes to Harlem* (made into a feature film), gained him a wide audience. The renowned author and social critic lived in Spain from the mid-'50s until his death in 1984.

HOSEA HUDSON (1898–1988) was a labor organizer and radical activist in the steel mills of Birmingham, Alabama, in the 1930s, 1940s, and 1950s. He recounted his experiences in *Black Worker in the Deep South* and *The Narrative of Hosea Hudson* (written by Nell Irvin Painter).

LANGSTON HUGHES (1902–67) was one of the most important writers of the Harlem Renaissance. Discovered in 1924 by Vachel Lindsay when he was working as a busboy in Washington, his first book, *The Weary Blues*, launched his career in 1925. He introduced Jesse B. Semple in 1943 in a newspaper column, and "Simple" proved to be among his most popular and enduring creations. *The Best of Simple*, a collection of his columns, was edited by Hughes himself. In 1961 he was inducted into the National Institute of Arts and Letters, and later he served on the executive board of P.E.N. American Center. Among his works are the autobiographical *The Big Sea* and *I Wonder as I Wander*, *Not Without Laughter*, *The Ways of White Folks*, *Mulatto* (a long-running Broadway play), four children's books, and his many poems.

EARL OFARI HUTCHINSON is a writer, lecturer, radio host commentator, and publisher. He holds a bachelor's degree in sociology, a master's degree in humanities, and a doctorate in social studies. He is the author of eight books, including *Let Your Motto Be Resistance*, *The Myth of Black*, *Black Fatherhood: The Guide to Male Parenting*, *Black Fatherhood II: Black Women Talk About Their Men*, and *The Assassination of the Black Male Image*, as well as the forthcoming *Blacks and Reds* and *The Presidential Betrayal of America*. His writings have appeared in the *Chicago Tribune*, *Los Angeles Times*, *San Francisco Examiner*, *Ebony*, and *Harpers*.

ICE T has sold over ten million records worldwide. Chosen by *Rolling Stone* readers as 1992's Best Male Rapper, he was the first California rapper to challenge the hegemony of the East Coast rappers, and is credited with the invention of L.A.-style gangsta rap. Since 1987, he has toured extensively in America, Europe, Japan, South America, and Australia. He had also starred in feature films, including *New Jack City*, *Ricochet*, and *Trespass*. His heavy-metal band, *Body Count*, released "Cop Killer" and rekindled the debate about censorship in the recording industry.

JAMES E. JACKSON is an editor and journalist, and the author of *The Bold, Bad '60s*, *Revolutionary Tracings*, *The View from Here*, and *U.S. Negroes in Battle*. A veteran of World War II, he has been an international correspondent and has reported on the U.S. Civil Rights struggle. A professional organizer of the Southern Negro Youth Congress and the Tobacco Workers' Union, he is the winner of the Joliot Curie Gold Medal for his contribution to peace and friendship among the people.

REVEREND JESSE JACKSON has been in the national spotlight since the early sixties when he was a trusted lieutenant of Martin Luther King, Jr. An outstanding orator and civil rights organizer, Jackson founded Operation Breadbasket. Jackson took national center stage in the political arena when he became the first African American candidate for the presidency in 1984 and 1988, and he emerged as a prominent spokesperson for Black America. As a roving ambassador for peace, he has played significant roles in the struggle against apartheid in South Africa and for democracy in Haiti. Currently, he is revitalizing and restructuring his Rainbow Coalition.

CHARLES JOHNSON, writer and artist, has gained wide critical acclaim with his complex, insightful novels and short stories. Winner of the National Book Award for his novel *Middle Passage*, Johnson has also written the novels *Faith and the Good Thing*, and *Oxherding Tale*. He also published *The Sorcerer's Apprentice*, a collection of short stories, and a book of criticism, *Being and Race: Black Writing Since 1970*. He is currently a professor in the English Department at the University of Washington, Seattle.

EARVIN "MAGIC" JOHNSON, with his thrill-a-minute, razzle-dazzle style on the basketball court, has more than lived up to his sobriquet. Magic burst onto the national scene in 1979 when he led Michigan State University to the NCAA title. His success continued in the professional ranks, as he orchestrated NBA championships for the L.A. Lakers in 1980, 1982, 1985, and

1987–88. He won three MVP awards and holds the assist record of 9,921. His legendary career is chronicled in his autobiography, *My Life.* At the start of the 1991–92 season Magic tested positive for the HIV virus and retired. Magic Johnson has been a tireless campaigner in the fight against AIDS and is the author of *What You Can Do to Avoid AIDS*.

JOHN H. JOHNSON is the nation's best known black publishing executive. As publisher of *Ebony*, *Jet*, and *EM* magazines and an entrepreneur in cosmetics and television programming, Johnson represents a classic American success story. He chronicles his outstanding achievements in his autobiography, *Succeeding Against the Odds* (written with Lerone Bennett, Jr.)

EDWARD P. JONES's first book, *Lost in the City*, was a critically acclaimed collection of short stories chronicling African American life in Washington, D.C. Nominated for a 1992 National Book Award, *Lost in the City* was the first short story collection to achieve this honor in six years. The writer attended College of the Holy Cross and the University of Virginia. He lives in Arlington, Virginia.

QUINCY JONES has mastered nearly every genre of music as an instrumentalist, composer, arranger, conductor, and producer. He began as a trumpeter in the big bands of Lionel Hampton and Dizzy Gillespie in the 1950s. By 1961 he was a musical director at Mercury Records, the first such position held by an African American. In 1964 he broke another color barrier, scoring the music for a major Hollywood film, *The Pawnbroker*. Since then, he has scored numerous films and television shows, including "Roots." As a producer, his accomplishments have been even more astounding. Michael Jackson's *Thriller*, which Jones produced, is the top-selling album of all time; and in 1985, Jones produced the American hunger relief anthem "We Are the World." Jones has won more than twenty Grammy awards, including those for his all-star album, *Back on the Block.*

MAULANA KARENGA, an award-winning activist-scholar, is widely known as the creator of the African American holiday Kwanzaa. His philosophy of Kawaida is an ongoing synthesis of the best of nationalist, Pan-Africanist, and socialist thought. He has written eight books, as well as numerous scholarly articles, including *Introduction to Black Studies*, 2nd Edition, *The African American Holiday of Kwanzaa: A Celebration of Family, Community and Culture*, and *The Book of Coming Forth Day By Day: The Ethics of the Declarations of Innocence.* He is currently a professor and chair of the Department of Black Studies at California State University, Long Beach.

WILLIAM MELVIN KELLEY published his first novel, *A Different Drummer*, in 1961, after attending Harvard University in the 1950s. Among his other novels are *A Drop of Patience*, *Dem*, and *Dunsfords Travels Everywhere*. *Dancers on the Shore*, a collection of short stories, was published in 1963. Kelley teaches at Sarah Lawrence College and lives in New York City.

RANDALL KENAN teaches writing at Sarah Lawrence College and Columbia University. A former editor at Alfred A. Knopf, Kenan is the author of an award-winning collection of short stories, *Let the Dead Bury Their Dead*, which was nominated for the 1992 National Book Award in Fiction, and a novel, *A Visitation of Spirits*. His other awards include a New York Foundation for the Arts Fellowship and a MacDowell Colony Lila Wallace Readers Digest Fellowship.

JOHN OLIVER KILLENS (1916–87) is best known as the founder and chair of the Harlem Writers' Guild Workshop. A teacher, activist, and writer, he was a professor of Creative Writing at Medgar Evers College in Brooklyn when he died in 1987. He is the author of five novels, including *Youngblood*, *And Then We Heard the Thunder*, based on his army experiences in the South Pacific, *Sippi*, and *The Cotillion*; a collection of political essays; a biography of Denmark Vesey; and a children's book as well as two screenplays, three plays, and numerous stories and essays.

DENNIS KIMBRO is the coauthor of the bestselling *Think and Grow Rich: A Black Choice*, with Napoleon Hill. His popular book, *Daily Motivations for African-American Success* was published in 1993. He is currently the director of the Center for Entrepreneurship at Clark Atlanta University.

MARTIN LUTHER KING, JR. (1929–68) was the leading spokesman of the nonviolent civil rights movement in the South in the 1960s. His passionate oratory and determined commitment to the struggle for justice and peace inspired millions of Americans. King, who in 1964 became the youngest recipient of the Nobel Peace Prize, was assassinated in 1968. His works include *Stride Toward Freedom*, *Why We Can't Wait*, and *A Testament of Hope: The Essential Writings and Speeches of Martin Luther King, Jr.* He is the only African American to have a holiday celebrated in his honor.

SPIKE LEE has almost singlehandedly revitalized the African American film industry with his provocative movies on Black American life, family, class, culture, politics, racism, sexism, and religion. The Brooklyn-born film director is the founder and director of his own film company, 40 Acres & a Mule Filmworks, and has produced a long string of hits including *She's Gotta Have It*, *School Daze*, *Do the Right Thing*, *Mo' Better Blues*, *Malcolm X*, and *Crooklyn*. His many honors include a Prix de Jeunesse from the Cannes Film Festival in 1986. He is also the coauthor or author of six books, including, with Ralph Wiley, *By Any Means Necessary: The Trials and Tribulations of the Making of "Malcolm X."*

JULIUS LESTER has been a writer, civil rights activist, musician and singer, and college professor. An award-winning author or editor of more than twenty books, Lester gained national attention with his 1968 book, *Look Out Whitey! Black Power's Gon' Get Your Mama!* His recent writings include *Falling Pieces of the Broken Sky*, *And All Our Wounds Forgiven*, and *The Last Tales of Uncle Remus*. He presently teaches at the University of Massachusetts at Amherst.

DAVID LEVERING LEWIS topped off his remarkable literary career in 1994 when he won three distinguished awards for his biography of W. E. B. Du Bois, including a Pulitzer Prize. He is the first Rutgers University professor to claim such an honor. At Rutgers, Dr. Lewis holds the Martin Luther King, Jr., chair in history and is currently working on the second volume of Du Bois's life. Among his several fellowships is a Guggenheim and an award from the National Humanities Center. Educated at Fisk and Columbia universities, he is the author of *King: A Biography*, *Prisoners of Honor*, *When Harlem Was in Vogue*, and *The Race to Fashoda*. He lives in Washington, D.C.

NATHANIEL MACKEY is a fascinating stylist who represents an almost singular effort to merge experimental expressions with jazz textures and improvisations. A poet and editor *(Hambone)*, he is the author of *Four for Trane*, *Septet for the End of Time*, and *Eroding Witness*. Recently, with Art Lange, he coedited *Moment's Notice: Jazz in Poetry and Prose*. He teaches literature at the University of California, Santa Cruz.

HAKI MADHUBUTI is the publisher and editor of Third World Press, founder of the Institute of Positive Education in Chicago, and professor of English and director of the Gwendolyn Brooks Center at Chicago State University. A cofounder of the Organization of Black American Culture Writer's Workshop, he has published numerous books of poetry and fiction, some under the name Don L. Lee, including *Think Black*, *Black Men: Obsolete, Single, Dangerous?*, *Say That the River Turns: The Impact of Gwendolyn Brooks*, and *Claiming the Earth: Race, Rage, Rape, Redemption*. Lecturer, community worker, and researcher, he has published widely in magazines, quarterlies, and newspapers. He lives in Chicago.

CLARENCE MAJOR is the author of seven novels and nine books of poetry. His three most recent novels are *Painted Turtle: Woman with Guitar*, *Such Was the Season*, and *My Amputations*. He has edited two anthologies, *The New Black Poetry* and *Calling the Wind: Twentieth-Century African-American Short Stories*. His many awards include a National Council on the Arts Award in 1970, a Fulbright (1981–83), and two Pushcart Prizes (1967, 1990). He reviews for the *Washington Post Book World* and has contributed to the *New York Times Book Review* and over a hundred other periodicals and anthologies. He is currently professor of African-American Literature and Creative Writing at the University of California, Davis.

RICHARD MAJORS received his Ph.D. in counseling psychology from the University of Illinois, Urbana, and was a clinical fellow in psychiatry at Harvard Medical School. He is cofounder and president of the National Council of African American Men (NCAAM), the first umbrella group in the United States for African American males, and is the founder and deputy editor of the *Journal of African American Men* (JAAM). He is coauthor of *Cool Pose: The Dilemmas of Black Manhood in America* and *The American Black Male: His Present Status and Future*. The recipient of many awards, his work has appeared in such magazines as *Time*, *Newsweek*, *American Vision*, *Jet*, and *Reader's Digest*. He lives in Washington, D.C.

MALCOLM X, along with Martin Luther King, Jr., stands as an unimpeachable sentinel of human and civil rights. Resurrecting himself from a life of crime, he became a powerful voice for Black America and its quest for freedom and self-determination. After leaving prison in the early 1950s, he joined the Nation of Islam and was soon the national spokesman for the organization, appearing in forums around the world. He visited Mecca and made two trips to Africa. In 1963, following the assassination of President Kennedy, he was silenced after violating Elijah Muhammad's order not to comment on the incident. In 1964 he broke with Elijah Muhammad and devoted his time to forming his own organization—the Organization of Afro-American Unity. In 1965, before it was fully conceived, he was assassinated. *The Autobiography of Malcolm X*, which he completed with Alex Haley, remains a classic.

MANNING MARABLE is a professor of History and Political Science, and the director of the Institute for Research in African-American Studies at Columbia University. The founding director of Colgate University's Africana and Hispanic Studies Program, he has written over one hundred articles in scholarly publications and has written eight books, including: *How Capitalism Underdeveloped Black America*, *Race Reform and Rebellion*, and *The Crisis of Color and Democracy*, as well as the forthcoming *Beyond Black and White* and *Speaking Truth to Power*. He also serves as an adviser to members of the Congressional Black Caucus and is a national co-chairperson of the Committees of Correspondence.

JARVIS MASTERS is a writer who lives in San Quentin Prison's Death Row. As a death row inmate, he has a unique perspective from which to explore morality, particularly in matters of life and death. He received a 1992 P.E.N. Center Writing Award for Prisoners for his poem, "Recipe for Prison Pruno," which tied for third place. A student of Buddhism for four years, he was given Buddhist Precepts by Chagdud Tulku Rinpoche in March 1991. He is a frequent contributor to the Buddhist publication *Turning Wheel* and has been published in *Men's Studies Review*, *Recovering*, *Men's Council Newsletter*, and *Wingspan: Journal of the Male Spirit*.

NATHAN MCCALL grew up in Portsmouth, Virginia. He studied journalism at Norfolk State University after serving three years in prison. He reported for the *Virginian Pilot-Ledger Star* and the *Atlanta Journal-Constitution* before moving to the *Washington Post* in 1989. He is the author of the bestselling *Makes Me Wanna Holler*, his 1994 autobiography.

CLAUDE MCKAY (1890–1948) was born in Jamaica and educated in the United States. A well-known poet and novelist of the Harlem Renaissance, as well as a prominent figure in the post-World War I radical press, his works include *Harlem Shadows* (poems), the novels *Home to Harlem* (a bestseller), *Banjo*, and *Banana Bottom*, and two autobiographical works, *A Long Way from Home* and *My Green Hills of Jamaica*.

REGINALD MCKNIGHT, a novelist and short story writer, has thoughtfully limned his experiences in Africa. This is best reflected in his novel *I Get on the Bus*, and *Moustapha's Eclipse*, a collection of short stories. He has won several literary awards. A graduate of Denver University, McKnight has taught at the University of Pittsburgh and is currently at the University of Maryland.

JAMES ALAN MCPHERSON was born in Savannah, Georgia, and attended Morgan State University, Harvard University, and the University of Iowa. McPherson has written two collections of short stories, *Hue and Cry*, published in 1969; and the Pulitzer Prize-winning *Elbow Room*, published in 1977. He has received several literary awards for his work, including a MacArthur Fellowship.

KENNETH MEEKS is the managing editor of *Black Elegance* magazine. A reporter for the *Amsterdam News* and *Black Ethnic Collectibles*, his work has also appeared in *Black Enterprise*, *Guideposts*, *Urban Profile*, and *Seek*. He writes primarily about people of color and their struggle in the 1990s. *Pledging Alpha* is his first published work of fiction. He lives in New York City, where he is currently working on a novella.

KWEISI MFUME represents Maryland's 7th Congressional District and serves as chairman of the Congressional Black Caucus for the 103rd Congress. A four-term member of Congress, Congressman Mfume serves on the Banking, Finance, and Urban Affairs Committee and the Small Business Committee. He is also chairman of the Joint Economic Committee and serves on the Ethics

Committee. He is the host of the weekly public affairs television show, "Bottom Line," slated for national syndication in 1995. He is the author of *No Free Ride*.

SYLVESTER MONROE is the Los Angeles correspondent for *Time*. He is the co-author of the 1988 nonfiction book *Brothers*. His work has also appeared in *Emerge*.

W. J. BRANDY MOORE, forty-nine, has been living with HIV for the past nine years. An AIDS activist of national acclaim, Mr. Moore is currently writing an archival book entitled, *The Black Men's History Project*. He is a health policy consultant and is skilled in the development of organizations that address social issues in the public sector. Mr. Moore founded the African American Men's Caucus in San Francisco, a group that works to assist African American men with issues of responsibility and survival.

WALTER MOSLEY is among the most celebrated writers in the country following the smashing success of his quartet of novels—*Devil in a Blue Dress*, *A Red Death*, *White Butterfly*, and *Black Betty*. He has given the Black mystery novel a distinctive but realistic spin as he plumbs the depths of a seamy Los Angeles. His fans eagerly await another episode in the life of his protagonist Easy Rawlins, and wonder what color he will fix in his title. Mosley's first non-Easy novel is the recent release, *RL's Dream*.

WILLARD MOTLEY (1909–65) was a novelist whose bestselling novel, *Knock on Any Door*, was made into a motion picture. His other novels include *Let No Man Write My Epitaph*, *We Fished All Night*, and *Let Noon Be Fair*.

JESS MOWRY was born in Mississippi in 1960 and was raised in Oakland, California, where he attended school through the eighth grade. In 1988 he bought a used typewriter at an auction and started writing. His first published story, "One Way," appeared in the literary magazine *Zyzzyva*. It was quickly followed by stories published in *Alchemy*, *Sequoia*, and the *Santa Clara Review*. Mowry's first book, *Rats in the Trees*, won the P.E.N. Oakland/Josephine Miles Award that year. He is also the author of *Children of the Night*, the critically acclaimed *Way Past Cool*, and *Six Out Seven*.

LEROY "SATCHEL" PAIGE was the oldest rookie (forty-two) and the first Black pitcher to make it to the major leagues. Easy-going, hard-throwing Satch earned his reputation toiling in the Negro Leagues where only the legend of Josh Gibson rivaled his feats. Satch joined the Cleveland Indians in 1948 and helped pitch them to the pennant and to victory in the World Series. He played until 1953, but made a memorable special appearance in 1965, pitching three innings for the Kansas City Athletics. Although he won only twenty-eight games in the majors, it is estimated that he pitched a total of 2,500 games during his career. In 1971 he was inducted into the Baseball Hall of Fame. He was seventy-six when he died in 1982.

GORDON PARKS is a gifted novelist, essayist, poet, composer and pianist, painter, and film director. His first national acclaim was as a photographer for *Life* magazine. His keen eye and winning personality were responsible for many award-winning photos, as well as lasting friendships with such disparate figures as Gloria Vanderbilt and Malcolm X. *The Learning Tree*, both the novel and the film he wrote and directed, forms the basis of his other three autobiographies—*A Choice of Weapons*, *To Smile in Autumn*, and *Voices in the Mirror*. In 1990 he premiered his ballet *Martin* and has completed his novel based on the life of the English painter J. M. W. Turner, and a book of his minimalist photographs.

ALEXS D. PATE is a writer and performance artist whose articles and essays have appeared in the *Washington Post*, *Essence*, *USA Today Weekend*, and *Hungry Mind Review*. He won the Best First Novelist Award from the Black Caucus of the American Library Association for his novel, *Losing Absalom*. He lives in Minneapolis.

RICHARD PERRY teaches literature and creative writing at Pratt Institute in Brooklyn. His first novel, *Changes*, was published in 1974. In 1985 he was the winner of the Quality Paperback Books' New Voice Award for his second novel, *Montgomery's Children*. His most recent novel, *No Other Tale to Tell*, appeared in 1994. He lives in Englewood Cliffs, New Jersey.

SIDNEY POITIER was the first African American man to win an Academy Award for his work in *Lilies of the Field* (1963). Among his major films are *The Blackboard Jungle* (1955), *The Defiant Ones* (1958), *The Bedford Incident* (1965), *Guess Who's Coming to Dinner* (1967), and *In the Heat of the Night* (1967). His autobiography, *This Life*, was published in 1980.

KEVIN POWELL is a staff writer at *Vibe* magazine. His articles, essays, and reviews have also appeared in such publications as *Rolling Stone*, *Essence*, and the *New York Times*. An award-winning poet, Kevin edited, with Ras Baraka, *In the Tradition: An Anthology of Young Black Writers*. He is currently at work on his first collection of essays, *Keepin' It Real*. His first volume of poetry, *recognize*, was published by Harlem River Press.

DUDLEY RANDALL is best known as a poet, but he is equally respected as the trailblazing publisher and founder of the legendary Broadside Press in the 1960s. He has edited several volumes of poetry, including his classic work, *Black Poets* (1971). A prolific poet, his poem "Booker T. and W. E. B." summarizes as well as any shelf of books the differences between these two great leaders. In 1981 his collection of poems, *A Litany of Friends*, was published.

ISHMAEL REED is well known for his innovative and often satirical fiction and his provocative essays. The author or editor of over twenty works of fiction, nonfiction and poetry, his most recent works include *Airing Dirty Laundry*, *Writin' is Fightin': Thirty-Seven Years of Boxing on Paper*, and *Japanese by Spring*. He is a cofounder of the Before Columbus Foundation, which gives the annual American Book Awards.

PAUL ROBESON (1898–1976) rose to prominence in the 1920s and 1940s as an actor and singer. His father, who had escaped from slavery, was a minister and his mother was a teacher. As a student at Rutgers College, Robeson became an All-American football player, a Phi Beta Kappa student, and the valedictorian of his graduating class. He received a law degree from Columbia University. His acting break came in 1923, when a director of the Provincetown Players asked him to audition for Eugene O'Neill's new drama, *All God's Chillun Have Wings*. His 1958 memoir, *Here I Stand*, written with Lloyd Brown, addressed, among other things, his involvement with socialism and communism.

JACK "JACKIE" ROBINSON was a gifted athlete of immense pride, courage, and fortitude. All of these attributes were instrumental in his breaking major league baseball's color barrier in 1947. Before joining the Brooklyn Dodgers, Robinson was a four-letter athlete at the University of California, starring in baseball, track, football, and basketball. He won Rookie of the Year honors with the Dodgers and led them to their first pennant since 1941. Robinson excelled in every facet of the game and won the MVP in 1949, leading the league in batting (.342) and stolen bases (37). He was as graceful in the field as he was potent with the bat and earned several Golden Glove awards. He was elected to the Baseball Hall of Fame in 1962. He died ten years later at the age of sixty-three.

RANDALL ROBINSON is the executive director of TransAfrica, a political action group that lobbies on behalf of Third World countries and is based in Washington, D.C.

J. A. ROGERS, historian, journalist, newspaper columnist, and writer, became the first Black war correspondent in the history of the United States when he was assigned to cover the Italo-Ethiopian War in 1935. He is peerless when it comes to his compilation of African Americans' notable contributions to world culture. The author of over fifteen works of nonfiction and fiction, an abbreviated list of his many books—*From "Superman" to Man*, *As Nature Leads*, *Africa's Gift to America*, *Sex and Race*, and *The World's Great Men of*

Color—only provides a glimpse of his massive research. Rogers is perhaps best noted for his claims that Beethoven, Alexander Hamilton, President Warren Harding, and several other presidents were of mixed blood. He died in 1966 at the age of eighty-three. His widow, Helga, continues to reprint his vast library.

KALAMU YA SALAAM is a writer, artist, actor, director, playwright, and editor. The author of eight plays and the recipient of numerous awards, his most recent work is *What Is Life?*, a collection of poetry and essays. A New Orleans native, Salaam is currently the producer and scriptwriter for Crescent City Sounds, a nationally syndicated weekly radio program of authentic New Orleans music.

YUSEF SALAAM has freelanced for the *Amsterdam News* for over fifteen years. His articles have appeared in *Essence*, *Black Enterprise*, *Players*, *Quarterly Black Review of Books*, and other publications. Salaam is the author of a book on Blacks in the martial arts, and *Capoeira: African-Brazilian Karate*. He is also the author of *Harry's Hair*, a children's book. He was the recipient of the William Monroe Trotter Journalism Award in 1992. He lives and teaches in Harlem.

ALBERT RACE SAMPLE is the author of *RaceHoss: Big Emma's Boy*. He was the first ex-convict in Texas to work out of the governor's office. A multi-recidivist, Sample was incarcerated for seventeen years. In 1976 he received a full pardon and restoration of civil rights. He has received numerous awards for his work in the field of corrections and rehabilitation and in 1984, he was appointed coordinator for the Travis County anti-DWI program. He lives in Austin, Texas.

BOBBY SEALE is the former chairman, surviving founder and national organizer of the Black Panther Party, U.S.A. He grew up in the Oakland–Berkeley communities, where he trained and worked as a carpenter in preparation for becoming an architect. He later joined the U.S. Air Force as a structural repairperson on high performance aircraft and then as a nondestruct inspector for the Gemini Missile Program. He is currently the creator–director of R.E.A.C.H., an organization dedicated to teaching community organizing. The author of several books, he is currently working with Warner Bros. on a feature film based on his book *Seize the Time*. Seale continues to lecture throughout the United States and is a volunteer community liaison with Temple University's Department of African and African American Studies.

CHARLIE SIFFORD, the first African American man to play professional golf, began his career in 1946. Sifford's autobiography, *Let Me Play*, published in 1992, chronicles his years on the pro golf circuit and the problems faced by black golfers. Nearly seventy, Sifford continues to tour as a golf professional, is a representative of the professional golf tour and the Senior PGA, and has appeared numerous times on national television news and sports specials. He lives in Kingwood, Texas.

BRENT STAPLES, the oldest son of nine children, grew up in a small industrial town near Philadelphia. He received a Ph.D. in psychology from the University of Chicago. Staples is currently a member of the editorial board of the *New York Times* and has served on the newspaper as assistant metropolitan editor and editor of the *Book Review*. He previously worked as a reporter for the *Chicago Sun-Times*. His latest book, *Parallel Time: Growing Up in Black and White*, was published in 1994.

SHELBY STEELE is a professor of English at San Jose State University in California. He received his doctorate in history from the University of Utah in 1974. He was the host of a PBS Special, "Seven Days in Bensonhurst," and his collection of essays, *The Content of Our Character*, won the National Book Critics Circle Award in 1990.

RON STODGHILL is an award-winning journalist on the staff of *Business Week*. He has also written for such publications as *Black Enterprise* and *Emerge*. He was a Davenport Fellow at the University of Missouri–Columbia, 1988; a Knight Foundation Fellow at the University of Maryland, 1991; and a Wharton Business Fellow at the University of Pennsylvania, 1993. He is currently working with Congressman Kweisi Mfume on the Congressman's memoir, *No Free Ride*.

WILLIAM STRICKLAND is an activist-scholar who is often sought for his expertise on political affairs. A member of the Massachusetts Black Hall of Fame, for several years he has been associate professor in the W. E. B. Du Bois Department of African American Studies at the University of Massachusetts at Amherst. He served as an academic consultant on the extraordinary T.V. series "Eyes on the Prize." Strickland is a widely published essayist and is a contributing editor to *Essence* magazine and *African World*, an international journal. In 1994 he coedited, with Cheryll Greene, *Malcolm X—Make It Plain*, which complemented a documentary by Blackslide Productions.

GEORGE EDWARD TAIT, a poet, musician, and a dynamic speaker with an emphasis on African-centered topics, has been a leader on the Harlem political and cultural front for many years. A founder of the Society of Afrikan Poets, Tait has sponsored readings, workshops, and helped promote the creative efforts of hundreds of writers through his reviews and critiques. He is the author of works including *At War: Selected Poems of George Edward Tait* and *A Song of the Sacrificial Goat*.

GREG TATE is one of the leading voices of the "New Black Aesthetic." His challenging wit and perceptive vision has continually captivated readers of current cultural trends in such magazines as *Vibe*, *Spin*, and *Down Beat*. He is currently a staff writer for the *Village Voice* and a founding member of the Black Rock Coalition. His provocative collection of essays, *Flyboy in the Buttermilk*, was published in 1992. He lives in Harlem.

CLYDE TAYLOR is a film critic and professor of English and Afro-American Studies at Tufts University. A frequent contributor to journals and magazines, his ground-breaking anthology, *Vietnam and Black America*, was published in 1973.

WALLACE TERRY, a New York native, was educated at Brown University, University of Chicago, and Harvard University. He covered the Vietnam War for two years while a *Time* magazine correspondent and also produced documentary films on Black marines for the U.S. Marine Corps. His landmark oral history of Black veterans in the Vietnam war, *Bloods*, was published in 1984. Recently, Terry has appeared as a radio and television commentator for CBS, *Post-Newsweek*, *The Evening Association*, and *In the Public Interest*.

HOWARD THURMAN (1900–81) was a theologian, a professor, and a renowned philosopher and writer. He served as Dean Emeritus at the Marsh Chapel, Boston University, until his death. In 1975, he was appointed Honorary Canon of the Cathedral of Saint John the Divine, New York City. In 1944, he founded the Church for the Fellowship of All Peoples in San Francisco, the first church to be completely integrated. The recipient of countless awards, his books include *Mysticism and the Experience of Love*, *The Inward Journey*, and his autobiography, *With Head and Heart*. He founded the Howard Thurman Educational Trust, a public foundation providing financial support for religious, charitable, scientific, literary, and educational causes.

WALLACE THURMAN (1902–34) was a playwright and novelist of the Harlem Renaissance. His novels were *The Blacker Berry* and *Infants of the Spring*. His play, *Harlem*, was produced at the Apollo Theater in 1929.

JEAN TOOMER's (1894–1967) classic experimental novel, *Cane*, was published in 1923. With this single book, a mosaic of poems, short stories, and sketches, Toomer created a hallmark of artistic achievement and racial expression. An inspiration to many American writers, Toomer attended the University of Wisconsin and the City College of New York. Although he studied various subjects, literature was his first love and he regularly contributed avant-garde poetry, sketches, and reviews to national magazines. His experience as a principal of a school in Georgia, which began in 1922, led to the writing of *Cane*. Although he continued to write both fiction and nonfiction, completing two more novels in addition to other works, his work was never again accepted for publication.

QUINCY TROUPE is a professor of Creative Writing and American and Caribbean Literature at the University of California, San Diego. He is the author of nine books, including *Weather Reports: New and Selected Poems* and a collection of essays, *Artists on the Cutting Edge*. He also edited *James Baldwin: The Legacy* and coauthored *Miles: The Autobiography*. He is the recipient of two American Book Awards and a Peabody Award for the Miles Davis Radio Project, which he wrote and coproduced. He is currently working on a memoir and on his fifth volume of poetry, *Avalanche*. He lives in La Jolla, California.

CHEO TYEHIMBA-TAYLOR is a staff writer at *Time* magazine. He is also editor and publisher of *Forward*, an African arts and culture journal. He has written for several publications including *Essence*, the *San Francisco Bay Guardian*, and the *Village Voice*. Coauthor, with Roland Gilbert, of *The Ghetto Solution*, he is currently completing his first screenplay. He lives in Brooklyn.

BRENT WADE is the author of *Company Man*. He graduated from the University of Maryland with a degree in English. Following a brief stint as a bricklayer, he worked in sales and marketing jobs for a number of businesses and corporations on both coasts, including AT&T, Westinghouse, and LSI Logic. He lives in Gambrills, Maryland, and is currently at work on a second novel.

DHORUBA BIN WAHAD served nineteen years in prison on controversial charges. Since his release in 1990, the former leader of the Black Panther Party has been a relentless advocate on behalf of political prisoners and P.O.W.s. Wahad is a powerful speaker and a prolific writer. In 1993 he traveled extensively in Europe and Africa, including the Seventh Pan-African Conference convened in Uganda, where he was delegate. He has recently established a base of operations in Accra, Ghana, with an aim of building an institution that will link the struggle of progressive Pan-Africanists and revolutionaries in the Diaspora with sympathetic governments in Africa.

BOOKER T. WASHINGTON (1858–1915) was born into slavery and rose to become the first president of Tuskegee Institute in Alabama. He argued that African Americans should give up their immediate demands for social equality and focus instead on economic development. For years, such arguments won him support from both the white and the Black community, and he dominated the Black political landscape. He met with dissension from many African American leaders, however, the most prominent of whom was W. E. B. Du Bois, who emphasized the need for equal educational opportunities. Still,

Washington had an indelible influence on such notables as Marcus Garvey. His classic autobiography, *Up from Slavery*, was published in 1901.

MEL WATKINS is a writer and former editor at the *New York Times Book Review* and editor of *Black Review* (1972), a paperback literary magazine. A graduate of Colgate University, he wrote the first and only comprehensive history of African American humor, *On the Real Side: Laughing, Lying, and Signifying—The Underground Tradition of African American Humor That Transformed American Culture, From Slavery to Richard Pryor.* His articles and reviews have appeared in numerous magazines, including *Southern Review*, *New York*, and *Entertainment Weekly*.

CORNEL WEST, a philosopher, teacher, and theologian, may be the most prominent intellectual in Black America. West participates in nearly a hundred forums a year, stressing his prophetic and liberation theology. His publications reflect his range of interests: *Prophecy Deliverance: An Afro-American Revolutionary Christianity*, *The American Evasion of Philosophy*, *Race Matters*, *Keeping Faith: Philosophy and Race in America*, and *Breaking Bread*, which was a dialogue with bell hooks. He received his doctorate from Princeton University and for several years later directed the school's African American Studies program. In 1994 he joined the staff of the African American Studies at Harvard University, where he earned his master of arts degree in 1975.

WALTER WHITE (1893–1955) was assistant secretary and then executive secretary of the NAACP during the years 1918 to 1955. White investigated numerous lynchings and race riots (sometimes passing as a white man to gain valuable information). He lobbied for a federal anti-lynching law and fought against racial discrimination in jobs, housing, and voting. *A Man Called White*, his autobiography, was published in 1948.

JOHN EDGAR WIDEMAN has produced a series of highly acclaimed works in his lengthy career, winning several literary awards such as the 1984 P.E.N./Faulkner Award for Fiction, the 1984 Dos Passos Prize for Literature, and a MacArthur Fellowship. A Rhodes scholar, he is currently a professor in the English Department at the University of Massachusetts. His novels include *A Glance Away*, *Hurry Home*, *The Lynchers*, *Hiding Place*, *Sent for You Yesterday*, *Reuben*, and *Philadelphia Fire*. He has also written two collections of short stories, *Dumballah* and *Fever*, and a memoir, *Brothers and Keepers*. His latest book, *Fatheralong: A Meditation on Fathers and Sons, Race and Society*, was published in 1994.

RALPH WILEY is best known for his controversial essays on culture, sports, and politics. He is the author of three collections of essays: *Why Black People*

Tend to Shout, *What Black People Should Do Now*, and the forthcoming *Dark Witness: When Black People Should Be Sacrificed (Again)*. He also wrote *Serenity: A Boxing Memoir* and coauthored, with Spike Lee, *By Any Means Necessary: The Trials and Tribulations of the Making of "Malcolm X."* A former *Sports Illustrated* writer, his work appeared in *Emerge* and *Premiere*. He lives in the greater Washington area.

JOHN A. WILLIAMS is the Paul Robeson Professor Emeritus of Rutgers University. The author of eleven published novels, among them *Sissie*, *Night Song*, *The Man Who Cried I Am*, and *!Click Song*, he is also the author of nine nonfiction books, including *If I Stop I'll Die: The Comedy and Tragedy of Richard Pryor* (with his son, Dennis A. Williams). In addition, he is the editor or coeditor of nine collections of writings. His articles have been published in various newspapers and magazines since 1947, including *The Nation*, the *New York Times*, *Ebony*, the *Village Voice*, and the *Washington Post*.

RICHARD WRIGHT (1908–60) wrote the classic novel, *Native Son*, which was published in 1940 and became the first novel by an African American to fully enter the mainstream of American literature. A bestseller and a Book-of-the-Month Club selection, *Native Son* was later a successful Broadway production. Wright's autobiographical *Black Boy* was published to critical acclaim in 1945. His success inspired other African American writers, including James Baldwin, Ralph Ellison, and Chester Himes.

SAMUEL F. YETTE, writer, professor, journalist, and photographer, was an associate editor of *Ebony* magazine. Yette, a former professor of Journalism at Howard University, is the author of *The Choice: The Issue of Black Survival in America*, which was published in 1971, and *Washington and Two Marches*, which he coauthored with his son, Frederick W. Yette. His articles and photographs have appeared in magazines and newspapers including *People*, *Time*, and *National Geographic*. He is currently the Washington correspondent and columnist for the *Richmond Free Press*.

Permission Acknowledgments

Grateful acknowledgment is made to the following for permission to reprint previously published material:

Addison-Wesley Publishing Company, Inc.: "First Poem for Linnet" from pp. 34–42 of *Daughters: On Family and Fatherhood* by Gerald Early. Copyright © 1994 by Gerald Early. Reprinted by permission of Addison-Wesley Publishing Company, Inc.

Africa World Press Inc.: Excerpt from pp. 94–101 of *Afrocentricity* by Molefi Kete Asante. Copyright © 1988. "The African Contribution to Technology and Science" by Dr. Yosef ben-Jochannan from pp. 55–62 of *New Dimensions in African History* edited by Dr. Yosef ben-Jochannan and Dr. John Henrik Clarke. Copyright © 1991. "The Africans in the New World: Their Contribution to Science, Invention and Technology" by Dr. John Henrik Clarke from pp. 63–71 of *Dimensions in African History* edited by Dr. Yosef ben-Jochannan and Dr. John Henrik Clarke. Copyright © 1991. Reprinted by permission of Africa World Press Inc.

Ernest Allen, Jr.: "Race and Gender Stereotyping in the Thomas Confirmation Hearings" by Ernest Allen, Jr. from *Court of Appeal: The Black Community Speaks Out on the Racial and Sexual Politics of Clarence Thomas vs. Anita Hill.* Reprinted by permission of the author.

Robert L. Allen: Preface from *The Port Chicago Mutiny* by Robert L. Allen. Reprinted by permission of the author.

Algonquin Books of Chapel Hill: Excerpt from *Company Man* by Brent Wade. Copyright © 1992 by Brent Wade. Reprinted by permission of Algonquin Books of Chapel Hill, a division of Workman Publishing Co., New York, NY.

Helga Rogers Andrews: "Third Day" from *From "Superman" to Man* by J. A. Rogers. Copyright 1941, renewed 1968, Helga M. Rogers. Reprinted by permission of Helga Rogers Andrews.

Archives of Claude McKay: Excerpt from *Selected Poems of Claude McKay.* Copyright © 1957 Harcourt, Brace. Reprinted by permission of the Archives of Claude McKay, Carl Cowl, Administrator.

Armistad: Excerpt from *Succeeding Against the Odds* by John H. Johnson with Lerone Bennett, Jr. Reprinted by permission of Armistad.

Jabari Asim: "Two Fools" by Jabari Asim. Reprinted by permission of the author.

Ballantine Books: "On the A-train to Venus with Isis" from *What Black People Should Do Now* by Ralph Wiley. Copyright © 1993 by HIP, Inc. Reprinted by permission of Ballantine Books, a division of Random House, Inc.

BasicBooks: Excerpt from *Faces at the Bottom of the Well* by Derrick Bell. Copyright © 1992 by BasicBooks, Inc. Excerpt from *Black Rage* by William H. Grier, M.D., and Price M. Cobbs, M.D. Copyright © 1968 by William H. Grier and Price M. Cobbs. Excerpt from *Reflections of an Affirmative Action Baby* by Stephen L. Carter. Copyright © 1991 by Stephen Carter. Reprinted by permission of BasicBooks, a division of HarperCollins Publishers, Inc.

Bantam Books: Excerpt from *Giant Steps* by Kareem Abdul-Jabbar. Copyright © 1983 by Kareem Abdul-Jabbar. Reprinted by permission of Bantam Books, a division of Bantam Doubleday Dell Publishing Group, Inc.

Nouk Bassomb: "IKOP MBOG: An Account of an African Child's Initiation" by Nouk Bassomb. Copyright © 1994 by Nouk Bassomb. Reprinted by permission of the author.

Beacon Press: Excerpt from *Race Matters* by Cornel West. Copyright © 1993 by Cornel West. Excerpt from *Here I Stand* by Paul Robeson. Copyright © 1958 by Paul Robeson. Excerpt from *Notes of a Native Son* by James Baldwin. Copyright © 1955, renewed 1983 by James Baldwin. Reprinted by permission of Beacon Press.

Playthell Benjamin: "Lush Life" from *Tall Tales from the Life and Times of Sug-*

arcane Hancock, Vol. I: Memoirs of a Sweet Colored Man by Playthell Benjamin. Copyright © 1994 by Playthell Benjamin. Reprinted by permission of the author.

Susan Bergholz Literary Services: Excerpt from "Anita" from *All-Night Visitors* by Clarence Major. Copyright © 1969 by Clarence Major. First published in *All-Night Visitors*, Olympia Press. Reprinted by permission of Susan Bergholz Literary Services, New York.

Georges Borchardt, Inc.: Excerpt from *Notes of a Hanging Judge: Essays and Reviews 1979–1989* by Stanley Crouch. Copyright © 1990 by Stanley Crouch. Reprinted by permission of Georges Borchardt, Inc. for the author.

British American Publishing, Ltd.: Excerpt from *Just Let Me Play* by Charlie Sifford with James Gullo. Copyright © 1992 by Charlie Sifford. Reprinted by permission of British American Publishing, Ltd.

Curtis Brown, Ltd.: Excerpt from *Beetlecreek* by William Demby. Copyright © 1967 by William Demby. Reprinted by permission of Curtis Brown, Ltd.

Lloyd L. Brown: Excerpt from *Iron City* by Lloyd L. Brown. *Iron City* was reprinted October 1994 by Northeastern University Press, Boston, MA. Copyright © 1994 by Lloyd L. Brown. Reprinted by permission of the author.

Wesley Brown: Excerpt from *Tragic Magic* by Wesley Brown. Reprinted by permission of the author.

Nick Chiles: Excerpt from *A Private War* by Nick Chiles. Reprinted by permission of the author.

Robert Chrisman: "Black Prisoners, White Law" by Robert Chrisman from *The Black Scholar.* Reprinted by permission of the author.

Coffee House Press: Excerpt from *Losing Absalom* by Alexs D. Pate, Coffee House Press, 1994. Copyright © 1994 by Alexs D. Pate. Reprinted by permission of the publisher.

Cottage Books: Excerpt from *The Choice: The Issue of Black Survival in America* by Samuel F. Yette. Originally published in 1971 by G.P. Putnam's Sons. (Republished by Cottage Books in 1982, ISBN: 0-911253-00-9, cloth; 0-911253-01-7, paper, Library of Congress Catalog 82-083686.) Reprinted by permission of Cottage Books.

Curtis Management Group: The "Speech to African Summit Conference—Cairo, Egypt" July 17, 1964 by Malcolm X from *Malcolm X: The Man and His Times*. TM/ © 1994 Dr. Betty Shabazz by Curtis Management Group, Indianapolis, IN.

Joan Daves Agency: "Where Do We Go from Here?" by Martin Luther King, Jr. from *The Essential Writings and Speeches of Martin Luther King, Jr.*, edited by James M. Washington. Copyright © 1967 by Martin Luther King, Jr. Reprinted by arrangement with The Heirs to the Estate of Martin Luther King, Jr., c/o Joan Daves Agency as agent for the proprietor. "Beyond Vietnam" by Martin Luther King, Jr. from *Vietnam and Black America* edited by Clyde Taylor. Copyright © 1967 by Martin Luther King, Jr. Reprinted by arrangement with The Heirs to the Estate of Martin Luther King, Jr., c/o Joan Daves Agency as agent for the proprietor.

Doubleday: Excerpt from *Vietnam and the Black American* by Clyde Taylor, editor. Copyright © 1973 by Clyde Taylor. Excerpt from *Invisible Life* by E. Lynn Harris. Copyright © 1991, 1994 by Clyde Taylor. "Enemy Territory" from *Dancers on the Shore* by William Melvin Kelley. Copyright © 1964 by William Melvin Kelley. Excerpt from *Sex and Racism in America* by Calvin C. Hernton. Copyright © 1965 by Calvin C. Hernton. Excerpt from *Music Is My Mistress* by Duke Ellington. Copyright © 1973 by Duke Ellington, Inc. "Dance of the Infidels" from *Lover Man* by Alston Anderson. Copyright © 1959 by Alston Anderson. Excerpt from *Blood on the Forge* by William Attaway. Copyright 1941 by Doubleday, a division of Bantam Doubleday Dell Publishing Group, Inc. All reprinted by permission of Doubleday, a division of Bantam Doubleday Dell Publishing Group, Inc.

Dutton Signet: Excerpt from *Vanishing Rooms* by Melvin Dixon. Copyright © 1991 by Melvin Dixon. Reprinted by permission of Dutton Signet, a division of Penguin Books USA Inc.

Michael Eric Dyson: Excerpt from *Reflecting Black* by Michael Eric Dyson. Reprinted by permission of the author.

Eakin Press: Excerpt from *Raceboss: Big Emma's Boy* by Albert Race Sample. Copyright © 1984 by Albert Race Sample. Published in the United States of America by Eakin Press, P.O. Box 23066, Austin, TX 78735. Reprinted by permission of Eakin Press.

The Ecco Press: Excerpt from *The Life and Loves of Mr. Jiveass Nigger* by Cecil Brown. Copyright © 1969 by Cecil Brown. Published by The Ecco Press in 1991. Reprinted by permission of The Ecco Press.

Harry Edwards: Excerpt from *The Struggle That Must Be* by Harry Edwards. Reprinted by permission of the author.

Minister Louis Farrakhan: Excerpt from *A Torchlight for America* by Louis Farrakhan. Reprinted by permission of the author.

Farrar, Straus & Giroux, Inc.: Excerpt from *Way Past Cool* by Jess Mowry. Copyright © 1992 by Jess Mowry. Reprinted by permission of Farrar, Straus & Giroux, Inc.

Robert Fleming: "Black Women" by Robert Fleming. Reprinted by permission of the author.

Roland J. Gilbert/Cheo Tyehimba-Taylor: "The Simba Six: The Men" from *The Ghetto Solution* by Roland J. Gilbert/Cheo Tyehimba-Taylor. Reprinted by permission of the authors.

Earl G. Graves, Ltd.: "The Men of Black Enterprise" by Earl G. Graves. Reprinted by permission of Earl G. Graves, Ltd.

Graywolf Press: "And He Was 25 Years Old . . ." from *Ten Seconds* by Louis Edwards. Copyright © 1991 by Louis Edwards. Reprinted by permission of Graywolf Press, Saint Paul, Minnesota.

Sam Greenlee: Excerpt from *The Spook Who Sat By the Door* by Sam Greenlee. Reprinted by permission of the author.

GRM Associates, Inc.: "Yet Do I Marvel" from *Color* by Countee Cullen. Copyright © 1925 by Harper & Brothers. Copyright renewed 1953 by Ida M. Cullen. Reprinted by permission of GRM Associates, Inc., Agents for the Estate of Ida M. Cullen.

Damu Hakim: "A Father's Lament" by Damu Hakim. Reprinted by permission of the author.

Alex P. Haley Estate: "There Are Days When I Wish It Hadn't Happened" by Alex P. Haley. Reprinted by permission of the Alex P. Haley Estate.

Ronald E. Hall: "Blacks Who Pass" from *The Complexion Connection* by Ronald E. Hall. Reprinted by permission of the author.

Harcourt Brace & Company: Excerpt from "This Far" in *Let the Dead Bury Their Dead* by Randall Kenan. Copyright © 1992 by Randall Kenan. Reprinted by permission of Harcourt Brace & Company.

Nathan Hare: "The Challenge of a Black Scholar" by Nathan Hare from *The Black Scholar*. Reprinted by permission of the author.

HarperCollins Publishers, Inc.: Excerpt from "Strong Men" from *The Collected Poems of Sterling A. Brown*, edited by Michael S. Harper. Copyright © 1932 by Harcourt Brace & Company. Copyright renewed 1960 by Sterling Brown. Excerpt from *The Rage of the Privileged Class* by Ellis Cose. Copyright © 1993 by Ellis Cose. Excerpt from *Black Boy: A Record of Childhood and Youth* by Richard Wright. Copyright 1937, 1942, 1944, 1945 by Richard Wright. Copyright renewed 1973 by Ellen Wright. Reprinted by permission of HarperCollins Publishers, Inc.

Essex Hemphill: Excerpt from "In An Afternoon Light" from *Brother to Brother:*

New Writings By Black Gay Men edited by Essex Hemphill. Reprinted by permission of the author.

The Napoleon Hill Foundation: Excerpt from *Think and Grow Rich: A Black Choice* by Dennis Kimbro and Napoleon Hill. Copyright © 1991 by the Napoleon Hill Foundation. Reprinted by permission of The Napoleon Hill Foundation.

Hill and Wang: "Father" from *The Big Sea* by Langston Hughes. Copyright © 1940 by Langston Hughes and copyright renewed © 1968 by Arna Bontemps and George Houston Bass. Reprinted by permission of Hill and Wang, a division of Farrar, Straus & Giroux, Inc.

Hill and Wang and Mark Paterson & Associates: "Back in New York" from *Treat It Gentle* by Sidney Bechet. Copyright © 1960 by Twayne Publishers Inc. and Cassell & Company Ltd. Reprinted by permission of Hill and Wang, a division of Farrar, Straus & Giroux, Inc., and Mark Paterson & Associates on behalf of the Sidney Bechet estate.

Henry Holt & Company, Inc.: Excerpt from *Brothers and Keepers* by John Edgar Wideman. Copyright © 1984 by John Edgar Wideman. Reprinted by permission of Henry Holt & Co., Inc.

Howard University Press: Excerpt from *And Then We Heard the Thunder* by John Oliver Killens. Copyright © 1962 by John Oliver Killens. Reprinted by permission of Howard University Press, Washington, DC.

Earl Ofari Hutchinson: "A Talk with Him" from *Black Fatherhood* by Earl Ofari Hutchinson. Reprinted by permission of the author.

Hyperion: Excerpt from *By Any Means Necessary: The Trials and Tribulations of the Making of Malcolm X . . .* by Spike Lee with Ralph Wiley. Copyright © 1992 by Spike Lee and Ralph Wiley. Reprinted by permission of the publisher, Hyperion.

International Publishers Company Inc.: Excerpt from *Black Worker in the Deep South: A Personal Record* by Hosea Hudson. Reprinted by permission of International Publishers Co. Inc.

James E. Jackson: "The Journey of Martin Luther King, Jr." by James E. Jackson. Reprinted by permission of the author.

Alfred A. Knopf, Inc.: Excerpt from *This Life* by Sidney Poitier. Copyright © 1980 by Sidney Poitier. Excerpt from *Days of Grace* by Arthur Ashe and Arnold Rampersad. Copyright © 1993 by Jeanne Moutoussamy-Ashe and Arnold Rampersad. Excerpt from *A Lesson Before Dying* by Ernest J. Gaines. Copyright © 1993 by Ernest J. Gaines. "Playing Hardball" from *Colored People: A Memoir* by Henry Louis Gates, Jr. Copyright © 1994 by Henry Louis Gates, Jr. Reprinted by permission of Alfred A. Knopf, Inc.

Little, Brown & Company: Excerpt from *Elbow Room* by James Alan McPherson. Copyright © 1974 by James Alan McPherson. Excerpt from *Falling Pieces of the Broken Sky* by Julius Lester. Copyright © 1990 by Julius Lester. Excerpt from *Shannon* by Gordon Parks. Copyright © 1988 by Gordon Parks. Excerpt from *I Get on the Bus* by Reginald McKnight. Copyright © 1990 by Reginald McKnight. Reprinted by permission of Little, Brown and Company.

Liveright Publishing Corporation: "Blood-Burning Moon" from *Cane* by Jean Toomer. Copyright © 1923 by Boni & Liveright, renewed 1951 by Jean Toomer. Reprinted by permission of Liveright Publishing Corporation.

Louisiana State University Press: "John Hope Franklin: A Life of Learning" from *Race and History: Selected Essays 1938–1988* by John Hope Franklin. Copyright © 1989 by Louisiana State University Press. Reprinted by permission of Louisiana State University Press.

Richard Majors: "Cool Pose: The Proud Signature of Black Survival" by Richard Majors. Reprinted by permission of the author.

Manning Marable: "Toward Black American Empowerment" by Manning Marable. Reprinted by permission of the author.

Jarvis Masters: "Scars" by Jarvis Masters. Reprinted by permission of the author.

Harold Matson Company, Inc.: Excerpt from *The Almost White Boy* by Willard Motley. Copyright © 1963 by Willard Motley, © renewed 1991. Reprinted by permission of Harold Matson Company, Inc.

Kweisi Mfume: "The State of Black America" by Kweisi Mfume. Reprinted by permission of the author.

Kenneth Meeks: "Pledging Alpha" by Kenneth Meeks. Reprinted by permission of the author.

W. J. Brandy Moore: "African American Males and Survival Against AIDS: Critical Alliances Beyond Accommodations" by W. J. Brandy Moore. Reprinted by permission of the author.

William Morrow & Company, Inc.: "A New Man" from *Lost in the City* by Edward P. Jones. Copyright © 1992 by Edward P. Jones. Excerpt from *Kwanzaa* by Eric V. Copage. Copyright © 1991 by Eric V. Copage. Excerpt from *Success Runs in Our Race* by George C. Fraser. Copyright © 1994 by George C. Fraser. Excerpt from *No Other Tale to Tell* by Richard Perry. Copyright © 1994 by Richard Perry. Excerpt from pp. 256–257 of *Brothers* by Sylvester Monroe and Peter Goldman with Vern E. Smith, Terry E. Johnson, Monroe Anderson, and Jacques Chenet. Text copyright © 1988 by Newsweek, Inc. Reprinted by permission of William Morrow & Company, Inc.

W. W. Norton & Company, Inc.: Excerpt from *White Butterfly: An Easy Rawlins Mystery* by Walter Mosley. Copyright © 1992 by Walter Mosley. Reprinted by permission of W. W. Norton & Company, Inc.

Harold Ober Associates Incorporated: "Who's Passing for Who?" from *Laughing to Keep from Crying* by Langston Hughes. Copyright © 1952 by Langston Hughes. Copyright renewed 1980 by George Houston Bass. Excerpt from *When Harlem Was in Vogue* by David Levering Lewis. Copyright © 1981 by David Levering Lewis. Reprinted by permission of Harold Ober Associates Incorporated.

Open Hand Publishing Inc.: Excerpt from *The Making of Black Revolutionaries* by James Forman. Published by Open Hand Publishing Inc. in 1985. Reprinted by permission of Open Hand Publishing Inc.

Pantheon Books: "Going Through Changes" from *The Death of Rhythm and Blues* by Nelson George. Copyright © 1988 by Nelson George. Excerpt from *Parallel Time: Growing Up Black and White* by Brent Staples. Copyright © 1994 by Brent Staples. Reprinted by permission of Pantheon Books, a division of Random House, Inc.

Playboy Enterprises, Inc.: "Playboy Interview: Cassius Clay," *Playboy* magazine (October 1964). Copyright © 1964, 1994 by Playboy. All Rights Reserved. Reprinted by permission of Playboy. "Playboy Interview: Quincy Jones," *Playboy* magazine (July 1990). Copyright © 1990 by Playboy. All Rights Reserved. Reprinted by permission of Playboy.

Kevin Powell: "Ghetto Bastard" by Kevin Powell. Copyright © 1992 by Kevin Powell. Reprinted by permission of the author.

Quarterly Review of Literature: "Juneteenth" by Ralph Ellison from *Quarterly Review of Literature, Volume XIII, 3–4*. Reprinted by permission of Quarterly Review of Literature.

Dudley Randall: "A Different Image" from *Cities Burning* by Dudley Randall. Reprinted by permission of the author.

Random House, Inc.: Excerpt from *Bloods: An Oral History of the Vietnam War By Black Veterans* by Wallace Terry. Copyright © 1984, 1992 by Wallace Terry. Excerpt from *Makes Me Wanna Holler: A Young Black Man in America* by Nathan McCall. Copyright © 1994 by Nathan McCall. Excerpt from *My Life* by Earvin "Magic" Johnson with William Novak. Copyright © 1992 by June Bug Enterprises. Excerpt from *The Autobiography of Malcolm X* by Malcolm X and Alex

Haley. Copyright © 1964 by Alex Haley and Malcolm X. Copyright © 1965 by Alex Haley and Betty Shabazz. Reprinted by permission of Random House, Inc.

Ishmael Reed: Excerpt from *Writin' Is Fightin'* by Ishmael Reed. Copyright © 1988 by Ishmael Reed. Reprinted by permission of the author.

Rachel Robinson: Excerpt from *I Never Had It Made* by Jackie Robinson and Alfred Duckett. Reprinted by permission of Rachel Robinson.

Randall Robinson: "Operation Island Storm" by Randall Robinson. Reprinted by permission of the author.

Kalamu ya Salaam: "What Is Life?" is excerpted from a manuscript, edited version appears in *What Is Life?* (Chicago: Third World Press). Reprinted by permission of the author.

Yusef Salaam: "Brer Rabbit Escapes Again" by Yusef Salaam. Reprinted by permission of the author.

Scribner: Excerpt from *Middle Passage* by Charles Johnson. Copyright © 1989 by Charles Johnson. Excerpt from *Adam Clayton Powell, Jr.: The Political Biography of an American Dilemma* by Charles V. Hamilton. Copyright © 1991 by Charles V. Hamilton. Reprinted by permission of Scribner, an imprint of Simon & Schuster.

Bobby Seale: Excerpt from *Seize the Time* by Bobby Seale. Reprinted by permission of the author.

Simon & Schuster, Inc.: Excerpt from *Manchild in the Promised Land* by Claude Brown. Copyright © 1965 by Claude Brown. Excerpt from *Miles: The Autobiography* by Miles Davis with Quincy Troupe. Copyright © 1989 by Miles Davis. Excerpt from *On the Real Side* by Mel Watkins. Copyright © 1994 by Mel Watkins. Excerpt from *Home Repairs* by Trey Ellis. Copyright © 1993 by Trey Ellis. Reprinted by permission of Simon & Schuster, Inc.

South End Press: Excerpt from *Keep Hope Alive: Jesse Jackson's 1988 Presidential Campaign* by Jesse Jackson. Reprinted by permission of South End Press.

St. Martin's Press, Inc.: Excerpt from *The Ice Opinion* by Ice T. Copyright © 1994 by Ice T and Heidi Siegmund. Excerpt from *The Content of Our Character* by Shelby Steele. Copyright © 1990 by Shelby Steele. Reprinted by permission of St. Martin's Press, Inc., New York, NY.

Ronald Stodghill II: Excerpt from *My Sparrow* by Ronald Stodghill II. Reprinted by permission of the author.

William Strickland: "The Future of Black Men" by William Strickland. Reprinted by permission of the author.

Sun & Moon Press: Excerpt from *DJBOT'S Baghostus's Run* by Nathaniel Mackey (Los Angeles: Sun & Moon Press, 1993). Copyright © 1993 by Nathaniel Mackey. Reprinted by permission of Sun & Moon Press.

George Edward Tait: "I Am a Black Man" from *At War: Selected Poems of George Edward Tait* by George Edward Tait. Reprinted by permission of the author.

Roslyn Targ Literary Agency, Inc.: Excerpt from *Lonely Crusade* by Chester Himes. Copyright © 1947, 1975 by Chester Himes. Reprinted by permission of Roslyn Targ Literary Agency, Inc., New York.

Greg Tate: "Silence, Exile, and Cunning: Miles Davis in Memoriam" from *Flyboy in the Buttermilk* by Greg Tate. Reprinted by permission of Greg Tate.

Third World Press: "Father's Place" from *Black Men: Obsolete, Single, Dangerous? The Afrikan American Family in Transition* by Haki R. Madhubuti (Chicago: Third World Press, 1990). Reprinted by permission of Third World Press.

Thunder's Mouth Press: Excerpt from *The LeRoi Jones/Amiri Baraka Reader* by Amiri Baraka. Copyright © 1991 by Amiri Baraka. Excerpt from *Goodbye Sweetwater* by Henry Dumas. Copyright © 1988 by Loretta Dumas and Eugene B. Redmond. Reprinted by permission of the publisher, Thunder's Mouth Press.

Howard Thurman Educational Trust: Excerpt from *For the Inward Journey* by Howard Thurman. Copyright © 1984 by Sue Bailey Thurman. Reprinted by permission of the Howard Thurman Educational Trust.

Quincy Troupe: "Poem for My Father" from *Weather Reports: New and Selected Poems* by Quincy Troupe. Reprinted by permission of the author.

University of Michigan Press: Excerpt from *The Walls of Jericho* by Rudolph Fisher. Copyright © 1928 by Alfred A. Knopf, copyright renewal © 1958 by Jane Ryder Fisher. Published in the United States of America by the University of Michigan Press. Reprinted by permission of the University of Michigan Press.

The University of Sankore Press: Excerpt from *The African-American Holiday of Kwanzaa: A Celebration of Family, Community & Culture* by Maulana Karenga. Copyright © 1989 by Maulana Karenga. Reprinted by permission of The University of Sankore Press.

Viking Penguin: "I Learn What I Am" from *A Man Called White* by Walter White. Copyright 1948 by Walter White, renewed © 1976 by the Estate of Walter White. Excerpt from *Another Good Loving Blues* by Arthur Flowers. Copyright © 1993 by Arthur Flowers. Excerpt from *Billy* by Albert French. Copyright © 1993 by Albert French. Reprinted by permission of Viking Penguin, a division of Penguin Books USA Inc.

Dhoruba Bin Wahad: Excerpt from *Still Black, Still Strong* by Dhoruba Bin Wahad. Reprinted by permission of the author.

John A. Williams: Excerpt from *The Man Who Cried I Am* by John A. Williams. © 1967, 1985. Reprinted by permission of the author.

WRS Publishing: Excerpt from *Fathers Behind Bars* by Arthur Hamilton, Jr. and William Banks. © 1993 WRS Publishing, Waco, Texas. Reprinted by permission of WRS Publishing.

Zebra Books: Excerpt from *Out of Bounds* by Jim Brown with Steve Delsohn. Copyright © 1989 by Jim Brown and Steve Delsohn. Published by Zebra Books, an imprint of Kensington Publishing Corp. Reprinted by permission of Zebra Books.

Herb Boyd: © Christopher Griffith

Robert L. Allen: © Janet Carter

About the Editors

Herb Boyd is the author of *African History for Beginners* and *Down the Glory Road*. An award-winning journalist, his articles have appeared in *Emerge*, *Class*, *Down Beat*, *Amsterdam News*, *Detroit Metro Times*, and *The Black Scholar*. He lives in New York City.

Robert L. Allen, Ph.D., is the author of *The Port Chicago Mutiny* and coeditor of *Court of Appeal.* He is senior editor of *The Black Scholar* and past board president of the Oakland Men's Project.